LEARNING QUICKBOOKS® PRO AND PREMIER ACCOUNTANT 2012

A Practical Approach

Terri E. Brunsdon, CPA, CITP, JD

PEARSON

Boston Columbus Indianapolis New York San Francisco Upper Saddle River
Amsterdam Cape Town Dubai London Madrid Milan Munich Paris Montreal Toronto
Delhi Mexico City Sao Paulo Sydney Hong Kong Seoul Singapore Taipei Tokyo

Editorial Director: Sally Yagan
Editor in Chief: Donna Battista
Acquisitions Editor: Victoria Warneck
Director of Editorial Services: Ashley Santora
Editorial Project Manager: Melissa Pellerano
Editorial Assistant: Jane Avery
VP/Director of Marketing: Patrice Jones
Marketing Manager: Alison Haskins
Marketing Assistant: Kimberly Lovato
Senior Managing Editor: Nancy H. Fenton
Associate Managing Editor: Karen Carter
Cover Designer: Anthony Gemmellaro
Cover Photo: leungchopan / Shutterstock.com
Executive Media Producer: Melissa Honig
Senior Manufacturing Buyer: Carol Melville
Media Procurement Specialist: Ginny Michaud
Text Permissions Supervisor: Michael Joyce
Permissions Specialist: Jill Dougan
Full-Service Project Management: GEX Publishing Services
Printer/Binder: Webcrafters Inc.
Cover Printer: Lehigh-Phoenix Color/Hagerstown
Text Font: Calibri

Library of Congress Cataloging-in-Publication Data

Brunsdon, Terri E.
Learning QuickBooks Pro and Premier accountant 2012 : a practical approach / Terri E. Brunsdon.
p. cm.
ISBN-13: 978-0-13-275167-4 (alk. paper)
ISBN-10: 0-13-275167-4
1. QuickBooks. 2. Small business–Accounting. 3. Small business–Finance–Computer programs. I. Title.
HF5679.B6636 2013
657'.9042028553–dc23
2012018216

12 11 10 9 8 7 6 5 4 3

ISBN-10: 0-13-275167-4
ISBN-13: 978-0-13-275167-4

TABLE OF CONTENTS

PREFACE

A Special Note to Students and Instructors from Terri Brunsdon
How This Textbook Teaches QuickBooks Pro and Premier Accountant 2012

Learning QuickBooks Pro and Premier Accountant 2012 is a comprehensive approach to teaching accounting concepts in a software environment. The text includes sample company data files designed to simulate real-world businesses. Students will gain "hands-on" experience in performing accounting tasks, tracing accounting entries, correcting accounting entries, producing financial statements, and analyzing company performance.

This text uses a "WHoW" approach to teaching accounting software. Students learn ***why*** a transaction is posted, ***how*** a transaction is posted, and ***what*** a transaction affected.

The "*Why*" aspect is demonstrated by preceding a task with discussions on the external events triggering accounting activities as well as any accounting concepts governing recognition of a transaction.

The "*How*" aspect is implemented by using step-by-step illustrations when recording transactions.

The "*What*" aspect is demonstrated in the **Manual Accounting Procedures *("MAPS")*** and ***Behind the Keys*** topics. Chapters begin with a MAPS illustration covering the subsidiary journals, ledgers, and accounts used when posting transactions in a manual system. These illustrations also explain the purpose of the audit trail in tracing posted transactions. After posting a transaction in the software, students will go *Behind the Keys* to trace their entries on subsidiary journals, ledgers, and accounts in the software. They will find that the software uses an audit trail that is similar to a manual system. After tracing entries, students learn the proper procedures for correcting a transaction. With *MAPS* and *Behind the Keys*, accounting software is less of a "black box" and students are able to recognize, locate, and correct posting errors.

This text also reinforces complex tasks by asking students to complete a self-guided ***You Try*** exercise immediately after completing a step-by-step illustration on the task. Solutions for these exercises are provided in Appendix E.

Finally, this text comes with online video tutorials that professors may use to visually illustrate certain topics. Topics that have an accompanying video are noted by placing a picture of a camera beside the name of the topic.

So What is New in this Edition of the Text?

The text has been significantly revised. Among these revisions are:

- **Redesigned Data Files.** This edition made significant changes to student data files. Each chapter and Practice Set now uses separate data files. Students download these data files from the Website at ***www.pearsonhighered.com/brunsdon.***

- **Additional Practice Sets.** The Practice Set at the end of Chapter 1 is redesigned. A Practice Set is added for the end of Chapter 2.

- **Additional Projects.** The Internet mini-projects added in the previous edition remain for this edition. These mini-projects appear at the end of Chapters 3 through 6 and 8 through 10. Students download instructions and data files for these projects from the Website at ***www.pearsonhighered.com/brundson.***

- **Additional Questions.** Additional multiple choice and true/false questions have been added at the end of certain chapters.

So What is New in this Version of the Software that Comes With the Text?

Overall, the software has few changes. Among these are a redesigned Help and Search feature. The text still comes with the Premier Accountant edition of the software. Because this text covers the Pro edition, students will still be asked to toggle to that edition. Appendix F still covers select features in the Premier Accountant Edition.

How Chapters Are Organized

- **Chapter 1** begins by explaining the role of accounting software. It then reviews activities such as downloading data files; opening and closing companies; backing up and restoring companies; working with QuickBooks help files; using shortcut keys; and practice navigating the QuickBooks interface.

- **Chapter 2** illustrates customizing QuickBooks preference options, reviewing the chart of accounts, printing, customizing, and exporting reports, emailing reports, and locating information using find, drilldown, and hyperlink features.

- **In Chapter 3** students post basic and compound journal entries before printing financial statements. This chapter is intended to make students comfortable with posting basic transactions, printing reports, and locating information before they tackle more complicated tasks such as posting sales, purchasing, and payroll transactions. After this chapter, the text branches into two distinct tracks that cover activities for either a service-based business or a merchandising business.

- **Chapters 4 through 7** use a cycle-based approach to illustrating sales, purchasing, payroll, and company activities for a service-based business. This tract focuses on a business that uses job costing so activities center on assigning costs to jobs. The track begins with a chapter on processing sales activities and proceeds to separate chapters for processing purchasing and payroll activities. The track concludes with a chapter on reviewing transactions, recording adjusting entries, printing financial statements, and closing the accounting period. After completing this series of chapters, students will have completed an entire accounting cycle for a service-based business and will have worked with job costing as well as service and non-inventory part items.

- **In Project 1,** students are asked to complete an entire accounting cycle for a service-based business. This project is a comprehensive review of the tasks covered in Chapters 4 through 7.

- **In Chapters 8 through 11,** the cycle-based approach is repeated, but this time for a merchandising business. This tract is distinguished from the previous tract because it covers in-depth topics on inventory. After completing this track, students have completed an entire accounting cycle for a merchandising business.

- **In Project 2,** students are asked to complete an entire accounting cycle for a merchandising. This project is a comprehensive review of the tasks covered in Chapters 8 through 11.

- **Chapter 12** provides an opportunity for students to create a merchandising business from scratch. After creating the data file, students are asked to complete an entire accounting cycle for the new business.

- **Appendix A** includes detailed instructions for installing the software. (See the Important Points about the Software topic that follows.)

- **Appendix B** includes comprehensive instructions for correcting posting errors.

- **Appendix C** repeats the data file backup and restore procedures illustrated in Chapter 1. It also covers making portable backup files and moving files between school and home.

- **Appendix D** contains a copy of the IRS Circular E tax tables discussed in the payroll chapters of the text.

- **Appendix E** contains solutions for the *You Try* exercises that appear throughout the text.

- **Appendix F** illustrates features found in the Premier Accountant Edition.

Note: The author recommends students complete Chapters 1 through 3 before either embarking on the service-based business or the merchandise business tracks.

Important Points about the Software

The QuickBooks software supplied with the textbook is currently not supported on a MAC operating system. Additionally, this software is a 140-day trial version, so it cannot be reused 140 days after installation.

Important Points on Technical Support for Installation

Instructions for installing the software are in Appendix A. The textbook does not cover problems in installing the software. Support for installation problems are found on Intuit's website at *www.quickbooks.com/support.*

Additionally, the Website at ***accountant.intuit.com/training_cpe/intuit_education_program/*** provides professors with information on purchasing a site license for use in the computer lab. Purchasing a site license provides additional benefits because professors gain access to specialized instructor resources from Intuit. Site licenses are valid for two years.

Features That Help Readers Really Learn the Software AND Accounting

The following icons are placed in the margin of topics and exercises to signal:

Step-by-step instructions for performing a task with illustrated solutions.

You Try exercises with solutions in Appendix E.

Manual Accounting Procedures *(MAPS)* illustrations.

Behind the Keys procedures for tracing posted entries.

Indicates a new feature in QuickBooks Pro 2012.

Web-based video tutorial is available to illustrate the topic.

LEARNING RESOURCES FOR STUDENTS

Online Student Resource Center located at *www.pearsonhighered.com/brunsdon*
These resources include:

- **Student data files for the text. Chapter 1 contains a table of the data files.**
- **Internet Mini-Projects**

TEACHING RESOURCES FOR INSTRUCTORS

Online Instructor's Resource Center located at *www.pearsonhighered.com/brunsdon*
Instructor files are located under the **"Instructor Resources"** link on the Website. These resources are password protected so contact your representative for access.
These resources include:

- **Instructor's Manual with teaching tips and solutions to multiple choice and true/false questions**
- **A sample syllabus**
- **PowerPoint slides**
- **Test bank files**
- **Online video tutorials for selected topics in each chapter**
- **Solution data files**
- **Solution reports in PDF and Excel formats**

Product Development

The author would like to thank Donna Battista, Victoria Warneck, Melissa Pellerano, and Karen Carter of Prentice Hall and Elisa Burchett for all the work they put into managing, editing, and accuracy checking this text.

About the Author

Terri Brunsdon is a Certified Public Accountant with a Juris Doctorate in Law, a Masters in Tax, and undergraduate degrees in accounting and computer programming. Terri has over twenty years of accounting experience and specializes in recommending and implementing accounting software solutions. In addition, Terri has six years of higher education experience in teaching accounting information systems and computer software applications. Terri is a member of the American Institute of Certified Public Accountants (AICPA) and is an AICPA Certified Information Technology Professional (CITP). She is also a member of the American Accounting Association, American Bar Association, Ohio Bar Association, and Ohio Society of Certified Public Accountants.

More Computerized Accounting Software Texts by Terri Brunsdon

If you like the teaching and learning approach of this book, don't forget to review these other Prentice Hall textbooks by Terri Brunsdon:

- *Learning Peachtree Complete Accounting*
- *Introduction to Microsoft Dynamics 10.0: Focus on Internal Controls*

Dedicated to my husband and best friend, Bill Brunsdon

CHAPTER 1 GET READY FOR QUICKBOOKS PRO 2012

LEARNING OBJECTIVES

This chapter introduces you to using QuickBooks Pro 2012 (QBP) by covering the following:

1. An introduction to accounting software and application software
2. Launching QBP and loading company data files
3. Opening and closing companies in QBP
4. Navigating the desktop
5. Customizing the icon bar
6. Using QuickBooks centers
7. Customizing company names
8. Using keyboard shortcuts
9. Using QuickBooks Help
10. Backing up company data files
11. Restoring sample data files
12. Moving data between school and home
13. Exiting the software

NOTE: BEFORE COMPLETING THE TASKS THAT FOLLOW, YOU MUST HAVE THE SOFTWARE INSTALLED ON YOUR COMPUTER. INSTRUCTIONS FOR INSTALLING THE SOFTWARE ARE IN APPENDIX A. THE TEXTBOOK DOES NOT COVER INSTALLATION PROBLEMS. SUPPORT FOR INSTALLATION PROBLEMS IS FOUND ON INTUIT'S WEBSITE AT *www.quickbooks.com/support*.

NOTE: THE SOFTWARE PROVIDED WITH THE TEXT DOES NOT WORK ON A MAC OPERATING SYSTEM. INTUIT DOES NOT CURRENTLY PROVIDE A FREE MAC VERSION FOR USE BY STUDENTS.

INTRODUCTION TO ACCOUNTING SOFTWARE

Accounting software simplifies capturing and posting accounting transactions. Although basic accounting procedures remain the same, accounting software eliminates tedious processes such as typing documents, manually posting and calculating transactions, and documenting the audit trail. The table that follows illustrates these differences.

Manual Accounting System	Computerized Accounting System
1. Business transaction occurs and is manually entered onto a source document.	1. Business transaction occurs and is entered into the accounting software.
2. Source document manually recorded in the subsidiary journal and posted to the subsidiary ledger and general ledger while documenting the audit trail.	2. Accounting software records transaction in the subsidiary journal and posts to subsidiary ledger and general ledger along with the audit trail.
3. Manually prepare trial balance.	3. Print computerized trial balance.
4. Record adjusting entries in the general journal and post entries to the general ledger.	4. Record adjusting entries in the general journal and software posts to the general ledger.
5. Manually prepare adjusted trial balance.	5. Reprint trial balance with adjusting entries.
6. Manually calculate and post closing entries.	6. Computer posts closing entries.
7. Manually prepare financial statements.	7. Print computerized financial statements.

Computerized accounting minimizes posting errors, thus protecting the validity of data. After correctly capturing an entry, the software coordinates posting, reporting, and the audit trail. In addition, the accountant can easily monitor transactions and analyze financial performance.

Naturally you need computer hardware and operating software to use computerized accounting software. Computer hardware encompasses the physical components such as keyboard, screen, hard drive, CD-ROM, mouse, memory, and printers. Operating software is the system software that translates user instructions to hardware components and application software. Microsoft's Windows XP, Windows 7, and Vista as well as Linux and UNIX are examples of operating software.

Application Software

Application software serves specific needs of the user and is installed over operating software. There are a wide variety of application software packages on the market, and the following table outlines a few of the more familiar packages alongside their purposes.

Application	Purpose
Microsoft Word	Word processing
Microsoft Excel	Financial analysis
Microsoft Access	Database
Microsoft Explorer	Internet browser
Microsoft Outlook	Email and contact manager
QuickBooks Pro	Accounting software

Application software must match the computer operating system software. Therefore, you will often find multiple versions of the same software for installation with particular operating software.

Accounting Software

Accounting software is application software that automates manual accounting procedures. This software is normally organized by activities with each activity representing a specific functional area of accounting such as customer activities or vendor activities. QBP segregates accounting activities into company (general journal entries), customer (sales, accounts receivable, and cash receipts), vendor (purchases, accounts payable, and cash disbursements), employee (payroll), and banking (deposits and checks) activities. A visual depiction of these activities is illustrated in Chapter 3 under the topic that discusses data integration.

DOWNLOADING AND OPENING DATA FILES

In this text, you will work with the following data files designed by the author. *(Note: There is an online video available for this topic.)* These data files are downloaded from the textbook **Website** at ***www.pearsonhighered.com/brunsdon/***. The following table lists when to use a data file.

Chapter	**Data File Name for Chapter**	**Data File Name for Practice Set**
Chapter 1	QB2012_Chp1_Stud	
Chapter 2	QB2012_Chp2_Stud	QB2012_Chp2_Stud
Chapter 3	QB2012_Chp3_Stud	QB2012_Chp3_PracSet_Stud
Chapter 4	QB2012_Chp4_Stud	QB2012_Chp4_PracSet_Stud
Chapter 5	QB2012_Chp5_Stud	QB2012_Chp5_PracSet_Stud
Chapter 6	QB2012_Chp6_Stud	QB2012_Chp6_PracSet_Stud
Chapter 7	QB2012_Chp7_Stud	QB2012_Chp7_PracSet_Stud
Chapter 8	QB2012_Chp8_Stud	QB2012_Chp8_PracSet_Stud
Chapter 9	QB2012_Chp9_Stud	QB2012_Chp9_PracSet_Stud
Chapter 10	QB2012_Chp10_Stud	QB2012_Chp10_PracSet_Stud
Chapter 11	QB2012_Chp11_Stud	QB2012_Chp11_PracSet_Stud
Chapter 12	You create a new data file	You use the data file you create
Project1	QB2012_Proj_1_Stud	
Project1	QB2012_Proj_2_Stud	

Steps to Downloading and Opening Data Files

1. Begin by downloading the data files from the textbook Website. Open your browser and type **www.pearsonhighered.com/brunsdon/**.

2. Click the **Student Data Files** link for the Learning QuickBooks 2012 textbook. Your browser will prompt you to save a file. Choose the **Save as** option so you can choose where to save the file.

   We recommend saving the downloaded file on the Desktop so you can easily locate it. To save in this location, click the **Desktop** icon on the left pane of the **Save As** window as illustrated next.

Figure 1:1

Click **Save** and a single compressed file is placed on your Desktop. This compressed file contains all the data files used in the text.

Close your browser window. You will next unzip the downloaded file.

To unzip the downloaded file, use your mouse to right click on the file saved to your desktop. Click **Extract All**.

The window illustrated in Figure 1:2 opens. You will now choose where to extract the files.

If your instructor provided a path for saving the files, enter this path in the field noted on the illustration.

If your instructor did not provide a path, we recommend using one of the following paths:

For **Windows Vista** users, enter:

C:\Users\Public\Documents\Intuit\QuickBooks\Company Files\

For **Windows 7** users, enter:

C:\Users\Public\Public Documents\Intuit\QuickBooks\Company Files\

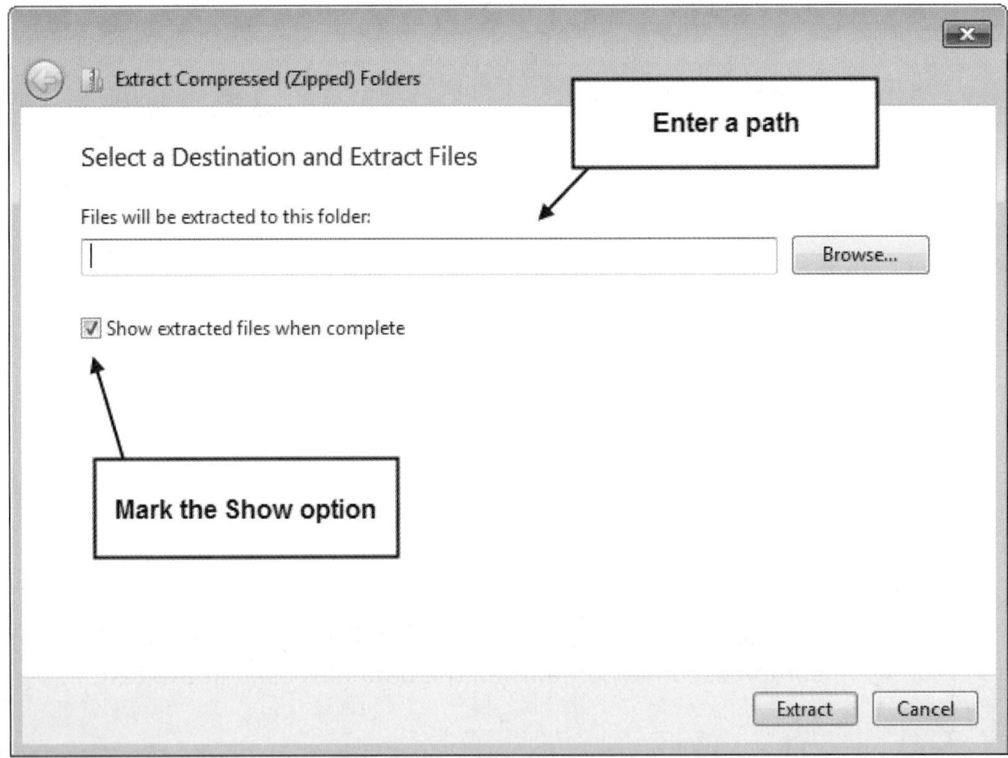

Figure 1:2

Click to mark the option that shows extracted files after extracting. Click **Extract**.

When finished, compare the files that were extracted to the list of files provided in the previous table. Close the window when finished and move to the next step.

3. You are now ready to open a data file in QuickBooks. **NOTE: BEFORE PROCEEDING, VERIFY THAT QUICKBOOKS IS INSTALLED ON YOUR COMPUTER. INSTRUCTIONS FOR INSTALLING QUICKBOOKS ARE LOCATED IN APPENDIX A.**

Begin by opening QuickBooks. You can do this by either double clicking the **icon** on your desktop (Figure 1:3) or by clicking the **Start** button on your computer, pointing to **All Programs** or **Programs**, and pointing to **QuickBooks** to select **QuickBooks Premier - Accountant Edition 2012.**

Figure 1:3

4. The first time you open QuickBooks, the software opens a window containing an **Express Start** button opens. This window offers to help you set up a new company. You will be opening one of the sample companies, so click **x** on the top right corner of the window to close it.

   Click **OK** if a window opens to explain how the software uses your internet connection.

   The following window now opens. Click the **Open or restore an existing company** button.

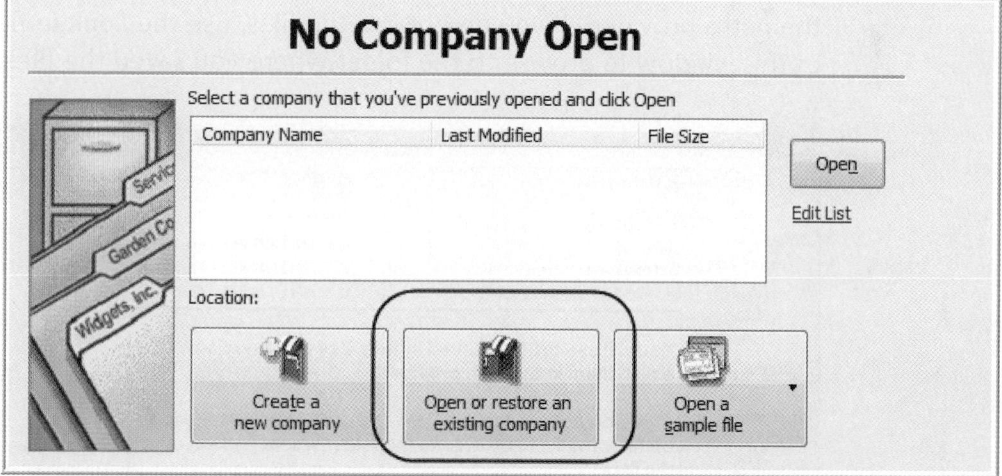

Figure 1:4

5. In the following window, verify that the **Open a company file** option is marked. Click **Next**.

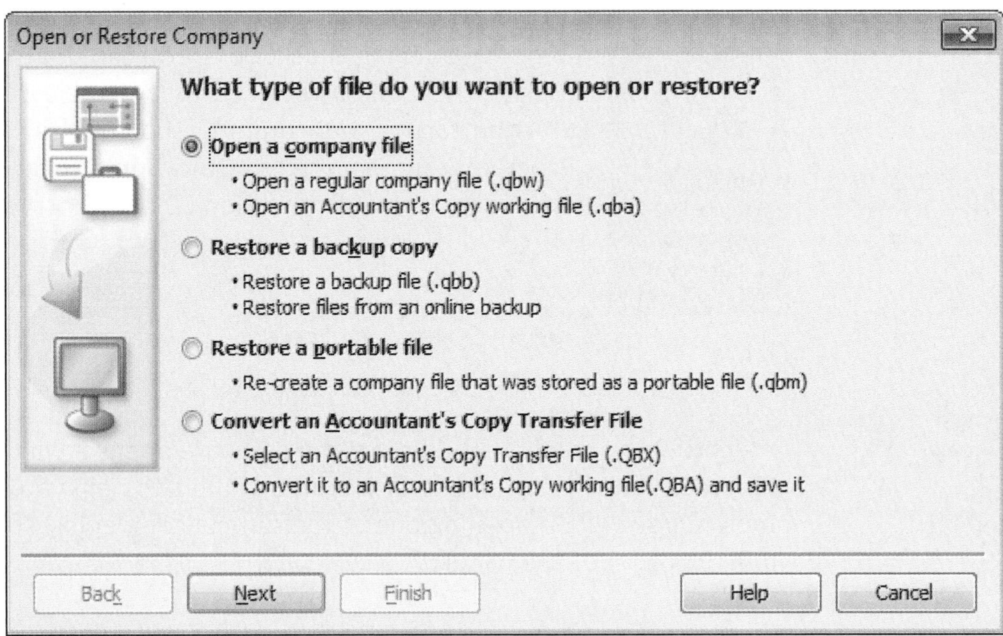

Figure 1:5

6. The **Open a Company** window opens. (See Figure 1:6.)

   You will see the files saved in **Step 2** of this exercise if you saved them in one of the paths provided. If you do not see the files, use the **Look in** field at the top of this window to browse to the folder where you saved the files.

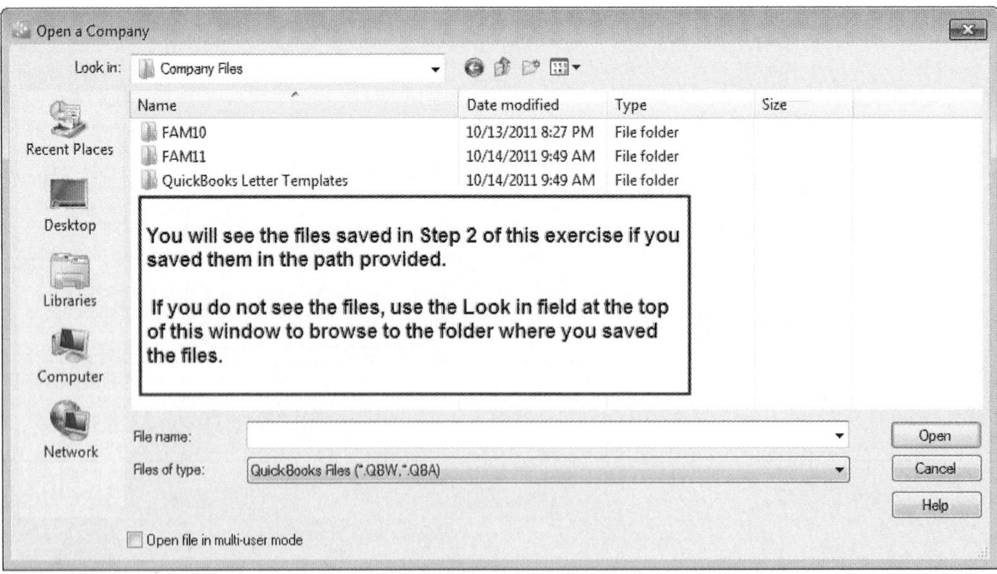

Figure 1:6

7. Click on the file named **QB2012_Chp1_Stud** to select it. Click **Open**.
   If you just installed QuickBooks, you may be prompted to register the software. Verify that you have an Internet connection before beginning registration. Follow the onscreen prompts to complete registration.

   You may be prompted to set up an external accountant user as illustrated next. Mark the **Don't show this again** option and click **No**.

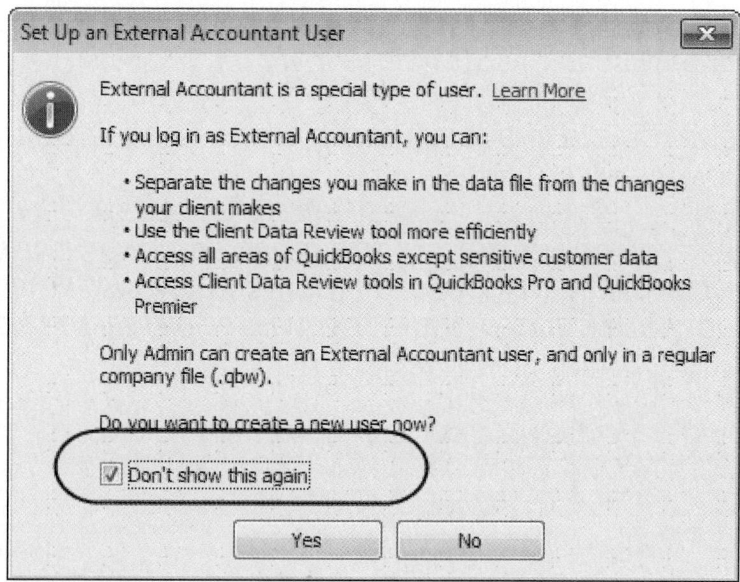

Figure 1:7

8. The **Accountant Center** is set to open each time you open a company. This center is new in 2012 and is only available in the Accountant Edition. If you do not want the center to open in the future, click to turn off the **Show Accountant Center when opening a company file** option.

   Close the center by clicking the **x** in the top right hand corner of the window.

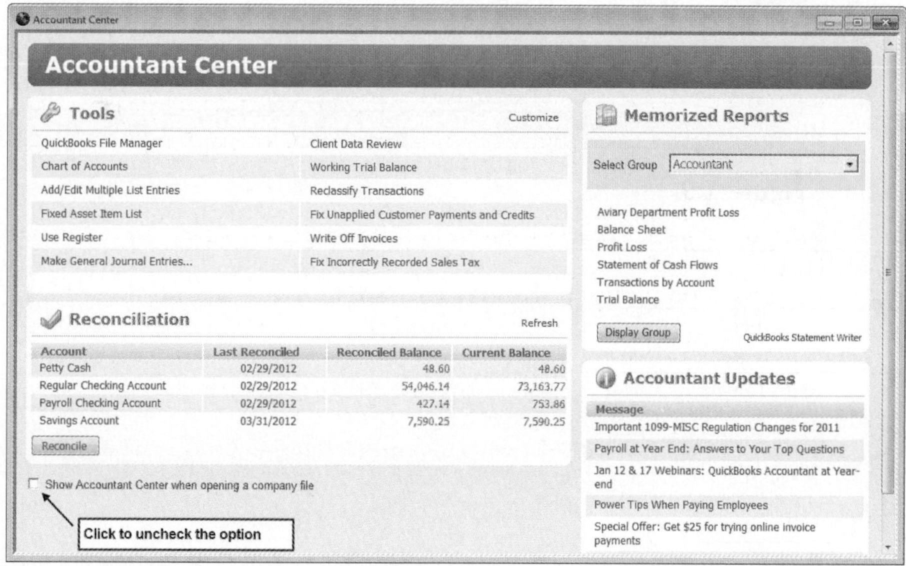

Figure 1:8

9. The **Accountant** edition of the software offers features not available to users of the **Pro** edition. This textbook focuses on the Pro edition, so we will instruct you to **toggle** to that edition at the beginning of each chapter. *(Note: Appendix F discusses some of the features available only in the Accountant edition.)*

TOGGLING THE SOFTWARE TO THE PRO EDITION

To toggle the software, click the **File** menu and choose **Toggle to Another Edition** as illustrated next.

NOTE: IF YOU EXIT THE SOFTWARE, YOU MUST AGAIN TOGGLE TO THE PRO EDITION UPON RETURNING.

NOTE: IF YOU DO NOT TOGGLE TO THE PRO EDITION, THERE IS NO EFFECT ON YOUR DATA. HOWEVER, SOME OF THE INSTRUCTIONS PROVIDED AND THE WINDOWS ILLUSTRATED IN THE TEXT WILL BE DIFFERENT FROM WHAT YOU EXPERIENCE IN THE SOFTWARE.

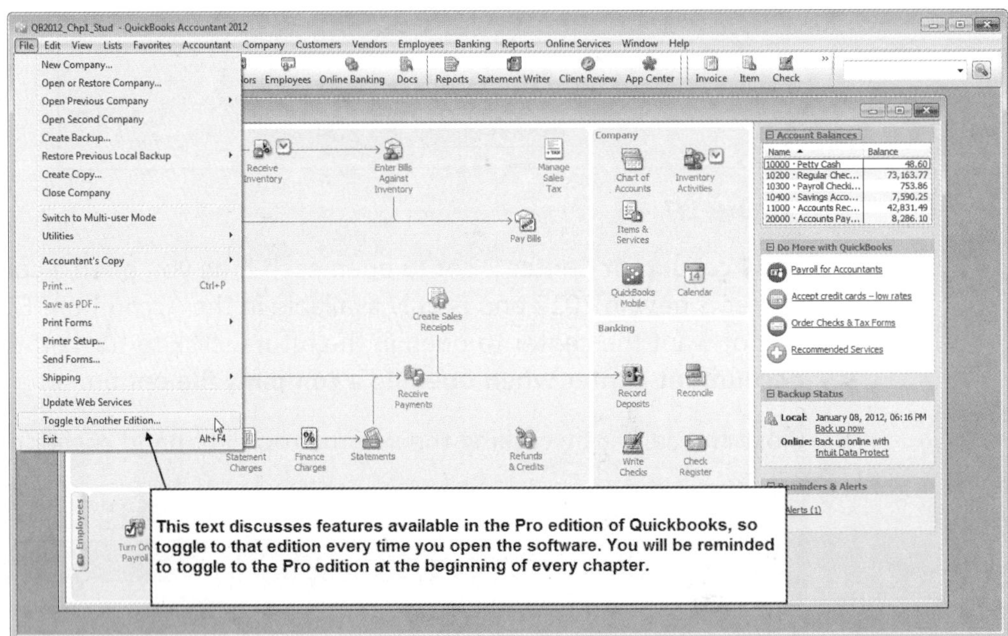

Figure 1:9

10. Click to select the **QuickBooks Pro** option as illustrated next. Click **Next**.

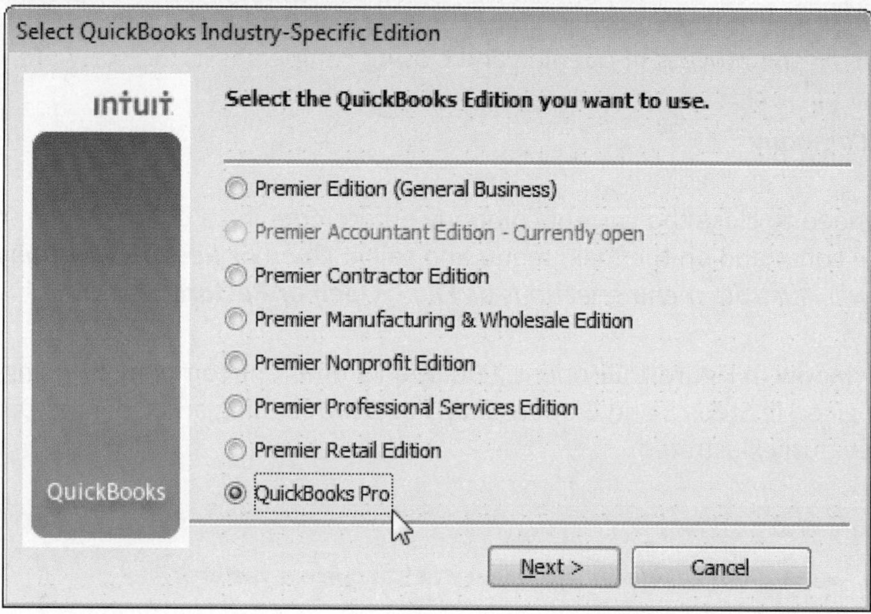

Figure 1:10

Finally, click **Toggle** (not illustrated). If prompted to back up your data, click **No**. Backing up your data is discussed later in the chapter.

The software closes and reopens in the Pro edition. You will always use the **Pro** edition in this text unless you are working in Appendix F.

Opening and Closing Companies

We now discuss the process of opening and closing companies in the software.

Opening a Company

You do not need to close the current company before opening a different one. You can simply click the ***File*** command on the main menu and select ***Open or Restore Company.*** *(Note: In the future, we will illustrate menu selections as **File>>Open or Restore Company**.)*

When the window in Figure 1:11 opens, you open a different company by using the same procedures given in Steps 5 and 6 of the Steps to Downloading and Opening Data Files exercise previously illustrated.

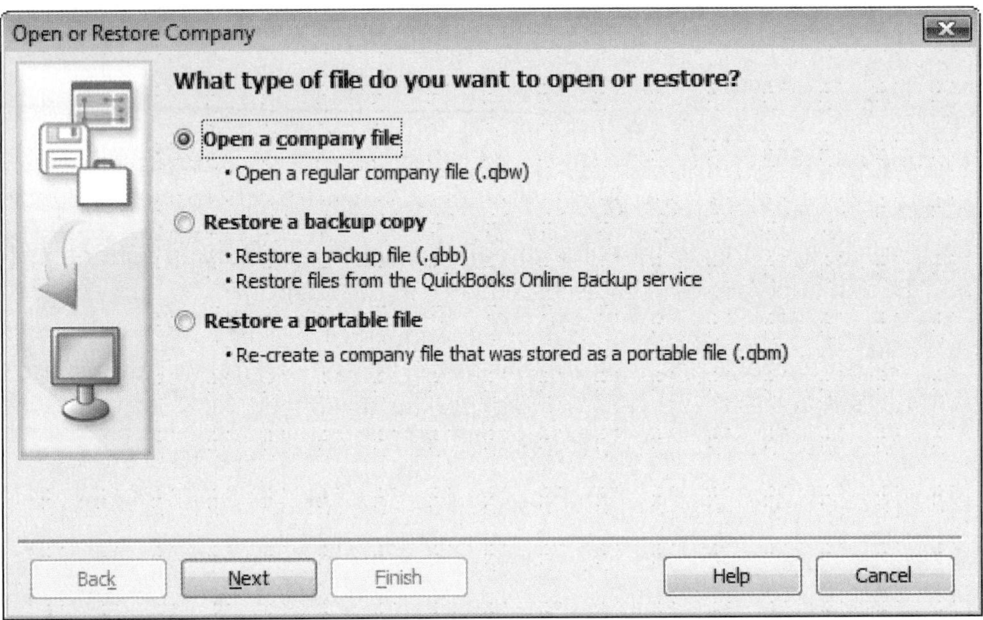

Figure 1:11

Opening Multiple Companies

You can also open two companies at the same time. This is done by opening the first company, which is called the Primary company. You then choose ***File>>Open Second Company*** on the main menu to open a Secondary company. The Secondary company is opened in a new window and some features of the software are restricted. None of these restrictions will affect transaction entry and reporting in the Secondary company. Please use caution if using this feature. Always make sure you are working in the correct company file.

Note: You may open a company and receive the message illustrated in Figure 1:12 or a similar message prompting you to update your software. Clicking Yes to update the software requires an active Internet connection, so verify that you are connected to the Internet before choosing to update the software. You can always click No and mark the option to turn off future messages without affecting tasks performed in the text.

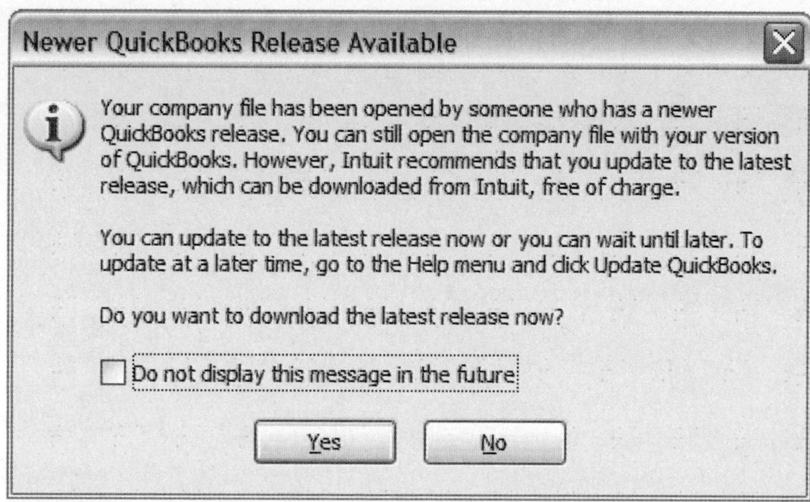

Figure 1:12

Closing a Company

To close the open company, click ***File>>Close Company*** on the main menu. QBP closes the company and opens the window previously illustrated in Figure 1:5. You can then either open a different company or exit the software. As previously discussed, it is not necessary to close a company before opening a different company.

THE QUICKBOOKS DESKTOP

You currently have the **QB2012_Chp1_Stud** company open. (*Note: You will see this name at the top of the QuickBooks window.)*

The desktop for this company is illustrated in Figure 1:13. Note that the **Home** page is open. If you do not see the Home page, click the **Home** icon on the Icon bar.

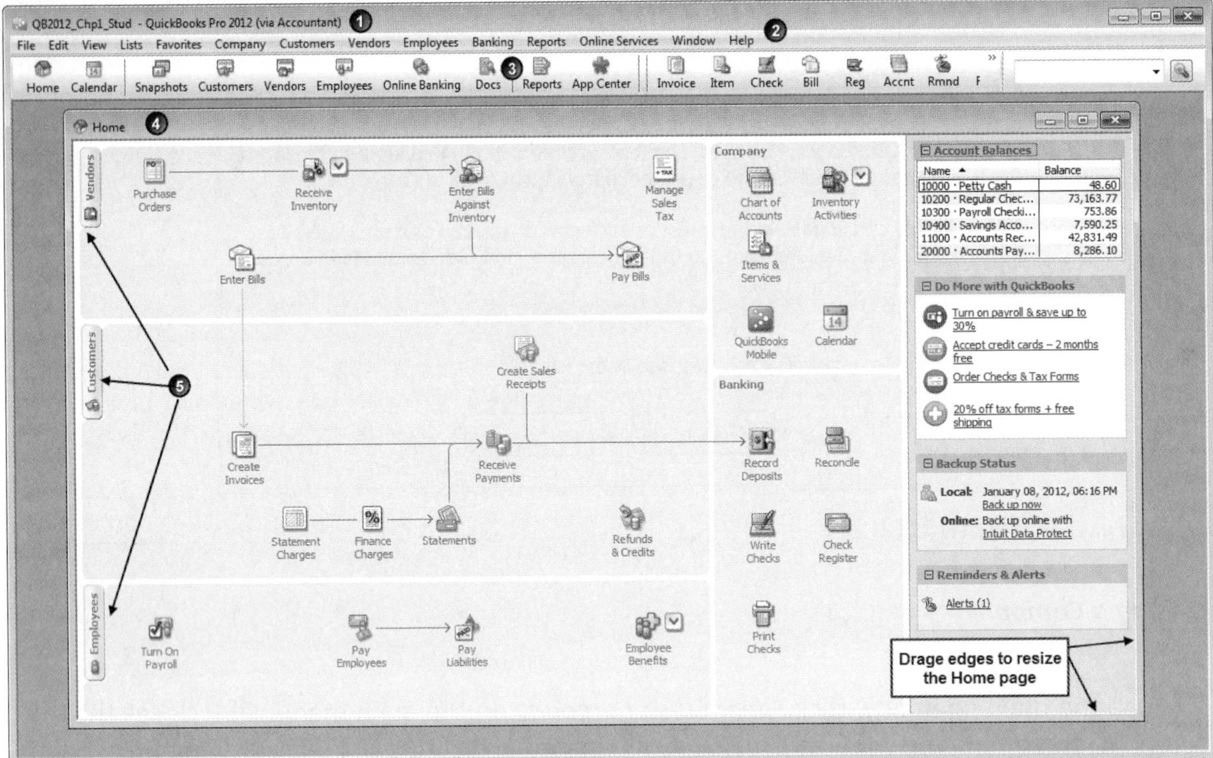

Figure 1:13

Figure 1:13 has been labeled for you to easily identify elements of the desktop. The table that follows explains these elements.

QUICKBOOKS DESKTOP ELEMENTS		
Section	**Name**	**Description**
1	Title Bar	Lists the name of the open company and shows that the company is open in QuickBooks Pro (via Accountant). ***This is where you verify the open company and verify that the software is toggled to the Pro edition.***
2	Main Menu	Menus for executing QBP commands.
3	Icon Bar	Quick access to frequently used tasks. Adding and deleting icons from this bar is explained later in the chapter.
4	Home Page	Icon access to vendor, customer, employee, company, and banking tasks with the workflow of tasks illustrated. Customizing the Home page is explained later in the chapter.
5	Center Icons	Icons for opening the Vendors, Customers, and Employees centers.

Before using the software, it also helps to understand using the main menu. The next table provides information on Main Menu commands.

MAIN MENU	
Menu Command	**Description**
File	Basic operations such as opening and closing companies, data backup, and recovery operations, printing, and printer setup.
Edit	Data manipulation features such as cut, copy, paste, delete, and undo. Submenus activate based on the task being performed. A calculator is also found here.
View	Submenus for displaying certain features on the desktop and for customizing the Icon Bar.
Lists	Submenus for viewing a list of the chart of accounts, inventory items, sales tax codes, payroll items, and memorized transactions.

MAIN MENU	
Menu Command	**Description**
Favorites	Menu for customizing links to frequently performed tasks.
Company	Submenus for company tasks such as entering company information, closing the accounting period, establishing budgets, and setting reminders and alerts.
Customers	Submenus for customer tasks such as invoicing, receiving payments, and printing customer statements.
Vendors	Submenus for vendor tasks such as entering billings, remitting payment, and managing inventory activities.
Employees	Submenus for employee tasks such as creating paychecks, entering time cards, and paying payroll liabilities.
Banking	Submenus for banking tasks such as making deposits, writing checks, and reconciling bank statements.
Reports	Submenus for printing reports.
Window	Submenus for arranging and activating open task windows when multi-tasking.
Help	Submenus for searching help files, updating the software, and viewing the license agreement and software version.

We next provide more information on using the Home page. (See Figure 1:14.)

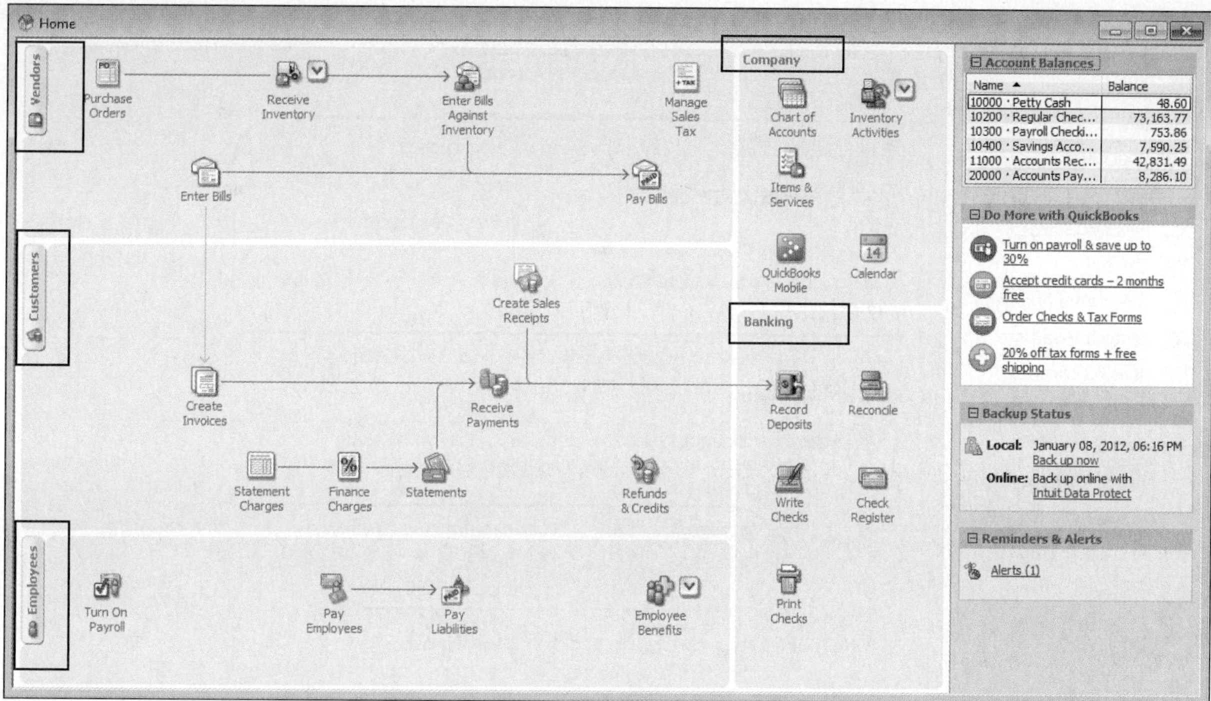

Figure 1:14

The **Home** page is divided into five distinct sections, namely **Vendors, Customers, Employees, Company,** and **Banking**. Each section contains icons for accessing specific tasks performed in that activity.

Arrows on the page depict the normal workflow of tasks. Focus on the **Vendors** section where you may begin a vendor transaction by entering a purchase order. After entering the order, you continue processing it by recording a vendor receipt or a bill. Only after recording the bill can you pay the vendor. The second row of icons shows that you may skip the purchase order step and begin a vendor transaction by entering a bill. Once again, the vendor is paid after recording the bill.

The arrows also depict the task workflow between activities. Notice that vendor bills will interface with customer invoices. In Chapter 4 we illustrate the interrelationship between customer invoices and vendor bills when you invoice a customer for vendor charges.

The **Home** page also displays checking and accounts receivable balances on the right. You can change the presence of certain icons on the Home page by customizing company preferences. To view company preferences, click **Edit** on the main menu and select **Preferences**, opening the window illustrated next. Click **Desktop View** on the left and click the **Company Preferences** tab on the right. (See Figure 1:15.)

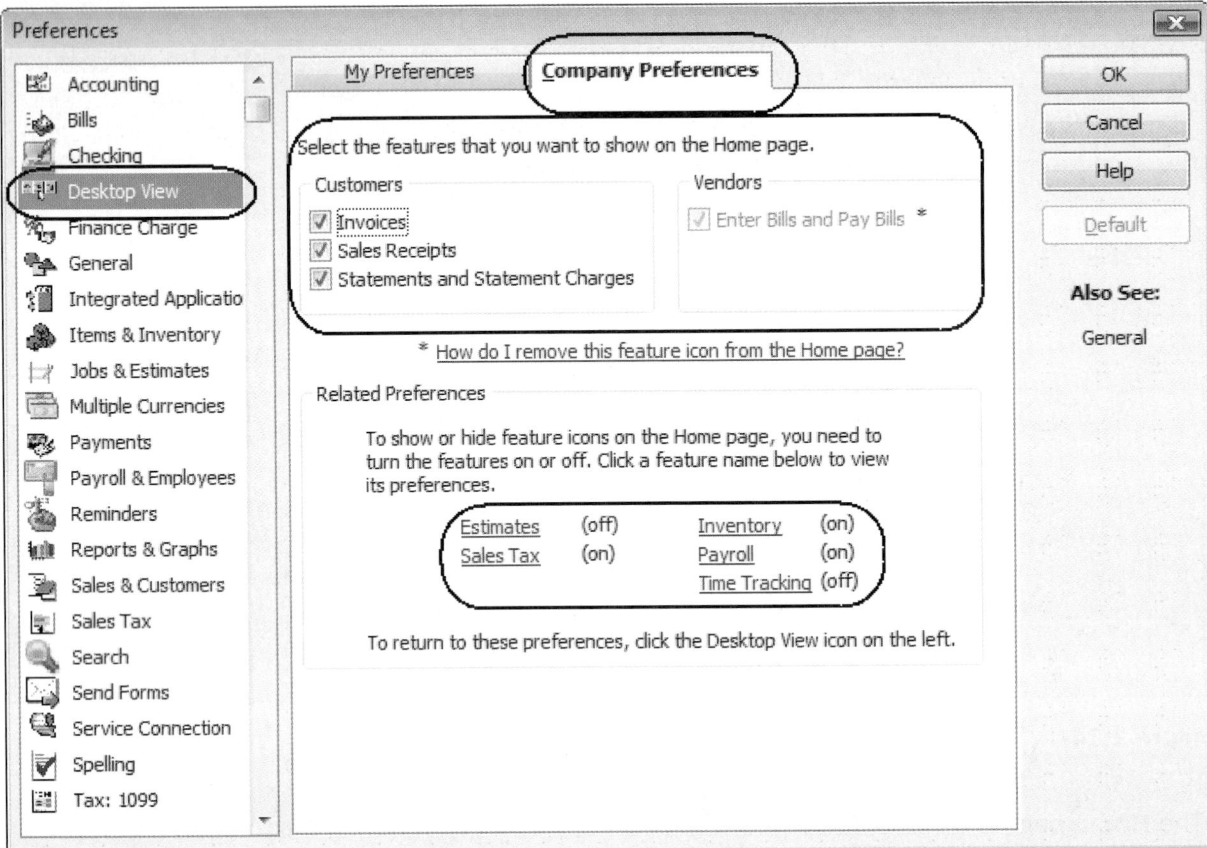

Figure 1:15

The **Related Preferences** section on this tab is used for turning on or off certain features in the software. For instance, you could turn on Estimates to begin using this feature. If this feature is turned on, the icon used to access it will be placed on the Home page. Click **OK** to exit this window.

Home page icons make it easier to access frequently performed tasks. However, as illustrated in Figure 1:15, you can only activate icons for the tasks listed under Related Preferences.

If you want a shortcut to frequently performed tasks that are not placed on the Home page, you can add shortcuts to the Favorites menu. In addition, you can add shortcuts to the Icon Bar, which is the subject of our next topic.

CUSTOMIZE THE ICON BAR

To begin customizing the Icon Bar, click ***View>>Customize Icon Bar*** on the main menu to open the window illustrated in Figure 1:16. Scroll to the top of the **Icon Bar Content** list.

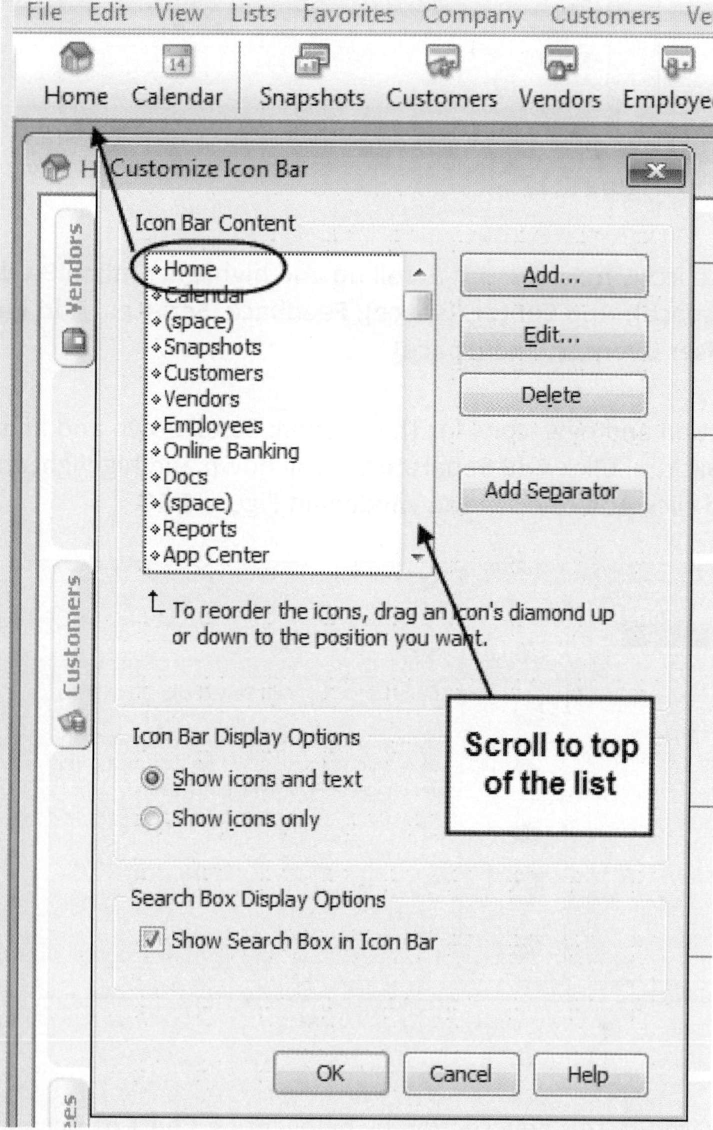

Figure 1:16

Notice that Home is first on the Icon Bar Content list and this matches the first icon appearing on the Icon Bar. Thus, this list displays the names and order of icons on the Icon Bar.

Let us change the ordering of the Check and Bill icons. Scroll down the list to locate the Bill icon. Using the mouse, click the diamond in front of **Bill** and drag it until a hash line appears above **Check**. (See Figure 1:17.) Release the mouse and the ordering changes.

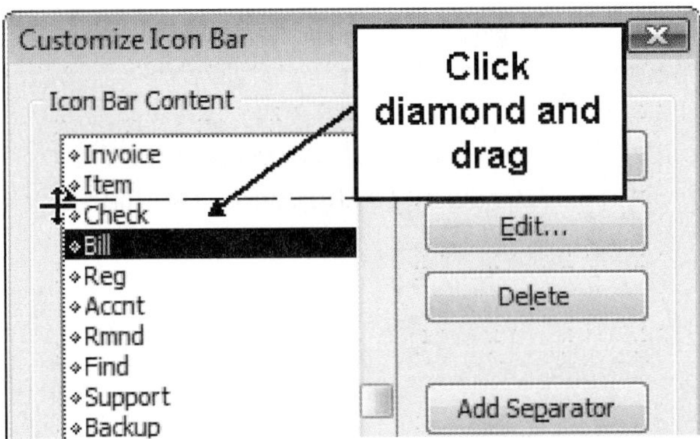

Figure 1:17

You will next remove icons from the bar. Scroll up and highlight **Online Banking**. Click **Delete**. Next delete **Docs, (space), App Center, (space), Feedback, Services, Add Payroll, Cards & eChecks, (space), User Licenses,** and **(space)**.

Now add a new section and new icons for this section. Scroll down and highlight the last item on the list named **Backup**. Click **Add Separator**. Scroll down and highlight the **(space)** separator you just added, and click **Add** to open the window in Figure 1:18.

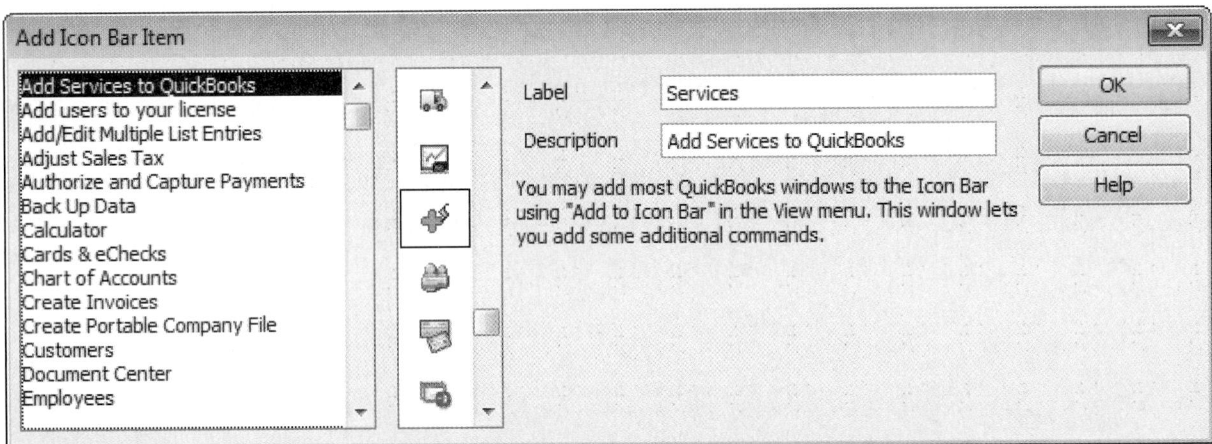

Figure 1:18

Now add the **Accnt** icon to this new section by highlighting **Chart of Accounts** on the list to the left. Notice that the icon to the right jumped to the picture for this item. The **Label** name will be Accnt. (See Figure 1:19.) Click **OK**. Click **OK** again to close the Customize Icon Bar window.

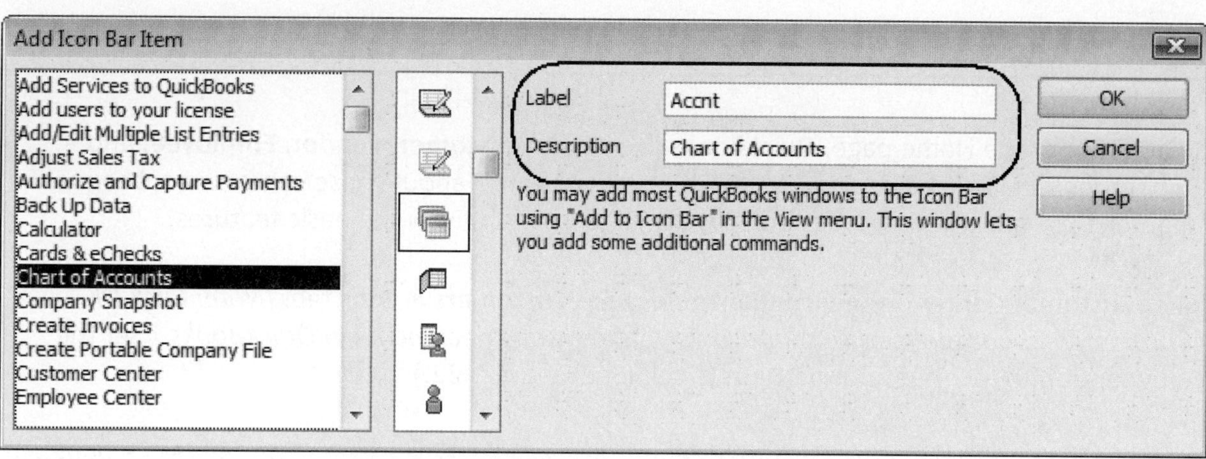

Figure 1:19

There is a different method for adding report shortcuts to the Icon Bar. Select ***Reports>>Memorized Reports>>Accountant>>Profit & Loss*** on the main menu. This action opens the income statement (not illustrated).

Now add the income statement to the Icon Bar. Click ***View>>Add "Profit & Loss" to Icon Bar*** on the main menu to open the window illustrated in Figure 1:20.

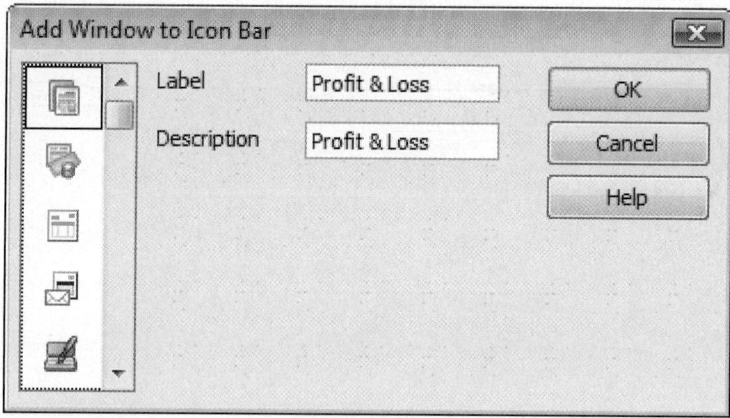

Figure 1:20

Change the **Label** to "P&L," click **OK**, and the report is added to the Icon Bar. Click **X** on the report to close it. Your Icon Bar will now resemble the bar in Figure 1:21.

Figure 1:21

QuickBooks Centers

In addition to the Home page, QuickBooks provides a **Customer, Vendor, Employee,** and **Report** center for managing activities. You will learn more about these centers in subsequent chapters. For now, we will focus on activating a center and viewing basic features.

Click **Customer Center** on the **Icon Bar.** Select the **Customers & Jobs** tab. *(Note: Click OK if prompted about the feature that allows you to attach documents in QuickBooks.)* Set the **Show** option to Invoices and the **Date** to All. (See Figure 1:22.)

(Note: You can also open the Customer Center by clicking Customers *on the Home page.)*

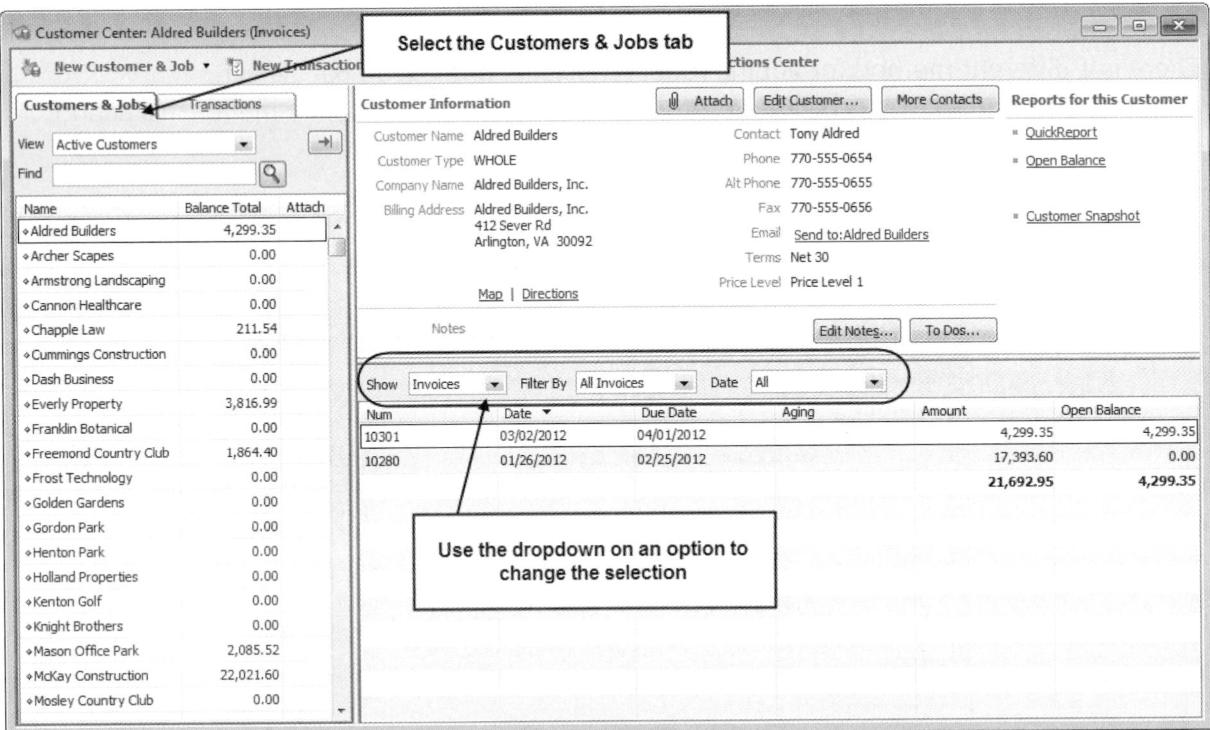

Figure 1:22

This center has a **Customers & Jobs** tab and a **Transactions** tab.

The **Customers & Jobs** tab lists customer accounts with balances to the left. Aldred Builders is the company currently highlighted on the left, so Aldred's account information and transactions appear on the right.

Transactions listed at the bottom are filtered by setting the **Show, Filter By**, and **Date** options. Figure 1:22 shows **Invoices** filtered by **All Invoices** on **All** dates. Option filters are changed by making a selection from the dropdown list.

IMPORTANT: QBP uses your computer system date to determine the current fiscal period. This applies not only when displaying transactions in centers, but also when producing reports. Hence, if your computer system date is in 2012, choosing a Date option of This Fiscal Year displays transactions recorded in 2012. However, if the system date is after 2012, you need to use the Date option of All when viewing transactions in a center or set a specific date range when viewing information on a report.

Change the **Show** option to **All Transactions**, keeping the **Date** option set to **All**. Also, if the transactions are not sorted by Type, click the column header to sort as shown. (See Figure 1:23.) You now see a payment on the list of transactions.

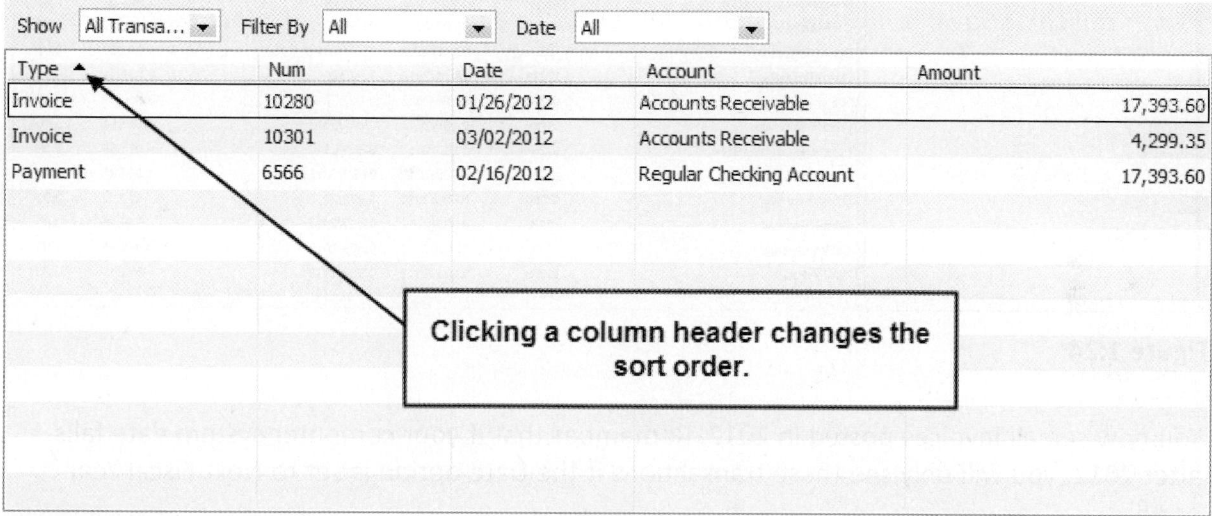

Figure 1:23

Next look at information displayed on the **Transactions** tab. Click this tab and select **Invoices** on the left so that the center displays sales invoices for all customers.

Make sure that the dropdown option for **Filter By** is **All Invoices** and the **Date** is filtered to **All**. (See Figure 1:24.)

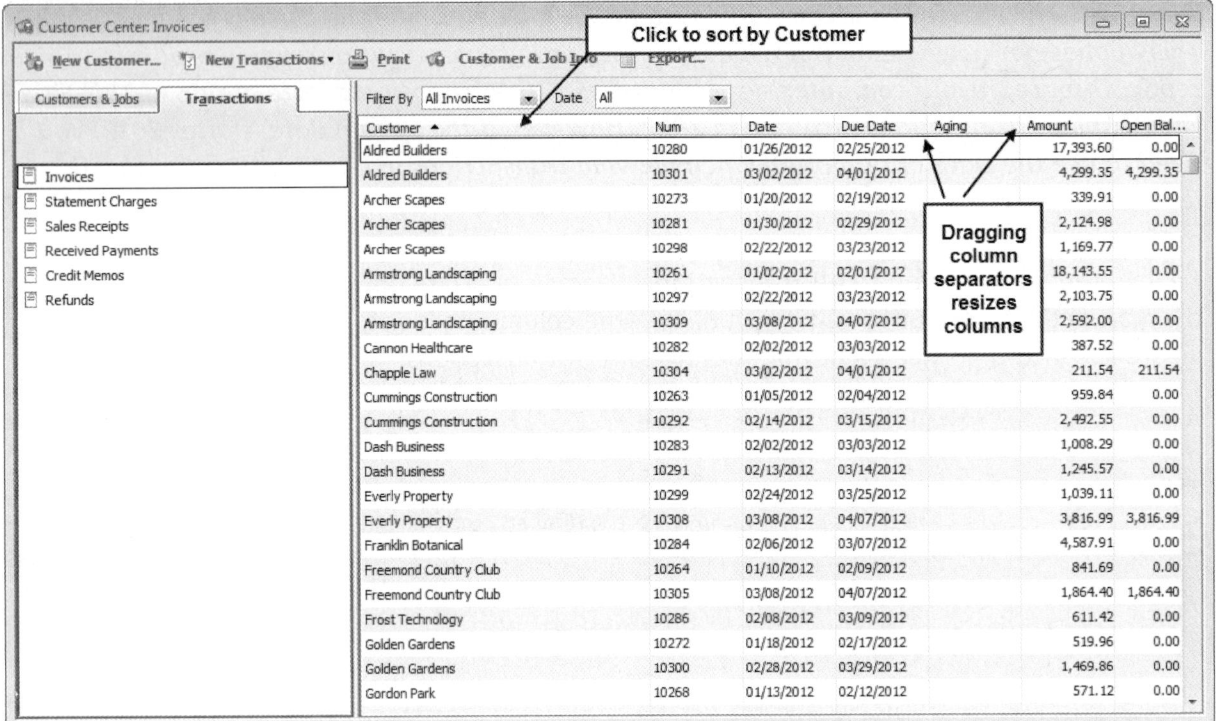

Customer	Num	Date	Due Date	Aging	Amount	Open Bal...
Aldred Builders	10280	01/26/2012	02/25/2012		17,393.60	0.00
Aldred Builders	10301	03/02/2012	04/01/2012		4,299.35	4,299.35
Archer Scapes	10273	01/20/2012	02/19/2012		339.91	0.00
Archer Scapes	10281	01/30/2012	02/29/2012		2,124.98	0.00
Archer Scapes	10298	02/22/2012	03/23/2012		1,169.77	0.00
Armstrong Landscaping	10261	01/02/2012	02/01/2012		18,143.55	0.00
Armstrong Landscaping	10297	02/22/2012	03/23/2012		2,103.75	0.00
Armstrong Landscaping	10309	03/08/2012	04/07/2012		2,592.00	0.00
Cannon Healthcare	10282	02/02/2012	03/03/2012		387.52	0.00
Chapple Law	10304	03/02/2012	04/01/2012		211.54	211.54
Cummings Construction	10263	01/05/2012	02/04/2012		959.84	0.00
Cummings Construction	10292	02/14/2012	03/15/2012		2,492.55	0.00
Dash Business	10283	02/02/2012	03/03/2012		1,008.29	0.00
Dash Business	10291	02/13/2012	03/14/2012		1,245.57	0.00
Everly Property	10299	02/24/2012	03/25/2012		1,039.11	0.00
Everly Property	10308	03/08/2012	04/07/2012		3,816.99	3,816.99
Franklin Botanical	10284	02/06/2012	03/07/2012		4,587.91	0.00
Freemond Country Club	10264	01/10/2012	02/09/2012		841.69	0.00
Freemond Country Club	10305	03/08/2012	04/07/2012		1,864.40	1,864.40
Frost Technology	10286	02/08/2012	03/09/2012		611.42	0.00
Golden Gardens	10272	01/18/2012	02/17/2012		519.96	0.00
Golden Gardens	10300	02/28/2012	03/29/2012		1,469.86	0.00
Gordon Park	10268	01/13/2012	02/12/2012		571.12	0.00

Figure 1:24

You now see all invoices posted in 2012. Remember that if your computer system date falls after 2012, you will only see these transactions if the Date option is set to Next Fiscal Year or All.

This exercise shows that the **Transactions** tab displays transactions by type and the **Customers & Jobs** tab displays transactions by customer.

Click **X** to close the Customer Center and complete the exercise that follows.

Practice Navigating QuickBooks

1. Click the **Vendors** icon on the **Home** page to open the Vendor Center. (See Figure 1:25.) *(Note: You can also click Vendor Center on the Icon Bar.)* This center operates similarly to the Customer center.

   The **Vendors** tab lists vendors and account balances to the left and filtered vendor information to the right. The **Transactions** tab displays all vendor transactions by type.

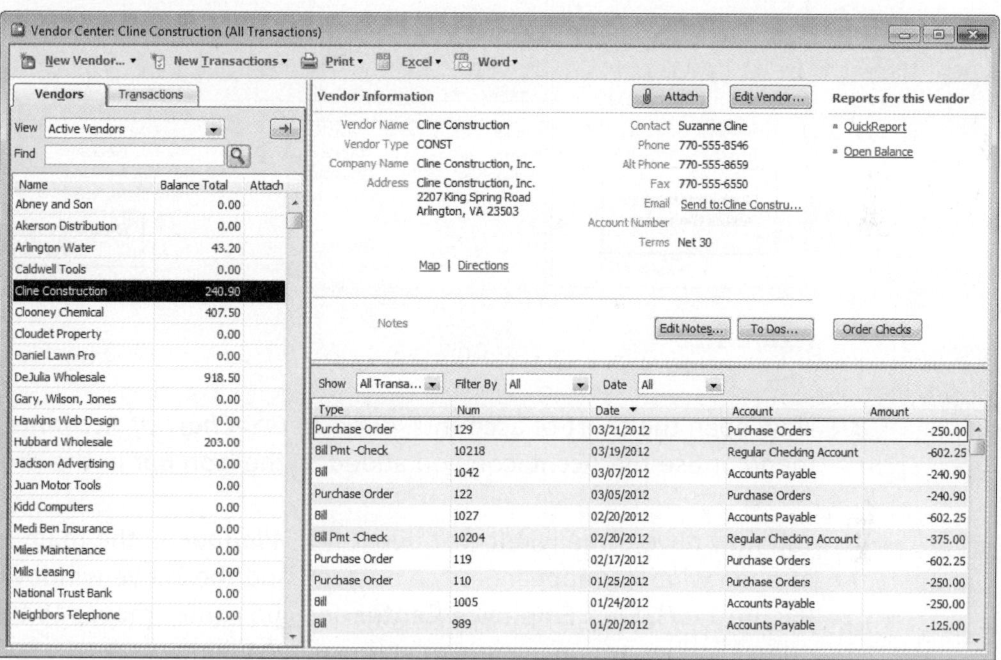

Figure 1:25

2. Click **Employee Center** on the Icon Bar and display the **Employees** tab. (See Figure 1:26.) You can resize a center using the mouse. To resize, place your cursor at the edge of the center until it changes to ⟺. Use the left mouse button and drag to resize. You can also resize sections of the center by dragging the separator bar.

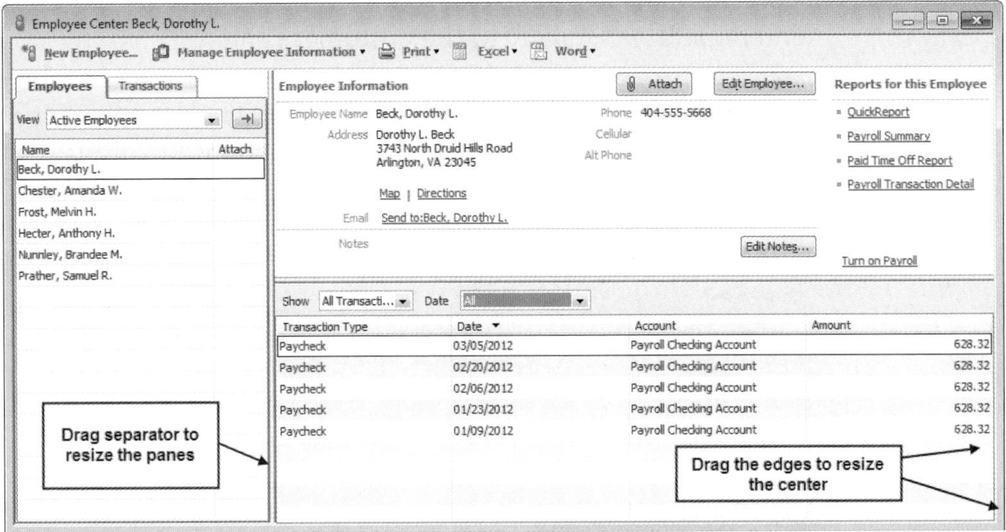

Figure 1:26

3. Now open the chart of accounts. Click ***Lists>>Chart of Accounts*** on the main menu or use the **Accnt** icon you added to the Icon Bar in the previous topic.

4. You now have three windows open. Click ***Window*** on the main menu. The list of open windows appears at the bottom, and the active window is checked (Figure 1:27). Click **Employee Center** and the center moves to the front of all open windows, meaning it is now the active window.

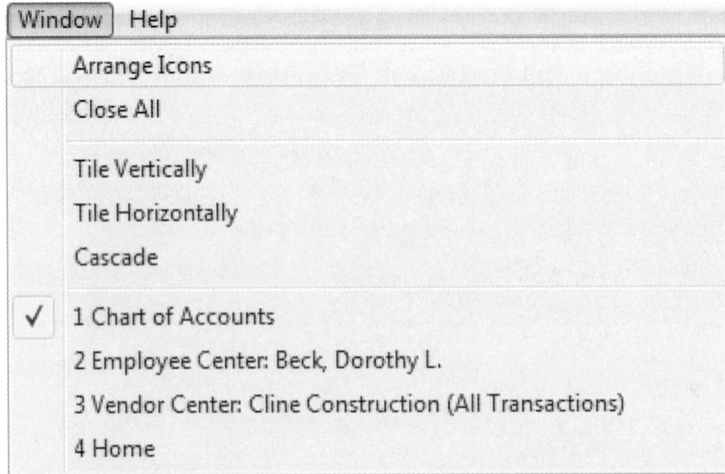

Figure 1:27

5. Click the **Minimize** button on the Employee Center. (See Figure 1:28.)

Figure 1:28

The center drops to the bottom of the screen and appears as illustrated in Figure 1:29. *(Note: It may be hidden behind the Home page if you are viewing the Home page in full screen.)*

Figure 1:29

The Restore button will reopen the window to its original size. The Maximize button will reopen the window to full screen.

6. Click ***View>Open Window List*** on the main menu and the list illustrated in Figure 1:30 appears to the left.

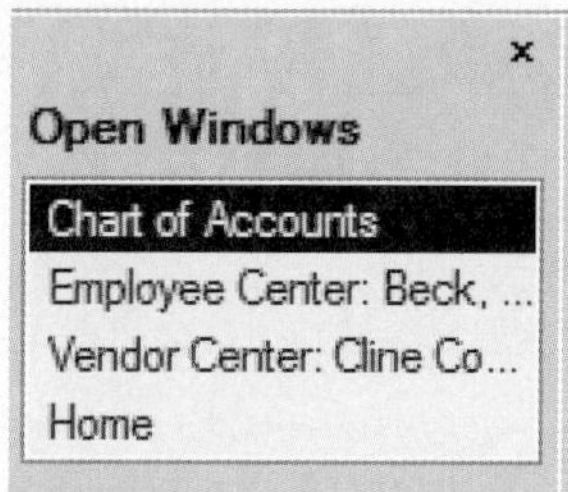

Figure 1:30

Keeping this list open will let you navigate between tasks. A task is activated by clicking it on the list. Clicking **X** will close the Open Windows list.

7. Click **Vendor Center** on the **Open Windows** list and then click **X** to close it. Do the same for the Employee Center and Chart of Accounts. You are now able to multitask in QBP.

Customize Company Names

Before working in a company, you need to customize the company's name to identify QBP reports and other output as yours. To customize the company name, click ***Company>>Company Information*** on the main menu. Refer to Figure 1:31 and add your initials to the **Company Name**.

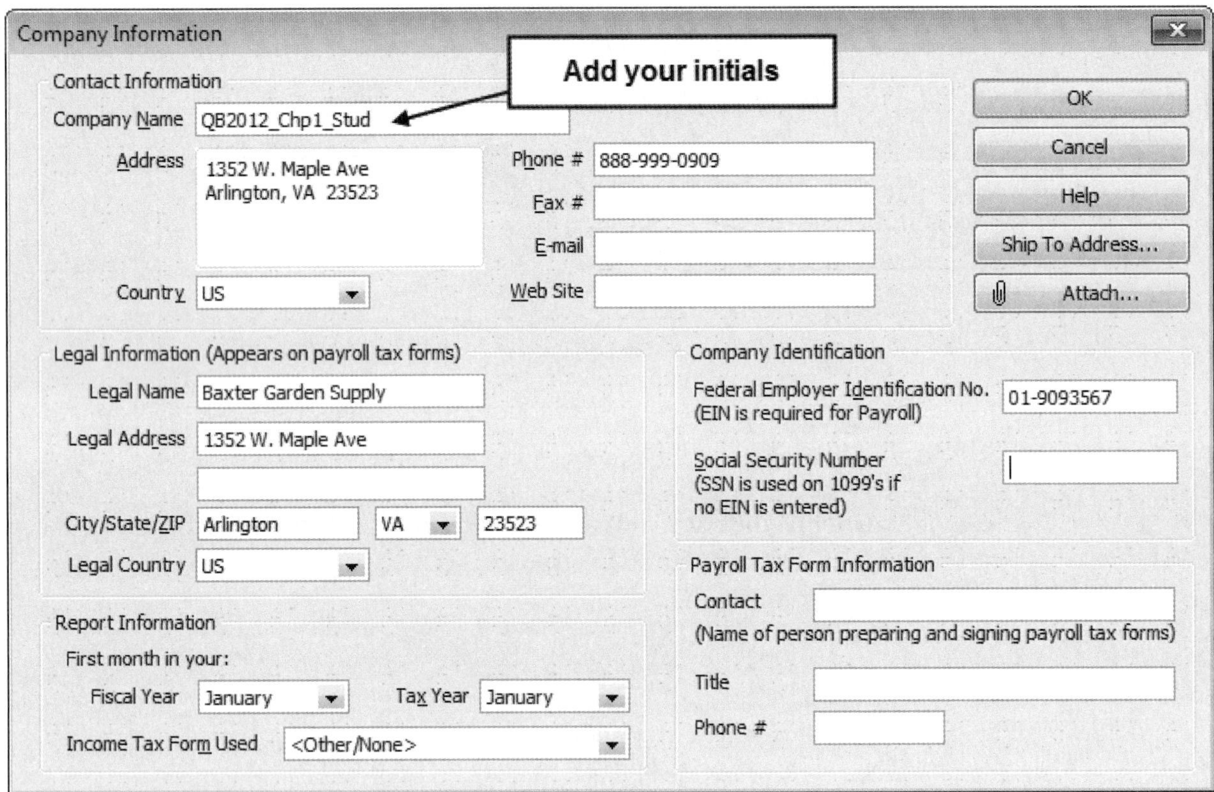

Figure 1:31

Before saving the changes, notice that the window shows the **Fiscal Year** and **Tax Year**. Both years begin in January, meaning that the company is on a calendar year accounting cycle. Click **OK** to save your changes. *(Note: Cancel will close the window without saving changes.)*

QuickBooks Keyboard Shortcuts

Keyboard shortcuts are a method of executing software commands without selecting a command from the menu. You may already be familiar with keyboard shortcuts by using other software applications. QBP sometimes lists the keyboard shortcut alongside the menu command. For instance, click ***Edit*** on the main menu and notice that **Ctrl+C** is the shortcut key for the **Copy** command. To use this shortcut, highlight the text to be copied, press and hold the Ctrl key on your keyboard, and then press the letter "C."

The following table lists frequently used keyboard shortcuts.

Editing Commands	Keyboard Action	Activity Commands	Keyboard Action
Cut highlighted text	Ctrl + X	Open help for the active window	F1
Copy highlighted text	Ctrl + C	Find transaction	Ctrl + F
Paste copied text	Ctrl + V	Create new transaction	Ctrl + N
Undo editing	Ctrl + Z	Open transaction journal	Ctrl + Y
Delete character to right of cursor	Del	Memorize transaction	Ctrl + M
Delete character to left of cursor	Backspace	Open chart of accounts list	Ctrl + A
Delete entire line	Ctrl + Del	Open dropdown list for an item	Ctrl + L
Delete entire transaction	Ctrl + D	Show list	Ctrl + S
Insert a new line	Ctrl + Ins	Open Quick Report for a transaction or to list items	Ctrl + Q
Move to next field	Tab	Print	Ctrl + P
Move to previous field	Shift + Tab		
Move to beginning of field	Home		
Move to end of field	End		
Move up or down a line	Up arrow or down arrow		

Date Shortcuts	Keyboard Action
Today	T
Date calendar	Alt + down arrow
Next day	+
Previous day	–

QuickBooks Help

Help on using QBP is only one click away. The shortcut key **F1** will open the help window pane illustrated in Figure 1:32. You can use the mouse to resize the pane. This window can also be opened by selecting ***Help>>QuickBooks Help*** on the main menu.

In 2012, QuickBooks help is again updated. The Help feature now acts like a web browser with hyperlinks. In addition, the window interacts seamlessly with Intuit's online community, so you can ask questions to other users of the software.

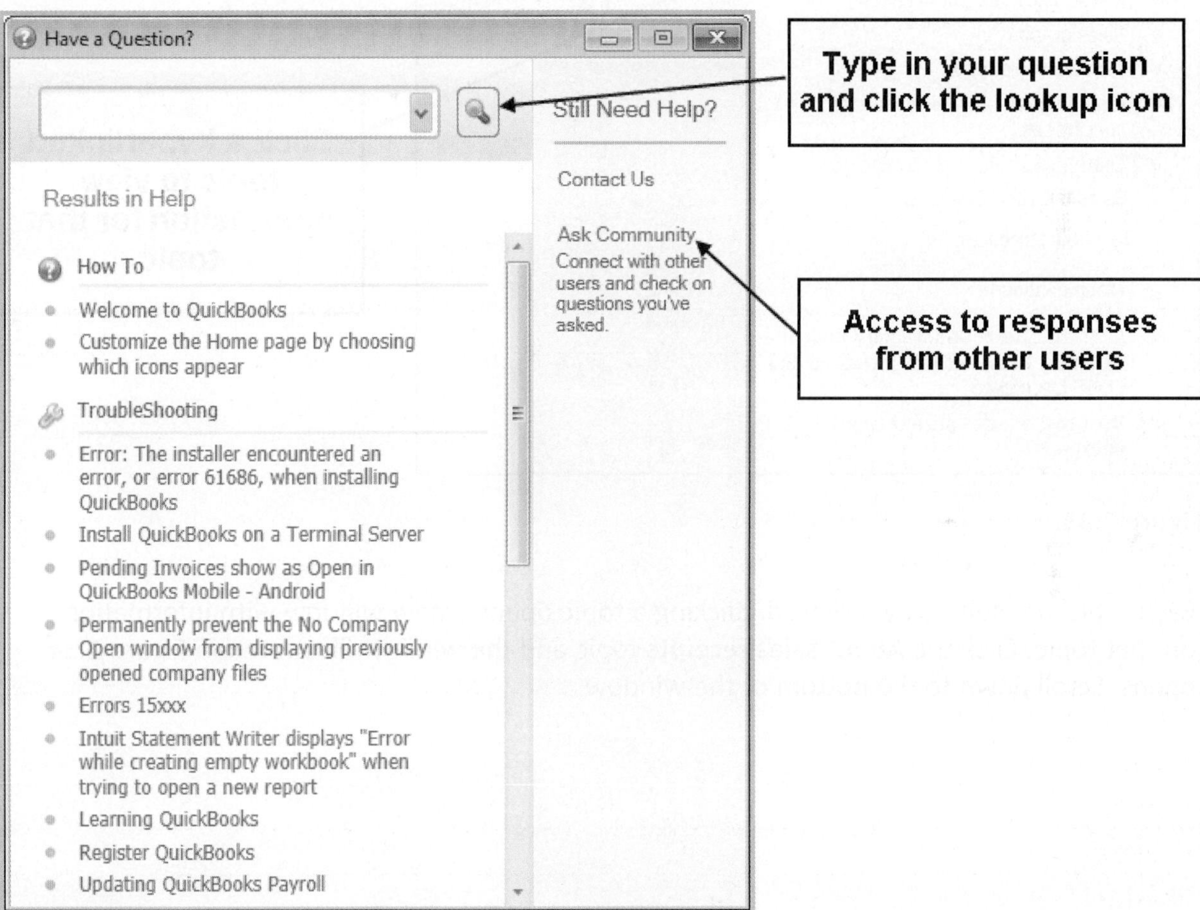

Figure 1:32

Practice using help. Type in **"sales"** and click the **lookup icon**. Figure 1:33 shows the results. Use the scroll bar to view all results.

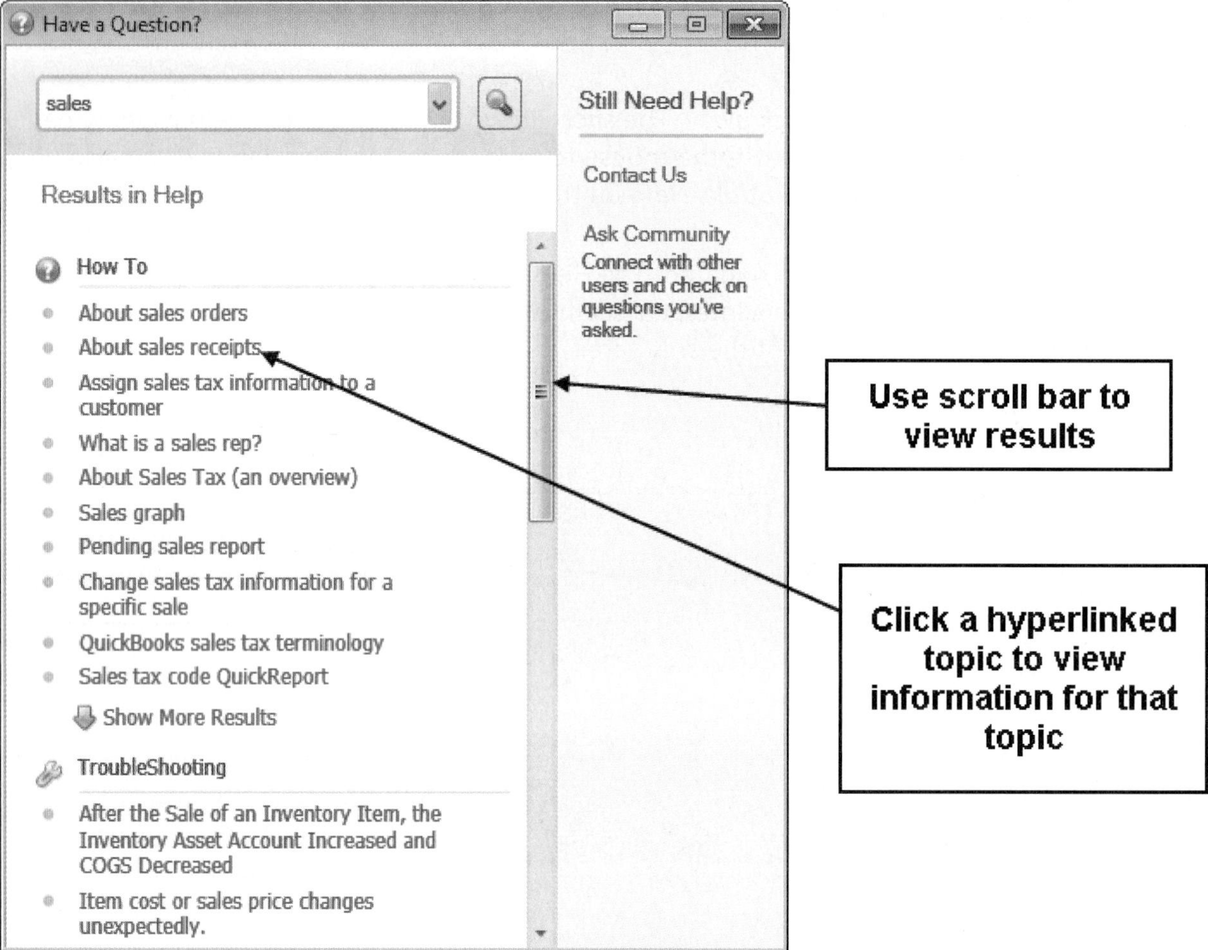

Figure 1:33

Each topic in results is hyperlinked. Clicking a topic opens a new window with information on that topic. Click the **About sales receipts** topic and the window illustrated in Figure 1:34 opens. Scroll down to the bottom of the window.

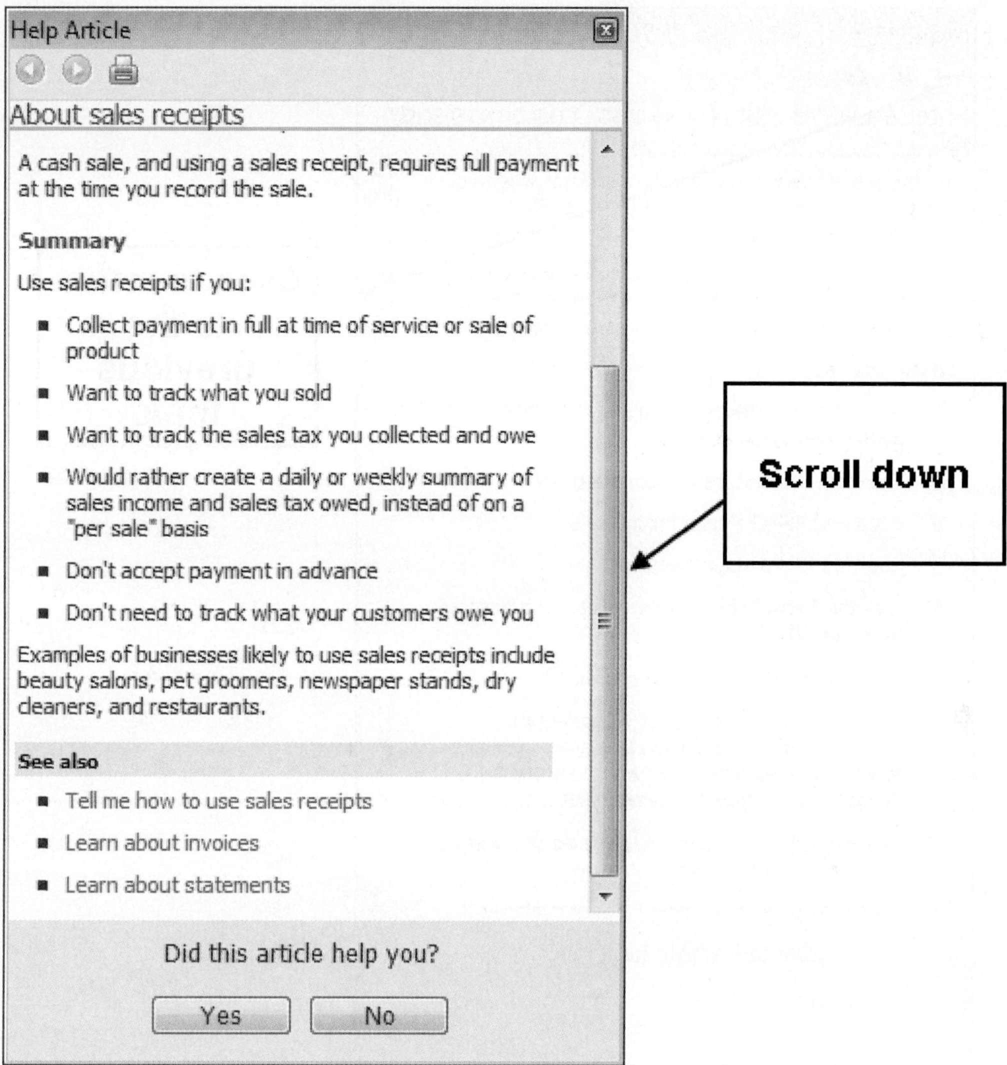

Figure 1:34

Referring to Figure 1:34, click the **Tell me how to use sales receipts** hyperlink to drilldown to specific information on using sales receipts. (See Figure 1:35.) You can move back to the previous topic by clicking the icon indicated on the next illustration.

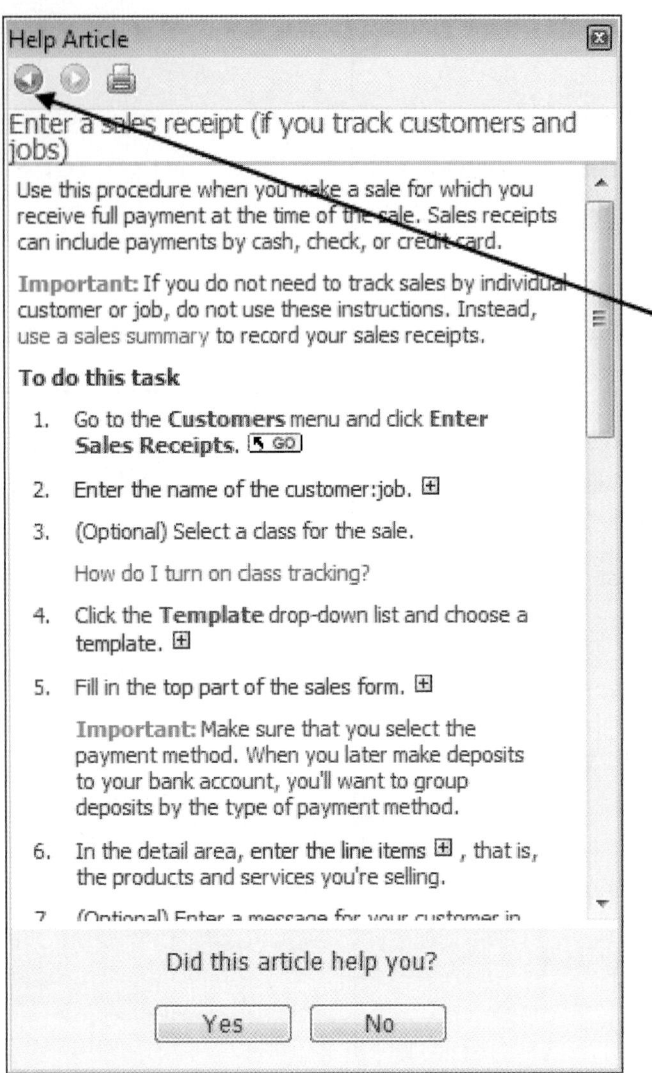
Help Article
Enter a sales receipt (if you track customers and jobs)
Use this procedure when you make a sale for which you receive full payment at the time of the sale. Sales receipts can include payments by cash, check, or credit card.
Important: If you do not need to track sales by individual customer or job, do not use these instructions. Instead, use a sales summary to record your sales receipts.
To do this task
1. Go to the Customers menu and click Enter Sales Receipts.
2. Enter the name of the customer:job.
3. (Optional) Select a class for the sale.
How do I turn on class tracking?
4. Click the Template drop-down list and choose a template.
5. Fill in the top part of the sales form.
Important: Make sure that you select the payment method. When you later make deposits to your bank account, you'll want to group deposits by the type of payment method.
6. In the detail area, enter the line items, that is, the products and services you're selling.
Did this article help you?
Yes
No
Click to return to the previous topic

Figure 1:35

Close the window illustrated in Figure 1:35 by clicking **x**.

Return to the **Have a Question?** window and scroll down to the Community section. (See Figure 1:36.)

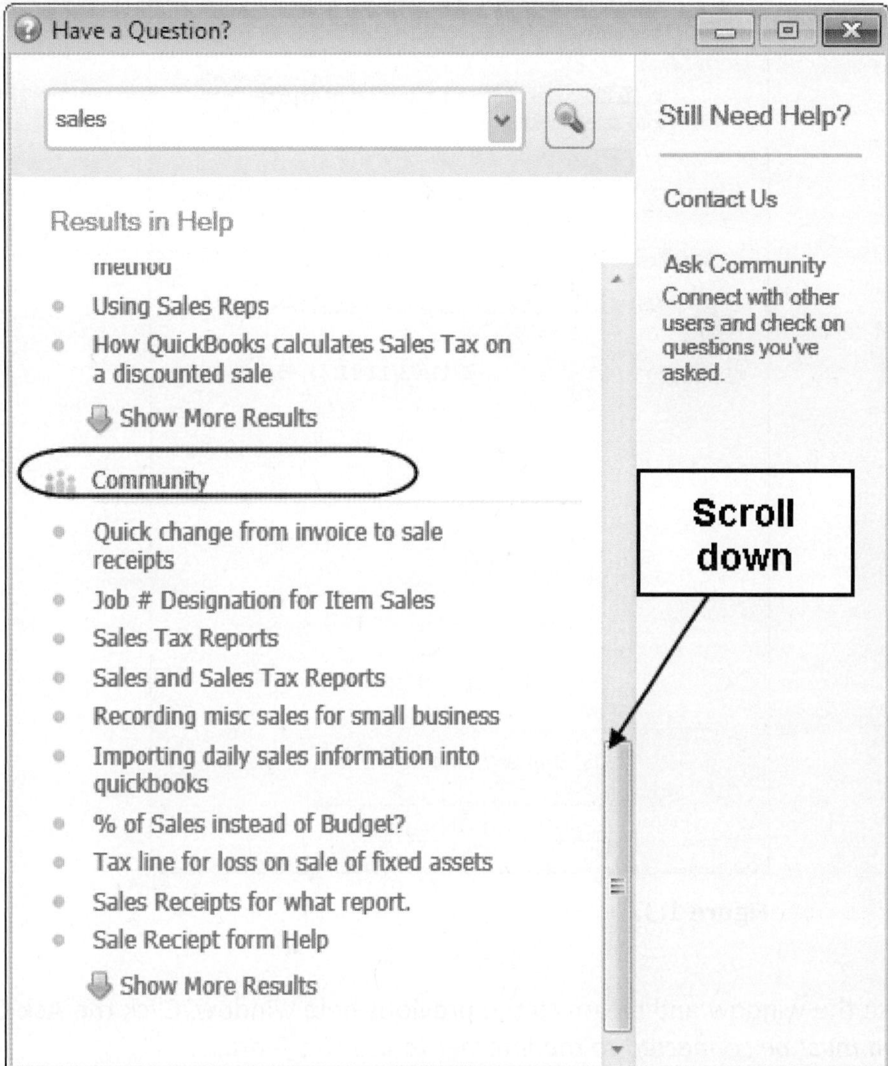

Figure 1:36

Click the **Quick change from invoice to sale receipts** topic and the window illustrated in Figure 1:37 opens. This window contains responses from other users, so the results will change based on user response.

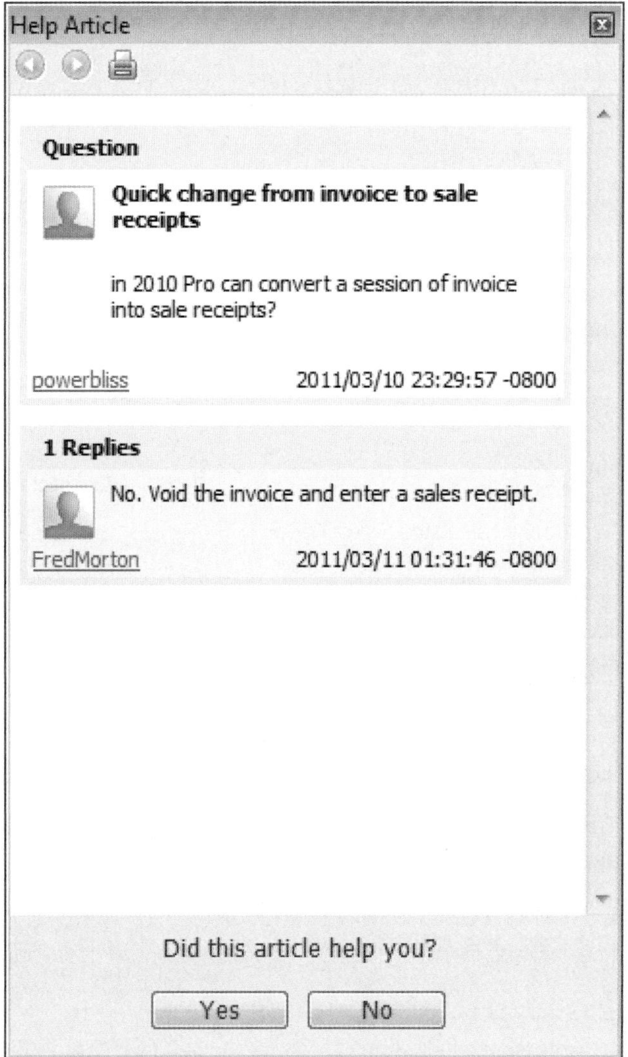

Figure 1:37

Click **x** to close the window and return to the previous help window. Click the **Ask Community** link. *Note: You must be connected to the Internet to use this feature*.

In this window (Figure 1:38.), you can submit your own question to other users.

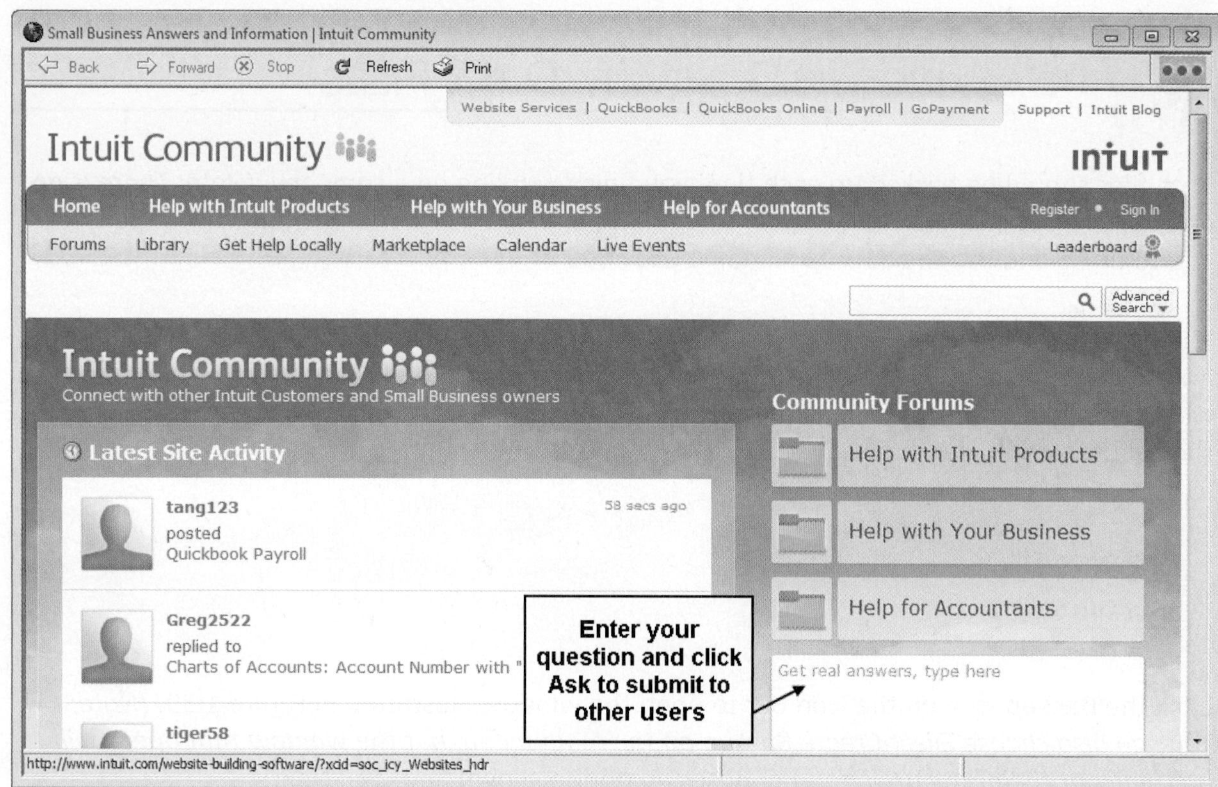

Figure 1:38

Click **x** to close the window illustrated in Figure 1:38. Click **x** to close the **Have a Question?** window. Note: The window may have minimized to your taskbar, so click it from task bar to activate and close the window.

BACKING UP COMPANY DATA FILES

Data files should be backed up each time you finish working on a company. *(Note: There is an online video available for this topic.)* At a minimum, perform a backup whenever the text tells you to do so and use the backup filename provided.

The backup utility will back up the company currently open in the software. Because this is now QB2012_Chp1_Stud, the steps that follow create a backup file for this company. You will create a backup file for remaining sample companies in the Practice Set at the end of the chapter.

❖ ***Backup Step 1***

Click the **Backup** icon on the Icon Bar to open the window illustrated in Figure 1:39. *(Note: You can also choose File>>Create Backup on the main menu, but the window that opens will not begin at the next illustration.)* Choose the option shown and click **Next**.

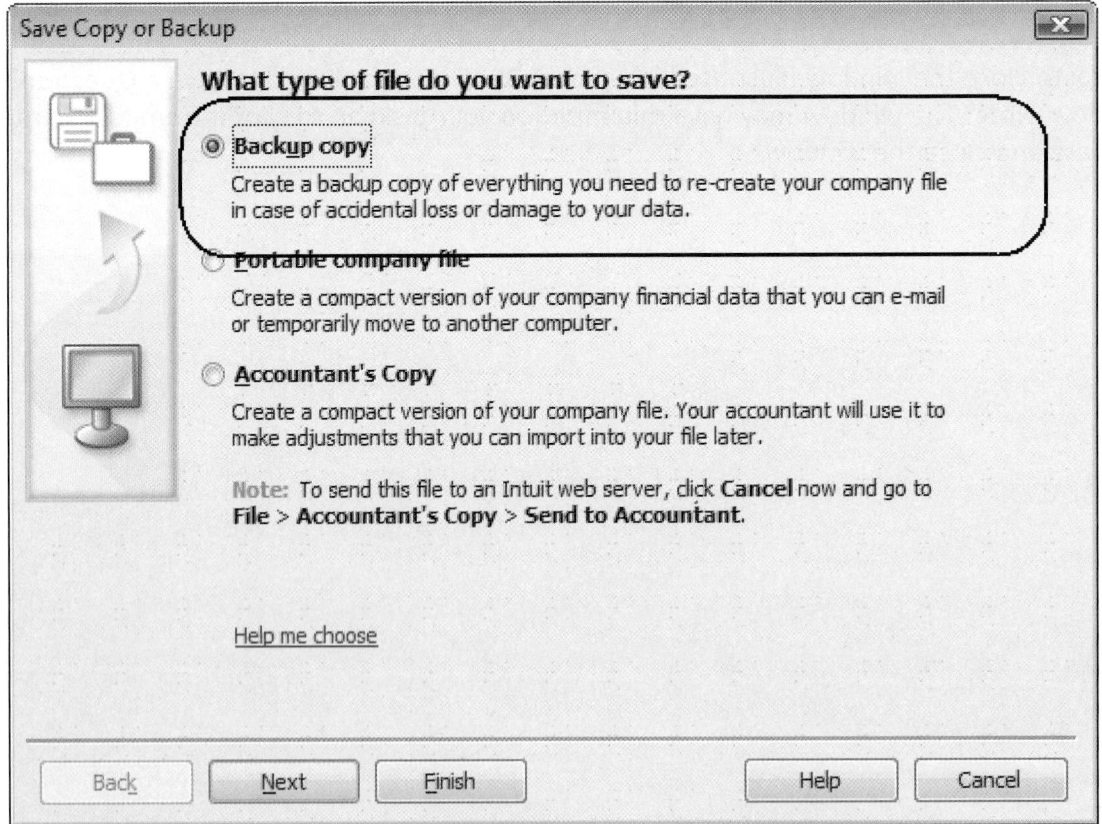

Figure 1:39

❖ ***Backup Step 2***

On the screen illustrated in Figure 1:40 select **Local backup**.

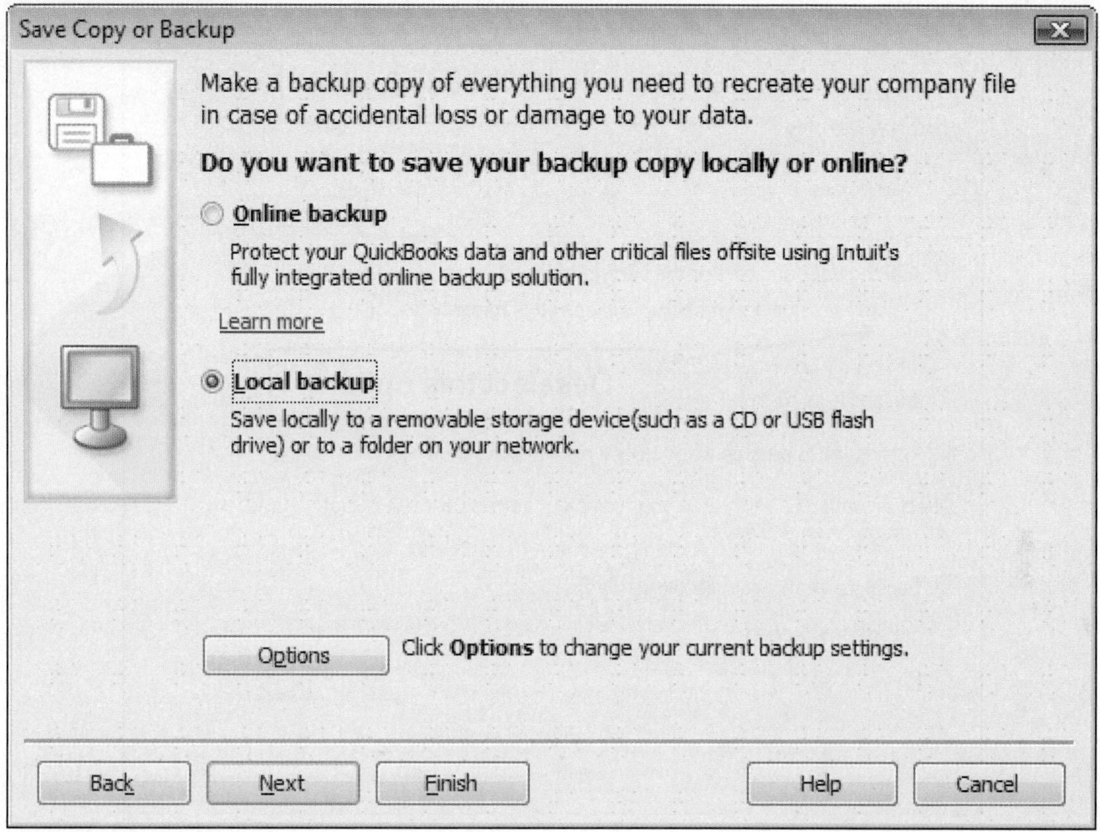

Figure 1:40

❖ *Backup Step 3*

Click **Options** to set options for storing the backup (Figure 1:41).

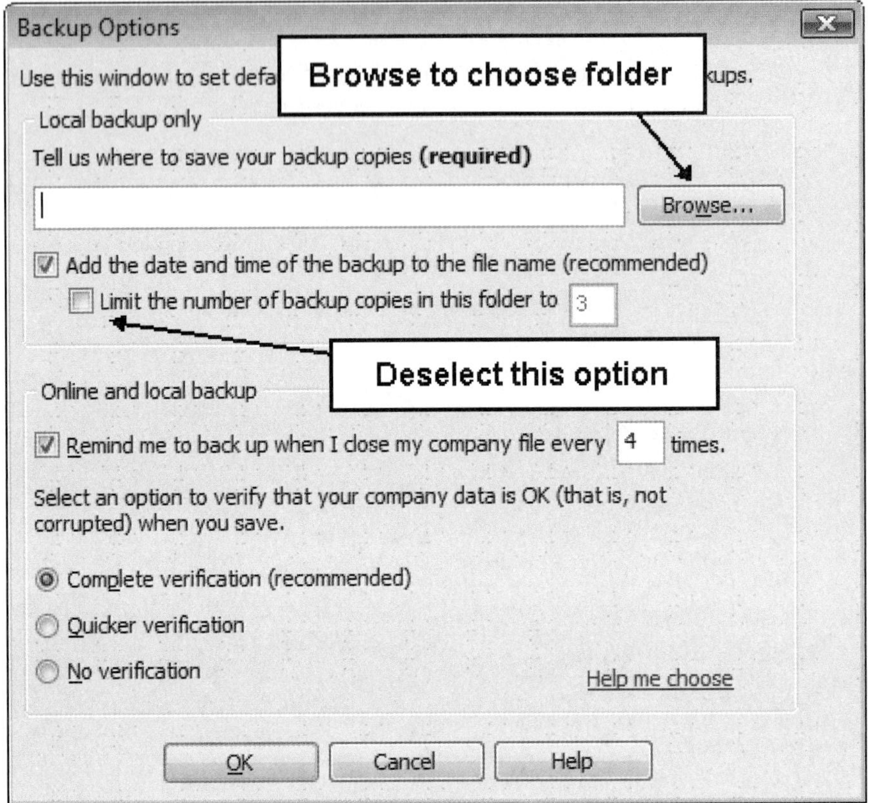

Figure 1:41

Clicking **Browse** will let you choose a folder on the hard drive to store the backup file. To make it easy to find the file in the future, double click the folder that displays **your name or username**.

You will then see a **Documents** or **My Documents** folder, depending on your operating system. (See Figure 1:42.) Double click to open this folder and click **OK**.

Note: You can also select the drive labeled CD-RW Drive. You can also select a USB drive, which is normally labeled "E." However, when storing backups to these devices you may need to use the instructions in Appendix C and create a portable backup to reduce the backup file size.

Figure 1:42

The window in Figure 1:43 shows the completed Backup Options window.

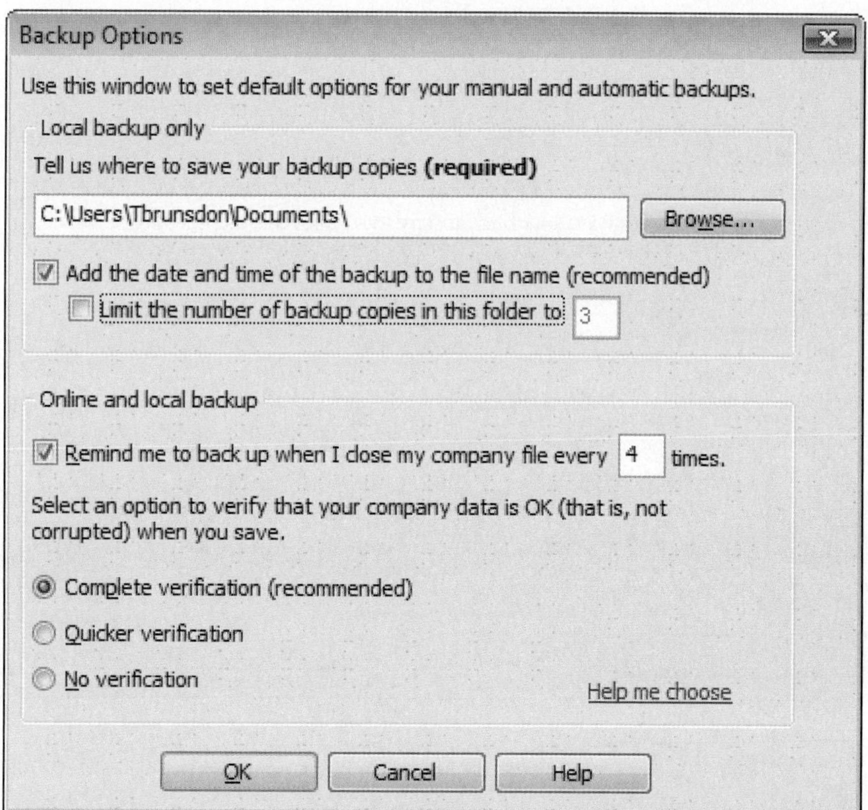

Figure 1:43

Click **OK** and you are prompted to change the location (Figure 1:44). Click **Use this Location.**

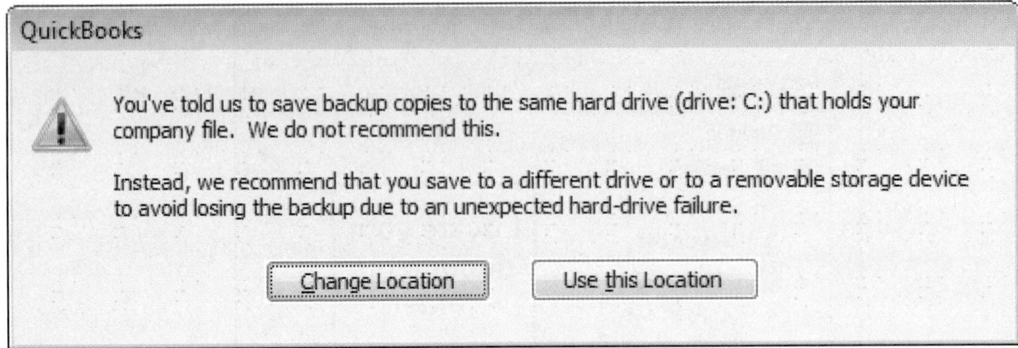

Figure 1:44

- ***Backup Step 4***

Click **Next**, select **Save it now** (Figure 1:45), and click **Next**.

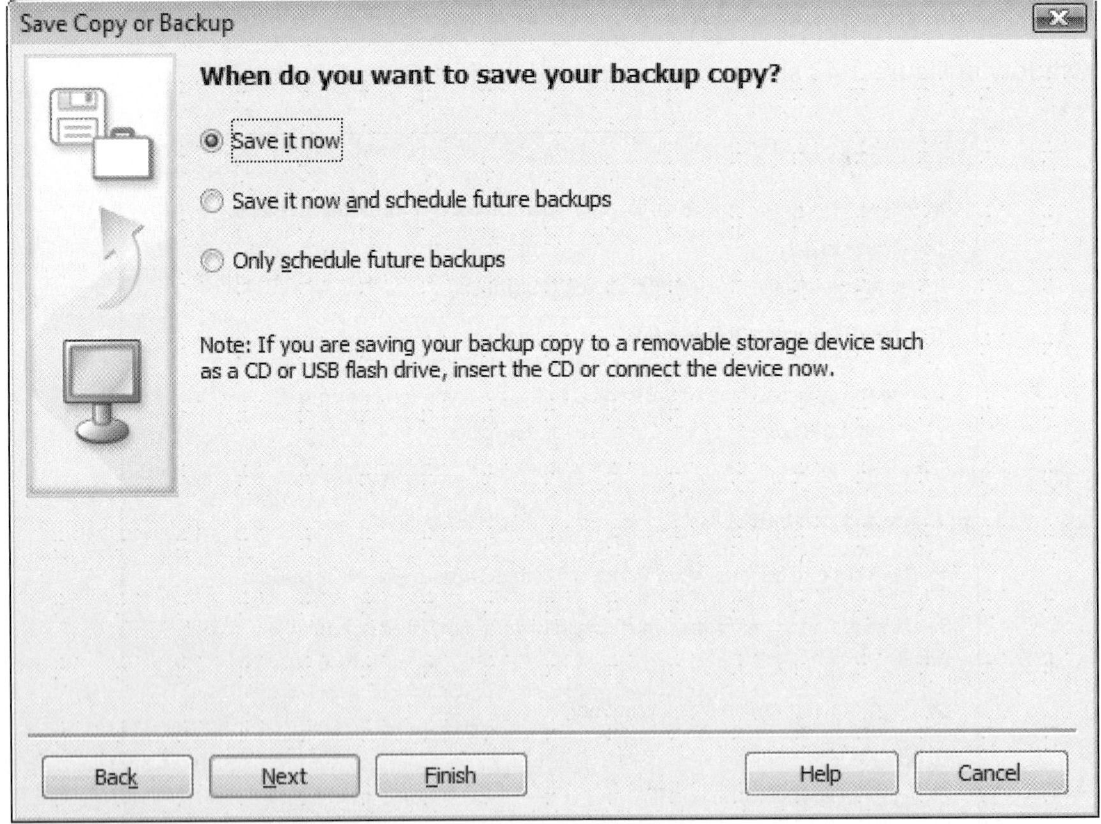

Figure 1:45

❖ ***Backup Step 5***

We suggest replacing the date portion of the backup file name with an extension that identifies the point where you stopped working in the file. Since you have completed this chapter, the window illustrated in Figure 1:46 shows the **File name** of ***QB2012_Chp1_Stud_Completed***. After entering a file name, click **Save**. *(Note: The software adds the QBB extension.)*

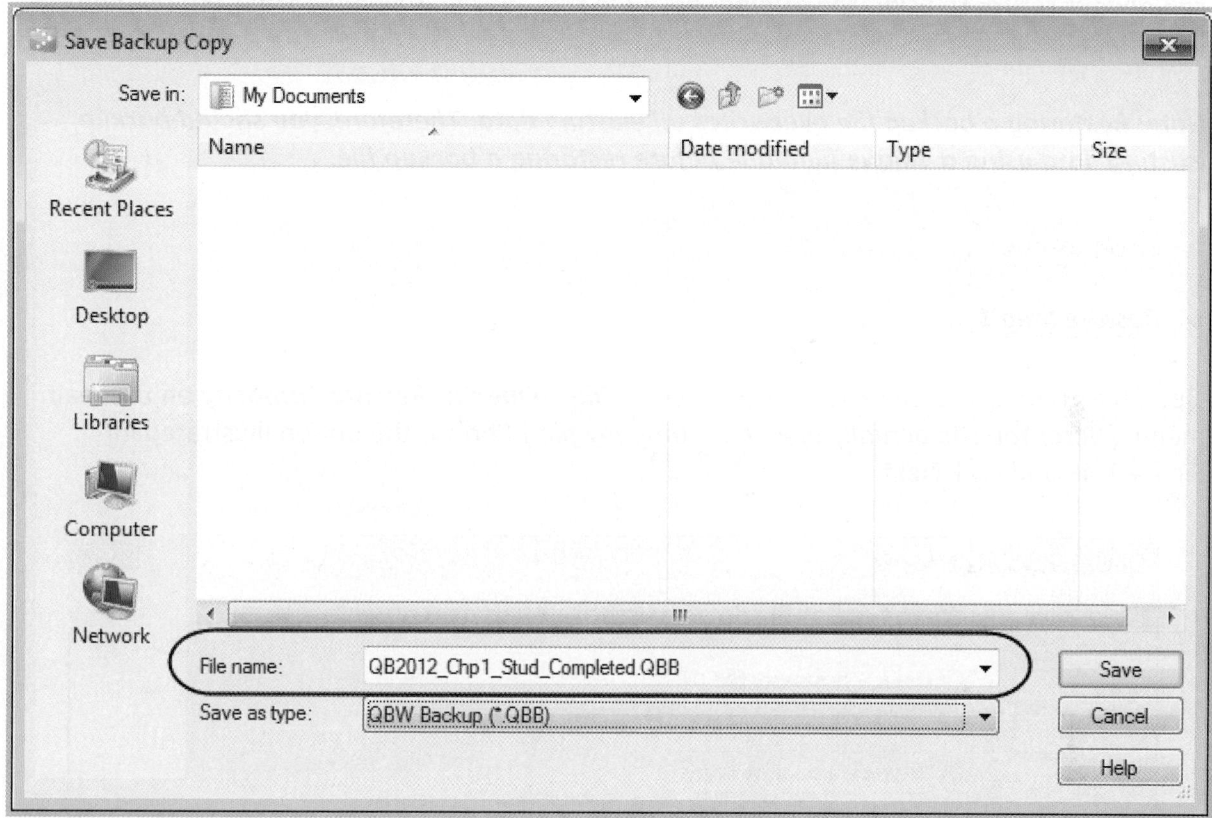

Figure 1:46

The company file closes and the backup begins. When Figure 1:47 appears the backup is complete. Click **OK** and the company file reopens.

Figure 1:47

RESTORING COMPANY DATA FILES

This topic covers situations where you need to restore a company backup file, for instance, when you want to restart a chapter or move data files between school and home. *(Note: If restoring a portable backup, refer to the instructions in Appendix C.)*

Note: You cannot restore previous work unless you have created a backup file; however, you can always return to using the original data file that was downloaded from the textbook Website.

Note: Restoring a backup file overwrites all existing data. Therefore, you should backup existing data using a unique filename before restoring a backup file.

❖ ***Restore Step 1***

Open the company to be restored by selecting ***File>>Open or Restore Company*** on the main menu. *(Note: You can actually open any company file.)* Choose the option illustrated in Figure 1:48 and click **Next**.

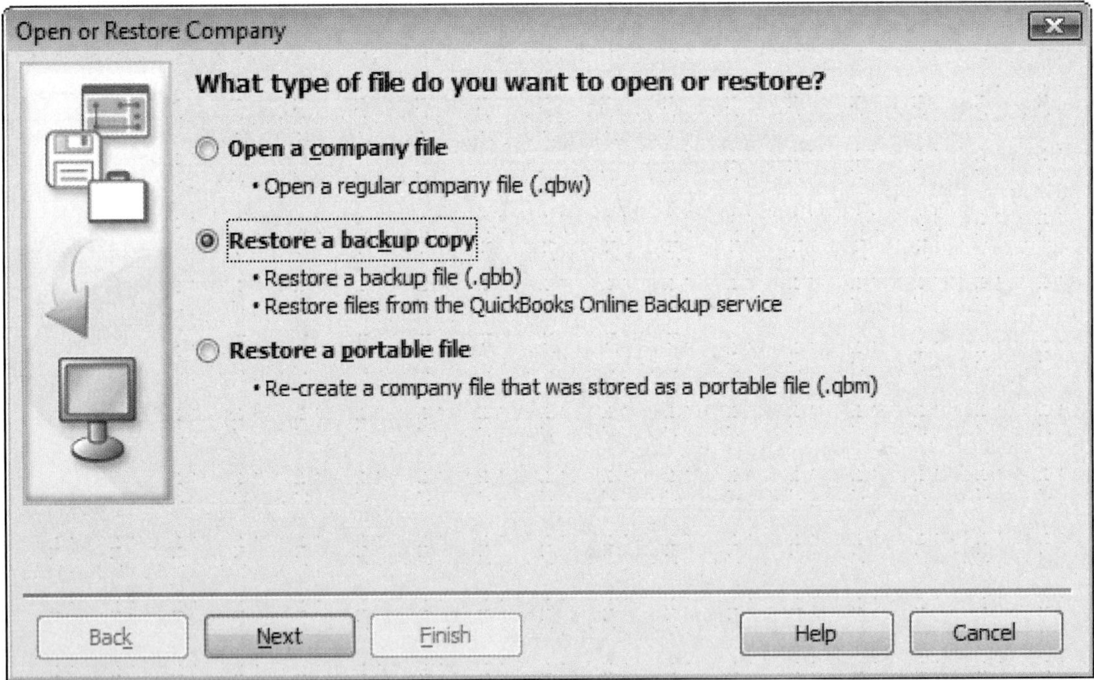

Figure 1:48

❖ ***Restore Step 2***

Select **Local backup** and click **Next** (Figure 1:49).

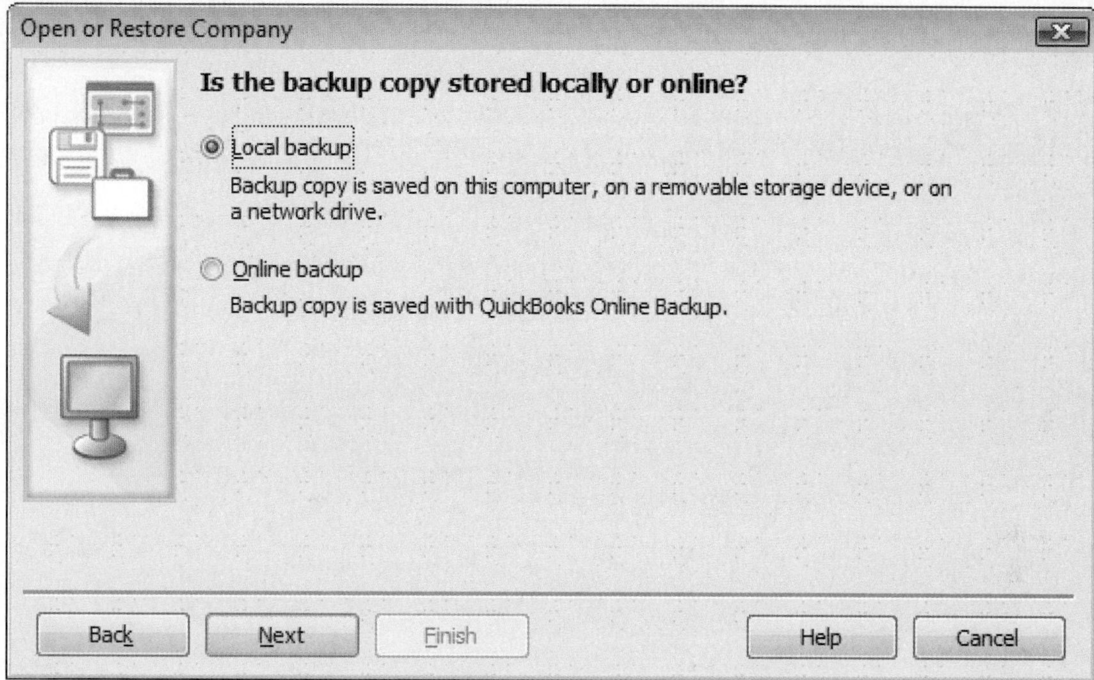

Figure 1:49

❖ ***Restore Step 3***

Highlight the backup file name and click **Open** (Figure 1:50).

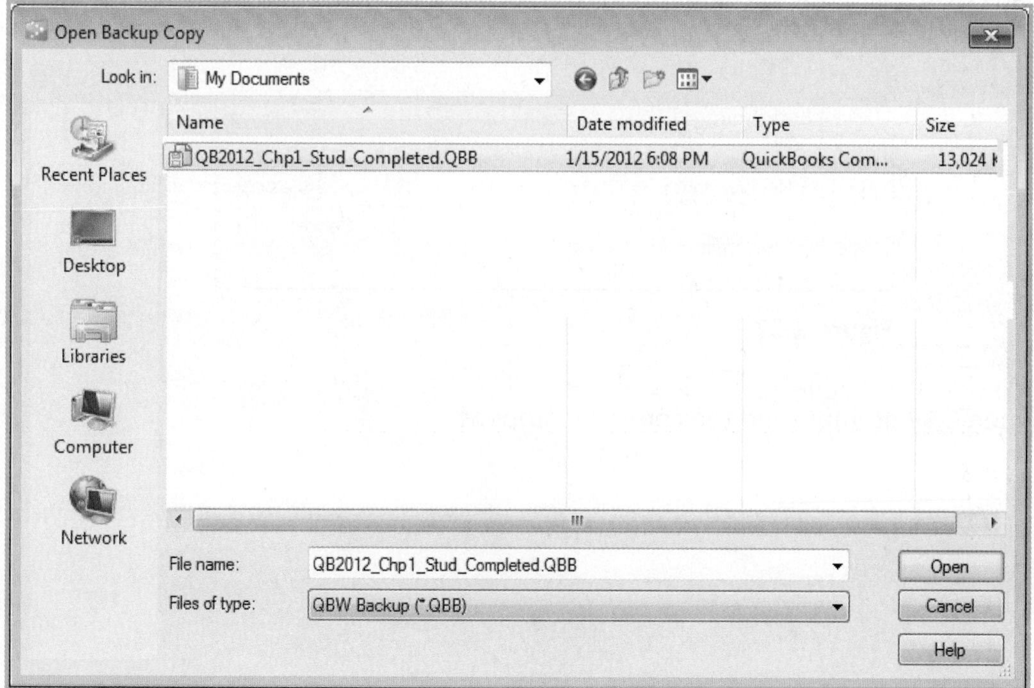

Figure 1:50

❖ ***Restore Step 4***

On the window illustrated in Figure 1:51 click **Next.**

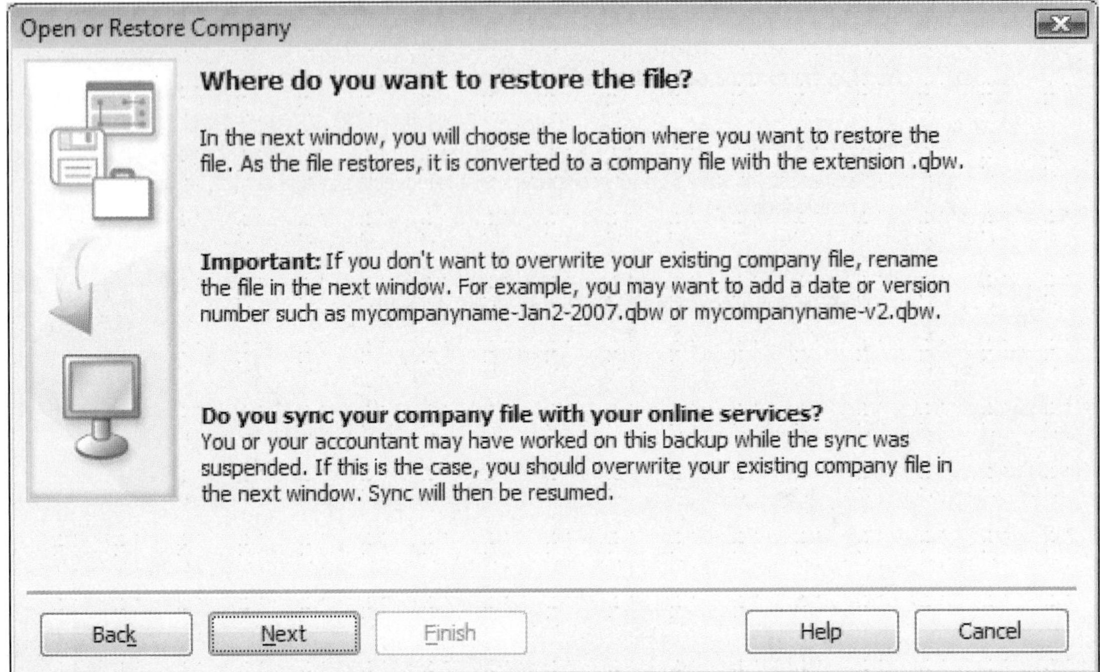

Figure 1:51

In the window that opens (not illustrated) highlight **QB2012_Chp1_Stud** and click **Save**. When QBP warns that the file already exists, click **Yes** to replace it.

The company closes and opens a confirmation screen to delete existing data by restoring data from the backup file (Figure 1:52). Type "YES" in all caps and click **OK**.

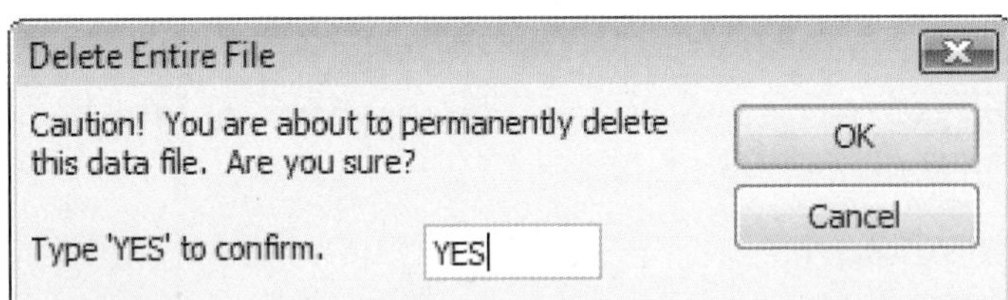

Figure 1:52

Click **OK** when QBP prompts and the company reopens.

MOVING DATA BETWEEN SCHOOL AND HOME

Using backup and restore procedures, you can move data files between home and school by following the next steps. *(Note: Use the portable backup and restore instructions in Appendix C if you need to reduce backup file sizes.)*

1. On the current machine, open each company to be moved and follow the steps in the *Backing Up Company Data Files* topic. For Backup Step 3, change the backup path to your USB or CD drive.

2. On the second machine, follow the steps in the *Restoring Company Data Files* topic. In Restore Step 3, change the data file path to your USB or CD drive. In Step 4, select the name of the company being restored.

EXITING QUICKBOOKS

Select ***File>>Exit*** on the main menu to close QBP. The next time you open the software, the company file that was open when exiting will reopen.

SUMMARY

In this chapter, you downloaded company data files from the textbook's Website to your computer and opened companies in the software. You learned to customize company names with your initials, worked with QBP's desktop, used the Home page and centers, and customized the Icon Bar. You also worked with QBP's help files and learned to back up and restore company data files.

Congratulations! You are now ready to move on to other tasks. In the next chapter, your focus shifts to working with other QBP features that prepare you for entering transactions.

END-OF-CHAPTER QUESTIONS

TRUE/FALSE

_____ 1. You can restore a company with a file you created in the Restore Company window.

_____ 2. Icons on the Icon Bar are shortcuts to frequently used tasks and reports.

_____ 3. Help for the software can be accessed by pressing F1.

_____ 4. You must close a company before exiting QBP.

_____ 5. Using just the restore utility, you can move your company files to a new computer.

_____ 6. QuickBooks is a type of operating software.

_____ 7. You prepare a trial balance only when using a manual accounting system.

_____ 8. A computer hard drive is considered computer hardware.

_____ 9. The data files used with the text must be downloaded from the textbook Website.

_____ 10. You can customize the Icon Bar.

MULTIPLE CHOICE

_____ 1. You can identify the open company in QBP by looking at the _____.

a. Main Menu
b. Title Bar
c. Icon Bar
d. Window Bar

_____ 2. Which of the following is considered operating software?

a. Microsoft Office Professional
b. LINUX
c. Microsoft Windows XP
d. Both b and c

_____ 3. Which main menu command will open a view of the chart of accounts?
   a. File
   b. Lists
   c. Customers
   d. Vendors

_____ 4. The Create Invoices icon appears on the _____ section of the Home page.
   a. Customers
   b. Banking
   c. Company
   d. Vendors

_____ 5. Which keyboard shortcut can be used to enter a new transaction?
   a. Ctrl + D
   b. Ctrl + S
   c. Ctrl + N
   d. Ctrl + L

_____ 6. ________ software is installed after installing ________ software.
   a. Operating, application
   b. Application, operating
   c. Hardware, operating
   d. Operating, accounting

_____ 7. The _________ tab in the Customer Center displays transactions by transaction type.
   a. Customers & Jobs
   b. Transactions
   c. both a and b
   d. neither a or b

_____ 8. QuickBooks contains a _____ center.
   a. Customer
   b. Employee
   c. Vendor
   d. all the above

PRACTICE SET

Answer the following questions.

1. In the Chapter 6 Practice Set, you will use the data file named ____________.

2. To open the Customize Icon Bar window, you choose the menu path of ________.

3. Before performing tasks in a data file, you must ________ the software to the Pro Edition.

4. The ________ on the software will show the name of the open company.

5. The shortcut key that opens the Customer center is ____________.

6. The Home page is divided into the Vendors, __________, Employees, ____________, and Banking sections.

7. The Vendor center contains the tabs named ____________ and ____________.

8. You add your initials to the end of a company name by selecting the menu path of ________.

9. If you have problems installing the software, you will find help at ______.

10. Using Help for assistance on the "vendor center" will provide a link to the "Vendor Center overview" help article. This help article provides another link to answer the common question of "Can I ______ a vendor?"

CHAPTER 2 QUICKBOOKS BASICS

LEARNING OBJECTIVES

You are probably ready to jump in and begin recording transactions, but accounting is more than posting entries. Accountants determine the "where and when" of transaction posting. For example, where is a rent bill posted (i.e., prepaid asset or expense account) and when is revenue posted (i.e., upon taking an order or shipping the goods). Understanding the where and when lets the accountant know what human intervention is needed to ensure financial statements are correct.

To understand the where and when in accounting software, you must understand how the software behaves behind the keys. This is why each chapter will review posting procedures in a manual accounting system and tracing entries behind the keys in the accounting software.

In this chapter, we look at options that control the overall posting behavior for the software. We also review other features used to locate and report on posted transactions. This chapter covers the following:

1. Viewing and printing the chart of accounts
2. Understanding the general ledger framework used to create general ledger accounts
3. Creating and managing general ledger accounts
4. Setting QBP preference options that control software behavior
5. Using drilldown, find, and search features to locate transactions
6. Using the reports menu and center
7. Printing, customizing, emailing and exporting reports
8. Closing accounting periods

<u>Begin by:</u>

- Opening the software.
- Opening the **QB2012_Chp2_Stud** data file. Add your initials to the end to the Company Name by clicking ***Company>>Company Information*** on the main menu. Click **OK** to save the changes.
- **Toggling the software to the PRO EDITION** by selecting ***File>>Toggle to Another Edition*** on the main menu and choosing **QuickBooks Pro** as the edition.

Chart of Account

Before looking at software settings and options, you need to become familiar with the basic foundation for all accounting entries, namely the chart of accounts.

Open the Chart of Accounts by selecting ***Lists>>Chart of Accounts*** on the main menu. The list displayed in Figure 2:1 shows the general ledger account numbers and names used by the company and the current account balances and account types. *(Note: Amounts with minus signs mean it is opposite the normal balance for the account type.)* Use the scroll bar to view accounts toward the bottom.

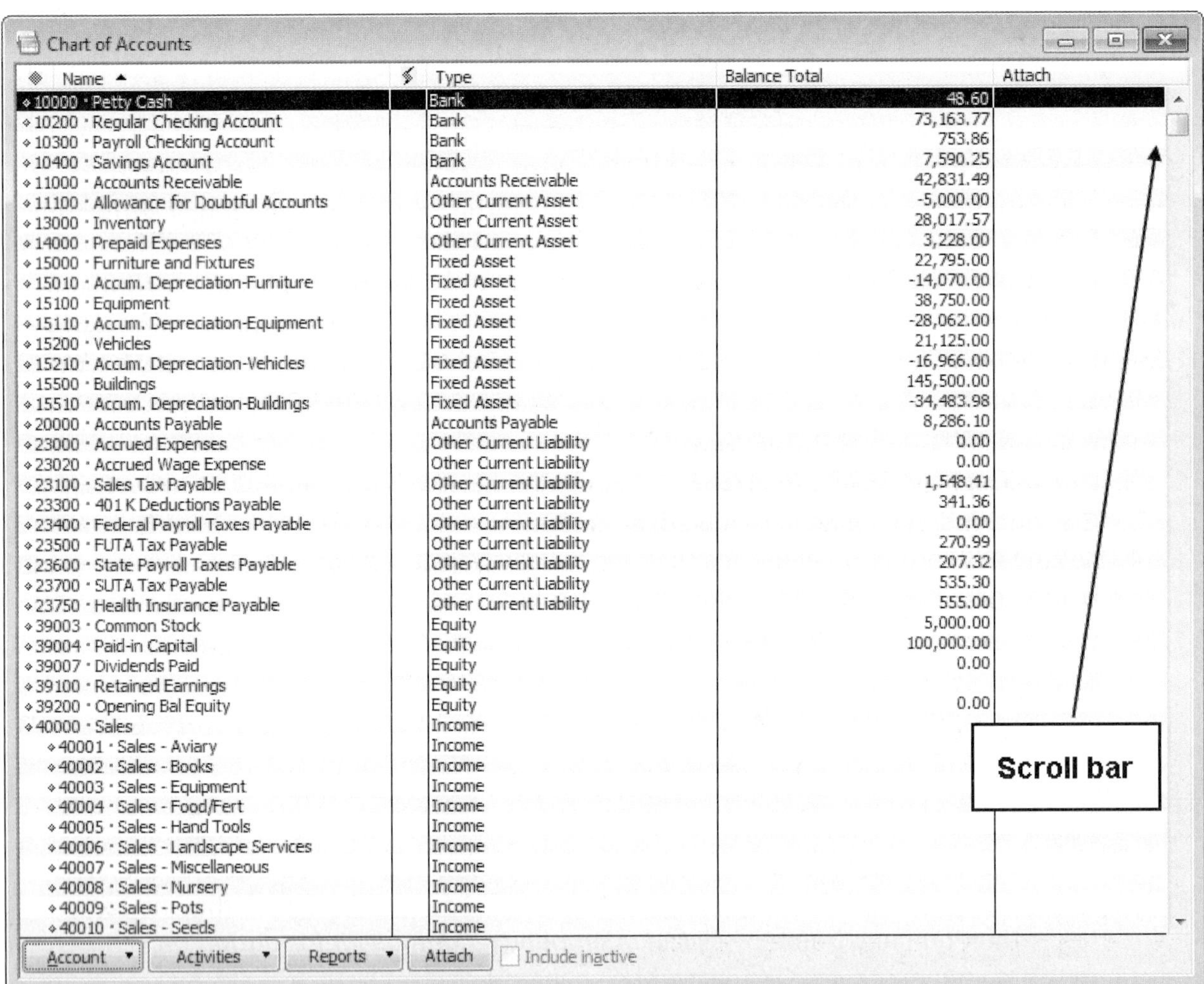

Name	Type	Balance Total	Attach
10000 · Petty Cash	Bank	48.60	
10200 · Regular Checking Account	Bank	73,163.77	
10300 · Payroll Checking Account	Bank	753.86	
10400 · Savings Account	Bank	7,590.25	
11000 · Accounts Receivable	Accounts Receivable	42,831.49	
11100 · Allowance for Doubtful Accounts	Other Current Asset	-5,000.00	
13000 · Inventory	Other Current Asset	28,017.57	
14000 · Prepaid Expenses	Other Current Asset	3,228.00	
15000 · Furniture and Fixtures	Fixed Asset	22,795.00	
15010 · Accum. Depreciation-Furniture	Fixed Asset	-14,070.00	
15100 · Equipment	Fixed Asset	38,750.00	
15110 · Accum. Depreciation-Equipment	Fixed Asset	-28,062.00	
15200 · Vehicles	Fixed Asset	21,125.00	
15210 · Accum. Depreciation-Vehicles	Fixed Asset	-16,966.00	
15500 · Buildings	Fixed Asset	145,500.00	
15510 · Accum. Depreciation-Buildings	Fixed Asset	-34,483.98	
20000 · Accounts Payable	Accounts Payable	8,286.10	
23000 · Accrued Expenses	Other Current Liability	0.00	
23020 · Accrued Wage Expense	Other Current Liability	0.00	
23100 · Sales Tax Payable	Other Current Liability	1,548.41	
23300 · 401 K Deductions Payable	Other Current Liability	341.36	
23400 · Federal Payroll Taxes Payable	Other Current Liability	0.00	
23500 · FUTA Tax Payable	Other Current Liability	270.99	
23600 · State Payroll Taxes Payable	Other Current Liability	207.32	
23700 · SUTA Tax Payable	Other Current Liability	535.30	
23750 · Health Insurance Payable	Other Current Liability	555.00	
39003 · Common Stock	Equity	5,000.00	
39004 · Paid-in Capital	Equity	100,000.00	
39007 · Dividends Paid	Equity	0.00	
39100 · Retained Earnings	Equity		
39200 · Opening Bal Equity	Equity	0.00	
40000 · Sales	Income		
40001 · Sales - Aviary	Income		
40002 · Sales - Books	Income		
40003 · Sales - Equipment	Income		
40004 · Sales - Food/Fert	Income		
40005 · Sales - Hand Tools	Income		
40006 · Sales - Landscape Services	Income		
40007 · Sales - Miscellaneous	Income		
40008 · Sales - Nursery	Income		
40009 · Sales - Pots	Income		
40010 · Sales - Seeds	Income		

Figure 2:1

These accounts are used to post accounting transactions and the balances appear on financial statements and other reports. After reading the topics that follow, you will be familiar with this company's Chart of Accounts and ready to record transactions.

PRINT THE CHART OF ACCOUNTS

Begin familiarizing yourself with the chart of accounts by printing it. Click the **Reports** button at the bottom of the Chart of Accounts list and select **Account Listing**. *(Note: You can also print this report by selecting **Reports>>List>>Account Listing** on the main menu.)*

The scroll bar to the right of the report will let you view accounts toward the bottom (Figure 2:2). You can resize report columns by selecting the column separator and dragging it.

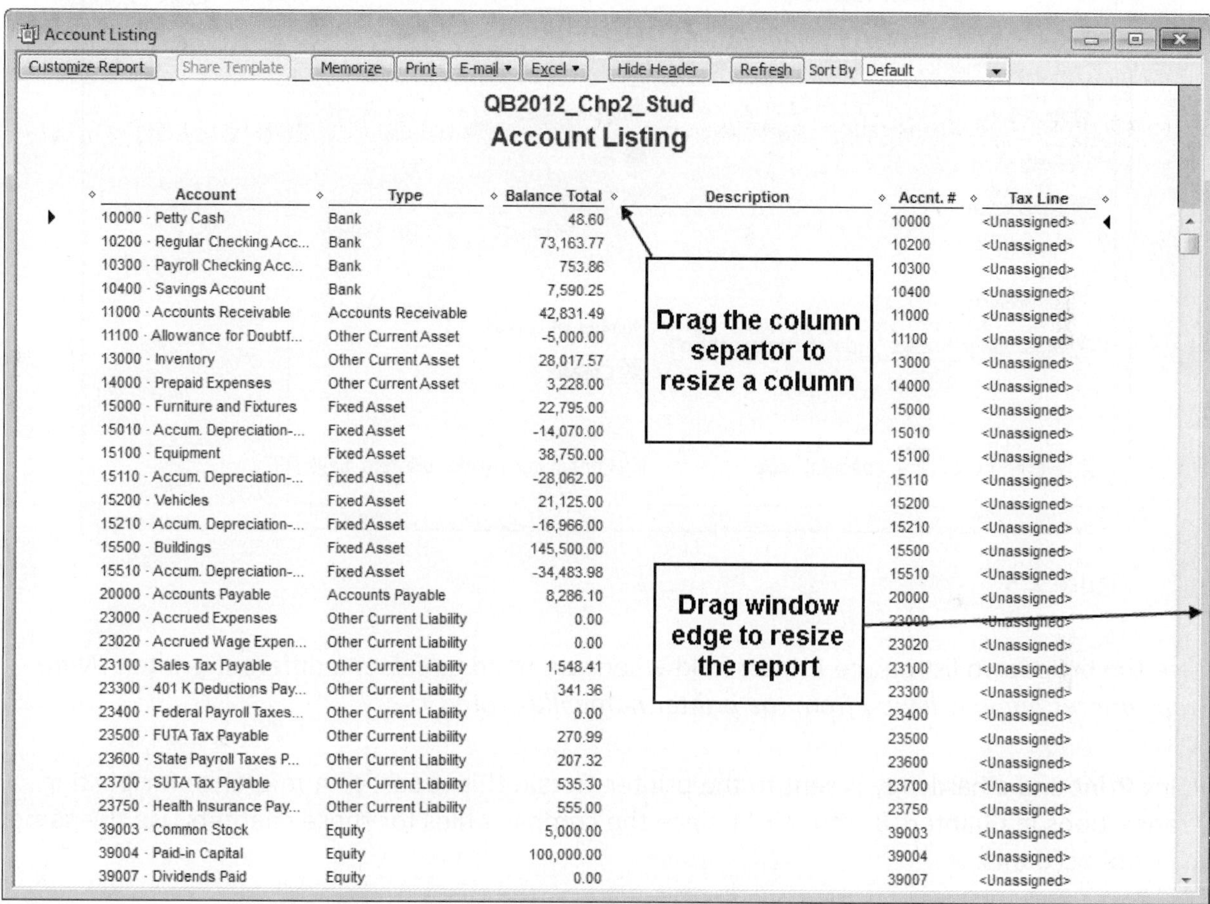

QB2012_Chp2_Stud

Account Listing

Account	Type	Balance Total	Description	Accnt. #	Tax Line
10000 · Petty Cash	Bank	48.60		10000	<Unassigned>
10200 · Regular Checking Acc...	Bank	73,163.77		10200	<Unassigned>
10300 · Payroll Checking Acc...	Bank	753.86		10300	<Unassigned>
10400 · Savings Account	Bank	7,590.25		10400	<Unassigned>
11000 · Accounts Receivable	Accounts Receivable	42,831.49		11000	<Unassigned>
11100 · Allowance for Doubtf...	Other Current Asset	-5,000.00		11100	<Unassigned>
13000 · Inventory	Other Current Asset	28,017.57		13000	<Unassigned>
14000 · Prepaid Expenses	Other Current Asset	3,228.00		14000	<Unassigned>
15000 · Furniture and Fixtures	Fixed Asset	22,795.00		15000	<Unassigned>
15010 · Accum. Depreciation-...	Fixed Asset	-14,070.00		15010	<Unassigned>
15100 · Equipment	Fixed Asset	38,750.00		15100	<Unassigned>
15110 · Accum. Depreciation-...	Fixed Asset	-28,062.00		15110	<Unassigned>
15200 · Vehicles	Fixed Asset	21,125.00		15200	<Unassigned>
15210 · Accum. Depreciation-...	Fixed Asset	-16,966.00		15210	<Unassigned>
15500 · Buildings	Fixed Asset	145,500.00		15500	<Unassigned>
15510 · Accum. Depreciation-...	Fixed Asset	-34,483.98		15510	<Unassigned>
20000 · Accounts Payable	Accounts Payable	8,286.10		20000	<Unassigned>
23000 · Accrued Expenses	Other Current Liability	0.00		23000	<Unassigned>
23020 · Accrued Wage Expen...	Other Current Liability	0.00		23020	<Unassigned>
23100 · Sales Tax Payable	Other Current Liability	1,548.41		23100	<Unassigned>
23300 · 401 K Deductions Pay...	Other Current Liability	341.36		23300	<Unassigned>
23400 · Federal Payroll Taxes...	Other Current Liability	0.00		23400	<Unassigned>
23500 · FUTA Tax Payable	Other Current Liability	270.99		23500	<Unassigned>
23600 · State Payroll Taxes P...	Other Current Liability	207.32		23600	<Unassigned>
23700 · SUTA Tax Payable	Other Current Liability	535.30		23700	<Unassigned>
23750 · Health Insurance Pay...	Other Current Liability	555.00		23750	<Unassigned>
39003 · Common Stock	Equity	5,000.00		39003	<Unassigned>
39004 · Paid-in Capital	Equity	100,000.00		39004	<Unassigned>
39007 · Dividends Paid	Equity	0.00		39007	<Unassigned>

Figure 2:2

Click the **Print** button and the printer dialog window opens (Figure 2:3).

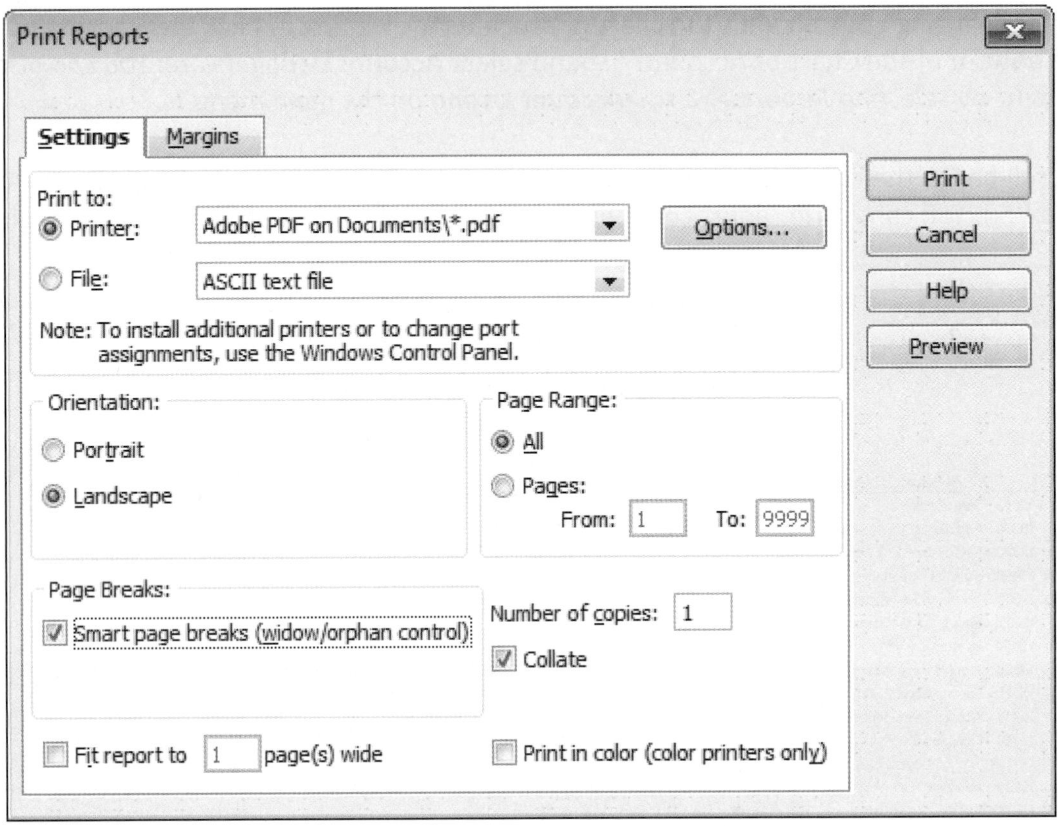

Figure 2:3

Use the dropdown list on the **Printer** field when you need to select a different printer. *(Note: Your printer name will vary from the printer name illustrated.)*

Click **Print** and a hardcopy is sent to the printer. Retain this report as a reference for posting transactions in Chapters 8 through 11 since the company files for these chapters use the same chart of accounts.

Click **X** to close the report. *(Note: If you resized report columns, QBP prompts to memorize the report before closing. Click* ***No.*** *You can turn off future prompts to save a report by clicking the* ***Do not display this message in the future*** *option before clicking No.)*

PRINTING THE CHART OF ACCOUNTS FOR OTHER SAMPLE COMPANIES

When you have time, print the Account Listing report for QB2012_Chp3_Stud so you can refer to it when posting transactions in Chapter 3.

Also, print the Account Listing report for QB2012_Chp4_Stud so you can refer to it when posting transactions in Chapters 4 through 7.

(Note: Solutions for this exercise are not provided in Appendix E.)

GENERAL LEDGER FRAMEWORK

Companies use a framework to design their chart of accounts. This framework uses account numbers along with descriptions. However, the question always becomes what number to assign as the account number.

The standard convention for numbering accounts is to use the first number to identify the type of account. The following table shows the standard convention for assigning account numbers. By understanding this convention, you will know to begin the account number on a checking account (i.e., an asset account) with the number "1."

First Digit in Account Number	Type of Account
1	Asset
2	Liability
3	Equity
4	Revenue
5	Cost of Goods Sold
6/7	Operating Expense
8	Other Income
9	Other Expense

Return to the Chart of Accounts window and review this company's chart of accounts. In QBP, the account number and description are found under the **Name** column. Note how the account **Type** correlates to the first number in an account number.

Knowing the framework used on account numbers aids you in selecting the account to use on a transaction.

General Ledger Accounts

After reviewing the account framework, now is a good time to discuss creating and managing general ledger accounts.

In the **Chart of Accounts** window, click **10000 Petty Cash**. Next, click the **Account** button at the bottom and select **Edit Account**. This action opens the window illustrated in Figure 2:4.

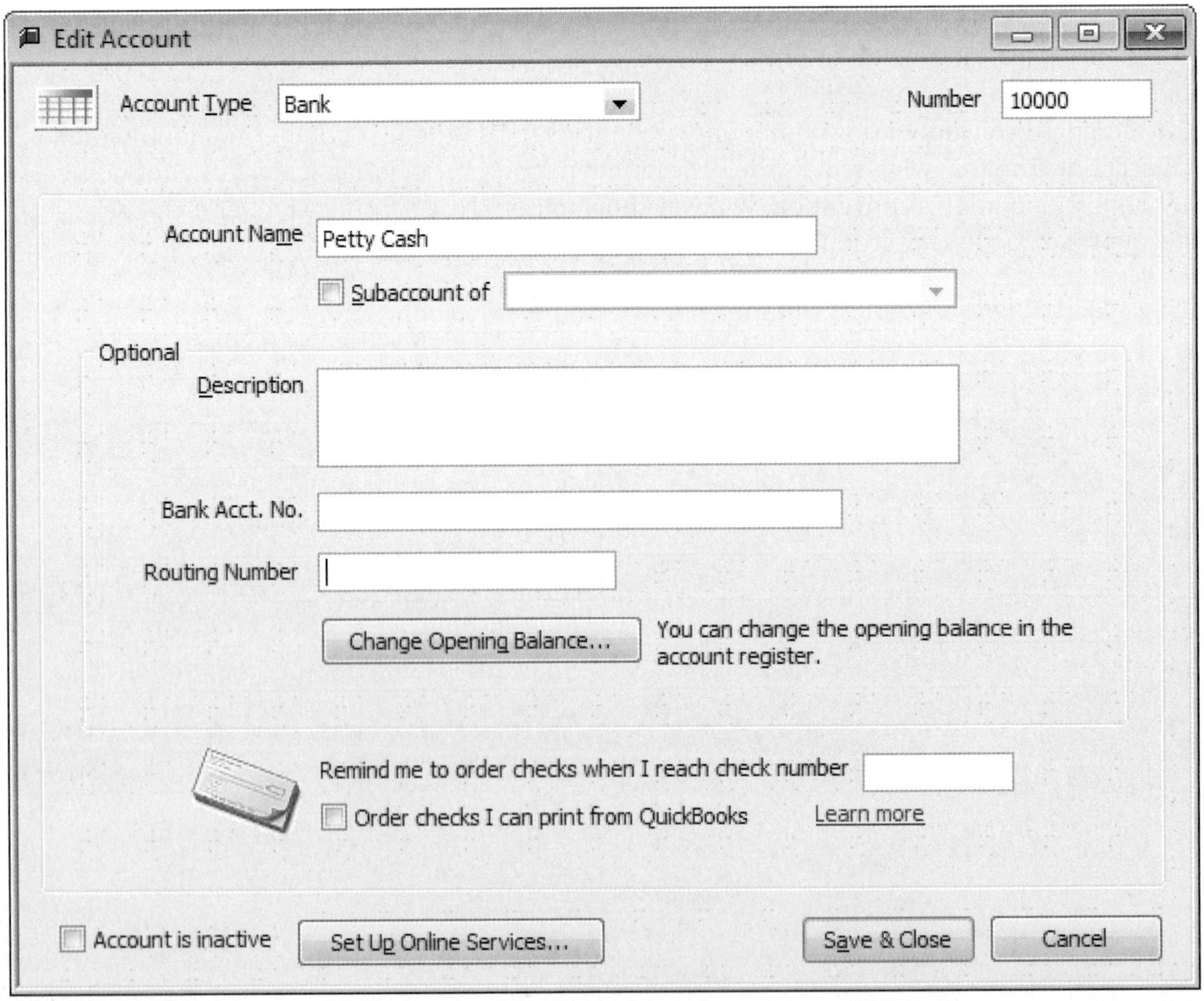

Figure 2:4

The following table explains the fields and buttons on an account.

Fields	Description
Account Type	Determines the account's normal balance (i.e., debit or credit) and the account's placement on financial reports. Selecting the dropdown list lets you view available account types and these types are explained in the next table. *Note: You may have to scroll up the list to see additional types.*
Number	Unique number used to implement the general ledger account framework.
Account Name	Unique name to describe the account. The name should be concise and properly spelled and capitalized because it appears on financial reports.
Subaccount of	Option for linking an account to a related account. Linked accounts appear indented on the Chart of Accounts List and will be grouped on financial reports. The sales accounts are examples of linked accounts.
Description	Optional text field to provide an additional description. This information does not appear on financial reports but will appear on the COA report.
Bank Acct. No. or Note	Bank and credit card account types contain a Bank Acct. No. field for storing the bank account number. All other accounts replace this field with the Note field.
Change Opening Balance	Opens an account's register, which can be used to enter beginning balances. Beginning balances are entered when transferring accounting data from another accounting system.
Account is inactive	Toggles the account from active to inactive. QBP will deny transaction posting to inactive accounts.

Click **X** to close the Petty Cash account. In the exercise that follows, you will create a new general ledger account. Before performing that task, go through an accounting refresher.

The next table lists QBP account types alongside the accounting categories covered in your accounting courses. The table also lists an account category's normal balance. *(Note: The table is organized in QBP's order for types on the dropdown list.)* You can see that asset, cost of sales, and expense accounts have normal balances of debit whereas liability, equity, and revenue accounts have normal balances of credit. The normal balance is important because it determines if a debit or credit increases the account balance; for instance, accounts with a normal debit balance are increased by posting a debit.

QBP Account Type	**Accounting Category**	**Normal Balance**
Bank	Asset	Debit *(Note: This type interfaces with the account reconciliation window.)*
Accounts Receivable	Asset	Debit
Other Current Assets	Asset	Debit
Fixed Asset	Asset	Debit
Other Asset	Asset	Debit
Accounts Payable	Liability	Credit
Credit Card	Liability	Credit *(Note: This type interfaces with the account reconciliation window.)*
Other Current Liability	Liability	Credit
Long-Term Liability	Liability	Credit
Equity	Equity	Credit
Income	Revenue	Credit
Cost of Goods Sold	Cost of Sales	Debit
Expense	Expense	Debit
Other Income	Income	Credit
Other Expense	Expense	Debit

STEPS FOR ADDING A NEW GENERAL LEDGER ACCOUNT

1. From the Chart of Accounts list click **Account** and select **New**.

2. You will be creating a new expense account for equipment rentals, so click **Expense**, as shown in Figure 2:5, and then click **Continue**.

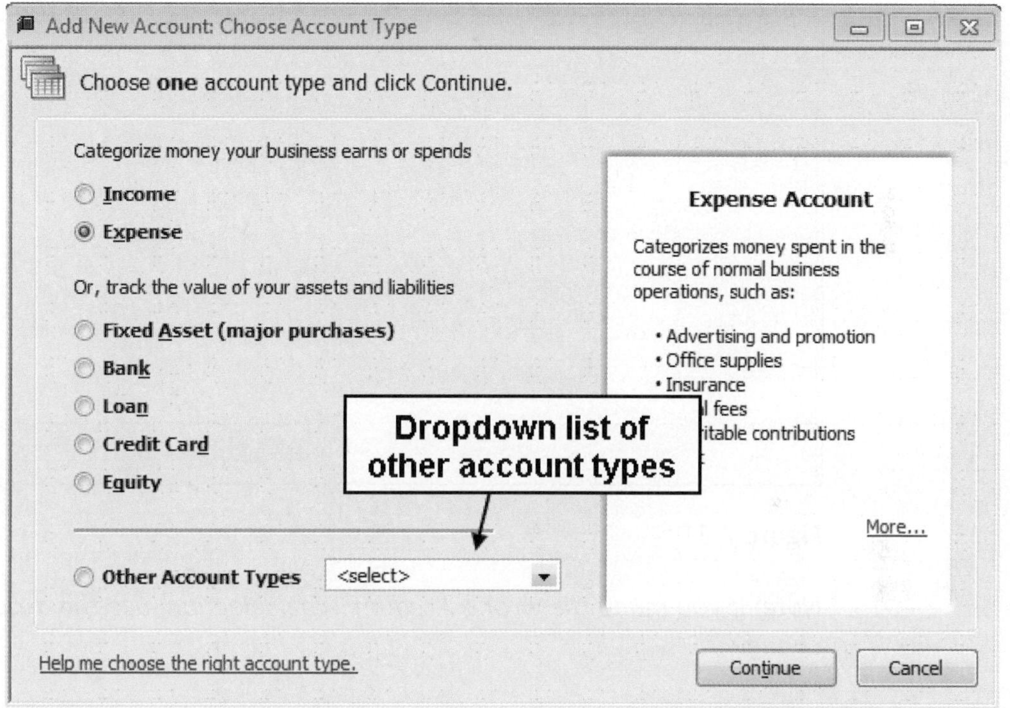

Figure 2:5

Note: When the account type does not appear as a listed option, use the dropdown list on Other Account Types to choose a type.

3. This account will appear right after rent expense for the office, so enter "71020" as the **Number**, as shown in Figure 2:6.

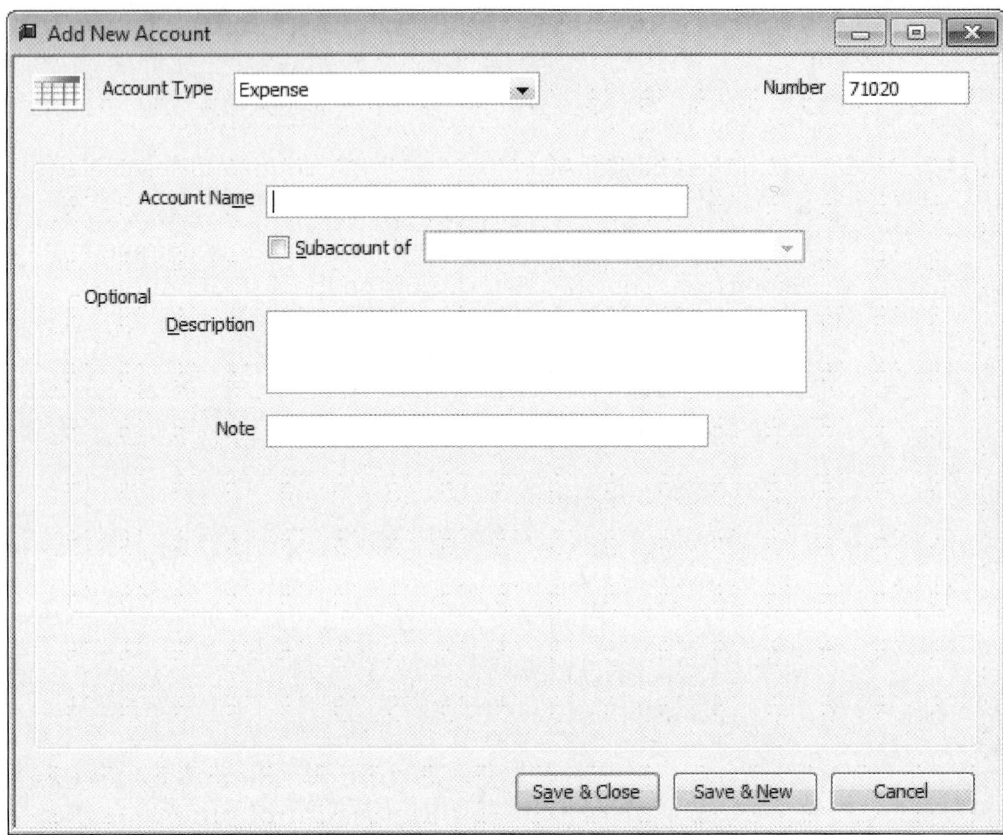

Figure 2:6

Note: If you made the wrong Account Type selection, use the dropdown list to change it.

4. Tab to **Account Name** and enter "Rent – Equipment".

5. Click the option box for **Subaccount** of and use the dropdown list to select account "71000 – Rent Expense". When finished, the new account appears as shown in Figure 2:7.

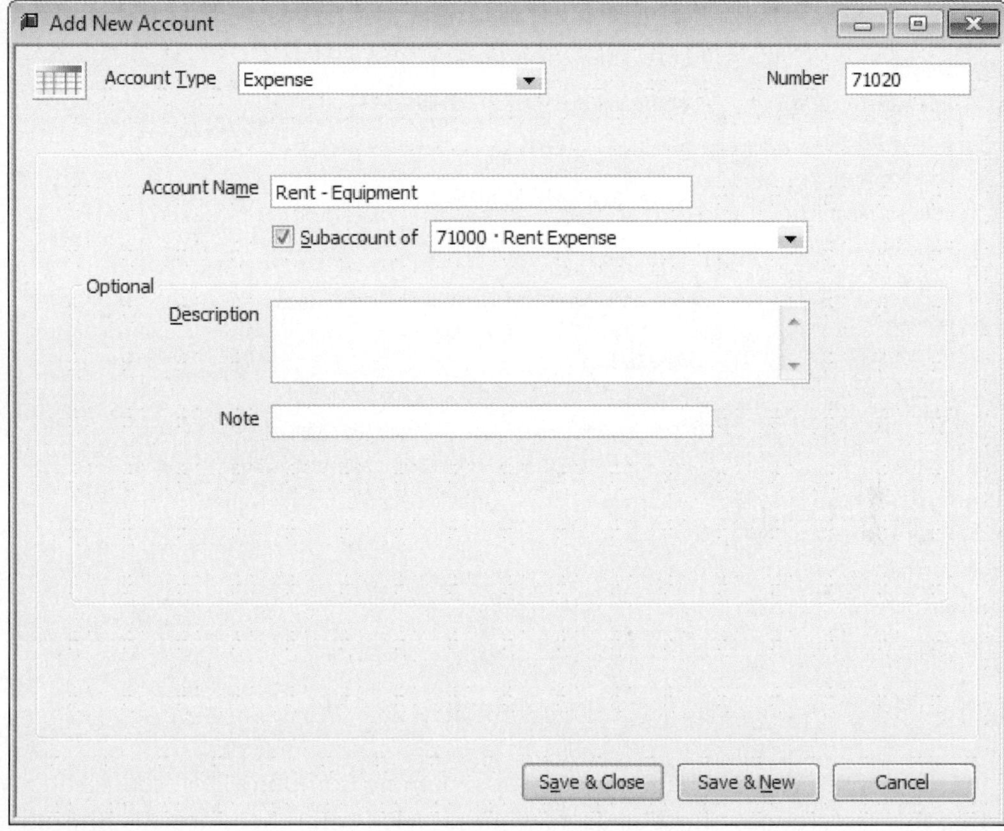

Figure 2:7

6. Click **Save & Close**. QBP returns to the Chart of Accounts. Scroll down to view the new account and then click **X** to close the Chart of Accounts.

QuickBooks Preference Options

In this topic, you manage options that control transaction processing. *(Note: There is an online video available for this topic.)*

Click ***Edit>>Preferences*** on the main menu, click the **Checking** preferences category to the left, and then select the **Company Preferences** tab. (See Figure 2:8.)

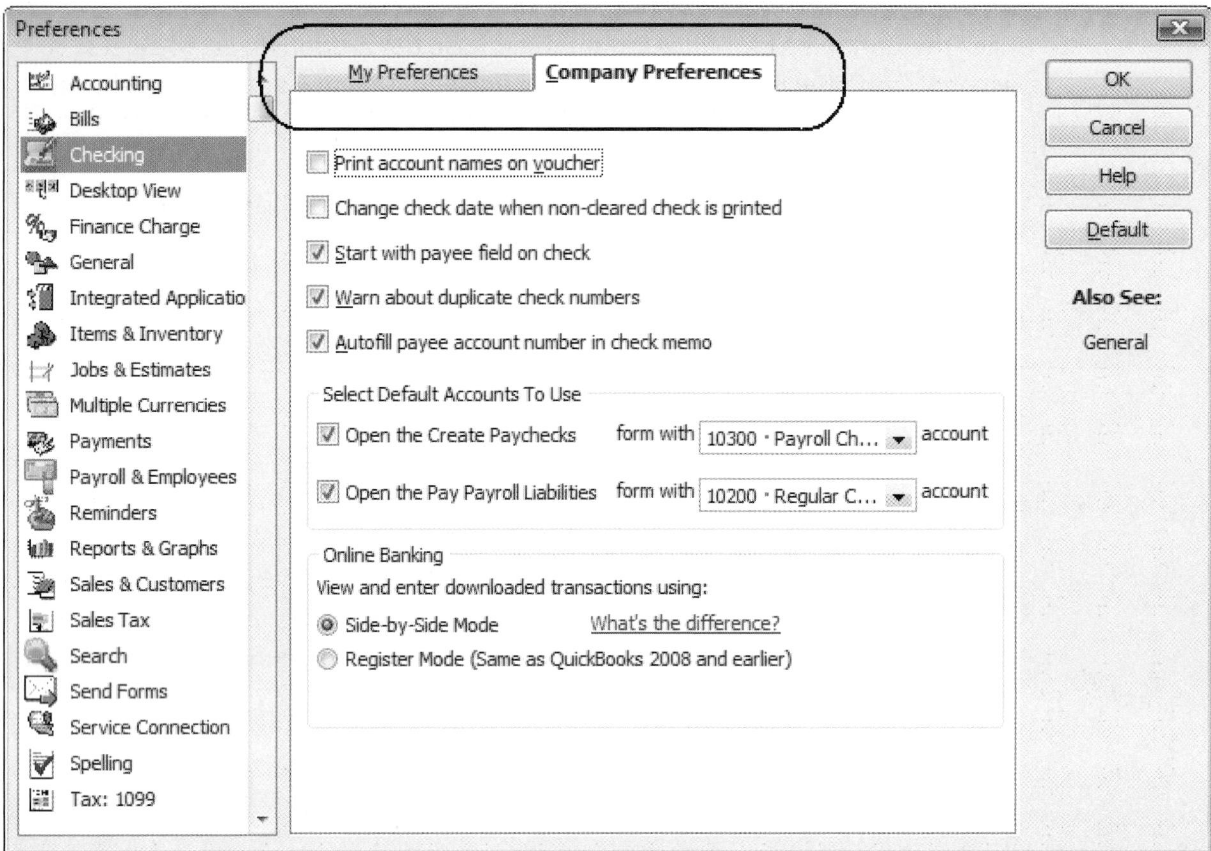

Figure 2:8

The Preferences window contains two tabs, namely Company Preferences and My Preferences. **Company Preferences** affect all users whereas **My Preferences** are customized for individual users. Company Preferences are stored with the company data file and will be copied to your machine when you load the sample databases. My Preferences are not stored within the data file and thus must be customized after opening it. My Preferences are saved only on the current machine.

Company Preferences

You will look at only a few of the company preferences to learn why certain activities behave in a particular fashion. ***Do not change any of these settings***.

Checking preferences (Figure 2:8) show that paychecks will post to 10300 Payroll Checking Account and payroll liability checks will post to 10200 Regular Checking.

Click **Accounting** and the Company Preferences tab shows that the company has activated general ledger account numbers.

Click **Bills** to see that vendor purchase discounts are automatically taken and the discount amount will post to 59500 Purchase Discounts.

My Preferences

Now focus on settings that control software behavior on your machine. ***You should set these options for each sample company.*** Furthermore, if you move data to a new machine, you may need to set these options again.

Go to the **My Preferences** tab for each preference discussed next. When you make changes, click a different category and QBP will prompt to save your changes. Click **Yes** to save the changes.

❖ Checking Preferences

Click **My Preferences** and select the regular checking account for each option illustrated in Figure 2:9. *(Note: The regular checking number may vary for each sample company.)* These options make sure that the correct checking account number defaults during transaction entry.

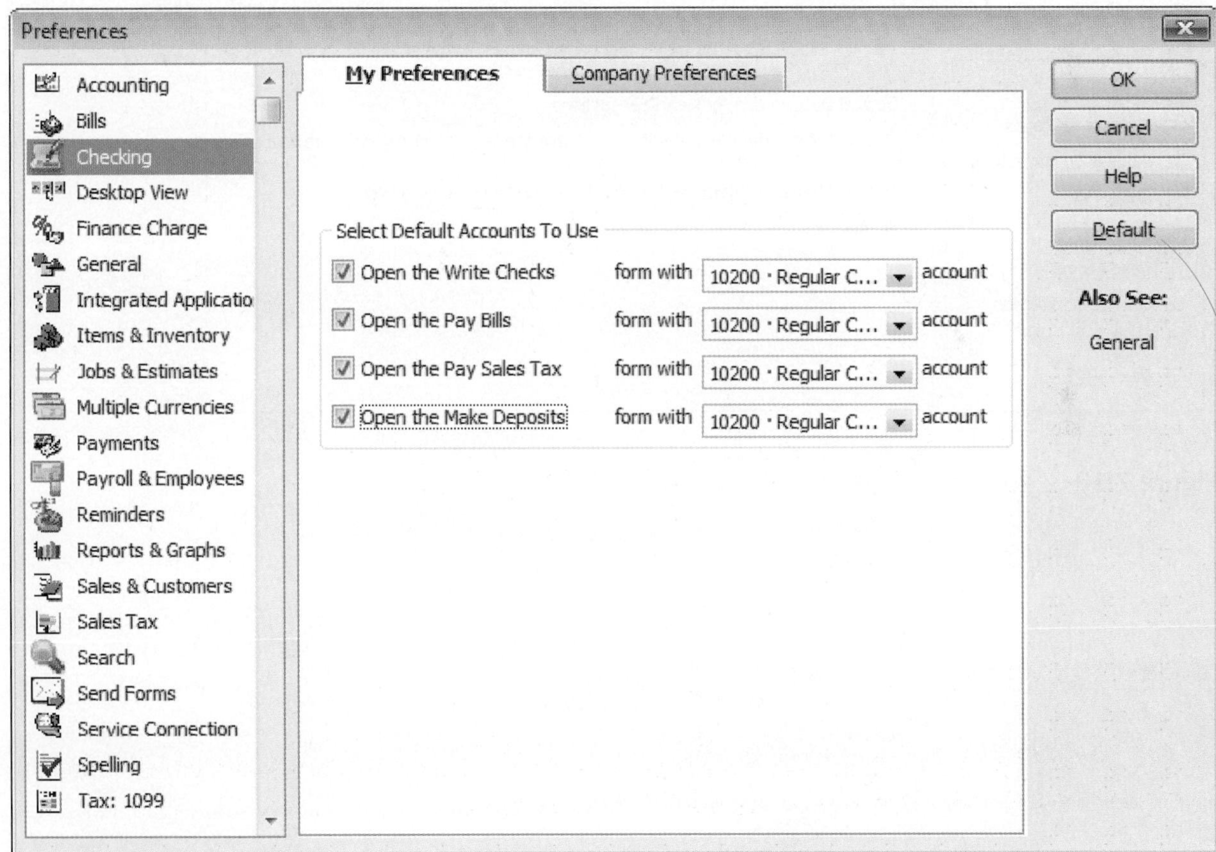

Figure 2:9

❖ General Preferences

Click **General** and verify the options shown in Figure 2:10. *(Note: Click **Save** if prompted to save any previous changes.)*

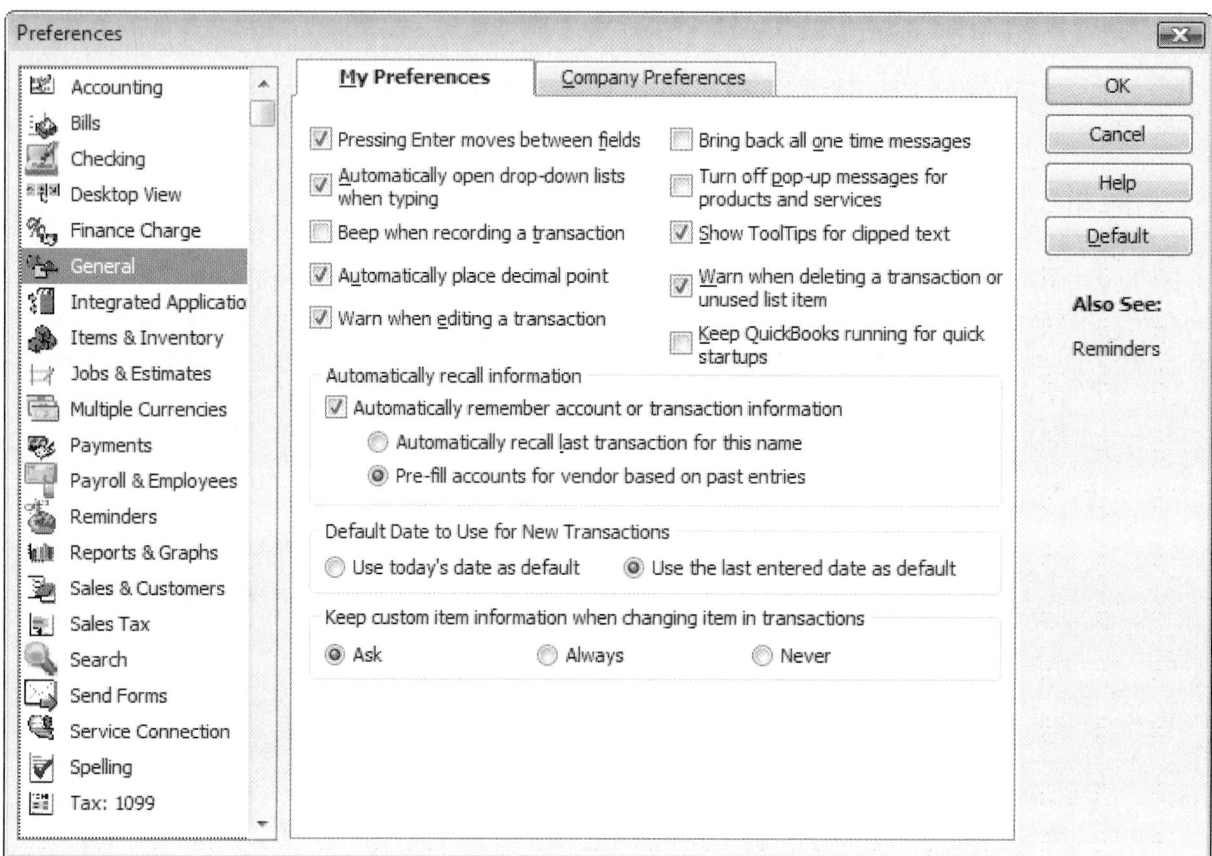

Figure 2:10

❖ Reports & Graphs Preferences

Click **Reports & Graphs** and verify that your options are the same as illustrated in Figure 2:11.

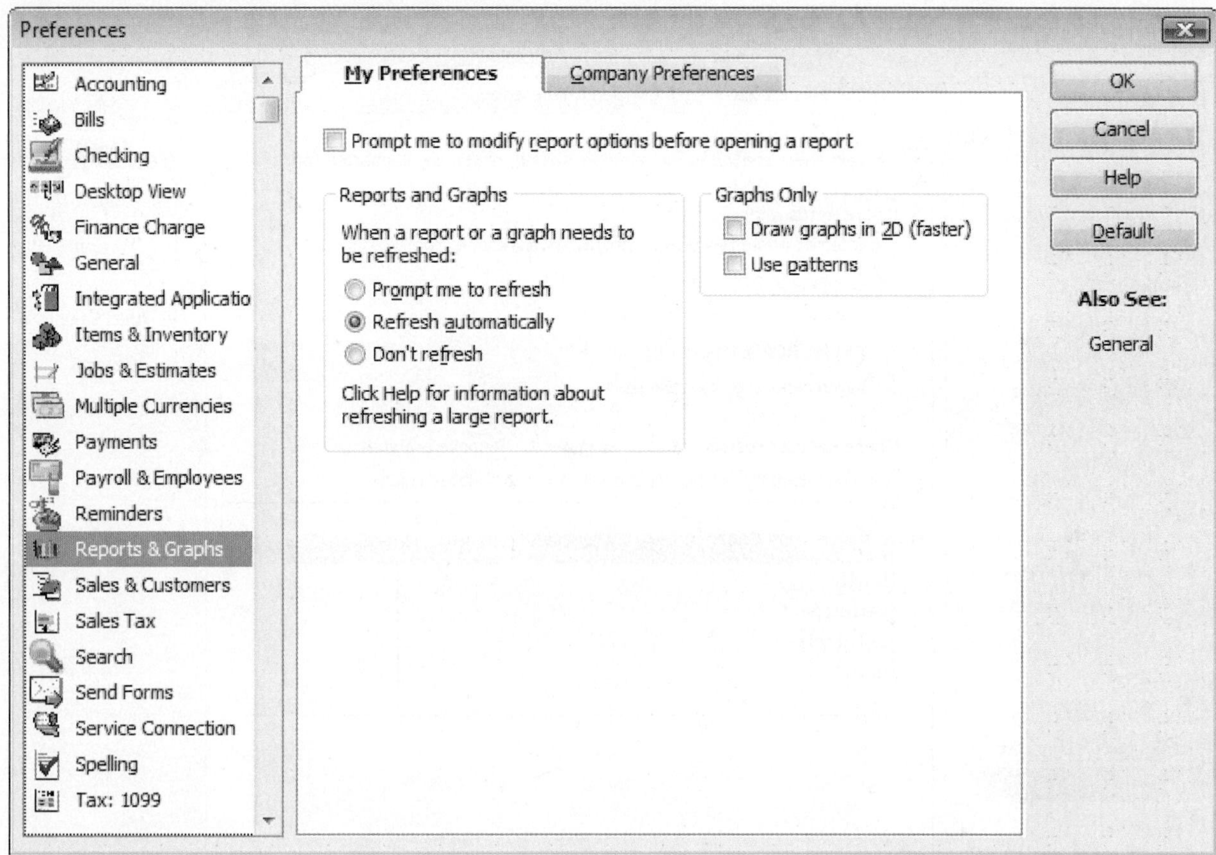

Figure 2:11

❖ Sales & Customers Preferences

Click **Sales & Customers** and verify that the option of **Ask what to do** is selected.

❖ Send Forms Preferences

Click **Send Forms** and make sure that the "**Auto-check the To be e-mailed**" checkbox is not selected.

❖ **Spelling Preferences**

Click **Spelling** if you want to customize spell check options (Figure 2:12).

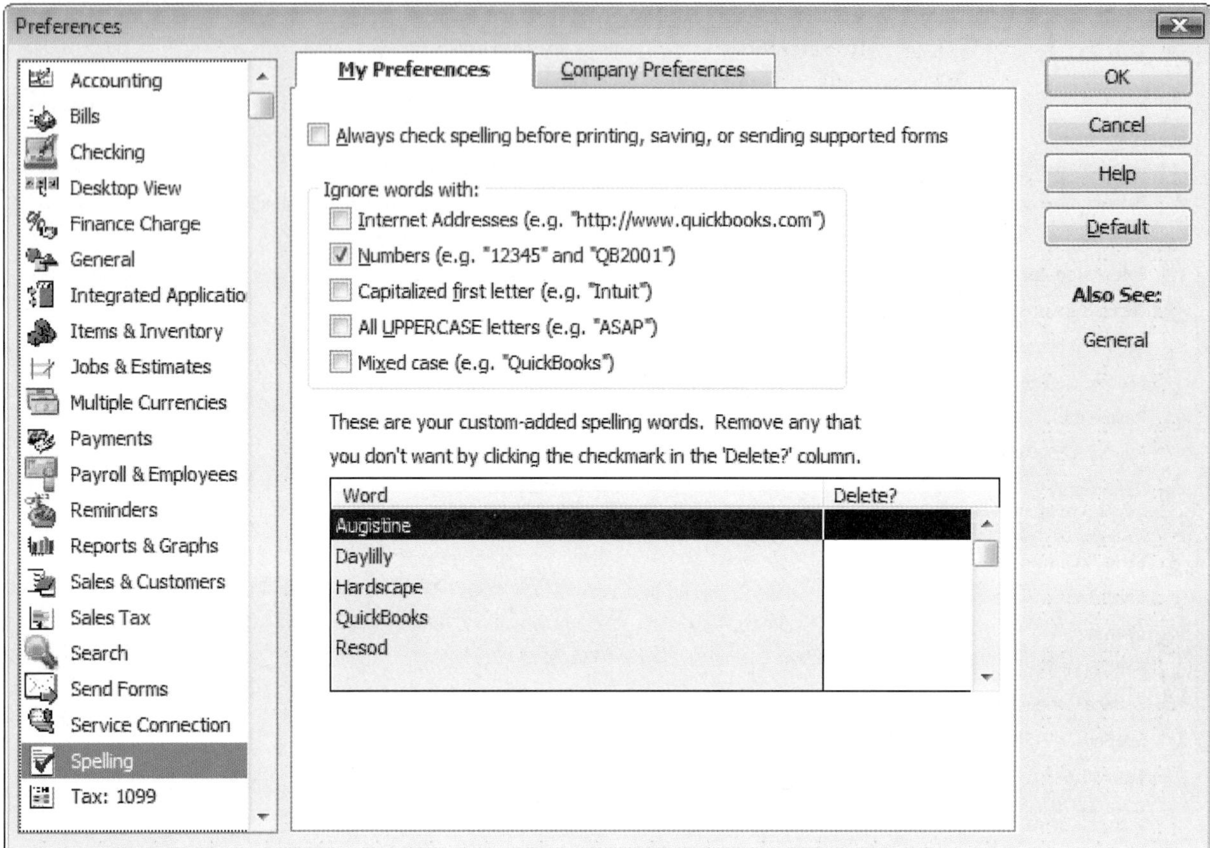

Figure 2:12

Click **OK** when finished. ***Remember you will need to set these options for each sample company***.

QUICKBOOKS DRILLDOWN FEATURES

Accounting software drilldown features offer a significant advantage over manual systems. Instead of sorting though general journal sheets, account ledgers, and other paperwork, you need only locate a transaction on a report or account and click to reopen the details. Let's begin by learning to use drilldown features on a report.

Open the Chart of Accounts list by using the keyboard shortcut of **Ctrl + A**. At the bottom of the list, click ***Reports>>Reports on All Accounts>>Other>>Trial Balance*** (Figure 2:13).

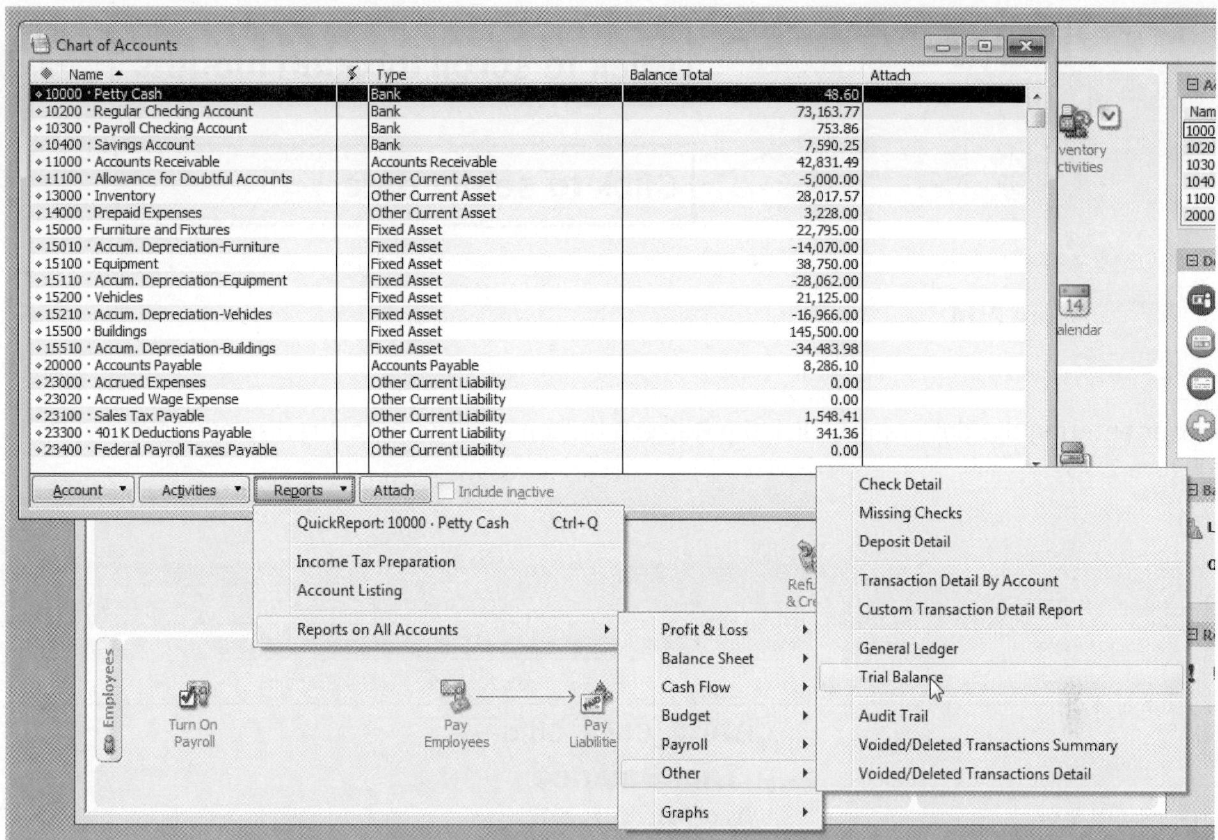

Figure 2:13

Set the date range on the report to **From 3/1/12** and **To 3/31/12**. The **From** date can be entered by typing "3/1/12" into the field or by clicking [calendar icon] to open the calendar feature. When using the calendar feature, dates are selected by scrolling through months to choose a date. (See Figure 2:14.)

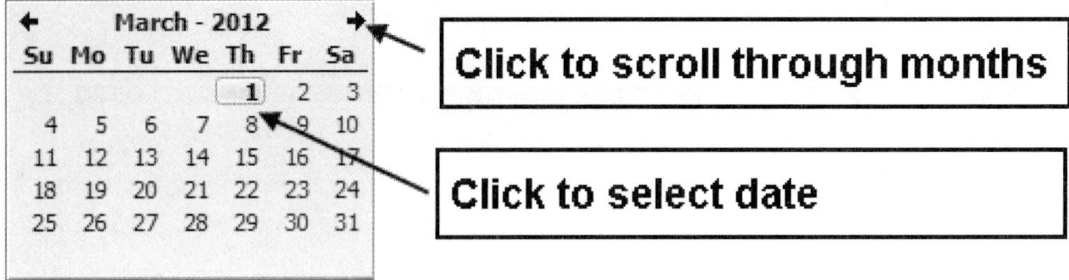

Figure 2:14

After entering the date range, click the **Refresh** button and the report redisplays as shown in Figure 2:15.

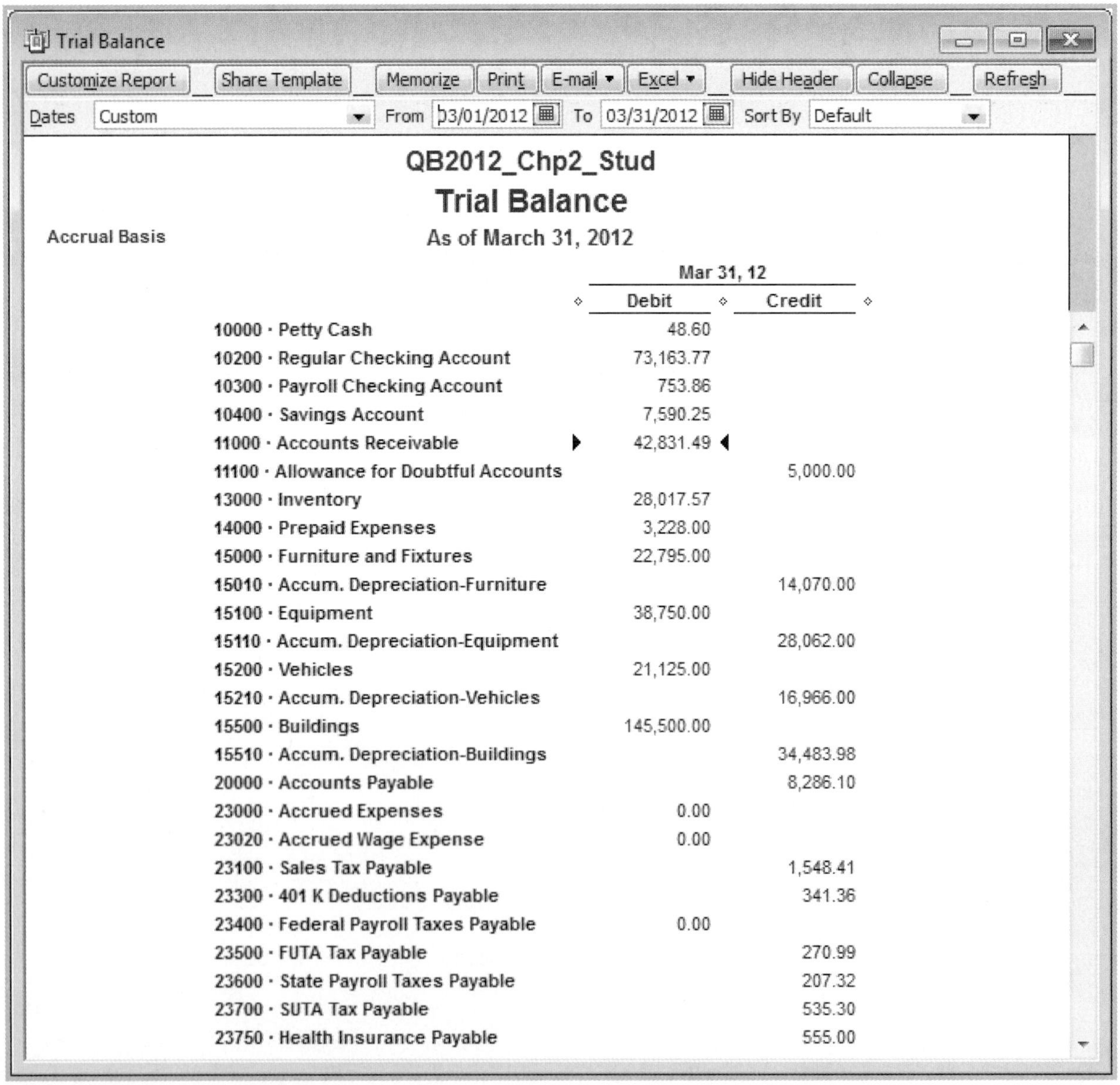

Trial Balance

Customize Report | Share Template | Memorize | Print | E-mail ▾ | Excel ▾ | Hide Header | Collapse | Refresh

Dates Custom | From 03/01/2012 | To 03/31/2012 | Sort By Default

QB2012_Chp2_Stud

Trial Balance

Accrual Basis

As of March 31, 2012

	Mar 31, 12	
	Debit	Credit
10000 · Petty Cash	48.60	
10200 · Regular Checking Account	73,163.77	
10300 · Payroll Checking Account	753.86	
10400 · Savings Account	7,590.25	
11000 · Accounts Receivable	42,831.49	
11100 · Allowance for Doubtful Accounts		5,000.00
13000 · Inventory	28,017.57	
14000 · Prepaid Expenses	3,228.00	
15000 · Furniture and Fixtures	22,795.00	
15010 · Accum. Depreciation-Furniture		14,070.00
15100 · Equipment	38,750.00	
15110 · Accum. Depreciation-Equipment		28,062.00
15200 · Vehicles	21,125.00	
15210 · Accum. Depreciation-Vehicles		16,966.00
15500 · Buildings	145,500.00	
15510 · Accum. Depreciation-Buildings		34,483.98
20000 · Accounts Payable		8,286.10
23000 · Accrued Expenses	0.00	
23020 · Accrued Wage Expense	0.00	
23100 · Sales Tax Payable		1,548.41
23300 · 401 K Deductions Payable		341.36
23400 · Federal Payroll Taxes Payable	0.00	
23500 · FUTA Tax Payable		270.99
23600 · State Payroll Taxes Payable		207.32
23700 · SUTA Tax Payable		535.30
23750 · Health Insurance Payable		555.00

Figure 2:15

We are looking for a March sales invoice to Holland Properties. Hold your mouse over the balance on **Accounts Receivable** until the mouse changes to . *(Note: When you see this symbol, the report contains a drilldown feature.)* Double click and the Transactions by Account report opens (Figure 2:16).

Transactions by Account

Customize Report | Share Template | Memorize | Print | E-mail ▾ | Excel ▾ | Hide Header | Expand | Refresh

Dates Custom From 03/01/2012 To 03/31/2012 Total By Account list Sort By Default

7:03 PM
01/16/12
Accrual Basis

QB2012_Chp2_Stud
Transactions by Account
As of March 31, 2012

Type	Date	Num	Adj	Name	Memo	Clr	Split	Debit	Credit	Balance
11000 · Accounts Receivable										39,175.15
Invoice	03/02/2012	10301		Aldred Builders			-SPLIT-	4,299.35		43,474.50
Invoice	03/02/2012	10302		Henton Park			-SPLIT-	3,596.10		47,070.60
Invoice	03/02/2012	10304		Chapple Law			-SPLIT-	211.54		47,282.14
Payment	03/02/2012	987		Henton Park			10200 · Regu...		5,124.52	42,157.62
Payment	03/02/2012	985		Mosley Country Club			10200 · Regu...		2,211.82	39,945.80
Invoice	03/06/2012	10303		Holland Properties			-SPLIT-	22,939.49		62,885.29
Payment	03/06/2012	666		Frost Technology			10200 · Regu...		611.42	62,273.87
Payment	03/06/2012	587		Dash Business			10200 · Regu...		1,245.57	61,028.30
Payment	03/06/2012	8766		Roberts Learning			10200 · Regu...		5,185.67	55,842.63
Payment	03/07/2012	7878		Rose University			10200 · Regu...		7,196.00	48,646.63
Payment	03/07/2012	6978		Williams Industries			10200 · Regu...		872.04	47,774.59
Invoice	03/08/2012	10305		Freemond Country...			-SPLIT-	1,864.40		49,638.99
Invoice	03/08/2012	10306		Smith Family Garden			-SPLIT-	3,228.90		52,867.89
Invoice	03/08/2012	10307		Stevenson Leasing			-SPLIT-	2,682.35		55,550.24
Invoice	03/08/2012	10308		Everly Property			-SPLIT-	3,816.99		59,367.23
Invoice	03/08/2012	10309		Armstrong Landsc...			-SPLIT-	2,592.00		61,959.23

Figure 2:16

You should see **Invoice 10303** to Holland Properties. Hold your mouse over this invoice and again double click to open the original invoice (Figure 2:17).

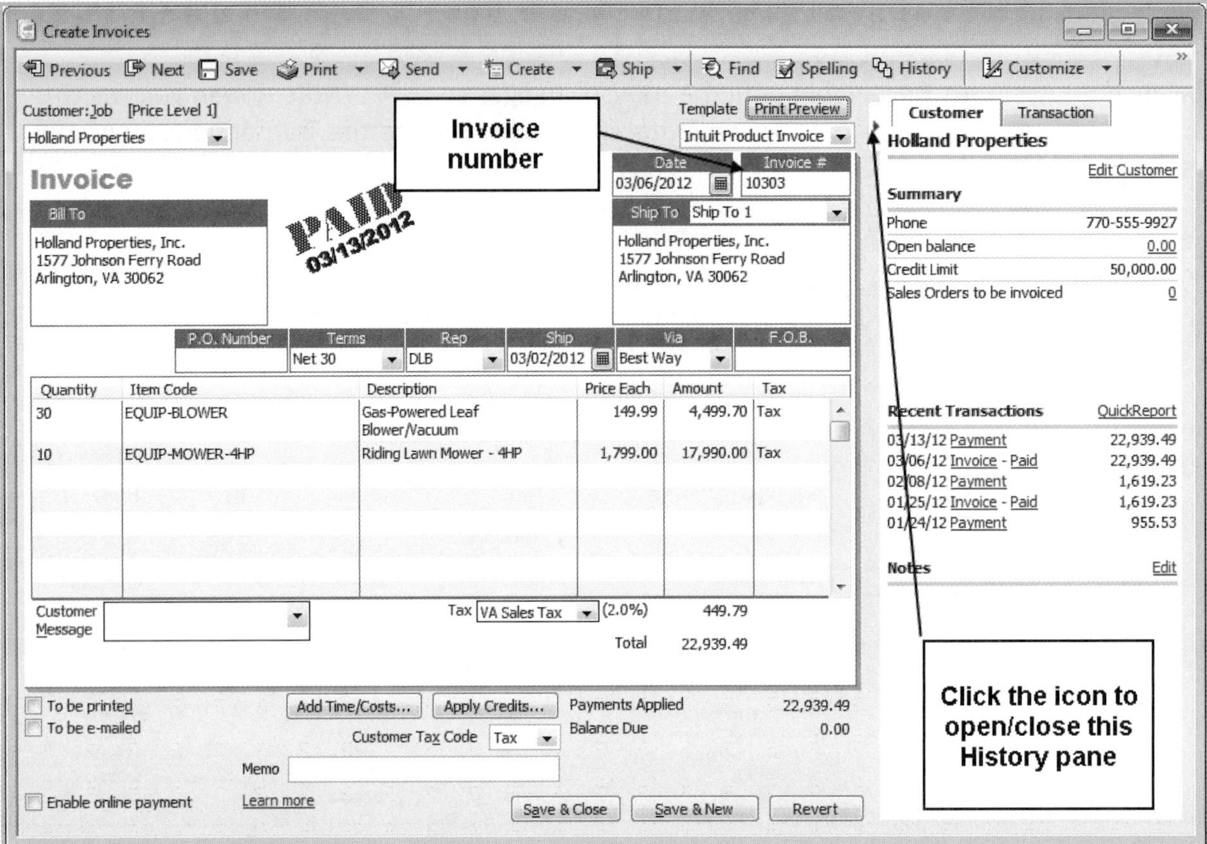

Figure 2:17

You have just used **report drilldown features** to locate an original transaction. Not all reports offer this feature. Drilldowns are only available when you see the magnifying glass.

So what information was gained by drilling down from the Trial Balance report to the Transaction by Account report to the invoice? First, you know that the invoice debited accounts receivable because you began your drill down from the accounts receivable account on the Trial Balance. Next, you know that it debited accounts receivable for $22,939.49 because this is the amount listed on the Transactions by Account report. Finally, you know the inventory items sold and the sales tax charged because this is shown on the invoice.

However, neither the reports nor the invoice tell you the general ledger sales accounts credited by the transaction because these accounts are defaulted from the inventory item sold and are not displayed. *(Note: You will learn about setting default inventory item sales accounts in Chapters 4 and 8.)* Therefore, the next report is used to show all the accounts affected by this invoice.

With the invoice still open, click ***Reports>>Transaction Journal*** on the main menu and the report in Figure 2:18 opens. You can now view all general ledger accounts affected by this transaction.

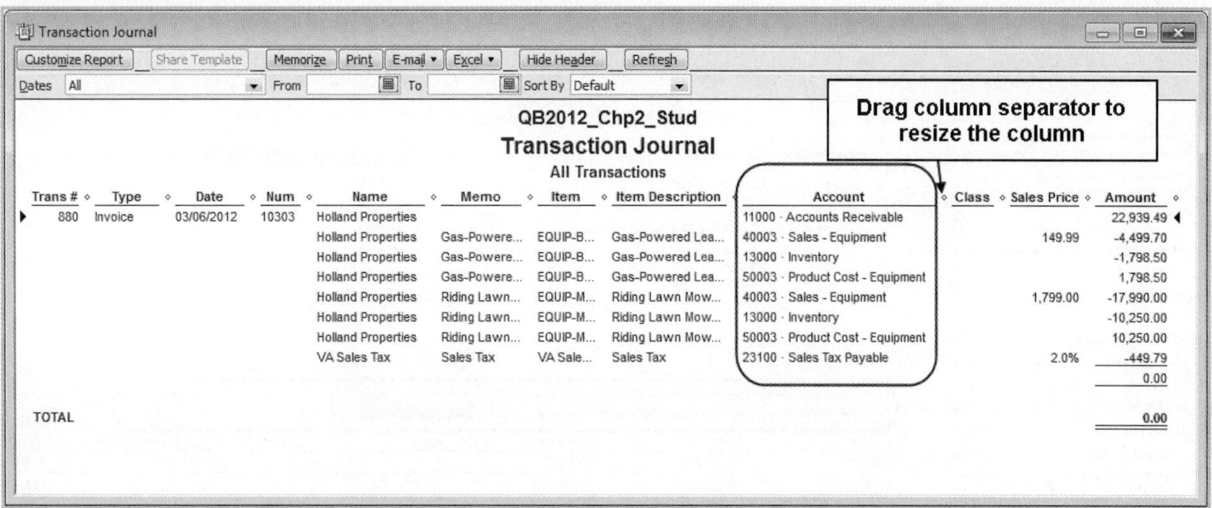

Figure 2:18

Close the Transaction Journal report, the Create Invoices window, the Transactions by Account report, the Trial Balance report, and the Chart of Accounts window by clicking **x** on each. QBP will prompt to save changes to the reports if you resized columns or entered custom dates (Figure 2:19). Click the option illustrated to turn off future messages and click **No**.

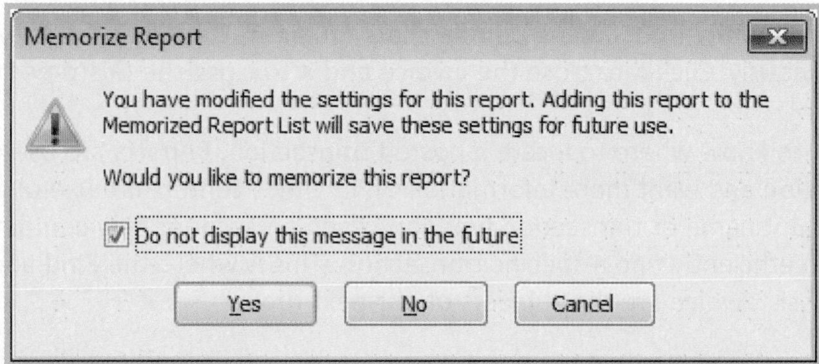

Figure 2:19

There is another way to locate the Holland invoice. This example assumes that you know the customer and invoice number. Click **Customers** on the Icon Bar, select the **Customers & Jobs** tab, and click **Holland Properties** on the left. On the right, change the **Show** option to "Invoices" and **Date** to "All." (See Figure 2:20.)

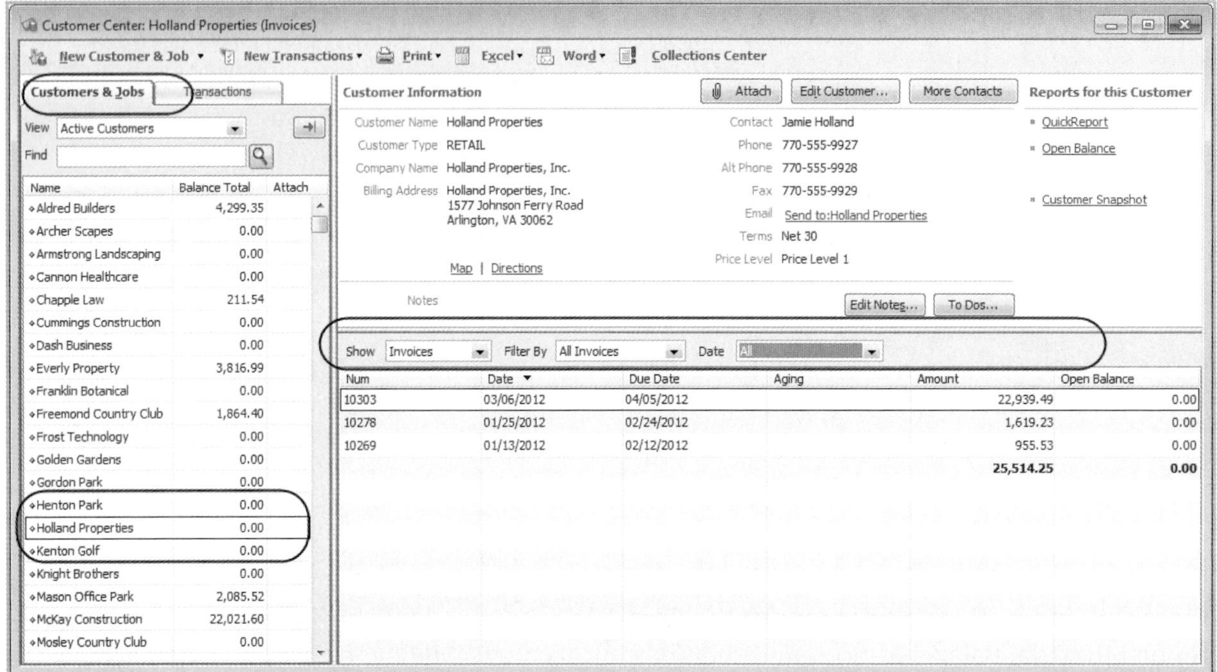

Figure 2:20

Highlight invoice number **10303** and double click. You are returned to the invoice transaction illustrated previously. Click **X** to close the invoice and **X** to close the Customer Center.

It is important to know where to locate a posted transaction. Reports are useful when you spot a transaction and want more information on it. QBP's centers are useful when you know the account name or transaction type; however, an account may contain too many transactions to efficiently find a specific transaction. This is where the **Find** and **Search** features can assist, which are the subjects of our next topic.

FIND OR SEARCH FOR TRANSACTIONS IN QUICKBOOKS

In this topic you will use the **Search** and **Find** features to locate Invoice 10303 issued to Holland Properties on March 6, 2012.

First use the **Search**. This feature appears as Search Company or Help on the right side of the Icon Bar. Type "10303" into the field and press enter or click the search icon. The results are illustrated next. Click **X** to close the pane.

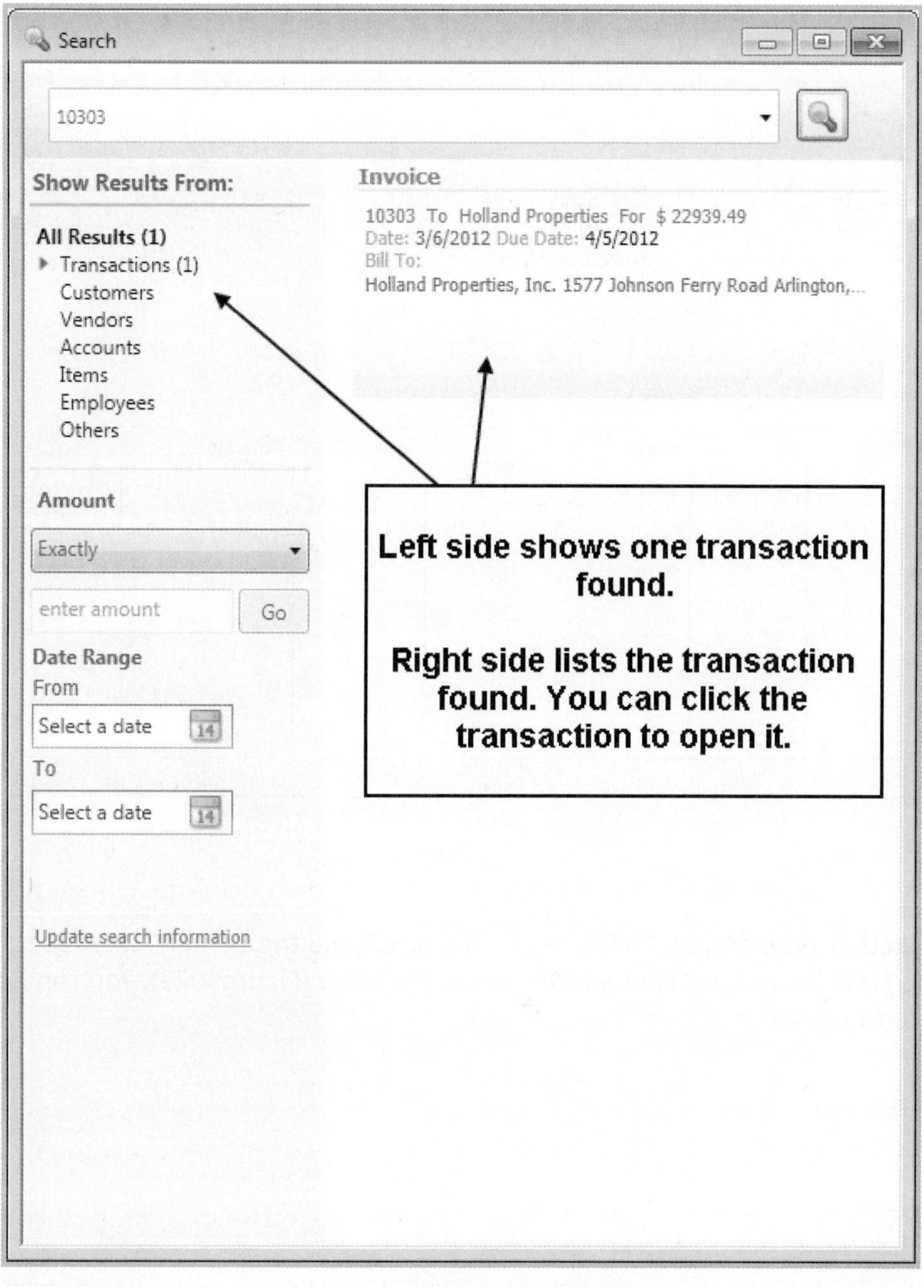

Figure 2:21

Now use the **Find** feature. Select ***Edit>>Find*** on the main menu or use the keyboard shortcut of **Ctrl + F**. Choose the **Simple** tab to view the window illustrated in Figure 2:22.

The Find window contains two tabs, one for performing a **Simple** search and the other for performing an **Advanced** search. We will use the simple approach first to locate Holland's invoice.

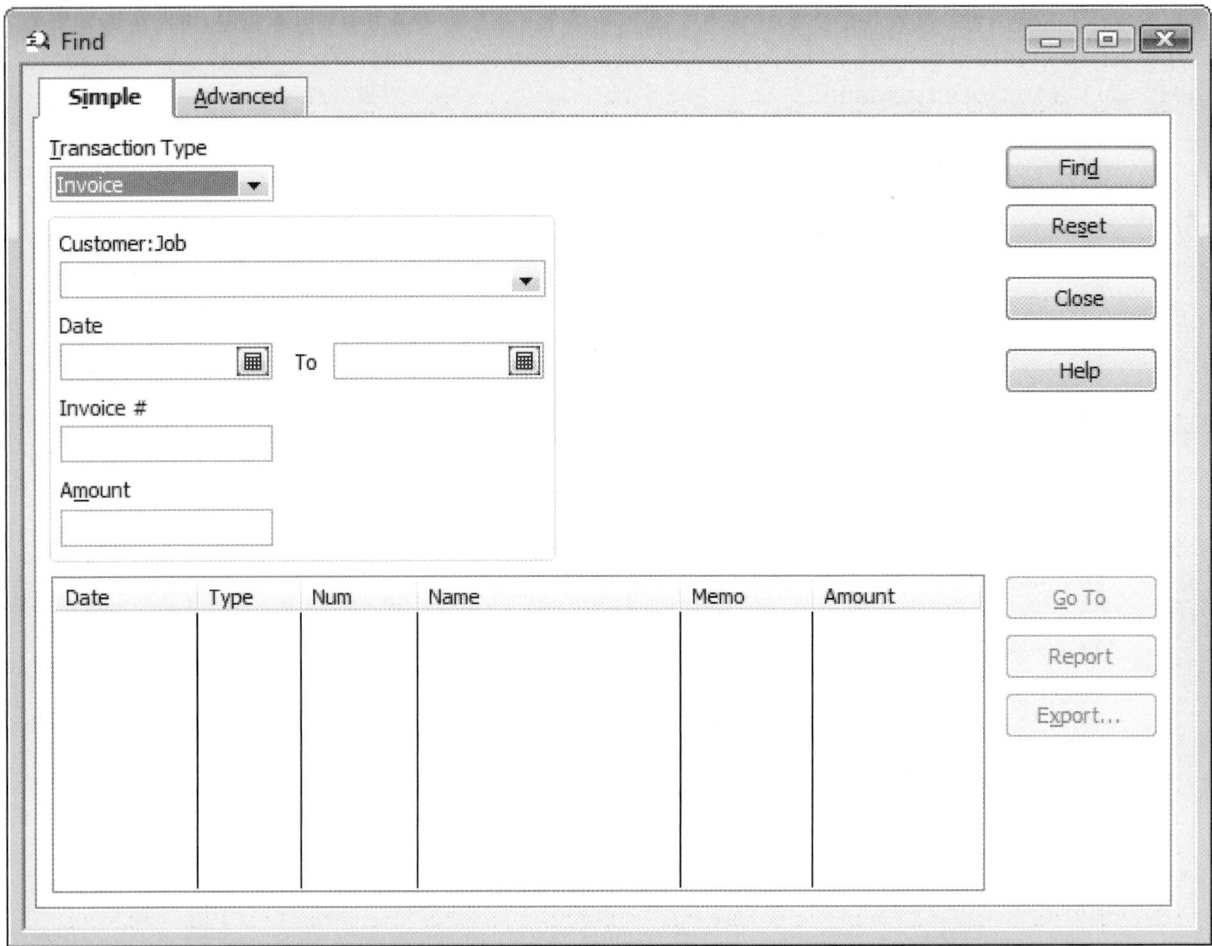

Figure 2:22

Click the **Transaction Type** dropdown list, select "Invoice," and then enter "3/6/12" to "3/6/12" in the **Date** fields. Click **Find** and the invoice is listed (Figure 2:23). You can double click the invoice to reopen it.

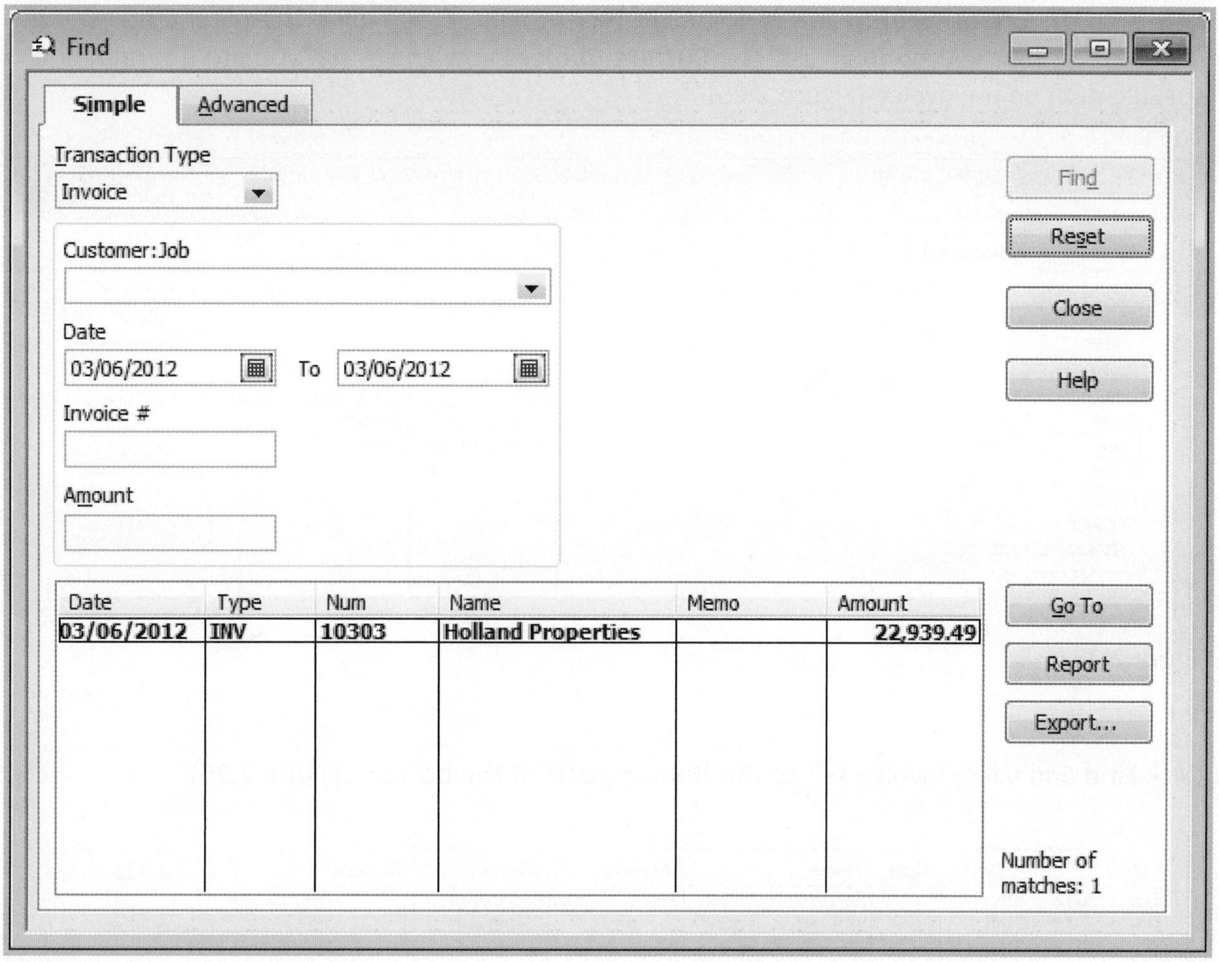

Figure 2:23

Now select the **Advanced** tab so we can illustrate using this method to locate other transactions containing one of the inventory items sold to Holland. Filter choices on this tab appear on the left and current filters appear on the right (Figure 2:24). Click **Transaction Type** under **Choose Filter** and, using the dropdown list, select Invoice to add it to the filters listed under **Current Choices**.

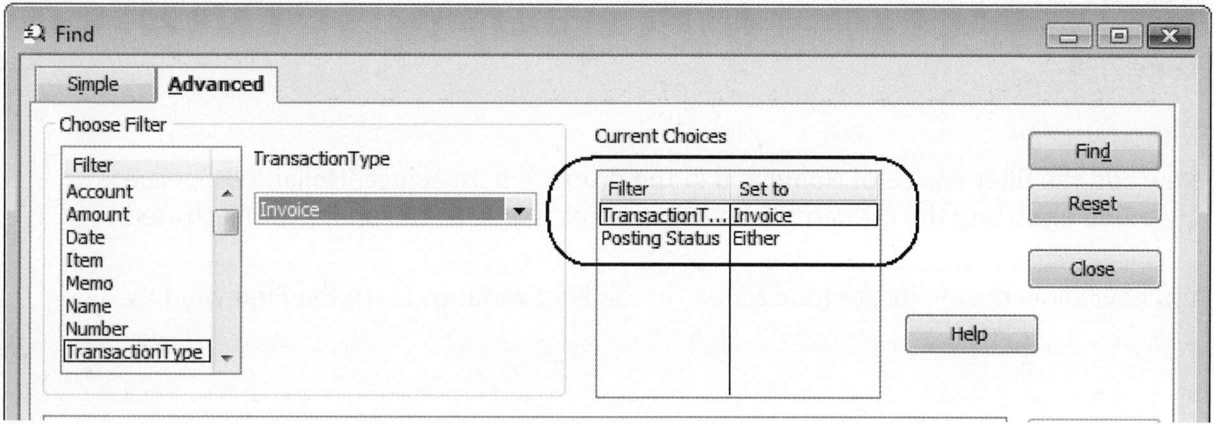

Figure 2:24

Return to the **Choose Filter** column. Highlight the **Item** filter and, under **Item**, look up "EQUIP-BLOWER" using the dropdown list. The **Current Choices** now show that you are filtering for a specific item on an invoice (Figure 2:25).

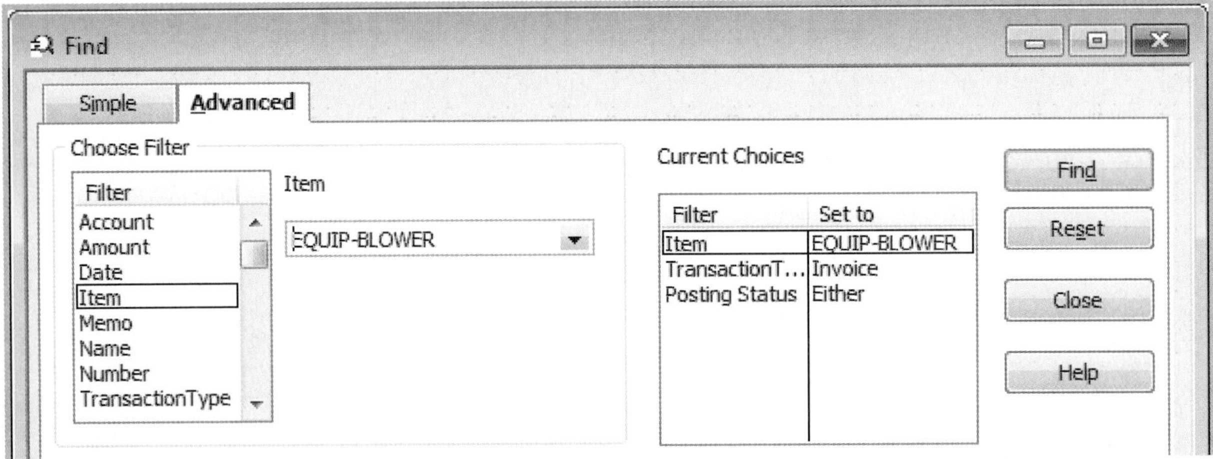

Figure 2:25

Click **Find** and every invoice selling this item appears at the bottom (Figure 2:26).

Date	Type	Num	Name	Account	Memo	Amount
03/15/2012	INV		Stevenson Leasing	Sales - Equi...	Gas-Power...	-749.95
03/15/2012	INV		Stevenson Leasing	Inventory	Gas-Power...	-299.75
03/15/2012	INV		Stevenson Leasing	Product Co...	Gas-Power...	299.75
03/08/2012	INV		Stevenson Leasing	Sales - Equi...	Gas-Power...	-2,249.85
03/08/2012	INV		Stevenson Leasing	Inventory	Gas-Power...	-899.25
03/08/2012	INV		Stevenson Leasing	Product Co...	Gas-Power...	899.25
03/08/2012	INV		Everly Property	Sales - Equi...	Gas-Power...	-2,249.85
03/08/2012	INV		Everly Property	Inventory	Gas-Power...	-899.25
03/08/2012	INV		Everly Property	Product Co...	Gas-Power...	899.25
03/06/2012	INV		Holland Properties	Sales - Equi...	Gas-Power...	-4,499.70
03/06/2012	INV		Holland Properties	Inventory	Gas-Power...	-1,798.50
03/06/2012	INV		Holland Properties	Product Co...	Gas-Power...	1,798.50
02/28/2012	INV		Golden Gardens	Sales - Equi...	Gas-Power...	-299.98
02/28/2012	INV		Golden Gardens	Inventory	Gas-Power...	-119.90
02/28/2012	INV		Golden Gardens	Product Co...	Gas-Power...	119.90

Go To

Report

Export...

Number of matches: 30

Figure 2:26

Now add the filter choice of **Name** and in the dropdown list select "Holland Properties." Click **Find** again and the list narrows to the invoices issued to Holland. (Not illustrated.)

You now know how to locate transactions in the Find window. Close the **Find** window.

THE REPORTS MENU AND REPORT CENTER

In this topic you learn to work with reports. Click ***Reports*** on the main menu to view the menu commands illustrated in Figure 2:27. This ▸ indicator on a menu means submenus are present.

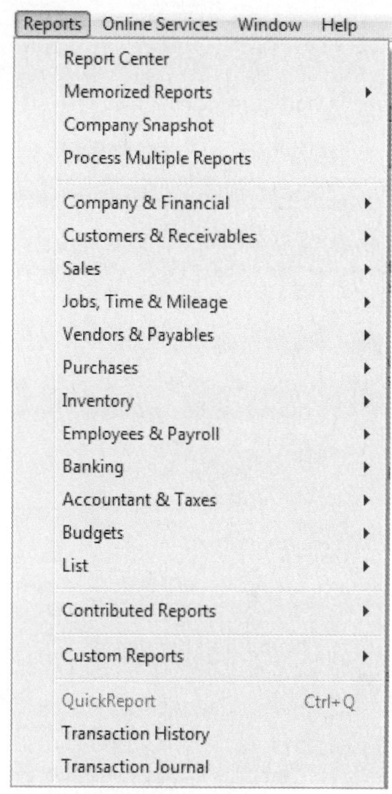

Figure 2:27

Reports are categorized by activities; therefore, you can generally locate a report by identifying the type of activity to report on. For instance, financial statements are found under the Company & Financial submenu whereas aged receivables reports are found under the Customers & Receivables submenu.

Reports that you customize will be located under the Memorized Reports submenu.

Click the **Report Center** submenu and the **Report Center** illustrated in Figure 2:28 opens. *(Note: Click the Close link to close the message about new contributed reports.)* Notice that categories on the left correspond to the submenus under the Reports menu.

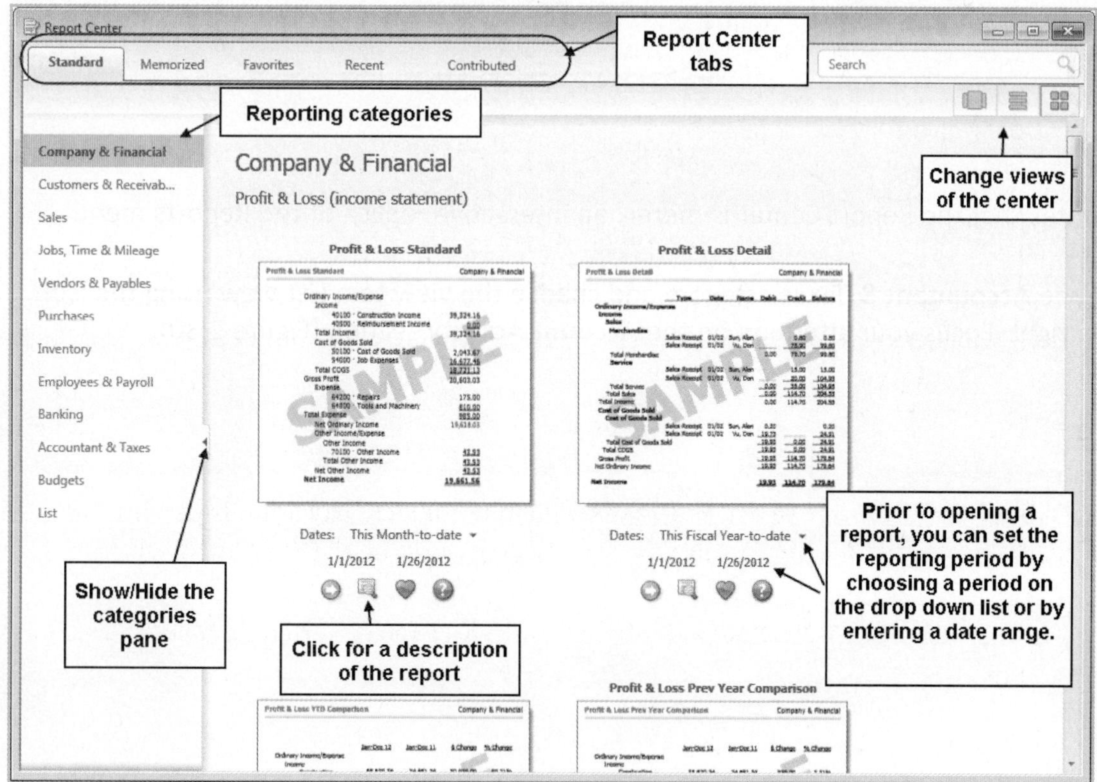

Figure 2:28

With the **Company & Financial** reporting category on the **Report Center** highlighted, you can click the **Company & Financial** submenu under the **Reports** menu (Figure 2:29) to see that reports on the center can also be opened from the menu.

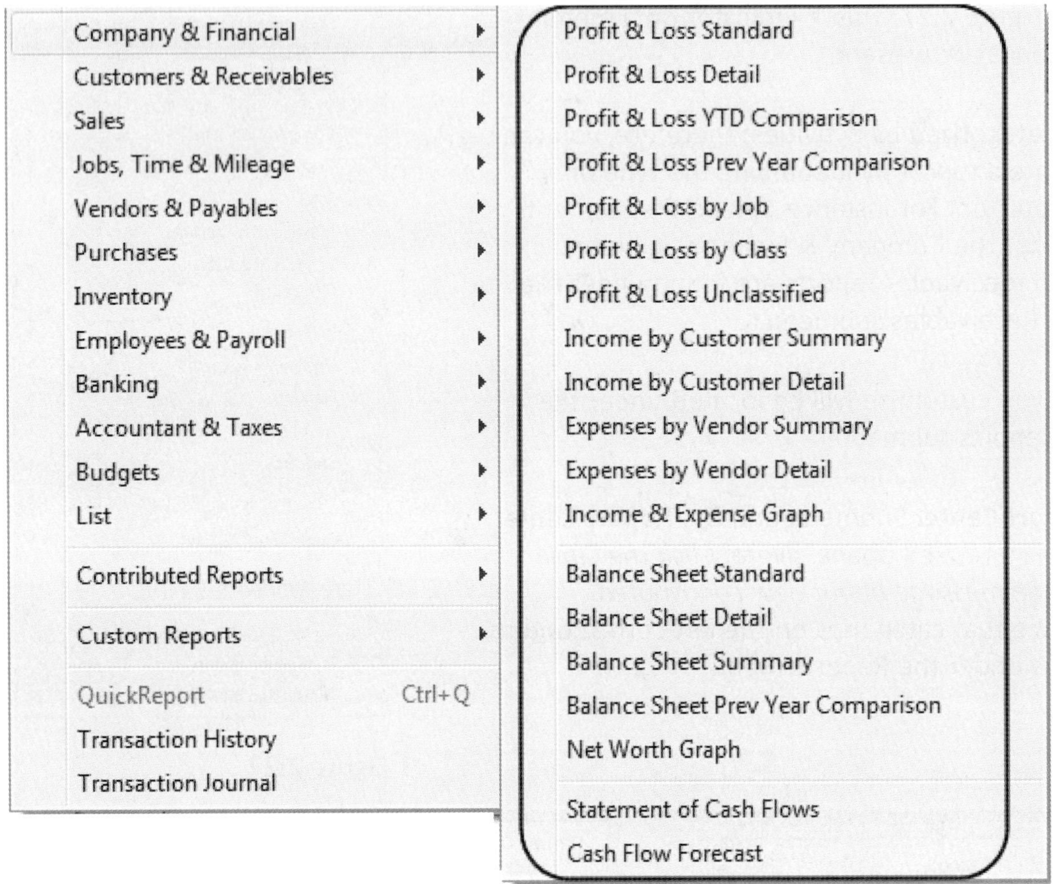

Figure 2:29

This illustrates that the Report Center is merely an interactive replica of the Reports menu.

Now click the **Accountant & Taxes** category and change the view to a List view using the icon on the top right. Focus your attention on the **Account Activity** section (Figure 2:30).

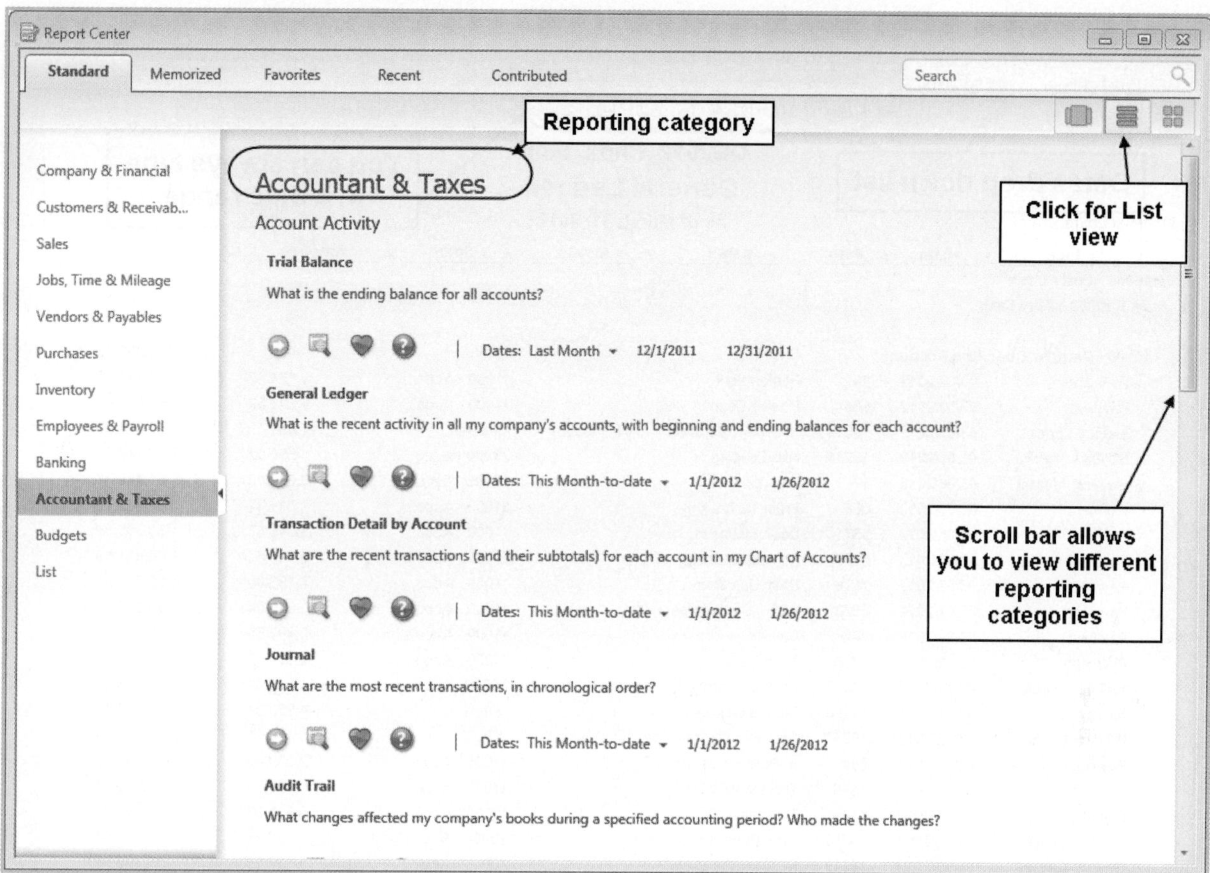

Figure 2:30

The **Audit Trail, Voided/Deleted Transactions Summary**, and **Detail** reports are control reports that document user activity in the software. In subsequent chapters, you will be asked to trace the audit trail for a posted transaction and to print reports that document this trail. We want to clarify that the Audit Trail report above does not document posted transactions. Instead, this report documents the activities of the users posting transactions.

Double click the **General Ledger** report to open it. *(Note: You may be prompted about collapsing and expanding transactions. You can turn off this message in the future using the Do not display this message in the future option. Click OK to proceed.)*

This report documents the audit trail on posted transactions. Set the reporting date range to **3/1/12** through **3/31/12**. *(Note: You can set a date range by clicking the existing date and typing a new date or use the dropdown list on the Dates field to select a reporting period. If you use the Dates field, remember that options for this field refer to the date on your computer to determine the period.)*

Click the **Refresh** button to open the report illustrated in Figure 2:31.

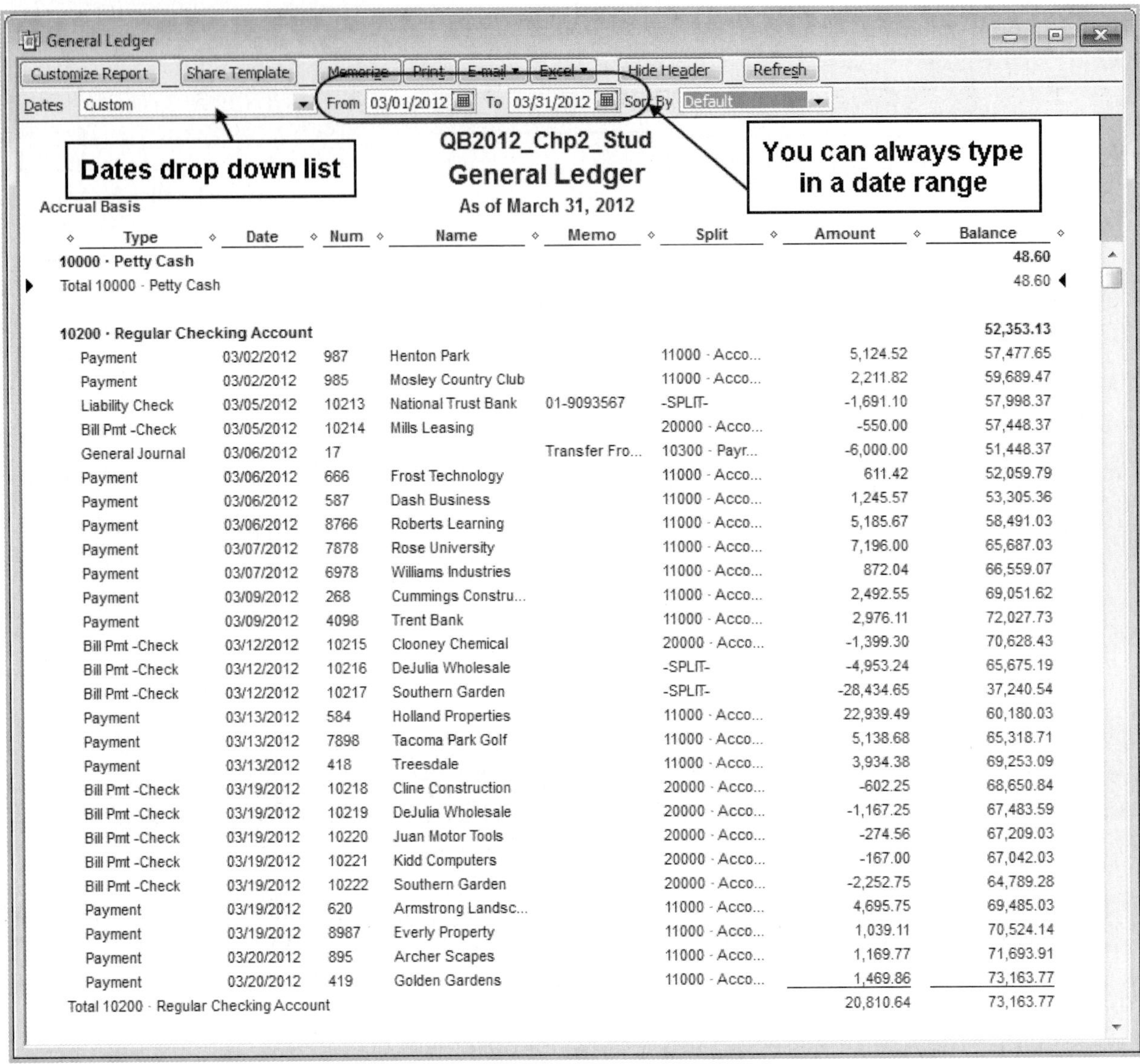

QB2012_Chp2_Stud
General Ledger
Accrual Basis
As of March 31, 2012

Type	Date	Num	Name	Memo	Split	Amount	Balance
10000 · Petty Cash							48.60
Total 10000 · Petty Cash							48.60
10200 · Regular Checking Account							52,353.13
Payment	03/02/2012	987	Henton Park		11000 · Acco...	5,124.52	57,477.65
Payment	03/02/2012	985	Mosley Country Club		11000 · Acco...	2,211.82	59,689.47
Liability Check	03/05/2012	10213	National Trust Bank	01-9093567	-SPLIT-	-1,691.10	57,998.37
Bill Pmt -Check	03/05/2012	10214	Mills Leasing		20000 · Acco...	-550.00	57,448.37
General Journal	03/06/2012	17		Transfer Fro...	10300 · Payr...	-6,000.00	51,448.37
Payment	03/06/2012	666	Frost Technology		11000 · Acco...	611.42	52,059.79
Payment	03/06/2012	587	Dash Business		11000 · Acco...	1,245.57	53,305.36
Payment	03/06/2012	8766	Roberts Learning		11000 · Acco...	5,185.67	58,491.03
Payment	03/07/2012	7878	Rose University		11000 · Acco...	7,196.00	65,687.03
Payment	03/07/2012	6978	Williams Industries		11000 · Acco...	872.04	66,559.07
Payment	03/09/2012	268	Cummings Constru...		11000 · Acco...	2,492.55	69,051.62
Payment	03/09/2012	4098	Trent Bank		11000 · Acco...	2,976.11	72,027.73
Bill Pmt -Check	03/12/2012	10215	Clooney Chemical		20000 · Acco...	-1,399.30	70,628.43
Bill Pmt -Check	03/12/2012	10216	DeJulia Wholesale		-SPLIT-	-4,953.24	65,675.19
Bill Pmt -Check	03/12/2012	10217	Southern Garden		-SPLIT-	-28,434.65	37,240.54
Payment	03/13/2012	584	Holland Properties		11000 · Acco...	22,939.49	60,180.03
Payment	03/13/2012	7898	Tacoma Park Golf		11000 · Acco...	5,138.68	65,318.71
Payment	03/13/2012	418	Treesdale		11000 · Acco...	3,934.38	69,253.09
Bill Pmt -Check	03/19/2012	10218	Cline Construction		20000 · Acco...	-602.25	68,650.84
Bill Pmt -Check	03/19/2012	10219	DeJulia Wholesale		20000 · Acco...	-1,167.25	67,483.59
Bill Pmt -Check	03/19/2012	10220	Juan Motor Tools		20000 · Acco...	-274.56	67,209.03
Bill Pmt -Check	03/19/2012	10221	Kidd Computers		20000 · Acco...	-167.00	67,042.03
Bill Pmt -Check	03/19/2012	10222	Southern Garden		20000 · Acco...	-2,252.75	64,789.28
Payment	03/19/2012	620	Armstrong Landsc...		11000 · Acco...	4,695.75	69,485.03
Payment	03/19/2012	8987	Everly Property		11000 · Acco...	1,039.11	70,524.14
Payment	03/20/2012	895	Archer Scapes		11000 · Acco...	1,169.77	71,693.91
Payment	03/20/2012	419	Golden Gardens		11000 · Acco...	1,469.86	73,163.77
Total 10200 · Regular Checking Account						20,810.64	73,163.77

Figure 2:31

The report lists March transactions posted to all general ledger accounts. Whenever you see "**-SPLIT-**" in the Split column, the transaction was posted to multiple accounts. For instance, the **Payment** from **Henton Park** on **3/2/2012** affected the 10200 Regular Checking Account (i.e., the account you are viewing) and the 11000 Accounts Receivable (i.e., the account listed in the Split column) whereas the **Bill Pmt-Check** to **DeJulia Wholesale** on **3/12/2012** affected the 10200 Regular Checking Account and multiple accounts listed as -SPLIT- under the Split column.

The following exercise steps through customizing this report. The steps will work when customizing any report.

STEPS TO CUSTOMIZING THE GENERAL LEDGER REPORT

1. Click **Customize Report** to open the window in Figure 2:32.

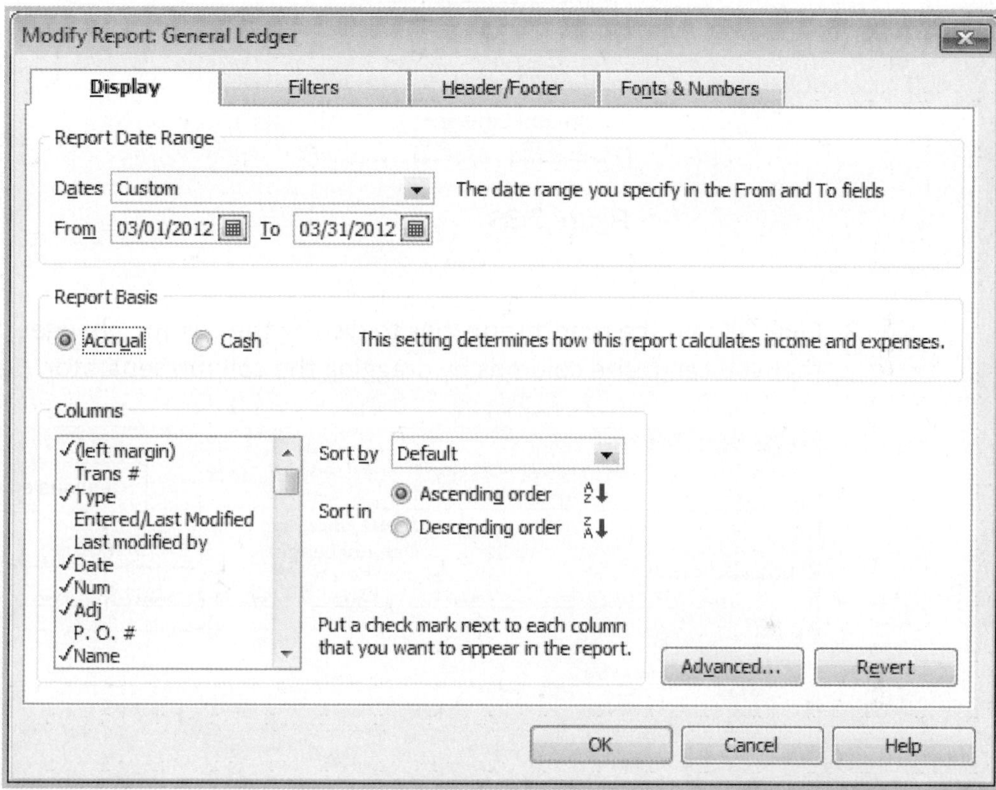

Figure 2:32

The **Display** tab sets the reporting period, columns, and sort order for the report. There is also an option for changing the **Report Basis** to **Cash** for companies that do not use the accrual method of accounting.

2. Scroll down the **Columns** section and locate the **Debit, Credit,** and **Amount** columns. Click **Debit** and **Credit** to activate these columns and click **Amount** to turn off the column. (See Figure 2:33.)

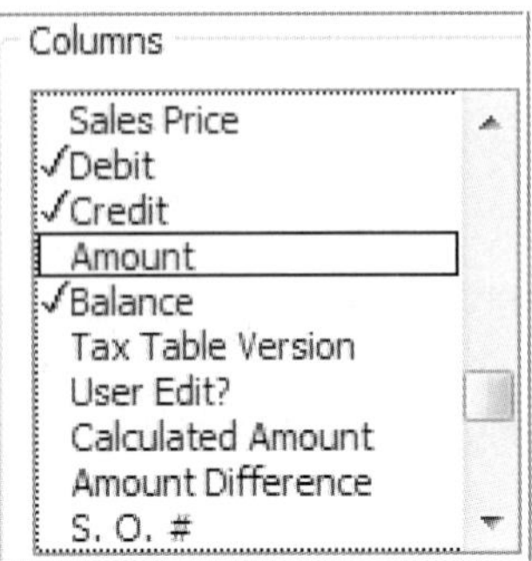

Figure 2:33

3. Click **OK** and the report refreshes to display the column changes. Remember that you can resize columns by dragging the column separator. (See Figure 2:34.)

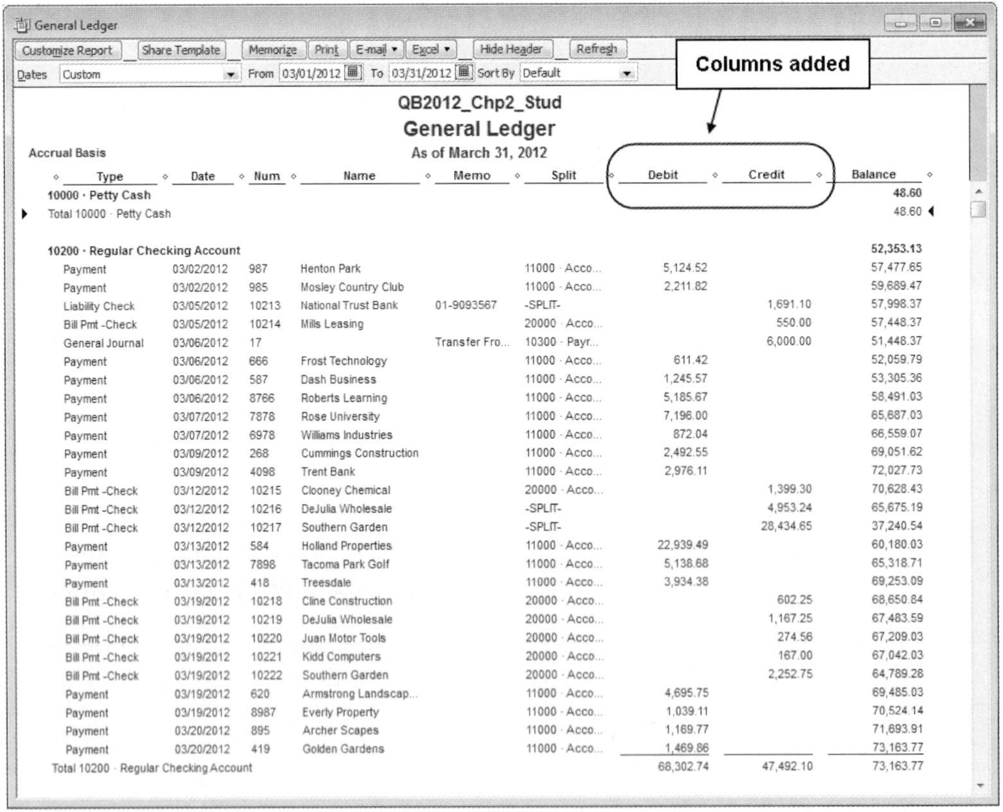

QB2012_Chp2_Stud
General Ledger
As of March 31, 2012
Accrual Basis

Type	Date	Num	Name	Memo	Split	Debit	Credit	Balance
10000 · Petty Cash								48.60
Total 10000 · Petty Cash								48.60
10200 · Regular Checking Account								52,353.13
Payment	03/02/2012	987	Henton Park		11000 · Acco...	5,124.52		57,477.65
Payment	03/02/2012	985	Mosley Country Club		11000 · Acco...	2,211.82		59,689.47
Liability Check	03/05/2012	10213	National Trust Bank	01-9093567	-SPLIT-		1,691.10	57,998.37
Bill Pmt -Check	03/05/2012	10214	Mills Leasing		20000 · Acco...		550.00	57,448.37
General Journal	03/06/2012	17		Transfer Fro...	10300 · Payr...		6,000.00	51,448.37
Payment	03/06/2012	666	Frost Technology		11000 · Acco...	611.42		52,059.79
Payment	03/06/2012	587	Dash Business		11000 · Acco...	1,245.57		53,305.36
Payment	03/06/2012	8766	Roberts Learning		11000 · Acco...	5,185.67		58,491.03
Payment	03/07/2012	7878	Rose University		11000 · Acco...	7,196.00		65,687.03
Payment	03/07/2012	6978	Williams Industries		11000 · Acco...	872.04		66,559.07
Payment	03/09/2012	268	Cummings Construction		11000 · Acco...	2,492.55		69,051.62
Payment	03/09/2012	4098	Trent Bank		11000 · Acco...	2,976.11		72,027.73
Bill Pmt -Check	03/12/2012	10215	Clooney Chemical		20000 · Acco...		1,399.30	70,628.43
Bill Pmt -Check	03/12/2012	10216	DeJulia Wholesale		-SPLIT-		4,953.24	65,675.19
Bill Pmt -Check	03/12/2012	10217	Southern Garden		-SPLIT-		28,434.65	37,240.54
Payment	03/13/2012	584	Holland Properties		11000 · Acco...	22,939.49		60,180.03
Payment	03/13/2012	7898	Tacoma Park Golf		11000 · Acco...	5,138.68		65,318.71
Payment	03/13/2012	418	Treesdale		11000 · Acco...	3,934.38		69,253.09
Bill Pmt -Check	03/19/2012	10218	Cline Construction		20000 · Acco...		602.25	68,650.84
Bill Pmt -Check	03/19/2012	10219	DeJulia Wholesale		20000 · Acco...		1,167.25	67,483.59
Bill Pmt -Check	03/19/2012	10220	Juan Motor Tools		20000 · Acco...		274.56	67,209.03
Bill Pmt -Check	03/19/2012	10221	Kidd Computers		20000 · Acco...		167.00	67,042.03
Bill Pmt -Check	03/19/2012	10222	Southern Garden		20000 · Acco...		2,252.75	64,789.28
Payment	03/19/2012	620	Armstrong Landscap...		11000 · Acco...	4,695.75		69,485.03
Payment	03/19/2012	8987	Everly Property		11000 · Acco...	1,039.11		70,524.14
Payment	03/20/2012	895	Archer Scapes		11000 · Acco...	1,169.77		71,693.91
Payment	03/20/2012	419	Golden Gardens		11000 · Acco...	1,469.86		73,163.77
Total 10200 · Regular Checking Account						68,302.74	47,492.10	73,163.77

Figure 2:34

4. Now filter the report to display selected accounts. Click **Customize Report** again and select the **Filters tab**. (See Figure 2:35.)

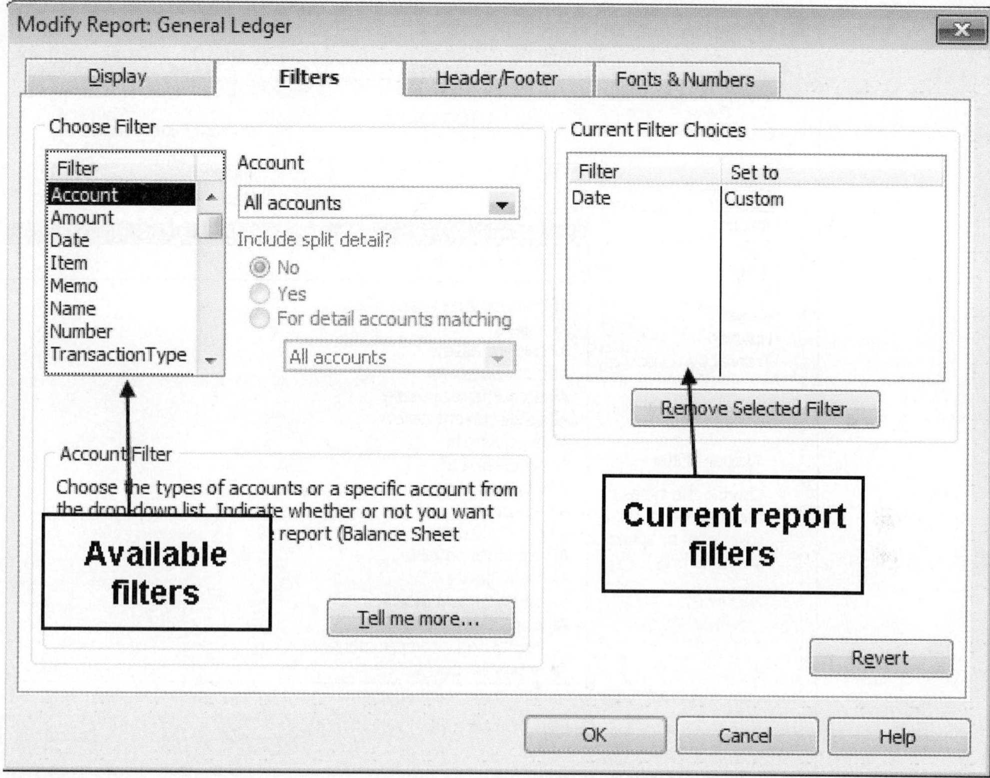

Figure 2:35

5. Highlight **Account** under **Choose Filter** and options for this filter are displayed to the right. Click the dropdown list to view these options (Figure 2:36).

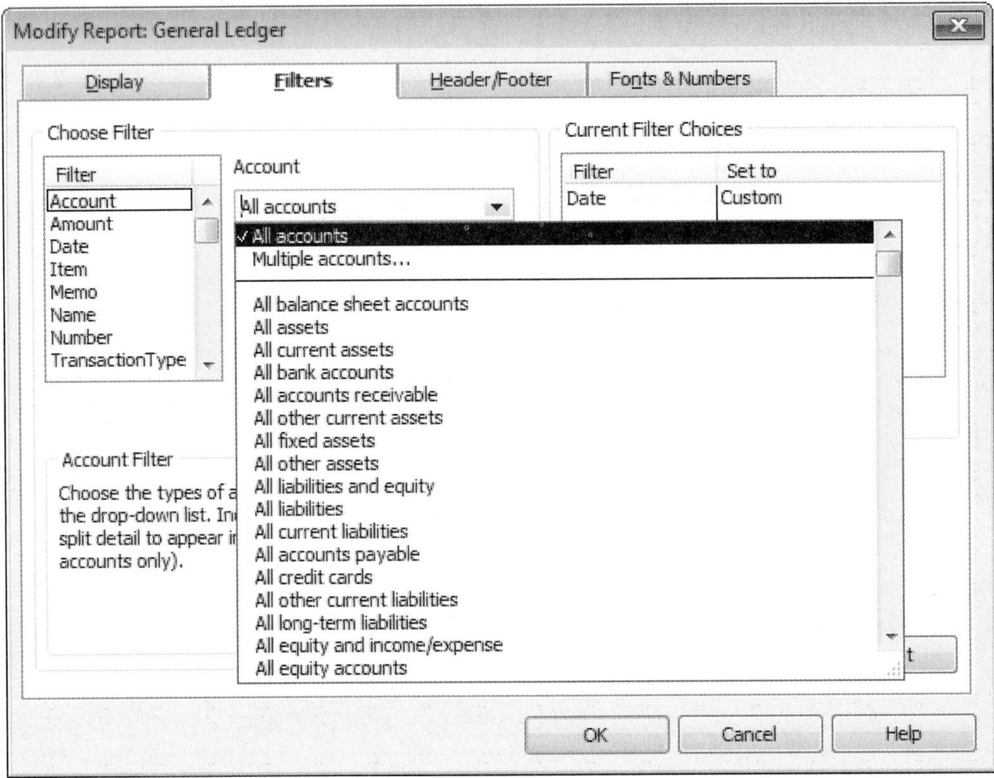

Figure 2:36

6. You are going to filter the general ledger report so that general ledger accounts 40001 and 40003 are the only accounts to display.

   In the filter box select **Multiple Accounts** and the window in Figure 2:37 opens.

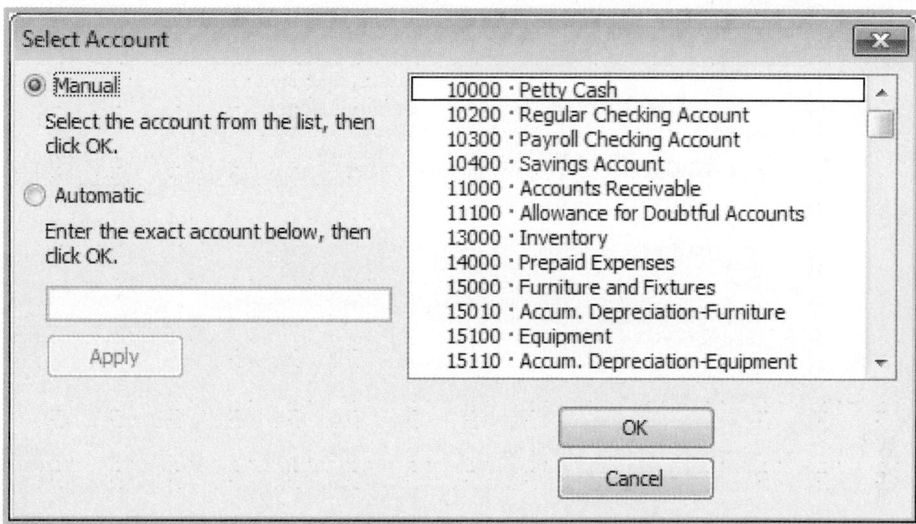

Figure 2:37

Scroll down and click **40001 Sales – Aviary** and **4003 Sales - Equipment** (Figure 2:38). Click **OK** after making these selections.

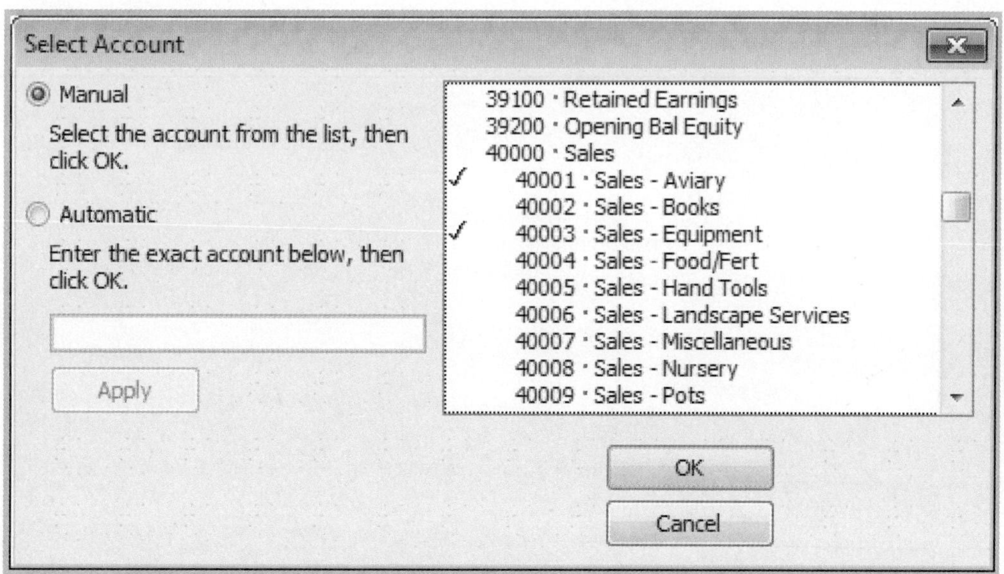

Figure 2:38

The **Current Filter Choices** now displays **Account** as an additional filter. Click **OK**.

7. Although the report still lists all accounts, these accounts do not display transactions. Scroll down to find that only the two filtered accounts display transactions (Figure 2:39).

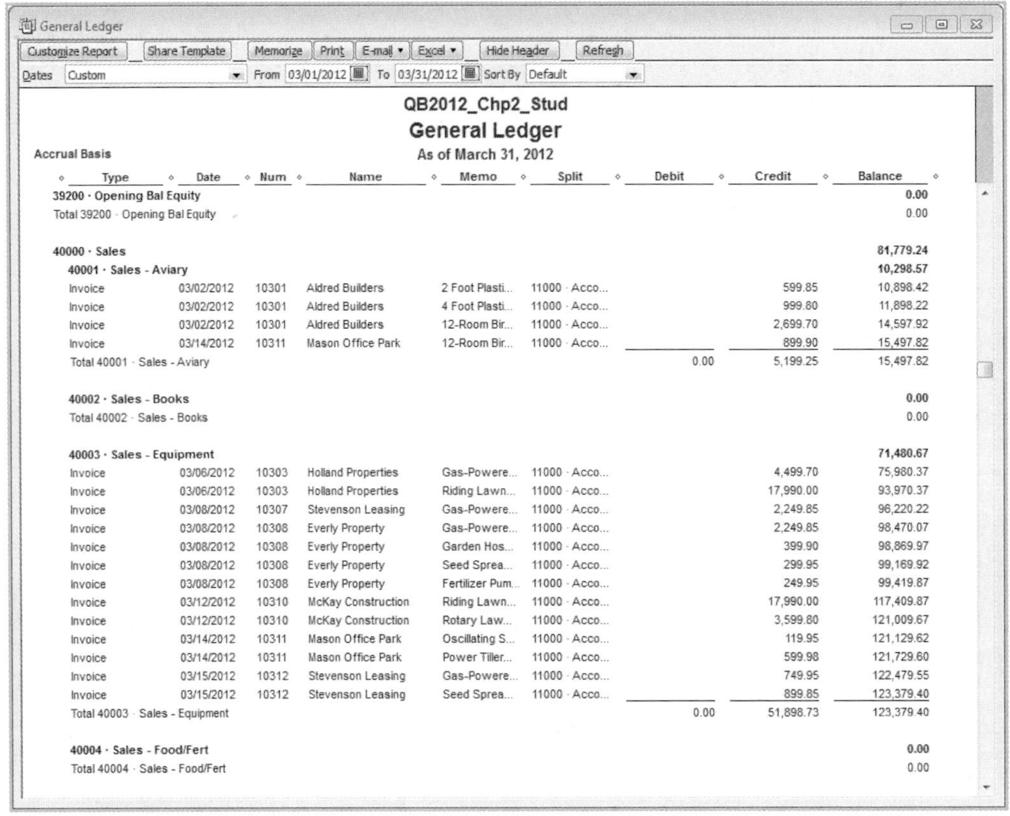

General Ledger

Customize Report | Share Template | Memorize | Print | E-mail | Excel | Hide Header | Refresh

Dates Custom From 03/01/2012 To 03/31/2012 Sort By Default

QB2012_Chp2_Stud

General Ledger

Accrual Basis — As of March 31, 2012

Type	Date	Num	Name	Memo	Split	Debit	Credit	Balance
39200 · Opening Bal Equity								**0.00**
Total 39200 · Opening Bal Equity								0.00
40000 · Sales								**81,779.24**
40001 · Sales - Aviary								**10,298.57**
Invoice	03/02/2012	10301	Aldred Builders	2 Foot Plasti...	11000 · Acco...		599.85	10,898.42
Invoice	03/02/2012	10301	Aldred Builders	4 Foot Plasti...	11000 · Acco...		999.80	11,898.22
Invoice	03/02/2012	10301	Aldred Builders	12-Room Bir...	11000 · Acco...		2,699.70	14,597.92
Invoice	03/14/2012	10311	Mason Office Park	12-Room Bir...	11000 · Acco...		899.90	15,497.82
Total 40001 · Sales - Aviary						0.00	5,199.25	15,497.82
40002 · Sales - Books								**0.00**
Total 40002 · Sales - Books								0.00
40003 · Sales - Equipment								**71,480.67**
Invoice	03/06/2012	10303	Holland Properties	Gas-Powere...	11000 · Acco...		4,499.70	75,980.37
Invoice	03/06/2012	10303	Holland Properties	Riding Lawn...	11000 · Acco...		17,990.00	93,970.37
Invoice	03/08/2012	10307	Stevenson Leasing	Gas-Powere...	11000 · Acco...		2,249.85	96,220.22
Invoice	03/08/2012	10308	Everly Property	Gas-Powere...	11000 · Acco...		2,249.85	98,470.07
Invoice	03/08/2012	10308	Everly Property	Garden Hos...	11000 · Acco...		399.90	98,869.97
Invoice	03/08/2012	10308	Everly Property	Seed Sprea...	11000 · Acco...		299.95	99,169.92
Invoice	03/08/2012	10308	Everly Property	Fertilizer Pum...	11000 · Acco...		249.95	99,419.87
Invoice	03/12/2012	10310	McKay Construction	Riding Lawn...	11000 · Acco...		17,990.00	117,409.87
Invoice	03/12/2012	10310	McKay Construction	Rotary Law...	11000 · Acco...		3,599.80	121,009.67
Invoice	03/14/2012	10311	Mason Office Park	Oscillating S...	11000 · Acco...		119.95	121,129.62
Invoice	03/14/2012	10311	Mason Office Park	Power Tiller...	11000 · Acco...		599.98	121,729.60
Invoice	03/15/2012	10312	Stevenson Leasing	Gas-Powere...	11000 · Acco...		749.95	122,479.55
Invoice	03/15/2012	10312	Stevenson Leasing	Seed Sprea...	11000 · Acco...		899.85	123,379.40
Total 40003 · Sales - Equipment						0.00	51,898.73	123,379.40
40004 · Sales - Food/Fert								**0.00**
Total 40004 · Sales - Food/Fert								0.00

Figure 2:39

8. Click **Customize Report** again and select the **Header/Footer** tab. Header options print at the top of report pages, whereas footer options print at the bottom. The Alignment option is used to left justify, right justify, or center report information on the page.

   Change the **Report Title** to "Customized General Ledger" (Figure 2:40).

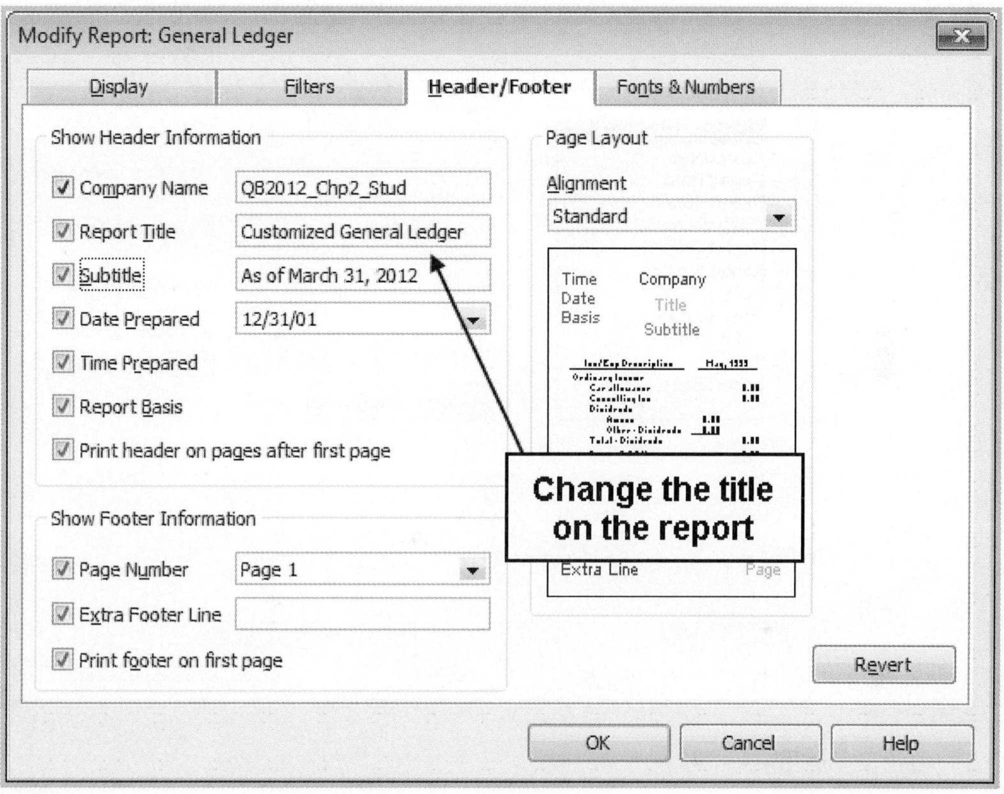

Figure 2:40

9. Click the **Fonts & Numbers** tab. The options illustrated in Figure 2:41 are used to change report fonts for data fields listed to the left. You can also change the appearance of negative numbers (i.e., options of Normally, In Parentheses, or With a Trailing Minus and In Bright Red).

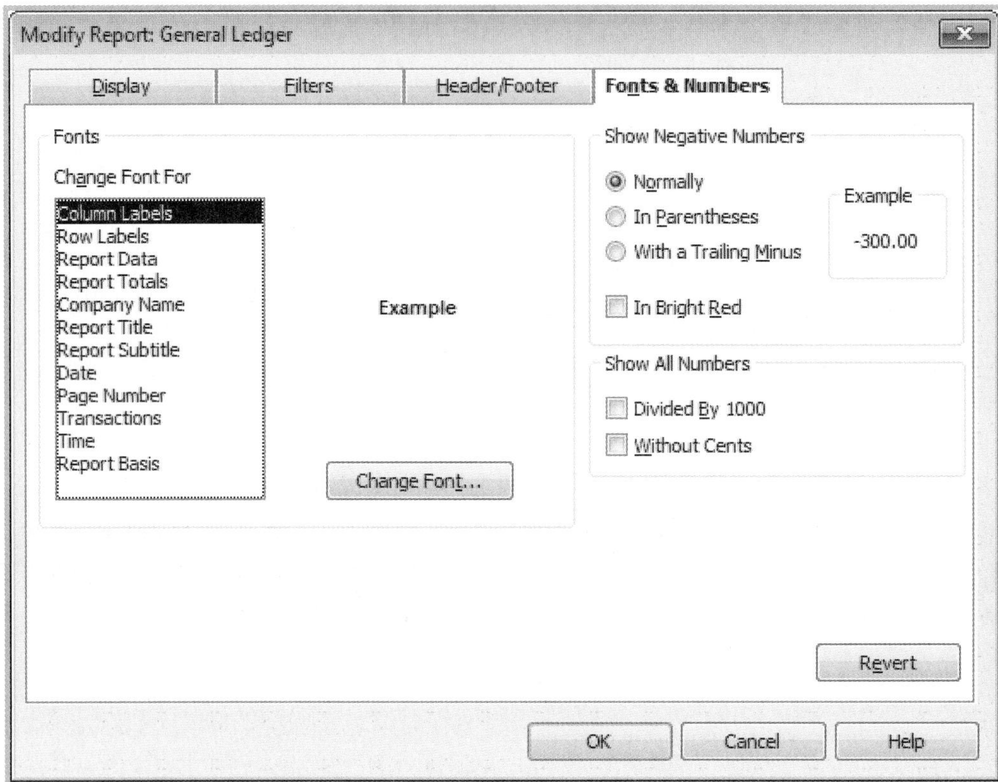

Figure 2:41

10. Click the **Filters** tab and highlight **Account** under Current Filter Choices. Click **Remove Selected Filter**.

11. Click **OK** and the report redisplays, listi ng transactions for all accounts. *(Note: If you click Print, the Print window will open to choose a printer. If you click Print again, the report will be sent to the printer.)*

12. You will now save the customized report. Click **Memorize** and, in the window that opens (Figure 2:42), verify that the **Name** is **Customized General Ledger**. Mark the option to **Save in Memorized Report Group** and look up the **Accountant** group. Click **OK** and close the report.

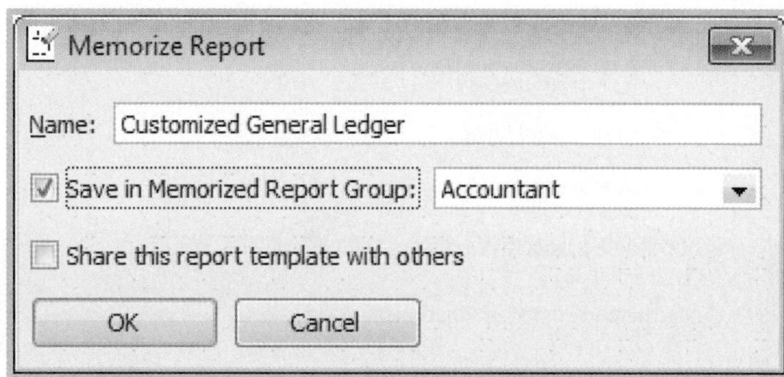

Figure 2:42

13. Click ***Reports>>Memorized Reports>>Accountant>>Customized General Ledger*** on the main menu and your customized report reopens. Thus, the Memorize Report window in the previous step created a new submenu item beneath the Accountant menu.

14. Now place this report on the Icon Bar so you can easily access it in the future. Click ***View>>Add "Customized General Ledger" to Icon Bar*** on the main menu.

    Change the **Label** to "Custom G/L" and click **OK**. Close the report and the Report Center.

EXPORTING AND EMAILING REPORTS

Your professor may want you to export reports to Excel and then email the workbook. Click ***Reports>>Company & Financial>>Profit & Loss Standard*** on the main menu to open the income statement.

Enter the reporting period of **1/1/12** to **3/31/12**. Click the **Excel** icon on the window toolbar and choose **Create New Worksheet** to open the window illustrated Figure 2:43.

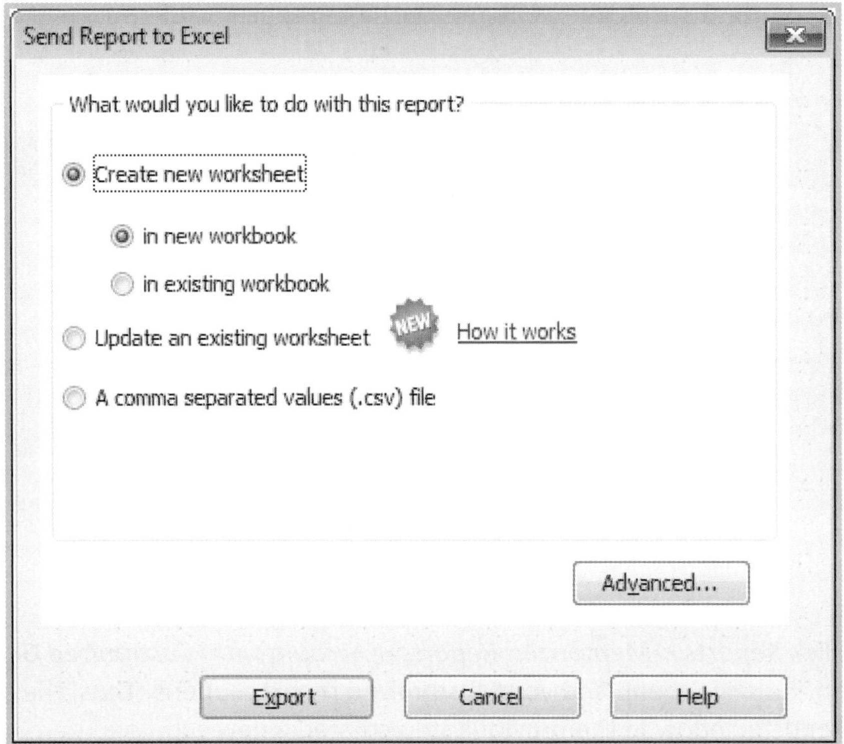

Figure 2:43

You have two choices under **Create new worksheet**. The first, **in new workbook**, will place the report on a worksheet in a new workbook file. The second, **in existing workbook**, will place the report on a new worksheet in an existing workbook file. *(Note: If you choose the second option, a field opens for you to choose the workbook file.)*

If you do not have Microsoft Excel software on your machine, then you can export the report to **a comma separated values (.csv) file**. This file type can then be copied to a machine that has Excel installed.

Keep the option illustrated in Figure 2:43 and click **Export**. A new Excel workbook is opened, containing two worksheets (Figure 2:44). *(Note: The workbook is illustrated in Excel 2007. Your workbook will look different if you are using an earlier version of Excel. We will provide Excel commands for 2007 and earlier versions.)*

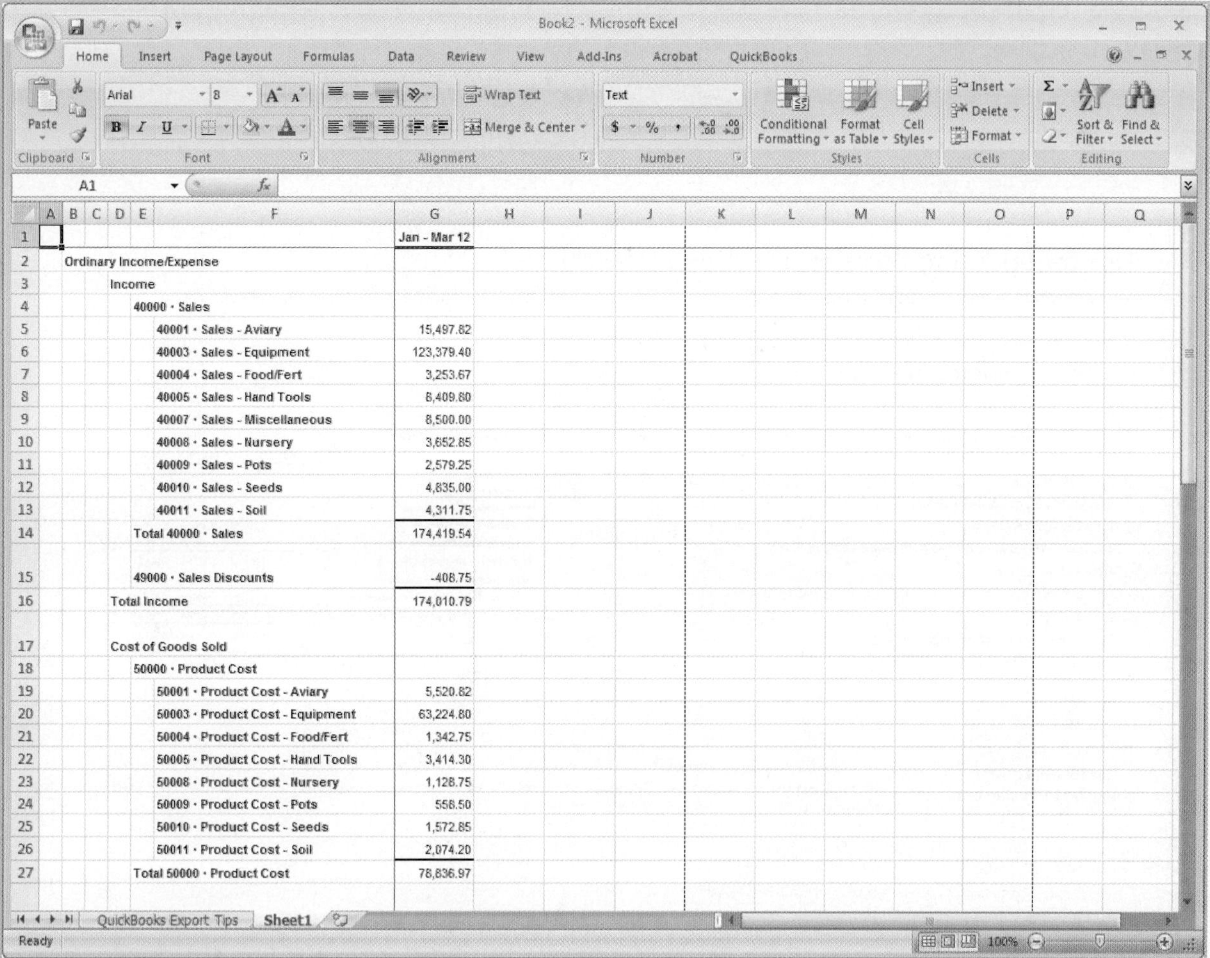

Account	Jan - Mar 12
Ordinary Income/Expense	
Income	
40000 · Sales	
40001 · Sales - Aviary	15,497.82
40003 · Sales - Equipment	123,379.40
40004 · Sales - Food/Fert	3,253.67
40005 · Sales - Hand Tools	8,409.80
40007 · Sales - Miscellaneous	8,500.00
40008 · Sales - Nursery	3,652.85
40009 · Sales - Pots	2,579.25
40010 · Sales - Seeds	4,835.00
40011 · Sales - Soil	4,311.75
Total 40000 · Sales	174,419.54
49000 · Sales Discounts	-408.75
Total Income	174,010.79
Cost of Goods Sold	
50000 · Product Cost	
50001 · Product Cost - Aviary	5,520.82
50003 · Product Cost - Equipment	63,224.80
50004 · Product Cost - Food/Fert	1,342.75
50005 · Product Cost - Hand Tools	3,414.30
50008 · Product Cost - Nursery	1,128.75
50009 · Product Cost - Pots	558.50
50010 · Product Cost - Seeds	1,572.85
50011 · Product Cost - Soil	2,074.20
Total 50000 · Product Cost	78,836.97

Figure 2:44

The worksheet named Sheet1 contains the exported data. Click to select this worksheet and scroll to the bottom. *(Hint: Use **CTRL + End** to jump to the end of the report.)*

Now click the worksheet named **QuickBooks Export Tips** (Figure 2:45). This worksheet provides information on using the export feature.

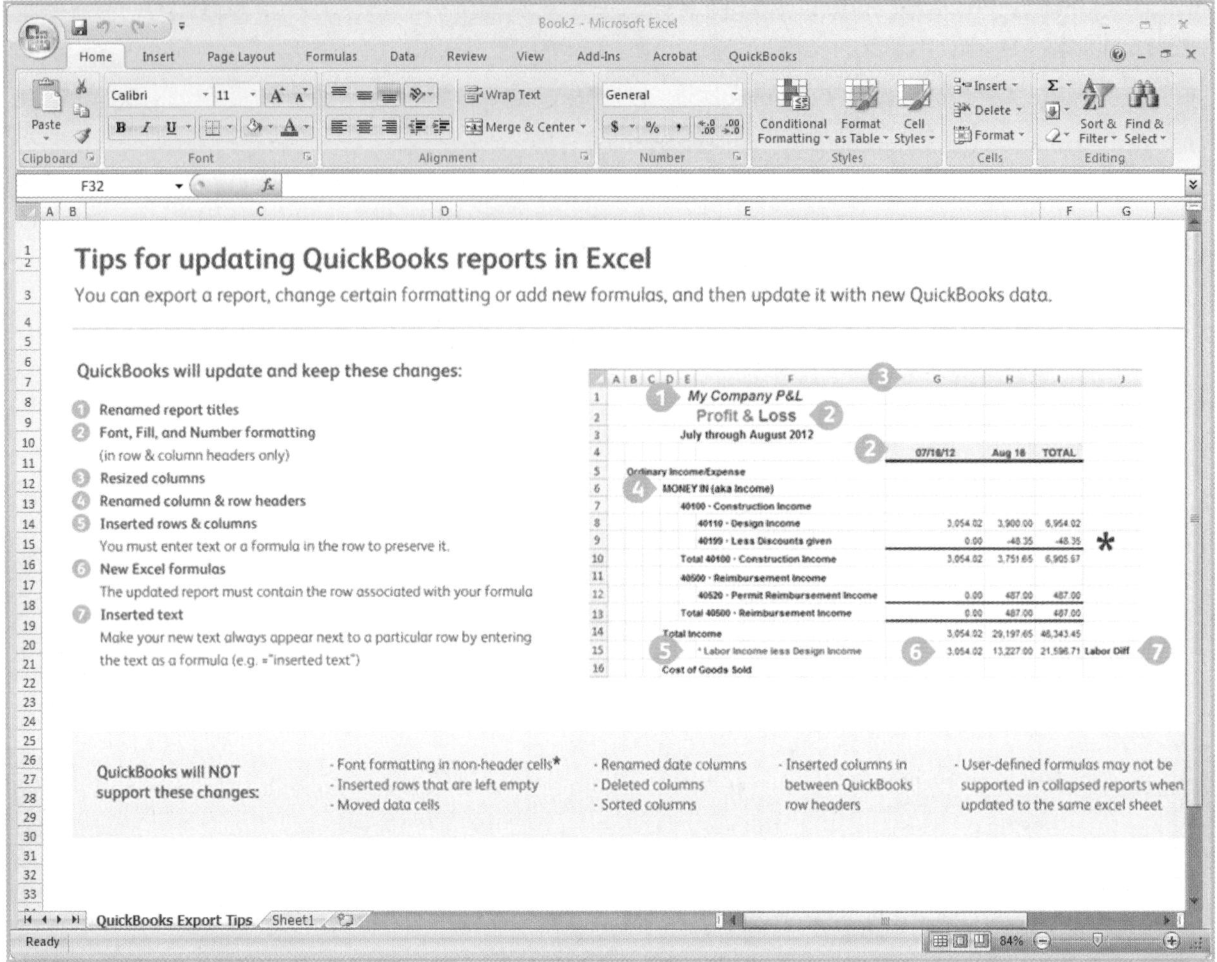

Figure 2:45

Click **X** to close the Excel workbook and click **No** to exit without saving.

Return to the **Profit & Loss** report. Click the **Excel** icon again and choose **Create New Worksheet**. Click the **Advanced** tab to review the options illustrated next.

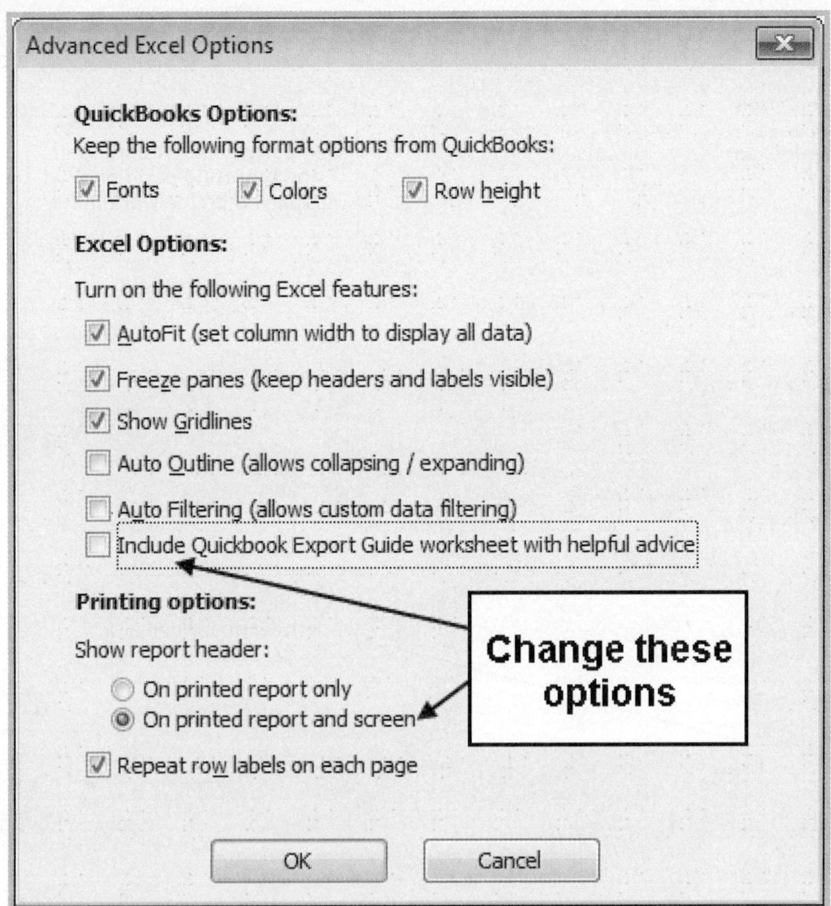

Figure 2:46

This tab contains options that determine how the data is exported into Excel.

QuickBooks Options: These options will preserve the fonts, colors, and row heights set by QuickBooks.

Excel Options: Activate the listed Excel features such as AutoFit, Freeze panes, and exporting the worksheet guide.

Printing options: Determines whether to place column headers into Excel's Page Setup where you can only view when printing the report or on the printed report and screen.

Set the **Advanced** options shown in Figure 2:46 and click **OK**. Click **Export** and view the results illustrated next.

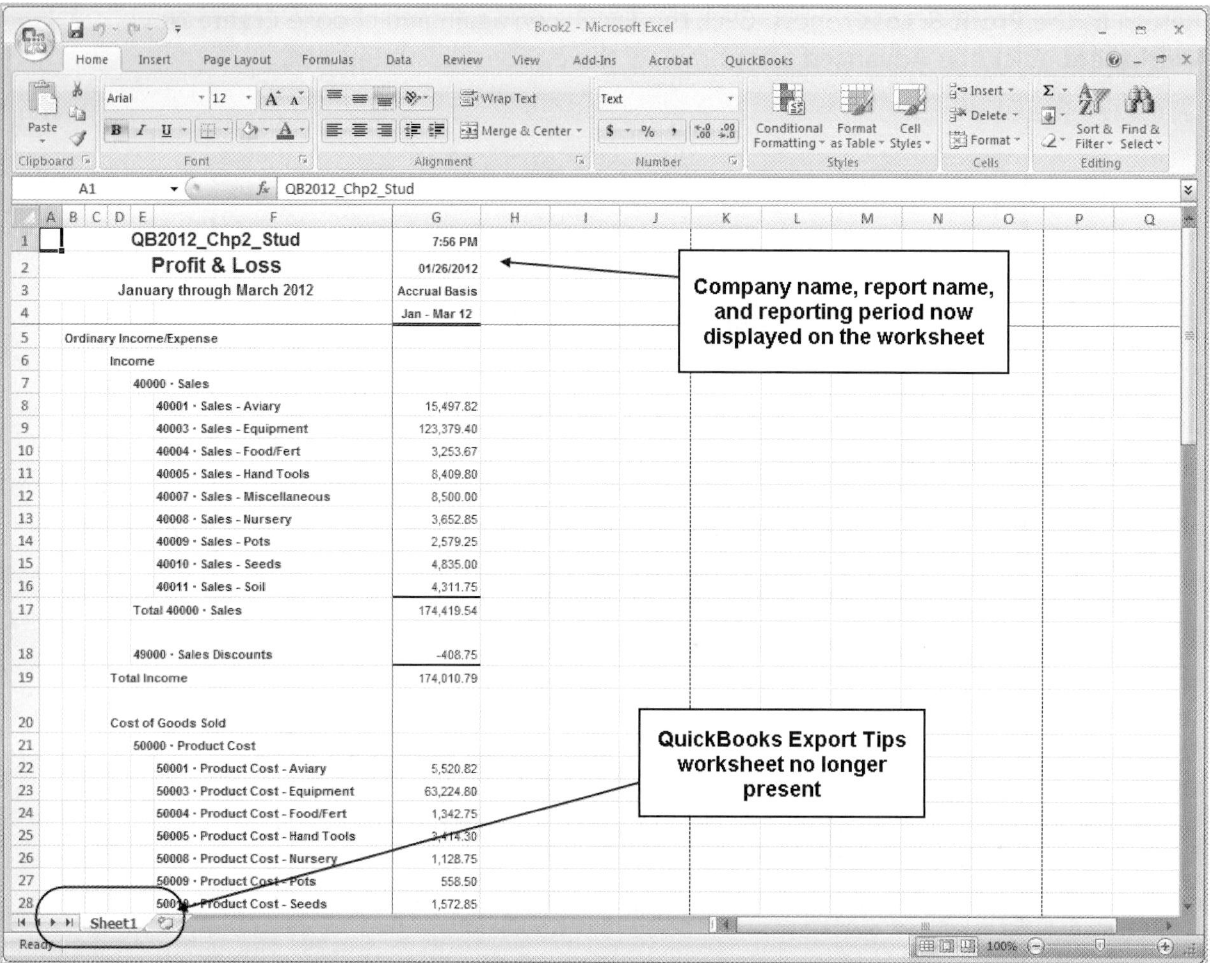

Figure 2:47

This time the workbook contains one worksheet with company information appearing in the top rows of the worksheet.

Save the new Excel workbook. Click this Office Icon and select ***Save As>>Excel Workbook*** (Figure 2:48). *(Note: You can save it as an Excel 97-2003 Workbook when needed. For earlier versions of Excel select File>>Save As on the main menu.)*

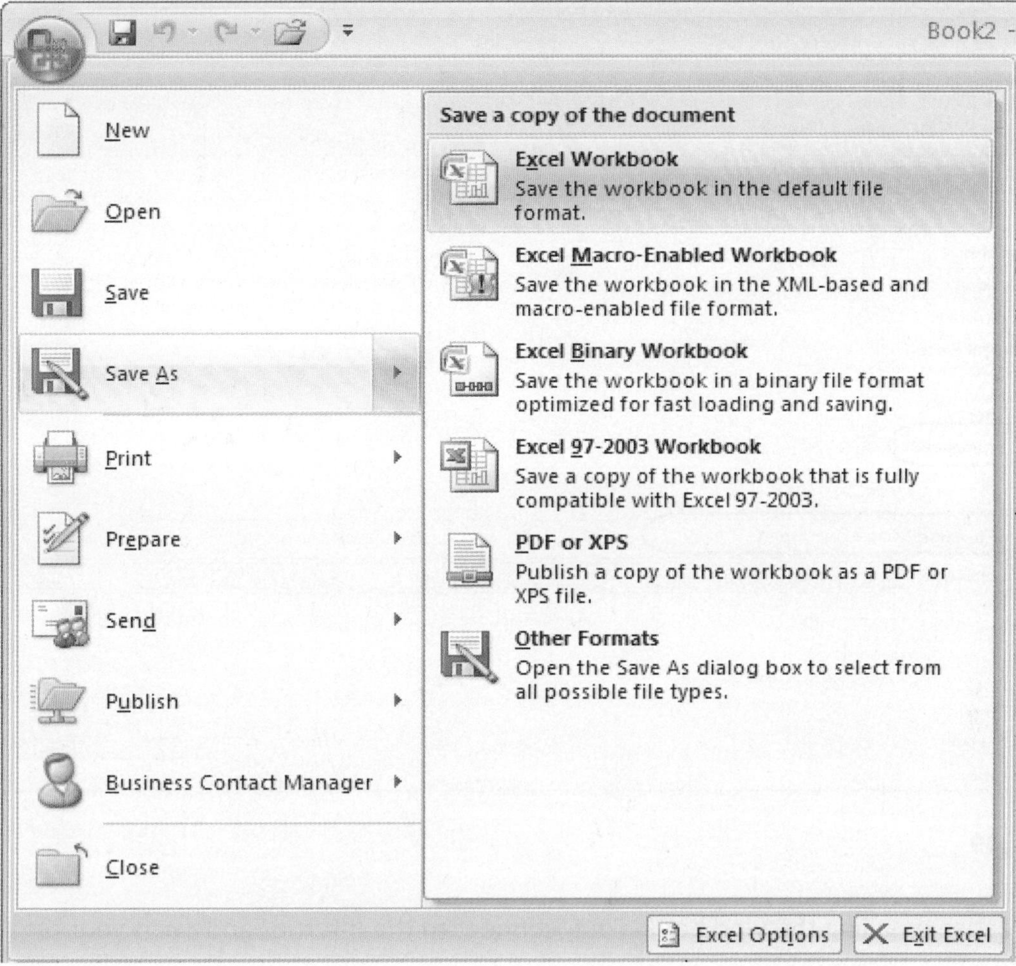

Figure 2:48

On the left, click **Documents** or My Documents if not using Windows 7. Change the **File name** to “Chp 2 Excel Export” as illustrated in Figure 2:49. *(Note: These instructions remain the same for earlier versions of Excel.)* Click **Save**.

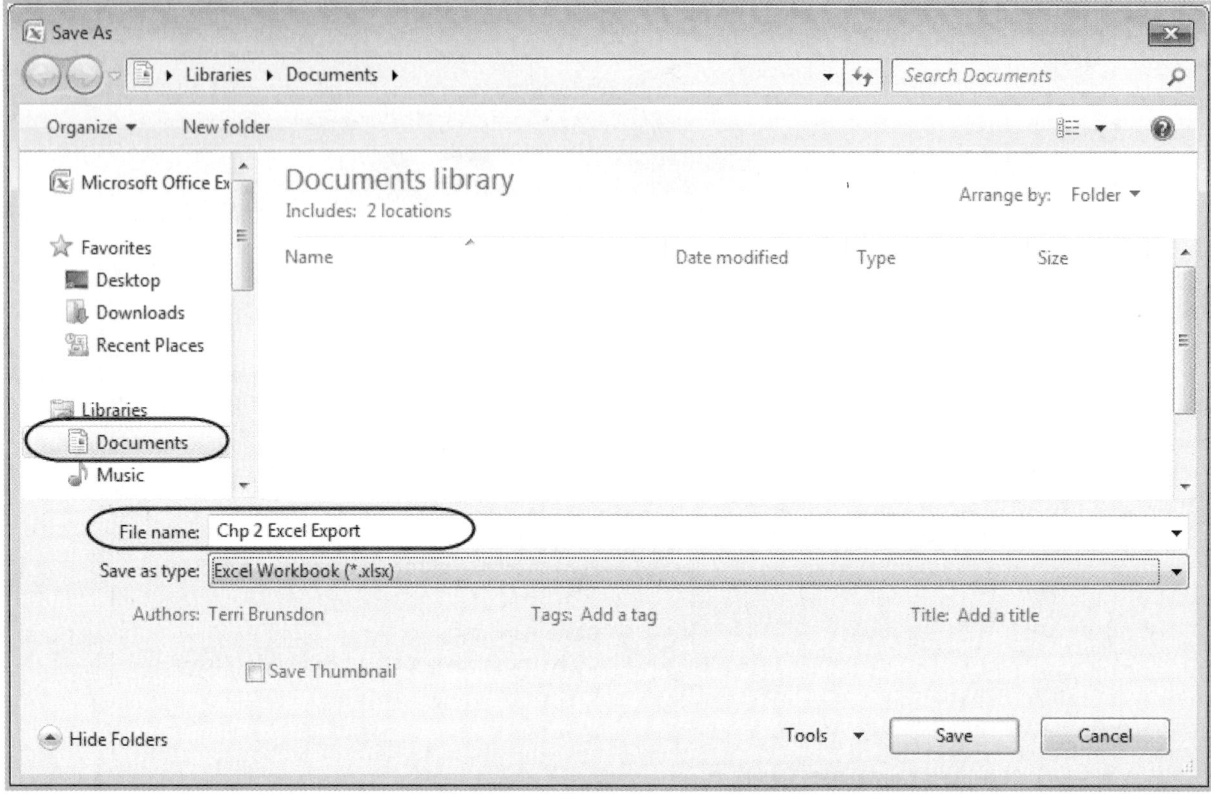

Figure 2:49

Now practice emailing the workbook. First, connect to the Internet and open your email software.

In Excel, click ***>> Send>>E-mail*** as shown in Figure 2:50. *(Note: For earlier versions of Excel click File>>Send To and select Mail Recipient (as Attachment).*

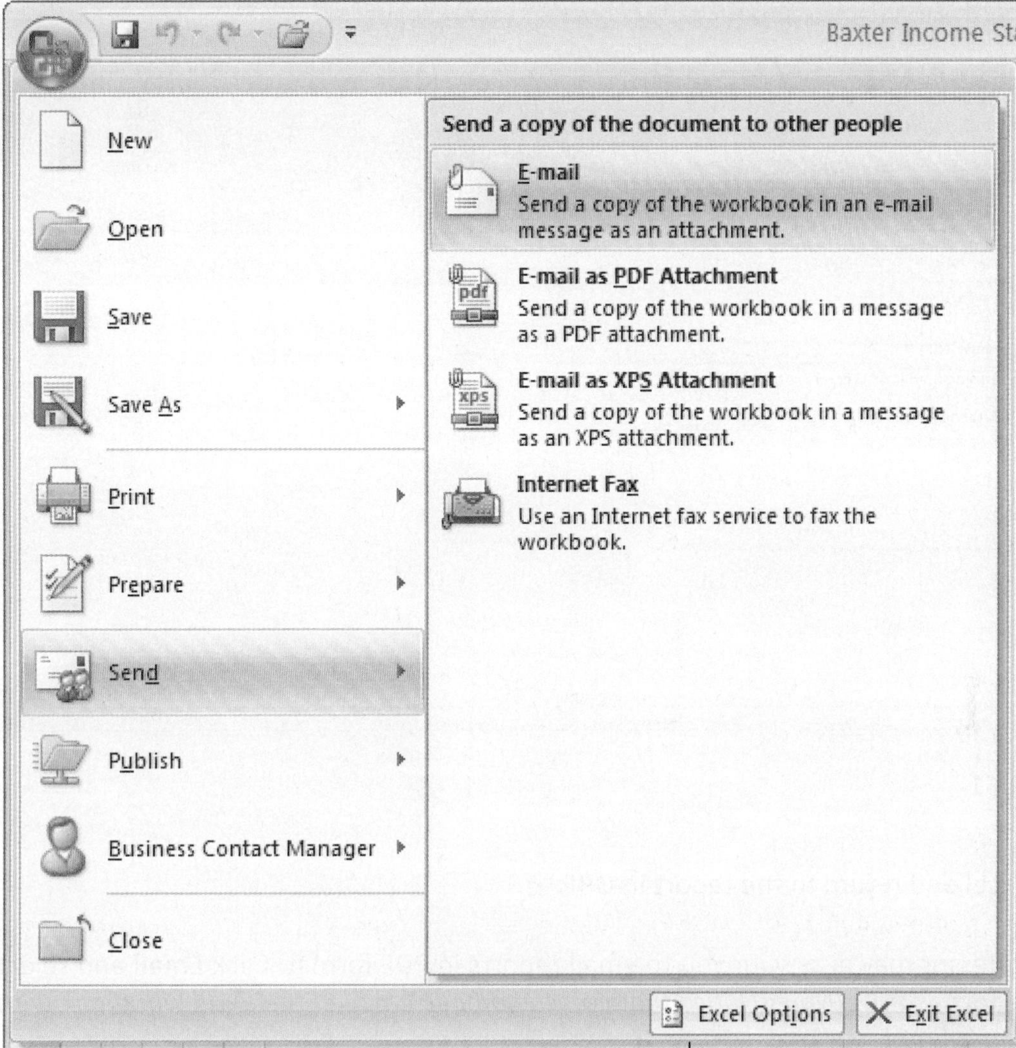

Figure 2:50

When the email message opens (Figure 2:51), enter your email address and click **Send**. Check your email later to verify delivery.

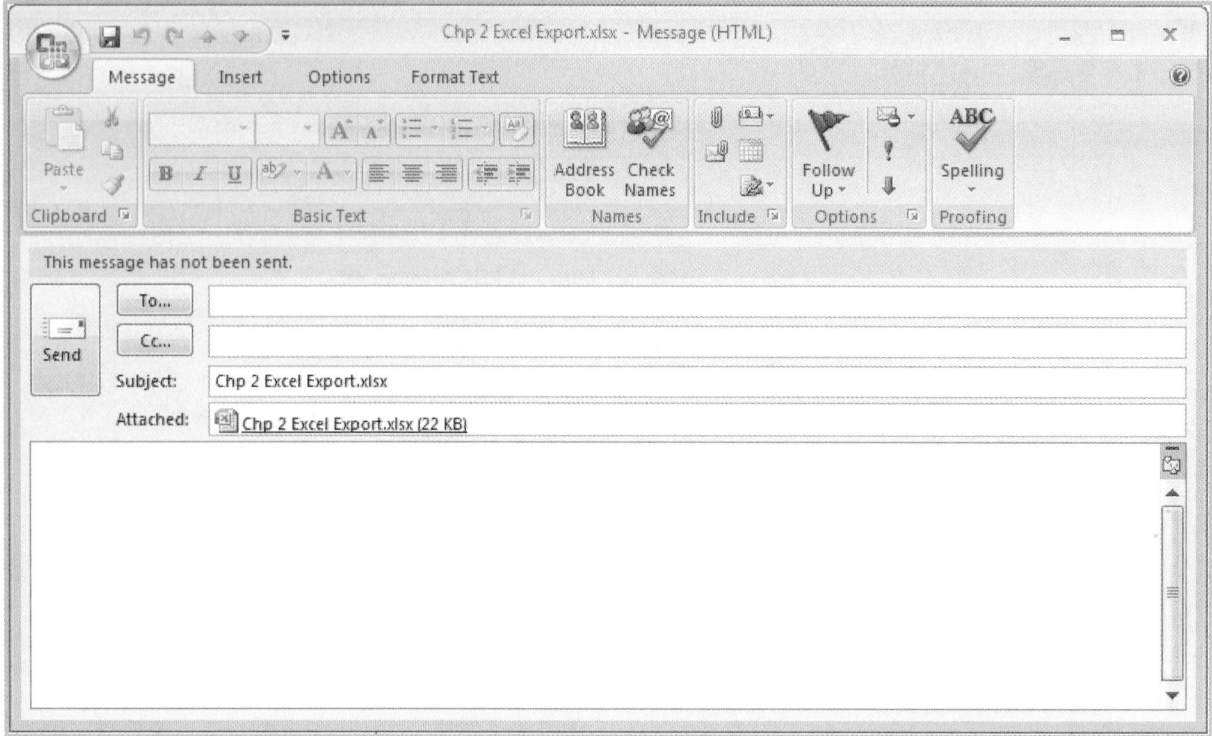

Figure 2:51

Close Excel and return to the report in QBP.

Your professor may also want you to email reports in PDF format. Click **Email** and select **Send report as PDF.** *(Note: Notice that you could have emailed the Excel workbook without exporting it first.)*

When the following Email Security message opens, mark the option of "Do not display this message in the future" and click **OK.** *(Note: If you also receive a message about sending E-mail using Outlook, click Close.)*

Figure 2:52

The email message now opens (Figure 2:53) with an attached PDF version of the report. Enter your email address and click **Send**. Check your email later to verify delivery.

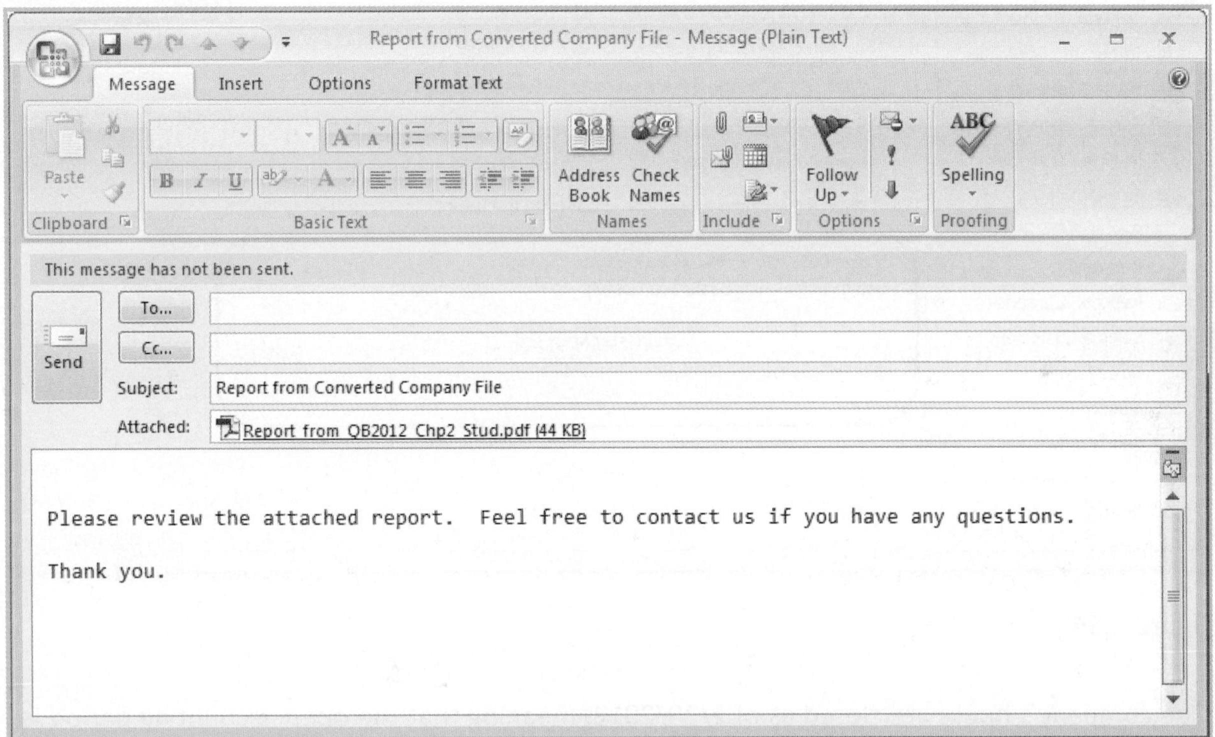

Figure 2:53

Close the report and continue to the next topic.

Accounting Periods

One final topic and you have covered QBP basics. Although the software will let you override this statement, you should only post transactions to the current accounting period. To locate the current period, click ***Company>>Set Closing Date*** on the main menu and open the Company Preferences tab illustrated in Figure 2:54.

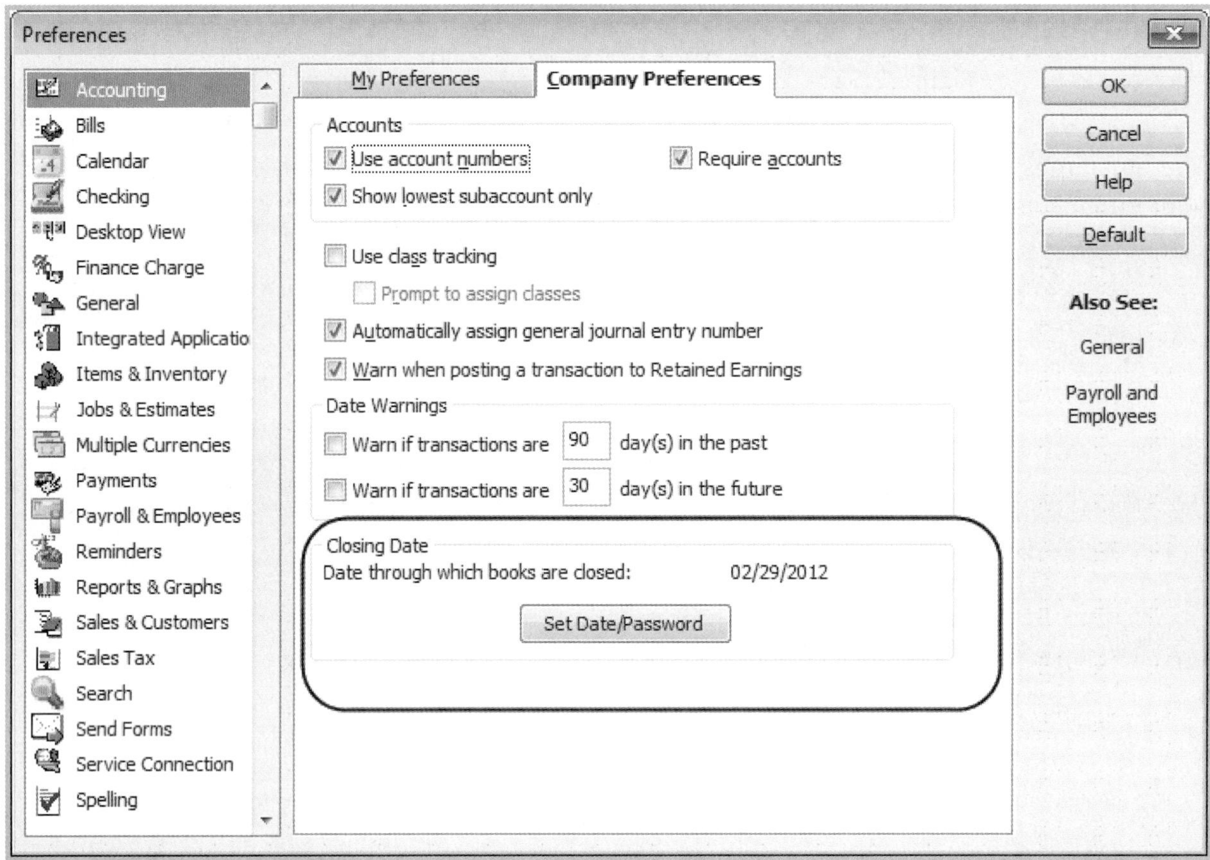

Figure 2:54

The company's books are closed as of 2/29/2012, meaning that the open accounting period is March 2012.

Click **Set Date/Password**. An accounting period is closed by entering a different date in the **Closing Date** field. (See Figure 2:55.)

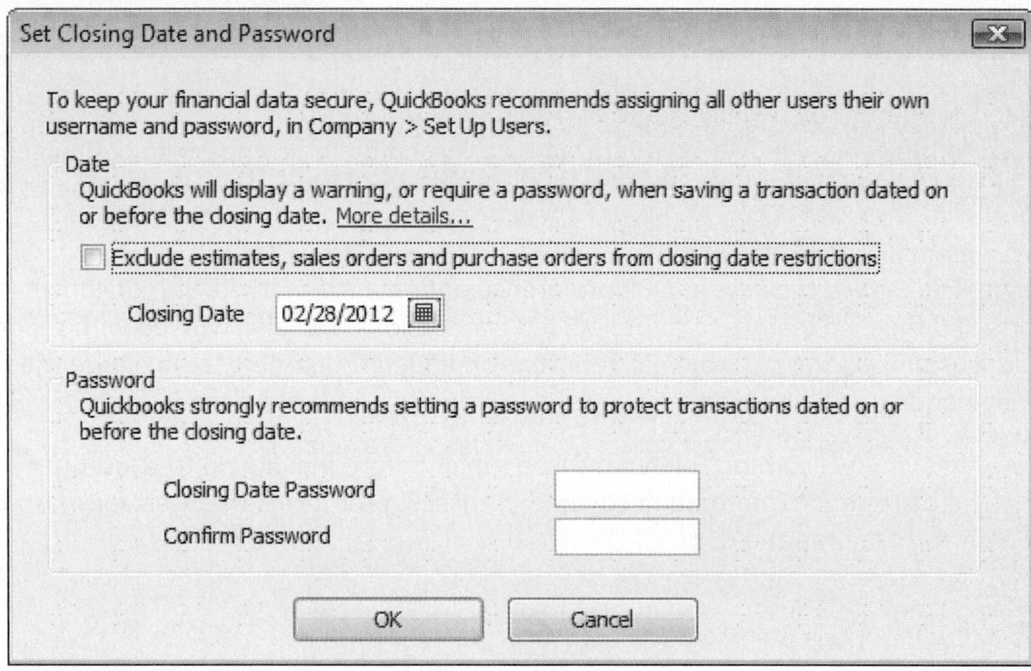

Figure 2:55

In the real world, you would also set a **Closing Date Password** to prevent users from posting to a closed period without first entering an authorization password. Because this window does not contain a password, QBP will merely warn when a user attempts to post an entry to a closed period. You can permit the posting to occur by clicking Yes on the warning window. Click **Cancel** to exit this window.

You should always close an accounting period after finalizing transactions and issuing financial reports. Closing the period protects the integrity of reported data by preventing erroneous postings to a reported period.

One last thought: Although you can prevent posting to prior months (closed periods), you cannot prevent posting to future months. Therefore, be very careful to enter correct dates on transactions.

You have now completed this chapter so ***backup the company file to a file named "QB2012_Chp2_Stud_Completed"***.

SUMMARY

You began the chapter by reviewing and printing the Chart of Accounts. You were then introduced to the general ledger account framework used by the company to define general ledger account numbers. With this information, you were able to create a new general ledger account.

You then looked *Behind the Keys* at QBP preference options. You worked with drilldown features on reports and the Find feature to locate posted transactions. You also worked with reports and learned to customize, export, and email reports. You ended by learning to recognize the open accounting period and by understanding why accounting periods are closed.

Make sure that you feel comfortable with these topics before moving on to subsequent chapters. The background information covered in this chapter forms the basis for many of the tasks you perform later in the text.

End-of-Chapter Questions

TRUE/FALSE

_____ 1. The account number used on a liability begins with "3."

_____ 2. The account type "Other Current Liability" would be assigned to the accounts payable account.

_____ 3. QBP will not let you post a transaction to a closed month.

_____ 4. QBP preference options control whether or not a decimal point will be required when entering a financial amount.

_____ 5. Exporting QBP reports to Excel requires owning the Excel software.

_____ 6. You can customize reports shown on the Report Center.

_____ 7. You can add new general ledger accounts using a button located at the top of the chart of accounts list.

_____ 8. You can email a report in Excel or PDF format.

_____ 9. The general ledger and trial balance reports contain the same information.

_____ 10. Using the Search feature to search for "10274" in the QB2012_Chp2_Stud data file will return a check written to Thurman Golf Course.

_____ 11. You can close an accounting period by selecting ***Company>>Close Accounting Period*** on the main menu.

_____ 12. The Report Center contains a reporting category named Budgets.

_____ 13. The Unpaid Bills Detail report is found under the Purchases category of the Report Center.

_____ 14. Reports that you customize and save are reopened using the ***Reports>> Memorized Reports*** menu.

_____ 15. You can open the Chart of Accounts window using a shortcut key.

MULTIPLE CHOICE

_____ 1. The chart of accounts for the QB2012_Chp2_Stud data file uses ____ as the account number for sales revenue.

a. 10200
b. 11000
c. 40000
d. 49000

_____ 2. The income statement can be printed using the ______.

a. Reports menu
b. Report Center
c. Lists menu
d. Both a and b

_____ 3. Referring to the chart of accounts for the QB2012_Chp2_Stud data file, which account number would be appropriate for an account named Consulting Expense?
   a. 15600
   b. 62610
   c. 30100
   d. 40100

_____ 4. Referring to the chart of accounts for the QB2012_Chp2_stud data file, which account would you use to record accounts payable liabilities?
   a. 11000
   b. 20000
   c. 50000
   d. 27000

_____ 5. Report filters are set by using the ______ button.
   a. Print
   b. Memorize
   c. Customize Report
   d. None of the above

_____ 6. Invoice number 10284 was issued to _____ and contained ______ items of Equip-Mower-3HP.
   a. Aldred Builders, 15
   b. Frost Technology, 10
   c. Franklin Botanical Gardens, 5
   d. None of the above

_____ 7. You can locate a posted check mailed to a vendor by using:
   a. The Search feature.
   b. The Find feature.
   c. The Vendors center.
   d. All of the above.

_____ 8. Clicking the Snapshots icon will _____.
   a. open a window containing three tabs
   b. show a graph of income and expense trends
   c. customers who owe money
   d. All of the above

_____ 9. Using the Lists menu will let you.
   a. view the Item List
   b. open a customer invoice
   c. modify a report
   d. None of the above

_____ 10. The Window menu is used to.
   a. select an open window
   b. tile open windows
   c. cascade open windows
   d. All of the above

Practice Set

In this practice set, you will use the Search and Find features and prepare reports. When preparing reports, you can use the Reports menu or the Report center.

Begin by:

- Opening the software.
- Opening the **QB2012_Chp2_Stud** file used while reading the chapter.
- **Toggling the software to the PRO EDITION** by selecting ***File>>Toggle to Another Edition*** on the main menu and choosing **QuickBooks Pro** as the edition.

Complete the following tasks.

1. Export the Purchases by Vendor Detail report to Excel. Use 2/1/12 through 2/29/12 as the date range and customize the report as follows:
   a. On the Filters tab, set the Name filter to Southern Garden;
   b. On the Header/Footer tab, change the Report Title to Southern Garden Purchases; and
   c. Resize the report columns so that all information in the columns is visible;
2. Practice using the Search feature and answer the following questions:
   a. How many transactions have been posted to McKay Construction? Provide information about these transactions.
   b. Explain what you find about Melvin Frost.
   c. How many bills have been posted for the item TOOL-HOE? What is the name of the vendor?
3. E-mail, as a PDF, the A/R Aging Summary report to yourself or, if instructed, to your professor. Use 2/29/12 as the date range.
4. Practice using the Find feature and answer the following questions:
   a. How many bills were posted from 2/12/12 through 2/20/12?
   b. How many transactions have been posted to the accounts receivable account?
5. Prepare the Profit & Loss Detail and the Profit & Loss YTD Comparison reports for the month of February 2012. Explain how these reports differ.

CHAPTER 3 GENERAL JOURNAL TRANSACTIONS AND REPORTS

LEARNING OBJECTIVES

This chapter introduces you to posting general journal entries and producing reports. In this chapter, you will:

1. Learn manual accounting procedures (*MAPS*) for recording general journal entries before posting entries in QBP
2. Post basic general journal entries
3. Go *Behind the Keys* of a posted transaction by reviewing the Journal and General Ledger reports
4. Learn to correct posted journal entries
5. Post compound journal entries and adjusting entries
6. Print the trial balance and financial statements
7. Close the accounting period
8. Review QBP data integration

Begin by:

- Opening the software.
- Opening the **QB2012_Chp3_Stud** data file. Add your initials to the end to the Company Name by clicking ***Company>>Company Information*** on the main menu. Click **OK** to save the changes.
- **Toggling the software to the PRO EDITION** by selecting ***File>>Toggle to Another Edition*** on the main menu and choosing **QuickBooks Pro** as the edition.

MANUAL ACCOUNTING PROCEDURES

In this chapter, we will call the company you are working with TEK. This company is a startup business that began operations on January 1, 2012. The company provides consulting services and, on January 2, 2012, made its first cash sale for $1,000.00.

Before posting transactions, you may find it helpful to use T-Accounts to visualize the entry. What follows is an illustration of the T-Accounts that will be used to post the sale. Notice that the entry will post as a $1,000.00 debit to the regular checking account and a $1,000.00 credit to the consulting income account.

Regular Checking Account

Dr.	Cr.
$1,000	

Consulting Income

Dr.	Cr.
	$1,000

Accountants with years of experience still rely on the use of T-Accounts to visualize the posting of complicated transactions. You may also find it helpful to rely on this method when encountering new and complicated exercises in the text.

We next acquaint you to the manual accounting procedures (*MAPS*) an accountant would use to post a cash sale if he or she were not using software. To post this transaction, the accountant begins by recording it on the general journal page illustrated in Figure 3:1.

Audit Trail

TEK Business

General Journal **Page 2**

Date	**Account Post Ref**	**Description**	**Debit**	**Credit**
1/2/2012	10100	Regular Checking Account	1,000.00	
	40000	Consulting Income		1,000.00

To record cash sale

Figure 3:1

Notice that the entry lists a transaction date, general ledger account numbers, and descriptions. In addition, the amount of the sale is recorded into the appropriate debit or credit column and the entry balances, meaning the debit amount equals the credit amount.

After recording the entry on the general journal, the accountant next posts it to the general ledger card for each account. These postings are illustrated in Figure 3:2.

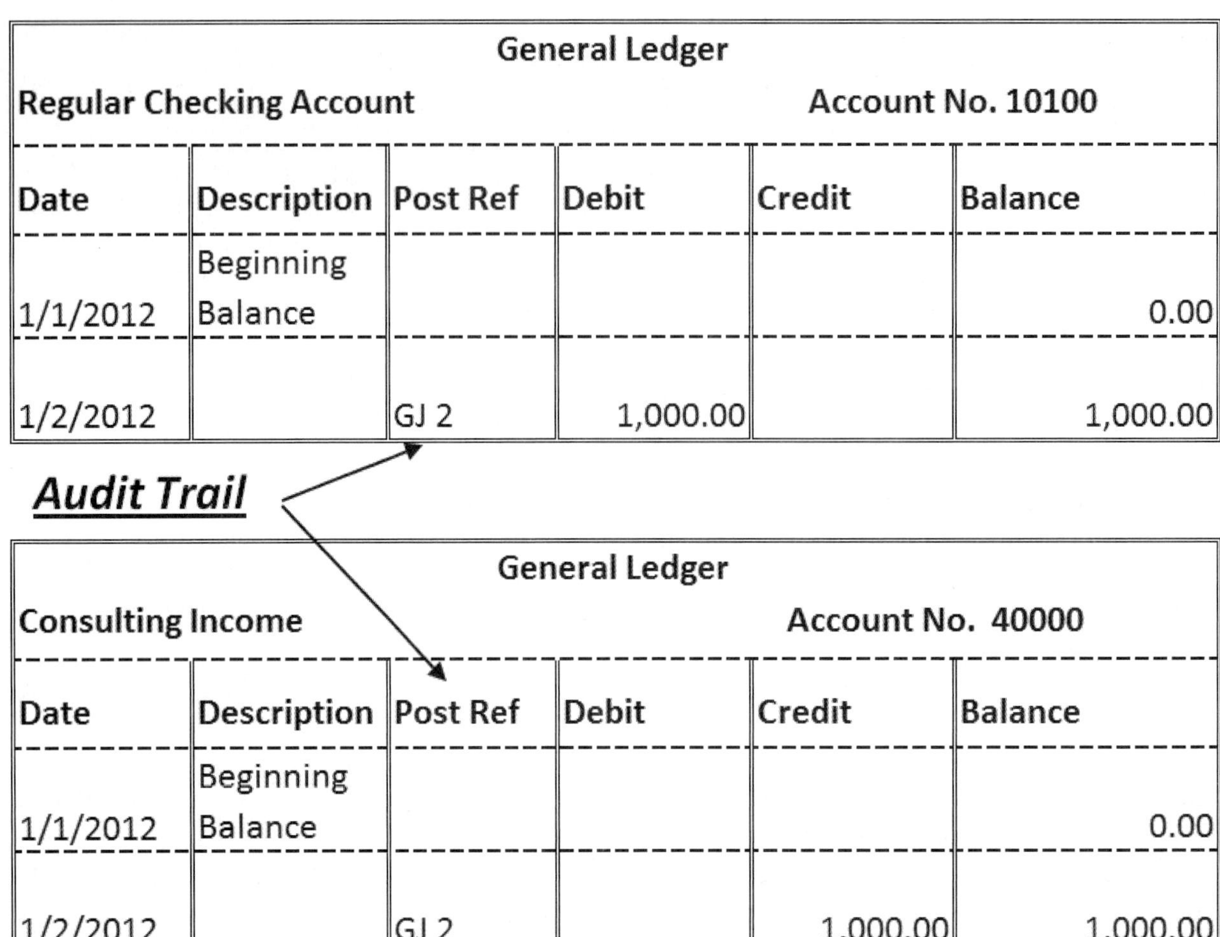

General Ledger					
Regular Checking Account				Account No. 10100	
Date	Description	Post Ref	Debit	Credit	Balance
1/1/2012	Beginning Balance				0.00
1/2/2012		GJ 2	1,000.00		1,000.00

General Ledger					
Consulting Income				Account No. 40000	
Date	Description	Post Ref	Debit	Credit	Balance
1/1/2012	Beginning Balance				0.00
1/2/2012		GJ 2		1,000.00	1,000.00

Figure 3:2

Notice that each general ledger card is headed with an account name and an account number. In addition, the amount is recorded under the debit or credit column that corresponds to the entry posted on the general journal.

Audit Trail

When posting transactions in an accounting system, whether the system is kept manually or in software, an audit trail for each transaction is also recorded so the transactions can be traced throughout the system.

In our illustration, the accountant entered GJ 2 under the Post Ref column of each general ledger card. This audit trail reference tells the accountant that the entry originated on page two of the general journal (i.e., GJ). Likewise, the account number on the general journal is the audit trail reference that tells the accountant which general ledger card to look at to see the transaction.

From this illustration, you see that the audit trail forms a path that the accountant can use to trace posted entries in the accounting system. Although we have illustrated a manual system, you will see later in the chapter that the software will record an audit trail.

Basic Journal Entries

In this topic, you will post the journal entry illustrated in the previous topic. Begin by reviewing the **Home** page. (See Figure 3:3.) Verify that the open company matches the illustration. Also, verify that you toggled the software by locating the words **QuickBooks Pro 2012 (via Accountant)** on the Title Bar.

(Note: There is an online video available for this topic.)

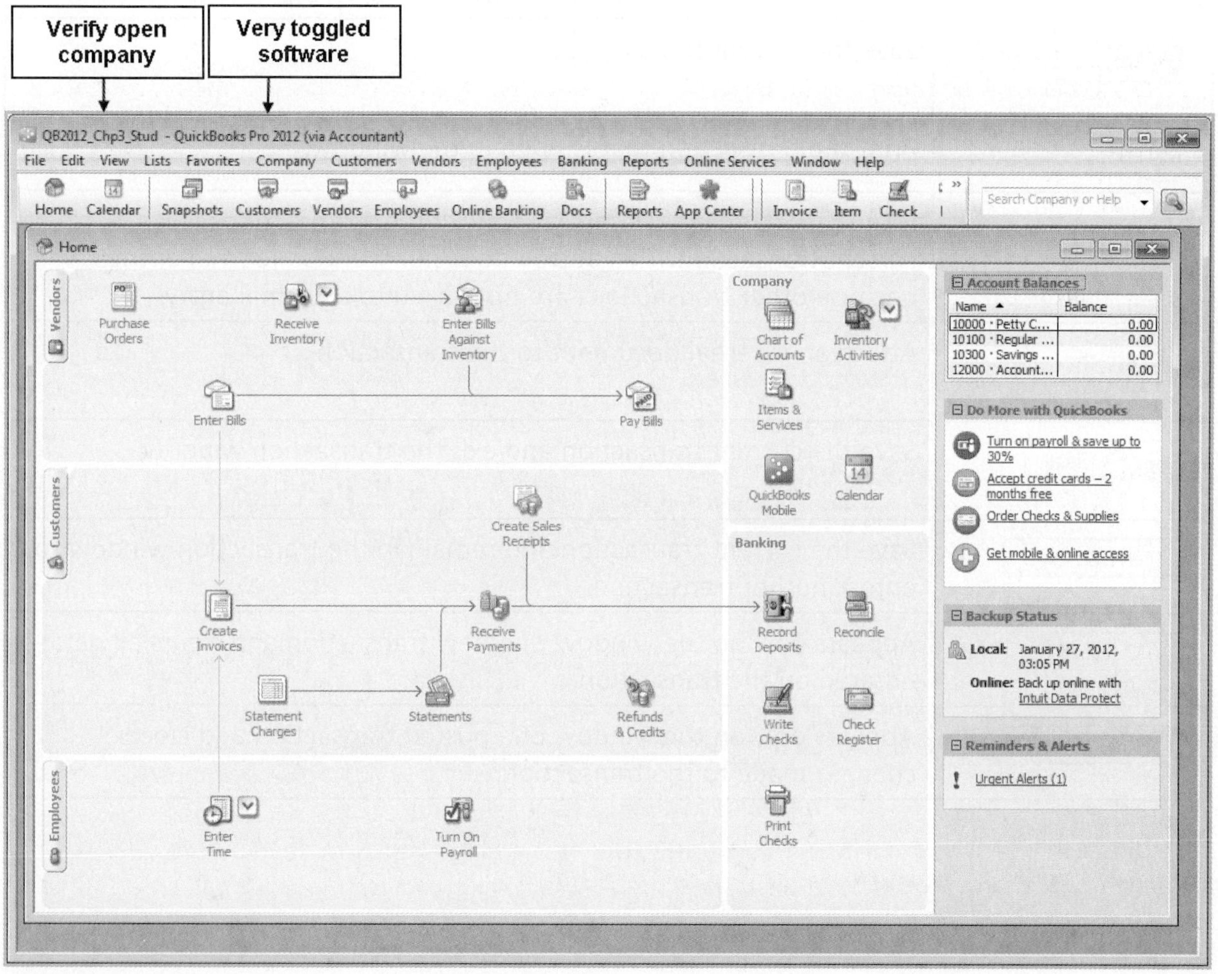

Verify open company

Very toggled software

Figure 3:3

Before completing the next exercise to post the journal entry, review the following data entry tips.

DATA ENTRY TIPS	
Edit	Main menu commands for inserting or deleting transaction lines.
Previous	Move to a previously posted transaction. If you are entering a new transaction, the transaction will be saved before moving to the previous transaction.
Next	Move to the next transaction. If you are entering a new transaction, the transaction will be saved before moving to the next transaction.
Save	Save the current transaction.
Print...	Print the transaction that is open in the window.
History	Open reports to view information for other transactions linked to the current transaction. This button does not work on journal entries because other transactions are not linked to a journal entry.
Attach	Attach an external document to the transaction.
Save & Close	Save the current transaction and exit the transaction window.
Save & New	Save the current transaction and remain in the transaction window to enter another transaction.
Clear	Appears only on the window of a new transaction and clears all data entered on the transaction.
Revert	Appears only on the window of a posted transaction and clears changes made to the transaction.

STEPS TO RECORDING A JOURNAL ENTRY

1. Click ***Company>>Make General Journal Entries*** on the main menu. Click **OK** if prompted by the Attach Documents to QuickBooks feature. If the window in Figure 3:4 opens, mark the option that turns off future messages and click **OK.**

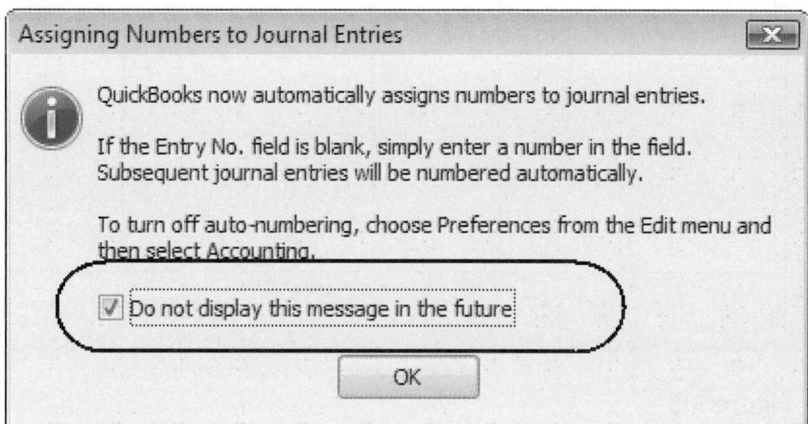

Figure 3:4

2. Change the transaction **Date** to 1/02/2012 as shown in Figure 3:5.

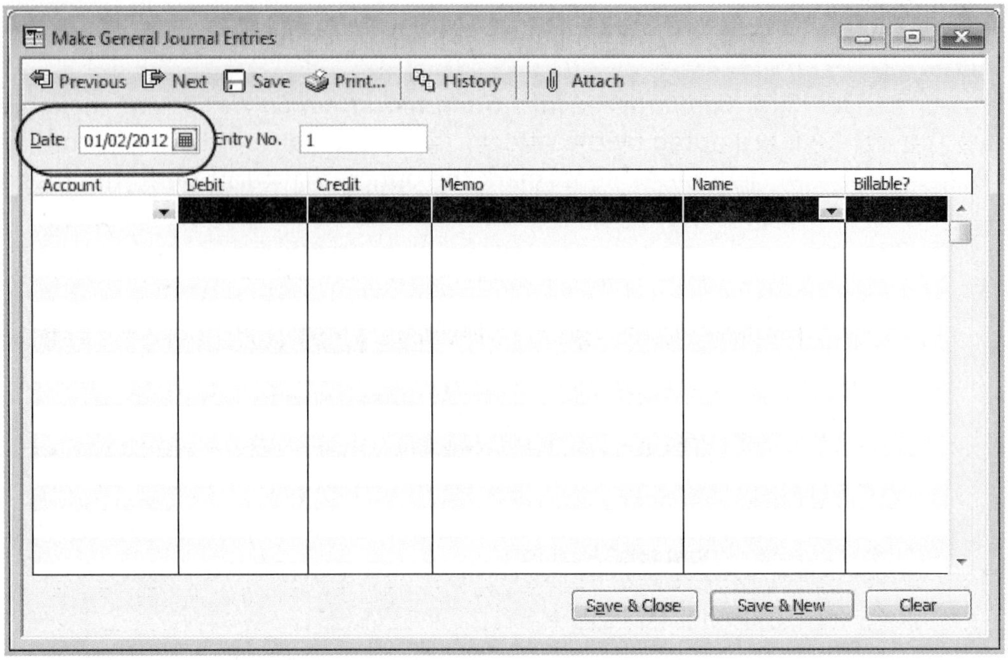

Figure 3:5

3. Press **Tab** and the cursor stops at **Entry No**. The message in Figure 3:4 explained that QBP will automatically assign entry numbers in sequential increments.

4. Press **Tab** and the cursor moves to the first line item on the entry, stopping at the **Account** field.

   This is where you enter the general ledger account number of "10100 Regular Checking Account".

   Place your cursor on the field separator until it looks like a plus sign and drag to widen the Account field (Figure 3:6).

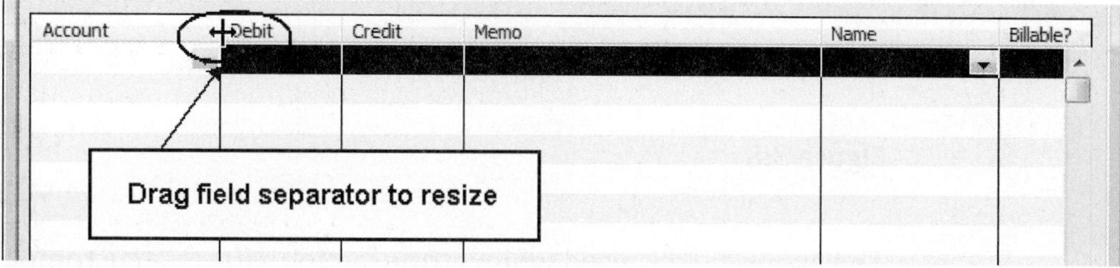

   Figure 3:6

   There are two methods for entering account numbers. You will use the first method in this step and the second method in a step that follows.

   With your cursor in the field, type "r" and QBP stops at the first account beginning with this letter (Figure 3:7), which happens to be the account you want.

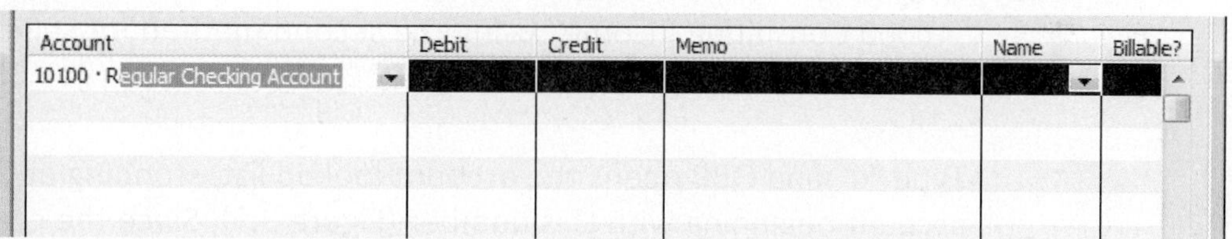

   Figure 3:7

5. Tab to **Debit** and type in "1000.00" because this is the cash amount of the sale.

   *Note: Recall in Chapter 2 that you turned on the Preference option for QBP to automatically enter the decimal point. Therefore, you could also type "100000" to enter this amount. You must turn this option on in each company file. To verify that the option is active, select **Edit>>Preferences** on the main menu, select the **General** category and the **My Preferences** tab. The **Automatically place decimal point** option should be selected. Click OK to close.*

6. Tab to **Memo** and enter the short description of "Cash sale." The Memo field is optional and used when you want to describe the transaction.

7. Now widen the General Journal window size. Place your cursor to the edge of the window until a double arrow appears and then drag to resize (Figure 3:8). You have now increased the size of all columns.

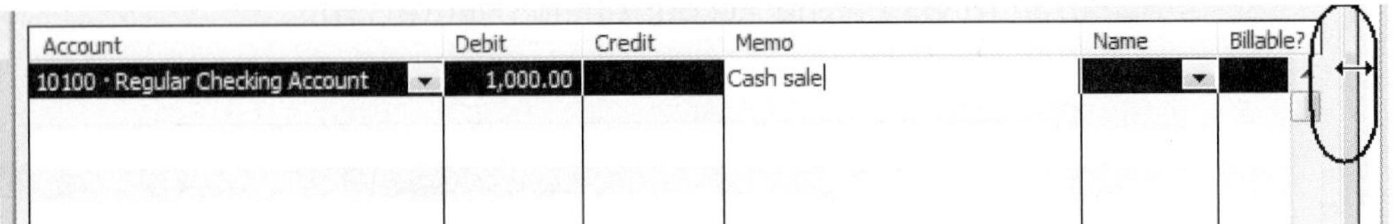

Figure 3:8

The **Name** field is used when a transaction affects a customer, vendor, or inventory account. Rarely should you use general journal entries to post these types of transactions; instead, you will learn to record these transactions using the accounting activities discussed in subsequent chapters.

The **Billable** field is used when the transaction amount will be billed to a customer. You will learn to record billable transactions in Chapters 4, 5, and 6.

8. **Tab** to the second row to enter the second **Account**. You will be selecting "40000 Consulting Income" using the second method for selecting account numbers.

   Type "4" and QBP opens the account lookup list, stopping at the first account beginning with this number (Figure 3:9). Since the correct account is already selected, press **Tab**. *(Note: You can select a different account by using your mouse or by pressing the down arrow on your keyboard to advance the account list.)*

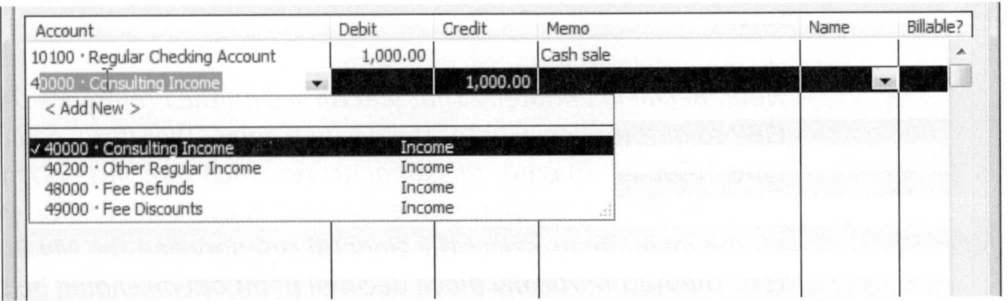

Figure 3:9

9. QBP has entered 1,000.00 into the **Credit** field because this is the amount needed to balance the entry. You can override the amount entered when needed and will do so in a different exercise. Since this is the correct credit amount, **Tab** to **Memo** and type "Cash sale".

10. The completed journal entry appears in Figure 3:10 and the entry balances. Unlike a manual system, QBP will not let you post an out-of-balance entry.

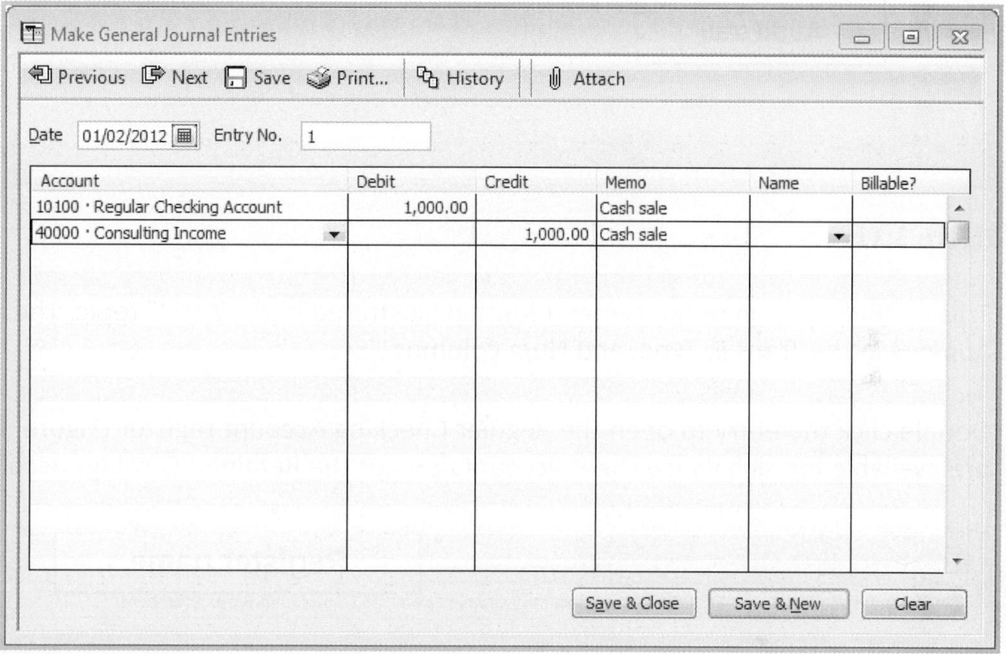

Figure 3:10

11. Click ***Save & Close*** at the bottom of the window and the entry posts.

On the Home page, review the Account Balances and notice that the balance for account 10100 Regular Checking has been updated to $1,000.00.

Behind The Keys Of A Posted Journal Entry

In this topic, you go *Behind the Keys* to trace the entries for the cash sale posted in the previous topic. Select ***Reports>>Accountant & Taxes>>Journal*** on the main menu. Enter the date range of **From 1/2/12** and **To 1/2/12** and refresh the report. (See Figure 3:11.)

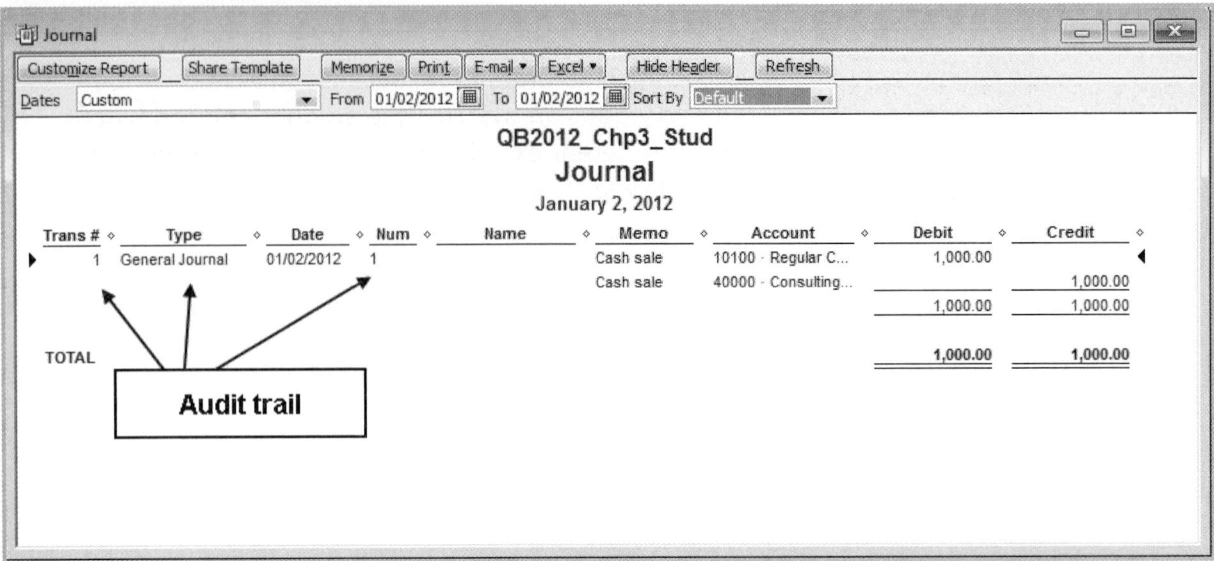

Figure 3:11

This is QBP's version of the General Journal illustrated in the *MAPS* topic. The audit trail appears in the Trans #, Type, and Num columns.

Double click the entry to open the Regular Checking Account register (Figure 3:12). Registers are available for all balance sheet accounts except the Retained Earnings account.

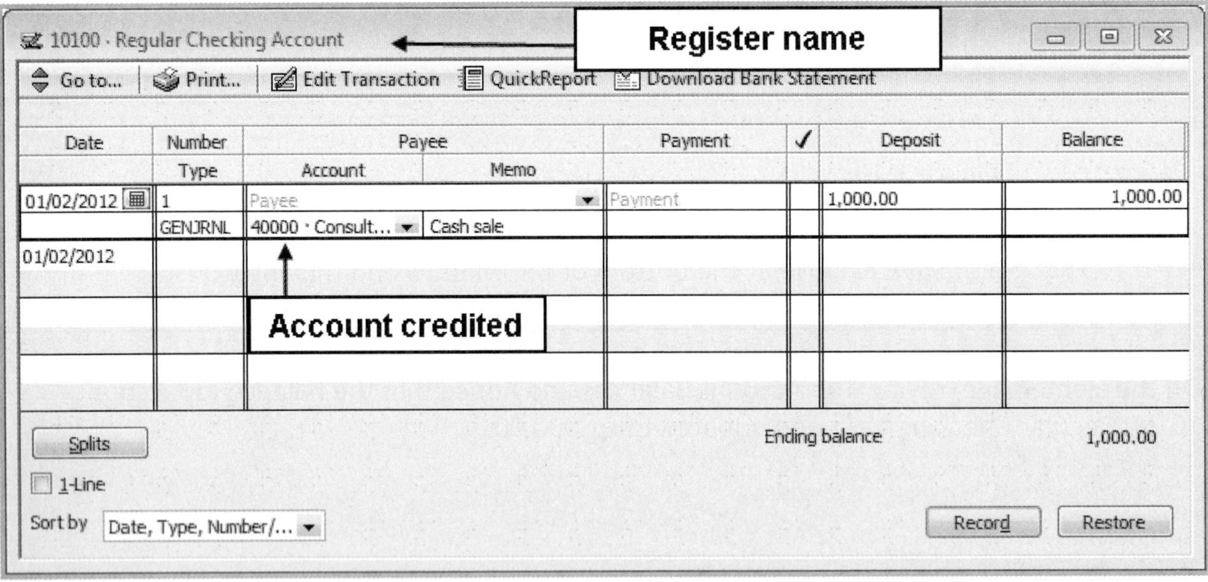

Figure 3:12

Figure 3:12 looks similar to your checkbook register. Notice that the sales amount appears as a deposit, meaning that the checking account was increased (debited) $1,000.00. The credit posted to 40000 Consulting Income and QBP entered GENJRNL and "1" as the audit trail code. Although you can record entries using the register, this method can be confusing and will not be used in the text.

Click **X** to close the register and **X** to close the Journal report. *(Note: You will be prompted to memorize the report. Mark the option to turn off future messages and click No.)*

You will now look for the entries posted to general ledger accounts. Select ***Reports>> Accountant & Taxes>>General Ledger*** on the main menu.

Follow the next steps to customize the report and add it to the icon bar because you will use this report often.

- Enter the date range of **1/1/12** to **1/31/12**.
- Click **Customize Report**. Add the **Debit** and **Credit** columns and remove the **Amount** column. Click **OK**.
- Resize the **Split** column so that the entire account number and name will display.
- Click **Memorize** and name the report "Custom General Ledger" and save in the **Accountant** memorized report group.
- Click ***View>>Add "Custom General Ledger" to Icon Bar*** on the main menu and enter "Custom G/L" as the **Label**. Click **OK**.

The customized report is shown in Figure 3:13, displaying entries recorded to 10100 Regular Checking Account and 40000 Consulting Income.

Audit trail

QB2012_Chp3_Stud

Custom General Ledger

Accrual Basis

As of January 31, 2012

Type	Date	Num	Name	Memo	Split	Debit	Credit	Balance
10000 · Petty Cash								**0.00**
Total 10000 · Petty Cash								0.00
10100 · Regular Checking Account								**0.00**
General Journal	01/02/2012	1		Cash sale	40000 · Consulting Income	1,000.00		1,000.00
Total 10100 · Regular Checking Account						1,000.00	0.00	1,000.00
10300 · Savings Account								**0.00**
Total 10300 · Savings Account								0.00
12000 · Accounts Receivable								**0.00**
Total 12000 · Accounts Receivable								0.00
12110 · Allowance for Doubtful Accounts								**0.00**
Total 12110 · Allowance for Doubtful Accounts								0.00
39007 · Owner's Draw								**0.00**
Total 39007 · Owner's Draw								0.00
40000 · Consulting Income								**0.00**
General Journal	01/02/2012	1		Cash sale	10100 · Regular Checking Ac...		1,000.00	-1,000.00
Total 40000 · Consulting Income						0.00	1,000.00	-1,000.00
40200 · Other Regular Income								**0.00**
Total 40200 · Other Regular Income								0.00
48000 · Fee Refunds								**0.00**
Total 48000 · Fee Refunds								0.00
49000 · Fee Discounts								**0.00**
Total 49000 · Fee Discounts								0.00

Figure 3:13

The audit trail code of **General Journal** is displayed in the Type column and the journal entry number in the **Num** column. You can also see where the **Memo** description appears.

Close this report and move to the next topic that explains correcting a posted journal entry.

Correcting a Posted Journal Entry

It is easy to correct a posted journal entry in QBP. First, locate the posted journal entry. *(Note: You could have opened it from the General Journal report illustrated in the previous topic.)* Type **Ctrl + F** to open the Find window and change the **Transaction Type** to "Journal." Next, type "1" in **Entry. No.**, and click **Find**.

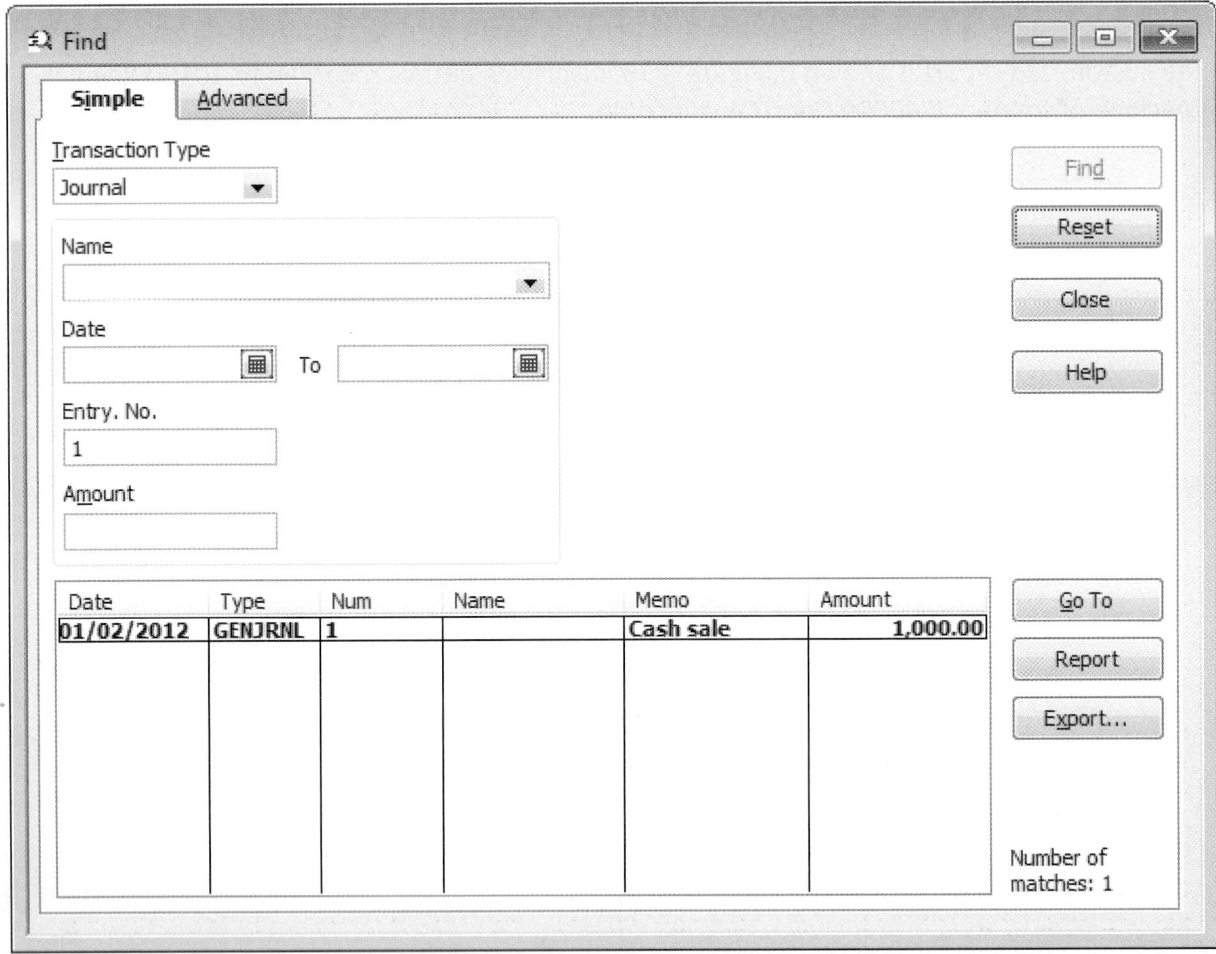

Figure 3:14

Double click the transaction displayed at the bottom to reopen the entry.

Now change the transaction. Place your cursor in the memo field for "4000 Consulting Income" and change the description to "Cash fees" (Figure 3:15).

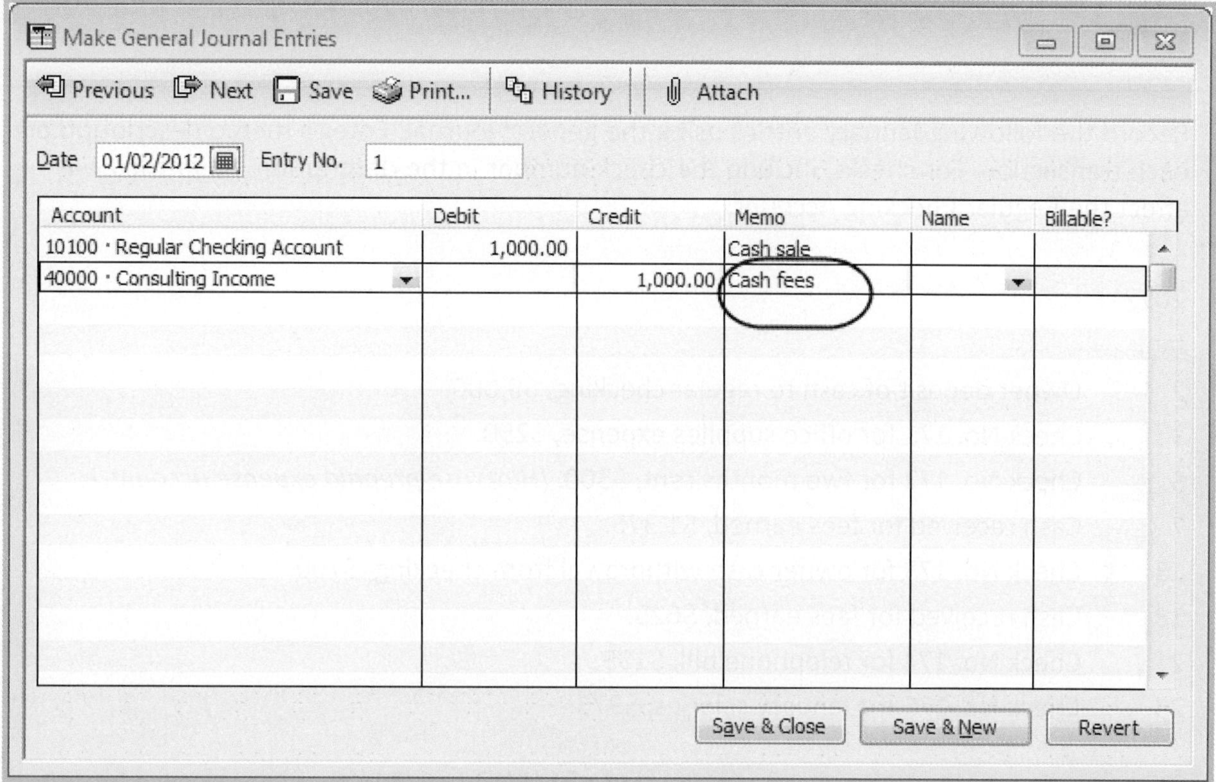

Figure 3:15

Click **Save & Close** to post the changes and exit the window. Click **Yes** when prompted to record the changes.

Close the **Find** window.

Click the **Custom G/L** icon button and reopen the report. Scroll down to account "40000 Consulting Income" and note the change in the Memo column.

Close the report and complete the next exercise.

RECORD TEK'S JANUARY TRANSACTIONS

Record the following January entries using the general journal. Enter a memo description on each transaction. For checks, include the check number in the description. All entries will affect the Regular Checking Account.

2012	
Jan.	
2	Owner deposit of cash to regular checking, $5,000.
3	Check No. 171 for office supplies expense, $250.
5	Check No. 172 for two months rent, $500. *(Hint: use prepaid expense account.)*
7	Cash received for fees earned, $1,375.
13	Check No. 173 for owner cash withdrawal from checking, $700.
18	Cash received for fees earned, $625.
21	Check No. 174 for telephone bill, $195.
24	Check No. 175 for January salaries, $975.

Print the January Journal report for the period of 1/1/12 to 1/24/12.

COMPOUND JOURNAL ENTRIES

Thus far, you have recorded journal entries using two accounts. Often accountants record compound journal entries affecting multiple accounts.

On January 28, TEK's owner made another investment in the company. She invested $7,000 in cash, a car valued at $10,000, and computer equipment valued at $12,000. Follow the next steps to record the transaction.

Steps to Record a Compound Journal Entry

1. Open a new journal entry.

2. Enter the date of "1/28/12".

3. Tab to **Account** on the first line and select "10100 Regular Checking Account". Tab to **Debit** and enter "7000.00". Tab to **Memo** and enter "Owner cash contribution".

4. Tab to **Account** on the second line and select "15200 Vehicle". Tab to **Debit** and enter "10000.00". Tab to **Memo** and enter "Owner car contribution". *(Note: You will override QBP's entry in the Credit field.)*

5. Tab to **Account** on the third line and select "15000 Office Equipment". Tab to **Debit** and enter "12000.00". Tab to **Memo** and enter "Owner computer contribution".

6. Tab to **Account** on the fourth line and select "39006 Owner's Contribution". QBP has entered "29,000.00" to the Credit field. *(Note: If you do not have this amount as a credit, check your previous entries.)*

7. Tab to **Memo** and enter "Owner contribution cash, car, computer". The completed entry appears in Figure 3:16.

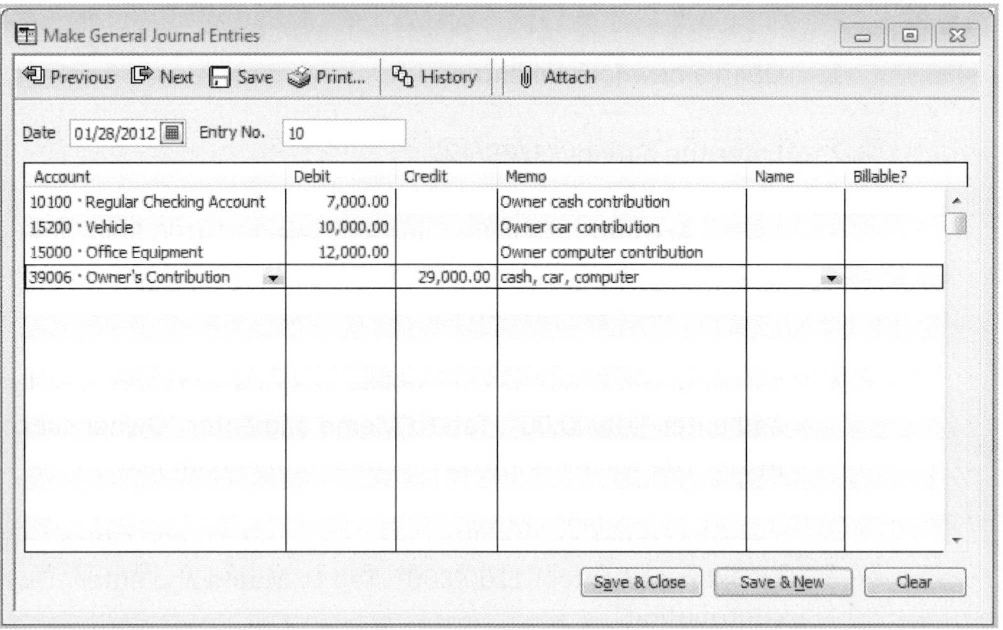

Figure 3:16

8. Click **Save & New**. *(Note: If you receive a message about fixed asset features, mark the option to turn off this message in the future and click OK.)*

Now complete the next exercise.

RECORD ADDITIONAL JOURNAL ENTRIES

Record the following journal entries and remember to enter a description for each transaction.

2012

Jan.

25 Check No. 176 for six months of vehicle insurance, $1,200. *(Hint: Use prepaid expense account.)*

26 Check No. 177 for office supplies expense, $210, and four desks, $3,250 recorded as office furniture.

27 Check No. 178 for electricity expense, $375.

28 Cash received for fees earned, $2,376.

Print the Journal report for 1/25/12 to 1/28/12.

ADJUSTING JOURNAL ENTRIES

Adjusting entries are journal entries that adjust account balances. These entries are used to post such transactions as expensing prepaid rent or recording depreciation expense.

After reviewing TEK's General Ledger report for January, the accountant asks you to post the following adjusting entries.

RECORD JANUARY ADJUSTING ENTRIES

Open the Journal Entry window and record the following adjusting entries for January 31, 2012.

a. Expense one month of the prepaid rent, $250.

b. Post January depreciation expense of $235.00 posted as follows.

Office equipment, $120

Office furniture, $30

Vehicles, $85.

Print the Journal report for January 31, 2012.

PRINT THE TRIAL BALANCE

The Trial Balance report differs from the General Ledger report because it lists accounts and balances without transaction detail. In addition, the report totals columns by debits and credits to make sure that general ledger accounts "balance." In a manual system, proving that the trial balance "balanced" was critical because it formed the basis for preparing financial statements.

In a computerized system, entries automatically balance. You have already seen that QBP will not post an out-of-balance entry. Therefore, accountants now use the trial balance to review account balances and to reconcile balances to external documents such as bank statements and asset reports.

Complete the following steps to print TEK's January Trial Balance report.

STEPS TO PRINT THE TRIAL BALANCE

1. Select ***Reports>>Accountant & Taxes>>Trial Balance*** from the main menu. Enter the dates of **From: 1/31/12** and **To 1/31/12**. The refreshed report is shown in Figure 3:17.

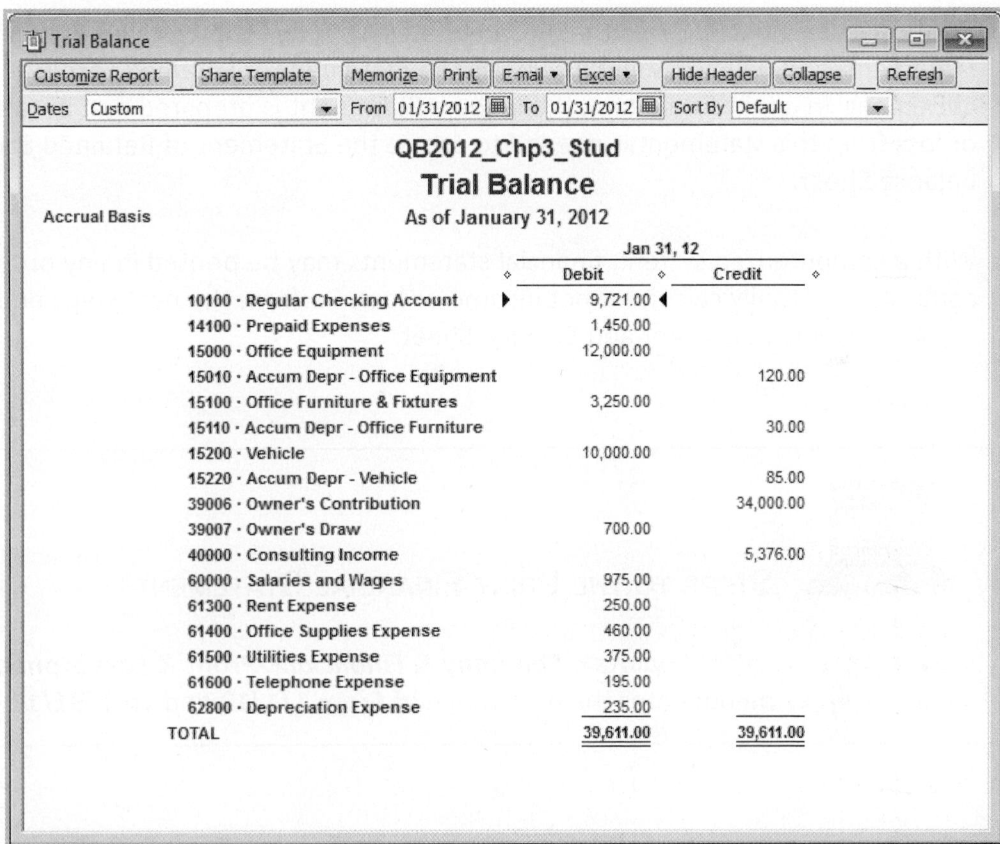

Trial Balance

Customize Report | Share Template | Memorize | Print | E-mail ▾ | Excel ▾ | Hide Header | Collapse | Refresh

Dates Custom From 01/31/2012 To 01/31/2012 Sort By Default

QB2012_Chp3_Stud

Trial Balance

Accrual Basis

As of January 31, 2012

	Jan 31, 12	
	Debit	Credit
10100 · Regular Checking Account	9,721.00	
14100 · Prepaid Expenses	1,450.00	
15000 · Office Equipment	12,000.00	
15010 · Accum Depr - Office Equipment		120.00
15100 · Office Furniture & Fixtures	3,250.00	
15110 · Accum Depr - Office Furniture		30.00
15200 · Vehicle	10,000.00	
15220 · Accum Depr - Vehicle		85.00
39006 · Owner's Contribution		34,000.00
39007 · Owner's Draw	700.00	
40000 · Consulting Income		5,376.00
60000 · Salaries and Wages	975.00	
61300 · Rent Expense	250.00	
61400 · Office Supplies Expense	460.00	
61500 · Utilities Expense	375.00	
61600 · Telephone Expense	195.00	
62800 · Depreciation Expense	235.00	
TOTAL	39,611.00	39,611.00

Figure 3:17

2. Click **Print**, choose a printer, and then click **Print** again to send the report to the printer. Click **X** to close the report and, when prompted, select the option to turn off future reminders on saving modified reports. Click **OK**.

PRINT FINANCIAL STATEMENTS

Financial statements include the Income Statement (sometimes called the Profit and Loss Statement) and Balance Sheet as well as the Statement of Retained Earnings and Cash Flow Statement. In a manual system, the Income Statement is prepared first because net income or loss from this statement is needed to create the Statement of Retained Earnings and Balance Sheet.

With a computerized system, financial statements may be printed in any order because the computer internally calculates net income or loss. Perform the next steps and print TEK's January Income Statement and Balance Sheet.

STEPS TO THE PRINT FINANCIAL STATEMENTS

1. Select ***Reports>>Company & Financial>>Profit & Loss Standard*** on the main menu. Enter the date range of **From 1/1/12** and **To 1/31/12**.

2. Click **Refresh** and the report Figure 3:18 in displays. Click **Print** to send the report to a printer. Recall from Chapter 2 that you can also email and export reports. Close this statement.

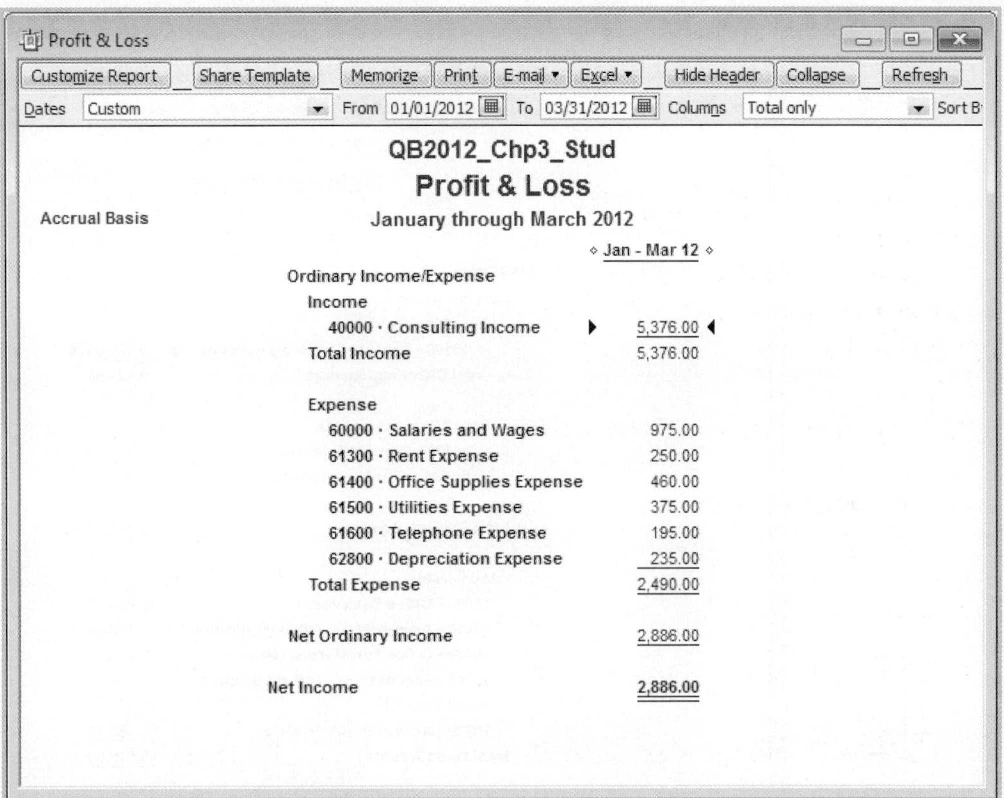

Figure 3:18

3. Select ***Reports>>Company & Financials>>Balance Sheet Standard*** on the main menu. Enter **1/31/12** as the date. The refreshed report displays as shown. Click **X** to close the report.

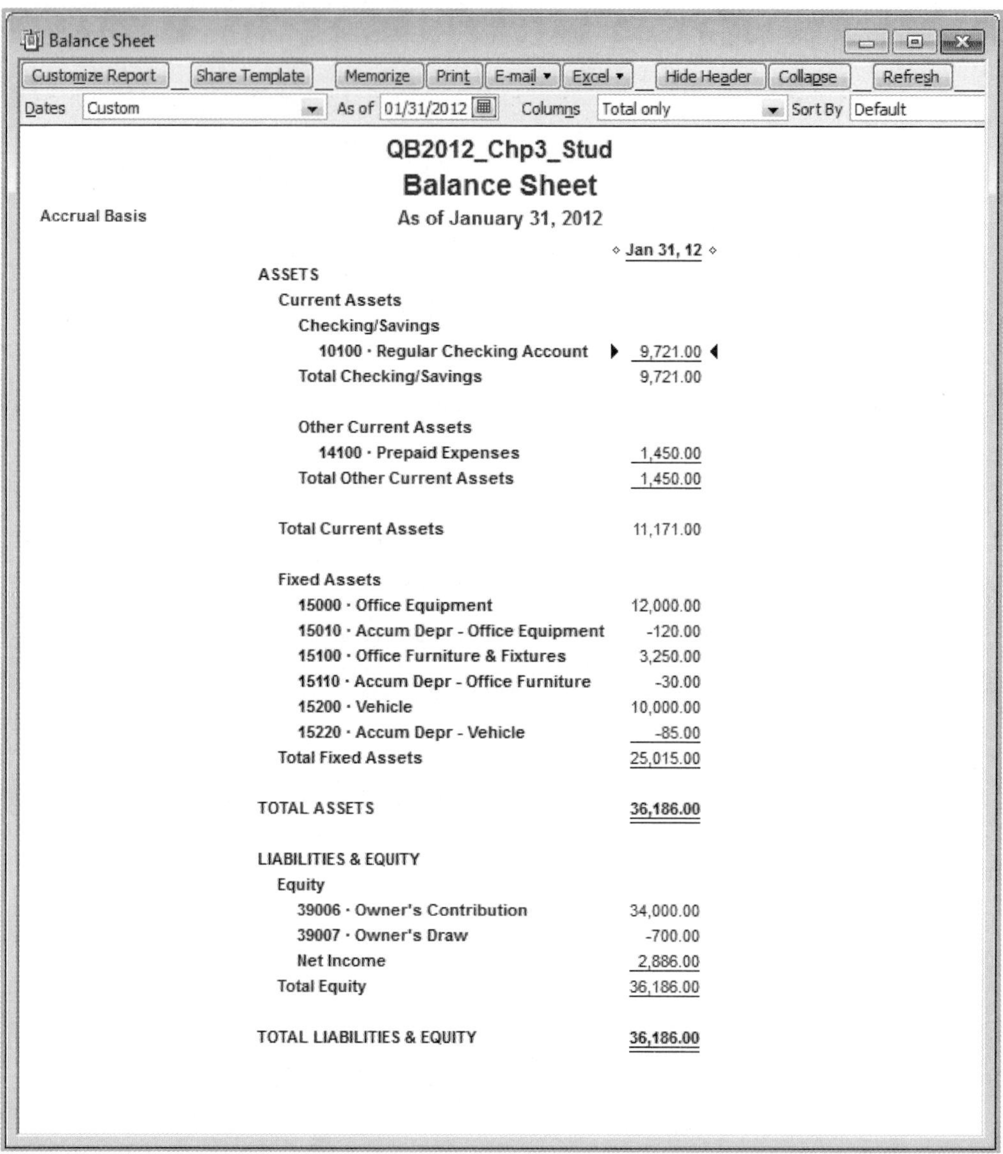

Figure 3:19

Close an Accounting Period

As stated in Chapter 2, you should always close the accounting period after issuing financial statements to protect the integrity of printed reports. After closing, QBP will warn when you attempt to post to a closed period.

With TEK's January reports issued, you are now ready to close the January accounting period.

Before closing, you should always make a backup of the company's data file.

Make a backup of the company data file to a backup file named "QB2012_Chp3_Stud_ Completed".

You will now close the January accounting period.

Steps to Close an Accounting Period

1. Click ***Company>>Set Closing Date*** on the main menu and the Company Preferences tab under Accounting preferences opens (Figure 3:20).

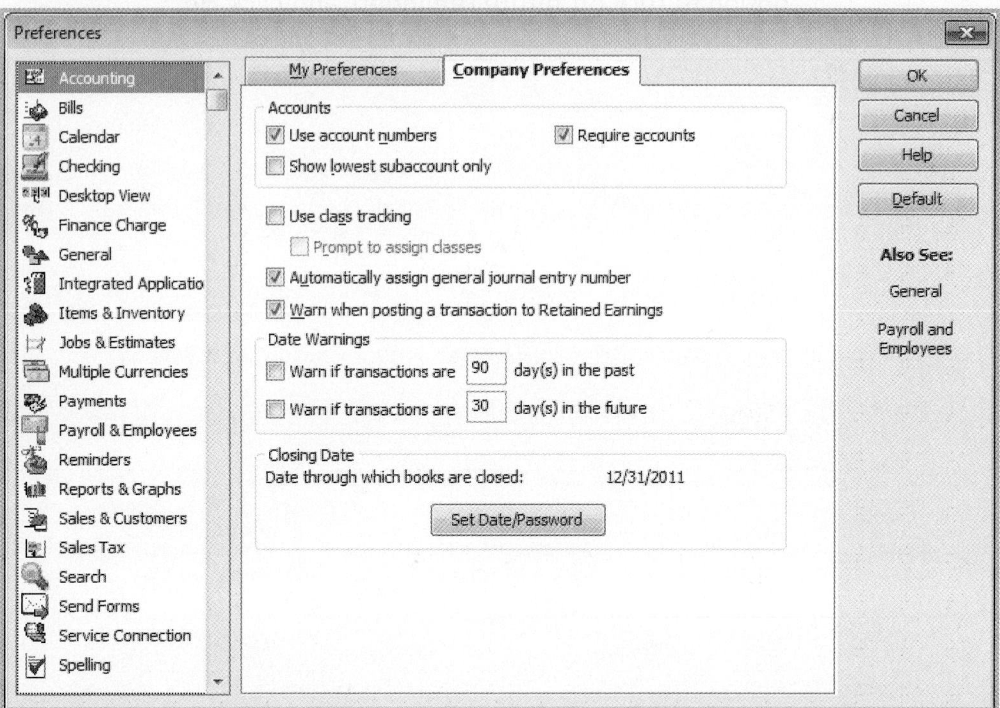

Figure 3:20

2. Click the **Set Date/Password** button and type "1/31/12" in the **Closing Date** field.

Figure 3:21

3. Click **OK**. A prompt appears to remind you to set a password. Mark the option to turn off future reminders and click **No**.

QUICKBOOKS DATA INTEGRATION

Data integration explains why QBP automatically posts transactions to general ledger accounts and customer, vendor, employee, and banking accounts. The next diagram visually depicts data integration.

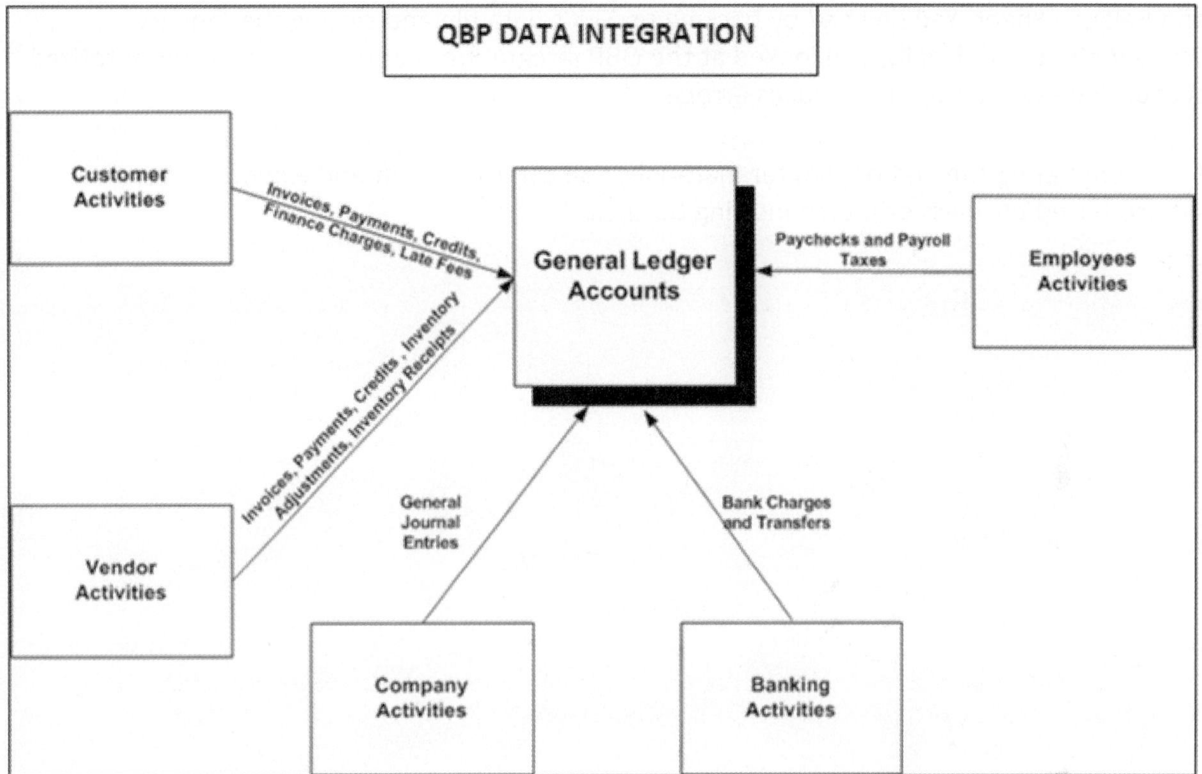

Figure 3:22

This diagram shows you that transactions posted in one activity flow through to the general ledger. Data integration saves time and reduces errors because you only enter data once instead of entering data in a subsidiary journal and then posting it to the general ledger. It also means that QBP automatically records the audit trail.

Subsequent chapters will focus on processing transactions for each activity depicted in the diagram. As in this chapter, you will begin by learning *MAPS* and then step through QBP transaction processing. Chapters 4 through 7 will cover customer, vendor, employee, and company/banking activities for a service-based business. Chapters 8 through Chapter 11 will focus on the same activities for a merchandising business.

SUMMARY

You began the chapter by looking at T-Accounts and *MAPS* for recording general journal entries. You then posted a general journal entry in QBP and went *Behind the Keys* of the posted transaction to trace the audit trail. You also posted compound journal entries and adjusting entries. You learned to correct entries and print the Trial Balance, Income Statement, and Balance Sheet. You finished by backing up TEK's data file and closing the January accounting period. Finally, you looked at the QBP integration that explains why computerized accounting saves times and reduces errors.

After completing the end-of-chapter materials, you can branch off and explore either the service-based business or merchandising business tracks.

END-OF-CHAPTER QUESTIONS

TRUE/FALSE

_____ 1. You should always back up a company's data file before closing an accounting period.

_____ 2. You view posted journal entries by selecting **Company>>Journal** on the main menu.

_____ 3. QBP will let you drilldown on the Trial Balance report to view transactions in an account.

_____ 4. You can create a journal entry from the Chart of Accounts.

_____ 5. The Save button on a journal entry posts the transaction.

_____ 6. QBP will let you delete a posted journal entry.

_____ 7. The Print icon on the Trial Balance report opens a window for selecting a printer to receive output.

_____ 8. Journal entries are automatically posted to general ledger accounts when saved.

_____ 9. QBP will let you reopen a posted journal entry to correct it.

_____ 10. The General Ledger report displays General Journal and the entry number as the audit trail of a posted journal entry.

MULTIPLE CHOICE

_____ 1. Which report will list the details of transactions by account?
  a. Journal
  b. Balance Sheet
  c. General Ledger
  d. Trial Balance

_____ 2. You can print a General Ledger report using __________.
  a. **Reports>>Accountants & Taxes>>General Ledger** on the main menu
  b. the Reports command on the Chart of Accounts
  c. Both a and b
  d. None of the above

______ 3. QBP will let you change a report by __________.

a. clicking the Customize Report icon
b. entering custom dates on the face of the report
c. changing the sort order on the face of the report
d. All of the above

______ 4. Adjusting journal entries are used to record __________.

a. depreciation expense
b. expired prepaid expense
c. Both a and b
d. None of the above

______ 5. Which report shows a company's financial position?

a. Balance Sheet
b. Chart of Accounts
c. Profit and Loss
d. General Ledger Trial Balance

______ 6. Which of the following reports will not let you enter a range of reporting dates?

a. General Ledger Trial Balance
b. Profit and Loss
c. Balance Sheet
d. Both a and b

______ 7. Which report is also known as the Income Statement?

a. Balance Sheet
b. Chart of Accounts
c. Profit and Loss
d. Trial Balance

Practice Set

In this practice set, you will record January accounting activities using general journal entries. Remember to enter a description on all transactions. Use the regular checking account for any transaction that affects cash.

Begin by:

- Opening the software.
- Opening the **QB2012_Chp3_PracSet_Stud** data file. Add your initials to the end to the Company Name by clicking ***Company>>Company Information*** on the main menu. Click **OK** to save the changes.
- **Toggling the software to the PRO EDITION** by selecting ***File>>Toggle to Another Edition*** on the main menu and choosing **QuickBooks Pro** as the edition.

1. Record the following transactions.

2012

Jan 1	Owner initial investment of $24,000: Cash $3,000 Office equipment $12,000 Office furniture $4,000 Vehicles $5,000
Jan 2	Check No. 178 for office supplies expense, $380.
Jan 3	Check No. 179 for six months of prepaid rent, $2,400.
Jan 5	Check No. 180 for advertising expense, $980. Check No. 181 to vehicle expenses, $1,700.
Jan 7	Cash received for fees earned, $7,625.
Jan 13	Check No. 182 for office salaries, $1,200.
Jan 14	Cash received for fees earned, $3,300.
Jan 17	Check No. 183 for donation to local charity, $300. Check No. 184 to owner, $1,300.
Jan 26	Check No. 185 for electricity expense, $350. Check No. 186 for office salaries, $1,200.

2. Record the following adjusting entries as of January 31.
    a. Expense one month of prepaid rent.
    b. January depreciation expense of $355 posted as follows:
        Office equipment, $170
        Office furniture, $65
        Vehicles, $120

3. Print the following January reports.
    a. Journal
    b. Trial Balance
    c. Profit and Loss
    d. Balance Sheet

4. ***Back up the company to a backup file named "QB2012_Chp3_PracSet_Stud_Completed". Close the January accounting period.***

INTERNET MINI-PROJECT

To complete this mini-project, go to the Website at ***www.pearsonhighered.com/brunsdon/*** and download the instruction file named **Young Accounting.pdf** and the data file named **Young Accounting.QBW**.

CHAPTER 4 CUSTOMER ACTIVITIES FOR A SERVICE-BASED BUSINESS

LEARNING OBJECTIVES

This chapter focuses on using the software to process customer activities for a service-based business. The chapter covers the following:

1. Manual accounting procedures (*MAPS*) for customer transactions
2. Using the Customer Center to perform customer-related tasks
3. Recording a basic sales invoice
4. Going *Behind the Keys* of a posted invoice to trace the entries
5. Learning to correct a posted invoice
6. Emailing a sales invoice
7. Managing customers and jobs
8. Understanding service and non-inventory part items
9. Invoicing job costs and printing job reports
10. Recording basic customer payments
11. Going *Behind the Keys* of a posted payment to trace the entries
12. Learning to correct a posted payment
13. Recording customer payments carrying a discount
14. Recording sales receipts
15. Recording customer credits
16. Reporting on customer activities and reconciling activities to the general ledger
17. Writing off customer invoices
18. Preparing customer statements

<u>Begin by:</u>

- Opening the software.
- Opening the **QB2012_Chp4_Stud** data file. Add your initials to the end to the Company Name by clicking ***Company>>Company Information*** on the main menu. Click **OK** to save the changes.
- **Toggling the software to the PRO EDITION** by selecting ***File>>Toggle to Another Edition*** on the main menu and choosing **QuickBooks Pro** as the edition.

In this chapter and the next three, we will call the company you are working with Astor Landscaping. This company provides landscaping and lawn maintenance services to residential and commercial customers. The company's current accounting period is March 2012.

MANUAL ACCOUNTING PROCEDURES

Before using the software, we will introduce you to using manual accounting procedures (*MAPS*) to process sales transactions. We begin at the point where a customer initiates a transaction.

On March 22, 2012, John Chester contacts Astor salesperson, Jan Folse, requesting seasonal lawn maintenance. John has used the company in the past. Jan quotes John a price of $80.00, plus tax, and schedules the service for March 25.

In a manual system, Jan writes up a service ticket, which an employee performing the service takes to the job. These tickets are not entered into the accounting records because the sale is not recognized until after performing the services. Recall that accrual accounting does not recognize revenue until earned and Astor does not earn the revenue until it provides the service.

On March 25, Jeff Henderson picks up the service ticket and heads to the job. After completing the service, Jeff has John sign the service ticket to acknowledge completion of the job and returns the signed ticket to Jan. Jan then forwards the ticket to the accountant, Judy White, who prepares the following invoice (Figure 4:1).

Astor Landscaping
1505 Pavilion Place, Suite C
Arlington, VA 30093

Date: 3/25/2012

Customer:

Mr. John Chester
2404 Pleasant Hill
Danville, VA 30096

INVOICE	No. 1036
Seasonal Lawn Maintenance March 25, 2012	$ 350.00
Sales Tax	17.50
Total	$ 367.50
Please remit balance within 30 days	

Figure 4:1

Judy next records the invoice, along with other invoices for that day, in the Sales Journal. Her entries to the Sales Journal for March 25 appear next.

Astor Landscaping						
Date: 3/25/2012			Sales Journal			Page 15
Customer	Post Ref	Description	Accounts Receivable (Debit)	Sales Landscape (Credit)	Sales Hardscape (Credit)	Sales Tax Payable (Credit)
John Chester	CHES001	Seasonal Maint. INV	367.50	350.00		17.50
DBH Enterprises	DBHE001	Landscaping / Maint. INV	3,383.15	290.00	2,916.78	176.37
Yango Software	YANG001	Seasonal Maint. INV	290.13		275.00	15.13
Totals:			$ 4,040.78	$ 640.00	$ 3,191.78	$ 209.00
Acct Ref:			(11000)	(41000)	(42000)	(22000)

Audit Trail

Figure 4:2

This shows that Judy recorded John's invoice as a debit to accounts receivable and as credits to landscape services and sales tax payable. At the end of the day, Judy totals each column on the Sales Journal and cross-foots the totals to verify that entries balance (i.e., debits equal credits). She then posts each invoice individually to a customer account and posts column totals to the general ledger accounts noted at the bottom.

Figure 4:3 shows Judy's entry to John's customer account. *(Note: Entries for other customer accounts are not illustrated.)*

John Chester
2404 Pleasant Hill
Danville, VA 30096 — **Acct No: CHES001**

Audit Trail

Date	Description	Post Ref	Debit	Credit	Balance
3/1/2012	Beginning Balance				0.00
3/25/2012	Seasonal Maint. INV 1036	SJ 15	367.50		367.50

Figure 4:3

Judy's entries to general ledger accounts are illustrated in Figure 4:4. *(Note: The entry to the sales tax payable account is not shown.)*

General Ledger					
Accounts Receivable				**Account No. 11000**	
Date	**Description**	**Post Ref**	**Debit**	**Credit**	**Balance**
3/24/2012	Balance Forward				96,273.96
3/25/2012		SJ 15	4,040.78		100,314.74

Audit Trail

General Ledger					
Sales Landscape				**Account No. 41000**	
Date	**Description**	**Post Ref**	**Debit**	**Credit**	**Balance**
3/24/2012	Balance Forward				22,240.00
3/25/2012		SJ 15		640.00	22,880.00

Audit Trail

General Ledger					
Sales Hardscape				**Account No. 42000**	
Date	**Description**	**Post Ref**	**Debit**	**Credit**	**Balance**
3/24/2012	Balance Forward				55,290.00
3/25/2012		SJ 15		3,191.78	58,481.78

Figure 4:4

As Judy posts, she also enters the posting references that form the audit trail. As explained in Chapter 3, the audit trail documents entries so you can later trace entries between subsidiary journals (i.e. the Sales Journal and General Journal), subsidiary ledgers (i.e. the customer account), and general ledger accounts. You can just imagine the posting errors that occur in a manual system. Judy could record an entry backwards (e.g., enter a debit as a credit), record an out-of-balance entry, or omit posting part or all of a transaction.

On the same day that Judy posts invoices, she also posts customer payments for outstanding invoices. These entries are recorded in a separate journal called the Cash Receipts Journal. Entries to the Cash Receipts Journal are illustrated in Figure 4:5.

Astor Landscaping

Date: 3/25/2012 **Cash Receipts Journal** **Page 3**

Customer	Check No.	Post Ref	Invoice No.	Regular Checking (Debit)	Accounts Receivable (Credit)	Sales Discounts (Debit)
O'Hara Homes	993	OHAR001	993	1,000.00	1,000.00	
Sycamore Homes	9832	SYCA001	1012	20,291.72	20,681.95	390.23
Totals:				**$ 21,291.72**	**$ 21,681.95**	**$ 390.23**
Acct Ref:				**(10200)**	**(11000)**	**(49000)**

Audit Trail

Figure 4:5

As with postings on the Sales Journal, Judy posts each check to the customer's account and column totals to the general ledger accounts. This time she will use the posting reference of CRJ (Cash Receipts Journal) along with the page number. *(Note: These postings are not illustrated.)*

With QBP, the accountant can eliminate many of the posting errors that occur in a manual system. You will see later in the chapter that sales invoices automatically post to the Sales Journal, customer account, and general ledger accounts upon saving. The same goes when saving customer payments. In addition, QBP records the audit trail and will not let you post an out-of-balance entry.

We next focus our attention to processing customer transactions in QBP.

Customer Center

The **Customer Center** is for processing and managing customer activities. Click the **Customers** button on the **Home** page or the **Customers** icon on the **Toolbar** to open the center. Set the options indicated in Figure 4:6. We now discuss using this center.

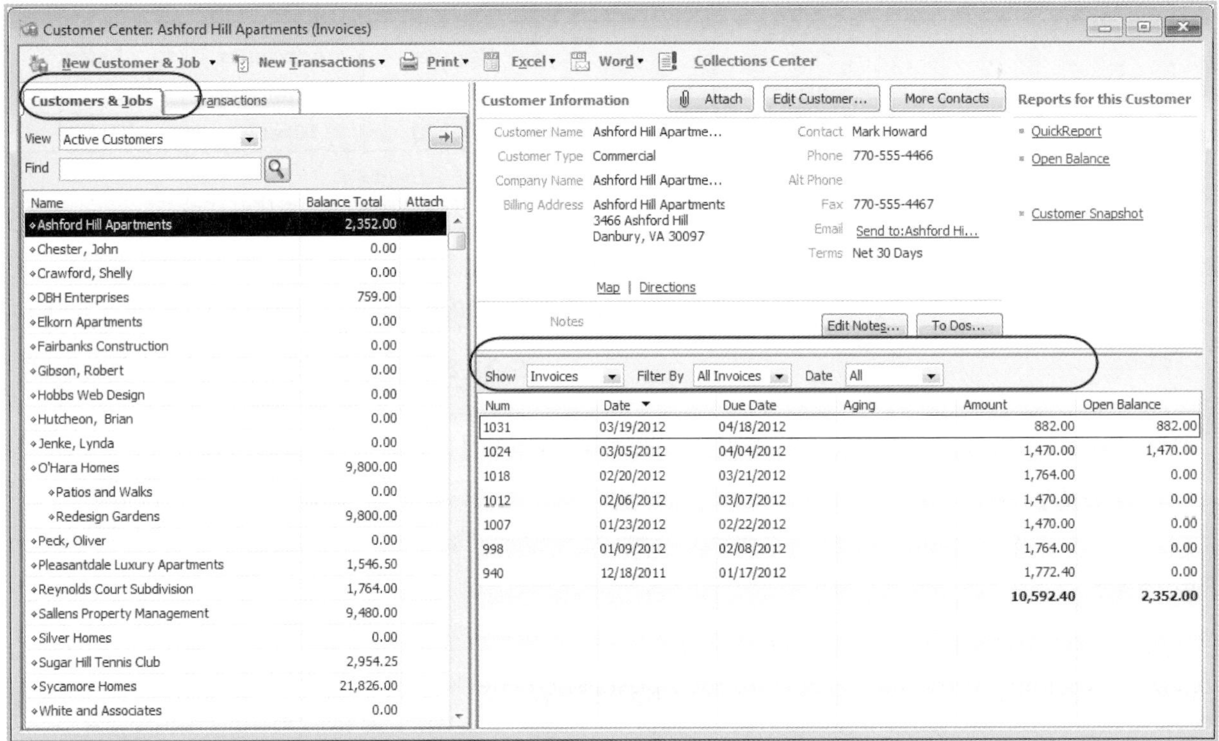

Figure 4:6

The **Customers & Jobs** tab lists transactions by customer account. Astor's customer accounts and balances appear to the left. The **View** option is used to toggle the listed customers to All Customers, Active Customers, or Customers with Open Balances. You are currently viewing Active Customers.

This [→|] button hides the Customer Information pane shown to the right. After hiding, this [|←] button appears on the far right for redisplaying the pane.

The **Customer Information** pane displays transactions for the account highlighted to the left. This account is currently Ashford Hill Apartments.

The **Edit Customer** button opens the account for editing customer information. The **Edit Notes** button lets you enter account notes. There are also hyperlinks for creating **Reports for this Customer**.

Ashford's transactions are listed at the bottom of its account information. The filter options of **Show**, **Filter By**, and **Date** determine the transactions displayed. Click ▾ to select a new option from the dropdown list. You are currently viewing **Invoices** that are **All Invoices** recorded on **All** dates. *(Remember that the fiscal year is based on your computer date.)*

Filter options work as follows:

- Show: Select the transaction type to list
- Filter By: Criteria based on transaction type
- Date: List all transactions for the type or only transactions recorded as of a specific date or range of dates

Now turn your attention to the buttons on the toolbar, which show tasks that can be performed while displaying the Customers & Jobs tab. These tasks include **New Customer & Job**, **New Transactions**, **Print**, **Excel**, and **Word**.

Each button has this ▾ dropdown symbol, meaning the button contains multiple tasks. The table that follows discusses the tasks you can perform. Many of these tasks will be performed on the customer account highlighted on the left.

Customers & Jobs Activities	Task	Description
New Customer & Job	New Customer	Create a new customer account.
	Add Job and Add Multiple Customer: Jobs	Create a new job for the highlighted customer or add a new job for multiple customers.
New Transactions	Invoices	Create a sales invoice for the highlighted customer.
	Sales Receipts	Record a sales transaction for the highlighted customer. Used when the customer is paying in full at time of sale. Do not use this task for invoicing the customer. Instead, use Invoices.
	Statement Charges	Open the highlighted customer's register and enter charges that will print on a statement. This is an alternate method for billing customers that bypasses creating an invoice. It can also be used to record finance charges. The text will not illustrate this method.
	Receive Payments	Record a payment from the highlighted customer.
	Credit Memos/Refunds	Issue a credit to the highlighted customer or refund a customer overpayment.

Customers & Jobs Activities	Task	Description
Print	Customer & Job List	Print a customer list with balances. The report cannot be customized, so this report is usually printed from the Reports menu.
	Customer & Job Information	Print account information and notes for the highlighted customer. The report cannot be customized, so this report is usually printed from the Reports menu.
	Customer & Job Transaction List	Print the highlighted customer's transactions for the current fiscal year. The report cannot be customized, so this report is usually printed from the Reports menu.
Excel	Export Customer List	Create an Excel workbook or comma separated values (.csv) file containing account information and balances for all customers.
	Export Transactions	Create an Excel workbook or comma separated values (.csv) file containing current fiscal year transactions for the highlighted customer.
	Import from Excel and Paste from Excel	Import or paste customer information and/or transactions from an Excel workbook or comma separated values (.csv) file.
Word	Customer communications	Create form letters for customers.
Collection Center	Reviewing collection information	Opens a window with information that assists in collecting from customers.

Next, turn your attention to the **Transactions** tab, which lists transactions by type instead of transactions by customer. Click to activate the tab and select the options indicated in the following illustration (Figure 4:7).

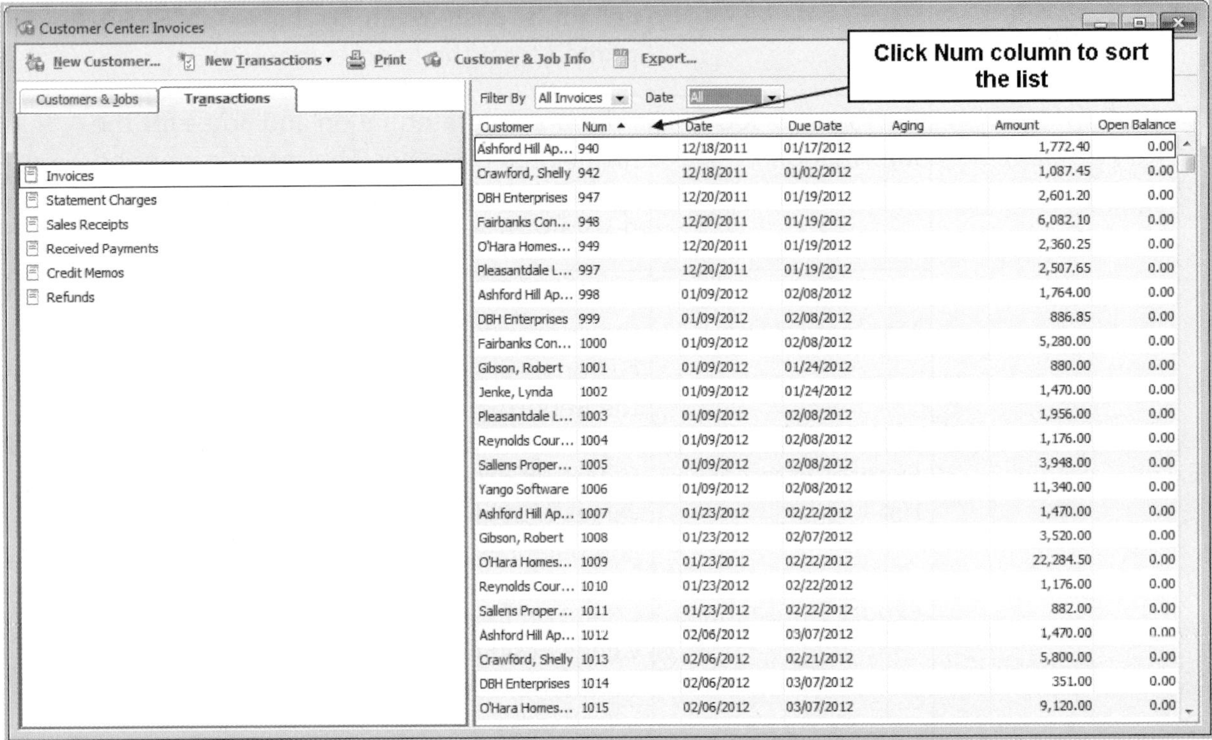

Figure 4:7

Transaction types are selected on the left. The **Invoices** type is currently highlighted and the information displayed on the right lists **All Invoices** for **All** dates. Once again, the transactions displayed depend on the filtering options. You can change the sort order by clicking a column header.

Tasks that can be performed on this tab are different from those that can be performed on the other tab. First, not all buttons have additional tasks, so clicking an activity immediately opens the task. The next table discusses tasks you can perform on the **Transactions** tab.

Button	Description
New Customer	Create a new customer account. Additional jobs can only be added from the Customers & Jobs tab.
New Transactions	Contains the same tasks found on the Customers & Jobs tab, but this time the user selects the customer.
Print	Print transactions listed to the right.
Customer & Job Info	Edit customer and job information for the customer attached to the transaction highlighted on the right.
Export	Create an Excel workbook or comma separated values (.csv) file containing transactions listed on the right.

As illustrated, you can perform a variety of customer activities from the Customer Center. You can initiate transactions, locate posted transactions, manage accounts, and create new accounts. **Close the Customer Center**.

In contrast, the icons on the customer section of the **Home** page (Figure 4:8) only initiate transactions, but offer quicker access to performing tasks. In addition, you can always use the ***Customers*** menu to perform customer activities.

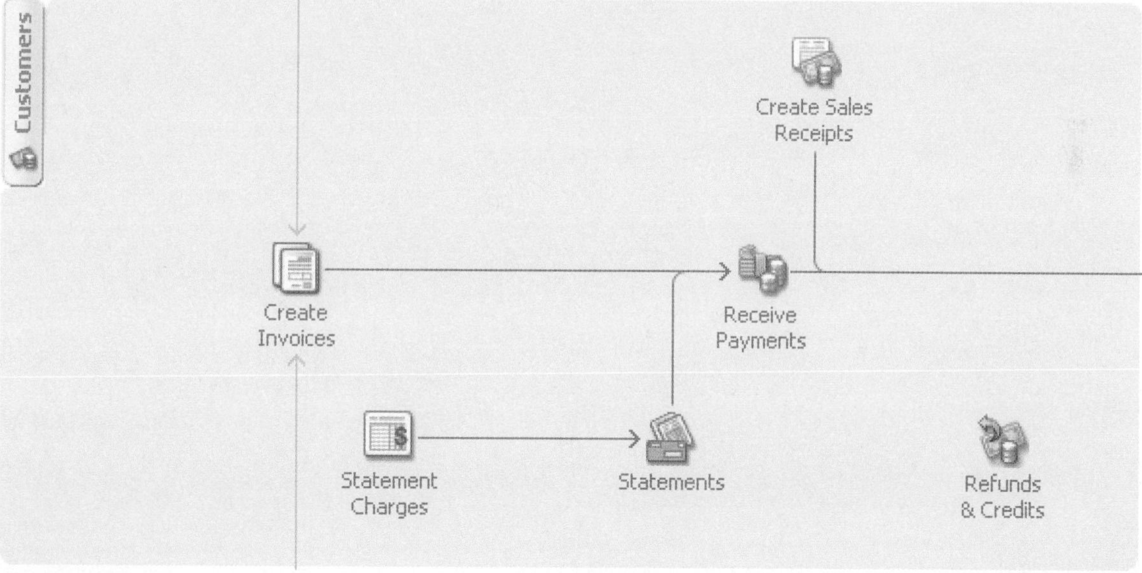

Figure 4:8

Now that you are familiar with locating customer activities, let us begin recording customer transactions.

Entering Sales Invoices

We now return to John Chester's transaction illustrated in the *MAPS* topic and record his invoice in QBP. Read the following data entry tips before completing the exercise that follows.

Data Entry Tips

Tip 1: The **Customer:Job** field links a transaction to a customer's account. The **Item** field links inventory items to a transaction. Customer accounts and items are also called master records. You will recognize a master record field because it contains look-ups for selecting a record.

Tip 2: You can either click the dropdown list on the **Customer:Job** or **Item** field to select a customer or item or begin typing the name of the customer or item to make a selection.

Tip 3: If you select the wrong customer or item, return to the field and change the selection. Click **Edit** on the main menu when you want to add or delete invoice line items.

Tip 4: QBP will create new master records "on the fly," meaning a new customer or item can be created while entering a transaction. Example: A new customer can be added by typing a customer name in the **Customer:Job** field and pressing tab. QBP will then prompt with the following:

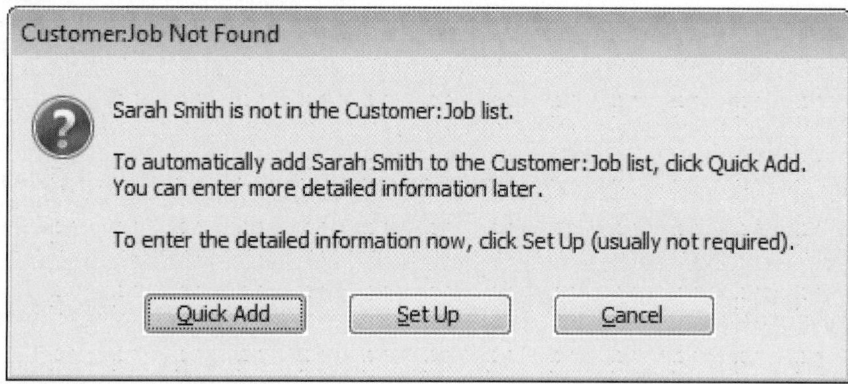

Figure 4:9

Clicking **Set Up** opens the New Customer window for entering all information on the new account. Clicking **Cancel** returns you to the **Customer:Job** field for selecting an existing customer. Clicking **Quick Add** creates the new account without opening the New Customer window. You will not want to use Quick Add because it does not allow you to enter an address or other information for the new account.

Tip 5: Figure 4:10 illustrates toolbar icons on the invoice window and a description of relevant icons follows the illustration.

Figure 4:10

Previous and **Next** scroll through posted invoices. QBP will prompt to save a new or modified transaction before moving to another transaction.

Save will save the current transaction and remain on the transaction.

Print sends the current invoice to a printer. The dropdown list for this icon contains an option for previewing an invoice before printing it and an option for printing multiple invoices.

Steps for Entering a Sales Invoice

1. On the **Home** page, click **Create Invoices** to open the invoice transaction window. *(Note: Click **No Thanks** if prompted about adding forms.)*

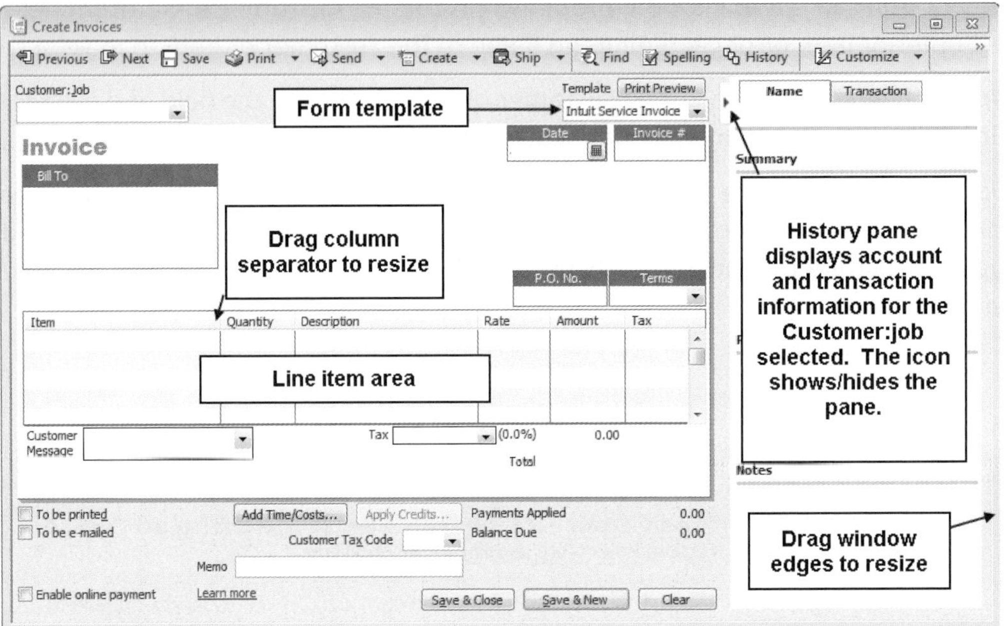

Figure 4:11

Make sure that the form template displays Intuit Service Invoice. This template is selected from the dropdown list. The service invoice template sets the columns displayed on the line items and other fields displayed on the form.

To resize the window, drag the edges using the mouse. To resize line item columns, drag the column separators.

The **History** pane displays Summary information, Recent Transactions, and Notes for the customer linked to the transaction. Clicking a hyperlinked item in the pane will open additional details.

2. Place your cursor in **Customer:Job** and look up "Chester, John". The **Bill To** and **Terms** information transfers from the customer account.

3. Place your cursor in **Date**. Type "3/25/12" because this is the day that the services were performed. *(Note: You can also select the date using the field's calendar feature.)*

   *(Note: The first time you open a transaction window, QBP will set the transaction date to your computer date. **BE CAREFUL** and always check transaction dates before saving.)*

4. Tab to **Invoice #** and the invoice number should be "1036."

5. Place your cursor in **Item** on the first line item. Look up and select "SEASONAL SERVICE – RESIDENTIAL" and QBP will display the item's description in the field.

   (Note: The lookup on Item signals that it links to a master record in the Items table.)

6. Tab to **Quantity** and enter "2". Click to select the **To be printed** option.

7. Press **Tab** and the completed invoice appears as illustrated in Figure 4:12.

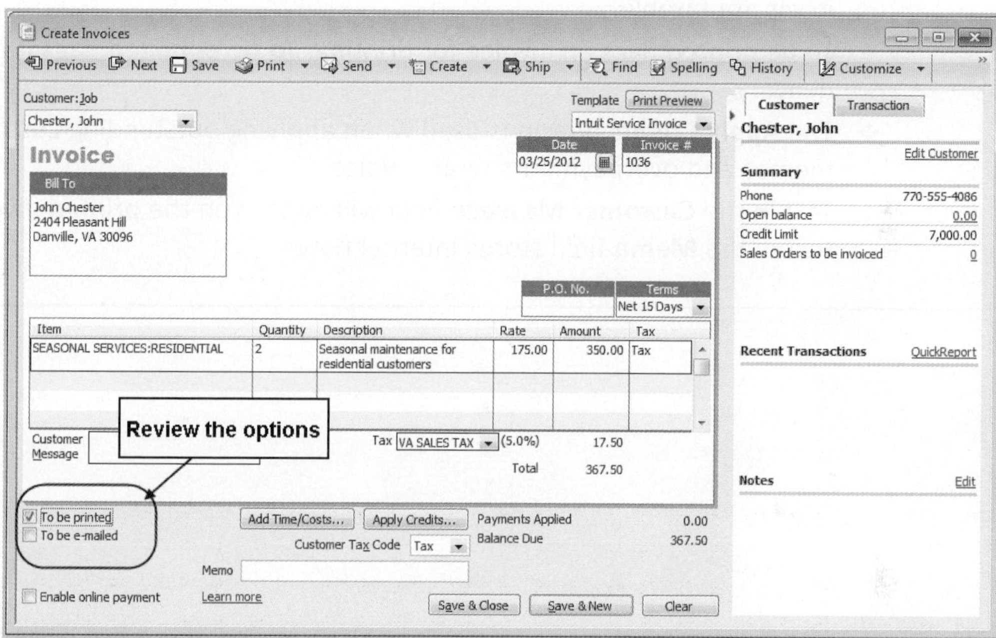

Figure 4:12

Before saving the invoice, review remaining fields in the window. You will normally not need to change data in these fields.

- **Description** and **Rate** defaulted from the item selected.
- **Amount** equals the **Quantity** times the **Rate**.
- The **Tax** column on a line item shows whether sales tax is normally charged on the item. You can mix taxable line items with nontaxable line items.
- The **Tax** field under the line items area (i.e., **VA SALES TAX**) sets the sales tax rate applied to taxable line items. The rate code defaults from the customer account.
- **Customer Tax Code** shows if sales to a particular customer are taxable. If the customer is not taxable, the invoice will not compute sales tax even when line items are taxable.
- ***To be printed*** flags an invoice for printing. ***To be e-mailed*** flags it for email delivery.
- The **Apply Credits** button is used when applying outstanding customer credit memos and overpayments to an invoice.
- Text in the **Customer Message** field will appear on the printed invoice whereas text in the **Memo** field stores internal notes.

8. Click the **dropdown list** on **Print** and select **Preview** to view the invoice (Figure 4:13) before sending it to the printer.

   (Note: If prompted about shipping labels, select the option that turns off future messages and click OK.)

   Scroll to the bottom of the invoice to view the total. You can click on the invoice to enlarge it.

   Click **Close** to return to the invoice transaction.

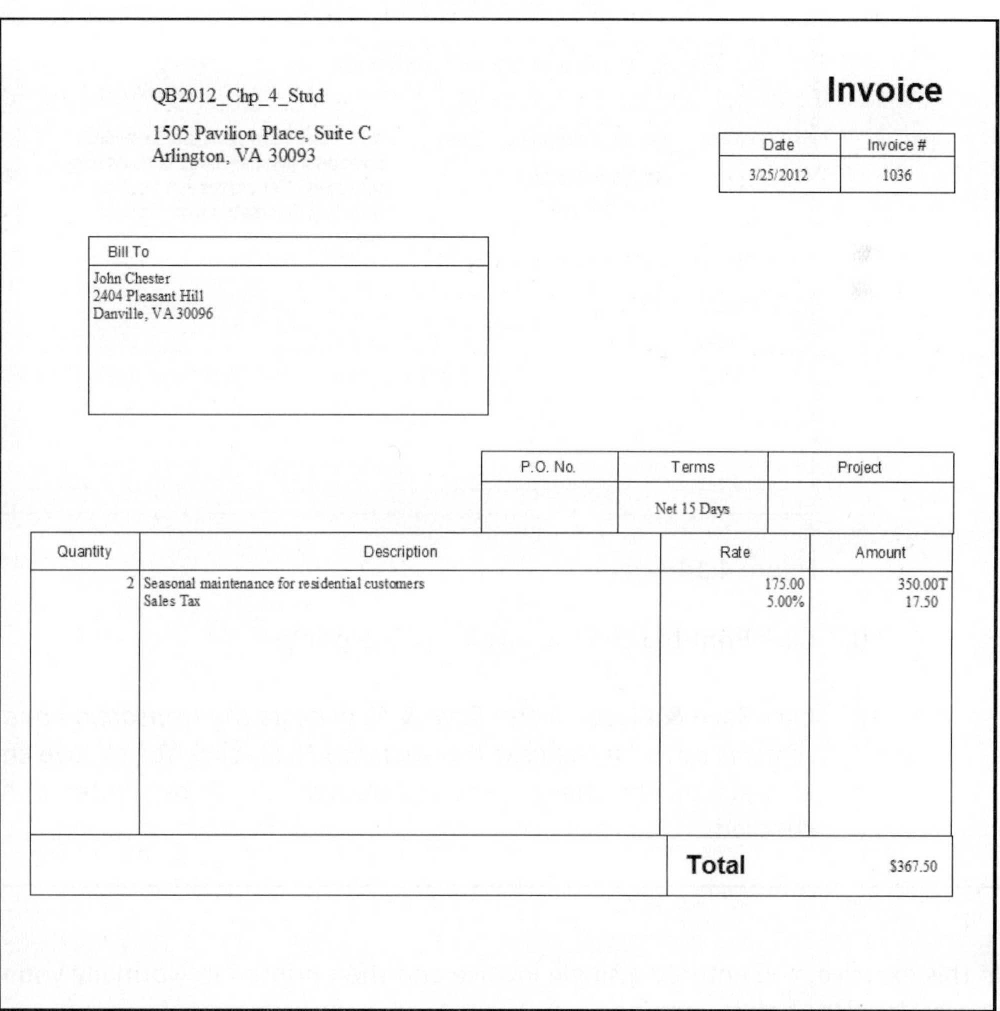

QB2012_Chp_4_Stud
1505 Pavilion Place, Suite C
Arlington, VA 30093

Invoice

Date	Invoice #
3/25/2012	1036

Bill To
John Chester
2404 Pleasant Hill
Danville, VA 30096

P.O. No.	Terms	Project
	Net 15 Days	

Quantity	Description	Rate	Amount
2	Seasonal maintenance for residential customers	175.00	350.00T
	Sales Tax	5.00%	17.50
		Total	$367.50

Figure 4:13

9. Click **Print** and QBP automatically saves the transaction before opening a window to select a printer (Figure 4:14). Use the dropdown list on **Printer name** if you need to select a different printer.

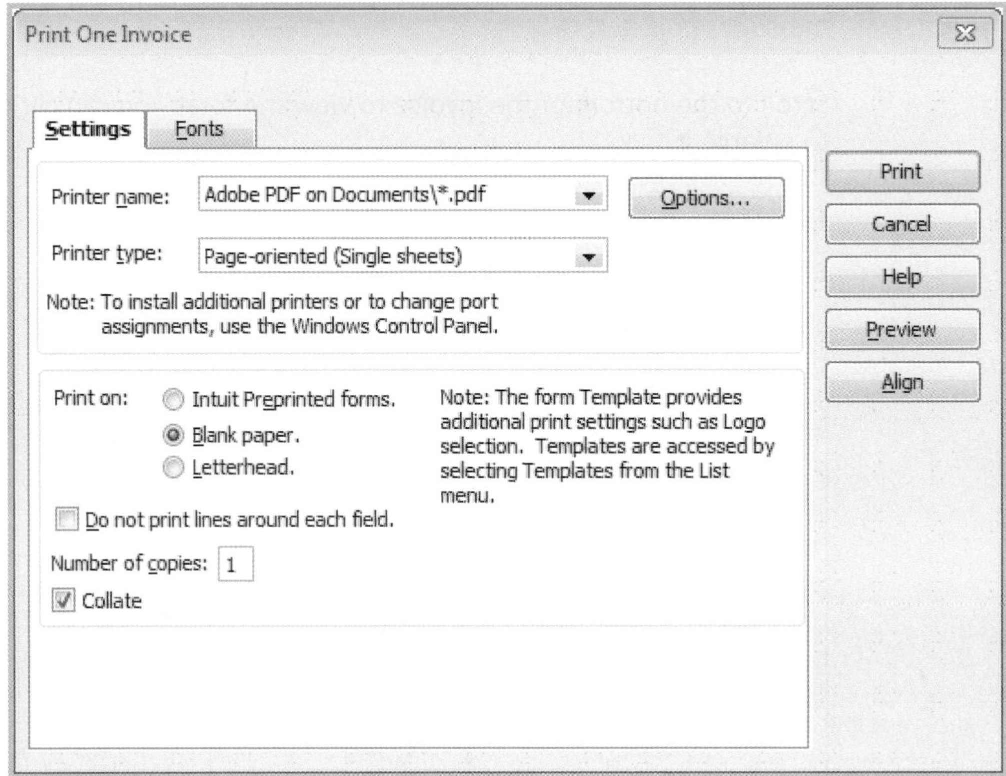

Figure 4:14

10. Click **Print** to send the invoice to the printer.

11. Click **Save & Close**. *(Note: Save & New posts the transaction and the window remains open for the next transaction.)* Next, click **Yes** to save changes to the transaction. The change occurred because the To be printed option is no longer checked.

In this exercise, you entered a single invoice and then printed it. Normally you will enter several invoices before printing.

To print multiple invoices, click the dropdown list on the **Print** icon and select **Print Batch**. QBP then displays every invoice that was marked ☑ To be printed in the Create Invoices window. You can then click to choose the invoices to print.

To reprint an invoice, reopen the invoice and click **Print**.

Behind the Keys of a Posted Sales Invoice

In this topic, you trace QBP's audit trail by locating the entries made when posting John's invoice in the previous topic. Remember that the audit trail in a manual system referenced the Sales Journal and the page number. Let us see how that compares with QBP's audit trail.

Trace the Audit Trail of a Posted Sales Invoice

1. First, open the Sales Journal by selecting **Reports>>Memorized Reports>>Accounting Journals>>Sales Journal** on the main menu.

2. Enter the date range of **From** 3/25/12 **To** 3/25/12. Click **Customize Report** and, on the **Filters** tab, set the **Name** filter to **Chester, John**. Click **OK** to refresh the report.

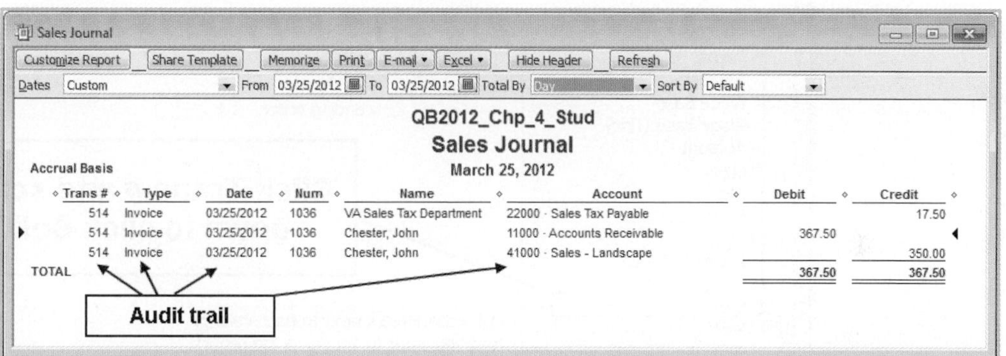

QB2012_Chp_4_Stud
Sales Journal
March 25, 2012

Accrual Basis

Trans #	Type	Date	Num	Name	Account	Debit	Credit
514	Invoice	03/25/2012	1036	VA Sales Tax Department	22000 · Sales Tax Payable		17.50
514	Invoice	03/25/2012	1036	Chester, John	11000 · Accounts Receivable	367.50	
514	Invoice	03/25/2012	1036	Chester, John	41000 · Sales - Landscape		350.00
TOTAL						367.50	367.50

Figure 4:15

Recall that the entries for John's invoice on the manual Sales Journal debited 11000 Accounts Receivable for $367.50, credited 41000 Sales Landscape for $350.00, and credited 22000 Sales Taxes Payable for $17.50. This is exactly what QBP shows as the entries.

Note the audit trail codes under **Type** and **Trans #** because we will refer to these codes again. *(Note: Your Trans # may differ because numbers are assigned based on activity in the software.)* Close this report without saving changes.

(Hint: You can reopen the original invoice by double clicking any of the entries shown on the report.)

3. Recall in the *MAPS* topic that after posting an invoice to the Sales Journal the invoice was then posted to the customer's account. You will now locate QBP's entries to John's customer account.

   Click **Reports>>Customers & Receivables>>Transaction List by Customer** on the main menu.

   Enter the date range of **From** 3/25/12 and **To** 3/25/12.

4. Click **Customize Report**. Select **Trans #** under **Columns** to display this audit trail code (Figure 4:16). Scroll down and click **Split** to uncheck this column. Click **OK** and the report displays. (See Figure 4:17.)

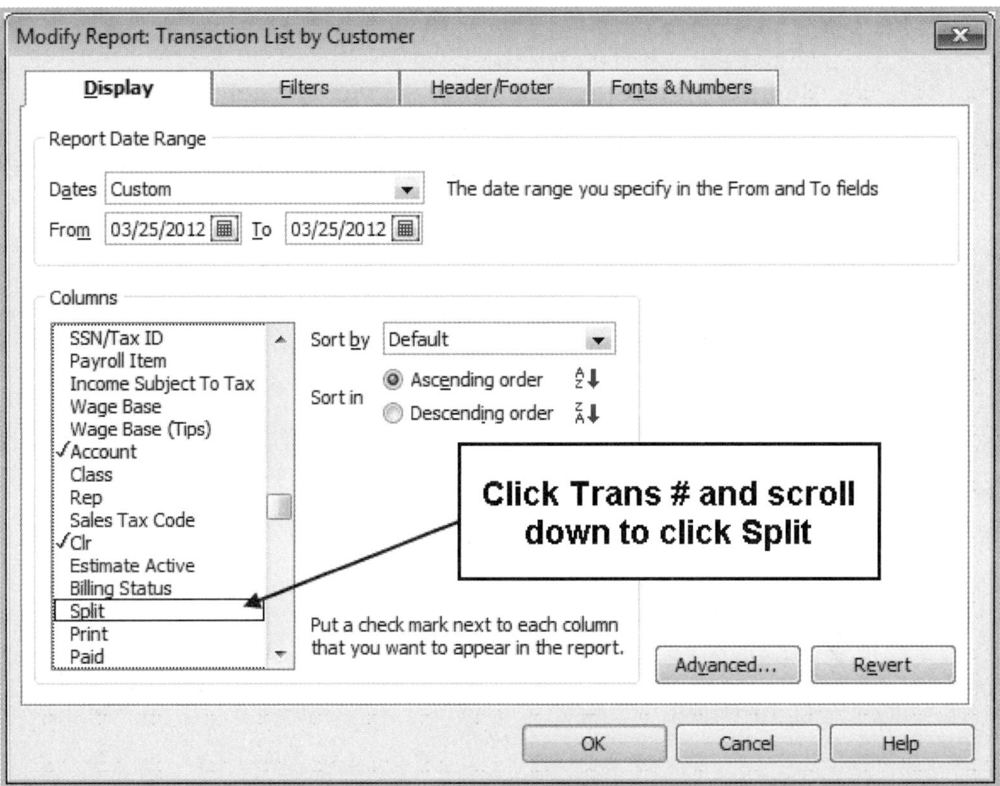

Figure 4:16

5. Notice that the **Trans #** and **Type** on John's account match the **Trans #** and **Type** on the Sales Journal. Close this report without saving changes.

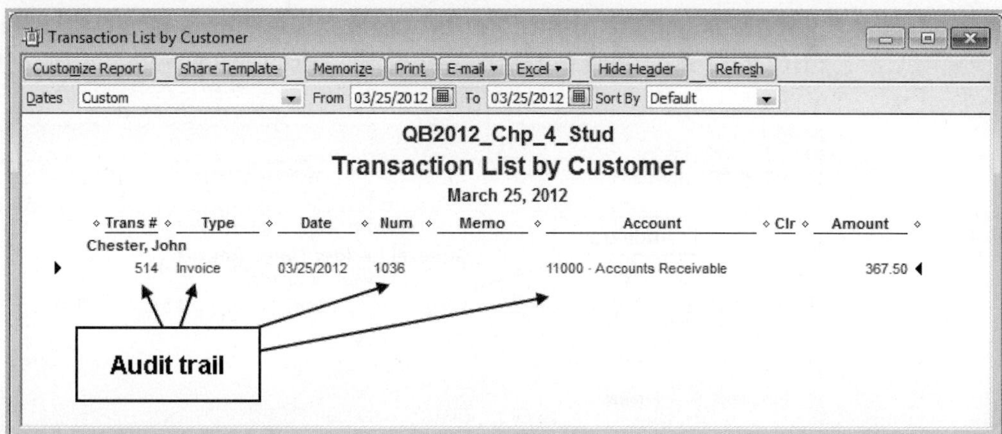

Figure 4:17

6. All that remains is tracing entries to the general ledger. Select ***Reports>>Memorized Reports>>Accounting Journals>>General Ledger Detail Report*** on the main menu. Enter the date range of **From** 3/25/12 and **To** 3/25/12. Click **Customize Report** and, on the **Filters** tab, set the **Name** filter to **Chester, John**. Click **Refresh** to redisplay as illustrated in Figure 4:18.

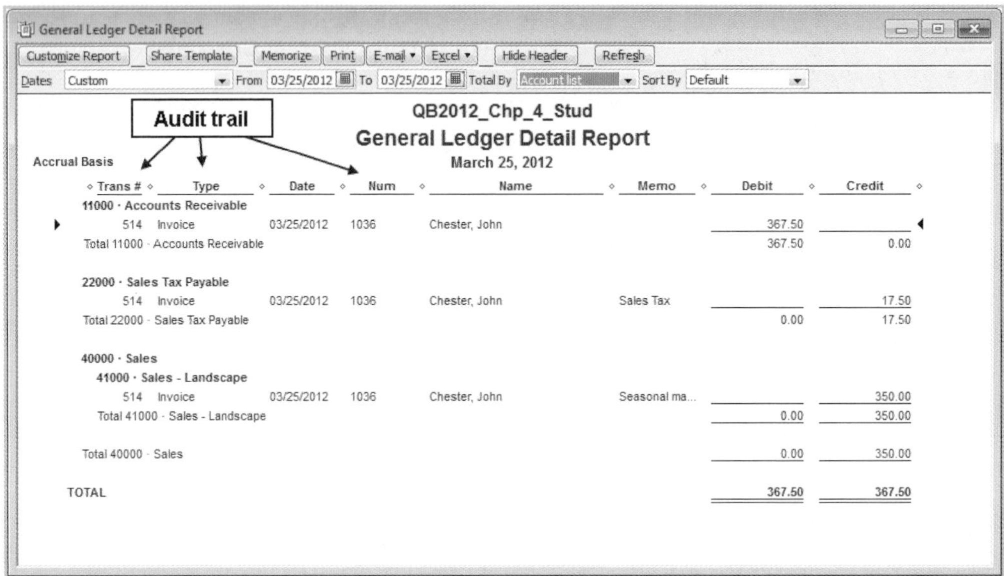

QB2012_Chp_4_Stud
General Ledger Detail Report
March 25, 2012

Accrual Basis

Trans #	Type	Date	Num	Name	Memo	Debit	Credit
11000 · Accounts Receivable							
514	Invoice	03/25/2012	1036	Chester, John		367.50	
Total 11000 · Accounts Receivable						367.50	0.00
22000 · Sales Tax Payable							
514	Invoice	03/25/2012	1036	Chester, John	Sales Tax		17.50
Total 22000 · Sales Tax Payable						0.00	17.50
40000 · Sales							
41000 · Sales - Landscape							
514	Invoice	03/25/2012	1036	Chester, John	Seasonal ma...		350.00
Total 41000 · Sales - Landscape						0.00	350.00
Total 40000 · Sales						0.00	350.00
TOTAL						367.50	367.50

Figure 4:18

Once again, you see that the **Trans #** and **Type** on John's entries match the Sales Journal audit trail. Close this report without saving changes.

You have now followed QBP's audit trail and can see the advantages to using a computerized accounting system. You were able to create a sales invoice and, upon saving the transaction, QBP posted entries to the Sales Journal, customer account, and general ledger accounts. In addition, the accountant is better equipped to answer customer inquiries, provide customer support, manage company sales, and analyze profitability.

Correcting Sales Invoices

This topic explains voiding and deleting invoices and correcting errors on **unpaid** invoices. *(Note: Refer to the instructions in Appendix B if correcting a paid invoice.)*

Note: There is an online video available for this topic.

Open the **Customer Center** and select the **Customers & Jobs** tab. Highlight John Chester's account and select the options shown in Figure 4:19.

Double click the listed invoice to reopen it. ***Do not make any changes to the invoice.***

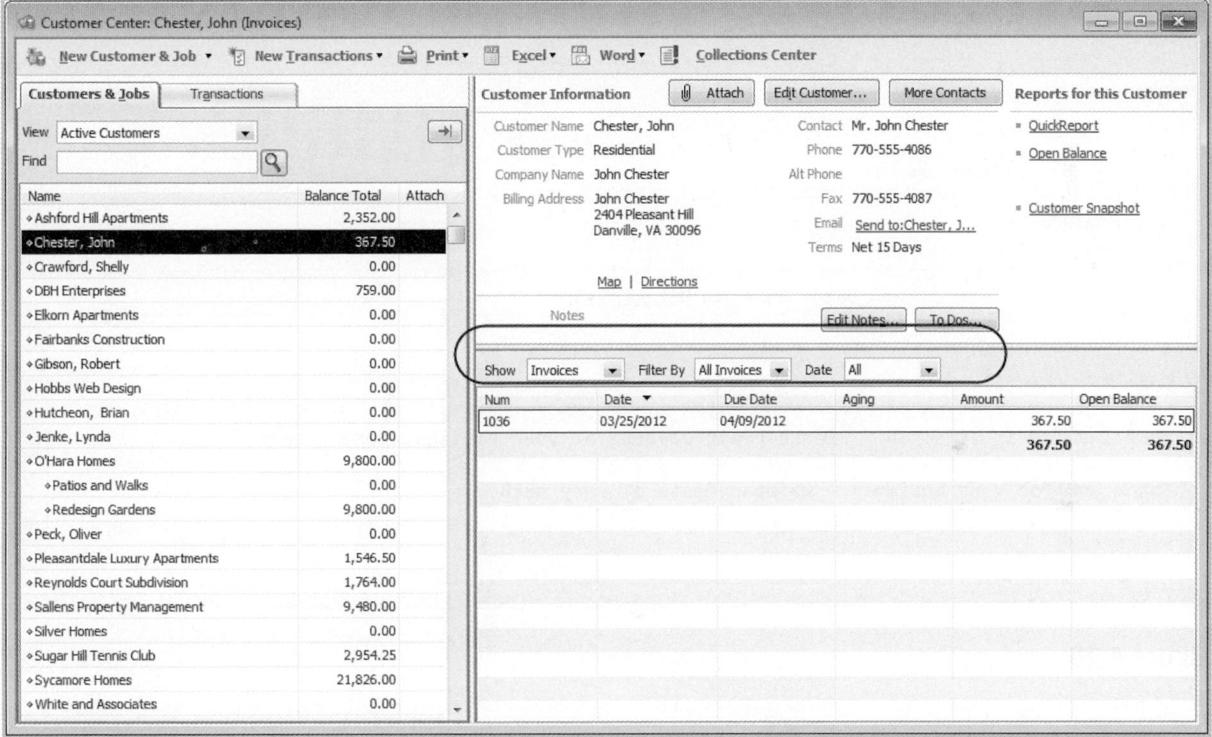

Figure 4:19

After reopening an invoice, you can void it by selecting ***Edit>>Void Invoice*** on the main menu. You can delete an invoice by selecting ***Edit>>Delete Invoice***. You can also make changes to an invoice and click **Save & Close** to record the changes.

Later in the chapter, you will learn to invoice customers for employee time and job materials. Once you invoice a customer for time and materials, you cannot reinvoice the same time and materials even if you delete or void the invoice. Therefore, you should print a copy of the invoice before deleting or voiding it so you can manually reenter time and material charges on a new invoice.

Keep this transaction open for the topic that follows.

QuickBooks Email Features

You will now use QBP's email features to send John's invoice to your email account. With the invoice open, click the dropdown list on **Send** and select **E-mail Invoice**. Click **Close** if a pop-up appears describing QBP's interaction with Microsoft's Outlook. ***(Note: You must be connected to the Internet to complete this exercise.)***

A message appears in your default email program. Figure 4:20 assumes your default email program is Microsoft Outlook.

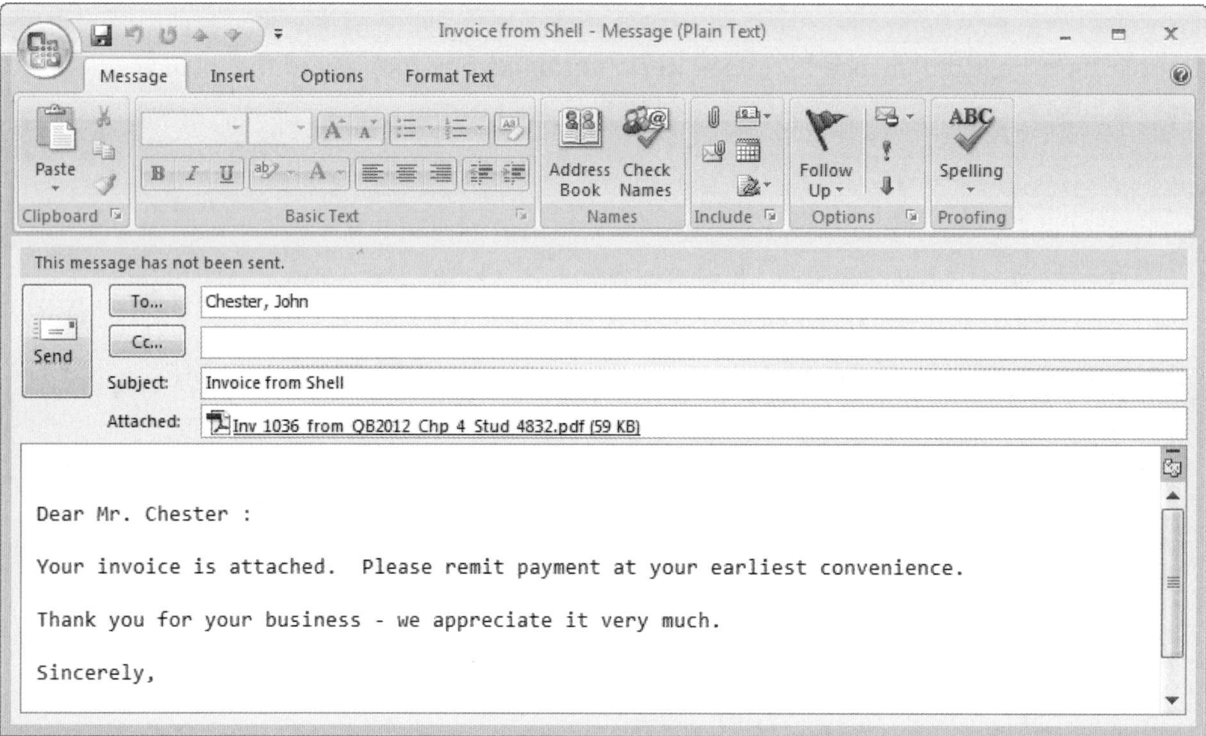

Figure 4:20

Enter your email address in the **To** field and, in **Subject**, replace the text "Invoice from Shell" with "Seasonal maintenance invoice". You can edit text in the body of the message when needed.

The invoice is attached as a PDF file. Click **Send**. You may get the message shown in Figure 4:21 and can turn off this message in the future by checking the Do not display this message in the future box. Click **OK** to close the message.

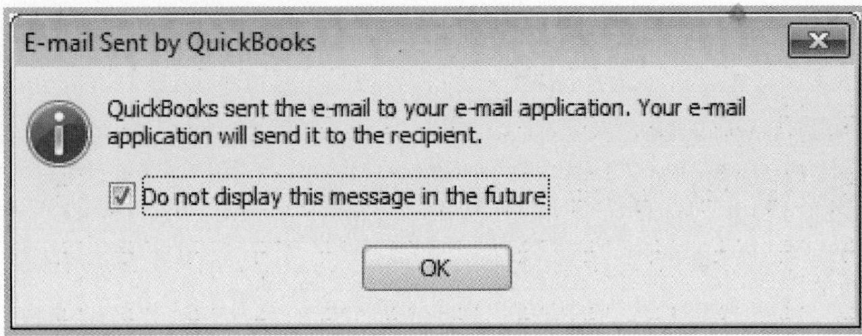

Figure 4:21

Check your email later to verify delivery. Click **X** to close John's invoice.

CUSTOMER AND JOB ACCOUNTS

This topic explains creating, editing, and deleting customers and jobs. You must use the **Customer Center** to manage customer and job accounts.

Open this center if it is not already open from the previous topic. On the **Customers & Jobs** tab, double click **Chester, John** to open his account. *(Note: If prompted with a message about adding and editing multiple list entries, mark the option to not display this message in the future and click **OK**.)* Now follow the next series of illustrations as we describe the tabs of the customer account.

Address Info Tab

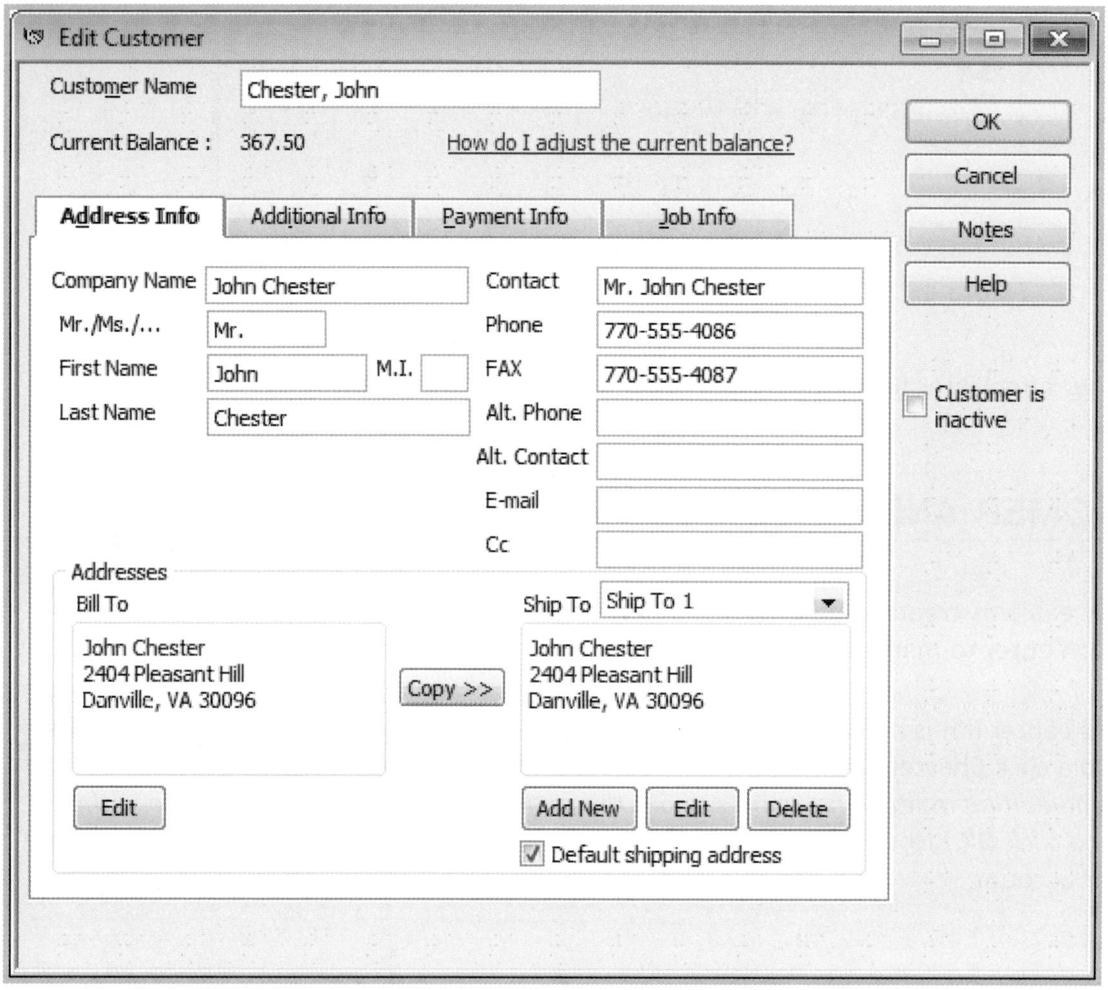

Figure 4:22

The **Address Info** tab stores basic customer information such as address, phone numbers, and email address. The **Bill To** address can be copied to the **Ship To** address by clicking the **Copy** button.

The **Ship To** address is important for companies shipping merchandise to customers because some customers may have one address for receiving invoices (Bill To) and another address for receiving orders (Ship To). When the customer has multiple locations, **Add New** opens the window illustrated in Figure 4:23 to enter additional addresses.

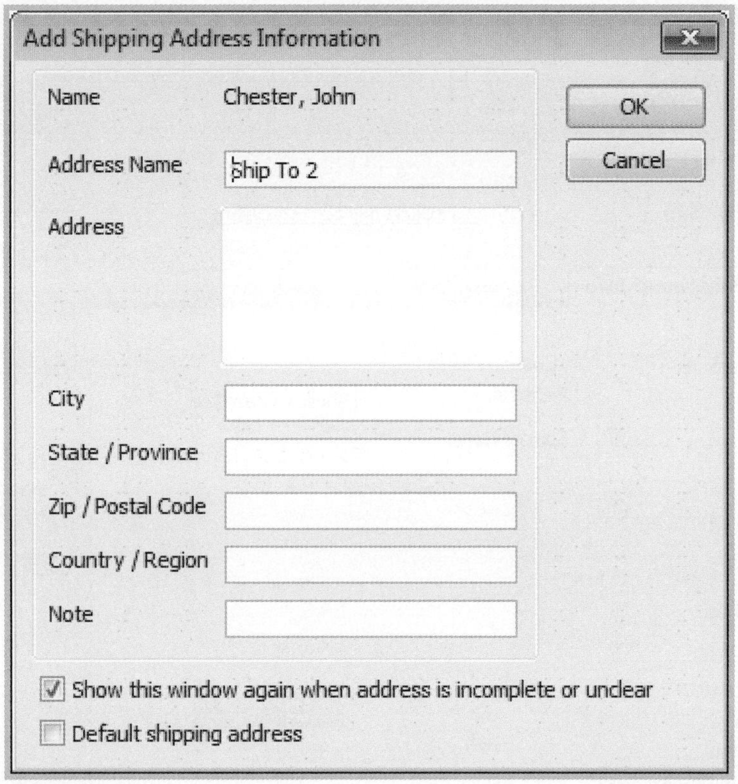

Add Shipping Address Information

Name Chester, John

Address Name Ship To 2

Address

City

State / Province

Zip / Postal Code

Country / Region

Note

OK

Cancel

Show this window again when address is incomplete or unclear

Default shipping address

Figure 4:23

You complete the window in Figure 4:23 by entering a unique name in **Address Name** and entering the address data. The **Default shipping address** option triggers an address to appear as the primary shipping address on invoices. Clicking **OK** will store the address.

Additional Info Tab

Edit Customer

Customer Name: Chester, John

Current Balance : 367.50 How do I adjust the current balance?

OK | Cancel | Notes | Help

Address Info | Additional Info | Payment Info | Job Info

Categorizing and Defaults

Type: Residential

Terms: Net 15 Days

Rep:

Preferred Send Method: Mail

Custom Fields

Referral: Shelley Crawford

Special Note:

Define Fields

Customer is inactive

Sales Tax Information

Tax Code: Tax

Tax Item: VA SALES TAX

Resale Number:

Figure 4:24

This tab stores customer defaults used during transaction entry. Defaults include the **Preferred Send Method** for invoices, customer payment **Terms**, and the **Tax Code** applied to sales transactions. The **Rep** field assigns an employee sales representative for tracking sales commissions and sales performance.

The **Type** field is optional and can be used to differentiate sales by customer characteristics. Astor uses the types of Commercial and Residential.

Click the dropdown list on **Terms** to open the terms illustrated in Figure 4:25.

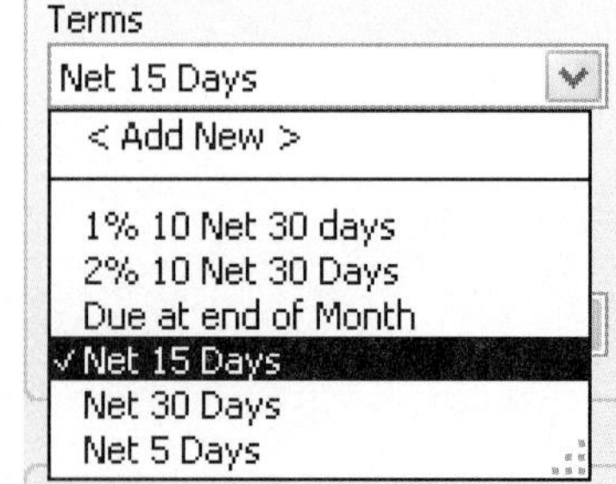

Figure 4:25

Terms establish invoice due dates and customer early payment discounts. The Net 15 Days terms make an invoice due 15 days from the invoice date. The 2% 10 Net 30 Days terms make the invoice due 30 days from the invoice date and grants a 2 percent discount when paying the total invoice within 10 days. *(Note: Discounts do not apply to sales tax.)*

Payment Info Tab

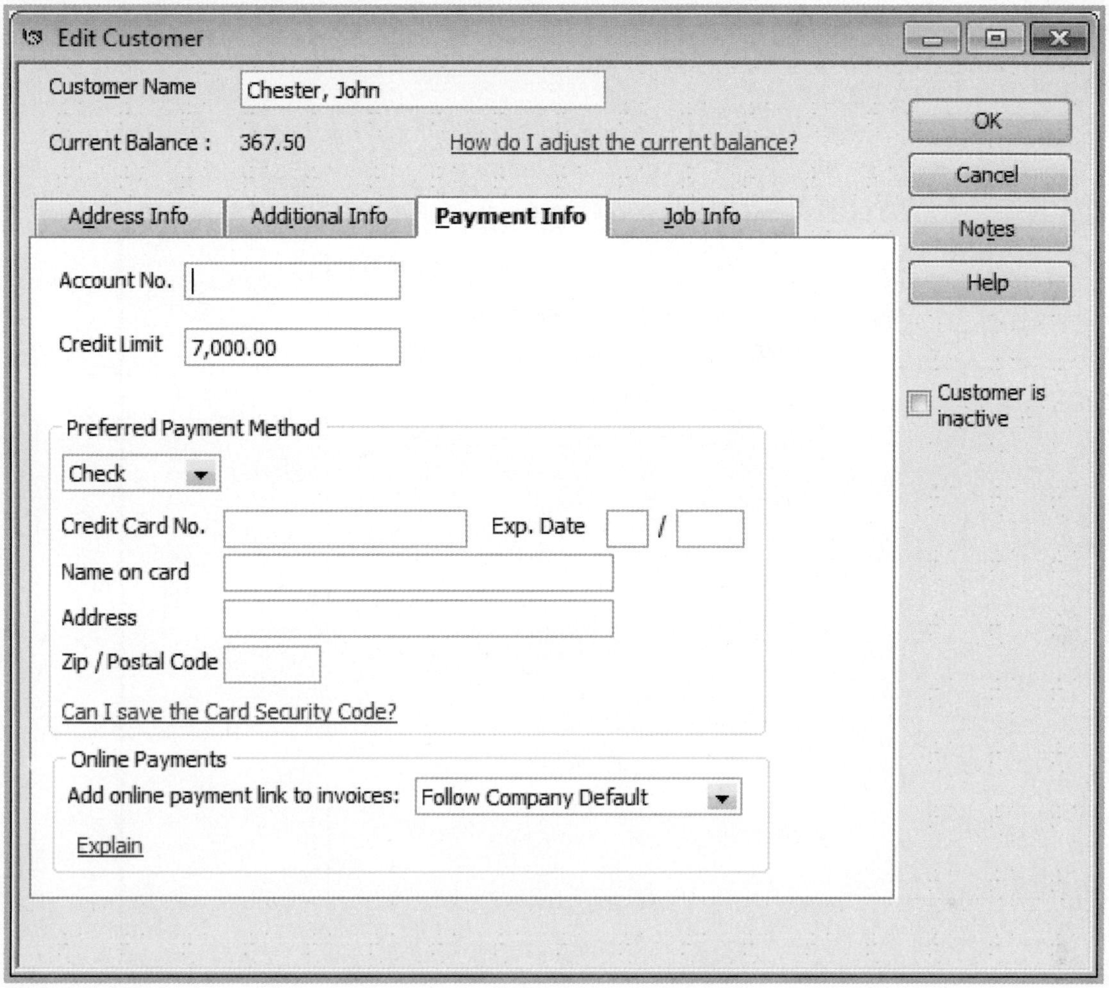

Edit Customer

Customer Name Chester, John

Current Balance : 367.50 How do I adjust the current balance?

OK
Cancel
Notes
Help

Address Info | Additional Info | **Payment Info** | Job Info

Account No.

Credit Limit 7,000.00

Customer is inactive

Preferred Payment Method

Check

Credit Card No. Exp. Date /

Name on card

Address

Zip / Postal Code

Can I save the Card Security Code?

Online Payments

Add online payment link to invoices: Follow Company Default

Explain

Figure 4:26

This tab stores a customer's **Credit Limit** and **Preferred Payment Method**. Setting a credit limit is important to managing bad debt. QBP will warn if saving a new invoice causes the customer's account balance to exceed the credit limit.

Job Info Tab

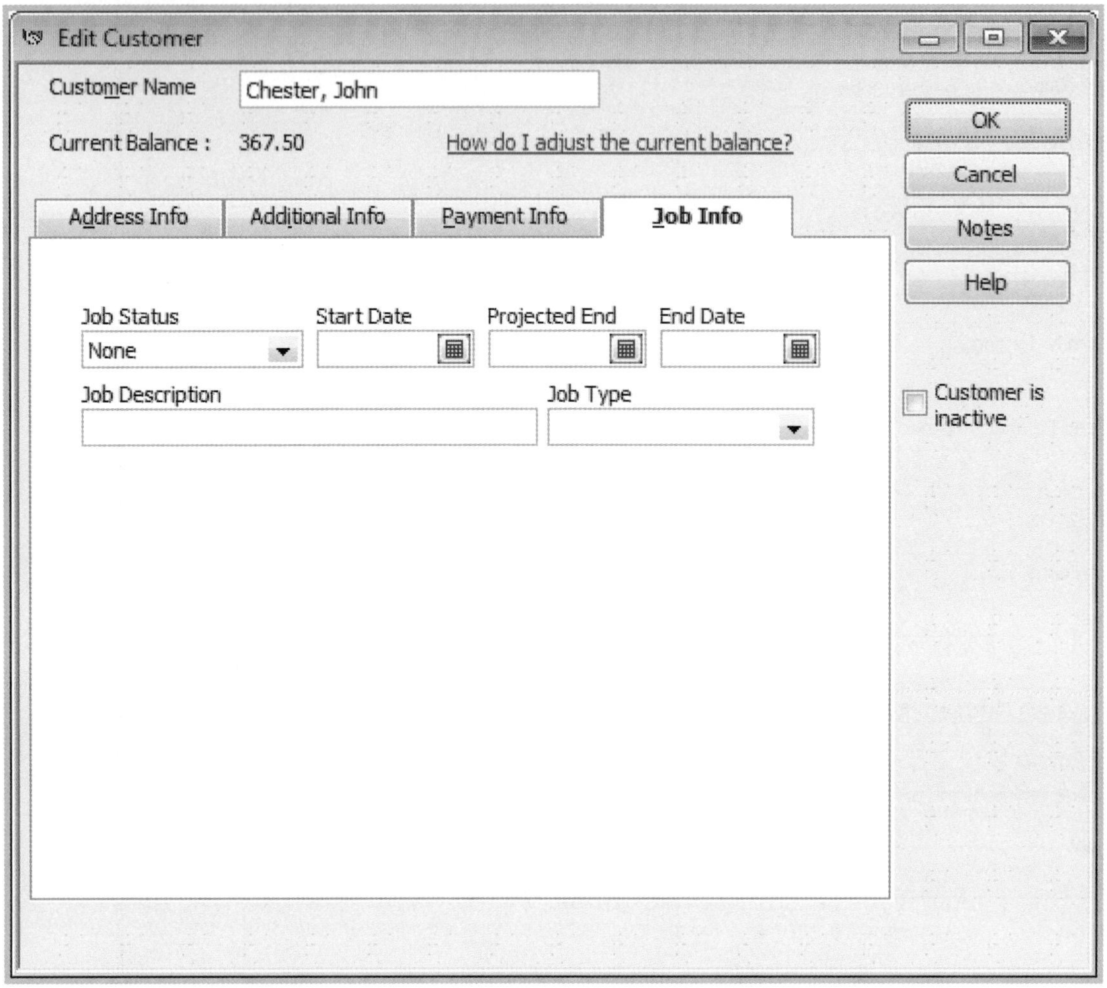

Figure 4:27

This tab implements customer job costing. By creating a job, you can track job revenue and costs such as vendor purchases and employee time. *(Note: Tracking job costs will be illustrated in Chapters 5 and 6.)* Implementing job costing means a company can analyze job profitability.

You can implement job costing without assigning a job to every customer. Sometimes the nature of the service will be short-term or nominal and the company does not find job costing beneficial. For instance, John's account does not have a job because his transaction involved a one-time service for seasonal maintenance.

Click **X** to close John's account and then double click **Ashford Hill Apartments**. Click the **Job Info** tab (Figure 4:28).

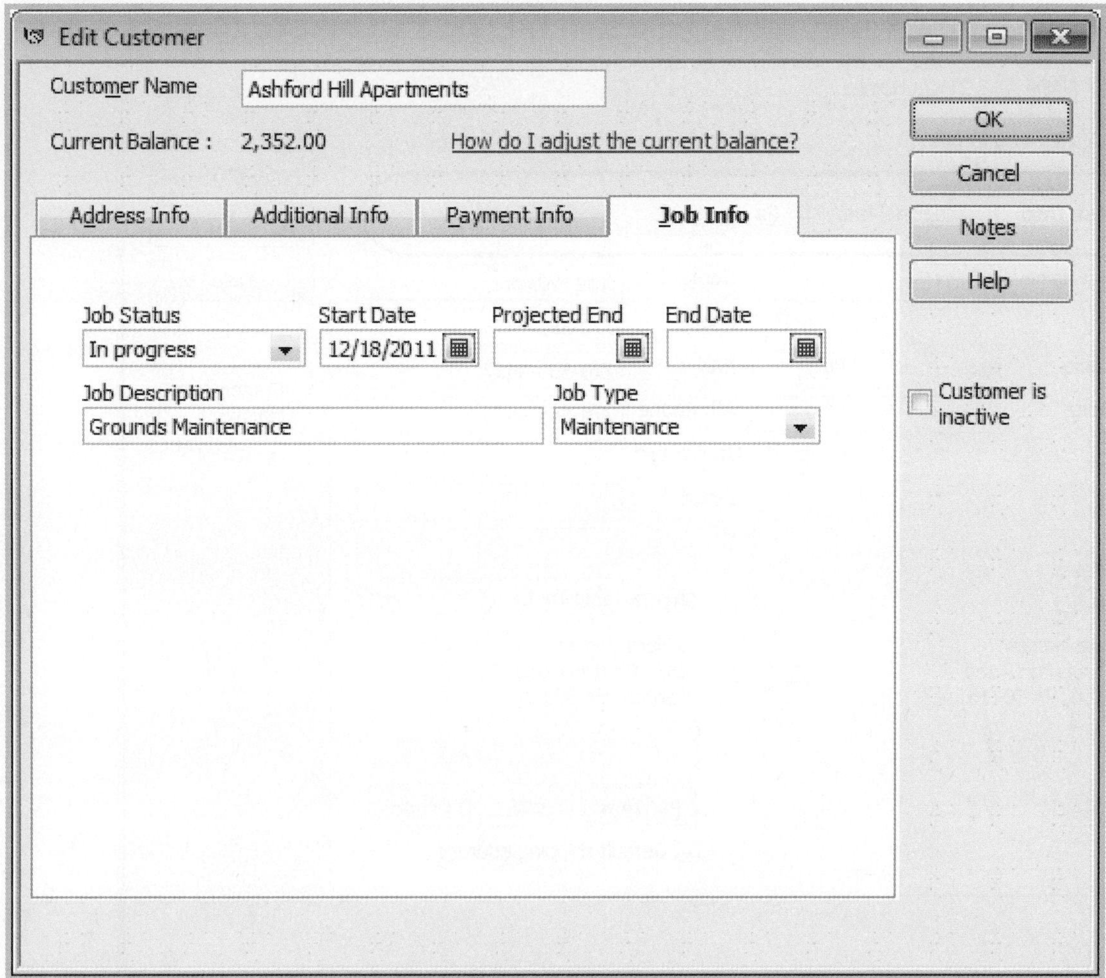

Figure 4:28

Ashford Hill has a job named "Grounds Maintenance." This Job is "In progress" and started on 12/18/2011. In addition, there is no projected end date because the service is ongoing grounds maintenance.

You can use the **Job Status** to monitor the progress on a job. The dropdown list for this field is shown in Figure 4:29.

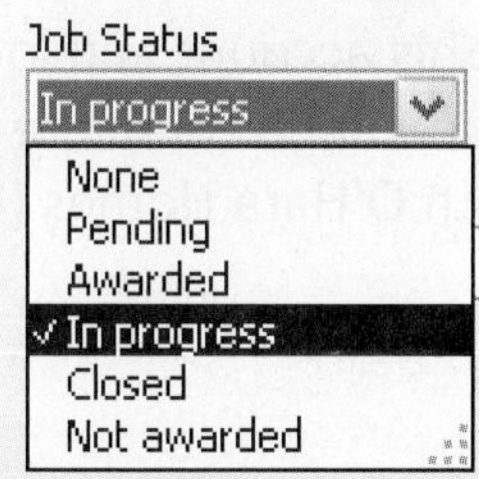

Figure 4:29

After completing a job, the accountant sets the job status to Closed and enters an End Date. When the job also contains a Projected End, the company can use this date to analyze how well it met the projection.

Job Type is optional but can improve analysis because different types of services often require different resources. Astor has created the job types of Construction, Design, Landscaping, and Maintenance.

Close Ashford Hill's account and double click **O'Hara Homes**. This account does not have a Job Info tab (Figure 4:30), but that does not mean there is not a customer job.

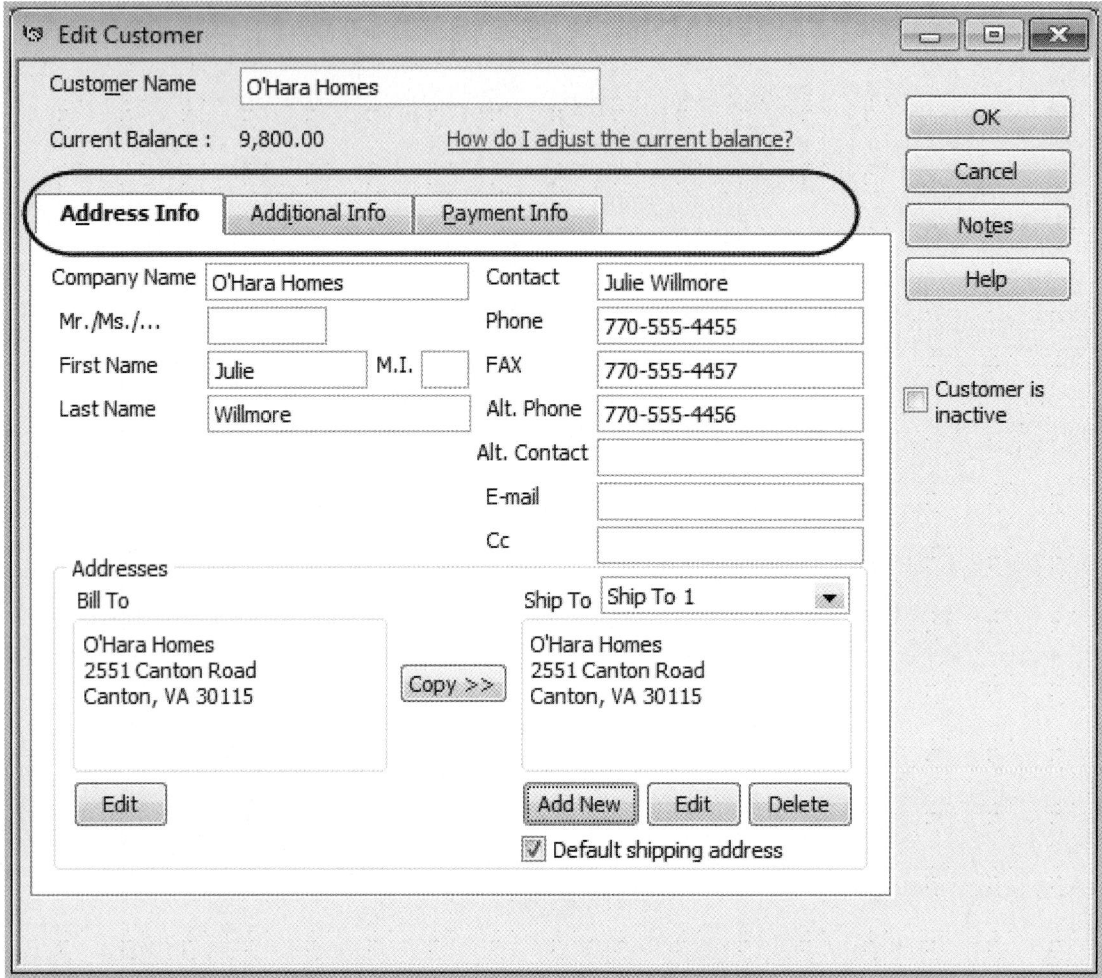

Figure 4:30

Close this account and look at the customer list on the left. There are two subitems beneath O'Hara Homes (Figure 4:31).

◆O'Hara Homes	9,800.00
◆Patios and Walks	0.00
◆Redesign Gardens	9,800.00

Figure 4:31

These subitems are the customer's jobs. When a customer has a single job, the job information is stored on the **Job Info** tab of the customer account. However, after adding more than one job, QBP removes the Job Info tab from the customer account and creates separate job accounts.

Double click **Patios and Walks** to open this job. Job accounts have the same tabs as a customer account and job information is entered on the **Job Info** tab (not illustrated). Close the Patios and Walks job.

Right click O'Hara Homes and select **Add Job**. In **Job Name**, enter "Test Job" (Figure 4:32).

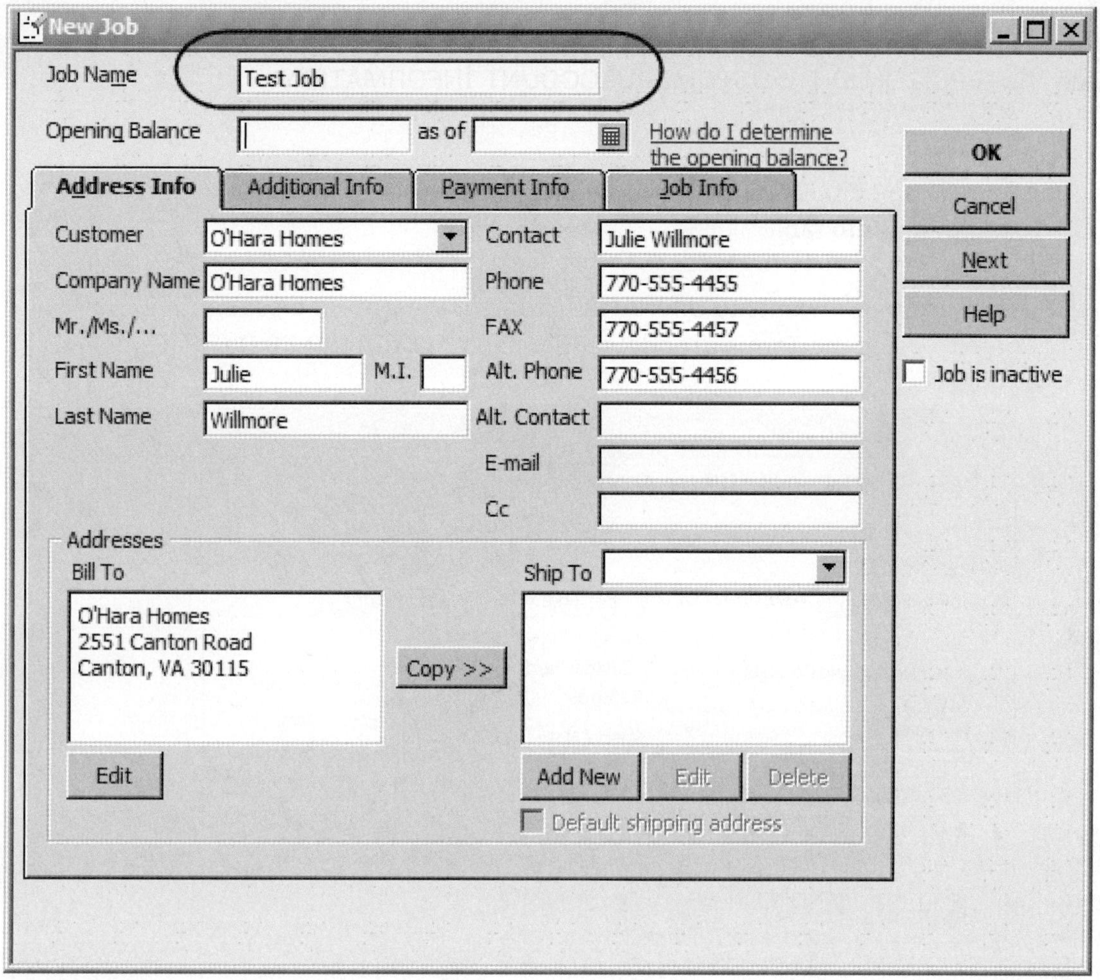

Figure 4:32

Customer account information has transferred to the job account so all you need to do is enter information on the Job Info tab. Click **OK** to save the job and it is placed beneath the Redesign Gardens job (Figure 4:33).

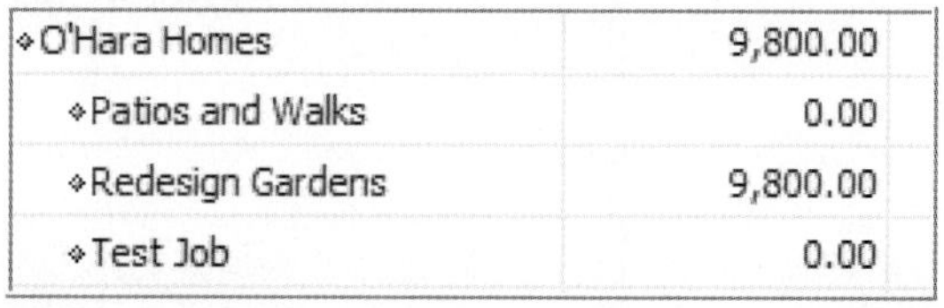

◆O'Hara Homes	9,800.00
◆Patios and Walks	0.00
◆Redesign Gardens	9,800.00
◆Test Job	0.00

Figure 4:33

Now highlight **Test Job** and select ***Edit>>Delete Customer:Job*** on the main menu. Click **OK** to confirm and the job is removed.

You have just created and deleted a job account. The next exercise walks through editing a customer account.

Steps to Edit Customer Account Information

1. You will be editing Ashford Hill's credit terms so open this account and click the **Additional Info** tab.

2. The accountant wants to offer Ashford an early payment discount of 2/10 net 30. Using the **Terms** dropdown list, select "2% 10 Net 30 Days" (Figure 4:34).

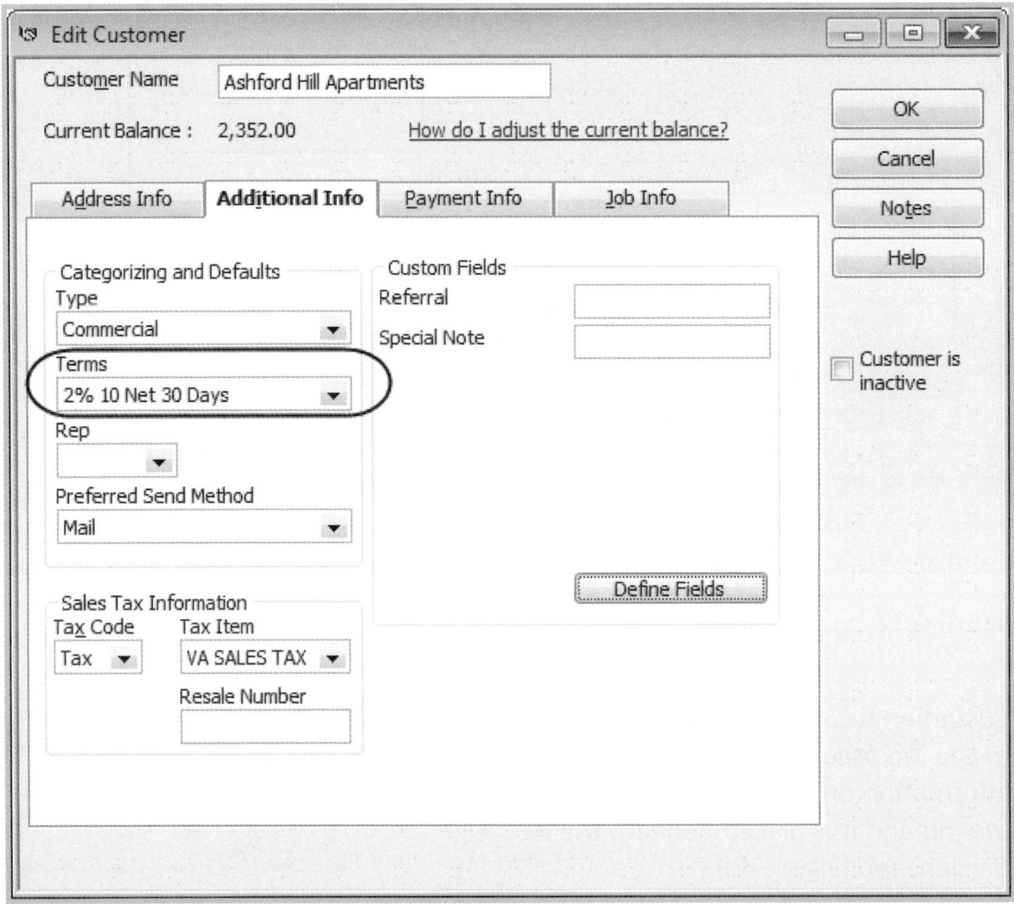

Figure 4:34

These terms mean that Ashford will receive a 2 percent discount on future invoices when paying the invoice in full within 10 days of the invoice date. Regardless, the invoice must be paid in full within 30 days.

3. Click **OK** to save the changes. Click **Yes** if QBP warns about modifying the account because this change does not affect previously posted transactions.

You will now add a new customer account.

Steps to Create a Customer Account

1. From the Customers & Jobs tab, click **New Customer & Job** and select **New Customer**.

2. Now enter the information illustrated in Figure 4:35.

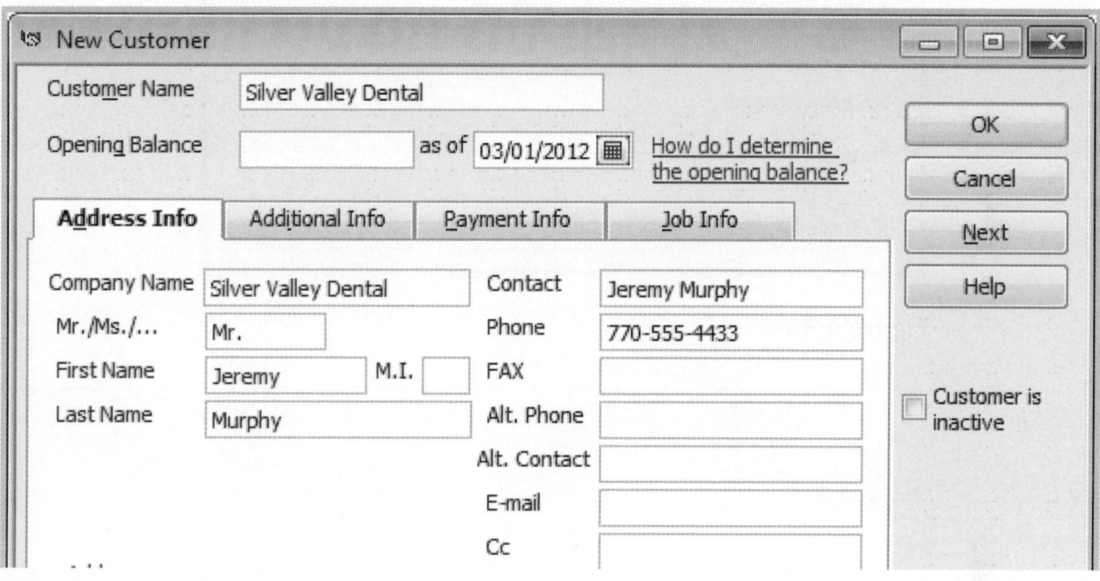

Figure 4:35

3. Click **Edit** on the **Bill To** field and enter the information illustrated in Figure 4:36. Click **OK**.

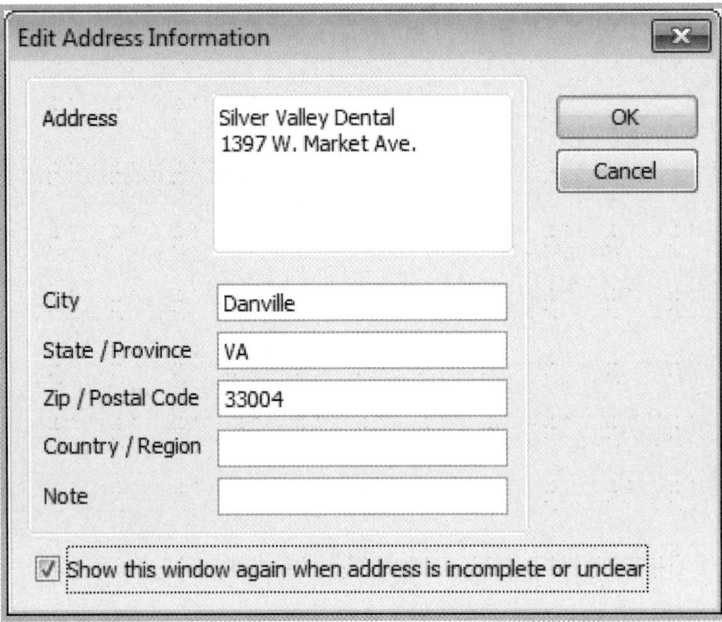

Figure 4:36

4. Click **Copy** to copy the **Bill To** address to the **Ship To** address. Click **OK** on the window that opens. The completed **Address Info** tab is shown in Figure 4:37.

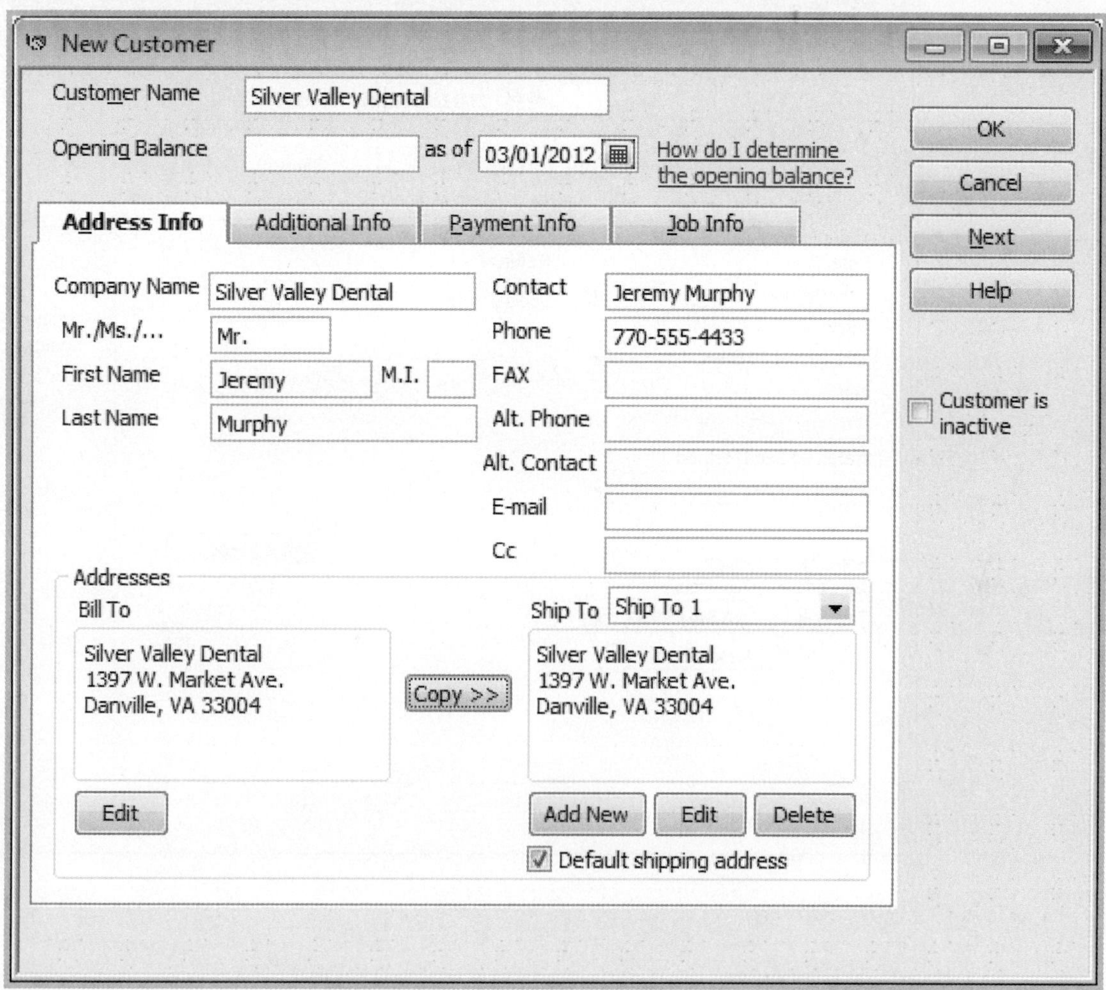

Figure 4:37

5. Click **Additional Info** and enter the information shown in Figure 4:38.

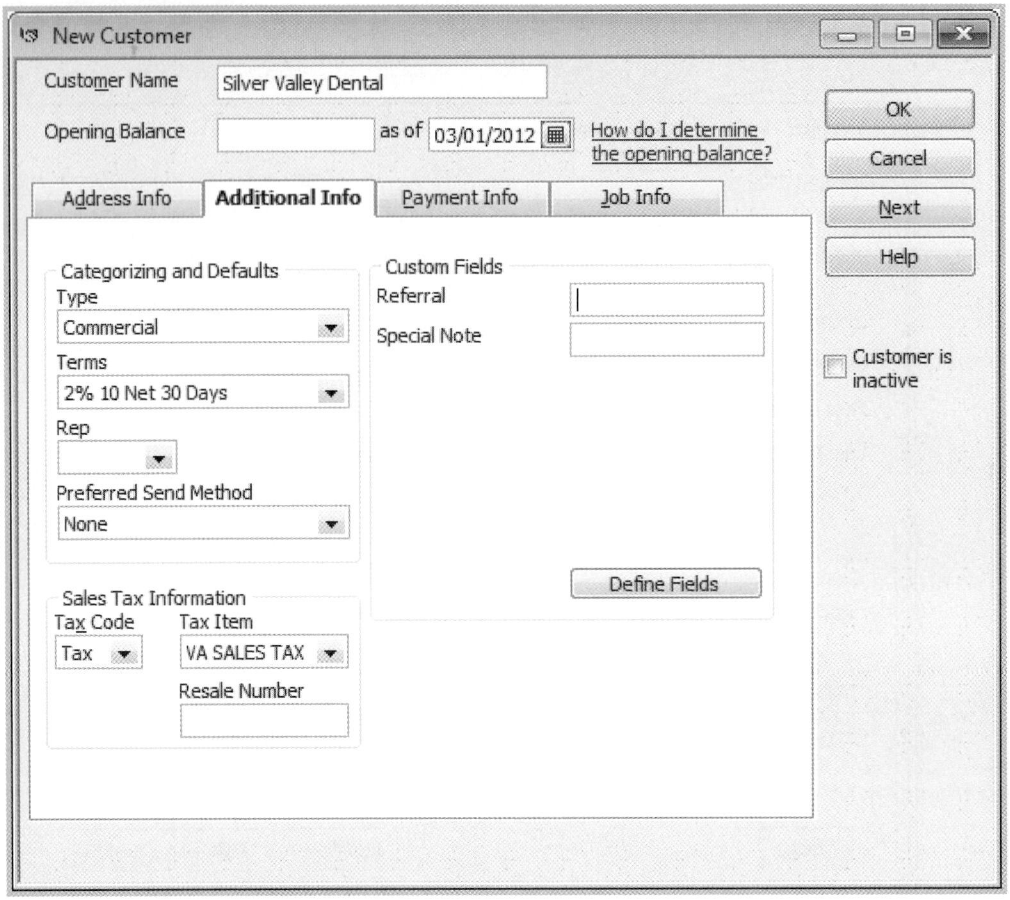

Figure 4:38

6. On the **Payment Info** tab enter "18,000.00" as the **Credit Limit**.

7. Enter the information shown in Figure 4:39 as the **Job Info**.

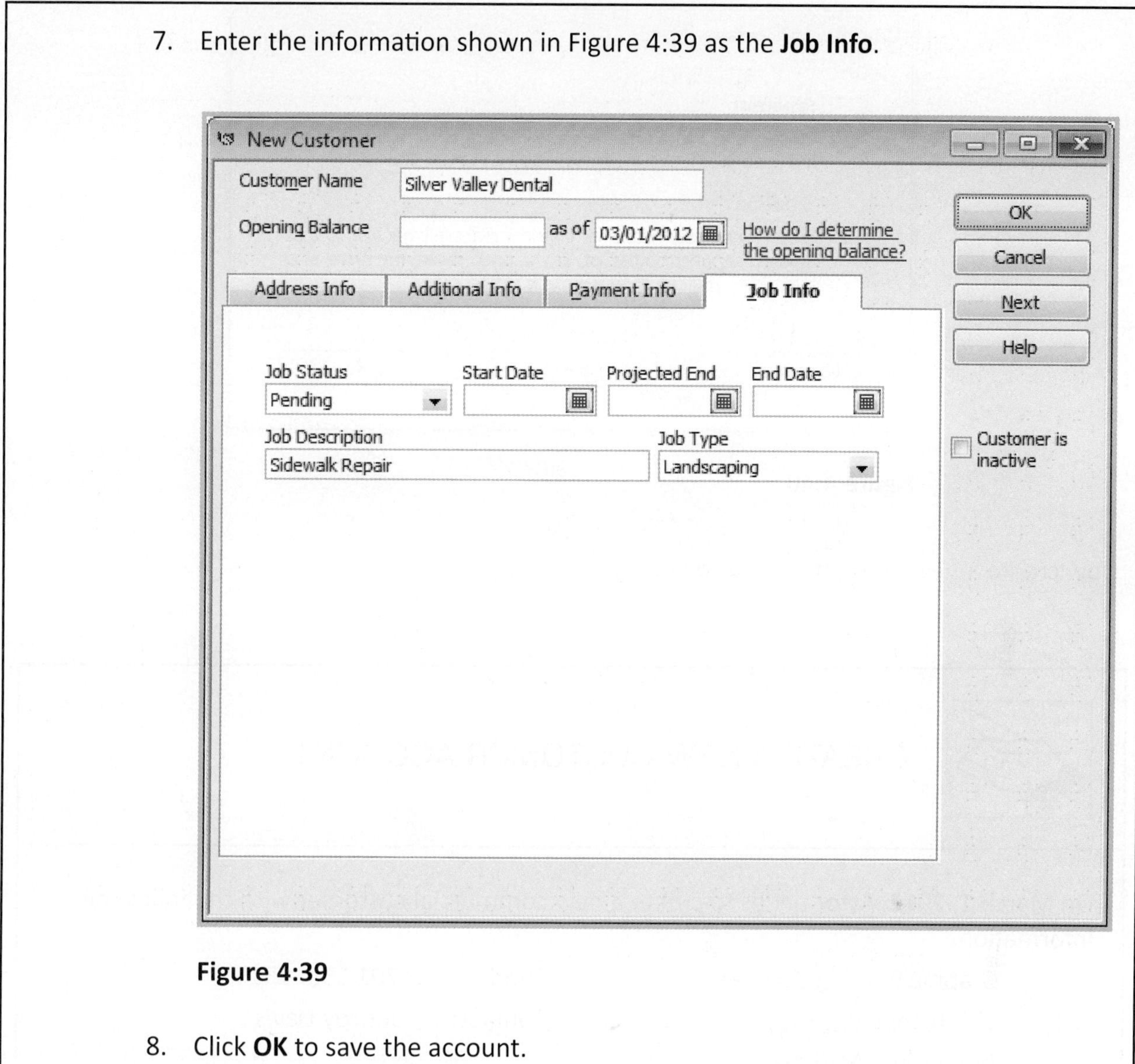

Figure 4:39

8. Click **OK** to save the account.

What happens when you try to delete an account with transaction history?

Highlight **Ashford Hill Apartments** and select ***Edit>>Delete Customer:Job*** on the main menu. QBP prompts, stating that it cannot delete an account with transaction history, but can make it inactive. (See Figure 4:40.) Inactivating the account denies future transactions while retaining account history. Click **Cancel**.

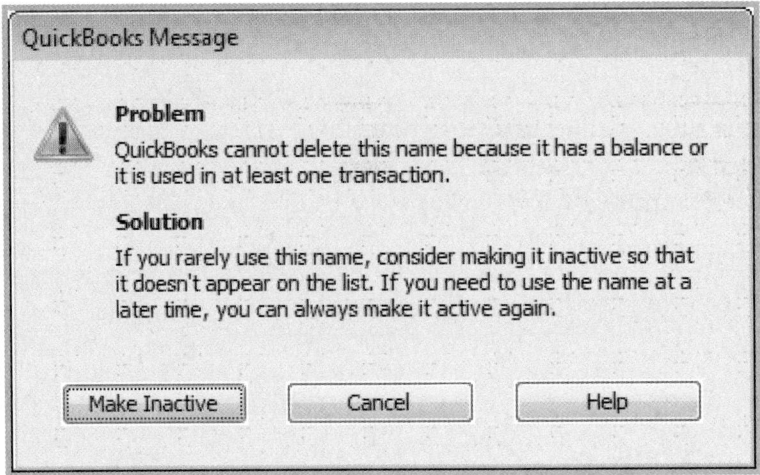

Figure 4:40

Now create a new account on your own.

CREATE A NEW CUSTOMER ACCOUNT

On March 1, 2012, Astor needs to create a new commercial customer with the following information.

Graphic Printing Services	Phone:	701 555–1515
127 Technology Way	Contact:	Jeffrey Davis
Arlington, VA 30097		

Credit Limit: $5,000.00

The customer pays VA sales tax and will be offered the terms of 2/10 Net 30 Days. The Preferred Send Method is Mail.

Job information: Pending Grounds Maintenance job, Maintenance job type.

Create this account.

UNDERSTANDING SERVICE AND NON-INVENTORY PART ITEMS

Service and non-inventory part items differ from the traditional inventory items used by a merchandising business. *(Note: Inventory items for a merchandiser are discussed in Chapter 8.)* Unlike goods sold by a merchandiser, services and job materials are not purchased until the work is performed. Thus, service-based businesses do not hold inventory. *(Note: Notice that Astor's inventory balance is zero.)*

QBP's service items are used to store sales prices and descriptions for labor costs that will be invoiced to customers. These items do not interact with inventory, thus do not track quantities on hand or purchasing costs. Recall that John Chester's invoice traced in a previous exercise recorded only sales revenue. Since cost of goods sold does not post at the time of sale, Astor must post these costs through another activity, namely the employee or vendor activities discussed in subsequent chapters.

QBP's non-inventory part items are used for invoicing job material purchases. Again, these items do not interact with inventory so quantities on hand and purchase costs are not tracked and cost of goods sold does not post when invoicing. Cost of goods sold posts only after recording a vendor receipt or bill for material purchases.

It is important to understand the posting of cost of goods sold; otherwise, you might prepare financial statements that do not match revenues with expenses. The following table explains the inventory, non-inventory part, and service items used in this text. After reviewing this table you will better understand when an item interacts with inventory and when cost of goods sold posts at the time of sale.

Item Class	Purpose
Inventory Part	Used to track goods purchased and held for resale. Tracks quantities and purchasing costs. Cost of goods sold posts at the time of invoicing. Cost of goods sold is calculated using the Average costing method. *(Note: QBP does not accommodate the LIFO and FIFO inventory costing methods.)*
Non-inventory Part	Used for job materials purchased but not tracked in inventory. Cost of goods sold posts when posting vendor bills or receipts for material purchases.
Service	Used for service labor costs provided by company employees or subcontractors. When provided by subcontractors, cost of goods sold posts when paying the contractor. When provided by employees, cost of goods sold posts when paying employees.
Sales Tax Item	Used to calculate sales tax for a single taxing agency.
Other Charge	Used for miscellaneous charges such as delivery and photocopying fees. Cost of goods sold posts when reimbursing the employee expense or paying a vendor.

Now look at the service and non-inventory part items used by Astor. Click **Item** on the toolbar to open the **Item List** illustrated in Figure 4:41. *(Note: You can also select **Lists>>Item List** on the main menu.)* Pay particular attention to the **Type** column.

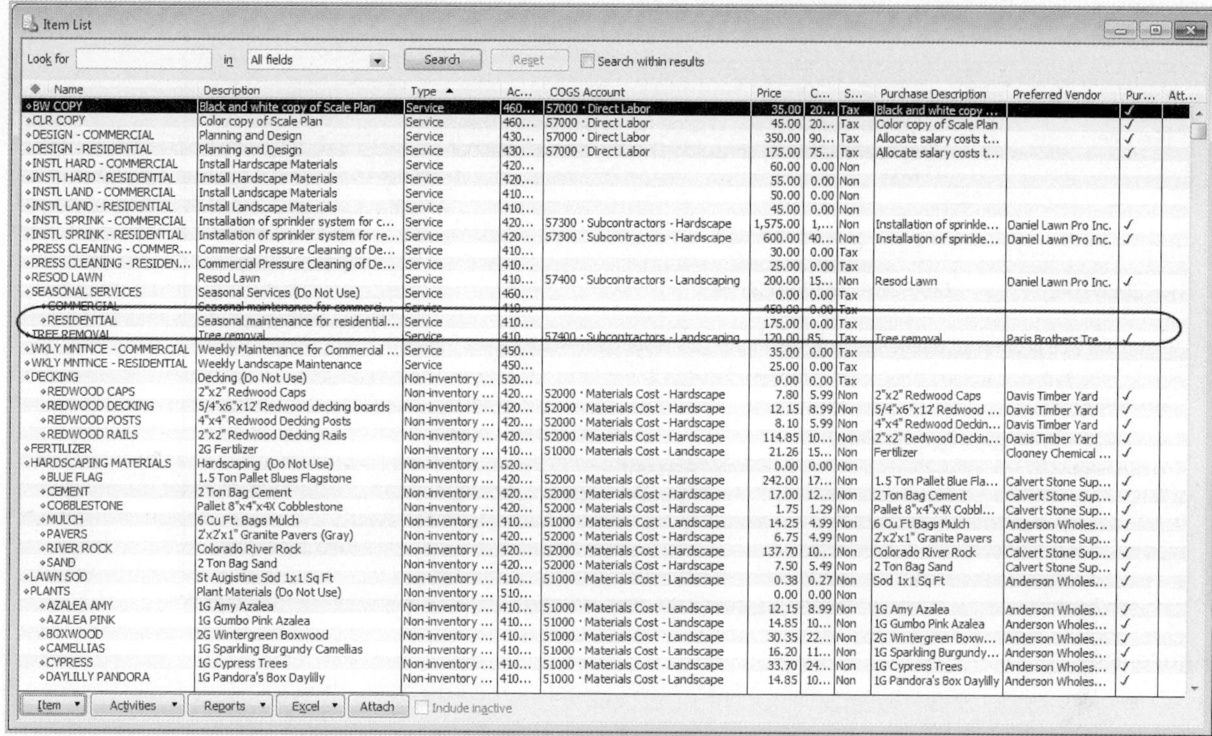

Name	Description	Type	Ac...	COGS Account	Price	C...	S...	Purchase Description	Preferred Vendor	Pur...	Att...
BW COPY	Black and white copy of Scale Plan	Service	460...	57000 · Direct Labor	35.00	20...	Tax	Black and white copy ...		✓	
CLR COPY	Color copy of Scale Plan	Service	460...	57000 · Direct Labor	45.00	20...	Tax	Color copy of Scale Plan		✓	
DESIGN - COMMERCIAL	Planning and Design	Service	430...	57000 · Direct Labor	350.00	90...	Tax	Allocate salary costs t...		✓	
DESIGN - RESIDENTIAL	Planning and Design	Service	430...	57000 · Direct Labor	175.00	75...	Tax	Allocate salary costs t...		✓	
INSTL HARD - COMMERCIAL	Install Hardscape Materials	Service	420...		60.00	0.00	Non				
INSTL HARD - RESIDENTIAL	Install Hardscape Materials	Service	420...		55.00	0.00	Non				
INSTL LAND - COMMERCIAL	Install Landscape Materials	Service	410...		50.00	0.00	Non				
INSTL LAND - RESIDENTIAL	Install Landscape Materials	Service	410...		45.00	0.00	Non				
INSTL SPRINK - COMMERCIAL	Installation of sprinkler system for c...	Service	420...	57300 · Subcontractors - Hardscape	1,575.00	1,...	Non	Installation of sprinkle...	Daniel Lawn Pro Inc.	✓	
INSTL SPRINK - RESIDENTIAL	Installation of sprinkler system for re...	Service	420...	57300 · Subcontractors - Hardscape	600.00	40...	Non	Installation of sprinkle...	Daniel Lawn Pro Inc.	✓	
PRESS CLEANING - COMMER...	Commercial Pressure Cleaning of De...	Service	410...		30.00	0.00	Tax				
PRESS CLEANING - RESIDEN...	Commercial Pressure Cleaning of De...	Service	410...		25.00	0.00	Tax				
RESOD LAWN	Resod Lawn	Service	410...	57400 · Subcontractors - Landscaping	200.00	15...	Non	Resod Lawn	Daniel Lawn Pro Inc.	✓	
SEASONAL SERVICES	Seasonal Services (Do Not Use)	Service	460...		0.00	0.00	Tax				
COMMERCIAL	Seasonal maintenance for commerci...	Service	410...		450.00	0.00	Tax				
RESIDENTIAL	Seasonal maintenance for residential...	Service	410...		175.00	0.00	Tax				
TREE REMOVAL	Tree removal	Service	410...	57400 · Subcontractors - Landscaping	120.00	85...	Tax	Tree removal	Paris Brothers Tre...	✓	
WKLY MNTNCE - COMMERCIAL	Weekly Maintenance for Commercial ...	Service	450...		35.00	0.00	Tax				
WKLY MNTNCE - RESIDENTIAL	Weekly Landscape Maintenance	Service	450...		25.00	0.00	Tax				
DECKING	Decking (Do Not Use)	Non-inventory ...	520...		0.00	0.00	Tax				
REDWOOD CAPS	2"x2" Redwood Caps	Non-inventory ...	420...	52000 · Materials Cost - Hardscape	7.80	5.99	Non	2"x2" Redwood Caps	Davis Timber Yard	✓	
REDWOOD DECKING	5/4"x6"x12' Redwood decking boards	Non-inventory ...	420...	52000 · Materials Cost - Hardscape	12.15	8.99	Non	5/4"x6"x12' Redwood ...	Davis Timber Yard	✓	
REDWOOD POSTS	4"x4" Redwood Decking Posts	Non-inventory ...	420...	52000 · Materials Cost - Hardscape	8.10	5.99	Non	4"x4" Redwood Deckin...	Davis Timber Yard	✓	
REDWOOD RAILS	2"x2" Redwood Decking Rails	Non-inventory ...	420...	52000 · Materials Cost - Hardscape	114.85	10...	Non	2"x2" Redwood Deckin...	Davis Timber Yard	✓	
FERTILIZER	2G Fertilizer	Non-inventory ...	410...	51000 · Materials Cost - Landscape	21.26	15...	Non	Fertilizer	Clooney Chemical ...	✓	
HARDSCAPING MATERIALS	Hardscaping (Do Not Use)	Non-inventory ...	520...		0.00	0.00	Non				
BLUE FLAG	1.5 Ton Pallet Blues Flagstone	Non-inventory ...	420...	52000 · Materials Cost - Hardscape	242.00	17...	Non	1.5 Ton Pallet Blue Fla...	Calvert Stone Sup...	✓	
CEMENT	2 Ton Bag Cement	Non-inventory ...	420...	52000 · Materials Cost - Hardscape	17.00	12...	Non	2 Ton Bag Cement	Calvert Stone Sup...	✓	
COBBLESTONE	Pallet 8"x4"x4X Cobblestone	Non-inventory ...	420...	52000 · Materials Cost - Hardscape	1.75	1.29	Non	Pallet 8"x4"x4X Cobbl...	Calvert Stone Sup...	✓	
MULCH	6 Cu Ft. Bags Mulch	Non-inventory ...	410...	51000 · Materials Cost - Landscape	14.25	4.99	Non	6 Cu Ft Bags Mulch	Anderson Wholes...	✓	
PAVERS	2'x2'x1" Granite Pavers (Gray)	Non-inventory ...	420...	52000 · Materials Cost - Hardscape	6.75	4.99	Non	2'x2'x1" Granite Pavers	Calvert Stone Sup...	✓	
RIVER ROCK	Colorado River Rock	Non-inventory ...	420...	52000 · Materials Cost - Hardscape	137.70	10...	Non	Colorado River Rock	Calvert Stone Sup...	✓	
SAND	2 Ton Bag Sand	Non-inventory ...	420...	52000 · Materials Cost - Hardscape	7.50	5.49	Non	2 Ton Bag Sand	Calvert Stone Sup...	✓	
LAWN SOD	St Augistine Sod 1x1 Sq Ft	Non-inventory ...	410...	51000 · Materials Cost - Landscape	0.38	0.27	Non	Sod 1x1 Sq Ft	Anderson Wholes...	✓	
PLANTS	Plant Materials (Do Not Use)	Non-inventory ...	510...		0.00	0.00	Non				
AZALEA AMY	1G Amy Azalea	Non-inventory ...	410...	51000 · Materials Cost - Landscape	12.15	8.99	Non	1G Amy Azalea	Anderson Wholes...	✓	
AZALEA PINK	1G Gumbo Pink Azalea	Non-inventory ...	410...	51000 · Materials Cost - Landscape	14.85	10...	Non	1G Gumbo Pink Azalea	Anderson Wholes...	✓	
BOXWOOD	2G Wintergreen Boxwood	Non-inventory ...	410...	51000 · Materials Cost - Landscape	30.35	22...	Non	2G Wintergreen Boxw...	Anderson Wholes...	✓	
CAMELLIAS	1G Sparkling Burgundy Camellias	Non-inventory ...	410...	51000 · Materials Cost - Landscape	16.20	11...	Non	1G Sparkling Burgundy...	Anderson Wholes...	✓	
CYPRESS	1G Cypress Trees	Non-inventory ...	410...	51000 · Materials Cost - Landscape	33.70	24...	Non	1G Cypress Trees	Anderson Wholes...	✓	
DAYLILLY PANDORA	1G Pandora's Box Daylilly	Non-inventory ...	410...	51000 · Materials Cost - Landscape	14.85	10...	Non	1G Pandora's Box Daylilly	Anderson Wholes...	✓	

Figure 4:41

We will now review a few of these items.

Service Items

Double click the **RESIDENTIAL** item under **SEASONAL SERVICES** to open the item illustrated in Figure 4:42.

As we review this item, refer back to the *Entering Sales Invoices* topic where you invoiced John Chester for 2 units of the item. Also refer back to the *Behind the Keys of a Posted Sales Invoice* topic where you traced entries made after posting John's invoice.

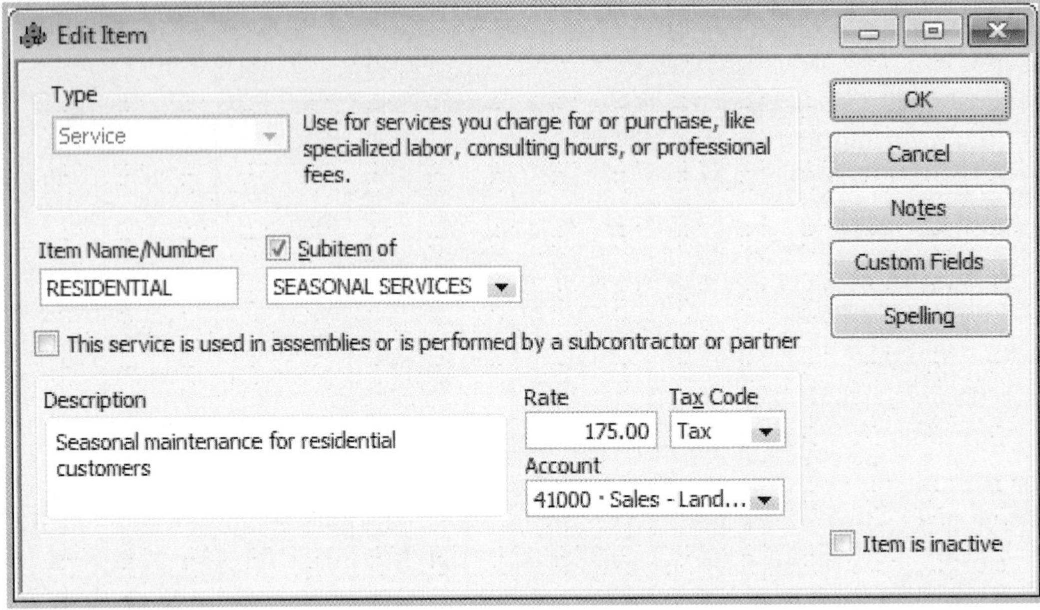

Figure 4:42

This item is for service labor costs provided by company employees. In addition, the item is a **Subitem of** SEASONAL SERVICES meaning it will be grouped with this category.

Rate is the fee charged customers for this service, explaining why John was invoiced $350.00 for 2 units.

Tax Code shows that these services are taxable. However, QBP also looks to the tax default assigned to the customer account before charging sales tax.

Account is the general ledger account used to post sales revenue for this item, explaining why John's invoice posted to 41000 Sales – Landscaping.

Notice that this item does not list an inventory general ledger account because service items are not inventoried. Likewise, because services items are not inventoried, cost of goods sold does not post at the time of sale. This explains why John's invoice posted only revenue entries.

Click **X** to close this item and open **DESIGN-COMMERCIAL**. (See Figure 4:43.)

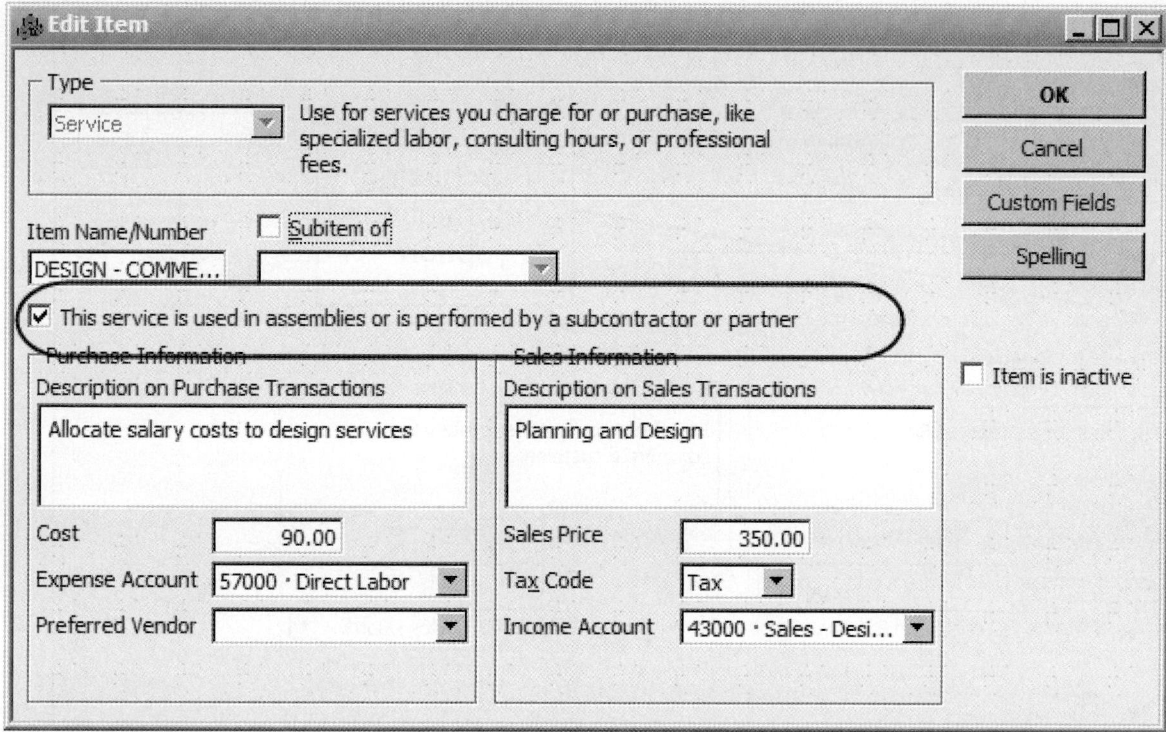

Figure 4:43

This is another labor service provided by employees. The item **Sales Price** is $350.00 and sales are taxable. Sales revenue for this item will post to **Income Account** 43000 Sales – Design Services.

Since these services are provided by salaried employees of the company, the option circled in Figure 4:43 is marked. This option opens the fields for entering standard costs or vendor purchase costs. In Chapter 5, you will use the $90.00 standard cost on this item to allocate salary expense for this service to the cost of goods sold **Expense Account** 57000-Direct Labor.

Close this item and open **INSTL SPRINK – COMMERCIAL**. (See Figure 4:44.)

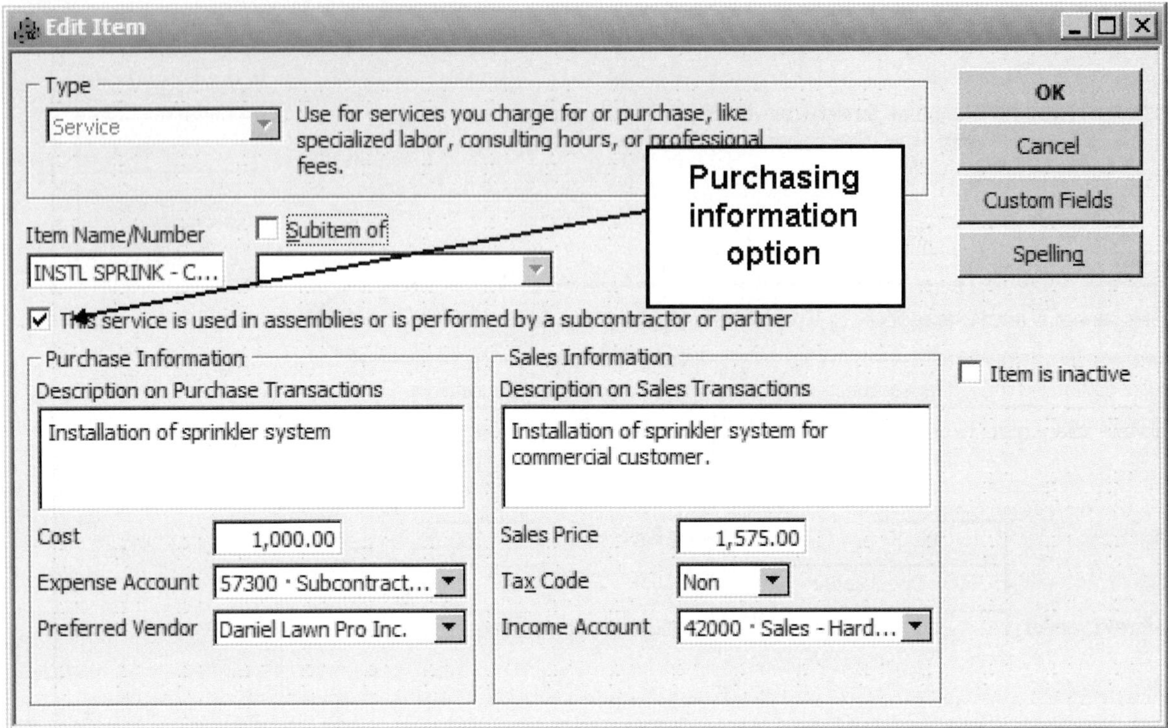

Figure 4:44

This is a labor service item purchased from **Preferred Vendor**, Daniel Lawn Pro Inc. Thus, the option for entering purchasing information is selected and the cost of goods sold **Expense Account** is entered. Cost of goods sold posts to "57300 Subcontractors - Hardscape" when recording a vendor bill for this item.

Charge Items

Close the preceding item and open **DELIVERY CHARGES**.

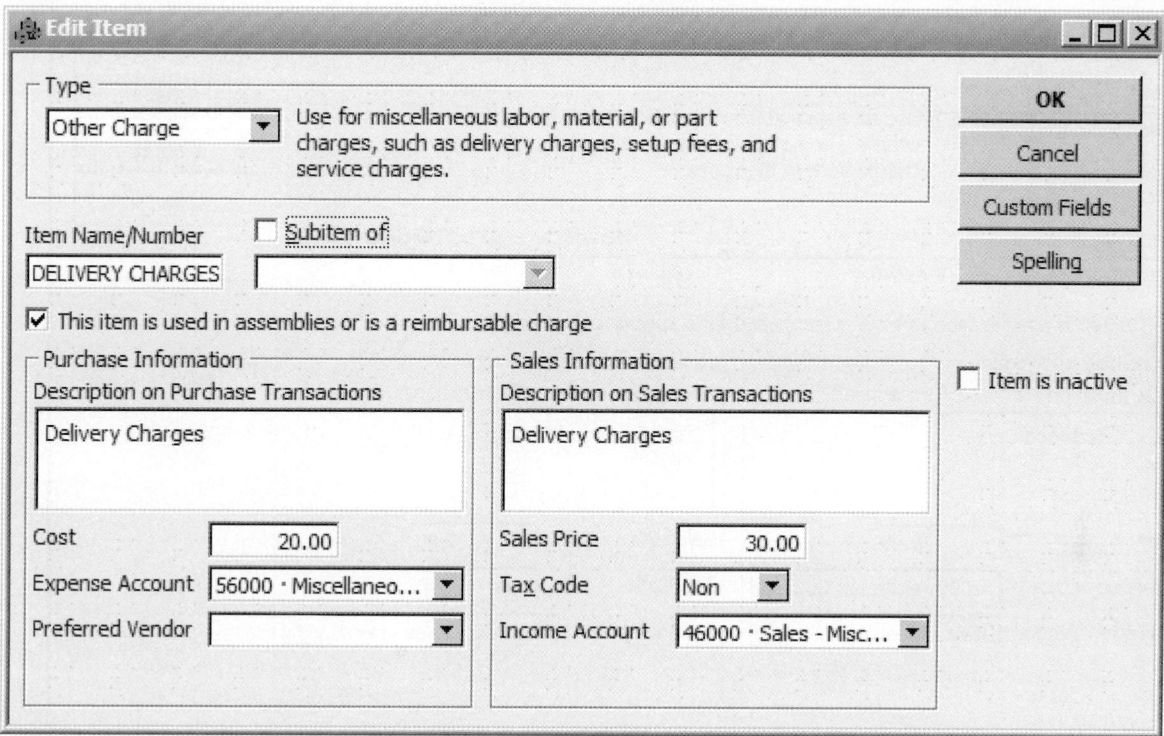

Figure 4:45

This charge item looks like the service item previously viewed; however, cost of goods sold for this item will post to an **Expense Account** when reimbursing employee expenses.

Non-inventory Part

Close the preceding item and open **REDWOOD CAPS**.

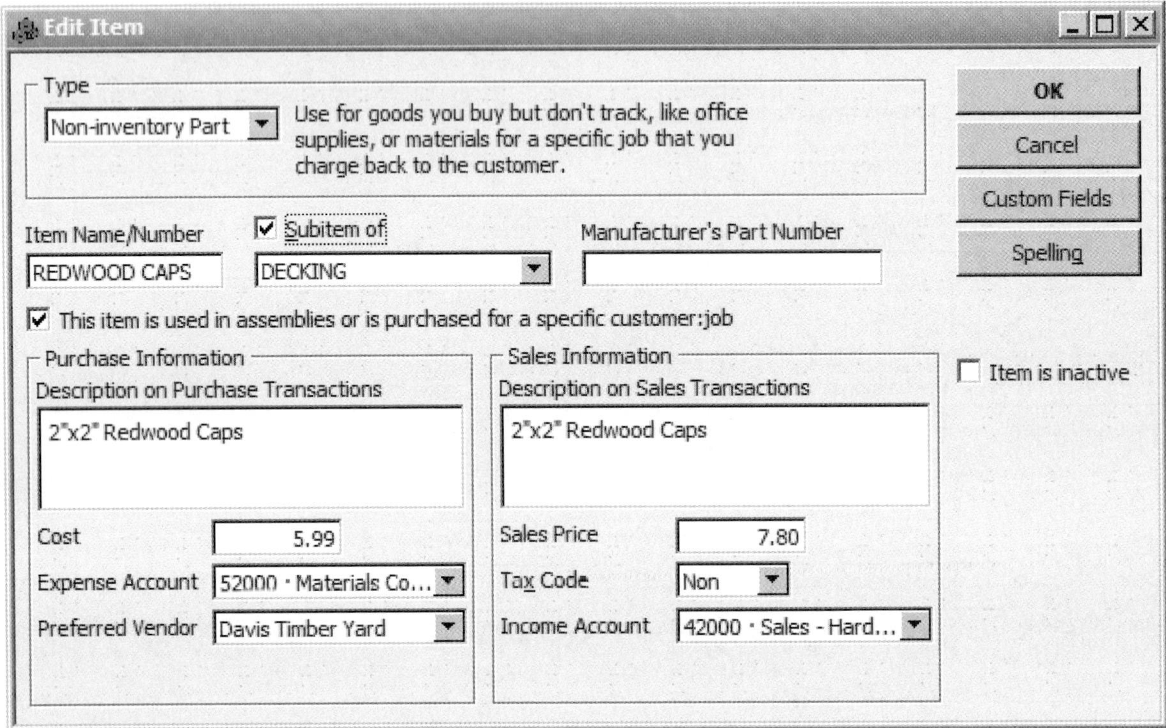

Figure 4:46

This is an item for job material purchases. Astor buys these caps from Davis Timber Yard, who charges $5.99 each. Astor then charges the customer $7.80 each.

Sales revenue for this item posts to 42000 Sales – Hardscape. Bills from the preferred vendor post to the costs of goods sold **Expense Account** 52000 Materials Cost – Hardscape.

Sales Tax Item

Close the preceding item and open **VA SALES TAX**.

Edit Item

Type: Sales Tax Item — Use to calculate a single sales tax at a specific rate that you pay to a single tax agency.

OK | Cancel | Spelling

Sales Tax Name: VA SALES TAX

Item is inactive

Description: Sales Tax

Tax Rate (%): 5.0%

Tax Agency (vendor that you collect for): VA Sales Tax Department

Figure 4:47

This item sets 5 percent as the sales tax rate for taxable items.

Close this item and the Item List and then move on to invoicing customer jobs.

INVOICING CUSTOMER JOBS

Earlier in the chapter, you created an invoice for John Chester before recording the costs associated with performing the service. However, service-based businesses normally bill customers for the time and materials involved with the job. In other words, invoices are created by transferring job material and labor costs.

The drawback to invoicing job costs is that costs must be recorded before invoicing can occur. Thus, it is important to record accounting transactions in a timely manner so that invoicing can occur as soon as possible. The earlier a company invoices the customer the quicker the cash is collected.

Let us now look at the steps used to invoice job costs. On March 29, 2012, Astor invoiced Silver Homes for job costs incurred to date. Complete the steps that follow to prepare this invoice.

STEPS TO INVOICING JOBS

1. Open a new sales invoice using **Create Invoices** on the **Home** page and select "Silver Homes" as the **Customer:Job**.

2. QBP prompts that the customer has billable job costs (Figure 4:48). Mark the first option and the preference option illustrated. Click **OK**.

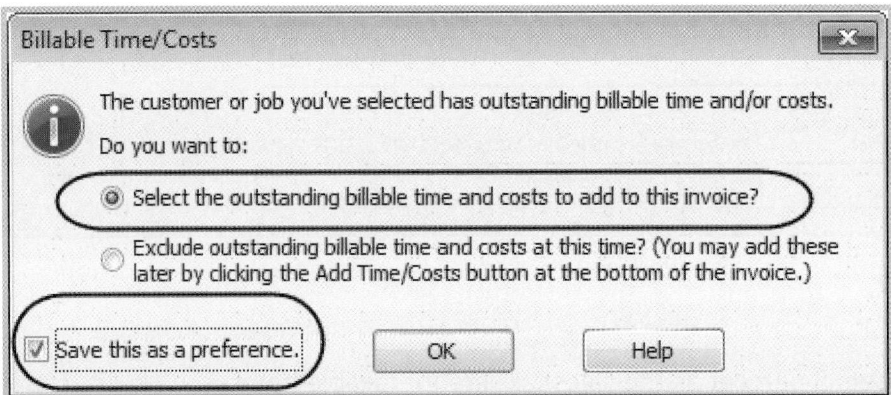

Figure 4:48

3. The **Choose Billable Time and Costs** window opens as illustrated next. In this window, you select the costs to invoice. Below this illustration is an explanation of the types of costs stored on each tab.

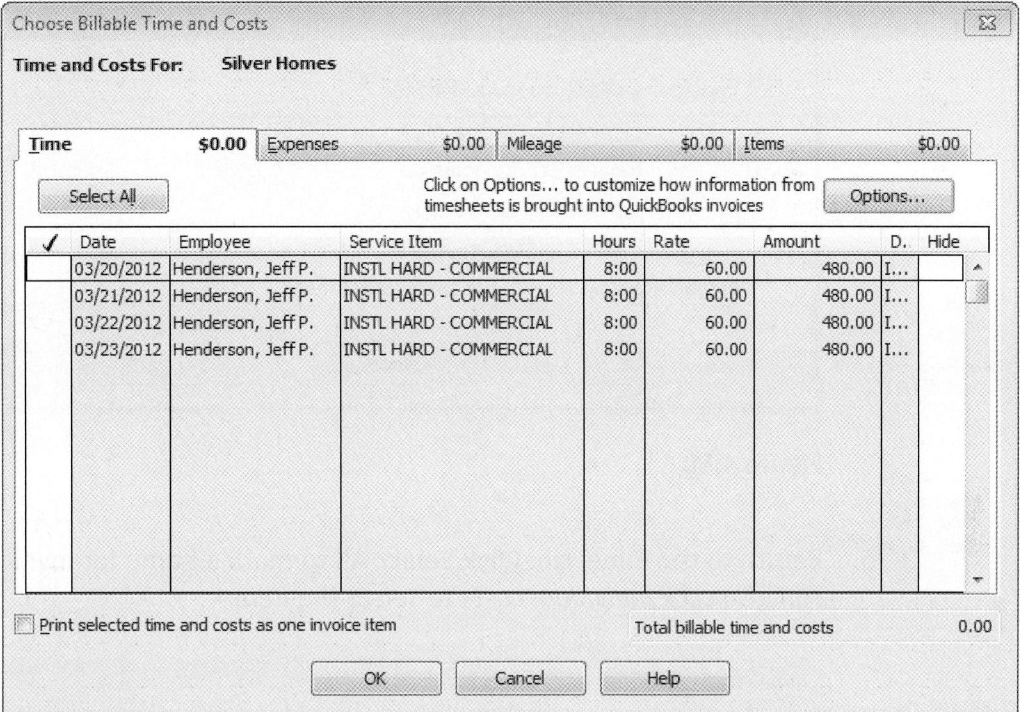

Figure 4:49

Time Tab
Employee time tickets assigned to the customer job.

Expenses Tab
Employee reimbursable expense tickets assigned to the customer job.

Mileage Tab
Employee mileage charges assigned to the customer job.

Items Tab
Vendor materials and subcontract labor bills assigned to the customer job.

In Chapter 5, you will learn to assign vendor invoices to jobs. In Chapter 6, you will learn to assign employee time and expenses to jobs. For now, remember to check each tab for costs that need to be invoiced to the customer.

4. On the **Time** tab, click the **Options** button. Before transferring employee time, make sure that the **Combine** option illustrated in Figure 4:50 is selected so that hours will be combined for similar activities. Click **OK**.

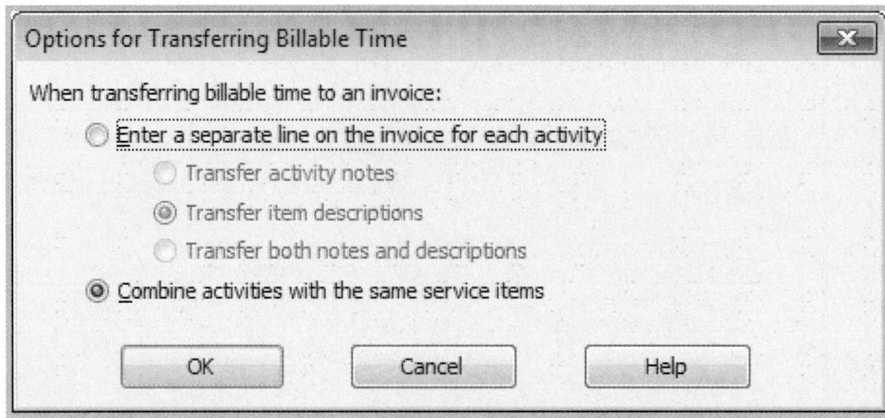

Figure 4:50

5. Return to the **Time** tab. Click **Select All** to mark all time for invoicing. *(Note: You can also click individual costs to select the item.)*

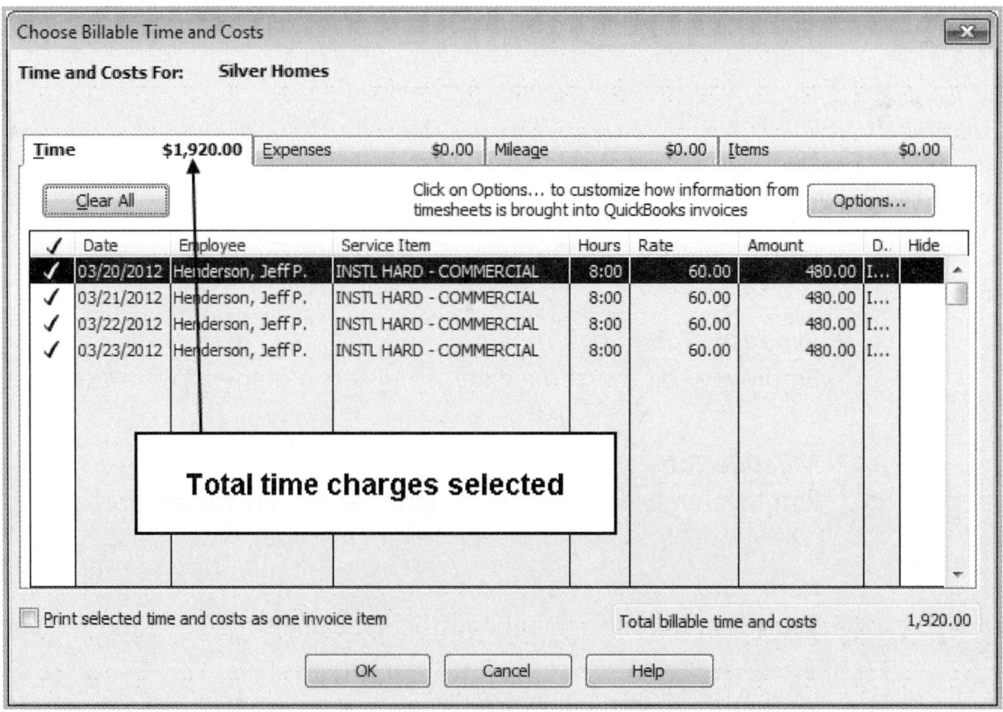

Figure 4:51

6. Select the **Items** tab and click **Select All**.

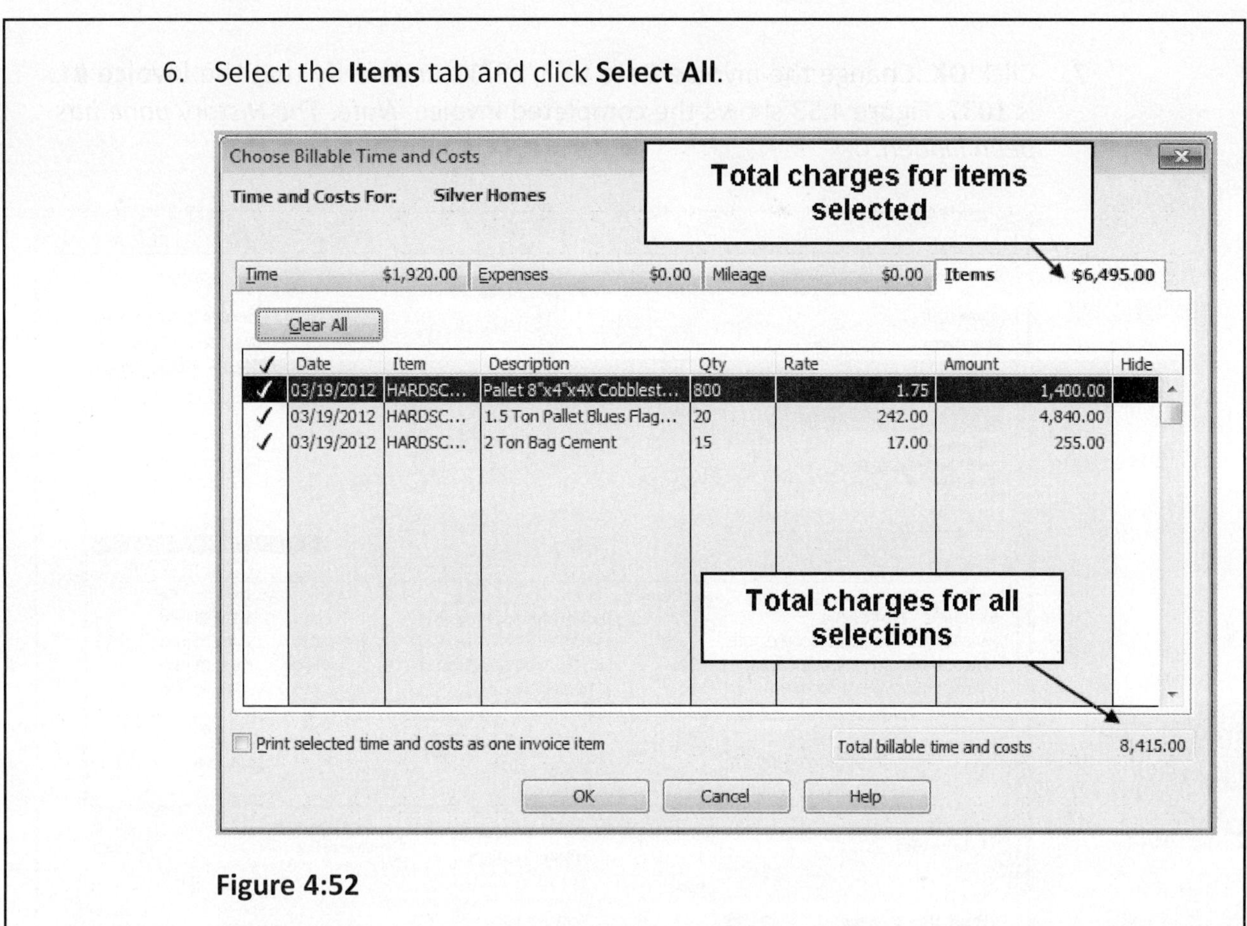

Figure 4:52

7. Click **OK**. Change the invoice **Date** to 3/29/12 and verify that the **Invoice #** is 1037. Figure 4:53 shows the completed invoice. *Note: The History pane has been hidden.*

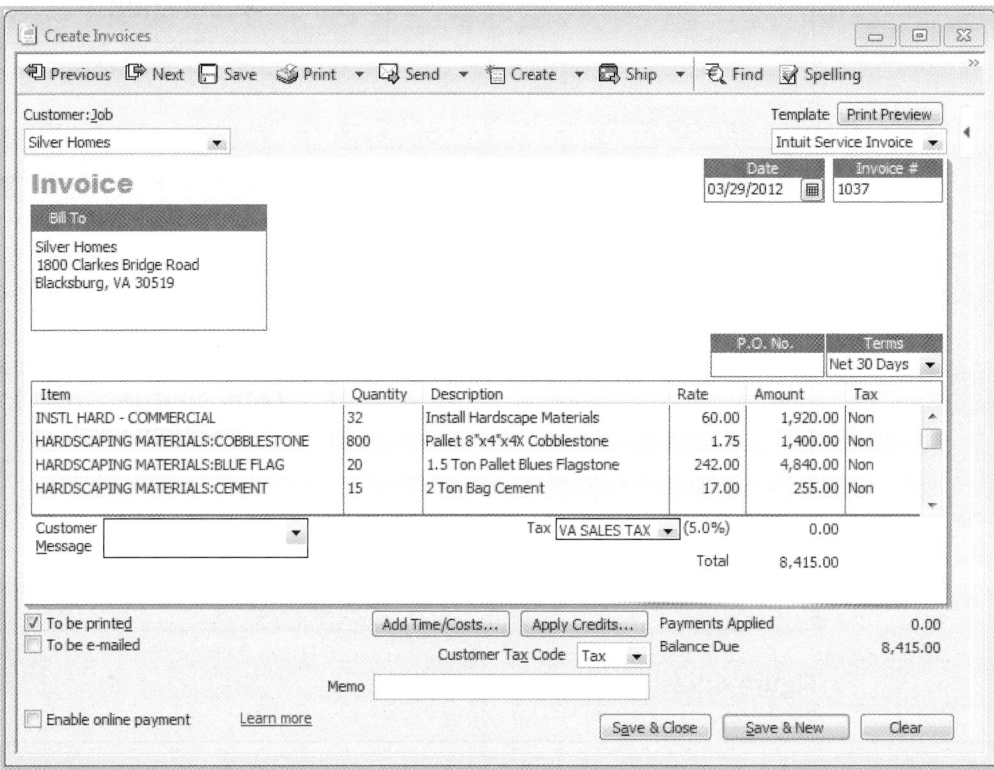

Figure 4:53

If you find a mistake, click **Add Time/Costs** to change your selections or **Clear** to start over.

A word of caution: After saving this invoice, you cannot transfer these costs again, even if you delete the invoice. So make sure that the totals are correct before moving to the next step.

8. Click **Save & Close**. *(Note: If a window opens to check the spelling of Hardscape, click Add to store this term in the dictionary.)*

Let us spend a few minutes discussing the importance of dates. QBP posts entries to the general ledger using the date on the invoice. This date is also called the posting date. The invoice date not only determines if the customer paid by the due date but also if the customer paid by the discount date. It is also important to use the correct posting date so that transactions post to the proper accounting period and financial statements are accurate. **Always pay careful attention to dates when entering transactions in QBP**.

INVOICE A CUSTOMER FOR JOB COSTS

On March 26, 2012, Astor invoices DBH Enterprises for the 8 hours of time worked on March 19, 2012. Prepare and print this invoice using invoice number 1038.

JOB REPORTING

After reading this topic, you will understand preparing and analyzing job cost reports. Follow the next instructions to prepare a job report.

Steps to Using Job Reports

1. Select ***Reports>>Report Center*** on the main menu. Change the view to a **List View** and choose the **Jobs, Time & Mileage** category. The Report Center provides a description for each type of job report. (Figure 4:54).

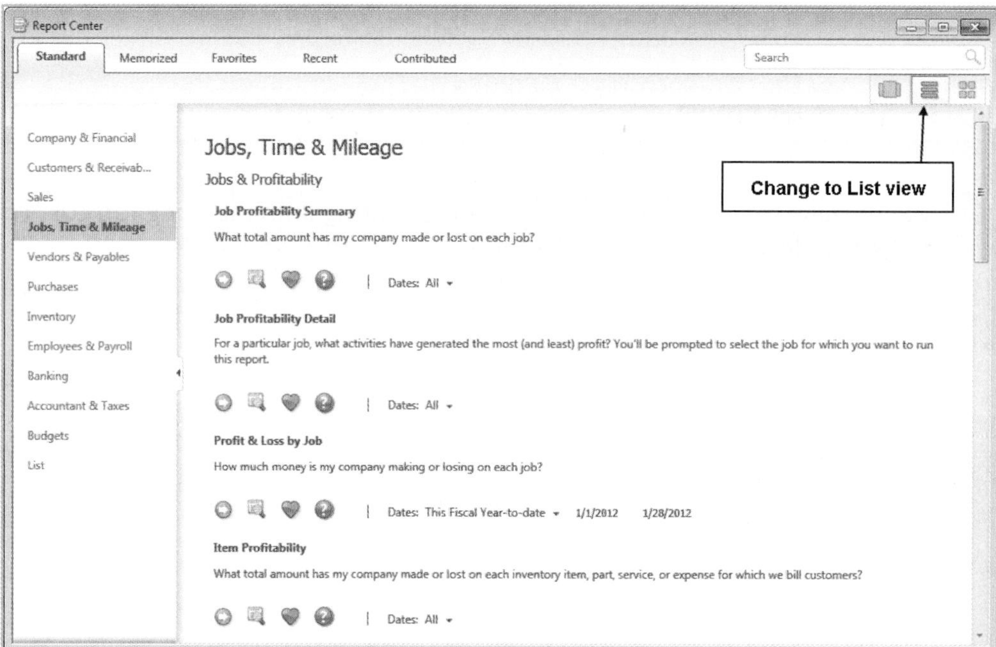

Figure 4:54

2. Click **Job Profitability Detail** and select **Fairbanks Construction** when prompted. Click **OK** and enter the date range of **1/1/12** through **1/31/12**.

   The report shows actual cost and actual revenue for this customer. You can double click on a number to open transactions behind it.

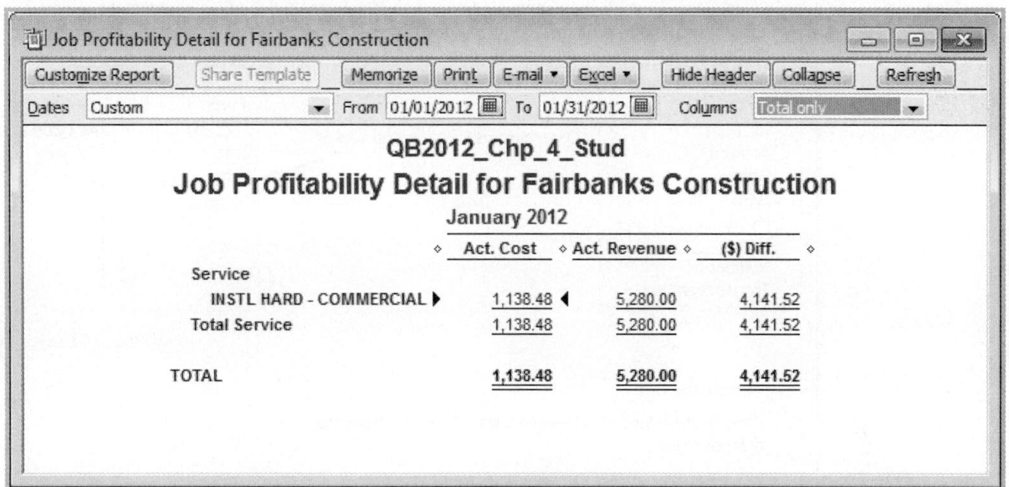

Figure 4:55

3. Click **Customize Report** and select the **Filters** tab. Under **Current Filter Choices**, highlight **Name** and use the dropdown list to the left of Current Filter Choices to select **O'Hara Homes Patios and Walk** job.

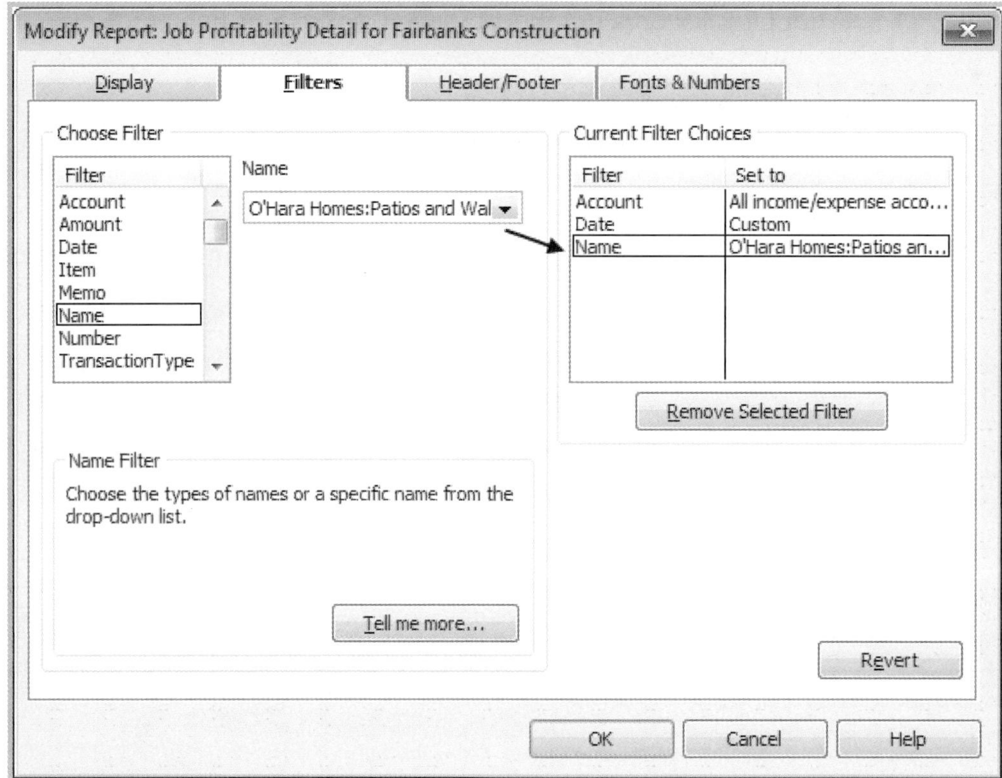

Figure 4:56

4. Click **OK** and the report redisplays as shown in Figure 4:57. Close the report without saving changes.

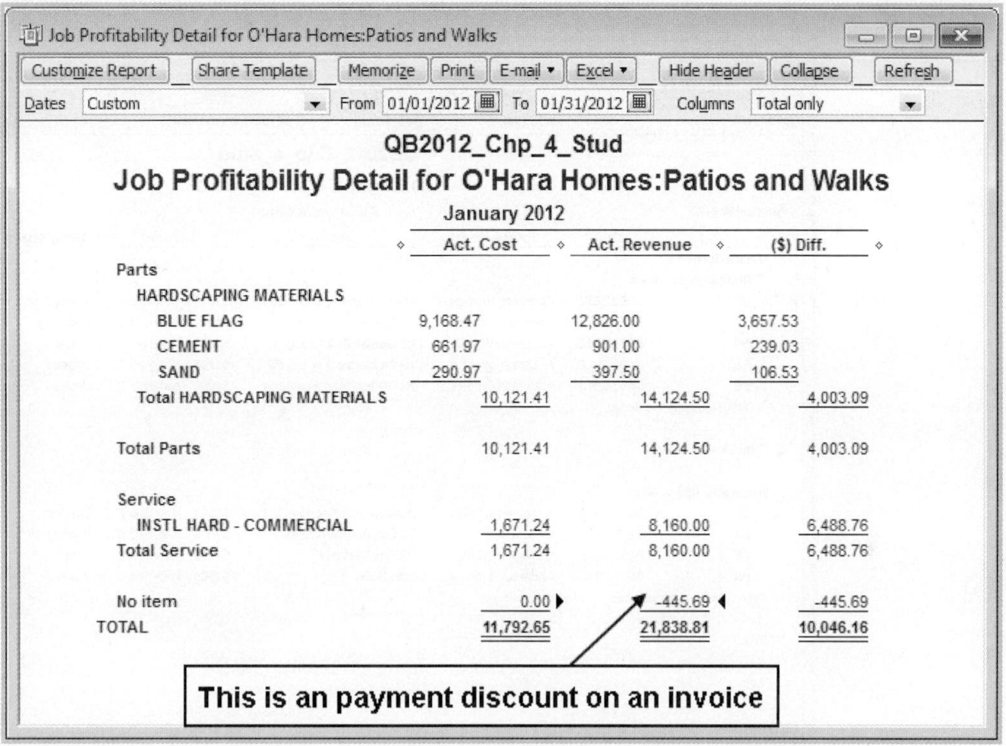

Figure 4:57

5. From the **Report Center**, scroll down and open the **Unbilled Costs by Job** report. This report lists vendor bills that need to be invoiced to customers (Figure 4:58). Close the report.

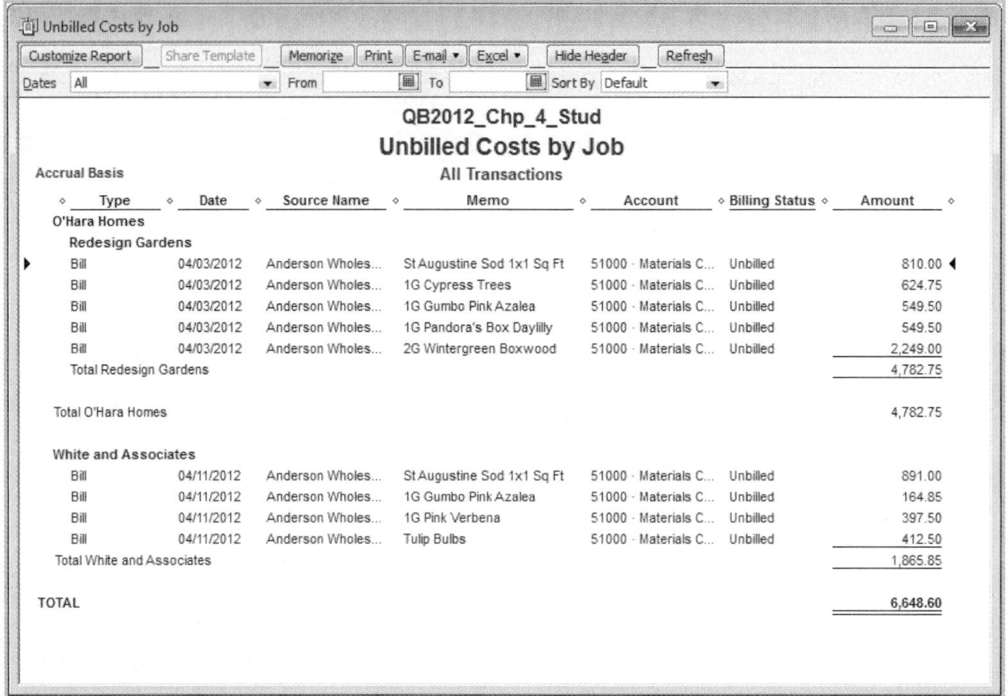

Unbilled Costs by Job

Customize Report | Share Template | Memorize | Print | E-mail | Excel | Hide Header | Refresh

Dates All | From | To | Sort By Default

QB2012_Chp_4_Stud

Unbilled Costs by Job

Accrual Basis

All Transactions

Type	Date	Source Name	Memo	Account	Billing Status	Amount
O'Hara Homes						
Redesign Gardens						
Bill	04/03/2012	Anderson Wholes...	St Augustine Sod 1x1 Sq Ft	51000 · Materials C...	Unbilled	810.00
Bill	04/03/2012	Anderson Wholes...	1G Cypress Trees	51000 · Materials C...	Unbilled	624.75
Bill	04/03/2012	Anderson Wholes...	1G Gumbo Pink Azalea	51000 · Materials C...	Unbilled	549.50
Bill	04/03/2012	Anderson Wholes...	1G Pandora's Box Daylilly	51000 · Materials C...	Unbilled	549.50
Bill	04/03/2012	Anderson Wholes...	2G Wintergreen Boxwood	51000 · Materials C...	Unbilled	2,249.00
Total Redesign Gardens						4,782.75
Total O'Hara Homes						4,782.75
White and Associates						
Bill	04/11/2012	Anderson Wholes...	St Augustine Sod 1x1 Sq Ft	51000 · Materials C...	Unbilled	891.00
Bill	04/11/2012	Anderson Wholes...	1G Gumbo Pink Azalea	51000 · Materials C...	Unbilled	164.85
Bill	04/11/2012	Anderson Wholes...	1G Pink Verbena	51000 · Materials C...	Unbilled	397.50
Bill	04/11/2012	Anderson Wholes...	Tulip Bulbs	51000 · Materials C...	Unbilled	412.50
Total White and Associates						1,865.85
TOTAL						6,648.60

Figure 4:58

6. Double click **Item Profitability** and enter the date range of **01/01/12** through **03/31/12**. Click **Customize Report** and use the **Display** tab to add the **($) Difference** column. Click **OK**.

   This report shows the profit made on each item. Close the report without saving changes.

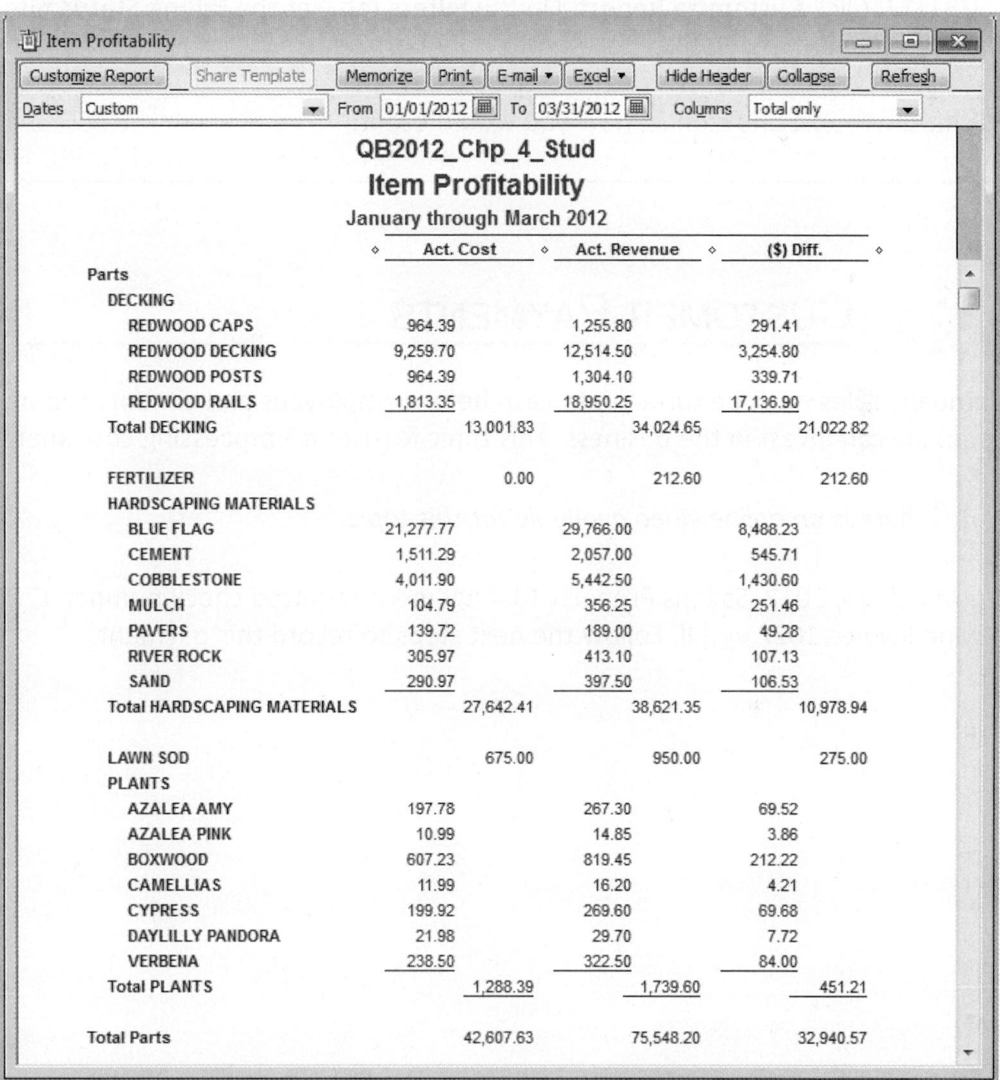

Item Profitability

Customize Report | Share Template | Memorize | Print | E-mail | Excel | Hide Header | Collapse | Refresh

Dates: Custom — From 01/01/2012 To 03/31/2012 — Columns: Total only

QB2012_Chp_4_Stud

Item Profitability

January through March 2012

	Act. Cost	Act. Revenue	($) Diff.
Parts			
DECKING			
REDWOOD CAPS	964.39	1,255.80	291.41
REDWOOD DECKING	9,259.70	12,514.50	3,254.80
REDWOOD POSTS	964.39	1,304.10	339.71
REDWOOD RAILS	1,813.35	18,950.25	17,136.90
Total DECKING	13,001.83	34,024.65	21,022.82
FERTILIZER	0.00	212.60	212.60
HARDSCAPING MATERIALS			
BLUE FLAG	21,277.77	29,766.00	8,488.23
CEMENT	1,511.29	2,057.00	545.71
COBBLESTONE	4,011.90	5,442.50	1,430.60
MULCH	104.79	356.25	251.46
PAVERS	139.72	189.00	49.28
RIVER ROCK	305.97	413.10	107.13
SAND	290.97	397.50	106.53
Total HARDSCAPING MATERIALS	27,642.41	38,621.35	10,978.94
LAWN SOD	675.00	950.00	275.00
PLANTS			
AZALEA AMY	197.78	267.30	69.52
AZALEA PINK	10.99	14.85	3.86
BOXWOOD	607.23	819.45	212.22
CAMELLIAS	11.99	16.20	4.21
CYPRESS	199.92	269.60	69.68
DAYLILLY PANDORA	21.98	29.70	7.72
VERBENA	238.50	322.50	84.00
Total PLANTS	1,288.39	1,739.60	451.21
Total Parts	42,607.63	75,548.20	32,940.57

Figure 4:59

CREATE A JOB REPORT

Prepare the **Time** report named **Time by Job Summary** for the date range of 3/1/12 to 3/31/12. Click **Customize Report**. On the **Filters** tab, set the **Billing Status** filter to **Unbilled** and the **Customer:Job** filter to Ashford Hill Apartments.

Print the report and explain how you would use it.

Customer Payments

Company sales must be turned into cash before employees and vendors can be paid or the company can invest in the business. This topic focuses on processing customer payments.

Note: There is an online video available for this topic.

On March 29, 2012, Sallens Property Management remitted check number 1786 for $4,800.00 paying Invoice 1022 in full. Follow the next steps to record this payment.

Steps to Process Customer Payments

1. On the **Home** page, click **Receive Payments**. *(Note: Click No Thanks if prompted about integrating payments.)* In **Received From**, select **Sallens Property Management** and enter the **Date** of 3/29/12.

   Click the **check mark** field in front of the first unpaid invoice listed at the bottom. You will receive the message illustrated in the next step.

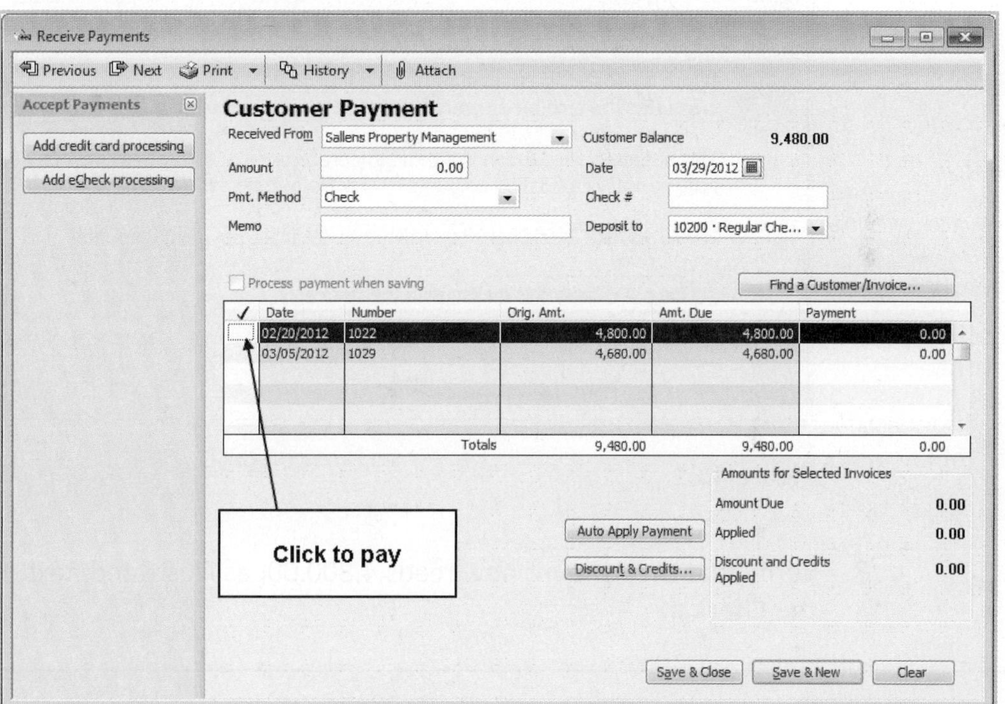

Figure 4:60

2. Because you did not enter an **Amount** before clicking the invoice, QBP asks if you want to continue automatically calculating the payment amount, meaning the Amount field in the window will be auto filled as you select invoices to pay.

   Mark the option illustrated to turn off future messages and click **Yes**.

   Note: If you mark No, you can turn the feature back on by clicking Edit>>Preferences to open the Preferences window. Select the Payments area on the left. On the Company Preferences tab, click the Automatically calculate payments options to turn the feature back on.

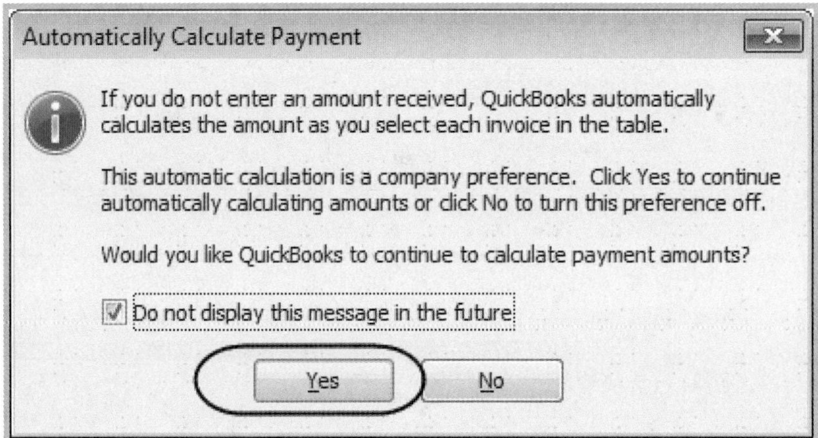

Figure 4:61

3. Verify that the **Amount** now reads 4,800.00, as illustrated next. Enter "1786" as the **Check #**.

4. The completed entry is shown in Figure 4:62.

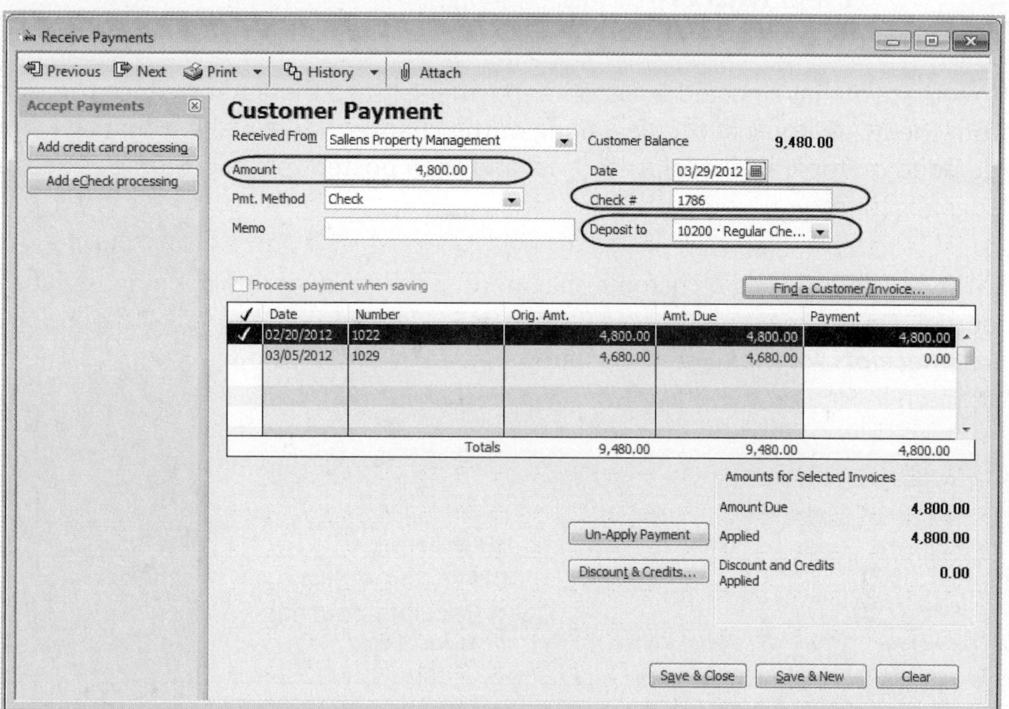

Figure 4:62

Notice that the payment will post (i.e., debit) to the **10200 Regular Checking** account. Also the **Pmt Method** has defaulted to **Check**.

If needed, the **Un-Apply Payment** button at the bottom is a quick way to clear selected invoices. You can also click an invoice to clear its selection.

5. Click **Save & Close** to post the payment.

BEHIND THE KEYS OF A POSTED CUSTOMER PAYMENT

Now that you have posted a customer payment, trace the audit trail for the transaction. Recall from the *MAPS* topic at the beginning of the chapter, we explained that a customer payment is recorded on the Cash Receipts Journal and then posted to the customer's account and general ledger accounts.

So let us begin tracing a customer payment in the software by opening the Cash Receipts Journal. On the main menu, select ***Reports>>Memorized Reports>>Accounting Journals>> Cash Receipts Journal***. Enter the date range of **3/29/12** through **3/29/12**. The refreshed report is shown in Figure 4:63.

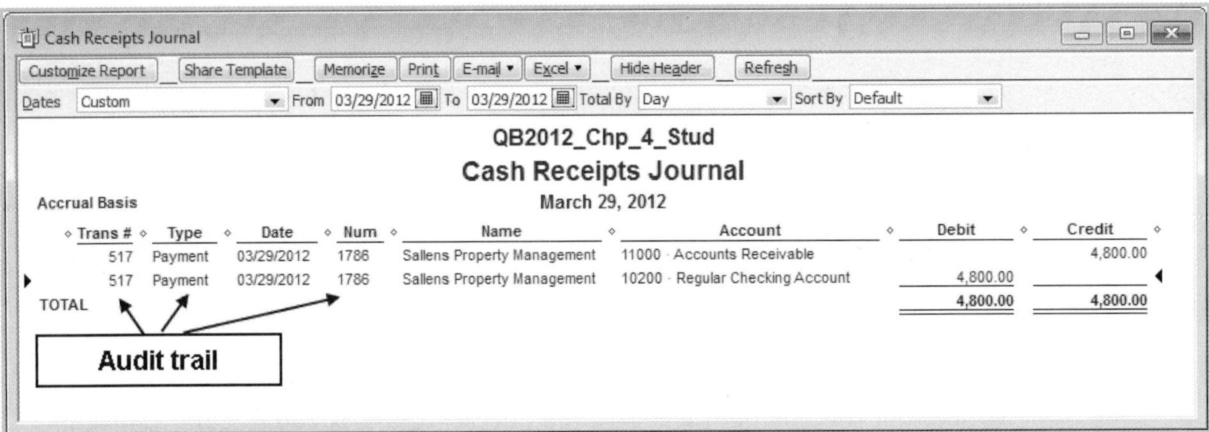

Cash Receipts Journal

Customize Report | Share Template | Memorize | Print | E-mail | Excel | Hide Header | Refresh

Dates Custom From 03/29/2012 To 03/29/2012 Total By Day Sort By Default

QB2012_Chp_4_Stud
Cash Receipts Journal
Accrual Basis March 29, 2012

Trans #	Type	Date	Num	Name	Account	Debit	Credit
517	Payment	03/29/2012	1786	Sallens Property Management	11000 · Accounts Receivable		4,800.00
517	Payment	03/29/2012	1786	Sallens Property Management	10200 · Regular Checking Account	4,800.00	
TOTAL						4,800.00	4,800.00

Figure 4:63

This report will display customer payments and other bank deposits. Note the **Trans #** and **Type**.

Close this report, discarding changes. On the main menu, select ***Reports>>Customers & Receivables>>Transaction List by Customer***.

Enter the date range of **3/29/12** through **3/29/12**. Click **Customize Report** and select **Trans #** under **Columns**. Click **OK**.

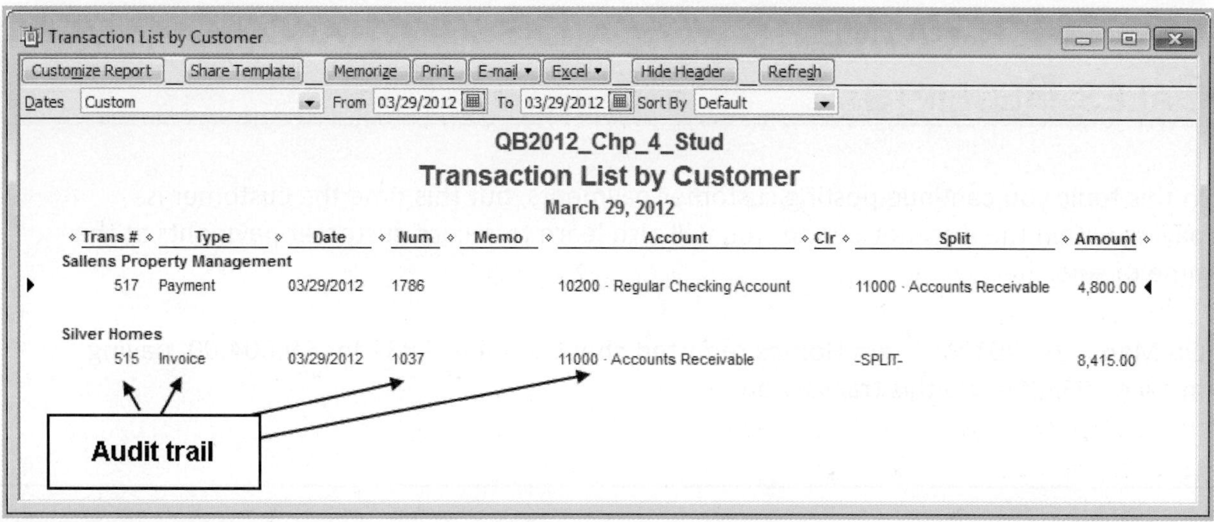

Figure 4:64

Figure 4:64 illustrates the report. The entry for the Payment transaction shows the same **Trans #** and **Type** as displayed on the Cash Receipts Journal.

Close this report and complete tracing entries by opening the memorized report named **General Ledger Detail Report**. Locate your entries made to general ledger accounts 10200 Regular Checking and 11000 Accounts Receivable (not illustrated).

Customer Payments with a Discount and Sales Receipts

In this topic you continue posting customer payments, but this time the customer is paying within the discount period. You will also learn to record customer payments at the time of sale.

On March 29, 2012, O'Hara Homes remitted check number 9832 for $9,604.00, paying Invoice 1033. Record this transaction.

Steps to Process Customer Payment with a Discount

1. On the **Home** page, click **Receive Payments** and select **O'Hara Homes**. Change the **Date** to "3/29/12" and enter "9832" as the **Check #**. Click the **check mark** field in front of invoice **1033**.

2. Figure 4:65 shows the entry thus far. Notice that the customer has an available discount.

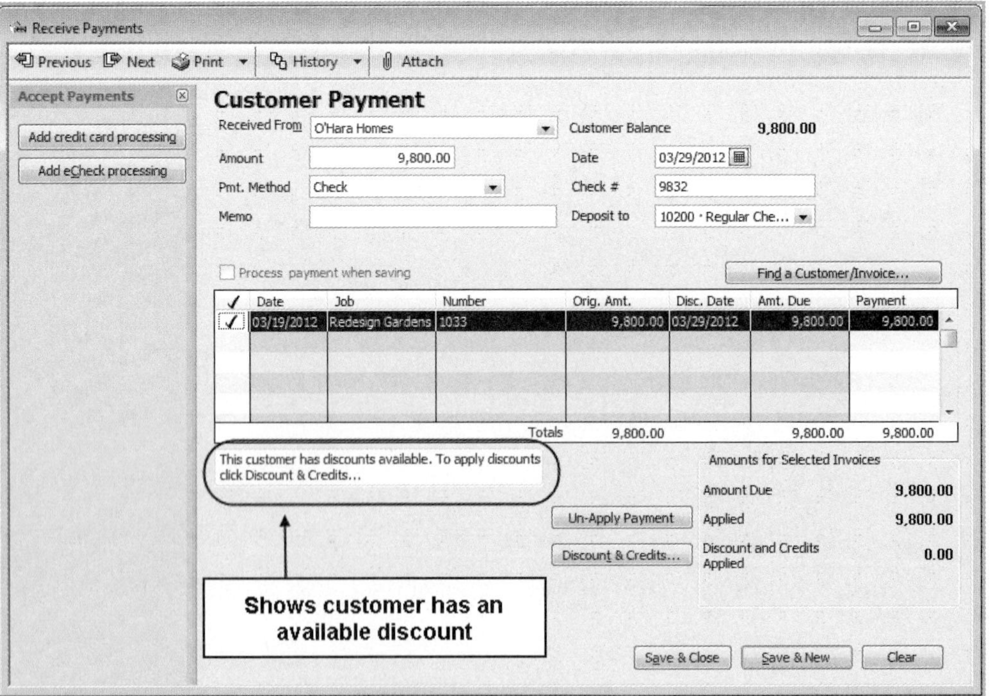

Figure 4:65

3. Click the **Discount and Credits** button to open the window illustrated in Figure 4:66.

   This window shows that the invoice has payment **Terms** of 2% 10 Net 30. The **Amount of Discount** is $196.00. The discount will post to the **Discount Account** of 49000 Sales Discounts.

   (Note: Notice that the window also contains a Credits tab, which is used when applying a customer's existing credit balances to an invoice.)

   Click **Done**.

Figure 4:66

4. Notice that clicking the Discount & Credits button applied the discount and reduced the payment Amount to $9,604.00. (See Figure 4:67.) Click **Save & Close**.

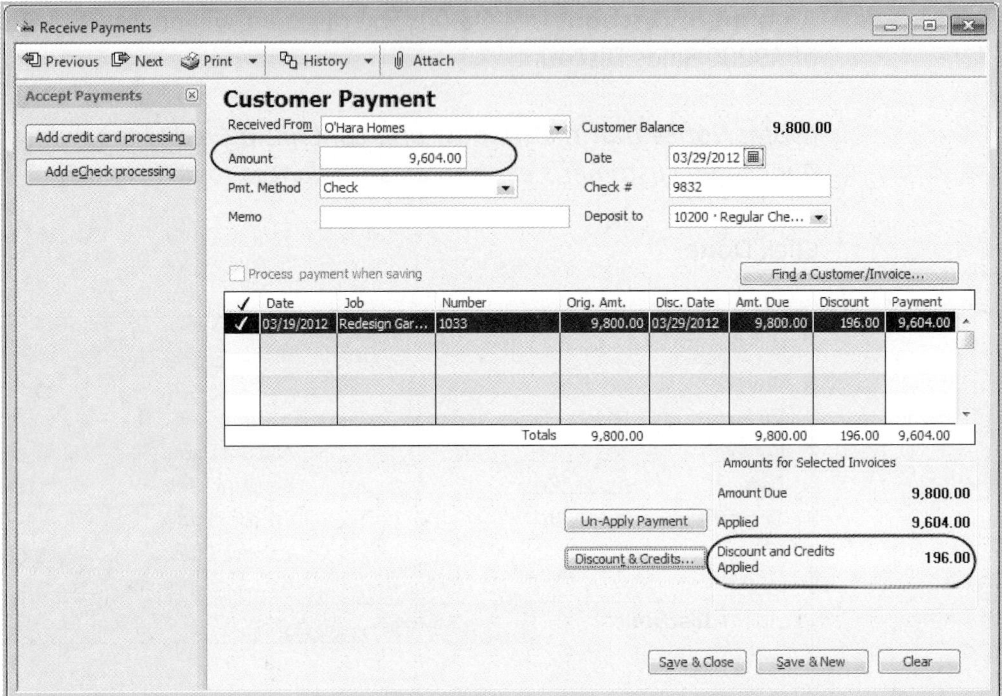

Figure 4:67

5. You will now record a cash sale to Elkorn Apartments.

   When a customer pays at the time of sale, you do not record an invoice. You record a sales receipt.

   On the **Home** page, click **Create Sales Receipts** and hide the History pane.

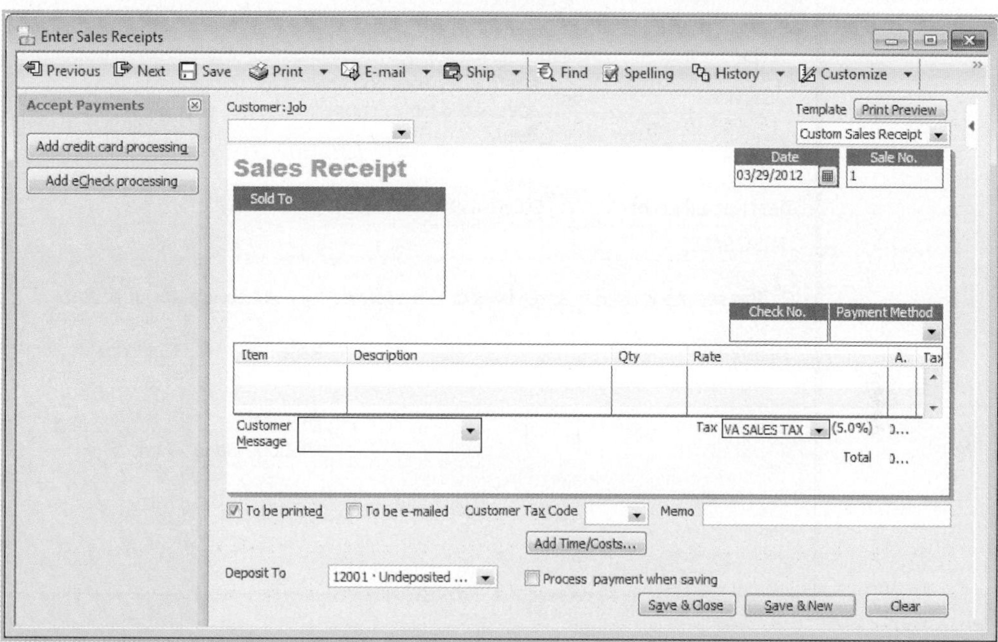

Figure 4:68

6. Select **Elkhorn Apartments** customer. Enter "3/29/12" as the **Date** and "736" as the **Check No.**

7. Place your cursor in the **Item** field and type in "MISC SALES" in the space provided. Press **Tab** and QBP prompts to create the item. Click **Yes**.

   Complete the item window as illustrated in Figure 4:69. You will not enter a Rate because the rate will vary. Click **OK**.

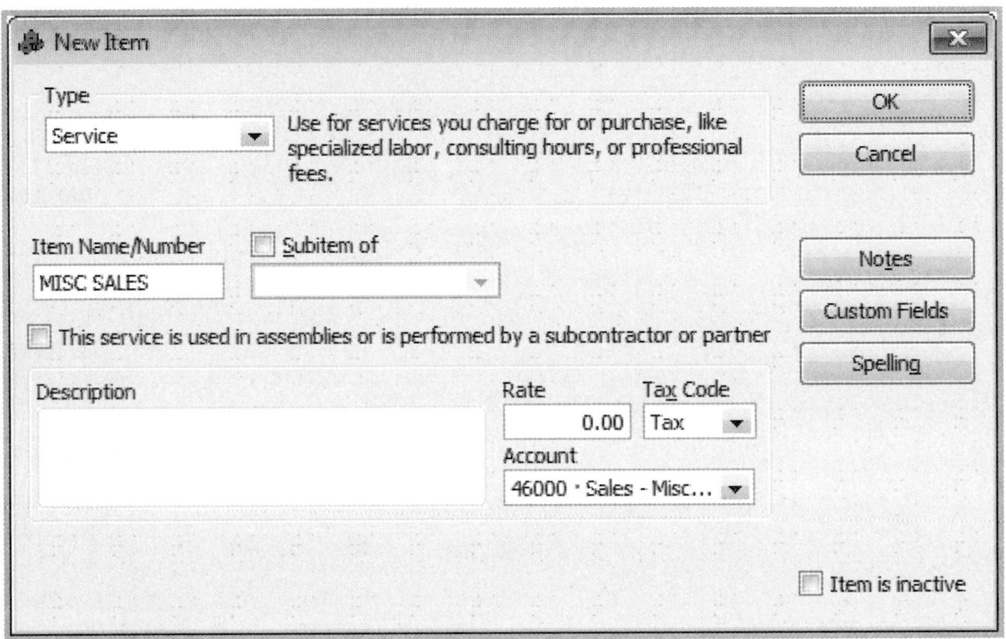

Figure 4:69

8. Return to the Enter Sales Receipts window and type in "Spot treatment for rose disease" as the **Description**. Enter "1" as the **Qty** and 150.00 as the **Rate**. Change the **Deposit To** field to "10200 Regular Checking."

   The completed entry is shown in Figure 4:70. This entry will be listed on the Cash Receipts Journal as a $157.50 debit to 10200 Regular Checking, a $150.00 credit to 46000 Sales Miscellaneous, and a $7.50 credit to 2200 Sales Tax Payable.

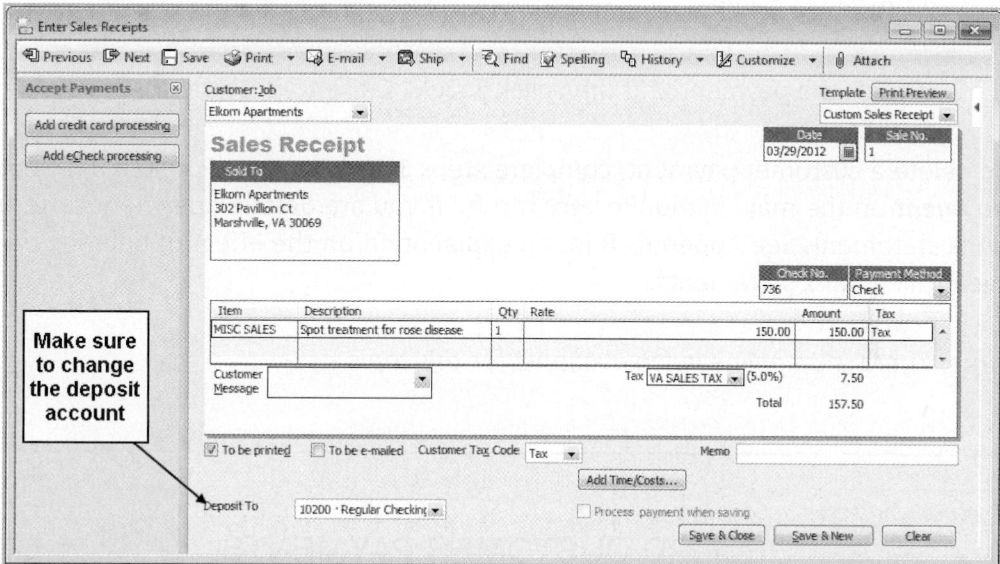

Figure 4:70

9. Click **Save & Close**.

CORRECTING CUSTOMER PAYMENTS

QBP permits editing and deleting customer payments. To correct a customer payment, you complete the following steps.

1. Using the Customer Center, locate the payment on the customer's account.
2. Double click the payment to reopen.
3. Edit the payment and then click Save & Close to post the changes.

To delete a customer payment, complete steps 1 and 2 above. For step 3, select ***Edit>>Delete Payment*** on the main menu. Be very careful if you are deleting payments after reconciling the bank statement. See Appendix B for an explanation on the effect of deleting deposits after reconciling bank statements.

Note: There is an online video available for this topic.

RECORD CUSTOMER PAYMENTS

On March 28, 2012, the following customer payments were received. Post the payments.

Ashford Hill Apartments, check number 2583 for $1,000.00, paying Invoice 1024. The customer is not paying in full so you must enter the payment amount and leave the remaining balance as an underpayment.

Sycamore Homes, check number 857 for $21,607.74, paying Invoice 1035 within the discount date.

Print the Cash Receipts Journal for the date range of 03/28/2012.

Customer Credits

Occasionally Astor may need to issue a credit against a customer invoice. In the exercise that follows, Astor is issuing a credit to Ashford Hill Apartments Homes for three hours of labor billed on Invoice 1031.

Steps to Enter a Customer Credit Memo

1. On the **Home** page, click **Refunds & Credits** and hide the History pane.

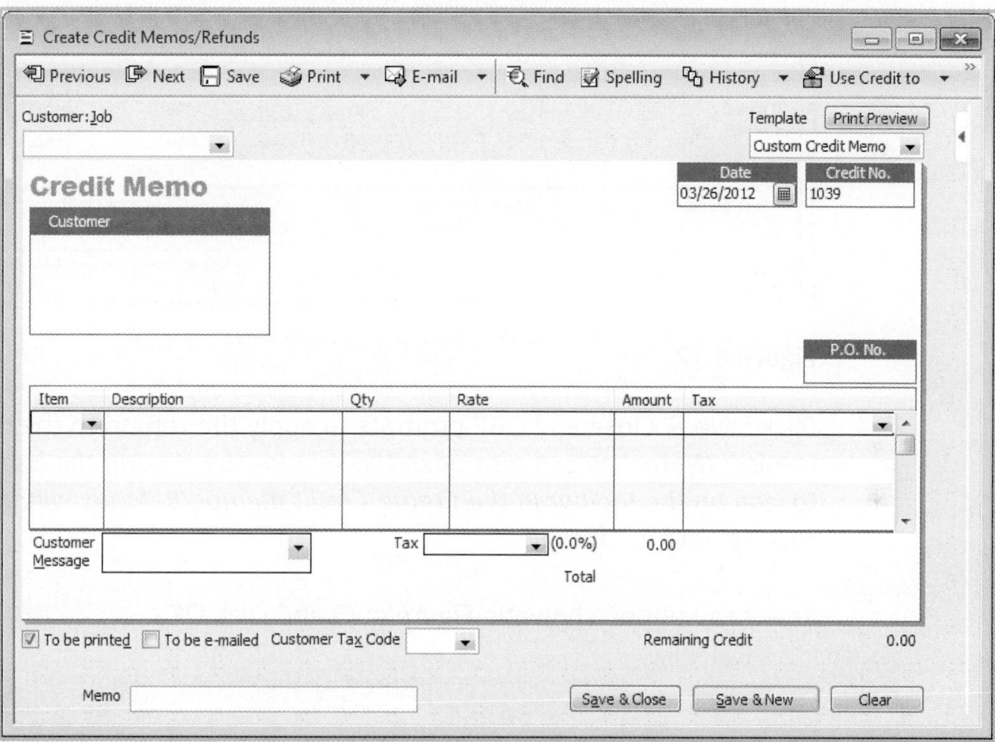

Figure 4:71

2. Select **Ashford Hill Apartments** and enter "3/26/12" as the **Date**.

3. In **Item**, select WKLY MNTNCE – COMMERCIAL and enter "3" as the **QTY**. Press **Tab** and the completed credit memo is shown in Figure 4:72.

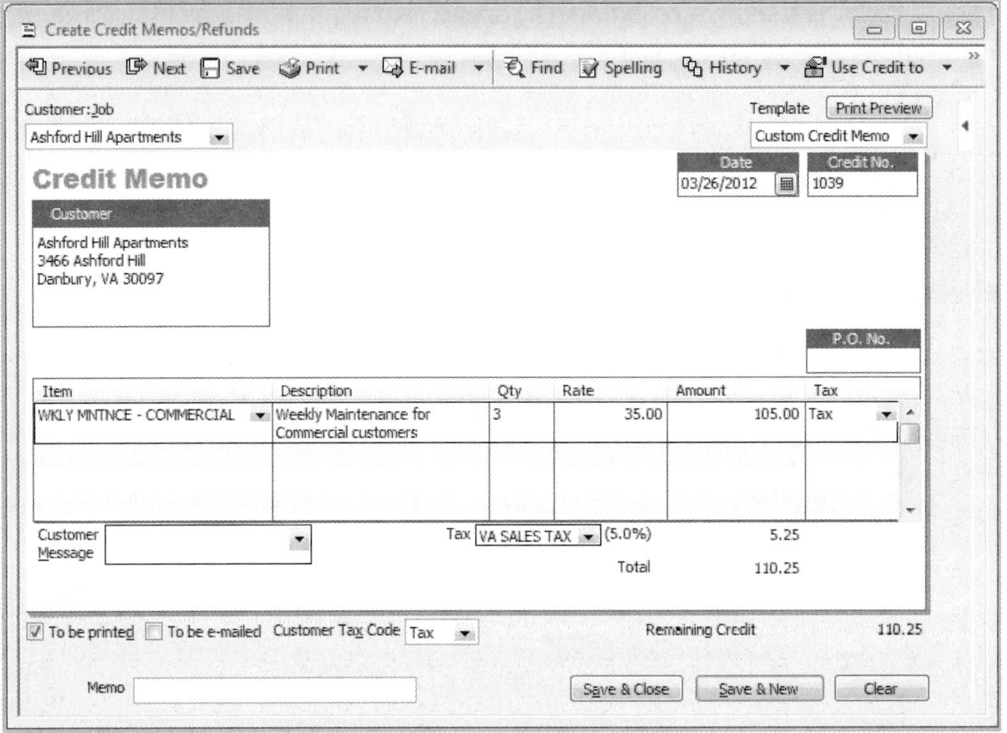

Figure 4:72

4. Click **Save & Close** and QBP prompts to apply the refund to the outstanding invoice. *(Note: You can also open this window by clicking the Use Credit to icon on the toolbar in the Create Credit memos/Refunds window before clicking Save & Close.)*

   Select the option shown in Figure 4:73 and click **OK**.

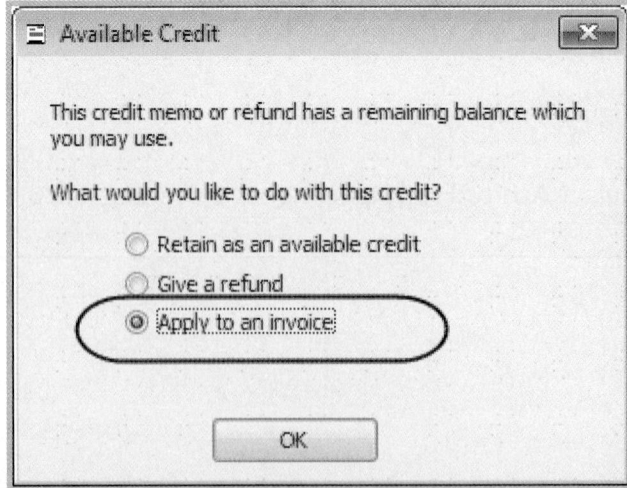

Figure 4:73

5. Click the **checkmark** field for Invoice 1024 to unapply the credit to this invoice. Click the **checkmark** field in front of Invoice 1031 to apply to this invoice. The completed window is illustrated next.

   Click **Done**. The credit is applied to the invoice and the window is closed.

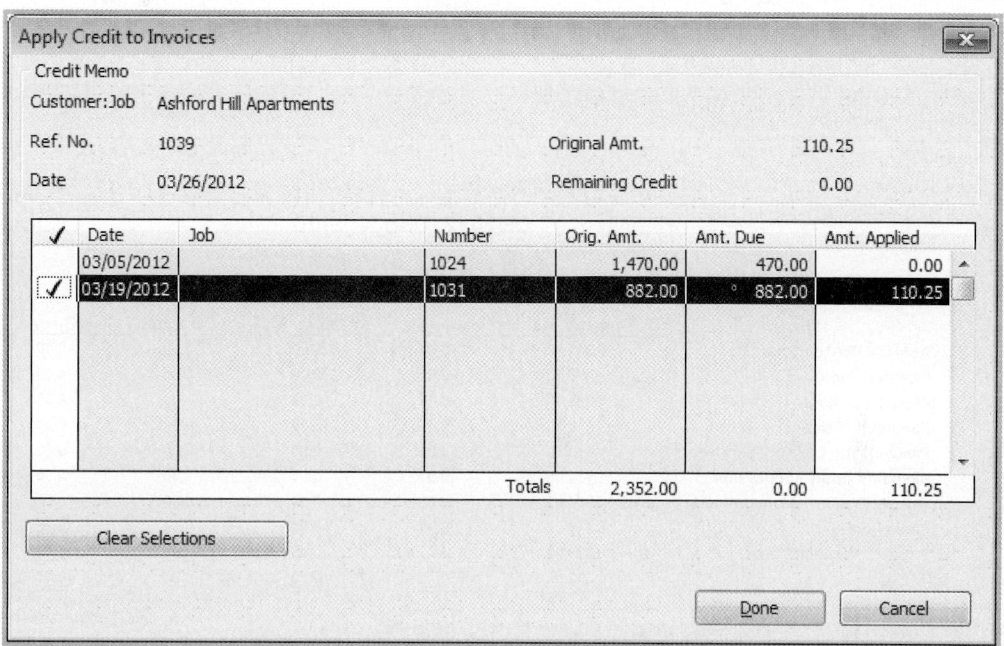

Figure 4:74

Customer Reporting and Reconciling Activities

QBP offers a variety of customer reports and these reports are available on the **Reports** menu and the **Report Center**. Open the center and select the **Customers & Receivables** area.

Double click **A/R Aging Summary** to open the accounts receivable aging report. Change the date to "3/31/12". Refresh and the report displays as illustrated in Figure 4:75.

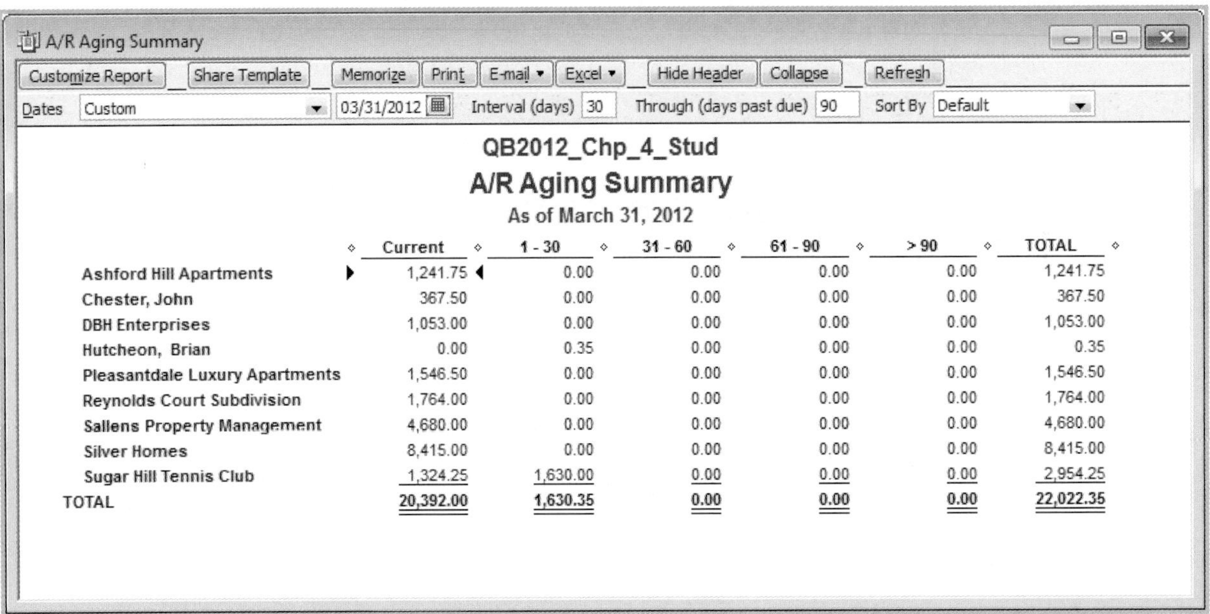

QB2012_Chp_4_Stud

A/R Aging Summary

As of March 31, 2012

	Current	1 - 30	31 - 60	61 - 90	> 90	TOTAL
Ashford Hill Apartments	1,241.75	0.00	0.00	0.00	0.00	1,241.75
Chester, John	367.50	0.00	0.00	0.00	0.00	367.50
DBH Enterprises	1,053.00	0.00	0.00	0.00	0.00	1,053.00
Hutcheon, Brian	0.00	0.35	0.00	0.00	0.00	0.35
Pleasantdale Luxury Apartments	1,546.50	0.00	0.00	0.00	0.00	1,546.50
Reynolds Court Subdivision	1,764.00	0.00	0.00	0.00	0.00	1,764.00
Sallens Property Management	4,680.00	0.00	0.00	0.00	0.00	4,680.00
Silver Homes	8,415.00	0.00	0.00	0.00	0.00	8,415.00
Sugar Hill Tennis Club	1,324.25	1,630.00	0.00	0.00	0.00	2,954.25
TOTAL	20,392.00	1,630.35	0.00	0.00	0.00	22,022.35

Figure 4:75

This report lists a summary of customer outstanding balances by age of the balance. *(Note: Your balances will differ from those illustrated if you have not completed all chapter exercises.)*

The report serves two important purposes. First, Astor uses it to monitor customer payments so it can manage company cash flow and mitigate the risk of making future sales to customers failing to pay.

Second, the company uses the report to reconcile customer activities with the accounts receivable control account. This task is performed by comparing the total on the report to the March ending balance in general ledger account 11000 Accounts Receivable. Close this report.

Now view the balance in accounts receivable. Open the **Trial Balance** report from the **Accountant & Taxes** category in the **Report Center** and filter the report to 3/31/12 (not illustrated). Scroll down and locate the balance in 11000 Accounts Receivable. The total on the A/R Aging report and the balance in Accounts Receivable on the Trial Balance must agree to verify proper recording of customer activities.

These balances can become out of balance when you improperly correct customer transactions. Therefore, always correct customer transactions by referring to the instructions in Appendix B.

You should reconcile the aged receivables report to the accounts receivable balance at the end of every month and prior to issuing financial reports. Close this report.

Return to the **Customers & Receivables** area to open the **A/R Aging Detail** report. Enter "3/31/12" as the date range (not illustrated). This report lists individual invoices by aging category.

Notice that there is an outstanding balance of $.35 on Invoice 1026 to Brian Hutcheon. You will write off the balance on this invoice in the next topic.

Close the report and the Report Center.

WRITE OFF A CUSTOMER INVOICE

In business, you will find that customers do not always pay. If the amount cannot be collect, you will need to write of the invoice.

In addition, like Brian Hutcheon, a customer may pay the wrong amount and, instead of calling the error to a customer's attention, the company decides to write off the invoice balance. The instructions that follow are used when you decide to write off the balance on an invoice after posting the payment.

(Note: Instead of writing off an invoice after posting the payment, you can write off the balance at the time of recording the payment. In Chapter 8, we illustrate writing off the balance on an invoice at the time of recording a payment.)

Steps to Write Off a Customer's Invoice

1. On the **Home** page, click **Receive Payments**. Complete the window as illustrated in Figure 4:76.

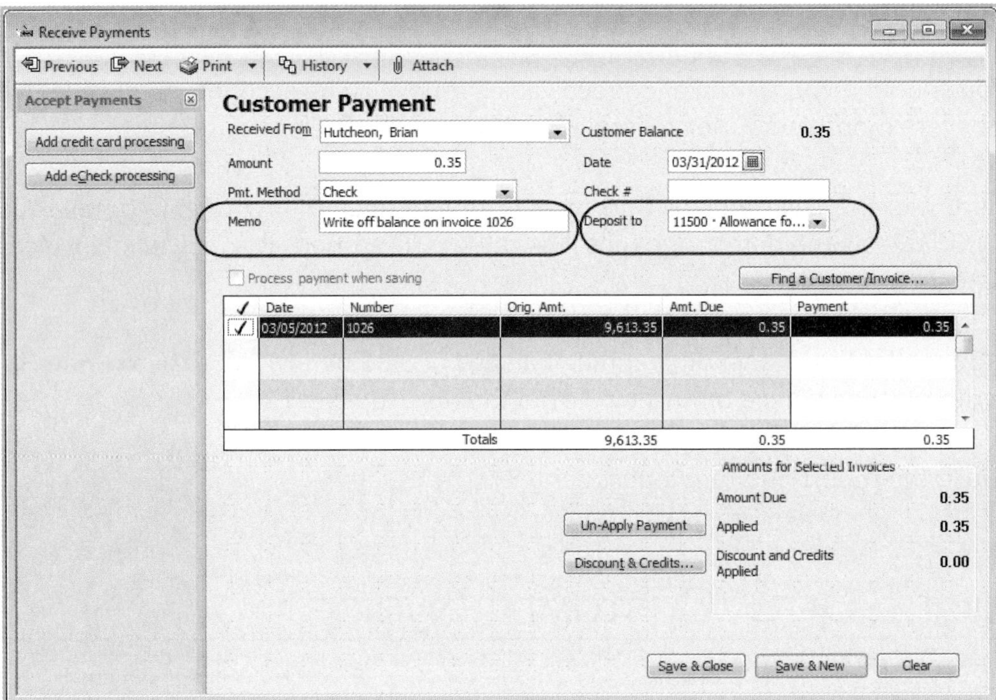

Figure 4:76

Notice that the **Deposit to** account has been changed to 11500 Allowance for Doubtful Accounts. When a company uses the allowance method of accounting for bad debts, bad debt expense is recognized when adjusting the allowance estimate and actual bad debt is written off to the estimated allowance.

2. Click **Save & Close**.

CUSTOMER STATEMENTS

Astor mails customer statements once a month. These statements list invoice and payment activity and prompt customers to pay.

Click **Statements** on the **Home** page to open the window illustrated in Figure 4:77. Enter the **Statement Date** of "3/31/12" and select the **All open transactions as of Statement Date** option. Click the **One Customer** option and use the drop down box to select "Ashford Hill Apartments."

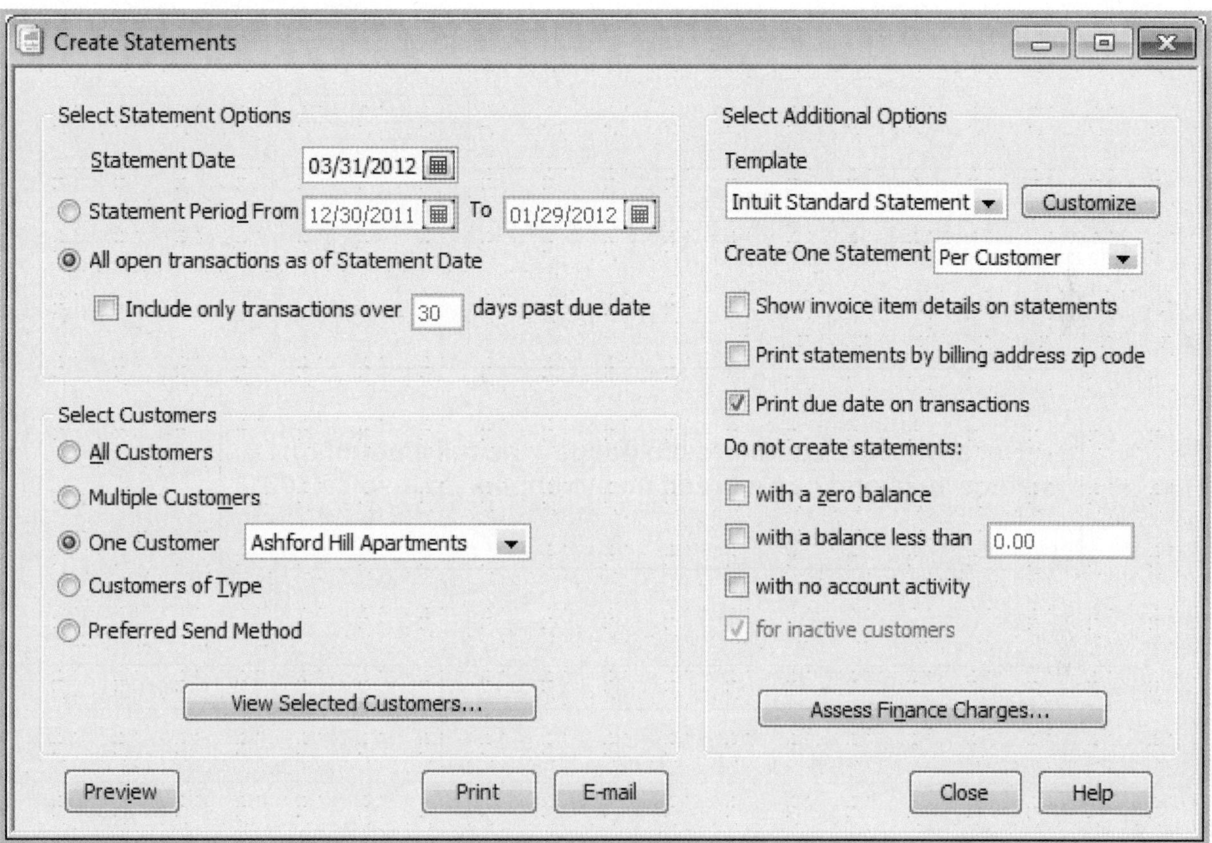

Figure 4:77

Click **Preview** and the statement is shown in Figure 4:78.

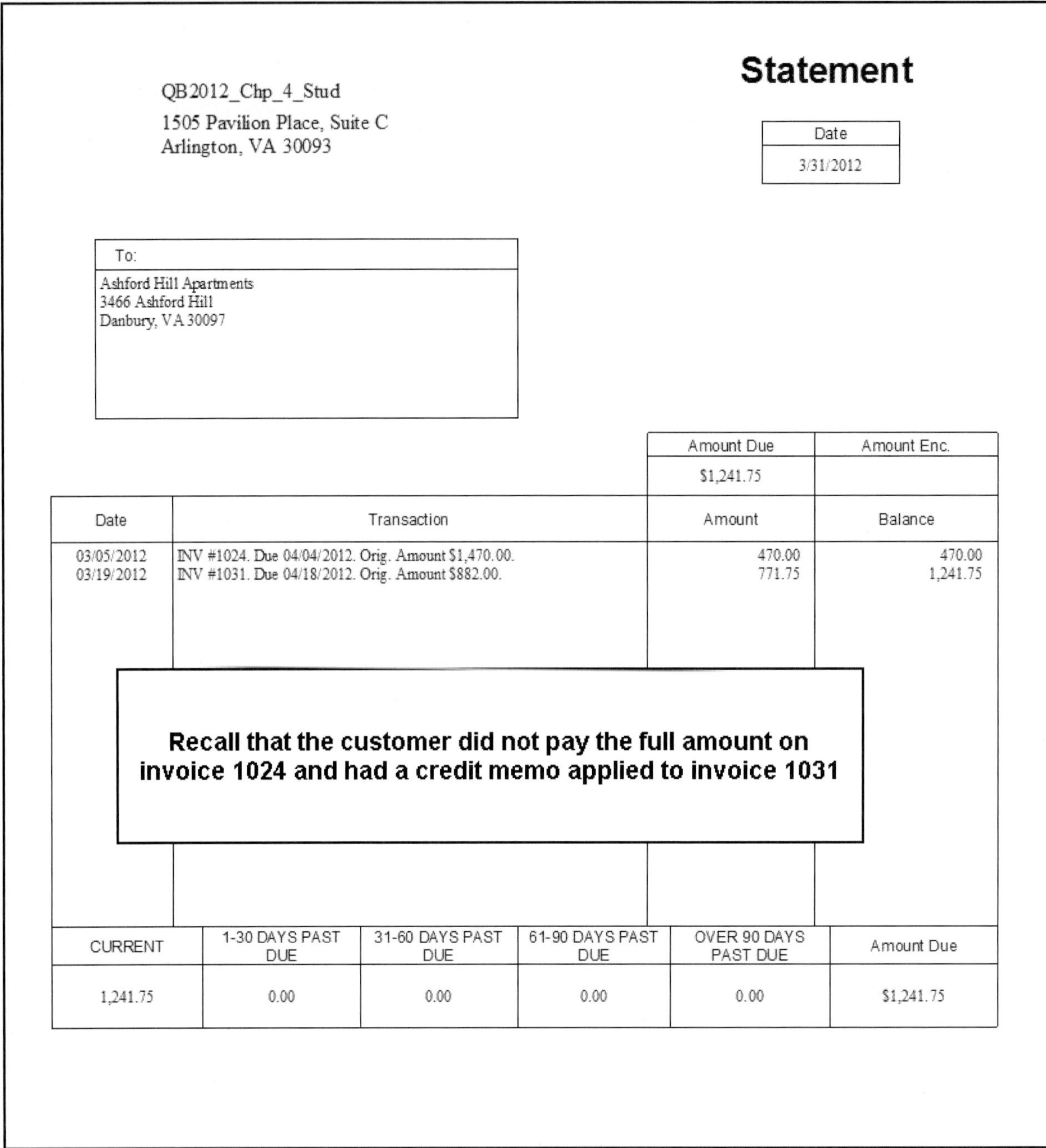

Statement

QB2012_Chp_4_Stud
1505 Pavilion Place, Suite C
Arlington, VA 30093

Date
3/31/2012

To:
Ashford Hill Apartments 3466 Ashford Hill Danbury, VA 30097

Amount Due	Amount Enc.
$1,241.75	

Date	Transaction	Amount	Balance
03/05/2012	INV #1024. Due 04/04/2012. Orig. Amount $1,470.00.	470.00	470.00
03/19/2012	INV #1031. Due 04/18/2012. Orig. Amount $882.00.	771.75	1,241.75

CURRENT	1-30 DAYS PAST DUE	31-60 DAYS PAST DUE	61-90 DAYS PAST DUE	OVER 90 DAYS PAST DUE	Amount Due
1,241.75	0.00	0.00	0.00	0.00	$1,241.75

Figure 4:78

Click **Print** and, when prompted to verify that statements printed correctly, click **Yes**.

If QBP prompts to remind you that statements can also be emailed, check the option to turn off future messages and click **OK**.

Click **Close** to exit the window.

You have now completed the chapter. ***Make a backup of the company data file to a backup file named "QB2012_Chp4_Stud_Completed".***

SUMMARY

In this chapter, you learned the *MAPS* for posting customer transactions before recording transactions in QBP. By understanding manual entries, you were able to trace QBP's *Behind the Keys* entries. Understanding how a transaction affects financial accounts is critical to posting transactions correctly and to tracing the audit trail of a posted transaction.

After completing this chapter, you are skilled in recording customer invoices, payments, and credit memos for a service-based business. You can manage the master accounts linked to transactions (i.e., customer accounts, jobs, and service and non-inventory items). You understand job reporting as well as other reports that let you monitor and document customer activities. With firm knowledge on processing customer activities, you are now ready to take on Astor's vendor activities in the next chapter.

End-of-Chapter Questions

TRUE/FALSE

_____ 1. The audit trail can be used to trace a transaction posting in the general ledger.

_____ 2. The Sales Journal report will list the general ledger account numbers affected by a sales invoice.

_____ 3. You can create a sales invoice by entering items directly on the invoice or by transferring job costs.

_____ 4. You can customize columns on the Item List using the Item button.

_____ 5. You can create a customer account "on the fly" while entering a sales invoice.

_____ 6. You should reconcile the aged receivables report to the balance in accounts receivable before printing financial statements.

_____ 7. In QBP, you can email sales invoices to customers.

_____ 8. You can delete a customer account that has transaction history.

_____ 9. The Item List can be exported to Excel.

_____ 10. You can correct a posted customer payment.

_____ 11. The A/R Aging Summary report lists customer payments.

_____ 12. The Open Invoices report is found under the Customers & Receivables reporting area.

_____ 13. Before saving a credit memo, you can apply the credit to an unpaid invoice.

_____ 14. When creating a new item for services sold by the company, you would select Inventory Part as the item Type.

_____ 15. You can open a memorized report in the Report Center.

MULTIPLE CHOICE

_____ 1. The _____ will tell you the balance on a customer invoice.
   a. Customer Center
   b. Customer Balance Detail report
   c. Collections report
   d. All of the above

_____ 2. One of the reports you can use to trace the audit trail on a posted sales invoice is the _____ report.
   a. Journal
   b. Transaction List by Customer
   c. Trial Balance
   d. A/R Aging Detail

_____ 3. When selling a(n) _____ item, cost of goods sold will post at the time of sale.

a. Service
b. Inventory Part
c. Non-inventory Part
d. All of the above

_____ 4. Use the _____ icon to record a customer payment on an invoice.

a. Receive Payments
b. Create Sales Receipts
c. Both a and b
d. None of the above

_____ 5. An accounts receivable aging report is used to _____.

a. monitor the age of customer invoices
b. reconcile customer activities with the general ledger
c. manage cash flow
d. All of the above

_____ 6. Customer statements may be printed from the _____.

a. Home page
b. Customers menu
c. Both a and b
d. None of the above

_____ 7. When Astor sells Fertilizer, QBP will post revenue to the general ledger account _____.

a. entered in the sales invoice window
b. stored on the item
c. Both a and b
d. None of the above

_____ 8. On the Customer Center, you can _____.

a. create a new invoice
b. edit a customer
c. Both a and b
d. None of the above

_____ 9. You can open the Customer Center using _____.

a. the Customers icon on the Home page
b. the Customers icon on the Icon Bar
c. the Customers menu
d. All of the above

_____ 10. You will use the _____ icon on the Home page to record a cash sale.

a. Create Sales Receipts
b. Create Invoices
c. Receive Payments
d. Statements

Practice Set

In this practice set, you will record customer activities for April 2012. Keep the following in mind:

- Unless otherwise instructed, accept all defaults on transactions, including default tax codes, default sales rates, and default terms.
- You will print sales invoices and reports in Step 2, so do not print transactions unless otherwise instructed and make sure all invoices are marked "***To be printed.***"

Begin by:

- Opening the software.
- Opening the **QB2012_Chp4_PracSet_Stud** data file. Add your initials to the end to the Company Name by clicking ***Company>>Company Information*** on the main menu. Click **OK** to save the changes.
- **Toggling the software to the PRO EDITION** by selecting ***File>>Toggle to Another Edition*** on the main menu and choosing **QuickBooks Pro** as the edition.

1. Record the following transactions.

2012

Apr 1	Record the following payments from customers: *(Note: If you select an invoice to pay before entering the amount, remember to click the option that turns off future messages and click Yes.)*
	Check number 6740 for $9,480.00 from Sallens Property Management, paying Invoices 1022 and 1029.
	Check number 2534 for $9,800.00 from O'Hara Homes, paying Invoice 1033.
Apr 2	Create Invoice 1036 for $4,560.00 to O'Hara Homes for the Redesign Gardens by selecting the time tickets dated March 19 to March 23. **Mark the To be printed option.** *(Note: When the Billable Time/Costs window opens, click the Save this as a preference option and click OK.)*

2012	
Apr 5	Create the following invoices. Invoice 1037 for $882.00, with tax, to Ashford Hill Apartments by transferring time tickets dated March 21 to March 23. Invoice 1038 for $8,415.00 to Silver Homes by transferring all time tickets and all job materials on the Items tab.
Apr 7	Record the following payments from customers: Check number 2518 for $2,352.00 from Ashford Hill Apartments, paying Invoices 1024 and 1031. Check number 955 for $465.00 from DBH Enterprises, paying Invoice 1025.
Apr 9	Record check number 7577 for $1,630.00 from Sugar Hill Tennis Club, paying Invoices 1023.
Apr 10	Prepare credit memo number 1039 for $100.00 issued to Pleasantdale Luxury Apartments for 2 hours of INSTL LAND–COMMERCIAL. Apply the credit to Invoice 1027. **Print the credit memo.**
Apr 13	Prepare the following invoices: Invoice 1040 for $1,764.00, with tax, to DBH Enterprises by transferring all time tickets. Invoice 1041 to for $10,502.50 to O'Hara Homes for the Redesign Gardens job by transferring all time tickets and all job material costs.
Apr 21	Record the following payments from customers: Check number 470 for $1,446.50 from Pleasantdale Luxury Apartments, paying Invoice 1027. Check number 2363 for $21,826.00 from Sycamore Homes, paying Invoice 1035. Check number 6725 for $1,324.25 from Sugar Hill Tennis Club, paying Invoice 1030.

2012

Apr 23 Prepare invoice 1042 for $2,569.25 to White and Associates for all job material costs.

Apr 26 Create the following new customer and job.

Customer information

Jordan Industries
575 N. Main Street
Arlington, VA 30022

Customer Type:	Commercial
Payment Terms:	Net 30 Days
Tax Code:	Tax
Tax Item:	VA SALES TAX
Credit Limit:	$10,000

Job information

Status:	Awarded
Start:	5/1/2012
Description:	New deck
Job Type:	Construction

Apr 26 Record a sales receipt from Jordan Industries for the following item using the Enter Sales Receipts window. Make sure the payment will post to the Deposit To account of 10200 Regular Checking. **Print the receipt.**

Check number:	725 for $1,500.00
Item:	INSTL HARD – COMMERCIAL
Qty:	25

2. Print the following.

   a. Invoices 1036 through 1042. You can print by using ***File>>Print Forms>>Invoices*** on the main menu. If you do not have six invoices selected, totaling $28,692.75, cancel out of the window and return to the invoices to verify that all invoices are marked *To be printed*.

   b. Cash Receipts Journal for April 1 to April 30.

   c. Sales Journal for April 1 to April 30.

   d. Job Profitability Summary for January 1 to April 30.

e. A/R Aging Detail report at April 30.

f. Customer statement dated April 30 for DBH Enterprises showing all open transactions. (Note: Use the One Customer option under Select Customers.)

3. ***Back up the data file to a backup file named "QB2012_Chp4_PracSet_Stud_Completed."***

Internet Mini-Project

To complete this mini-project, go to the Website at ***www.pearsonhighered.com/brunsdon/*** and download the instruction file named **Cathy Gardens.pdf** and the data file named **Cathy Gardens.QBW**.

CHAPTER 5 VENDOR ACTIVITIES FOR A SERVICE-BASED BUSINESS

LEARNING OBJECTIVES

In this chapter, you process vendor activities, including placing orders for goods and services, recording vendor bills for goods and services, and remitting vendor payments. While performing these activities, you will:

1. Review the *MAPS* for vendor transactions before posting transactions in QBP
2. Learn to use the Vendor Center to manage vendor activities
3. Record vendor purchase orders and assign purchases to jobs
4. Correct a purchase order
5. Record vendor bills and receipts for items on purchase orders
6. Go *Behind the Keys* to view posted bills and receipts
7. Learn to correct bills and receipts
8. Record vendor bills for previously posted receipts
9. Learn to manage vendor accounts
10. Record vendor bills for expenses
11. Learn to memorize vendor bills
12. Pay vendors
13. Go *Behind the Keys* to view vendor payments
14. Learn to correct vendor payments
15. Learn to write checks without recording a vendor bill
16. Pay sales tax
17. Enter vendor credits
18. Prepare and analyze vendor reports and reconcile vendor activities to the general ledger

Begin by:

- Opening the software.
- Opening the **QB2012_Chp5_Stud** data file. Add your initials to the end to the Company Name by clicking ***Company>>Company Information*** on the main menu. Click **OK** to save the changes.
- **Toggling the software to the PRO EDITION** by selecting ***File>>Toggle to Another Edition*** on the main menu and choosing **QuickBooks Pro** as the edition.

MANUAL ACCOUNTING PROCEDURES

As in the previous chapter, you begin by learning the manual accounting procedures (*MAPS*) for vendor activities before posting transactions in QBP. These procedures help you learn to trace your transactions.

Before continuing it helps to explain that Astor sometimes uses a purchase order (PO) for ordering job materials. POs authorize purchases and document the price for the quantities ordered. An Astor employee, with authorization to order materials, creates and signs the PO before sending it to the vendor. Thereafter, either an employee will pick up the materials at the vendor's location or the vendor will deliver the materials to a job site.

The vendor's bill is normally included with the materials. This bill is forwarded to the accounting department. Before recording the bill, the accountant matches it with the PO. This matching process verifies that the purchase was authorized and confirms that billed quantities and prices equal PO terms.

On March 18, 2012, Seth Ruland issues a PO for materials to be used on a job for John Chester. He manually prepares the document, signs it, and faxes it to Clooney Chemical Supply. A copy of the PO is sent to Judy in accounting, who files the document for matching with the vendor bill. POs do not trigger accounting recognition because the liability does not occur until receipt of the materials.

On March 22, Jeff Henderson picks up the materials with the vendor bill. At the end of the day, the bill is dropped off to Judy in accounting. Judy matches the PO with the bill illustrated in Figure 5:1.

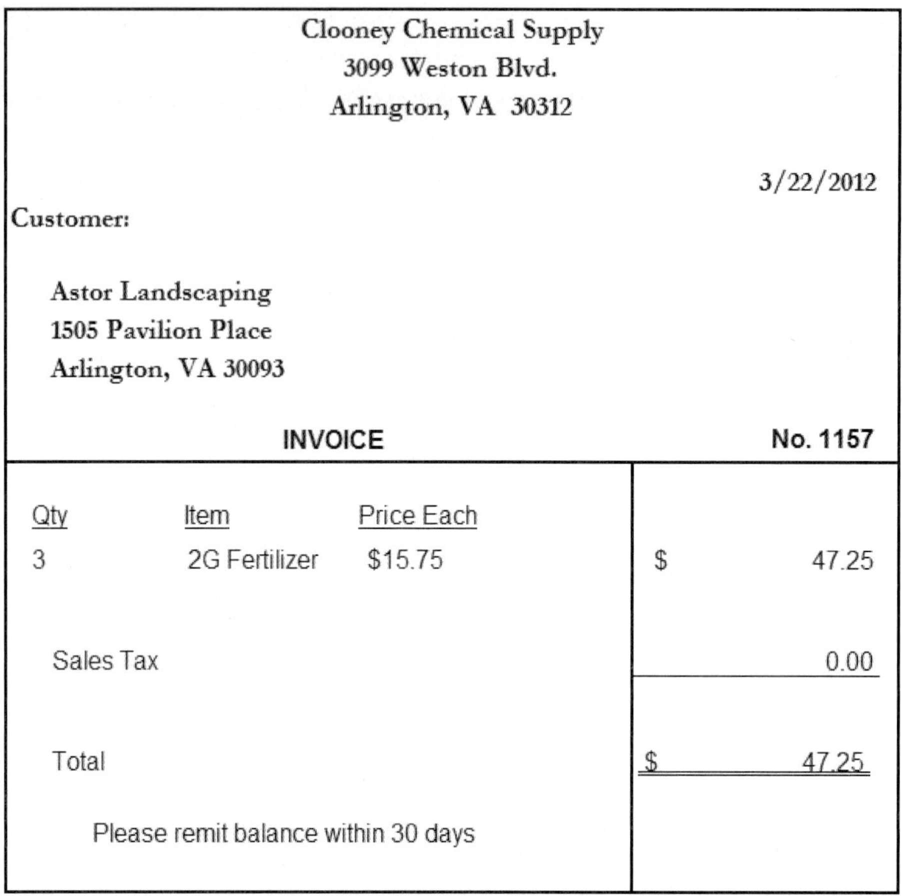

Clooney Chemical Supply
3099 Weston Blvd.
Arlington, VA 30312

3/22/2012

Customer:

Astor Landscaping
1505 Pavilion Place
Arlington, VA 30093

INVOICE No. 1157

Qty	Item	Price Each		
3	2G Fertilizer	$15.75	$	47.25
Sales Tax				0.00
Total			$	47.25

Please remit balance within 30 days

Figure 5:1

Judy then records the transaction on the Purchases Journal illustrated in Figure 5:2.

Astor Landscaping

Date: 3/22/2012 **Purchases Journal** **Page 5**

Vendor	Post Ref	Description	Accounts Payable (Credit)	Materials Cost Landscape (Debit)	Office Supplies Expense (Debit)	Utilities Expense (Debit)
Clooney Chemical	CLOO001	Maintenance Job INV 1157	47.25	47.25		
Georgia Gas Co.	GEOR002	March Utilities	143.17			143.17
Office Maxters	OFFI001	Office Supplies INV 7631	237.25		237.25	
Totals:			**$ 427.67**	**$ 47.25**	**$ 237.25**	**$ 143.17**
Acct Ref:			**(20000)**	**(51000)**	**(63000)**	**(71100)**

Audit Trail

Figure 5:2

Just like on the Sales Journal in Chapter 4, Judy totals journal columns and cross-foots totals to verify that entries balance (i.e., debits equal credits). Judy then posts each invoice to the vendor's account and posts column totals to the general ledger accounts listed at the bottom.

Judy's entry to Clooney's account is illustrated in Figure 5:3. *(Note: Entries for other vendor accounts are not illustrated.)*

Clooney Chemical Supply
3099 Weston Blvd. ***Audit Trail***
Arlington, Va 30312 Acct No: CLOO001

Date	Description	Post Ref	Debit	Credit	Balance
3/1/2012	Beginning Balance				0.00
3/22/2012	John Chester Maintenance Job INV 1157	PJ 5		47.25	47.25

Figure 5:3

Judy's entries to general ledger accounts are illustrated in Figure 5:4. *(Note: The entry for utilities is not shown.)*

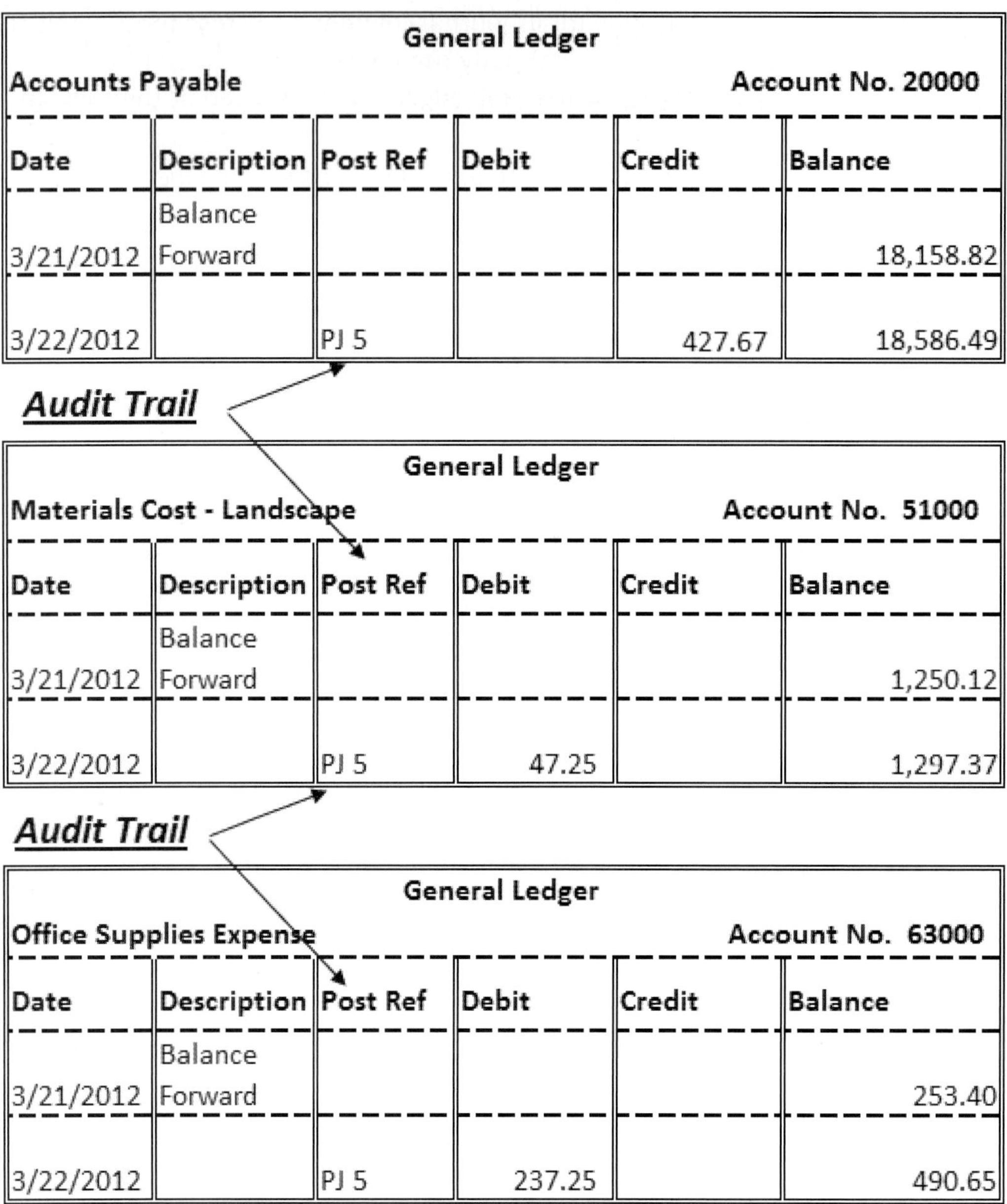

General Ledger

Accounts Payable — Account No. 20000

Date	Description	Post Ref	Debit	Credit	Balance
3/21/2012	Balance Forward				18,158.82
3/22/2012		PJ 5		427.67	18,586.49

General Ledger

Materials Cost - Landscape — Account No. 51000

Date	Description	Post Ref	Debit	Credit	Balance
3/21/2012	Balance Forward				1,250.12
3/22/2012		PJ 5	47.25		1,297.37

General Ledger

Office Supplies Expense — Account No. 63000

Date	Description	Post Ref	Debit	Credit	Balance
3/21/2012	Balance Forward				253.40
3/22/2012		PJ 5	237.25		490.65

Figure 5:4

On a different day, Judy reviews vendor bills and prepares checks for bills that are due. Judy also prepares a check to buy postage. These checks are recorded in the Cash Disbursements Journal illustrated in Figure 5:5.

Astor Landscaping						
Date: 3/25/2012			**Cash Disbursements Journal**			**Page 7**
Vendor	**Check No.**	**Post Ref**	**Invoice No.**	**Regular Checking (Credit)**	**Accounts Payable (Debit)**	**Postage (Debit)**
Neighbors Telephone	440	PAIN001	March Phone	262.43	262.43	
Calvert Stone	441	CALV001	32532	4,937.35	4,937.35	
Clooney Chemical	442	CLOO001	1062	10.00	10.00	
Postage	443	POST001	March Postage	150.00		150.00
Totals:				**$ 5,359.78**	**$ 5,209.78**	**$ 150.00**
Acct Ref:				**(10200)**	**(20000)**	**(63100)**

Audit Trail

Figure 5:5

Like in the Purchases Journal, columns are totaled and cross-footed. Each check is then posted to a vendor account and column totals are posted to general ledger accounts. This time, Judy will use CDJ (Cash Disbursements Journal) along with the page number as the posting reference. *(Note: These postings are not illustrated.)*

As discussed in Chapter 4, the manual method is fraught with opportunities to make posting errors. Judy could enter an amount incorrectly, post an entry backwards, or forget to post it altogether.

With an understanding of *MAPS* for vendor activities, you are now ready to use QBP for recording vendor transactions. The topic that follows will introduce you to the center focused on these activities.

Vendor Center

The Vendor Center is for vendor activities. Click **Vendors** on the **Home** page to open this center (Figure 5:6) and set the options illustrated.

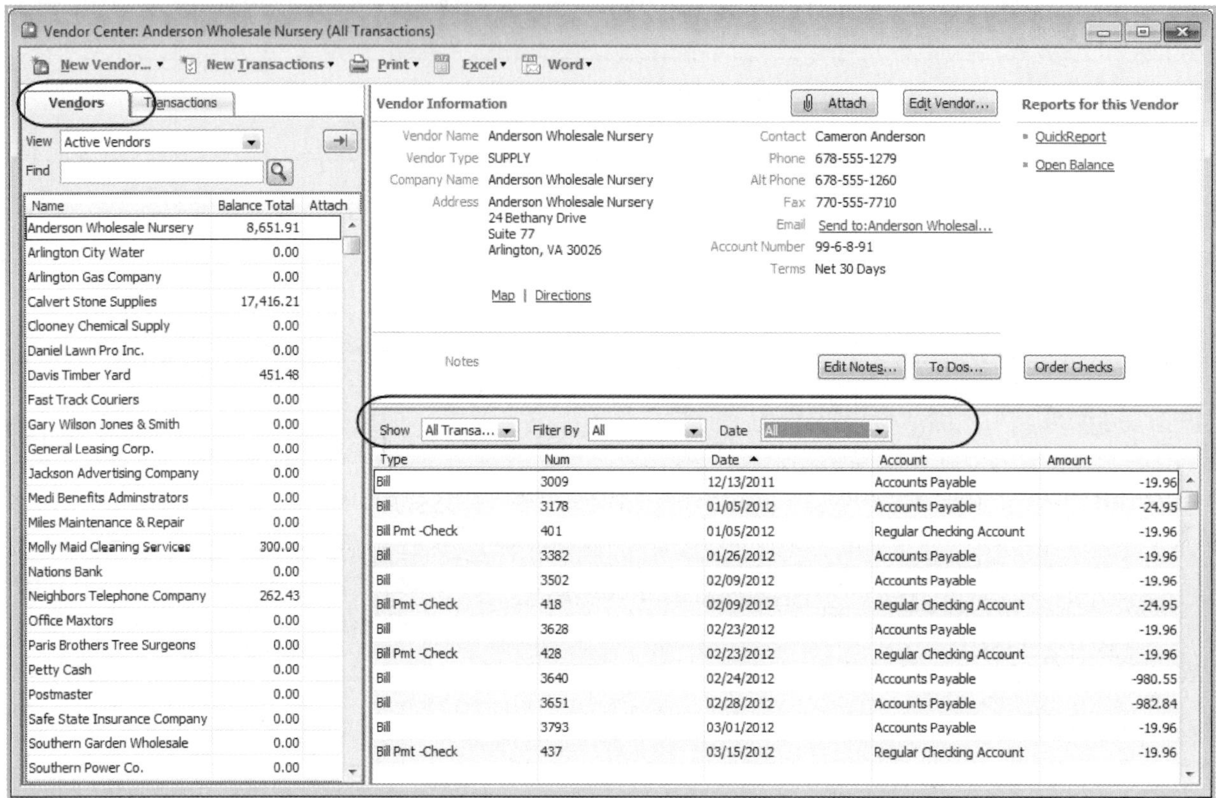

Figure 5:6

The **Vendors** tab lists transactions by vendor account. Astor's vendor accounts and balances appear to the left. The **View** option contains selections for viewing All Vendors, Active Vendors, or Vendors with Open Balances. You are currently viewing Active Vendors.

This [→|] button hides the Vendor Information pane shown to the right. After hiding, this [|←] button is located on the far right for redisplaying the information pane.

The **Vendor Information** pane displays transactions for the account highlighted on the left. This account is currently Anderson Wholesale Nursery.

The **Edit Vendor** button is used to edit Anderson's account information. The **Edit Notes** button is for entering account notes. There are also hyperlinks for creating **Reports for this Vendor**.

Anderson's transactions are listed at the bottom of its account information. The filtering options of **Show**, **Filter By**, and **Date** determine the transactions listed. Click ⌄ to access an option's dropdown list for changing selections. You are currently viewing **All Transactions** for **All Dates**. *(Note: Remember, if using fiscal year as the date then this is based on your computer date.)*

Filtering options work as follows:

- ❖ Show: Select the transaction type to display
- ❖ Filter By: Filtering criteria for the type
- ❖ Date: List all transactions for the type or only transactions recorded as of a specific date or range of dates

Now turn your attention to activities that can be performed while the Vendor tab is active. These activities are **New Vendor**, **New Transactions**, **Print**, **Excel**, and **Word**.

Each activity has this ▾ button for choosing a specific task. The table that follows discusses the tasks by activity. Most actions will operate on the vendor account highlighted on the left.

Vendors Activities	Tasks	Description
New Vendor	New Vendor and Add Multiple Vendors	Create a new vendor account or multiple vendor accounts.
New Transactions	Enter Bills	Record a vendor bill for the highlighted vendor.
	Pay Bills	Open a window to select vendor bills to pay.
	Purchase Orders	Create a purchase order for the highlighted vendor.
	Receive Items and Enter Bill	Receive and enter bill for items on a PO issued to the highlighted vendor.
	Receive Items	Receive, without entering a bill, the items on a PO issued to the highlighted vendor.
	Enter Bill for Received Items	Enter a bill for a receipt from the highlighted vendor.

Vendors Activities	**Tasks**	**Description**
Print	Vendor List	Print a vendor list with balances. The report cannot be customized, so this report is usually printed from the Reports menu.
	Vendor Information	Print account information and notes for the highlighted vendor The report cannot be customized, so this report is usually printed from the Reports menu.
	Vendor Transaction List	Print the highlighted vendor's transactions for the current fiscal year. The report cannot be customized, so this report is usually printed from the Reports menu.
Excel	Export Vendor List	Create an Excel workbook or comma separated values (.csv) file containing all vendor information along with account balances.
	Export Transactions	Create an Excel workbook or comma separated values (.csv) file containing current fiscal year transactions for the highlighted vendor.
	Import from Excel and Paste from Excel	Import or paste vendor information or transactions from an Excel workbook or comma separated values (.csv) file.
Word		Create form letters for communicating with a vendor.

Next, turn your attention to the **Transactions** tab, which lists transactions by type instead of transactions by vendor. Click to activate the tab illustrated in Figure 5:7.

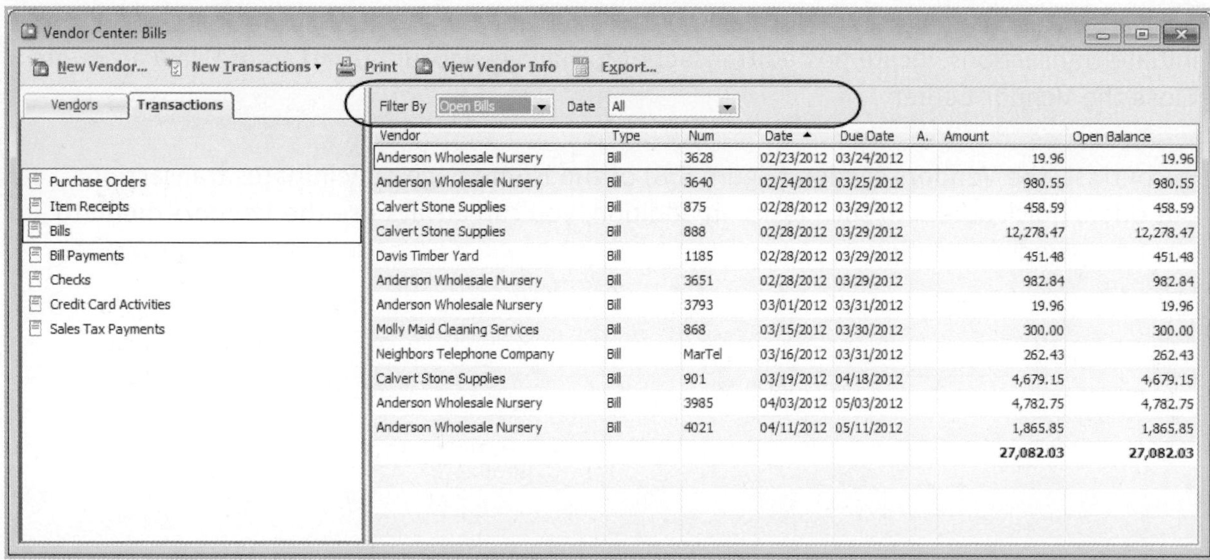

Figure 5:7

Transaction types are chosen on the left. Click **Bills** and then use the dropdown list on **Filter By** to select **Open Bills** and the dropdown on **Date** to select **All**. Your center now matches the illustration in Figure 5:7. You can sort the list by clicking a column name.

Activities that can be performed from this tab are different from activities performed on the previous tab. First, only the New Transactions activity offers multiple tasks so, clicking other activities immediately opens the task. The following table discusses activities on this tab.

Transactions Activities	Description
New Vendor	Create a new vendor account.
New Transactions	Contains the same tasks as the Vendors tab but the user must select the customer.
Print	Print the transactions listed to the right.
View Vendor Info	Edit the vendor account associated with the transaction highlighted on the right.
Export	Create an Excel workbook or comma separated values (.csv) file containing transactions listed on the right.

This illustrates that you can perform a variety of activities from the **Vendor Center**. You can initiate transactions, locate posted transactions, manage accounts, and create new accounts. Close the Vendor Center.

In contrast, the **Vendors** section (Figure 5:8) of the **Home** page only initiates transactions, but offers quick access to such tasks. In addition, you can always use the ***Vendors*** menu to per form vendor activities.

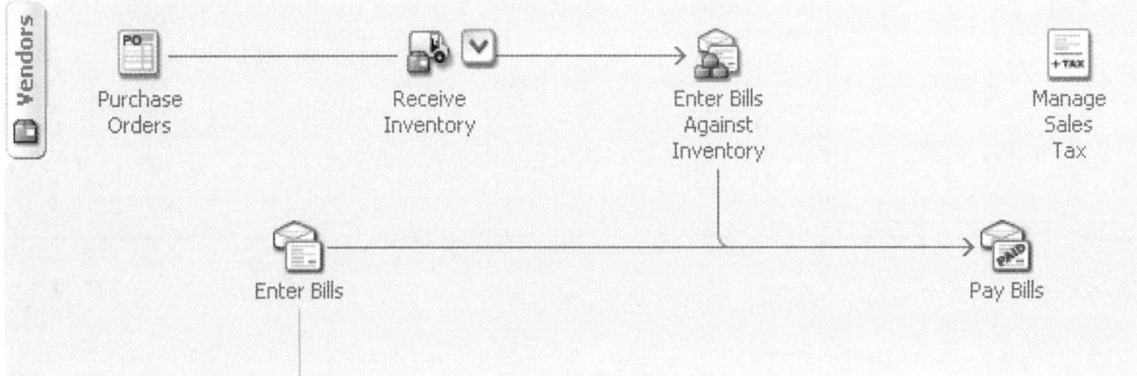

Figure 5:8

Now that you are familiar with locating vendor activities, let us begin recording vendor transactions. Close the Vendor Center.

PURCHASE ORDERS

As previously discussed, POs authorize vendor purchases. Recall from the *MAPS* topic that Seth created a PO for John Chester's landscape maintenance job. Follow the next steps to capture the transaction in QBP.

STEPS TO CREATE A PURCHASE ORDER

1. On the **Home** page, click the **Purchase Orders** icon to open Figure 5:9. Hide the History pane.

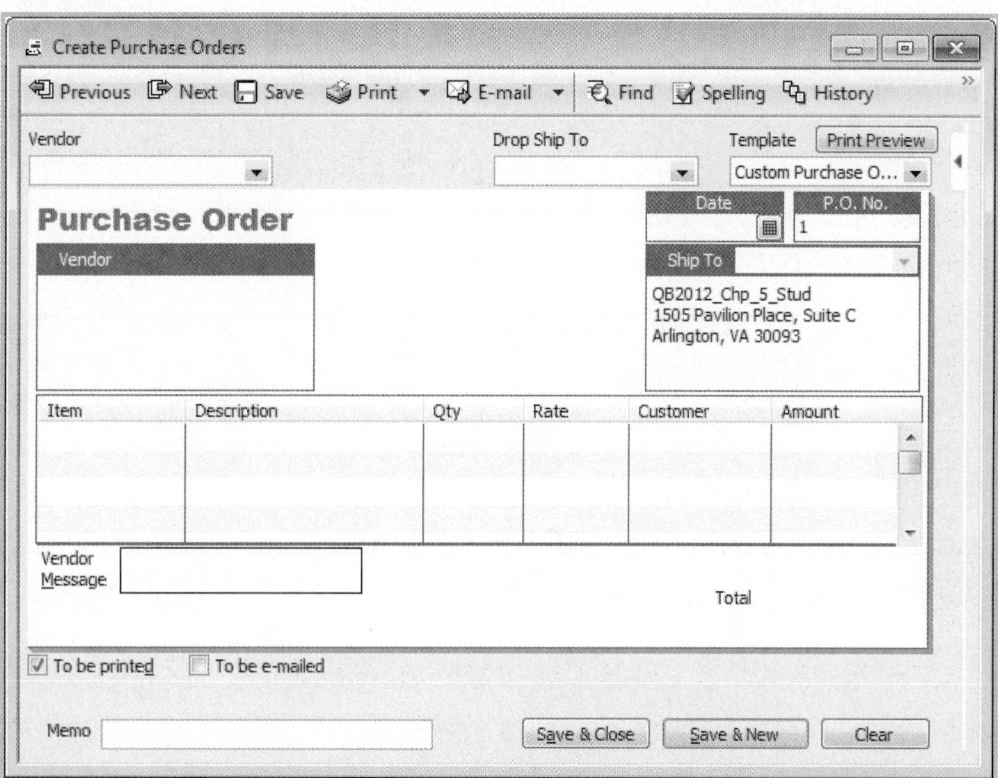

Figure 5:9

2. In **Vendor**, look up and select "Clooney Chemical Supply." Leave **Drop Ship To** empty because an Astor employee will pick up the order. Enter "3/18/12" in the **Date** field and "180" in the **P.O. No.** field.

3. In **Item**, look up and select "FERTILIZER." Tab to **Qty** and enter "3" into the field. For **Customer**, look up and select "Chester, John" to assign this cost to the job.

   Figure 5:10 shows the completed PO.

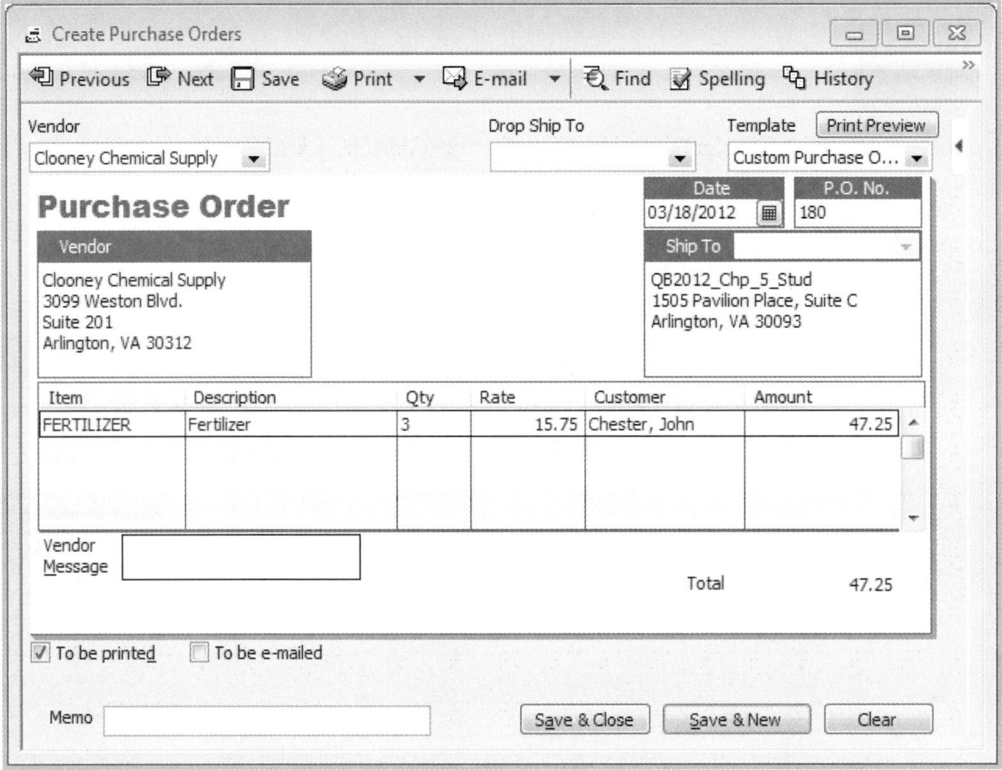

Figure 5:10

4. Click the look up on **Print** and select **Preview**. When prompted with information on shipping labels, select the option to turn off future messages and click **OK**.

   Figure 5:11 shows the previewed PO.

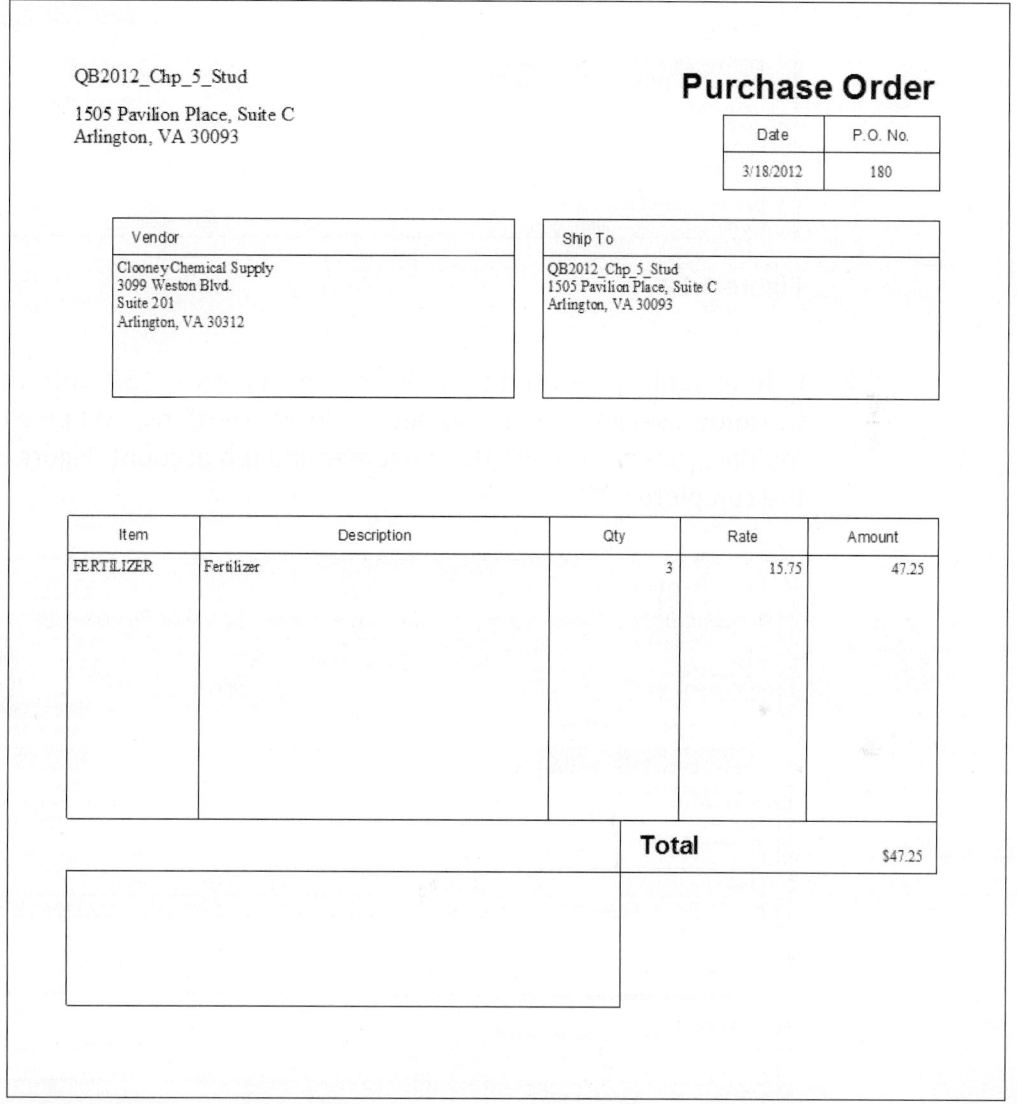

QB2012_Chp_5_Stud

1505 Pavilion Place, Suite C
Arlington, VA 30093

Purchase Order

Date	P.O. No.
3/18/2012	180

Vendor	Ship To
CloneyChemical Supply 3099 Weston Blvd. Suite 201 Arlington, VA 30312	QB2012_Chp_5_Stud 1505 Pavilion Place, Suite C Arlington, VA 30093

Item	Description	Qty	Rate	Amount
FERTILIZER	Fertilizer	3	15.75	47.25
			Total	$47.25

Figure 5:11

5. Click **Print** to send the order to the default printer.

   Note: When you want to select a different printer, click Close to exit the preview window and click Print on the transaction window.

6. Click **Save & New** and click **Yes** to save the changes. *(Note: The change occurred because QBP removed the checkmark from To be printed.)*

7. Enter the information shown in Figure 5:12.

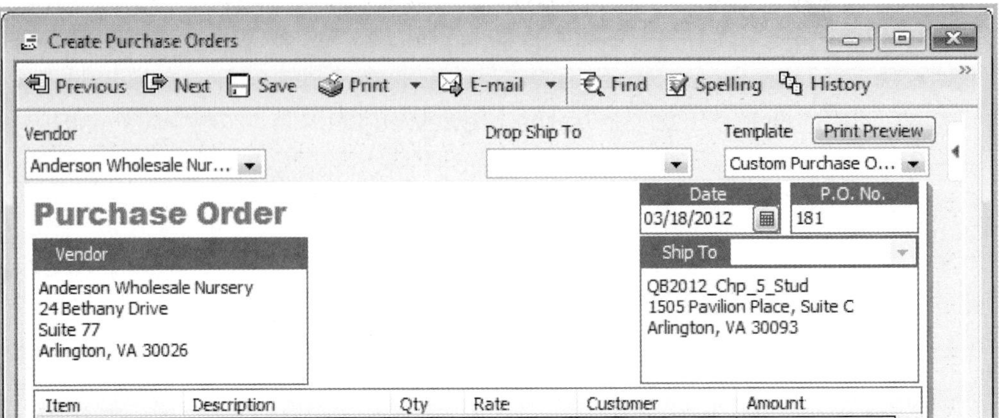

Figure 5:12

8. In **Item**, look up and select "PAVERS." In **Qty**, enter "50" into the field. In **Customer**, select "O'Hara Homes: Redesign Gardens." When a customer has multiple jobs, you select the customer and job account. Figure 5:13 shows the completed PO.

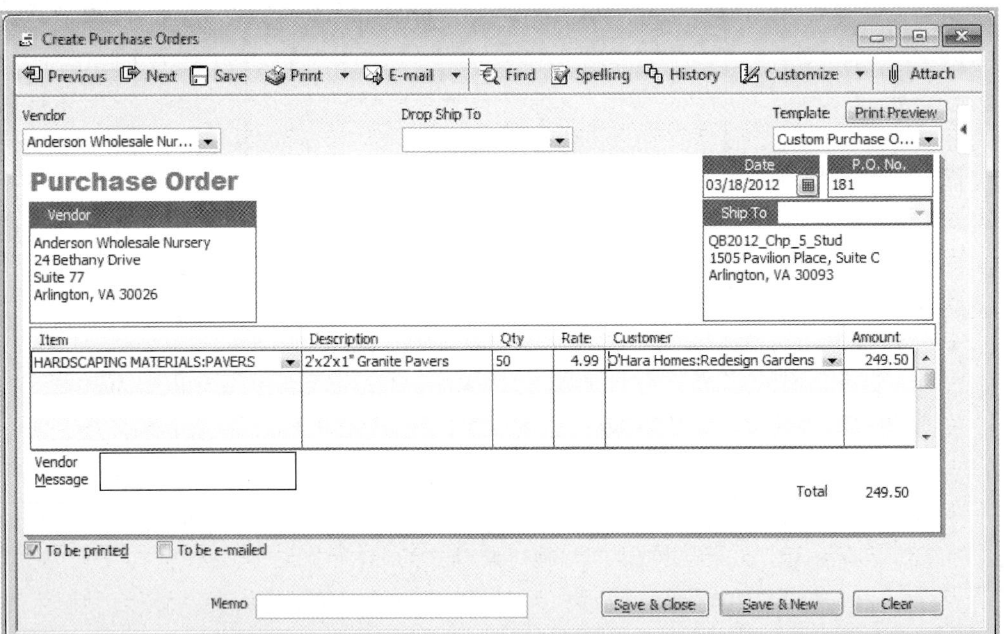

Figure 5:13

9. Click **Print**, select a printer, and click **Print** again.

10. Click **Save & Close** and click **Yes** to save the changes.

    POs do not post entries to the general ledger because POs are merely commitments to purchase. Accounting recognition occurs after receiving the items on the PO.

Correcting a Purchase Order

You can correct information for an item on a PO as long as the items have not been received.

First, locate the PO using the **Vendor Center**. Click **Vendors** on the **Home** page to open the center.

Next, select the **Transactions** tab and click **Purchase Orders** on the left.

Finally, locate **Clooney Chemical's** transaction on the right and double click to reopen (Figure 5:14). Notice that after saving the PO, QBP added the **Rcv'd** and **Clsd** columns.

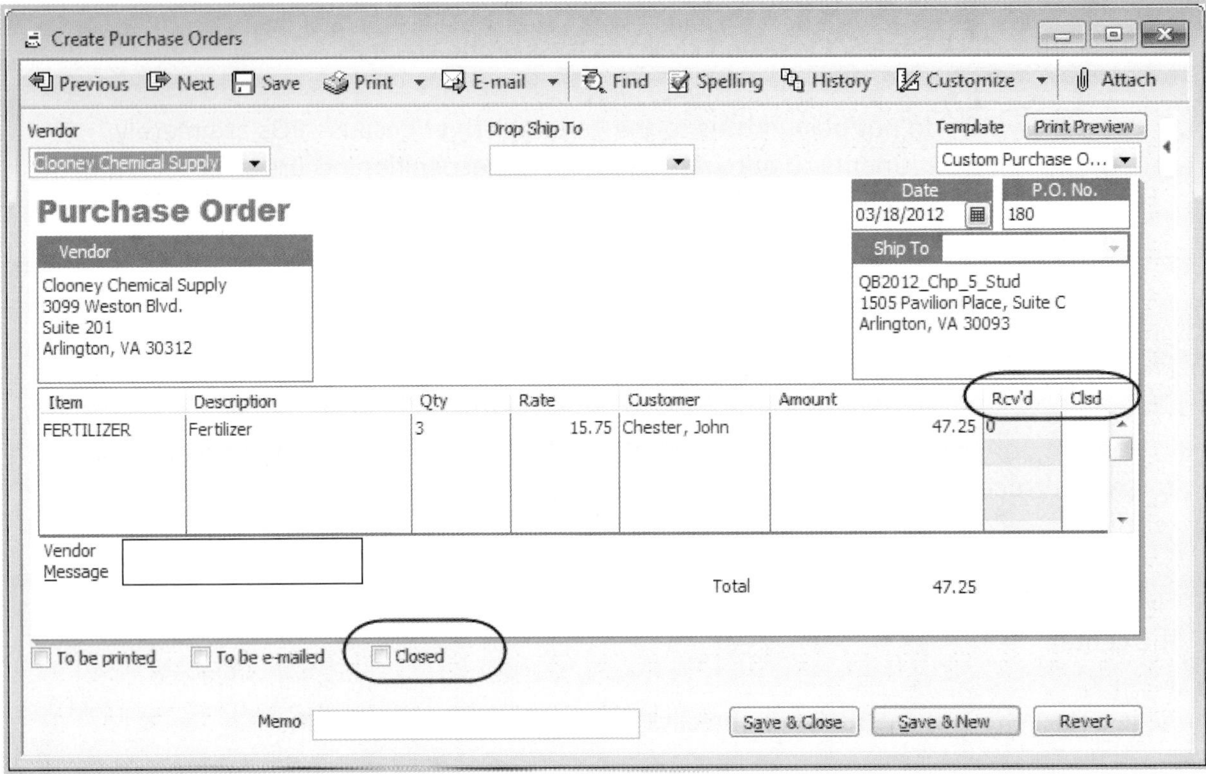

Figure 5:14

The **Rcv'd** field stores the quantity received for each line item. When all quantities on a line item have been received, QBP marks the line item as **Clsd.**

Notice that there is also a **Closed** option for the entire PO located at the bottom. QBP marks this option after receiving all line items in full.

As long as all line items remain open, you can change information and even delete the PO. If needed, POs are deleted by using ***Edit>>Delete Purchase Order*** on the main menu.

Click **X** to exit the PO window. Now try the next exercise.

ENTER PURCHASE ORDERS

On March 23, 2012, Astor issued the following POs for items needed to complete Sugar Hill Tennis Club's landscape job. Two POs were required because items were ordered from separate vendors. Enter the POs and exit the transaction window. Remember to use correct transaction dates and verify that POs are marked **To be printed**.

PO 182 for $199.60, issued to Calvert Stone Supplies for the following billable materials.

Item	Qty	Rate	Customer
Mulch	40	$ 4.99	Sugar Hill Tennis Club

PO 183 for $764.60, issued to Southern Garden Wholesale for the following billable materials.

Item	Qty	Rate	Customer
Boxwood	30	$ 22.49	Sugar Hill Tennis Club
Azalea Amy	10	$ 8.99	Sugar Hill Tennis Club

Print the POs by selecting ***File>>Print Forms>>Purchase Orders*** on the main menu. When the window illustrated in Figure 5:15 opens, POs are selected and ready for printing. Click **OK**, choose a printer, and then click **Print**. After printing, click **OK** to close the confirmation window.

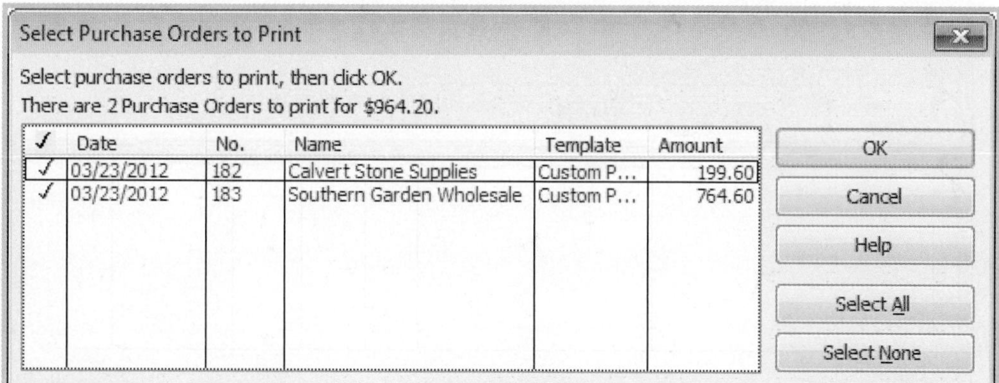

Figure 5:15

VENDOR BILLS AND RECEIPTS FOR PURCHASE ORDERS

From the *MAPS* topic, you will recall that Jeff picked up the chemicals along with the vendor bill from Clooney Chemical Supply on March 22. Jeff then turned the bill over to Judy, who matched it with the PO before posting the bill to the Purchases Journal.

Judy now performs this matching process as she enters the vendor bill. Follow the next instructions to record the bill from Clooney Chemical Supply.

Note: There is an online video for this topic.

STEPS TO RECORD A VENDOR BILL FOR ITEMS ON A PURCHASE ORDER

1. On the **Home** page, click **Receive Inventory** and choose **Receive Inventory with Bill** to open the window illustrated in Figure 5:16. Hide the History pane.

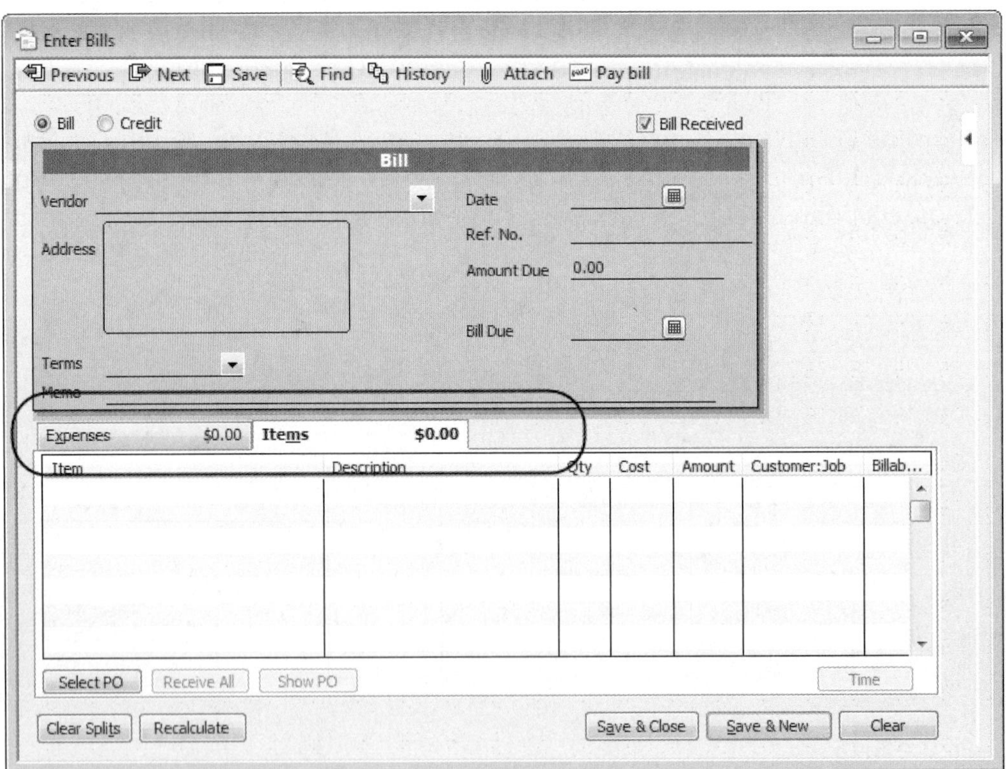

Figure 5:16

Notice that there are two tabs. The **Expenses** tab is used for non-inventory purchases such as utility and insurance bills. The **Items** tab is for recording inventory purchases.

2. In **Vendor**, look up and select "Clooney Chemical Supply." Click **Yes** when QBP prompts to receive against the PO.

3. In the window that opens (Figure 5:17), click **PO No 180** and click **OK**.

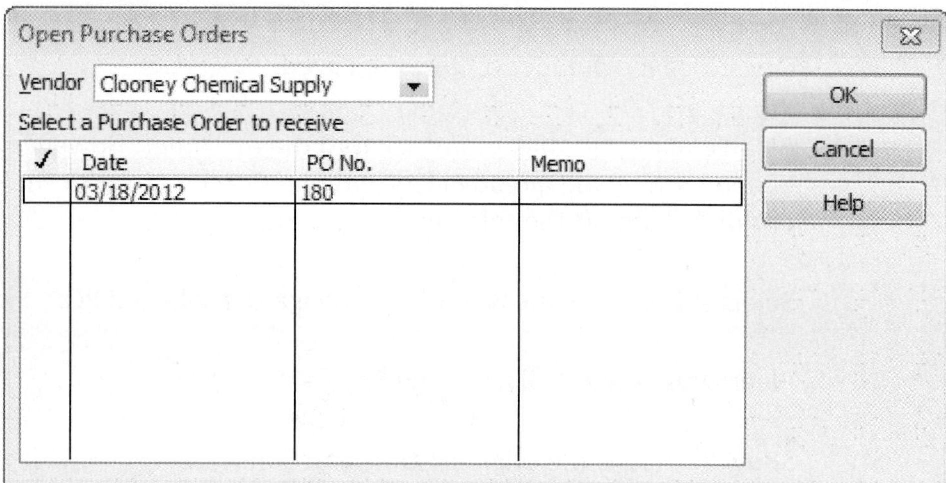

Figure 5:17

4. Change the **Date** to "3/22/12." Enter Clooney's invoice number "78265" into the **Ref. No.** field. Figure 5:18 shows the bill thus far.

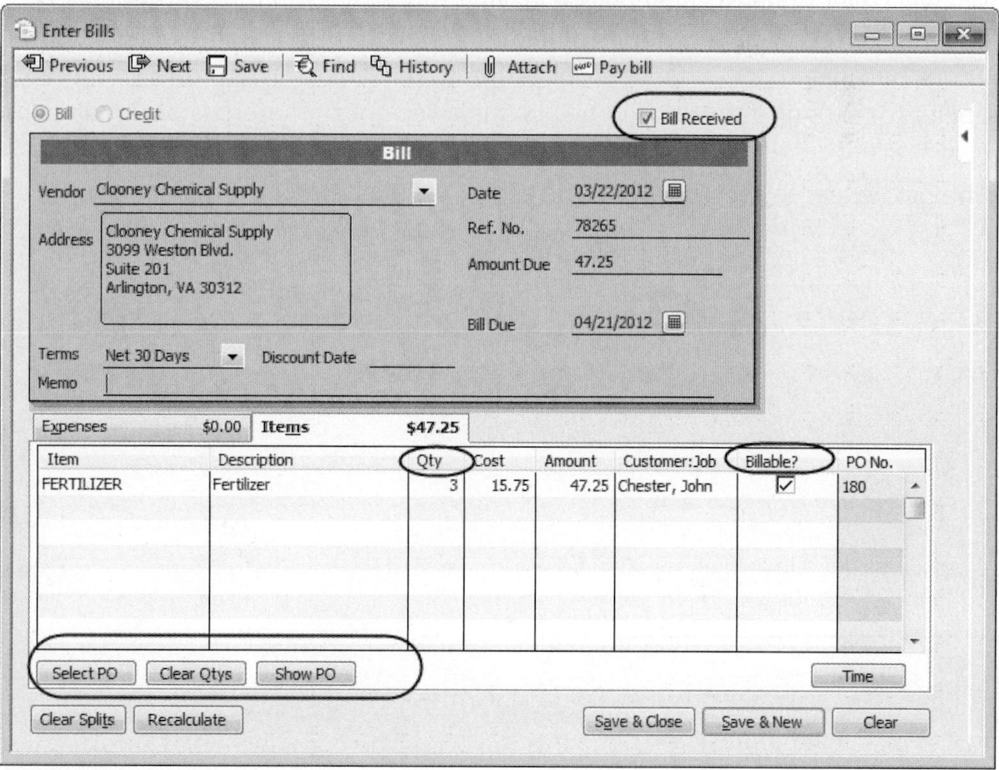

Figure 5:18

5. Before saving, review the following fields on this transaction.

   Bill Received, when marked, means that this transaction records a vendor bill for the PO. In the next exercise, you will unmark this field to record a vendor receipt.

   Qty stores the number of items received.

   Billable marks this bill for invoicing to the customer. However, recall in Chapter 4 that you already invoiced John Chester. So **click** the **Billable option** to turn off the selection.

   Select PO reopens the window to change the selected PO.

   Clear Qtys deletes values in the Qty field.

   Show PO opens the original PO transaction.

6. Click **Save & Close**.

We will cover one last thing before leaving this topic. You may sometimes receive items on a PO prior to receiving a vendor's bill. Remember that the liability occurs upon receipt of the goods because this is when the obligation to pay arises. Therefore, you need to have the ability to recognize the liability by posting a receipt of materials prior to receiving the bill.

The next exercise records a vendor receipt for PO items.

Steps to Record a Vendor Receipt for Items on a Purchase Order

1. Click **Receive Inventory** and this time select **Receive Inventory without Bill** to open Figure 5:19.

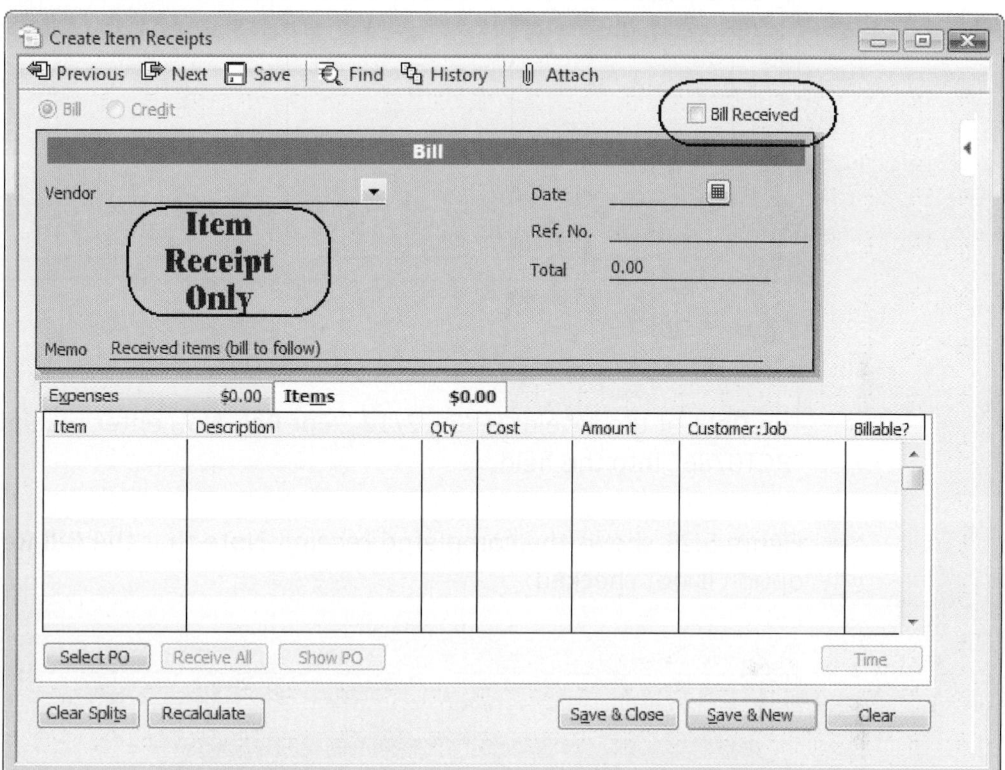

Figure 5:19

You will again find two tabs; however, this time the **Bill Received** option is not marked and the **Memo** states that this is a receipt with a bill to follow.

2. In **Vendor**, look up and select "Anderson Wholesale Nursery." Click **Yes** when QBP prompts to receive against the PO.

3. As shown in Figure 5:20 click **PO No 181** and then click **OK**.

Open Purchase Orders

Vendor Anderson Wholesale Nursery

Select a Purchase Order to receive

✓	Date	PO No.	Memo
✓	03/18/2012	181	

OK

Cancel

Help

Figure 5:20

4. The **Date** of the receipt is "3/22/12." For **Ref. No.**, enter receipt number "RCT0786" into the field.

   Figure 5:21 shows the completed receipt. Note that the **Bill Received** option is not checked.

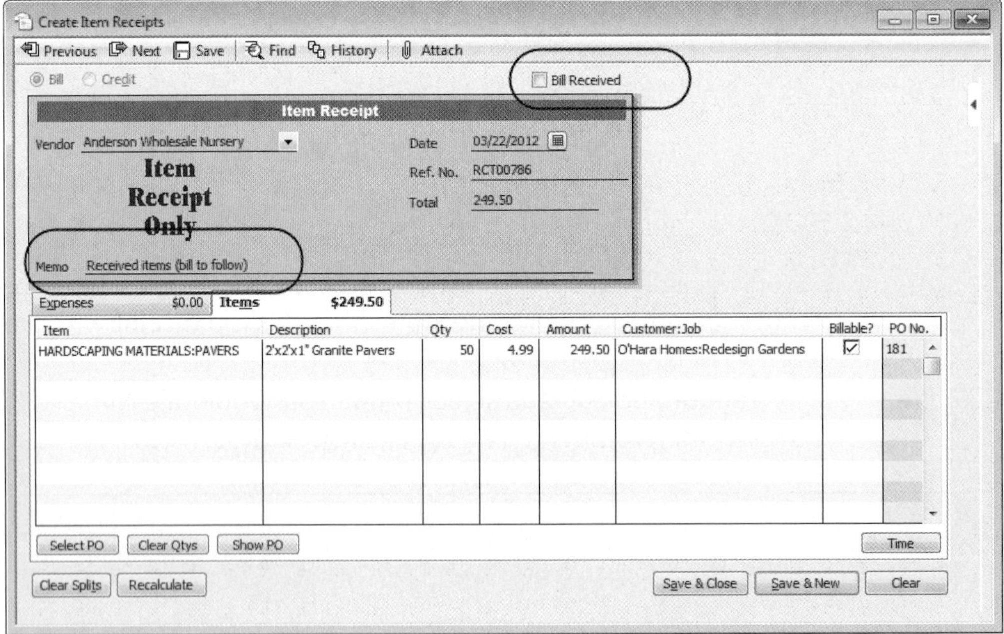

Figure 5:21

5. Click **Save & Close**.

Behind the Keys of a Posted Vendor Receipt and Bill

Transactions in the previous topic posted entries to the Purchases Journal, vendor accounts, and general ledger. Follow the next steps to trace those entries.

Steps to Trace the Entries for a Vendor Bill and a Vendor Receipt

1. First, open the Purchases Journal report by selecting ***Reports>>Memorized Reports>>Accounting Journals>>Purchases Journal*** on the main menu. Enter the date range of **3/22/12** through **3/22/12**.

   Figure 5:22 shows this report, listing only transactions with the "Bill" **Type**.

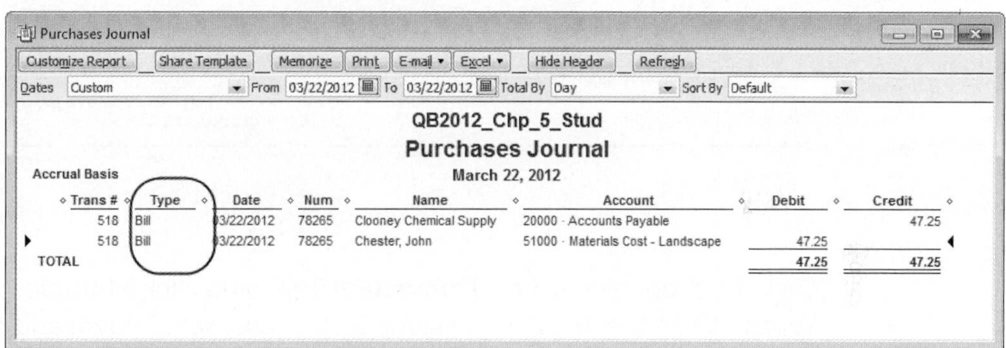

Purchases Journal

Customize Report | Share Template | Memorize | Print | E-mail | Excel | Hide Header | Refresh

Dates Custom From 03/22/2012 To 03/22/2012 Total By Day Sort By Default

QB2012_Chp_5_Stud

Purchases Journal

March 22, 2012

Accrual Basis

Trans #	Type	Date	Num	Name	Account	Debit	Credit
518	Bill	03/22/2012	78265	Clooney Chemical Supply	20000 · Accounts Payable		47.25
518	Bill	03/22/2012	78265	Chester, John	51000 · Materials Cost - Landscape	47.25	
TOTAL						47.25	47.25

Figure 5:22

Note: The vendor name prints next to the accounts payable entry whereas the customer job name prints next to the cost of goods sold entry. This makes it easier to recognize entries on the general ledger report.

2. Click **Customize Report** so we can add the "Item Receipt" **Type** to the report. Select the **Filters** tab and click **Transaction Type** under **Filter**.

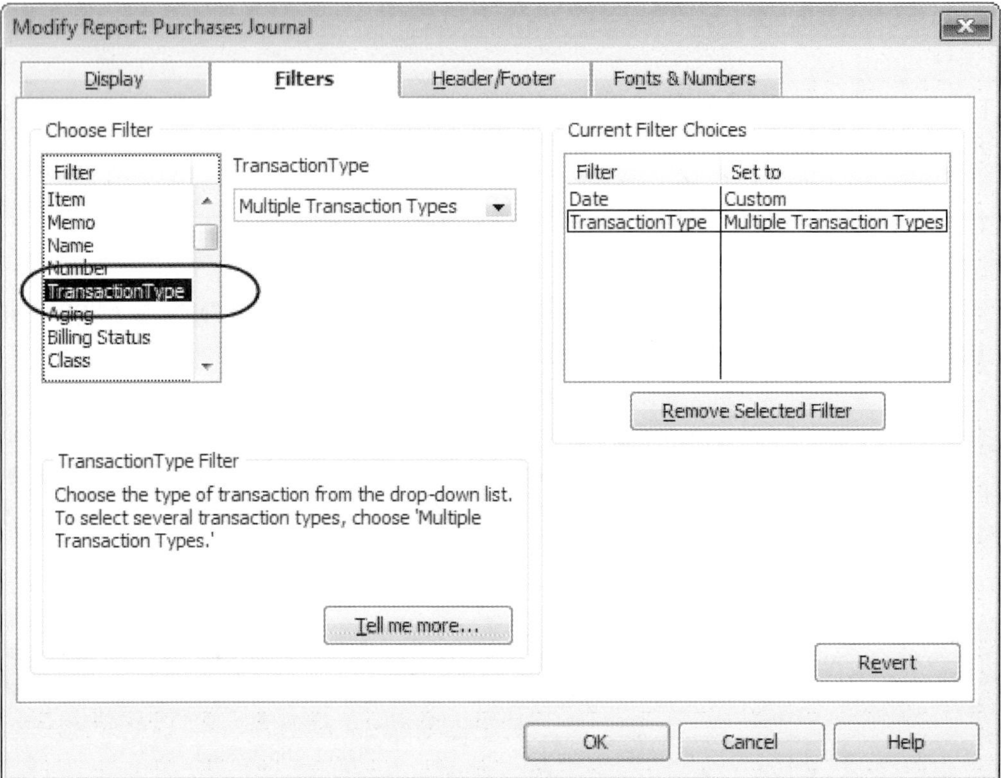

Figure 5:23

Click the dropdown list on **Transaction Type** and click **Multiple Transaction Types**. When the window in Figure 5:24 opens, scroll down and click **Item Receipt** to add it to the report.

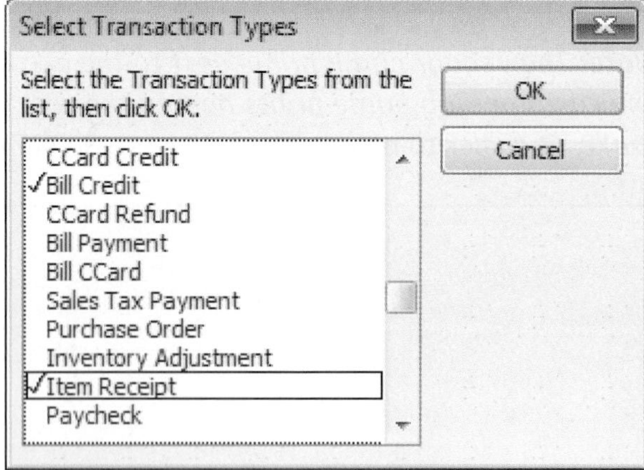

Figure 5:24

3. Click **OK** to close the selection window. Click **OK** on the modify report window and the report refreshes (Figure 5:25). Although Item Receipts posted to accounts payable, you cannot pay receipt transactions until the bill is posted.

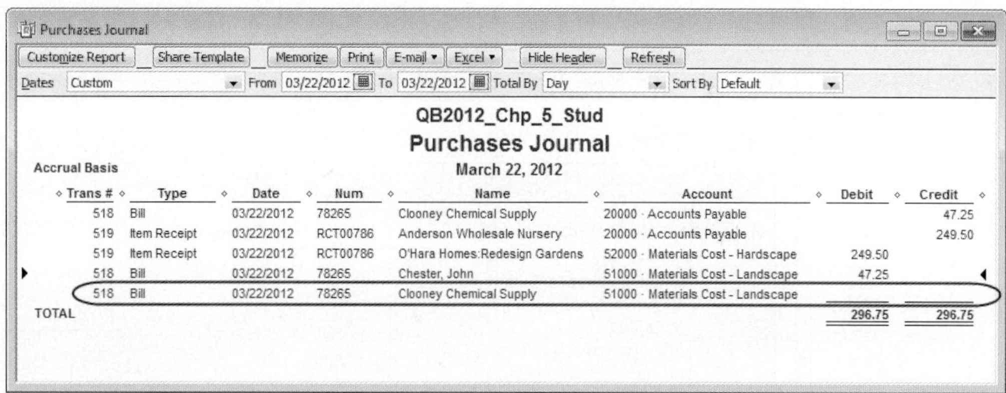

QB2012_Chp_5_Stud
Purchases Journal
Accrual Basis March 22, 2012

Trans #	Type	Date	Num	Name	Account	Debit	Credit
518	Bill	03/22/2012	78265	Clooney Chemical Supply	20000 · Accounts Payable		47.25
519	Item Receipt	03/22/2012	RCT00786	Anderson Wholesale Nursery	20000 · Accounts Payable		249.50
519	Item Receipt	03/22/2012	RCT00786	O'Hara Homes:Redesign Gardens	52000 · Materials Cost - Hardscape	249.50	
518	Bill	03/22/2012	78265	Chester, John	51000 · Materials Cost - Landscape	47.25	
518	Bill	03/22/2012	78265	Clooney Chemical Supply	51000 · Materials Cost - Landscape		
TOTAL						296.75	296.75

Figure 5:25

Notice that in our example the Clooney bill added an extra transaction line without a financial amount. We created this situation on purpose. Although this does not create a problem, it can be confusing if you cannot identify the source of the entry. We now explain why this occurred.

4. When we double click our Clooney transaction to reopen it and look at the **Expenses** tab, we find account 51000 Materials Cost – Landscape under Account. *(Note: This is for illustrative purposes only. Your transaction will not have this account present.)*

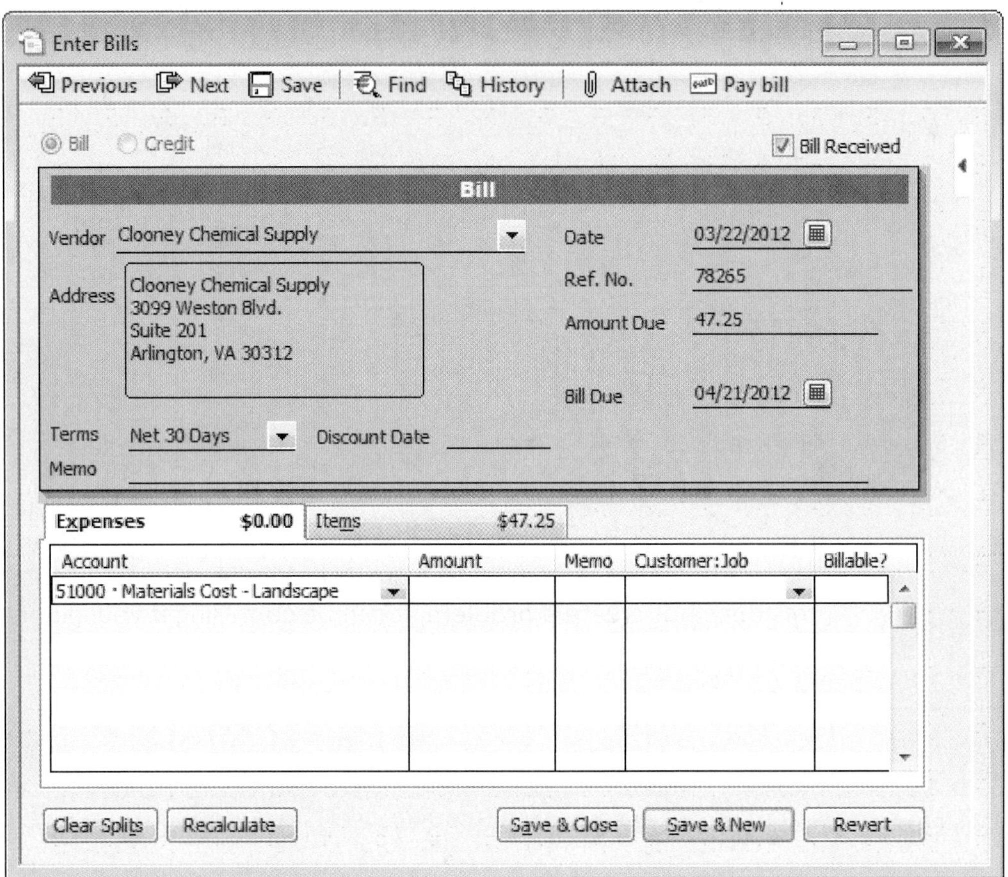

Figure 5:26

You will see later in the chapter that this tab is used to enter vendor expense bills. QBP will sometimes remember the general ledger accounts previously used on this tab. The presence of an account on the Expenses tab will cause a zero transaction line to post. The line item is removed by highlighting the account and pressing **Delete** on the keyboard.

The following explains turning off the account remember feature.

*The account "remember" feature is turned off by selecting **Edit>> Preferences** on the main menu and turning off the option illustrated in Figure 5:27. You do not need to do this.*

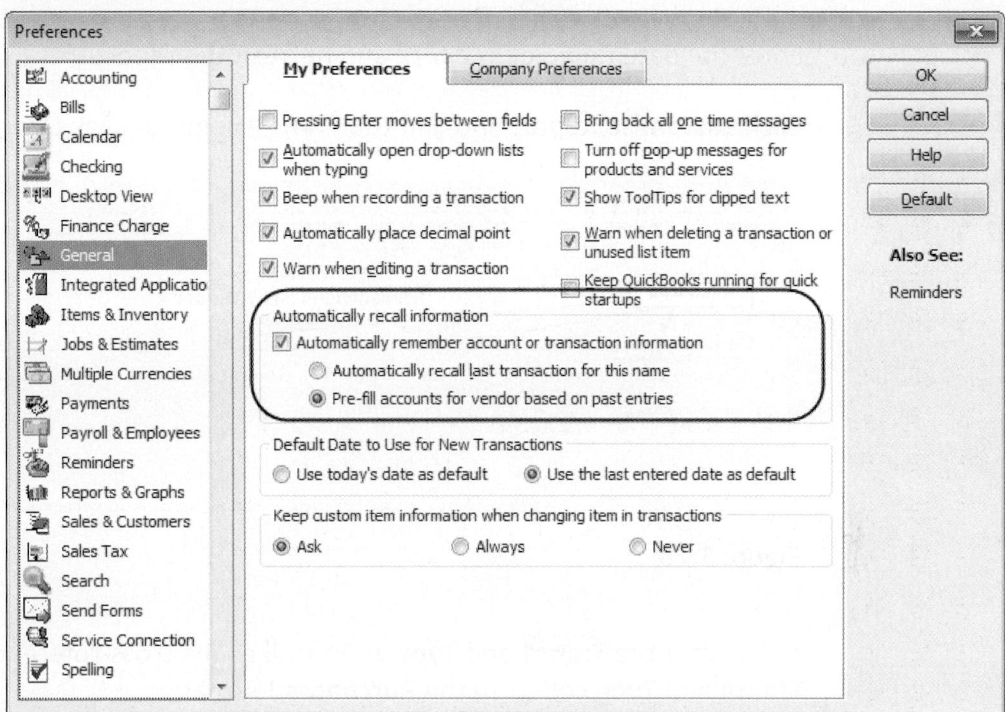

Figure 5:27

Before closing the Purchases Journal, click **Memorize** and click **Replace** to save the modified report. Click **X** to close the Purchases Journal.

5. Now trace entries posted to the vendor accounts.

   Select ***Reports>>Vendors & Payables>>Transaction List by Vendor*** on the main menu.

   Enter the date range of **3/22/12** and **Refresh** the report.

   Click **Customize Report** and add the **Trans #** column. Click **OK**.

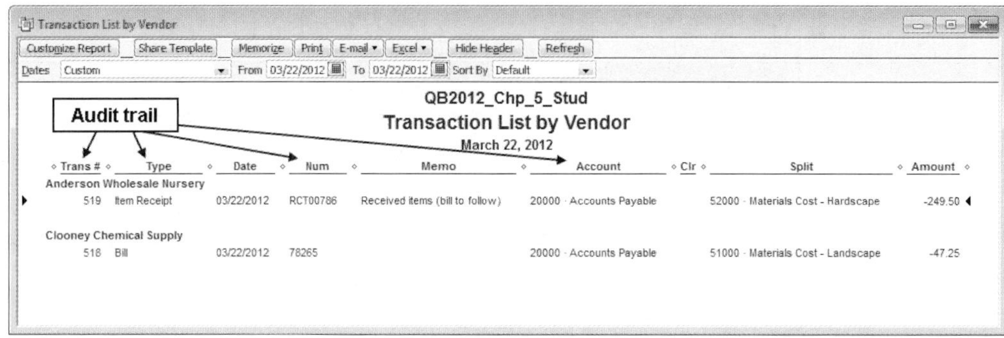

Figure 5:28

Notice that the **Trans#** and **Type** audit trail codes cross-reference to the **Trans#** and **Type** codes on the **Purchases Journal**.

Close this report.

6. Finally, verify QBP's entries to the general ledger.

Select ***Reports>>Memorized Reports>>Accounting Journals>>General Ledger Detail Report*** on the main menu.

Enter **3/22/12** as the date range. Click **Customize Report** and, on the **Filters** tab, set the **Transaction Type** to **Multiple Transaction Types** and choose the **Bill** and **Item Receipt** types. Click **OK** and **OK** to return to the report illustrated next.

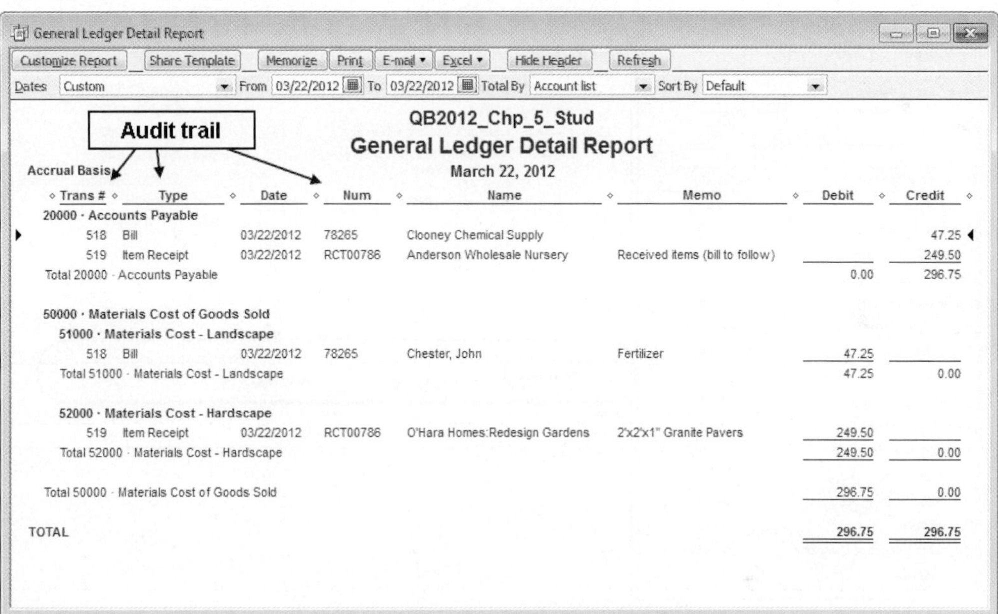

QB2012_Chp_5_Stud
General Ledger Detail Report
March 22, 2012

Accrual Basis

Trans #	Type	Date	Num	Name	Memo	Debit	Credit
20000 · Accounts Payable							
518	Bill	03/22/2012	78265	Clooney Chemical Supply			47.25
519	Item Receipt	03/22/2012	RCT00786	Anderson Wholesale Nursery	Received items (bill to follow)		249.50
Total 20000 · Accounts Payable						0.00	296.75
50000 · Materials Cost of Goods Sold							
51000 · Materials Cost - Landscape							
518	Bill	03/22/2012	78265	Chester, John	Fertilizer	47.25	
Total 51000 · Materials Cost - Landscape						47.25	0.00
52000 · Materials Cost - Hardscape							
519	Item Receipt	03/22/2012	RCT00786	O'Hara Homes:Redesign Gardens	2'x2'x1" Granite Pavers	249.50	
Total 52000 · Materials Cost - Hardscape						249.50	0.00
Total 50000 · Materials Cost of Goods Sold						296.75	0.00
TOTAL						296.75	296.75

Figure 5:29

In Figure 5:29, you finally see cost of goods sold entries. Recall when explaining service and non-inventory items in Chapter 4, we stated that service based businesses post cost of goods sold when paying employees and posting vendor bills and receipts.

Close the report when finished.

Correcting a Vendor Receipt or Bill

QBP permits modifying and deleting vendor receipts and bills. Use the **Vendor Center** to locate transactions. *Note: There is an online video for this topic.*

Open this center and, on the **Vendors** tab, highlight **Anderson Wholesale Nursery**. Filter to **Show Item Receipts** for **All** dates (Figure 5:30).

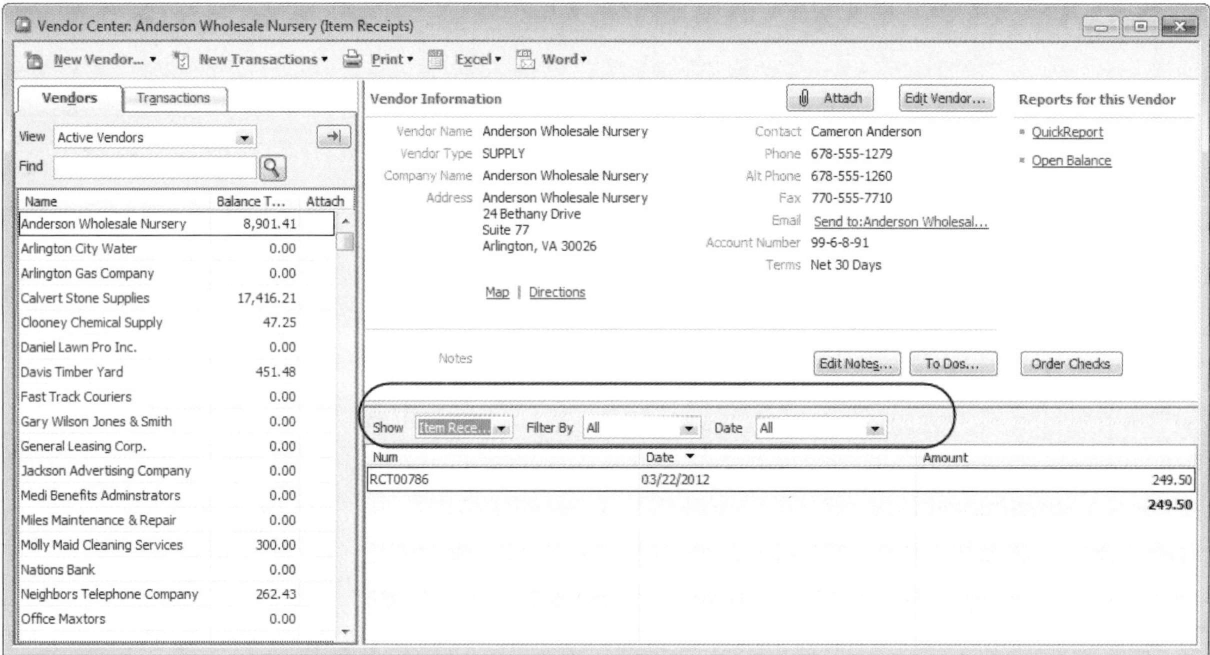

Figure 5:30

After reopening a receipt or bill, you can modify it and save the changes. You can also delete bills and receipts using ***Edit*** on the main menu. After deleting, QBP will reinstate any POs used to create the transaction so you can receive items again.

Caution: You should not modify or delete paid bills because the payment will no longer match the bill. Instead, void the payment and then delete the bill. We will show you how to void payments later in the chapter.

Remember Appendix B provides a complete set of instructions on correcting QBP transactions.

ENTER VENDOR RECEIPTS AND BILLS FOR PURCHASE ORDERS

On March 25, 2012, items were received on the following POs. Post the following transactions and click **Yes** if prompted to exceed a vendor's credit limit.

Bill: Calvert Stone Supplies Invoice 2346 for all items on PO 182.

Receipt: Southern Garden Wholesale Receipt RCT5132 for 30 Boxwoods on PO 183.

Print the Purchases Journal for March 25 and list both Bills and Item Receipts.

VENDOR BILLS FOR VENDOR RECEIPTS

You still need to post the vendor bill for Anderson Wholesale Nursery's receipt recorded on March 22. The following instructions show you the steps to turn a receipt into a bill so you can pay the vendor.

Note: There is an online video for this topic.

Steps to Record a Vendor Bill for a Receipt

1. On the **Home** page, click **Enter Bills Against Inventory**. As shown in Figure 5:31 look up and select **Anderson Wholesale Nursery**.

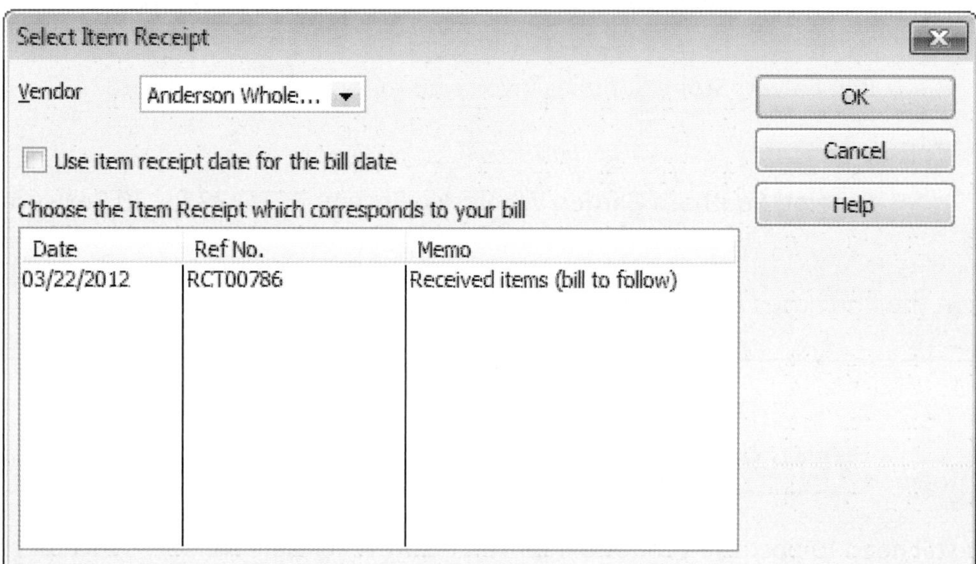

Figure 5:31

2. Highlight the receipt and click **OK**. Change the **Date** to "3/24/12" and enter "8213" as the **Ref. No.** Click **Save & Close** and click **Yes** to change the transaction.

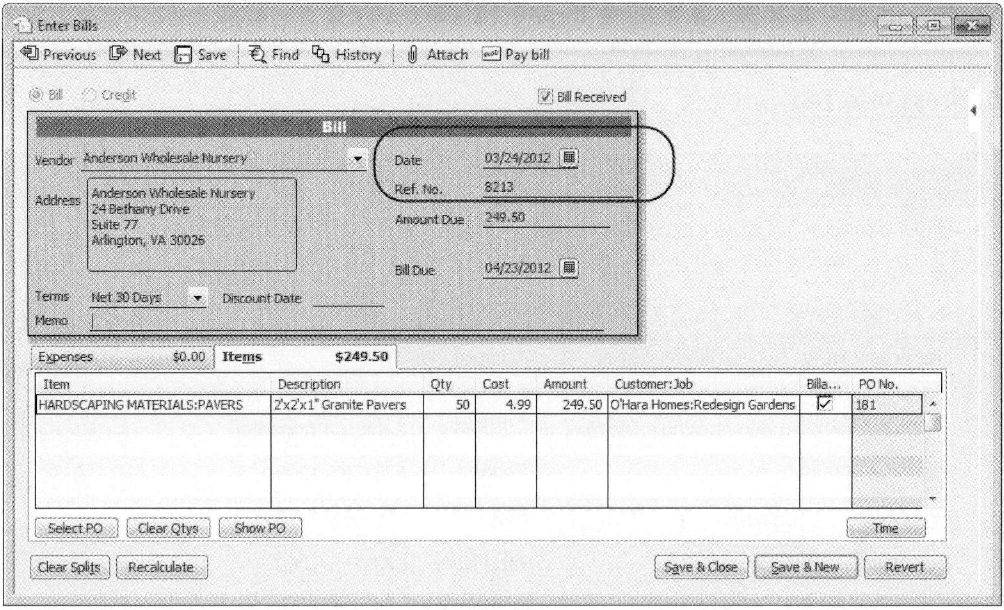

Figure 5:32

ENTER VENDOR BILL FOR VENDOR RECEIPT

The company received Invoice 7631, dated March 28, 2012, for $683.69 from Southern Garden Wholesale. The bill is for RCT5132.

This bill is for all the boxwoods and for one of the Amy Azaleas that was received since recording the vendor receipt. You need to add the Azaleas to the bill. Click the **Select PO** button in the Enter Bills window to open the PO. Click **OK** to add the line item to the bill. Change the **QTY** on the line item to 1. Also, change the **Amount Due** to match the bill from the vendor.

Print the Purchases Journal for March 28.

Vendor Accounts

This topic explains creating, editing, and deleting vendor accounts. Open the **Vendor Center**, select the **Vendors** tab, and double click **Anderson Wholesale Nursery** to open the account. Now follow below as we describe tabs on the vendor account.

Address Info Tab

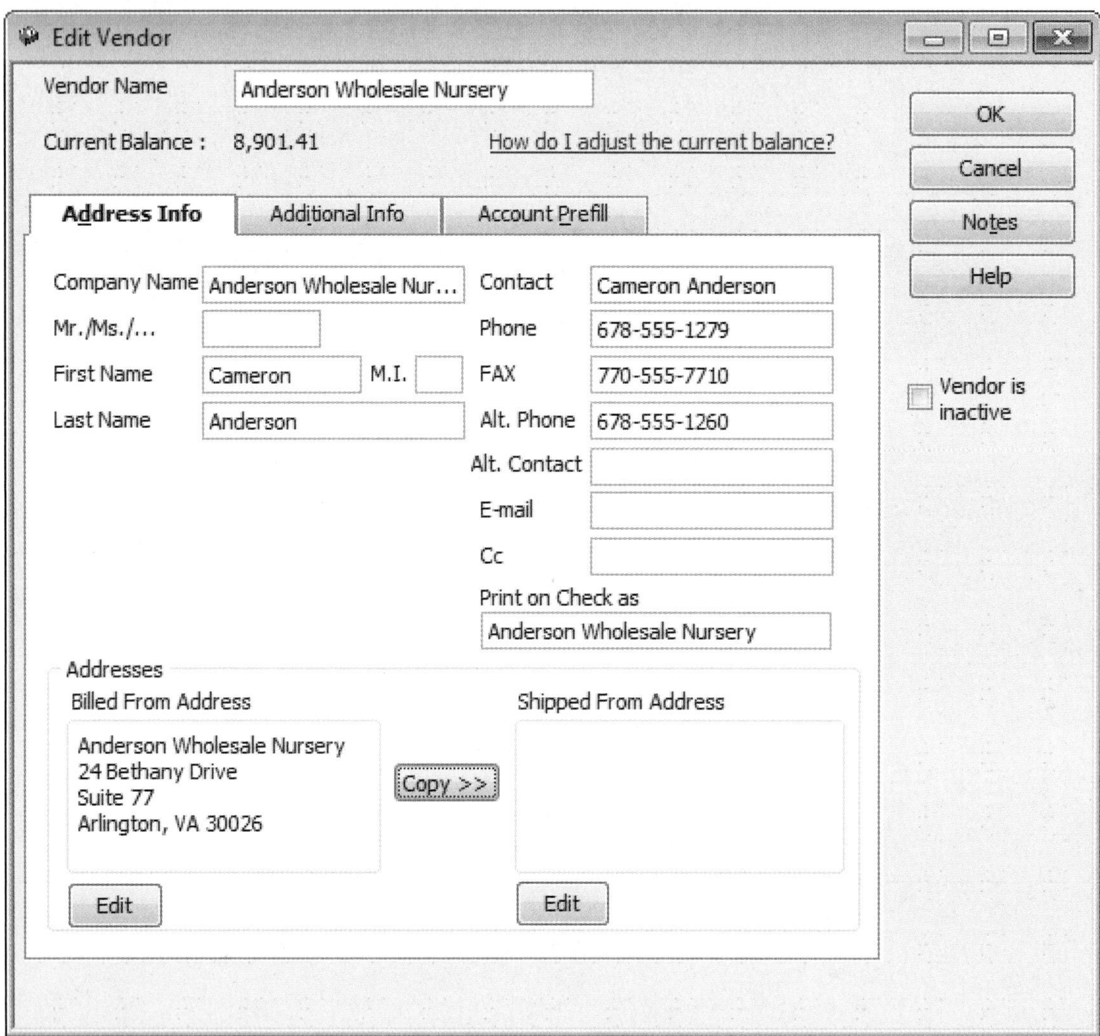

Figure 5:33

This tab stores basic vendor information such as address, phone numbers, and contacts (Figure 5:33).

Additional Info Tab

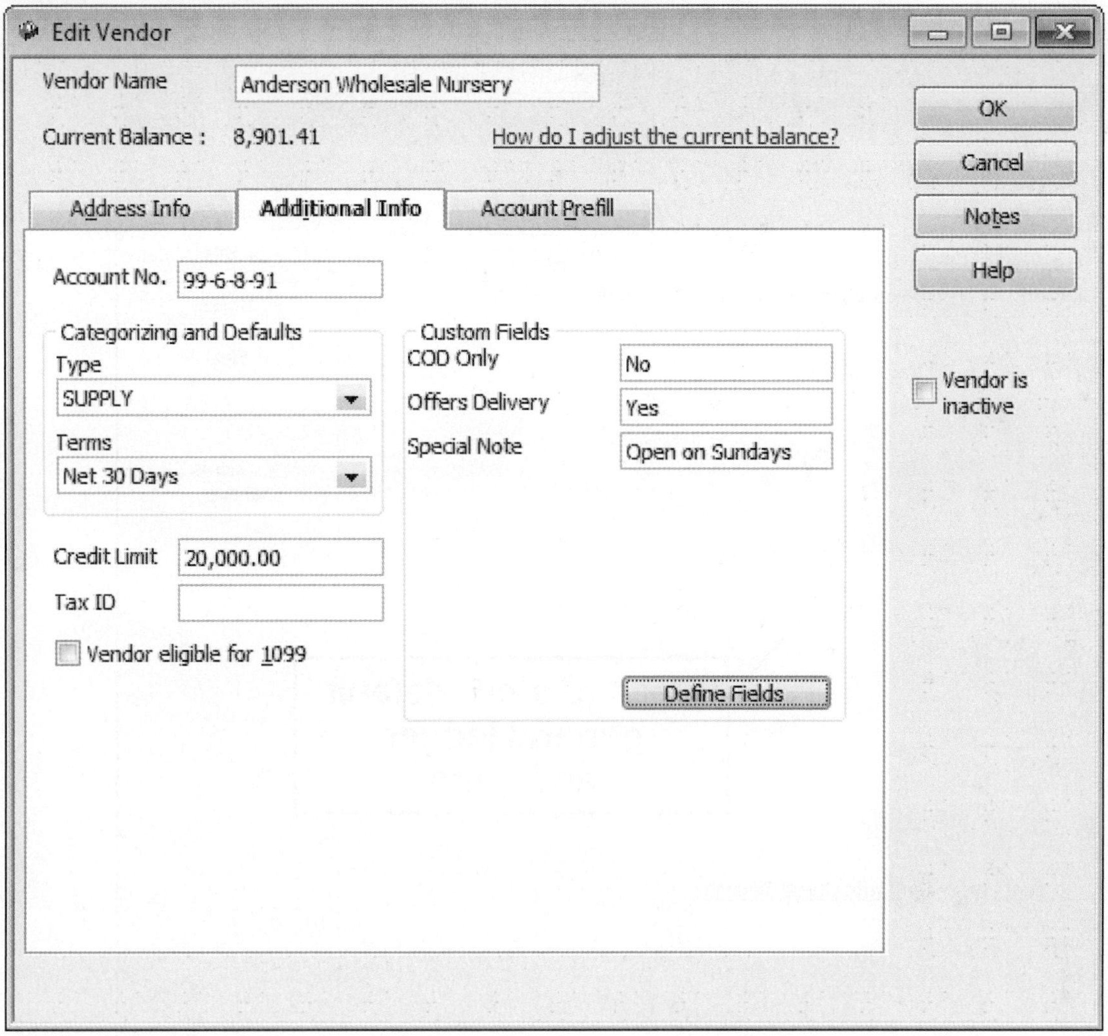

Edit Vendor

Vendor Name	Anderson Wholesale Nursery
Current Balance :	8,901.41

How do I adjust the current balance?

OK
Cancel
Notes
Help

Address Info | Additional Info | Account Prefill

Account No. 99-6-8-91

Categorizing and Defaults
Type: SUPPLY
Terms: Net 30 Days

Credit Limit 20,000.00
Tax ID

Vendor eligible for 1099

Custom Fields

COD Only	No
Offers Delivery	Yes
Special Note	Open on Sundays

Define Fields

Vendor is inactive

Figure 5:34

This tab stores vendor transaction defaults and fields for vendor reporting (Figure 5:34).

Account No. is optional and stores the account number used by the vendor.

Type is optional and is used to group reports by vendor characteristics. You can click the dropdown list to view the types used by Astor.

Terms on the vendor serve the same role as terms on the customer by controlling vendor bill due dates and early payment discounts.

Credit Limit on the vendor serves the same function as on the customer by controlling vendor purchases.

Vendor eligible for 1099 triggers a vendor for IRS tax reporting. When selected, QBP tracks annual payments for reporting on Form 1099. The IRS requires the annual filing of Form 1099 for subcontractor payments that exceed $600. Information on 1099 reporting requirements is available at www.irs.gov.

Tax ID stores a vendor's social security number or federal ID number for Form 1099 reporting.

Account Prefill Tab

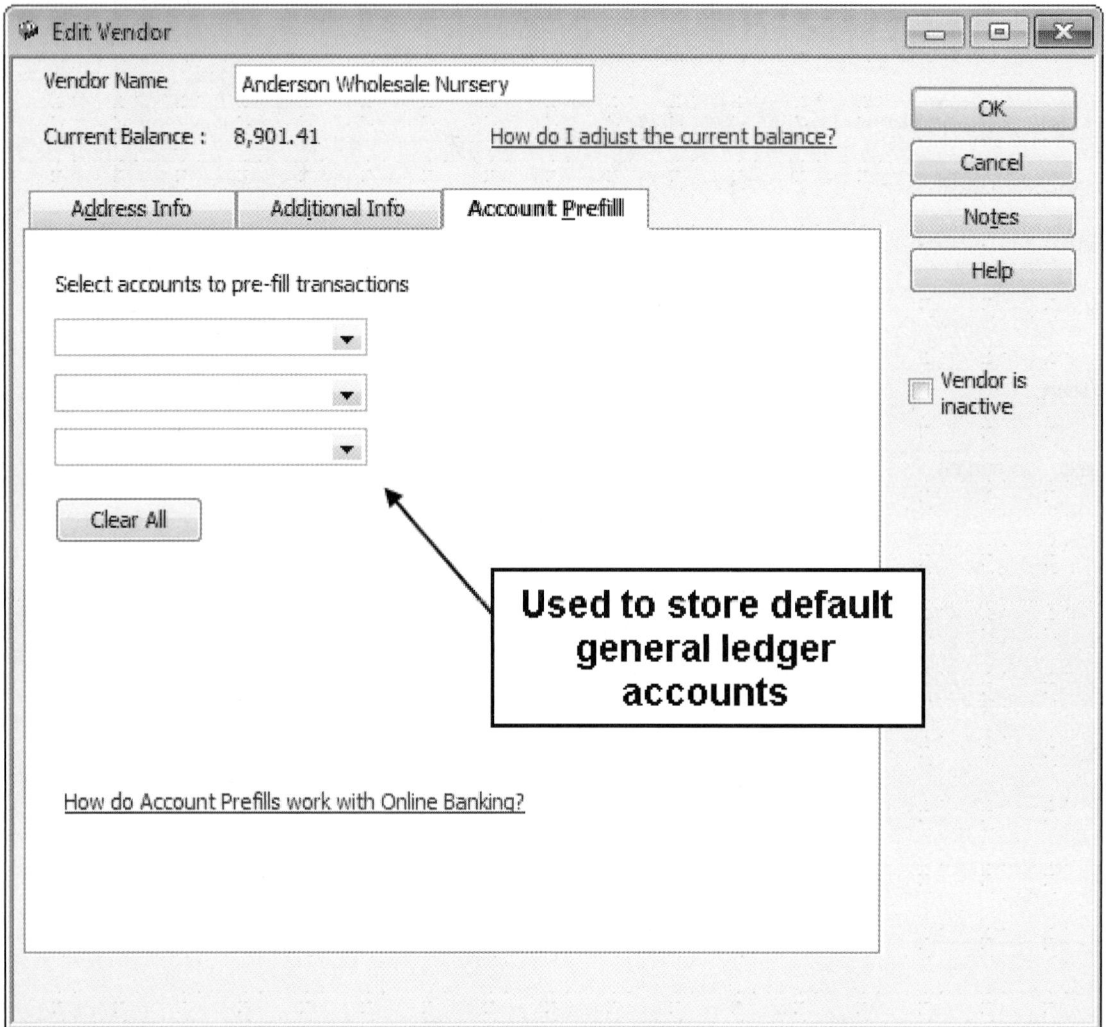

Figure 5:35

This tab (Figure 5:35) stores up to three default general ledger expense accounts. If a vendor has prefilled accounts, QBP will automatically enter the accounts on the Expenses tab of the Enter Bills window.

Anderson Wholesale Nursery does not have prefill accounts because it is a supplier of inventory so purchases from this vendor use the default account assigned to the inventory item. You can open the Petty Cash vendor if you want to view prefilled accounts.

Click **X** to close the account. Now practice editing vendor accounts by completing the next exercise.

Steps to Edit Vendor Account Information

1. Open the account for **Davis Timber Yard**. You will change the account terms to calculate a 1 percent discount when paying invoices within 10 days of the invoice date.
2. Select the **Additional Info** tab and look up the terms illustrated in Figure 5:36.

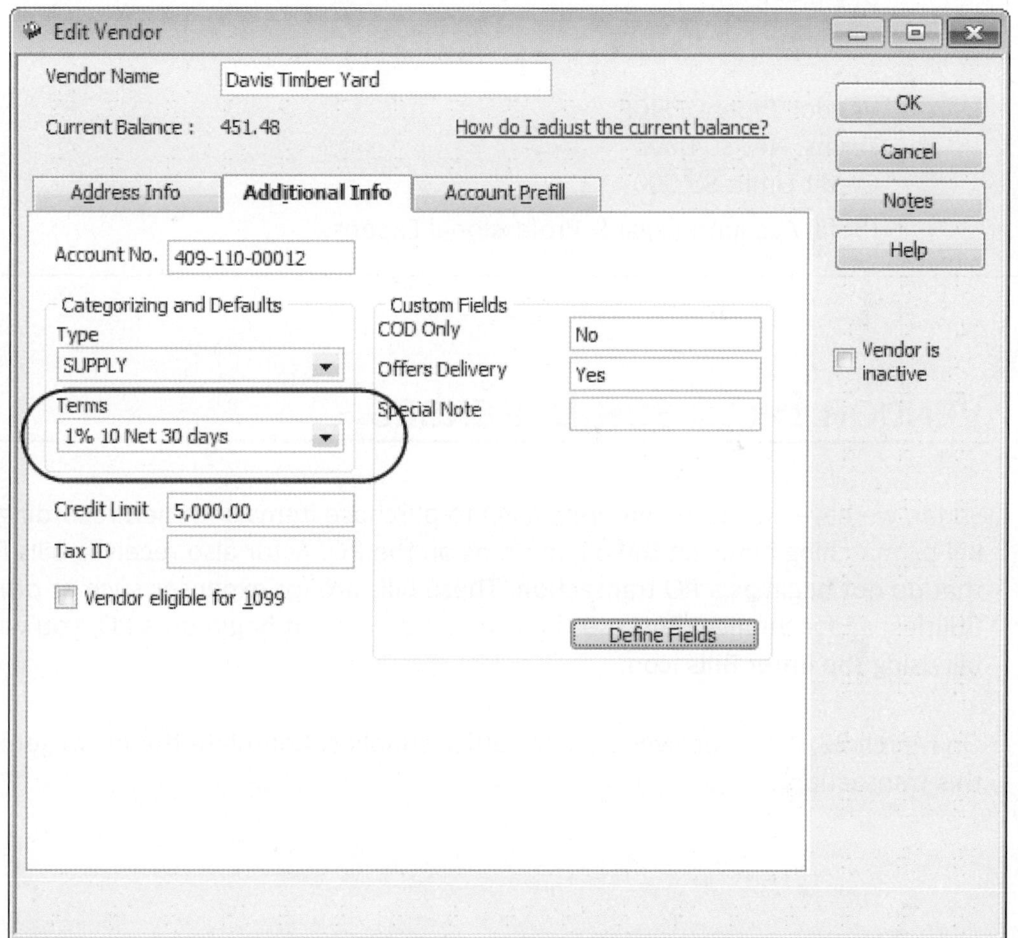

Figure 5:36

3. Click **OK**. Click **Yes** when warned that modifying the account could impact previously filed tax returns because this change applies only to future transactions.

You can delete vendors by highlighting a vendor account and selecting ***Edit>>Delete Vendor*** on the main menu. Like customers, you cannot delete accounts with transaction history, so use the **Vendor is inactive** option if you need to deny future transactions.

Adding vendors is similar to adding customers. Practice creating a new vendor in the exercise that follows.

CREATE A NEW VENDOR ACCOUNT

On March 26, Astor opened an account with the following vendor. Create the vendor account.

Jackson Hyland Tax Service
P.O. Box 8276
Arlington, VA 30010

Vendor Type: OFFICE
Terms: Net 30 Days
Credit Limit: $5,000
Prefill Account: Legal & Professional Expense

Vendor Bills for Expenses

So far, we have illustrated entering a PO to purchase items and then recording the vendor bill by matching items on the bill to items on the PO. Astor also receives bills for expenses that do not begin as a PO transaction. These bills are for expenses such as office supplies, utilities, and insurance. Because the transaction did not begin on a PO, you will record the bill using the **Enter Bills** icon.

On March 22, Astor receives a bill for office supplies. Complete the next exercise to record this transaction.

STEPS FOR ENTERING VENDOR BILLS FOR EXPENSES

1. On the **Home** page, click **Enter Bills**. In **Vendor**, look up and select "Office Maxtors." Change the **Date** to "3/22/12" and click the **Expenses** tab. (See Figure 5:37.)

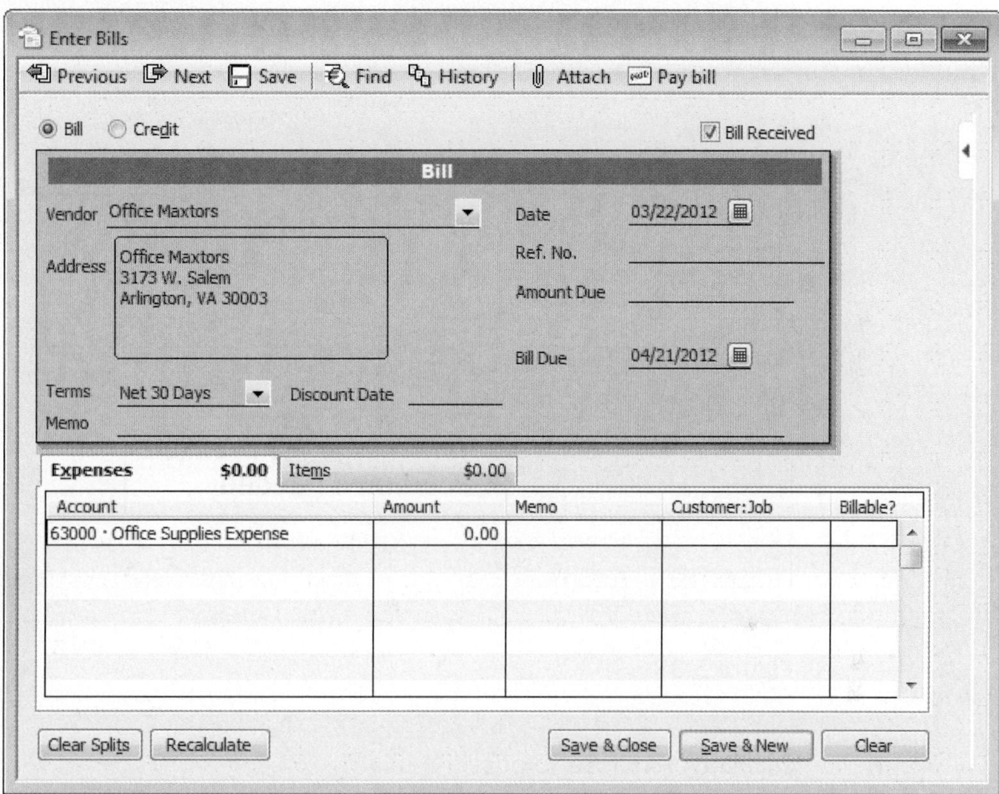

Figure 5:37

You now see the advantage to assigning prefilled accounts because 63000 Office Supplies Expense is already present.

2. Enter "575" as the **Ref. No.**

3. Enter "125.76" as the **Amount**. Tab to **Memo** and type "Paper supplies" into the field. These bills are not usually assigned to a **Customer:Job** so the completed transaction is shown in Figure 5:38.

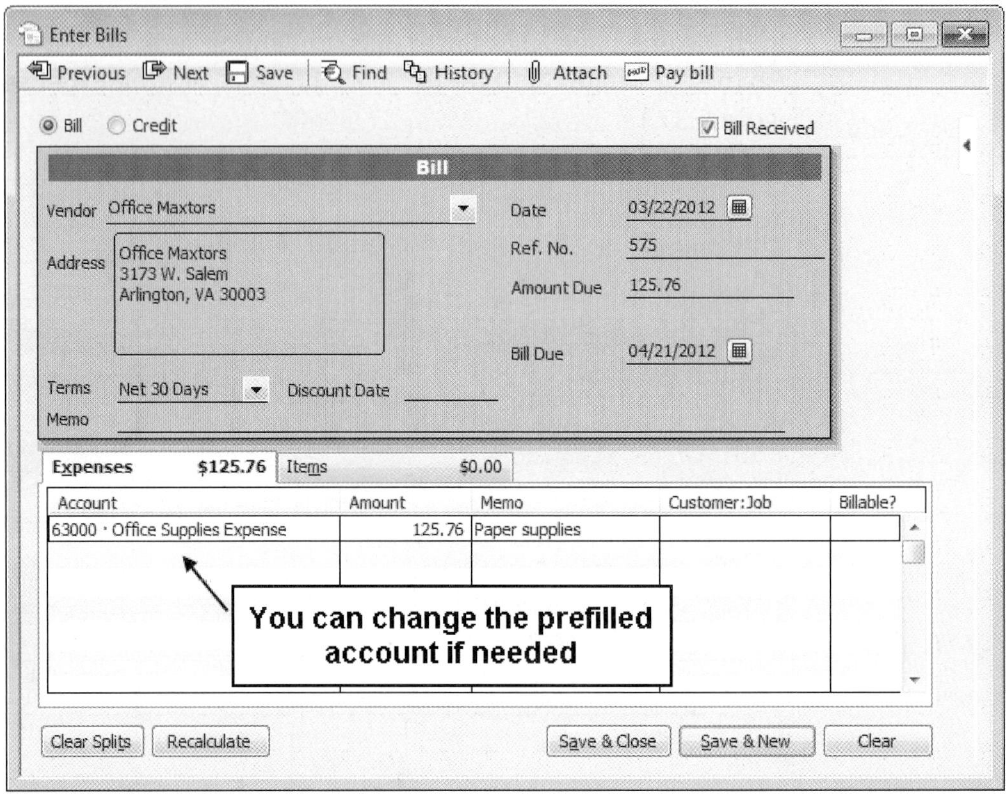

Figure 5:38

4. Click **Save & Close** to post the bill.

The exercise that follows provides more practice on entering vendor bills for expenses.

ENTER VENDOR BILLS FOR EXPENSES

On March 25, Astor received a bill dated March 18, 2012 from Jackson Hyland Tax Service. You created this vendor in the previous *You Try* exercise. The bill is for $762.00 for first quarter tax advice. Record this entry.

Hints:

There are a couple of points to this exercise. First, you always use the date on the vendor bill, not the date of receiving the bill, as the date on the transaction. Generally, you will receive bills after the date the vendor prepared the bill.

Second, you often encounter bills that do not include an invoice number, particularly bills for utility and professional expenses. Therefore, you must create an invoice number that lets you later identify the transaction. For instance, you can use "MarElec" as the invoice number for March electricity.

MEMORIZED VENDOR BILLS

QBP will let you memorize vendor bills. This feature is especially useful for bills that repeat. You can memorize while creating a new bill. You can also open a posted bill and memorize it.

The accountant received a bill for monthly advertising. In the following exercise, you will create and memorize this recurring bill.

STEPS TO CREATE A MEMORIZED VENDOR BILL

1. Click **Enter Bills** on the Home page and enter the information illustrated in Figure 5:39.

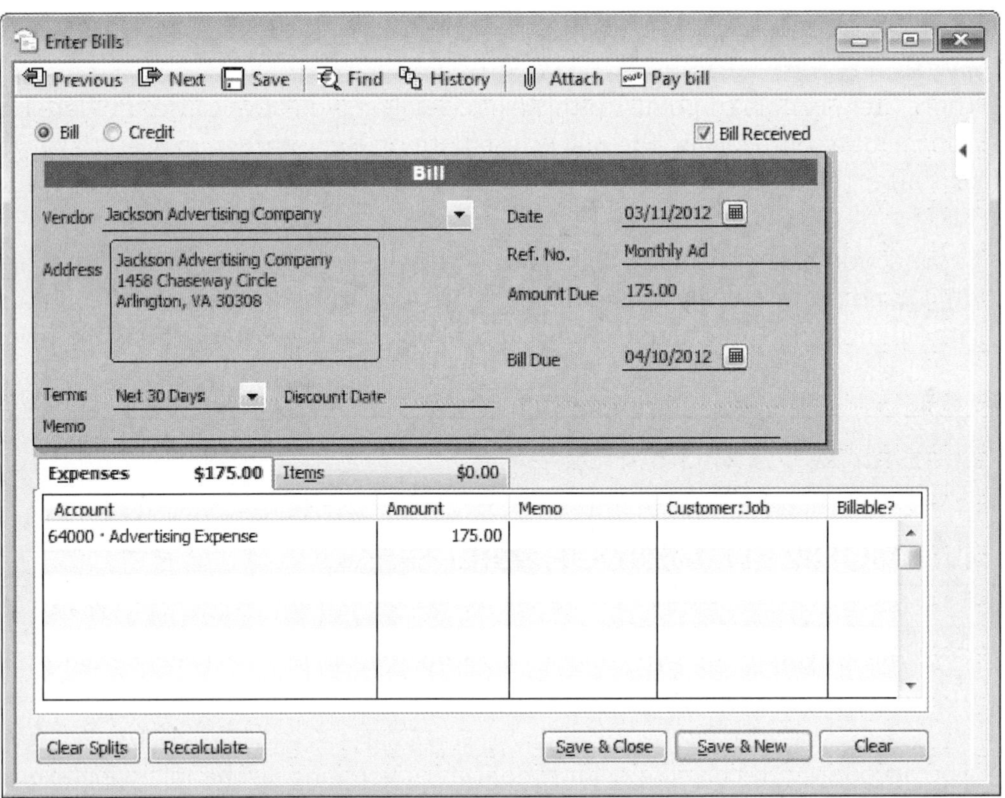

Figure 5:39

2. On the main menu, select ***Edit>>Memorize Bill*** to open Figure 5:40.

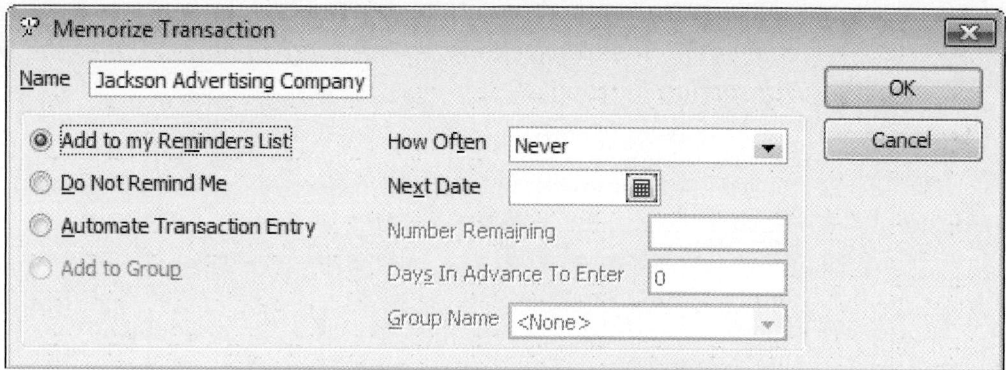

Figure 5:40

You can instruct QBP to remind you to post the bill or automatically post the bill. Select **Do Not Remind Me** as illustrated in Figure 5:41.

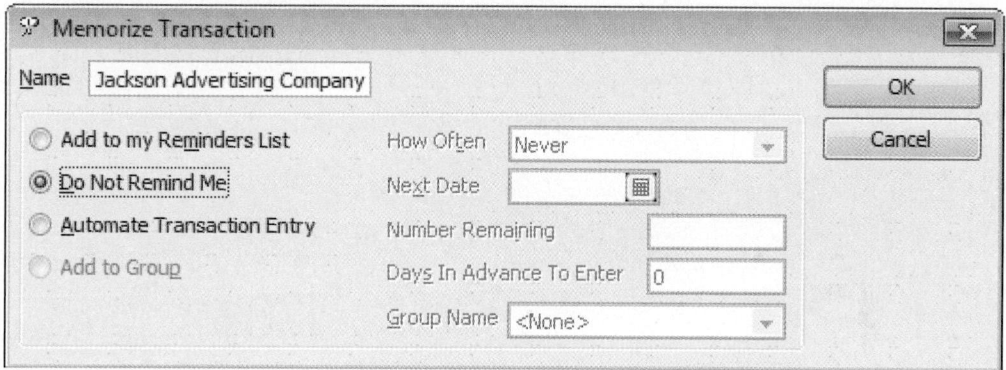

Figure 5:41

Click **OK** and then click **Save & Close** on the March bill.

3. You will now locate this memorized transaction. Select ***Lists>>Memorized Transaction List*** on the main menu to open the Memorized Transaction List illustrated next. *(Note: You can change a memorized transaction by highlighting the transaction and selecting an option under the **Memorized Transaction** button.)*

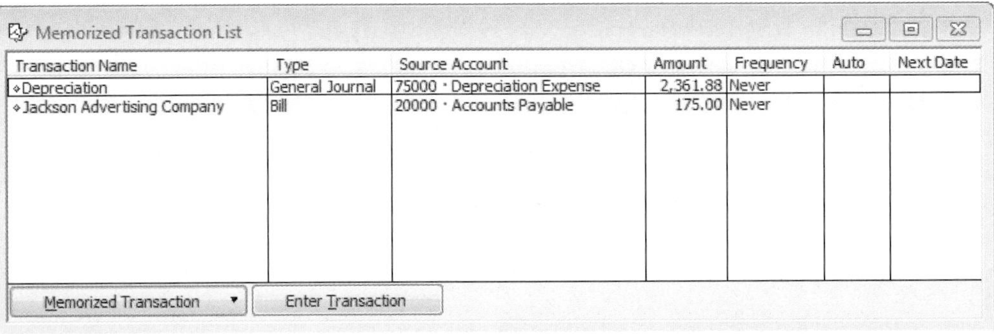

Memorized Transaction List

Transaction Name	Type	Source Account	Amount	Frequency	Auto	Next Date
◆Depreciation	General Journal	75000 · Depreciation Expense	2,361.88	Never		
◆Jackson Advertising Company	Bill	20000 · Accounts Payable	175.00	Never		

Figure 5:42

4. You will now post the April bill for Jackson. Highlight the transaction and click the **Enter Transaction** button. Enter the **Date** and **Ref. No.** illustrated. (See Figure 5:43.) Click **Save & Close**.

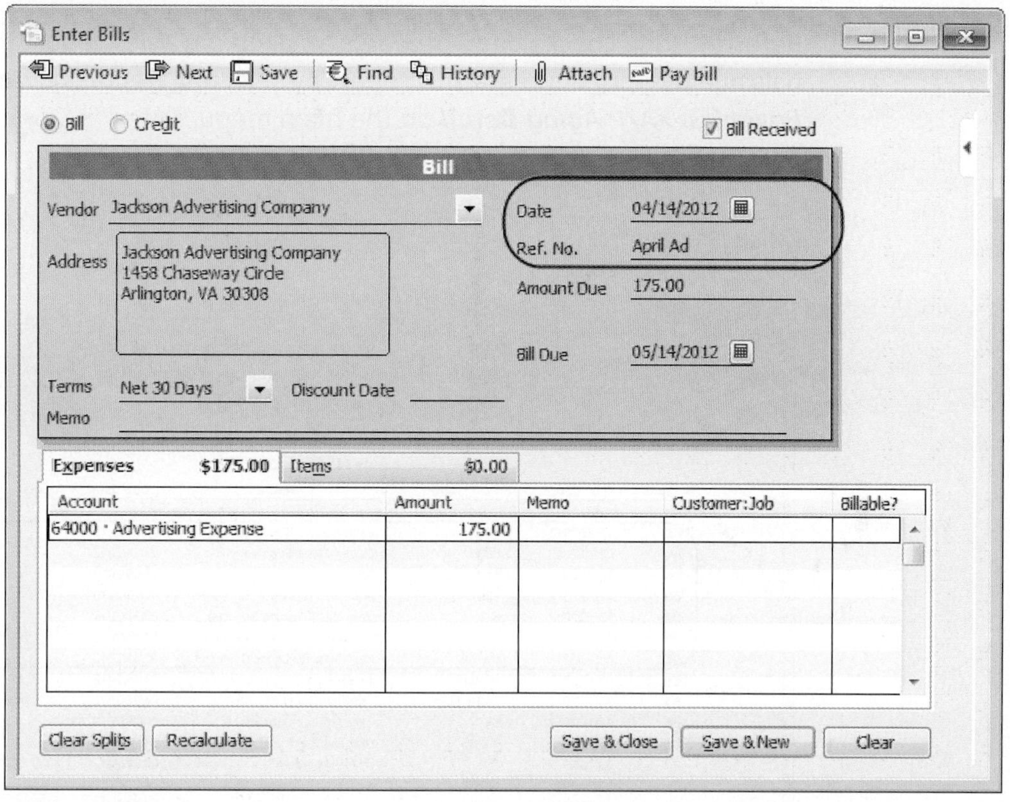

Figure 5:43

5. Click **X** to close the list.

VENDOR PAYMENTS

You are now ready to pay vendor bills. In the following exercise you create checks dated March 26 to pay vendor bills due by April 2.

Steps to Pay Vendors

1. Before cutting checks, Judy prepares an aged payables report to review bills due by April 2. Create this report by selecting ***Reports>>Vendors & Payables>>A/P Aging Detail*** on the main menu. Enter "3/26/12" as the date. The bills due by April 2 are marked in Figure 5:44.

   Close the report.

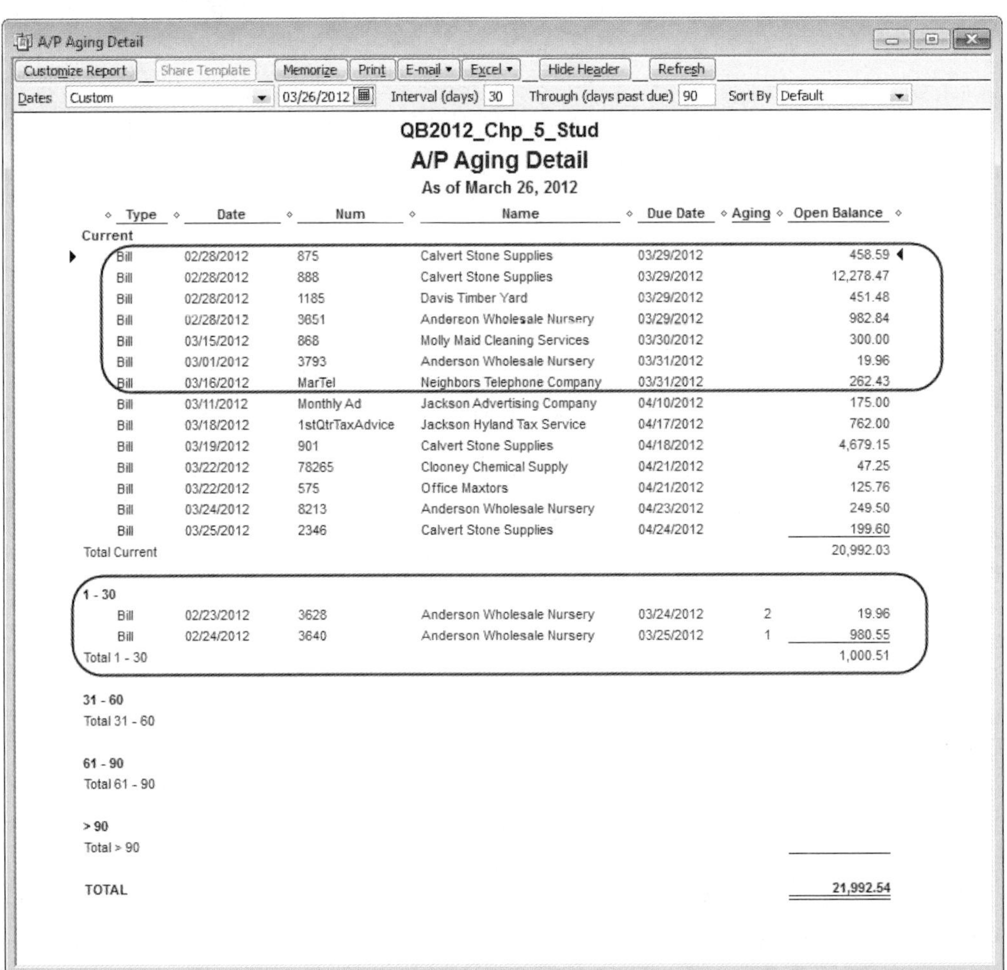

QB2012_Chp_5_Stud
A/P Aging Detail
As of March 26, 2012

Type	Date	Num	Name	Due Date	Aging	Open Balance
Current						
Bill	02/28/2012	875	Calvert Stone Supplies	03/29/2012		458.59
Bill	02/28/2012	888	Calvert Stone Supplies	03/29/2012		12,278.47
Bill	02/28/2012	1185	Davis Timber Yard	03/29/2012		451.48
Bill	02/28/2012	3651	Anderson Wholesale Nursery	03/29/2012		982.84
Bill	03/15/2012	868	Molly Maid Cleaning Services	03/30/2012		300.00
Bill	03/01/2012	3793	Anderson Wholesale Nursery	03/31/2012		19.96
Bill	03/16/2012	MarTel	Neighbors Telephone Company	03/31/2012		262.43
Bill	03/11/2012	Monthly Ad	Jackson Advertising Company	04/10/2012		175.00
Bill	03/18/2012	1stQtrTaxAdvice	Jackson Hyland Tax Service	04/17/2012		762.00
Bill	03/19/2012	901	Calvert Stone Supplies	04/18/2012		4,679.15
Bill	03/22/2012	78265	Clooney Chemical Supply	04/21/2012		47.25
Bill	03/22/2012	575	Office Maxtors	04/21/2012		125.76
Bill	03/24/2012	8213	Anderson Wholesale Nursery	04/23/2012		249.50
Bill	03/25/2012	2346	Calvert Stone Supplies	04/24/2012		199.60
Total Current						20,992.03
1 - 30						
Bill	02/23/2012	3628	Anderson Wholesale Nursery	03/24/2012	2	19.96
Bill	02/24/2012	3640	Anderson Wholesale Nursery	03/25/2012	1	980.55
Total 1 - 30						1,000.51
31 - 60						
Total 31 - 60						
61 - 90						
Total 61 - 90						
> 90						
Total > 90						
TOTAL						21,992.54

Figure 5:44

2. Click **Pay Bills** on the Home page. Enter "4/2/12" into the **Due on or before** field. Verify that the **To be printed** option is selected. Enter "3/26/12" as the **Payment Date**. (See Figure 5:45.)

   Note: The Due on or before option shows only bills due by the date entered. It will not show bills with discounts that may expire before you pay bills again. To see these bills, use the Show all bills option and review the dates listed in the Disc. Date column.

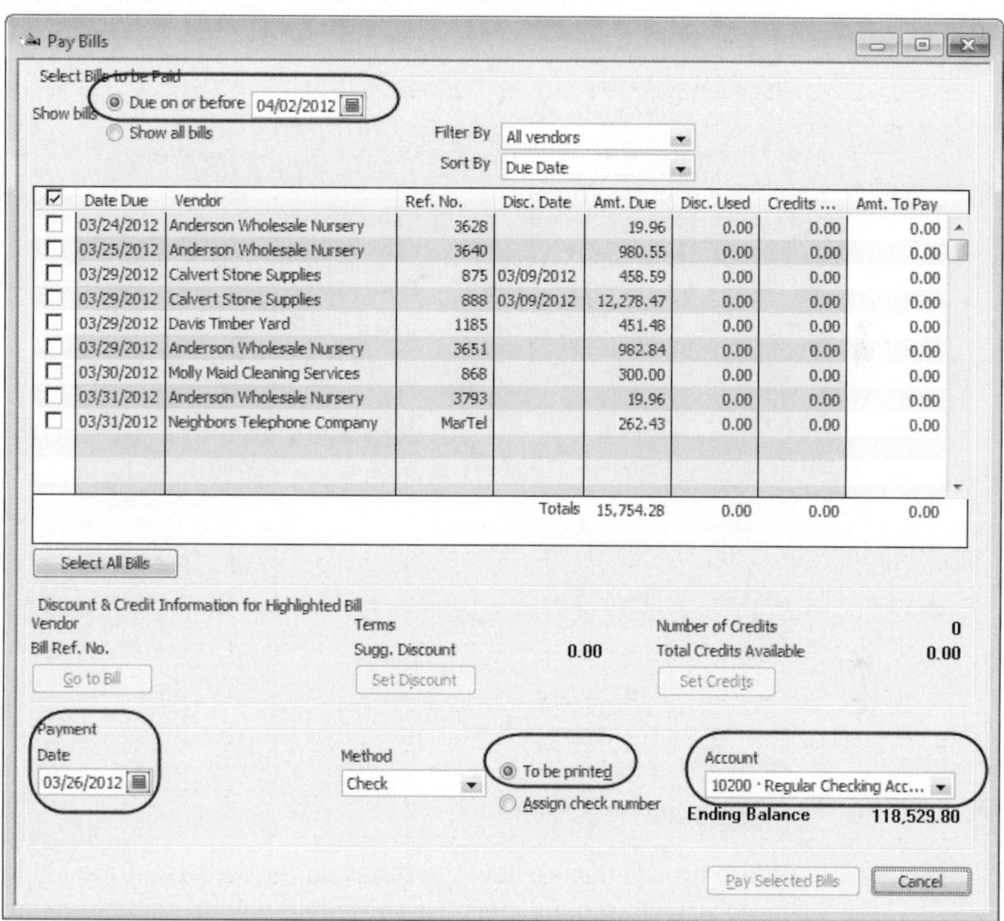

Figure 5:45

Before continuing, note that these checks will post a credit to the 10200 Regular Checking Account.

3. Click **Select All Bills** to mark the bills for payment as illustrated in Figure 5:46. Paying these bills will post a credit to the regular checking account and a debit the accounts payable account.

   (Note: After selecting bills, use the Clear Selections button to unmark all bills. You can unmark an individual bill by clicking the check mark field in front of the bill. You can also change the amount to pay a vendor by entering a different amount in the ***Amt. To Pay*** *column.)*

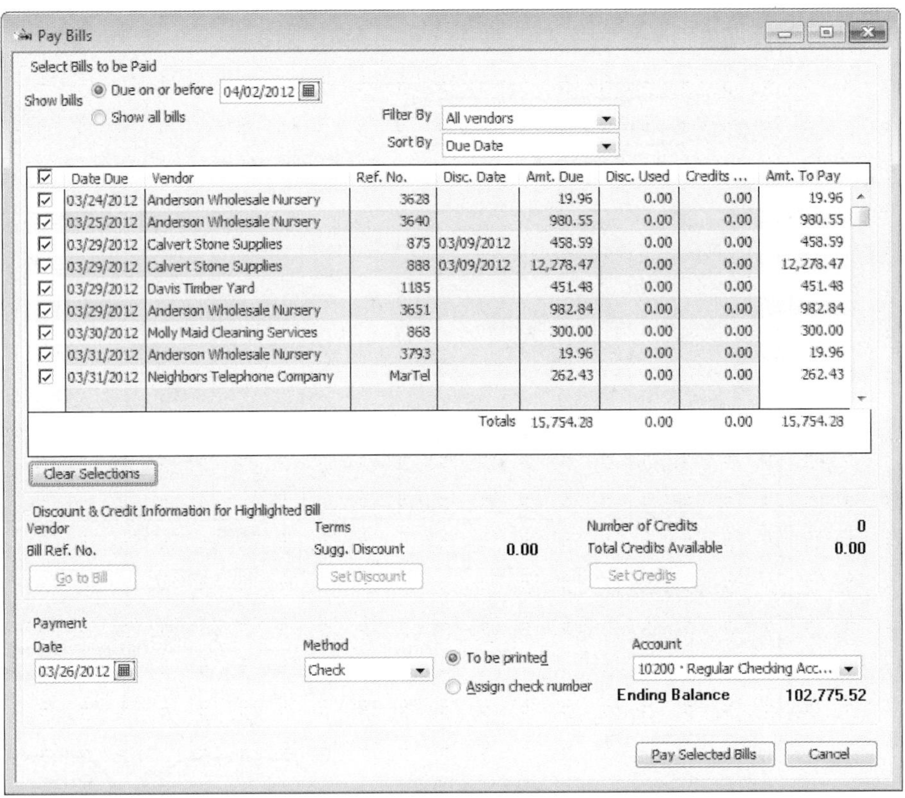

Figure 5:46

Before proceeding, review the dates under the **Disc. Date** column. The company has lost two discounts because these bills will be paid after the discount date. If paying a bill with a discount, the discount amount credits the default account set on the Company Preferences tab for Bills. (See Figure 5:47.)

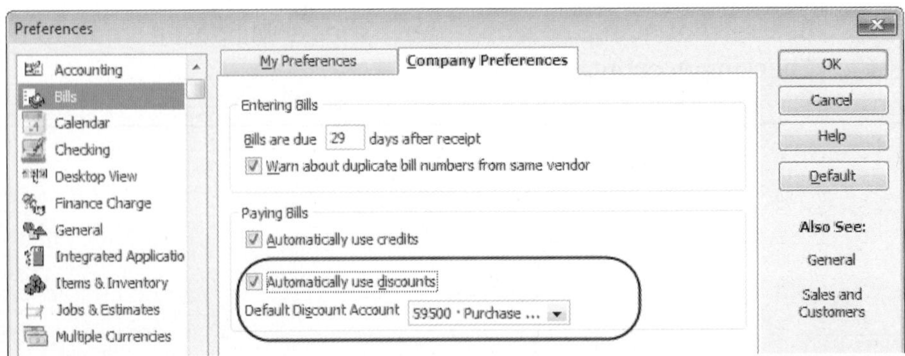

Figure 5:47

4. Click **Pay Selected Bills** to open the window illustrated in Figure 5:48. Use the scroll bar to review other payments.

   Note: If needed, you can click Done and return to printing later using Print Forms on the File menu. You can also add additional bills by clicking Pay More Bills.

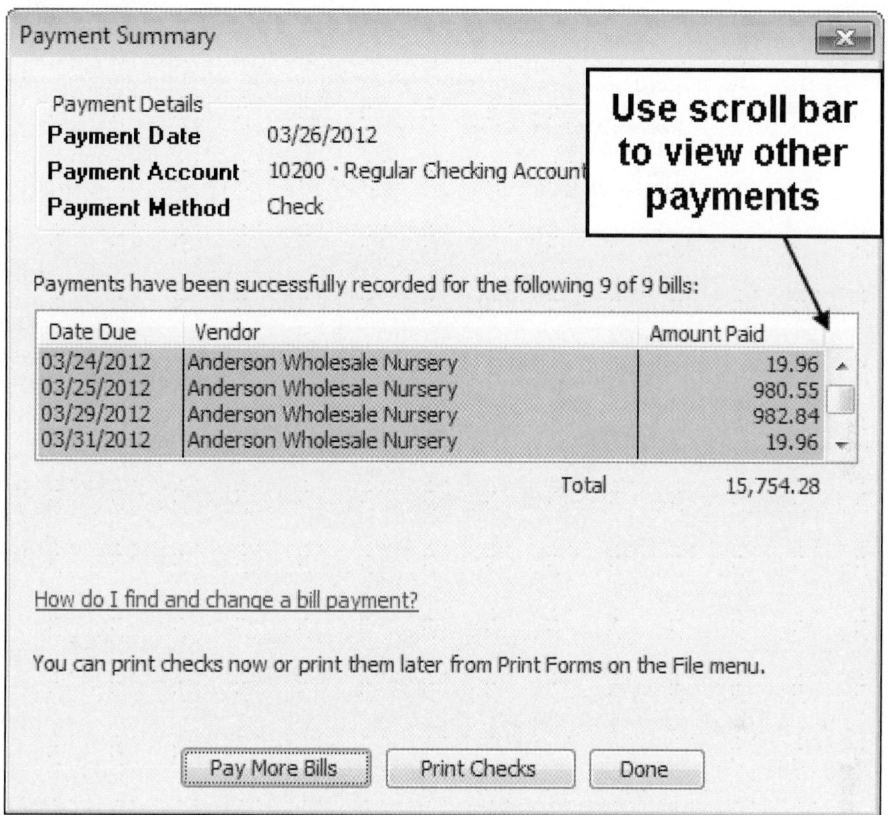

Figure 5:48

5. Click **Print Checks** and the window in Figure 5:49 opens. Confirm that "439" is the check number.

   Notice that QBP has combined vendor bills so that only five checks will be used to pay the bills.

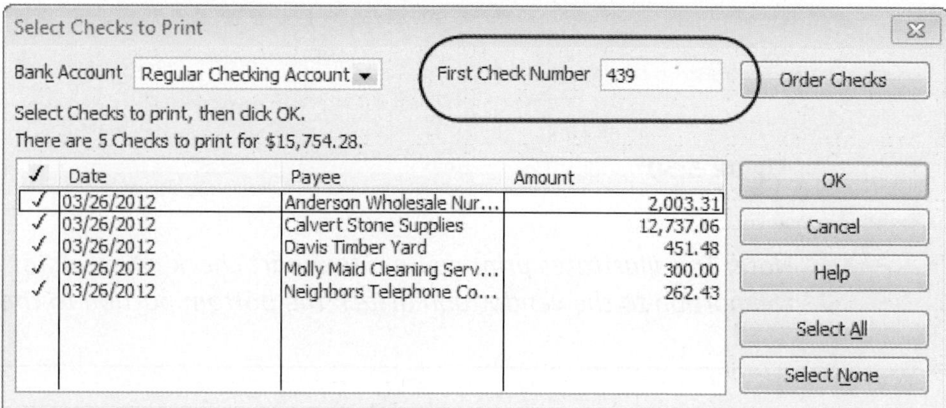

Figure 5:49

6. Click **OK** and the printer selection window opens. Select a printer and click **Print**. Figure 5:50 shows the first check printed.

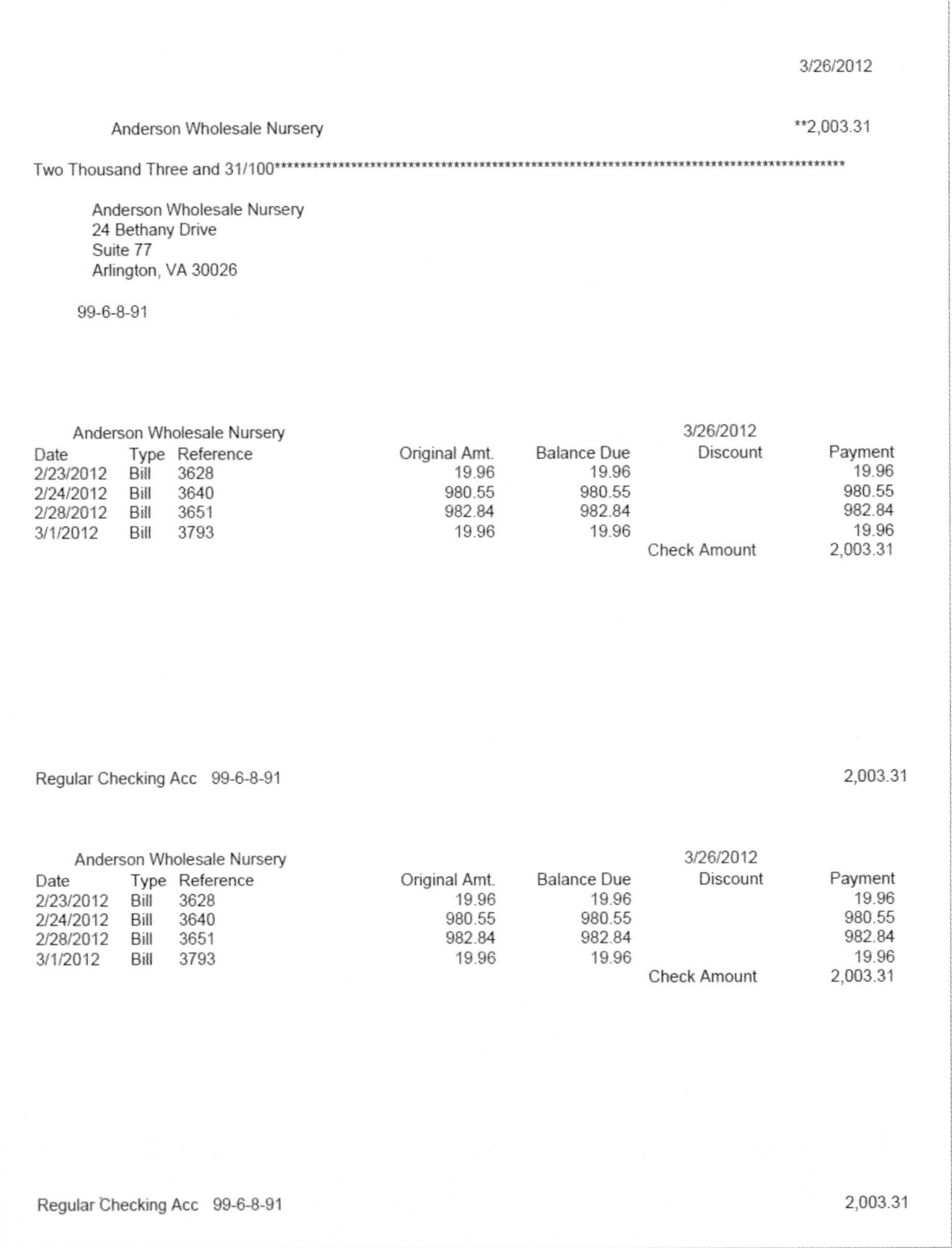

3/26/2012

Anderson Wholesale Nursery **2,003.31

Two Thousand Three and 31/100***

Anderson Wholesale Nursery
24 Bethany Drive
Suite 77
Arlington, VA 30026

99-6-8-91

Anderson Wholesale Nursery 3/26/2012

Date	Type	Reference	Original Amt.	Balance Due	Discount	Payment
2/23/2012	Bill	3628	19.96	19.96		19.96
2/24/2012	Bill	3640	980.55	980.55		980.55
2/28/2012	Bill	3651	982.84	982.84		982.84
3/1/2012	Bill	3793	19.96	19.96		19.96
					Check Amount	2,003.31

Regular Checking Acc 99-6-8-91 2,003.31

Anderson Wholesale Nursery 3/26/2012

Date	Type	Reference	Original Amt.	Balance Due	Discount	Payment
2/23/2012	Bill	3628	19.96	19.96		19.96
2/24/2012	Bill	3640	980.55	980.55		980.55
2/28/2012	Bill	3651	982.84	982.84		982.84
3/1/2012	Bill	3793	19.96	19.96		19.96
					Check Amount	2,003.31

Regular Checking Acc 99-6-8-91 2,003.31

Figure 5:50

Note: This illustrates printing on a two-part check where Astor can send the top portion to the vendor and attach the bottom portion to the paid bill.

7. QBP next confirms check printing (Figure 5:51). If checks did not print properly, click **Select All** and click **OK** so you can reprint the checks.

   Click **OK**.

Print Checks - Confirmation

If your checks printed correctly, click OK.

What if my checks printed in reverse order?

If you need to reprint any checks, select them and click OK. Then return to the Select Checks to Print window to reprint them.

Reprint	Check No.	Payee	Amount
	439	Anderson Wholesale Nursery	2,003.31
	440	Calvert Stone Supplies	12,737.06
	441	Davis Timber Yard	451.48
	442	Molly Maid Cleaning Services	300.00
	443	Neighbors Telephone Company	262.43

Select All

What if my checks printed incorrectly?

Cancel OK

Figure 5:51

Behind the Keys of a Posted Vendor Payment

Now trace the audit trail for the checks printed in the previous topic. On the main menu, select ***Reports>>Memorized Reports>>Accounting Journals>>Cash Disbursement Journal***. Change the date range to **3/26/12.** Note QBP's audit trail under the **Trans #** and **Type** columns. Close the report. (See Figure 5:52.)

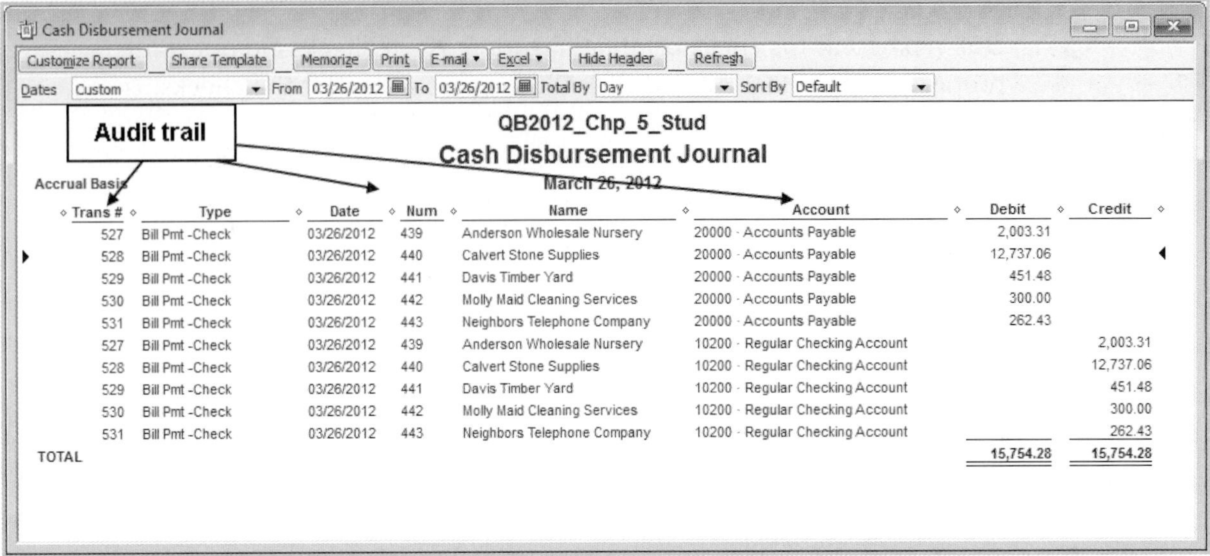

Cash Disbursement Journal

Customize Report | Share Template | Memorize | Print | E-mail | Excel | Hide Header | Refresh

Dates Custom From 03/26/2012 To 03/26/2012 Total By Day Sort By Default

QB2012_Chp_5_Stud

Cash Disbursement Journal

March 26, 2012

Accrual Basis

Trans #	Type	Date	Num	Name	Account	Debit	Credit
527	Bill Pmt -Check	03/26/2012	439	Anderson Wholesale Nursery	20000 · Accounts Payable	2,003.31	
528	Bill Pmt -Check	03/26/2012	440	Calvert Stone Supplies	20000 · Accounts Payable	12,737.06	
529	Bill Pmt -Check	03/26/2012	441	Davis Timber Yard	20000 · Accounts Payable	451.48	
530	Bill Pmt -Check	03/26/2012	442	Molly Maid Cleaning Services	20000 · Accounts Payable	300.00	
531	Bill Pmt -Check	03/26/2012	443	Neighbors Telephone Company	20000 · Accounts Payable	262.43	
527	Bill Pmt -Check	03/26/2012	439	Anderson Wholesale Nursery	10200 · Regular Checking Account		2,003.31
528	Bill Pmt -Check	03/26/2012	440	Calvert Stone Supplies	10200 · Regular Checking Account		12,737.06
529	Bill Pmt -Check	03/26/2012	441	Davis Timber Yard	10200 · Regular Checking Account		451.48
530	Bill Pmt -Check	03/26/2012	442	Molly Maid Cleaning Services	10200 · Regular Checking Account		300.00
531	Bill Pmt -Check	03/26/2012	443	Neighbors Telephone Company	10200 · Regular Checking Account		262.43
TOTAL						15,754.28	15,754.28

Figure 5:52

Select ***Reports>>Vendors & Payables>>Transaction List by Vendor*** to open the report listing transactions posted to vendor accounts. Enter **3/26/12** as the date range and customize the report to add the **Trans #** column. (See Figure 5:53.)

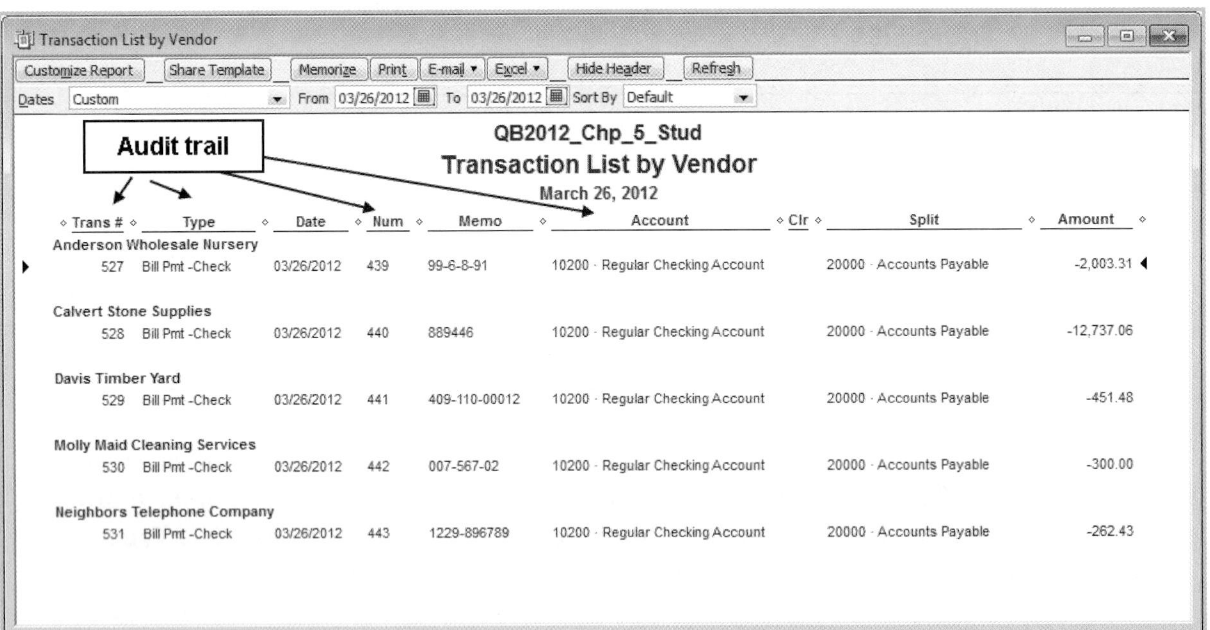

Transaction List by Vendor

Customize Report | Share Template | Memorize | Print | E-mail | Excel | Hide Header | Refresh

Dates Custom From 03/26/2012 To 03/26/2012 Sort By Default

QB2012_Chp_5_Stud

Transaction List by Vendor

March 26, 2012

Trans #	Type	Date	Num	Memo	Account	Clr	Split	Amount
Anderson Wholesale Nursery								
527	Bill Pmt -Check	03/26/2012	439	99-6-8-91	10200 · Regular Checking Account		20000 · Accounts Payable	-2,003.31
Calvert Stone Supplies								
528	Bill Pmt -Check	03/26/2012	440	889446	10200 · Regular Checking Account		20000 · Accounts Payable	-12,737.06
Davis Timber Yard								
529	Bill Pmt -Check	03/26/2012	441	409-110-00012	10200 · Regular Checking Account		20000 · Accounts Payable	-451.48
Molly Maid Cleaning Services								
530	Bill Pmt -Check	03/26/2012	442	007-567-02	10200 · Regular Checking Account		20000 · Accounts Payable	-300.00
Neighbors Telephone Company								
531	Bill Pmt -Check	03/26/2012	443	1229-896789	10200 · Regular Checking Account		20000 · Accounts Payable	-262.43

Figure 5:53

The audit trail of **Trans #** and **Type** on this report matches the audit trail in the **Cash Disbursements Journal**. Close this report and complete tracing entries by opening the **General Ledger Detail Report**. Locate your entries in accounts 10200 Regular Checking and 20000 Accounts Payable (not illustrated). Close the report.

Write Checks Without a Vendor Bill

In QBP, you can write checks without entering a vendor bill first. This is useful if you need to write a check to a vendor that requests cash upon delivery. Sometimes the vendor account will also be new so you can add it "on the fly." *(Note: Remember "on the fly" means creating a new account while entering a transaction.)*

Complete the next exercise that records a check for office party food.

Steps to Add a Vendor On the Fly While Writing a Check Without a Vendor Bill

1. Click **Write Checks** under the **Banking** section of the **Home** page. Enter "444" as the check **No**. Enter "3/26/12" as the **Date**.

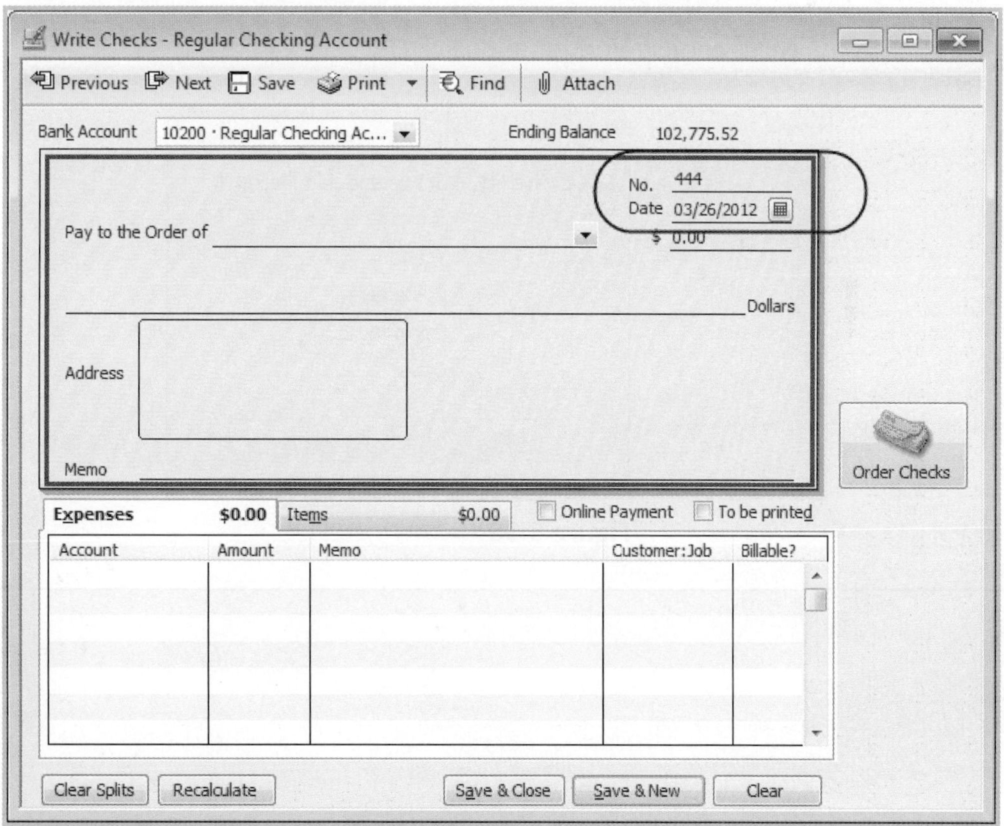

Figure 5:54

2. The vendor is not on file so place your cursor in **Pay to the Order of** and type "Joe's Grocery".

   Press **Tab**. When QBP prompts to create the account (Figure 5:55), click **Set Up**.

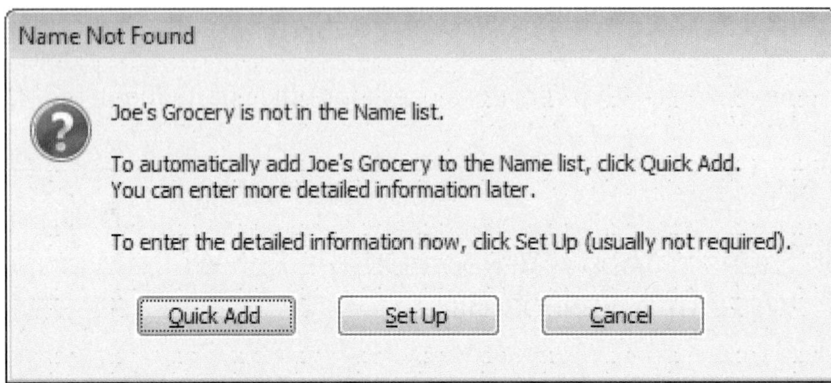

Figure 5:55

   Next, choose **Vendor** and click **OK**.

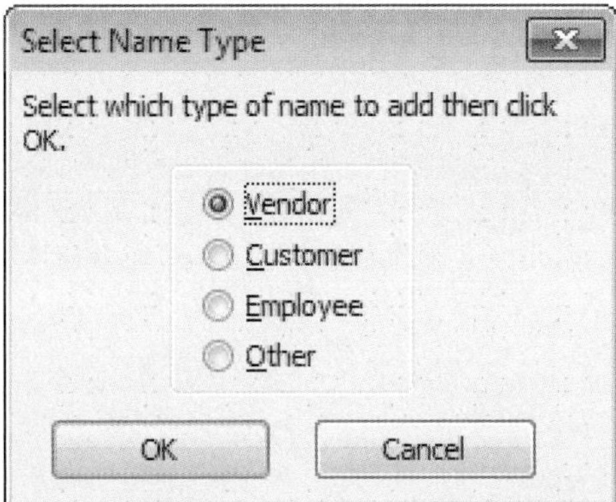

Figure 5:56

3. Use information in the next series of figures to create the vendor account.

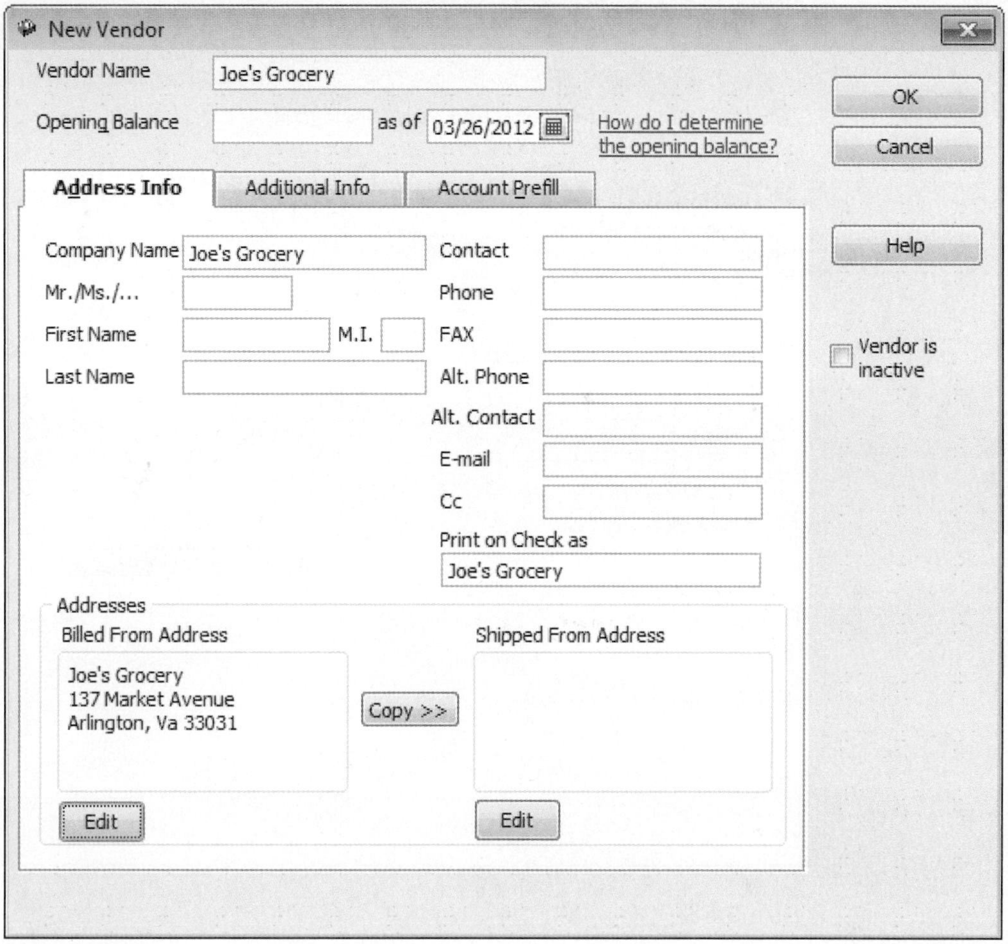

New Vendor

Vendor Name: Joe's Grocery

Opening Balance: as of 03/26/2012 — How do I determine the opening balance?

OK | Cancel | Help

Address Info | Additional Info | Account Prefill

Company Name: Joe's Grocery
Mr./Ms./...
First Name — M.I.
Last Name

Contact
Phone
FAX
Alt. Phone
Alt. Contact
E-mail
Cc
Print on Check as: Joe's Grocery

Vendor is inactive

Addresses

Billed From Address:
Joe's Grocery
137 Market Avenue
Arlington, Va 33031

Copy >>

Shipped From Address

Edit | Edit

Figure 5:57

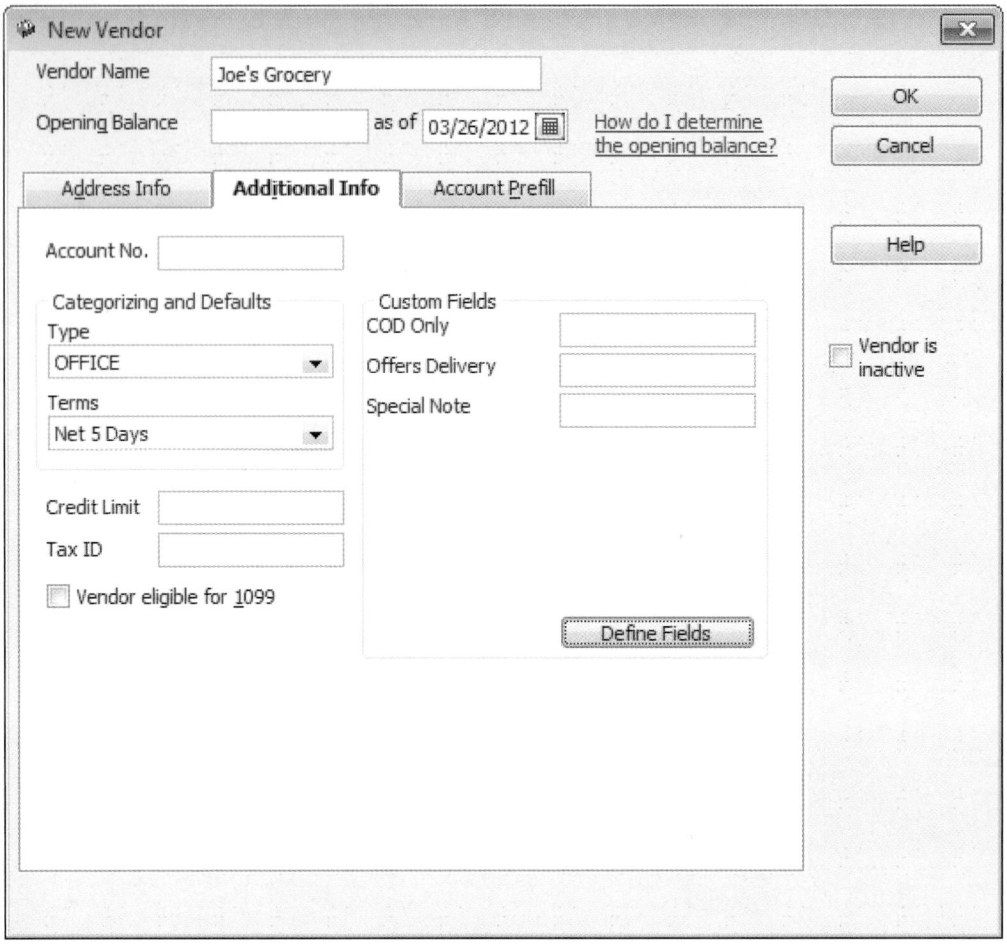

New Vendor

Vendor Name	Joe's Grocery	
Opening Balance	as of 03/26/2012	How do I determine the opening balance?

OK
Cancel
Help

Address Info | Additional Info | Account Prefill

Account No.

Categorizing and Defaults
Type: OFFICE
Terms: Net 5 Days

Custom Fields
COD Only
Offers Delivery
Special Note

Define Fields

Credit Limit
Tax ID
Vendor eligible for 1099

Vendor is inactive

Figure 5:58

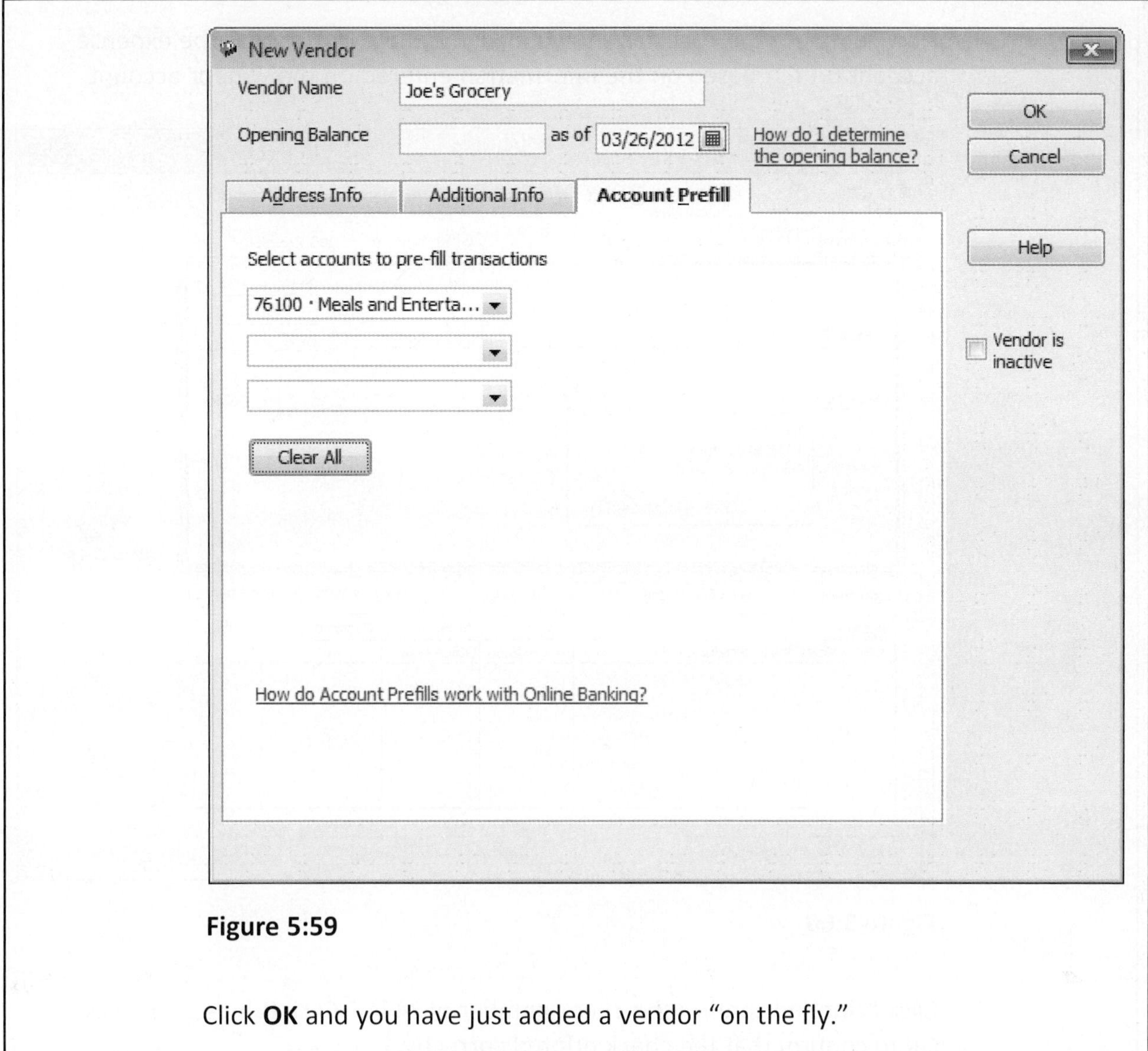

Figure 5:59

Click **OK** and you have just added a vendor "on the fly."

4. Now complete the check as shown in Figure 5:60. Notice that the expense account prefills based on the information entered on the vendor account.

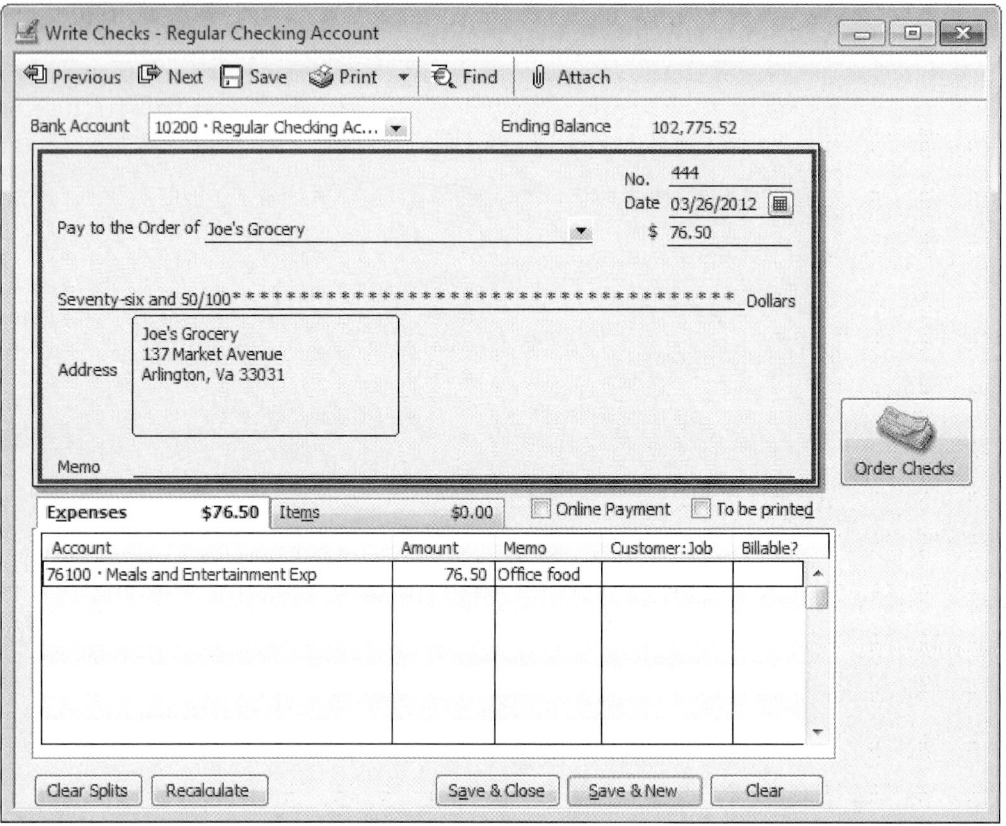

Figure 5:60

5. Click **Print** and confirm the check number of "444." Click **Print** again. Click **OK** to confirm that the check printed correctly.

6. Click **Save & Close**.

VOIDING VENDOR PAYMENTS

QBP will let you reopen a vendor payment and change check data. Although this changes data in the software, the printed check remains incorrect, so do not alter check data. Instead, you correct an error by voiding the check and reissuing it. The following instructions illustrate voiding a vendor check.

STEPS TO VOIDING A VENDOR PAYMENT

1. In this exercise, you will void check number "432" cut to General Leasing Corp on March 1. Open the **Vendor Center** and locate **Bill Payments** for this vendor's account. (See Figure 5:61.)

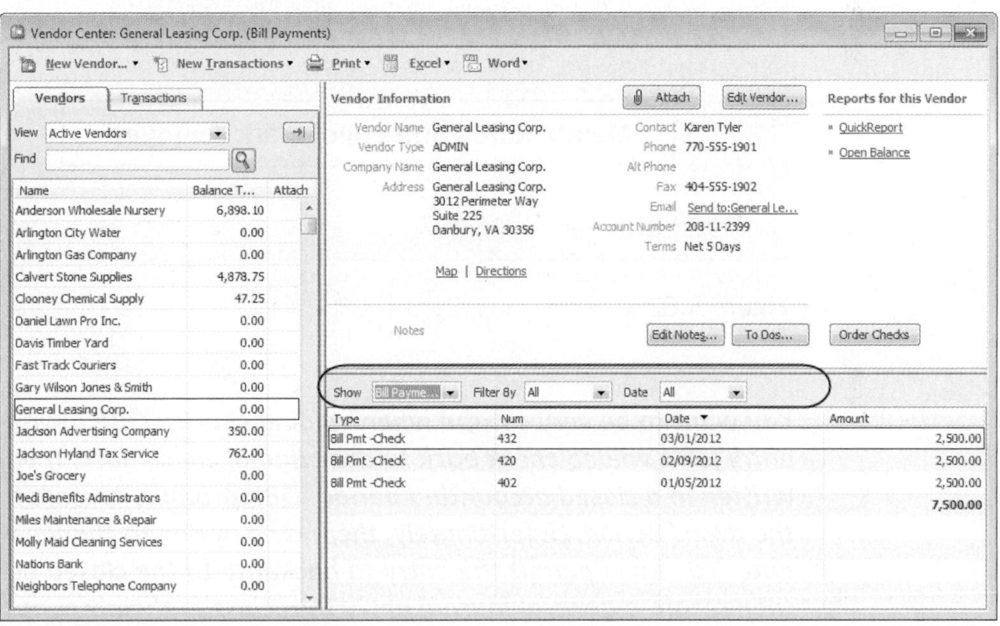

Figure 5:61

2. Double click to reopen the check. On the main menu, select ***Edit>>Void Bill Pmt – Check***.

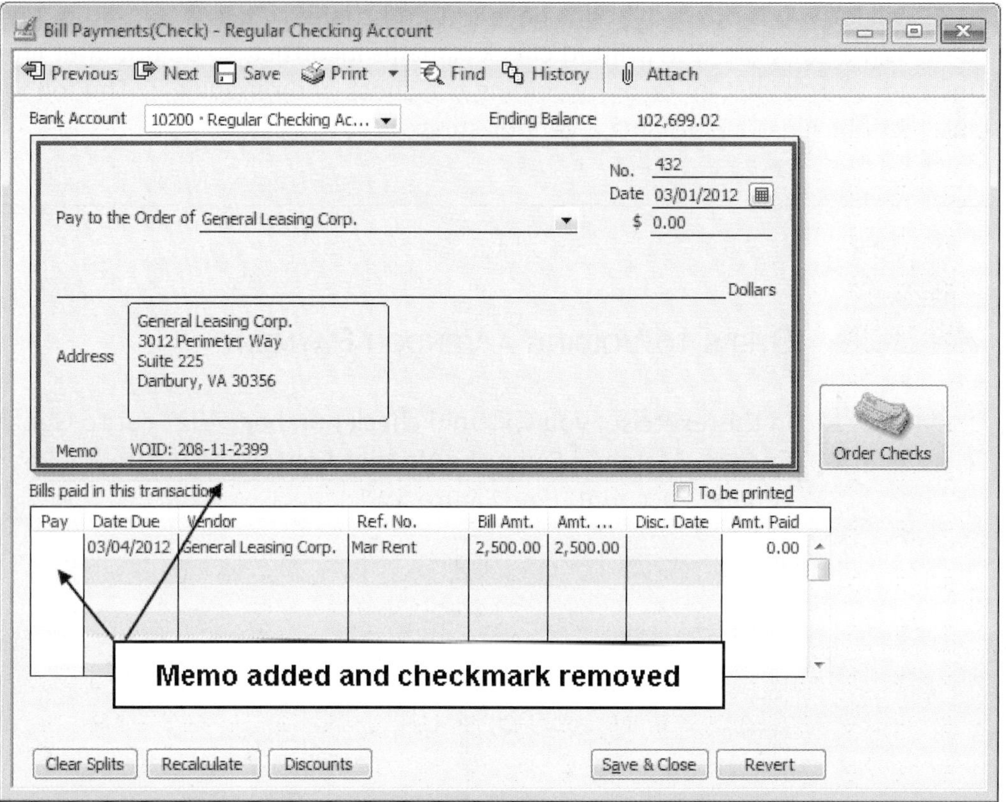

Figure 5:62

You want to be very careful when voiding checks. QBP always posts the entry for a voided check back to the original check date. If voiding a check written in a closed accounting period, QBP prompts to post the entry to the closed period. Unfortunately, there is no option to change the posting date. You must permit the entry to backdate to the closed period and then record a general journal entry to reclassify the amount to the open accounting period.

3. Click **Save & Close**. When prompted (Figure 5:63), click **Yes**.

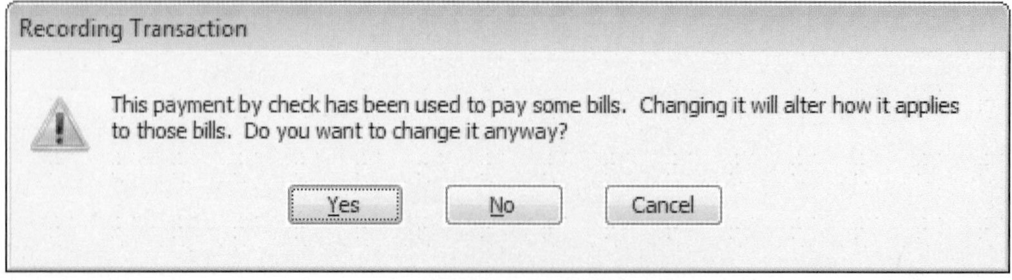

Figure 5:63

4. View the results of your action. Select ***Reports>>Memorized Reports>>Accounting Journals>>General Ledger Detail Report*** on the main menu. Enter **3/1/12** as the date range. Notice that QBP voided the check as of the check date (Figure 5:64). Close the report.

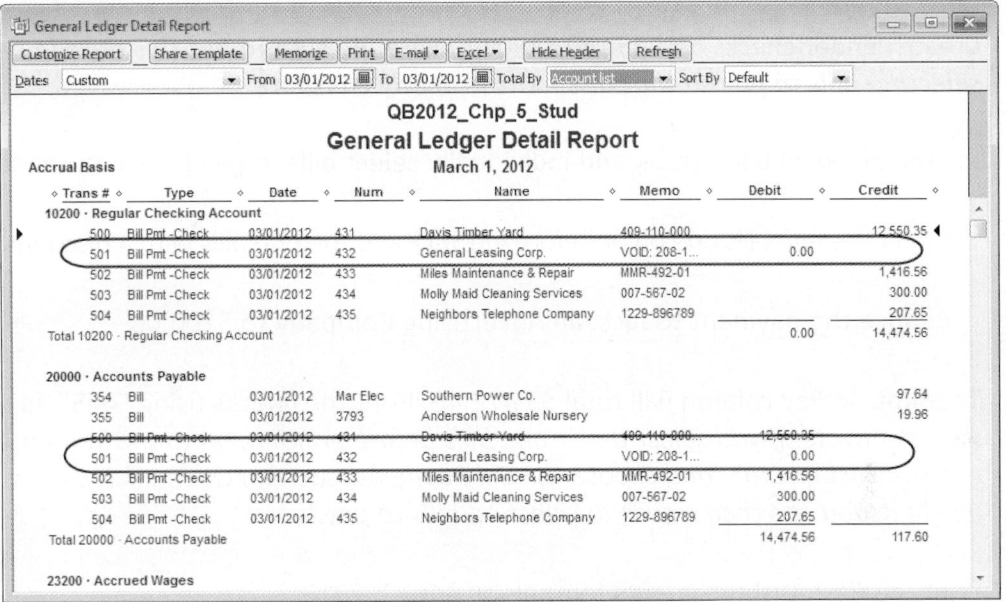

General Ledger Detail Report

Customize Report | Share Template | Memorize | Print | E-mail | Excel | Hide Header | Refresh

Dates Custom From 03/01/2012 To 03/01/2012 Total By Account list Sort By Default

QB2012_Chp_5_Stud

General Ledger Detail Report

Accrual Basis

March 1, 2012

Trans #	Type	Date	Num	Name	Memo	Debit	Credit
10200 · Regular Checking Account							
500	Bill Pmt -Check	03/01/2012	431	Davis Timber Yard	409-110-000		12,550.35
501	Bill Pmt -Check	03/01/2012	432	General Leasing Corp.	VOID: 208-1...	0.00	
502	Bill Pmt -Check	03/01/2012	433	Miles Maintenance & Repair	MMR-492-01		1,416.56
503	Bill Pmt -Check	03/01/2012	434	Molly Maid Cleaning Services	007-567-02		300.00
504	Bill Pmt -Check	03/01/2012	435	Neighbors Telephone Company	1229-896789		207.65
Total 10200 · Regular Checking Account						0.00	14,474.56
20000 · Accounts Payable							
354	Bill	03/01/2012	Mar Elec	Southern Power Co.			97.64
355	Bill	03/01/2012	3793	Anderson Wholesale Nursery			19.96
500	Bill Pmt -Check	03/01/2012	431	Davis Timber Yard	409-110-000...	12,550.35	
501	Bill Pmt -Check	03/01/2012	432	General Leasing Corp.	VOID: 208-1...	0.00	
502	Bill Pmt -Check	03/01/2012	433	Miles Maintenance & Repair	MMR-492-01	1,416.56	
503	Bill Pmt -Check	03/01/2012	434	Molly Maid Cleaning Services	007-567-02	300.00	
504	Bill Pmt -Check	03/01/2012	435	Neighbors Telephone Company	1229-896789	207.65	
Total 20000 · Accounts Payable						14,474.56	117.60
23200 · Accrued Wages							

Figure 5:64

5. Return to the vendor's account and view **Bills**. The March bill has an open balance so it can be reselected for payment. You will pay this bill in the next exercise.

Close the **Vendor Center**.

PAY VENDORS

Create vendor checks dated April 3, 2012. ***Note: Be sure to put this date in before selecting bills to pay so that discounts properly calculate.***

Use the Show all bills option and individually select bills to pay based on the following.

Select the two bills due on or before 4/15/12 and the two bills with a discount date in April.

Reduce the payment to Jackson Advertising Company to $100.00.

The Amt. To Pay column will total $3,472.46. Print the checks using "445" as the first check number. *(Note: If you select the wrong bills before printing, go to the Vendor Center, select the Transactions tab, and choose the Bill Payments section. Open each unprinted check and delete it. You can then return to selecting bills to pay.)*

Print the Cash Disbursements Journal for April 3, 2012.

PAYING SALES TAX

At the end of every month, Astor must remit sales tax collected from customers. QBP tracks sales tax collections and the following shows you how to remit it.

STEPS TO PAYING SALES TAX

1. Click **Manage Sales Tax** in the Vendors section of the **Home** page to open the window in Figure 5:65.

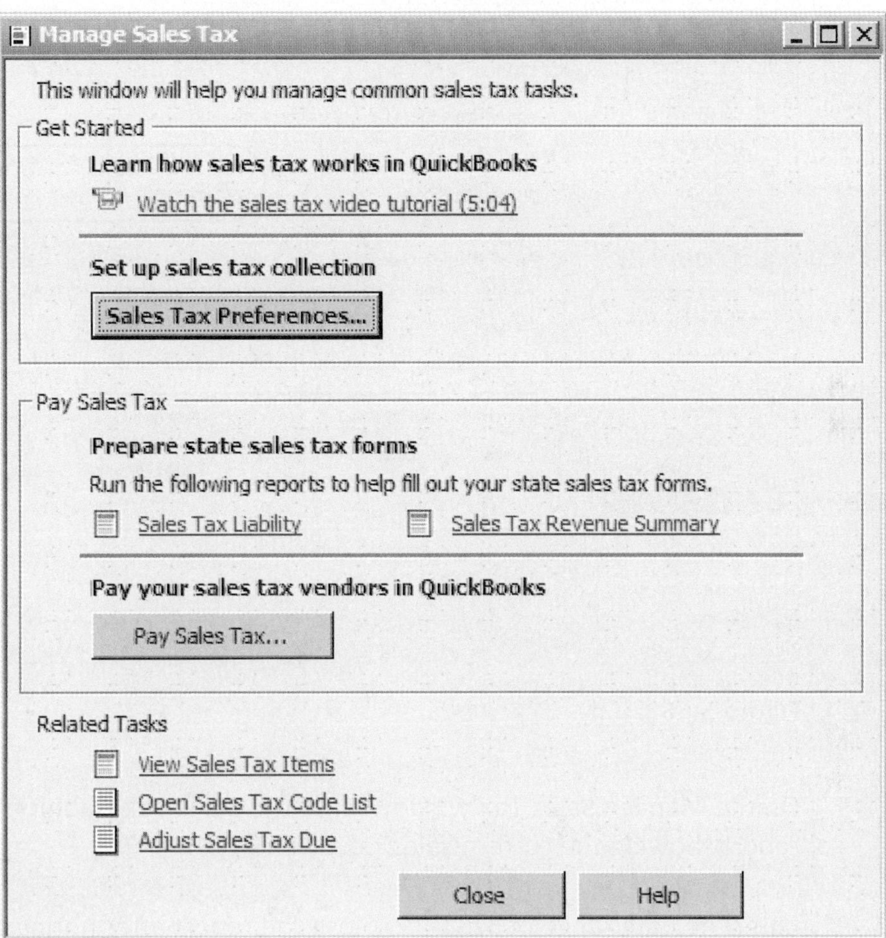

Figure 5:65

2. Click **Sales Tax Preferences**. Figure 5:66 shows that Astor collects Virginia sales tax, owes the tax after the customer pays the invoice, and remits sales tax monthly.

   Click **Cancel** to exit.

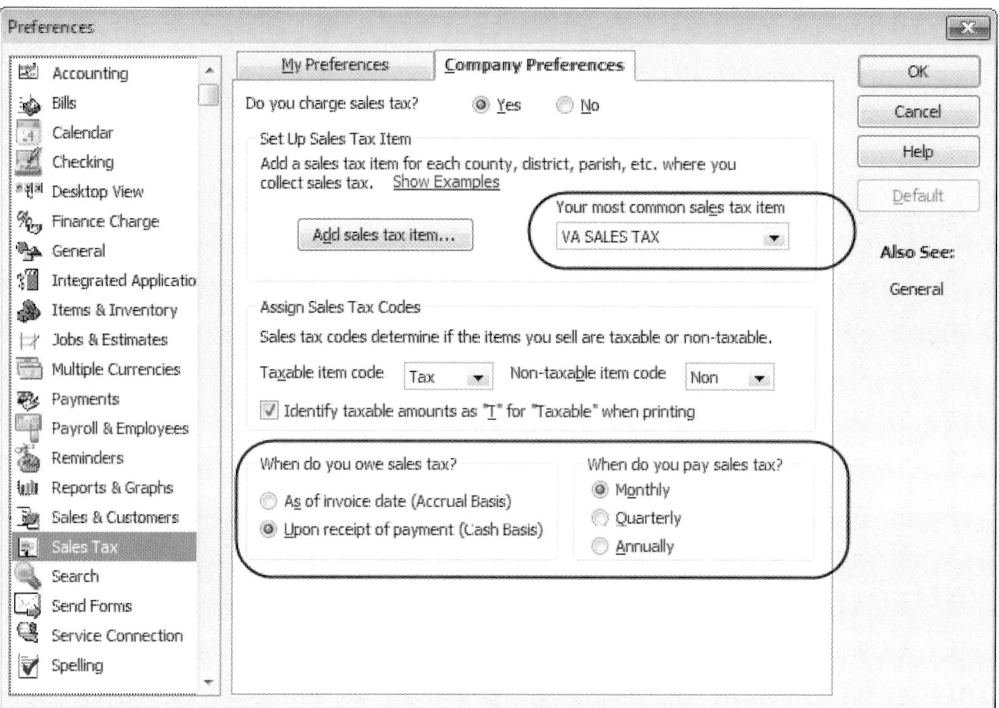

Figure 5:66

3. On the **Manage Sales Tax** window, click the **Sales Tax Liability** link to view a report showing the current sales tax owed.

   Enter the date range of **3/31/12**. Close the report after noting the amount to pay under Sales Tax Payable (Figure 5:67).

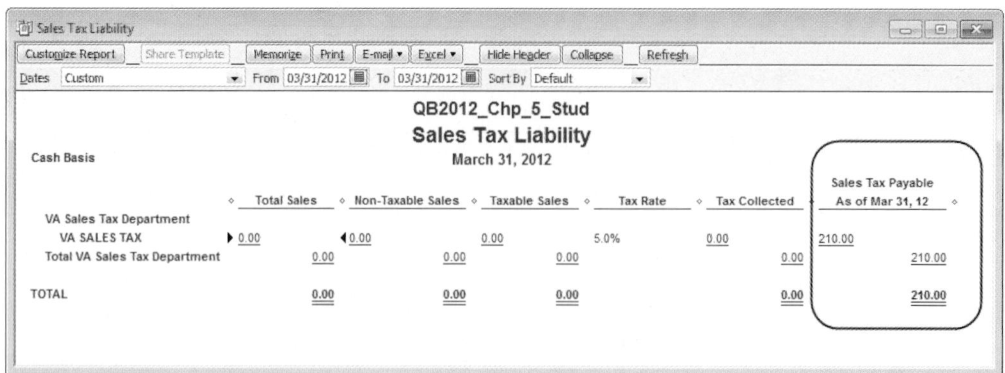

Figure 5:67

4. Click the **Pay Sales Tax** button. Enter the **Check Date** as "4/4/12" and the **Show sales tax due through** date as "3/31/12." Click the **Pay** field . Select the **To be printed** option.

   The **Amt. Due** in Figure 5:68 now matches the amount due on the previous report.

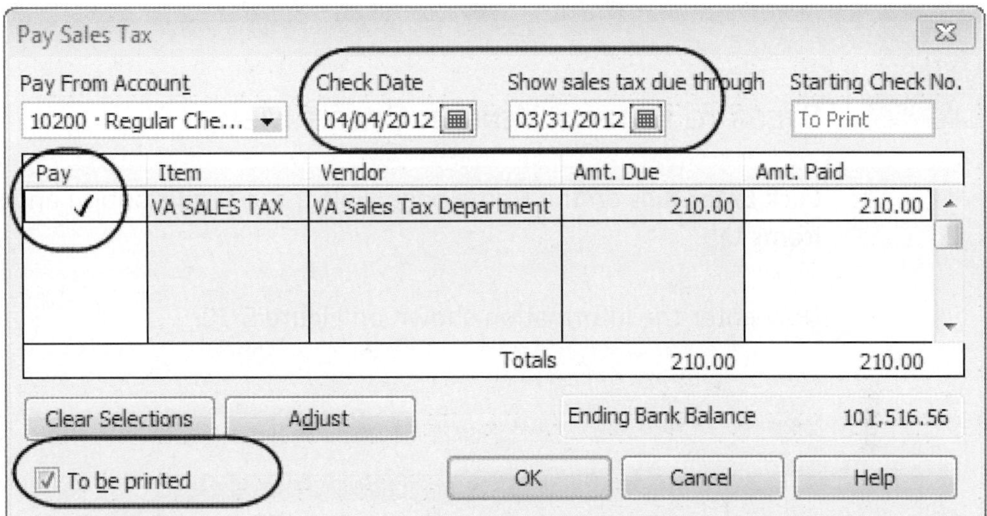

Figure 5:68

5. Click **OK**. Return to the Manage Sales Tax window and **Close** it.

6. You will now print the check. Click **Print Checks** under the **Banking** section of the Home page.

   Confirm that "449" is the check number. Click **OK**. Click **Print** in the Print Checks window. Click **OK** in the confirmation window.

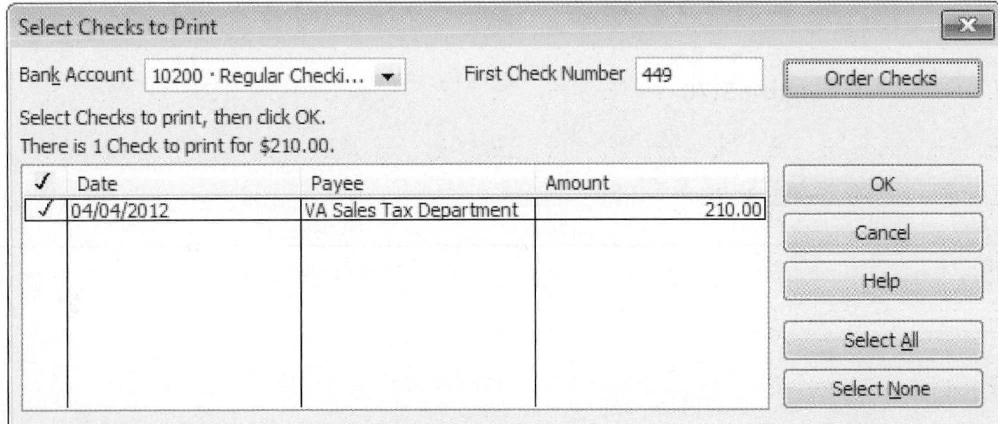

Figure 5:69

VENDOR CREDITS

Just as Astor issues credits to customers, vendors issue credits to Astor. Follow the next steps to record a credit for returning 10 granite pavers to Anderson Wholesale Nursery billed on Invoice 8213.

STEPS TO ENTER A VENDOR CREDIT MEMO

1. Click **Enter Bills** on the Home page. Select the **Credit** option and select the **Items** tab.

   Now enter the information shown on Figure 5:70.

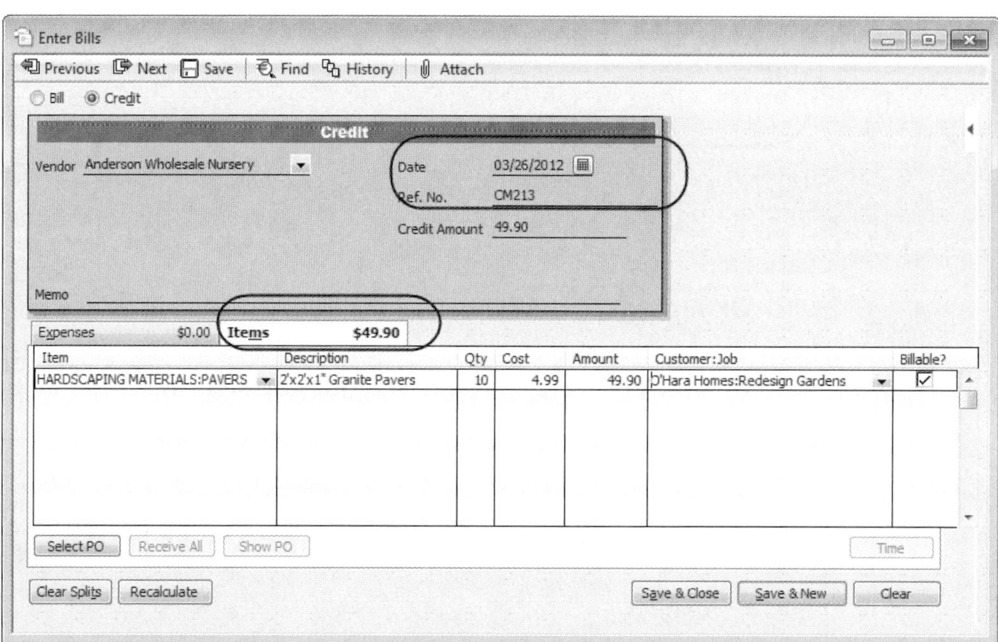

Figure 5:70

2. Click **Save & Close**.

3. Open the **Vendor Center** and view the **Bills** in Anderson's account. You should see the credit memo shown in Figure 5:71.

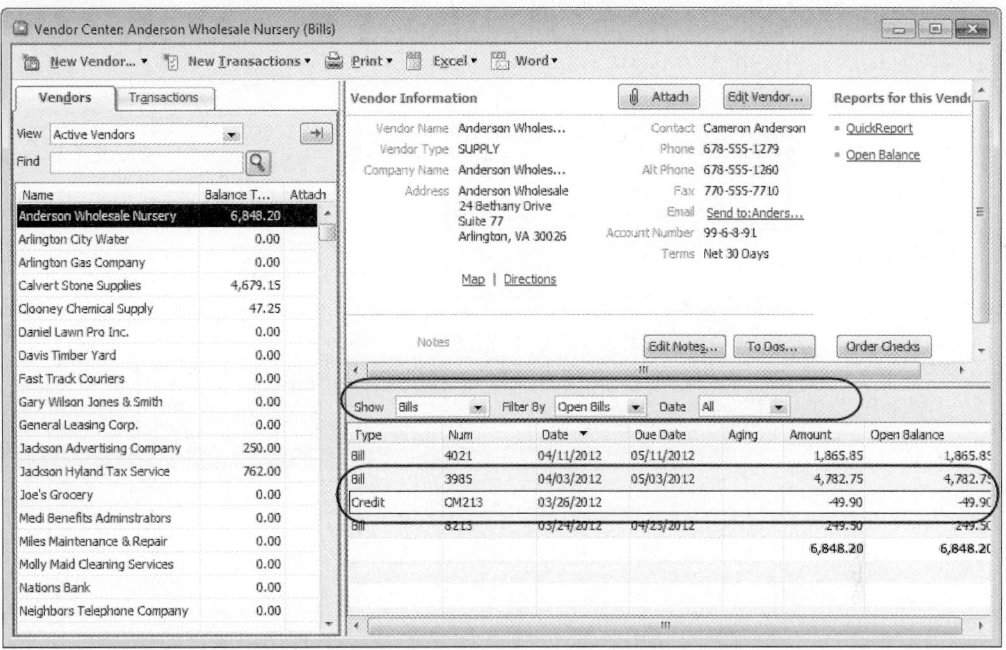

Figure 5:71

4. Now see what happens the next time you pay Anderson. Click the **New Transactions** button on the Vendor Center and select **Pay Bills**.

   Highlight any bill from Anderson and the window will display an available credit of $49.90 (Figure 5:72).

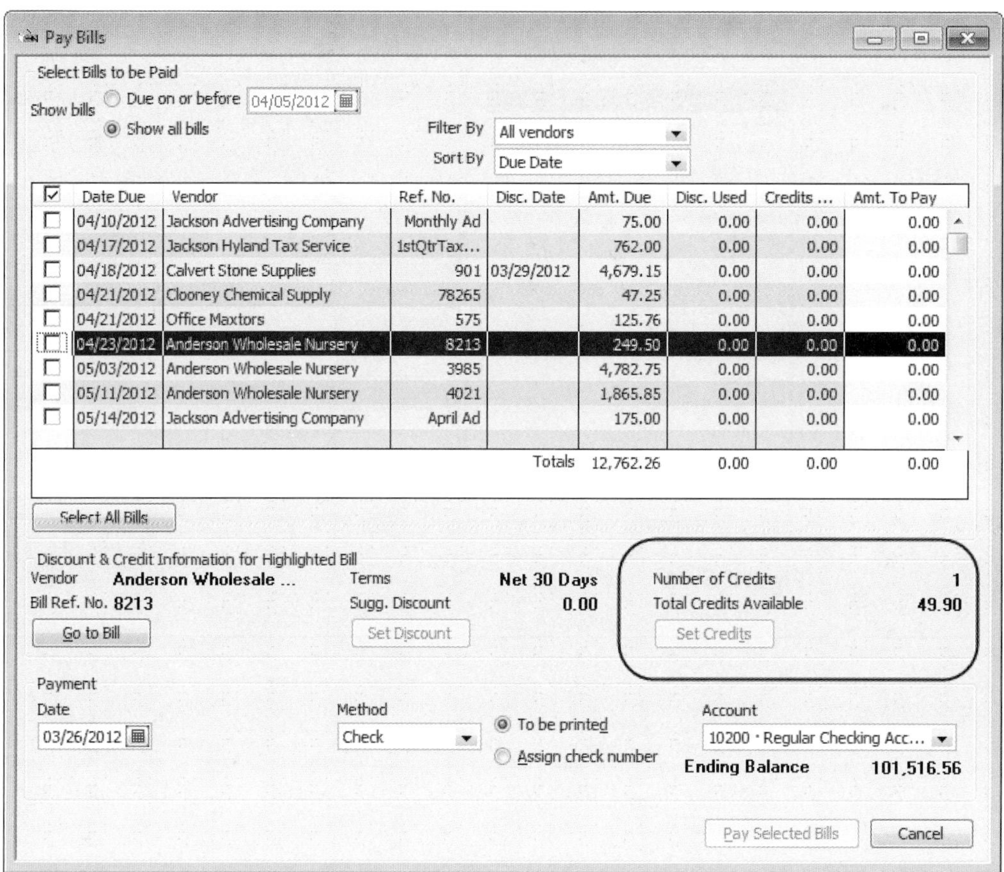

Figure 5:72

Now click to select Anderson's Invoice 8213. The credit will be applied to the bill selected and the amount applied will appear in the **Credits Used** column. *(Note: You can apply the credit to any bill.)*

Click **Cancel** and close the Vendor Center.

VENDOR REPORTING AND RECONCILING ACTIVITIES

QBP offers a variety of purchasing and vendor reports on the **Report Center**. Open the **Report Center** using the icon on the toolbar and select the **Vendors & Payables** category. You have already opened many of these reports using the Reports menu.

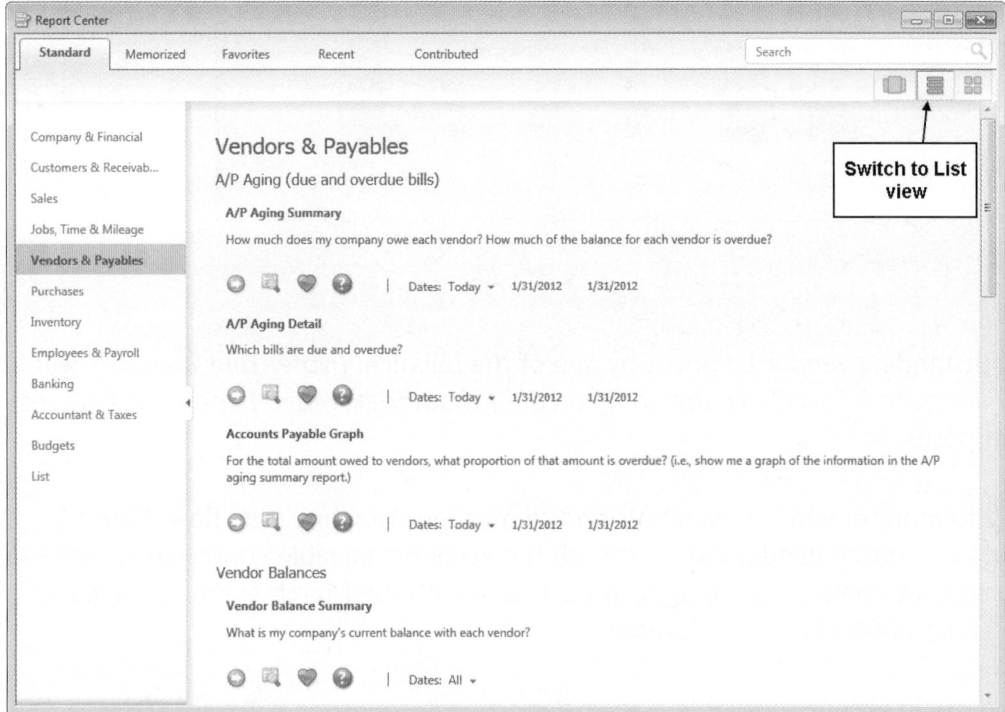

Figure 5:73

We will begin with **A/P Aging** reports. Double click to open the **A/P Aging Summary** and change the date to **3/31/12**. The report is illustrated in Figure 5:74.

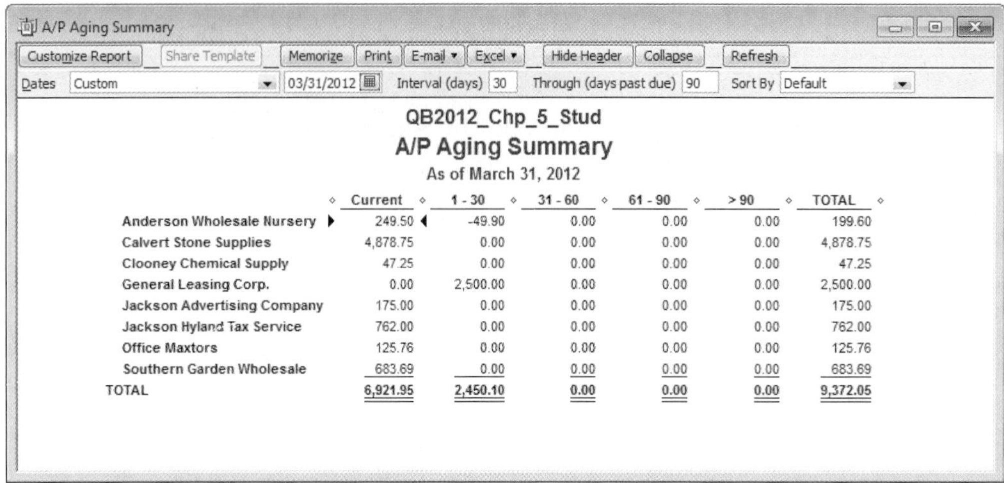

QB2012_Chp_5_Stud
A/P Aging Summary
As of March 31, 2012

	Current	1 - 30	31 - 60	61 - 90	> 90	TOTAL
Anderson Wholesale Nursery	249.50	-49.90	0.00	0.00	0.00	199.60
Calvert Stone Supplies	4,878.75	0.00	0.00	0.00	0.00	4,878.75
Clooney Chemical Supply	47.25	0.00	0.00	0.00	0.00	47.25
General Leasing Corp.	0.00	2,500.00	0.00	0.00	0.00	2,500.00
Jackson Advertising Company	175.00	0.00	0.00	0.00	0.00	175.00
Jackson Hyland Tax Service	762.00	0.00	0.00	0.00	0.00	762.00
Office Maxtors	125.76	0.00	0.00	0.00	0.00	125.76
Southern Garden Wholesale	683.69	0.00	0.00	0.00	0.00	683.69
TOTAL	6,921.95	2,450.10	0.00	0.00	0.00	9,372.05

Figure 5:74

This report lists outstanding vendor balances by age of the balance. *(Note: Your balances will differ from those illustrated if you have not completed all chapter exercises.)* The report serves two important purposes.

First, Astor uses it to monitor vendor payments and to manage company cash flow. Second, the report is used to reconcile vendor balances with the accounts payable control account. This task is performed by comparing the aging report total with the March ending balance in general ledger account 20000 Accounts Payable.

Now view the balance in accounts payable. Select ***Reports>>Accountant & Taxes>>Trial Balance*** on the main menu and filter the report for **3/31/12**. Scroll down and locate the balance in 20000 Accounts Payable. The total on the A/P Aging report and the balance in Accounts Payable must agree to ensure proper recording of vendor activities.

These amounts will not reconcile when you improperly correct vendor transactions. Therefore, you should always refer to the instructions in Appendix B when correcting transactions. You should reconcile the aged payables report to the accounts payable account at the end of every month and prior to issuing financial reports.

Close all open reports and then open the **A/P Aging Detail** report. Change the date to **3/31/12** and refresh the report. This report (Figure 5:75) lists invoices by invoice age.

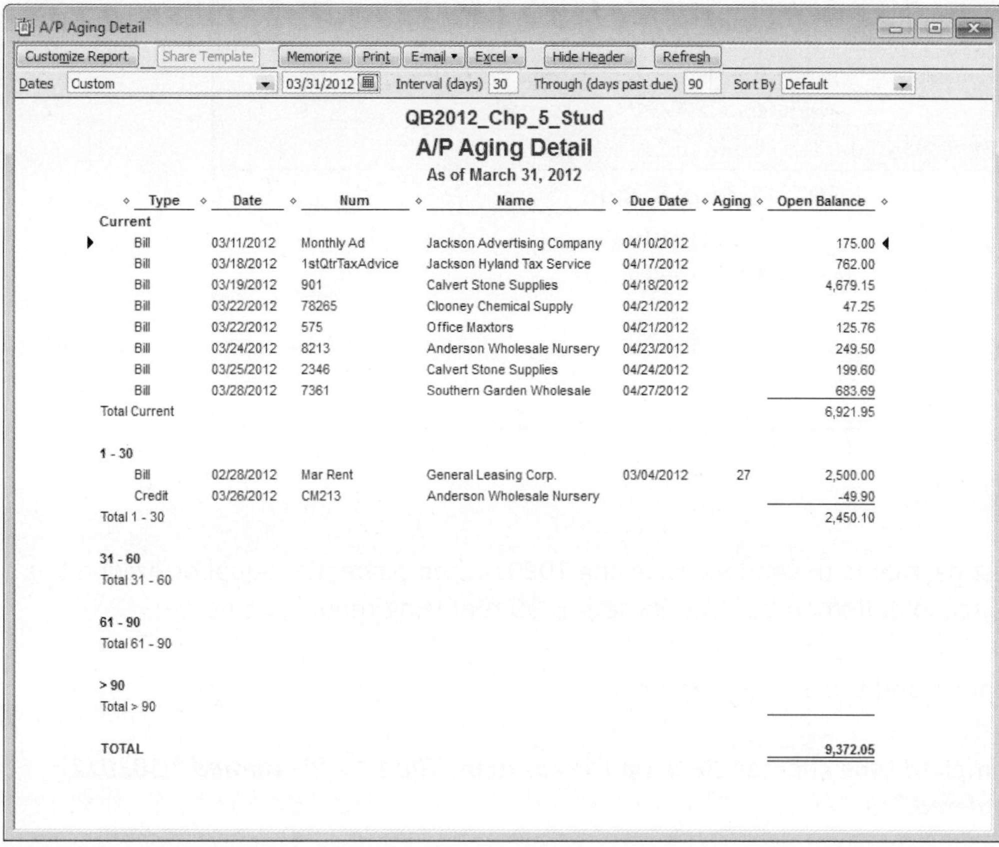
A/P Aging Detail

Customize Report | Share Template | Memorize | Print | E-mail | Excel | Hide Header | Refresh

Dates Custom 03/31/2012 Interval (days) 30 Through (days past due) 90 Sort By Default

QB2012_Chp_5_Stud

A/P Aging Detail

As of March 31, 2012

Type	Date	Num	Name	Due Date	Aging	Open Balance
Current						
Bill	03/11/2012	Monthly Ad	Jackson Advertising Company	04/10/2012		175.00
Bill	03/18/2012	1stQtrTaxAdvice	Jackson Hyland Tax Service	04/17/2012		762.00
Bill	03/19/2012	901	Calvert Stone Supplies	04/18/2012		4,679.15
Bill	03/22/2012	78265	Clooney Chemical Supply	04/21/2012		47.25
Bill	03/22/2012	575	Office Maxtors	04/21/2012		125.76
Bill	03/24/2012	8213	Anderson Wholesale Nursery	04/23/2012		249.50
Bill	03/25/2012	2346	Calvert Stone Supplies	04/24/2012		199.60
Bill	03/28/2012	7361	Southern Garden Wholesale	04/27/2012		683.69
Total Current						6,921.95
1 - 30						
Bill	02/28/2012	Mar Rent	General Leasing Corp.	03/04/2012	27	2,500.00
Credit	03/26/2012	CM213	Anderson Wholesale Nursery			-49.90
Total 1 - 30						2,450.10
31 - 60						
Total 31 - 60						
61 - 90						
Total 61 - 90						
> 90						
Total > 90						
TOTAL						9,372.05

Figure 5:75

Close the A/P Aging Detail report. Finally, open the **1099 Summary** report and enter the date range of **1/1/12** through **3/31/12**. (See Figure 5:76.)

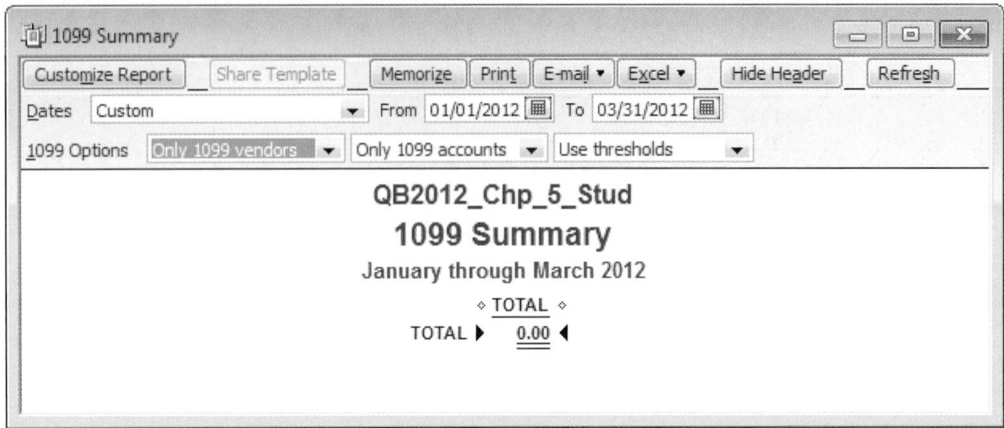

Figure 5:76

This report will list payments to vendors receiving 1099s when payments equal or exceed the $600 reporting threshold. Remember the IRS sets 1099 reporting requirements.

Close all open reports and the Report Center.

You have now completed the chapter. ***Back up the company file to a file named "QB2012_Chp5_Stud_Completed."***

SUMMARY

You began the chapter by learning to post transactions in a manual accounting system. You then posted *MAPS* transactions in QBP. You also learned to use the Vendor Center to manage vendor activities.

You have recorded POs and receipts of items on a PO. You posted vendor bills for receipts and vendor bills for expenses. You also paid vendors, voided payments, and recorded vendor credits.

Finally, you reconciled vendor transactions to the general ledger and worked with a variety of accounts payable reports that analyze activities. You are now ready to focus on the payroll activities covered in Chapter 6.

END-OF-CHAPTER QUESTIONS

TRUE/FALSE

_____ 1. You can enter a void date when voiding a vendor payment.

_____ 2. The Expenses tab on a vendor bill is used for recording inventory purchases.

_____ 3. You must first enter a PO before creating a vendor bill.

_____ 4. Vendor bills assigned to a customer job can be invoiced to the customer after posting the bill. *(Note: Relies on knowledge gained in Chapter 4.)*

_____ 5. Purchase orders are used to verify items on a vendor's bill.

_____ 6. QBP marks a PO "Closed" when all items have been received.

_____ 7. QBP will let you email POs and payments to vendors.

_____ 8. You can delete a vendor account with transaction history.

_____ 9. The Purchases Journal report will list vendor payments.

_____ 10. QBP will let you make changes to a posted vendor payment.

_____ 11. In the Vendor Center, you can view all Item Receipts on the Transactions tab.

_____ 12. You can pay bills from the Vendor Center.

_____ 13. You can add a new customer in the Vendor Center.

_____ 14. You enter vendor credits by selecting the Enter Bills icon on the Home page.

_____ 15. You use the Enter Bills Against Inventory icon on the Home page to record a vendor receipt.

MULTIPLE CHOICE

_____ 1. Which icon(s) will initiate a new vendor transaction?

a. Purchase Orders
b. Receive Inventory
c. Enter Bills
d. Both a and c

_____ 2. The Manage Sales Tax icon will let you _____.

a. create a report for reviewing sales tax liability
b. create a check for sales tax owed
c. view sales tax setup information
d. All of the above

_____ 3. Reconciling vendor activities means that the balance on the aged payables report equals the balance(s) in the _____.
   a. Accounts Payable account
   b. Accrued Liabilities account
   c. Both a and b
   d. None of the above

_____ 4. Which report lets you analyze all transactions for a vendor account?
   a. Vendor Balance Summary
   b. Transaction List by Vendors
   c. Vendor Balance Detail
   d. Both b and c

_____ 5. If you want to pay a vendor less than the full amount on a vendor bill, you can reduce the amount to pay in the _____ window.
   a. Enter Bills
   b. Pay Bills
   c. Enter Bills Against Inventory
   d. Both a and b

_____ 6. Which report ages by vendor account balances?
   a. A/P Aging Summary
   b. b. A/P Aging Detail
   c. c. Both a and b
   d. d. None of the above

_____ 7. Clicking _____ will create checks without a vendor bill.
   a. Pay Bills
   b. Receive Inventory
   c. Write Checks
   d. Enter Bills

_____ 8. To view the age of all unpaid bills, you can view the _____ report.
   a. A/P Aging Summary
   b. A/P Aging Detail
   c. Vendor Balance Summary
   d. Both a and b

_____ 9. All the following statements on POS are true, except _____.
   a. you can pay the amount due on a PO
   b. you can receive items against a PO
   c. you can record a vendor bill against a PO
   d. you can enter items on a PO

_____ 10. The Manage Sales Tax window will let you do all the following, except _____.
   a. open the Sales Tax preferences window
   b. view the Sales Tax Liability report
   c. pay sales taxes
   d. record sales taxes

PRACTICE SET

In this practice set, you will record vendor activities for April 2012. Keep the following in mind:

- Unless otherwise instructed, accept all defaults assigned from the vendor account.
- You will print reports in Step 2, so do not print transactions unless otherwise instructed.

Begin by:

- Opening the software.
- Opening the **QB2012_Chp5_PracSet_Stud** data file. Add your initials to the end to the Company Name by clicking ***Company>>Company Information*** on the main menu. Click **OK** to save the changes.
- Toggling the software to the PRO EDITION by selecting *File>>Toggle to Another Edition* on the main menu and choosing QuickBooks Pro as the edition.

1. Record the following transactions.

2012

Apr 1 Post Safe State Insurance Company bill for six months of prepaid insurance, $1,200.00.

Apr 2 Add the following Non-inventory Part. Make sure to mark the option of *This item is used in assemblies or is purchased for a specific customer:job.*

Item name:	ARBORVITAE
Subitem of:	PLANTS
Purchase description:	2G Arborvitae
Purchase cost:	$40.00
Expense account:	51000 Materials Cost - Landscape
Preferred vendor:	Anderson Wholesale Nursery
Sales description:	2G Arborvitae
Sales price:	$52.00
Tax code:	Tax
Income account:	41000 Sales - Landscape

Record the following vendor bills for job materials. *(Note: There are no existing POs on file so you will not be matching the bills to a PO.)*

Anderson Wholesale Nursery Invoice 7383 dated April 1, $2,318.00, for O'Hara Homes Redesign Gardens job.

Qty	Item	Cost
20	Verbena	$ 15.90
50	Arborvitae	$ 40.00

Paris Brothers Tree Surgeons Invoice 4263 dated April 1, $1,020.00 for O'Hara Homes Redesign Gardens job.

Qty	Item	Cost
12	Tree removal	$ 85.00

2012

Apr 7 Post Davis Timber Yard's Invoice 9033 dated April 5, $3,775.70 for White and Associates job.

Qty	Item	Cost
400	Redwood Decking	$ 8.99
15	Redwood Posts	$ 5.99
15	Redwood Caps	$ 5.99

Pay $21,453.43 to vendors for bills with a due date or discount date before April 19. First check number is 439.

Apr 14 Post Miles Maintenance & Repair Invoice 1762 for $275.00 dated April 12 for auto repairs. Verify the account number for the transaction.

Apr 15 Issue PO 176 for $449.50 to Davis Timber Yard containing the following item for the White and Associates job. **Print the PO.**

Qty	Item	Cost
50	Redwood Decking	$ 8.99

Post Anderson Wholesale Nursery Invoice 3766 for $9.98 dated April 14 for the DBH Enterprises job.

Qty	Item	Cost
2	Mulch	$ 4.99

Apr 18 Post the following bills for expenses dated April 18.

Arlington City Water	April water	$110.00
Neighbors Telephone Co.	April phone	$230.00
Arlington Gas Company	April gas	$175.80
Southern Power Co.	April electric	$162.50

Apr 19 Write and print check number 445 to Postmaster for postage expense $150.00.

Post Davis Timber Yard Invoice 6261, $449.50, dated April 18, for all items on PO 176.

2012

Apr 20 Add the following new vendor.

Metropolitan Supplies
672 N. Main Street
Arlington, VA 30010

Vendor Type:	OFFICE
Payment terms:	Net 30 Days
Expense Account:	63000 Office Supplies Expense

Post Metropolitan Supplies Invoice 6565, dated April 19, for office supply expense $137.20.

Apr 26 Post Anderson Wholesale Nursery credit memo CM7383, $80.00, dated April 20, for returning 2 Arborvitae on Invoice 7383 for the O'Hara Homes Redesign Garden job. Credit memo is billable to the job.

Apr 28 Pay $8,899.05 to vendors for bills with a due date or discount date before May 3. First check number is 446.

Write check number 452 for $210.00 for April sales tax.

2. Print the following reports.

    a. Purchases Journal for April transactions

    b. Cash Disbursements Journal for April transactions. Customize the report to add the Transaction Type of Check to existing transaction types.

    c. Open Purchase Orders report for April transactions. Customize the Received filter option to include Either.

    d. A/P Aging Detail report for April 30.

    e. Job Profitability Summary report for April transactions.

3. ***Back up the company file to a backup file named QB2012_Chp5_Prac_Set_Stud_Completed."***

Internet Mini-Project

To complete this mini-project, go to the Website at ***www.pearsonhighered.com/brunsdon/*** and download the instruction file named **Max Repair.pdf** and the data file named **Max Repair. QBW**.

CHAPTER 6 PAYROLL ACTIVITIES FOR A SERVICE-BASED BUSINESS

LEARNING OBJECTIVES

In this chapter, you perform payroll activities for the company we call Astor. You will:

1. Review the *MAPS* for processing paychecks before using the software
2. Review setting up payroll items to understand the impact these items have on processing payroll
3. Learn to use the Employee Center to manage employees and transactions
4. Record employee time and print time reports
5. Prepare paychecks
6. Go *Behind the Keys* to view posted paychecks
7. Learn to correct paychecks
8. Learn to allocate wages for salaried employees to jobs
9. Remit payroll tax liabilities to government taxing agencies
10. Create and interpret payroll reports, including Form 941 and W-2s

Begin by:

- Opening the software.
- Opening the **QB2012_Chp6_Stud** data file. Add your initials to the end to the Company Name by clicking ***Company>>Company Information*** on the main menu. Click **OK** to save the changes.
- **Toggling the software to the PRO EDITION** by selecting ***File>>Toggle to Another Edition*** on the main menu and choosing **QuickBooks Pro** as the edition.

MANUAL ACCOUNTING PROCEDURES

Astor pays its employees biweekly (every two weeks). Employees are paid either an annual salary or hourly wage. Salaried employees are paid the same amount each pay period. Hourly employees are paid for the hours worked during the pay period. Hourly employees document their hours on a timesheet and note the hours spent on a job so Astor can invoice time to its customers.

You will soon learn that payroll in a manual accounting system is tedious and time consuming. First, you must calculate the gross pay for each employee. For hourly employees, gross pay is calculated by totaling timesheet hours for the pay period and multiplying total hours by the hourly pay rate. For salaried employees, gross pay remains the same each pay period and is calculated by dividing the annual salary by the number of pay periods in the year. The number of pay periods in the year is 26 for Astor.

After calculating gross pay, you next calculate net pay. Net pay equals gross pay minus total payroll tax withholdings and total voluntary deductions. The following tables explain payroll tax withholdings and voluntary deductions.

Employee Tax Withholdings	**Description**
Federal Income Tax	Employee federal income taxes withheld on taxable wages. Taxable wages exclude employee contributions to a 401K or IRA retirement plan. IRS Circular E sets the guidelines for withholding federal income taxes. Using this table is explained later.
Social Security (FICA)	Employee taxes withheld on gross wages and paid to the federal government to fund Social Security retirement. Gross wages include employee contributions to a 401K or IRA retirement plan. The IRS has historically taxed gross wages, below the annual cap, at 6.2 percent (0.062). This cap is changed each year. For 2012, the cap is $110,100. *(Note: In 2011 and 2012, a 2 percent reduction is in effect, making the percentage 4.2 percent (.042). The text will continue to use the 6.2 percent rate.)*
Medicare (FICA)	Employee taxes withheld on gross wages and paid to the federal government to fund Medicare health insurance. Gross wages include employee contributions to a 401K or IRA retirement plan. The IRS taxes gross wages at 1.45 percent (0.0145) with no annual wage cap.
State Income Tax	Employee state income taxes withheld on taxable wages (i.e., gross wages minus contributions to a 401K or IRA retirement plan). Each state publishes guidelines for withholding state income taxes. ***Astor withholds 3 percent (0.03) of gross wages.***

Employee Voluntary Deductions	Description
Retirement Plans	Voluntary contributions to an employer-sponsored retirement plan. Retirement plans include 401K and IRA plans. These contributions are deducted from gross wages to determine federal and state taxable wages. ***Aster does not sponsor a retirement plan***.
Health Insurance	Health insurance premiums deducted from pay when the employer requires its employees to pay for a portion of health insurance costs. ***Astor does not require employees to share this cost***.
Contributions	Deductions from net pay for charitable contributions made by the employee.

Astor also pays taxes on employee compensation and provides additional compensation by providing health insurance. The following tables explain typical employer tax liabilities and other forms of employee compensation.

Employer Payroll Taxes	Description
Social Security (FICA) and Medicare (FICA)	Employer portion of Social Security and Medicare taxes paid on gross wages. The employer tax equals the tax paid by employees. *(Exception: In 2011 and 2012, the employer does not receive the 2% reduction given to employees.)*
Federal Unemployment (FUTA)	Employer tax on gross wages paid to the federal government for subsidizing state unemployment compensation funds. Historically, employers have paid 0.8 percent (0.008) on the first $7,000 of annual gross wages paid to each employee. In July 2011, the rate was reduced to 0.6 percent (0.006); however, employers in states with higher than normal unemployment pay an adjusted rate that is higher. For simplicity, the text will continue to illustrate the historical rate.
State Unemployment (SUTA)	Employer tax on gross wages paid to the state for funding compensation for unemployed workers. Typically, the tax rate is based on an employer's unemployment history and/or business type and will be capped after reaching an annual limit on gross wages. ***For Astor, the rate is 1.5 percent (0.015) of the first $8,000 of annual wages paid to each employee***.
Worker's Compensation	Employer tax paid to the state to fund compensating injured workers. Typically, states set the tax rates based on risk factors in an employee's job. ***The text does not illustrate worker's compensation tax***.

Additional Compensation	Description
Retirement Plans	Employer contributions to a company-sponsored 401K or IRA retirement plan. Typically, companies match contributions based on employee participation in the plan. ***Astor does not sponsor a retirement plan***.
Health Insurance	Employer premiums for health insurance. Employers may pay all premiums or require employees to share in this cost. ***Astor pays all health insurance premiums for employees eligible to participate in the plan***.

Each pay period the accountant prepares an Excel spreadsheet called the Payroll Register to calculate employee net pay. The register illustrated in Figure 6:1 covers the two-week pay period of February 20 to March 4.

Astor Landscaping
Paychecks for Pay Period 2/20/2012 thru 3/04/2012

Check No.	Employee	Filing Status	Allow.	Pay Type	Pay Rate	Regular Hrs	O.T. Hours	Gross Pay	Federal Income Tax	Soc. Sec. (FICA) Tax	Medicare Tax	VA State Tax	Net Pay
721	Dillion, Roy J.	Single	1	Hourly Wage	12.00	80.00		960.00	95.00	59.52	13.92	28.80	762.76
722	Folse, Jan B.	Single	1	Hourly Office	10.00	80.00		800.00	71.00	49.60	11.60	24.00	643.80
723	Greene, Kellie I.	Married	1	Salary	2,346.15			2,346.15	256.00	145.46	34.02	70.38	1,840.29
724	Hardman, Alan	Single	2	Hourly Wage	12.00	78.00		936.00	69.00	58.03	13.57	28.08	767.32
725	Henderson, Jeff P.	Married	1	Hourly Wage	12.00	80.00		960.00	53.00	59.52	13.92	28.80	804.76
726	Ramez, Victor M.	Single	0	Hourly Wage	10.00	75.00		750.00	83.00	46.50	10.88	22.50	587.12
727	Ruland, Seth N.	Married	0	Salary	3,103.85			3,103.85	429.00	192.44	45.01	93.12	2,344.28
	Totals					**393.00**	**0.00**	**9,856.00**	**1,056.00**	**611.07**	**142.92**	**295.68**	**7,750.33**
	Tax Basis								**Circular E**	**6.20%**	**1.45%**	**3.00%**	
	G/L Accounts							**57000 / 60000**	**23400**	**23400**	**23400**	**23600**	**10300**

Figure 6:1

The Payroll Register shows that Kellie Greene claims the federal filing status of Married (M) with one withholding allowance. Kellie's federal income tax withholding for this pay period is calculated by referring to the payroll tax withholding table illustrated in Figure 6:2.

(Note: These tables are for instructional purposes only and are excerpts from the Internal Revenue Service's Circular E publication, which is updated annually. To obtain a current edition of this publication, visit www.irs.gov.)

MARRIED Persons—**BIWEEKLY** Payroll Period

(For Wages Paid in)

If the wages are–		And the number of withholding allowances claimed is—										
At least	But less than	0	1	2	3	4	5	6	7	8	9	10
		The amount of income tax to be withheld is—										
$1,380	$1,400	$132	$112	$92	$72	$54	$41	$27	$14	$1	$0	$0
1,400	1,420	135	115	95	75	56	43	29	16	3	0	0
1,420	1,440	138	118	98	78	58	45	31	18	5	0	0
1,440	1,460	141	121	101	81	61	47	33	20	7	0	0
1,460	1,480	144	124	104	84	64	49	35	22	9	0	0
1,480	1,500	147	127	107	87	67	51	37	24	11	0	0
1,500	1,520	150	130	110	90	70	53	39	26	13	0	0
1,520	1,540	153	133	113	93	73	55	41	28	15	1	0
1,540	1,560	156	136	116	96	76	57	43	30	17	3	0
1,560	1,580	159	139	119	99	79	59	45	32	19	5	0
2,280	2,300	267	247	227	207	187	166	146	126	106	86	66
2,300	2,320	270	250	230	210	190	169	149	129	109	89	69
2,320	2,340	273	253	233	213	193	172	152	132	112	92	72
2,340	2,360	276	256	236	216	196	175	155	135	115	95	75
2,360	2,380	279	259	239	219	199	178	158	138	118	98	78
2,380	2,400	282	262	242	222	202	181	161	141	121	101	81
2,400	2,420	285	265	245	225	205	184	164	144	124	104	84
2,420	2,440	288	268	248	228	208	187	167	147	127	107	87
2,440	2,460	291	271	251	231	211	190	170	150	130	110	90
2,460	2,480	294	274	254	234	214	193	173	153	133	113	93
2,480	2,500	297	277	257	237	217	196	176	156	136	116	96
2,500	2,520	300	280	260	240	220	199	179	159	139	119	99
2,520	2,540	303	283	263	243	223	202	182	162	142	122	102
2,540	2,560	306	286	266	246	226	205	185	165	145	125	105
2,560	2,580	309	289	269	249	229	208	188	168	148	128	108
2,580	2,600	312	292	272	252	232	211	191	171	151	131	111
2,600	2,620	315	295	275	255	235	214	194	174	154	134	114
2,620	2,640	318	298	278	258	238	217	197	177	157	137	117
2,640	2,660	321	301	281	261	241	220	200	180	160	140	120
2,660	2,680	324	304	284	264	244	223	203	183	163	143	123
2,680	2,700	327	307	287	267	247	226	206	186	166	146	126
$2,700 and over		Use Table 2(b) for a **MARRIED person** on page 38. Also see the instructions on page 36.										

Figure 6:2

Figure 6:2 is the IRS table for employees paid biweekly and claiming the Married (M) filing status. There are separate IRS tables for employees claiming the Single (S) filing status and separate tables for married and single employees paid on a weekly or monthly basis.

Kellie's $256.00 federal income tax withholding amount is found at the point where her taxable pay of $2,346.15 intersects with her one claimed withholding allowance. Because Kellie does not contribute to a 401K or IRA retirement plan, her taxable pay equals her gross pay.

Kellie's Social Security tax withholding of $145.46 equals her gross pay times 6.2 percent (0.062). Her Medicare tax withholding of $34.02 equals gross pay times 1.45 percent (0.0145).

The state tax withholding of $70.38 is 3 percent (0.03) of her taxable pay.

Kellie has no deductions for health insurance premiums, retirement plan contributions, or charitable contributions. In fact, premiums are not deducted from any employee's paycheck because Astor pays the full cost of health insurance. There are no deductions for retirement plans because Astor does not sponsor a plan. Finally, there are no employees making charitable contributions through payroll.

Accordingly, Kellie's net pay of $1,840.29 equals her gross pay minus the sum of her total tax withholdings.

The accountant also computed the employer payroll tax liabilities for the pay period, illustrated in Figure 6:3.

Astor Landscaping
Employer Costs for Pay Period 2/20/2012 thru 3/04/2012

Employee	ER Soc Sec FICA	ER Medicare	ER FUTA	ER SUTA	Health Insurance
Dillion, Roy J.	59.52	13.92	7.68	14.40	0.00
Folse, Jan B.	49.60	11.60	6.40	12.00	60.00
Greene, Kellie I.	145.46	34.02	0.00	0.00	60.00
Hardman, Alan	58.03	13.57	7.49	14.04	0.00
Henderson, Jeff P.	59.52	13.92	7.68	14.40	0.00
Ramez, Victor M.	46.50	10.88	6.00	11.25	0.00
Ruland, Seth N.	192.44	45.01	0.00	0.00	60.00
Totals	**611.07**	**142.92**	**35.25**	**66.09**	**180.00**
Tax Basis	**6.20%**	**1.45%**	**0.8%**	**1.50%**	
G/L Accounts	23400 / 61000	23400 / 61000	23500 / 61000	23700 / 61000	23800 / 60600

Figure 6:3

After computing employee pay and employer payroll tax liabilities, the accountant creates paychecks and records the general journal entries illustrated in Figure 6:4. *(Note: General ledger accounts are listed on the worksheets. The expense recorded to 57000 Direct Labor is the gross pay for employees paid by hourly wage.)*

Audit Trail

Astor Landscaping
General Journal **Page 5**

Date	Account Post Ref	Description	Debit	Credit
3/5/2012	57000	Direct Labor	4,406.00	
	60000	Salaries Expense	5,450.00	
	23400	Federal Payroll Tax Liabilities		1,809.99
	23600	State Payroll Taxes Payable		295.68
	10300	Payroll Checking Account		7,750.33
To record employee paychecks				
3/5/2012	61000	Payroll Tax Expense	855.33	
	60600	Employee Benefit Exp.	180.00	
	23400	Federal Payroll Tax Liabilities		753.99
	23500	FUTA Tax Payable		35.25
	23700	SUTA Tax Payable		66.09
	23800	Medical Insurance Payable		180.00
To record employer payroll tax expense				

Figure 6:4

The journal entries are then posted to the general ledger accounts affected by the transactions (Figure 6:5). *(Note: Only two general ledger accounts are illustrated.)*

General Ledger					
Payroll Checking Account				Account No. 10300	
Date	Description	Post Ref	Debit	Credit	Balance
3/4/2012	Balance Forward				7,900.00
3/5/2012		GJ 5		7,750.33	149.67

Audit Trail

General Ledger					
Federal Payroll Tax Liabilities				Account No. 23400	
Date	Description	Post Ref	Debit	Credit	Balance
3/4/2012	Balance Forward				-
3/5/2012		GJ 5		1,809.99	1,809.99
3/5/2012		GJ 5		753.99	2,563.98

Figure 6:5

As explained in previous chapters, the audit trail is recorded while posting to general ledger accounts.

With an understanding of *MAPS* for paycheck activities, you are now ready to perform these activities in QBP.

Understanding Payroll Items

A series of setup steps is performed before a company can use QBP for processing payroll. The accountant has already completed these steps; however, it will help for you to understand payroll setup.

Begin by opening the Payroll Item List. Select ***Lists>>Payroll Item List*** on the main menu to open the window illustrated in Figure 6:6.

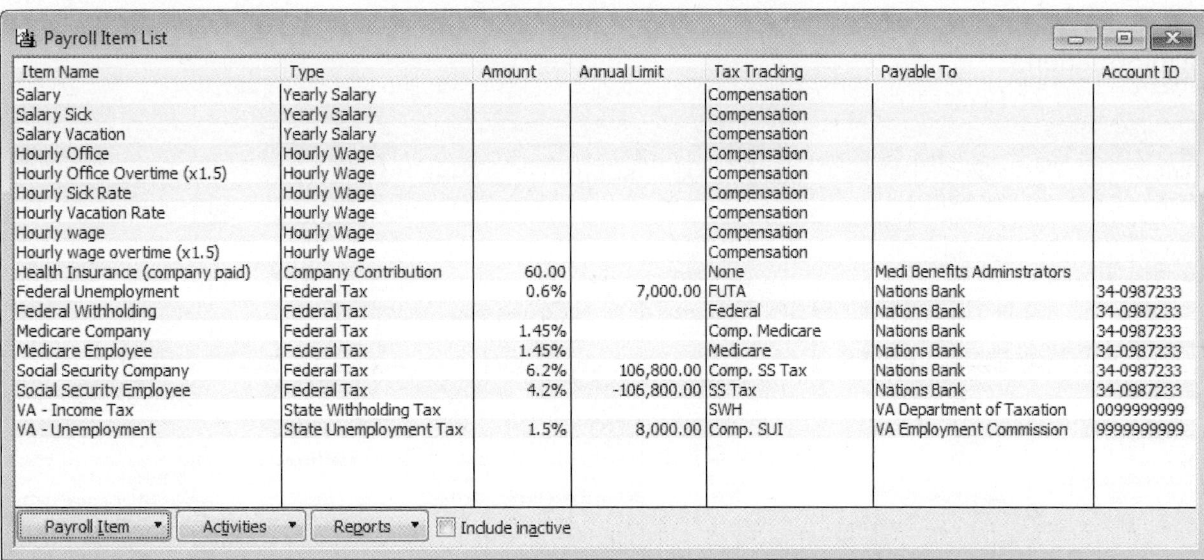

Payroll Item List

Item Name	Type	Amount	Annual Limit	Tax Tracking	Payable To	Account ID
Salary	Yearly Salary			Compensation		
Salary Sick	Yearly Salary			Compensation		
Salary Vacation	Yearly Salary			Compensation		
Hourly Office	Hourly Wage			Compensation		
Hourly Office Overtime (x1.5)	Hourly Wage			Compensation		
Hourly Sick Rate	Hourly Wage			Compensation		
Hourly Vacation Rate	Hourly Wage			Compensation		
Hourly wage	Hourly Wage			Compensation		
Hourly wage overtime (x1.5)	Hourly Wage			Compensation		
Health Insurance (company paid)	Company Contribution	60.00		None	Medi Benefits Adminstrators	
Federal Unemployment	Federal Tax	0.6%	7,000.00	FUTA	Nations Bank	34-0987233
Federal Withholding	Federal Tax			Federal	Nations Bank	34-0987233
Medicare Company	Federal Tax	1.45%		Comp. Medicare	Nations Bank	34-0987233
Medicare Employee	Federal Tax	1.45%		Medicare	Nations Bank	34-0987233
Social Security Company	Federal Tax	6.2%	106,800.00	Comp. SS Tax	Nations Bank	34-0987233
Social Security Employee	Federal Tax	4.2%	-106,800.00	SS Tax	Nations Bank	34-0987233
VA - Income Tax	State Withholding Tax			SWH	VA Department of Taxation	0099999999
VA - Unemployment	State Unemployment Tax	1.5%	8,000.00	Comp. SUI	VA Employment Commission	9999999999

Payroll Item ▼ | Activities ▼ | Reports ▼ | Include inactive

Figure 6:6

Figure 6:6 shows the payroll items used to record compensation, payroll tax withholdings, and payroll tax liabilities. Salary and wage types post employee compensation whereas federal and state types post employee tax withholdings and employer tax liabilities.

Next, you will add columns to the list so that general ledger accounts are displayed for each item. Click **Payroll Item** at the bottom of the list and select **Customize Columns**.

Under Available Columns, highlight **Expense Account** and click **Add**. Do the same for **Liability Account**. Under Chosen Columns, highlight **Account ID** and click **Remove**. The completed window is illustrated in Figure 6:7.

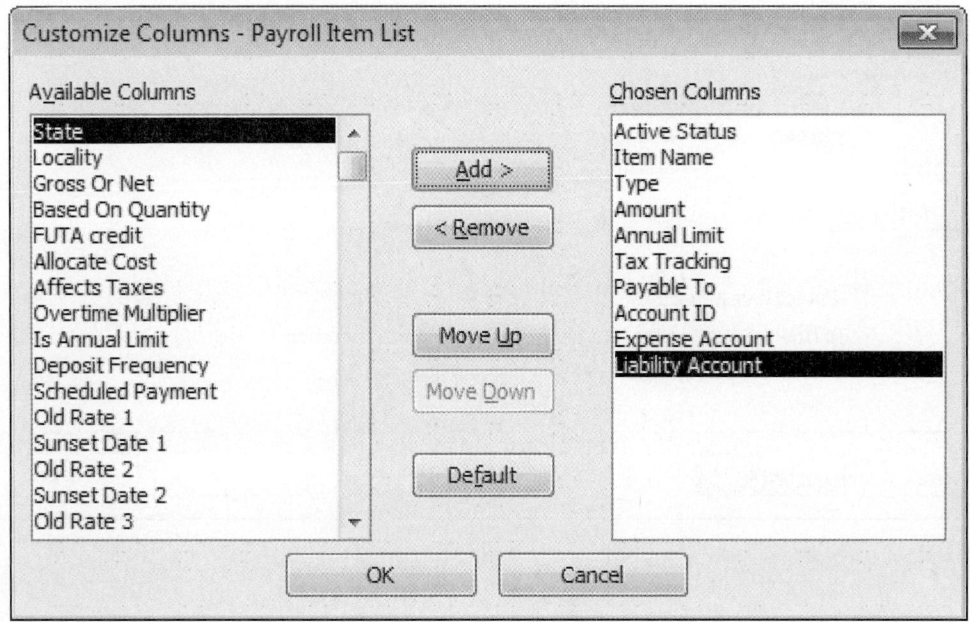

Figure 6:7

Click **OK** to view the list with the added columns (Figure 6:8). You have to resize columns to view all information.

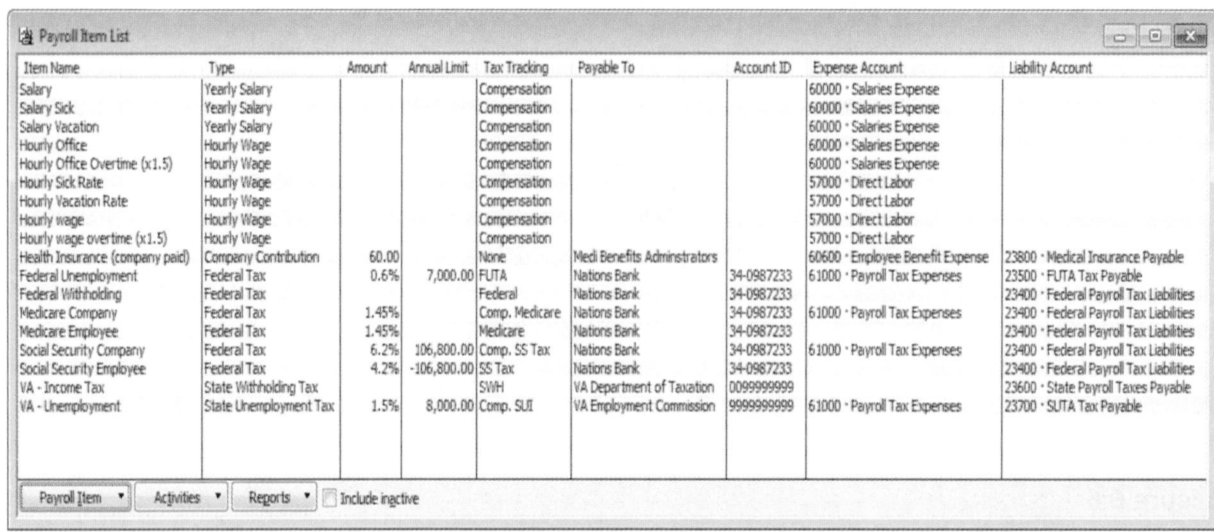

Payroll Item List

Item Name	Type	Amount	Annual Limit	Tax Tracking	Payable To	Account ID	Expense Account	Liability Account
Salary	Yearly Salary			Compensation			60000 · Salaries Expense	
Salary Sick	Yearly Salary			Compensation			60000 · Salaries Expense	
Salary Vacation	Yearly Salary			Compensation			60000 · Salaries Expense	
Hourly Office	Hourly Wage			Compensation			60000 · Salaries Expense	
Hourly Office Overtime (x1.5)	Hourly Wage			Compensation			60000 · Salaries Expense	
Hourly Sick Rate	Hourly Wage			Compensation			57000 · Direct Labor	
Hourly Vacation Rate	Hourly Wage			Compensation			57000 · Direct Labor	
Hourly wage	Hourly Wage			Compensation			57000 · Direct Labor	
Hourly wage overtime (x1.5)	Hourly Wage			Compensation			57000 · Direct Labor	
Health Insurance (company paid)	Company Contribution	60.00		None	Medi Benefits Adminstrators		60600 · Employee Benefit Expense	23800 · Medical Insurance Payable
Federal Unemployment	Federal Tax	0.6%	7,000.00	FUTA	Nations Bank	34-0987233	61000 · Payroll Tax Expenses	23500 · FUTA Tax Payable
Federal Withholding	Federal Tax			Federal	Nations Bank	34-0987233		23400 · Federal Payroll Tax Liabilities
Medicare Company	Federal Tax	1.45%		Comp. Medicare	Nations Bank	34-0987233	61000 · Payroll Tax Expenses	23400 · Federal Payroll Tax Liabilities
Medicare Employee	Federal Tax	1.45%		Medicare	Nations Bank	34-0987233		23400 · Federal Payroll Tax Liabilities
Social Security Company	Federal Tax	6.2%	106,800.00	Comp. SS Tax	Nations Bank	34-0987233	61000 · Payroll Tax Expenses	23400 · Federal Payroll Tax Liabilities
Social Security Employee	Federal Tax	4.2%	-106,800.00	SS Tax	Nations Bank	34-0987233		23400 · Federal Payroll Tax Liabilities
VA - Income Tax	State Withholding Tax			SWH	VA Department of Taxation	0099999999		23600 · State Payroll Taxes Payable
VA - Unemployment	State Unemployment Tax	1.5%	8,000.00	Comp. SUI	VA Employment Commission	9999999999	61000 · Payroll Tax Expenses	23700 · SUTA Tax Payable

Payroll Item ▾ Activities ▾ Reports ▾ Include inactive

Figure 6:8

Refer to these accounts as we go through the setup of payroll items.

Double click the **Salary** item. The window in Figure 6:9 is used to define the item's name or to inactivate the item. Click **Next**.

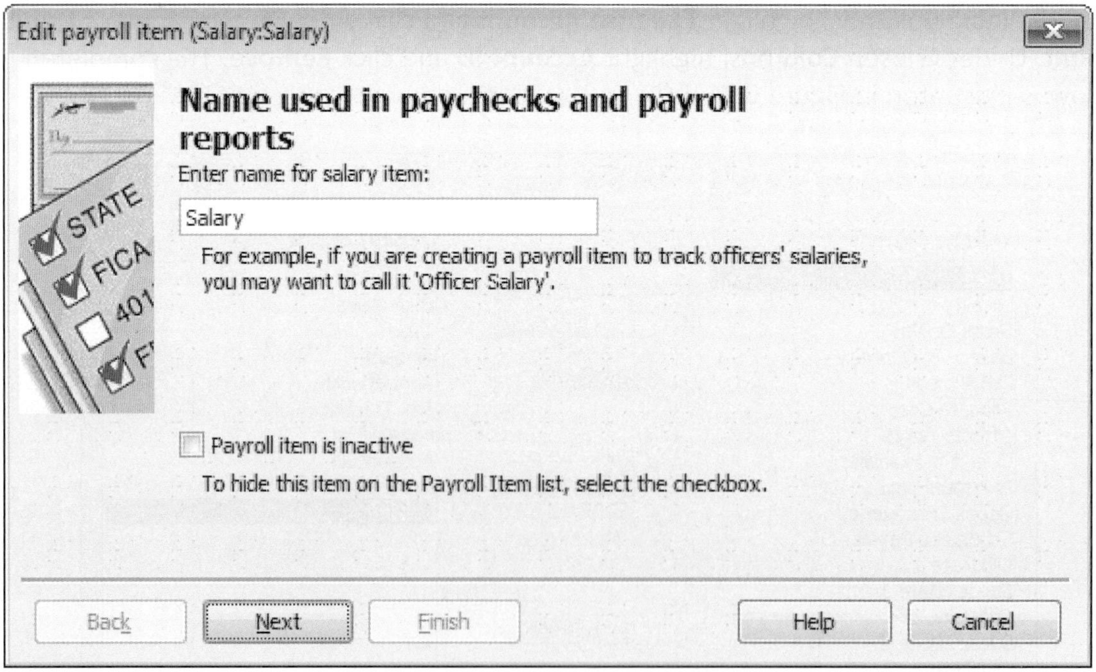

Figure 6:9

The window in Figure 6:10 sets the default general ledger account used when posting a salaried employee's gross pay. The account displayed matches the expense account listed on the Payroll Item List. Click **Cancel**.

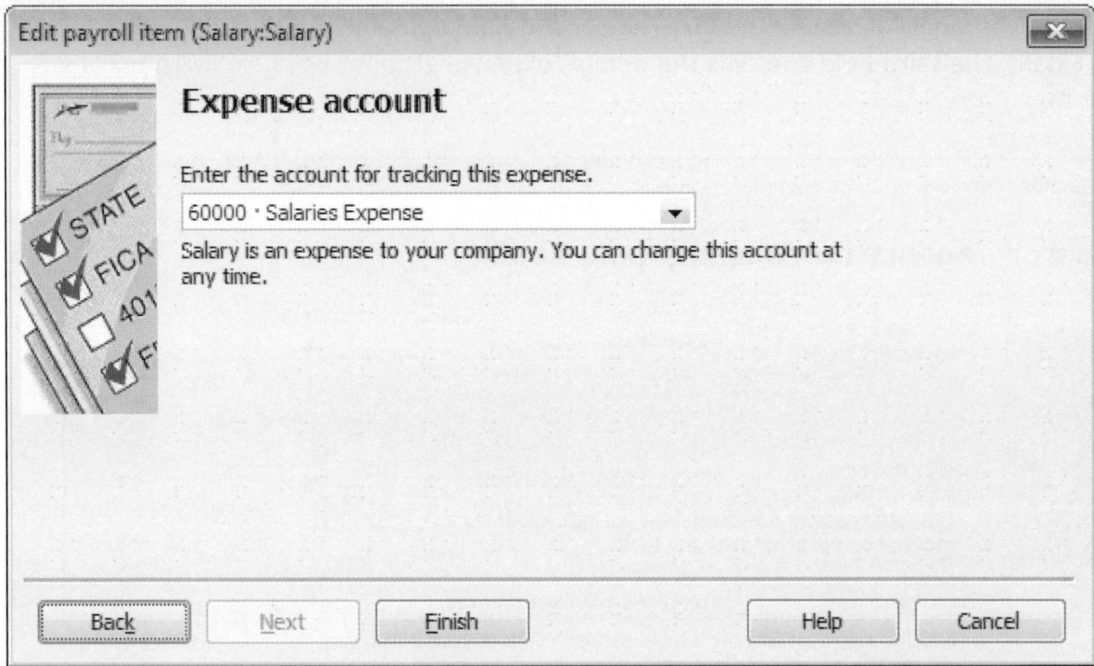

Figure 6:10

Return to the **Payroll Item List** and note that Astor has two categories of wage compensation.

Yearly Salary items are for employees paid an annual salary. Gross pay for these items post to 60000 Salaries Expense.

Hourly Wage items are for employees paid an hourly wage for work performed on customer jobs. Astor will bill customers for these hours. Gross pay for these items post to 57000 Direct Labor (i.e., a cost of goods sold account).

Double click **Federal Unemployment** to open the item. Once again, the first screen names the item so click **Next**.

Figure 6:11 shows the defaults the software uses on this item. The first field contains the default vendor account for paying the tax. The second field contains the default liability account. Finally, the third field contains the default expense account because FUTA tax is an employer tax.

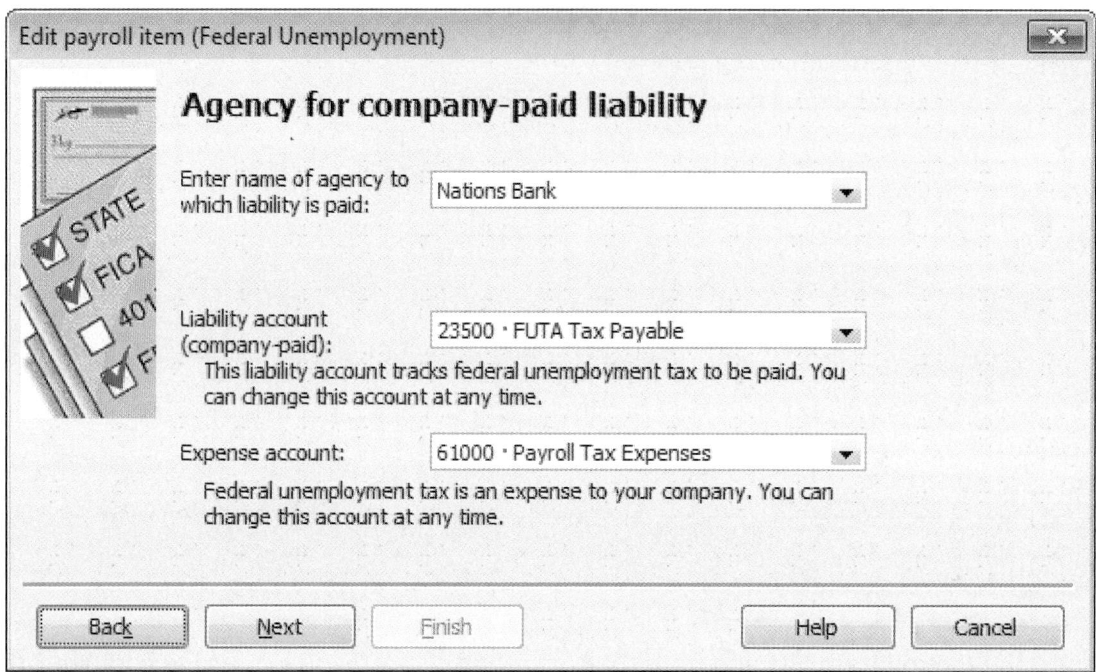

Figure 6:11

Click **Next**. This window (Figure 6:12) is used to set the tax rate. You can refer back to the tables presented earlier in the chapter for more information on this rate.

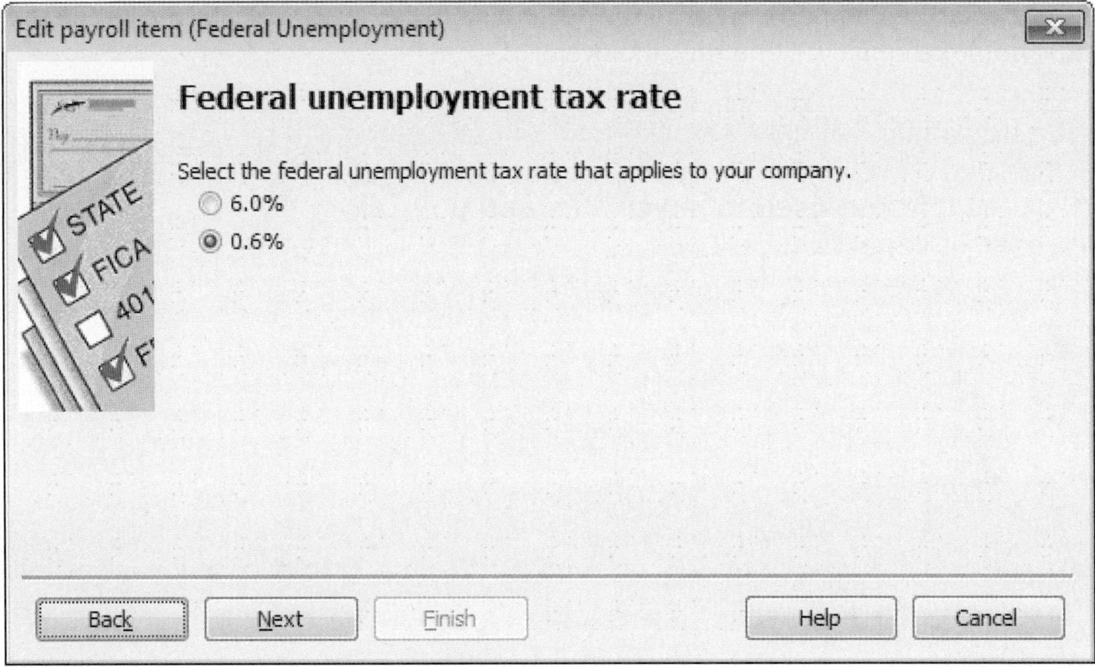

Figure 6:12

Click **Next**. This window (Figure 6:13) sets the compensation items subject to FUTA tax. Generally, all compensation is FUTA taxable. For more information on FUTA taxes, visit www.irs.gov.

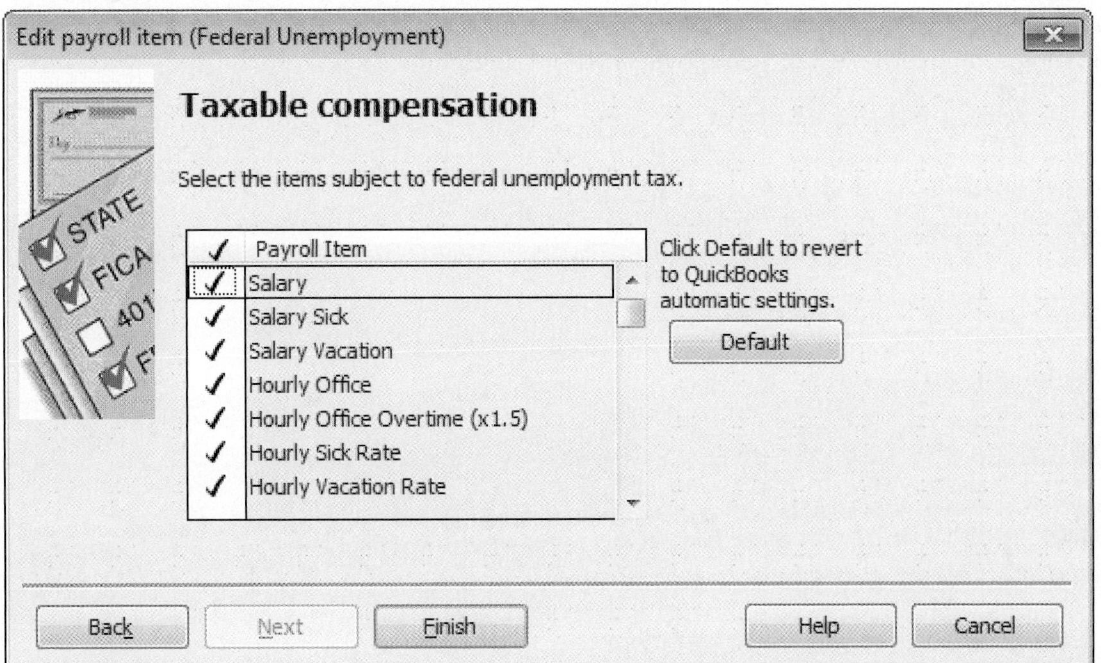

Figure 6:13

Click **Cancel**.

Now open **Medicare Company**. This window (Figure 6:14) names two items because Medicare is paid by both the employee and the employer.

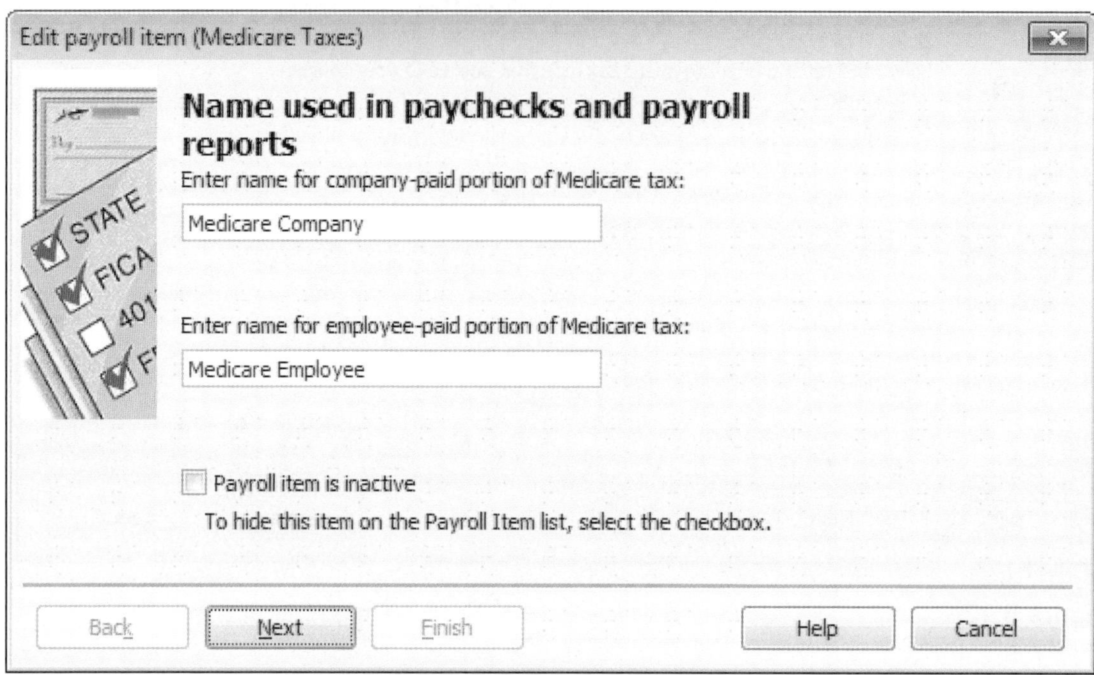

Figure 6:14

Click **Next**. Once again, you find a window (Figure 6:15) for setting the general ledger posting accounts and the vendor for paying taxes. However, this time you set just the liability accounts for posting employer taxes and employee withholdings.

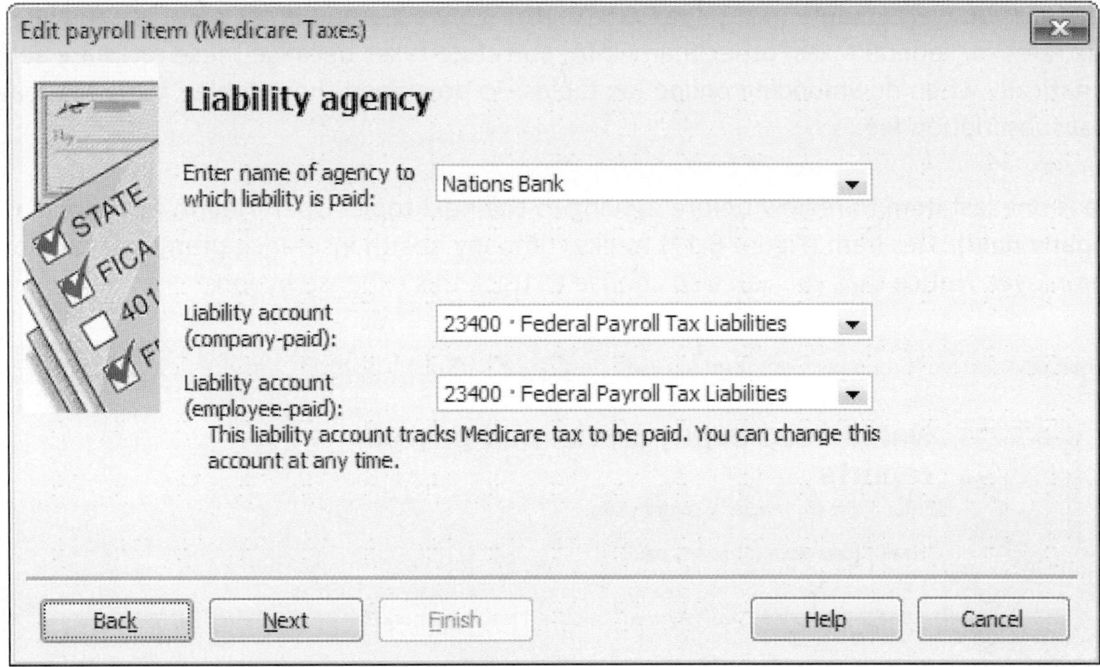

Figure 6:15

Click **Next**. Figure 6:16 shows where you set the employer tax expense account.

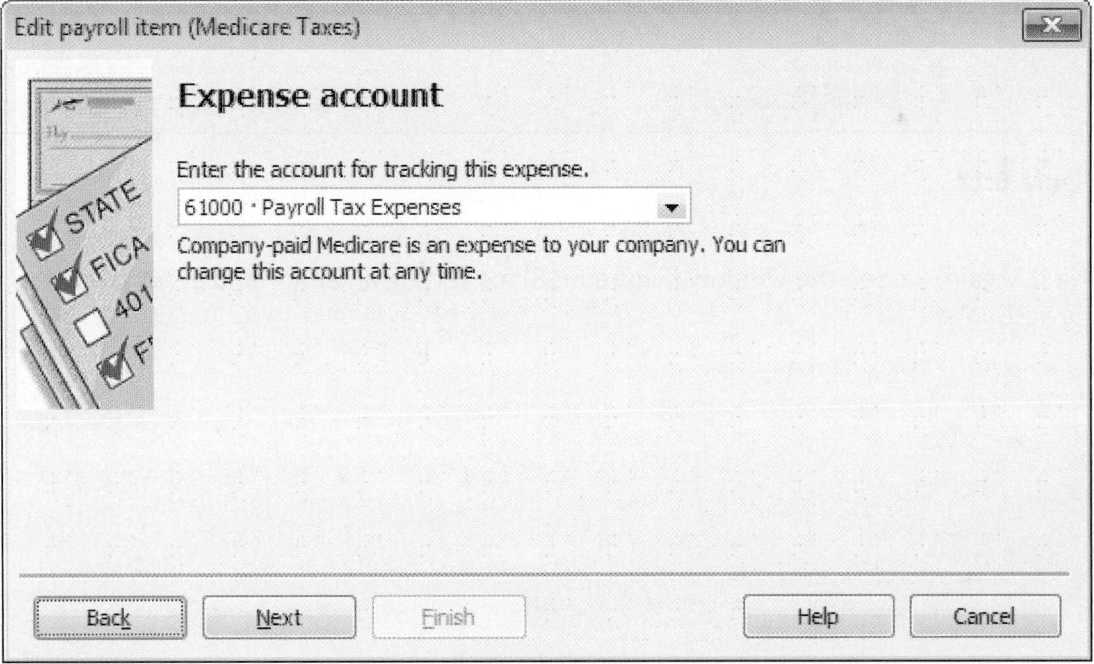

Figure 6:16

Click **Cancel**.

Notice that you were unable to set a tax rate on the previous item. In fact, you are unable to set tax rates for federal taxes, other than FUTA, and state taxes because these rates are set automatically when downloading online tax tables. To download these tables, you must pay an annual subscription fee.

There is one last item to review before moving to the next topic. Open **Health Insurance (company paid)**. This item (Figure 6:17) tracks company health insurance premiums paid by the employer. Notice that you can also choose to track this expense by job.

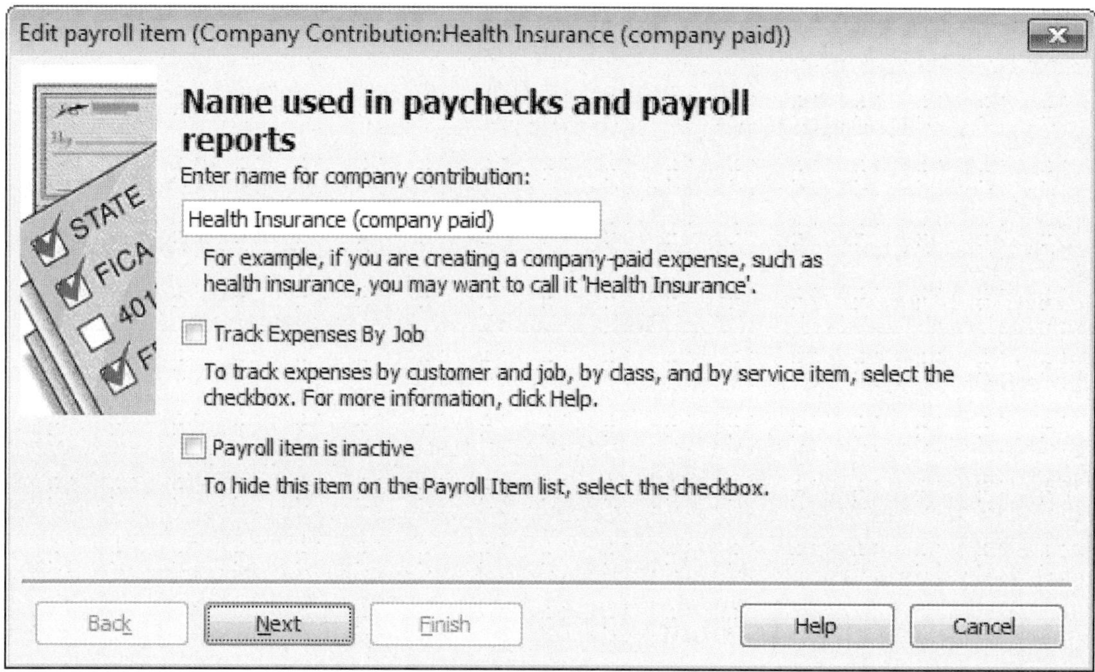

Figure 6:17

Click **Next**. Again, we see the window (Figure 6:18) for setting a vendor and general ledger posting accounts.

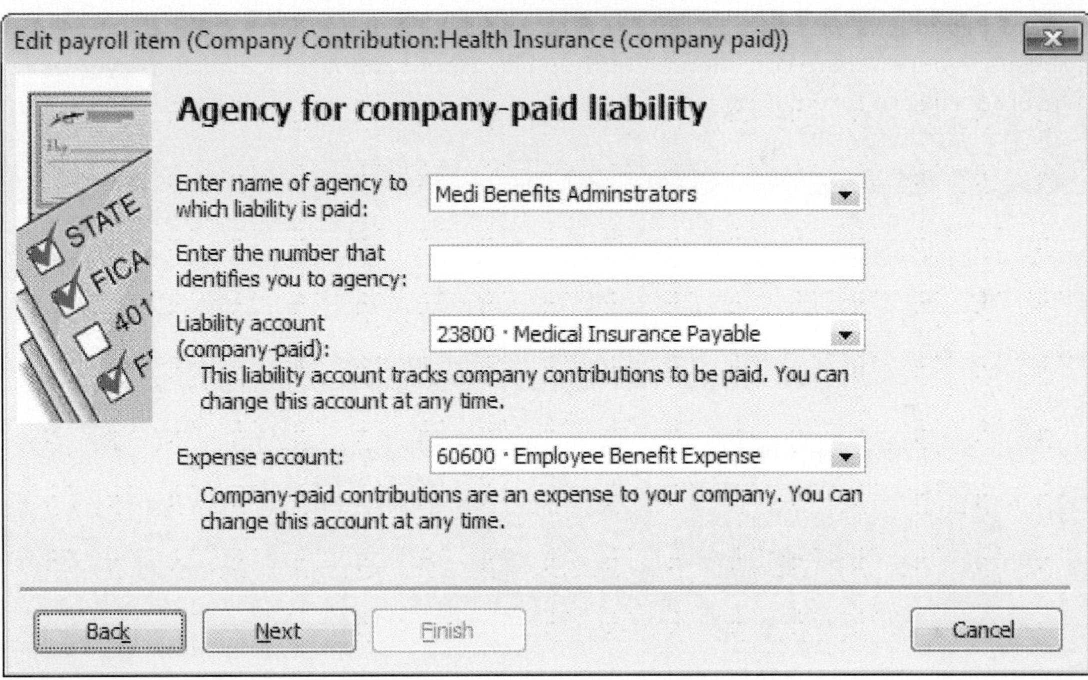

Figure 6:18

Click **Next**. In this window (Figure 6:19), you choose whether to print company contributions for health insurance on employee W-2s.

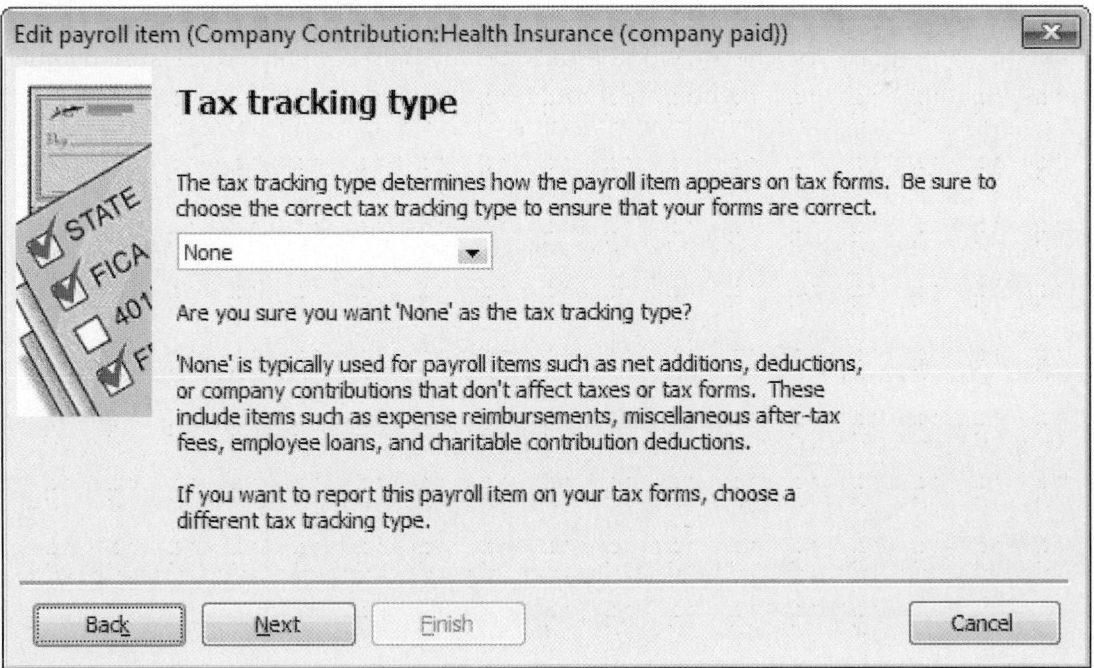

Figure 6:19

Click **Next**. This window (Figure 6:20) is for setting any taxes that apply to the company-paid benefit because benefits are considered additional compensation. Typically, employer-paid health insurance is not taxed.

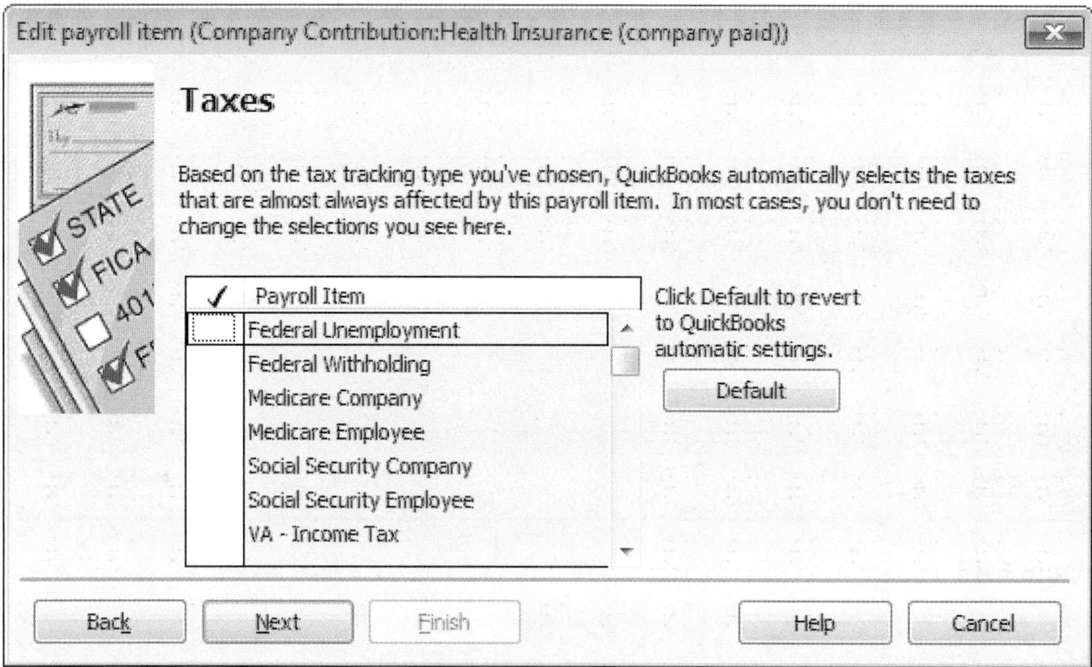

Figure 6:20

Click **Next**. In Figure 6:21, you choose whether a company-paid benefit is calculated by quantity or percentage. If neither, you can enter an amount on the window that follows.

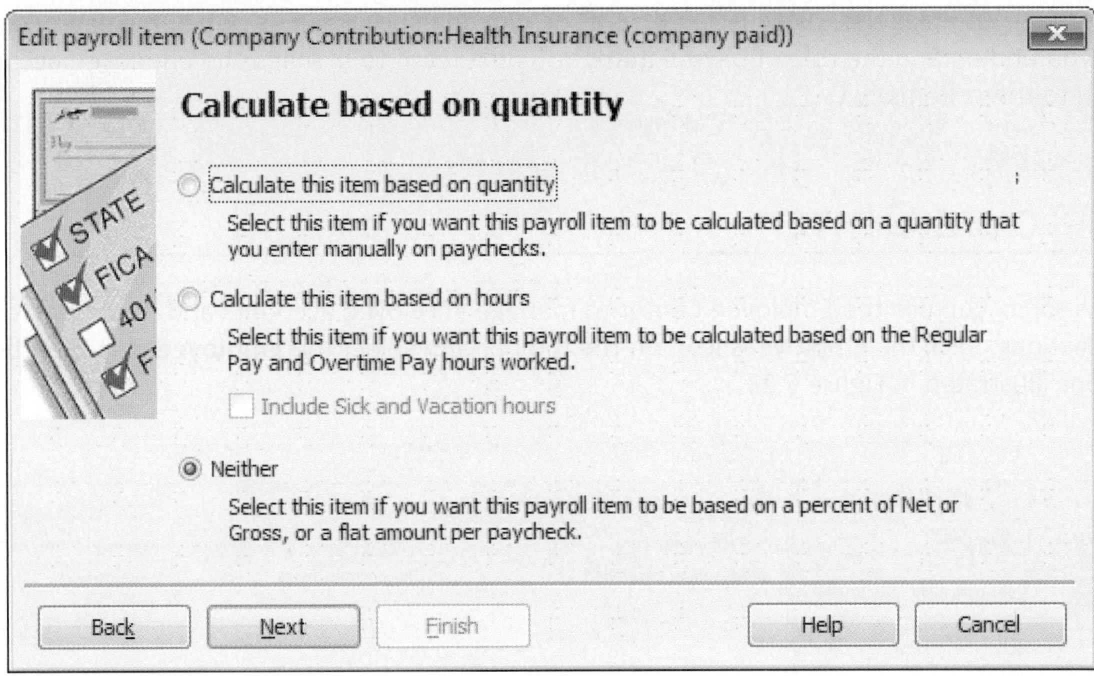

Figure 6:21

Click **Next**. In this window (Figure 6:22), you enter the amount.

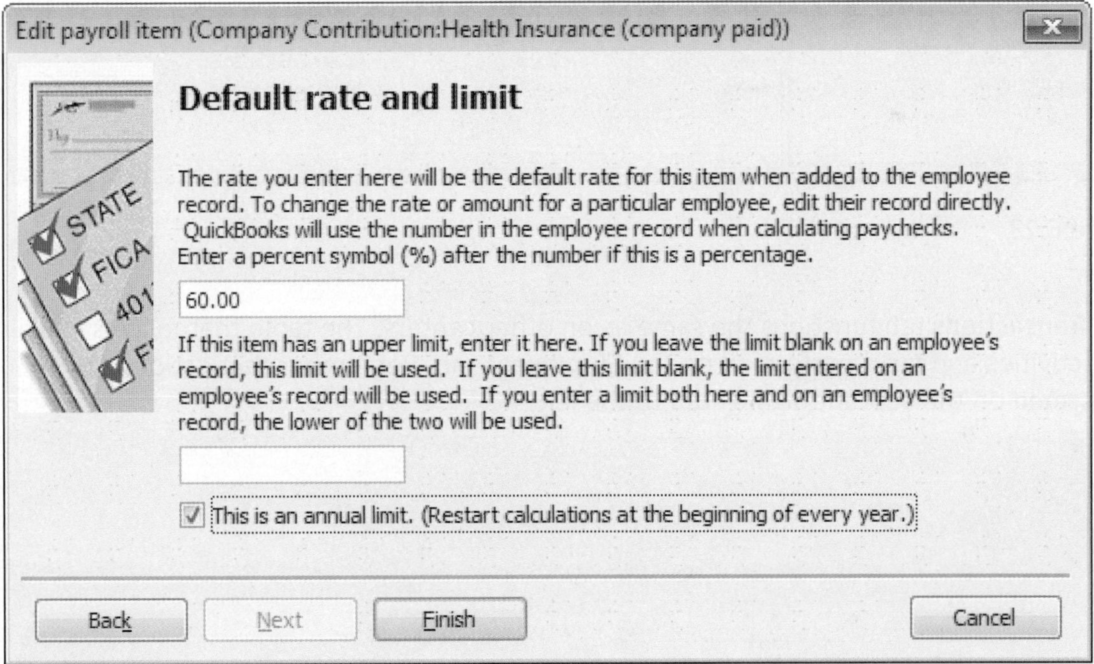

Figure 6:22

Click **Cancel** and then close the Payroll Item List.

With all the complexities just illustrated, you see why many companies outsource payroll. Now that you understand the role of payroll items you next learn to manage the employee accounts linked to these items.

EMPLOYEE CENTER

In this topic, you use the Employee Center to manage employee accounts and locate payroll transactions. Click the **Employees** icon on the toolbar and select the **Employees** tab. Set the options illustrated in Figure 6:23.

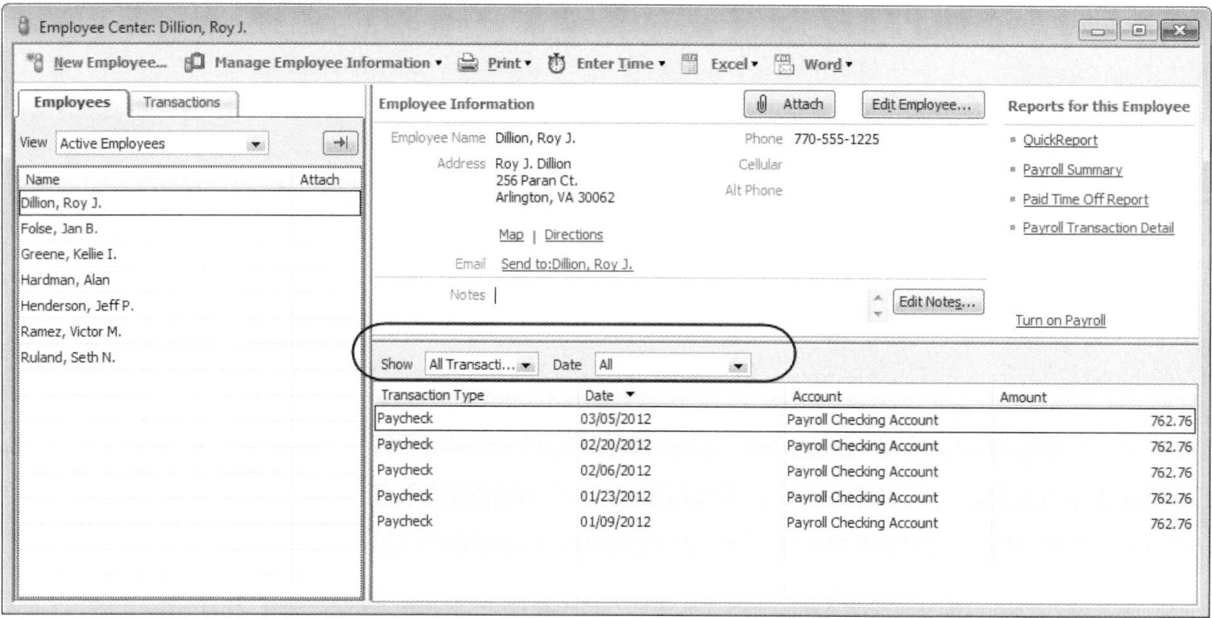

Figure 6:23

The **Transactions** tab functions the same as on other centers. The table that follows explains the activities and tasks performed on the **Employees** tab. Remember that actions are performed on the account highlighted to the left.

Employees Activities	Task	Description
New Employee		Create a new employee account.
Manage Employee Information	Add/Edit Sales Rep	Manage existing employee accounts.
	Change New Employee Default Settings	Enter defaults to be assigned to new employee accounts.
Print	Print Paychecks	Print paychecks.
	Print/Send Paystubs	Print only pay stubs. This is used when checks are deposited directly to employee bank accounts.
	Employee List/Employee Information/Employee Transaction List	Print an employee list, information, or transactions. These reports cannot be customized so use the Reports menu to print this information.
Enter Time	Use Weekly Timesheet	Record employee time for an entire week.
	Time/Enter Single Activity	Record employee time for a single day or single activity.
Excel	Export Employee List	Export employee information to an Excel workbook or comma separated values (.csv) file.
	Export Transactions	Export paycheck transactions for the highlighted employee to an Excel workbook or comma separated values (.csv) file.
	Summarize Payroll Data in Excel	Extract payroll data for analysis in Excel.
Word		Create form letters for communicating with employees.

The Employee Center is helpful for managing employees and the next topic walks through this activity.

MANAGING EMPLOYEES

Double click Roy Dillion's account to open it. *(Note: You can also click the Edit Employee button to the right.)*

An employee account contains three different tabs for entering information. You choose a tab by selecting it from the dropdown list on **Change tabs**. (See Figure 6:24.) As illustrated, the tab names are **Personal Info**, **Payroll and Compensation Info**, and **Employment Info**.

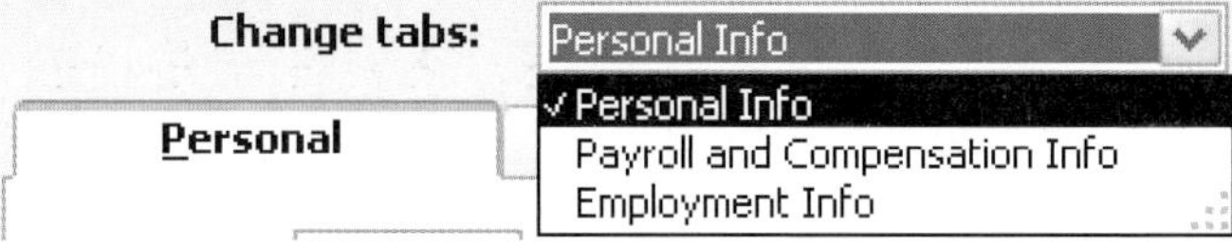

Figure 6:24

Select the **Personal Info** tab. As illustrated in Figure 6:25, this tab contains three sub-tabs, namely **Personal**, **Address and Contact**, and **Additional Info**. We next illustrate the information stored on each sub-tab.

The **Personal** sub-tab illustrated next stores an employee's name, social security number, and birth date.

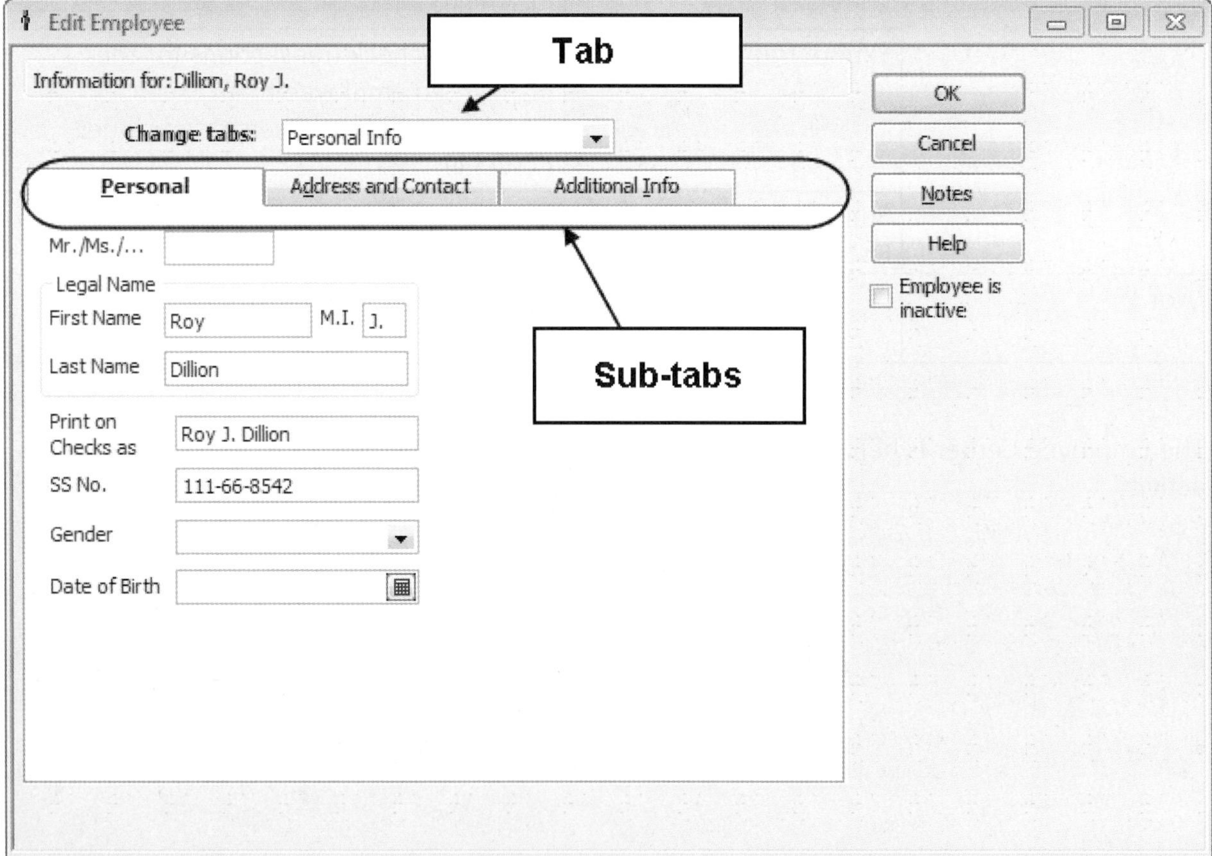

Figure 6:25

The **Address and Contact** sub-tab illustrated next stores basic contact information on the employee.

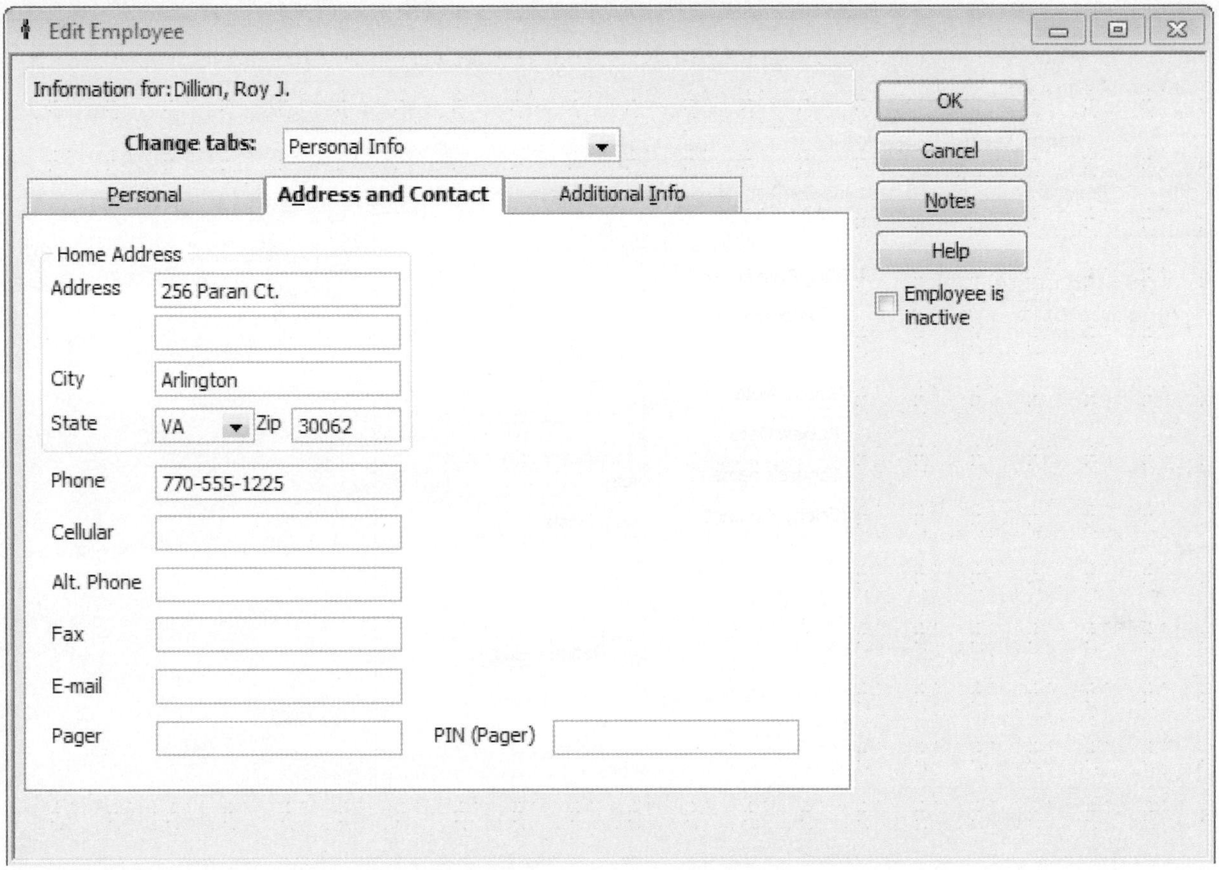

Edit Employee

Information for: Dillion, Roy J.

Change tabs: Personal Info

Personal | Address and Contact | Additional Info

OK
Cancel
Notes
Help
Employee is inactive

Home Address
Address: 256 Paran Ct.
City: Arlington
State: VA Zip: 30062
Phone: 770-555-1225
Cellular
Alt. Phone
Fax
E-mail
Pager
PIN (Pager)

Figure 6:26

The **Additional Info** sub-tab illustrated next stores miscellaneous information such as job position.

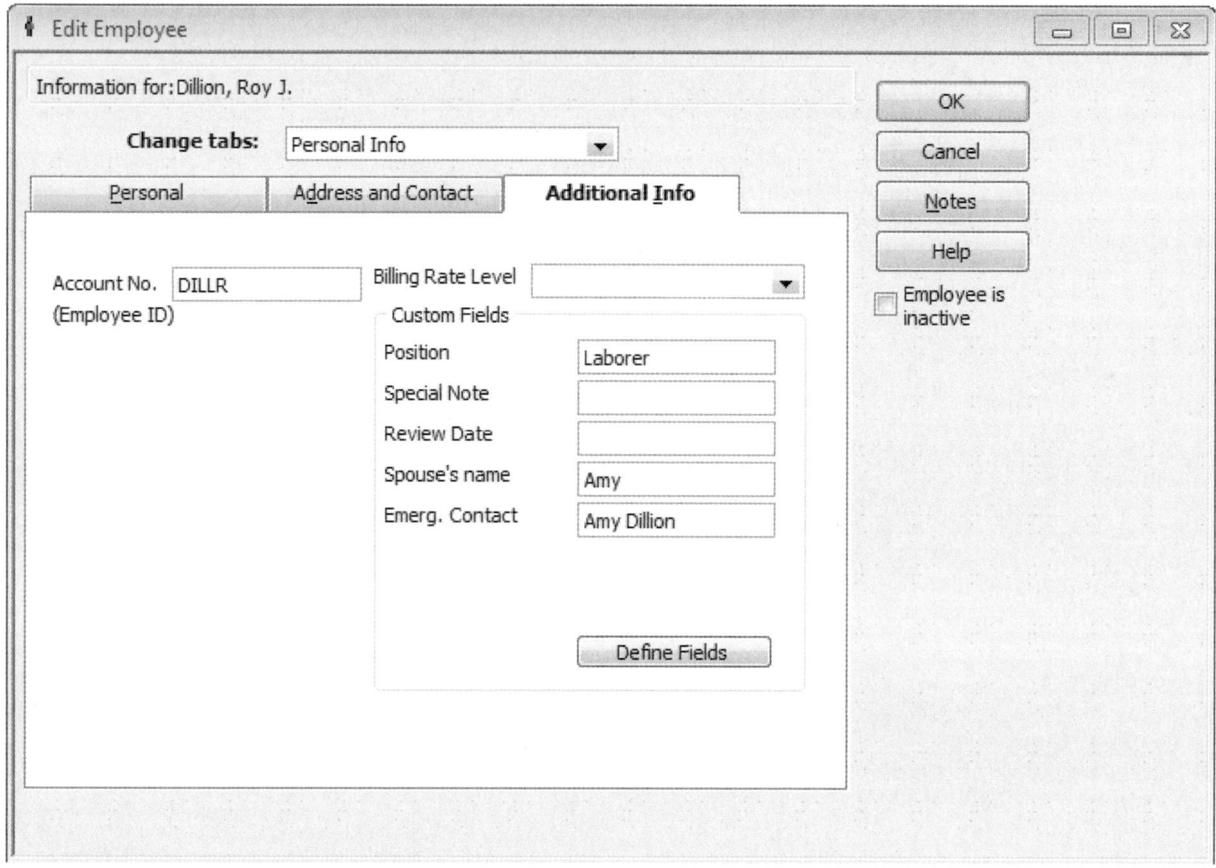

Figure 6:27

Now select the **Payroll and Compensation Info** tab by choosing it from the dropdown list under **Change tabs**. As illustrated next, this tab contains one sub-tab, namely **Payroll Info**. This is where you enter the employee's pay and tax information.

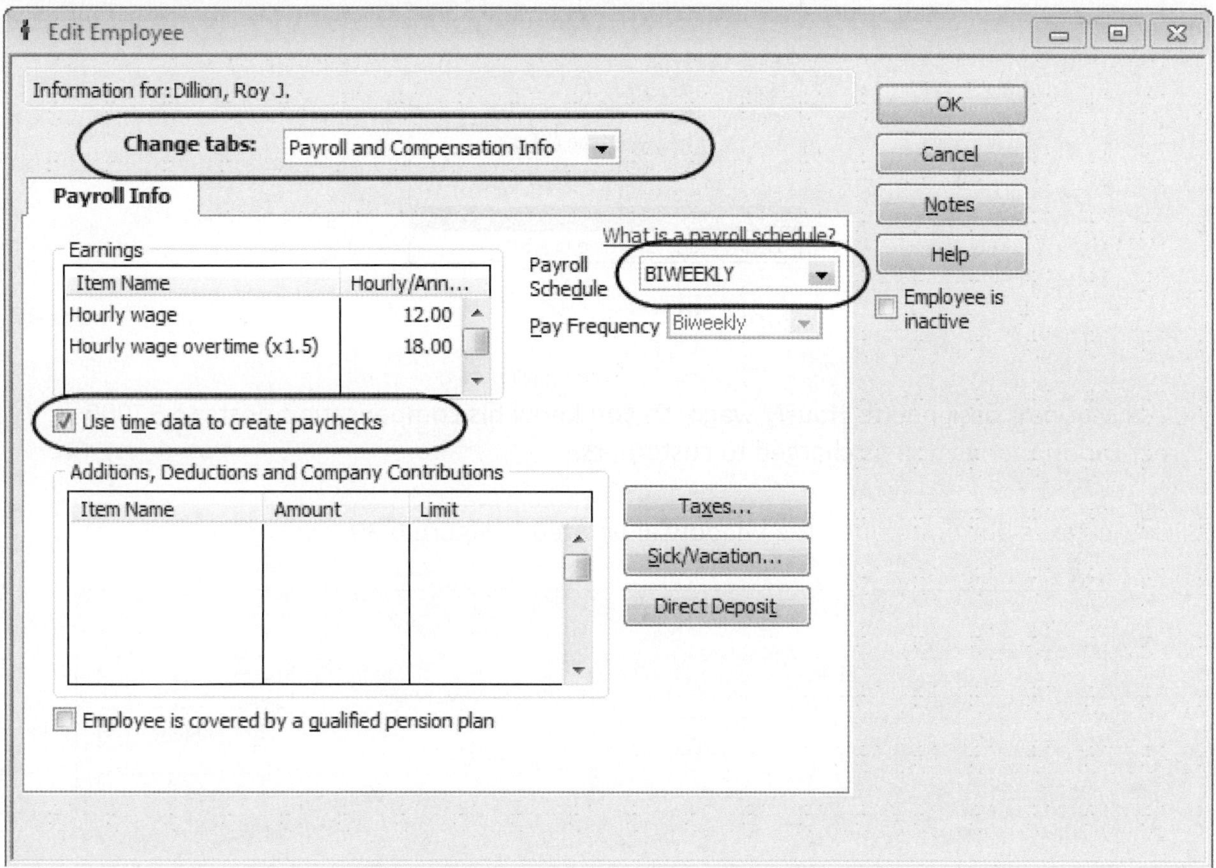

Figure 6:28

In Figure 6:28, we see that Roy is paid **BIWEEKLY**. His **Hourly wage** is $12.00 and his **Hourly wage overtime (x1.5)** is $18.00.

Also note, Roy's account is set to **Use time data to create paychecks,** meaning you must enter Roy's timesheet into the software before preparing a paycheck.

Now focus on the **Item Name** column. Click **Hourly Wage** and select the dropdown to view the list illustrated in Figure 6:29. This is a list of all pay type items previously viewed on the Payroll Item List.

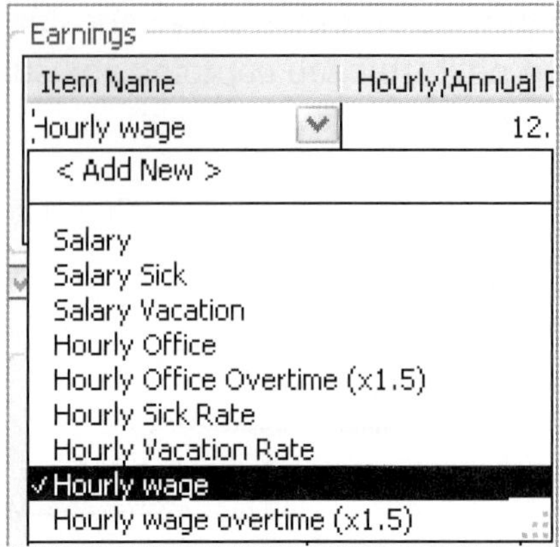

Figure 6:29

Roy's account is assigned to **Hourly wage**, so you know his compensation posts to 57000 Direct Labor and his time is charged to customers.

Click the **Taxes** button to open the window illustrated in Figure 6:30.

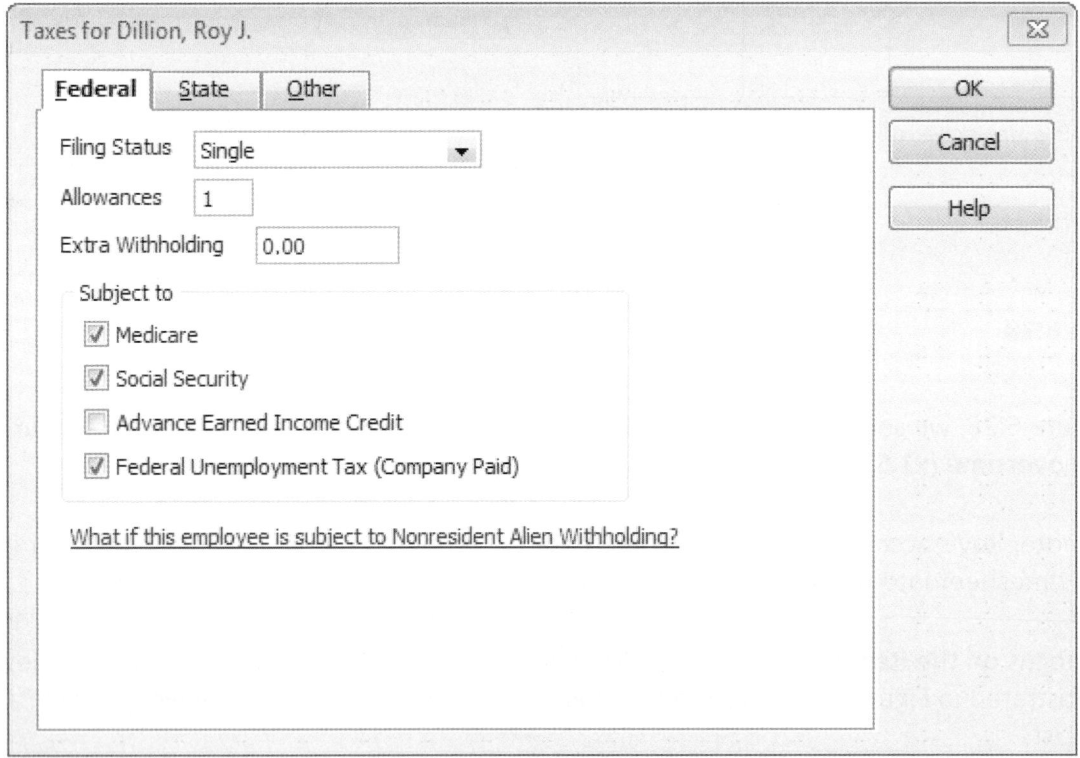

Figure 6:30

QBP looks to this window for instructions on calculating Roy's federal, state, and other taxes. The **Federal** tab illustrated shows he claims the federal **Filing Status** of **Single** and one withholding **Allowance**. We also see that his compensation is **Subject to** Medicare and Social Security tax withholdings and Medicare, Social Security, and FUTA taxes.

The **State** tab, not illustrated, is for entering state tax instructions. The **Other** tab, not illustrated, is for entering city or local tax instructions.

Click **Cancel** to exit the window.

Finally, change the category to **Employment Info**. The tab, illustrated next, stores the employee hire date as well as the last day an employee worked for the company.

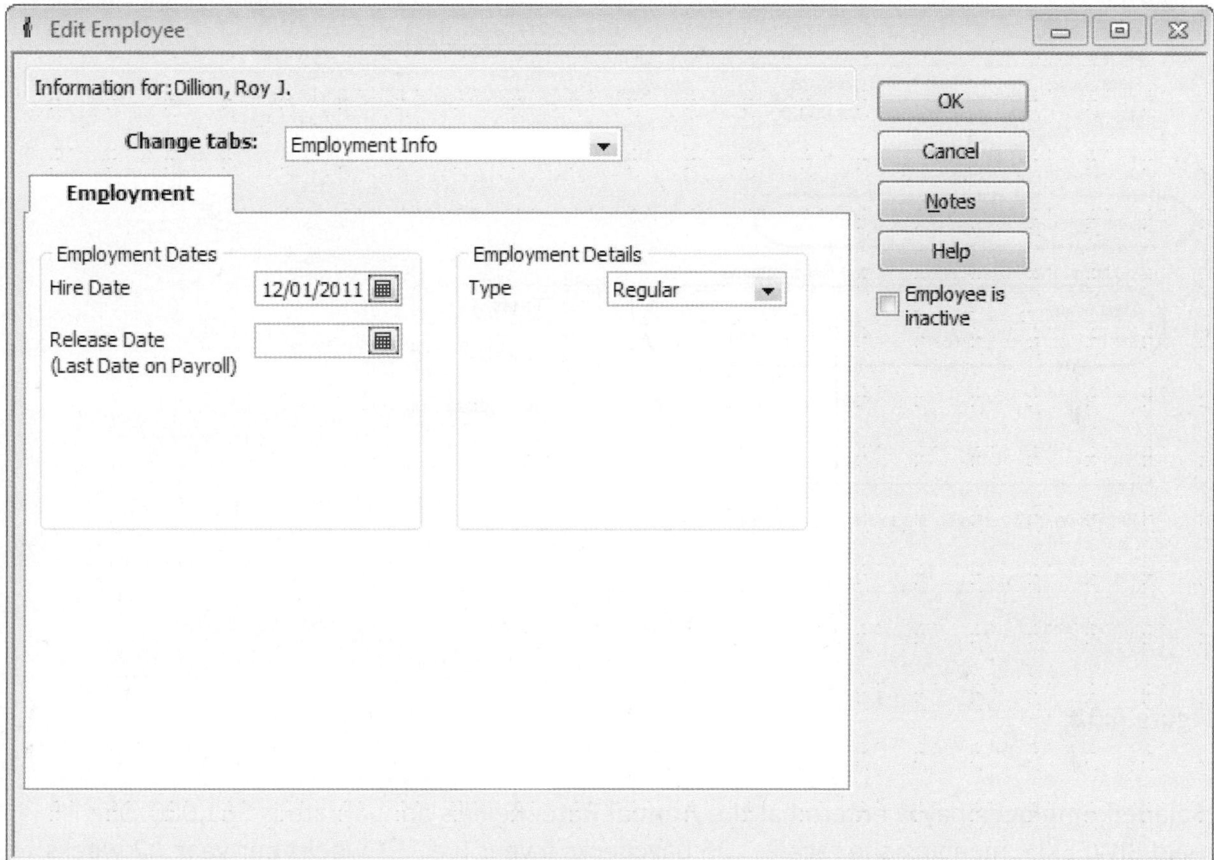

Figure 6:31

Click **Cancel** to close Roy's account.

Before leaving this topic, open Kellie Greene's account to view pay information for a salaried employee. After opening, change the tab category to **Payroll and Compensation Info**.

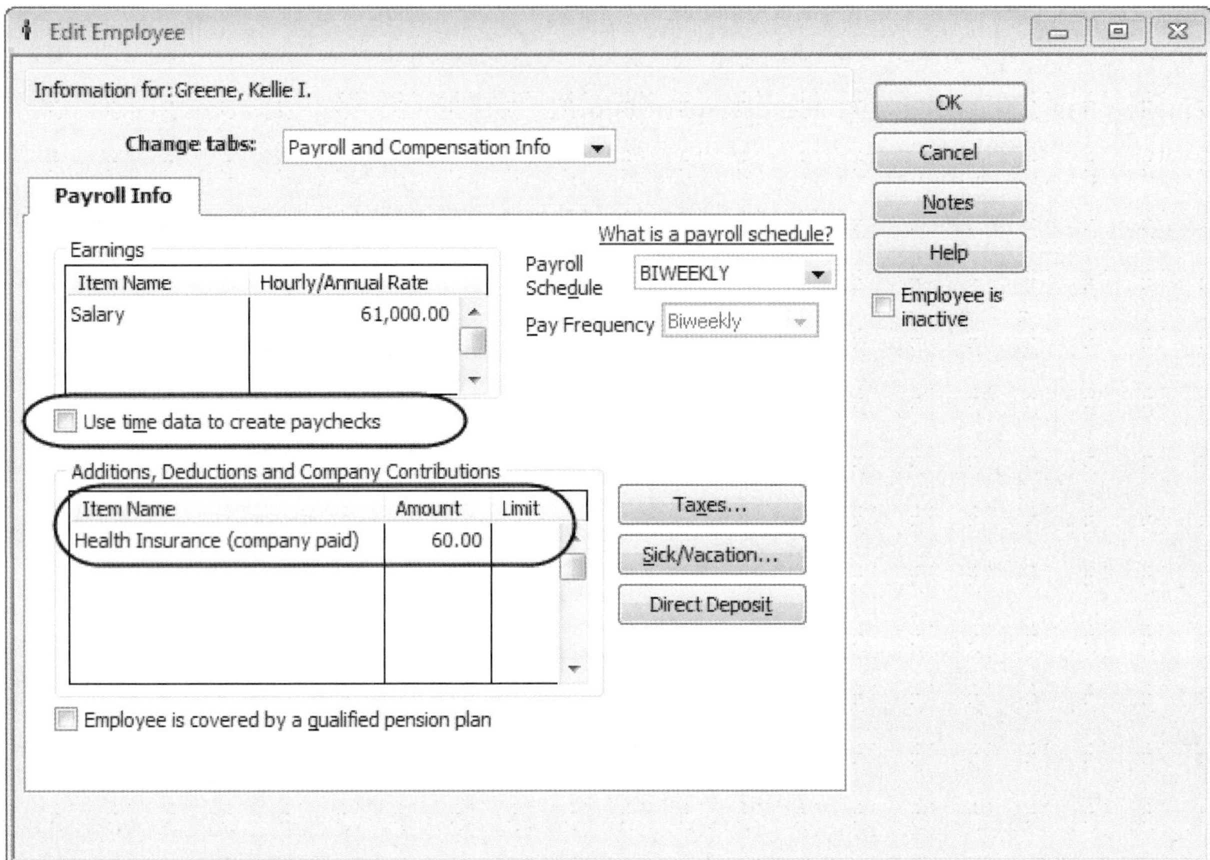

Figure 6:32

Salaried employee pay is entered at the **Annual Rate**. Kellie's annual rate is $61,000. She is paid BIWEEKLY, meaning she receives 26 paychecks a year (i.e., 52 weeks per year / 2 weeks per pay period). Accordingly, her gross pay each pay period is $2,346.15 (i.e., $61,000 / 26).

In addition, she does not use time data to create paychecks because pay for a salaried employee is not based on the hours worked.

Finally, she participates in the company's health insurance plan, so the **Health Insurance (company paid)** payroll item is assigned to her account.

Click **Cancel** to exit Kellie's account.

You are now ready to create a new employee. Click the **New Employee** button on the Employee Center.

Astor hired Jack Zickefoose to work as a laborer on customer jobs. Follow the next steps to create the account.

Enter his **Personal** information as shown on Figure 6:33.

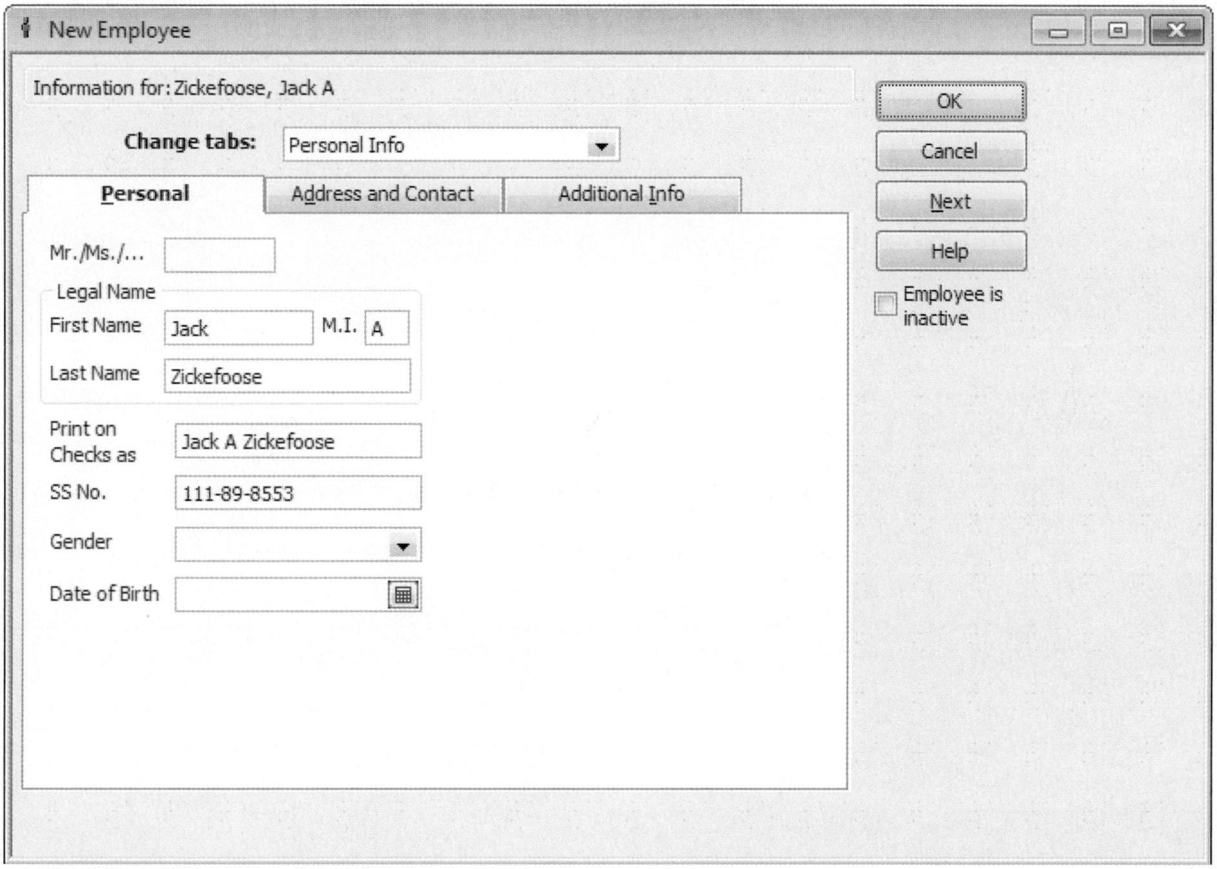

New Employee

Information for: Zickefoose, Jack A

Change tabs: Personal Info

Personal | Address and Contact | Additional Info

Mr./Ms./...

Legal Name

First Name: Jack M.I.: A

Last Name: Zickefoose

Print on Checks as: Jack A Zickefoose

SS No.: 111-89-8553

Gender

Date of Birth

OK

Cancel

Next

Help

Employee is inactive

Figure 6:33

Click the **Address and Contact** sub-tab and enter the information shown in Figure 6:34.

Information for:	Zickefoose, Jack A
Change tabs:	Personal Info
Tabs	Personal / **Address and Contact** / Additional Info
Home Address – Address	9123 Appleton Way
City	Arlington
State	VA
Zip	30076
Phone	
Cellular	
Alt. Phone	
Fax	
E-mail	
Pager	
PIN (Pager)	

New Employee — Buttons: OK, Cancel, Next, Help; Employee is inactive

Figure 6:34

On the **Additional Info** tab, enter the information shown in Figure 6:35.

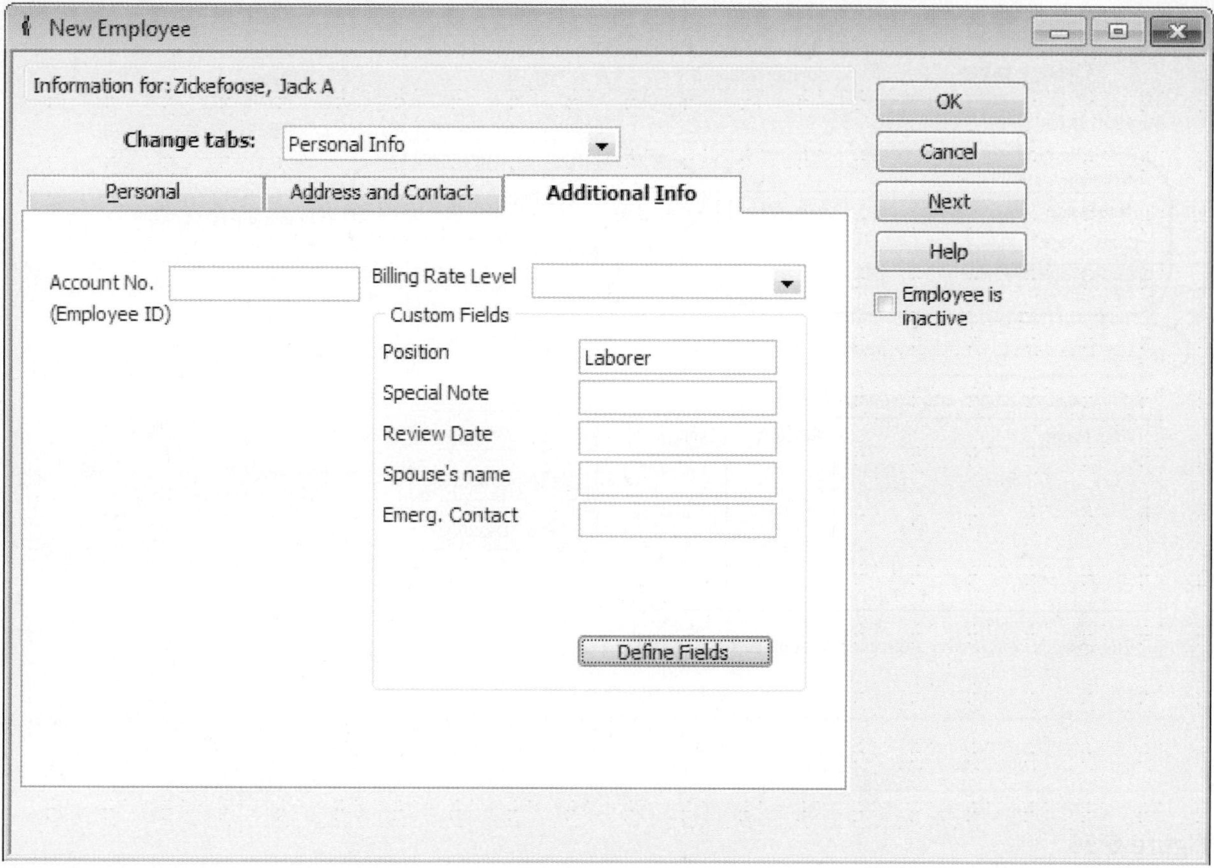

Figure 6:35

Change the tab to **Payroll and Compensation Info** and enter the information illustrated in Figure 6:36 using the instructions that follow.

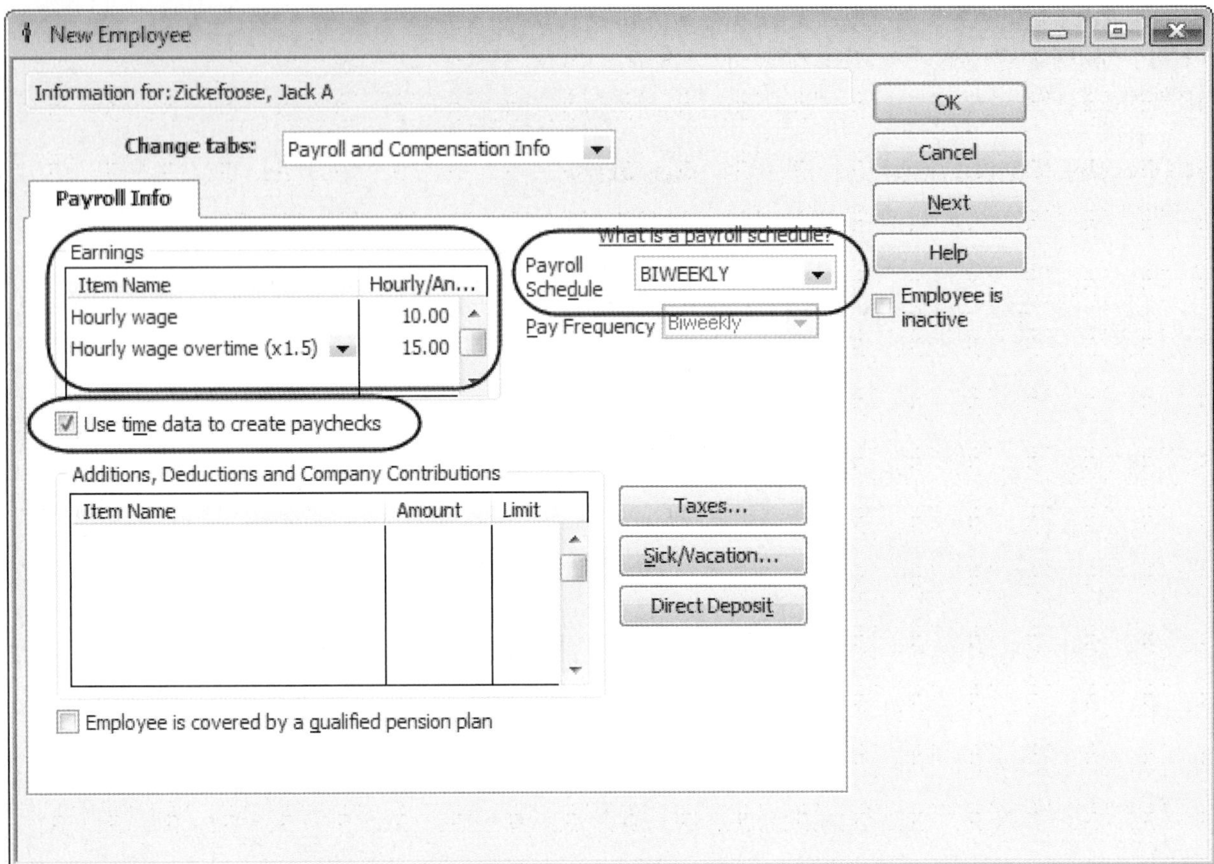

Figure 6:36

Enter Jack's salary information using the next steps:

1. Place your cursor in **Item Name** and look up **Hourly wage**.
2. Tab to **Hourly/Annual Rate** and enter 10.00.
3. Place your cursor in the next row for **Item Name** and select **Hourly wage overtime (x1.5)**. QBP will fill in the rate of 15.00.
4. Use your cursor and select **BIWEEKLY** in the **Payroll Schedule**.
5. Verify that **Use time data to create paychecks** is selected.

Click the **Taxes** button and use the following steps to enter Jack's federal and state withholding information:

1. On the **Federal** tab shown in Figure 6:37, look up and select **Married** as the **Filing Status**.
2. Enter "1" in **Allowances**.

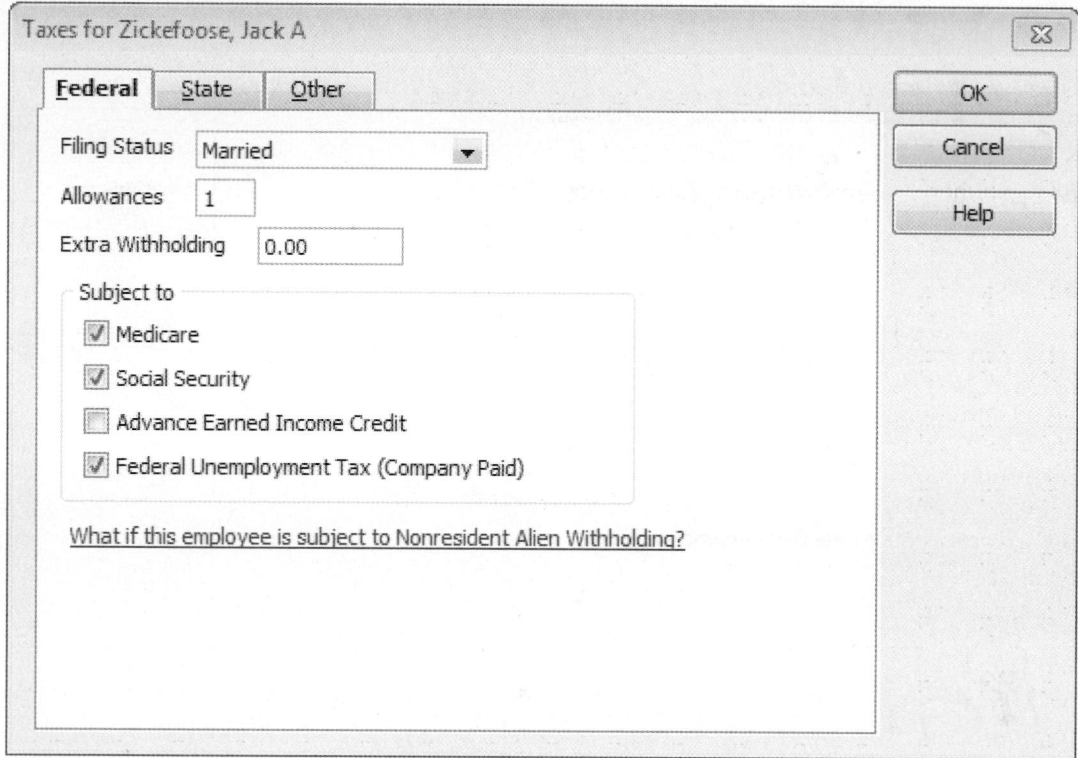

Figure 6:37

3. Click the **State** tab. (See Figure 6:38.)
4. In **State Worked**, look up **VA** as the **State**. Leave the **SUI (Company Paid)** option unchanged. (Note: This option calculates Astor's state unemployment tax expense.)
5. In **State Subject to Withholding**, look up **VA** as the **State**. (Note: This state will vary when an employee lives in one state but works in a different state.)
6. When finished, click **OK**.

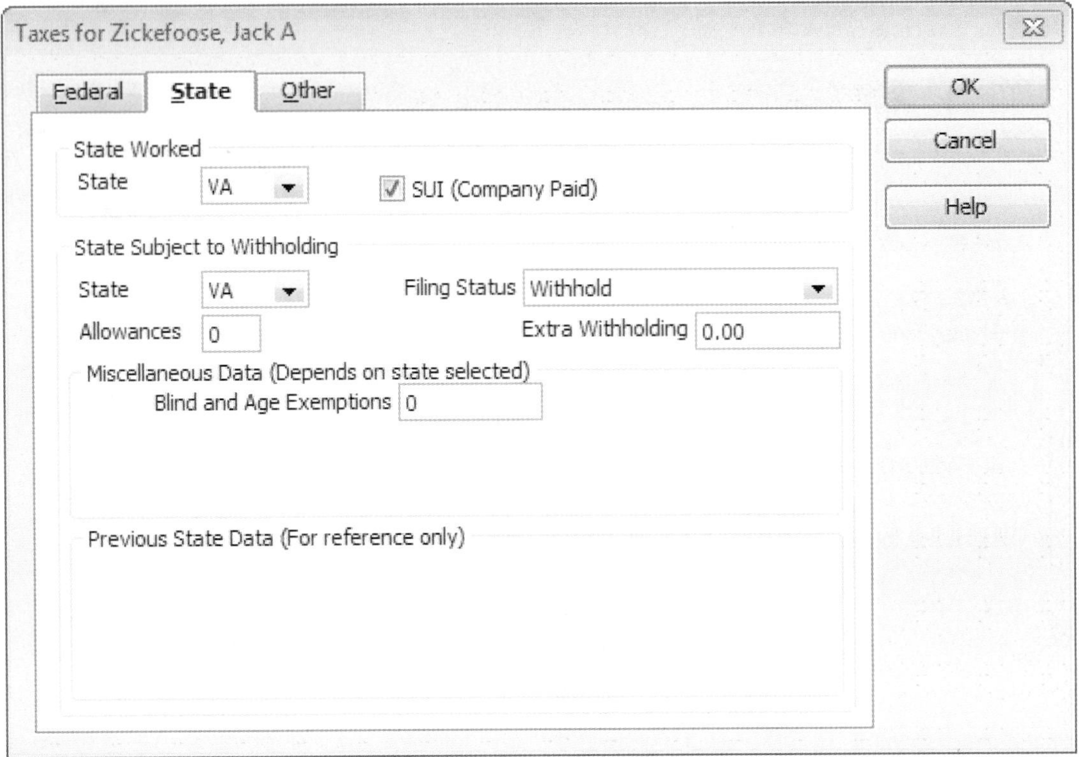

Figure 6:38

Now change the tab to **Employment Info** and enter Jack's hire date. (See Figure 6:39.)

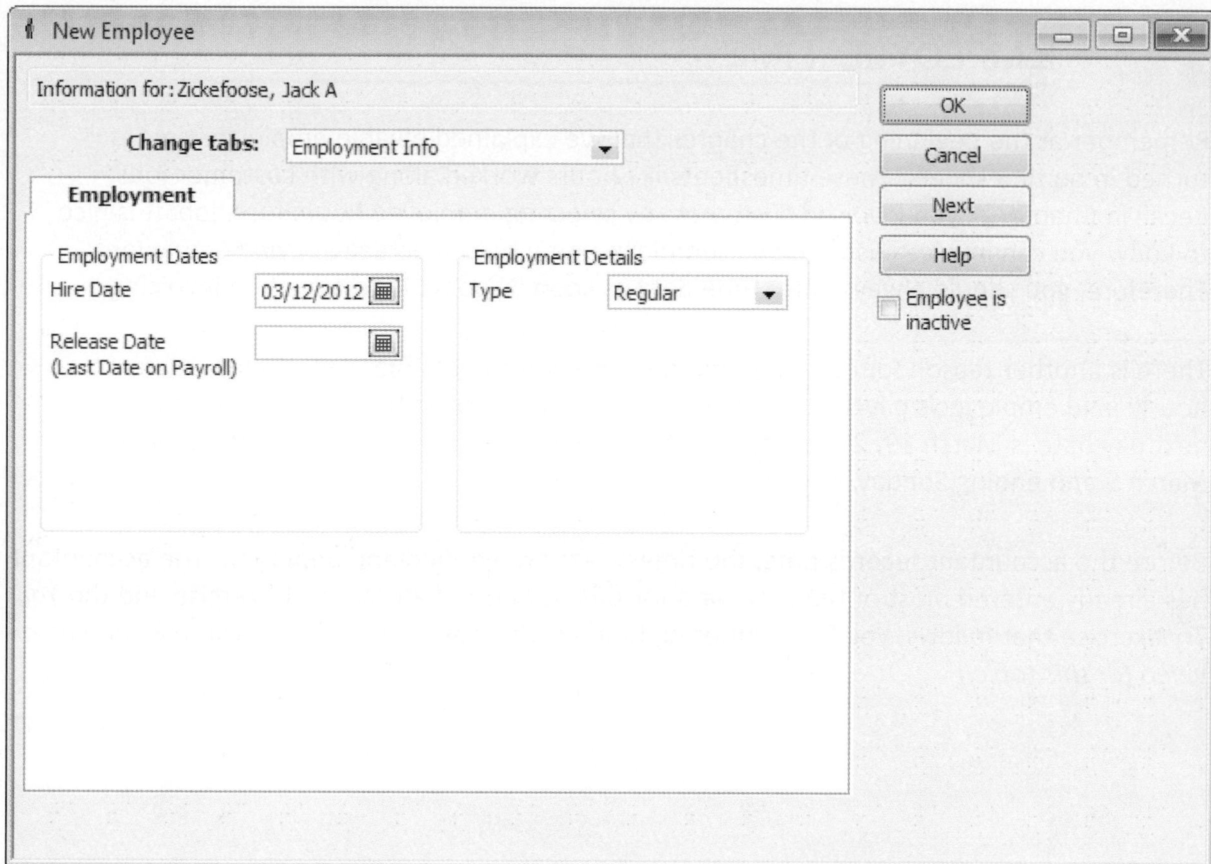

Figure 6:39

Click **OK** to save Jack's account. If prompted to setup local taxes and sick/vacation time, click **Leave As Is**.

Close the Employee Center.

Besides creating, you also need to know about terminating an employee. You cannot delete an employee account that has paycheck history. Instead, you enter a termination date in the **Release Date** field on the **Employment** tab and mark the **Employee is inactive** option.

Now that you understand managing employee accounts, you are ready to begin entering time data for hourly employees.

EMPLOYEE TIME

Remember at the beginning of the chapter that we explained billable employee time is turned in on timesheets. These timesheets list hours worked along with customer jobs. Recall in Chapter 4, you invoiced customers by selecting employee hours for a job. It is nice to know you can invoice customers for employee time before actually paying employees. Therefore, you should always enter time data as soon as possible to speed up invoicing.

There is another reason for entering time data as soon as possible. You cannot create an hourly paid employee's paycheck until hours for the pay period have been entered. Astor's next pay date is March 19, 2012, covering the two-week pay period beginning Monday, March 5 and ending Sunday, March 18.

Before the accountant records time, the timesheets are verified and approved. The accountant has already entered most of the time data for this pay period. In the next exercise and the *You Try* exercise that follows, you finish entering time for this pay period. *(Note: There is an online video for this topic.)*

STEPS TO RECORDING EMPLOYEE TIME DATA

1. On the Home page, click **Enter Time** and select **Use Weekly Timesheet**. In **Name**, look up Hardman, Alan. Using the calendar, scroll through and select March 12, 2012 (i.e., the day that begins the pay week).

   Figure 6:40 shows Alan's hours that have been entered for the week. Notice that the columns with hours are headed by the day and date.

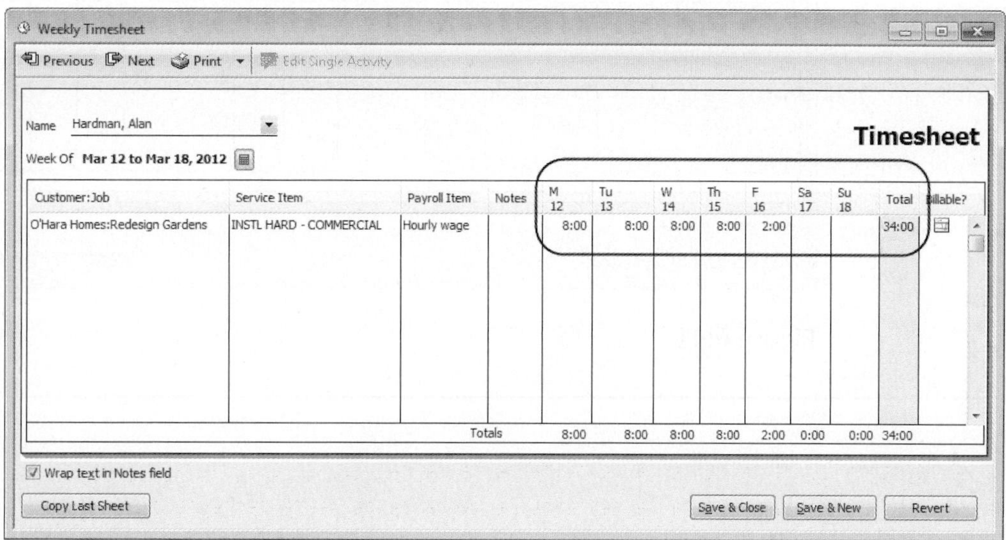

Figure 6:40

2. Alan worked 6 additional hours on Friday for a different customer job. Place your cursor in **Customer:Job** on the second line and look up **Ashford Hill Apartments.**

3. Tab to **Service Item** and look up the service item of **WKLY MNTNCE – COMMERCIAL**.

4. The **Payroll Item** remains **Hourly wage**. *(Note: You select Hourly wage overtime (x1.5) when hours are for overtime.)*

5. Place your cursor in the Friday (**F**) column and enter "6."

   Press Tab and Alan's timesheet for the week is complete (Figure 6:41). Notice that the hours you added are **Billable** to the customer.

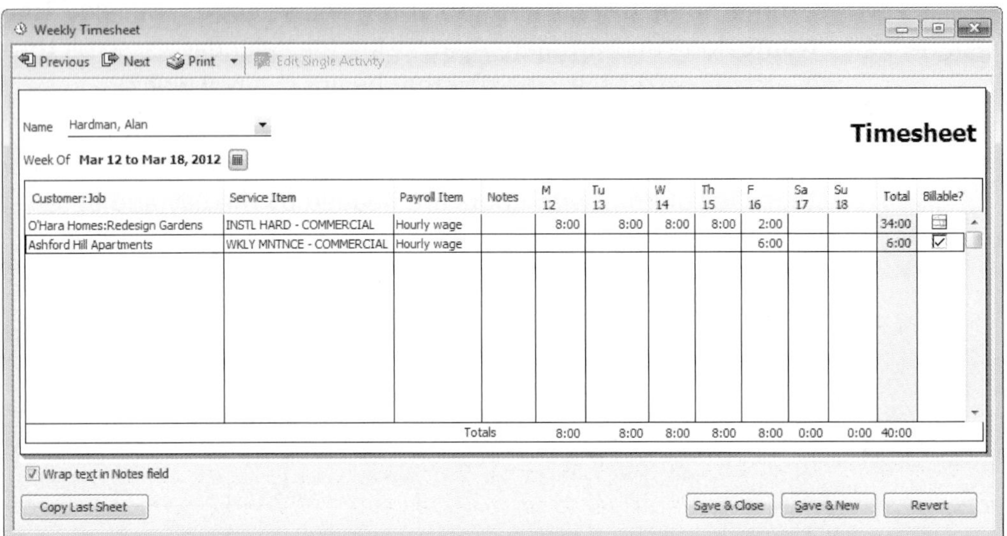

Figure 6:41

6. Click **Save & New** so you can enter a timesheet for Jack Zickefoose for the same week. Refer to the following information and verify that all hours are marked Billable.

<u>Line 1:</u>

Customer:Job:	O'Hara Homes:Redesign Gardens
Service Item:	INSTL LAND – COMMERCIAL
Payroll Item:	Hourly wage
M through F:	Enter 8 for each day

<u>Line 2:</u>

Customer:Job:	O'Hara Homes:Redesign Gardens
Service Item:	INSTL LAND – COMMERCIAL
Payroll Item:	Hourly wage overtime (x1.5)
Friday, 21:	2

Figure 6:42 shows the completed timesheet.

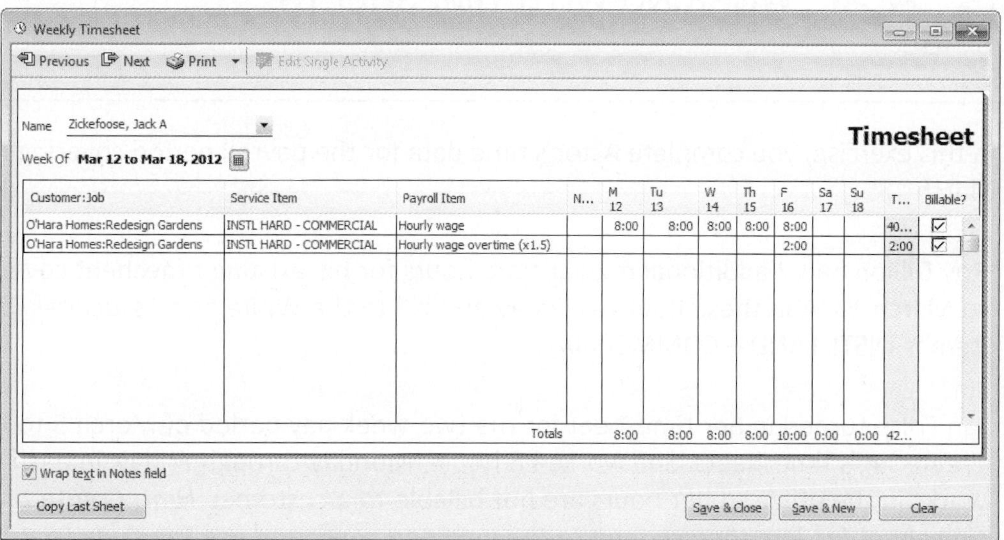

Figure 6:42

We want to point out other information before leaving this window.

The **Previous** and **Next** buttons scroll through an employee's recorded timesheets.

The **Copy Last Sheet** button transfers information from the most recent timesheet onto a new timesheet. This can save data entry time.

You can delete a timesheet in the window by selecting ***Edit>>Delete Timesheet*** on the main menu. You should not delete time that has been invoiced to the customer, meaning a time entry that shows this ▤ symbol in the Billable column.

7. Click **Save & Close**.

WORKING WITH TIMESHEETS

In this exercise, you complete Astor's time data for the payroll period covering March 5 to March 18.

Roy Dillion had 2 additional regular time hours for his existing timesheet covering March 12 to March 18. Add these hours to Friday and bill to the White and Associates job. The billing item is INSTL LAND – COMMERCIAL.

Jan Folse turned in her timesheet for the two-week pay period of March 5 to March 18. Create Jan's timesheets. She worked 8 hours, Monday through Friday, in each week. Jan works in the office so her hours are not billable to a customer. ***Hint: Create the first timesheet for Jan, then change to the next pay week and use the Copy Last Sheet button.***

Employee Time Reports

After recording time, Judy prints an employee time report to verify that hours and job information were entered correctly. Follow the next steps to create this report.

Steps to Create an Employee Time Report

1. Select ***Reports>>Jobs, Time & Mileage>>Time by Name*** on the main menu. Enter the date range of **3/5/12** to **3/18/12** (i.e., the biweekly pay period). (See Figure 6:43.)

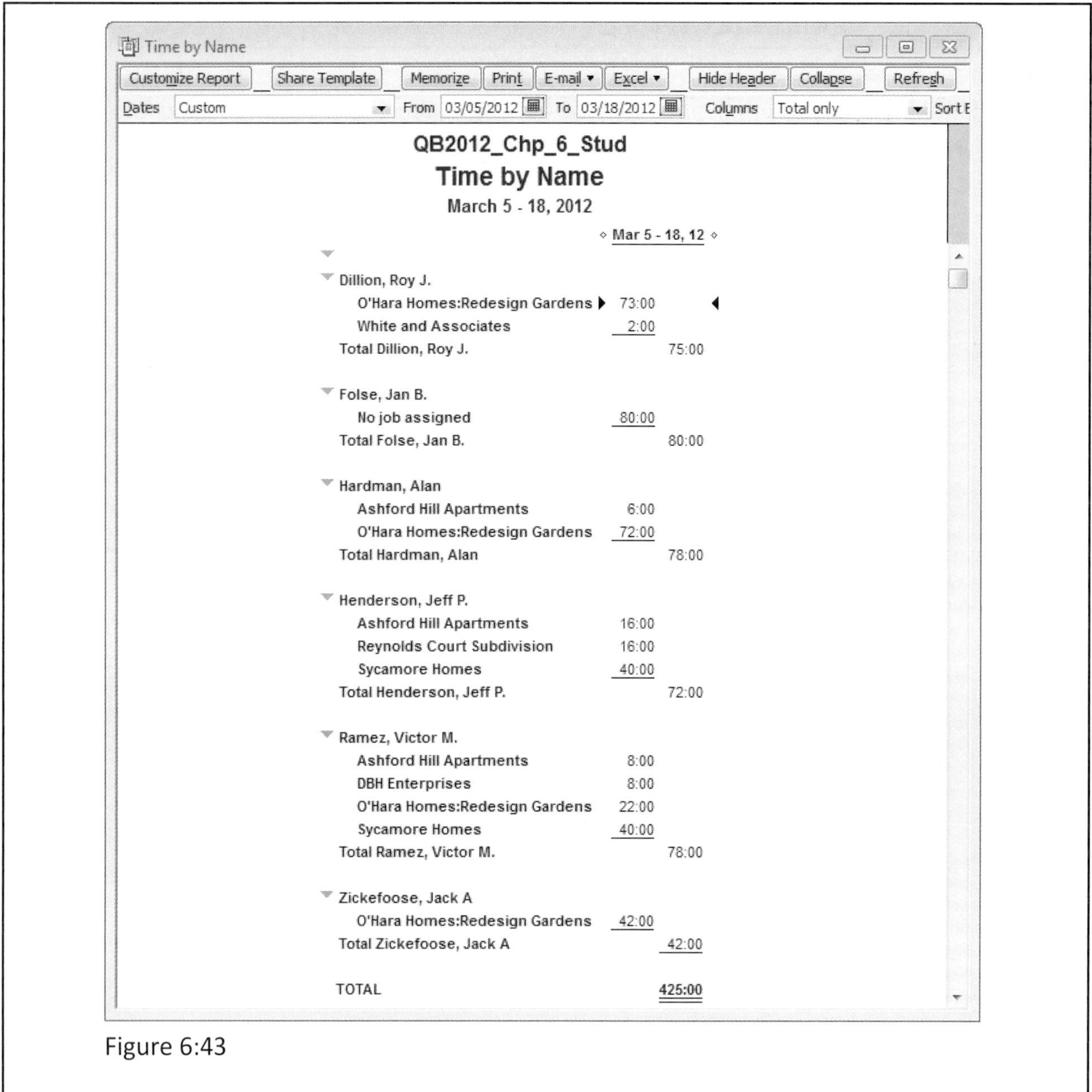
Time by Name

Customize Report | Share Template | Memorize | Print | E-mail | Excel | Hide Header | Collapse | Refresh

Dates: Custom | From 03/05/2012 | To 03/18/2012 | Columns: Total only | Sort B

QB2012_Chp_6_Stud

Time by Name

March 5 - 18, 2012

	Mar 5 - 18, 12	
Dillion, Roy J.		
O'Hara Homes:Redesign Gardens	73:00	
White and Associates	2:00	
Total Dillion, Roy J.		75:00
Folse, Jan B.		
No job assigned	80:00	
Total Folse, Jan B.		80:00
Hardman, Alan		
Ashford Hill Apartments	6:00	
O'Hara Homes:Redesign Gardens	72:00	
Total Hardman, Alan		78:00
Henderson, Jeff P.		
Ashford Hill Apartments	16:00	
Reynolds Court Subdivision	16:00	
Sycamore Homes	40:00	
Total Henderson, Jeff P.		72:00
Ramez, Victor M.		
Ashford Hill Apartments	8:00	
DBH Enterprises	8:00	
O'Hara Homes:Redesign Gardens	22:00	
Sycamore Homes	40:00	
Total Ramez, Victor M.		78:00
Zickefoose, Jack A		
O'Hara Homes:Redesign Gardens	42:00	
Total Zickefoose, Jack A		42:00
TOTAL		425:00

Figure 6:43

After verifying the hours, you are ready to pay employees. Close the report and move to the next topic.

PAYING EMPLOYEES

With employee time entered and verified, it is now time to pay employees. Since you are not subscribed to Intuit's payroll service, you are not able to use the automatic tax calculation feature of the software. *(Remember there is a fee for this service.)* Instead, you will create paychecks using information illustrated in the following spreadsheet. Although this takes additional time, there are benefits to understanding this method since some companies may not subscribe to the payroll service.

(Note: There is an online video for this topic.)

Figure 6:44 shows the payroll register for the pay period ended March 18. Notice that total hours for hourly paid employees is 425 (regular hours of 423 plus 2 hours of overtime). This total reconciles to the Time by Name report viewed in the previous topic.

Astor Landscaping
Paychecks for Pay Period 3/05/2012 thru 3/18/2012

Check No.	Employee	Filing Status	Allow.	Pay Type	Pay Rate	Regular Hrs	O.T. Hours	Gross Pay	Federal Income Tax	Sec. (FICA) Tax	Medicare Tax	VA State Tax	Net Pay
728	Dillion, Roy J.	Single	1	Hourly Wage	12.00	75.00		900.00	86.00	55.80	13.05	27.00	718.15
729	Folse, Jan B.	Single	1	Hourly Office	10.00	80.00		800.00	71.00	49.60	11.60	24.00	643.80
730	Greene, Kellie I.	Married	1	Salary	2,346.15			2,346.15	256.00	145.46	34.02	70.38	1,840.29
731	Hardman, Alan	Single	2	Hourly Wage	12.00	78.00		936.00	69.00	58.03	13.57	28.08	767.32
732	Henderson, Jeff P.	Married	1	Hourly Wage	12.00	72.00		864.00	43.00	53.57	12.53	25.92	728.98
733	Ramez, Victor M.	Single	0	Hourly Wage	10.00	78.00		780.00	89.00	48.36	11.31	23.40	607.93
734	Ruland, Seth N.	Married	0	Salary	3,103.85			3,103.85	429.00	192.44	45.01	93.12	2,344.28
735	Zickefoose, Jack A.	Married	1	Hourly Wage	10.00	40.00	2.00	430.00	0.00	26.66	6.24	12.90	384.20
	Totals					423.00	2.00	10,160.00	1,043.00	629.92	147.33	304.80	8,034.95
	Tax Basis								Circular E	6.20%	1.45%	3.00%	
	G/L Accounts							57000 / 60000	23400	23400	23400	23600	10300

Figure 6:44

Figure 6:45 shows the payroll register for employer costs.

Astor Landscaping
Employer Costs for Pay Period 3/05/2012 thru 3/18/2012

Employee	ER Soc Sec FICA	ER Medicare	ER FUTA	ER SUTA	Health Insurance
Dillion, Roy J.	55.80	13.05	7.20	13.50	0.00
Folse, Jan B.	49.60	11.60	6.40	12.00	60.00
Greene, Kellie I.	145.46	34.02	0.00	0.00	60.00
Hardman, Alan	58.03	13.57	7.49	14.04	0.00
Henderson, Jeff P.	53.57	12.53	6.91	12.96	0.00
Ramez, Victor M.	48.36	11.31	6.24	11.70	0.00
Ruland, Seth N.	192.44	45.01	0.00	0.00	60.00
Zickefoose, Jack A.	26.66	6.24	3.44	6.45	0.00
Totals	**629.92**	**147.33**	**37.68**	**70.65**	**180.00**
Tax Basis	**6.20%**	**1.45%**	**0.8%**	**1.50%**	
G/L Accounts	**23400 / 61000**	**23400 / 61000**	**23500 / 61000**	**23700 / 61000**	**23800 / 60600**

Figure 6:45

Now follow the next steps to create employee paychecks using the spreadsheet information.

STEPS TO CREATE EMPLOYEE PAYCHECKS

1. Click **Pay Employees** on the **Home** page.

   Set the **Pay Period Ends** date to 3/18/12 and click **Yes** when prompted to fill in hours for this pay period. Set the **Check Date** to 3/19/12 and verify that the **Bank Account** is 10300 Payroll Checking. (See Figure 6:46.)

   Review the hours in the window and note that these hours match the hours shown on the worksheet.

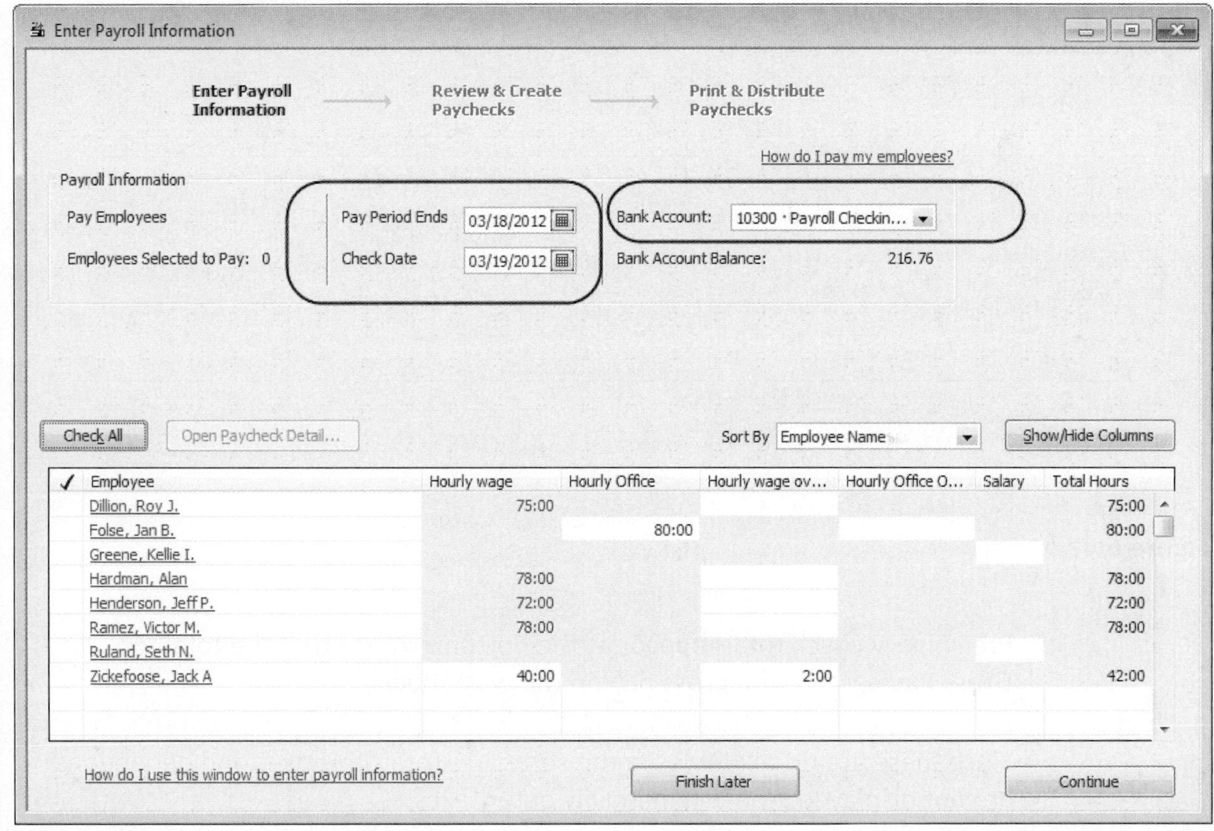

Figure 6:46

Do not worry that the payroll checking balance does not show enough to cover payroll. Companies normally do not carry large balances in the payroll account. Instead, funds are transferred on payday to cover the amount of payroll. In the next chapter, you will transfer funds from the regular checking account into this account.

2. Click **Check All** to select all employees and then click **Continue**.

   Verify that the **Print paychecks from QuickBooks** option is selected (Figure 6:47).

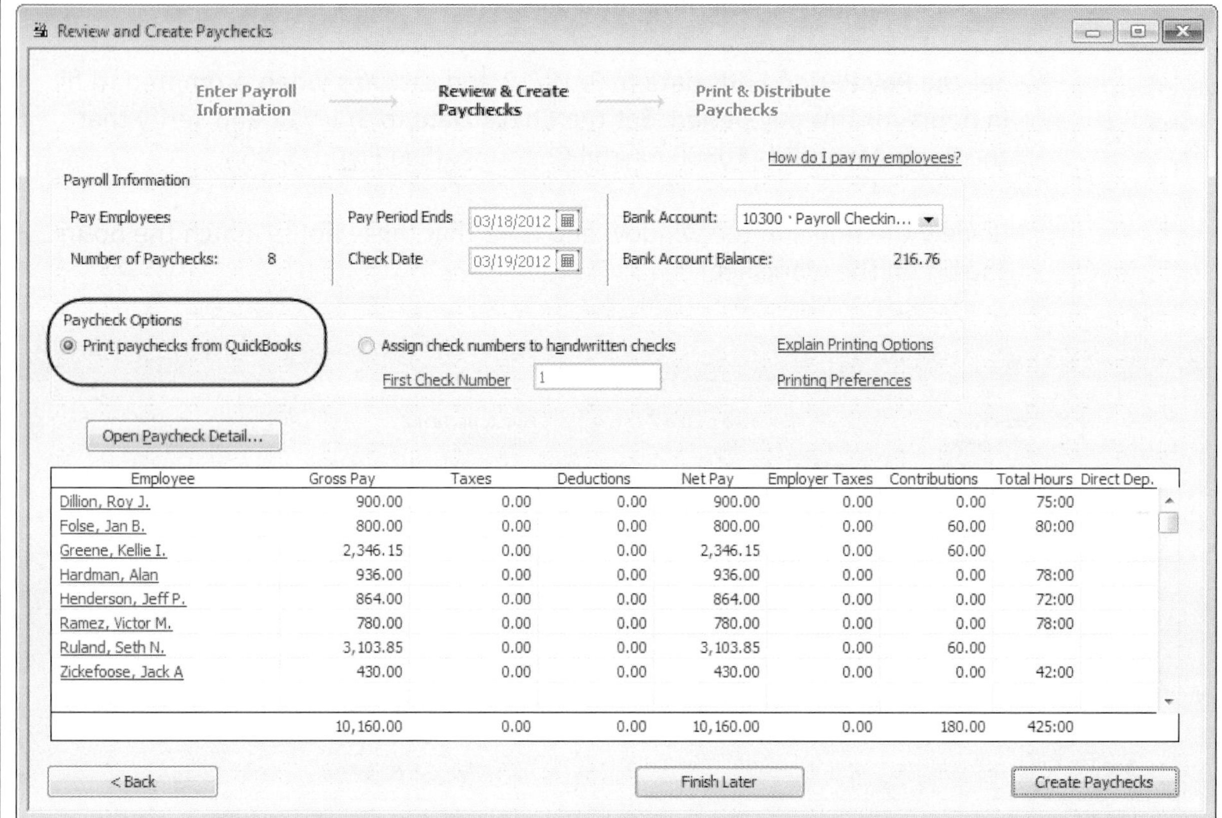

Employee	Gross Pay	Taxes	Deductions	Net Pay	Employer Taxes	Contributions	Total Hours	Direct Dep.
Dillion, Roy J.	900.00	0.00	0.00	900.00	0.00	0.00	75:00	
Folse, Jan B.	800.00	0.00	0.00	800.00	0.00	60.00	80:00	
Greene, Kellie I.	2,346.15	0.00	0.00	2,346.15	0.00	60.00		
Hardman, Alan	936.00	0.00	0.00	936.00	0.00	0.00	78:00	
Henderson, Jeff P.	864.00	0.00	0.00	864.00	0.00	0.00	72:00	
Ramez, Victor M.	780.00	0.00	0.00	780.00	0.00	0.00	78:00	
Ruland, Seth N.	3,103.85	0.00	0.00	3,103.85	0.00	60.00		
Zickefoose, Jack A	430.00	0.00	0.00	430.00	0.00	0.00	42:00	
	10,160.00	0.00	0.00	10,160.00	0.00	180.00	425:00	

Figure 6:47

Preliminary check totals appear at the bottom. Notice that the total for **Gross Pay** agrees with gross pay on the worksheet.

Since there are no tax tables in the software, totals for taxes and deductions are not displayed. You will manually enter taxes.

3. Click **Dillion, Roy J.** or click **Open Paycheck Detail** to open paycheck details. Step 4 illustrates entering information into the fields circled in Figure 6:48. *(Note: The information entered is gathered from the payroll spreadsheets.)*

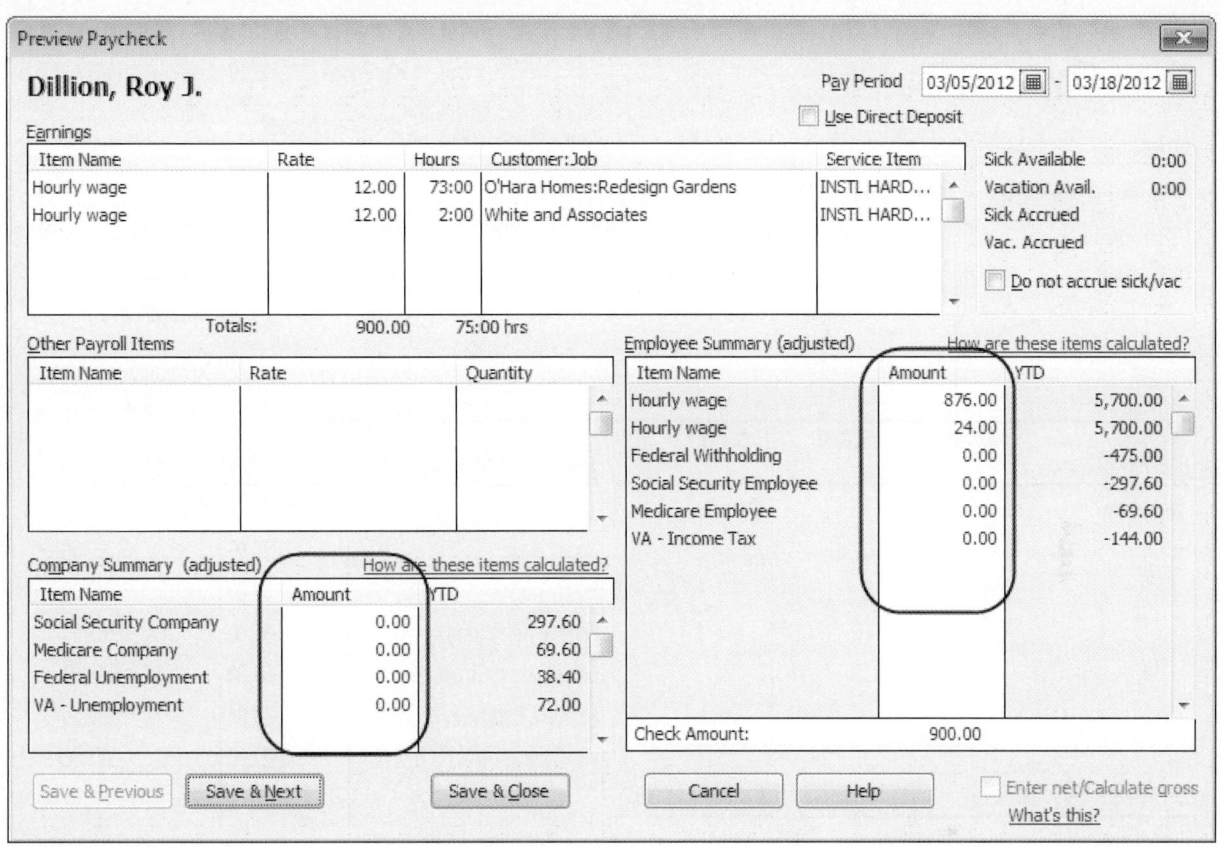

Figure 6:48

4. Under **Company Summary**, place your cursor in **Social Security Company** and enter "55.80."

   Tab to **Medicare Company** and enter "13.05." Now enter these remaining employer taxes:

Federal Unemployment (FUTA)	7.20
VA-Unemployment (SUTA)	13.50

5. Tab to **Employee Summary** and enter the amounts on the worksheet. *(Note: You will enter a positive amount and then QBP converts it to a negative amount.)*

Federal Withholding	86.00
Social Security Employee	55.80
Medicare Employee	13.05
VA – Income Tax	27.00

6. Figure 6:49 shows Roy's completed paycheck. His **Check Amount** agrees with the net pay amount on the worksheet.

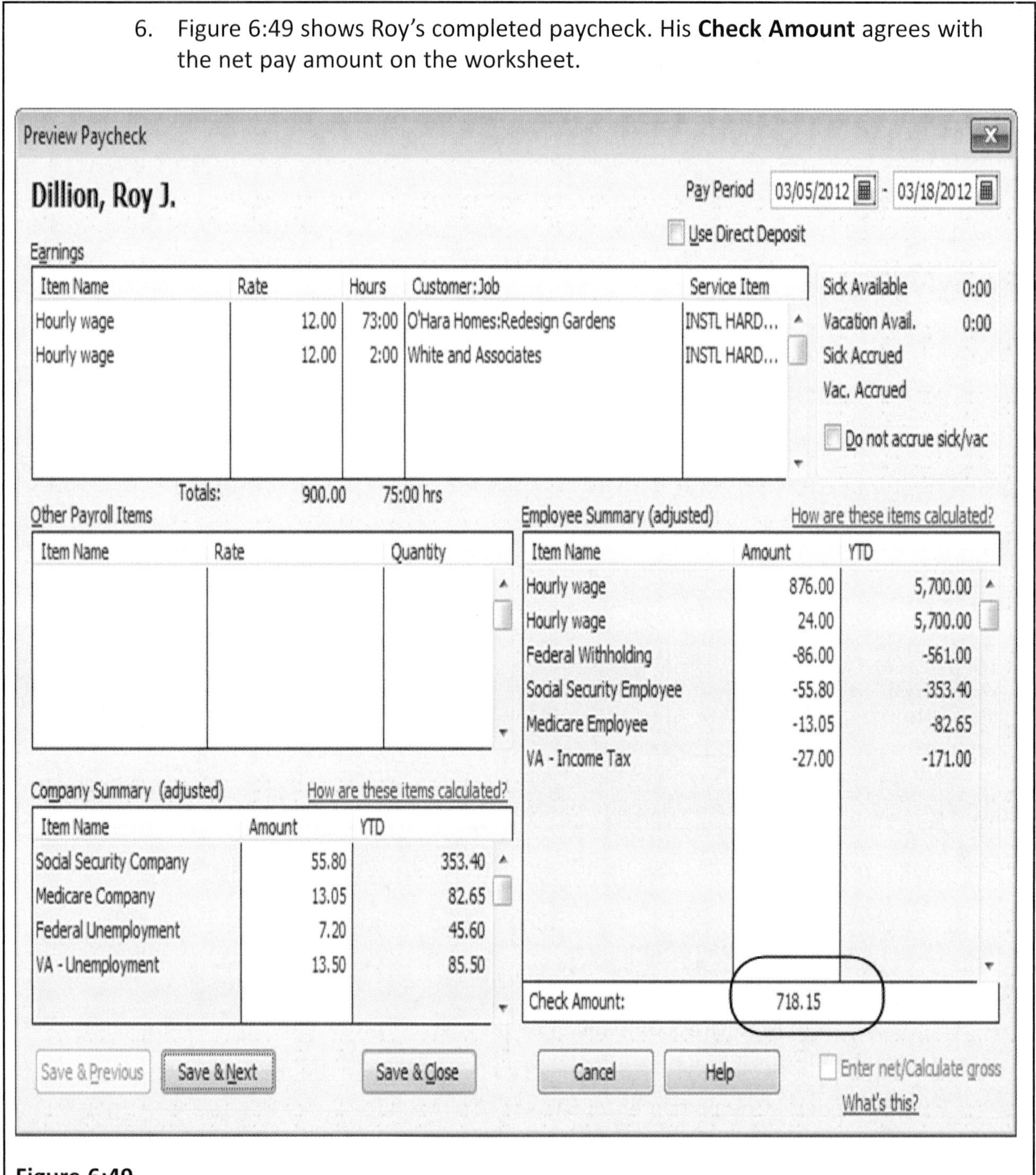

Figure 6:49

7. Click **Save & Next** and enter the following paycheck information for **Jan Folse**.

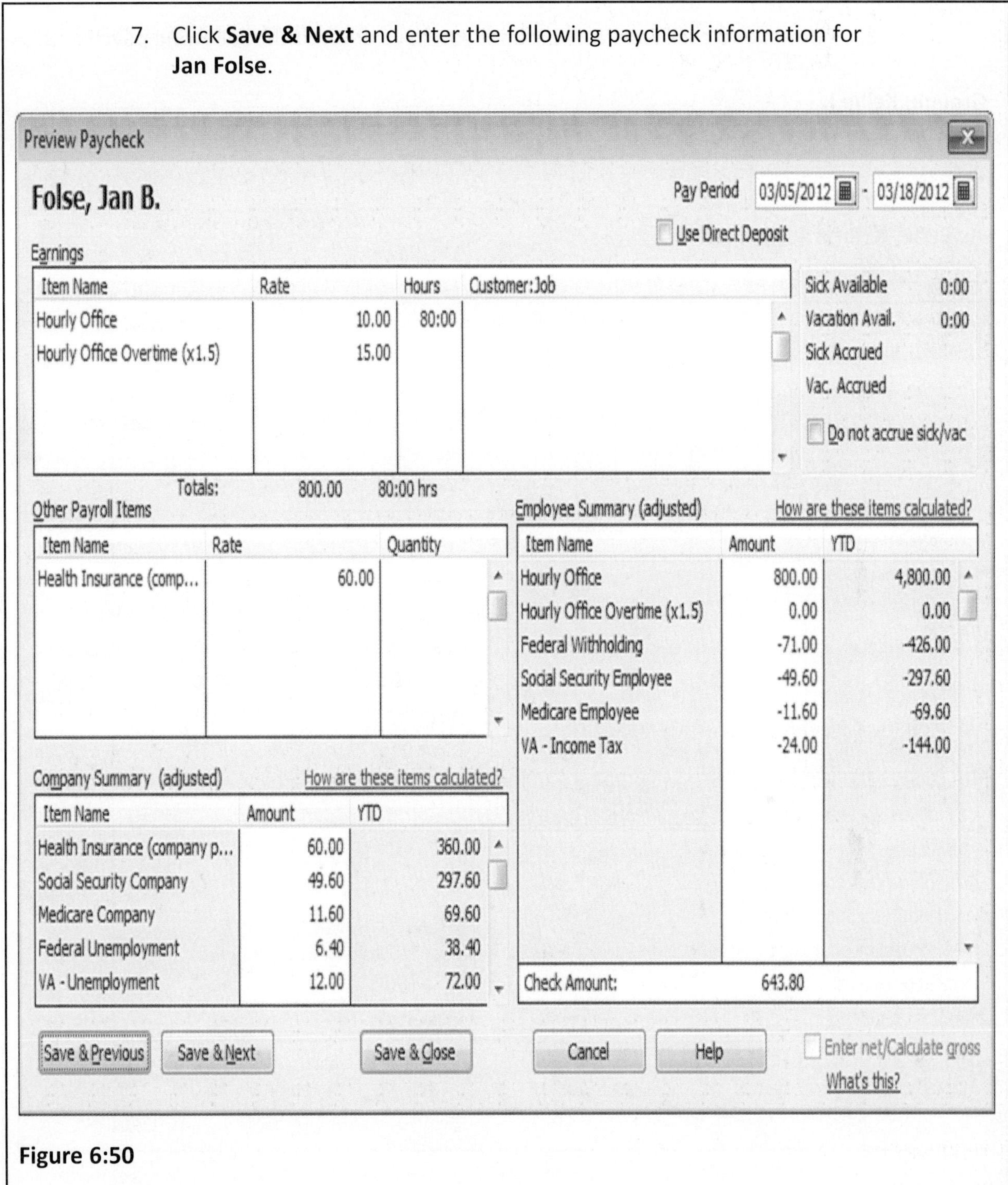

Figure 6:50

8. Continue to click **Save & Next** until you have entered the following paychecks.

Greene, Kellie I.

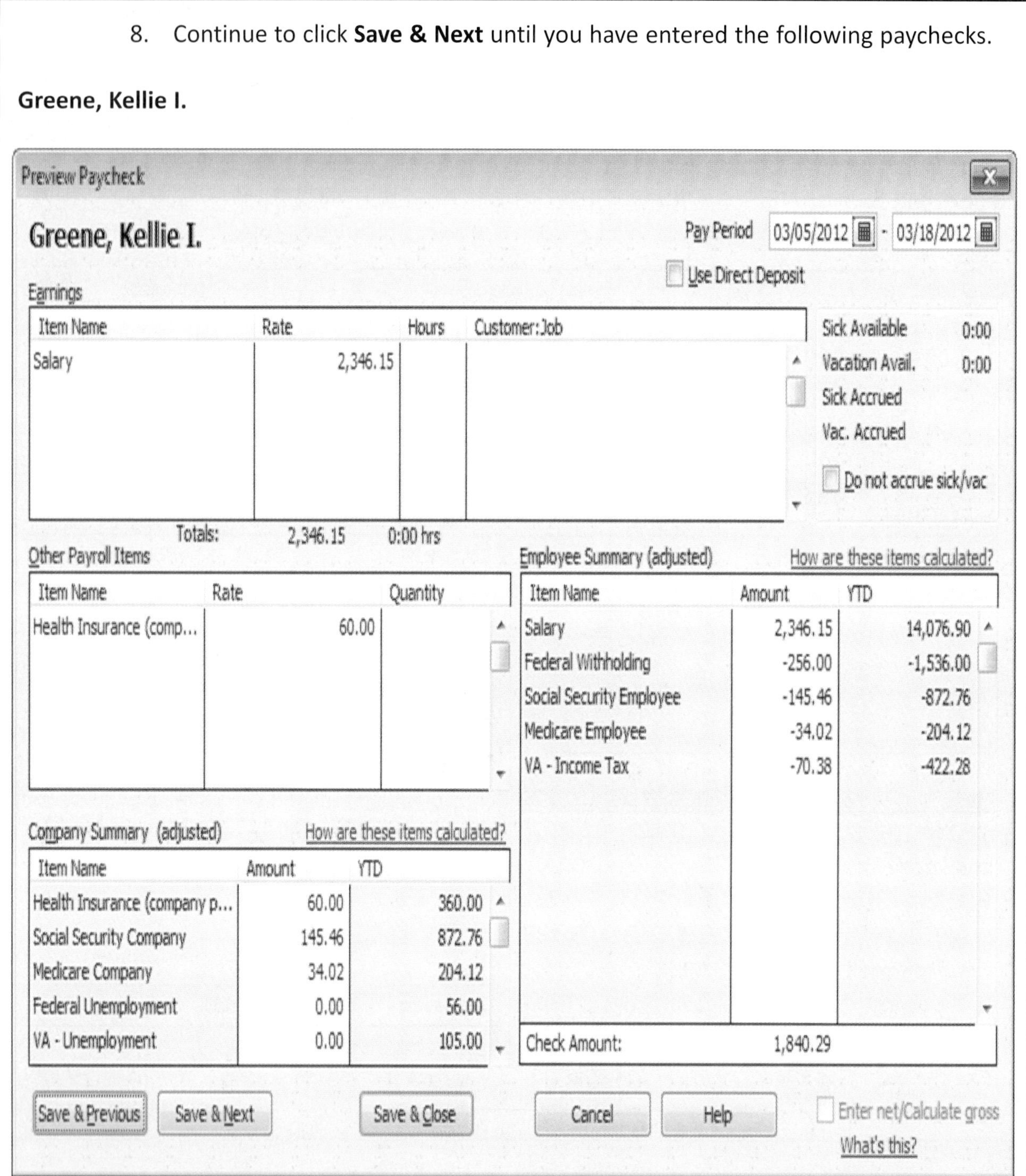

Figure 6:51

(Notice that unemployment taxes for this check are zero because Kellie's year-to-date wages exceed the taxable limit for this year.)

Hardman, Alan

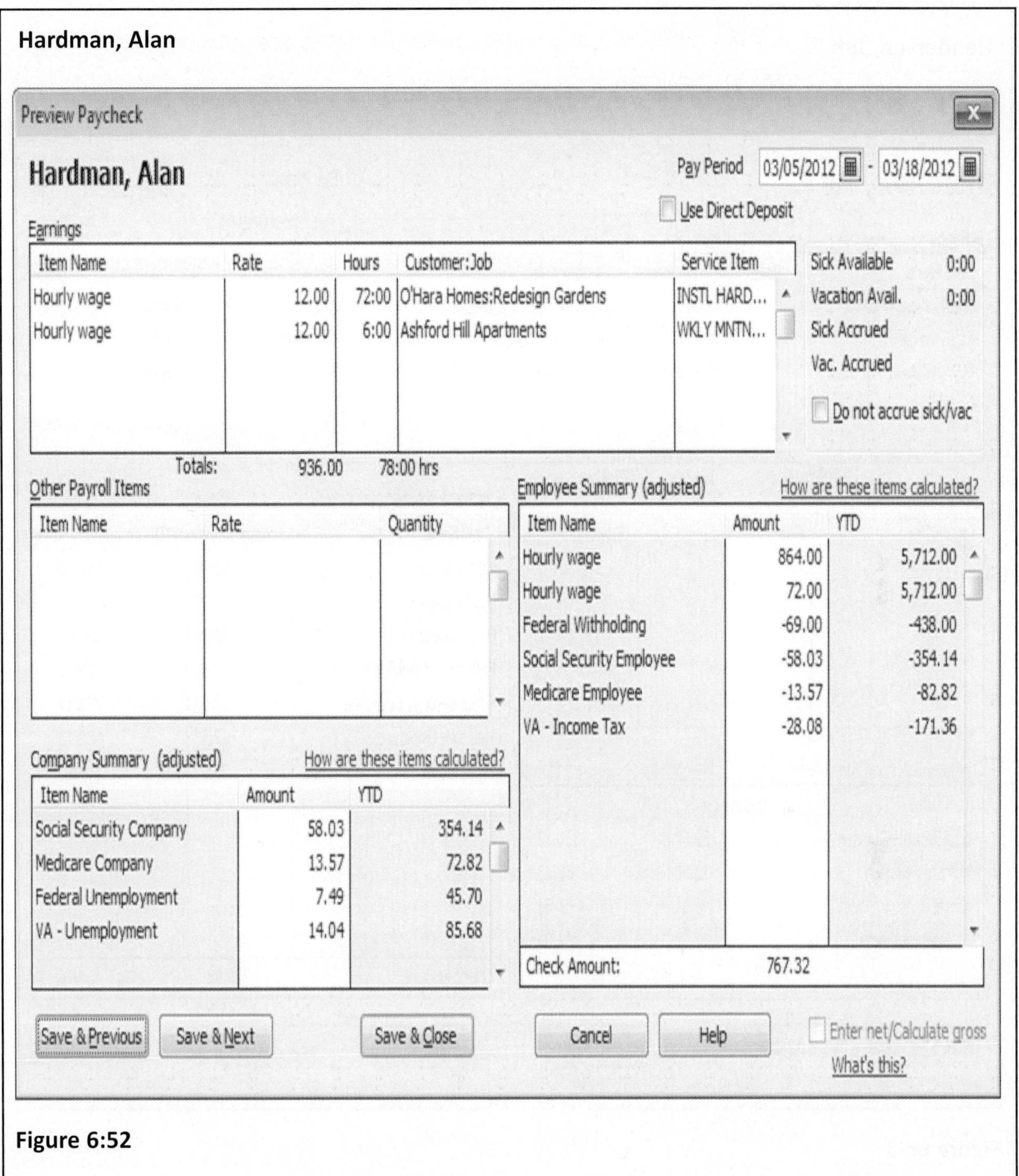

Figure 6:52

Henderson, Jeff P.

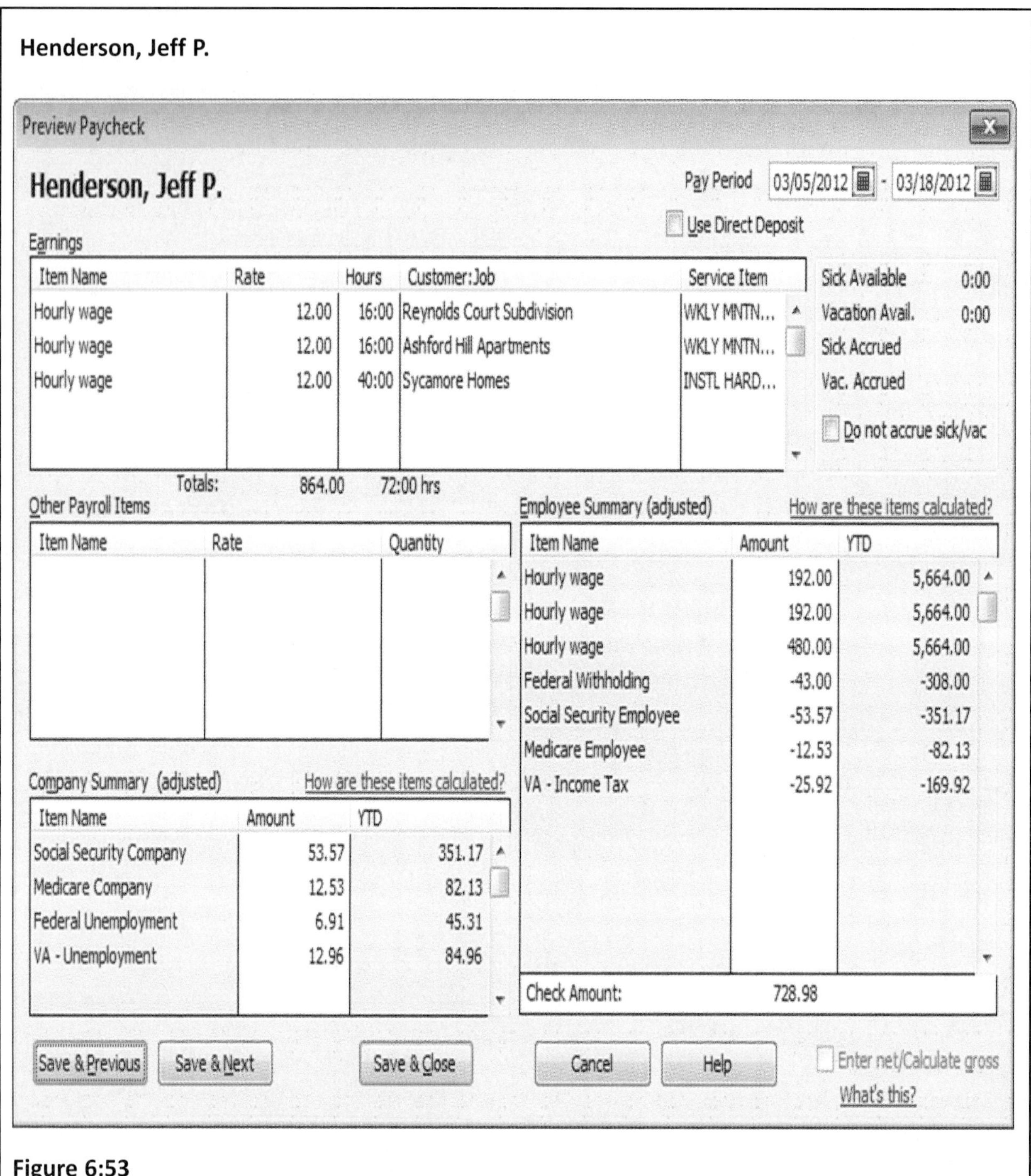

Figure 6:53

Ramez, Victor M.

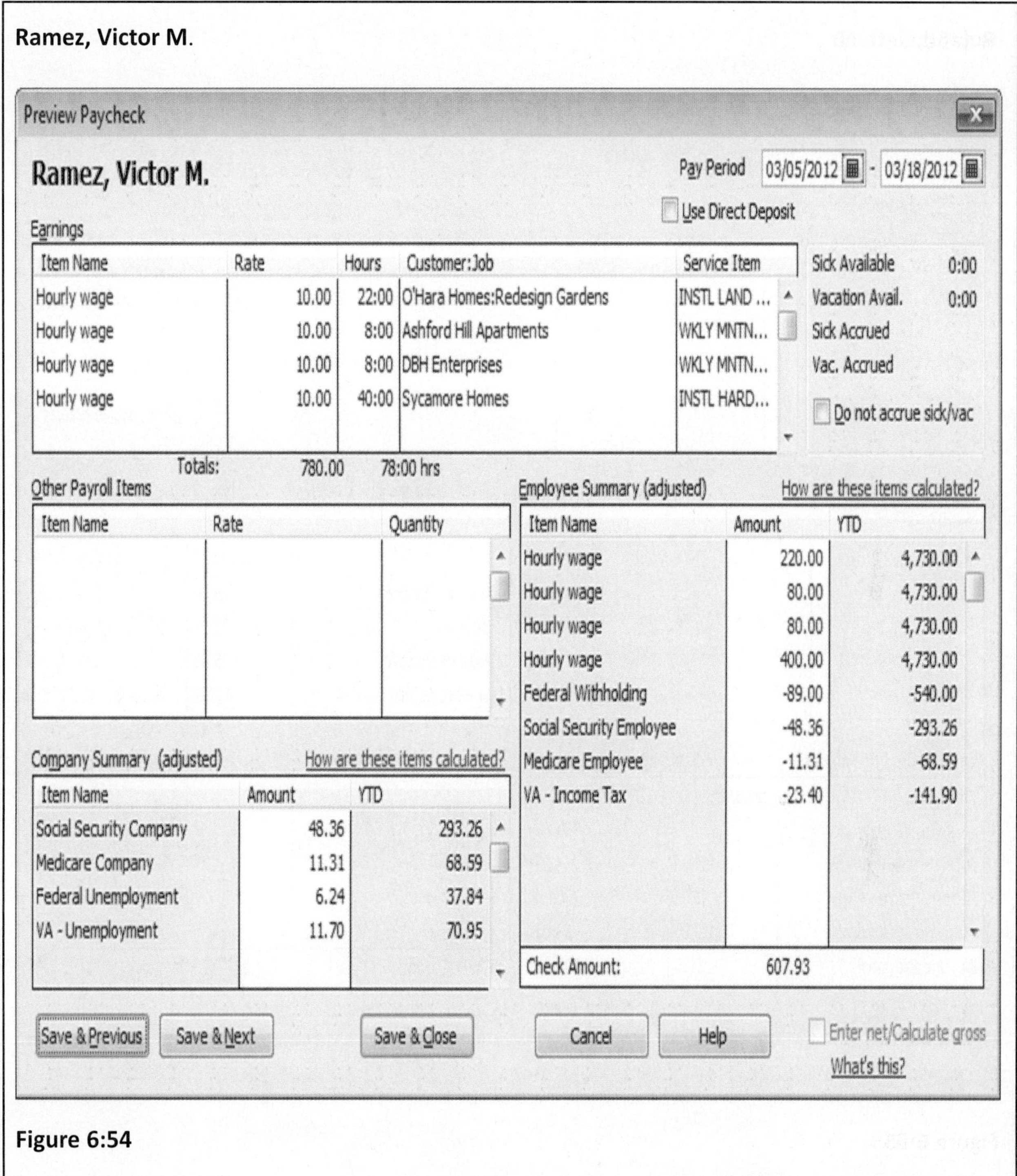

Preview Paycheck

Ramez, Victor M.

Pay Period 03/05/2012 - 03/18/2012

Use Direct Deposit

Earnings

Item Name	Rate	Hours	Customer:Job	Service Item
Hourly wage	10.00	22:00	O'Hara Homes:Redesign Gardens	INSTL LAND ...
Hourly wage	10.00	8:00	Ashford Hill Apartments	WKLY MNTN...
Hourly wage	10.00	8:00	DBH Enterprises	WKLY MNTN...
Hourly wage	10.00	40:00	Sycamore Homes	INSTL HARD...
Totals:	780.00	78:00 hrs		

Sick Available 0:00
Vacation Avail. 0:00
Sick Accrued
Vac. Accrued
Do not accrue sick/vac

Other Payroll Items

Item Name	Rate	Quantity

Employee Summary (adjusted) How are these items calculated?

Item Name	Amount	YTD
Hourly wage	220.00	4,730.00
Hourly wage	80.00	4,730.00
Hourly wage	80.00	4,730.00
Hourly wage	400.00	4,730.00
Federal Withholding	-89.00	-540.00
Social Security Employee	-48.36	-293.26
Medicare Employee	-11.31	-68.59
VA - Income Tax	-23.40	-141.90

Check Amount: 607.93

Company Summary (adjusted) How are these items calculated?

Item Name	Amount	YTD
Social Security Company	48.36	293.26
Medicare Company	11.31	68.59
Federal Unemployment	6.24	37.84
VA - Unemployment	11.70	70.95

Save & Previous | Save & Next | Save & Close | Cancel | Help

Enter net/Calculate gross
What's this?

Figure 6:54

Ruland, Seth N.

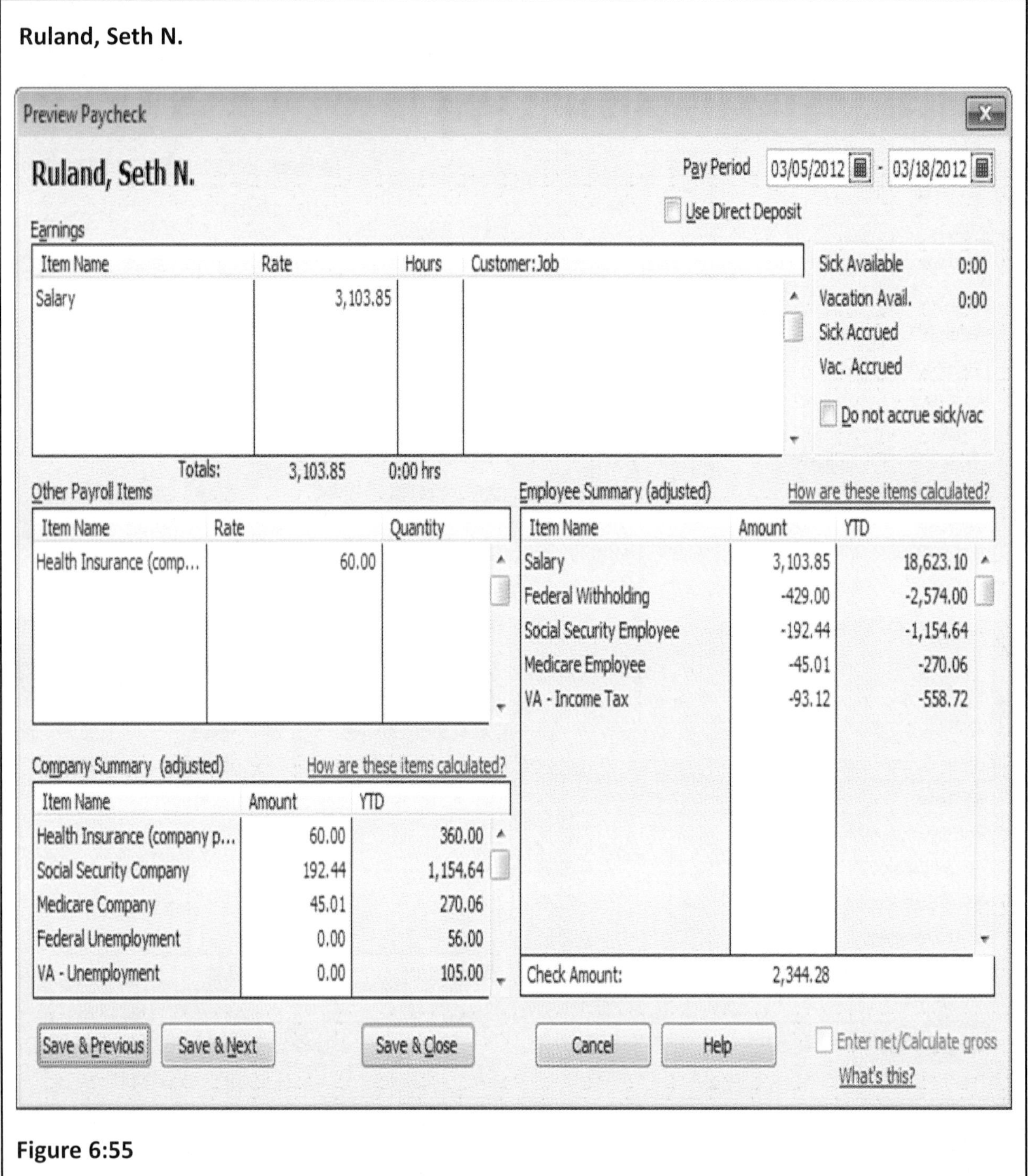

Figure 6:55

Zickefoose, Jack A.

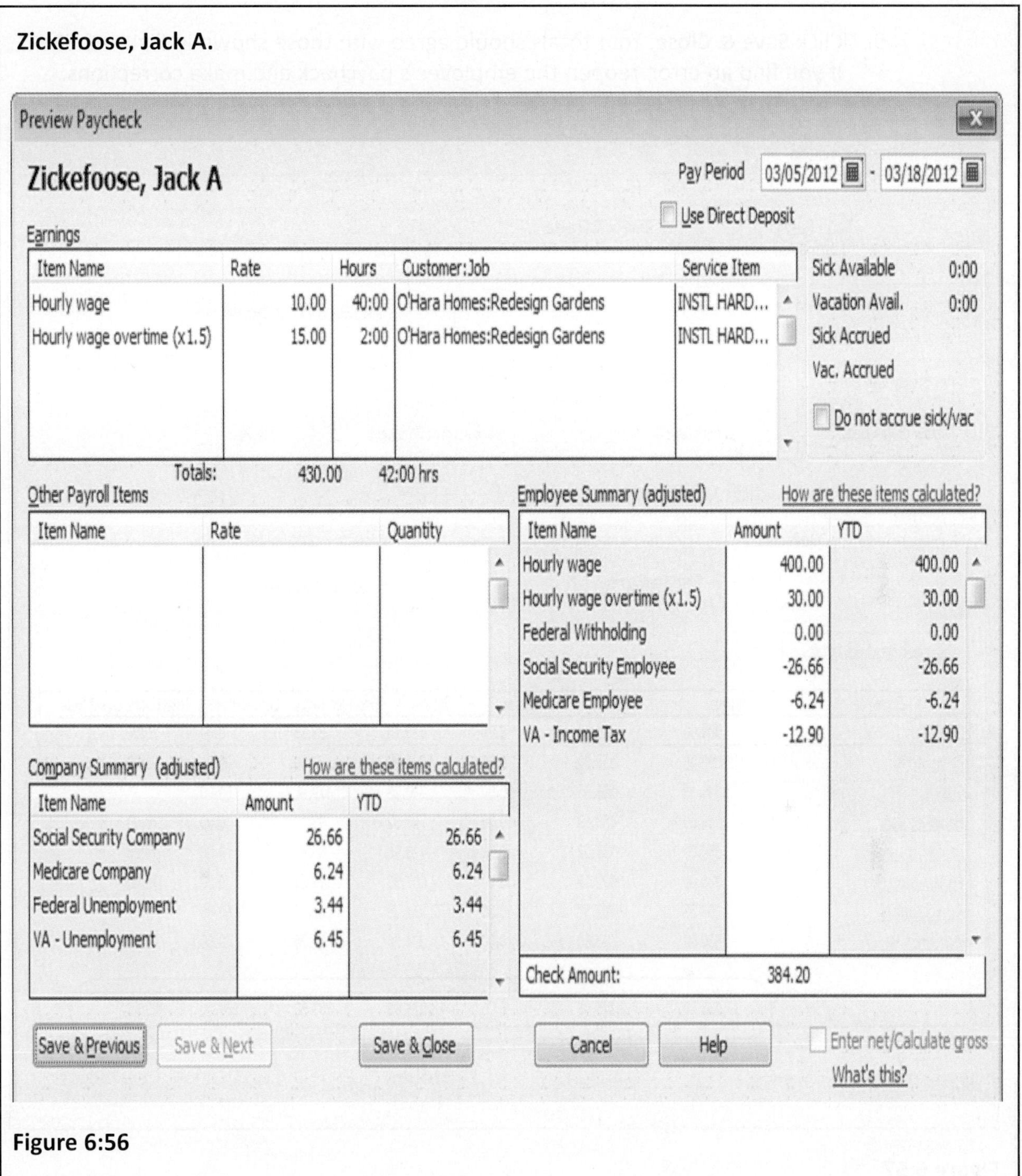
Preview Paycheck

Zickefoose, Jack A

Pay Period 03/05/2012 - 03/18/2012

Use Direct Deposit

Earnings

Item Name	Rate	Hours	Customer:Job	Service Item
Hourly wage	10.00	40:00	O'Hara Homes:Redesign Gardens	INSTL HARD...
Hourly wage overtime (x1.5)	15.00	2:00	O'Hara Homes:Redesign Gardens	INSTL HARD...
Totals:	430.00	42:00 hrs		

Sick Available 0:00
Vacation Avail. 0:00
Sick Accrued
Vac. Accrued
Do not accrue sick/vac

Other Payroll Items

Item Name	Rate	Quantity

Employee Summary (adjusted) How are these items calculated?

Item Name	Amount	YTD
Hourly wage	400.00	400.00
Hourly wage overtime (x1.5)	30.00	30.00
Federal Withholding	0.00	0.00
Social Security Employee	-26.66	-26.66
Medicare Employee	-6.24	-6.24
VA - Income Tax	-12.90	-12.90

Check Amount: 384.20

Company Summary (adjusted) How are these items calculated?

Item Name	Amount	YTD
Social Security Company	26.66	26.66
Medicare Company	6.24	6.24
Federal Unemployment	3.44	3.44
VA - Unemployment	6.45	6.45

Save & Previous | Save & Next | Save & Close | Cancel | Help | Enter net/Calculate gross | What's this?

Figure 6:56

9. Click **Save & Close**. Your totals should agree with those shown in Figure 6:60. If you find an error, reopen the employee's paycheck and make corrections.

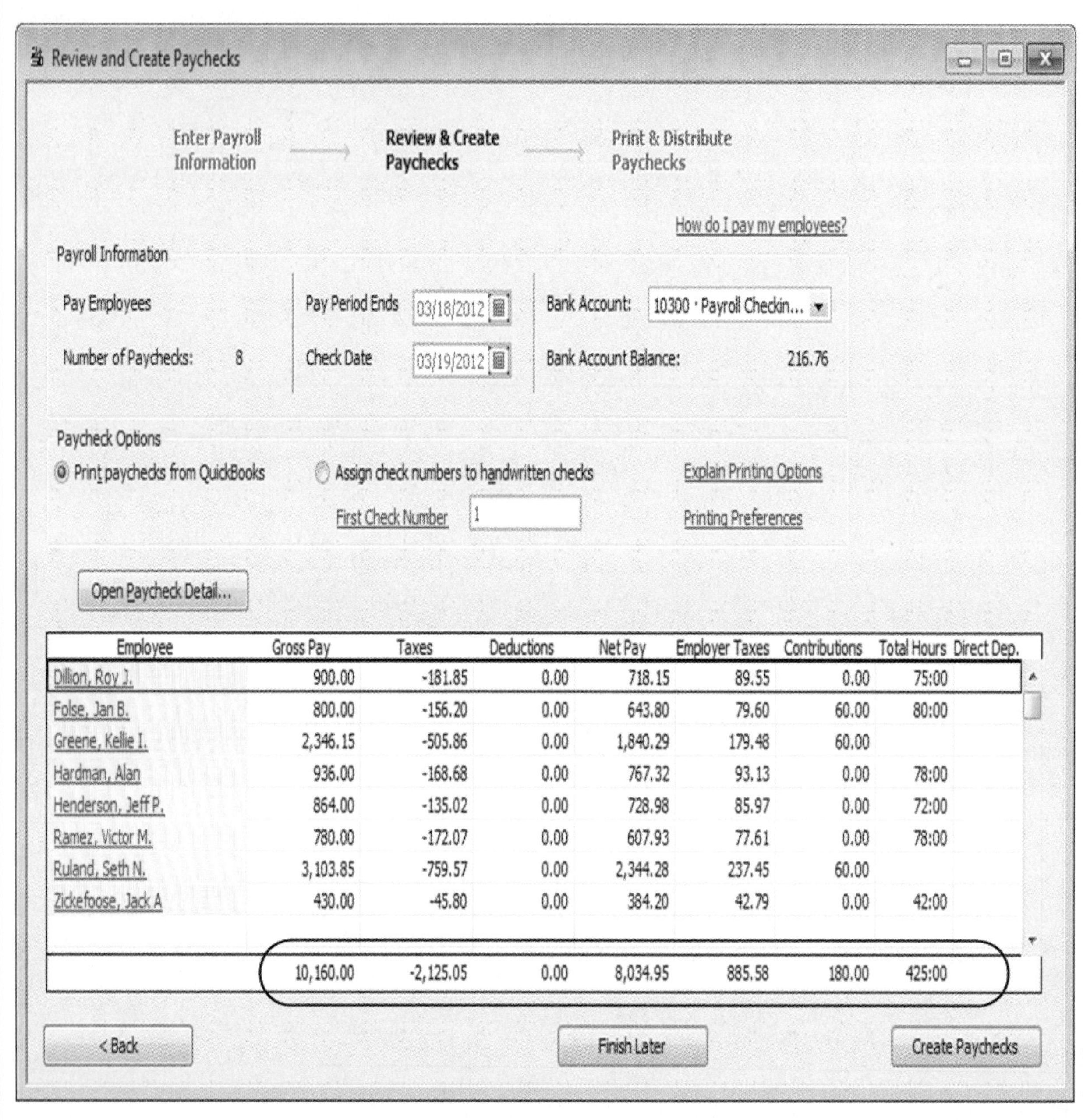

Employee	Gross Pay	Taxes	Deductions	Net Pay	Employer Taxes	Contributions	Total Hours	Direct Dep.
Dillion, Roy J.	900.00	-181.85	0.00	718.15	89.55	0.00	75:00	
Folse, Jan B.	800.00	-156.20	0.00	643.80	79.60	60.00	80:00	
Greene, Kellie I.	2,346.15	-505.86	0.00	1,840.29	179.48	60.00		
Hardman, Alan	936.00	-168.68	0.00	767.32	93.13	0.00	78:00	
Henderson, Jeff P.	864.00	-135.02	0.00	728.98	85.97	0.00	72:00	
Ramez, Victor M.	780.00	-172.07	0.00	607.93	77.61	0.00	78:00	
Ruland, Seth N.	3,103.85	-759.57	0.00	2,344.28	237.45	60.00		
Zickefoose, Jack A	430.00	-45.80	0.00	384.20	42.79	0.00	42:00	
	10,160.00	-2,125.05	0.00	8,034.95	885.58	180.00	425:00	

Figure 6:57

10. Click **Create Paychecks** and QBP informs you that 8 paychecks have been created and are ready for printing.

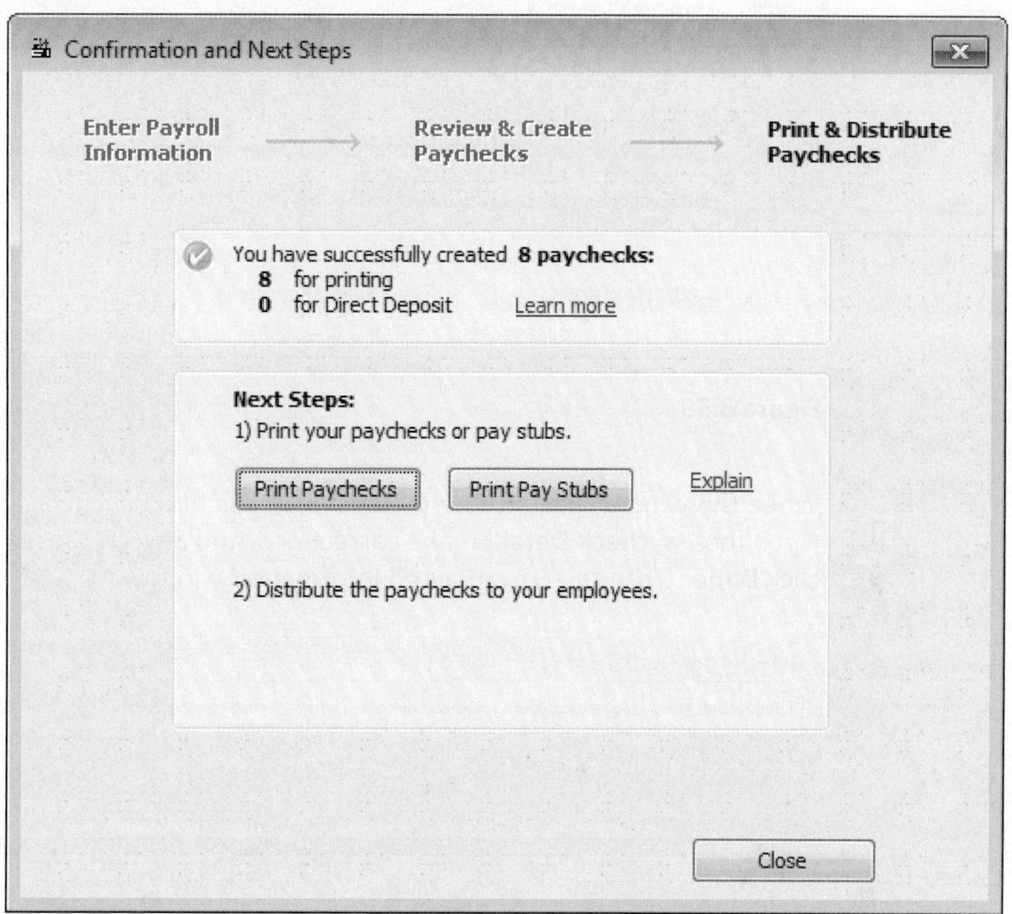

Figure 6:58

Note: If you find a mistake after clicking Create Paychecks, DO NOT click Print Paychecks on the window illustrated in Figure 6:58. Instead, click Close, return to Step 1, and reenter the pay ending and check dates. Click Check All and QBP will prompt as shown in Figure 6:59. Click Find Existing Paychecks.

If there are no mistakes, proceed to Step 11.

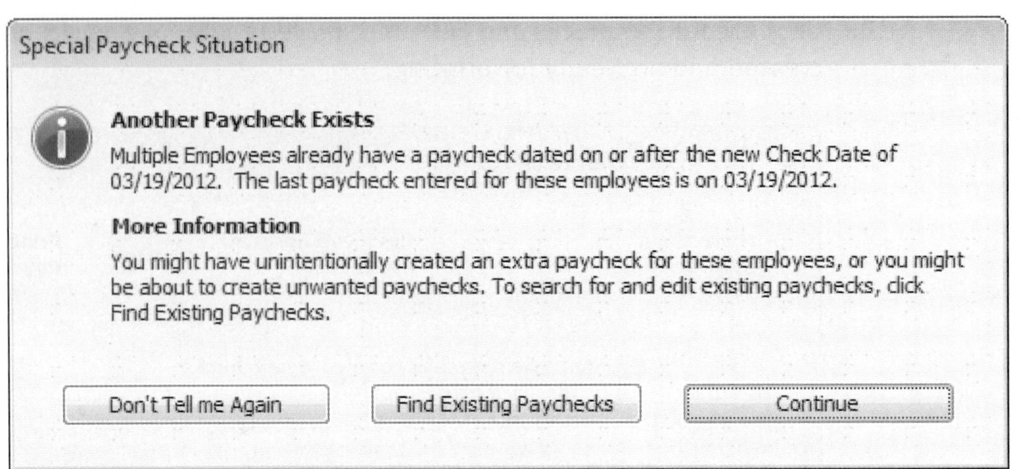

Figure 6:59

When the window illustrated next opens, highlight a paycheck and click **Edit**. Open the **Paycheck Detail**, make corrections, and **Save & Close**. When finished, click **Done**. Close the Enter Payroll Information window.

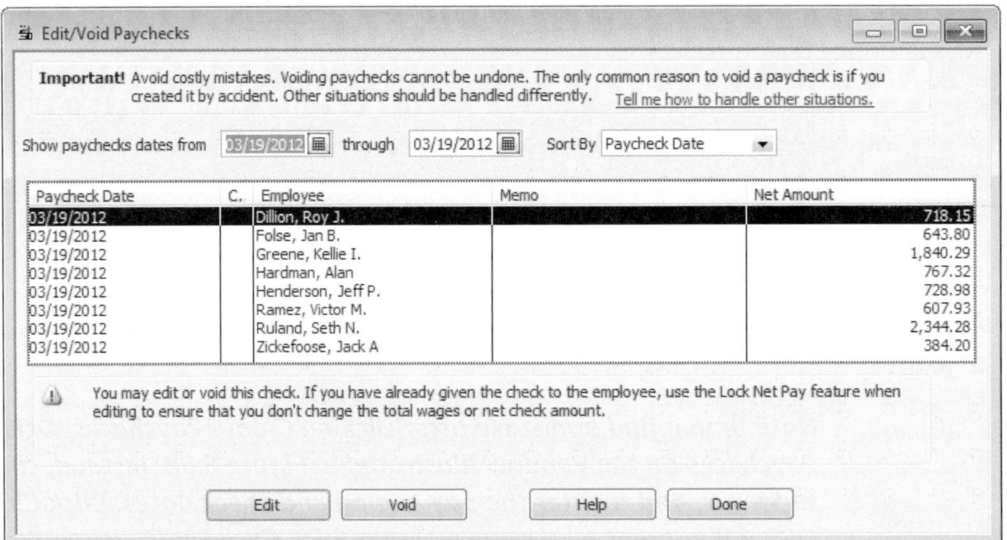

Figure 6:60

To return to printing paychecks, click ***File>>Print Forms>>Paychecks*** on the main menu. This opens the window illustrated in the next step.

11. Click **Print Paychecks**. The first check number should be 728 and all checks should be marked for printing.

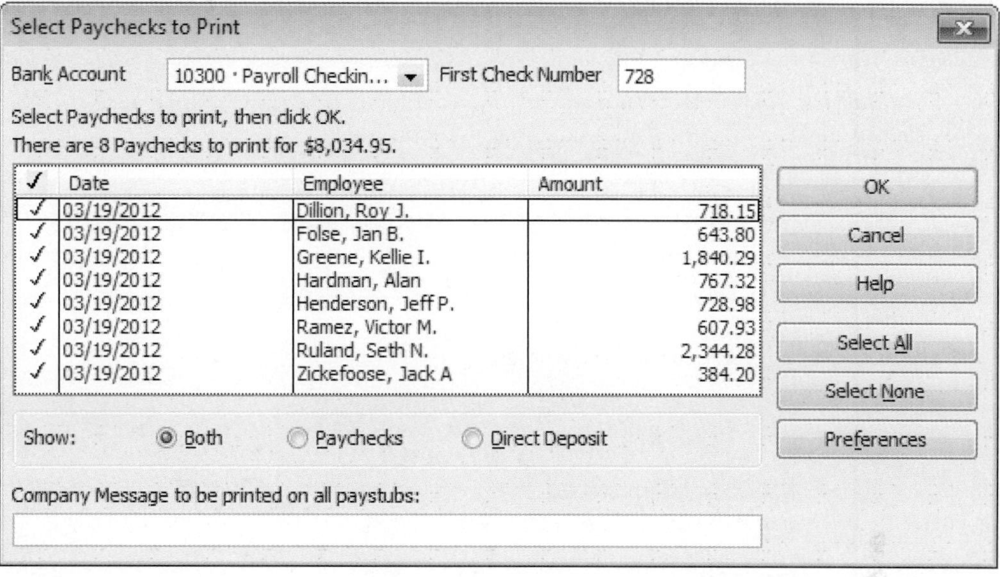

✓	Date	Employee	Amount
✓	03/19/2012	Dillion, Roy J.	718.15
✓	03/19/2012	Folse, Jan B.	643.80
✓	03/19/2012	Greene, Kellie I.	1,840.29
✓	03/19/2012	Hardman, Alan	767.32
✓	03/19/2012	Henderson, Jeff P.	728.98
✓	03/19/2012	Ramez, Victor M.	607.93
✓	03/19/2012	Ruland, Seth N.	2,344.28
✓	03/19/2012	Zickefoose, Jack A	384.20

Figure 6:61

12. Click **OK**. Select a printer and then click **Print**. Figure 6:62 shows the first paycheck.

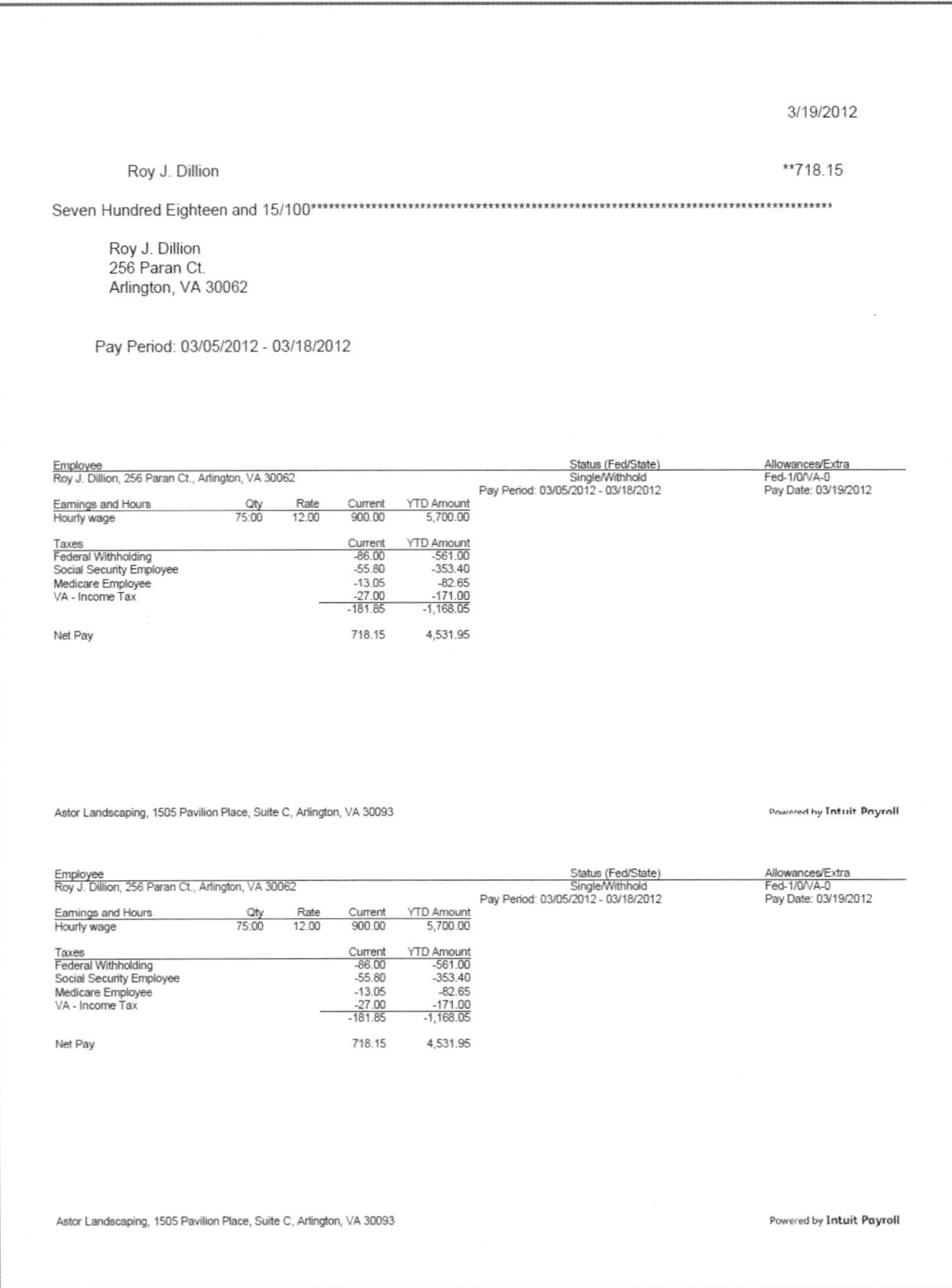

3/19/2012

Roy J. Dillion **718.15

Seven Hundred Eighteen and 15/100***

Roy J. Dillion
256 Paran Ct.
Arlington, VA 30062

Pay Period: 03/05/2012 - 03/18/2012

Employee	Status (Fed/State)	Allowances/Extra
Roy J. Dillion, 256 Paran Ct., Arlington, VA 30062	Single/Withhold	Fed-1/0/VA-0
	Pay Period: 03/05/2012 - 03/18/2012	Pay Date: 03/19/2012

Earnings and Hours	Qty	Rate	Current	YTD Amount
Hourly wage	75:00	12.00	900.00	5,700.00

Taxes	Current	YTD Amount
Federal Withholding	-86.00	-561.00
Social Security Employee	-55.80	-353.40
Medicare Employee	-13.05	-82.65
VA - Income Tax	-27.00	-171.00
	-181.85	-1,168.05
Net Pay	718.15	4,531.95

Astor Landscaping, 1505 Pavilion Place, Suite C, Arlington, VA 30093 Powered by Intuit Payroll

Employee	Status (Fed/State)	Allowances/Extra
Roy J. Dillion, 256 Paran Ct., Arlington, VA 30062	Single/Withhold	Fed-1/0/VA-0
	Pay Period: 03/05/2012 - 03/18/2012	Pay Date: 03/19/2012

Earnings and Hours	Qty	Rate	Current	YTD Amount
Hourly wage	75:00	12.00	900.00	5,700.00

Taxes	Current	YTD Amount
Federal Withholding	-86.00	-561.00
Social Security Employee	-55.80	-353.40
Medicare Employee	-13.05	-82.65
VA - Income Tax	-27.00	-171.00
	-181.85	-1,168.05
Net Pay	718.15	4,531.95

Astor Landscaping, 1505 Pavilion Place, Suite C, Arlington, VA 30093 Powered by Intuit Payroll

Figure 6:62

13. After printing, QBP confirms that checks printed correctly. *(Note: If prompted to subscribe to a payroll service, select* ***No, and don't show me this message again*** and click ***OK***.*)* If needed, click **Close** on the confirmation window.

You have just printed paychecks. Now trace the entries that posted.

BEHIND THE KEYS OF A POSTED PAYCHECK

You will now trace the entries made when printing paychecks in the previous topic.

STEPS TO TRACING PAYCHECK ENTRIES

1. Click **Reports** on the Icon bar. Select the **Employees & Payroll** category and open the **Payroll Transaction Detail** report. Enter **3/19/12** as the date range.

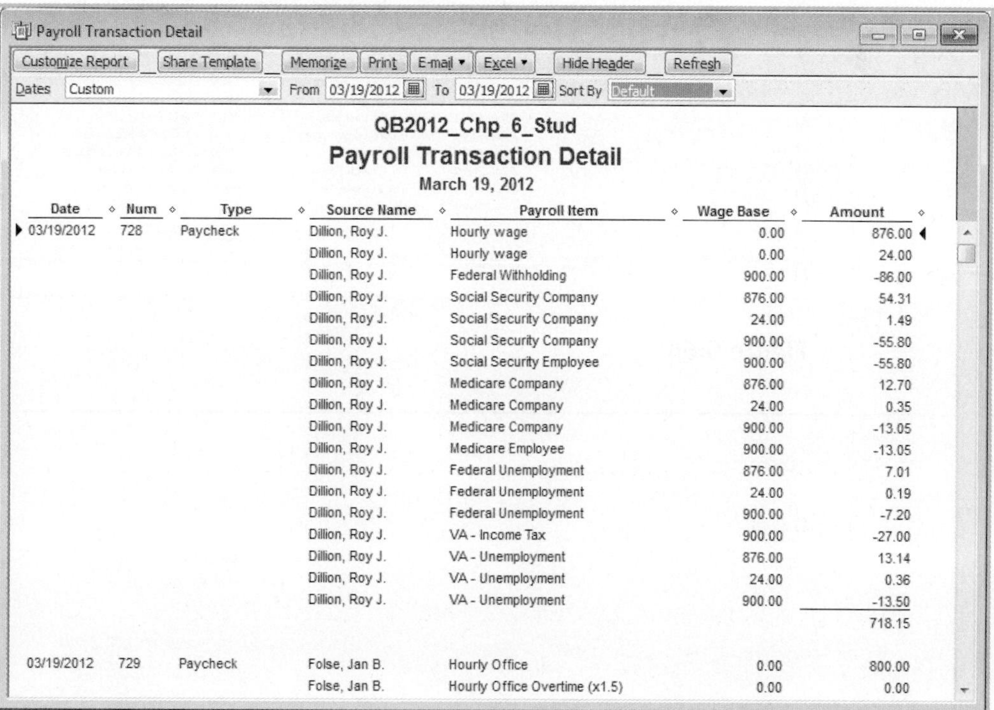

QB2012_Chp_6_Stud

Payroll Transaction Detail

March 19, 2012

Date	Num	Type	Source Name	Payroll Item	Wage Base	Amount
03/19/2012	728	Paycheck	Dillion, Roy J.	Hourly wage	0.00	876.00
			Dillion, Roy J.	Hourly wage	0.00	24.00
			Dillion, Roy J.	Federal Withholding	900.00	-86.00
			Dillion, Roy J.	Social Security Company	876.00	54.31
			Dillion, Roy J.	Social Security Company	24.00	1.49
			Dillion, Roy J.	Social Security Company	900.00	-55.80
			Dillion, Roy J.	Social Security Employee	900.00	-55.80
			Dillion, Roy J.	Medicare Company	876.00	12.70
			Dillion, Roy J.	Medicare Company	24.00	0.35
			Dillion, Roy J.	Medicare Company	900.00	-13.05
			Dillion, Roy J.	Medicare Employee	900.00	-13.05
			Dillion, Roy J.	Federal Unemployment	876.00	7.01
			Dillion, Roy J.	Federal Unemployment	24.00	0.19
			Dillion, Roy J.	Federal Unemployment	900.00	-7.20
			Dillion, Roy J.	VA - Income Tax	900.00	-27.00
			Dillion, Roy J.	VA - Unemployment	876.00	13.14
			Dillion, Roy J.	VA - Unemployment	24.00	0.36
			Dillion, Roy J.	VA - Unemployment	900.00	-13.50
						718.15
03/19/2012	729	Paycheck	Folse, Jan B.	Hourly Office	0.00	800.00
			Folse, Jan B.	Hourly Office Overtime (x1.5)	0.00	0.00

Figure 6:63

2. Now customize the report to show additional information. Click **Customize Report** and

   On the Display tab:

   Add columns: Trans #, Account, Debit, Credit
   Remove columns: Wage Base, Amount

   On the Filters tab, under Current Filter Choices:
   Click **Detail Level** and remove the filter.
   Click **Payroll Item** and remove the filter.

   On the Header/Footer tab:
   Type "Payroll Journal" as the **Report Title** and click **OK**.

   Figure 6:64 shows the customized report listing all accounts affected by paycheck. Notice that the accounts affected match the accounts set on the payroll items discussed in the *Payroll Items* topic.

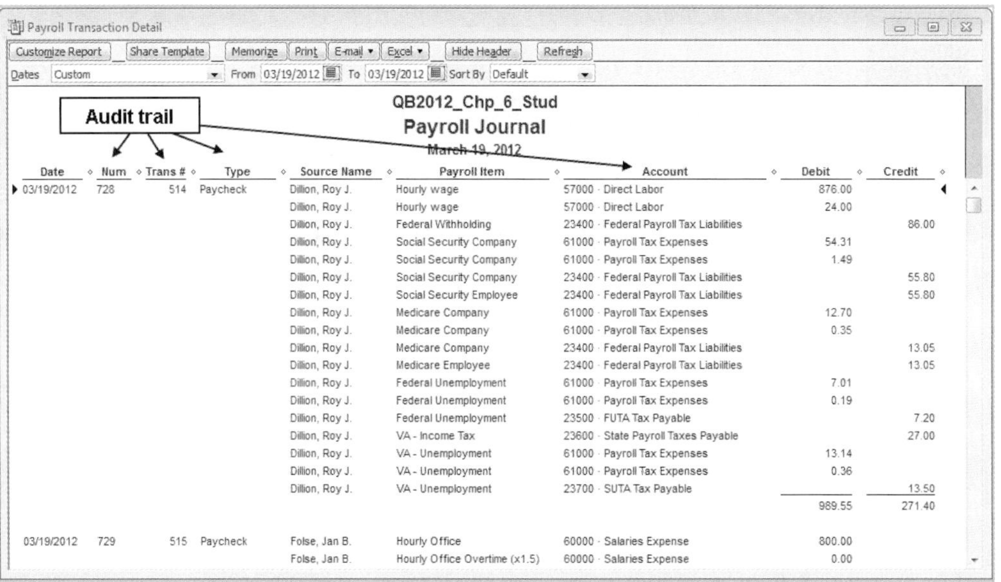

QB2012_Chp_6_Stud
Payroll Journal
March 19, 2012

Date	Num	Trans #	Type	Source Name	Payroll Item	Account	Debit	Credit
03/19/2012	728	514	Paycheck	Dillion, Roy J.	Hourly wage	57000 · Direct Labor	876.00	
				Dillion, Roy J.	Hourly wage	57000 · Direct Labor	24.00	
				Dillion, Roy J.	Federal Withholding	23400 · Federal Payroll Tax Liabilities		86.00
				Dillion, Roy J.	Social Security Company	61000 · Payroll Tax Expenses	54.31	
				Dillion, Roy J.	Social Security Company	61000 · Payroll Tax Expenses	1.49	
				Dillion, Roy J.	Social Security Company	23400 · Federal Payroll Tax Liabilities		55.80
				Dillion, Roy J.	Social Security Employee	23400 · Federal Payroll Tax Liabilities		55.80
				Dillion, Roy J.	Medicare Company	61000 · Payroll Tax Expenses	12.70	
				Dillion, Roy J.	Medicare Company	61000 · Payroll Tax Expenses	0.35	
				Dillion, Roy J.	Medicare Company	23400 · Federal Payroll Tax Liabilities		13.05
				Dillion, Roy J.	Medicare Employee	23400 · Federal Payroll Tax Liabilities		13.05
				Dillion, Roy J.	Federal Unemployment	61000 · Payroll Tax Expenses	7.01	
				Dillion, Roy J.	Federal Unemployment	61000 · Payroll Tax Expenses	0.19	
				Dillion, Roy J.	Federal Unemployment	23500 · FUTA Tax Payable		7.20
				Dillion, Roy J.	VA - Income Tax	23600 · State Payroll Taxes Payable		27.00
				Dillion, Roy J.	VA - Unemployment	61000 · Payroll Tax Expenses	13.14	
				Dillion, Roy J.	VA - Unemployment	61000 · Payroll Tax Expenses	0.36	
				Dillion, Roy J.	VA - Unemployment	23700 · SUTA Tax Payable		13.50
							989.55	271.40
03/19/2012	729	515	Paycheck	Folse, Jan B.	Hourly Office	60000 · Salaries Expense	800.00	
				Folse, Jan B.	Hourly Office Overtime (x1.5)	60000 · Salaries Expense	0.00	

Figure 6:64

Click **Memorize** and confirm the information in Figure 6:65. Click **OK** and close the report.

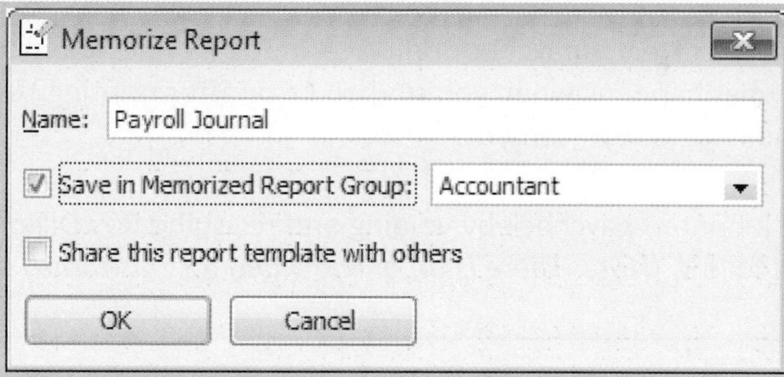

Figure 6:65

3. To view a report looking something like our payroll register in Excel, open the **Employee Earnings Summary** report. Enter **3/19/12** as the date range.

   Use the scroll bars to view additional information. This report should reconcile to the Excel payroll register.

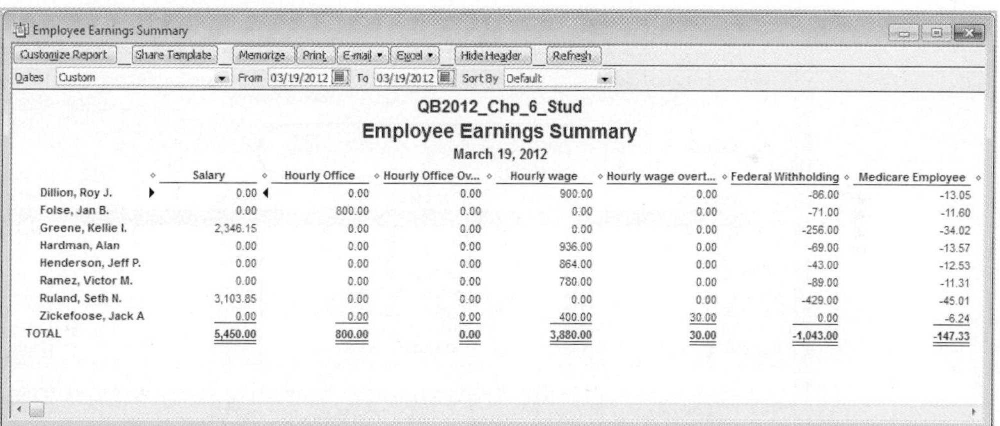

QB2012_Chp_6_Stud
Employee Earnings Summary
March 19, 2012

	Salary	Hourly Office	Hourly Office Ov...	Hourly wage	Hourly wage overt...	Federal Withholding	Medicare Employee
Dillion, Roy J.	0.00	0.00	0.00	900.00	0.00	-86.00	-13.05
Folse, Jan B.	0.00	800.00	0.00	0.00	0.00	-71.00	-11.60
Greene, Kellie I.	2,346.15	0.00	0.00	0.00	0.00	-256.00	-34.02
Hardman, Alan	0.00	0.00	0.00	936.00	0.00	-69.00	-13.57
Henderson, Jeff P.	0.00	0.00	0.00	864.00	0.00	-43.00	-12.53
Ramez, Victor M.	0.00	0.00	0.00	780.00	0.00	-89.00	-11.31
Ruland, Seth N.	3,103.85	0.00	0.00	0.00	0.00	-429.00	-45.01
Zickefoose, Jack A	0.00	0.00	0.00	400.00	30.00	0.00	-6.24
TOTAL	5,450.00	800.00	0.00	3,880.00	30.00	-1,043.00	-147.33

Figure 6:66

4. Remember that you complete tracing entries to the general ledger by displaying the ***Reports>>Memorized Reports>>Accounting Journals>>General Ledger Detail Report***.

5. Close all open reports and the Report Center.

Correcting Employee Paychecks

We told you how to correct a paycheck before printing it while you were entering paycheck data. However, what happens when you find an error after printing? Well, you must then void the paycheck and issue a replacement.

Practice voiding a printed paycheck by voiding and reissuing Roy Dillion's most recent paycheck in the steps that follow. *(Note: There is an online video for this topic.)*

Steps to Voiding a Printed Paycheck

1. Select ***Employees>>Edit/Void Paychecks*** on the main menu. Enter the date range of **3/19/12**. You now see the paychecks issued on this date (Figure 6:67).

   Highlight Roy's check and click **Void**.

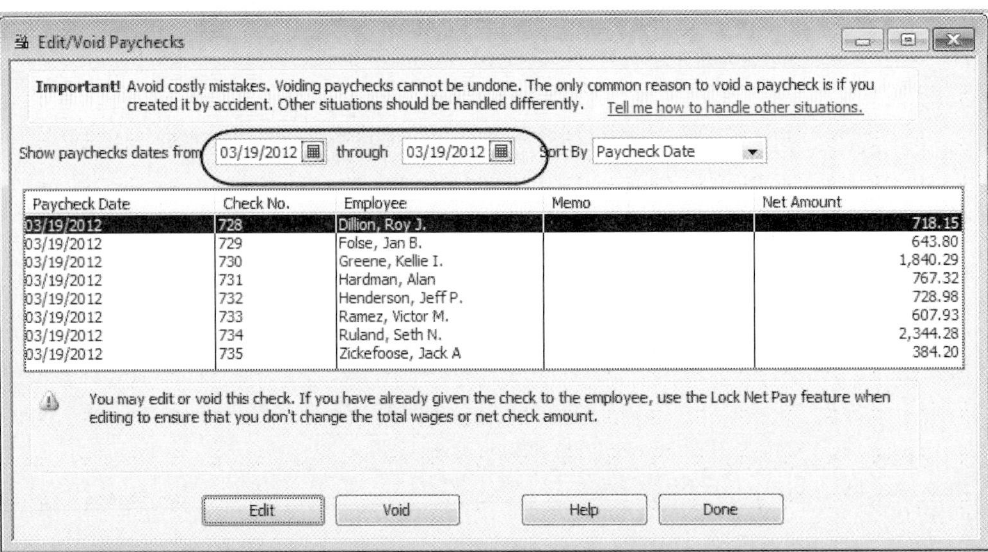

Figure 6:67

2. The window updates, showing Roy's paycheck as void. Click **Done**.

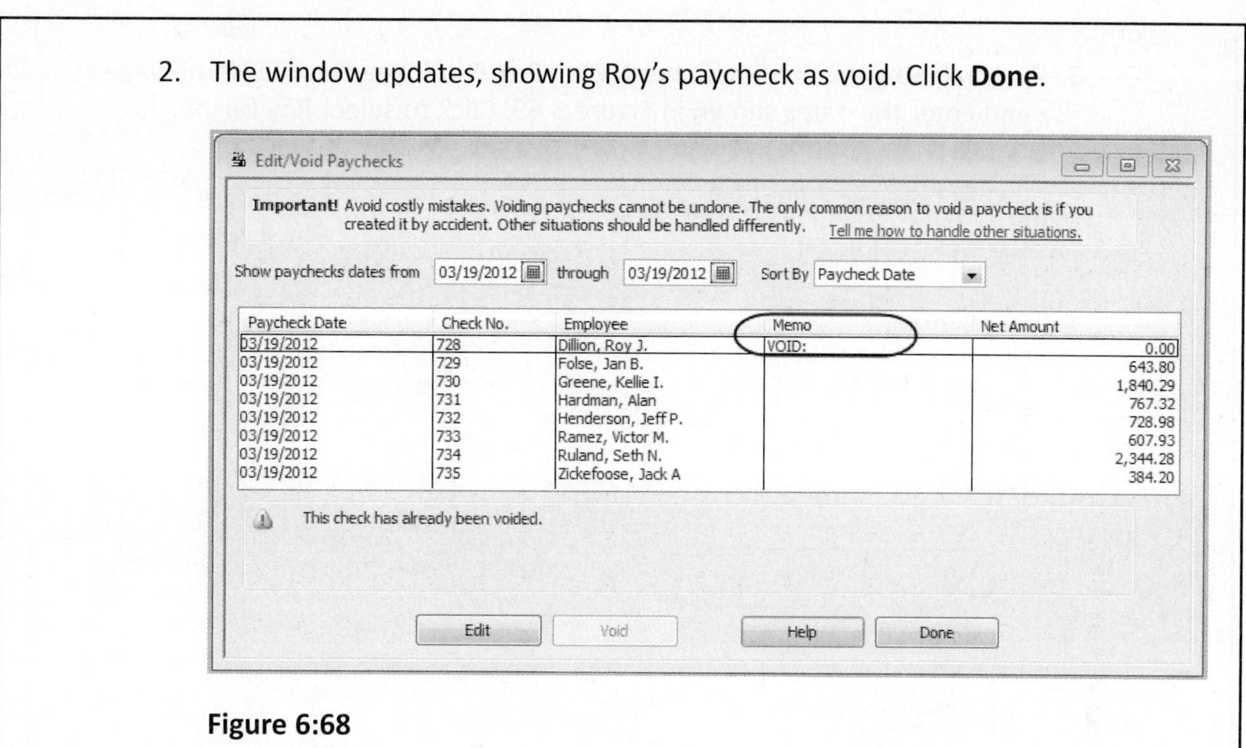

Figure 6:68

3. You will now reissue Roy's check. Click **Pay Employees** on the Home page and enter the dates shown in Figure 6:69. Click to select Roy Dillion.

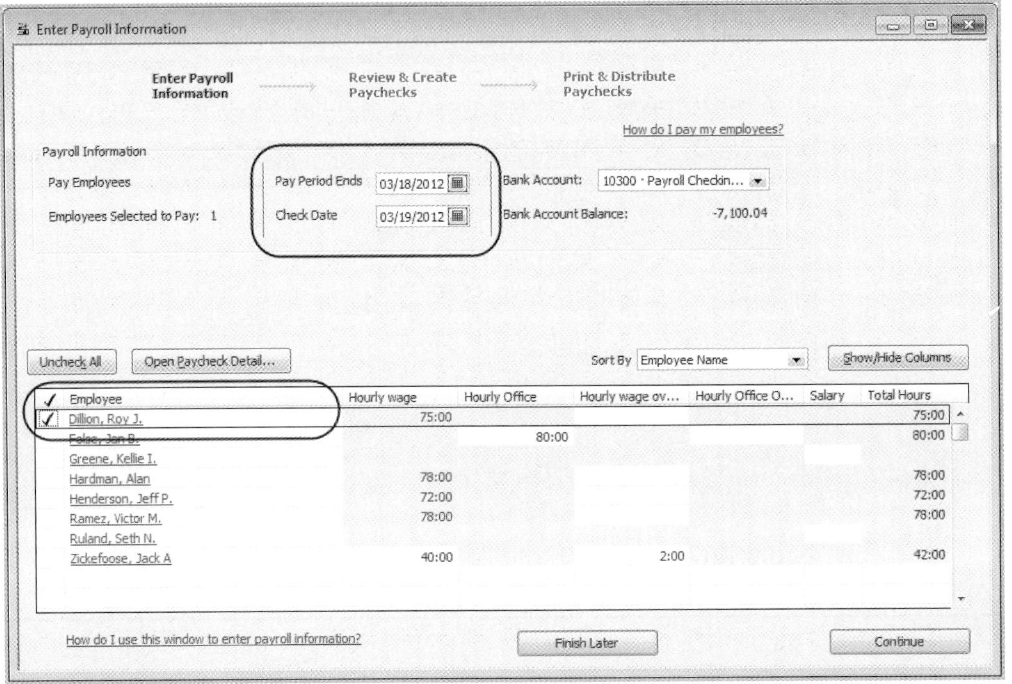

Figure 6:69

4. Click **Continue**. Click to open Roy's paycheck and enter his paycheck information again. (See Figure 6:70.)

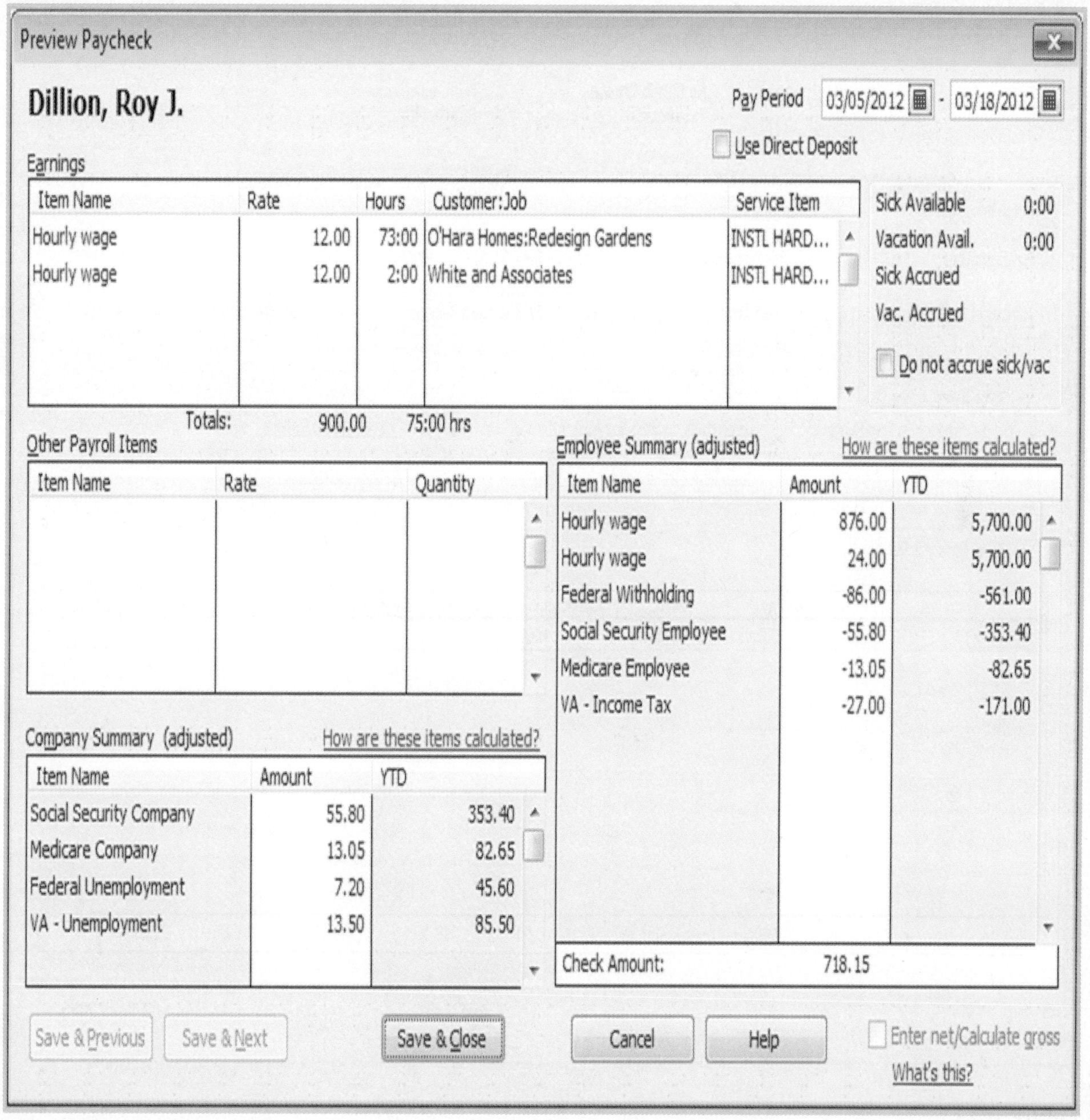

Preview Paycheck

Dillion, Roy J.

Pay Period 03/05/2012 - 03/18/2012

Use Direct Deposit

Earnings

Item Name	Rate	Hours	Customer:Job	Service Item
Hourly wage	12.00	73:00	O'Hara Homes:Redesign Gardens	INSTL HARD...
Hourly wage	12.00	2:00	White and Associates	INSTL HARD...
Totals:	900.00	75:00 hrs		

Sick Available 0:00
Vacation Avail. 0:00
Sick Accrued
Vac. Accrued
Do not accrue sick/vac

Other Payroll Items

Item Name	Rate	Quantity

Employee Summary (adjusted) How are these items calculated?

Item Name	Amount	YTD
Hourly wage	876.00	5,700.00
Hourly wage	24.00	5,700.00
Federal Withholding	-86.00	-561.00
Social Security Employee	-55.80	-353.40
Medicare Employee	-13.05	-82.65
VA - Income Tax	-27.00	-171.00

Check Amount: 718.15

Company Summary (adjusted) How are these items calculated?

Item Name	Amount	YTD
Social Security Company	55.80	353.40
Medicare Company	13.05	82.65
Federal Unemployment	7.20	45.60
VA - Unemployment	13.50	85.50

Save & Previous | Save & Next | Save & Close | Cancel | Help | Enter net/Calculate gross | What's this?

Figure 6:70

5. Click **Save & Close**. Figure 6:71 shows Roy's updated check.

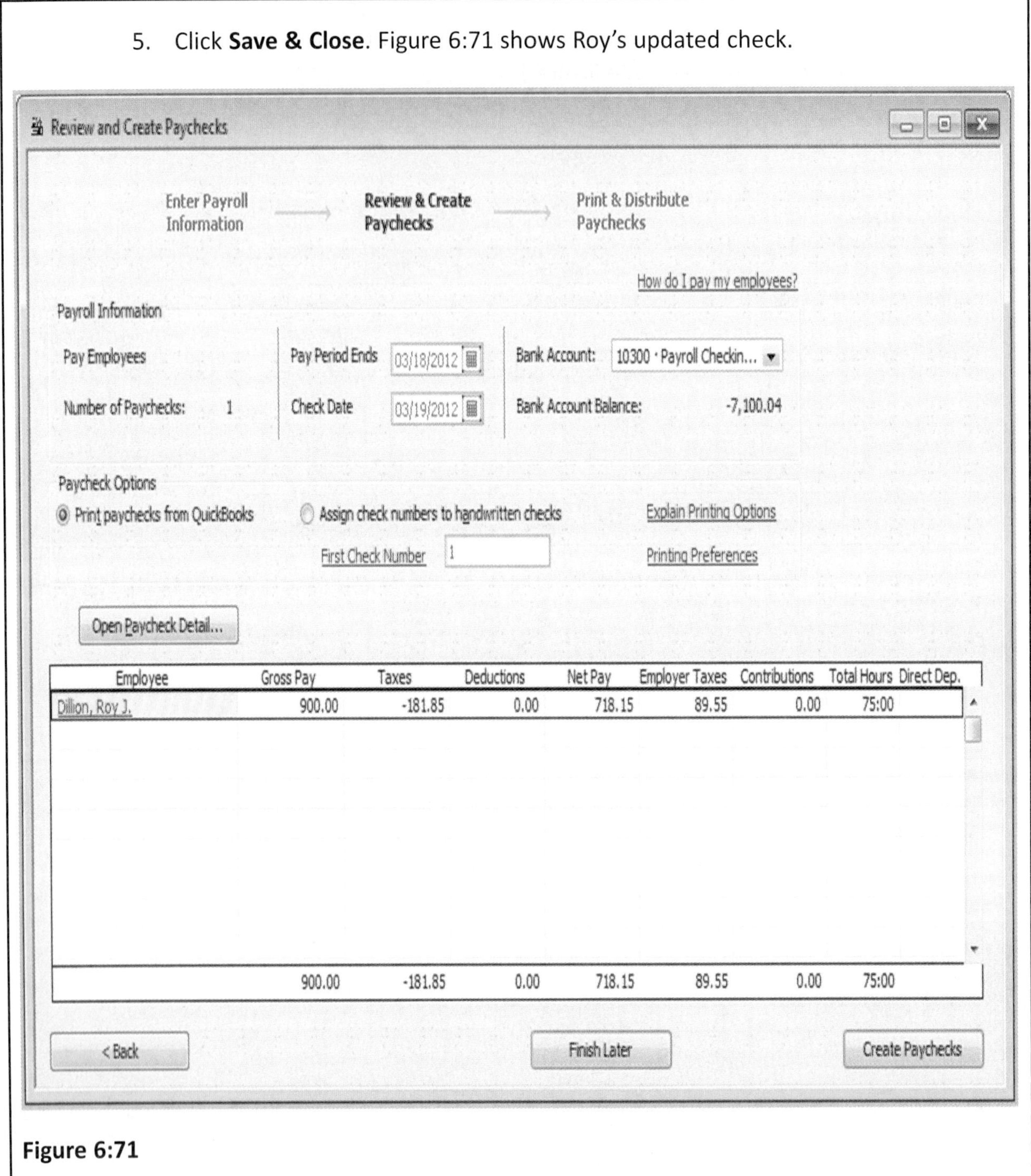

Figure 6:71

6. Click **Create Paychecks** and then click **Print Paychecks**. The first check number should be 736. Click **OK**, select a printer, and click **Print**.

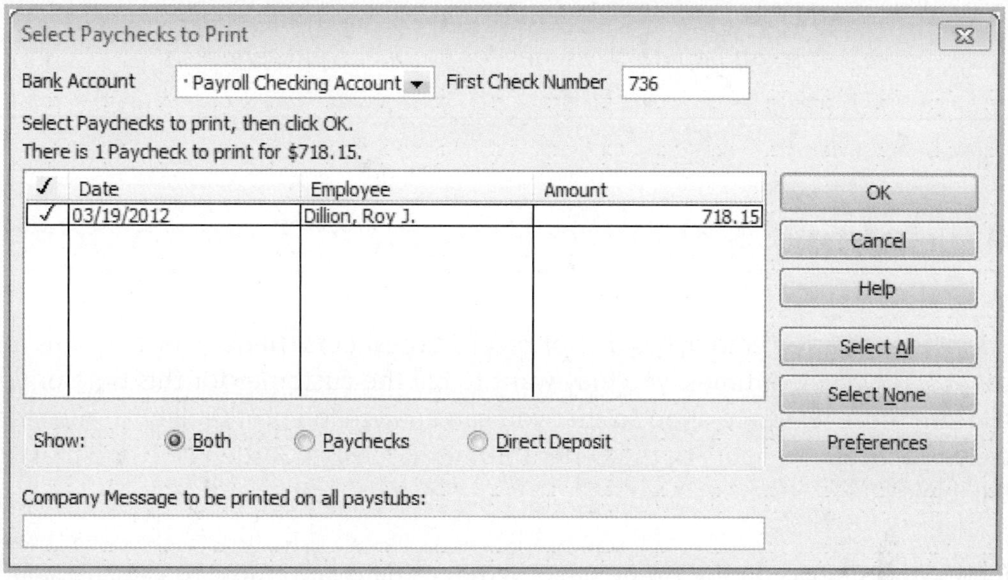

Select Paychecks to Print

Bank Account: Payroll Checking Account   First Check Number: 736

Select Paychecks to print, then click OK.
There is 1 Paycheck to print for $718.15.

✓	Date	Employee	Amount
✓	03/19/2012	Dillion, Roy J.	718.15

OK | Cancel | Help | Select All | Select None | Preferences

Show: Both   Paychecks   Direct Deposit

Company Message to be printed on all paystubs:

Figure 6:72

7. Click **OK** in the print confirmation window and then **Close** the print confirmation window.

   (Note: If you receive a message to subscribe to payroll tax tables, select No and turn off pop-up messages for products and services.)

Allocating Salaried Employee Time to Jobs

Recall that salaried employees do not record timesheets. Hence, these wages are not assigned to jobs. However, at times, you may want to bill the customer for this time or you may want to allocate these wages to a job so that you can analyze job profitability. In the steps that follow, we will allocate 16 hours to the O'Hara Homes Redesign Gardens job and mark this time as billable.

Click **Write Checks** on the Home page. When using this window to allocate salaries, you will not enter a payee or a check number. In addition, you will enter information on the **Items** tab and the **Expenses** tab.

Enter "3/19/12" as the **Date**, click **To be Printed** to turn off the option, and delete the check number appearing in the **No** field.

Now enter the information shown on Figure 6:73 onto the **Items** tab. *Note: The Design-Commercial service item has been created to allocate salary costs.* (See Figure 6:74.)

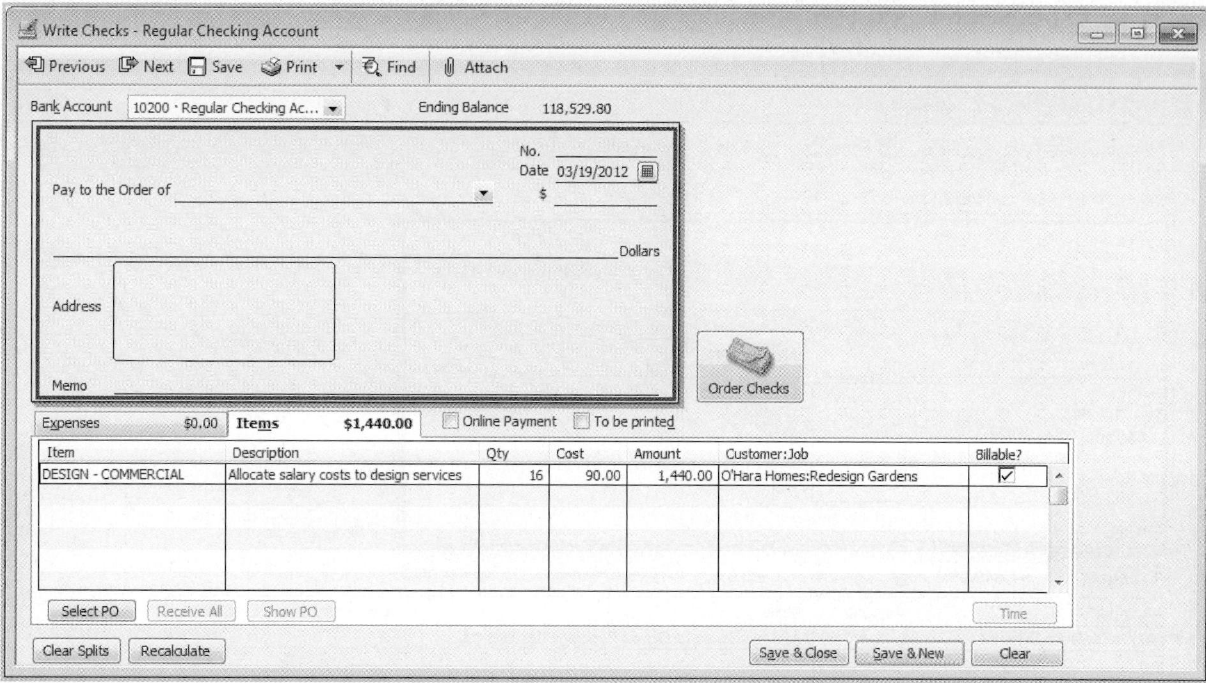

Figure 6:73

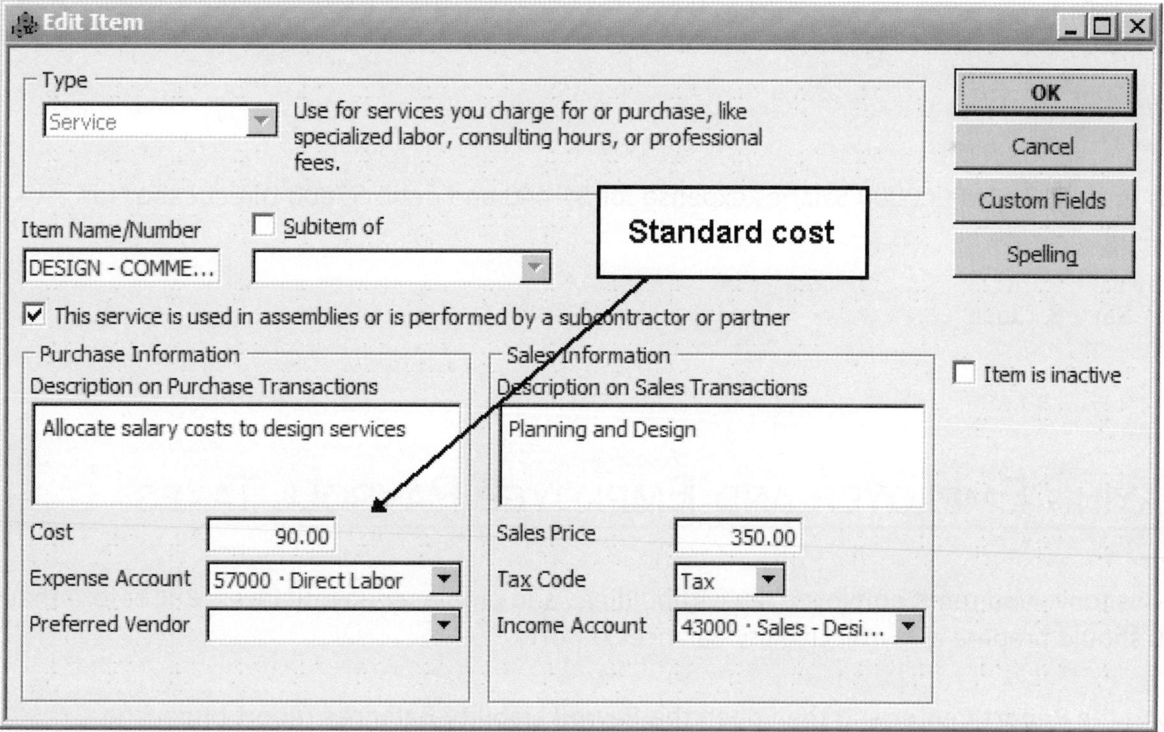

Figure 6:74

Click the **Expenses** tab and enter the information shown in Figure 6:75.

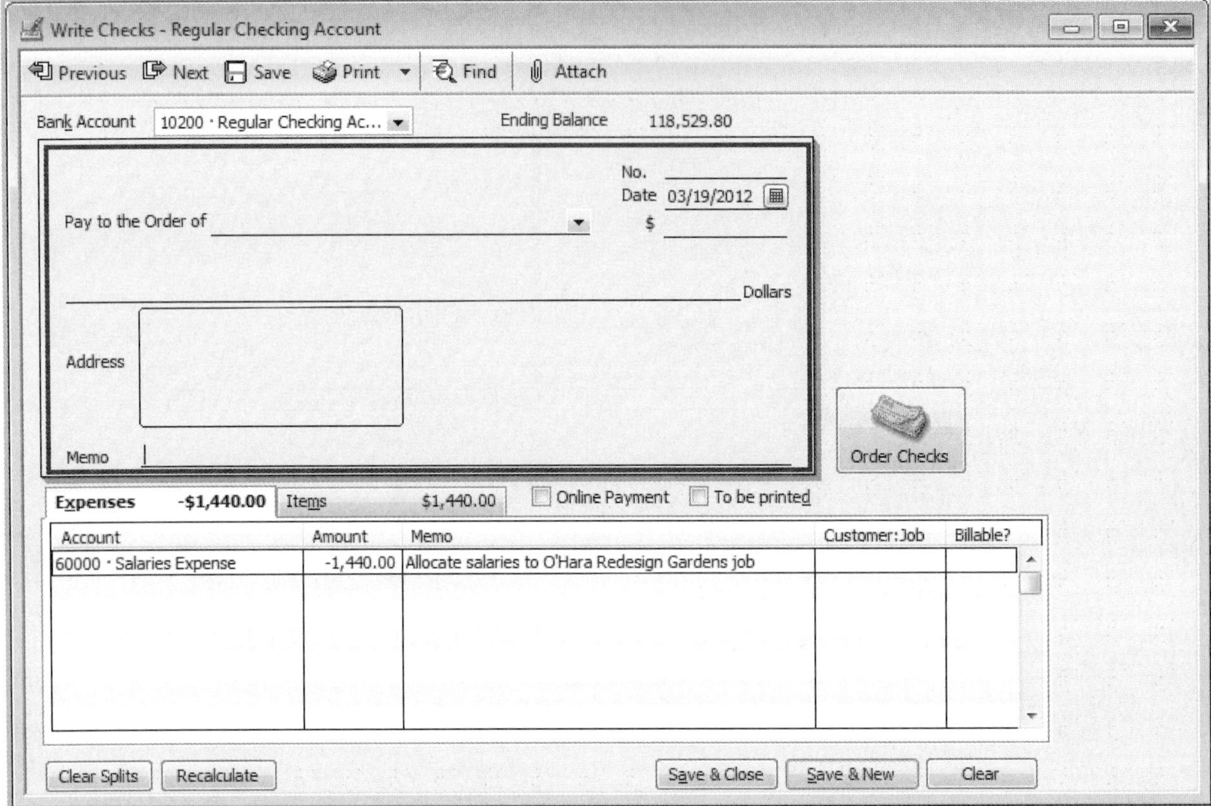

Figure 6:75

This entry will credit 60000 Salaries expense for $1,440 and debit 57000 Direct Labor for $1,440.

Click **Save & Close**.

PAYING EMPLOYER AND EMPLOYEE PAYROLL TAXES

In this topic, you remit employee tax withholdings and employer payroll taxes. But before that, you should prepare a Payroll Liability Balances report.

Open the **Report Center** and then open the **Payroll Liability Balances** report under the **Employees & Payroll** category.

Enter the date range of 1/1/12 to 3/31/12 to view the report illustrated in Figure 6:76.

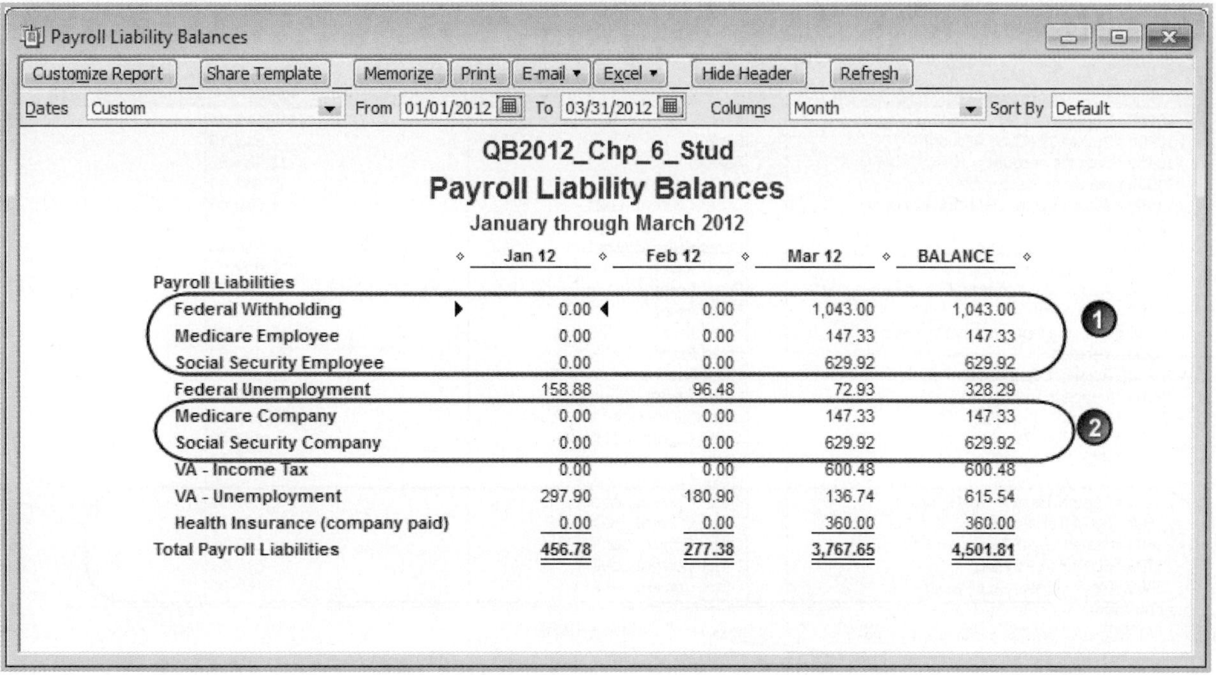

Payroll Liability Balances

Customize Report | Share Template | Memorize | Print | E-mail | Excel | Hide Header | Refresh

Dates Custom From 01/01/2012 To 03/31/2012 Columns Month Sort By Default

QB2012_Chp_6_Stud

Payroll Liability Balances

January through March 2012

	Jan 12	Feb 12	Mar 12	BALANCE
Payroll Liabilities				
Federal Withholding	0.00	0.00	1,043.00	1,043.00
Medicare Employee	0.00	0.00	147.33	147.33
Social Security Employee	0.00	0.00	629.92	629.92
Federal Unemployment	158.88	96.48	72.93	328.29
Medicare Company	0.00	0.00	147.33	147.33
Social Security Company	0.00	0.00	629.92	629.92
VA - Income Tax	0.00	0.00	600.48	600.48
VA - Unemployment	297.90	180.90	136.74	615.54
Health Insurance (company paid)	0.00	0.00	360.00	360.00
Total Payroll Liabilities	456.78	277.38	3,767.65	4,501.81

Figure 6:76

Payroll taxes are due on the dates set by taxing agencies. For Astor, federal tax, FICA, and Medicare taxes are due within three days of paying employees. State income tax for the current month is due the first of the next month. Federal and state unemployment taxes are due at the end of every quarter.

The balances marked as 1 on the report are for federal tax withholdings. The balances marked as 2 are for federal employer taxes. The total for federal payroll taxes is $2,597.50.

Now verify that report balances reconcile with balances in the general ledger accounts. Press **Ctrl + A** on the keyboard to open the chart of accounts. (See Figure 6:77.)

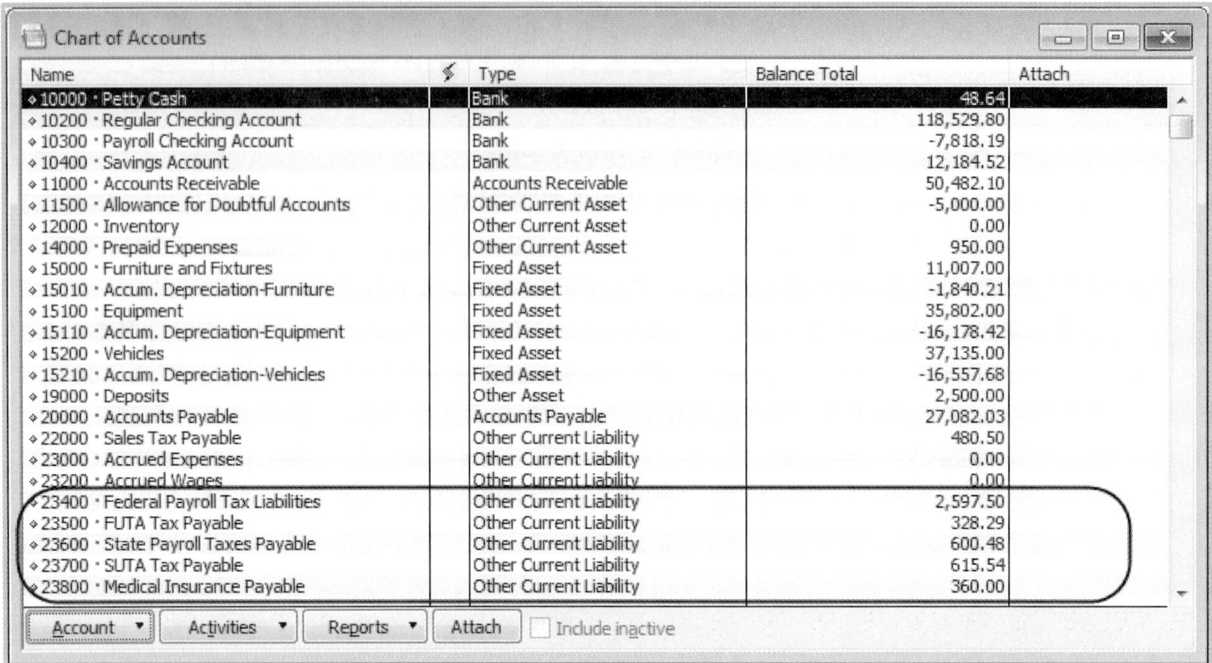

Chart of Accounts

Name	Type	Balance Total	Attach
10000 · Petty Cash	Bank	48.64	
10200 · Regular Checking Account	Bank	118,529.80	
10300 · Payroll Checking Account	Bank	-7,818.19	
10400 · Savings Account	Bank	12,184.52	
11000 · Accounts Receivable	Accounts Receivable	50,482.10	
11500 · Allowance for Doubtful Accounts	Other Current Asset	-5,000.00	
12000 · Inventory	Other Current Asset	0.00	
14000 · Prepaid Expenses	Other Current Asset	950.00	
15000 · Furniture and Fixtures	Fixed Asset	11,007.00	
15010 · Accum. Depreciation-Furniture	Fixed Asset	-1,840.21	
15100 · Equipment	Fixed Asset	35,802.00	
15110 · Accum. Depreciation-Equipment	Fixed Asset	-16,178.42	
15200 · Vehicles	Fixed Asset	37,135.00	
15210 · Accum. Depreciation-Vehicles	Fixed Asset	-16,557.68	
19000 · Deposits	Other Asset	2,500.00	
20000 · Accounts Payable	Accounts Payable	27,082.03	
22000 · Sales Tax Payable	Other Current Liability	480.50	
23000 · Accrued Expenses	Other Current Liability	0.00	
23200 · Accrued Wages	Other Current Liability	0.00	
23400 · Federal Payroll Tax Liabilities	Other Current Liability	2,597.50	
23500 · FUTA Tax Payable	Other Current Liability	328.29	
23600 · State Payroll Taxes Payable	Other Current Liability	600.48	
23700 · SUTA Tax Payable	Other Current Liability	615.54	
23800 · Medical Insurance Payable	Other Current Liability	360.00	

Figure 6:77

Scroll down to 23400 Federal Payroll Tax Liabilities to find that the account balance equals the report balance. You can also compare other payroll liability balances to the report.

Close the report, the Report Center, and the Chart of Accounts.

After reconciling balances, you are ready to pay the taxes. In the next exercise, you will create a check paying federal payroll tax and health insurance liabilities.

STEPS TO PAYING PAYROLL TAXES

1. Click **Pay Liabilities** on the **Home** page. Enter the date range of **1/01/12** to **3/31/12** to view all liabilities for the quarter and then click **OK**.

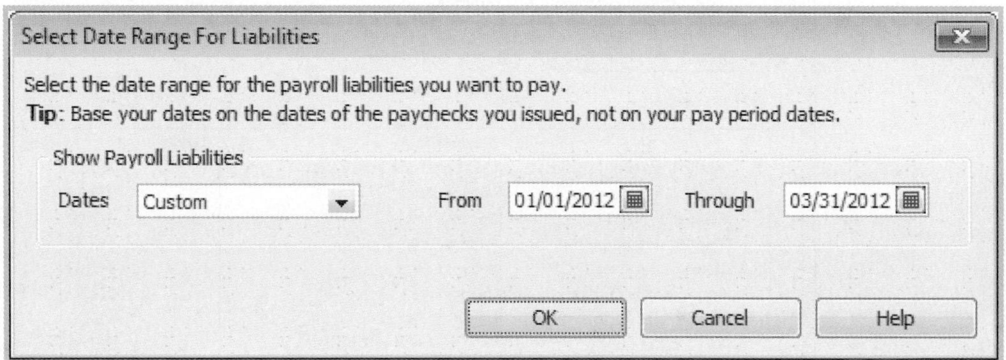

Figure 6:78

2. Enter **3/22/12** as the **Check Date**. Verify that **To be printed** is marked and that 10200 Regular Checking is the **Bank Account**.

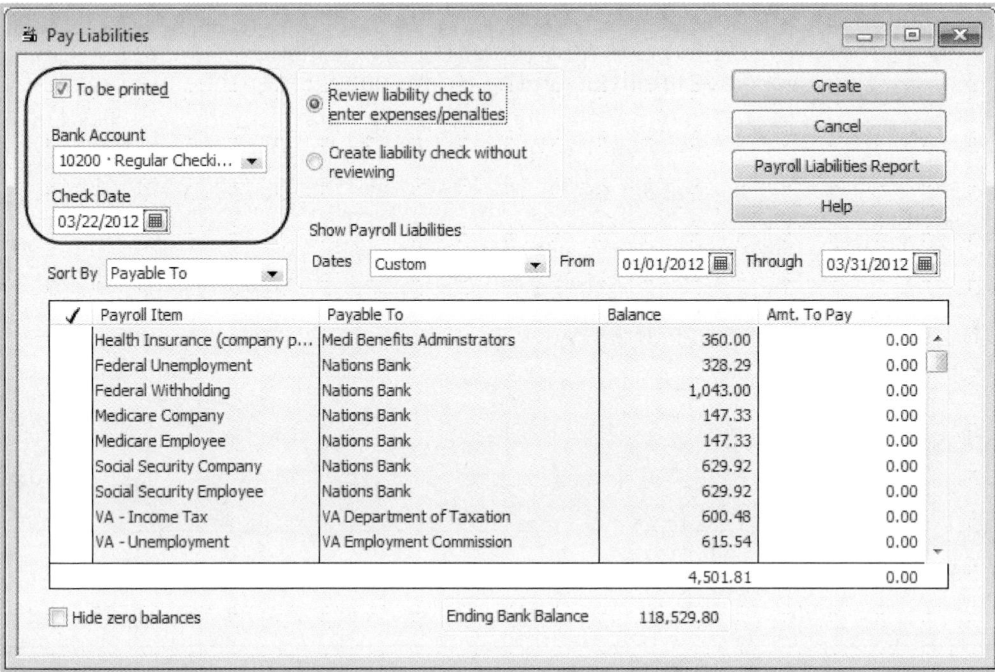

Figure 6:79

This window lists vendor accounts with balances. You now see why vendors were entered on payroll tax and company benefit items.

Also, notice that you can print payroll liability reports from this window by clicking the **Payroll Liabilities Report** button.

3. You next select the items to pay. Click the **Health Insurance (company paid)**, **Federal Withholding**, **Medicare Company**, **Medicare Employee**, **Social Security Company** and **Social Security Employee** items.

   The total payments are listed under the **Amt. To Pay** column.

   Before creating the checks, make sure that the **Review** option is selected in Figure 6:80.

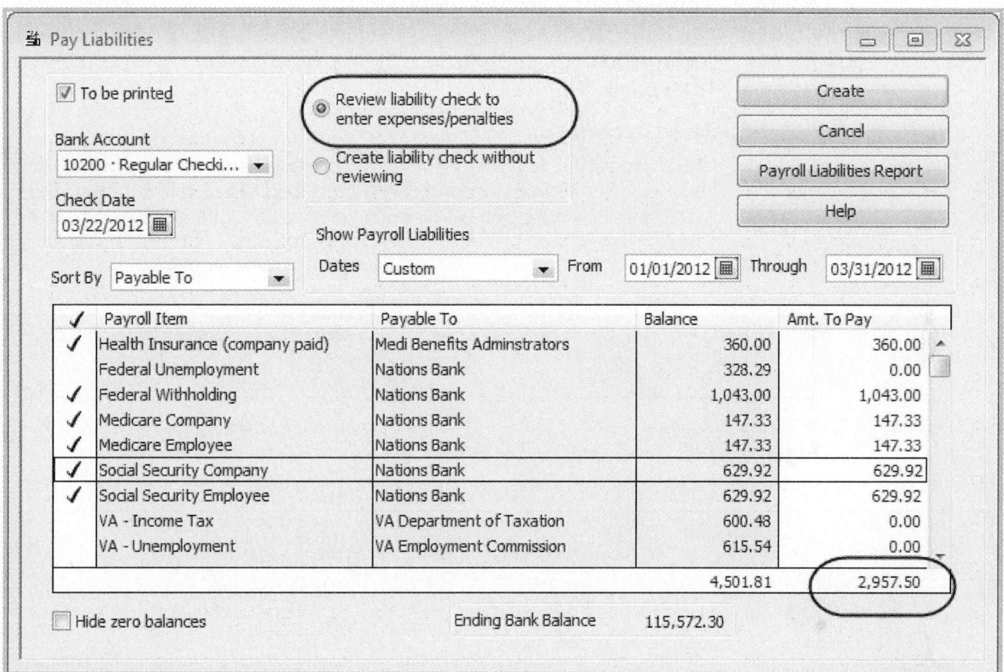

Figure 6:80

4. Click **Create**. The warning in Figure 6:81 is issued because the check is dated before the Through date on Figure 6:80. However, notice that the message states this can be appropriate, especially when prepaying a liability.

   Click **Continue**.

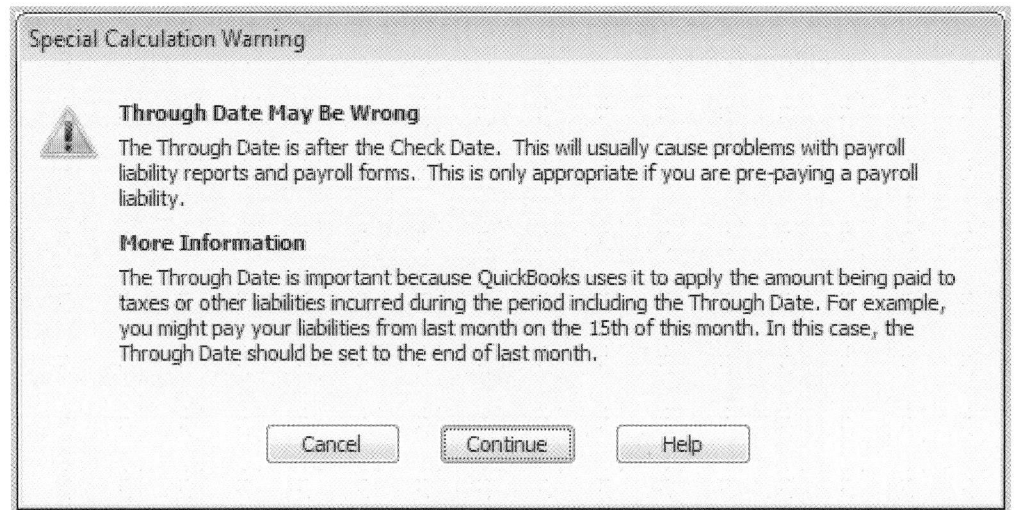

Figure 6:81

5. Because the **Review liability check to enter expenses/penalties** option was selected in Figure 6:80, the check for health insurance opens (Figure 6:82) so you can review and enter additional information if needed. For instance, if the bill contained additional fees, you could add these fees to the Expenses tab.

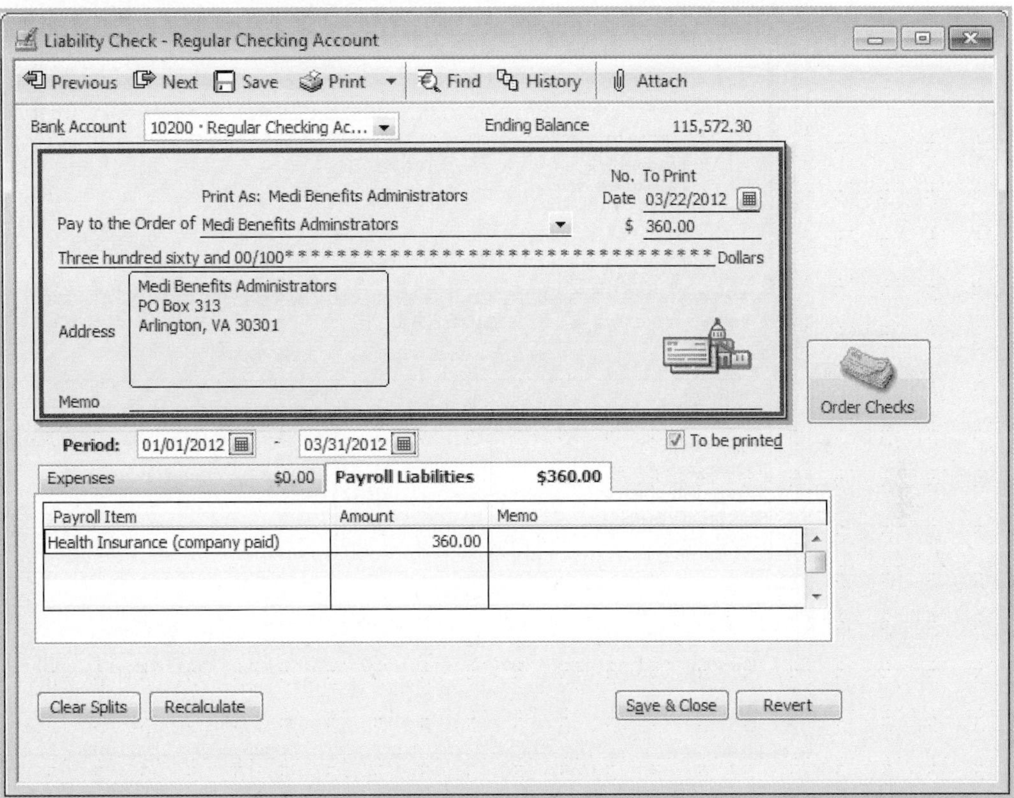

Figure 6:82

6. Click **Next** and the second check opens.

Liability Check - Regular Checking Account

Previous Next Save Print Find History Attach

Bank Account 10200 · Regular Checking Ac... Ending Balance 115,572.30

No. To Print
Date 03/22/2012
Pay to the Order of Nations Bank $ 2,597.50
Two thousand five hundred ninety-seven and 50/100*********************** Dollars

Address
Nations Bank
11000 Main Street
Arlington, VA 30022

Memo 100023365564400

Order Checks

Period: 01/01/2012 - 03/31/2012 To be printed

Expenses $0.00 Payroll Liabilities $2,597.50

Payroll Item	Amount	Memo
Federal Withholding	1,043.00	
Medicare Company	147.33	
Medicare Employee	147.33	
Social Security Company	629.92	
Social Security Employee	629.92	

Clear Splits Recalculate Save & Close Revert

Figure 6:83

7. You will now print the checks. Click the **Print** dropdown list and select **Print Batch**. Verify that both payments are marked and use "439" as the **First Check Number**.

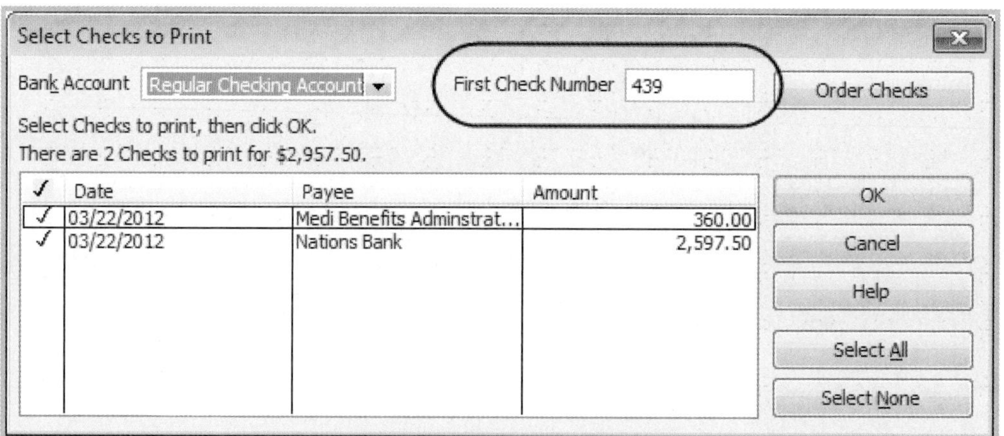

Figure 6:84

8. Click **OK**. Select a printer and click **Print**. Click **OK** in the print confirmation window. Click **Save & Close** to exit the Liability Check window.

Now complete the next exercise to finish paying tax liabilities for March and the first quarter of 2012.

CREATE CHECKS FOR PAYROLL TAXES

Reopen the Pay Liabilities window and enter the date range of 1/01/12 to 3/31/12.

Create checks dated 4/01/12 for FUTA, VA-Income Tax, and VA-Unemployment taxes.

Print the checks using the first check number of 441. The checks will total $1,554.31.

Print the Check Detail report for April 1, 2012.

QUARTERLY AND YEAR-END PAYROLL REPORTING

At the end of each quarter, Astor prepares payroll tax reports for each taxing agency. These reports list employee wages and reconcile employee tax withholdings and employer tax liabilities with taxes paid during the quarter.

For federal taxes, the quarterly report is called Form 941. We will now show you how to prepare this report based on information from QBP.

Open the **Report Center** and select the **Employees and Payroll** category. Run the **Employee Earnings Summary** for 1/01/12 to 3/31/12. (See Figure 6:85.) Print and close the report.

QB2012_Chp_6_Stud

Employee Earnings Summary

January through March 2012

	Salary	Hourly Office	Hourly Office Overtime...	Hourly wage	Hourly wage overtime...	Federal Withholding
Dillion, Roy J.	0.00	0.00	0.00	5,700.00	0.00	-561.00
Folse, Jan B.	0.00	4,800.00	0.00	0.00	0.00	-426.00
Greene, Kellie I.	14,076.90	0.00	0.00	0.00	0.00	-1,536.00
Hardman, Alan	0.00	0.00	0.00	5,712.00	0.00	-438.00
Henderson, Jeff P.	0.00	0.00	0.00	5,664.00	0.00	-308.00
Ramez, Victor M.	0.00	0.00	0.00	4,730.00	0.00	-540.00
Ruland, Seth N.	18,623.10	0.00	0.00	0.00	0.00	-2,574.00
Zickefoose, Jack A	0.00	0.00	0.00	400.00	30.00	0.00
TOTAL	32,700.00	4,800.00	0.00	22,206.00	30.00	-6,383.00
	1	1		1	1	2

	Medicare Employee	Social Security Employee	Federal Unemployment	Medicare Company	Social Security Company
Dillion, Roy J.	-82.65	-353.40	45.60	82.65	353.40
Folse, Jan B.	-69.60	-297.60	38.40	69.60	297.60
Greene, Kellie I.	-204.12	-872.76	56.00	204.12	872.76
Hardman, Alan	-82.82	-354.14	45.70	72.82	354.14
Henderson, Jeff P.	-82.13	-351.17	45.31	82.13	351.17
Ramez, Victor M.	-68.59	-293.26	37.84	68.59	293.26
Ruland, Seth N.	-270.06	-1,154.64	56.00	270.06	1,154.64
Zickefoose, Jack A	-6.24	-26.66	3.44	6.24	26.66
TOTAL	-866.21	-3,703.63	328.29	856.21	3,703.63
	4	3		4	3

	VA - Income Tax	VA - Unemployment	Health Insurance (com..	TOTAL
Dillion, Roy J.	-171.00	85.50	0.00	5,099.10
Folse, Jan B.	-144.00	72.00	360.00	4,700.40
Greene, Kellie I.	-422.28	105.00	360.00	12,639.62
Hardman, Alan	-171.36	85.68	0.00	5,224.02
Henderson, Jeff P.	-169.92	84.96	0.00	5,316.35
Ramez, Victor M.	-141.90	70.95	0.00	4,156.89
Ruland, Seth N.	-558.72	105.00	360.00	16,011.38
Zickefoose, Jack A	-12.90	6.45	0.00	426.99
TOTAL	-1,792.08	615.54	1,080.00	53,574.75

Figure 6:85

Next, run the **Payroll Transactions by Payee** for 01/01/12 to 3/31/12, listing the total federal tax payments for the first quarter. (See Figure 6:86.) Print and close the report.

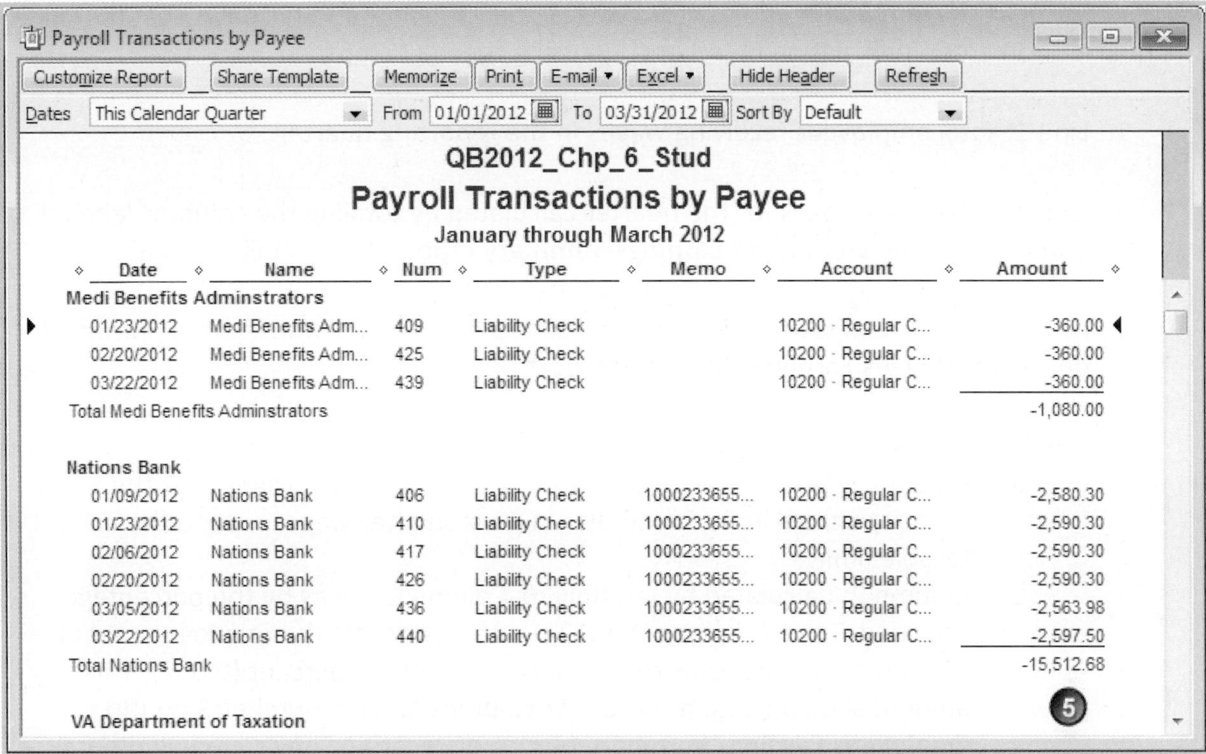

Payroll Transactions by Payee

Customize Report | Share Template | Memorize | Print | E-mail ▾ | Excel ▾ | Hide Header | Refresh

Dates: This Calendar Quarter | From 01/01/2012 | To 03/31/2012 | Sort By Default

QB2012_Chp_6_Stud

Payroll Transactions by Payee

January through March 2012

Date	Name	Num	Type	Memo	Account	Amount
Medi Benefits Adminstrators						
01/23/2012	Medi Benefits Adm...	409	Liability Check		10200 · Regular C...	-360.00
02/20/2012	Medi Benefits Adm...	425	Liability Check		10200 · Regular C...	-360.00
03/22/2012	Medi Benefits Adm...	439	Liability Check		10200 · Regular C...	-360.00
Total Medi Benefits Adminstrators						-1,080.00
Nations Bank						
01/09/2012	Nations Bank	406	Liability Check	1000233655...	10200 · Regular C...	-2,580.30
01/23/2012	Nations Bank	410	Liability Check	1000233655...	10200 · Regular C...	-2,590.30
02/06/2012	Nations Bank	417	Liability Check	1000233655...	10200 · Regular C...	-2,590.30
02/20/2012	Nations Bank	426	Liability Check	1000233655...	10200 · Regular C...	-2,590.30
03/05/2012	Nations Bank	436	Liability Check	1000233655...	10200 · Regular C...	-2,563.98
03/22/2012	Nations Bank	440	Liability Check	1000233655...	10200 · Regular C...	-2,597.50
Total Nations Bank						-15,512.68
VA Department of Taxation						

Figure 6:86

You will next place numbers from these reports onto Form 941. For purposes of this example, we downloaded a Form 941 from the Internal Revenue Service Website (www.irs.gov).

The top of Form 941 (Figure 6:87) contains basic company information such as EIN, Business name, Business address, and the reporting quarter.

Form **941 for** : **Employer's QUARTERLY Federal Tax Return** 950108

(Rev. January) Department of the Treasury — Internal Revenue Service OMB No. 1545-0029

(EIN) Employer identification number: 3 4 – 0 9 8 7 2 3 3

Name *(not your trade name)*: Astor Landscaping

Trade name *(if any)*:

Address: 1505 Pavilion Place (Number, Street, Suite or room number)

Arlington (City) VA (State) 30093 (ZIP code)

Read the separate instructions before you fill out this form. Please type or print within the boxes.

Report for this Quarter of (Check one.)

- [x] 1: January, February, March
- [ ] 2: April, May, June
- [ ] 3: July, August, September
- [ ] 4: October, November, December

Figure 6:87

Part I of Form 941 (Figure 6:88) reports gross wages, tax liabilities, and tax payments during the quarter. You enter information in this section using the next steps:

1. Line 1: Total employees receiving wages in the reporting quarter.

2. Line 2: Total gross wages for the quarter calculated by totaling the columns labeled number 1 on the **Employees Earnings Summary** report shown in Figure 6:85.

3. Line 3: Total federal tax withholdings calculated from the column labeled number 2 on the **Employees Earnings Summary** report.

4. Line 5a:
    a. Column 1: Gross wages from Form 941 Line 2 minus wages over the Social Security annual limit. Recall that taxes stop after wages exceed the annual taxable limit.
    b. Column 2: Calculated by multiplying Column 1 wages by the percentage provided. The 12.4 percent (0.124) rate represents the employee rate of 6.2 percent (0.062) plus the employer rate of 6.2 percent (0.062). This amount should equal the total for columns labeled number 3 on the **Employees Earnings Summary** report, disregarding any rounding differences in the cents.

5. Line 5c:
    a. Column 1: Gross wages from Form 941 Line 2.
    b. Column 2: Calculated by multiplying Column 1 wages by the percentage provided. The 2.9 percent (0.029) rate represents the employee rate of 1.45 percent (0.0145) plus the employer rate of 1.45 percent (0.0145). This amount should equal the total for columns labeled number 4 on the **Employees Earnings Summary** report, disregarding any rounding differences in the cents. *(Note: The report is $10.00 lower than the amount calculated on Form 941 and we will illustrate correcting this error later in the chapter.)*

6. Line 5d: The total of Lines 5a plus 5c, column 2. This is the total FICA and Medicare taxes due this quarter.

7. Line 7a: The rounding difference that occurs because Form 941 calculates FICA and Medicare as a percentage of total wages whereas the taxes were actually calculated on individual paychecks.

8. Line 11: Total payroll tax payments labeled number 5 on the **Payroll Transactions by Payee** report (Figure 6:86).

Part 1: Answer these questions for this quarter.

1 Number of employees who received wages, tips, or other compensation for the pay period including: *Mar. 12* (Quarter 1), *June 12* (Quarter 2), *Sept. 12* (Quarter 3), *Dec. 12* (Quarter 4)	1		8
2 Wages, tips, and other compensation	2	❶	59,736.00
3 Total income tax withheld from wages, tips, and other compensation	3	❷	6,383.00
4 If no wages, tips, and other compensation are subject to social security or Medicare tax		☐ Check and go to line 6.	

5 Taxable social security and Medicare wages and tips:

	Column 1		Column 2
5a Taxable social security wages	❶ 59,736.00	× .124 =	❸ 7,407.26
5b Taxable social security tips	.	× .124 =	.
5c Taxable Medicare wages & tips	❶ 59,736.00	× .029 =	❹ 1,732.34

5d Total social security and Medicare taxes (*Column 2,* lines 5a + 5b + 5c = line 5d)	5d		9,139.60
6 Total taxes before adjustments (lines 3 + 5d = line 6)	6		15,522.60

7 **TAX ADJUSTMENTS** (read the instructions for line 7 before completing lines 7a through 7g):

7a Current quarter's fractions of cents	0.08
7b Current quarter's sick pay	.
7c Current quarter's adjustments for tips and group-term life insurance	.
7d Current year's income tax withholding (attach Form 941c)	.
7e Prior quarters' social security and Medicare taxes (attach Form 941c)	.
7f Special additions to federal income tax (attach Form 941c)	.
7g Special additions to social security and Medicare (attach Form 941c)	.

7h **TOTAL ADJUSTMENTS** (combine all amounts: lines 7a through 7g)	7h		0.08
8 Total taxes after adjustments (combine lines 6 and 7h)	8		15,522.68
9 Advance earned income credit (EIC) payments made to employees	9		.
10 Total taxes after adjustment for advance EIC (line 8 – line 9 = line 10)	10		15,522.68
11 Total deposits for this quarter, including overpayment applied from a prior quarter	11	❺	15,512.68
12 Balance due (If line 10 is more than line 11, write the difference here.) For information on how to pay, see the instructions.	12		10.00
13 Overpayment (If line 11 is more than line 10, write the difference here.) .		Check one	☐ Apply to next return. ☐ Send a refund.

▶ You **MUST** fill out both pages of this form and **SIGN** it. **Next ➔**

For Privacy Act and Paperwork Reduction Act Notice, see the back of the Payment Voucher. Cat. No. 17001Z Form **941** (Rev. 1-)

Figure 6:88

After completing Part 1, you complete Parts 2 through 5 using the next instructions. (See Figure 6:89.)

1. Part 2:
   a. Line 14: The code for the state where the company makes tax deposits.
   b. Line 15: Check the box that the company was a semiweekly depositor for the quarter. This also means that Schedule B must be completed and attached to Form 941. (See Figure 6:90.)

2. Part 5: Sign and date.

Name (not your trade name) Astor Landscaping | Employer identification number (EIN) 34-0987233

Part 2: Tell us about your deposit schedule and tax liability for this quarter.

If you are unsure about whether you are a monthly schedule depositor or a semiweekly schedule depositor, see *Pub. 15 (Circular E)*, section 11.

14 [V][A] Write the state abbreviation for the state where you made your deposits OR write "MU" if you made your deposits in *multiple* states.

15 Check one: ☐ Line 10 is less than $2,500. Go to Part 3.

☐ You were a monthly schedule depositor for the entire quarter. Fill out your tax liability for each month. Then go to Part 3.

Tax liability: Month 1 [.]

Month 2 [.]

Month 3 [.]

Total liability for quarter [.] Total must equal line 10.

☑ You were a semiweekly schedule depositor for any part of this quarter. Fill out *Schedule B (Form 941): Report of Tax Liability for Semiweekly Schedule Depositors,* and attach it to this form.

Part 3: Tell us about your business. If a question does NOT apply to your business, leave it blank.

16 If your business has closed or you stopped paying wages . . . . ☐ Check here, and

enter the final date you paid wages [/ /].

17 If you are a seasonal employer and you do not have to file a return for every quarter of the year . . ☐ Check here.

Part 4: May we speak with your third-party designee?

Do you want to allow an employee, a paid tax preparer, or another person to discuss this return with the IRS? (See the instructions for details.)

☐ Yes. Designee's name [ ]

Select a 5-digit Personal Identification Number (PIN) to use when talking to IRS. ☐☐☐☐☐

☐ No.

Part 5: Sign here. You MUST fill out both pages of this form and SIGN it.

Under penalties of perjury, I declare that I have examined this return, including accompanying schedules and statements, and to the best of my knowledge and belief, it is true, correct, and complete.

✗ Sign your name here [ ] Print your name here [ ] Print your title here [ ]

Date [/ /] Best daytime phone [( ) -]

Figure 6:89

Finally, Schedule B (Figure 6:90) is completed when a company makes semiweekly deposits. The information for this form is gathered from the **Payroll Transactions by Payee** report (Figure 6:86). The IRS will use this information to verify that employers pay all taxes by the due date. Astor is required to pay tax liabilities within 3 days of paying employees. You should know that failure to pay taxes by the due date will result in IRS-imposed penalties and interest.

Schedule B (Form 941):

990306

Report of Tax Liability for Semiweekly Schedule Depositors

(Rev. January) Department of the Treasury — Internal Revenue Service OMB No. 1545-0029

(EIN) Employer identification number: 3 4 – 0 9 8 7 2 3 3

Name *(not your trade name)*: Astor Landscaping

Calendar year: 2 0 1 2 (Also check quarter)

Report for this Quarter ... **(Check one.)**

- ✓ 1: January, February, March
- ☐ 2: April, May, June
- ☐ 3: July, August, September
- ☐ 4: October, November, December

Use this schedule to show your TAX LIABILITY for the quarter; DO NOT use it to show your deposits. You must fill out this form and attach it to Form 941 (or Form 941-SS) if you are a semiweekly schedule depositor or became one because your accumulated tax liability on any day was $100,000 or more. Write your daily tax liability on the numbered space that corresponds to the date wages were paid. See Section 11 in *Pub. 15 (Circular E), Employer's Tax Guide,* for details.

Month 1

Day	Amount	Day	Amount	Day	Amount	Day	Amount
1	.	9	2,590.30	17	.	25	.
2	.	10	.	18	.	26	.
3	.	11	.	19	.	27	.
4	.	12	.	20	.	28	.
5	.	13	.	21	.	29	.
6	.	14	.	22	.	30	.
7	.	15	.	23	2,590.30	31	.
8	.	16	.	24	.		

Tax liability for Month 1: 5,180.60

Month 2

Day	Amount	Day	Amount	Day	Amount	Day	Amount
1	.	9	.	17	.	25	.
2	.	10	.	18	.	26	.
3	.	11	.	19	.	27	.
4	.	12	.	20	2,590.30	28	.
5	.	13	.	21	.	29	.
6	2,590.30	14	.	22	.	30	.
7	.	15	.	23	.	31	.
8	.	16	.	24	.		

Tax liability for Month 2: 5,180.60

Month 3

Day	Amount	Day	Amount	Day	Amount	Day	Amount
1	.	9	.	17	.	25	.
2	.	10	.	18	.	26	.
3	.	11	.	19	2,597.50	27	.
4	.	12	.	20	.	28	.
5	2,563.98	13	.	21	.	29	.
6	.	14	.	22	.	30	.
7	.	15	.	23	.	31	.
8	.	16	.	24	.		

Tax liability for Month 3: 5,161.48

Fill in your total liability for the quarter (Month 1 + Month 2 + Month 3) = Total tax liability for the quarter ▶
Total must equal line 10 on Form 941 (or line 8 on Form 941-SS).

Total liability for the quarter: 15,522.68

For Paperwork Reduction Act Notice, see separate instructions. Cat. No. 11967Q **Schedule B (Form 941)** Rev. 1-

Figure 6:90

Now that we have illustrated preparing Form 941, you will fix the $10.00 error on Medicare taxes. *(Note: Rounding differences are not fixed in the software.)* The error occurred when recording Alan Hardman's paycheck number 696 on January 9, 2012. Employer Medicare was reported as $3.92 and should have been $13.92.

This error is located by returning to the **Employees Earnings Summary** report and double clicking Alan Hardman's hourly wage amount to open the **Transactions by Payroll Item** report. Modify the **Payroll Item** filter to show only **Medicare Company** and **Medicare Employee**. (See Figure 6:91.)

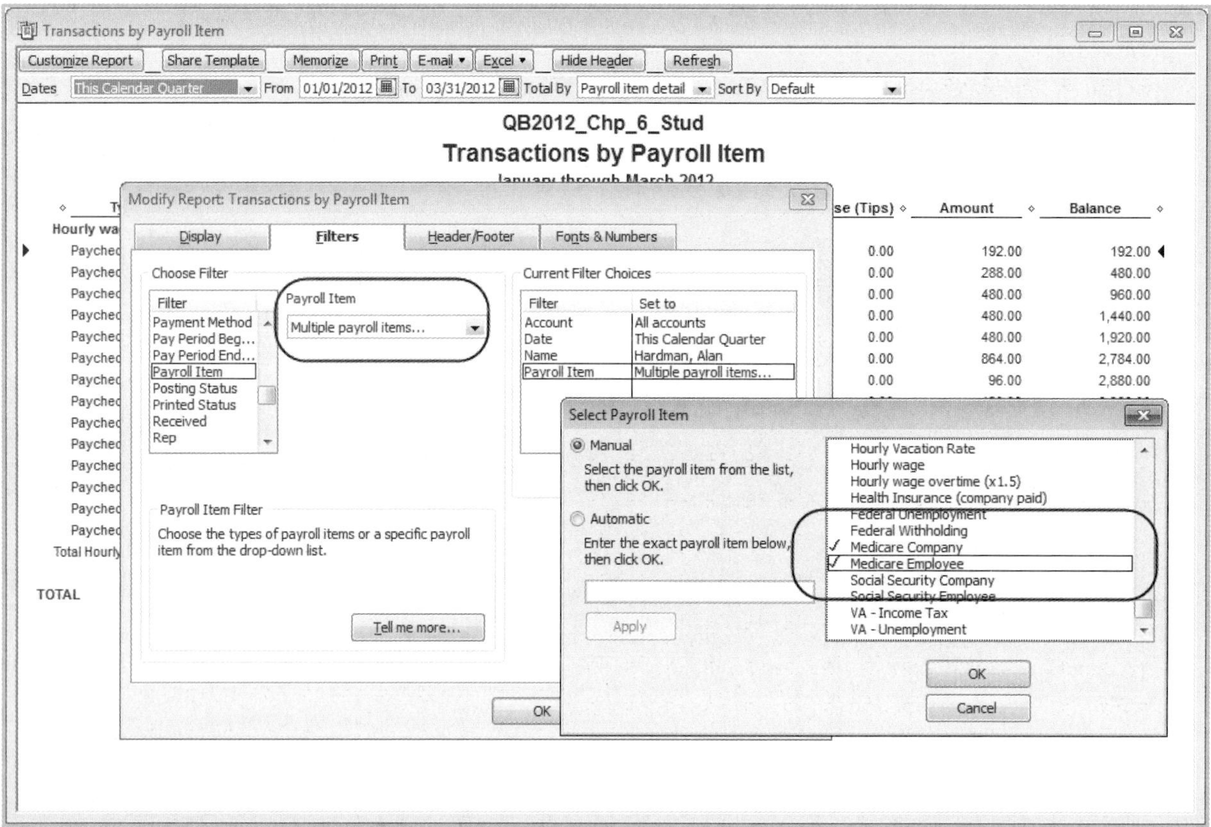

Figure 6:91

Click **OK** after setting the filter and the report refreshes as shown in Figure 6:92.

Transactions by Payroll Item

Customize Report | Share Template | Memorize | Print | E-mail ▾ | Excel ▾ | Hide Header | Refresh

Dates: This Calendar Quarter | From 01/01/2012 | To 03/31/2012 | Total By: Payroll item detail | Sort By: Default

QB2012_Chp_6_Stud

Transactions by Payroll Item

January through March 2012

Type	Date	Num	Name	Income Subject To Tax	Wage Base	Wage Base (Tips)	Amount	Balance
Medicare Employee								
Paycheck	01/09/2012	696	Hardman, Alan	960.00	960.00	0.00	-13.92	-13.92
Paycheck	01/23/2012	703	Hardman, Alan	960.00	960.00	0.00	-13.92	-27.84
Paycheck	02/06/2012	710	Hardman, Alan	960.00	960.00	0.00	-13.92	-41.76
Paycheck	02/20/2012	717	Hardman, Alan	960.00	960.00	0.00	-13.92	-55.68
Paycheck	03/05/2012	724	Hardman, Alan	936.00	936.00	0.00	-13.57	-69.25
Paycheck	03/19/2012	731	Hardman, Alan	936.00	936.00	0.00	-13.57	-82.82
Total Medicare Employee				5,712.00	5,712.00	0.00	-82.82	-82.82
Medicare Company								
Paycheck	01/09/2012	696	Hardman, Alan	192.00	192.00	0.00	0.78	0.78
Paycheck	01/09/2012	696	Hardman, Alan	288.00	288.00	0.00	1.18	1.96
Paycheck	01/09/2012	696	Hardman, Alan	480.00	480.00	0.00	1.96	3.92
Paycheck	01/23/2012	703	Hardman, Alan	480.00	480.00	0.00	6.96	10.88
Paycheck	01/23/2012	703	Hardman, Alan	480.00	480.00	0.00	6.96	17.84
Paycheck	02/06/2012	710	Hardman, Alan	864.00	864.00	0.00	12.53	30.37
Paycheck	02/06/2012	710	Hardman, Alan	96.00	96.00	0.00	1.39	31.76
Paycheck	02/20/2012	717	Hardman, Alan	480.00	480.00	0.00	6.96	38.72
Paycheck	02/20/2012	717	Hardman, Alan	480.00	480.00	0.00	6.96	45.68
Paycheck	03/05/2012	724	Hardman, Alan	456.00	456.00	0.00	6.61	52.29
Paycheck	03/05/2012	724	Hardman, Alan	216.00	216.00	0.00	3.13	55.42
Paycheck	03/05/2012	724	Hardman, Alan	264.00	264.00	0.00	3.83	59.25
Paycheck	03/19/2012	731	Hardman, Alan	864.00	864.00	0.00	12.53	71.78
Paycheck	03/19/2012	731	Hardman, Alan	72.00	72.00	0.00	1.04	72.82
Total Medicare Company				5,712.00	5,712.00	0.00	72.82	72.82
TOTAL				11,424.00	11,424.00	0.00	-10.00	-10.00

Figure 6:92

You must now check the Medicare calculation to determine whether the employee or the employer tax is incorrect. Multiplying $960.00 by the tax rate of 0.0145 shows that $13.92 is the correct amount. *(Note: You also find the $10.00 difference at the bottom of the report.)*

You will now record an adjustment. Select ***Employees>>Payroll Taxes and Liabilities>>Adjust Payroll Liabilities*** on the main menu.

We want the adjustment to post in March so enter the **Date** of 3/31/12. Enter 1/9/12 in the **Effective Date** because this is the date the error occurred.

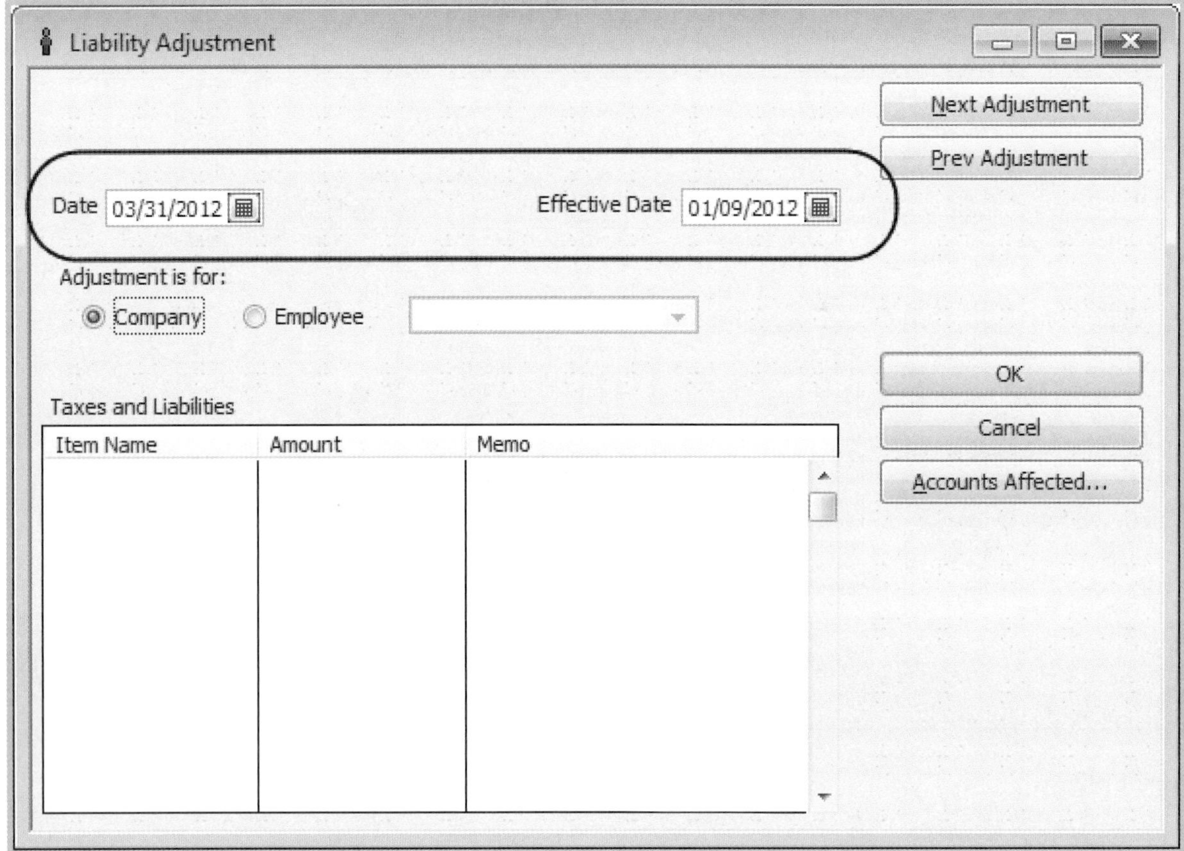

Figure 6:93

Although the error occurred on the company's Medicare liability, you still want to adjust the paycheck so select **Employee** and look up **Hardman, Alan**.

Place your cursor in **Item Name** and select **Medicare Company**. Tab to **Amount** and enter "10.00" in the space provided.

Click the **Accounts Affected** button and verify that **Affect liability and expense accounts** is selected so that the adjustment increases the Medicare liability and posts a credit to the liability account on the general ledger. Click **OK** to exit the window.

Figure 6:94 shows the completed adjustment. Click **OK** to post it.

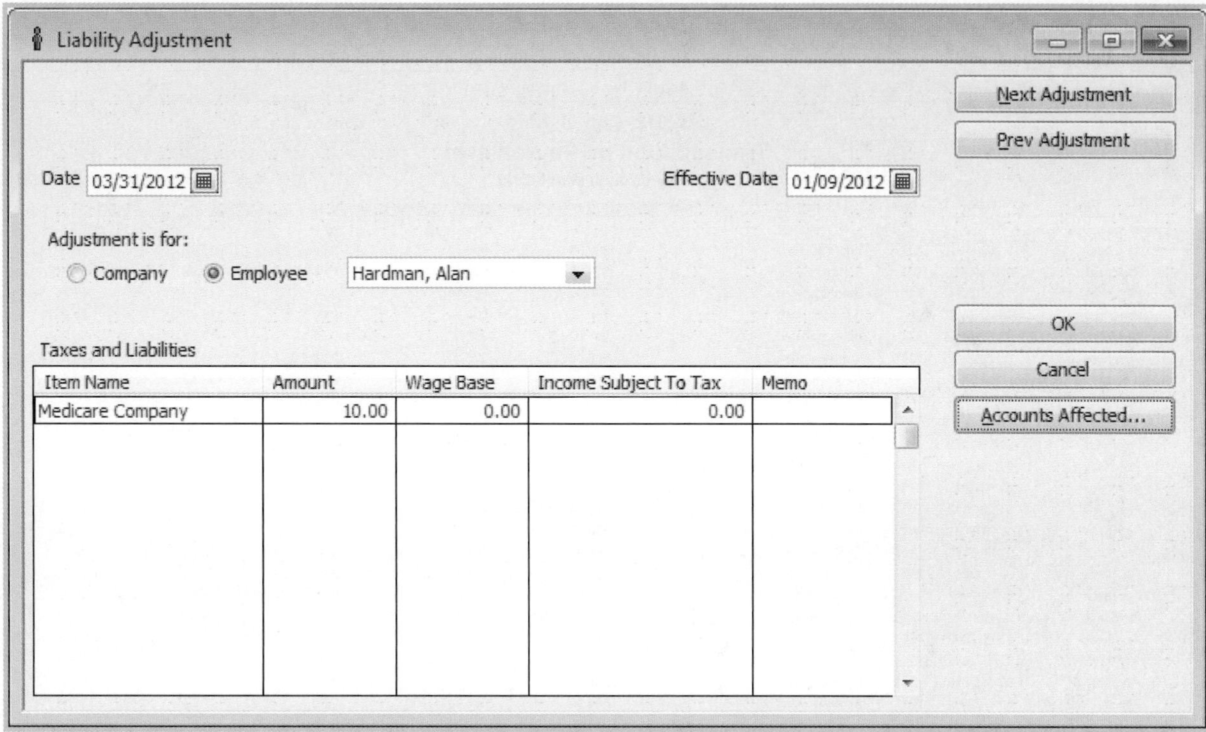

Figure 6:94

Return to the **Transactions by Payroll Item** report and notice the entry posted to the general ledger as of 3/31/12 (Figure 6:95). If you had entered 1/9/12 in the Date field, the change would have been made as of the paycheck date; however, this would also cause the entry to backdate to a closed period. Remember that you do not want to post entries to a closed accounting period because it changes reported financial results. The Effective Date will adjust the liability amount on Form 941 as of January.

Finally, you could have selected the Company option instead of Employee to make the adjustment. However, you would not be able to see that the adjustment was related to Alan's paycheck.

Transactions by Payroll Item

Customize Report | Share Template | Memorize | Print | E-mail ▾ | Excel ▾ | Hide Header | Refresh

Dates: This Calendar Quarter | From 01/01/2012 | To 03/31/2012 | Total By: Payroll item detail | Sort By: Default

QB2012_Chp_6_Stud

Transactions by Payroll Item

January through March 2012

Type	Date	Num	Name	Income Subject To Tax	Wage Base	Wage Base (Tips)	Amount	Balance
Medicare Employee								
Paycheck	01/09/2012	696	Hardman, Alan	960.00	960.00	0.00	-13.92	-13.92
Paycheck	01/23/2012	703	Hardman, Alan	960.00	960.00	0.00	-13.92	-27.84
Paycheck	02/06/2012	710	Hardman, Alan	960.00	960.00	0.00	-13.92	-41.76
Paycheck	02/20/2012	717	Hardman, Alan	960.00	960.00	0.00	-13.92	-55.68
Paycheck	03/05/2012	724	Hardman, Alan	936.00	936.00	0.00	-13.57	-69.25
Paycheck	03/19/2012	731	Hardman, Alan	936.00	936.00	0.00	-13.57	-82.82
Total Medicare Employee				5,712.00	5,712.00	0.00	-82.82	-82.82
Medicare Company								
Paycheck	01/09/2012	696	Hardman, Alan	192.00	192.00	0.00	0.78	0.78
Paycheck	01/09/2012	696	Hardman, Alan	288.00	288.00	0.00	1.18	1.96
Paycheck	01/09/2012	696	Hardman, Alan	480.00	480.00	0.00	1.96	3.92
Paycheck	01/23/2012	703	Hardman, Alan	480.00	480.00	0.00	6.96	10.88
Paycheck	01/23/2012	703	Hardman, Alan	480.00	480.00	0.00	6.96	17.84
Paycheck	02/06/2012	710	Hardman, Alan	864.00	864.00	0.00	12.53	30.37
Paycheck	02/06/2012	710	Hardman, Alan	96.00	96.00	0.00	1.39	31.76
Paycheck	02/20/2012	717	Hardman, Alan	480.00	480.00	0.00	6.96	38.72
Paycheck	02/20/2012	717	Hardman, Alan	480.00	480.00	0.00	6.96	45.68
Paycheck	03/05/2012	724	Hardman, Alan	456.00	456.00	0.00	6.61	52.29
Paycheck	03/05/2012	724	Hardman, Alan	216.00	216.00	0.00	3.13	55.42
Paycheck	03/05/2012	724	Hardman, Alan	264.00	264.00	0.00	3.83	59.25
Paycheck	03/19/2012	731	Hardman, Alan	864.00	864.00	0.00	12.53	71.78
Paycheck	03/19/2012	731	Hardman, Alan	72.00	72.00	0.00	1.04	72.82
Liability Adjust	03/31/2012		Hardman, Alan	0.00	0.00	0.00	10.00	82.82
Total Medicare Company				5,712.00	5,712.00	0.00	82.82	82.82
TOTAL				11,424.00	11,424.00	0.00	0.00	0.00

Figure 6:95

Close all open reports and the Report Center.

We just illustrated preparing one quarterly report. There are also quarterly reporting requirements for state tax withholdings and state unemployment tax that were not illustrated.

Besides quarterly reports, Astor files annual reports in January. Form 940, reporting FUTA taxes, must be prepared and submitted to the IRS. In addition, W-2s must be printed and distributed to employees by January 31.

Figure 6:96 shows an uncompleted Form W-2. These forms are mailed to the Social Security Administration along with a Form W-3 (Figure 6:97), which serves to reconcile total wages and taxes on the W-2 forms.

When you subscribe to QBP's payroll tax service, you can then prepare quarterly and annual tax reports in the software.

22222	Void ☐	a Employee's social security number	For Official Use Only ► OMB No. 1545-0008	
b Employer identification number (EIN)			1 Wages, tips, other compensation	2 Federal income tax withheld
c Employer's name, address, and ZIP code			3 Social security wages	4 Social security tax withheld
			5 Medicare wages and tips	6 Medicare tax withheld
			7 Social security tips	8 Allocated tips
d Control number			9 Advance EIC payment	10 Dependent care benefits
e Employee's first name and initial	Last name	Suff.	11 Nonqualified plans	12a See instructions for box 12
			13 Statutory employee ☐ Retirement plan ☐ Third-party sick pay ☐	12b
			14 Other	12c
				12d
f Employee's address and ZIP code				

15 State	Employer's state ID number	16 State wages, tips, etc.	17 State income tax	18 Local wages, tips, etc.	19 Local income tax	20 Locality name

Form **W-2** Wage and Tax Statement

Department of the Treasury—Internal Revenue Service

For Privacy Act and Paperwork Reduction Act Notice, see back of Copy D.

Copy A For Social Security Administration — Send this entire page with Form W-3 to the Social Security Administration; photocopies are **not** acceptable.

Cat. No. 10134D

Do Not Cut, Fold, or Staple Forms on This Page — Do Not Cut, Fold, or Staple Forms on This Page

Figure 6:96

DO NOT STAPLE

33333 a Control number For Official Use Only ▶ OMB No. 1545-0008

b Kind of Payer ▶ 941 Military 943 944 CT-1 Hshld. emp. Medicare govt. emp. Third-party sick pay

1 Wages, tips, other compensation 2 Federal income tax withheld

3 Social security wages 4 Social security tax withheld

c Total number of Forms W-2 d Establishment number

5 Medicare wages and tips 6 Medicare tax withheld

e Employer identification number (EIN)

7 Social security tips 8 Allocated tips

f Employer's name

9 Advance EIC payments 10 Dependent care benefits

11 Nonqualified plans 12 Deferred compensation

13 For third-party sick pay use only

14 Income tax withheld by payer of third-party sick pay

g Employer's address and ZIP code

h Other EIN used this year

15 State Employer's state ID number

16 State wages, tips, etc. 17 State income tax

18 Local wages, tips, etc. 19 Local income tax

Contact person Telephone number ( ) For Official Use Only

Email address Fax number ( )

Under penalties of perjury, I declare that I have examined this return and accompanying documents, and, to the best of my knowledge and belief, they are true, correct, and complete.

Signature ▶ Title ▶ Date ▶

Form **W-3** Transmittal of Wage and Tax Statements

Department of the Treasury Internal Revenue Service

Send this entire page with the entire Copy A page of Form(s) W-2 to the Social Security Administration.

Figure 6:97

You have now completed the chapter. ***Back up the company file to a file named "QB2012_ Chp6_Stud_Completed."***

SUMMARY

You began this chapter with an overview of payroll processing in a manual system. We first explained the types of employee withholdings and voluntary deductions as well as the types of employer payroll taxes and additional forms of compensation. You also learned to calculate payroll taxes and withholdings.

You next looked at the different types of payroll items in QBP. This helped you to understand how payroll items track wages, employee withholdings, and employer taxes. You also saw that payroll items determine the general ledger account used when posting paychecks.

You then worked with the Employee Center to manage employee accounts and view payroll transactions. You created a new employee and learned the procedures for terminating an employee.

You were then ready to begin processing payroll. You first entered employee time and then prepared a report to verify the accuracy of the data entered. After that you entered data to create paychecks and printed the checks. You even allocated salary expense to a job.

Finally, you printed checks for payroll tax liabilities and reviewed quarterly and annual tax filing requirements. You learned to prepare Form 941 and reviewed W-2 and W-3 forms.

In the next chapter, you focus on finalizing the March accounting period by recording adjusting entries, printing financial statements, and closing the accounting period.

End-of-Chapter Questions

TRUE/FALSE

_____ 1. The IRS provides separate withholding tax tables for paying employees monthly and for paying employees biweekly.

_____ 2. Only employees pay Social Security and Medicare taxes.

_____ 3. The Federal Tax payroll item will track FUTA tax liabilities.

_____ 4. You can modify hours on an employee's timesheet as long as you have not paid the employee for the hours.

_____ 5. After voiding a paycheck, you can reissue it using the same timesheet hours.

_____ 6. Unemployment taxes are paid by employees.

_____ 7. You delete an employee account to stop paying the employee.

_____ 8. An employee's net pay will equal the gross pay minus payroll tax withholdings and voluntary deductions.

_____ 9. If you purchase the payroll tax service, you do not have to manually enter payroll tax withholdings.

_____ 10. You can enter time as a single activity or as a timesheet.

MULTIPLE CHOICE

_____ 1. The _____ report is used to complete Form 941.

a. Employee Earnings Summary
b. Payroll Liability Balances
c. Payroll Transactions by Payee
d. Both a and c

_____ 2. You can locate the check number for an employee's paycheck on the _____.

a. Employee Center
b. Payroll Transaction Detail report
c. Check Detail report
d. All of the above

_____ 3. An employee's withholding for Social Security tax _____ is of an employee's gross pay.

a. 1.45 percent
b. 6.2 percent
c. 7.65 percent
d. Employees do not pay Social Security taxes.

_____ 4. Per the IRS tax table, the withholding amount for a biweekly paid employee with gross wages of $960 claiming the Married filing status with four allowances will be _____. *(Note: See Appendix D for complete payroll tax withholding tables.)*

a. $10
b. $12
c. $35
d. $32

_____ 5. An employee with gross pay of $830 will have a net pay of _____. Assume the employee is paid biweekly, claims Married with three allowances, and pays state taxes of 2 percent of gross pay.

a. $712.90
b. $739.90
c. $737.90
d. $715.90

_____ 6. All the following are true when using the Enter Payroll Information window, except _____.

a. You can select a bank account
b. You can enter a timesheet
c. You can choose not to pay an employee
d. You can enter the check date

_____ 7. When using the Pay Liabilities window, all the following are true, except _____.

a. You can pay Medicare tax withholdings
b. You can pay employer FUTA taxes
c. You can adjust payroll liabilities
d. You can pay state tax withholdings

_____ 8. Timesheets are recorded so the company can _____.

a. Pay employees for the hours worked
b. Bill customers for the hours worked
c. Report on hours worked by each employee
d. All the above

_____ 9. You can print a _____ report to review how much time an employee has spent on a customer job.

a. Time by Name
b. Time by Item
c. Time by Job
d. Time by Customer

______ 10. The Employment tab on an employee account contains all the following fields, except.

a. Release Date
b. Hire Date
c. Pay Rate
d. Type

PRACTICE SET

In this Practice Set, you complete the following payroll activities for March and April.

Begin by:

- Opening the software.
- Opening the **QB2012_Chp6_PracSet_Stud** data file. Add your initials to the end to the Company Name by clicking ***Company>>Company Information*** on the main menu. Click **OK** to save the changes.
- **Toggling the software to the PRO EDITION** by selecting ***File>>Toggle to Another Edition*** on the main menu and choosing **QuickBooks Pro** as the edition.

1. Record the following transactions.

2012

Mar 19 Enter the following weekly timesheets for Jan Folse.

Employee ID: Folse, Jan **Mar 5 to Mar 11, 2012**

Customer:Job	Service Item	Payroll Item	M 5	Tu 6	W 7	Th 8	F 9	Sa 10	Su 11	Total	Billable
			8.00	8.00	8.00	8.00	8.00			**40.00**	No

Employee ID: Folse, Jan **Mar 12 to Mar 18, 2012**

Customer:Job	Service Item	Payroll Item	M 12	Tu 13	W 14	Th 15	F 16	Sa 17	Su 18	Total	Billable
			8.00	8.00	8.00	8.00	8.00			**40.00**	No

Mar 19 Create the following paychecks for the pay period ending 3/18/12. Click Yes if prompted to update hours.

Astor Landscaping
Paychecks for Pay Period 3/05/2012 thru 3/18/2012

Check No.	Employee	Filing Status	Allow	Pay Type	Pay Rate	Reg Hrs	OT Hrs	Gross Pay	Federal Income Tax	Soc. Sec. (FICA) Tax	Medicare Tax	VA State Tax	Net Pay
728	Dillion, Roy J.	Single	1	Hrly Wage	12.00	73.00		876.00	80.00	54.31	12.70	26.28	702.71
729	Folse, Jan B.	Single	1	Hrly Office	10.00	80.00		800.00	71.00	49.60	11.60	24.00	643.80
730	Greene, Kellie I.	Married	1	Salary	2,346.15			2,346.15	256.00	145.46	34.02	70.38	1,840.29
731	Hardman, Alan	Single	2	Hrly Wage	12.00	72.00		864.00	60.00	53.57	12.53	25.92	711.98
732	Henderson, Jeff P.	Married	1	Hrly Wage	12.00	72.00		864.00	43.00	53.57	12.53	25.92	728.98
733	Ramez, Victor M.	Single	0	Hrly Wage	10.00	78.00		780.00	89.00	48.36	11.31	23.40	607.93
734	Ruland, Seth N.	Married	0	Salary	3,103.85			3,103.85	429.00	192.44	45.01	93.12	2,344.28
	Totals					375.00	0.00	9,634.00	1,028.00	597.31	139.70	289.02	7,579.97
	Tax Basis								Circular E	6.20%	1.45%	3.00%	
	G/L Accounts								23400	23400	23400	23600	10300

Astor Landscaping
Employer Costs for Pay Period 3/05/2012 thru 3/18/2012

Employee	ER Soc Sec FICA	ER Medicare	ER FUTA	ER SUTA	Health Insurance
Dillion, Roy J.	54.31	12.70	7.01	13.14	0.00
Folse, Jan B.	49.60	11.60	6.40	12.00	60.00
Greene, Kellie I.	145.46	34.02	0.00	0.00	60.00
Hardman, Alan	53.57	12.53	6.91	12.96	0.00
Henderson, Jeff P.	53.57	12.53	6.91	12.96	0.00
Ramez, Victor M.	48.36	11.31	6.24	11.70	0.00
Ruland, Seth N.	192.44	45.01	0.00	0.00	60.00
Totals	597.31	139.70	33.47	62.76	180.00
Tax Basis	6.20%	1.45%	0.8%	1.50%	
G/L Accounts	23400 / 61000	23400 / 61000	23500 / 61000	23700 / 61000	23800 / 60600

The next illustration shows totals after entering the paychecks. Print the paychecks on first check number 728.

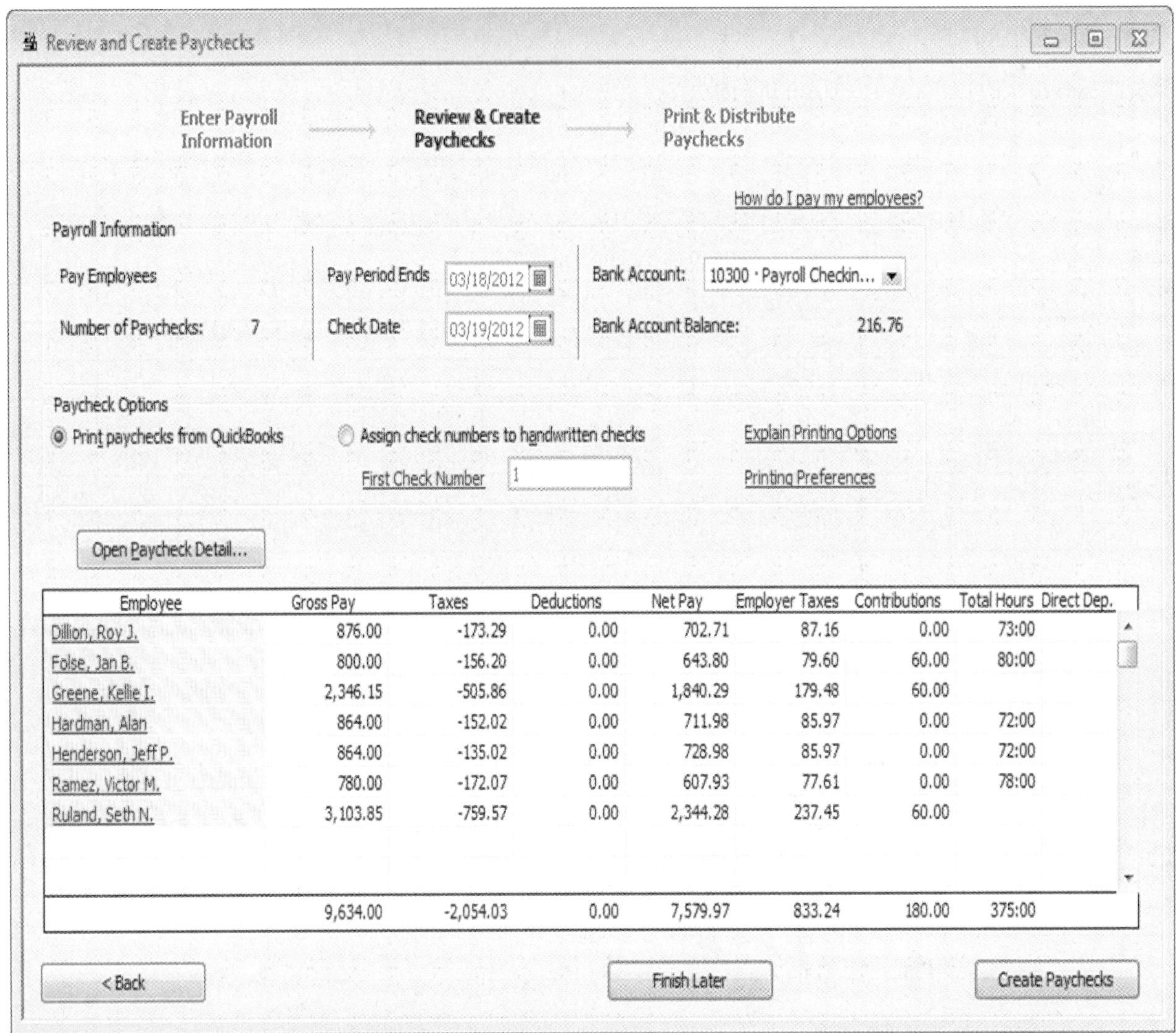

Employee	Gross Pay	Taxes	Deductions	Net Pay	Employer Taxes	Contributions	Total Hours	Direct Dep.
Dillion, Roy J.	876.00	-173.29	0.00	702.71	87.16	0.00	73:00	
Folse, Jan B.	800.00	-156.20	0.00	643.80	79.60	60.00	80:00	
Greene, Kellie I.	2,346.15	-505.86	0.00	1,840.29	179.48	60.00		
Hardman, Alan	864.00	-152.02	0.00	711.98	85.97	0.00	72:00	
Henderson, Jeff P.	864.00	-135.02	0.00	728.98	85.97	0.00	72:00	
Ramez, Victor M.	780.00	-172.07	0.00	607.93	77.61	0.00	78:00	
Ruland, Seth N.	3,103.85	-759.57	0.00	2,344.28	237.45	60.00		
	9,634.00	-2,054.03	0.00	7,579.97	833.24	180.00	375:00	

Mar 19 Print check number 439 to Nations Bank for $2,502.02 for federal withholding and Medicare and Social Security taxes for the liability period of 1/01/12 to 3/19/12.

2012

Apr 1 Print checks for the following payroll liabilities from 1/01/12 to 3/31/12. The first check number is 440 and checks total $1,876.43.

Medi Benefits Administrators for health insurance	$360.00
Nations Bank for FUTA taxes	$324.08
VA Department of Taxation for VA income tax	$584.70
VA Employment Commission for SUTA taxes	$607.65

Apr 2 Enter the following timesheets for Alan Hardman. Note: The first timesheet is added to his existing timesheet, bringing total hours to 40.

Employee ID: Hardman, Alan **Mar 19 to Mar 25, 2012**

Customer:Job	Service Item	Payroll Item	M 19	Tu 20	W 21	Th 22	F 23	Sa 24	Su 25	Total	Billable
Sallens Property Management	INSTL HARD - COMMERCIAL	Hourly Wage	4.00							4.00	Yes
		Totals	**4.00**	-	-	-	-			**4.00**	

Employee ID: Hardman, Alan **Mar 26 to Apr 1, 2012**

Customer:Job	Service Item	Payroll Item	M 26	Tu 27	W 28	Th 29	F 30	Sa 31	Su 1	Total	Billable
O'Hara Homes: Redesign Gardens	INSTL HARD - COMMERCIAL	Hourly Wage	8.00	8.00	8.00	8.00	8.00			40.00	Yes
O'Hara Homes: Redesign Gardens	INSTL HARD - COMMERCIAL	Hourly Wage Overtime	2.00							2.00	Yes
		Totals	**10.00**	**8.00**	**8.00**	**8.00**	**8.00**			**42.00**	

Apr 2 Create the following paychecks for the pay period ending 4/01/12.

Astor Landscaping
Paychecks for Pay Period 3/19/2012 thru 4/01/2012

Check No.	Employee	Filing Status	Allow.	Pay Type	Pay Rate	Reg Hrs	OT Hrs	Gross Pay	Federal Income Tax	Soc. Sec. (FICA) Tax	Medicare Tax	VA State Tax	Net Pay
735	Dillion, Roy J.	Single	1	Hrly Wage	12.00	80.00		960.00	95.00	59.52	13.92	28.80	762.76
736	Folse, Jan B.	Single	1	Hrly Office	10.00	80.00		800.00	71.00	49.60	11.60	24.00	643.80
737	Greene, Kellie I.	Married	1	Salary	2,346.15			2,346.15	256.00	145.46	34.02	70.38	1,840.29
738	Hardman, Alan	Single	2	Hrly Wage	12.00	80.00	2.00	996.00	78.00	61.75	14.44	29.88	811.93
739	Henderson, Jeff P.	Married	1	Hrly Wage	12.00	80.00		960.00	53.00	59.52	13.92	28.80	804.76
740	Ramez, Victor M.	Single	0	Hrly Wage	10.00	64.00		640.00	47.00	39.68	9.28	19.20	524.84
741	Ruland, Seth N.	Married	0	Salary	3,103.85			3,103.85	429.00	192.44	45.01	93.12	2,344.28
	Totals					384.00	2.00	9,806.00	1,029.00	607.97	142.19	294.18	7,732.66
	Tax Basis								Circular E	6.20%	1.45%	3.00%	
	G/L Accounts								23400	23400	23400	23600	10300

Astor Landscaping
Employer Costs for Pay Period 3/19/2012 thru 4/01/2012

Employee	ER Soc Sec FICA	ER Medicare	ER FUTA	ER SUTA	Health Insurance
Dillion, Roy J.	59.52	13.92	7.68	14.40	0.00
Folse, Jan B.	49.60	11.60	6.40	12.00	60.00
Greene, Kellie I.	145.46	34.02	0.00	0.00	60.00
Hardman, Alan	61.75	14.44	7.97	14.94	0.00
Henderson, Jeff P.	59.52	13.92	7.68	14.40	0.00
Ramez, Victor M.	39.68	9.28	5.12	9.60	0.00
Ruland, Seth N.	192.44	45.01	0.00	0.00	60.00
Totals	**607.97**	**142.19**	**34.85**	**65.34**	**180.00**
Tax Basis	**3.00%**	**0.00%**	**0.8%**	**1.50%**	
G/L Accounts	**23400 / 61000**	**23400 / 61000**	**23500 / 61000**	**23700 / 61000**	**23800 / 60600**

The next illustration shows the totals after entering paychecks. Print the paychecks on the first check number 735.

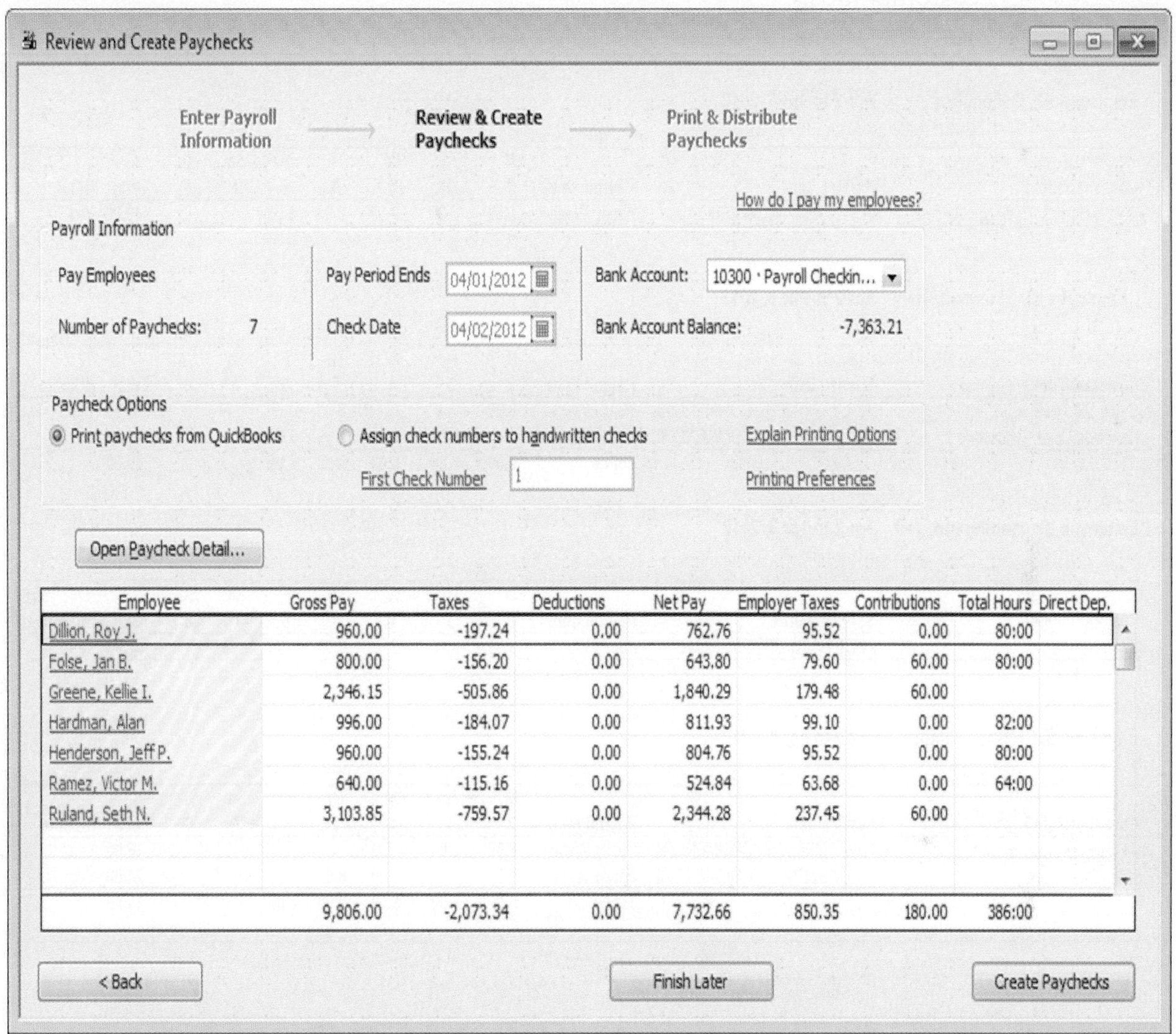

Employee	Gross Pay	Taxes	Deductions	Net Pay	Employer Taxes	Contributions	Total Hours	Direct Dep.
Dillion, Roy J.	960.00	-197.24	0.00	762.76	95.52	0.00	80:00	
Folse, Jan B.	800.00	-156.20	0.00	643.80	79.60	60.00	80:00	
Greene, Kellie I.	2,346.15	-505.86	0.00	1,840.29	179.48	60.00		
Hardman, Alan	996.00	-184.07	0.00	811.93	99.10	0.00	82:00	
Henderson, Jeff P.	960.00	-155.24	0.00	804.76	95.52	0.00	80:00	
Ramez, Victor M.	640.00	-115.16	0.00	524.84	63.68	0.00	64:00	
Ruland, Seth N.	3,103.85	-759.57	0.00	2,344.28	237.45	60.00		
	9,806.00	-2,073.34	0.00	7,732.66	850.35	180.00	386:00	

Apr 2 Print check number 444 to Nations Bank for $2,529.32 for federal withholding and Medicare and Social Security taxes for the payroll liability period of 1/01/12 to 4/04/12.

Apr 9 Enter the following timesheets. Print a Time by Name report and verify the total hours. Print a Time by Job Detail report and verify the hours assigned to customer jobs.

Employee ID: Dillion, Roy **Apr 2 to Apr 8, 2012**

Customer/JobID	Service Item	Payroll Item	M 2	Tu 3	W 4	Th 5	F 6	Sa 7	Su 8	Total	Billable
O'Hara Homes: Redesign Gardens	INSTL LAND - COMMERCIAL	Hourly Wage	8.00	8.00	8.00	8.00	8.00			**40.00**	Yes

Employee ID: Hardman, Alan **Apr 2 to Apr 8, 2012**

Customer/JobID	Service Item	Payroll Item	M 2	Tu 3	W 4	Th 5	F 6	Sa 7	Su 8	Total	Billable
Sugar Hill Tennis Club	WKLY MNTNCE - COMMERCIAL	Hourly Wage	8.00			8.00				**16.00**	Yes
Reynolds Court Subdivision	WKLY MNTNCE - COMMERCIAL	Hourly Wage		8.00	8.00		8.00			**24.00**	Yes
		Totals	**8.00**	**8.00**	**8.00**	**8.00**	**8.00**			**40.00**	

Employee ID: Henderson, Jeff **Apr 2 to Apr 8, 2012**

Customer/JobID	Service Item	Payroll Item	M 2	Tu 3	W 4	Th 5	F 6	Sa 7	Su 8	Total	Billable
Silver Homes	INSTL HARD - COMMERCIAL	Hourly Wage	8.00	8.00	8.00	8.00				32.00	Yes

Employee ID: Ramez, Victor **Apr 2 to Apr 8, 2012**

Customer/JobID	Service Item	Payroll Item	M 2	Tu 3	W 4	Th 5	F 6	Sa 7	Su 8	Total	Billable
Ashford Hill Apartments	WKLY MNTNCE - COMMERCIAL	Hourly Wage	8.00	8.00						**16.00**	Yes
DBH Enterprises	WKLY MNTNCE - COMMERCIAL	Hourly Wage			8.00	8.00	8.00			**24.00**	Yes
		Totals	**8.00**	**8.00**	**8.00**	**8.00**	**8.00**			**40.00**	

Total Hours	152.00

Apr 9 Add the following new employee. Make sure to use time data to create paychecks.

Name:	David R. Bellows	
Address:	873 Trumpet St., Arlington, VA 30026	
Soc Sec:	111-00-3232	
Position:	Laborer	
Hired:	4/09/12	
Pay Info:	BIWEEKLY payroll schedule	
	Hourly wage:	$12.00
	Hourly wage overtime:	$18.00
Tax Info:	Federal:	Single, 0 Allowances
	State:	VA for state worked and state withholding

Apr 16 Terminate Alan Hardman. Release date is April 4/16/12.

Apr 16 Enter the following timesheets. Print a Time by Name report and verify the total hours. Print a Time by Job Detail report and verify the hours assigned to customer jobs.

Employee ID: Bellows, David **Apr 9 to Apr 15, 2012**

Customer/JobID	Service Item	Payroll Item	M 9	Tu 10	W 11	Th 12	F 13	Sa 14	Su 15	Total	Billable
Sugar Hill Tennis Club	WKLY MNTNCE - COMMERCIAL	Hourly Wage	8.00	8.00	8.00					24.00	Yes
Reynolds Court Subdivision	WKLY MNTNCE - COMMERCIAL	Hourly Wage				8.00	8.00			16.00	Yes
		Totals	8.00	8.00	8.00	8.00	8.00			40.00	

Employee ID: Dillion, Roy **Apr 9 to Apr 15, 2012**

Customer/JobID	Service Item	Payroll Item	M 9	Tu 10	W 11	Th 12	F 13	Sa 14	Su 15	Total	Billable
O'Hara Homes: Redesign Gardens	INSTL LAND - COMMERCIAL	Hourly Wage	8.00	8.00	8.00	8.00	8.00			40.00	Yes

Employee ID: Henderson, Jeff **Apr 9 to Apr 15, 2012**

Customer/JobID	Service Item	Payroll Item	M 9	Tu 10	W 11	Th 12	F 13	Sa 14	Su 15	Total	Billable
Silver Homes	INSTL HARD - COMMERCIAL	Hourly Wage	8.00	8.00	8.00	8.00	8.00			40.00	Yes

Employee ID: Ramez, Victor **Apr 9 to Apr 15, 2012**

Customer/JobID	Service Item	Payroll Item	M 9	Tu 10	W 11	Th 12	F 13	Sa 14	Su 15	Total	Billable
Ashford Hill Apartments	WKLY MNTNCE - COMMERCIAL	Houly Wage	8.00	8.00						16.00	Yes
DBH Enterprises	WKLY MNTNCE - COMMERCIAL	Houly Wage			8.00	6.00	8.00			22.00	Yes
		Totals	8.00	8.00	8.00	6.00	8.00			38.00	

Total Hours 158.00

Apr 16 Create the following paychecks for the pay period ending 4/15/12. Manually change the hours for Jan Folse to 78.

Astor Landscaping
Paychecks for Pay Period 4/02/2012 thru 4/15/2012

Check No.	Employee	Filing Status	Allow.	Pay Type	Pay Rate	Reg Hrs	OT Hrs	Gross Pay	Federal Income Tax	Soc. Sec. (FICA) Tax	Medicare Tax	VA State Tax	Net Pay
742	Bellows, David R	Single	0	Hrly Wage	12.00	40.00		480.00	43.00	29.76	6.96	14.40	385.88
743	Dillion, Roy J.	Single	1	Hrly Wage	12.00	80.00		960.00	95.00	59.52	13.92	28.80	762.76
744	Folse, Jan B.	Single	1	Hrly Office	10.00	78.00		780.00	68.00	48.36	11.31	23.40	628.93
745	Greene, Kellie I.	Married	1	Salary	2,346.15			2,346.15	256.00	145.46	34.02	70.38	1,840.29
746	Hardman, Alan	Single	2	Hrly Wage	12.00	40.00		480.00	11.00	29.76	6.96	14.40	417.88
747	Henderson, Jeff P.	Married	1	Hrly Wage	12.00	72.00		864.00	43.00	53.57	12.53	25.92	728.98
748	Ramez, Victor M.	Single	0	Hrly Wage	10.00	78.00		780.00	68.00	48.36	11.31	23.40	628.93
749	Ruland, Seth N.	Married	0	Salary	3,103.85			3,103.85	429.00	192.44	45.01	93.12	2,344.28
	Totals					388.00	0.00	9,794.00	1,013.00	607.23	142.02	293.82	7,737.93
	Tax Basis								Circular E	6.20%	1.45%	3.00%	
	G/L Accounts								23400	23400	23400	23600	10300

Astor Landscaping
Employer Costs for Pay Period 4/02/2012 thru 4/15/2012

Employee	ER Soc Sec (FICA)	ER Medicare	ER FUTA	ER SUTA	Health Insurance
Bellows, David R	29.76	6.96	3.84	7.20	0.00
Dillion, Roy J.	59.52	13.92	2.91	5.46	0.00
Folse, Jan B.	48.36	11.31	6.24	11.70	60.00
Greene, Kellie I.	145.46	34.02	0.00	0.00	60.00
Hardman, Alan	29.76	6.96	2.91	5.46	0.00
Henderson, Jeff P.	53.57	12.53	3.01	5.64	0.00
Ramez, Victor M.	48.36	11.31	6.24	11.70	0.00
Ruland, Seth N.	192.44	45.01	0.00	0.00	60.00
Totals	**607.23**	**142.02**	**25.15**	**47.16**	**180.00**
Tax Basis	**6.20%**	**1.45%**	**0.8%**	**1.50%**	
G/L Accounts	**23400 / 61000**	**23400 / 61000**	**23500 / 61000**	**23700 / 61000**	**23750 / 60300**

The next illustration shows totals after entering the paychecks. Print the paychecks using the first check number 742.

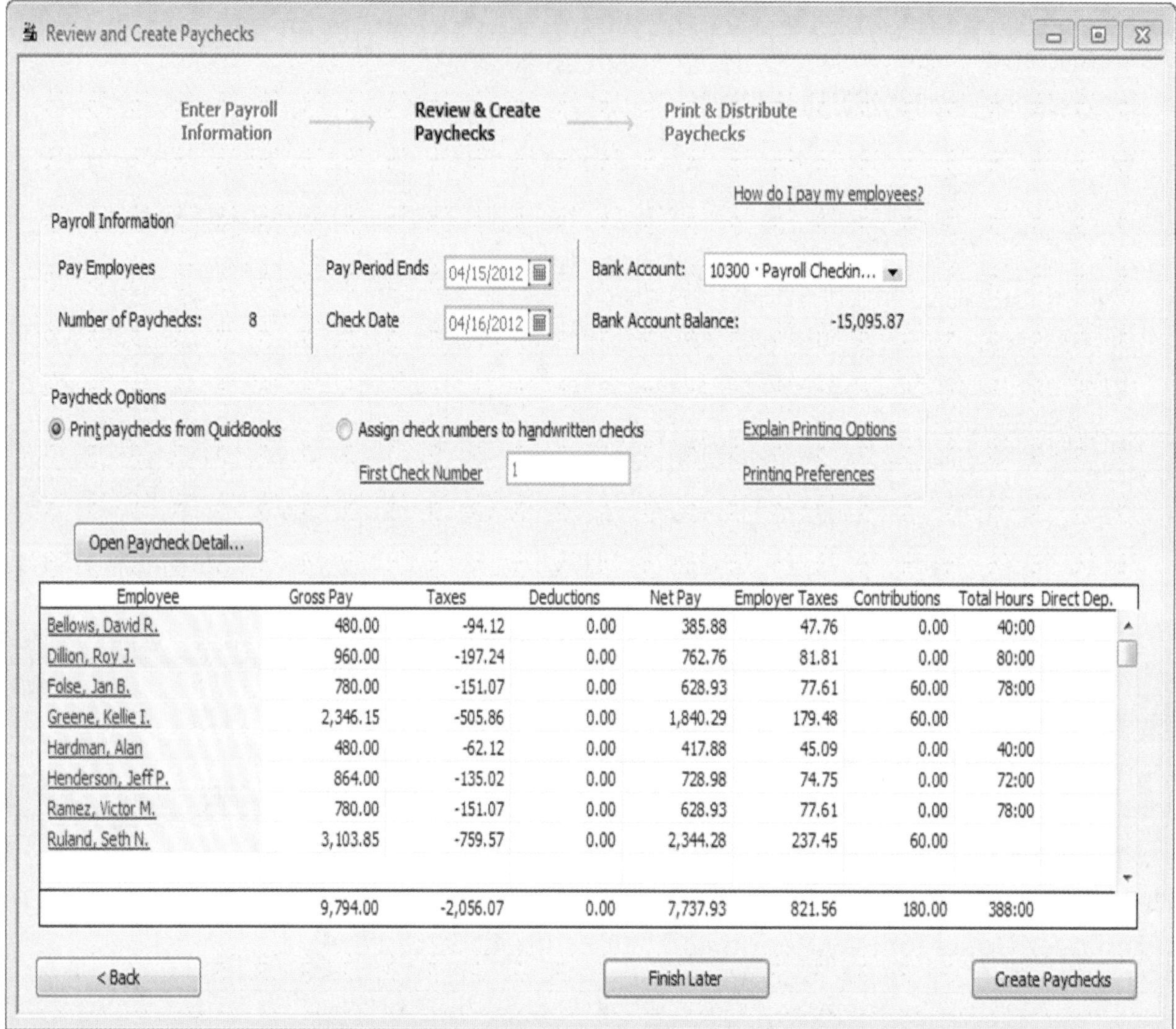

Employee	Gross Pay	Taxes	Deductions	Net Pay	Employer Taxes	Contributions	Total Hours	Direct Dep.
Bellows, David R.	480.00	-94.12	0.00	385.88	47.76	0.00	40:00	
Dillion, Roy J.	960.00	-197.24	0.00	762.76	81.81	0.00	80:00	
Folse, Jan B.	780.00	-151.07	0.00	628.93	77.61	60.00	78:00	
Greene, Kellie I.	2,346.15	-505.86	0.00	1,840.29	179.48	60.00		
Hardman, Alan	480.00	-62.12	0.00	417.88	45.09	0.00	40:00	
Henderson, Jeff P.	864.00	-135.02	0.00	728.98	74.75	0.00	72:00	
Ramez, Victor M.	780.00	-151.07	0.00	628.93	77.61	0.00	78:00	
Ruland, Seth N.	3,103.85	-759.57	0.00	2,344.28	237.45	60.00		
	9,794.00	-2,056.07	0.00	7,737.93	821.56	180.00	388:00	

Apr 16 Print check number 445 to Nations Bank for $2,511.50 for federal withholding and Medicare and Social Security taxes for the payroll liability period of 1/01/12 to 4/16/12.

Apr 30 Print checks for the following payroll liabilities from 1/01/12 to 4/30/12. The first check number is 446 and checks total $948.00.

Medi Benefits Administrators for health insurance	$360.00
VA Department of Taxation for VA income tax	$588.00

2. Print the following reports to document activities:

    a. Payroll Transactions by Payee filtered for 3/19/12 to 4/30/12.

    b. Payroll Liability Balances report filtered for 4/01/12 to 4/30/12.

3. ***Back up the company file to a backup file named "QB2012_Chp6_Prac_Set_Stud_ Completed."***

INTERNET MINI-PROJECT

This mini-project asks you to prepare a Form 940 and the instructions are downloaded from the textbook Website at ***www.pearsonhighered.com/brunsdon/***. Download the files named **PrepareForm940.pdf** and **MillisForm940.pdf**.

CHAPTER 7 CLOSE THE ACCOUNTING PERIOD FOR A SERVICE-BASED BUSINESS

LEARNING OBJECTIVES

In this chapter, you complete the accounting cycle for March 2012. You will:

1. Analyze transactions posted in March
2. Review a preclosing checklist
3. Post adjusting entries
4. Reconcile bank accounts
5. Print financial statements
6. Close the accounting period

Begin with:

- Opening the software.
- Opening the **QB2012_Chp7_Stud** data file. Add your initials to the end to the Company Name by clicking ***Company>>Company Information*** on the main menu. Click **OK** to save the changes.
- **Toggling the software to the PRO EDITION** by selecting ***File>>Toggle to Another Edition*** on the main menu and choosing **QuickBooks Pro** as the edition.

ANALYZE TRANSACTIONS

In Chapter 3, you learned to post general journal entries. You will use journal entries in this chapter to adjust account balances and accrue expenses.

Before making adjustments, it is important to analyze posted transactions. Begin your analysis by reviewing the **General Ledger** report that follows.

Open the report by selecting ***Reports>>Accountant and Taxes>>General Ledger*** on the main menu. Enter the date range of **3/01/12** to **3/31/12**. (See Figure 7.1.)

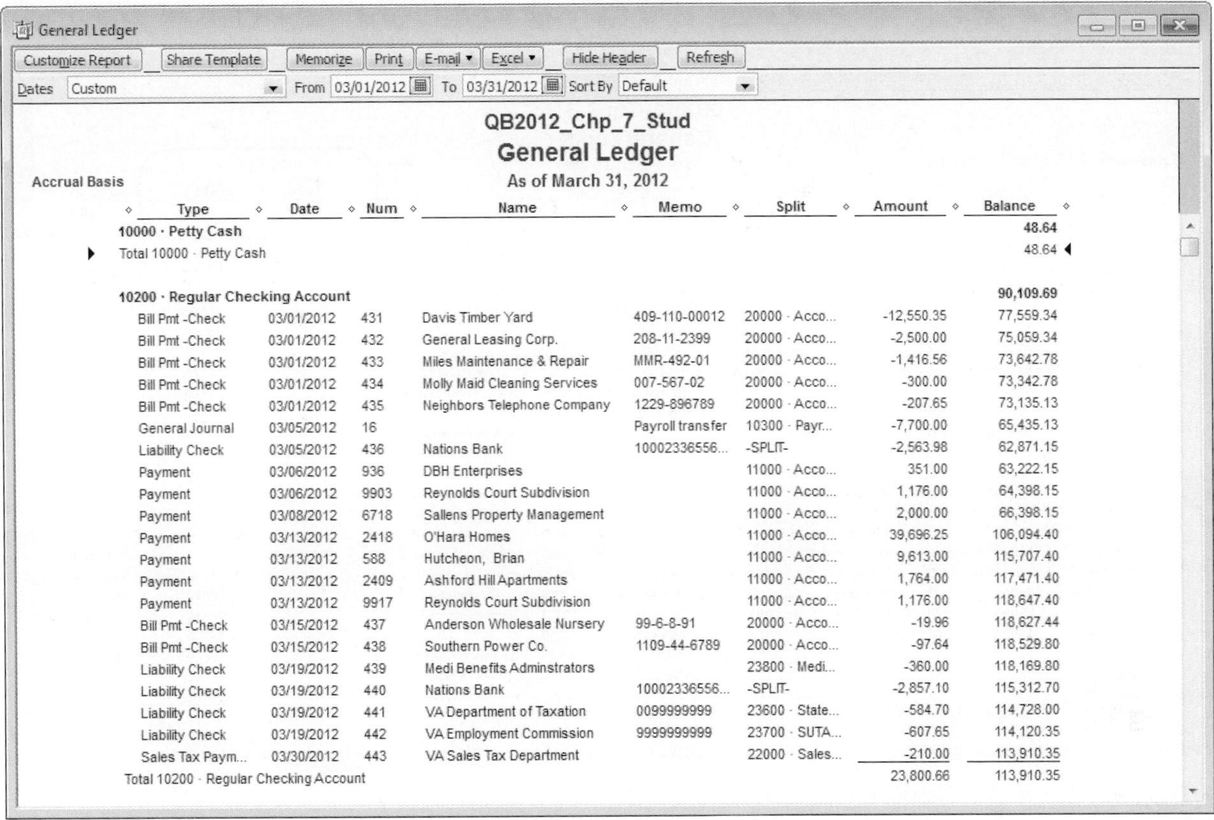

QB2012_Chp_7_Stud

General Ledger

Accrual Basis

As of March 31, 2012

Type	Date	Num	Name	Memo	Split	Amount	Balance
10000 · Petty Cash							**48.64**
Total 10000 · Petty Cash							48.64
10200 · Regular Checking Account							**90,109.69**
Bill Pmt -Check	03/01/2012	431	Davis Timber Yard	409-110-00012	20000 · Acco...	-12,550.35	77,559.34
Bill Pmt -Check	03/01/2012	432	General Leasing Corp.	208-11-2399	20000 · Acco...	-2,500.00	75,059.34
Bill Pmt -Check	03/01/2012	433	Miles Maintenance & Repair	MMR-492-01	20000 · Acco...	-1,416.56	73,642.78
Bill Pmt -Check	03/01/2012	434	Molly Maid Cleaning Services	007-567-02	20000 · Acco...	-300.00	73,342.78
Bill Pmt -Check	03/01/2012	435	Neighbors Telephone Company	1229-896789	20000 · Acco...	-207.65	73,135.13
General Journal	03/05/2012	16		Payroll transfer	10300 · Payr...	-7,700.00	65,435.13
Liability Check	03/05/2012	436	Nations Bank	10002336556...	-SPLIT-	-2,563.98	62,871.15
Payment	03/06/2012	936	DBH Enterprises		11000 · Acco...	351.00	63,222.15
Payment	03/06/2012	9903	Reynolds Court Subdivision		11000 · Acco...	1,176.00	64,398.15
Payment	03/08/2012	6718	Sallens Property Management		11000 · Acco...	2,000.00	66,398.15
Payment	03/13/2012	2418	O'Hara Homes		11000 · Acco...	39,696.25	106,094.40
Payment	03/13/2012	588	Hutcheon, Brian		11000 · Acco...	9,613.00	115,707.40
Payment	03/13/2012	2409	Ashford Hill Apartments		11000 · Acco...	1,764.00	117,471.40
Payment	03/13/2012	9917	Reynolds Court Subdivision		11000 · Acco...	1,176.00	118,647.40
Bill Pmt -Check	03/15/2012	437	Anderson Wholesale Nursery	99-6-8-91	20000 · Acco...	-19.96	118,627.44
Bill Pmt -Check	03/15/2012	438	Southern Power Co.	1109-44-6789	20000 · Acco...	-97.64	118,529.80
Liability Check	03/19/2012	439	Medi Benefits Adminstrators		23800 · Medi...	-360.00	118,169.80
Liability Check	03/19/2012	440	Nations Bank	10002336556...	-SPLIT-	-2,857.10	115,312.70
Liability Check	03/19/2012	441	VA Department of Taxation	0099999999	23600 · State...	-584.70	114,728.00
Liability Check	03/19/2012	442	VA Employment Commission	9999999999	23700 · SUTA...	-607.65	114,120.35
Sales Tax Paym...	03/30/2012	443	VA Sales Tax Department		22000 · Sales...	-210.00	113,910.35
Total 10200 · Regular Checking Account						23,800.66	113,910.35

Figure 7:1

This report differs from the General Ledger Detail Report you have been using to document the audit trail because it also lists beginning and ending account balances.

Customize this report so that transactions appear in debit and credit columns. Click **Customize Report**. On the **Display** tab, add the **Debit** and **Credit** columns and remove the **Amount** column. Click **OK.**

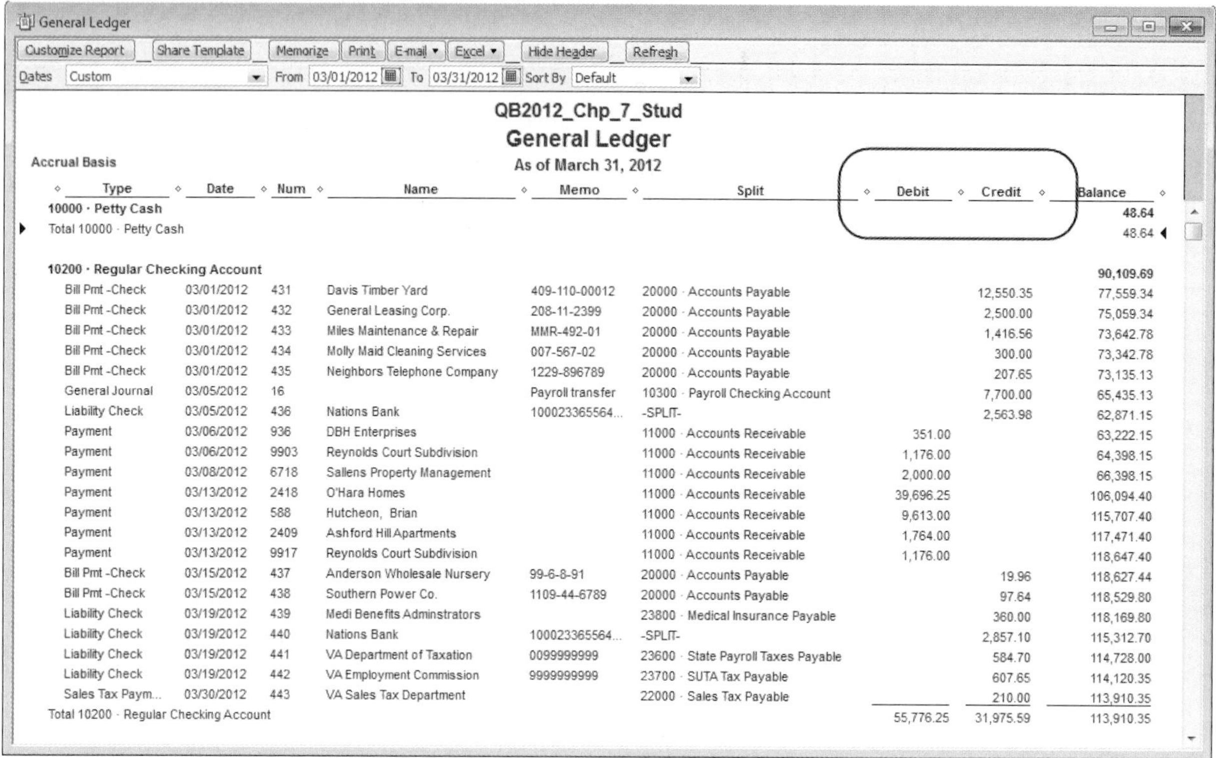

General Ledger

Customize Report | Share Template | Memorize | Print | E-mail | Excel | Hide Header | Refresh

Dates: Custom From 03/01/2012 To 03/31/2012 Sort By Default

QB2012_Chp_7_Stud
General Ledger
As of March 31, 2012

Accrual Basis

Type	Date	Num	Name	Memo	Split	Debit	Credit	Balance
10000 · Petty Cash								**48.64**
Total 10000 · Petty Cash								48.64
10200 · Regular Checking Account								**90,109.69**
Bill Pmt -Check	03/01/2012	431	Davis Timber Yard	409-110-00012	20000 · Accounts Payable		12,550.35	77,559.34
Bill Pmt -Check	03/01/2012	432	General Leasing Corp.	208-11-2399	20000 · Accounts Payable		2,500.00	75,059.34
Bill Pmt -Check	03/01/2012	433	Miles Maintenance & Repair	MMR-492-01	20000 · Accounts Payable		1,416.56	73,642.78
Bill Pmt -Check	03/01/2012	434	Molly Maid Cleaning Services	007-567-02	20000 · Accounts Payable		300.00	73,342.78
Bill Pmt -Check	03/01/2012	435	Neighbors Telephone Company	1229-896789	20000 · Accounts Payable		207.65	73,135.13
General Journal	03/05/2012	16		Payroll transfer	10300 · Payroll Checking Account		7,700.00	65,435.13
Liability Check	03/05/2012	436	Nations Bank	100023365564...	-SPLIT-		2,563.98	62,871.15
Payment	03/06/2012	936	DBH Enterprises		11000 · Accounts Receivable	351.00		63,222.15
Payment	03/06/2012	9903	Reynolds Court Subdivision		11000 · Accounts Receivable	1,176.00		64,398.15
Payment	03/08/2012	6718	Sallens Property Management		11000 · Accounts Receivable	2,000.00		66,398.15
Payment	03/13/2012	2418	O'Hara Homes		11000 · Accounts Receivable	39,696.25		106,094.40
Payment	03/13/2012	588	Hutcheon, Brian		11000 · Accounts Receivable	9,613.00		115,707.40
Payment	03/13/2012	2409	Ashford Hill Apartments		11000 · Accounts Receivable	1,764.00		117,471.40
Payment	03/13/2012	9917	Reynolds Court Subdivision		11000 · Accounts Receivable	1,176.00		118,647.40
Bill Pmt -Check	03/15/2012	437	Anderson Wholesale Nursery	99-6-8-91	20000 · Accounts Payable		19.96	118,627.44
Bill Pmt -Check	03/15/2012	438	Southern Power Co.	1109-44-6789	20000 · Accounts Payable		97.64	118,529.80
Liability Check	03/19/2012	439	Medi Benefits Adminstrators		23800 · Medical Insurance Payable		360.00	118,169.80
Liability Check	03/19/2012	440	Nations Bank	100023365564...	-SPLIT-		2,857.10	115,312.70
Liability Check	03/19/2012	441	VA Department of Taxation	0099999999	23600 · State Payroll Taxes Payable		584.70	114,728.00
Liability Check	03/19/2012	442	VA Employment Commission	9999999999	23700 · SUTA Tax Payable		607.65	114,120.35
Sales Tax Paym...	03/30/2012	443	VA Sales Tax Department		22000 · Sales Tax Payable		210.00	113,910.35
Total 10200 · Regular Checking Account						55,776.25	31,975.59	113,910.35

Figure 7:2

Remember that the Split column shows the corresponding account used on a transaction. If the term "SPLIT" appears, multiple accounts were involved. What follows are the steps performed to analyze the report.

First, scroll through the report to look for transactions that may indicate a posting error. In particular, scroll to account **71100 Utilities Expense** and notice that the March telephone bill for $262.43 posted to utilities instead of posting to account **71200 Telephone Expense**.

You will now reclassify the expense. Double click the entry to reopen it and use the lookup on **Account** to select **71200 Telephone Expense**. (See Figure 7.3.)

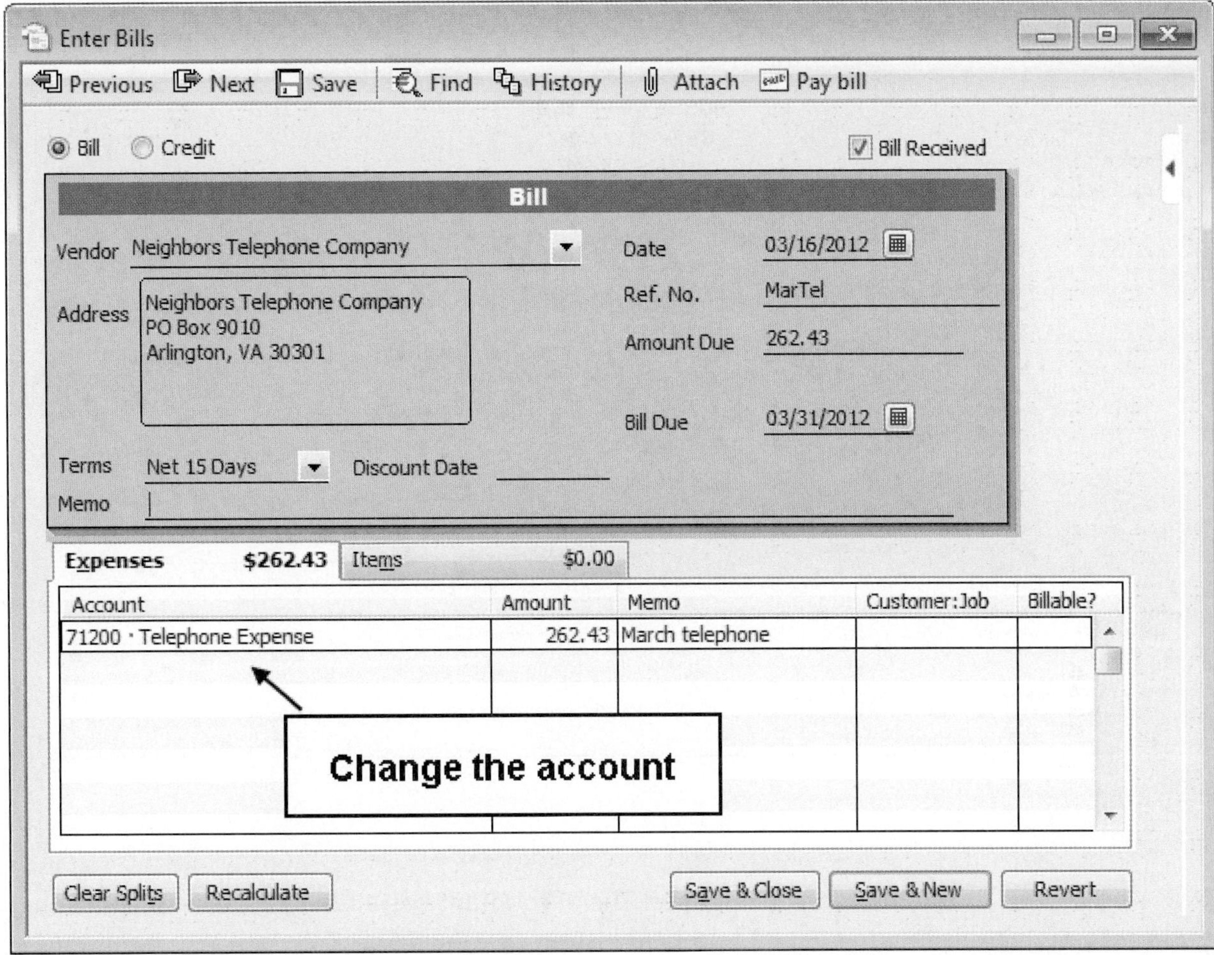

Figure 7:3

Click **Save & Close** and **Yes** when prompted to confirm changes. That is how easy it is to reclassify a posting error for expenses.

The next step is to review the report for missing transactions. In particular, scroll to account **10300 Payroll Checking** and notice that the bank balance is negative. This is because the bank transfer covering the last payroll has not been recorded. (See Figure 7.4.) You will record this adjusting entry in the exercise that follows.

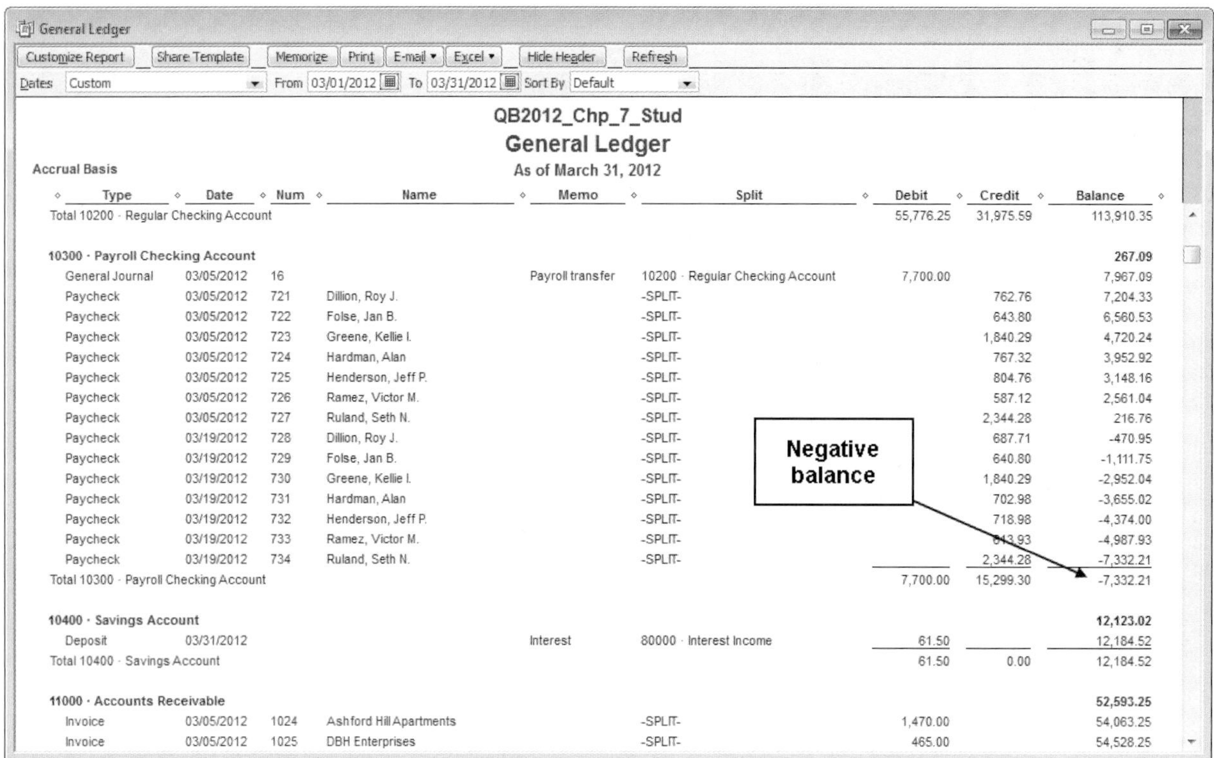

General Ledger

Customize Report | Share Template | Memorize | Print | E-mail ▾ | Excel ▾ | Hide Header | Refresh

Dates Custom | From 03/01/2012 | To 03/31/2012 | Sort By Default

QB2012_Chp_7_Stud
General Ledger
As of March 31, 2012

Accrual Basis

Type	Date	Num	Name	Memo	Split	Debit	Credit	Balance
Total 10200 · Regular Checking Account						55,776.25	31,975.59	113,910.35
10300 · Payroll Checking Account								**267.09**
General Journal	03/05/2012	16		Payroll transfer	10200 · Regular Checking Account	7,700.00		7,967.09
Paycheck	03/05/2012	721	Dillion, Roy J.		-SPLIT-		762.76	7,204.33
Paycheck	03/05/2012	722	Folse, Jan B.		-SPLIT-		643.80	6,560.53
Paycheck	03/05/2012	723	Greene, Kellie I.		-SPLIT-		1,840.29	4,720.24
Paycheck	03/05/2012	724	Hardman, Alan		-SPLIT-		767.32	3,952.92
Paycheck	03/05/2012	725	Henderson, Jeff P.		-SPLIT-		804.76	3,148.16
Paycheck	03/05/2012	726	Ramez, Victor M.		-SPLIT-		587.12	2,561.04
Paycheck	03/05/2012	727	Ruland, Seth N.		-SPLIT-		2,344.28	216.76
Paycheck	03/19/2012	728	Dillion, Roy J.		-SPLIT-		687.71	-470.95
Paycheck	03/19/2012	729	Folse, Jan B.		-SPLIT-		640.80	-1,111.75
Paycheck	03/19/2012	730	Greene, Kellie I.		-SPLIT-		1,840.29	-2,952.04
Paycheck	03/19/2012	731	Hardman, Alan		-SPLIT-		702.98	-3,655.02
Paycheck	03/19/2012	732	Henderson, Jeff P.		-SPLIT-		718.98	-4,374.00
Paycheck	03/19/2012	733	Ramez, Victor M.		-SPLIT-		613.93	-4,987.93
Paycheck	03/19/2012	734	Ruland, Seth N.		-SPLIT-		2,344.28	-7,332.21
Total 10300 · Payroll Checking Account						7,700.00	15,299.30	-7,332.21
10400 · Savings Account								**12,123.02**
Deposit	03/31/2012			Interest	80000 · Interest Income	61.50		12,184.52
Total 10400 · Savings Account						61.50	0.00	12,184.52
11000 · Accounts Receivable								**52,593.25**
Invoice	03/05/2012	1024	Ashford Hill Apartments		-SPLIT-	1,470.00		54,063.25
Invoice	03/05/2012	1025	DBH Enterprises		-SPLIT-	465.00		54,528.25

Figure 7:4

Now scroll down to **14000 Prepaid Expenses**. The accountant has already posted the adjusting entry recognizing this month's expired prepaid insurance. Double click the entry to open the transactions. (See Figure 7.5.)

*(Note: If a message appears letting you know that QBP can automatically assign journal entry numbers, click the option to turn off future messages and click **OK**.)*

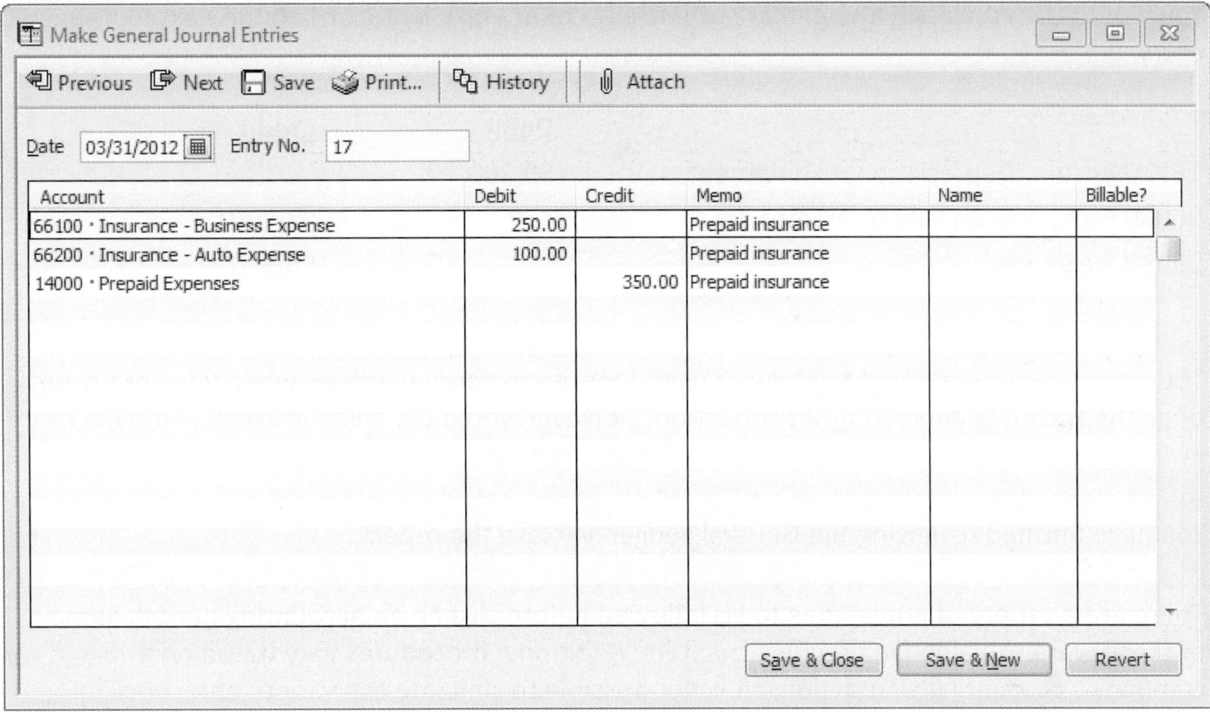
Make General Journal Entries

Date 03/31/2012 Entry No. 17

Account	Debit	Credit	Memo	Name	Billable?
66100 · Insurance - Business Expense	250.00		Prepaid insurance		
66200 · Insurance - Auto Expense	100.00		Prepaid insurance		
14000 · Prepaid Expenses		350.00	Prepaid insurance		

Figure 7:5

Figure 7.5 illustrates recording an adjusting entry for prepaid expense. Click **X** to close the entry.

As you scroll past prepaid expenses, look for March entries to accumulated depreciation. These entries have not been recorded so you will record them in the exercise that follows.

Now is a good time to talk about using a suspense account. Scroll to the bottom of the General Ledger report and locate the **99999 Suspense** account. This account is used when you need to post an entry but do not have all the information necessary to complete it.

For instance, assume the company sold equipment costing $15,000 and received $8,500 in cash. You cannot delay recording cash on the sale; however, you do not have final depreciation on the equipment to finalize gain or loss on the sale. This is where the entry can be posted using the suspense account. The following illustrates the journal entry to post the transaction using the suspense account.

	Debit	Credit
10200 Regular Checking Account	$8,500	
99999 Suspense	$6,500	
15100 Equipment		$15,000

When you later calculate that $8,000 was previously posted to the accumulated equipment depreciation account and that final depreciation is $9,200, the following journal entry records the depreciation adjustment.

	Debit	Credit
75000 Depreciation Expense	$1,200	
15110 Accum. Depreciation – Equipment		$1,200

You would then reclassify the earlier suspense account entry by recording the next journal entry.

	Debit	**Credit**
15110 Accum. Depreciation – Equipment	$9,200	
90000 Gain/Loss on Sale of Assets		$2,700
99999 Suspense		$6,500

Thus, the suspense account becomes a useful tool for recording entries when you are unsure of all the accounts affected by a transaction. However, you must diligently review the balance in the suspense account to make sure entries are finalized.

You have finished reviewing the General Ledger so close the report.

There are a variety of procedures to be followed before closing an accounting period. Some of these were explained in previous chapters. Additional procedures vary based on a company's accounting transactions. It is not possible to simulate the variety of reconciling procedures you may encounter in practice. Instead, we have prepared the following preclosing checklist to help guide you in the future.

Preclosing Checklist	
Review Pending Transactions	Review pending sales to verify all sales income has been recognized.
	Review pending purchases to verify all expenses have been recognized.
	Review payroll tax liability accounts to ensure timely payment.
Reconciliation Procedures	Reconcile all bank statements.
	Reconcile the A/R aging report to the accounts receivable control account (performed in Chapters 4 and 8).
	Reconcile the inventory valuation report to the inventory control account (performed in Chapter 8).
	Reconcile fixed asset reports to fixed asset control accounts Often fixed asset costs and depreciation will be tracked outside the software. QBP can track fixed asset costs and depreciation but this feature is not illustrated.
	Reconcile the A/P aging report to the accounts payable control account (performed in Chapters 5 and 9).
Adjusting Entries	Post petty cash transactions.
	Review prepaid expenses for expired costs.
	Review accrued liability accounts such as wages and taxes payable.
	Review expenses in the prior period to identify expenses that need to be recognized in the current period—for example, missing utility bills or recurring rent transactions.
	Review posted expenses for prepaid costs and for fixed assets expensed to office supplies.

ADJUSTING ENTRIES

In this topic, you post Astor's remaining adjusting entries for March. The accountant has already posted entries for expired prepaid expense and recurring rent. This means that you need to post entries transferring funds to payroll checking, replenishing petty cash and recognizing depreciation and accrued wage expense.

In the exercise that follows, you post the bank transfer and depreciation entries. In the *You Try* exercise that follows, you post an entry for accrued wages expense and print a check for petty cash.

When posting depreciation, keep in mind that this is an estimate of expense based on ending assets held in the prior year. The estimate may be revised during the year for current year acquisitions or dispositions. Any difference between estimated and actual expense is recorded at the end of the fiscal year.

STEPS TO ENTER ADJUSTING ENTRIES

1. You will record the payroll transfer first. Select ***Banking>>Transfer Funds*** on the main menu and enter the information illustrated in Figure 7.6. Click **Save & Close**.

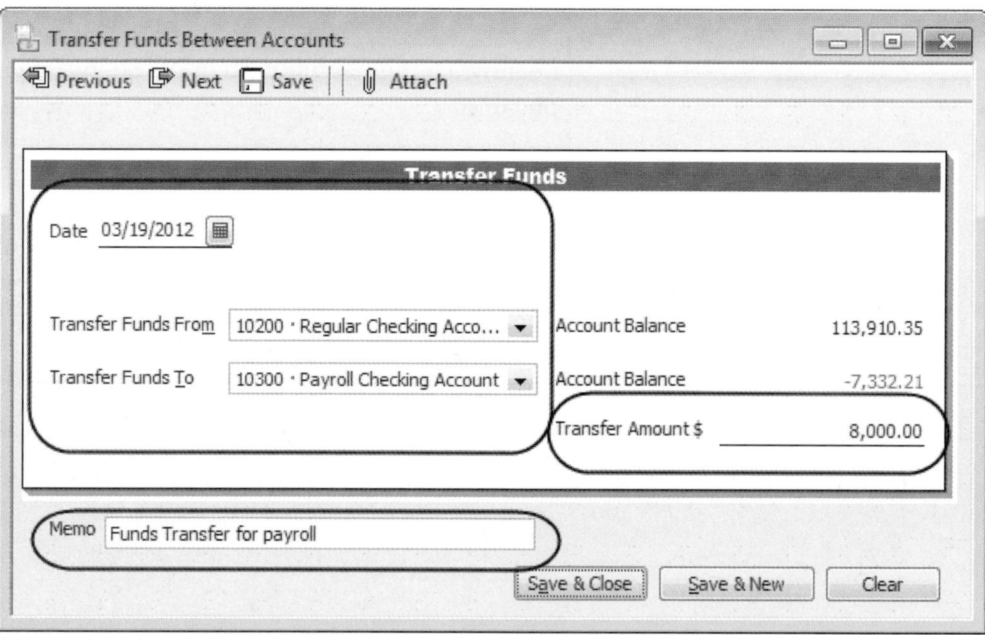

Figure 7:6

2. Adjusting entries are often saved as memorized transactions, especially when such transactions repeat every month. Check to see if the accountant has created a memorized entry for accumulated depreciation.

   Select ***Lists>>Memorized Transactions List*** on the main menu to find a memorized depreciation transaction.

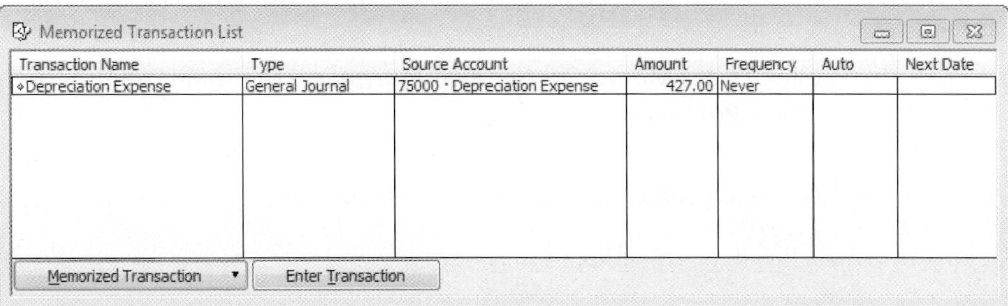

Figure 7:7

3. Highlight the entry and click the **Enter Transaction** button. Depreciation Expense. *(Note: If prompted that transaction affects a closed period, click Yes.)* Change the **Date** to 3/31/12. (See Figure 7.8.)

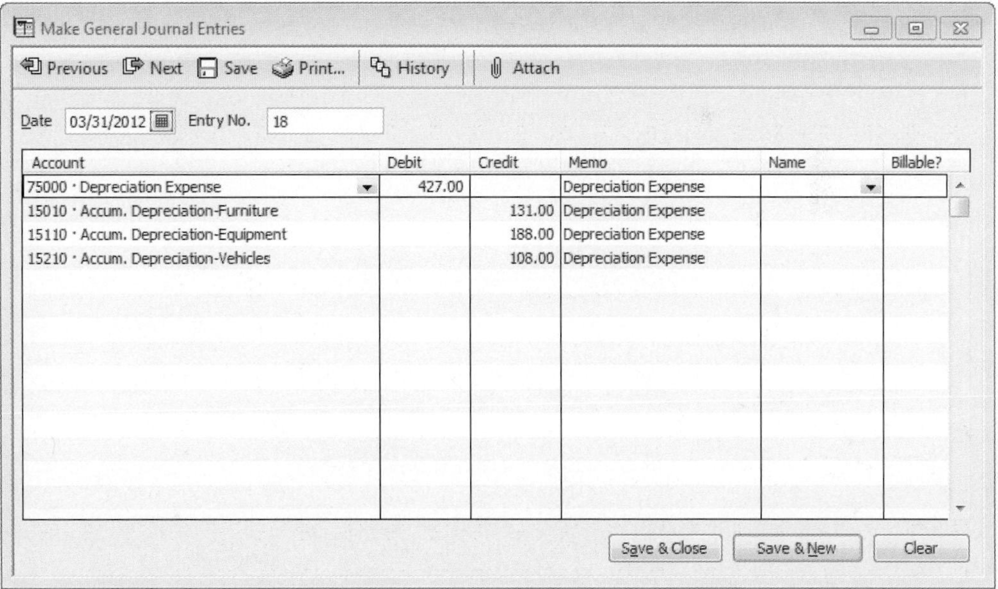

Figure 7:8

4. The accountant wants to revise the estimate for furniture depreciation.

   Change the **Debit** for 75000 Depreciation Expense to 436.00.

   Change the **Credit** for 15010 Accum. Depreciation-Furniture to 140.00.

5. Before you post this entry, replace the existing memorized transaction.

   Click ***Edit>>Memorize General Journal*** on the main menu. When QBP prompts, select **Replace**.

6. Now click **Save & Close**. *(Note: You can turn off future messages on fixed assets.)*

   When you return to the Memorized Transaction List, the Amount has been updated.

   Close the Memorized Transaction List.

FINISH RECORDING MARCH ADJUSTING ENTRIES

You will be recording accrued wages for March and printing a check to replenish petty cash.

Print check number 444 on March 31 to Petty Cash for $376.26. The check is expensed as follows:

Office Supplies Expense	$163.83
Travel Expense	$103.76
Meals and Entertainment Expense	$108.67

Before posting accrued wages, calculate the amount to accrue using the following steps.

a. Open the Employee Earnings Summary report to determine the average weekly wage expense. Enter 3/1/12 to 3/31/12 as the date range. Compute the total for the Salary, Hourly Office, and Hourly Wage columns and divide by 4 (i.e., the number of pay weeks in March). The weekly average is $4,872.50, computed as (10,900.00 + 1,600.00 + 6,990.00) / 4.

b. Next, compute a daily average by dividing the weekly average by 5 working days. The daily average is $974.50. Rounded to the nearest dollar, makes the daily average equal to $975.00.

c. Finally, multiply the rounded daily average by the number of days to accrue. For March, this is 10 days because the last pay period ended on March 18. The amount to accrue is $9,750.00.

Now post a journal entry recording March accrued wages using the 60000 Salaries Expense and 23200 Accrued Wages accounts.

RECONCILE BANK ACCOUNTS

After posting adjusting entries, you are ready to reconcile the bank accounts. The accountant has already reconciled the savings account. The steps that follow help you reconcile the regular checking account. Thereafter, you reconcile the payroll checking account in the *You Try* exercise that follows. *(Note: There is an online video for this topic.)*

On the Home page, click **Reconcile** under **Banking**. The reconciliation process begins by selecting the bank account.

Note: The Begin Reconciliation window always opens to the first bank account on the Chart of Accounts; therefore, you need to choose the account after opening the window. (See Figure 7.9.)

Figure 7:9

Astor has received the following March bank statement for the regular checking account. The next exercise walks through reconciling this account.

Astor Landscaping
Bank Statement March 31, 2012

Beginning Balance for March				$ 91,195.75
March Deposits				
	Mar 6, 2012		351.00	
	Mar 6, 2012		1,176.00	
	Mar 8, 2012		2,000.00	
	Mar 13, 2012		9,613.00	
	Mar 13, 2012		1,764.00	
	Mar 13, 2012		39,696.25	
	Mar 13, 2012		1,176.00	
Total Deposits for March				55,776.25
March Checks Cleared				
	Mar 1, 2012	428	19.96	
	Mar 1, 2012	429	178.10	
	Mar 2, 2012	430	888.00	
	Mar 5, 2012	431	12,550.35	
	Mar 5, 2012	432	2,500.00	
	Mar 5, 2012	433	1,416.56	
	Mar 6, 2012	434	300.00	
	Mar 6, 2012	435	207.65	
	Mar 18, 2012	436	2,563.98	
	Mar 20, 2012	437	19.96	
	Mar 20, 2012	438	97.64	
	Mar 25, 2012	440	2,857.10	
Total Cleared Checks for March				23,599.30
Less Bank Transfers	Mar 5, 2012		7,700.00	
	Mar 19, 2012		8,000.00	
Total March Transfers				15,700.00
March Service Charges				60.00
Ending Bank Balance March 31, 2012				$ 107,612.70

Figure 7:10

Steps to Reconcile the Checking Account

1. Select **10200 Regular Checking** as the Account to reconcile.

   Referring to the bank statement, enter the **Ending Balance, Date**, and **Service Charge** as shown in Figure 7.11. Verify that service charges will post to 73000 Bank Charges.

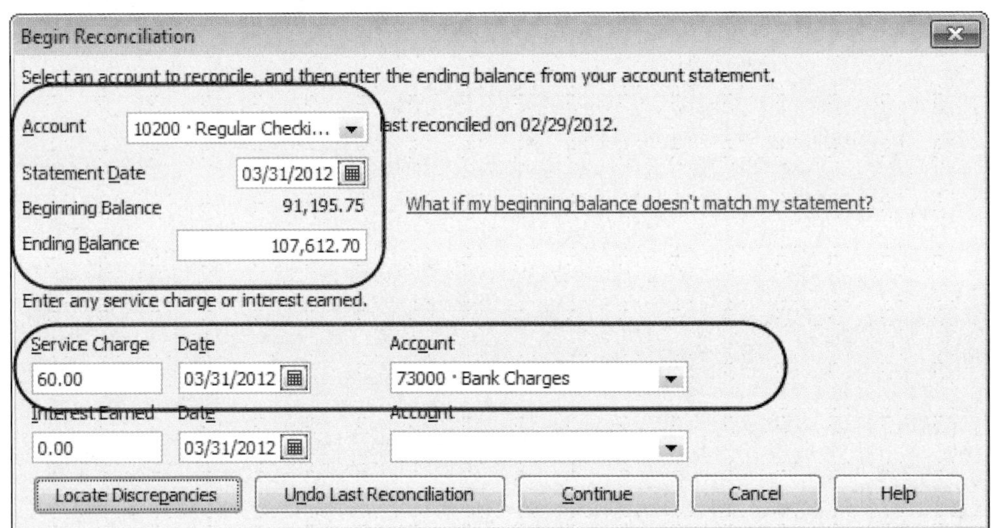

Figure 7:11

2. Click **Continue** to proceed to the screen where you mark the deposits and checks that have cleared the March bank statement.

Drag to resize columns

You can use this option if there are transactions in a subsequent month

Reconcile - Regular Checking Account

For period: 03/31/2012

Hide transactions after the statement's end date

Checks and Payments

✓	Date ▲	Chk #	Payee	Amount
	02/23/2012	428	Anderson Wholesale Nursery	19.96
	02/23/2012	429	Office Maxtors	178.10
	02/29/2012	430	VA Sales Tax Department	888.00
	03/01/2012	431	Davis Timber Yard	12,550.35
	03/01/2012	432	General Leasing Corp.	2,500.00
	03/01/2012	433	Miles Maintenance & Repair	1,416.56
	03/01/2012	434	Molly Maid Cleaning Services	300.00
	03/01/2012	435	Neighbors Telephone Company	207.65
	03/05/2012	16		7,700.00
	03/05/2012	436	Nations Bank	2,563.98
	03/15/2012	437	Anderson Wholesale Nursery	19.96
	03/15/2012	438	Southern Power Co.	97.64
	03/19/2012			8,000.00
	03/19/2012	439	Medi Benefits Adminstrators	360.00
	03/19/2012	440	Nations Bank	2,857.10
	03/19/2012	441	VA Department of Taxation	584.70
	03/19/2012	442	VA Employment Commission	607.65
	03/30/2012	443	VA Sales Tax Department	210.00
	03/31/2012	444	Petty Cash	376.26

Deposits and Other Credits

✓	Date ▲	Chk #	Memo	Type	Amount
	03/06/2012	936		PMT	351.00
	03/06/2012	9903		PMT	1,176.00
	03/08/2012	6718		PMT	2,000.00
	03/13/2012	588		PMT	9,613.00
	03/13/2012	2409		PMT	1,764.00
	03/13/2012	2418		PMT	39,696.25
	03/13/2012	9917		PMT	1,176.00

Highlight Marked | Mark All | Unmark All | Go To | Columns to Display...

Beginning Balance	91,195.75
Items you have marked cleared	
0 Deposits and Other Credits	0.00
0 Checks and Payments	0.00

Modify

Service Charge	-60.00
Interest Earned	0.00
Ending Balance	107,612.70
Cleared Balance	91,135.75
Difference	16,476.95

Reconcile Now | Leave

Figure 7:12

3. We will now explain using this window.

   Modify reopens the Begin Reconciliation window illustrated in Step 1 to adjust your entries.

   Outstanding checks and bank transfers are listed on the left. On the right are deposits and void checks.

   Clicking a transaction marks the item as cleared. *(Note: You can also click the Mark All button and then click individual checks and deposits that have not cleared.)*

   You can double click a transaction to reopen it.

   The Columns to Display button customizes data displayed in the columns.

   At the top right of the window, is the **Hide transactions after the statement's end date** option that will turn off displaying transactions in a subsequent month.

4. Click **Mark All** and refer to the totals listed at the bottom of the window. (See Figure 7.13.) The total for **Deposits** and **Other Credits** will equal the total for deposits on the bank statement. You will now work on the checks.

Figure 7:13

5. Refer back to the bank statement and click to deselect checks in the Reconcile window that have not cleared the statement. When finished, your results will compare to the results illustrated in Figure 7.14.

   The total for **Checks**, **Payments**, and **Service Charges** will equal the sum of bank transfers, service charges, and cleared checks on the bank statement.

   You cannot complete the next step until the **Difference** equals zero.

   If you have difficulty reconciling an account, the **Leave** button saves your work and closes the reconciliation window. You can return later to complete the reconciliation.

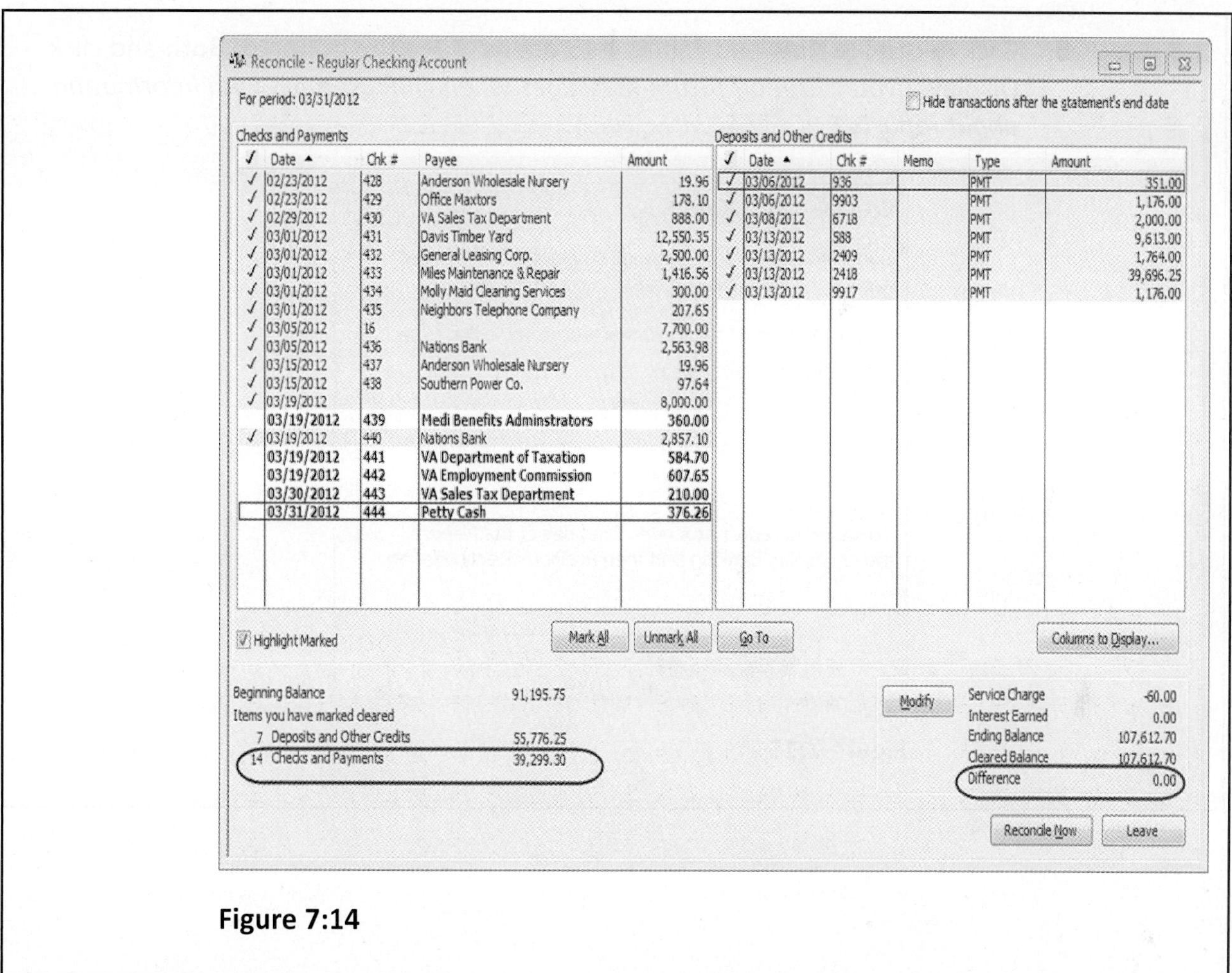
Reconcile - Regular Checking Account
For period: 03/31/2012
Hide transactions after the statement's end date
Checks and Payments
✓ Date Chk # Payee Amount
✓ 02/23/2012 428 Anderson Wholesale Nursery 19.96
✓ 02/23/2012 429 Office Maxtors 178.10
✓ 02/29/2012 430 VA Sales Tax Department 888.00
✓ 03/01/2012 431 Davis Timber Yard 12,550.35
✓ 03/01/2012 432 General Leasing Corp. 2,500.00
✓ 03/01/2012 433 Miles Maintenance & Repair 1,416.56
✓ 03/01/2012 434 Molly Maid Cleaning Services 300.00
✓ 03/01/2012 435 Neighbors Telephone Company 207.65
✓ 03/05/2012 16 7,700.00
✓ 03/05/2012 436 Nations Bank 2,563.98
✓ 03/15/2012 437 Anderson Wholesale Nursery 19.96
✓ 03/15/2012 438 Southern Power Co. 97.64
✓ 03/19/2012 8,000.00
03/19/2012 439 Medi Benefits Adminstrators 360.00
✓ 03/19/2012 440 Nations Bank 2,857.10
03/19/2012 441 VA Department of Taxation 584.70
03/19/2012 442 VA Employment Commission 607.65
03/30/2012 443 VA Sales Tax Department 210.00
03/31/2012 444 Petty Cash 376.26
Deposits and Other Credits
✓ Date Chk # Memo Type Amount
✓ 03/06/2012 936 PMT 351.00
✓ 03/06/2012 9903 PMT 1,176.00
✓ 03/08/2012 6718 PMT 2,000.00
✓ 03/13/2012 588 PMT 9,613.00
✓ 03/13/2012 2409 PMT 1,764.00
✓ 03/13/2012 2418 PMT 39,696.25
✓ 03/13/2012 9917 PMT 1,176.00
Highlight Marked
Mark All
Unmark All
Go To
Columns to Display...
Beginning Balance 91,195.75
Items you have marked cleared
7 Deposits and Other Credits 55,776.25
14 Checks and Payments 39,299.30
Modify
Service Charge -60.00
Interest Earned 0.00
Ending Balance 107,612.70
Cleared Balance 107,612.70
Difference 0.00
Reconcile Now
Leave

Figure 7:14

6. Click **Reconcile Now** and Figure 7.15 opens. Keep the option of **Both** and click **Display**. *(Note: Turn off future messages when QBP prompts with information about reports.)*

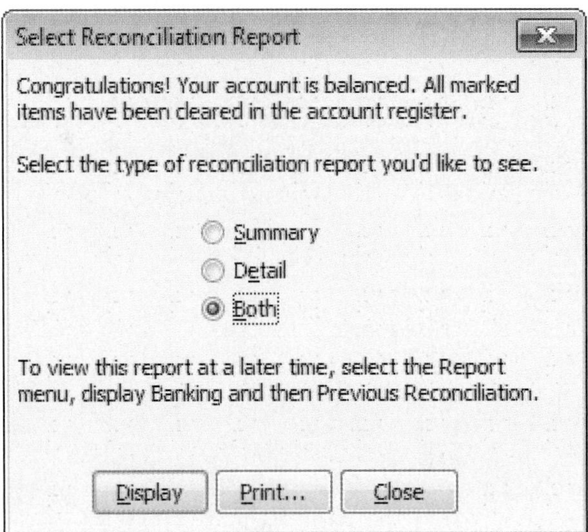

Figure 7:15

7. Figure 7.16 shows the **Reconciliation Summary** report. The **Cleared Balance** agrees with the ending balance on the March bank statement. You will not print this statement because there is no information on individual items. Close the report.

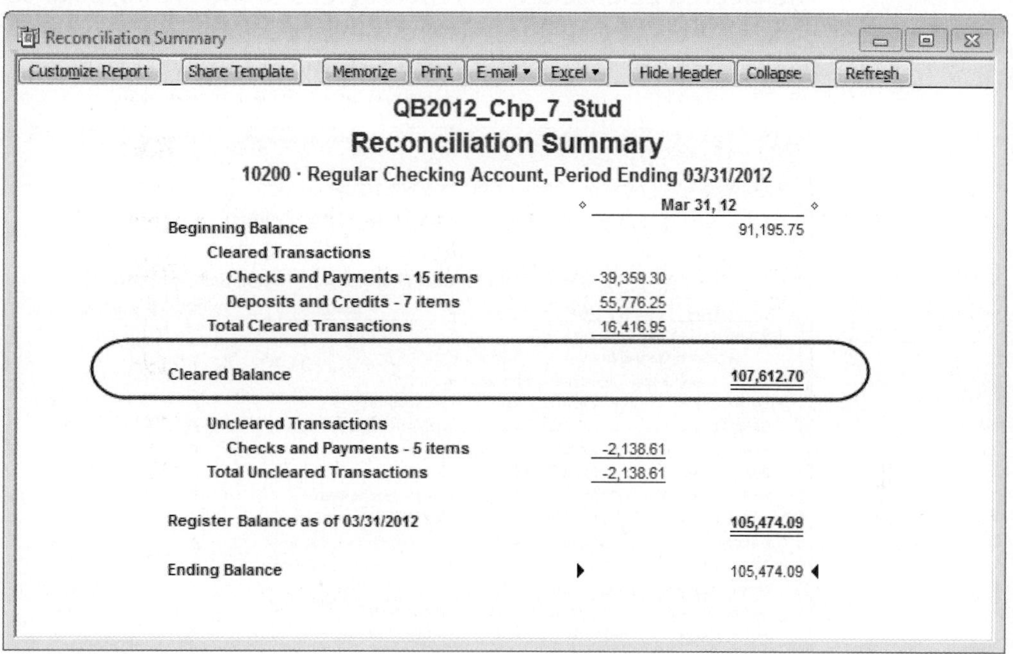

QB2012_Chp_7_Stud

Reconciliation Summary

10200 · Regular Checking Account, Period Ending 03/31/2012

		Mar 31, 12
Beginning Balance		91,195.75
Cleared Transactions		
Checks and Payments - 15 items	-39,359.30	
Deposits and Credits - 7 items	55,776.25	
Total Cleared Transactions	16,416.95	
Cleared Balance		107,612.70
Uncleared Transactions		
Checks and Payments - 5 items	-2,138.61	
Total Uncleared Transactions	-2,138.61	
Register Balance as of 03/31/2012		105,474.09
Ending Balance		105,474.09

Figure 7:16

8. You now see the **Reconciliation Detail** report, which was located behind the summary report. You will always want to print this report because it provides information on individual transactions.

   The **Cleared Balance** on the report agrees to the ending balance on the March bank statement. Beneath this are transactions that should clear on the April bank statement.

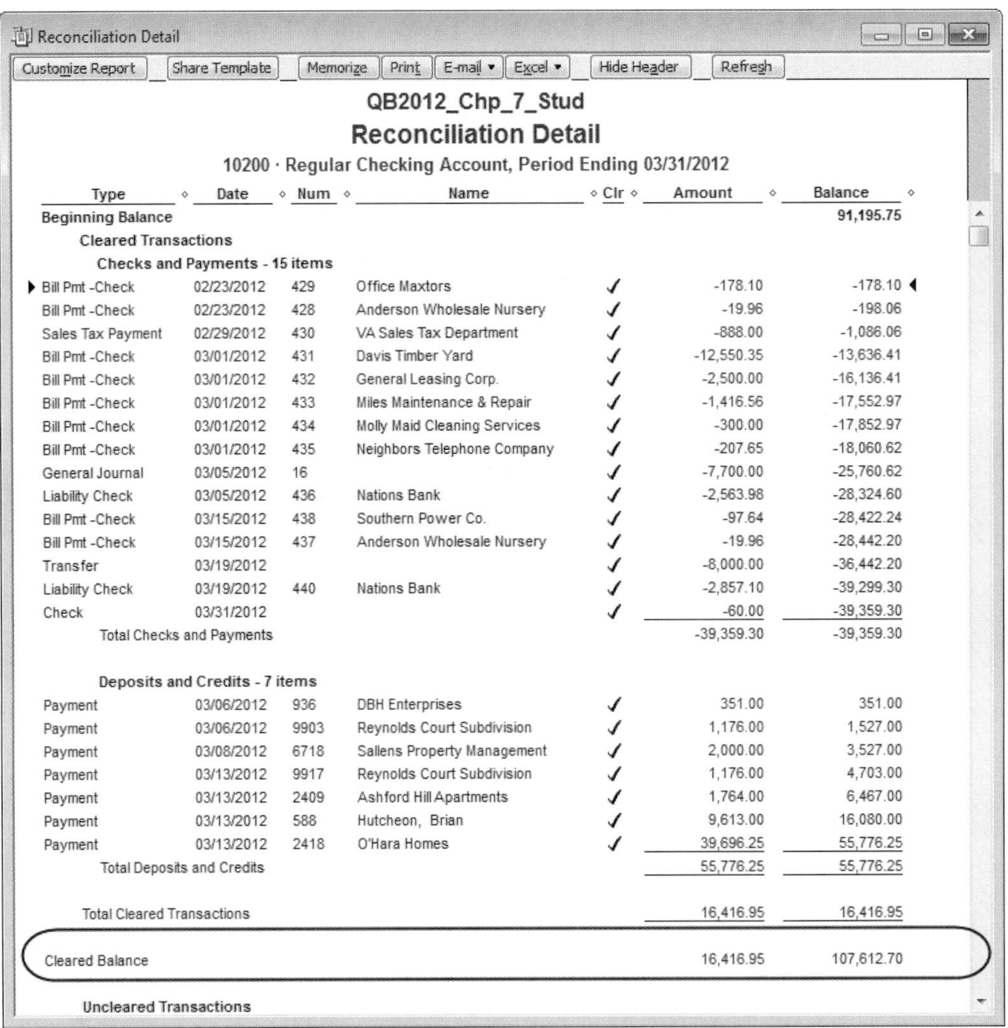

Reconciliation Detail

Customize Report | Share Template | Memorize | Print | E-mail ▾ | Excel ▾ | Hide Header | Refresh

QB2012_Chp_7_Stud

Reconciliation Detail

10200 · Regular Checking Account, Period Ending 03/31/2012

Type	Date	Num	Name	Clr	Amount	Balance
Beginning Balance						91,195.75
Cleared Transactions						
Checks and Payments - 15 items						
Bill Pmt -Check	02/23/2012	429	Office Maxtors	✓	-178.10	-178.10
Bill Pmt -Check	02/23/2012	428	Anderson Wholesale Nursery	✓	-19.96	-198.06
Sales Tax Payment	02/29/2012	430	VA Sales Tax Department	✓	-888.00	-1,086.06
Bill Pmt -Check	03/01/2012	431	Davis Timber Yard	✓	-12,550.35	-13,636.41
Bill Pmt -Check	03/01/2012	432	General Leasing Corp.	✓	-2,500.00	-16,136.41
Bill Pmt -Check	03/01/2012	433	Miles Maintenance & Repair	✓	-1,416.56	-17,552.97
Bill Pmt -Check	03/01/2012	434	Molly Maid Cleaning Services	✓	-300.00	-17,852.97
Bill Pmt -Check	03/01/2012	435	Neighbors Telephone Company	✓	-207.65	-18,060.62
General Journal	03/05/2012	16		✓	-7,700.00	-25,760.62
Liability Check	03/05/2012	436	Nations Bank	✓	-2,563.98	-28,324.60
Bill Pmt -Check	03/15/2012	438	Southern Power Co.	✓	-97.64	-28,422.24
Bill Pmt -Check	03/15/2012	437	Anderson Wholesale Nursery	✓	-19.96	-28,442.20
Transfer	03/19/2012			✓	-8,000.00	-36,442.20
Liability Check	03/19/2012	440	Nations Bank	✓	-2,857.10	-39,299.30
Check	03/31/2012			✓	-60.00	-39,359.30
Total Checks and Payments					-39,359.30	-39,359.30
Deposits and Credits - 7 items						
Payment	03/06/2012	936	DBH Enterprises	✓	351.00	351.00
Payment	03/06/2012	9903	Reynolds Court Subdivision	✓	1,176.00	1,527.00
Payment	03/08/2012	6718	Sallens Property Management	✓	2,000.00	3,527.00
Payment	03/13/2012	9917	Reynolds Court Subdivision	✓	1,176.00	4,703.00
Payment	03/13/2012	2409	Ashford Hill Apartments	✓	1,764.00	6,467.00
Payment	03/13/2012	588	Hutcheon, Brian	✓	9,613.00	16,080.00
Payment	03/13/2012	2418	O'Hara Homes	✓	39,696.25	55,776.25
Total Deposits and Credits					55,776.25	55,776.25
Total Cleared Transactions					16,416.95	16,416.95
Cleared Balance					16,416.95	107,612.70
Uncleared Transactions						

Figure 7:17

9. If you need to print the report, click the **Print** button on the report, select a printer, and click **Print**. Close the report without printing it.

You can reprint reconciliation reports by selecting ***Reports>>Banking>>Previous Reconciliation*** on the main menu. You then choose the options illustrated in Figure 7.18 and click **Display**.

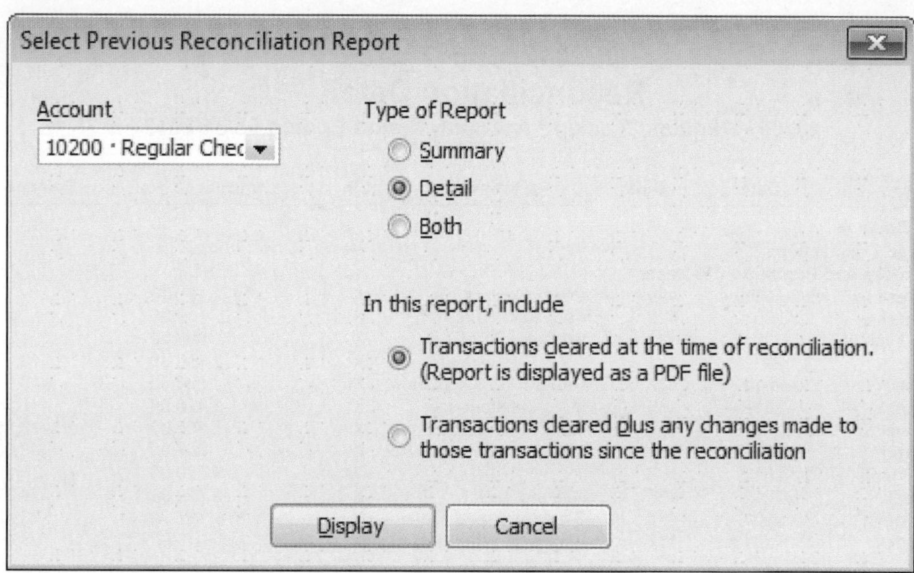

Figure 7:18

The report opens in PDF format (Figure 7.19), which can be saved to your local hard drive by selecting ***File>>Save As*** on the PDF menu. You can only print the most recent reconciliation using this method.

Close the report.

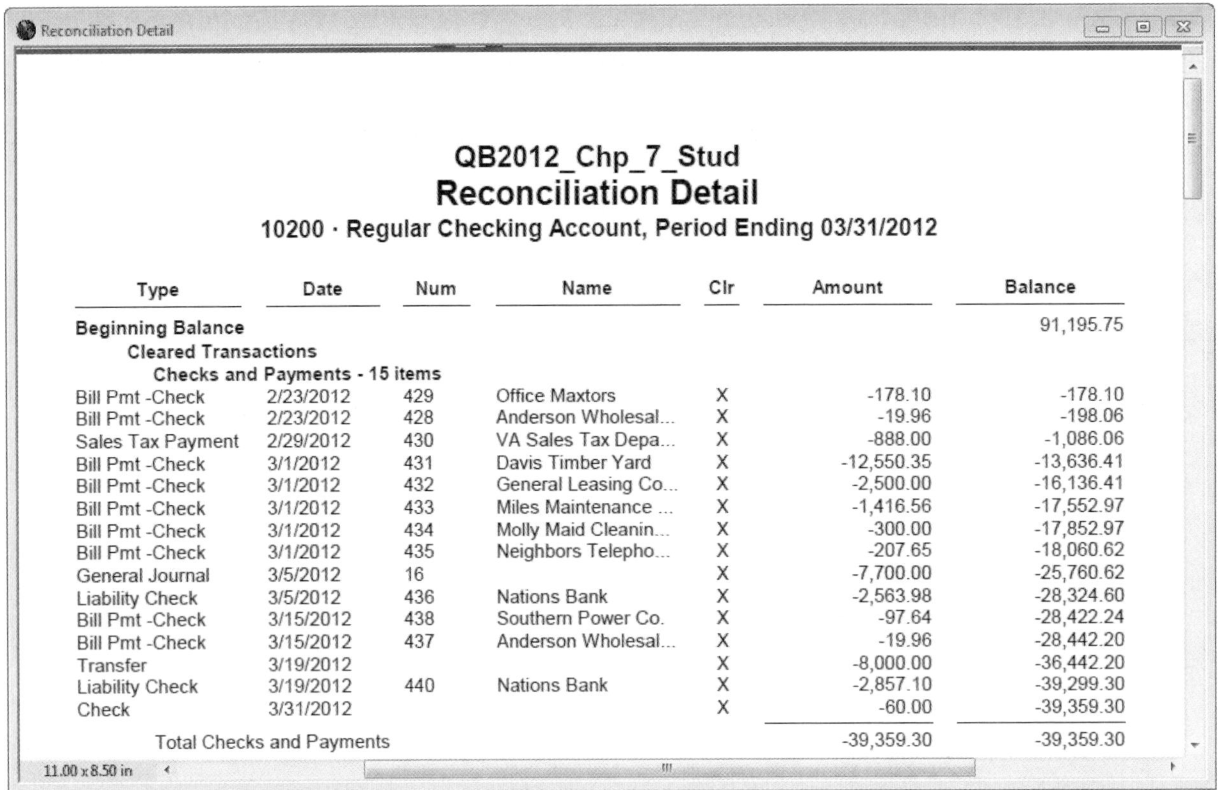
Reconciliation Detail

QB2012_Chp_7_Stud
Reconciliation Detail
10200 · Regular Checking Account, Period Ending 03/31/2012

Type	Date	Num	Name	Clr	Amount	Balance
Beginning Balance						91,195.75
Cleared Transactions						
Checks and Payments - 15 items						
Bill Pmt -Check	2/23/2012	429	Office Maxtors	X	-178.10	-178.10
Bill Pmt -Check	2/23/2012	428	Anderson Wholesal...	X	-19.96	-198.06
Sales Tax Payment	2/29/2012	430	VA Sales Tax Depa...	X	-888.00	-1,086.06
Bill Pmt -Check	3/1/2012	431	Davis Timber Yard	X	-12,550.35	-13,636.41
Bill Pmt -Check	3/1/2012	432	General Leasing Co...	X	-2,500.00	-16,136.41
Bill Pmt -Check	3/1/2012	433	Miles Maintenance ...	X	-1,416.56	-17,552.97
Bill Pmt -Check	3/1/2012	434	Molly Maid Cleanin...	X	-300.00	-17,852.97
Bill Pmt -Check	3/1/2012	435	Neighbors Telepho...	X	-207.65	-18,060.62
General Journal	3/5/2012	16		X	-7,700.00	-25,760.62
Liability Check	3/5/2012	436	Nations Bank	X	-2,563.98	-28,324.60
Bill Pmt -Check	3/15/2012	438	Southern Power Co.	X	-97.64	-28,422.24
Bill Pmt -Check	3/15/2012	437	Anderson Wholesal...	X	-19.96	-28,442.20
Transfer	3/19/2012			X	-8,000.00	-36,442.20
Liability Check	3/19/2012	440	Nations Bank	X	-2,857.10	-39,299.30
Check	3/31/2012			X	-60.00	-39,359.30
Total Checks and Payments					-39,359.30	-39,359.30

11.00 x 8.50 in

Figure 7:19

RECONCILE THE PAYROLL CHECKING ACCOUNT

The March bank statement for the payroll checking account has arrived. All paychecks and deposits have cleared. Bank charges for March are $28.30 and the ending bank statement balance is $639.49.

Reconcile the account and print the Detail Reconciliation report.

Financial Reports

You have now completed the preclosing checklist and are ready to print the trial balance and financial statements.

The trial balance is printed first so you can perform one final check of account balances. Select ***Reports>>Accountant and Taxes>>Trial Balance*** on the main menu and enter 3/31/12 as the date range. (See Figure 7.20.)

QB2012_Chp_7_Stud
Trial Balance
As of March 31, 2012

Accrual Basis

	Mar 31, 12	
	Debit	Credit
10000 · Petty Cash	48.64	
10200 · Regular Checking Account	105,474.09	
10300 · Payroll Checking Account	639.49	
10400 · Savings Account	12,184.52	
11000 · Accounts Receivable	50,482.10	
11500 · Allowance for Doubtful Accounts		5,000.00
14000 · Prepaid Expenses	950.00	
15000 · Furniture and Fixtures	11,007.00	
15010 · Accum. Depreciation-Furniture		1,980.21
15100 · Equipment	35,802.00	
15110 · Accum. Depreciation-Equipment		16,366.42
15200 · Vehicles	37,135.00	
15210 · Accum. Depreciation-Vehicles		16,665.68
19000 · Deposits	2,500.00	
20000 · Accounts Payable		22,933.43
22000 · Sales Tax Payable		270.50
23200 · Accrued Wages		9,750.00
23400 · Federal Payroll Tax Liabilities	0.00	
23500 · FUTA Tax Payable	0.00	
23600 · State Payroll Taxes Payable	0.00	
23700 · SUTA Tax Payable	0.00	
23800 · Medical Insurance Payable	0.00	
30000 · Common Stock		8,200.00
39100 · Paid-in Capital		20,000.00
39500 · Retained Earnings		107,644.03
41000 · Sales - Landscape		34,258.45
42000 · Sales - Hardscape		127,784.75
45000 · Sales - Maintenance Services		17,080.00
49000 · Sales Discounts	445.69	
51000 · Materials Cost - Landscape	2,068.18	
52000 · Materials Cost - Hardscape	40,539.45	
57000 · Direct Labor	21,710.00	
57400 · Subcontractors - Landscaping	3,000.00	
60000 · Salaries Expense	42,350.00	
60600 · Employee Benefit Expense	1,080.00	
61000 · Payroll Tax Expenses	5,451.33	
63000 · Office Supplies Expense	417.23	
63100 · Postage Expense	217.84	
66100 · Insurance - Business Expense	750.00	
66200 · Insurance - Auto Expense	300.00	
71000 · Rent Expense	7,500.00	
71100 · Utilities Expense	743.44	
71200 · Telephone Expense	746.26	
72100 · Rep & Maint - Building Expense	900.00	
72300 · Rep & Maint - Auto Expense	1,416.56	
73000 · Bank Charges	243.30	
75000 · Depreciation Expense	1,290.00	
76000 · Travel Expense	383.58	
76100 · Meals and Entertainment Exp	337.07	
80000 · Interest Income		179.30
TOTAL	388,112.77	388,112.77

Figure 7:20

In a manual accounting system, this report was critical to proving that debits equaled credits before preparing financial statements. You will recall the manual sales journal entries illustrated in Chapter 4 and how this journal was cross-footed before posting entries to customer and general ledger accounts. You also remember the manual purchasing entries in Chapter 5 and the manual payroll entries in Chapter 6. Now you understand why this report is called a "trial" balance. Imagine the number of trials it took before the books balanced because of the number of errors that could occur in a manual system. In fact, an unadjusted trial balance was prepared before posting adjusting entries and then an adjusted closing trial balance was prepared before preparing financial statements.

Today the trial balance still verifies that accounts balance; however, it more likely functions as a tool for reconciling account balances to external source documents and reports. In fact, you used the report to tie the balance on the A/R aging report back to the balance in Accounts Receivable and to tie other report balances back to the general ledger.

Close the trial balance so we can next focus on financial statements.

Open the **Report Center**. As shown in Figure 7.21, QBP refers to the Income Statement as the Profit & Loss Statement.

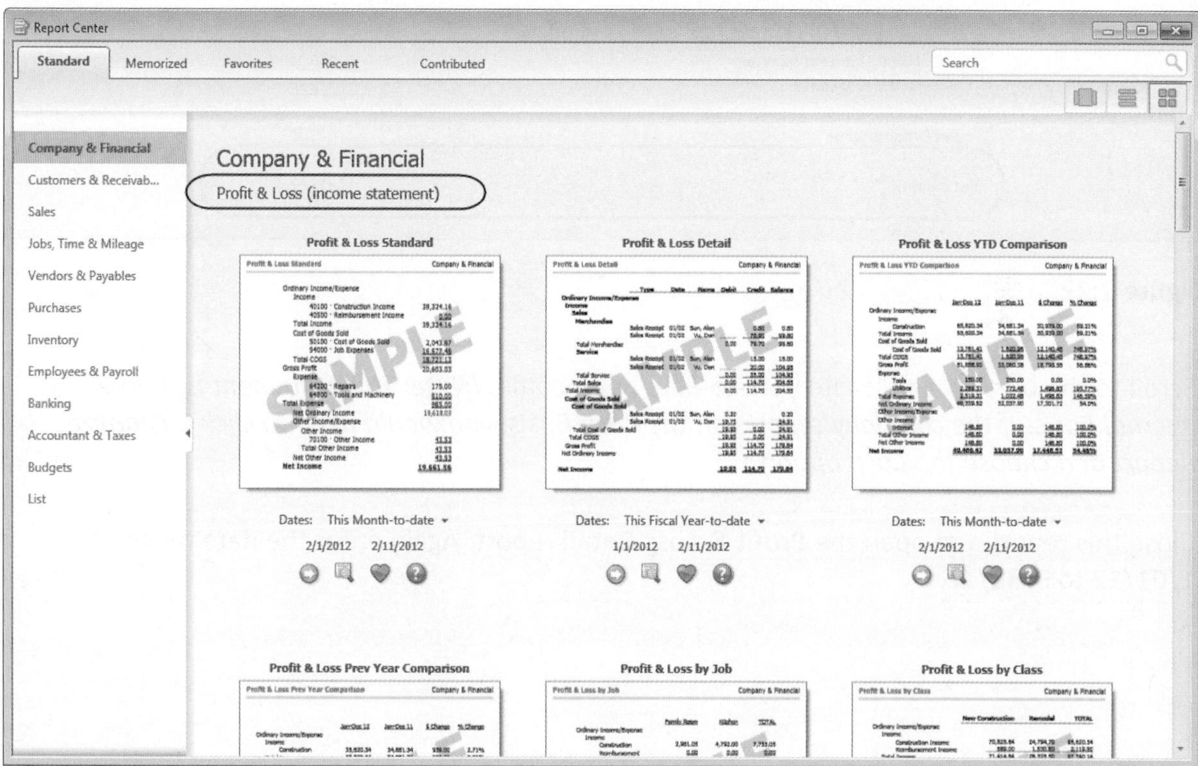

Figure 7:21

Open the **Profit & Loss Standard** statement and enter the date range of 1/01/12 to 3/31/12. (See Figure 7.22.)

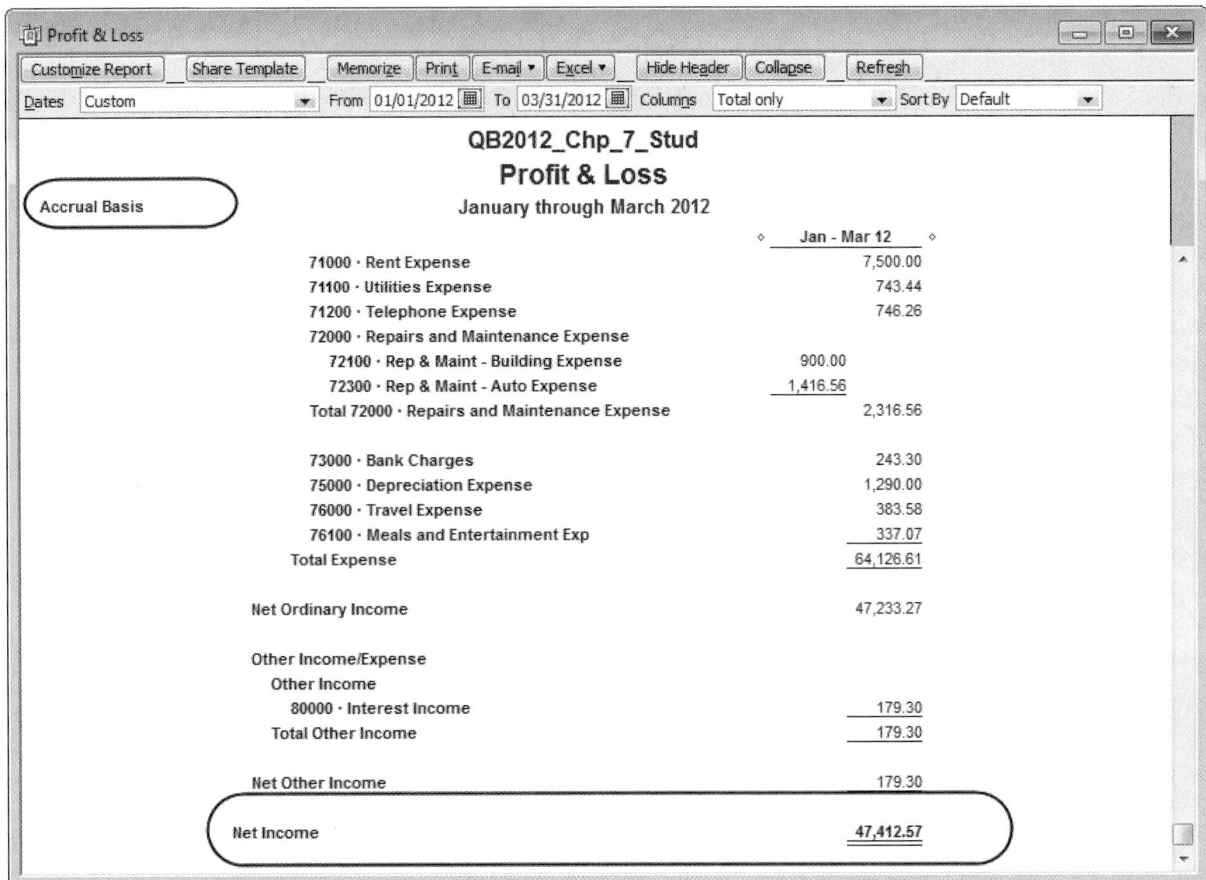

Figure 7:22

Scroll to the bottom and locate year-to-date net income. *(Note: This statement is on the Accrual Basis. If the company reports on the Cash Basis, you would need to click Customize Report and choose the Cash option.)*

Close this report and open the **Profit & Loss Detail** report. Again enter the date range of **1/01/12** to **3/31/12**.

The report in Figure 7.23 lists individual transactions affecting Income Statement accounts. Close this report.

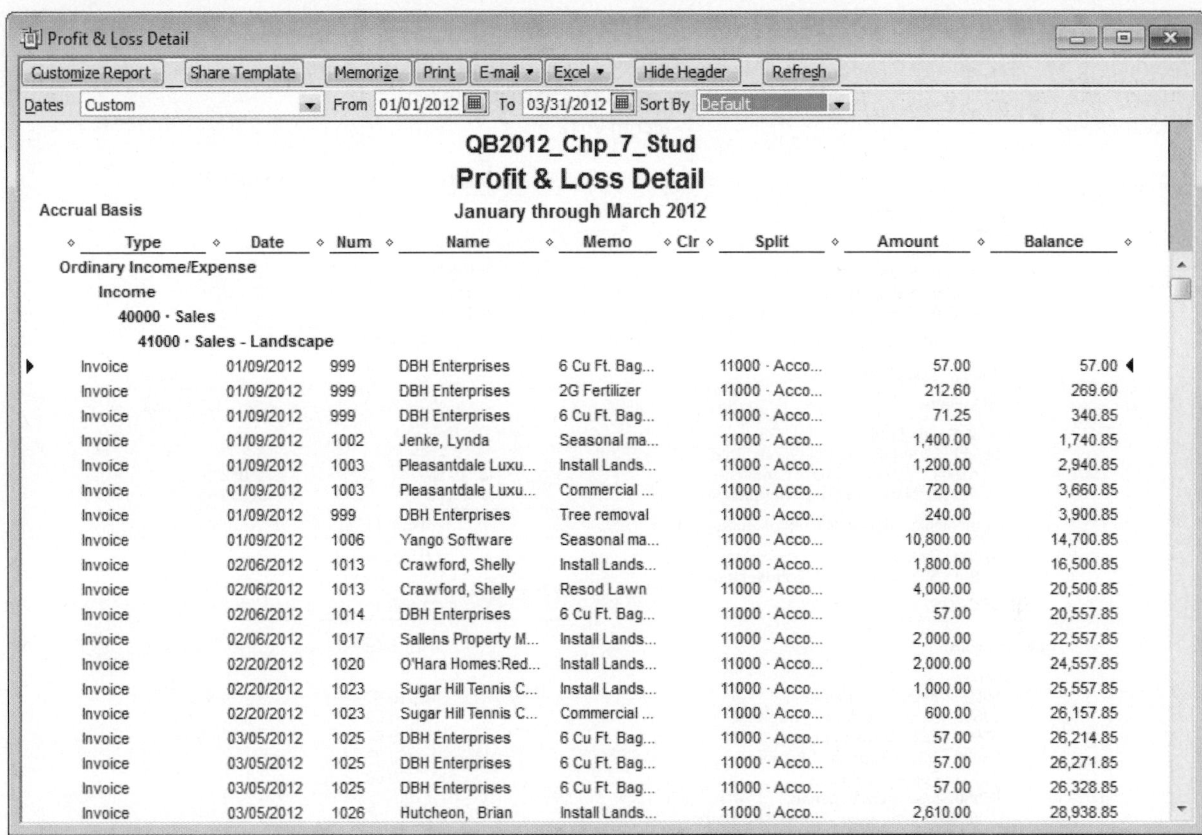

Profit & Loss Detail

Customize Report | Share Template | Memorize | Print | E-mail ▾ | Excel ▾ | Hide Header | Refresh

Dates Custom From 01/01/2012 To 03/31/2012 Sort By Default

QB2012_Chp_7_Stud

Profit & Loss Detail

Accrual Basis — January through March 2012

Type	Date	Num	Name	Memo	Clr	Split	Amount	Balance
Ordinary Income/Expense								
Income								
40000 · Sales								
41000 · Sales - Landscape								
Invoice	01/09/2012	999	DBH Enterprises	6 Cu Ft. Bag...		11000 · Acco...	57.00	57.00
Invoice	01/09/2012	999	DBH Enterprises	2G Fertilizer		11000 · Acco...	212.60	269.60
Invoice	01/09/2012	999	DBH Enterprises	6 Cu Ft. Bag...		11000 · Acco...	71.25	340.85
Invoice	01/09/2012	1002	Jenke, Lynda	Seasonal ma...		11000 · Acco...	1,400.00	1,740.85
Invoice	01/09/2012	1003	Pleasantdale Luxu...	Install Lands...		11000 · Acco...	1,200.00	2,940.85
Invoice	01/09/2012	1003	Pleasantdale Luxu...	Commercial ...		11000 · Acco...	720.00	3,660.85
Invoice	01/09/2012	999	DBH Enterprises	Tree removal		11000 · Acco...	240.00	3,900.85
Invoice	01/09/2012	1006	Yango Software	Seasonal ma...		11000 · Acco...	10,800.00	14,700.85
Invoice	02/06/2012	1013	Crawford, Shelly	Install Lands...		11000 · Acco...	1,800.00	16,500.85
Invoice	02/06/2012	1013	Crawford, Shelly	Resod Lawn		11000 · Acco...	4,000.00	20,500.85
Invoice	02/06/2012	1014	DBH Enterprises	6 Cu Ft. Bag...		11000 · Acco...	57.00	20,557.85
Invoice	02/06/2012	1017	Sallens Property M...	Install Lands...		11000 · Acco...	2,000.00	22,557.85
Invoice	02/20/2012	1020	O'Hara Homes:Red...	Install Lands...		11000 · Acco...	2,000.00	24,557.85
Invoice	02/20/2012	1023	Sugar Hill Tennis C...	Install Lands...		11000 · Acco...	1,000.00	25,557.85
Invoice	02/20/2012	1023	Sugar Hill Tennis C...	Commercial ...		11000 · Acco...	600.00	26,157.85
Invoice	03/05/2012	1025	DBH Enterprises	6 Cu Ft. Bag...		11000 · Acco...	57.00	26,214.85
Invoice	03/05/2012	1025	DBH Enterprises	6 Cu Ft. Bag...		11000 · Acco...	57.00	26,271.85
Invoice	03/05/2012	1025	DBH Enterprises	6 Cu Ft. Bag...		11000 · Acco...	57.00	26,328.85
Invoice	03/05/2012	1026	Hutcheon, Brian	Install Lands...		11000 · Acco...	2,610.00	28,938.85

Figure 7:23

Now open the **Profit & Loss YTD Comparison** report. This time enter the date range of **3/01/12** to **3/31/12** and scroll to the bottom of the report.

QB2012_Chp_7_Stud
Profit & Loss YTD Comparison
March 2012

Accrual Basis

	Mar 12	Jan - Mar 12
Ordinary Income/Expense		
Income		
40000 · Sales		
41000 · Sales - Landscape	8,100.60	34,258.45
42000 · Sales - Hardscape	40,844.00	127,784.75
45000 · Sales - Maintenance Services	4,480.00	17,080.00
Total 40000 · Sales	53,424.60	179,123.20
49000 · Sales Discounts	0.00	-445.69
Total Income	53,424.60	178,677.51
Cost of Goods Sold		
50000 · Materials Cost of Goods Sold		
51000 · Materials Cost - Landscape	19.96	2,068.18
52000 · Materials Cost - Hardscape	4,679.15	40,539.45
Total 50000 · Materials Cost of Goods Sold	4,699.11	42,607.63
57000 · Direct Labor	6,990.00	21,710.00
57400 · Subcontractors - Landscaping	0.00	3,000.00
Total COGS	11,689.11	67,317.63
Gross Profit	41,735.49	111,359.88
Expense		
60000 · Salaries Expense	16,250.00	42,350.00
60600 · Employee Benefit Expense	360.00	1,080.00
61000 · Payroll Tax Expenses	1,688.57	5,451.33
63000 · Office Supplies Expense	163.83	417.23
63100 · Postage Expense	0.00	217.84
66000 · Insurance Expense		
66100 · Insurance - Business Expense	250.00	750.00
66200 · Insurance - Auto Expense	100.00	300.00
Total 66000 · Insurance Expense	350.00	1,050.00
71000 · Rent Expense	2,500.00	7,500.00
71100 · Utilities Expense	97.64	743.44
71200 · Telephone Expense	262.43	746.26
72000 · Repairs and Maintenance Expense		
72100 · Rep & Maint - Building Expense	300.00	900.00
72300 · Rep & Maint - Auto Expense	0.00	1,416.56
Total 72000 · Repairs and Maintenance Expense	300.00	2,316.56
73000 · Bank Charges	88.30	243.30
75000 · Depreciation Expense	436.00	1,290.00
76000 · Travel Expense	103.76	383.58
76100 · Meals and Entertainment Exp	108.67	337.07
Total Expense	22,709.20	64,126.61
Net Ordinary Income	19,026.29	47,233.27
Other Income/Expense		
Other Income		
80000 · Interest Income	61.50	179.30
Total Other Income	61.50	179.30
Net Other Income	61.50	179.30
Net Income	**19,087.79**	**47,412.57**

Figure 7:24

The **Profit & Loss YTD Comparison** report compares March income to year-to-date income. As you know, the Income Statement paints a company's financial picture over a period. This report informs the owners that approximately forty percent of year-to-date income was generated in March.

QBP creates the Income Statement using general ledger account types. You will recall setting types when creating general ledger accounts in Chapter 3. You will now see these types mapped to the Income Statement.

Press **Ctrl + A** on the keyboard to open the **Chart of Accounts**. Refer to the **Profit & Loss YTD Comparison** report and the **Type** column on the **Chart of Accounts** as we explain type mapping on the Income Statement.

Income account types appear under the Income category on the statement; **Cost of Goods Sold** account types appear under Cost of Goods Sold, and so forth. Within these categories, account balances are listed individually.

Types serve the same purpose on the Balance Sheet. Close the Income Statement and open the **Balance Standard Sheet** report. (See Figure 7.25.) This statement reports a company's financial position on a specific date. Enter **3/31/12** as the date. Take the time to scroll through accounts on the Balance Sheet and compare the placement of accounts to types on the Chart of Accounts.

QB2012_Chp_7_Stud
Balance Sheet
As of March 31, 2012

Accrual Basis

	Mar 31, 12
ASSETS	
Current Assets	
Checking/Savings	
10000 · Petty Cash	48.64
10200 · Regular Checking Account	105,474.09
10300 · Payroll Checking Account	639.49
10400 · Savings Account	12,184.52
Total Checking/Savings	118,346.74
Accounts Receivable	
11000 · Accounts Receivable	50,482.10
Total Accounts Receivable	50,482.10
Other Current Assets	
11500 · Allowance for Doubtful Accounts	-5,000.00
14000 · Prepaid Expenses	950.00
Total Other Current Assets	-4,050.00
Total Current Assets	164,778.84
Fixed Assets	
15000 · Furniture and Fixtures	11,007.00
15010 · Accum. Depreciation-Furniture	-1,980.21
15100 · Equipment	35,802.00
15110 · Accum. Depreciation-Equipment	-16,366.42
15200 · Vehicles	37,135.00
15210 · Accum. Depreciation-Vehicles	-16,665.68
Total Fixed Assets	48,931.69
Other Assets	
19000 · Deposits	2,500.00
Total Other Assets	2,500.00
TOTAL ASSETS	**216,210.53**
LIABILITIES & EQUITY	
Liabilities	
Current Liabilities	
Accounts Payable	
20000 · Accounts Payable	22,933.43
Total Accounts Payable	22,933.43
Other Current Liabilities	
22000 · Sales Tax Payable	270.50
23200 · Accrued Wages	9,750.00
Total Other Current Liabilities	10,020.50
Total Current Liabilities	32,953.93
Total Liabilities	32,953.93
Equity	
30000 · Common Stock	8,200.00
39100 · Paid-in Capital	20,000.00
39500 · Retained Earnings	107,644.03
Net Income	47,412.57
Total Equity	183,256.60
TOTAL LIABILITIES & EQUITY	**216,210.53**

Figure 7:25

Close the Balance Sheet and the Chart of Accounts.

Next, open the **Statement of Cash Flows** and enter the date range of **3/01/12** to **3/31/12**.

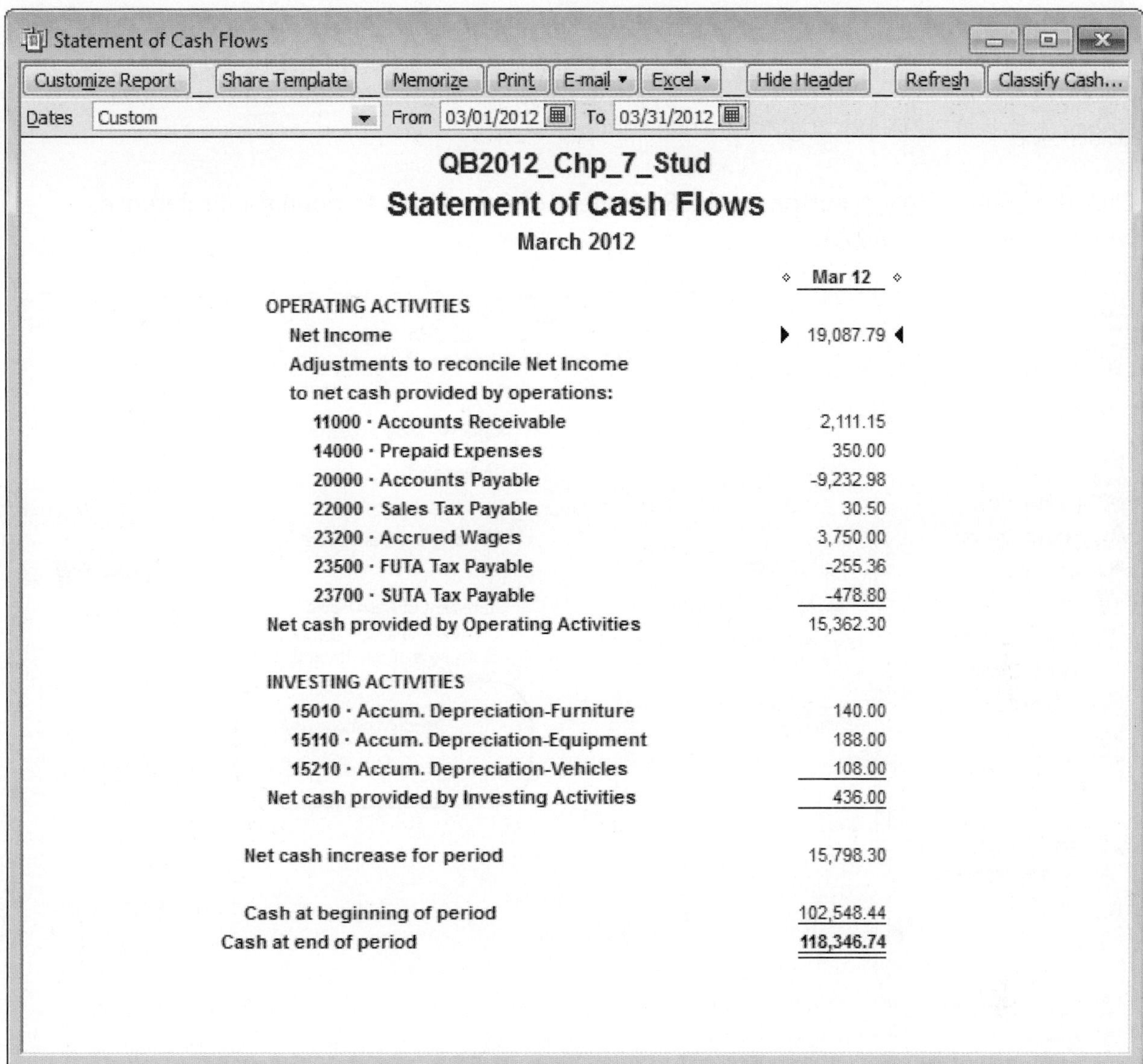
Statement of Cash Flows

Customize Report | Share Template | Memorize | Print | E-mail | Excel | Hide Header | Refresh | Classify Cash...

Dates Custom From 03/01/2012 To 03/31/2012

QB2012_Chp_7_Stud

Statement of Cash Flows

March 2012

	Mar 12
OPERATING ACTIVITIES	
Net Income	19,087.79
Adjustments to reconcile Net Income to net cash provided by operations:	
11000 · Accounts Receivable	2,111.15
14000 · Prepaid Expenses	350.00
20000 · Accounts Payable	-9,232.98
22000 · Sales Tax Payable	30.50
23200 · Accrued Wages	3,750.00
23500 · FUTA Tax Payable	-255.36
23700 · SUTA Tax Payable	-478.80
Net cash provided by Operating Activities	15,362.30
INVESTING ACTIVITIES	
15010 · Accum. Depreciation-Furniture	140.00
15110 · Accum. Depreciation-Equipment	188.00
15210 · Accum. Depreciation-Vehicles	108.00
Net cash provided by Investing Activities	436.00
Net cash increase for period	15,798.30
Cash at beginning of period	102,548.44
Cash at end of period	**118,346.74**

Figure 7:26

This may be your first exposure to the Statement of Cash Flows so we will spend some time explaining its importance.

This statement reports cash activities by operations, investing, and financing. Operating cash is generated by day-to-day activities of the business such as collecting on accounts receivable and reducing accounts payable. Investing is the cash effect of buying or selling company assets such as equipment or buildings. Finally, financing is the cash effect of borrowing or repaying loans. *(Note: Astor does not have any financing activities for this year.)*

After reviewing the report, the accountant notices that accumulated depreciation accounts are appearing under investing activities when these accounts should appear under operating activities because depreciation is a noncash activity added back to net income. Follow the next steps to correct the reporting of these accounts.

Click the Classify Cash... button on the Statement of Cash Flows to open the Preferences window. (See Figure 7:27.)

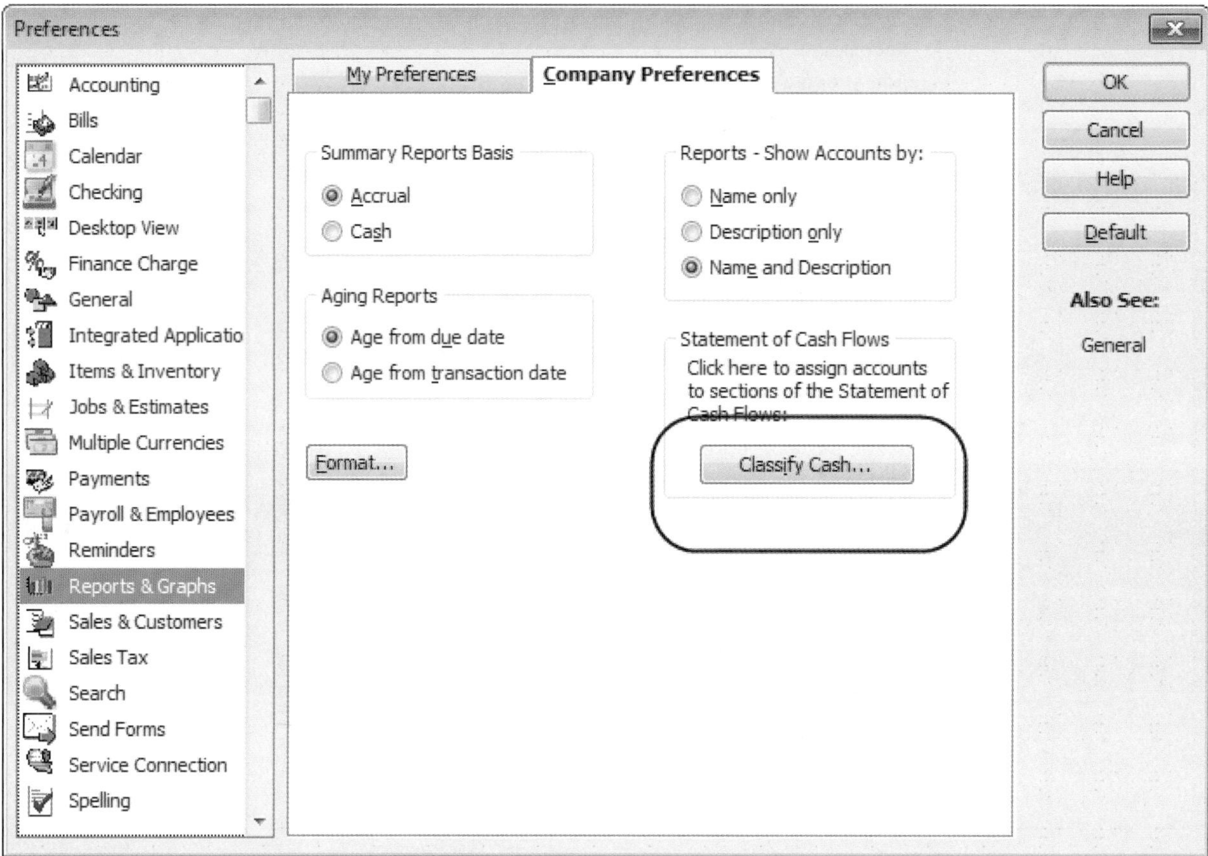

Figure 7:27

Click the **Classify Cash** button on the **Company Preferences** tab to open the window in Figure 7.28.

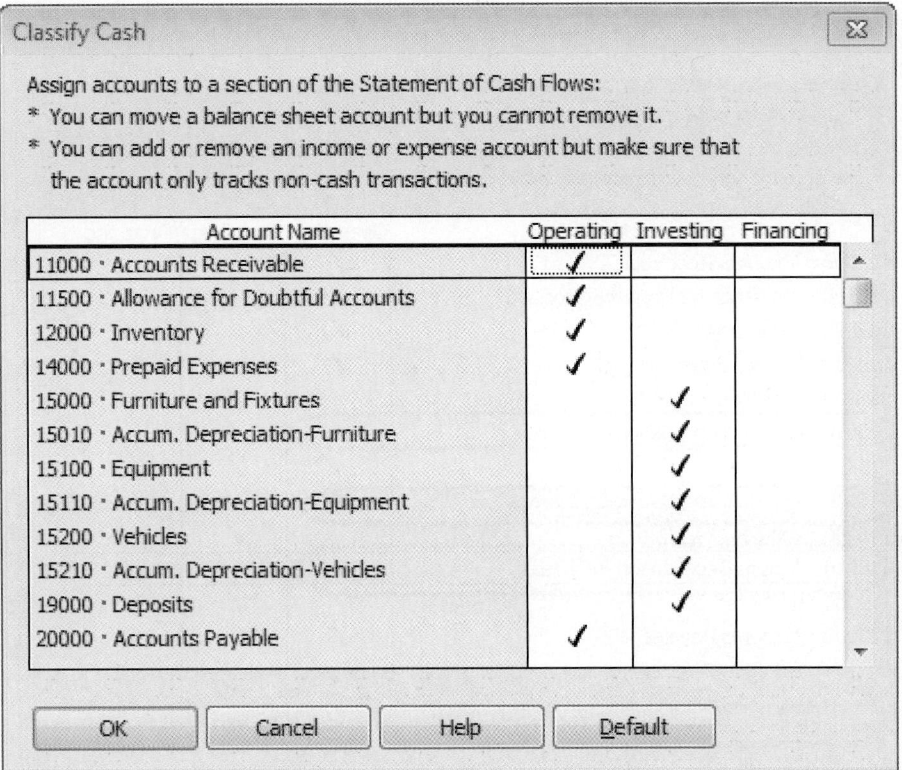

Figure 7:28

In this window, you map accounts to categories on the Statement of Cash Flows. Notice that accumulated depreciation accounts are currently mapped to the Investing category.

Click the **Operating** column on each accumulated depreciation account to move the checkmark into this category. When finished, categories are changed to those shown in Figure 7.29.

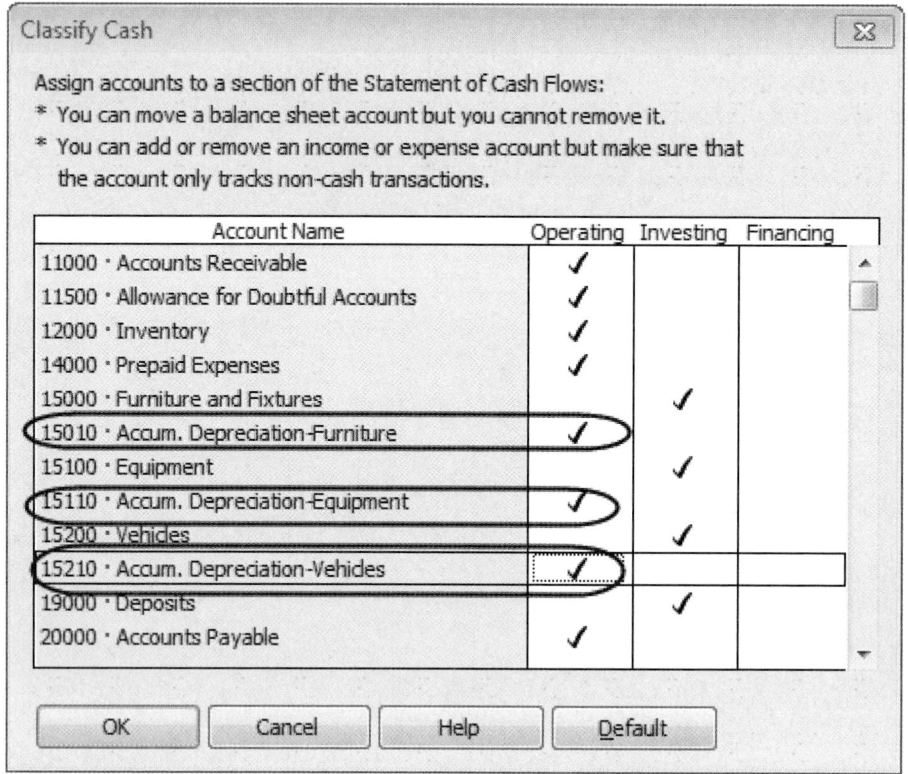

Figure 7:29

Before saving the changes, scroll down and notice that you do not map Income Statement accounts to the Statement of Cash Flows. Instead, these accounts already appear in the Net Income line of the statement.

Click **OK** to save these changes and click **OK** to close the Preferences window.

Return to the Statement of Cash Flows and note the changes. (See Figure 7.30.)

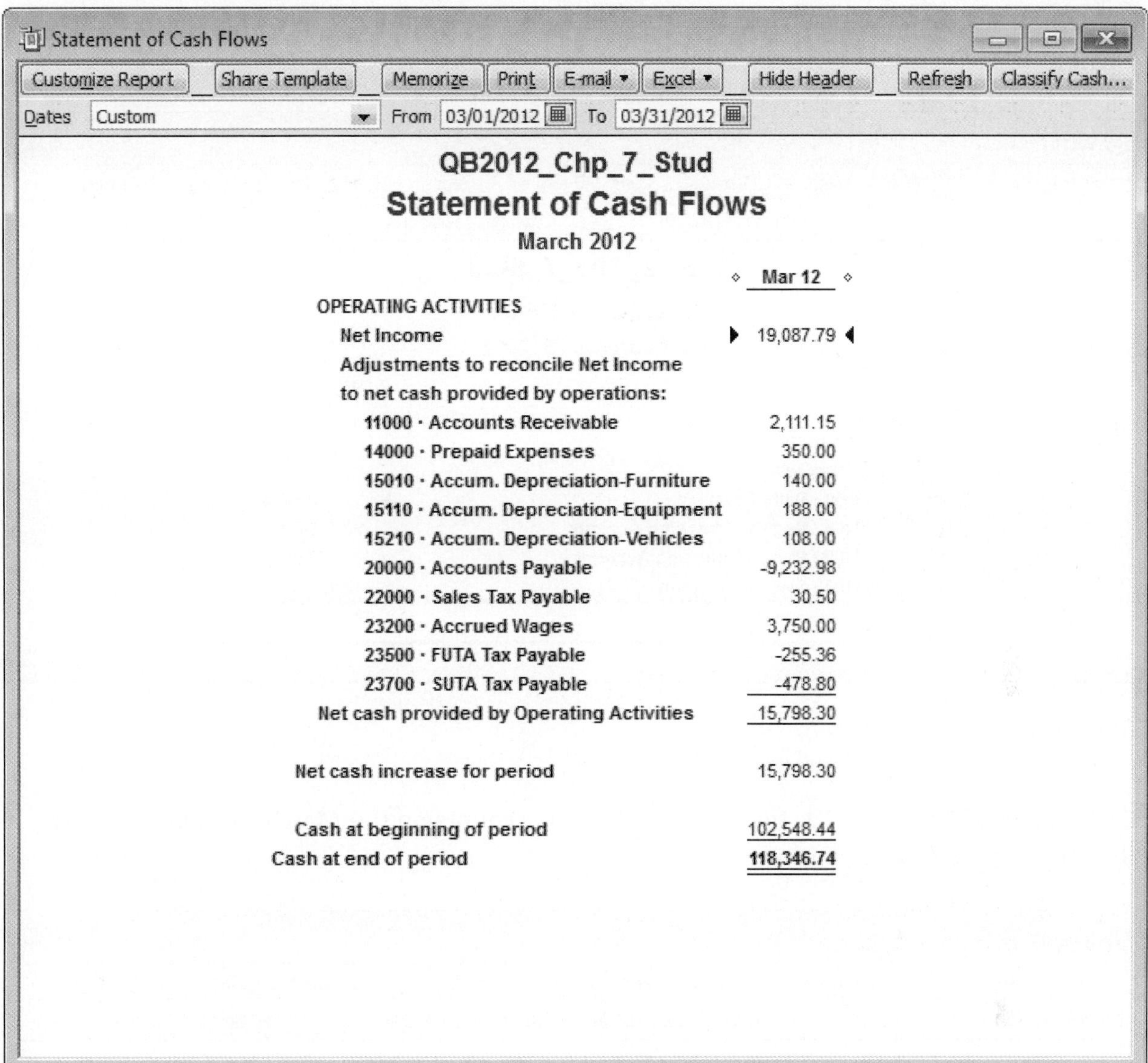

Statement of Cash Flows

Customize Report | Share Template | Memorize | Print | E-mail ▾ | Excel ▾ | Hide Header | Refresh | Classify Cash...

Dates Custom From 03/01/2012 To 03/31/2012

QB2012_Chp_7_Stud
Statement of Cash Flows
March 2012

	Mar 12
OPERATING ACTIVITIES	
Net Income	19,087.79
Adjustments to reconcile Net Income to net cash provided by operations:	
11000 · Accounts Receivable	2,111.15
14000 · Prepaid Expenses	350.00
15010 · Accum. Depreciation-Furniture	140.00
15110 · Accum. Depreciation-Equipment	188.00
15210 · Accum. Depreciation-Vehicles	108.00
20000 · Accounts Payable	-9,232.98
22000 · Sales Tax Payable	30.50
23200 · Accrued Wages	3,750.00
23500 · FUTA Tax Payable	-255.36
23700 · SUTA Tax Payable	-478.80
Net cash provided by Operating Activities	15,798.30
Net cash increase for period	15,798.30
Cash at beginning of period	102,548.44
Cash at end of period	118,346.74

Figure 7:30

We now focus on interpreting this statement. The statement begins with **Net Income** from the March Income Statement and adjusts this number to arrive at net income on a cash basis.

Noncash items, such as depreciation, are added back and the cash changes for operating asset and liability accounts are calculated to obtain the **Net cash provided by Operating Activities**. Net positive cash from operations is a critical point of analysis. Companies that continually fail to generate cash from operations will eventually need to borrow to fund day-to-day activities, such as paying employees and vendors.

Net cash flow from operations is then adjusted for cash changes from investing and financing activities to arrive at the **Net cash increase for period**. *(Note: This could be a net cash decrease.)*

Focus now on the bottom section of the report. **Cash at beginning of period** equals the February 29 total for all cash accounts on the **Balance Sheet**. (See Figure 7.31.)

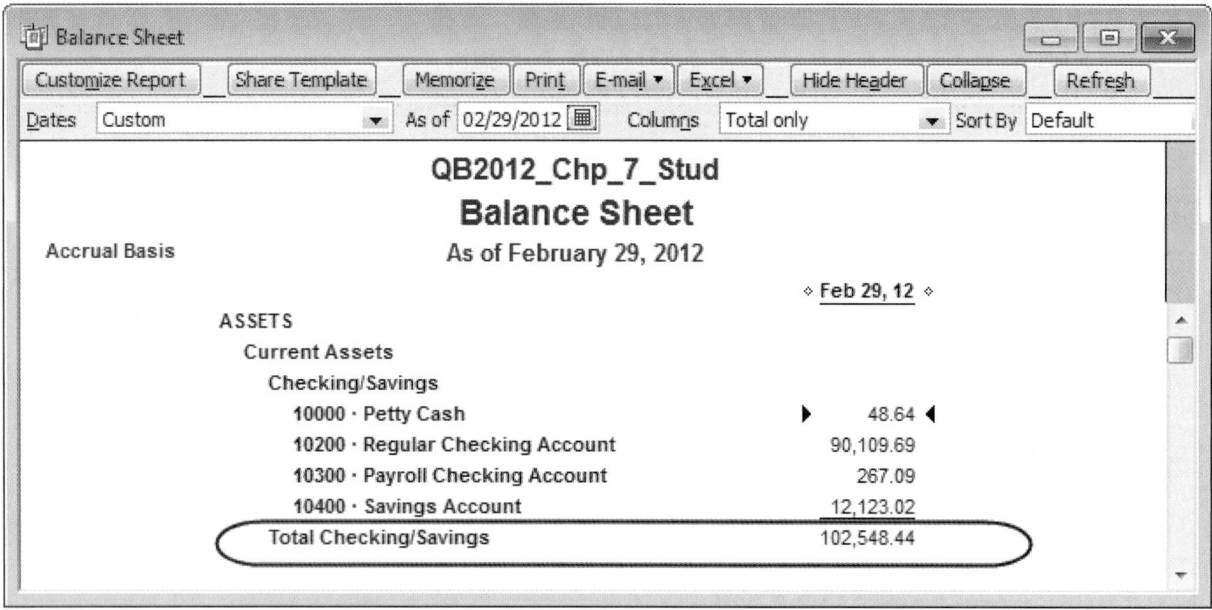

Figure 7:31

Cash at end of Period equals the total for all cash accounts on the March 31 Balance Sheet shown in Figure 7.32.

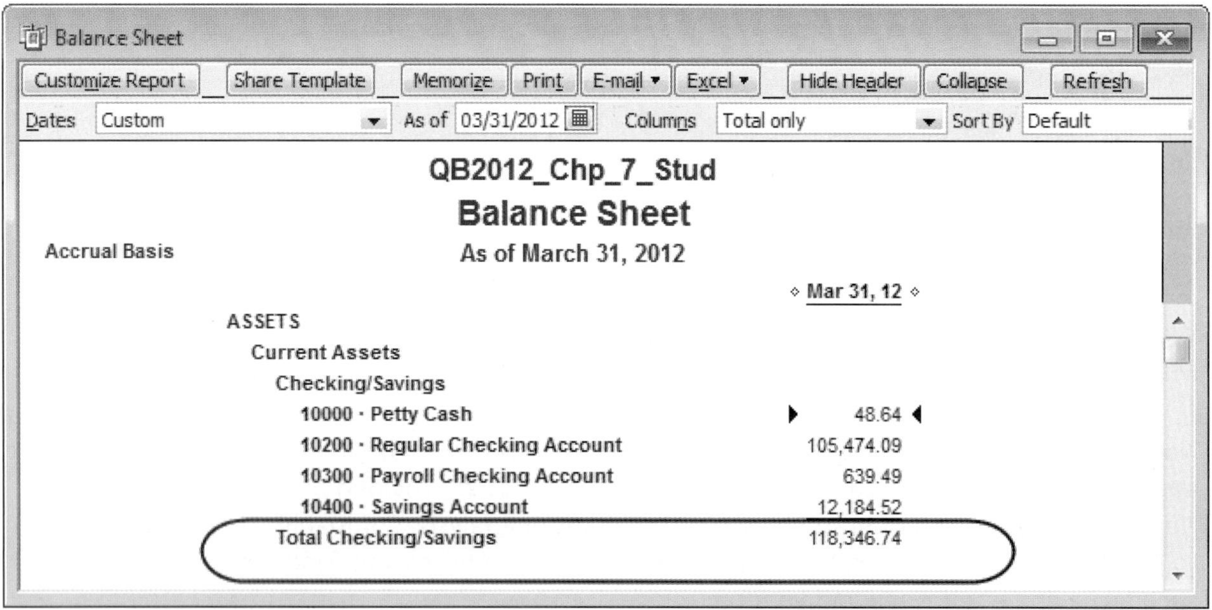

Figure 7:32

The difference between these amounts matches the **Net cash increase for period.**

Close this statement and the Report Center. After printing financial statements, you are ready to close the accounting period.

CLOSING THE ACCOUNTING PERIOD

Closing the period is important to prevent posting transactions that affect issued financial statements. You do not want to send March financial statements to owners or the bank and subsequently have an entry erroneously posted to March.

You should always back up a data file before closing the period so create a ***backup of the data file to a backup file named "QB2012_Ch7_Stud_Completed."***

Now select ***Company>>Set Closing Date*** on the main menu to open the Preferences window illustrated in Figure 7.33.

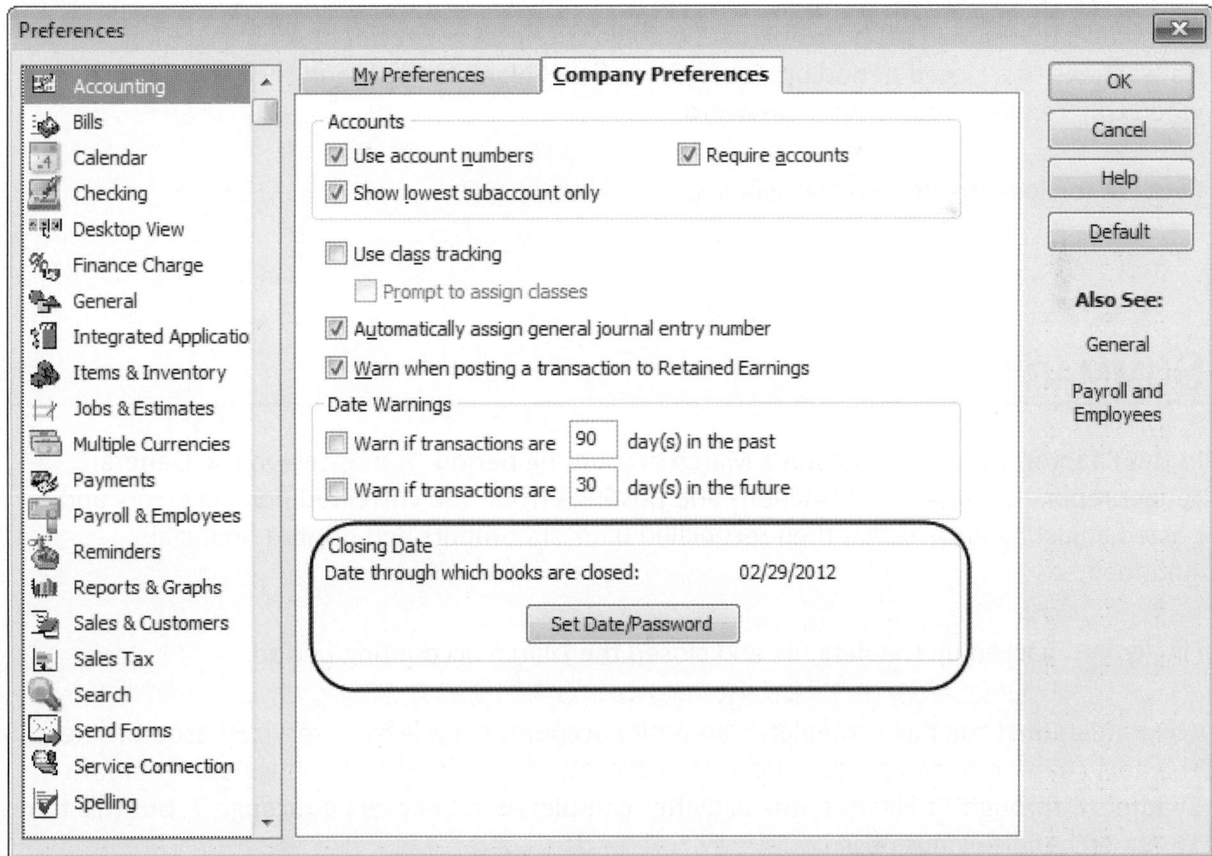

Figure 7:33

This window shows that the books are closed through February 29, 2012. Click **Set Date/Password** and enter the date illustrated in Figure 7.34.

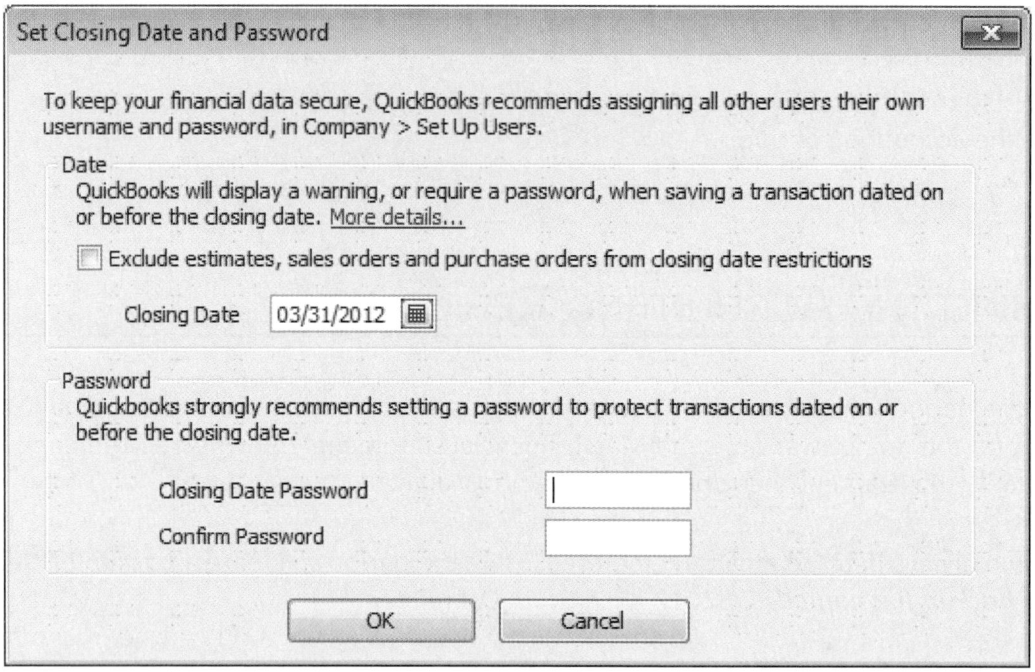

Set Closing Date and Password

To keep your financial data secure, QuickBooks recommends assigning all other users their own username and password, in Company > Set Up Users.

Date
QuickBooks will display a warning, or require a password, when saving a transaction dated on or before the closing date. More details...

Exclude estimates, sales orders and purchase orders from closing date restrictions

Closing Date 03/31/2012

Password
Quickbooks strongly recommends setting a password to protect transactions dated on or before the closing date.

Closing Date Password

Confirm Password

OK Cancel

Figure 7:34

In practice, you should set a closing date password to prevent accidentally backdating transactions to a closed period but leave these fields blank for now and click **OK**. Click **No** when QBP reminds you to set a password.

Click **OK** to close the Preferences window.

SUMMARY

In this chapter, you finalized Astor's March accounting period. You reviewed the General Ledger report for missing transactions and posting errors. You corrected posting errors and posted adjusting entries. You then reconciled bank statements and printed financial statements.

Finally, you backed up the data file and closed the March accounting period.

Congratulations! You have completed an entire accounting cycle for a service-based business. The next chapter presents a comprehensive project for a service-based business. Thereafter, Chapters 8 through 11 illustrate the activities completed in Chapters 4 through 7, but this time for a merchandising business.

End-of-Chapter Questions

TRUE/FALSE

_____ 1. Closing the accounting period prevents posting to a closed month.

_____ 2. The Statement of Cash Flows ties back to the sum of cash account balances on the Balance Sheet.

_____ 3. QBP will track fixed asset costs and calculate monthly depreciation.

_____ 4. Depreciation journal entries are usually posted by using memorized transactions.

_____ 5. The General Ledger report will let you analyze transaction details posted for the month.

_____ 6. The Transfer Funds Between Accounts window is used to record a bank transfer from one bank account to a different bank account.

_____ 7. If a journal entry posted to the wrong general ledger account, you must void the entry and post a new entry to correct the mistake.

_____ 8. The SPLIT column on the General Ledger report will display the term SPLIT when a transaction has posted to more than one general ledger account.

_____ 9. You can save time recording adjusting entries by using a memorized transaction.

_____ 10. The only time you can print a bank reconciliation report is immediately after reconciling the bank account.

MULTIPLE CHOICE

_____ 1. A company's Net Income/Net Loss will be listed on the _____ report.

a. Statement of Cash Flows
b. Income Statement
c. Statement of Retained Earnings
d. All of the above

_____ 2. The Cash Flow Statement will report changes in cash by _____.

a. Operations
b. Financing
c. Investing
d. All of the above

_____ 3. Which financial statement is a "snapshot" of financial position at a point in time?
   a. Balance Sheet
   b. Income Statement
   c. Statement of Retained Earnings
   d. Both b and c

_____ 4. To accrue utility expense, you would _____.
   a. Post a journal entry that debited accrued expense and credited utility expense.
   b. Post a journal entry that credited accrued expense and debited utility expense
   c. Post a journal entry that debited accounts payable and credited utility expense
   d. None of the above

_____ 5. Which of the following is part of preclosing procedures?
   a. Review pending transactions
   b. Post adjusting entries
   c. Reconcile account balances
   d. All of the above

_____ 6. You can open the Bank Reconciliation window using _____.
   a. The Reconcile icon on the Home page
   b. Banking>>Reconcile on the main menu
   c. The Reconciliation icon on the Home page
   d. Both a and b

_____ 7. The Banking area on the Report Center contains all the following reports, except _____.
   a. Reconcilement
   b. Deposit Detail
   c. Check Detail
   d. Missing Checks

_____ 8. All of the following statements are true, except _____.
   a. an income statement is the same as a profit and loss
   b. the income statement lists the value for total assets
   c. the statement of cash flow reports the cash inflow and outflow for a period of time
   d. the balance sheet reports the total amount for equity

PRACTICE SET

In this practice set, you will perform the activities needed to close the March and April accounting periods.

Begin by:

- Opening the software.
- Opening the **QB2012_Chp7_PracSet_Stud** data file. Add your initials to the end to the Company Name by clicking ***Company>>Company Information*** on the main menu. Click **OK** to save the changes.
- **Toggling the software to the PRO EDITION** by selecting ***File>>Toggle to Another Edition*** on the main menu and choosing **QuickBooks Pro** as the edition.

1. Record the following transactions to close the March accounting period.

2012

Mar 19	Transfer $8,500.00 from regular checking to payroll checking.
Mar 31	Reconcile the Regular Checking Account for March 31 using the statement that follows. *(Note: This statement is different from the statement illustrated in the chapter.)* Print the Detail Reconciliation report.
	Reconcile the Payroll Checking Account for March 31. The ending statement balance is $1,157.79. All March checks and deposits have cleared and the monthly bank charge is $10.00. Print the Detail Reconciliation report. *(Remember that April paychecks are in this account.)*
	Post the memorized depreciation entry using the depreciation estimates on the transaction.
	Accrue $9,000.00 for wages expense.
	Print the Balance Sheet Standard, Profit & Loss Standard, and Statement of Cash Flows for March.

Close the March accounting period.

Astor Landscaping
Bank Statement March 31, 2012

Beginning Balance for March				$ 91,195.75
March Deposits				
	Mar 6, 2012		351.00	
	Mar 6, 2012		1,176.00	
	Mar 8, 2012		2,000.00	
	Mar 13, 2012		9,613.00	
	Mar 13, 2012		1,764.00	
	Mar 13, 2012		39,696.25	
	Mar 13, 2012		1,176.00	
	Mar 28, 2012		9,480.00	
	Mar 30, 2012		2,954.25	
Total Deposits for March				68,210.50
March Checks Cleared				
	Mar 1, 2012	428	19.96	
	Mar 1, 2012	429	178.10	
	Mar 2, 2012	430	888.00	
	Mar 5, 2012	431	12,550.35	
	Mar 5, 2012	432	2,500.00	
	Mar 5, 2012	433	1,416.56	
	Mar 6, 2012	434	300.00	
	Mar 6, 2012	435	207.65	
	Mar 18, 2012	436	2,563.98	
	Mar 20, 2012	437	19.96	
	Mar 25, 2012	438	97.64	
Total Cleared Checks for March				20,742.20
Less Bank Transfers	Mar 5, 2012		7,700.00	
	Mar 19, 2012		8,500.00	
Total March Transfers				16,200.00
March Service Charges				70.00
Ending Bank Balance March 31, 2012				$ 122,394.05

2. Perform the following activities and close the April accounting period.

2012

Apr 1 Reverse the March 31 journal entry for accrued salaries for $9,000.00.

Apr 2 Transfer $7,000.00 from regular checking to payroll checking to cover paychecks printed on April 2.

Apr 16 Transfer $7,200.00 from regular checking to payroll checking to cover paychecks printed on April 16.

Apr 23 Post a journal entry for the following equipment sale:

Equipment cost: $2,300.00
Accumulated Depreciation on equipment: $ 1,100.00
Cash deposited to regular checking: $750.00

Apr 30 Post the following adjusting journal entries:

Accrued Wages $9,600.00
Expense prepaid business insurance $250.00
Expense prepaid auto insurance $100.00

Post the memorized depreciation entry after revising equipment depreciation to $190.00. Replace the previous memorized transaction.

2012

Write check 460 out of Regular Checking Account to Petty Cash for $150.00 to replenish the fund for meals and entertainment expense spent in April.

Reconcile the Regular Checking Account for April using the statement that follows. Print the Detail Reconciliation report.

Reconcile the Payroll Checking Account for April. The ending statement balance is $291.48. All checks and deposits have cleared and the monthly bank charge is $20.00. Print the Detail Reconciliation report.

Reconcile the Savings Account for April. Interest income is $63.00 and the ending balance is $12,247.52. Do not print a reconciliation report.

Print the Balance Sheet Standard, Profit & Loss Standard, and Statement of Cash Flows for April.

Create a backup file named "QB2012_Chp7_PracSet_Stud_Completed" and close the April accounting period.

Astor Landscaping
Bank Statement April 30, 2012

Beginning Balance for April				$ 122,394.05
April Deposits				
	Apr 4, 2012		2,523.00	
	Apr 4, 2012		2,352.00	
	Apr 6, 2012		1,546.50	
	Apr 12, 2012		24,561.25	
	Apr 17, 2012		21,826.00	
	Apr 23, 2012		750.00	
	Apr 25, 2012		36,587.17	
Total Deposits for April				90,145.92
April Checks Cleared				
	Apr 2, 2012	439	360.00	
	Apr 2, 2012	440	2,857.10	
	Apr 4, 2012	441	584.70	
	Apr 4, 2012	442	607.65	
	Apr 6, 2012	443	210.00	
	Apr 12, 2012	444	1,414.02	
	Apr 12, 2012	445	2,003.31	
	Apr 12, 2012	446	118.00	
	Apr 13, 2012	447	12,737.06	
	Apr 14, 2012	448	451.48	
	Apr 14, 2012	449	2,500.00	
	Apr 14, 2012	450	300.00	
	Apr 14, 2012	451	262.43	
	Apr 20, 2012	452	360.00	
	Apr 22, 2012	453	3,582.24	
	Apr 22, 2012	454	574.56	
	Apr 27, 2012	455	227.00	
	Apr 27, 2012	456	16,712.05	
	Apr 27, 2012	457	300.00	
	Apr 27, 2012	458	275.00	
Total Cleared Checks for April				46,436.60
Less Bank Transfers				
	Apr 2, 2012		7,000.00	
	Apr 16, 2012		7,200.00	
Total April Transfers				14,200.00
April Service Charges				65.00
Ending Bank Balance April 30, 2012				$ 151,838.37

PROJECT 1 COMPREHENSIVE EXAM FOR A SERVICE-BASED BUSINESS

In this exam, you will record February 2012 transactions for a company named Eragon Electrical Contracting. This is a service-based business that designs and installs electrical systems for new construction and older buildings under renovation. Eragon focuses primarily on commercial buildings although it will also perform residential work on large projects. You will be entering all transactions for the month of February, including month-end adjusting entries.

All checks received from customers are deposited into the Regular Checking Account. You will only print when instructed and will not be asked to print POs and invoices.

Begin by:

- Opening the software.
- Opening the **QB2012_Proj1_Stud** data file. Add your initials to the end to the Company Name by clicking ***Company>>Company Information*** on the main menu. Click **OK** to save the changes.
- **Toggling the software to the PRO EDITION** by selecting ***File>>Toggle to Another Edition*** on the main menu and choosing **QuickBooks Pro** as the edition.

Feb 1

Issue the following Purchase Orders (POs).

PO 1803 to Parcells Electric for $797.40 for the following items.

Qty	Item	Rate	Job
2	Switch 30 Amp	218.95	Alamo
10	Breaker 30 Amp	35.95	Red Bird

PO 1804 to RJM Electric for $1,678.00 for the following item.

Qty	Item	Rate	Job
40	Wire 100 Ft.	41.95	Fox and Hound

PO 1805 to Spade Hardware for $244.40 for the following items.

Qty	Item	Rate	Job
5	Timer Outdoor	18.96	Mendez
10	Timer Air Condition	14.96	Mendez

Enter a bill for $1,100.00 to Brays Property Management for February office and warehouse rental. Print the rent check on check number 1214.

<table>
<tr><td>Feb 2</td><td>Received bills for the following job materials.

All items on PO 1800 to Parcells Electric. Invoice 8901 for $1,048.75 dated Feb 1.

All items on PO 1801 to RJM Electrical Supplies. Invoice 23890 for $582.75 dated Feb 1.

Only five rolls of wire on PO 1802 to Spade Hardware. Invoice 109 for $209.75 dated Feb 1.</td></tr>
<tr><td></td><td>Received the remaining job materials on PO 1802 to Spade Hardware. Invoice 121 for $209.75 dated Feb 2.</td></tr>
<tr><td></td><td>Issue PO 1806 to RJM Electric for $2,517.00 for the following item.

Qty | Item | Rate | Job
60 | Wire 100 Ft. | 41.95 | Wellington</td></tr>
<tr><td></td><td>Received the following checks. (Note: Verify that checks will post to the Regular Checking Account.)

Check number 1395 for $839.00 from Fox and Hound Apartments paying Invoice 1205.

Check number 151 for $6,700.26 from Jessie Johnson paying Invoice 1203.</td></tr>
<tr><td></td><td>Pay $5,614.65 for all bills due on or before Feb 12. Print the checks starting on check number 1215.</td></tr>
<tr><td></td><td>Hired the following electrician on January 30, who is paid biweekly with hourly time ticket hours. (Note: Mark the Use time data to create paychecks option.)

James Munson
321 Park Springs Blvd.
Arlington, TX 76017
SS# 111-08-0754
Taxes: Federal is Married with two allowances and State is Texas
Pay rate: Hourly wage $35.00, Hourly wage overtime $52.50</td></tr>
</table>

<table>
<tr><td>Feb 3</td><td>Issue the following POs.

PO 1807 to Spade Hardware for $674.55 for the following items.

<table>
<tr><td>Qty</td><td>Item</td><td>Rate</td><td>Job</td></tr>
<tr><td>20</td><td>Switch Beach</td><td>14.99</td><td>Mendez</td></tr>
<tr><td>25</td><td>Switch Granite</td><td>14.99</td><td>Mendez</td></tr>
</table>

PO 1808 to Parcells Electric for $1,148.50 for the following items.

<table>
<tr><td>Qty</td><td>Item</td><td>Rate</td><td>Job</td></tr>
<tr><td>10</td><td>Breaker 50 Amp</td><td>42.95</td><td>Alamo</td></tr>
<tr><td>20</td><td>Breaker 30 Amp</td><td>35.95</td><td>Alamo</td></tr>
</table>
</td></tr>
<tr><td></td><td>Create invoice numbers 1215 through 1218 for customers with activity during the week of Jan 23 to Jan 29. Perform the following steps to identify customers for billing.

a. For labor hours, print the Time by Job Detail report. Modify the report to add the Billing Status filter and set the filter to Unbilled. Memorize the report for future use.
b. For material costs, print the Unbilled Costs by Job report.

Before creating invoices, verify that the invoice template is set to Eragon Electrical Invoice Template. In addition, when transferring employee time, select the option to Combine activities with the same service items.</td></tr>
<tr><td>Feb 4</td><td>Received bills for the following job materials.

All items on PO 1804 to RJM Electric. Invoice 24803 for $1,678.00 dated Feb 4.
All items on PO 1805 to Spade Hardware. Invoice 137 for $244.40 dated Feb 3.
All items on PO 1803 to Parcells Electric. Invoice 8975 for $797.40 dated Feb 4.</td></tr>
</table>

Feb 6

Record a vendor credit on reference number CM8975 issued by Parcells Electric for $359.50 and dated Feb 4. The credit is for returning 10 items of Breaker 30 Amp on Invoice 8975 for the Red Bird job.

Enter James Munson's time ticket for the week of Jan 30 to Feb 5. All hours are for regular time and are billable.

Service Item	Job	Hours
Residential Remodel	Mendez	8 hours Wed through Fri

Add the following hours to Vu Tran's time ticket for the week of Jan 31 to Feb 6. Hours are billable.

Service Item	Job	Hours
Commercial Installation	Fox and Hound	4 hours of overtime on Saturday

Prepare a **Time by Name** report for Jan 23 to Feb 5. Verify that 24 hours are listed for James Munson, 4 overtime hours for Vu Tran, and total time equals 348 hours.

Create paychecks for the biweekly pay period ending on Feb 5 by referring to the spreadsheets that follow. (*Hint: Enter 2/05/12 as the* ***Pay Period Ends Date.)***

Confirm that the hours selected for payment equal the hours on the Time by Name report. Print the paychecks on beginning check number 847.

Pay the liabilities from 1/01/12 to 2/06/12 for all Federal Withholding, Medicare, and Social Security taxes. Print as check number 1219 for $4,636.64 from the Regular Checking Account.

Transfer $12,300.00 from the Regular Checking Account to the Payroll Checking Account to cover payroll.

Eragon Electrical Contracting
Pay Period 1/23/2012 thru 2/05/2012

Employee	Filing Status	Allow	Pay Type	Pay Rate	Regular Hrs	OT Hrs	Gross Pay	Federal Income Tax	Soc. Sec. (FICA) Tax	Medicare Tax	Net Pay
Eragon, Ernest	Married	5	Salary	3,000.00			3,000.00	443.00	186.00	43.50	2,327.50
Hardisty, Warren	Married	2	Salary	2,500.00			2,500.00	260.00	155.00	36.25	2,048.75
Jameson, Mike	Married	2	Hourly	25.75	80.00		2,060.00	194.00	127.72	29.87	1,708.41
Munson, James	Married	2	Hourly	35.00	24.00		840.00	27.00	52.08	12.18	748.74
Rodriguez, Jamie	Married	3	Hourly	25.75	80.00		2,060.00	174.00	127.72	29.87	1,728.41
Tran, Vu	Single	1	Hourly	35.00	80.00	4.00	3,010.00	685.00	186.62	43.65	2,094.73
Wilson, Chuck	Single	1	Hourly	28.00	80.00		2,240.00	450.00	138.88	32.48	1,618.64
Totals					**344.00**	**4.00**	**15,710.00**	**2,233.00**	**974.02**	**227.80**	**12,275.18**
Tax Basis								**Circular E**	**6.20%**	**1.45%**	
G/L Accounts							**57000 / 60000**	**23400**	**23400**	**23400**	**10300**

Eragon Electrical Contracting
Employer Costs for Period 1/23/2012 thru 2/05/2012

Employee	ER Soc. Sec. (FICA)	ER Medicare	ER FUTA	ER SUTA
Eragon, Ernest	186.00	43.50	16.00	90.00
Hardisty, Warren	155.00	36.25	20.00	75.00
Jameson, Mike	127.72	29.87	16.48	61.80
Munson, James	52.08	12.18	6.72	25.20
Rodriguez, Jamie	127.72	29.87	16.48	61.80
Tran, Vu	186.62	43.65	24.08	90.30
Wilson, Chuck	138.88	32.48	17.92	67.20
Totals	**974.02**	**227.80**	**117.68**	**471.30**
Tax Basis	6.20%	1.45%	0.8%	3.0%
G/L Accounts	23400 / 61000	23400 / 61000	23500 / 61000	23700 / 61000

<table>
<tr><td rowspan="2">Feb 7</td><td>Received the following checks.

Check number 1087 for $2,280.00 from River Run Housing paying Invoice 1206.
Check number 131 for $10,104.00 from TAM Apartments paying Invoice 1204.
Check number 803 for $960.00 from Fred Thompson paying Invoice 1202.</td></tr>
<tr><td>Pay $4,648.70 for all bills due on or before Feb 19. Print checks on beginning check number 1220.</td></tr>
<tr><td rowspan="3">Feb 9</td><td>Received check number 3247 for $10,915.30 from TMI Properties paying Invoices 1200 and 1201.</td></tr>
<tr><td>Issue and print PO 1809 to Spade Hardware for $149.90 for following item.

<table><tr><td>Qty</td><td>Item</td><td>Rate</td><td>Job</td></tr><tr><td>10</td><td>Switch Beach</td><td>14.99</td><td>Fox and Hound</td></tr></table></td></tr>
<tr><td>Create invoice numbers 1219 through 1225 for customers with activity during the week of Jan 30 to Feb 5. Identify customers for invoicing by printing the reports previously illustrated.

After checking with the owner for approval, you allow Fox and Hound to exceed its credit limit.</td></tr>
<tr><td rowspan="3">Feb 11</td><td>Received bills for the following job materials.

All items on PO 1806 to RJM Electric. Invoice 24897 for $2,517.00 dated Feb 10.
All items on PO 1807 to Spade Hardware. Invoice 135 for $674.55 dated Feb 11.</td></tr>
<tr><td>Issue PO 1810 to RJM Electric for $629.25 for following item.

<table><tr><td>Qty</td><td>Item</td><td>Rate</td><td>Job</td></tr><tr><td>15</td><td>Wire 100 Ft</td><td>41.95</td><td>Red Bird</td></tr></table></td></tr>
<tr><td>Create the following vendor.

Bart's Automotive
3318 Pioneer Parkway
Arlington, TX 76019
Terms: Net 30
Account Prefill: 72300 Repairs – Auto Expenses

Enter bill number 5663 dated Feb 11 for $573.95 from Bart's Automotive for auto repairs.</td></tr>
</table>

<table>
<tr><td rowspan="3">Feb 15</td><td>Enter James Munson's time ticket for the week of Feb 6 to Feb 12. All hours are for regular time and are billable.
<table><tr><th>Service Item</th><th>Job</th><th>Hours</th></tr><tr><td>Residential Remodel</td><td>Mendez</td><td>8 hours Mon through Fri</td></tr></table></td></tr>
<tr><td>Received all items on PO 1810 to RJM Electric. Invoice 25002 for $629.25 dated Feb 15.</td></tr>
<tr><td>Create invoice numbers 1226 through 1230 for customers with activity during the week of Feb 6 to Feb 12. Identify customers for invoicing by printing the reports previously provided.

After checking with the owner for approval, you allow Jackson Property Management to exceed its credit limit.</td></tr>
<tr><td rowspan="2">Feb 18</td><td>Received check number 1192 for $7,323.95 from River Run Housing paying Invoice 1211.</td></tr>
<tr><td>Signed a contract for a new residential remodeling job for David White to begin on March 1.

Create a customer using the following information.

David White
3851 Southpark Drive
Arlington, TX 76011
Type: RESID
Terms: Net 30

Create a job using the following information.
Job Name: White Residential Remodel</td></tr>
</table>

<table>
<tr><td>Feb 20</td><td>Enter the following timesheets for the week of Feb 13 to Feb 19. All hours are billable.

<table>
<tr><th>Employee</th><th>Job</th><th>Service Item</th><th>Hours</th></tr>
<tr><td>Mike Jameson</td><td>Wellington</td><td>Design Labor</td><td>8 hours Mon through Fri</td></tr>
<tr><td rowspan="2">Jamie Rodriguez</td><td>Red Bird</td><td>Commercial Remodel</td><td>8 hours Mon through Thur</td></tr>
<tr><td>Wellington</td><td>Commercial Installation</td><td>8 hours on Fri</td></tr>
<tr><td>Vu Tran</td><td>River Run</td><td>Commercial Installation</td><td>8 hours Mon through Fri</td></tr>
<tr><td>Chuck Wilson</td><td>Fox and Hound</td><td>Commercial Installation</td><td>8 hours Mon through Fri</td></tr>
<tr><td>James Munson</td><td>Mendez</td><td>Residential Remodel</td><td>8 hours Mon through Fri</td></tr>
</table>
</td></tr>
<tr><td></td><td>Prepare a Time by Name report for Feb 6 to Feb 19. Verify that all employees worked 80 hours and total time equals 400 hours.

Create paychecks for the biweekly pay period ending on Feb 19 by referring to the spreadsheets that follow.

Confirm that the hours selected for payment equal the hours on the Time by Name report. Print the paychecks on beginning check number 854.

Pay the liabilities from 1/01/12 to 2/20/12 for all Federal Withholding, Medicare, and Social Security taxes. Print as check number 1222 for $5,275.38 from the Regular Checking Account.

Transfer $13,500.00 from the Regular Checking Account to the Payroll Checking Account to cover payroll.</td></tr>
</table>

Eragon Electrical Contracting
Pay Period 2/06/2012 thru 2/19/2012

Employee	Filing Status	Allow	Pay Type	Pay Rate	Regular Hrs	OT Hrs	Gross Pay	Federal Income Tax	Soc. Sec. (FICA) Tax	Medicare Tax	Net Pay
Eragon, Ernest	Married	5	Salary	3,000.00			3,000.00	443.00	186.00	43.50	2,327.50
Hardisty, Warren	Married	2	Salary	2,500.00			2,500.00	260.00	155.00	36.25	2,048.75
Jameson, Mike	Married	2	Hourly	25.75	80.00		2,060.00	194.00	127.72	29.87	1,708.41
Munson, James	Married	2	Hourly	35.00	80.00		2,800.00	460.00	173.60	40.60	2,125.80
Rodriguez, Jamie	Married	3	Hourly	25.75	80.00		2,060.00	174.00	127.72	29.87	1,728.41
Tran, Vu	Single	1	Hourly	35.00	80.00		2,800.00	623.00	173.60	40.60	1,962.80
Wilson, Chuck	Single	1	Hourly	28.00	80.00		2,240.00	450.00	138.88	32.48	1,618.64
Totals					**400.00**	**0.00**	**17,460.00**	**2,604.00**	**1,082.52**	**253.17**	**13,520.31**
Tax Basis								**Circular E**	**6.20%**	**1.45%**	
G/L Accounts							**57000 / 60000**	**23400**	**23400**	**23400**	**10300**

Eragon Electrical Contracting
Employer Costs for Period 2/06/2012 thru 2/19/2012

Employee	ER Soc. Sec. (FICA)	ER Medicare	ER FUTA	ER SUTA
Eragon, Ernest	186.00	43.50	0.00	0.00
Hardisty, Warren	155.00	36.25	4.00	45.00
Jameson, Mike	127.72	29.87	16.21	61.80
Munson, James	173.60	40.60	22.40	84.00
Rodriguez, Jamie	127.72	29.87	16.48	61.80
Tran, Vu	173.60	40.60	1.84	36.90
Wilson, Chuck	138.88	32.48	17.92	67.20
Totals	1,082.52	253.17	78.85	356.70
Tax Basis	6.20%	1.45%	0.8%	3.0%
G/L Accounts	23400 / 61000	23400 / 61000	23500 / 61000	23700 / 61000

<table>
<tr><td>Feb 21</td><td>Pay $2,295.40 for bills due on or before March 4. Print checks on beginning check number 1223.</td></tr>
<tr><td>Feb 23</td><td>Received the following checks.
Check number 3302 for $1,397.50 from TMI Properties paying Invoice 1214.
Check number 842 for $4,800.00 from Fred Thompson paying invoice 1213.
Check number 181 for $2,880.00 from Jessie Johnson paying Invoice 1210.</td></tr>
<tr><td></td><td>The owner asks that you increase the credit limits for Jackson Property Management to $40,000.00 and for River Run Housing, Jose Mendez, and Fox and Hound Apartments to $30,000.00.</td></tr>
<tr><td></td><td>Create invoice numbers 1231 through 1235 for customers with activity during the week of Feb 13 to Feb 19. Identify customers for invoicing by printing the reports previously illustrated.</td></tr>
<tr><td>Feb 24</td><td>Received the following checks.
Check number 6387 for $9,768.75 from Jackson Property Management paying Invoices 1208 and 1209.
Check number 1237 for $8,918.00 from Fox and Hound paying Invoice 1207.</td></tr>
<tr><td></td><td>Enter the following bills dated Feb 24.
Arlington Utilities — Feb Water — $265.00
Southwestern Bell Telephone — Feb Phone — $450.00
TXU Electric — Feb Elect — $775.00</td></tr>
</table>

<table>
<tr><td>EOM</td><td>Prepare the following end of month adjusting entries.

Refer to the Jan 31 entry and record February depreciation expense.

Refer to the Jan 31 entry and adjust prepaid expenses for expired February insurance.

Accrue $8,730.00 for wages. Reverse this entry on Mar 1.

Write check number 1226 to Cash for $141.40 to replenish petty cash fund for the following expenses.
Office Supplies Expense $38.95
Meals and Entertainment $84.50
Postage $17.95

Prepare the following bank reconciliations and print the detail reconciliation report.

Regular Checking Account statement provided next.

Payroll Checking Account statement balance is $159.51. Monthly service charge is $25.00. All checks and transfers have cleared.

Print a February Trial Balance report and review for accuracy.

Print the Aged Receivables and Aged Payables Detail reports as of Feb. 29 and reconcile Accounts Receivable and Accounts Payable account balances to the trial balance.

Print the Payroll Liability Balances report for 1/01/12 to 2/29/12. Reconcile report totals to the appropriate payroll liability accounts on the trial balance.

Print the Job Profitability Summary for February.

Print the following February financial statements.
Profit & Loss Standard
Balance Sheet Standard
Statement of Cash Flows</td></tr>
<tr><td colspan="2">Backup the company data file using the backup file name of QB2012_Proj1_Stud_Completed.</td></tr>
</table>

Eragon Electrical Contracting
Bank Statement February 29, 2012

Beginning Balance from January Statement				$ 89,159.00
February Deposits				
	Feb 2, 2012		839.00	
	Feb 2, 2012		6,700.26	
	Feb 7, 2012		960.00	
	Feb 7, 2012		2,280.00	
	Feb 7, 2012		10,104.00	
	Feb 9, 2012		10,915.30	
	Feb 18, 2012		7,323.95	
	Feb 23, 2012		1,397.50	
	Feb 23, 2012		2,880.00	
	Feb 23, 2012		4,800.00	
	Feb 24, 2012		8,918.00	
	Feb 24, 2012		9,768.75	
Total Deposits for February				66,886.76
February Checks Cleared				
	Feb 1, 2012	1205	499.65	
	Feb 1, 2012	1206	2,127.25	
	Feb 1, 2012	1207	1,679.45	
	Feb 1, 2012	1208	789.46	
	Feb 1, 2012	1209	100.00	
	Feb 1, 2012	1210	450.00	
	Feb 1, 2012	1211	750.00	
	Feb 4, 2012	1212	300.00	
	Feb 4, 2012	1213	173.85	
	Feb 4, 2012	1214	1,100.00	
	Feb 4, 2012	1215	372.25	
	Feb 4, 2012	1216	1,048.65	
	Feb 5, 2012	1217	1,048.75	
	Feb 5, 2012	1218	3,145.00	
	Feb 7, 2012	1219	4,636.64	
	Feb 7, 2012	1220	3,404.75	
	Feb 7, 2012	1221	1,243.95	
	Feb 21, 2012	1222	5,275.38	
	Feb 21, 2012	1223	1,048.75	
Total Cleared Checks for February				29,193.78
Less Bank Transfers				
	Feb 6, 2012		12,300.00	
	Feb 20, 2012		13,500.00	
Total February Transfers				25,800.00
February Service Charges				75.00
Ending Bank Balance February 29, 2012				$ 100,976.98

CHAPTER 8 CUSTOMER ACTIVITIES FOR A MERCHANDISING BUSINESS

LEARNING OBJECTIVES

In Chapter 4, you performed customer activities for a service-based business. For these types of businesses, the invoicing process centers on billing customers for the time and materials used on a job.

In this chapter, you work with a merchandising business, where invoicing centers on selling merchandise. Consequently, you will see more attention paid to inventory items. The chapter covers the following:

1. Manual accounting procedures (*MAPS*) for customer transactions
2. Using the Customer Center to perform customer-related tasks
3. Recording invoices for sales of merchandise
4. Going *Behind the Keys* to review the entries for a posted sales invoice
5. Learning procedures to correct an invoice
6. Emailing sales invoices
7. Managing customers
8. Understanding inventory items and pricing levels
9. Preparing and reviewing inventory reports
10. Taking a physical count to reconcile external inventory to the software
11. Recording inventory adjustments
12. Recording sales receipts
13. Handling sales of out-of-stock inventory
14. Recording basic customer payments
15. Going *Behind the Keys* to review the entries for a posted customer payment
16. Recording customer payments carrying a discount
17. Correcting errors after posting customer payments
18. Recording customer credits
19. Reporting on and reconciling customer activities to the general ledger
20. Writing off customer invoices
21. Preparing customer statements

In this chapter and the following three chapters, we will refer to the company you are working with as Baxter Garden Supply. This company sells garden supplies to retail and wholesale customers. The company's current accounting period is March 2012.

<u>Begin by:</u>

- Opening the software.
- Opening the **QB2012_Chp8_Stud** data file. Add your initials to the end to the Company Name by clicking ***Company>>Company Information*** on the main menu. Click **OK** to save the changes.
- **Toggling the software to the PRO EDITION** by selecting ***File>>Toggle to Another Edition*** on the main menu and choosing **QuickBooks Pro** as the edition.

MANUAL ACCOUNTING PROCEDURES

Before illustrating customer transactions in the software, we want to review the manual accounting procedures (*MAPS*) for processing customer activities. Regardless of whether an accounting system is kept manually or on a computer, the sales process begins with a customer order for merchandise.

On March 18, 2012, Knight Brothers Nurseries contacts the company salesperson, Brandee Nunnley, requesting shipment of 10 hand sprayer/misters and 15 hose-end sprayers. Brandee quotes the customer a total sales price of $294.15. She writes up a sales order, sending a copy of the order to the customer and a copy to the company accountant. She also writes up a picking ticket, sending this to the warehouse.

In the warehouse, an employee fills and ships the order. On March 22, Al Duke fills the order, indicating the quantities shipped on the picking ticket. The items are boxed with a copy of the picking ticket and the order is shipped to the customer. Another copy of the picking ticket is forwarded to the accountant.

In the accounting department, Melvin matches the picking ticket with the sales order. This matching process tells Melvin it is time to prepare the invoice illustrated in Figure 8:1.

Baxter Garden Supply
1305 Maple Ave
Arlington, VA 23523

Date: 3/22/2012

Customer:

Knight Brothers
5682 Main Street
Arlington, VA 30004

INVOICE No. 10313

Qty	Description		
10	Hand Sprayer/Mister	$	99.90
15	Hose-End Sprayer		194.25
Subtotal			294.15
Sales Tax			-
Total		$	294.15
	Terms: Net 30		

Figure 8:1

Melvin next records the invoice, along with other invoices issued that day, in the Sales Journal for March 22 (Figure 8:2).

Baxter Garden Supply

Date: 3/22/2012		**Sales Journal**			**Page 8**
Customer	**Post Ref**	**Description**	**Accounts Receivable (Debit)**	**Sales Equipment (Credit)**	**Sales Tax Payable (Credit)**
Knight Brothers	KNIG001	Invoice 10313	294.15	294.15	
Cummings Construction	CUMM001	Invoice 10314	3,768.25	3,504.47	263.78
Dash Business Systems	DASH001	Invoice 10315	4,326.00	4,023.18	302.82
Totals:			**$ 8,388.40**	**$ 7,821.80**	**$ 566.60**
Acct Ref:			**(11000)**	**(40003)**	**(23100)**

Audit Trail

Figure 8:2

Melvin entered Knight's invoice as a debit to accounts receivable and a credit to equipment sales. At day's end, Melvin totals Sales Journal columns and cross-foots the totals to verify that entries balance (i.e., debits equal credits). He then posts each invoice to the customer's account and posts column totals to the general ledger accounts noted at the bottom.

Melvin's entry to Knight's customer account is illustrated in Figure 8:3. *(Note: Entries for other customer accounts are not illustrated.)*

Knight Brothers					
5682 Main Street		*Audit Trail*			
Arlington, VA 30004				Acct No:	KNIG001
Date	**Description**	**Post Ref**	**Debit**	**Credit**	**Balance**
3/1/2012	Beginning Balance				0.00
3/22/2012	Invoice 10313	SJ 8	294.15		294.15

Figure 8:3

Melvin's entries to general ledger accounts are shown in Figure 8:4.

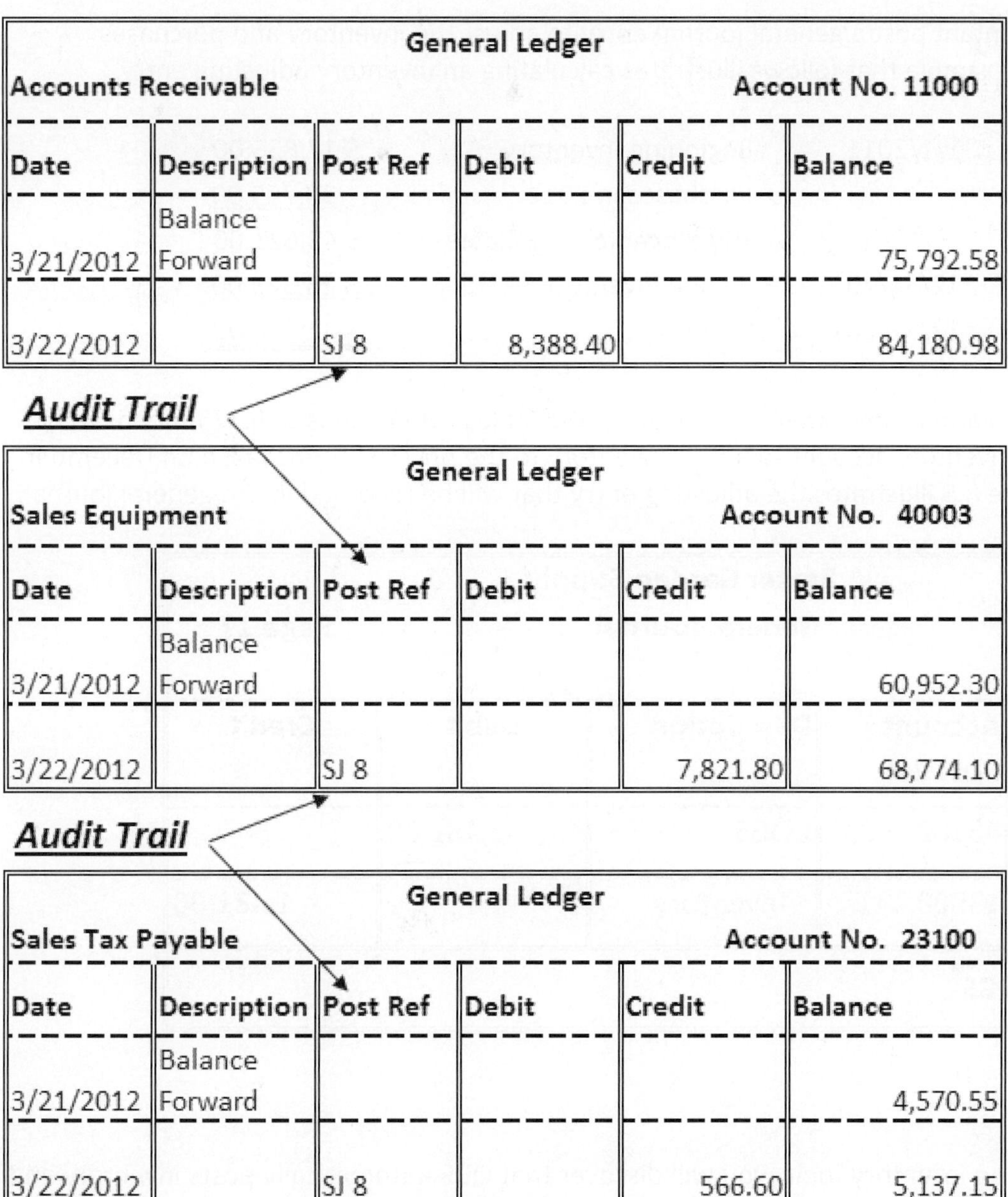

General Ledger

Accounts Receivable — **Account No. 11000**

Date	Description	Post Ref	Debit	Credit	Balance
3/21/2012	Balance Forward				75,792.58
3/22/2012		SJ 8	8,388.40		84,180.98

Audit Trail

General Ledger

Sales Equipment — **Account No. 40003**

Date	Description	Post Ref	Debit	Credit	Balance
3/21/2012	Balance Forward				60,952.30
3/22/2012		SJ 8		7,821.80	68,774.10

Audit Trail

General Ledger

Sales Tax Payable — **Account No. 23100**

Date	Description	Post Ref	Debit	Credit	Balance
3/21/2012	Balance Forward				4,570.55
3/22/2012		SJ 8		566.60	5,137.15

Figure 8:4

As Melvin posts, he is also entering the posting references that form the audit trail. An audit trail documents entries from the Sales Journal to general ledger accounts, from the Sales Journal to customer accounts, and vice versa. You can imagine the posting errors that could occur in a manual system. Melvin could record an entry backwards (e.g., enter a debit as a credit), record an out-of-balance entry, omit an entry, or forget to enter the audit trail.

Notice that Melvin did not post an entry for costs of goods sold and inventory when recording Knight's invoice because he does not know the specific cost for the items sold. In a manual system, inventory purchases are recorded to the purchases account instead of the inventory account. Only after conducting a physical inventory count to determine the quantities on hand does the accountant post a general journal entry to adjust the inventory and purchases accounts. The example that follows illustrates calculating an inventory adjusting entry.

1/1/2011	Beginning Inventory		$ 17,856.00
	Purchases in 2011	+	30,765.00
	Total Inventory Available		$ 48,621.00
12/31/2011	Ending Inventory	–	$ 16,375.00
12/31/2011	COGS		$ 32,246.00

The above calculation shows that a credit of $1,481.00 ($17,856 minus $16,375) needs to be posted to the inventory account to adjust inventory to the physical count taken on December 31, 2011. Figure 8:5 illustrates the adjusting entry that will be recorded in the general journal.

Baxter Garden Supply **General Journal**				**Page 17**
Date	**Account Post Ref**	**Description**	**Debit**	**Credit**
12/31/2011	45100	COGS	1,481.00	
	13000	Inventory		1,481.00
To record COGS				

Figure 8:5

After reading the inventory topic, you will discover that QBP automatically posts inventory and cost of goods sold entries at the time of sale (i.e., when saving an invoice).

On the same day as posting sales invoices, Melvin posts customer payments on outstanding invoices. These transactions are recorded on the Cash Receipts Journal shown in Figure 8:6.

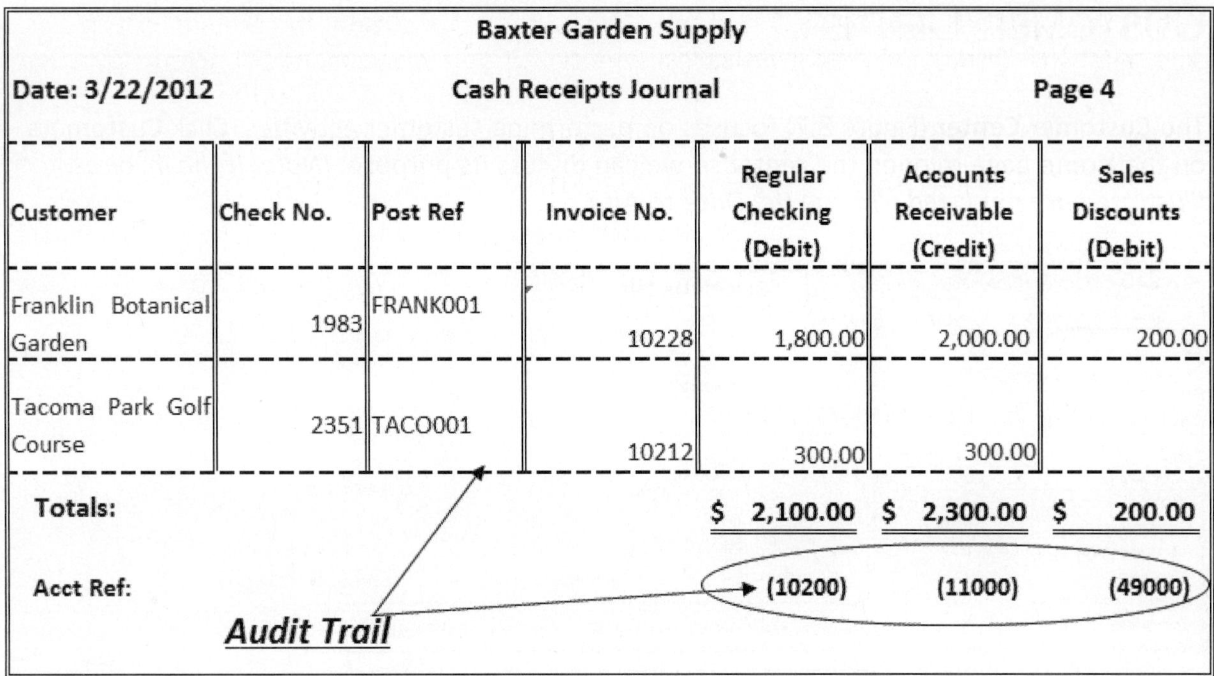

Baxter Garden Supply

Date: 3/22/2012 — Cash Receipts Journal — Page 4

Customer	Check No.	Post Ref	Invoice No.	Regular Checking (Debit)	Accounts Receivable (Credit)	Sales Discounts (Debit)
Franklin Botanical Garden	1983	FRANK001	10228	1,800.00	2,000.00	200.00
Tacoma Park Golf Course	2351	TACO001	10212	300.00	300.00	
Totals:				**$ 2,100.00**	**$ 2,300.00**	**$ 200.00**
Acct Ref:				**(10200)**	**(11000)**	**(49000)**

Figure 8:6

As with the Sales Journal, Melvin posts each check to a customer account and column totals to general ledger accounts. This time he will use the posting reference of CRJ (Cash Receipts Journal) along with the page number. *(Note: These postings are not illustrated.)*

With QBP, most posting errors are eliminated. You will see in subsequent topics that sales invoices and customer payments are posted when saving. In addition, QBP posts entries recorded in the Sales and Cash Receipts Journals to the customer's account and general ledger accounts. QBP also records the audit trail and does not post out-of-balance entries.

We next focus your attention on processing customer transactions in QBP.

Customer Center

The **Customer Center** (Figure 8:7) focuses on performing customer activities. Click **Customers** on the **Home** page to open the center so we can discuss its purpose. *(Note: If the invoices illustrated are not listed, change the **Date** to **All**.)*

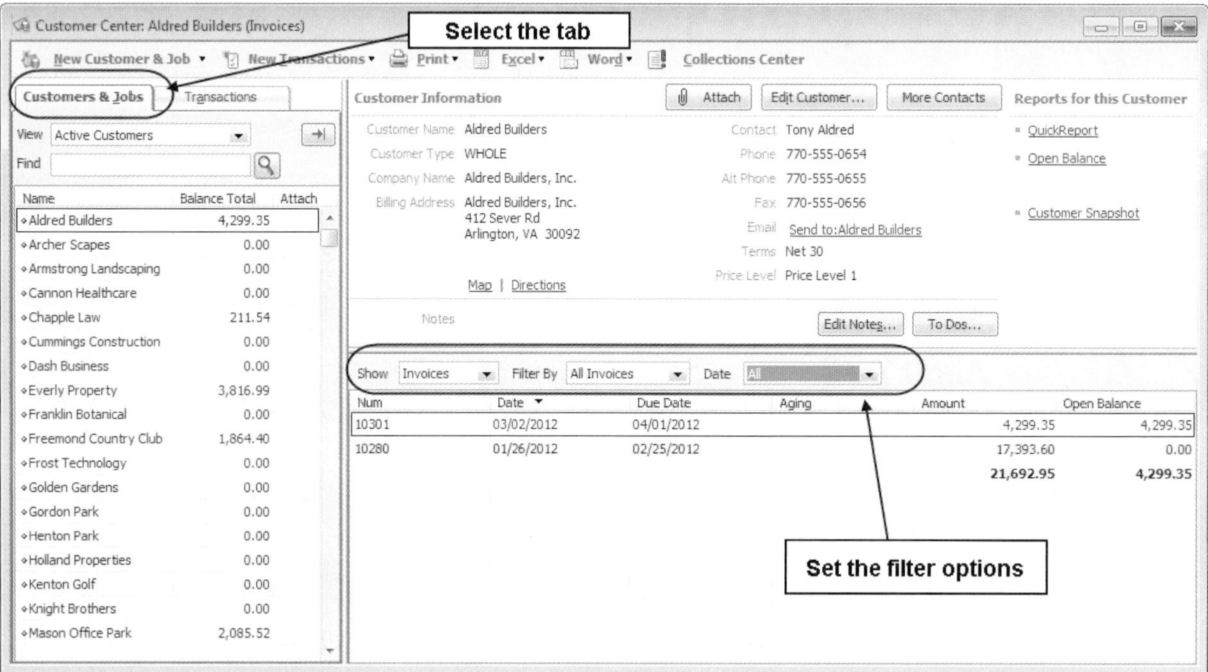

Figure 8:7

The **Customers & Jobs** tab lists transactions by customer account. Baxter's customer accounts and balances appear to the left. The **View** option will toggle accounts to All Customers, Active Customers, or Customers with Open Balances. You are currently viewing Active Customers.

This →| button hides the Customer Information pane shown to the right. After hiding, this |← button appears on the far right for redisplaying the pane.

The **Customer Information** pane displays transactions for the account highlighted on the left. This account is currently Aldred Builders.

The **Edit Customer** button opens the account for editing information. The **Edit Notes** button lets you enter account notes. There are also hyperlinks for creating **Reports for this Customer.**

Aldred's transactions are listed at the bottom of the account information. The filter options of **Show, Filter By,** and **Date** determine the transactions displayed. Click to access an option's dropdown list to change selections. You are currently viewing **Invoices** that are **All Invoices** recorded on **All** dates. *(Remember that the software refers to your computer system date when choosing the fiscal year option.)*

Filter options work as follows:

- Show: Select the transaction type to list
- Filter By: Criteria based on transaction type
- Date: List all transactions for the type or only transactions recorded as of a specific date or range of dates

Now turn your attention to the task buttons for activities that can be performed while displaying the Customers & Jobs tab. These buttons are **New Customer & Job**, **New Transactions**, **Print**, **Excel**, and **Word.**

Each button has this dropdown symbol, meaning the button lists multiple tasks. The next table discusses tasks for each button. Many of the tasks will be performed on the customer account highlighted on the left.

Customers & Jobs Activities	Task	Description
New Customer & Job	New Customer	Create a new customer account.
	Add Job and Add Multiple Customer: Jobs	Create a new job for the highlighted customer or add a new job for multiple customers.
New Transactions	Invoices	Create a sales invoice for the highlighted customer.
	Sales Receipts	Record a sales transaction for the highlighted customer. Used when the customer is paying in full at the time of sale. Do not use this task for invoicing the customer. Instead, use Invoices.
	Statement Charges	Open the highlighted customer's register and enter charges that will print on a statement. This is an alternate method for billing customers that bypasses creating an invoice. It can also be used to record finance charges. The text will not illustrate this method.
	Receive Payments	Record a payment from the highlighted customer.
	Credit Memos/ Refunds	Issue a credit to the highlighted customer or refund a customer overpayment.

Customers & Jobs Activities	Task	Description
Print	Customer & Job List	Print a customer list with balances. The report cannot be customized, so this report is usually printed from the Reports menu.
	Customer & Job Information	Print account information and notes for the highlighted customer. The report cannot be customized, so this report is usually printed from the Reports menu.
	Customer & Job Transaction List	Print the highlighted customer's transactions for the current fiscal year. The report cannot be customized, so this report is usually printed from the Reports menu.
Excel	Export Customer List	Create an Excel workbook or comma separated values (.csv) file containing account information and balances for all customers.
	Export Transactions	Create an Excel workbook or comma separated values (.csv) file containing current fiscal year transactions for the highlighted customer.
	Import from Excel and Paste from Excel	Import or paste customer information and/or transactions from an Excel workbook or comma separated values (.csv) file.
Word	Customer communications	Create form letters for customers.
Collection Center	Reviewing collection information	Opens a window with information that assists in collecting from customers.

Next, turn your attention to the **Transactions** tab, which lists transactions by type instead of by customer. Click to activate the tab and select the options illustrated next.

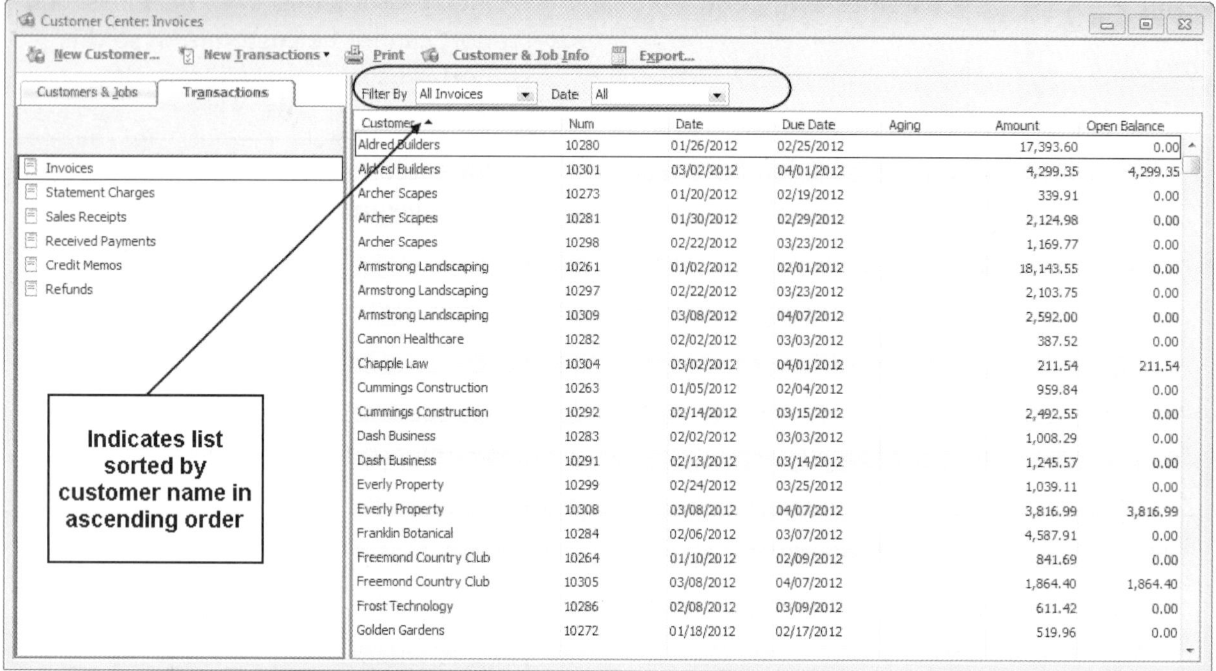

Figure 8:8

Transaction types are chosen to the left. The **Invoices** type is currently highlighted and the information displayed on the right lists **All Invoices** for **All** dates. Once again, the transactions displayed depend on the filtering options. You can also sort the list by clicking a column header.

Tasks that can be performed on this tab is active are different from those performed on the previous tab. First, not all buttons contain a dropdown list of additional tasks, so clicking a button immediately opens the task. The next table discusses tasks for the **Transactions** tab.

Button	Description
New Customer	Create a new customer account.
New Transactions	Contains the same tasks found on the Customers & Jobs tab, but this time the user selects the customer.
Print	Print transactions listed to the right.
Customer & Job Info	Edit customer and job information for the customer attached to the transaction highlighted on the right.
Export	Create an Excel workbook or comma separated values (.csv) file containing transactions listed on the right.

As illustrated, you can perform a variety of customer activities from the Customer Center. You can initiate transactions, locate posted transactions, manage accounts, and create new accounts. **Close the Customer Center.**

In contrast, the icons on the customer section of the **Home** page (Figure 8:9) only initiate transactions, but offers quicker access to tasks. In addition, you can always use the ***Customers*** menu to perform customer activities.

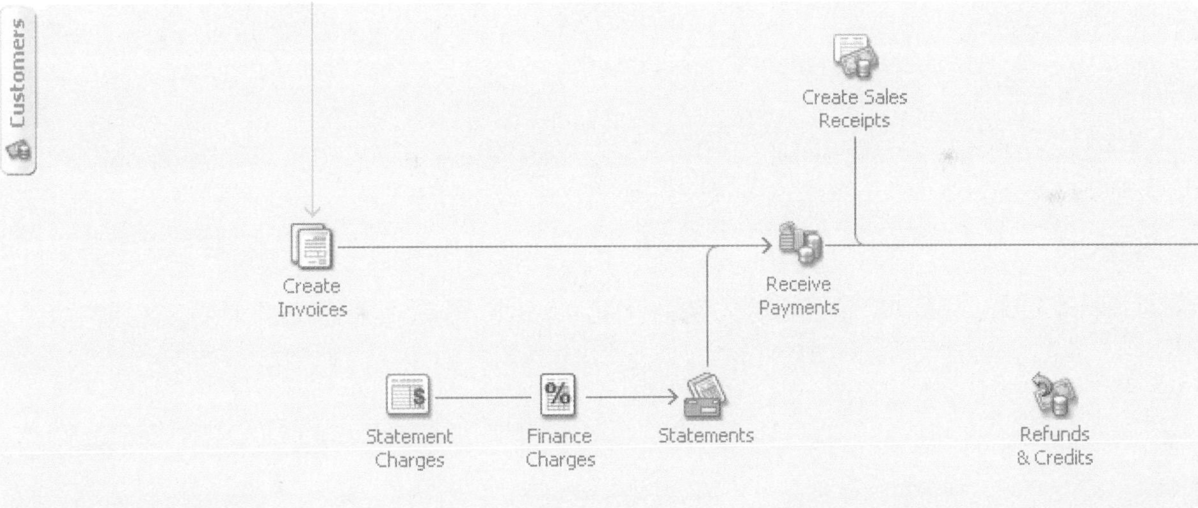

Figure 8:9

Now that you are familiar with locating customer activities, let us begin recording customer transactions.

ENTERING SALES INVOICES

Recall the Knight Brothers invoice illustrated in the *MAPS* topic. We will now record this invoice in the software. Before that, read the data entry tips that follow. *(Note: There is an online video available for this topic.)*

Data Entry Tips

Tip 1: The **Customer:Job** field links a transaction to a customer's account. The **Item** field links inventory items to a transaction. Customer accounts and items are also called master records. You will recognize a master record field because it contains lookups for selecting a record.

Tip 2: You can either click the dropdown list on the **Customer:Job** or **Item** field to select a customer or item or begin typing the name of the customer or item to make a selection.

Tip 3: If you select the wrong customer or item, return to the field and change the selection. Click **Edit** on the main menu when you want to add or delete invoice line items.

Tip 4: QBP will create new master records "on the fly," meaning a new customer or item can be created while entering a transaction. Example: A new customer can be added by typing a customer name in the **Customer:Job** field and pressing tab. QBP will then prompt with the following:

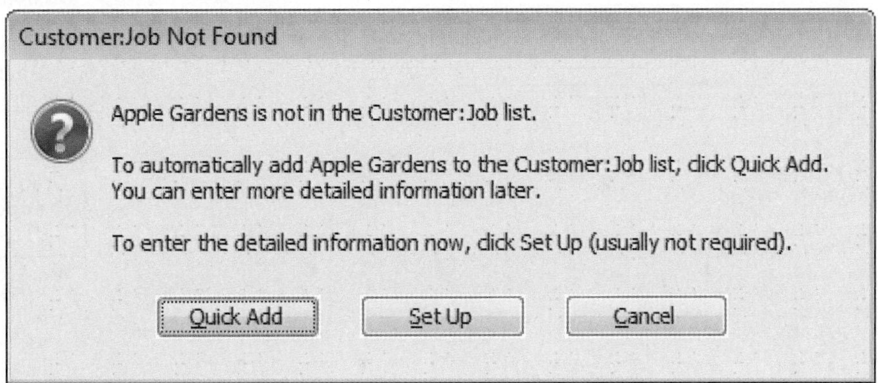

Figure 8:10

Clicking **Set Up** opens the New Customer window for entering all information on the new account. Clicking **Cancel** returns you to the Customer:Job field for selecting an existing customer. Clicking **Quick Add** creates the new account without opening the New Customer window. You will not want to Quick Add because it does not allow you to enter address or other information for the new account.

Tip 5: Figure 8:11 illustrates toolbar icons on the invoice window and a description of relevant icons follows the illustration.

Figure 8:11

Previous and **Next** scroll through posted invoices. QBP will prompt to save a new or modified transaction before moving to another transaction.

Save will save the current transaction and remain on the transaction.

Print sends the current invoice to a printer. The dropdown list for this icon contains an option for previewing an invoice before printing it and an option for printing multiple invoices.

STEPS FOR ENTERING A SALES INVOICE

1. On the **Home** page, click **Create Invoices** to open the invoice transaction window. *(Note: Click **No Thanks** if prompted about adding forms.)*

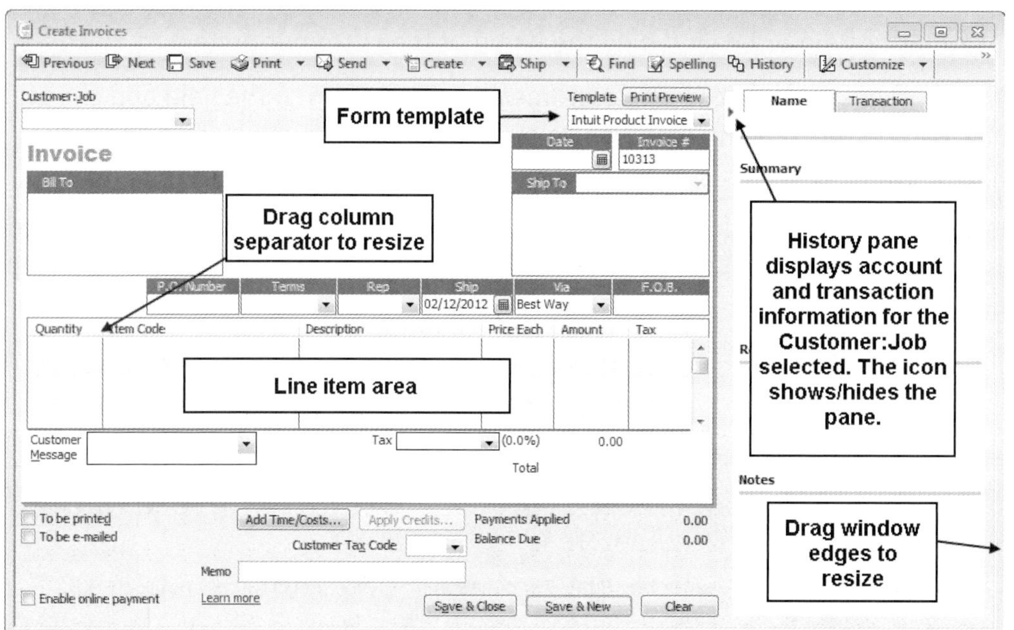

Figure 8:12

Make sure that the form template reads Intuit Product Invoice. You change the template using the dropdown list. The product invoice template sets the columns for line items and other fields displayed on the form.

To resize the window, drag the edges using the mouse. To resize line item columns, drag the column separators.

The **History** pane displays Summary information, Recent Transactions, and Notes for the customer linked to the transaction. Clicking a hyperlinked item in the pane will open additional details.

2. Place your cursor in **Customer:Job** and look up "Knight Brothers." The **Bill To, Ship To, Terms,** and **Rep** information transfers from the customer account.

3. Place your cursor in **Date.** Type "3/22/12" because this is the day the order was filled and shipped. *(Note: You can also select the date using the field's calendar icon.)*

   *(Note: The first time you open a transaction window QBP sets the transaction date to your computer date. **BE CAREFUL** and always check transaction dates before saving.)*

4. Tab to **Invoice #** and the invoice number should be "10313."

5. Place your cursor in **Quantity** on the first line item and enter "10". Press **Tab.**

6. You are now in the **Item Code** field. Use the lookup list to select "SPRAYER-HAND." Turn off future information on assigning sales taxes and click **OK.**

   (Note: QBP will open a window explaining that the sales tax code for the customer is automatically assigned, but can be changed if needed. Select the option to turn off future messages and click OK.)

   (Note: The lookup on Item Code signals that this field links to a master record in the Items table.)

7. Tab to **Quantity** on the second line item and enter "15" into the field. Tab to the **Item Code** and look up "SPRAYER-HOSE."

8. Verify that the **To be printed** option is checked. The completed invoice appears in Figure 8:13.

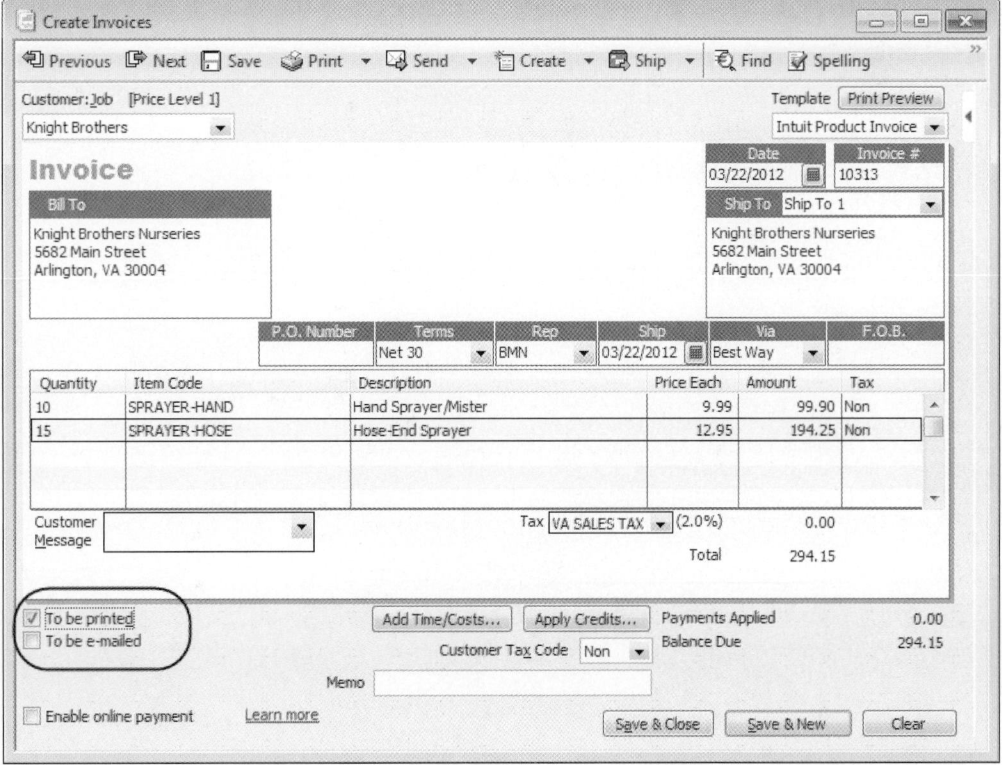

Figure 8:13

Before saving, review remaining fields in the window. You will normally not need to change data in these fields.

- **Description** and **Price Each** default from the inventory item selected.
- **Amount** equals the **Quantity** times **Price Each.**
- The **Tax** column on a line item shows whether sales tax is normally charged on the item. You can mix taxable line items with nontaxable line items.
- The **Tax** field under the line items (i.e., **VA SALES TAX**) is the sales tax rate applied to taxable line items. This rate code defaults from the customer account.
- **Customer Tax Code** shows when sales to a particular customer are taxable. If the customer is not taxable, the invoice will not compute sales tax even when line items are taxable.
- ***To be printed*** flags an invoice for printing. ***To be e-mailed*** flags it for email delivery.
- The **Apply Credits** button is used when applying outstanding customer credit memos and overpayments to the invoice.
- Text in the **Customer Message** field will appear on the printed invoice whereas text in the **Memo** field stores internal notes.

9. Click the **dropdown list** on **Print** and select **Preview** to view the invoice (Figure 8:14) before sending it to the printer.

   (Note: If prompted about shipping labels, select the option that turns off future messages and click OK.)

   Scroll to the bottom of the invoice to view the total. You can click on the invoice to enlarge it.

   Click **Close** to return to the invoice transaction.

QB2012_Chp8_Stud

1352 W. Maple Ave
Arlington, VA 23523

Invoice

Date	Invoice #
3/22/2012	10313

Bill To	Ship To
Knight Brothers Nurseries 5682 Main Street Arlington, VA 30004	Knight Brothers Nurseries 5682 Main Street Arlington, VA 30004

P.O. Number	Terms	Rep	Ship	Via	F.O.B.	Project
	Net 30	BMN	3/22/2012	Best Way		

Quantity	Item Code	Description	Price Each	Amount
10	SPRAYER-HAND	Hand Sprayer/Mister	9.99	99.90
15	SPRAYER-HOSE	Hose-End Sprayer	12.95	194.25
			Total	$294.15

Figure 8:14

10. Click **Print.** QBP saves the invoice and opens a window for selecting a printer (Figure 8:15). Use the dropdown list on **Printer name** if you need to select a different printer.

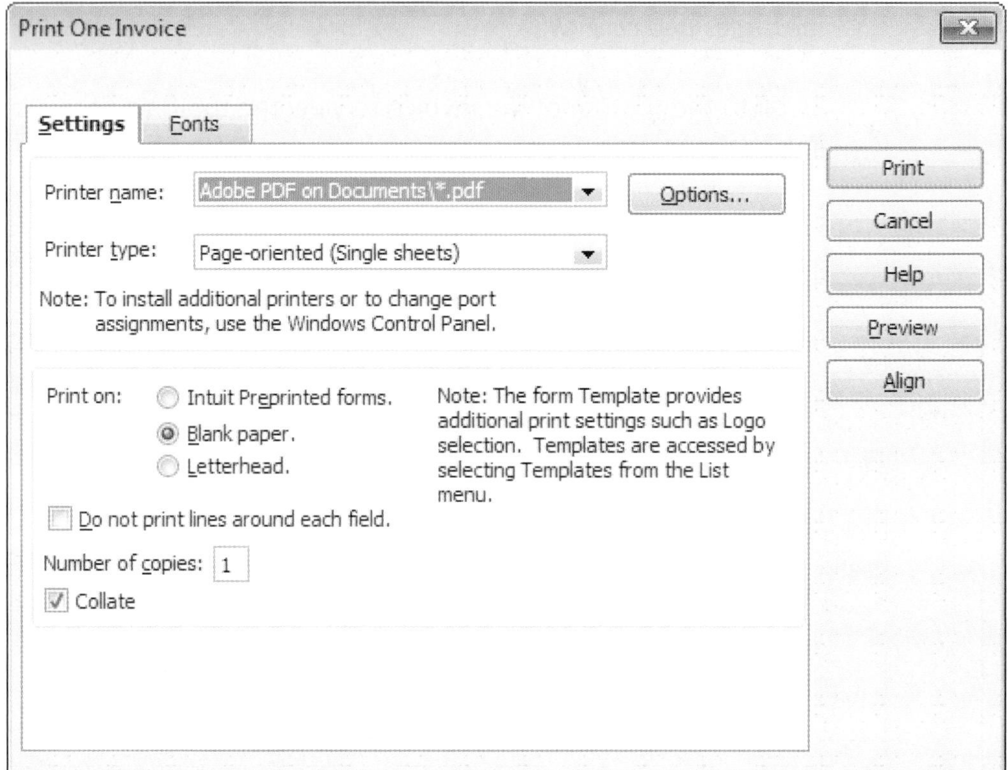

Figure 8:15

11. Click **Print** to send the invoice to the printer.

12. Click **Save & Close**. *(Note: Save & New posts the transaction and the window remains open for the next transaction.)* Click **Yes** to save changes to the transaction. The change occurred because the To be printed option is no longer checked.

In this exercise you entered a single invoice and then printed it. Normally you will enter several invoices before printing.

To print multiple invoices, click the dropdown list on the Print icon and select Print Batch. QBP then displays every invoice marked ☑ To be printed. You then click to choose the invoices to print.

To reprint an invoice, reopen the invoice and click **Print.**

Behind the Keys of a Posted Sales Invoice

In this topic, you will trace QBP's audit trail by locating the entries made when posting Knight Brothers' invoice. Remember that the audit trail in a manual system referenced the Sales Journal and the page number. Let us see how that compares with QBP'S audit trail.

Trace the Audit Trail of a Posted Sales Invoice

1. First, open the Sales Journal by selecting ***Reports>>Memorized Reports>>Accounting Journals>>Sales Journal*** on the main menu.

2. Enter the date range of **3/22/12** through **3/22/12.**

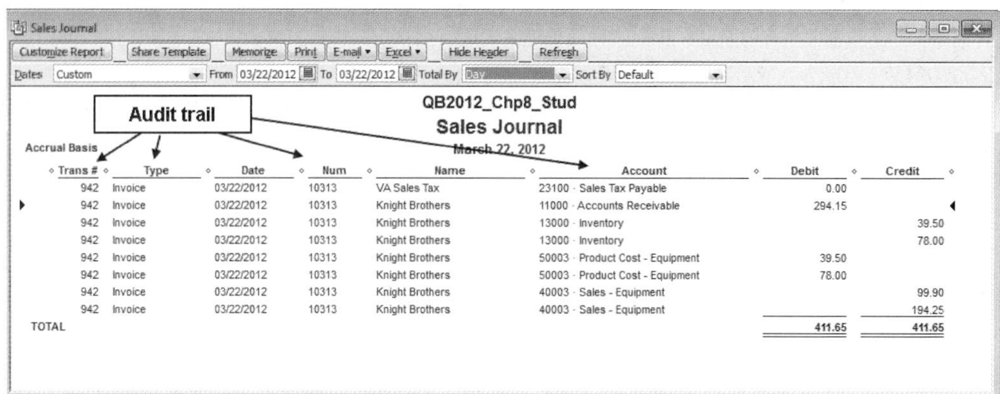

QB2012_Chp8_Stud
Sales Journal
March 22, 2012

Trans #	Type	Date	Num	Name	Account	Debit	Credit
942	Invoice	03/22/2012	10313	VA Sales Tax	23100 · Sales Tax Payable	0.00	
942	Invoice	03/22/2012	10313	Knight Brothers	11000 · Accounts Receivable	294.15	
942	Invoice	03/22/2012	10313	Knight Brothers	13000 · Inventory		39.50
942	Invoice	03/22/2012	10313	Knight Brothers	13000 · Inventory		78.00
942	Invoice	03/22/2012	10313	Knight Brothers	50003 · Product Cost - Equipment	39.50	
942	Invoice	03/22/2012	10313	Knight Brothers	50003 · Product Cost - Equipment	78.00	
942	Invoice	03/22/2012	10313	Knight Brothers	40003 · Sales - Equipment		99.90
942	Invoice	03/22/2012	10313	Knight Brothers	40003 · Sales - Equipment		194.25
TOTAL						411.65	411.65

Figure 8:16

Recall that manual sales journal entries debited 11000 Accounts Receivable and credited 40003 Sales - Equipment for $294.15. Although QBP recorded sales entries to the same accounts, it posted each line item as a separate sales entry. QBP also posted cost of goods sold and inventory entries for the items sold.

Note the audit trail codes under **Type** and **Tran #** because we will refer to them later. *(Note: Your Trans # may differ because numbers are assigned based on activity in the software.)*

Close this report without saving changes.

(Hint: You can reopen the original invoice by double clicking any of the entries shown on the report.)

As explained in the *MAPS* topic, cost of goods sold entries are not recorded in a manual system because companies do not have the resources to identify inventory costs at the time of sale. Instead, cost of goods sold is recorded after taking a physical count of quantities on hand. Furthermore, companies using a manual system do not have immediate access to accurate on-hand inventory.

You will see in the inventory topic to follow that QBP tracks item cost and quantities on hand. As a result, companies have more timely financial information because cost of goods sold posts and quantities on hand adjust when invoicing.

3. Recall in the *MAPS* topic that after posting an invoice to the Sales Journal the invoice was then posted to the customer's account. You will now locate QBP's entries to Knight Brothers' customer account.

   Click ***Reports>>Customers & Receivables>>Transaction List by Customer*** on the main menu.

   Enter the date range of **3/22/12** through **3/22/12.**

4. Click **Customize Report.** Select **Trans #** under **Columns** to print this audit trail code (Figure 8:17). Scroll down and click **Split** to uncheck this column.

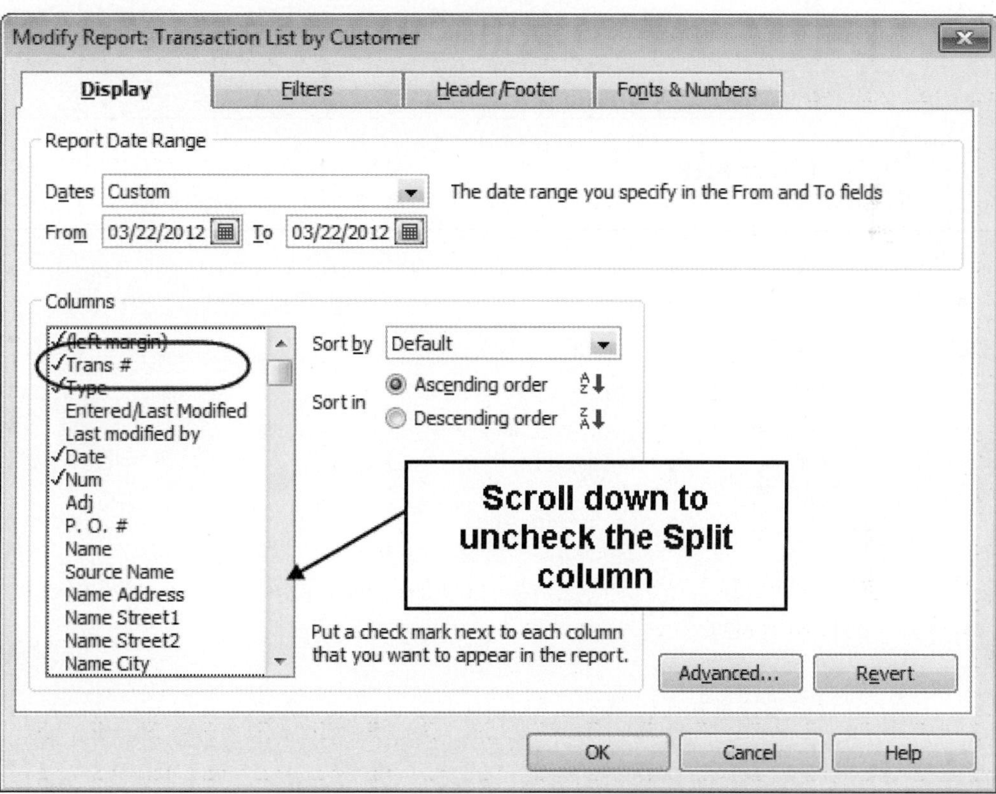

Figure 8:17

5. Click **OK** and the report displays as illustrated next. Notice that the **Trans #** and **Type** on the transaction matches the **Trans #** and **Type** on the Sales Journal. Close this report without saving changes.

Figure 8:18

6. All that remains is tracing entries in the general ledger. Select ***Reports>> Memorized Reports>>Accounting Journals>>General Ledger Detail Report*** on the main menu. Enter the date range of **3/22/12** through **3/22/12.**

   Customize the report by setting the **Transaction Type** on the **Filters** tab to "**Invoice**" and the report redisplays as illustrated in Figure 8:19.

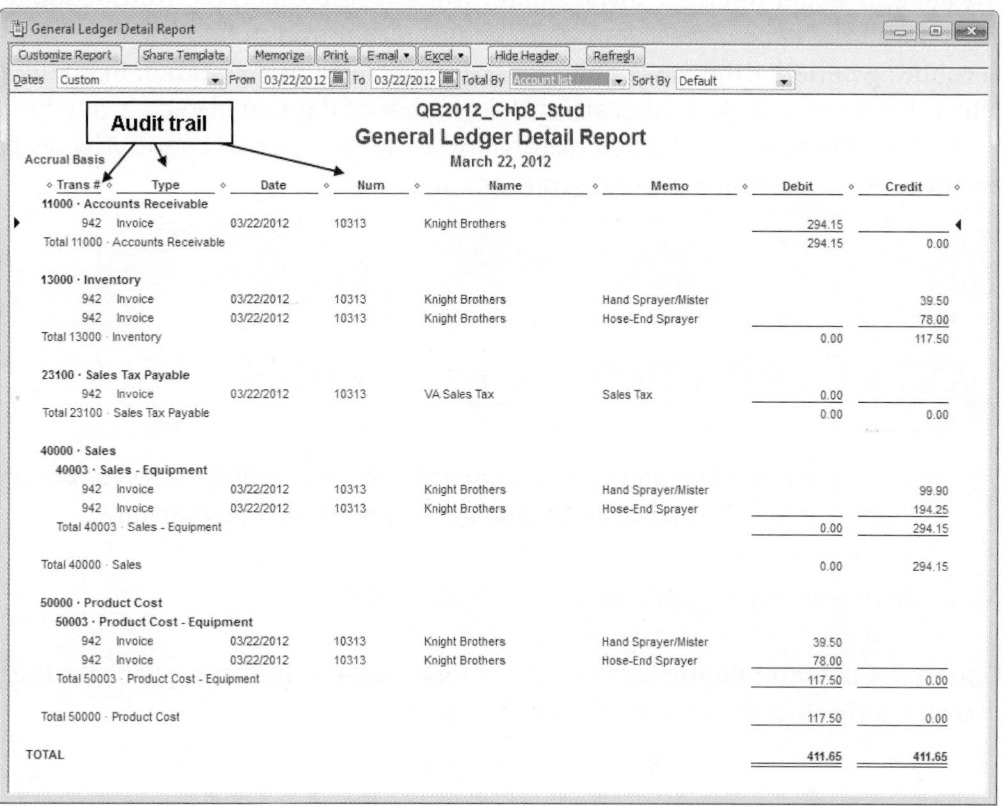

QB2012_Chp8_Stud
General Ledger Detail Report
March 22, 2012

Accrual Basis

Trans #	Type	Date	Num	Name	Memo	Debit	Credit
11000 · Accounts Receivable							
942	Invoice	03/22/2012	10313	Knight Brothers		294.15	
Total 11000 · Accounts Receivable						294.15	0.00
13000 · Inventory							
942	Invoice	03/22/2012	10313	Knight Brothers	Hand Sprayer/Mister		39.50
942	Invoice	03/22/2012	10313	Knight Brothers	Hose-End Sprayer		78.00
Total 13000 · Inventory						0.00	117.50
23100 · Sales Tax Payable							
942	Invoice	03/22/2012	10313	VA Sales Tax	Sales Tax	0.00	
Total 23100 · Sales Tax Payable						0.00	0.00
40000 · Sales							
40003 · Sales - Equipment							
942	Invoice	03/22/2012	10313	Knight Brothers	Hand Sprayer/Mister		99.90
942	Invoice	03/22/2012	10313	Knight Brothers	Hose-End Sprayer		194.25
Total 40003 · Sales - Equipment						0.00	294.15
Total 40000 · Sales						0.00	294.15
50000 · Product Cost							
50003 · Product Cost - Equipment							
942	Invoice	03/22/2012	10313	Knight Brothers	Hand Sprayer/Mister	39.50	
942	Invoice	03/22/2012	10313	Knight Brothers	Hose-End Sprayer	78.00	
Total 50003 · Product Cost - Equipment						117.50	0.00
Total 50000 · Product Cost						117.50	0.00
TOTAL						411.65	411.65

Figure 8:19

Once again, you see that the **Trans #** and **Type** on Knight Brothers' entries match the Sales Journal audit trail. Close this report without saving changes.

You have now followed QBP's audit trail and can see the advantages to using a computerized accounting system. You were able to capture a sales invoice and QBP posted entries to the Sales Journal, customer account, and general ledger when saving it. In addition, the accountant is better equipped to answer customer inquiries, provide customer support, manage company sales, and analyze profitability.

Let us spend a few minutes discussing the importance of invoice dates. QBP posts entries to the general ledger using the invoice date, which is also called the transaction date. It is important to use the correct transaction date so that transactions post to the proper accounting period; otherwise, financial statements will be misstated. In addition, invoice dates affect due dates and due dates affect the number of days an invoice is outstanding, which can then affect the customer's credit history and early payment discount. **Always pay careful attention to dates when entering transactions in QBP.**

Correcting Sales Invoices

This topic explains voiding and deleting invoices and correcting errors on **unpaid** invoices. *(Note: Refer to the instructions in Appendix B if correcting a paid invoice.)*

Note: There is an online video available for this topic.

Open the **Customer Center** and select the **Customers & Jobs** tab. Highlight **Knight Brothers'** account and select the options shown in Figure 8:20.

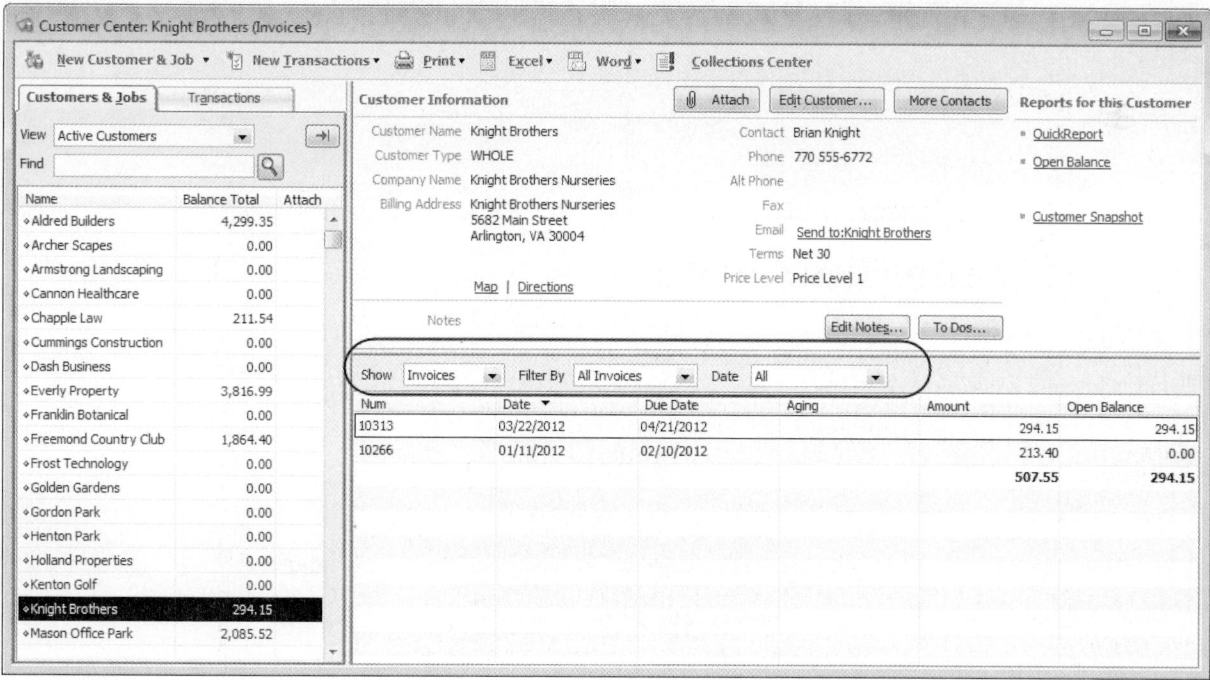

Figure 8:20

Double click the listed invoice to reopen it. ***Do not make any changes to the invoice,*** but note that you can void the invoice by selecting ***Edit>>Void Invoice*** on the main menu and delete it by selecting ***Edit>>Delete Invoice.*** You can also modify the invoice and repost it by clicking **Save & Close.**

Keep this transaction open for the topic that follows.

QuickBooks Email Features

As we showed you in Chapter 4, you can email invoices to the customer. With the invoice open from the previous topic, click the dropdown list on **Send** Send and select **E-mail Invoice.** Click **Close** if prompted with information about using Outlook. ***(Note: You must be connected to the Internet to complete this exercise.)***

A message appears with the invoice attached as shown in Figure 8:21.

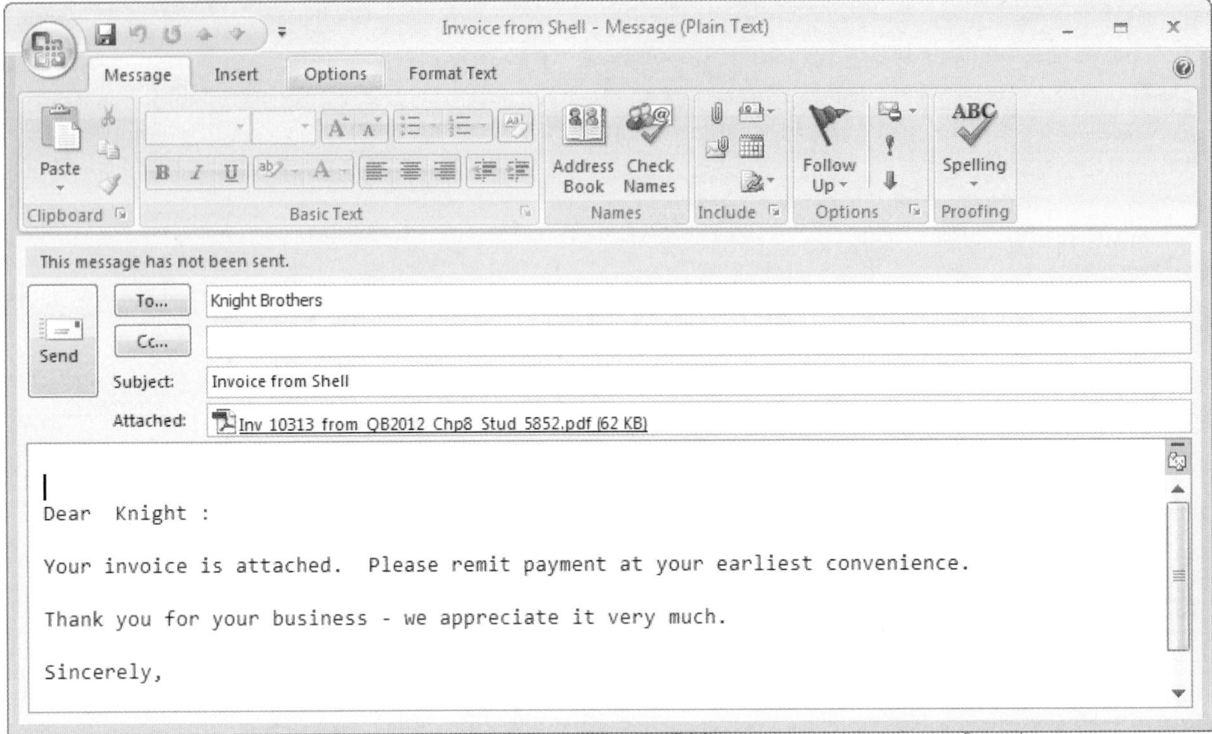

Figure 8:21

Enter your email address in the **To** field and, in **Subject**, replace the text "Invoice from Shell" with "Merchandise invoice". Change the body's salutation to "Dear Knight Brothers".

Click **Send.** You may get the message shown in Figure 8:22 and can turn off this message in the future by checking the Do not display this message in the future box and clicking OK to close the message.

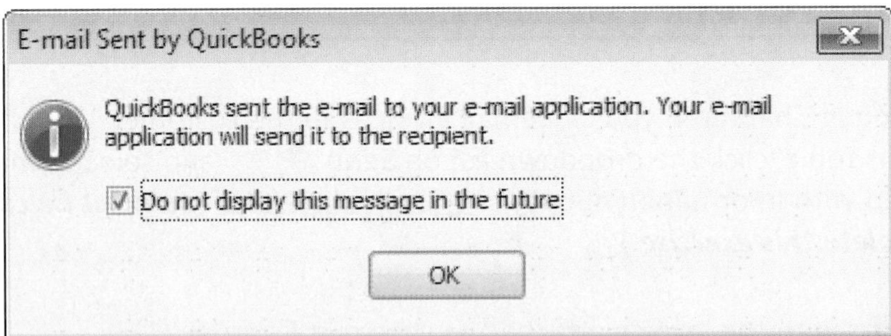

Figure 8:22

Check your email later to verify delivery. Click **X** to close Knight's invoice.

CUSTOMER ACCOUNTS

This topic explains creating, editing, and deleting customer accounts for a merchandising company, which means you will not use the Job Info tab. *(Note: Chapter 4 illustrates using this tab). The customer account contains job information used for implementing job costing.* You use the **Customer Center** to manage customer accounts.

Open this center if it is not still open from the previous topic. Select the **Customers & Jobs** tab and double click **Knight Brothers** to open the account. *(Note: If prompted with a message about adding and editing multiple list entries, mark the option to not display this message in the future and click* ***OK.)*** Now follow below as we describe the tabs of the customer account.

Address Info Tab

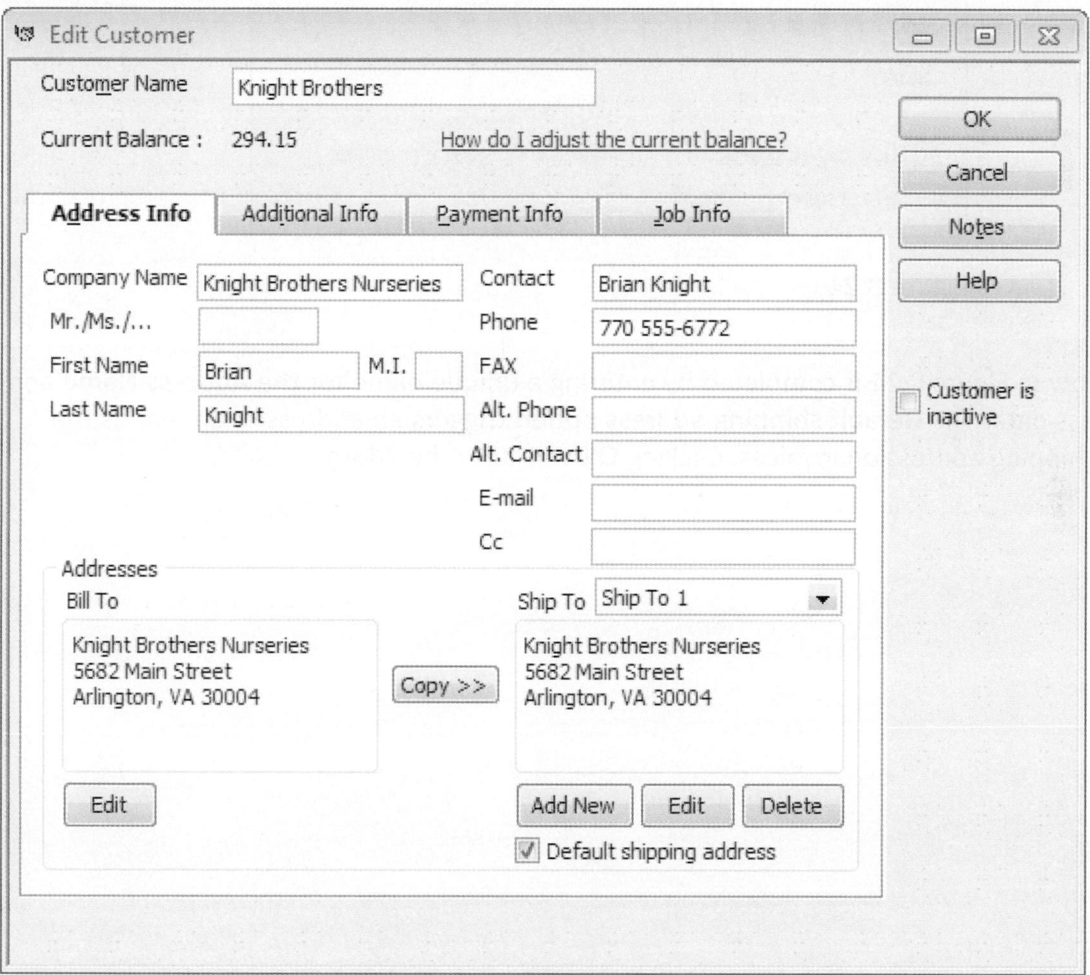

Figure 8:23

The **Address Info** tab stores basic customer information such as address, phone numbers, and email address. The **Bill To** address can be copied to the **Ship To** address by clicking the **Copy** button.

The **Ship To** address is important for companies shipping merchandise to customers because some customers may have one address for receiving invoices (Bill To) and another address for receiving orders (Ship To). When the customer has multiple locations, **Add New** opens the window illustrated in Figure 8:24 to enter additional addresses.

Figure 8:24

The window in Figure 8:24 is completed by entering a unique name for the **Address Name** and the address data. The **Default shipping address** option triggers an address to appear as the primary shipping address on invoices. Clicking **OK** will store the address.

Additional Info Tab

Figure 8:25

This tab stores customer defaults used during transaction entry. Defaults include the **Preferred Send Method** for invoices, customer payment **Terms** and the **Tax Code** applied to sales transactions. The **Rep** field assigns an employee sales representative for tracking sales commissions and sales performance.

The **Type** field is optional and can be used to differentiate sales by customer characteristics. Baxter uses the types of Retail and Whole.

Click the dropdown list on **Terms** to open the terms illustrated in Figure 8:26.

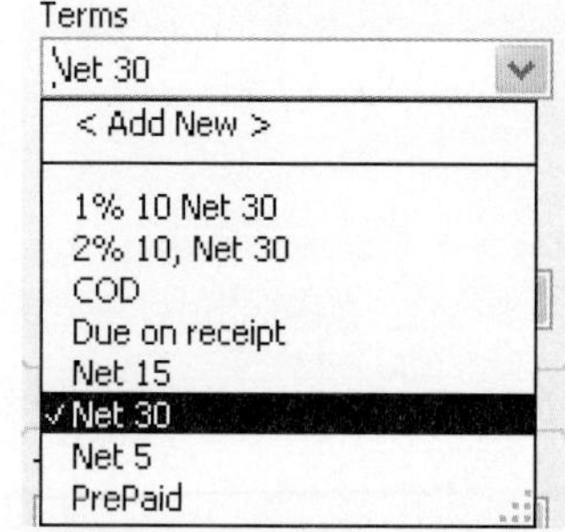

Figure 8:26

Terms establish invoice due dates and customer early payment discounts. The Net 15 terms make an invoice due 15 days from the invoice date. The 2% 10, Net 30 terms make the invoice due 30 days from the invoice date, but grants a 2 percent discount when paying the total invoice within 10 days. *(Note: Discounts do not apply to sales tax.)*

Payment Info Tab

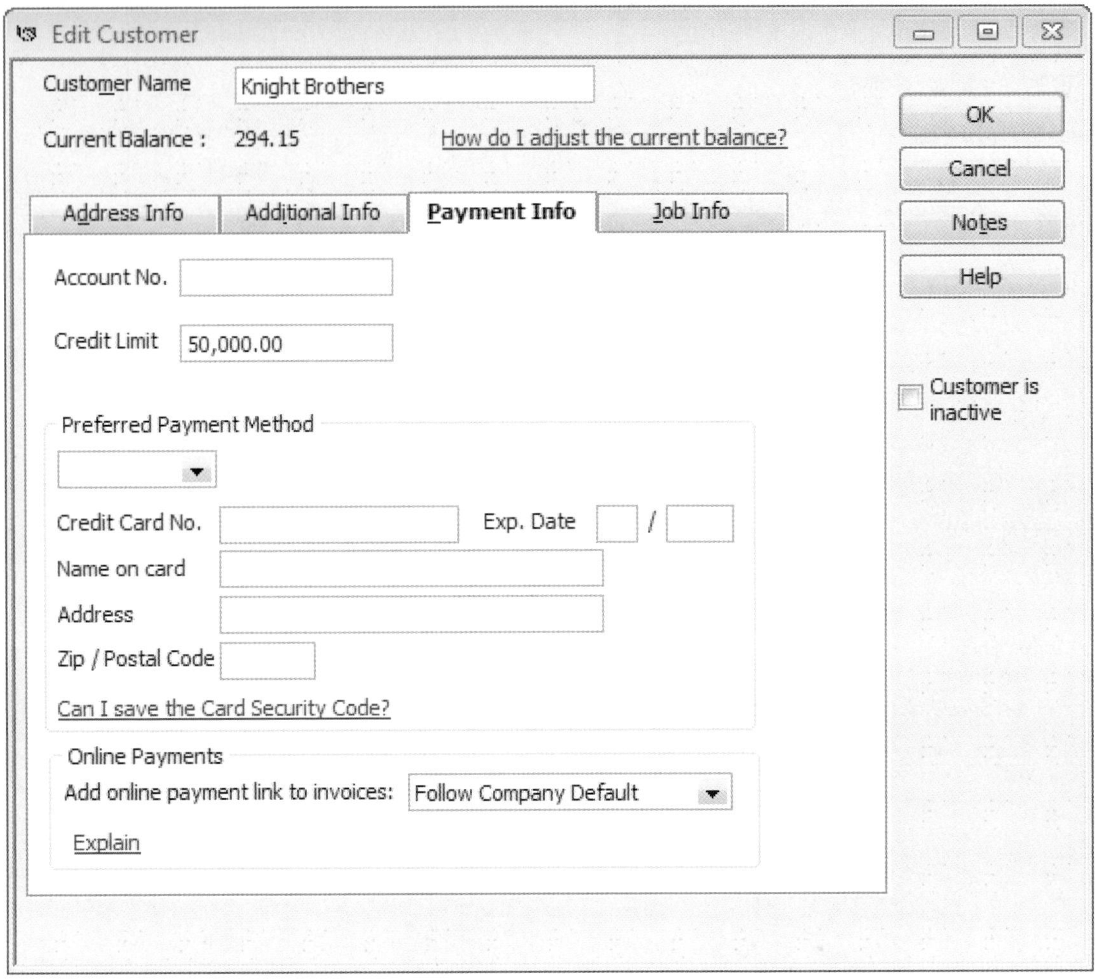

Edit Customer

Customer Name: Knight Brothers

Current Balance : 294.15 How do I adjust the current balance?

Address Info | Additional Info | Payment Info | Job Info

Account No.

Credit Limit 50,000.00

Preferred Payment Method

Credit Card No. Exp. Date /

Name on card

Address

Zip / Postal Code

Can I save the Card Security Code?

Online Payments

Add online payment link to invoices: Follow Company Default

Explain

OK

Cancel

Notes

Help

Customer is inactive

Figure 8:27

This tab stores a customer's **Credit Limit** and **Preferred Payment Method**. Setting a credit limit is important to managing bad debt. QBP will warn when saving a new invoice causes the customer's account balance to exceed the credit limit.

Job Info Tab

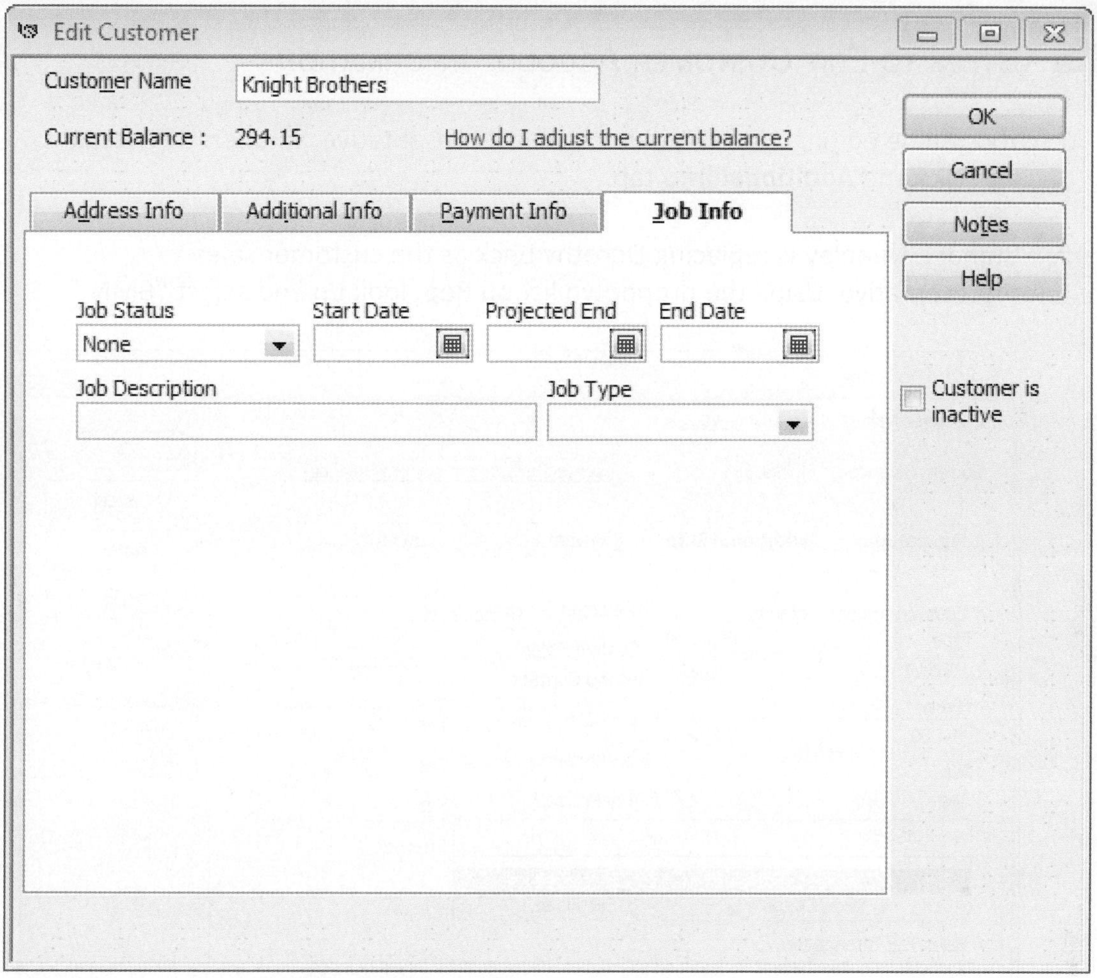

Figure 8:28

This tab implements QBP job costing and is discussed in Chapter 4. Baxter, as a merchandiser, does not use job costing.

Click **X** to close Knight's account without making changes.

The next exercise walks through editing a customer account.

Steps to Edit Customer Account Information

1. You will be editing Aldred Builders' sales representative, so open this account and click the **Additional Info** tab.

2. Brandee Nunnley is replacing Dorothy Beck as the customer sales representative. Using the dropdown list on **Rep**, look up and select "BMN."

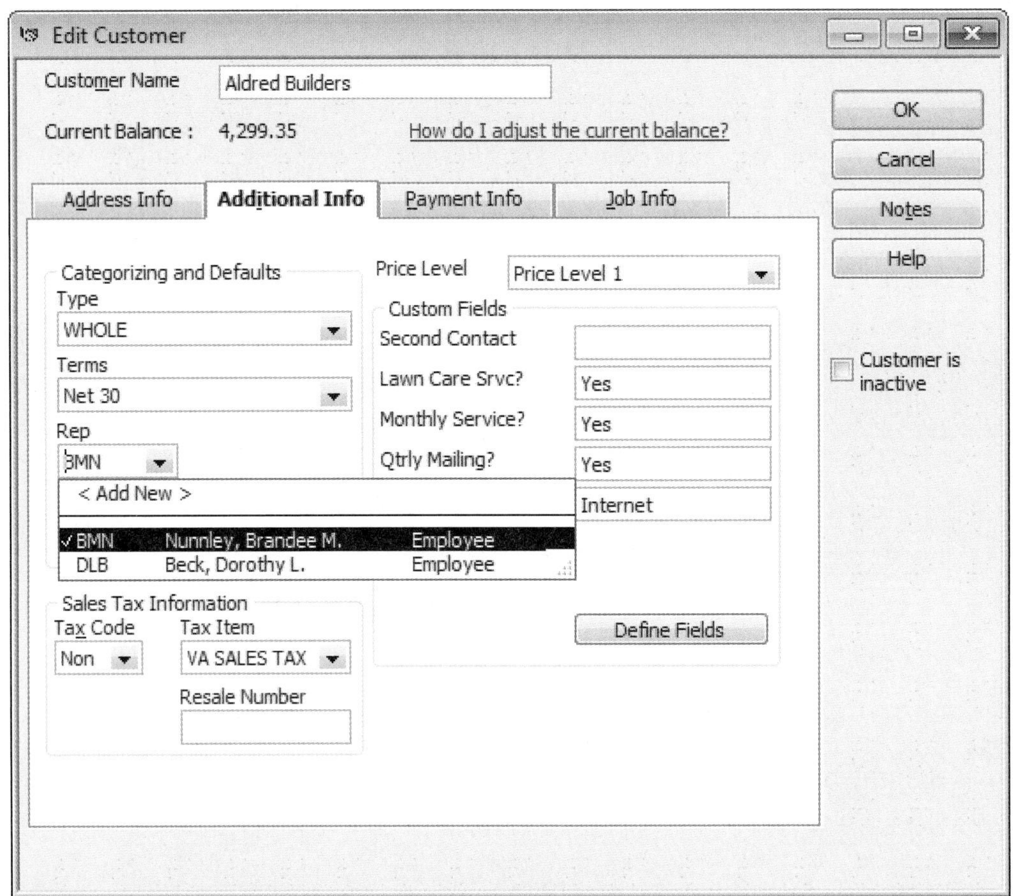

Figure 8:29

3. Click **OK** to save the changes. Click **Yes** if QBP warns about modifying the account because this change only affects future transactions.

You will now add a new customer account.

Steps To Create a Customer Account

1. From the Customers & Jobs tab, click **New Customer & Job** and select **New Customer.**

2. Enter the information illustrated in Figure 8:30.

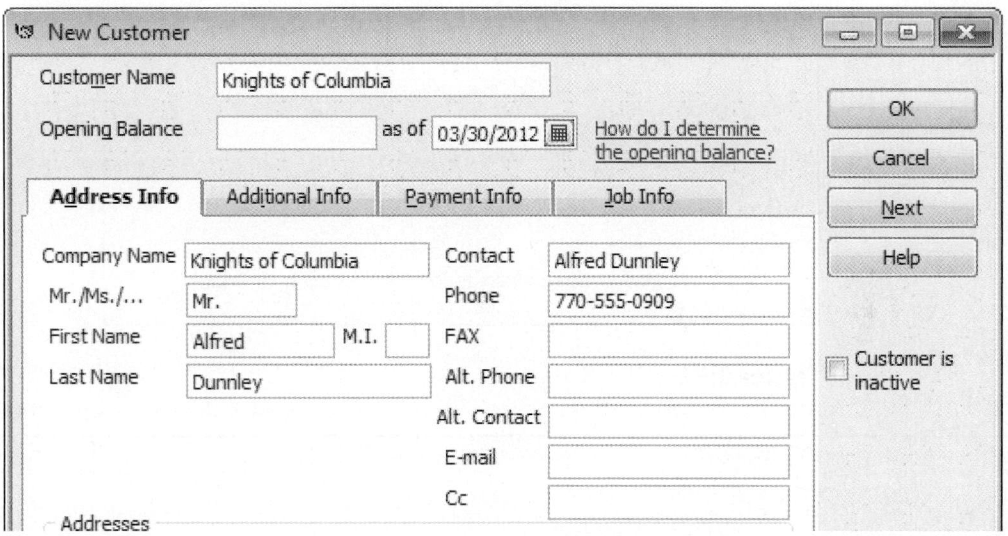

Figure 8:30

3. Click **Edit** on the **Bill To** field and enter the following information. Click **OK.**

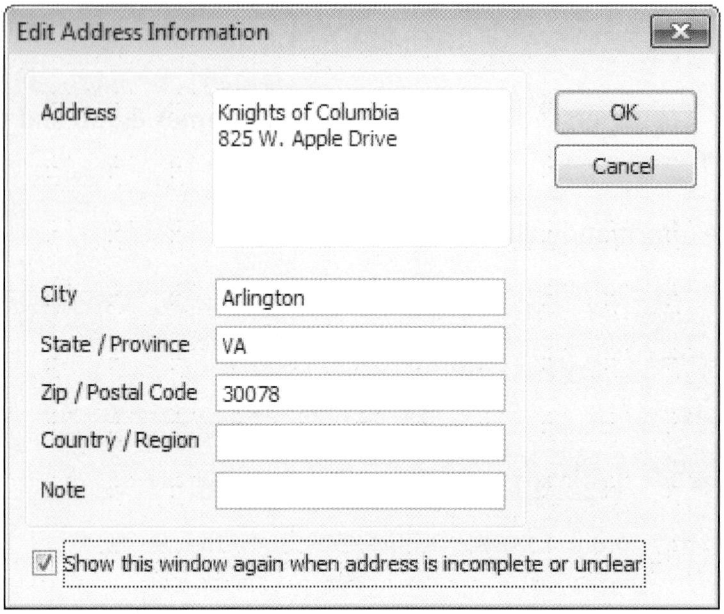

Edit Address Information

Address	Knights of Columbia 825 W. Apple Drive
City	Arlington
State / Province	VA
Zip / Postal Code	30078
Country / Region	
Note	

OK

Cancel

☑ Show this window again when address is incomplete or unclear

Figure 8:31

4. Click **Copy** to insert the **Bill To** address into the **Ship To** address. Click **OK** on the window that opens. The completed **Address Info** tab is shown in Figure 8:32.

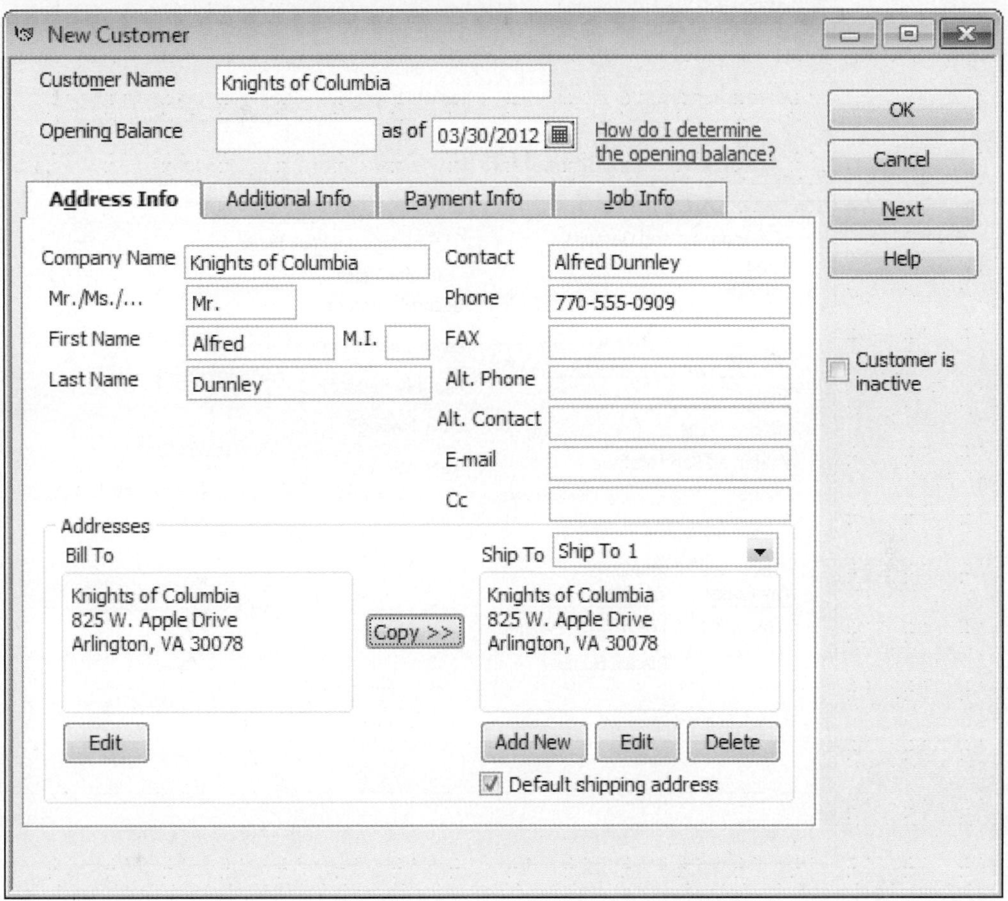

Figure 8:32

5. Click **Additional Info** and enter the information in Figure 8:33.

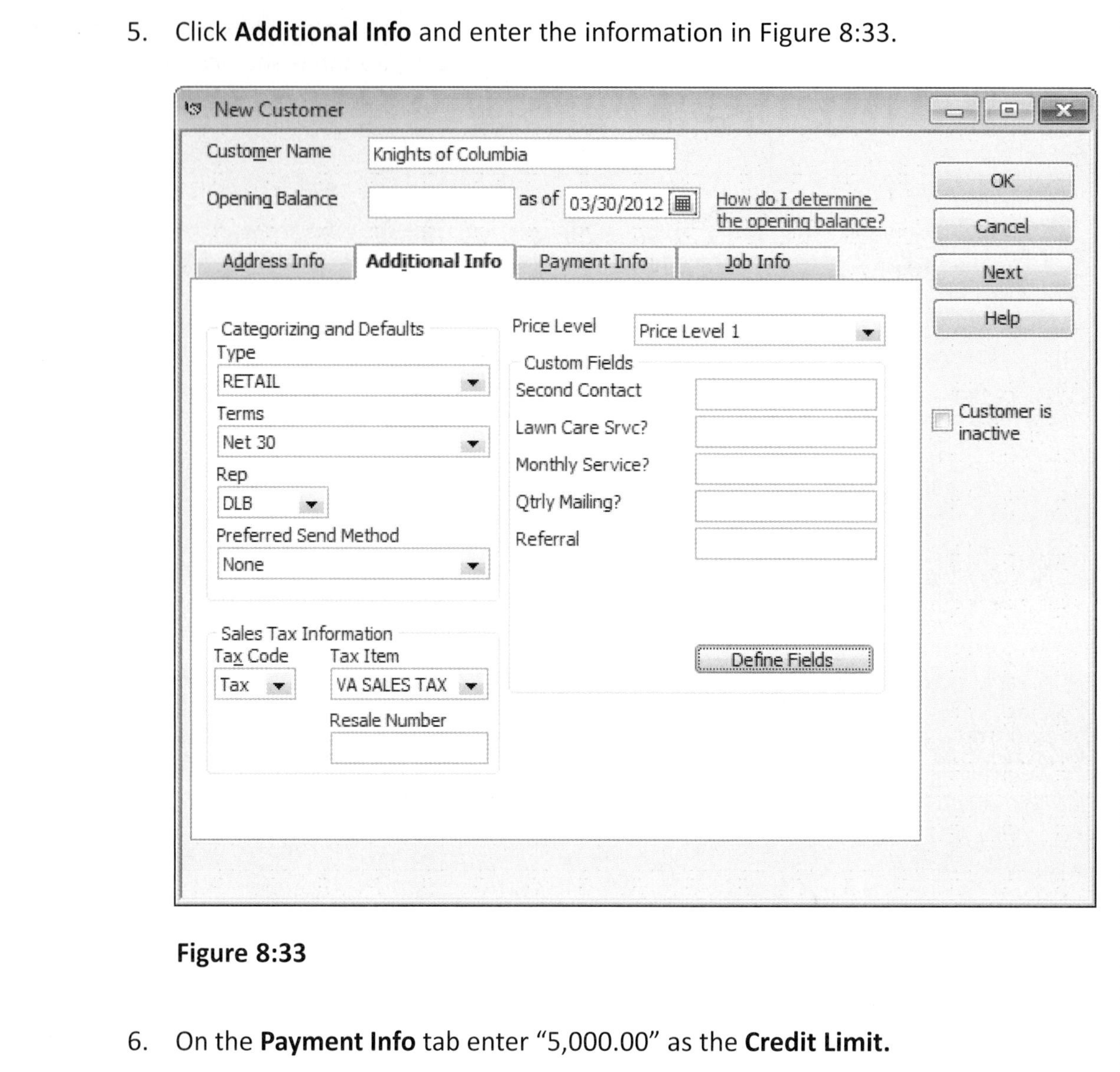

Figure 8:33

6. On the **Payment Info** tab enter "5,000.00" as the **Credit Limit.**

7. Click **OK**.

What happens when you try to delete an account with transaction history?

Highlight **Mosley Country Club** and select ***Edit>>Delete Customer:Job*** on the main menu. QBP prompts, stating that it cannot delete an account with transaction history, but can make it inactive. (See Figure 8:34.) Inactivating the account denies future transactions while retaining account history. Click **Cancel.**

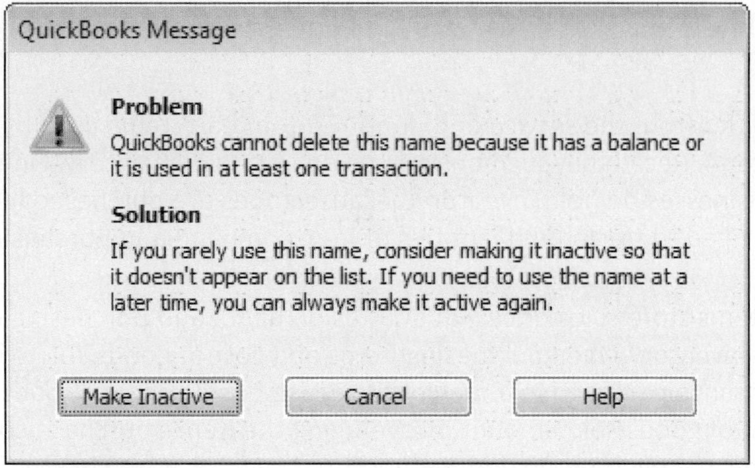

Figure 8:34

Now create a new account on your own.

CREATE A NEW CUSTOMER ACCOUNT

On March 2, 2012, Baxter needs to create a new wholesale customer with the following information.

Frost Garden Center	Phone:	701 555-1515
127 Frost Avenue	Fax:	701 555-1518
Danville, VA 30765	Contact:	Jeffrey Davis

Credit Limit:	$15,000.00
Preferred Payment Method:	Check
Sales Rep:	Brandee Nunnley
Price Level:	Price Level 1

The customer does not pay sales tax and will be offered the terms of 1/10 Net 30.

Understanding Inventory Items

Inventory items differ from the service and non-inventory part items used by a service-based business in Chapter 4. Recall that such businesses do not hold inventory. On the other hand, merchandising businesses do hold inventory because goods are purchased in advance of sale. These businesses need to track the quantities of items on hand and purchasing costs.

QBP's inventory items store sales prices, quantities on hand, and purchasing costs. The software posts to inventory when purchasing items and cost of goods sold when selling items. Recall that Knight's invoice traced in a previous exercise posted cost of goods sold. QBP calculates the cost of goods sold amount by averaging the item's purchase costs. *(Note: QBP only accommodates the average costing method.)*

It is important to understand the posting of cost of goods sold; otherwise you might prepare financial statements that do not match revenues with expenses. The following table explains the inventory, non-inventory part, and service items used in this text. After reviewing this table, you will better understand when an item class interacts with inventory and when the item posts cost of goods sold at the time of sale.

Item Class	Purpose
Inventory Part	Used to track goods purchased and held for resale. Tracks quantities and purchasing costs. Cost of goods sold posts at the time of invoicing. Cost of goods sold is calculated using the Average costing method. *(Note: QBP does not accommodate the LIFO and FIFO inventory costing methods.)*
Non-inventory Part	Used for job materials purchased but not tracked in inventory. Cost of goods sold posts when posting vendor bills or receipts for material purchases.
Service	Used for service labor costs provided by company employees or subcontractors. When provided by subcontractors, cost of goods sold posts when paying the contractor. When provided by employees, cost of goods sold posts when paying employees.
Sales Tax Item	Used to calculate sales tax for a single taxing agency.
Other Charge	Used for miscellaneous charges such as delivery and photocopying fees. Cost of goods sold posts when reimbursing the employee expense or paying a vendor.

Now look at the inventory items sold by Baxter. Click **Item** on the toolbar to open the Item List illustrated in Figure 8:35. *(Note: You can also select **Lists>>Item List** on the main menu.)* Pay particular attention to the **Type** column.

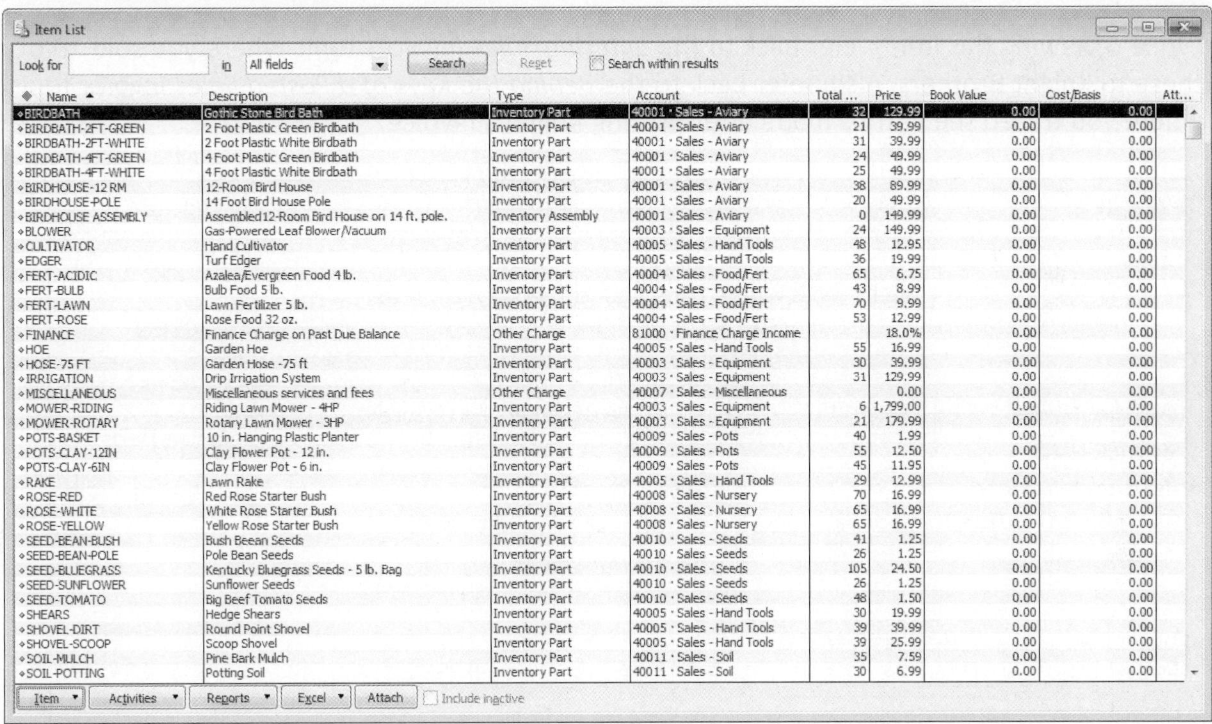

Name	Description	Type	Account	Total ...	Price	Book Value	Cost/Basis	Att...
BIRDBATH	Gothic Stone Bird Bath	Inventory Part	40001 · Sales - Aviary	32	129.99	0.00	0.00	
BIRDBATH-2FT-GREEN	2 Foot Plastic Green Birdbath	Inventory Part	40001 · Sales - Aviary	21	39.99	0.00	0.00	
BIRDBATH-2FT-WHITE	2 Foot Plastic White Birdbath	Inventory Part	40001 · Sales - Aviary	31	39.99	0.00	0.00	
BIRDBATH-4FT-GREEN	4 Foot Plastic Green Birdbath	Inventory Part	40001 · Sales - Aviary	24	49.99	0.00	0.00	
BIRDBATH-4FT-WHITE	4 Foot Plastic White Birdbath	Inventory Part	40001 · Sales - Aviary	25	49.99	0.00	0.00	
BIRDHOUSE-12 RM	12-Room Bird House	Inventory Part	40001 · Sales - Aviary	38	89.99	0.00	0.00	
BIRDHOUSE-POLE	14 Foot Bird House Pole	Inventory Part	40001 · Sales - Aviary	20	49.99	0.00	0.00	
BIRDHOUSE ASSEMBLY	Assembled12-Room Bird House on 14 ft. pole.	Inventory Assembly	40001 · Sales - Aviary	0	149.99	0.00	0.00	
BLOWER	Gas-Powered Leaf Blower/Vacuum	Inventory Part	40003 · Sales - Equipment	24	149.99	0.00	0.00	
CULTIVATOR	Hand Cultivator	Inventory Part	40005 · Sales - Hand Tools	48	12.95	0.00	0.00	
EDGER	Turf Edger	Inventory Part	40005 · Sales - Hand Tools	36	19.99	0.00	0.00	
FERT-ACIDIC	Azalea/Evergreen Food 4 lb.	Inventory Part	40004 · Sales - Food/Fert	65	6.75	0.00	0.00	
FERT-BULB	Bulb Food 5 lb.	Inventory Part	40004 · Sales - Food/Fert	43	8.99	0.00	0.00	
FERT-LAWN	Lawn Fertilizer 5 lb.	Inventory Part	40004 · Sales - Food/Fert	70	9.99	0.00	0.00	
FERT-ROSE	Rose Food 32 oz.	Inventory Part	40004 · Sales - Food/Fert	53	12.99	0.00	0.00	
FINANCE	Finance Charge on Past Due Balance	Other Charge	81000 · Finance Charge Income		18.0%	0.00	0.00	
HOE	Garden Hoe	Inventory Part	40005 · Sales - Hand Tools	55	16.99	0.00	0.00	
HOSE-75 FT	Garden Hose -75 ft	Inventory Part	40003 · Sales - Equipment	30	39.99	0.00	0.00	
IRRIGATION	Drip Irrigation System	Inventory Part	40003 · Sales - Equipment	31	129.99	0.00	0.00	
MISCELLANEOUS	Miscellaneous services and fees	Other Charge	40007 · Sales - Miscellaneous		0.00	0.00	0.00	
MOWER-RIDING	Riding Lawn Mower - 4HP	Inventory Part	40003 · Sales - Equipment	6	1,799.00	0.00	0.00	
MOWER-ROTARY	Rotary Lawn Mower - 3HP	Inventory Part	40003 · Sales - Equipment	21	179.99	0.00	0.00	
POTS-BASKET	10 in. Hanging Plastic Planter	Inventory Part	40009 · Sales - Pots	40	1.99	0.00	0.00	
POTS-CLAY-12IN	Clay Flower Pot - 12 in.	Inventory Part	40009 · Sales - Pots	55	12.50	0.00	0.00	
POTS-CLAY-6IN	Clay Flower Pot - 6 in.	Inventory Part	40009 · Sales - Pots	45	11.95	0.00	0.00	
RAKE	Lawn Rake	Inventory Part	40005 · Sales - Hand Tools	29	12.99	0.00	0.00	
ROSE-RED	Red Rose Starter Bush	Inventory Part	40008 · Sales - Nursery	70	16.99	0.00	0.00	
ROSE-WHITE	White Rose Starter Bush	Inventory Part	40008 · Sales - Nursery	65	16.99	0.00	0.00	
ROSE-YELLOW	Yellow Rose Starter Bush	Inventory Part	40008 · Sales - Nursery	65	16.99	0.00	0.00	
SEED-BEAN-BUSH	Bush Beean Seeds	Inventory Part	40010 · Sales - Seeds	41	1.25	0.00	0.00	
SEED-BEAN-POLE	Pole Bean Seeds	Inventory Part	40010 · Sales - Seeds	26	1.25	0.00	0.00	
SEED-BLUEGRASS	Kentucky Bluegrass Seeds - 5 lb. Bag	Inventory Part	40010 · Sales - Seeds	105	24.50	0.00	0.00	
SEED-SUNFLOWER	Sunflower Seeds	Inventory Part	40010 · Sales - Seeds	26	1.25	0.00	0.00	
SEED-TOMATO	Big Beef Tomato Seeds	Inventory Part	40010 · Sales - Seeds	48	1.50	0.00	0.00	
SHEARS	Hedge Shears	Inventory Part	40005 · Sales - Hand Tools	30	19.99	0.00	0.00	
SHOVEL-DIRT	Round Point Shovel	Inventory Part	40005 · Sales - Hand Tools	39	39.99	0.00	0.00	
SHOVEL-SCOOP	Scoop Shovel	Inventory Part	40005 · Sales - Hand Tools	39	25.99	0.00	0.00	
SOIL-MULCH	Pine Bark Mulch	Inventory Part	40011 · Sales - Soil	35	7.59	0.00	0.00	
SOIL-POTTING	Potting Soil	Inventory Part	40011 · Sales - Soil	30	6.99	0.00	0.00	

Figure 8:35

The columns for Book Value and Cost/Basis show no values; however, you can view average cost data after opening an item.

Now customize the Item List. Click the **Item** button at the bottom and select **Customize Columns**. On the right, highlight **Book Value** and click **Remove.** Use the same procedures to remove the **Cost/Basis** and **Attach** columns. On the left, highlight **Preferred Vendor** and click **Add.** Click **OK** and the list refreshes.

We will now review a few of these items.

Inventory Part

Scroll down and highlight **SPRAYER-HAND.** Double click to open the item (Figure 8:36).

While reviewing this item, refer back to the *Entering Sales Invoices* topic where you sold 10 of these to Knight Brothers. Also, refer back to the *Behind the Keys of a Posted Sales Invoice* topic where you traced the entries made after posting Knight's invoice.

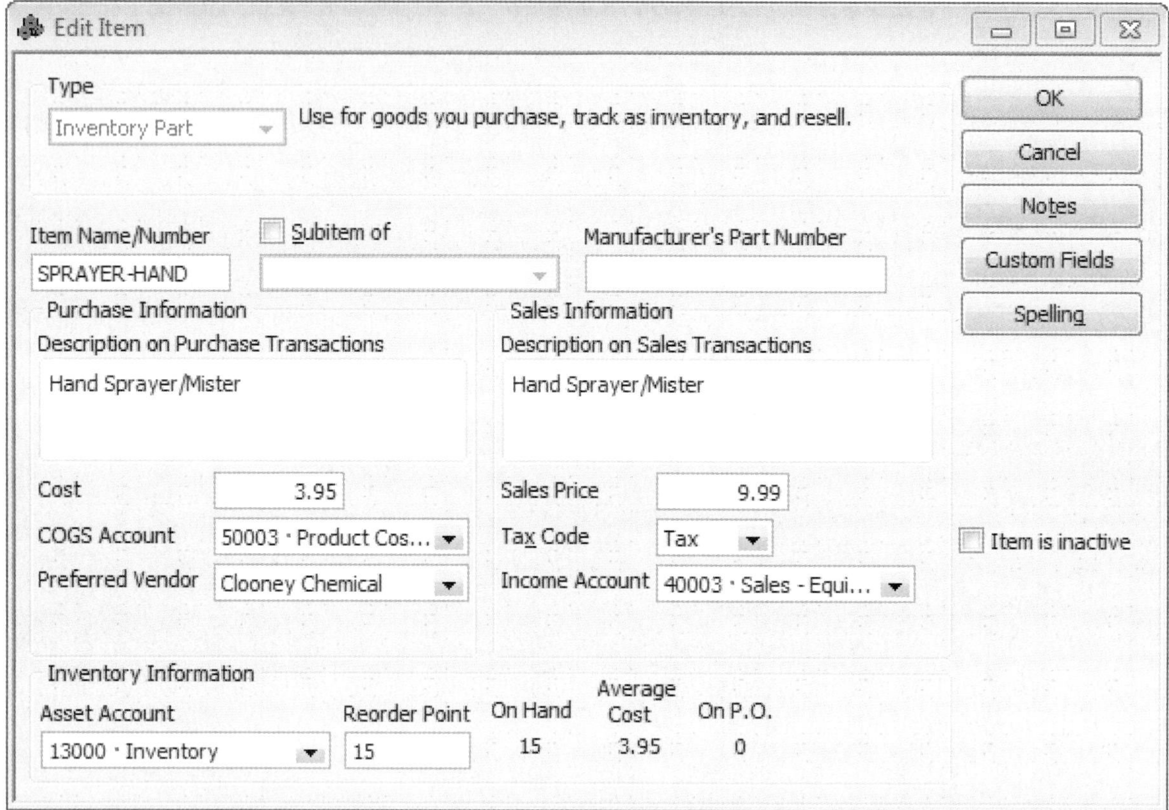

Figure 8:36

Purchase Information describes the item to vendors on purchase orders.

Sales Information is the description that appears on customer invoices.

Cost is the price paid vendors when purchasing the item. In Chapter 9, you will see that this Cost autofills as the purchase price on vendor purchase orders and bills.

COGS Account is the account used for posting cost of goods sold. For this item, cost of goods sold posts to account 50003 Product Cost-Equipment and can be verified by reviewing the Sales Journal printed after posting Knight's invoice. *(Note: Click the dropdown list on this field to view the account's full name.)*

Sales Price autofills as the sales price on invoices, explaining why Knight's invoice charged $9.99 for this item.

Tax Code shows that sales of this item are normally taxable. However, remember that QBP looks to the tax default on a customer account before charging sales tax.

Income Account is the account used for posting sales revenue, explaining why Knight's invoice posted revenue to 40003 Sales-Equipment.

Next, focus your attention on the **Inventory Information** section.

Purchases of this item debit **Asset Account** 13000 Inventory whereas sales of the item credit this account.

The **Reorder Point** on this item is 15 and the **On Hand** quantity is 15. This information indicates that a purchase order should be issued to restock the item.

Avg. Cost is $3.95, explaining why $39.50 was posted to cost of goods sold when Knight's invoice posted the sale of ten of these items. The average cost adjusts as items are purchased.

Finally, there are no items currently on order to vendors (**On P.O.**).

Click **X** to close this item.

Inventory Assembly

Now open **BIRDHOUSE-ASSEMBLY.**

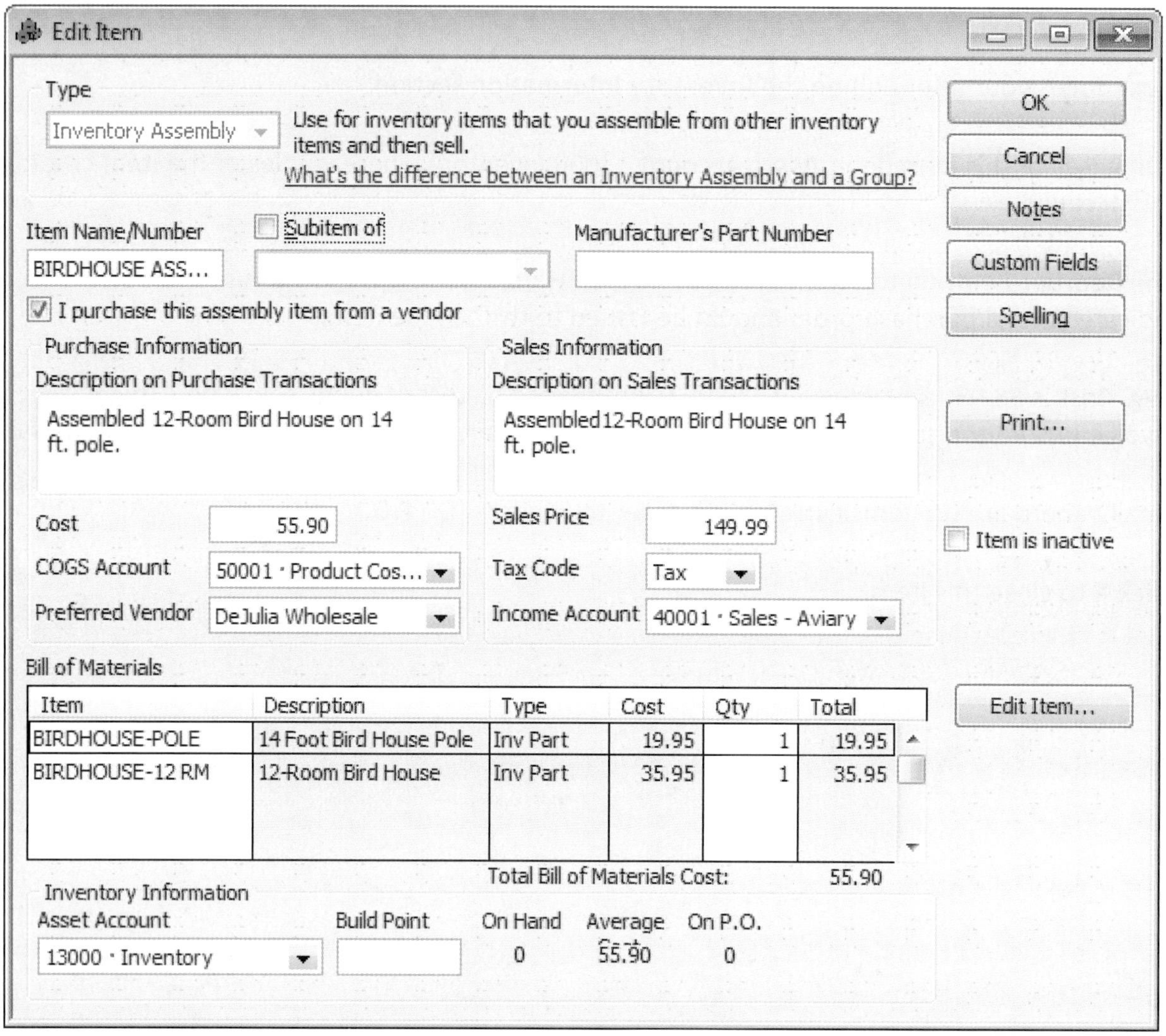

Item	Description	Type	Cost	Qty	Total
BIRDHOUSE-POLE	14 Foot Bird House Pole	Inv Part	19.95	1	19.95
BIRDHOUSE-12 RM	12-Room Bird House	Inv Part	35.95	1	35.95

Figure 8:37

This is an assembly item that combines the two individual items listed under **Bill of Materials.** Furthermore, this item is restocked by purchasing the individual items.

Sales Tax Item

Close the previous item and open **VA SALES TAX.**

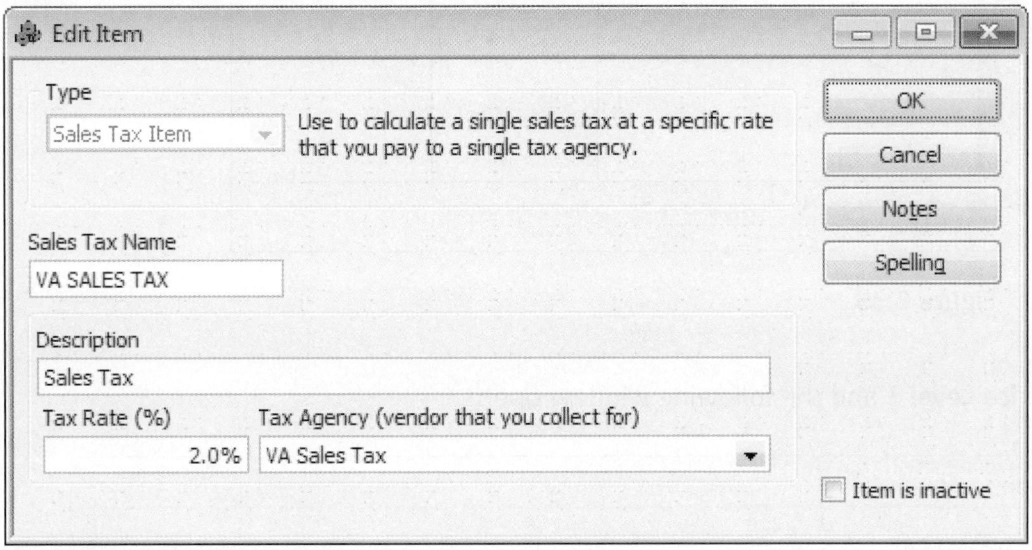

Figure 8:38

This item sets a 2 percent sales tax on taxable items.

Close this item and close the Item List. We will next discuss inventory pricing and price levels.

INVENTORY PRICING AND PRICE LEVELS

Baxter could offer a different sales price on the same item by instituting price levels. Companies sometimes offer preferred pricing (i.e., lower sales prices) to customers buying large quantities of an item. You should recall assigning a price level to the customer account created in an earlier exercise.

You can view the price level feature by selecting ***Lists>>Price Level List*** on the main menu to open the window illustrated next.

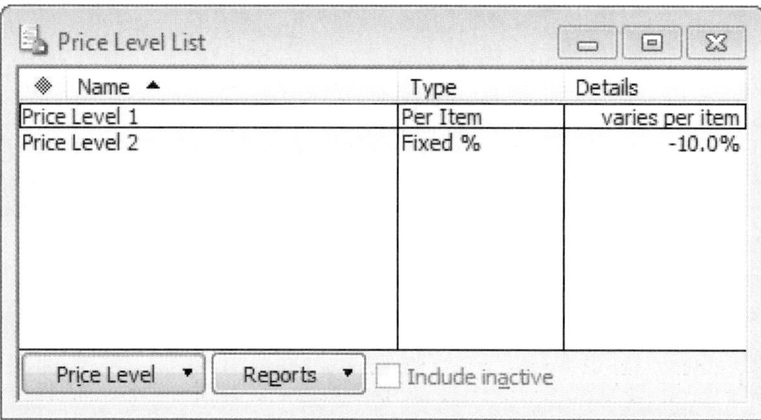

Figure 8:39

Double click **Price Level 1** and the following window opens.

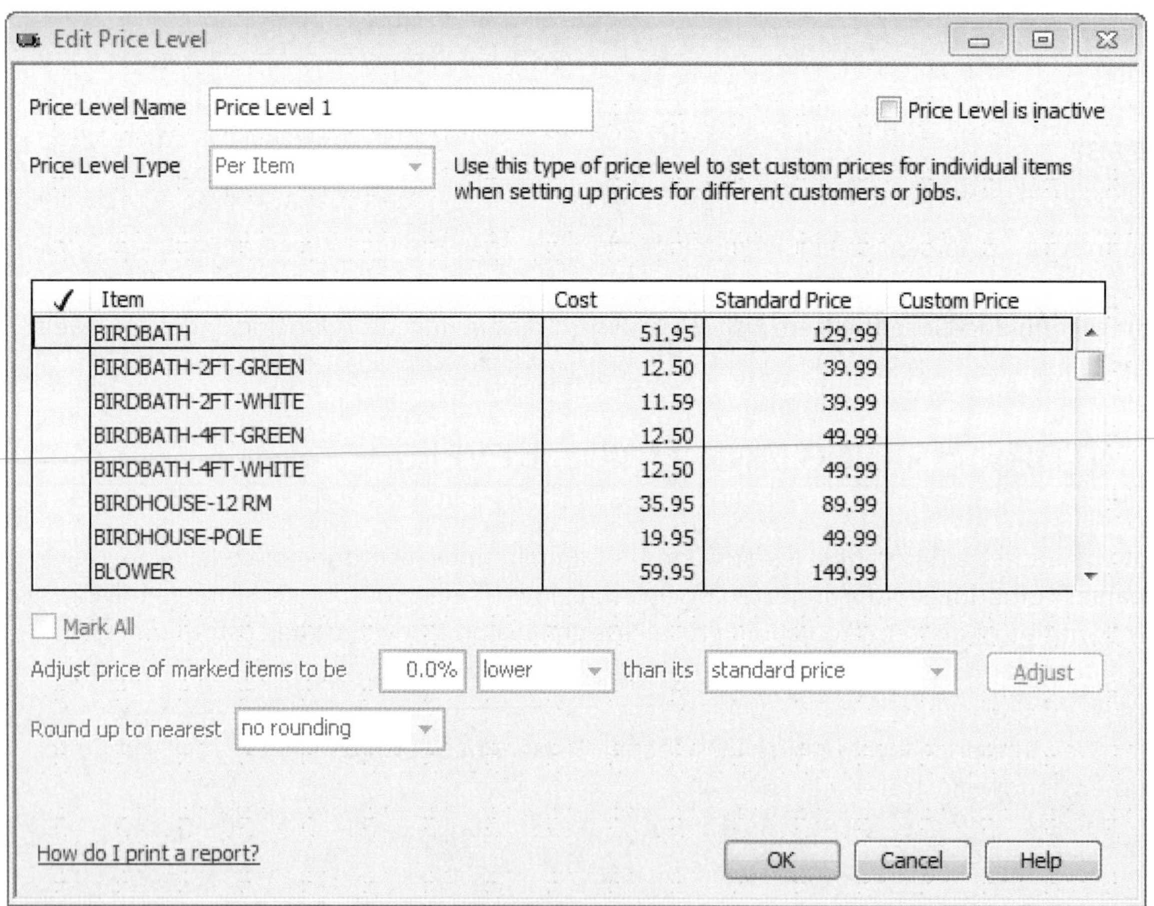

Figure 8:40

Click **Cancel** to close this list and double click **Price Level 2** to open the window illustrated in Figure 8:41.

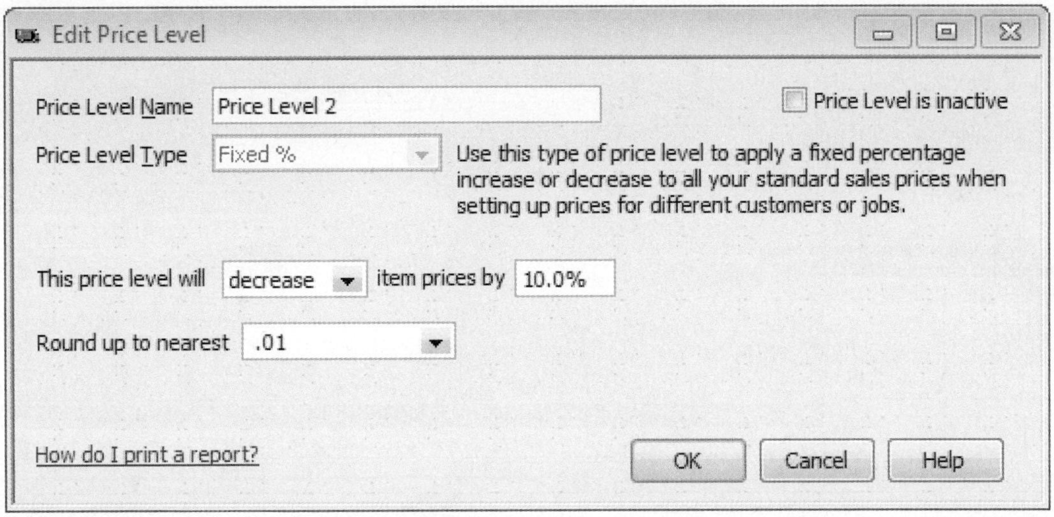

Figure 8:41

This level decreases the sales price of an item by 10 percent, rounding the amount to the nearest penny. Now look at using price levels on an invoice.

Click **X** to close the Edit Price Level window and **X** to close the Price Level List. On the **Home** page, click **Create Invoices** and select **Aldred Builders.** Enter "1" in **Quantity** and select **Item Code** "BIRDBATH" (i.e., the first item on the inventory list).

Click the dropdown list on **Price Each** to view the sales price at Price Level 2. (See Figure 8:42.)

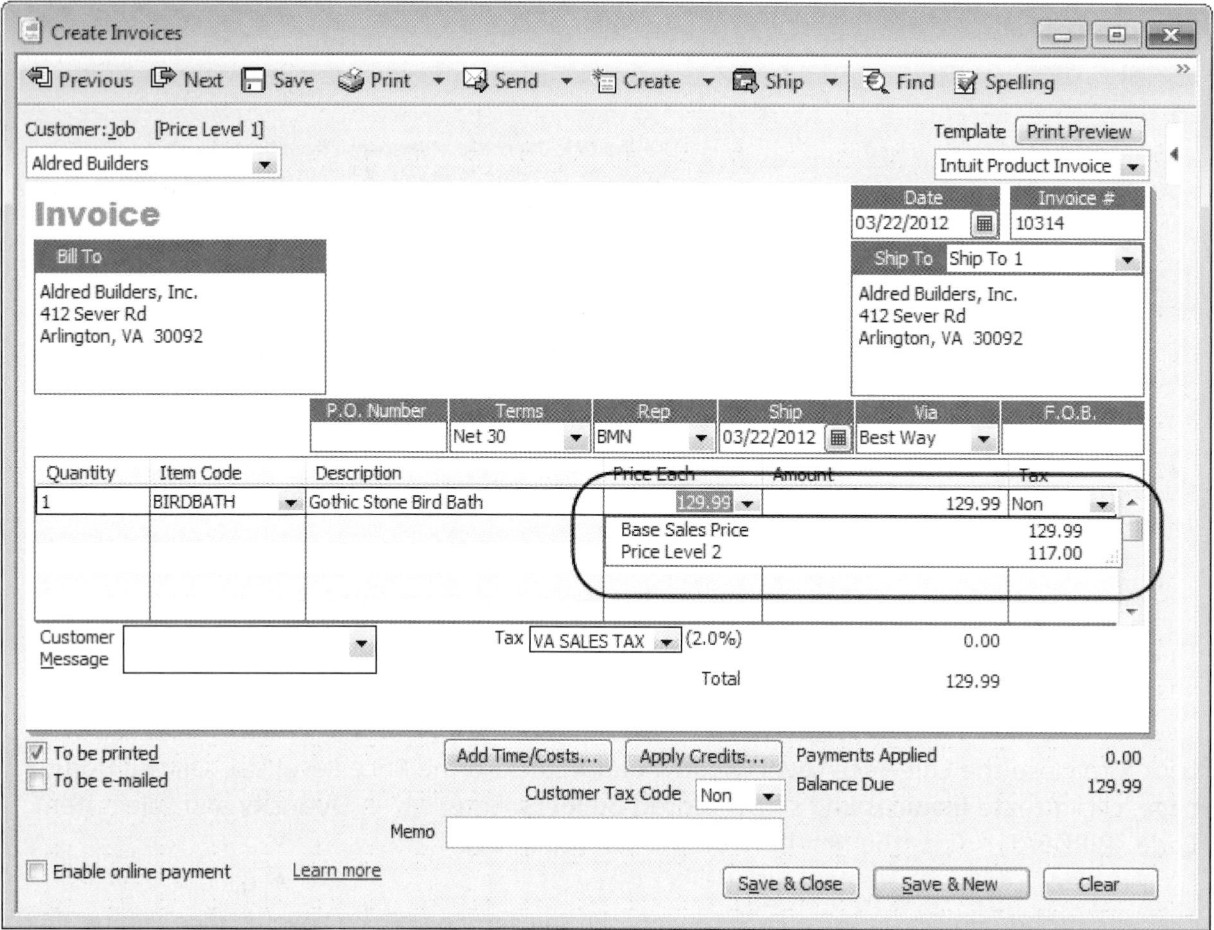

Figure 8:42

Aldred Builders' account is assigned to Price Level 1 so the price defaults to the Base Sales Price. You can, if needed, override the default by selecting a different price level on the invoice or by changing the customer's default price level.

Click **Clear** and then **X** to close the invoice window.

Now look at ways to adjust sales prices.

One method is to open the Item List and then the item. After opening, you can enter a new price and save the item. However, this method would be time consuming if changing prices for multiple items, so let us look at another method.

Select ***Customers>>Change Item Prices*** on the main menu. Choose **Inventory Part** as the **Item Type**. The Change Item Prices window now appears as illustrated next.

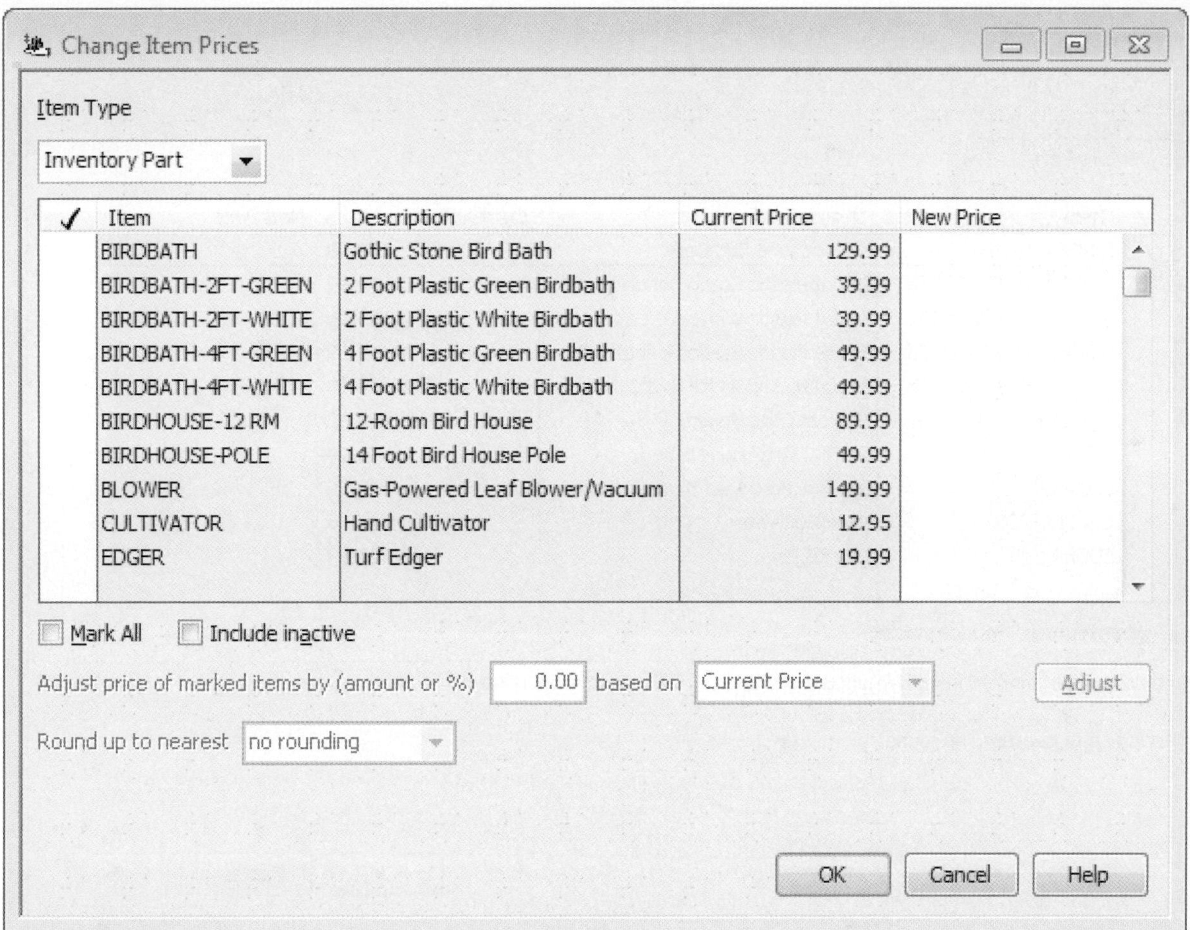

Figure 8:43

You begin by selecting the items to change. Items are selected by clicking the ✓ column on an item or by clicking **Mark All** to select all items.

Click the ✓ column on the first item as illustrated next.

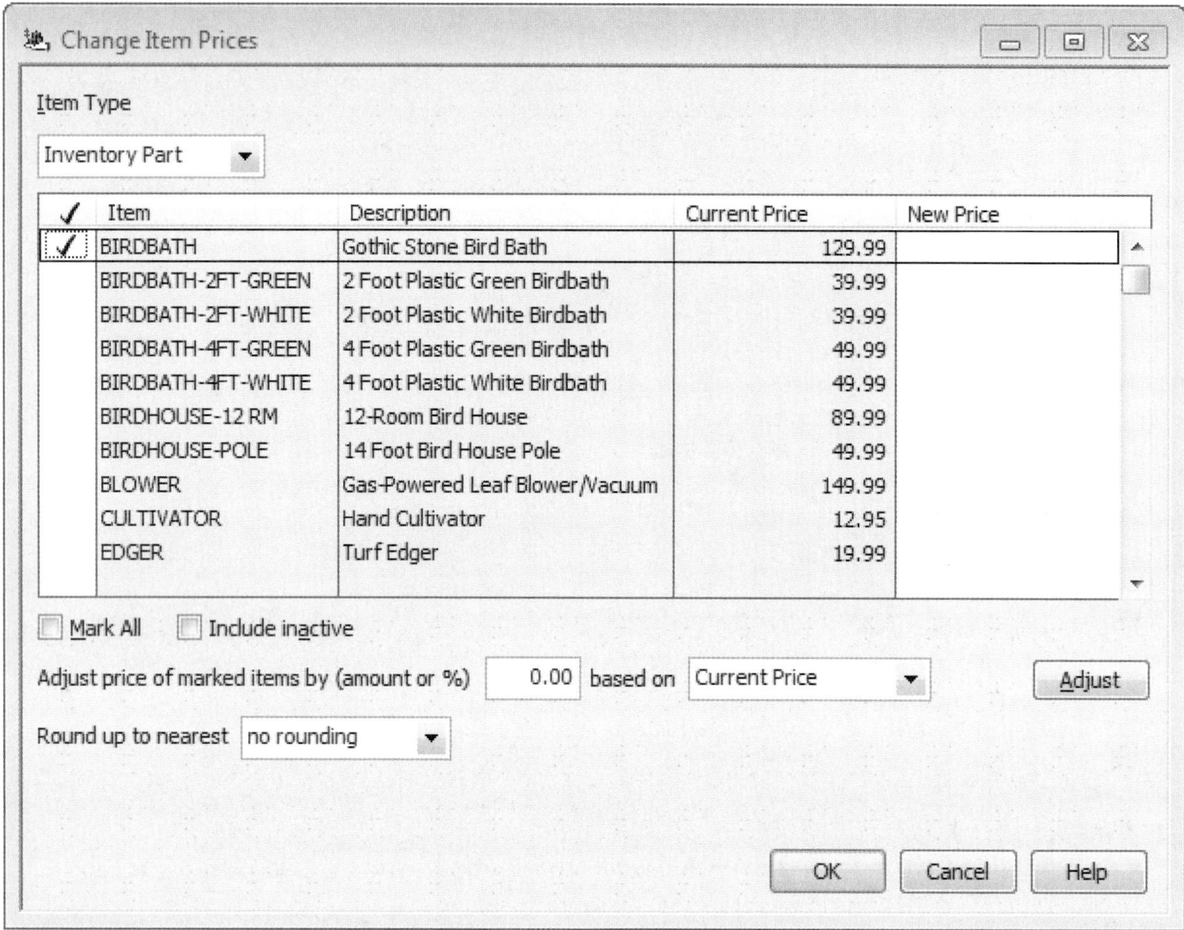

Figure 8:44

After selecting the item, you can change its sales price by either entering a new value in the **New Price** column or by using the adjust price options at the bottom of the window.

Let us use the adjust price options. Raise the item sales price 10 percent above the **Current Price** by entering the criteria illustrated next.

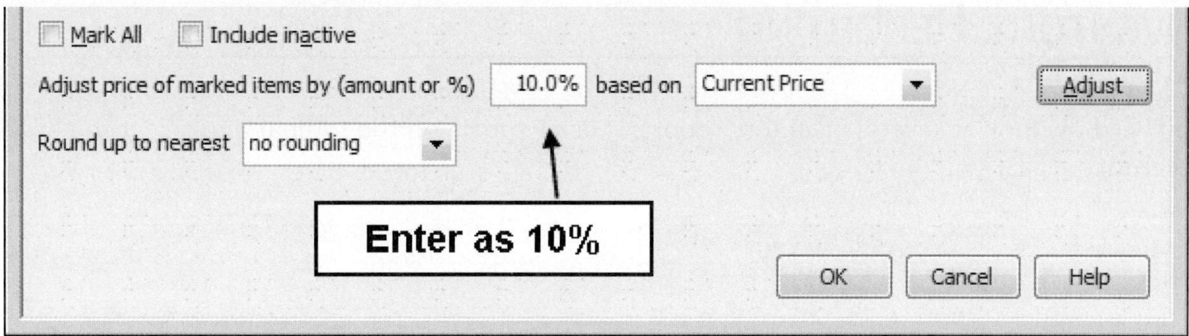

Figure 8:45

Click **Adjust** and the new sales price is $142.99. We could also round the new sales price to the nearest dollar. Click the dropdown list on round and select **1.00.** Click **Adjust** and the new price changes to $143.00 as illustrated next.

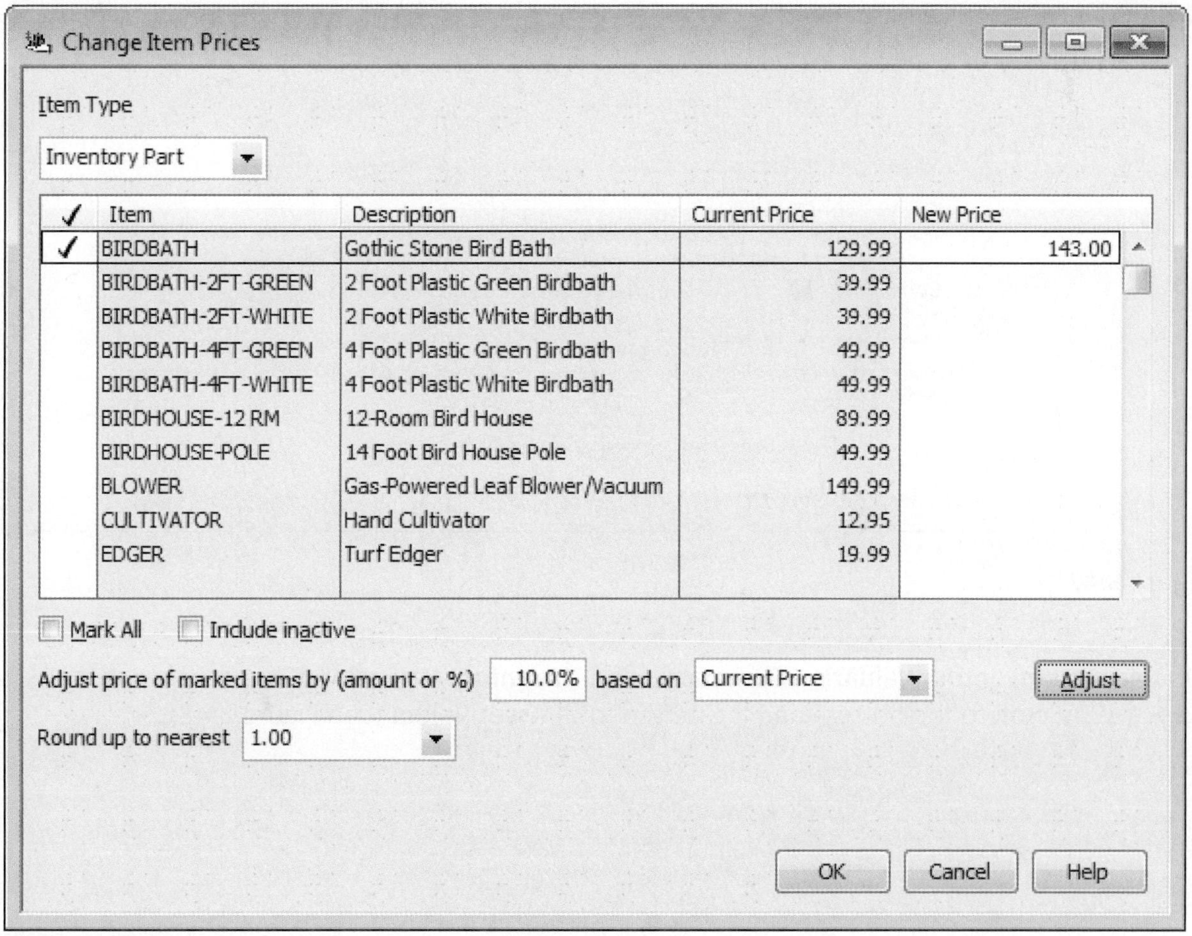

Change Item Prices

Item Type

Inventory Part

✓	Item	Description	Current Price	New Price
✓	BIRDBATH	Gothic Stone Bird Bath	129.99	143.00
	BIRDBATH-2FT-GREEN	2 Foot Plastic Green Birdbath	39.99	
	BIRDBATH-2FT-WHITE	2 Foot Plastic White Birdbath	39.99	
	BIRDBATH-4FT-GREEN	4 Foot Plastic Green Birdbath	49.99	
	BIRDBATH-4FT-WHITE	4 Foot Plastic White Birdbath	49.99	
	BIRDHOUSE-12 RM	12-Room Bird House	89.99	
	BIRDHOUSE-POLE	14 Foot Bird House Pole	49.99	
	BLOWER	Gas-Powered Leaf Blower/Vacuum	149.99	
	CULTIVATOR	Hand Cultivator	12.95	
	EDGER	Turf Edger	19.99	

Mark All Include inactive

Adjust price of marked items by (amount or %) 10.0% based on Current Price Adjust

Round up to nearest 1.00

OK Cancel Help

Figure 8:46

If you saved these changes, new sales of the item would be at $143.00. **Do not save the changes.** Instead, click **Cancel** to exit the window.

Inventory Reporting

You will now look at several inventory reports. Click **Reports** on the toolbar and select the **Inventory** area.

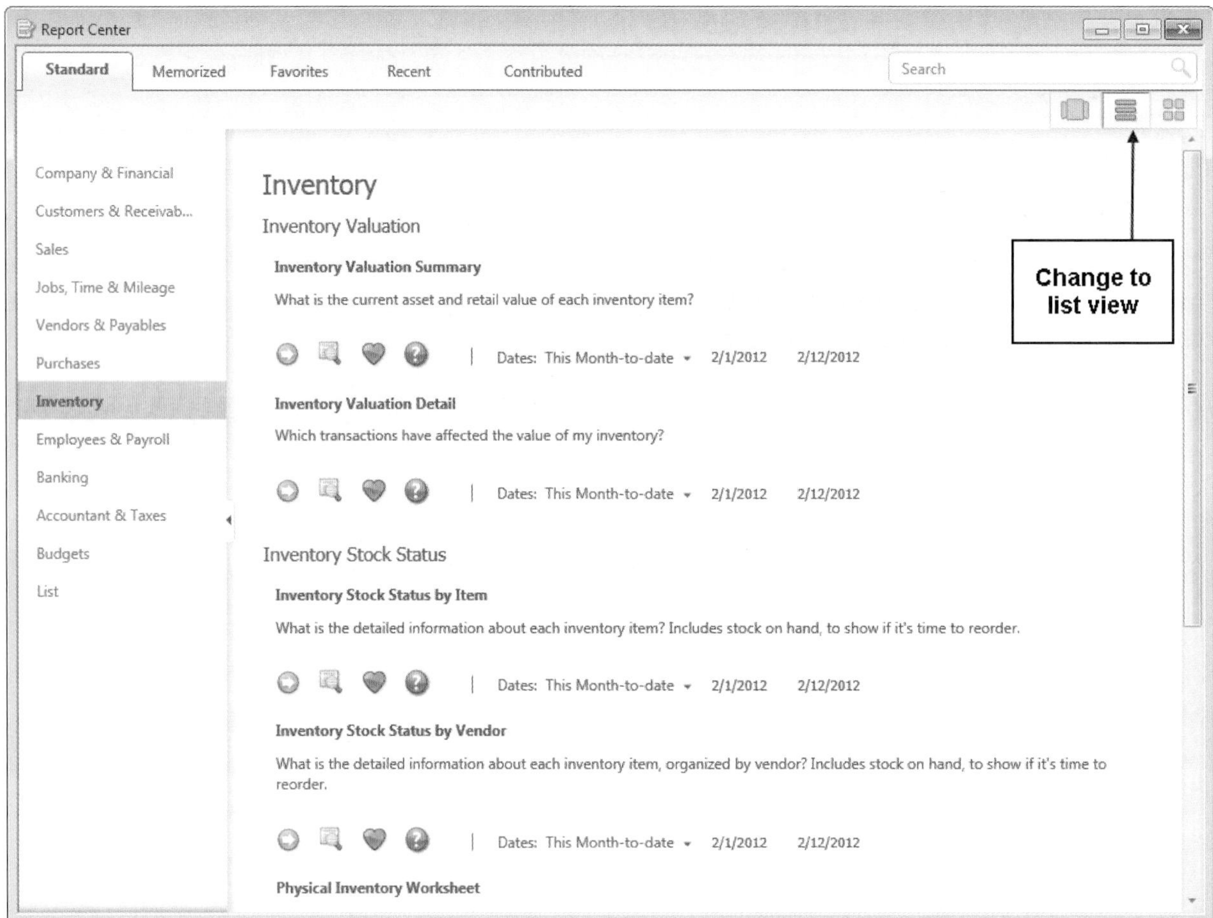

Figure 8:47

Double click **Inventory Valuation Summary** under **Inventory Valuation.** Change the date to "3/31/12." Scroll to the bottom and locate the total **Asset Value.** (See Figure 8:48.)

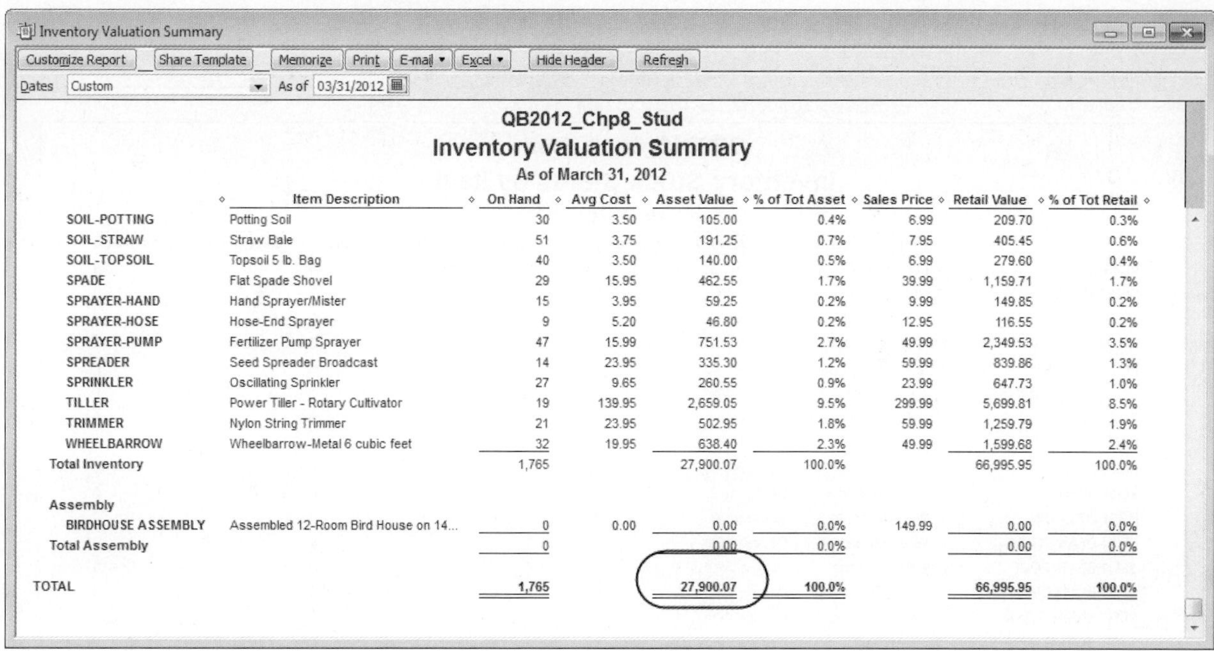

QB2012_Chp8_Stud

Inventory Valuation Summary

As of March 31, 2012

	Item Description	On Hand	Avg Cost	Asset Value	% of Tot Asset	Sales Price	Retail Value	% of Tot Retail
SOIL-POTTING	Potting Soil	30	3.50	105.00	0.4%	6.99	209.70	0.3%
SOIL-STRAW	Straw Bale	51	3.75	191.25	0.7%	7.95	405.45	0.6%
SOIL-TOPSOIL	Topsoil 5 lb. Bag	40	3.50	140.00	0.5%	6.99	279.60	0.4%
SPADE	Flat Spade Shovel	29	15.95	462.55	1.7%	39.99	1,159.71	1.7%
SPRAYER-HAND	Hand Sprayer/Mister	15	3.95	59.25	0.2%	9.99	149.85	0.2%
SPRAYER-HOSE	Hose-End Sprayer	9	5.20	46.80	0.2%	12.95	116.55	0.2%
SPRAYER-PUMP	Fertilizer Pump Sprayer	47	15.99	751.53	2.7%	49.99	2,349.53	3.5%
SPREADER	Seed Spreader Broadcast	14	23.95	335.30	1.2%	59.99	839.86	1.3%
SPRINKLER	Oscillating Sprinkler	27	9.65	260.55	0.9%	23.99	647.73	1.0%
TILLER	Power Tiller - Rotary Cultivator	19	139.95	2,659.05	9.5%	299.99	5,699.81	8.5%
TRIMMER	Nylon String Trimmer	21	23.95	502.95	1.8%	59.99	1,259.79	1.9%
WHEELBARROW	Wheelbarrow-Metal 6 cubic feet	32	19.95	638.40	2.3%	49.99	1,599.68	2.4%
Total Inventory		1,765		27,900.07	100.0%		66,995.95	100.0%
Assembly								
BIRDHOUSE ASSEMBLY	Assembled 12-Room Bird House on 14...	0	0.00	0.00	0.0%	149.99	0.00	0.0%
Total Assembly		0		0.00	0.0%		0.00	0.0%
TOTAL		1,765		27,900.07	100.0%		66,995.95	100.0%

Figure 8:48

The total on this report must equal the total in the general ledger inventory control account. *(Note: Your total will differ if you have not completed previous exercises.)*

Check the balance in your inventory account by selecting ***Reports>>Accountants & Taxes>>Trial Balance*** on the main menu. Enter "3/31/12" as the date range and scroll down to account 13000 Inventory. Compare the balance on your Inventory Valuation Summary report with your balance in 13000 Inventory.

This reconciliation procedure makes sure that sales and purchases of inventory have posted to the correct general ledger accounts. The report and general ledger can become "out of balance" when you fail to properly correct transactions. Therefore, always check the steps in Appendix B when correcting a posted transaction.

Close the Trial Balance and return to the inventory report. The amount for the **Retail Value** shows the sales value of on-hand inventory.

Close this report and open the **Inventory Stock Status by Item** report. Enter the date range of **3/31/12** through **3/31/12**. (See Figure 8:49.)

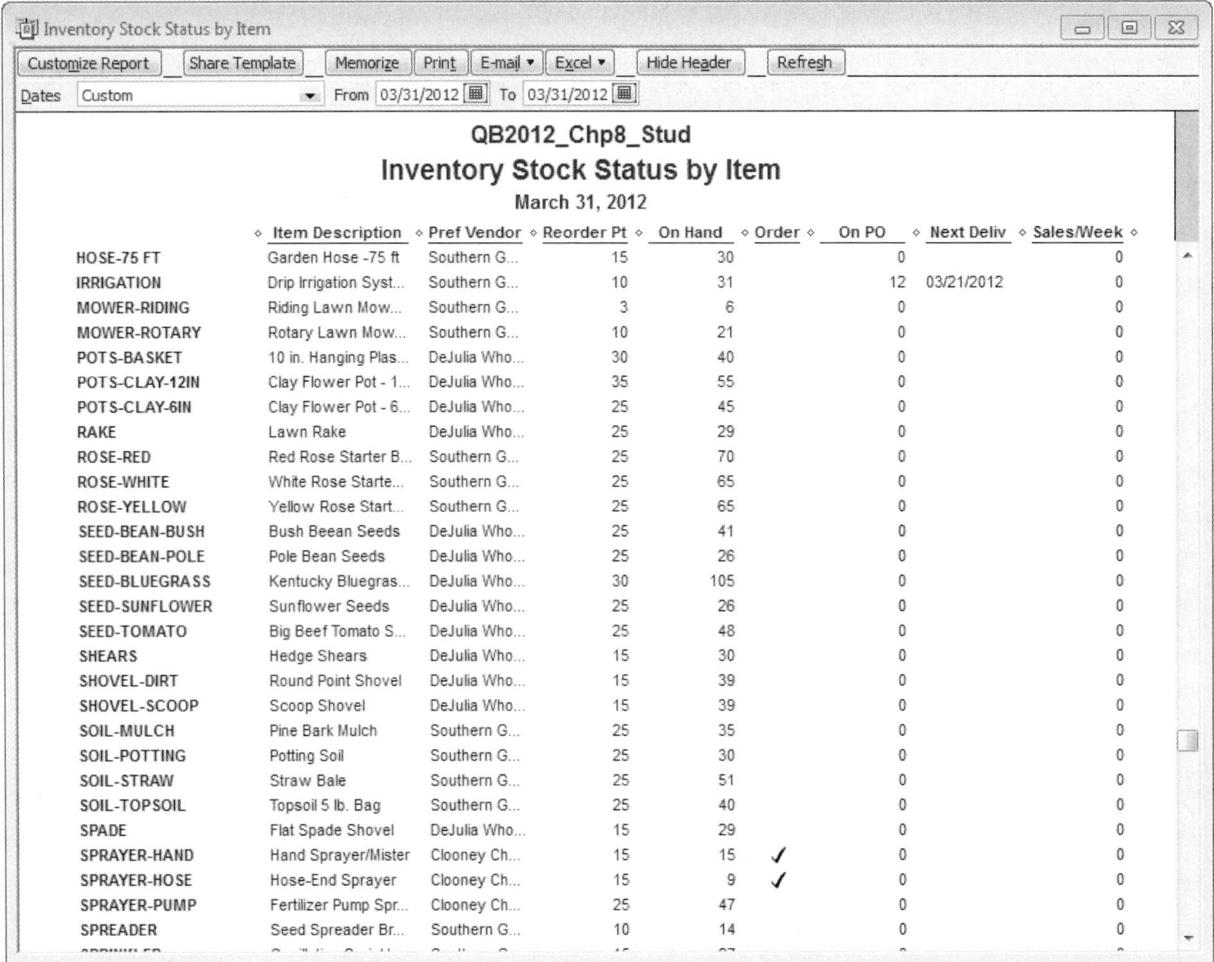

Inventory Stock Status by Item

Customize Report | Share Template | Memorize | Print | E-mail ▾ | Excel ▾ | Hide Header | Refresh

Dates Custom From 03/31/2012 To 03/31/2012

QB2012_Chp8_Stud

Inventory Stock Status by Item

March 31, 2012

	Item Description	Pref Vendor	Reorder Pt	On Hand	Order	On PO	Next Deliv	Sales/Week
HOSE-75 FT	Garden Hose -75 ft	Southern G...	15	30		0		0
IRRIGATION	Drip Irrigation Syst...	Southern G...	10	31		12	03/21/2012	0
MOWER-RIDING	Riding Lawn Mow...	Southern G...	3	6		0		0
MOWER-ROTARY	Rotary Lawn Mow...	Southern G...	10	21		0		0
POTS-BASKET	10 in. Hanging Plas...	DeJulia Who...	30	40		0		0
POTS-CLAY-12IN	Clay Flower Pot - 1...	DeJulia Who...	35	55		0		0
POTS-CLAY-6IN	Clay Flower Pot - 6...	DeJulia Who...	25	45		0		0
RAKE	Lawn Rake	DeJulia Who...	25	29		0		0
ROSE-RED	Red Rose Starter B...	Southern G...	25	70		0		0
ROSE-WHITE	White Rose Starte...	Southern G...	25	65		0		0
ROSE-YELLOW	Yellow Rose Start...	Southern G...	25	65		0		0
SEED-BEAN-BUSH	Bush Beean Seeds	DeJulia Who...	25	41		0		0
SEED-BEAN-POLE	Pole Bean Seeds	DeJulia Who...	25	26		0		0
SEED-BLUEGRASS	Kentucky Bluegras...	DeJulia Who...	30	105		0		0
SEED-SUNFLOWER	Sunflower Seeds	DeJulia Who...	25	26		0		0
SEED-TOMATO	Big Beef Tomato S...	DeJulia Who...	25	48		0		0
SHEARS	Hedge Shears	DeJulia Who...	15	30		0		0
SHOVEL-DIRT	Round Point Shovel	DeJulia Who...	15	39		0		0
SHOVEL-SCOOP	Scoop Shovel	DeJulia Who...	15	39		0		0
SOIL-MULCH	Pine Bark Mulch	Southern G...	25	35		0		0
SOIL-POTTING	Potting Soil	Southern G...	25	30		0		0
SOIL-STRAW	Straw Bale	Southern G...	25	51		0		0
SOIL-TOPSOIL	Topsoil 5 lb. Bag	Southern G...	25	40		0		0
SPADE	Flat Spade Shovel	DeJulia Who...	15	29		0		0
SPRAYER-HAND	Hand Sprayer/Mister	Clooney Ch...	15	15	✓	0		0
SPRAYER-HOSE	Hose-End Sprayer	Clooney Ch...	15	9	✓	0		0
SPRAYER-PUMP	Fertilizer Pump Spr...	Clooney Ch...	25	47		0		0
SPREADER	Seed Spreader Br...	Southern G...	10	14		0		0

Figure 8:49

This report can be used to determine items that need to be reordered. If **On Hand** quantities are less than or equal to **Reorder Pt** quantities, a checkmark appears in the **Order** column. Recall that the reorder point is set on individual items.

It is important to monitor this report to ensure sufficient stock levels exist to fill customer orders.

Close the report and click the **Physical Inventory Worksheet.** Before opening it, use the **Dates** option and select **All.**

The report illustrated in Figure 8:50 can be distributed to employees conducting a physical inventory count. To protect the integrity of the count, you should remove the On Hand quantities column before distributing it.

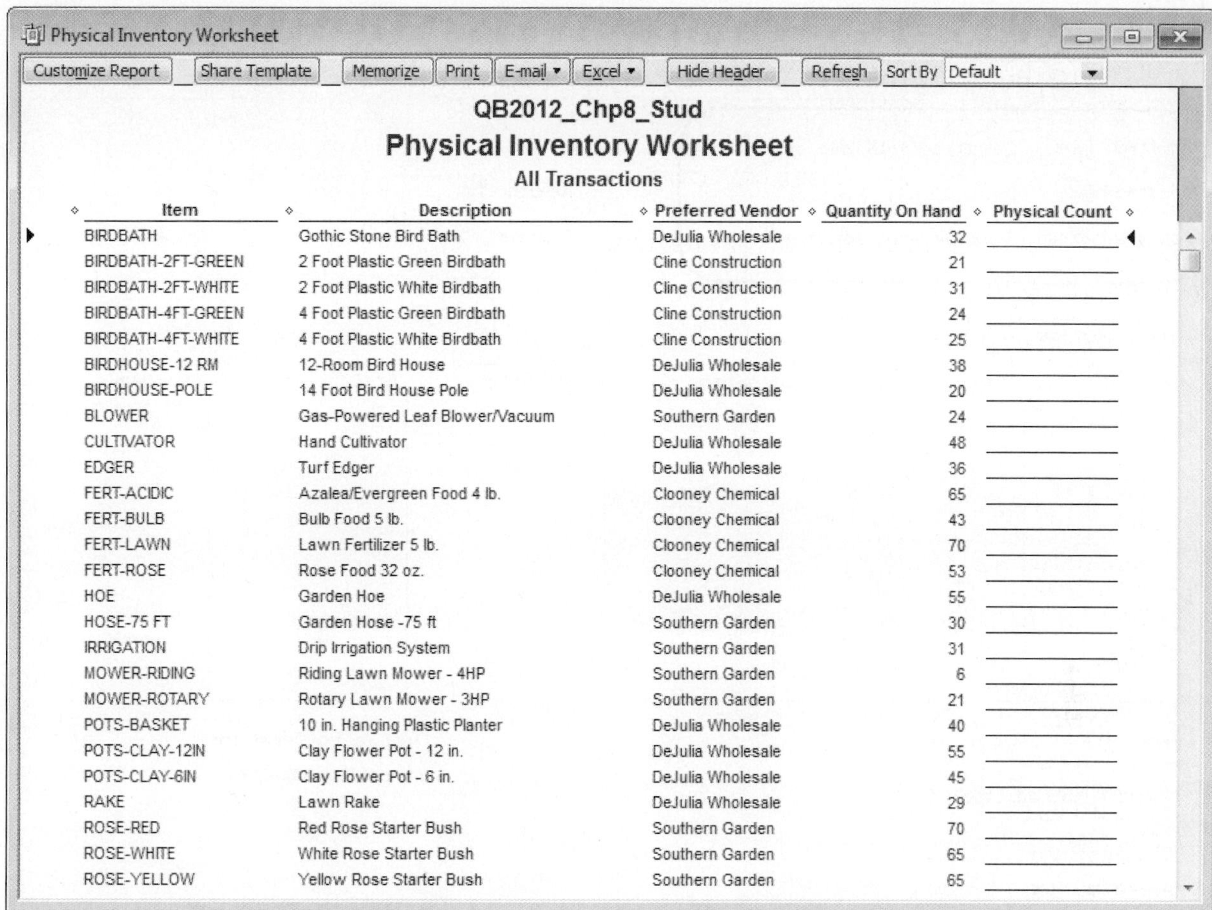

QB2012_Chp8_Stud
Physical Inventory Worksheet
All Transactions

Item	Description	Preferred Vendor	Quantity On Hand	Physical Count
BIRDBATH	Gothic Stone Bird Bath	DeJulia Wholesale	32	
BIRDBATH-2FT-GREEN	2 Foot Plastic Green Birdbath	Cline Construction	21	
BIRDBATH-2FT-WHITE	2 Foot Plastic White Birdbath	Cline Construction	31	
BIRDBATH-4FT-GREEN	4 Foot Plastic Green Birdbath	Cline Construction	24	
BIRDBATH-4FT-WHITE	4 Foot Plastic White Birdbath	Cline Construction	25	
BIRDHOUSE-12 RM	12-Room Bird House	DeJulia Wholesale	38	
BIRDHOUSE-POLE	14 Foot Bird House Pole	DeJulia Wholesale	20	
BLOWER	Gas-Powered Leaf Blower/Vacuum	Southern Garden	24	
CULTIVATOR	Hand Cultivator	DeJulia Wholesale	48	
EDGER	Turf Edger	DeJulia Wholesale	36	
FERT-ACIDIC	Azalea/Evergreen Food 4 lb.	Clooney Chemical	65	
FERT-BULB	Bulb Food 5 lb.	Clooney Chemical	43	
FERT-LAWN	Lawn Fertilizer 5 lb.	Clooney Chemical	70	
FERT-ROSE	Rose Food 32 oz.	Clooney Chemical	53	
HOE	Garden Hoe	DeJulia Wholesale	55	
HOSE-75 FT	Garden Hose -75 ft	Southern Garden	30	
IRRIGATION	Drip Irrigation System	Southern Garden	31	
MOWER-RIDING	Riding Lawn Mower - 4HP	Southern Garden	6	
MOWER-ROTARY	Rotary Lawn Mower - 3HP	Southern Garden	21	
POTS-BASKET	10 in. Hanging Plastic Planter	DeJulia Wholesale	40	
POTS-CLAY-12IN	Clay Flower Pot - 12 in.	DeJulia Wholesale	55	
POTS-CLAY-6IN	Clay Flower Pot - 6 in.	DeJulia Wholesale	45	
RAKE	Lawn Rake	DeJulia Wholesale	29	
ROSE-RED	Red Rose Starter Bush	Southern Garden	70	
ROSE-WHITE	White Rose Starter Bush	Southern Garden	65	
ROSE-YELLOW	Yellow Rose Starter Bush	Southern Garden	65	

Figure 8:50

Close the report and the Report Center before moving on to the tasks performed after conducting a physical count.

PHYSICAL INVENTORY

Although QBP tracks inventory quantities, Baxter still conducts a physical count to confirm that actual quantities agree with QBP quantities. The Physical Inventory Worksheet previously illustrated is distributed to employees taking a physical count. These employees enter the actual quantities counted and the completed report is returned to the accounting department for comparison with QBP.

On the main menu, select ***Vendors>>Inventory Activities>>Adjust Quantity/Value on Hand*** to open the window illustrated in Figure 8:51. Choose the **Adjustment Type** of "Quantity and Total Value," enter the **Adjustment Date** of "3/31/12," and change the **Adjustment Account** to "58500 Inventory Adjustments." In the pop-up window that opens, click **Do not display this message in the future** and click **OK.**

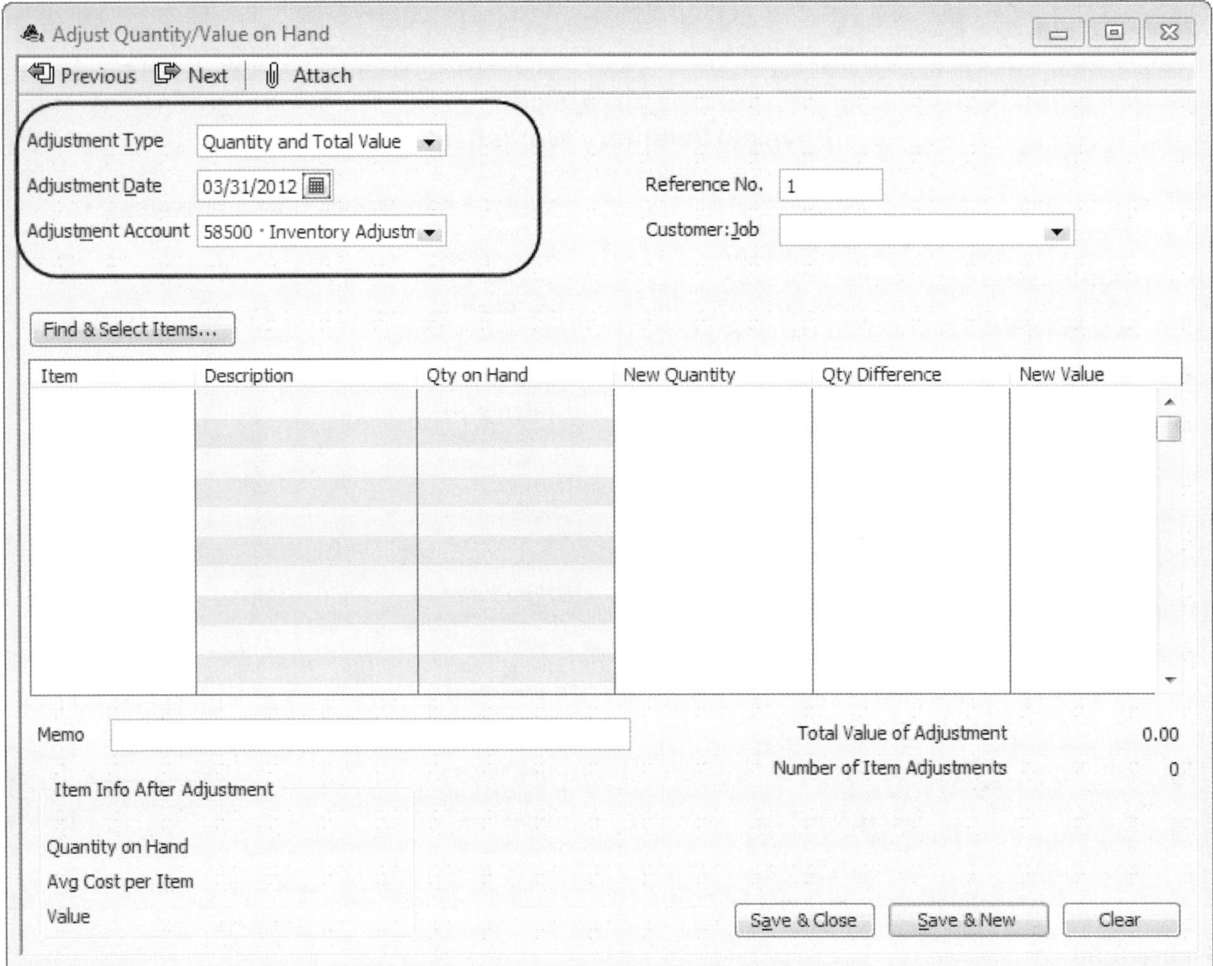

Figure 8:51

The accountant noticed that the physical count for the EDGER item is 35, but the software quantity is 36. It is not unusual for actual quantities to vary slightly from software quantities. Perhaps an item was discarded because it was damaged. However, large discrepancies should be investigated because it may indicate a problem with control over inventory.

You will now record the adjustment that is needed to reconcile QBP quantities to the physical count. Click **Find & Select Items** and click the **checkmark** field on "EDGER." Click **Add Selected Items** to return to the Adjust Quantity/Value on Hand window. In the **New Quantity** column, enter "35" as illustrated next.

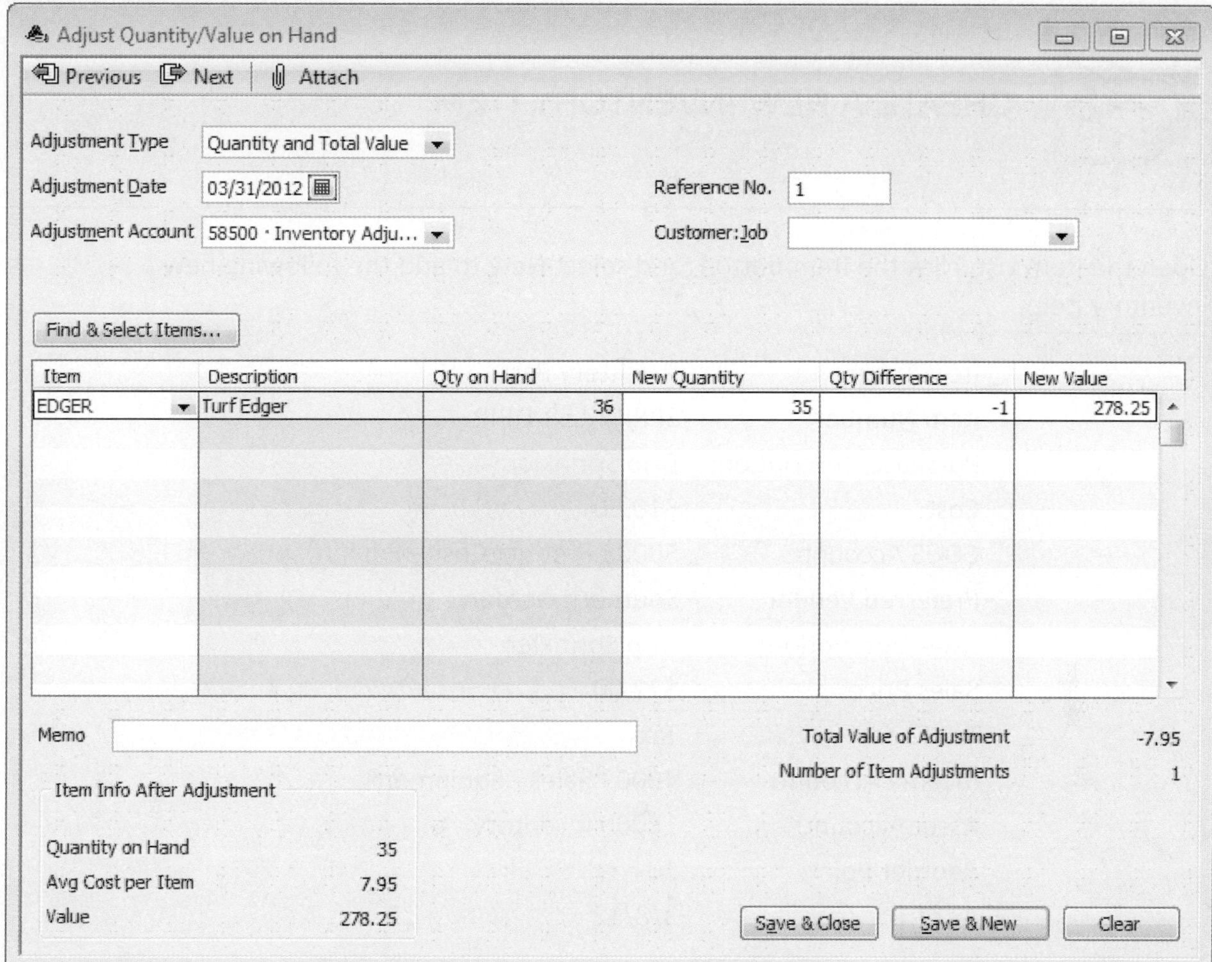

Figure 8:52

This adjustment will debit the Adjustment Account of 58500 Inventory Adjustment and credit 13000 Inventory for $7.95.

Click **Save & Close** to post the adjustment.

Now complete the next exercise to add a new inventory item.

CREATE A NEW INVENTORY ITEM

Open the Item List, click the Item button, and select New to add the following new inventory item.

Item Type:	Inventory Part
Item Number:	SPRINKLER-DRIP
Purchase Description:	Drip Sprinkler
Cost:	$10.50
COGS Account:	50003 Product Cost – Equipment
Preferred Vendor:	Southern Garden
Sales Description:	Drip Sprinkler
Sales Price:	$22.00
Tax Code:	Tax
Income Account:	40003 Sales - Equipment
Asset Account:	13000 Inventory
Reorder Point:	10
As of:	3/8/12

Print an Item Listing report filtered to display only the new item. Add the Account, Purchase Description, Asset Account, and COGS Account columns to the report and delete the Quantity on Hand and Quantity on Purchase Orders columns.

Storefront Sale of Merchandise

On March 24, Baxter made a storefront sale of merchandise. With these sales, customers usually come into the store and pay for items at the time of sale. Therefore, these transactions are recorded using the **Create Sales Receipts** icon.

Follow the next steps to record this sale.

Steps to Record a Storefront Sale of Merchandise

1. On the **Home** page, click **Create Sales Receipts,** hide the History pane, and enter the following information. *(Note: Click No Thanks if QBP prompts on integrated payment processing.)*

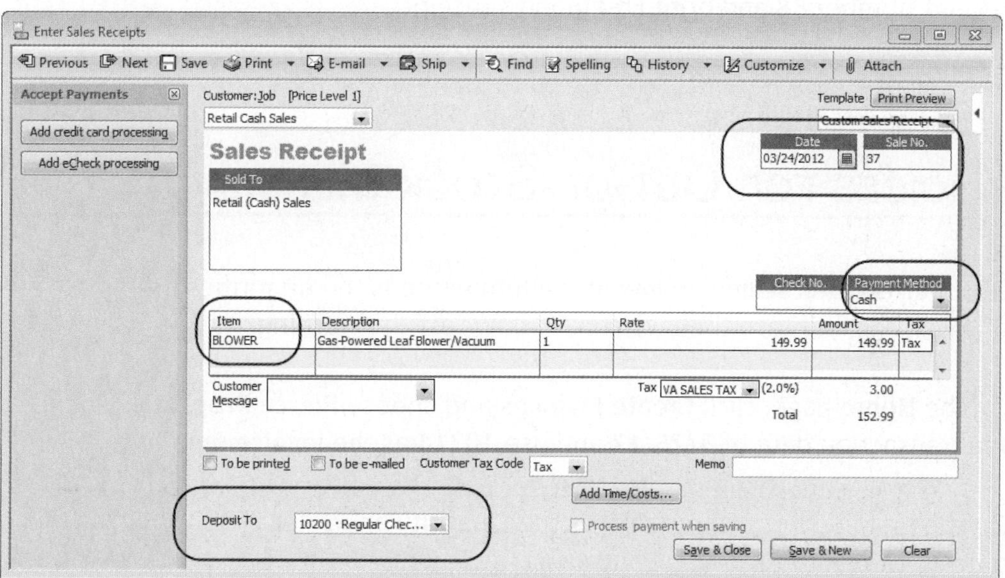

Figure 8:53

2. Click **Save & Close.**

Note: The debit will post to the regular checking account instead of the accounts receivable account because this is not a sale on account.

ENTER A STOREFRONT SALE OF MERCHANDISE

On March 24, 2012, Freemond Country Club picked up 30 bags of topsoil, item SOIL-TOPSOIL. The customer paid with check number 8925 at the time of purchase. Record the sale on receipt number 38 and print Freemond's receipt.

INVOICES FOR OUT-OF-STOCK MERCHANDISE

QBP warns when selling an inventory item exceeds the quantities on-hand. You can override this warning and save the invoice. We now test the warning.

On the **Home** page, click **Create Invoices** and choose **Pierce Properties** as the customer. Enter the transaction date of **3/25/12** and use **10314** as the invoice number.

On the first line item, enter "**25**" as the **Quantity** and select "**BLOWER**" as the item. QBP warns of insufficient stock to fill the invoice. (See Figure 8:54.)

Figure 8:54

Click **OK** and refer to the invoice in Figure 8:55.

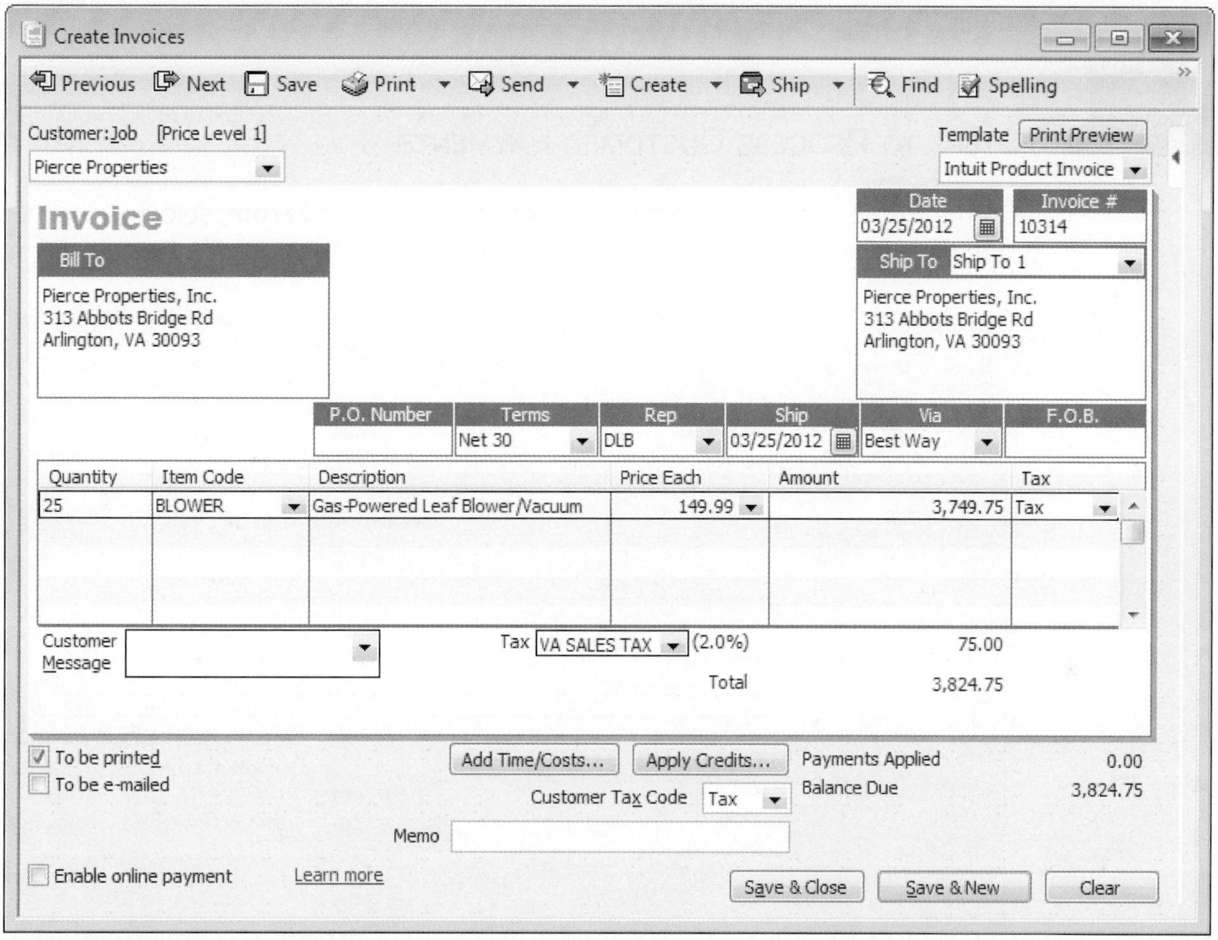

Create Invoices

Previous Next Save Print Send Create Ship Find Spelling

Customer:Job [Price Level 1] Pierce Properties

Template Print Preview Intuit Product Invoice

Invoice

Date 03/25/2012 Invoice # 10314

Bill To
Pierce Properties, Inc.
313 Abbots Bridge Rd
Arlington, VA 30093

Ship To Ship To 1
Pierce Properties, Inc.
313 Abbots Bridge Rd
Arlington, VA 30093

P.O. Number	Terms	Rep	Ship	Via	F.O.B.
	Net 30	DLB	03/25/2012	Best Way	

Quantity	Item Code	Description	Price Each	Amount	Tax
25	BLOWER	Gas-Powered Leaf Blower/Vacuum	149.99	3,749.75	Tax

Customer Message

Tax VA SALES TAX (2.0%) 75.00

Total 3,824.75

To be printed
To be e-mailed

Add Time/Costs... Apply Credits...

Payments Applied 0.00
Balance Due 3,824.75

Customer Tax Code Tax

Memo

Enable online payment Learn more

Save & Close Save & New Clear

Figure 8:55

Click **Save & Close.** Normally you will not sell items without sufficient stock. However, if you receive an insufficient quantity message when working on end-of-chapter exercises, override the warning and save the invoice.

CUSTOMER PAYMENTS

Companies can have thousands of dollars in sales, but without collecting the cash on the sale, continuing operations are threatened. In other words, sales must be realized in cash before the company can pay employees and vendors or invest in the business. This topic focuses on processing customer payments on account. *(Note: There is an online video for this topic.)*

On March 26, Stevenson Leasing remitted check number 875 for $5,303.19, paying Invoices 10307 and 10312 in full. Follow the next steps to record this payment.

Steps to Process Customer Payments

1. On the **Home** page, click **Receive Payments**. In **Received From**, select "Stevenson Leasing." Enter the **Date** of "3/26/12" as illustrated in Figure 8:56

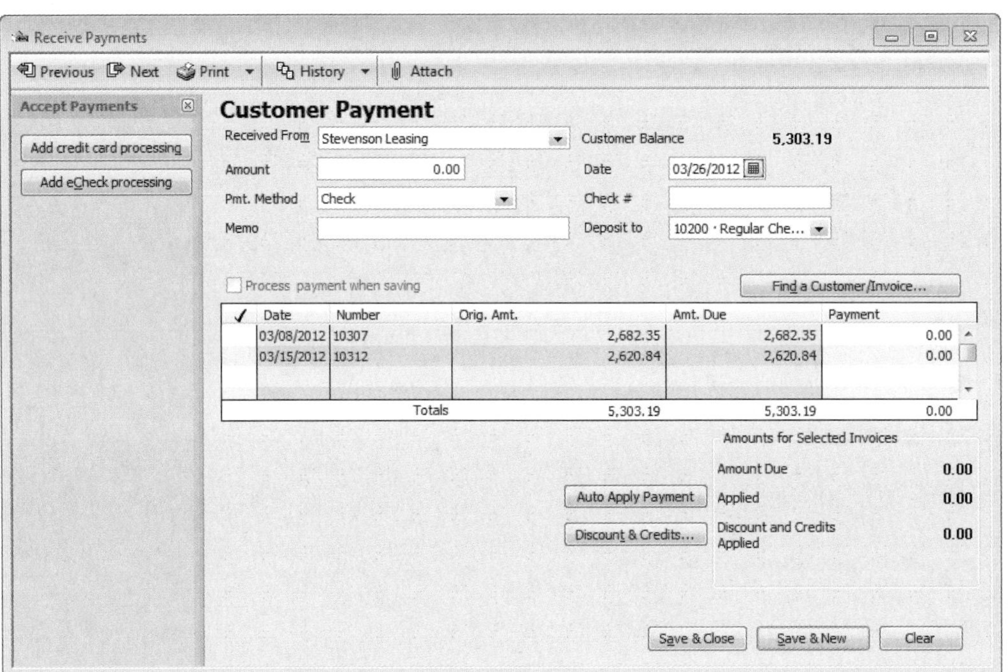

Figure 8:56

2. Now click invoice **10307.** You are prompted as illustrated next because you did not enter an **Amount** first. Mark the option to turn off future messages and click **Yes** so that the Amount will fill in automatically as you select invoices to pay.

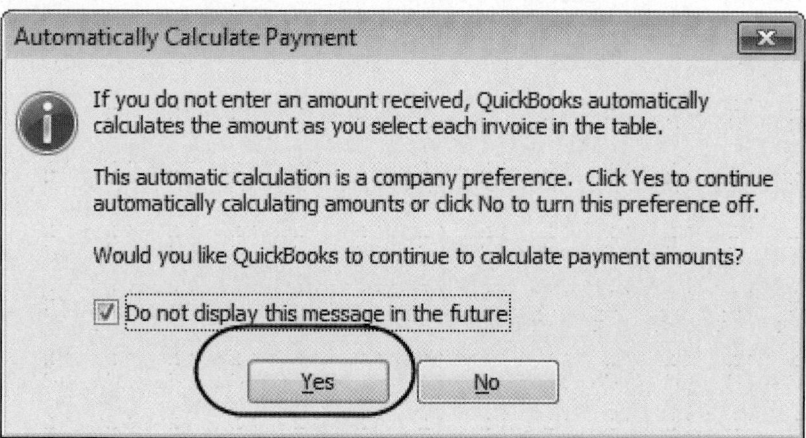

Figure 8:57

3. Click invoice **10312** and the **Amount** shows $5,303.19 as the payment. Enter "875" as the **Check #**.

4. The completed entry is illustrated in Figure 8:58.

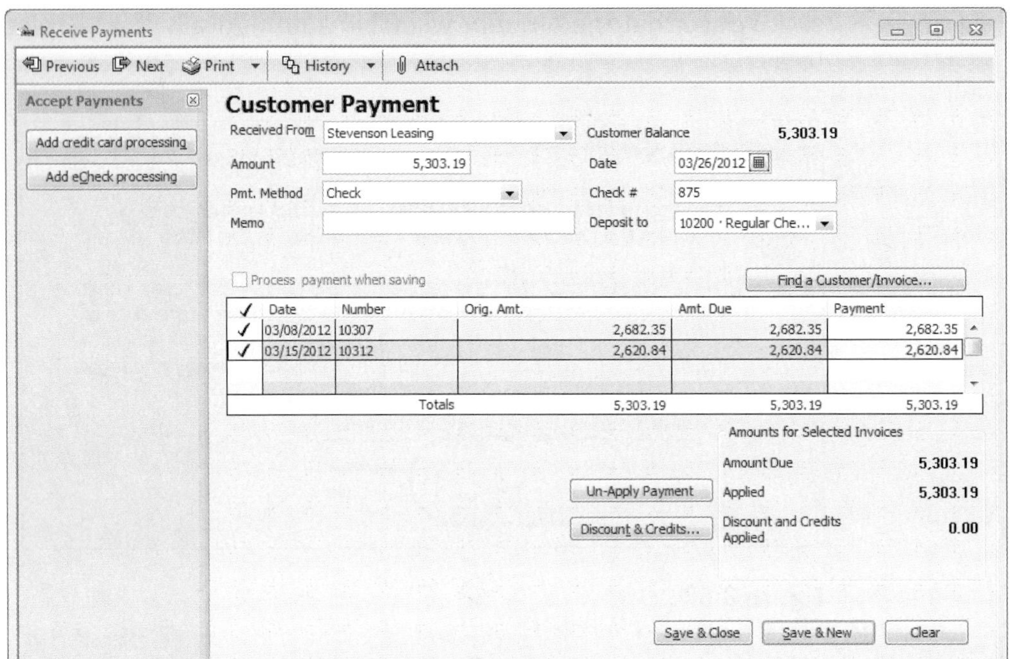

Figure 8:58

Notice that the payment will post (i.e., debit) to **10200 Regular Checking** and the **Pmt Method** defaulted to **Check.**

If needed, the **Un-Apply Payment** button at the bottom is a quick way to clear selected invoices. You can also click an invoice to clear its selection.

5. Click **Save & Close** to post the payment.

Behind the Keys of a Posted Customer Payment

Now trace the audit trail for the payment posted in the previous topic. Recall that in the *MAPS* topic at the beginning of the chapter, we explained that customer payments are recorded on the Cash Receipts Journal then posted to customer accounts and general ledger accounts.

So let us begin by opening the Cash Receipts Journal. On the main menu, select **Reports>>** ***Memorized Reports>>Accounting Journals>>Cash Receipts Journal.*** Enter the date range of **3/26/12.** The refreshed report is shown in Figure 8:59.

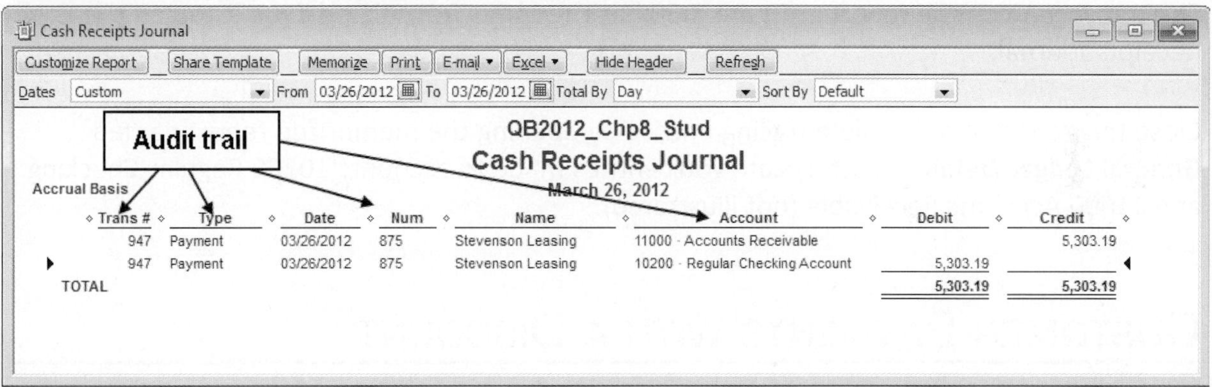

QB2012_Chp8_Stud
Cash Receipts Journal
March 26, 2012
Accrual Basis

Trans #	Type	Date	Num	Name	Account	Debit	Credit
947	Payment	03/26/2012	875	Stevenson Leasing	11000 · Accounts Receivable		5,303.19
947	Payment	03/26/2012	875	Stevenson Leasing	10200 · Regular Checking Account	5,303.19	
TOTAL						5,303.19	5,303.19

Figure 8:59

Note the **Trans #** and **Type** for the payment. *(Note: Your Trans # number may vary based on the number of transactions recorded thus far.)* Now trace this entry to the customer's account.

Close the report, discarding any changes. On the main menu, select ***Reports>>Customers & Receivables>>Transaction List by Customer.***

Enter the date range of **3/26/12.** Click **Customize Report** and select **Trans #** under **Columns.** Click **OK.**

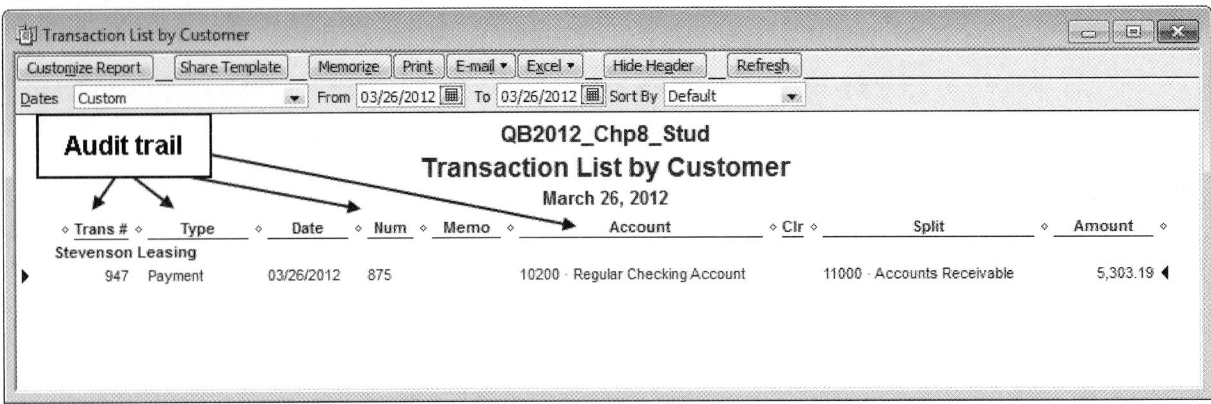

Figure 8:60

The transaction on the report in Figure 8:60 has the same **Trans #** and **Type** listed on the Cash Receipts Journal.

Close this report and complete tracing entries by opening the memorized report named **General Ledger Detail Report**. Locate your entries made to accounts 10200 Regular Checking and 11000 Accounts Receivable (not illustrated).

Customer Payments with a Discount

In this topic, you continue posting customer payments. This time the customer is paying within the discount period.

On March 24, Mason Office Park paid Invoice 10311 with check number 995 for $2,064.66. We next record this transaction.

Steps to Process Customer Payment with a Discount

1. On the **Home** page, click **Receive Payments** and select **Mason Office Park**. Enter “3/24/12” as the **Date**. Enter “995” as the **Check #**. Click Invoice **10311** to select it for payment.

2. Notice in the next illustration that the customer has discounts available.

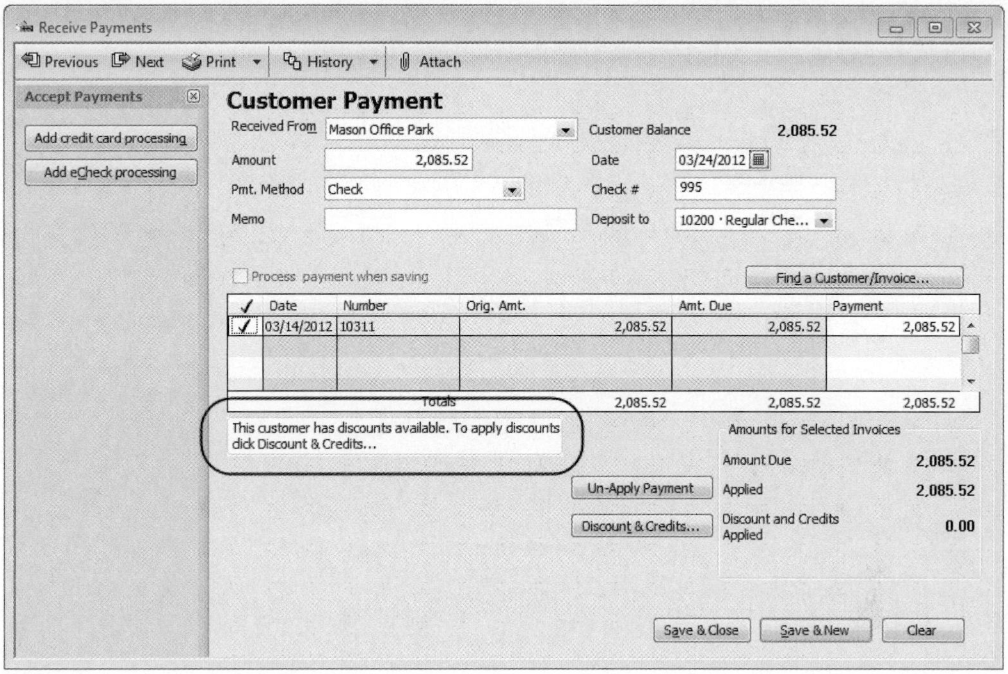

Figure 8:61

3. To apply the discount, click the **Discount and Credits** button to open the window illustrated next. Verify the **Discount Account** illustrated and click **Done.**

Figure 8:62

4. The completed entry is shown in Figure 8:63. Click **Save & Close.**

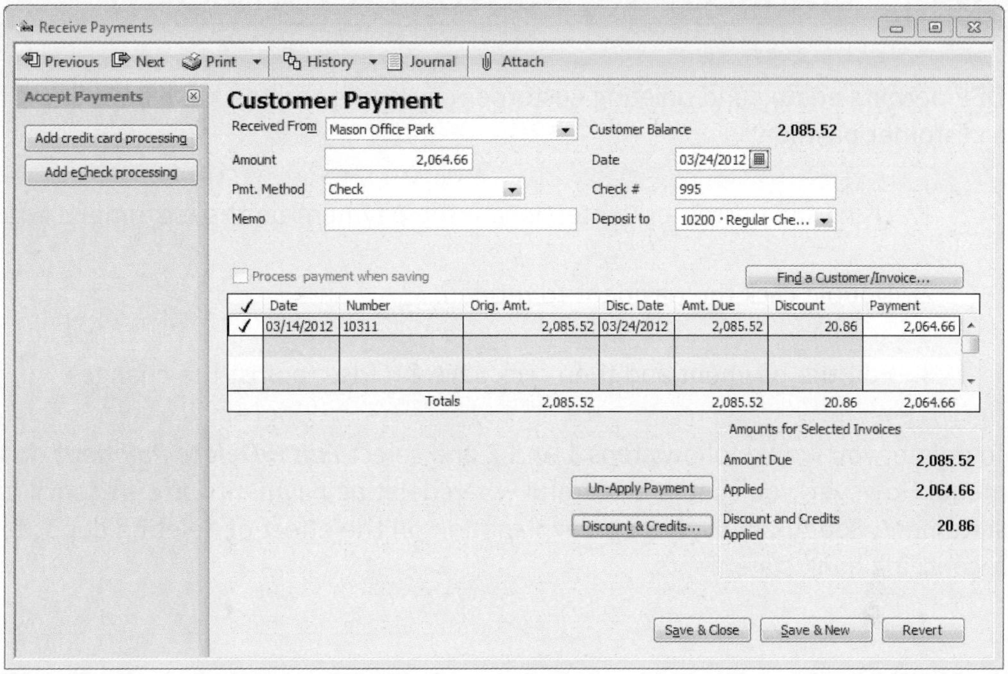

Figure 8:63

Correcting Customer Payments

QBP permits editing and deleting customer payments and the next steps show how to correct a customer payment.

1. Using the Customer Center, locate the payment on the customer's account.
2. Double click the payment to reopen.
3. Edit the payment and then click Save & Close to post the changes.

To delete, you would follow steps 1 and 2 and select ***Edit>>Delete Payment*** on the main menu. However, you should be careful when deleting payments after reconciling the bank statement. See Appendix B for an explanation on the effect of deleting deposits after reconciling bank statements.

RECORD CUSTOMER PAYMENTS

On March 28, 2012, the following payments were deposited:

Chapple Law, check nwumber 8565 for $211.54 for Invoice 10304

Everly Property, check number 9092 for $3,000.00 on Invoice 10308

Note: Everly Property did not pay the invoice in full so change the Amount and keep the option of Leave this as an underpayment.

Post these payments. Print the Cash Receipts Journal filtered for the date range of 3/28/12.

CUSTOMER CREDITS

Occasionally Baxter may need to issue a credit for returned inventory. In the exercise that follows, Baxter issues a credit to Smith Family Garden Center for returning three spades on Invoice 10306.

STEPS TO ENTER A CUSTOMER CREDIT MEMO

1. On the **Home** page, click **Refunds & Credits** and hide the History pane.

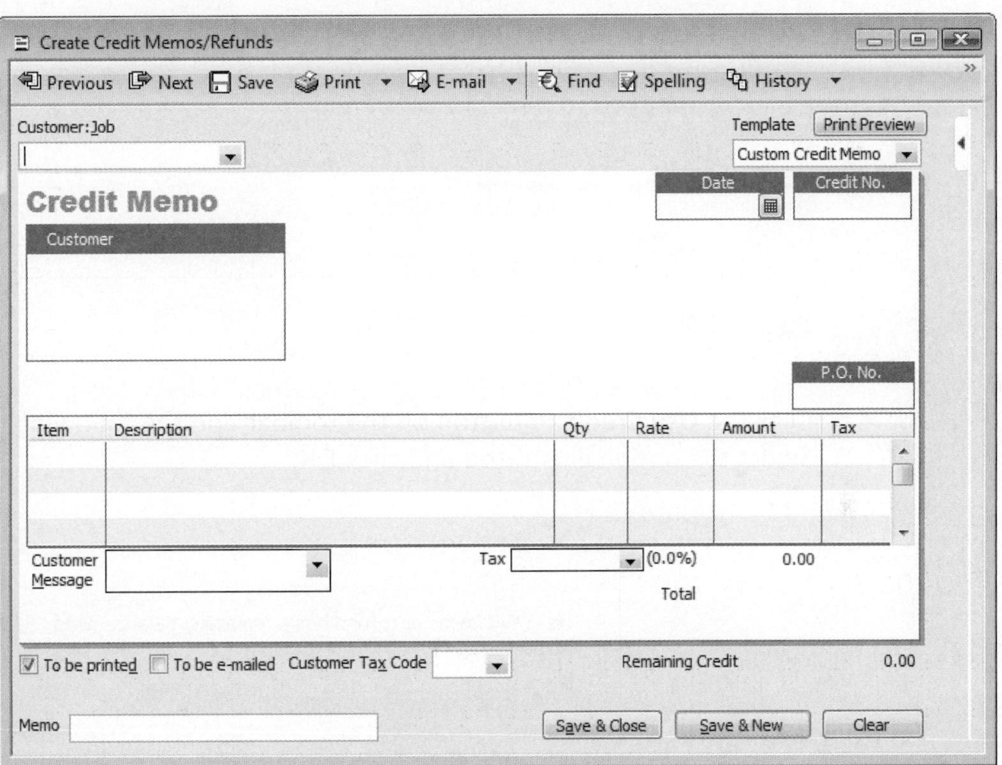

Figure 8:64

2. Select **Smith Family Garden Center** and enter "3/29/12" as the **Date.**

3. In **Item**, select "SPADE" and enter "3" as the **QTY.** The completed credit is shown in Figure 8:65.

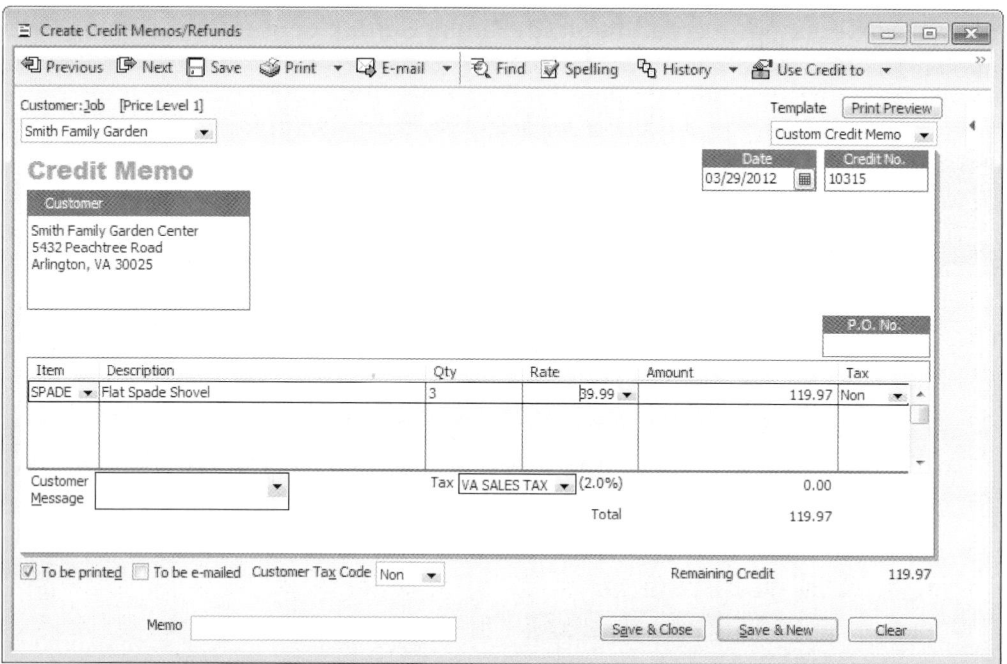

Figure 8:65

4. Click the **Use Credit to** button on the toolbar and the following window opens. Select the option illustrated and click **OK.**

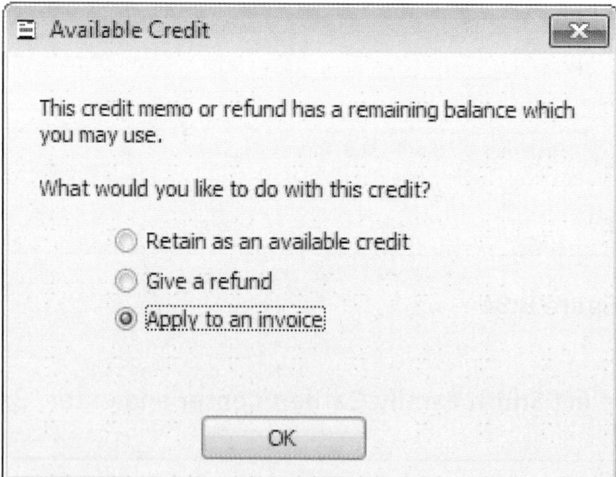

Figure 8:66

5. The window illustrated next shows the credit will be applied to Invoice 10306. Click **Done.** Click **Save & Close** on the Create Credit Memos/Refunds window.

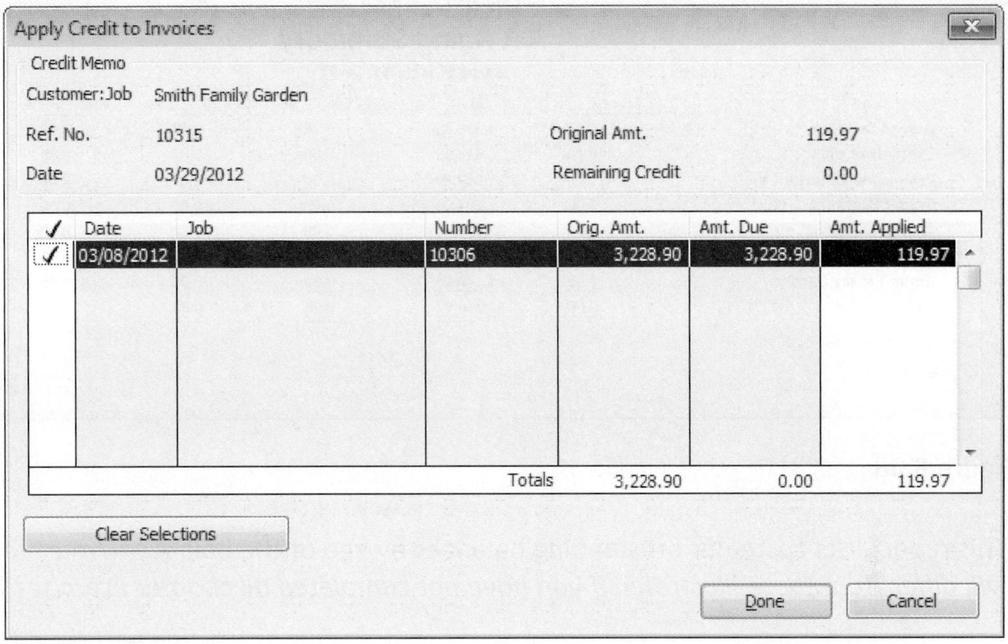

Apply Credit to Invoices

Credit Memo

Customer:Job Smith Family Garden

Ref. No. 10315 Original Amt. 119.97

Date 03/29/2012 Remaining Credit 0.00

✓	Date	Job	Number	Orig. Amt.	Amt. Due	Amt. Applied
✓	03/08/2012		10306	3,228.90	3,228.90	119.97
			Totals	3,228.90	0.00	119.97

Clear Selections

Done Cancel

Figure 8:67

Customer Reporting and Reconciling Activities

QBP offers a variety of customer reports and these reports can be viewed from the **Report Center**. Open this center and select the **Customers & Receivables** area.

Double click the **A/R Aging Summary** report category to open the accounts receivable aging report. Change the date to “3/31/12.” Refresh and the report displays as illustrated in Figure 8:68.

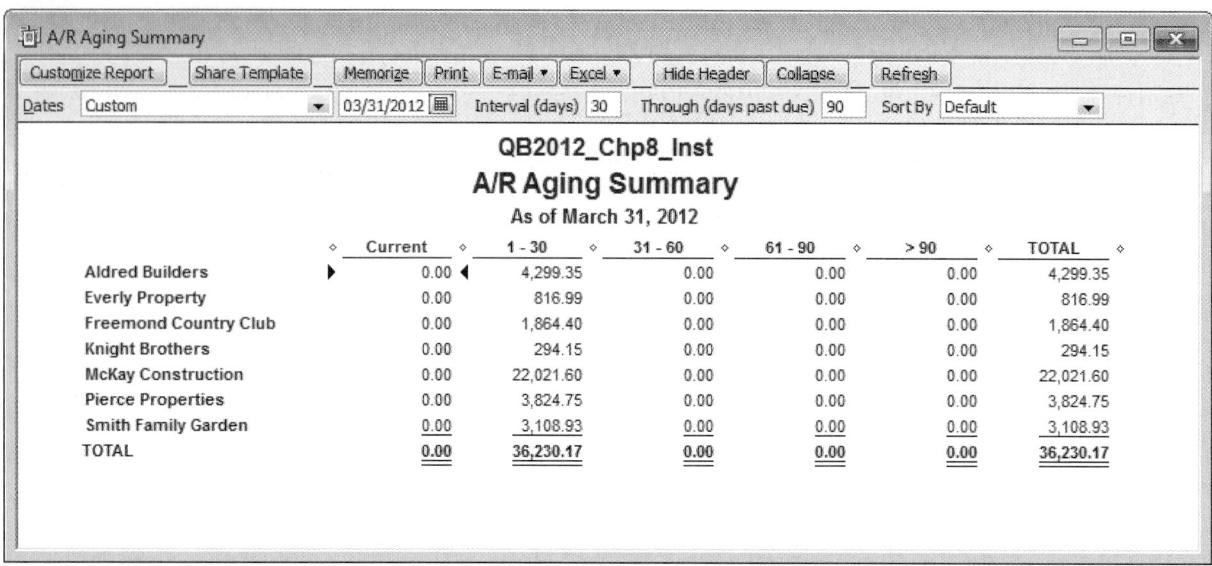
A/R Aging Summary

Customize Report | Share Template | Memorize | Print | E-mail | Excel | Hide Header | Collapse | Refresh

Dates: Custom | 03/31/2012 | Interval (days) 30 | Through (days past due) 90 | Sort By Default

QB2012_Chp8_Inst

A/R Aging Summary

As of March 31, 2012

	Current	1 - 30	31 - 60	61 - 90	> 90	TOTAL
Aldred Builders	0.00	4,299.35	0.00	0.00	0.00	4,299.35
Everly Property	0.00	816.99	0.00	0.00	0.00	816.99
Freemond Country Club	0.00	1,864.40	0.00	0.00	0.00	1,864.40
Knight Brothers	0.00	294.15	0.00	0.00	0.00	294.15
McKay Construction	0.00	22,021.60	0.00	0.00	0.00	22,021.60
Pierce Properties	0.00	3,824.75	0.00	0.00	0.00	3,824.75
Smith Family Garden	0.00	3,108.93	0.00	0.00	0.00	3,108.93
TOTAL	0.00	36,230.17	0.00	0.00	0.00	36,230.17

Figure 8:68

This report lists customer outstanding balances by age of the balance. *(Note: Your balances will differ from those illustrated if you have not completed all chapter exercises.)*

The report serves two important purposes. First, Baxter uses it to monitor customer payments and manage company cash flow, thus, mitigating the risk of future sales to customers failing to pay.

Second, this report is used to reconcile customer activities to the accounts receivable control account. This task is performed by comparing the report's total amount due with the March ending balance in general ledger account 11000 Accounts Receivable. Close this report.

Now view the balance in accounts receivable. Open the **Trial Balance** report from the **Accountant & Taxes** category in the **Report Center** and filter the report for 3/31/12 (not illustrated). Scroll down and locate the balance in 11000 Accounts Receivable. The total on the A/R Aging report and the balance in Accounts Receivable on the Trial Balance must agree to verify proper recording of customer activities.

These balances can become out of balance when you improperly correct customer transactions. Therefore, always correct customer transactions by referring to the instructions in Appendix B.

You should reconcile the aged receivables report to the accounts receivable balance at the end of every month and prior to issuing financial reports. Close this report.

Return to the **A/R Aging** category to open the **A/R Aging Detail** report (not illustrated). This report lists invoices by invoice age. Close this report and the Report Center.

Write Off a Customer Invoice

You will find that customers do not always pay. Furthermore, customers sometimes pay the wrong amount. Instead of calling a payment error to the customer's attention, Baxter has decided to write off the invoice balance.

The instructions that follow write off an invoice balance while recording the payment. The instructions in Chapter 4 illustrated writing off the balance after posting the payment.

STEPS TO WRITE OFF A CUSTOMER'S INVOICE

1. On the **Home** page, click **Receive Payments**. Complete the window as illustrated in Figure 8:69.

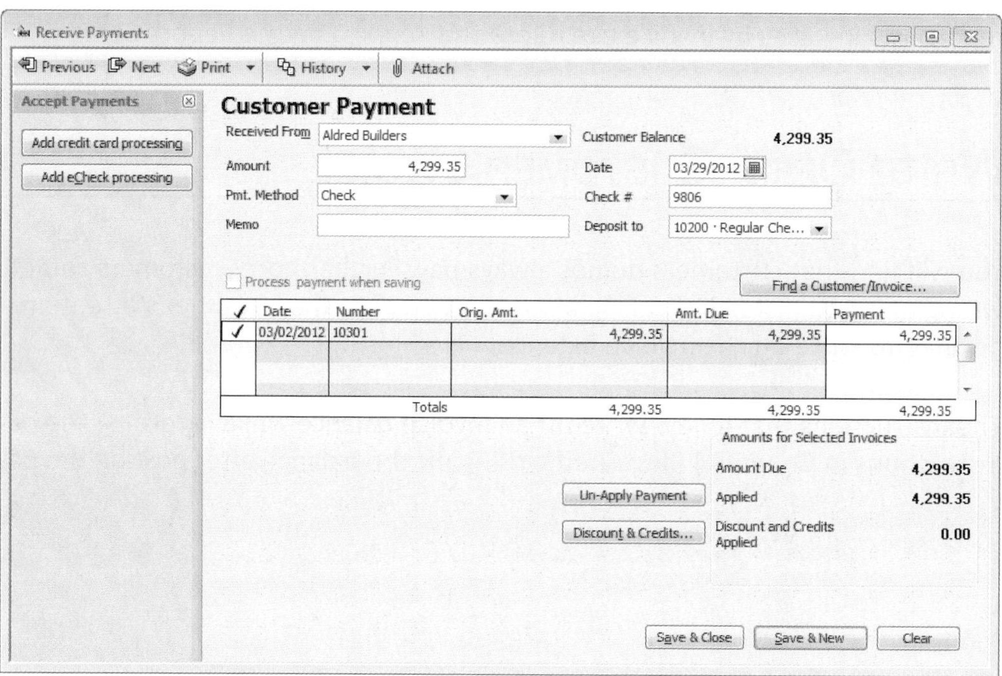

Figure 8:69

2. Now change **Amount** to "4,299.25" and the following information appears at the bottom of the Receive Payments window. Choose the option illustrated.

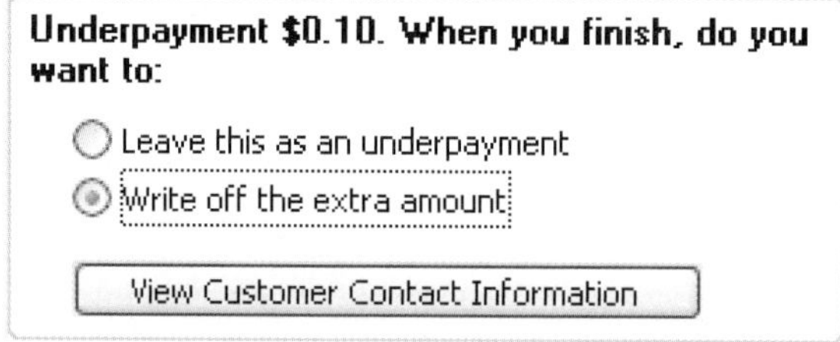

Figure 8:70

3. Click **Save & Close** and the window illustrated next opens for you to enter the posting account for the adjustment. Select the account shown and click **OK.**

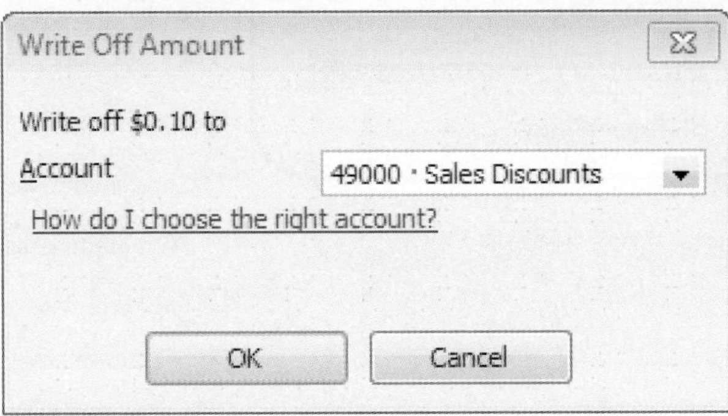

Figure 8:71

Note: If writing off a bad debt invoice then you would use 11100 Allowance for Doubtful Accounts.

CUSTOMER STATEMENTS

Baxter mails customer statements once a month. These statements list invoice and payment activity and prompt customers to pay.

Click **Statements** on the Home page to open the window illustrated in Figure 8:72. Enter the date and options illustrated.

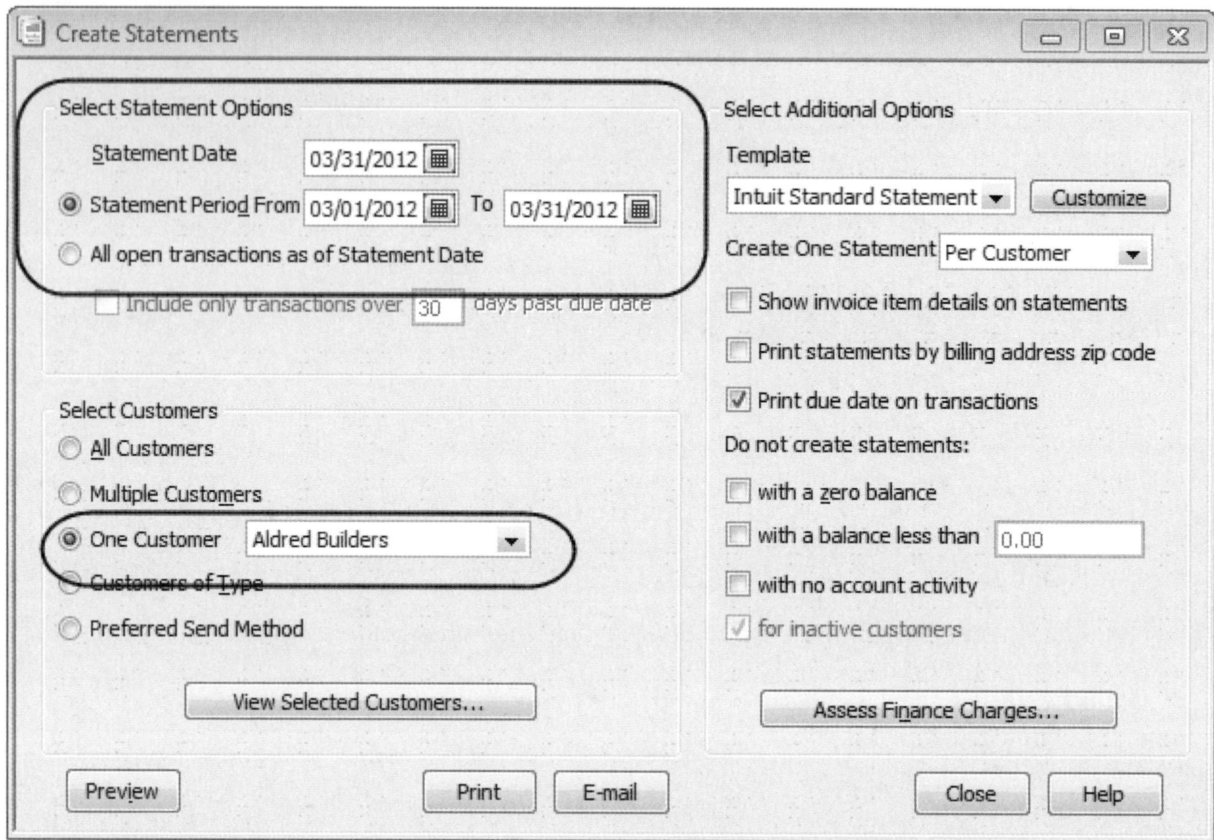

Figure 8:72

Click **Preview** and the first statement appears. (See Figure 8:73.)

Statement

QB2012_Chp8_Stud
1352 W. Maple Ave
Arlington, VA 23523

Date
3/31/2012

To:
Aldred Builders, Inc. 412 Sever Rd Arlington, VA 30092

Amount Due	Amount Enc.
$0.00	

Date	Transaction	Amount	Balance
02/29/2012	Balance forward		0.00
03/02/2012	INV #10301. Due 04/01/2012.	4,299.35	4,299.35
03/29/2012	PMT #9806.	-4,299.25	0.10
03/29/2012	Discount #9806.	-0.10	0.00

CURRENT	1-30 DAYS PAST DUE	31-60 DAYS PAST DUE	61-90 DAYS PAST DUE	OVER 90 DAYS PAST DUE	Amount Due
0.00	0.00	0.00	0.00	0.00	$0.00

Figure 8:73

Click **Print** and, when prompted to verify that statements printed correctly, click **Yes**.

When QBP prompts to remind you that statements can also be emailed, check the option to turn off future messages and click **OK.**

Click **Close** to exit the window.

You have now completed the chapter. ***Make a backup of the data file to a backup file named "QB2012_Chp8_Stud_Completed."***

SUMMARY

In this chapter, you learned *MAPS* for customer transactions before entering transactions in QBP. By understanding manual entries, you were able to anticipate QBP's *Behind the Keys* entries. Understanding a transaction's effect on financial accounts is critical to posting transactions correctly and to tracing the audit trail of a posted transaction.

After completing this chapter, you are skilled in recording customer invoices, payments, and credit memos for a merchandising business. You can manage the master accounts linked to transactions (i.e., customer accounts and inventory items). You understand the customer, inventory, and sales reports that let you monitor and document customer activities. With firm knowledge on processing customer activities, you are now ready to take on vendor activities in the next chapter.

END-OF-CHAPTER QUESTIONS

TRUE/FALSE

_____ 1. When saving an invoice containing inventory items, QBP will post cost of goods sold.

_____ 2. The Sales Journal report will display customer credit memo transactions.

_____ 3. When a customer pays for inventory at the time of sale, QBP posts entries to the inventory account but not to accounts receivable.

_____ 4. When adjusting an inventory item, decreasing the quantity on hand will post a credit to the inventory account.

_____ 5. Companies do not need to conduct a physical inventory count because QBP stores on-hand inventory quantities.

_____ 6. QBP uses the date entered on a customer payment to determine if a customer will receive a discount.

_____ 7. You can email sales invoices in QBP.

_____ 8. Customer statements list the age of an invoice.

_____ 9. QBP offers the LIFO, FIFO, and average cost methods of valuing inventory.

_____ 10. You must delete the original customer payment transaction and reenter it to correct the transaction date.

_____ 11. The menu command for adjusting inventory quantities is found under the Customers menu.

_____ 12. You can open the Create Invoices window from the Home page and from the Customers menu.

_____ 13. You can open the Create Statements window from the Home page but not from the Customers menu.

_____ 14. The Create Credit Memos/Refunds window contains a History pane.

_____ 15. You can use the Transactions tab on the Customer Center to view all recorded credit memos.

MULTIPLE CHOICE

_____ 1. Saving a sales invoice containing inventory items will post entries to the _____ accounts.
   a. Sales and accounts receivable
   b. Sales, accounts receivable, and cost of goods sold
   c. Sales, accounts receivable, cost of goods sold, and inventory
   a. None of the above

_____ 2. Saving a cash sale of merchandise will post entries to the _____ accounts.
   a. Cash, accounts receivable, and sales
   b. Cash, accounts receivable, inventory, and cost of goods sold
   c. Cash, sales, inventory, and cost of goods sold
   d. None of the above

_____ 3. Saving a credit memo posts entries to the _____ accounts.
   a. Sales and accounts receivable
   b. Sales, accounts receivable, and cost of goods sold
   c. Sales, accounts receivable, and inventory
   d. Sales, accounts receivable, cost of goods sold, and inventory

_____ 4. Which report will let you analyze the retail value of inventory?
   a. Inventory Valuation Summary
   b. Inventory Valuation Detail
   c. Inventory Stock Status by Item
   d. Both a and b

_____ 5. An inventory valuation report can be used to _____.
   a. View the cost value of an item
   b. Reconcile inventory values to the general ledger
   c. See on-hand quantities as of a specific date
   d. All of the above

_____ 6. Reports needed to document the audit trail of a posted sales invoice are the _____.
   a. General Journal and Sales Journal
   b. General Ledger Detail Report, Transaction List by Customer, and Sales Journal
   c. General Ledger, Customer Transaction History, and Cash Receipts Journal
   d. General Journal, Transaction List by Customer, and Sales Journal

_____ 7. The A/R Aging Summary report _____.
   a. Is used to reconcile customer balances with the accounts receivable account
   b. Lists customer balances by aging categories
   c. Both a and b
   d. None of the above

_____ 8. The A/R Aging Summary report is located in the _____ area of the Report Center.
   a. Company & Financial
   b. Sales
   c. Customers & Receivables
   d. Vendors & Payables

_____ 9. Which report will show the age of each invoice owed by a customer?
   a. A/R Aging Detail
   b. A/R Aging Summary
   c. Both a and b
   d. None of the above

_____ 10. Which report is reviewed to identify inventory items that need to be reordered?
   a. Inventory Valuation Detail
   b. Inventory Stock Status by Item
   c. Physical Inventory Worksheet
   d. Inventory Valuation Summary

PRACTICE SET

In this practice set, you will record customer activities for April 2012. Keep the following in mind:

- Unless otherwise instructed, accept all defaults on transactions, including default tax codes, default sales rates, and default terms.
- You will print sales invoices and reports in Step 2, so do not print transactions unless otherwise instructed and make sure all invoices are marked "***To be printed.***"

<u>Begin by:</u>

- Opening the software.
- Opening the **QB2012_Chp8_PracSet_Stud** data file. Add your initials to the end to the Company Name by clicking ***Company>>Company Information*** on the main menu. Click **OK** to save the changes.
- **Toggling the software to the PRO EDITION** by selecting ***File>>Toggle to Another Edition*** on the main menu and choosing **QuickBooks Pro** as the edition.

1. Record the following transactions.

2012

Apr 1 Receive check number 1077 for $211.54 from Chapple Law paying Invoice 10304 in full. *(When prompted on automatically calculating payments, mark the option to turn off future messages and click Yes.)*

Apr 2 Issue Invoice 10313 to Rose University for $519.88 for the following items. *(When prompted about sales tax codes, mark the option to turn off future messages and click OK. Also, remember to mark the To be printed option.)*

QTY	Item	Price Each
2	SPREADER	$ 59.99
10	HOSE-75 FT	$ 39.99

Apr 5 Issue Invoice 10314 to Knight Brothers for $3,199.50 for the following items.

QTY	Item	Price Each
30	SHEARS	$ 19.99
20	IRRIGATION	129.99

Apr 7 Issue Invoice 10315 to Franklin Botanical for $2,019.42, with tax, for the following items.

QTY	Item	Price Each
10	BLOWER	$ 149.99
8	TRIMMER	59.99

Receive check number 750 for $1,864.40 from Freedmond Country Club paying Invoice 10305.

Receive check number 255 for $3,228.00 from Smith Family Garden paying Invoice 10306. Write off the $ 0.90 underpayment to the 49000 Sales Discounts account.

Apr 9 Issue Invoice 10316 to Smith Family Garden for $4,612.30 for the following items.

QTY	Item	Price Each
10	TILLER	$ 299.99
10	SPREADER	59.99
50	POTS-CLAY-12IN	11.25 (Price Level 2)

2012

Apr 13 Issue Invoice 10317 to Saia's Neighborhood for $4,619.10 for the following items.

QTY	Item	Price Each
30	SOIL-TOPSOIL	$ 6.99
30	ROSE-RED	16.99
30	BIRDBATH	129.99

Post to the Retail Cash Sales account a sale for the following items on receipt number 37 for $713.80, with tax. ***Print the receipt.***

QTY	Item	Price Each
10	EDGER	$ 19.99
10	WHEELBARROW	49.99

Apr 16 Receive check number 735 for $4,299.35 from Aldred Builders paying Invoice 10301 in full.

Issue credit memo 10318 for $305.98, with tax, to Stevenson Leasing for returning 2 BLOWER items on Invoice 10312. ***Print the credit memo.***

Apr 21 Receive the following checks:

Check number 995 for $2,085.52 from Mason Office Park paying Invoice 10311 in full.

Check number 6725 for $4,997.21 from Stevenson Leasing paying Invoices 10307 and 10312 in full.

Apr 22 Issue Invoice 10319 to Golden Gardens for $4,345.63 for the following items.

QTY	Item	Price Each
2	MOWER-RIDING	$ 1,799.00
20	ROSE-YELLOW	16.99
17	SPRINKLER	23.99

2012

Apr 26 Create the following new customer.

Rose Gardens Supply
603 W. Arndale Street
Centerville, VA 30004

Customer Type:	WHOLE
Payment Terms:	Net 30
Tax Code:	Non
Price Level:	Price Level 1
Credit Limit:	$20,000.00

Issue Invoice 10320 to the new customer for $149.85 for the following item.

QTY	Item	Price Each
15	FERT-LAWN	$ 9.99

2. Print the following.

   a. Invoices 10313 through 10320. You can print using ***File>>Print Forms>>Invoices*** on the main menu. If you do not have seven invoices, totaling $19,015.68, verify that all invoices are marked "To be printed" and the invoices contain the correct items.

   b. Cash Receipts Journal for April 1 to April 30.

   c. Sales Journal for April 1 to April 30.

   d. Inventory Valuation Summary for April 30. Explain how you would use this report.

   e. A/R Aging Detail report at April 30. Explain how you would use this report.

   f. Customer statement dated April 30 for Rose Gardens Supply showing all open transactions. *(Note: Use the One Customer option under Select Customers.)*

3. ***Back up the data file to a backup file named "QB2012_Chp8_PracSet_Stud_Completed."***

Internet Mini-Project

To complete this mini-project, go to the Website at ***www.pearsonhighered.com/brunsdon/*** and download the instruction file named **Alex Tools.pdf** and the data file named **Alex Tools.QBW.**

CHAPTER 9 VENDOR ACTIVITIES FOR A MERCHANDISING BUSINESS

LEARNING OBJECTIVES

In this chapter, you process vendor activities, which include ordering goods, entering vendor bills and receipts of goods, and remitting vendor payments. While performing these activities, you will:

1. Review the *MAPS* for vendor transactions before posting transactions in the software
2. Learn to use the Vendor Center to manage vendor activities
3. Record vendor purchase orders for inventory
4. Learn to correct purchase orders
5. Record vendor bills and receipts for items on purchase orders
6. Go *Behind the Keys* to view posted bill and receipt transactions
7. Learn to correct a vendor bill
8. Record a vendor bill for a posted receipt
9. Learn to manage vendor accounts
10. Record vendor bills for expenses
11. Learn to memorize vendor bills
12. Pay vendors
13. Go *Behind the Keys* to view posted payments
14. Learn to correct vendor payments
15. Write a check to a vendor bill without entering a bill
16. Pay sales tax
17. Record vendor credits
18. Prepare and analyze vendor, purchasing, and inventory reports
19. Reconcile vendor activities to the general ledger

Begin by:

- Opening the software.
- Opening the **QB2012_Chp9_Stud** data file. Add your initials to the end to the Company Name by clicking ***Company>>Company Information*** on the main menu. Click **OK** to save the changes.
- **Toggling the software to the PRO EDITION** by selecting ***File>>Toggle to Another Edition*** on the main menu and **choosing QuickBooks Pro** as the edition.

Manual Accounting Procedures

As in the previous chapter, you begin by learning the manual accounting procedures (*MAPS*) for posting vendor activities before using the software. These procedures help you to understand the process of posting transactions since the software uses a similar process.

We begin by explaining the process of using purchase orders (POs) to authorize purchases of inventory. POs are documents that list item numbers, quantities, and prices for orders to a vendor. These documents serve as a control over purchasing inventory.

In a manual system, the warehouse creates POs to restock inventory. PO's are sent to a Baxter employee having authorization to order inventory. This employee signs the POs before placing the order with the vendor.

The vendor refers to the PO when filling the items. After filling, the vendor ships the items and encloses either a packing receipt or a bill. When the shipment arrives in Baxter's warehouse, an employee inspects the quality and quantities of items received, noting any discrepancies on the vendor document. This document is sent to the accounting department, where it is matched with the PO. If the vendor document is a packing receipt, the accounting department files it until a vendor bill arrives. Once the bill arrives, the PO and packing receipt are matched to the bill and the vendor is paid. If the vendor document is a bill, it is matched to the PO before paying the vendor.

On March 17, 2012, Sam Prather signs a PO to be sent to Southern Garden. The PO is for 20 items of IRRIGATION at $59.95 each. A copy of the PO is sent to Melvin in accounting, who files the document until matched with the vendor document sent with the shipment. POs do not trigger accounting recognition because the liability does not occur until after receiving the items.

The vendor's shipment arrives on March 18. Inventory clerk, Al Duke, inspects the merchandise before placing items on warehouse shelves. Al sends the packing receipt to Melvin, who matches it to the PO and files both documents until the bill arrives.

On March 22, Melvin receives the following bill.

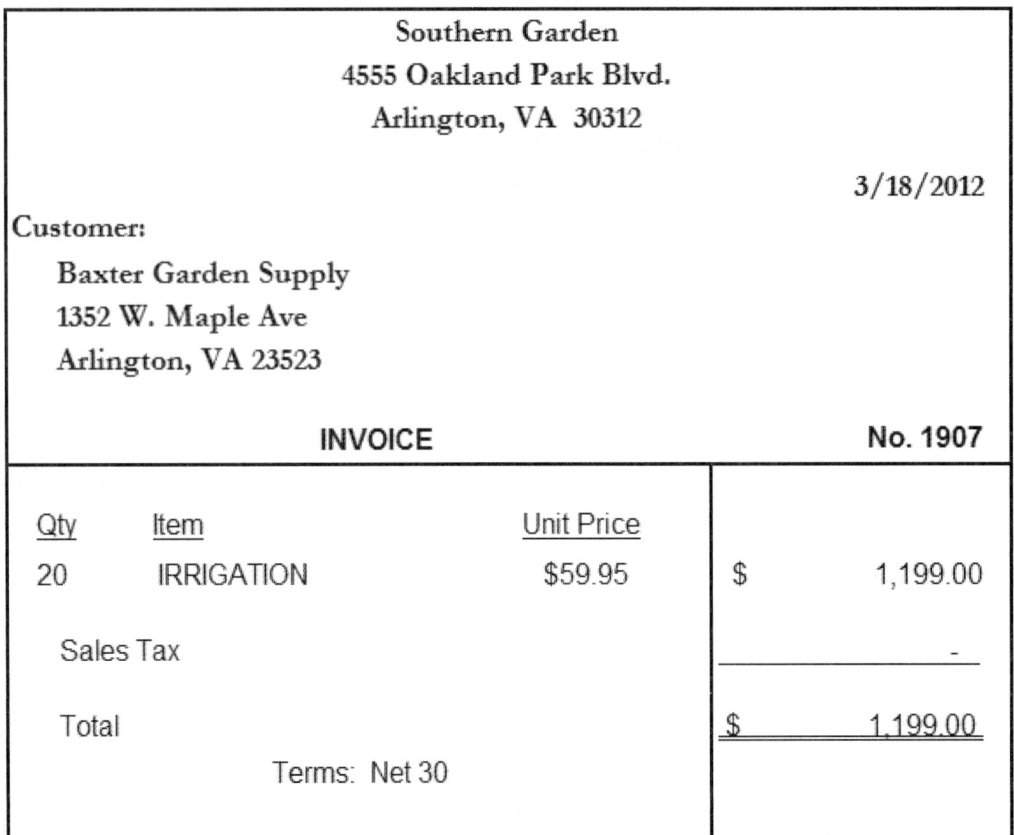

Southern Garden
4555 Oakland Park Blvd.
Arlington, VA 30312

3/18/2012

Customer:

Baxter Garden Supply
1352 W. Maple Ave
Arlington, VA 23523

INVOICE No. 1907

Qty	Item	Unit Price		
20	IRRIGATION	$59.95	$	1,199.00
	Sales Tax			-
	Total		$	1,199.00

Terms: Net 30

Figure 9:1

Melvin matches the bill with the receipt and the PO and enters the bill in the Purchases Journal. Melvin's entries to the Purchases Journal on March 22 appear in Figure 9:2.

Note: Technically the liability to Southern Garden was incurred on March 18 (i.e., the day the merchandise was received). However, manual accounting procedures do not accommodate such semantics. It would be tedious to record the receipt and then to record the bill. Instead, bills are recorded to the Purchases Journal on the date of receiving the bill.

Baxter Garden Supply					
Date: 3/22/2012		Purchases Journal			Page 4
Vendor	Post Ref	Description	Accounts Payable (Credit)	Purchases (Debit)	Utilities Expense (Debit)
Southern Garden	SOUT001	Invoice 1907	1,199.00	1,199.00	
Neighbors Telephone	NEIGH001	March Phone	237.05		237.05
Hubbard Wholesale	HUBB001	Invoice 877	677.00	677.00	
Totals:			$ 2,113.05	$ 1,876.00	$ 237.05
Acct Ref:			(20000)	(50000)	(71100)

Audit Trail

Figure 9:2

Like the procedures used to enter transactions in Chapter 8, Melvin totals journal columns and cross-foots totals to verify that en-tries balance (i.e., debits equal credits). He then posts each invoice to the vendor's account and posts column totals to general ledger accounts listed at the bottom.

Melvin's entry to Southern Garden's vendor account is illustrated in Figure 9:3. *(Note: Entries for other vendor accounts are not illustrated.)*

Southern Garden 4555 Oakland Park Blvd. **Audit Trail** Arlington, Va 30312				Acct No:	SOUT001
Date	**Description**	**Post Ref**	**Debit**	**Credit**	**Balance**
3/1/2012	Beginning Balance				0.00
3/22/2012	Invoice 1907	PJ 4		1,199.00	1,199.00

Figure 9:3

Melvin's entries to general ledger accounts follow. *(Note: The entry for utilities is not shown.)*

General Ledger

Accounts Payable **Account No. 20000**

Date	Description	Post Ref	Debit	Credit	Balance
3/21/2012	Balance Forward				51,506.21
3/22/2012		PJ 4		2,113.05	53,619.26

Audit Trail

General Ledger

Purchases **Account No. 50000**

Date	Description	Post Ref	Debit	Credit	Balance
3/21/2012	Balance Forward				24,668.25
3/22/2012		PJ 4	1,876.00		26,544.25

Figure 9:4

The next day, Melvin reviews vendor bills and prepares checks for bills that are due. He also prepares a check to buy postage. Melvin records these checks on the Cash Disbursements Journal shown in Figure 9:5.

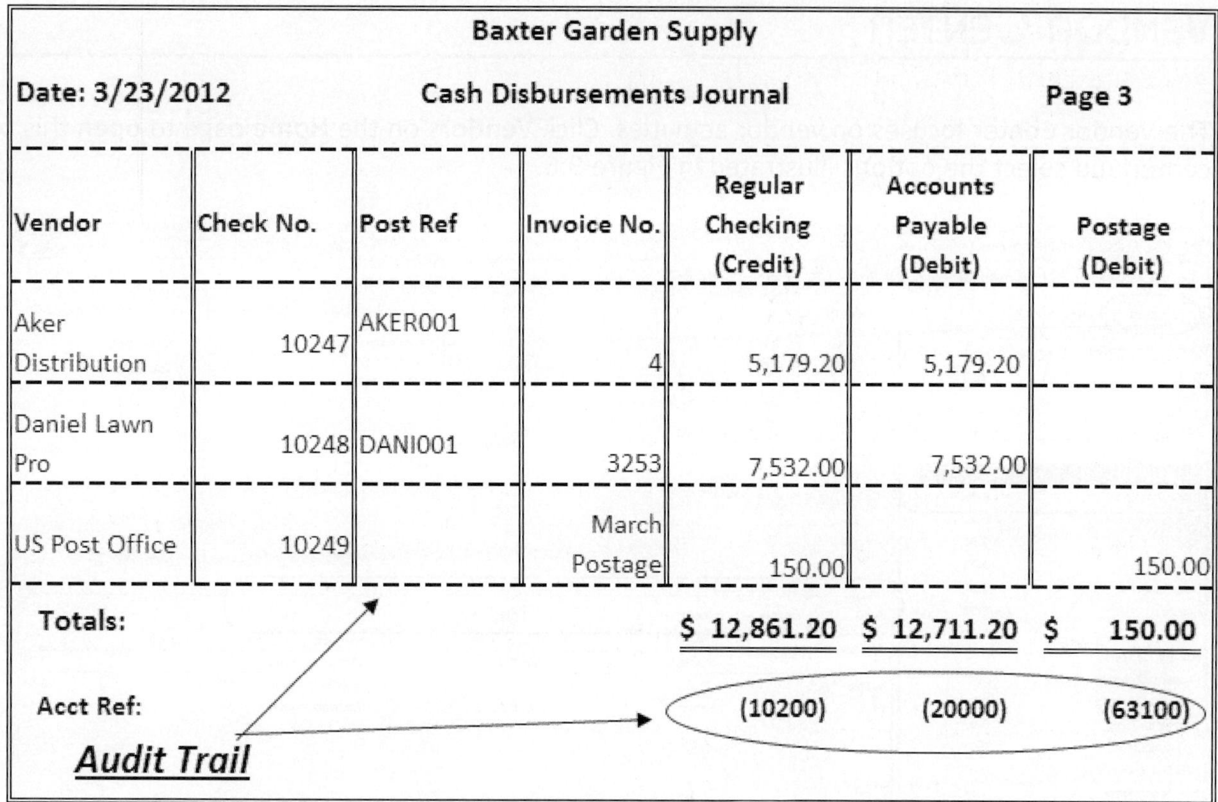

Baxter Garden Supply

Date: 3/23/2012 **Cash Disbursements Journal** **Page 3**

Vendor	Check No.	Post Ref	Invoice No.	Regular Checking (Credit)	Accounts Payable (Debit)	Postage (Debit)
Aker Distribution	10247	AKER001	4	5,179.20	5,179.20	
Daniel Lawn Pro	10248	DANI001	3253	7,532.00	7,532.00	
US Post Office	10249		March Postage	150.00		150.00
Totals:				**$ 12,861.20**	**$ 12,711.20**	**$ 150.00**
Acct Ref:				**(10200)**	**(20000)**	**(63100)**

Figure 9:5

Like in the Purchases Journal, Melvin posts each check to a vendor account and column totals to general ledger accounts. He will use the posting reference of CDJ (Cash Disbursements Journal) along with the page number. *(Note: These postings are not illustrated.)*

As discussed in Chapter 8, the manual method is fraught with opportunities to make posting errors. Melvin could enter an amount incorrectly, post an entry backwards, or forget to post it altogether.

With an understanding of *MAPS* for vendor activities, you are now ready to use QBP for processing vendor transactions. The topic that follows will introduce you to the center for these activities.

Vendor Center

The Vendor Center focuses on vendor activities. Click **Vendors** on the **Home** page to open this center and select the options illustrated in Figure 9:6.

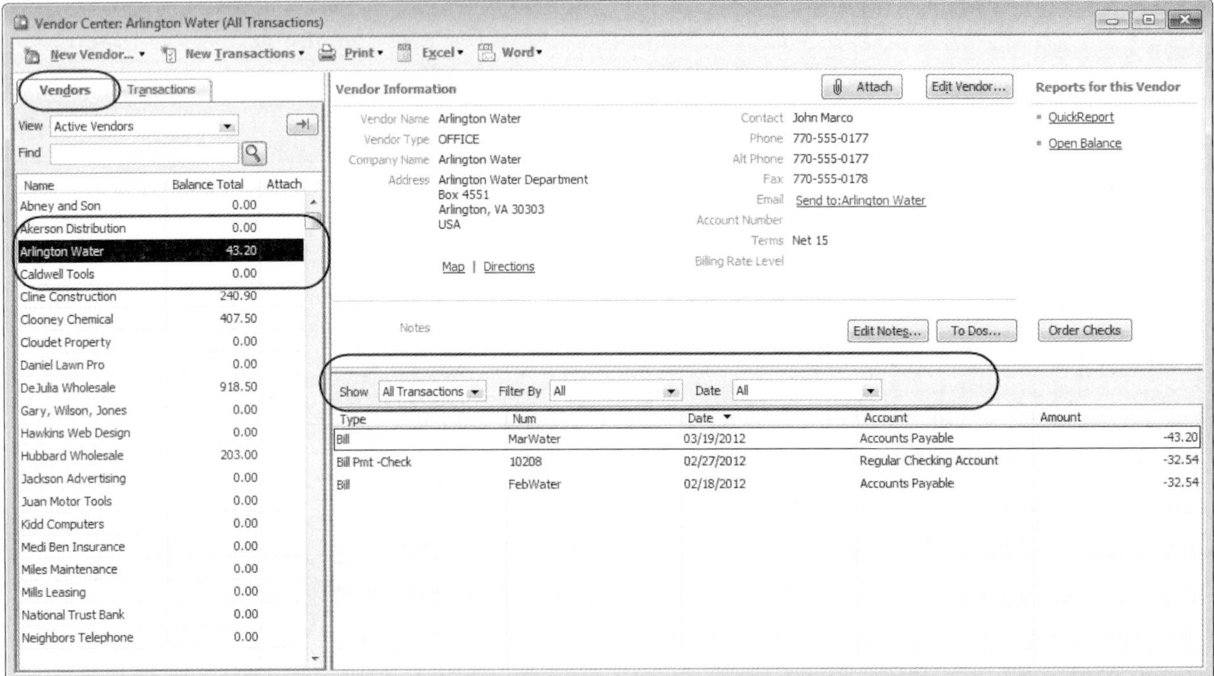

Figure 9:6

The **Vendors** tab lists transactions by vendor account. Baxter's vendor accounts and balances appear to the left. The **View** option contains selections for viewing All Vendors, Active Vendors, or Vendors with Open Balances. You are currently viewing Active Vendors.

This →| button hides the Vendor Information pane shown to the right. After hiding, this |← button is located on the far right for redisplaying the information pane.

The **Vendor Information** pane displays transactions for the account highlighted on the left. This account is currently Arlington Water.

The **Edit Vendor** button will open an account for editing. The **Edit Notes** button is for entering account notes. There are also hyperlinks for creating **Reports for this Vendor**.

Transactions for the highlighted company are listed at the bottom of the account information. The filtering options of **Show, Filter By,** and **Date** determine the transactions that are displayed. Click ⌄ to access an option's dropdown list to change selections. You are currently viewing **All Transactions** for **All Dates**. *(Note: Remember, the Date option of Fiscal Year looks to your computer date to determine the year.)*

Filtering options work as follows:

- ❖ Show: Selects the transaction type to display
- ❖ Filter By: Filters criteria for the type
- ❖ Date: Lists all transactions for the type or only transactions recorded as of a specific date or range of dates

Now turn your attention to activities that can be performed while the Vendor tab is active. These activities are **New Vendor, New Transactions, Print, Excel,** and **Word**.

Each activity has this ⌄ button for choosing a specific task. The table that follows discusses tasks by activity. Most actions will operate on the vendor account highlighted on the left.

Vendors Activities	**Tasks**	**Description**
New Vendor	New Vendor and Add Multiple Vendors	Create a new vendor account or multiple vendor accounts.
New Transactions	Enter Bills	Record a vendor bill for the highlighted vendor.
	Pay Bills	Open a window to select vendor bills to pay.
	Purchase Orders	Create a purchase order for the highlighted vendor.
	Receive Items and Enter Bills	Receive items and enter a bill for items on a PO issued to the highlighted vendor.
	Receive Items	Enter a receipt for items on a PO issued to the highlighted vendor.
	Enter Bill for Received Items	Enter a bill for a receipt from the highlighted vendor.

Vendors Activities	Tasks	Description
Print	Vendor List	Print a vendor list with balances. The report cannot be customized, so this report is usually printed from the Reports menu.
	Vendor Information	Print account information and notes for the highlighted vendor. The report cannot be customized, so this report is usually printed from the Reports menu.
	Vendor Transaction List	Print the highlighted vendor's transactions for the current fiscal year. The report cannot be customized, so this report is usually printed from the Reports menu.
Excel	Export Vendor List	Create an Excel workbook or comma separated values (.csv) file containing all vendor information along with account balances.
	Export Transactions	Create an Excel workbook or comma separated values (.csv) file containing current fiscal year transactions for the highlighted vendor.
	Import from Excel and Paste from Excel	Import or paste vendor information or transactions from an Excel workbook or comma separated values (.csv) file.
Word		Create form letters for communicating with a vendor.

Next, turn your attention to the **Transactions** tab, which lists transactions by type instead of transactions by vendor. Click to activate the tab and select the options illustrated in Figure 9:7.

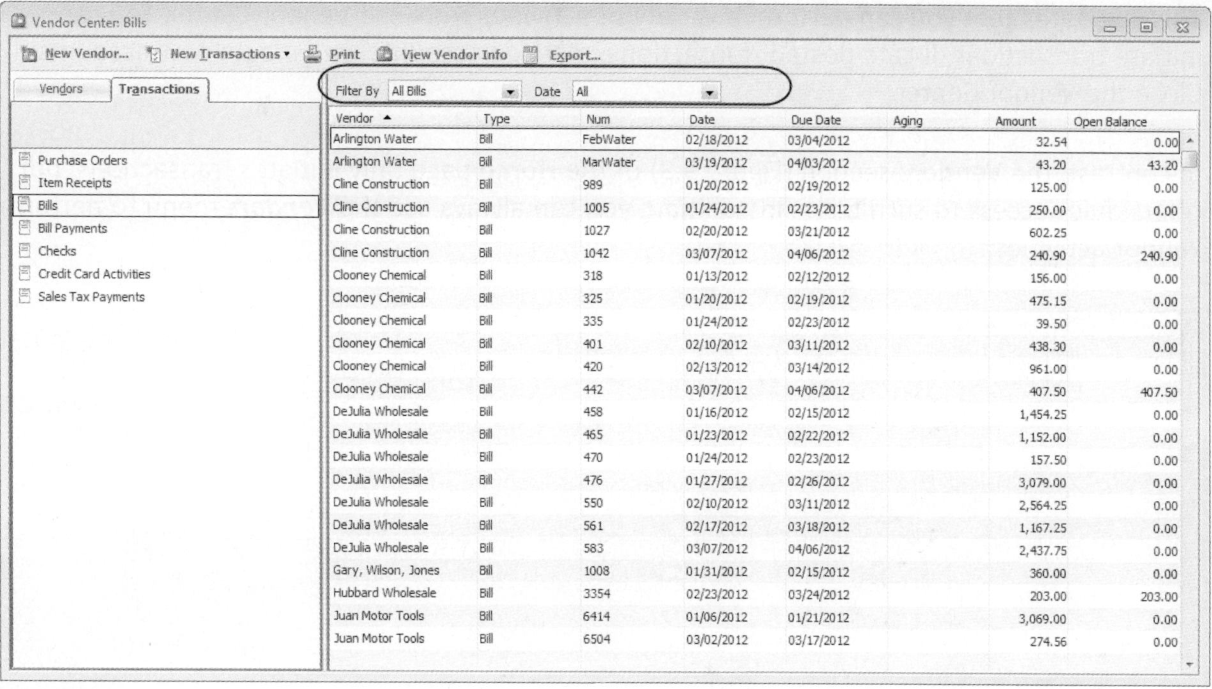

Figure 9:7

Transaction types are chosen on the left. You can sort the list by clicking a column name.

Activities that can be performed on this tab are different from those performed on the previous tab. First, only the New Transactions activity offers multiple tasks so clicking other activities immediately opens the task. The following table discusses activities on this tab.

Transactions Activities	Description
New Vendor	Create a new vendor account.
New Transactions	Contains the same tasks as the Vendors tab but the user must select the customer.
Print	Print the transactions listed to the right.
View Vendor Info	Edit the vendor account associated with the transaction highlighted on the right.
Export	Create an Excel workbook or comma separated values (.csv) file containing transactions listed on the right.

This illustrates that you can perform a variety of activities from the Vendor Center. You can initiate transactions, locate posted transactions, manage accounts, and create new accounts. Close the Vendor Center.

In contrast, the **Vendors** section (Figure 9:8) of the **Home** page only initiates transactions, but offers quick access to such tasks. In addition, you can always use the ***Vendors*** menu to perform vendor activities.

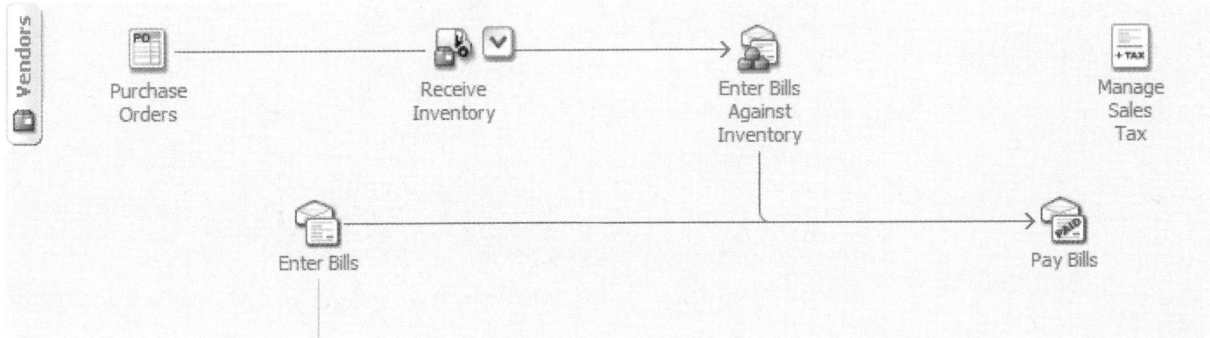

Figure 9:8

Now that you are familiar with locating vendor activities, let us begin recording vendor transactions.

Purchase Orders

As previously discussed, POs authorize vendor purchases. Recall from the *MAPS* topic that Sam created a PO to restock drip sprinklers. Follow the next steps and capture this transaction in QBP. *(Note: There is an online video for this topic.)*

Steps to Create a Purchase Order

1. On the **Home** page, click the **Purchase Orders** icon to open the window illustrated in Figure 9:9. Hide the History pane.

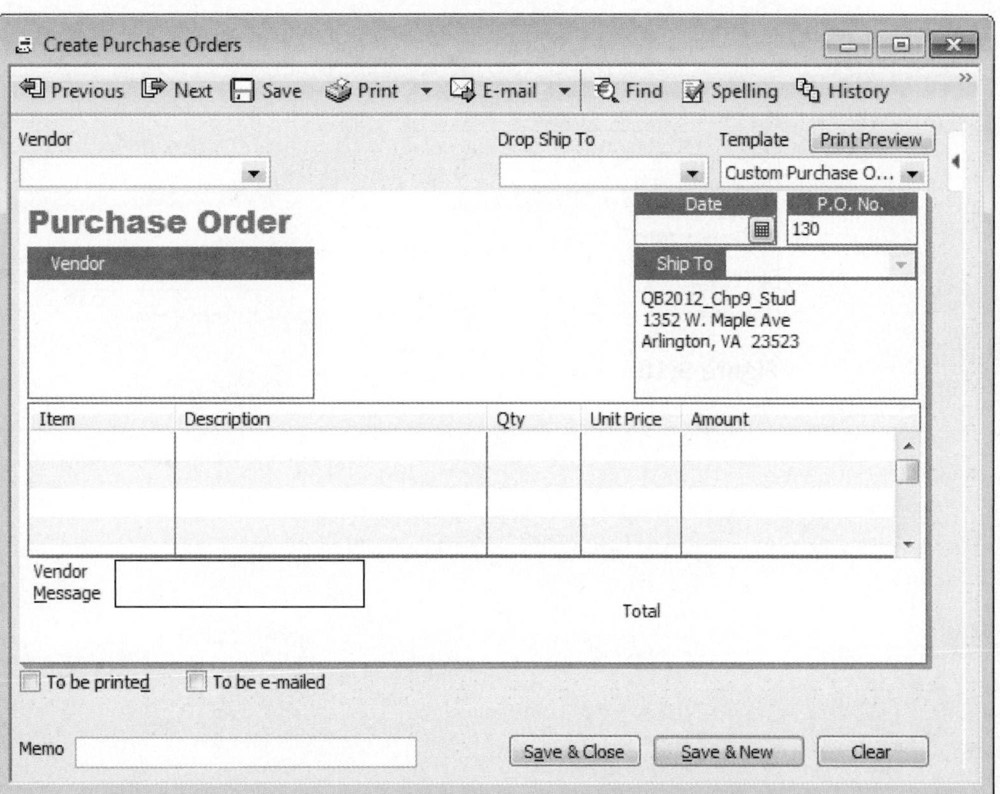

Figure 9:9

2. In **Vendor ID**, look up and select "Southern Garden." Enter "3/17/12" as the **Date**. Keep "130" as the **P.O. No**.

3. In **Item**, look up and select "IRRIGATION." Tab to **Qty** and enter "20" into the field. Mark the **To be printed** option. Figure 9:10 shows the completed PO.

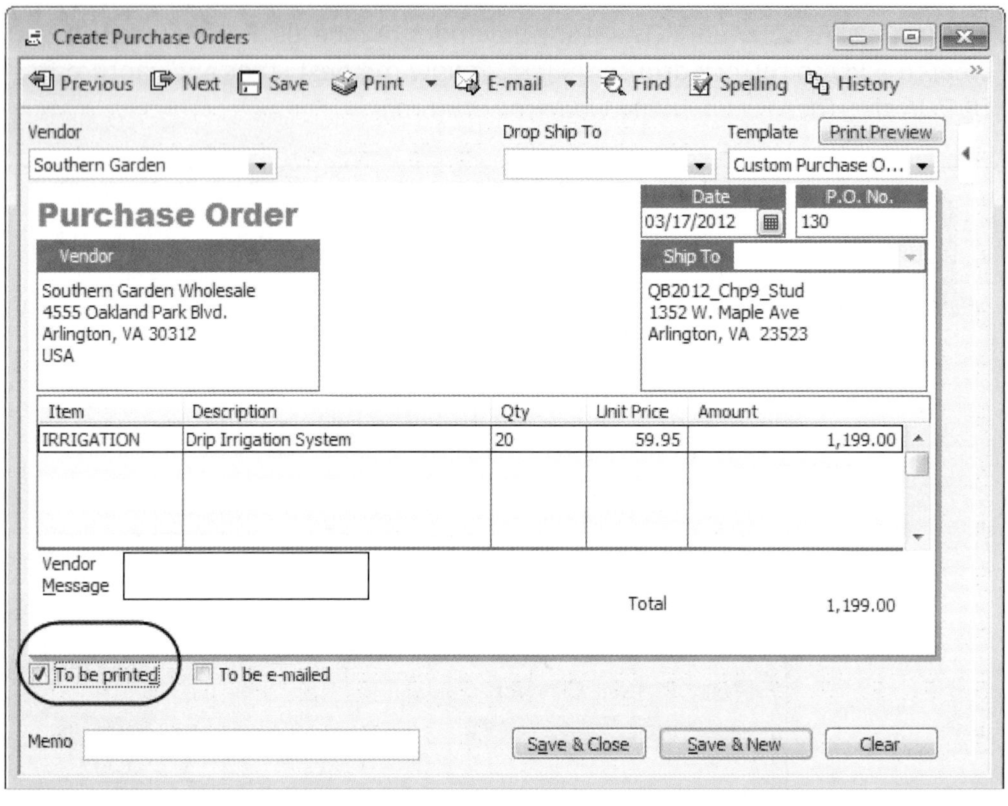

Figure 9:10

4. Click the dropdown on **Print** and select **Preview**. If prompted with information on shipping labels, select the option to turn off future messages, and click **OK**.

   Figure 9:11 shows the previewed PO.

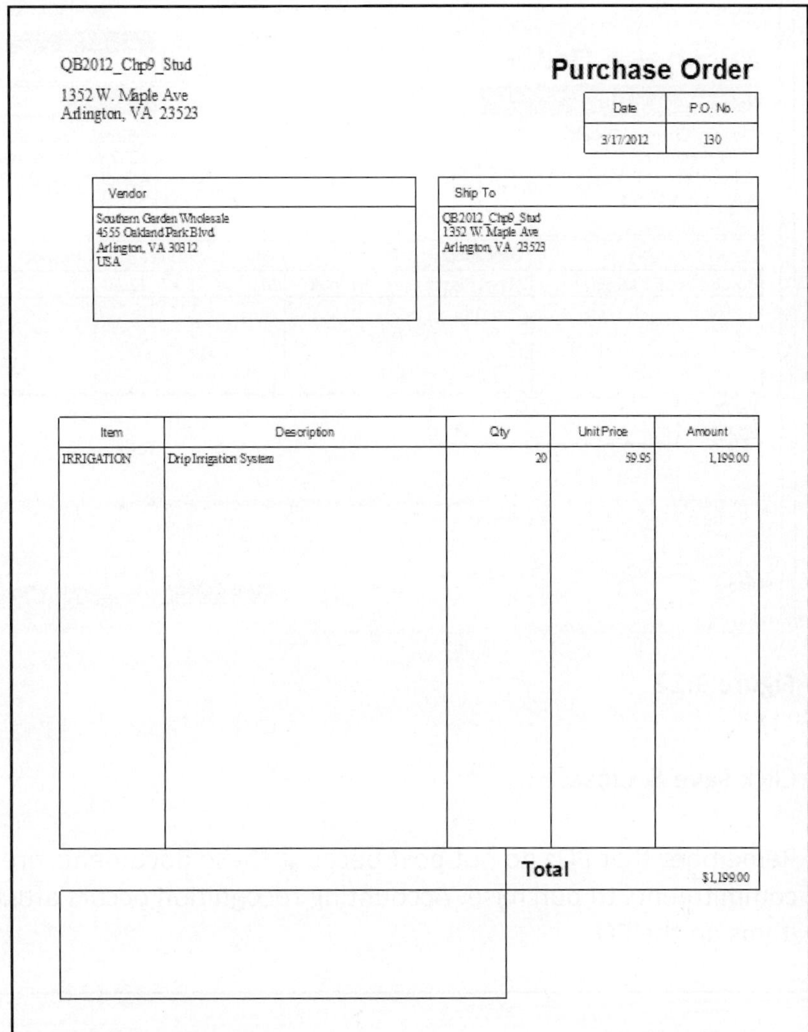
QB2012_Chp9_Stud
1352 W. Maple Ave
Arlington, VA 23523

Purchase Order

Date	P.O. No.
3/17/2012	130

Vendor	Ship To
Southern Garden Wholesale 4555 Oakland Park Blvd Arlington, VA 30312 USA	QB2012_Chp9_Stud 1352 W. Maple Ave Arlington, VA 23523

Item	Description	Qty	Unit Price	Amount
IRRIGATION	Drip Irrigation System	20	59.95	1,199.00
			Total	$1,199.00

Figure 9:11

5. Click **Print** to send the order to the default printer.

   Note: If you want to select a different printer then click Close to exit the preview window and click Print on the transaction window.

6. Click **Save & New** and click **Yes** to save the changes. *(Note: The change occurred because QBP removed the checkmark from To be printed.)*

7. Enter the information shown in Figure 9:12.

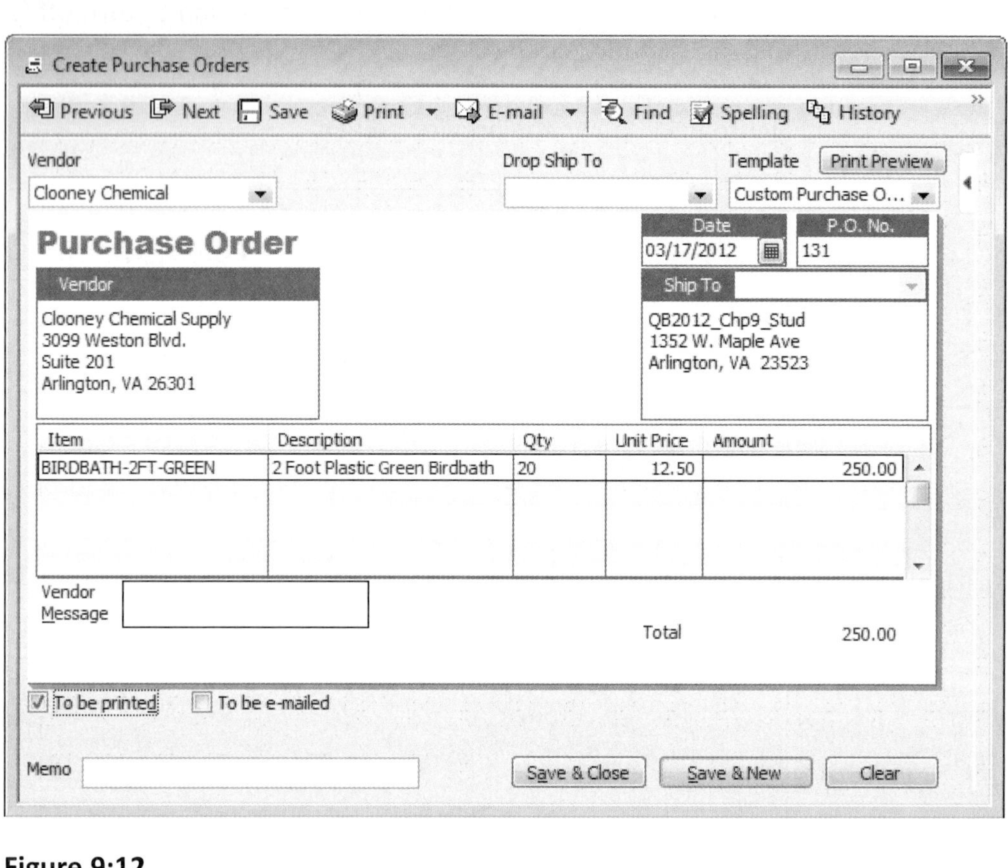

Figure 9:12

8. Click **Save & Close.**

   Remember that POs do not post because these documents are merely commitments to purchase. Accounting recognition occurs after receiving items on the PO.

Correcting a Purchase Order

You can correct information for an item on a PO as long as the items have not been received.

First, locate the PO using the **Vendor Center**. Click **Vendors** on the **Home** page to open the center.

Next, select the **Transactions** tab and click **Purchase Orders** on the left.

Finally, locate the **Clooney Chemical** transaction on the right and double click to reopen (Figure 9:13). Notice that after saving the PO, QBP added the **Rcv'd** and **Clsd** columns.

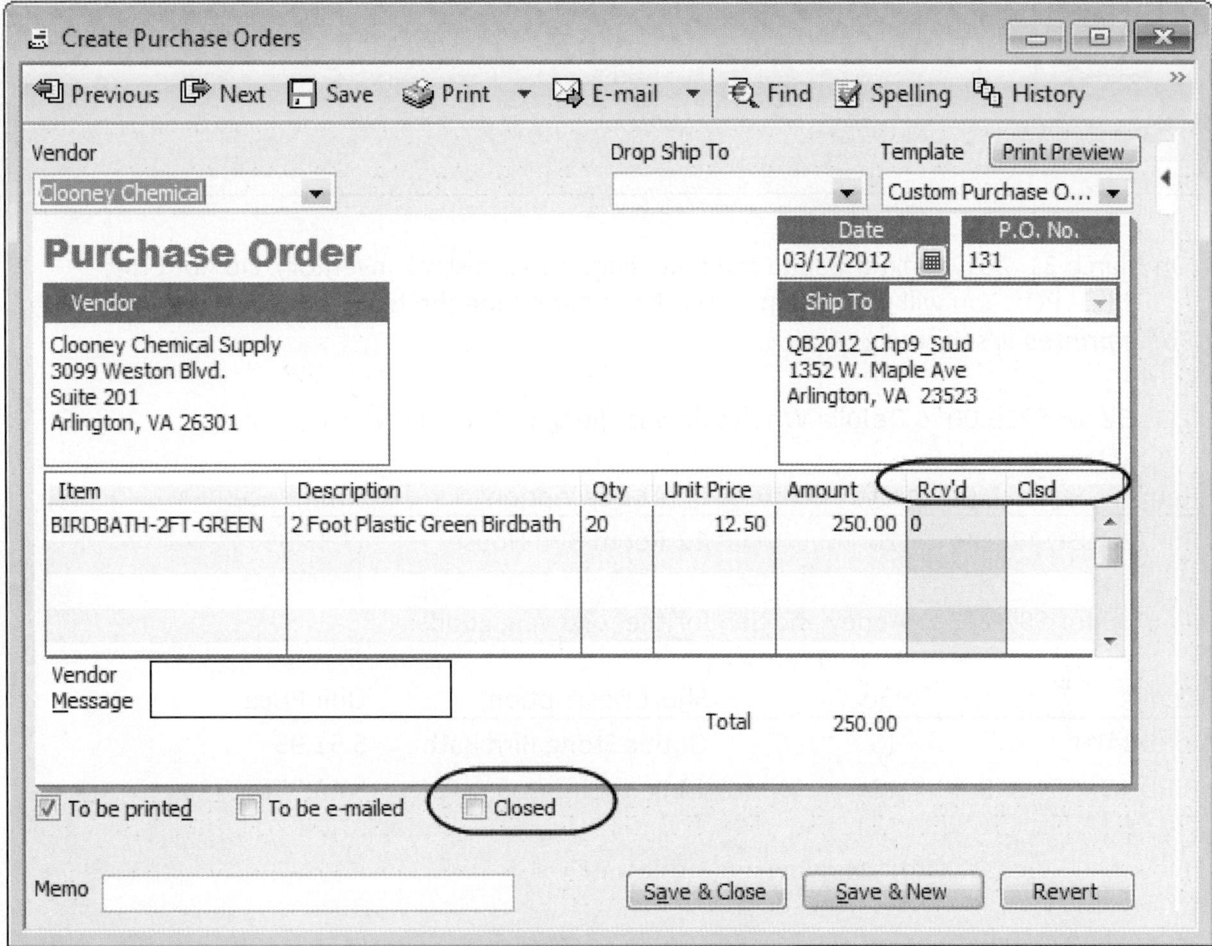

Figure 9:13

The **Rcv'd** field stores the quantity received for each line item. When all quantities on a line item have been received, QBP marks the line item **Clsd**.

Notice that there is also a **Closed** option for the entire PO located at the bottom. QBP marks this option after receiving all line items in full.

As long as all line items remain open, you can change information and even delete the PO. If needed, POs are deleted by using ***Edit>>Delete Purchase Order*** on the main menu.

Click **X** to exit the PO window. Now try the next exercise.

ENTER PURCHASE ORDERS

On March 21, 2012, Baxter issued the following POs to restock inventory. Do not print individual POs. You will print them altogether after saving the transactions so verify that ***To be printed*** is selected.

PO 132 for $719.00 to DeJulia Wholesale Suppliers for the following goods:

Item	Qty	Short Description	Unit Price
BIRDHOUSE-12RM	20	12-Room Bird House	$ 35.95

PO 133 for $978.75 to Abney and Son for the following goods:

Item	Qty	Short Description	Unit Price
BIRDBATH	15	Gothic Stone Bird Bath	$ 51.95
BIRDHOUSE POLE	10	14 Foot Bird House Pole	$ 19.95

Close the Purchase Order window and print the POs.

To print the POs, select ***File>>Print Forms>>Purchase Orders*** on the main menu. Verify that both POs are selected and click **OK**. Select a printer and click **Print**.

After printing, click **OK** in the print confirmation window.

VENDOR RECEIPTS AND BILLS FOR PURCHASE ORDERS

From the *MAPS* topic, you will recall that vendors ship orders to Baxter's warehouse enclosing a packing receipt or a bill with the merchandise. When Southern Garden's order arrived, Al inspected the merchandise and sent the packing receipt to Melvin in accounting. Melvin filed the receipt until the vendor's bill arrived.

With QBP, Melvin now records the packing receipt as a receipt of inventory. Two benefits flow from immediately recording the receipt. First, inventory assets are recorded when possession takes place and quantities of on-hand inventory are immediately updated. Second, the liability is recognized when the obligation to pay occurs.

Follow the next steps and record Baxter's receipt of Southern Garden's shipment of merchandise ordered on PO 130. *(Note: There is an online video for this topic.)*

STEPS TO RECORD A VENDOR RECEIPT FOR ITEMS ON A PURCHASE ORDER

1. Click **Receive Inventory** on the Home page and select **Receive Inventory without Bill** to open the window in Figure 9:14. Hide the History pane.

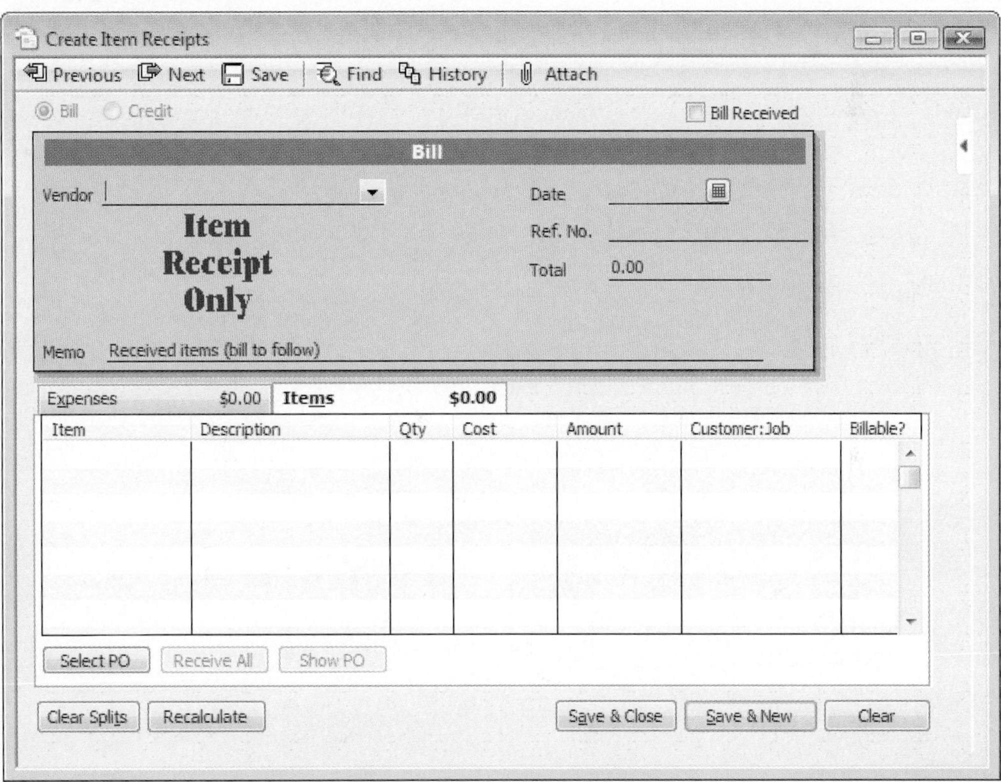

Figure 9:14

Note that there are two tabs. The **Expenses** tab is for recording non-inventory purchases such as utility and insurance bills. The **Items** tab is for recording receipt of inventory items.

On receipt transactions, the **Bill Received** option will not be marked and the **Memo** will indicate that this is a receipt transaction with bill to follow.

2. In **Vendor**, look up and select "Southern Garden." Click **Yes** when QBP prompts to receive against the PO.

3. In the window illustrated in Figure 9:15, click **PO No 130** and click **OK**.

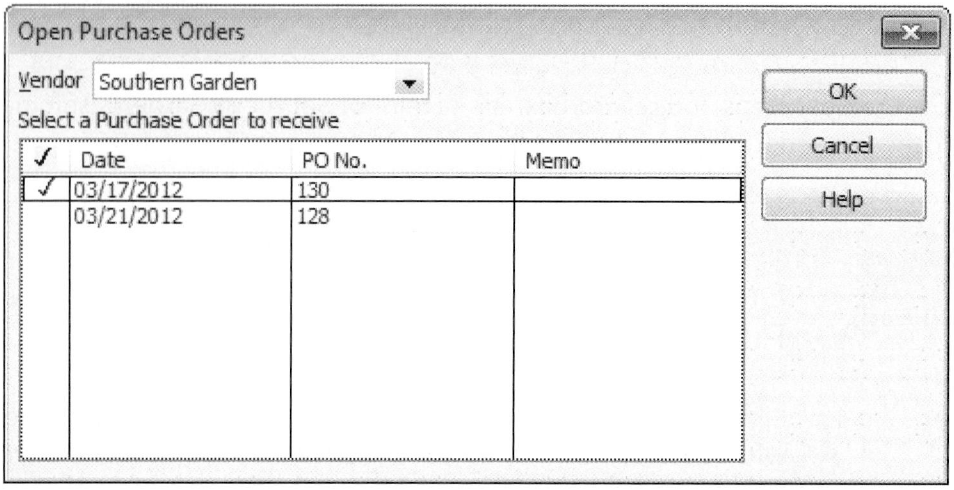

Open Purchase Orders

Vendor Southern Garden

OK

Cancel

Help

Select a Purchase Order to receive

✓	Date	PO No.	Memo
✓	03/17/2012	130	
	03/21/2012	128	

Figure 9:15

4. The **Date** of receipt is 3/12/12. In **Ref. No.,** enter "RCT3217" because this is the vendor's receipt number.

Figure 9:16 shows the completed receipt.

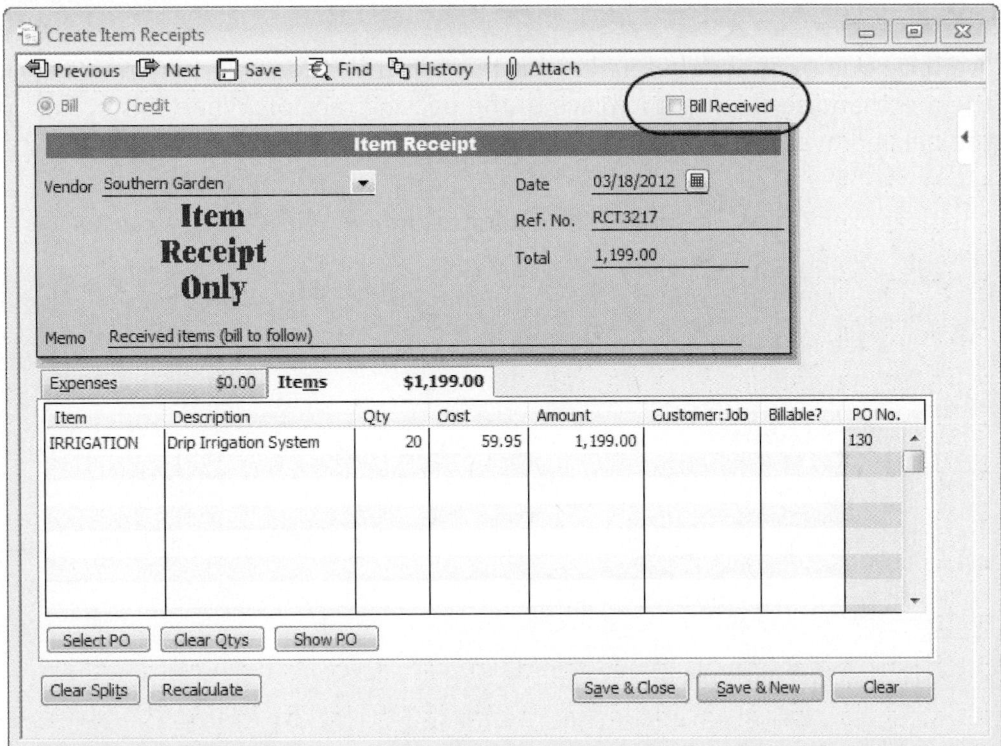

Figure 9:16

Before saving, review the following fields on this transaction.

Qty stores the number of items received.

Customer:Job and **Billable** are job costing fields that were illustrated in Chapter 5 and will not be used in this chapter.

Select PO reopens the window to change the selected PO.

Clear Qtys deletes values in the Qty field.

Show PO opens the original PO transaction.

5. Click **Save & Close.**

This transaction posted entries to the inventory and accounts payable accounts. You will trace these entries in the next topic.

Unlike the manual system where the vendor bill was recorded to the Purchases Journal on March 22 (i.e., the day the bill arrived), Baxter now recognizes the transaction on the actual date of incurring the liability (i.e., March 18).

We have one more task before leaving this topic. Vendors will sometimes enclose a bill with the merchandise shipment in place of the packing receipt. When this occurs, you will record the bill and bypass recording the receipt.

The next exercise records a vendor bill for PO items.

STEPS TO RECORD A VENDOR BILL FOR ITEMS ON A PURCHASE ORDER

1. On the **Home** page, click **Receive Inventory** and this time select **Receive Inventory with Bill** to open the window illustrated in Figure 9:17.

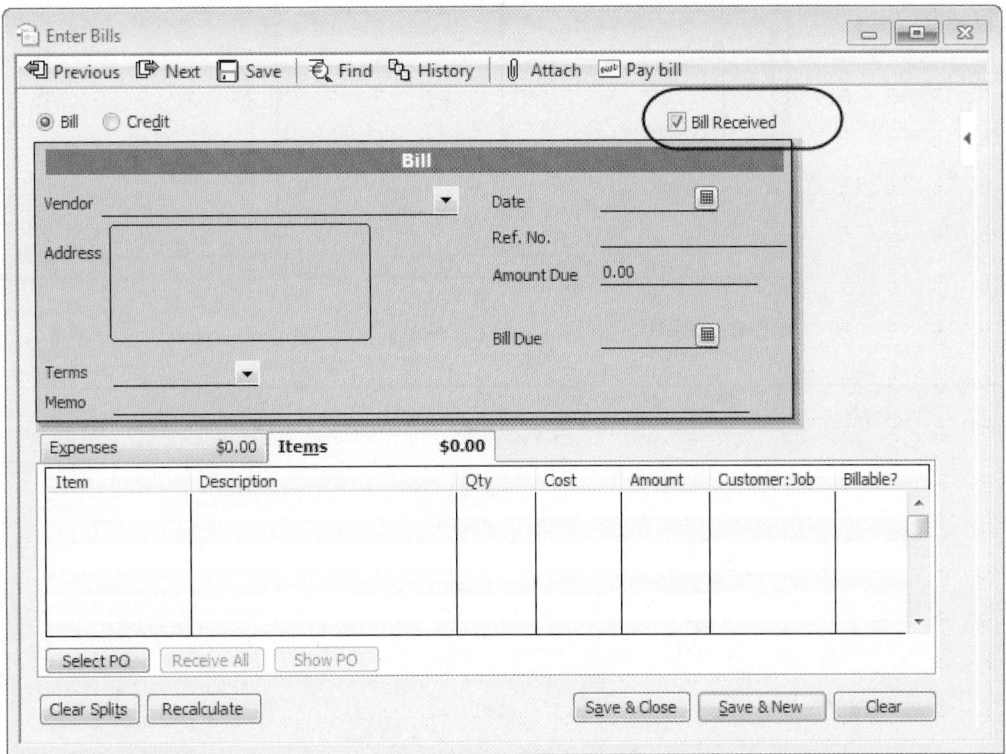

Figure 9:17

2. Look up "Clooney Chemical" as the **Vendor**. Click **Yes** when QBP prompts to receive against the PO.

3. In the next window (Figure 9:18), click **PO No 131** and click **OK**.

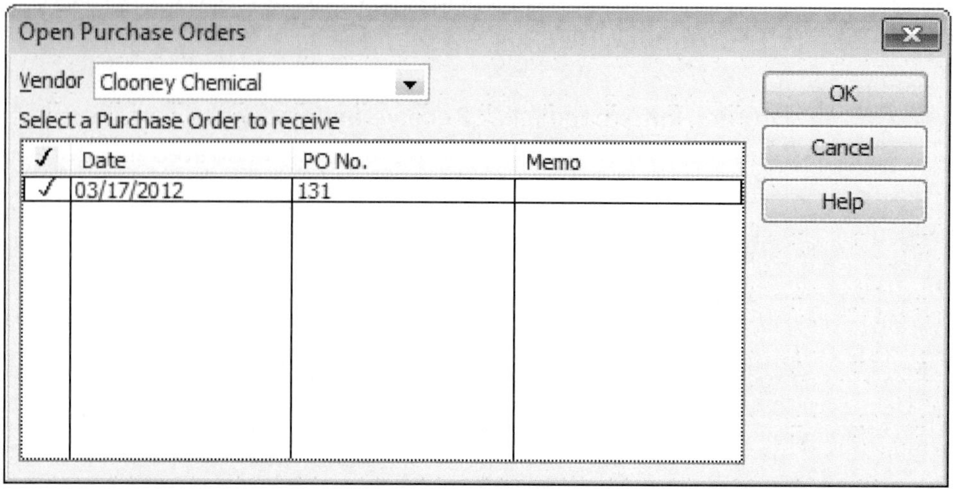

Figure 9:18

4. Baxter also received these goods on March 18, so enter this as the **Date**. Enter Clooney's invoice number of "1265" in the **Ref. No**. field.

   Figure 9:19 shows the bill you have entered. Notice that **Bill Received** is marked.

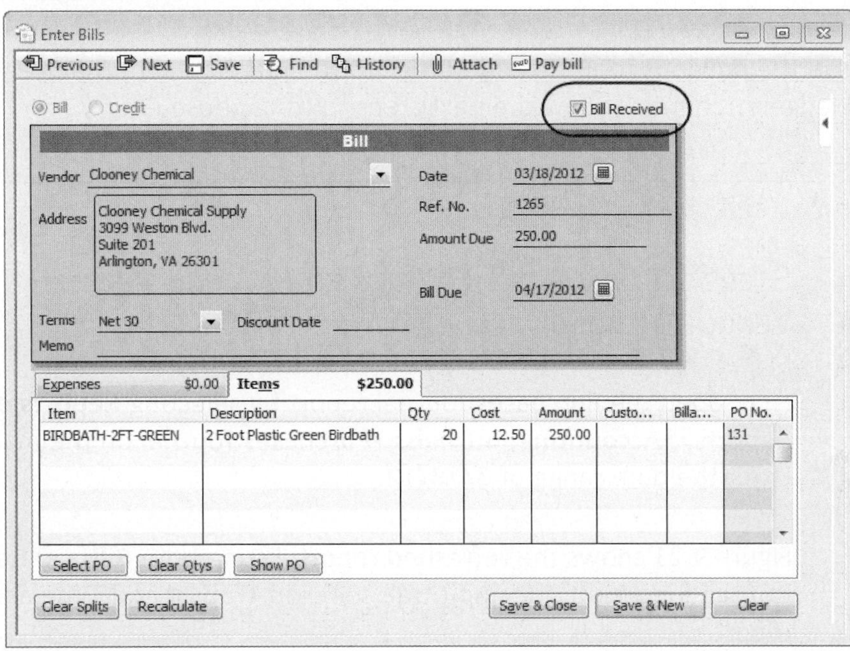

Figure 9:19

5. Click the **Expenses** tab. If a bill has other charges, such as shipping, these can be entered by selecting **Account** and entering the **Amount.**

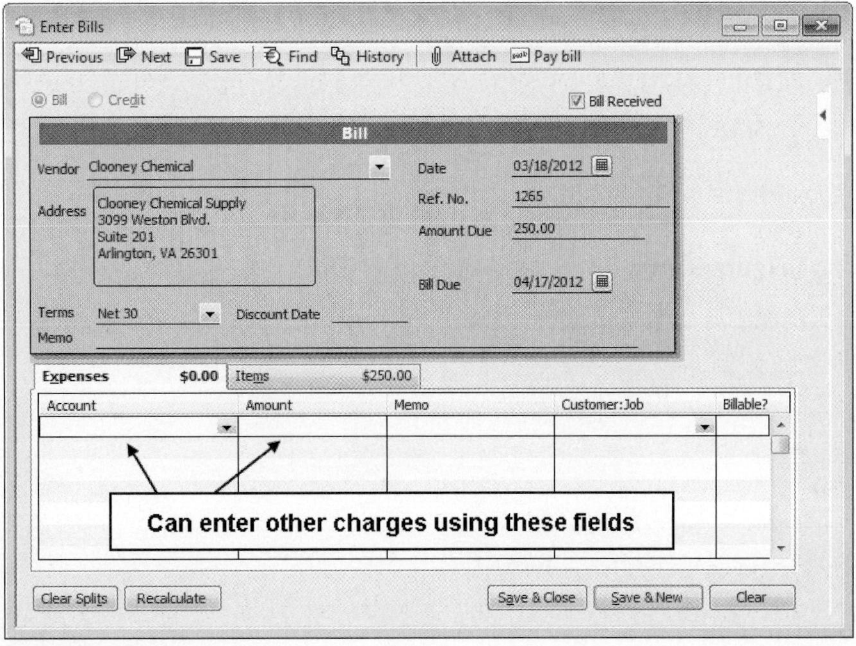

Figure 9:20

6. Click **Save & Close**.

BEHIND THE KEYS OF A POSTED VENDOR RECEIPT AND BILL

Transactions in the previous topic posted entries to the Purchases Journal, vendor accounts, and general ledger accounts. Follow the next steps to trace those entries.

STEPS TO TRACE THE ENTRIES FOR A VENDOR BILL AND A VENDOR RECEIPT

1. First, open the Purchases Journal report by selecting **Reports>>Memorized Reports>>Accounting Journals>>Purchases Journal** on the main menu. Enter the date range of **3/18/12**.

   Figure 9:21 shows the refreshed report, listing both **Bill** and **Item Receipt** transactions. Note the audit trail codes in **Trans #** and **Type** and close the report.

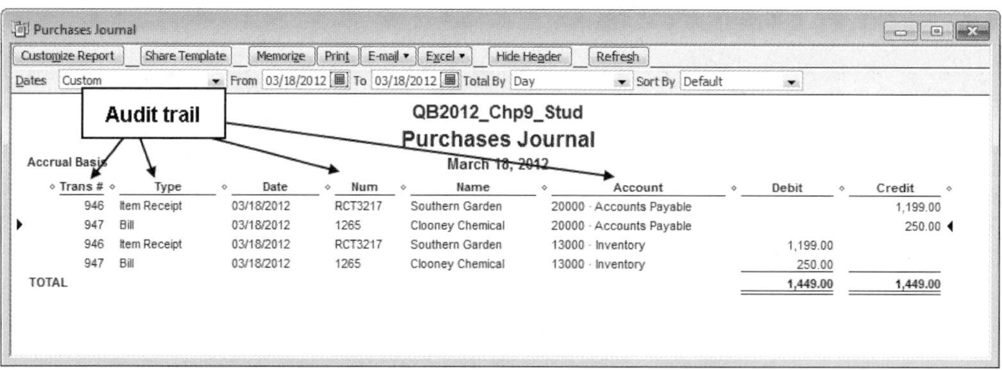

QB2012_Chp9_Stud

Purchases Journal

March 18, 2012

Accrual Basis

Trans #	Type	Date	Num	Name	Account	Debit	Credit
946	Item Receipt	03/18/2012	RCT3217	Southern Garden	20000 · Accounts Payable		1,199.00
947	Bill	03/18/2012	1265	Clooney Chemical	20000 · Accounts Payable		250.00
946	Item Receipt	03/18/2012	RCT3217	Southern Garden	13000 · Inventory	1,199.00	
947	Bill	03/18/2012	1265	Clooney Chemical	13000 · Inventory	250.00	
TOTAL						1,449.00	1,449.00

Figure 9:21

2. Now trace the entries to vendor accounts.

Select ***Reports>>Vendors & Payables>>Transaction List by Vendor*** on the main menu. Enter the date range of **3/18/12**.

Click **Customize Report** and add the **Trans #** column. Click **OK** and the report appears as illustrated in Figure 9:22.

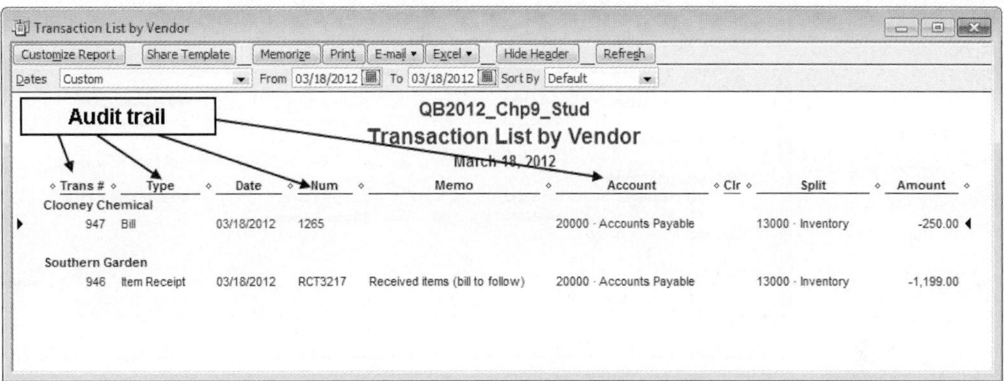

Figure 9:22

Notice that the **Trans #** and **Type** audit trail codes cross-reference to the audit trail codes in the **Purchases Journal**.

Close this report.

3. Finally, verify QBP's entries to the general ledger.

   Select ***Reports>>Memorized Reports>>Accounting Journals>>General Ledger Detail Report*** on the main menu. Enter **3/18/12** as the date range.

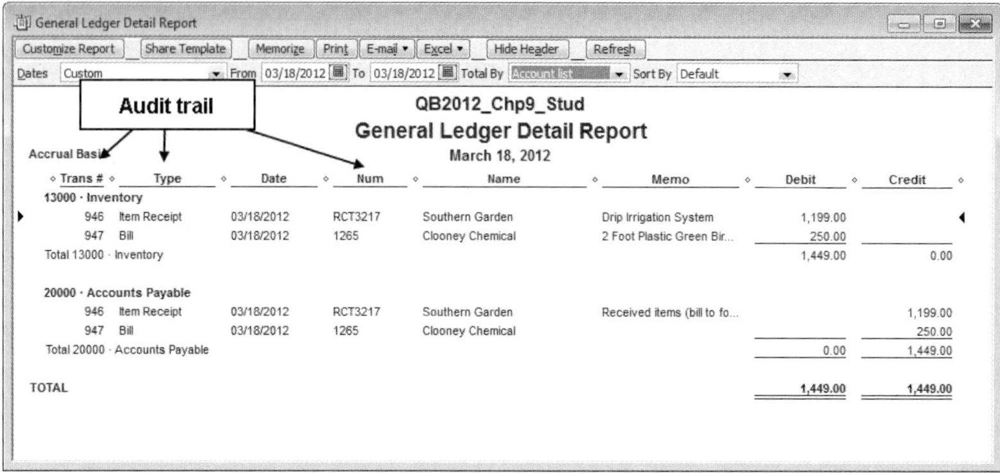

QB2012_Chp9_Stud
General Ledger Detail Report
March 18, 2012

Accrual Basis

Trans #	Type	Date	Num	Name	Memo	Debit	Credit
13000 · Inventory							
946	Item Receipt	03/18/2012	RCT3217	Southern Garden	Drip Irrigation System	1,199.00	
947	Bill	03/18/2012	1265	Clooney Chemical	2 Foot Plastic Green Bir...	250.00	
Total 13000 · Inventory						1,449.00	0.00
20000 · Accounts Payable							
946	Item Receipt	03/18/2012	RCT3217	Southern Garden	Received items (bill to fo...		1,199.00
947	Bill	03/18/2012	1265	Clooney Chemical			250.00
Total 20000 · Accounts Payable						0.00	1,449.00
TOTAL						1,449.00	1,449.00

Figure 9:23

You can locate your entries by looking for the audit trail code. Close the report when finished.

CORRECTING A VENDOR RECEIPT OR BILL

QBP permits modifying and deleting vendor receipts and bills. Use the **Vendor Center** to locate transactions. *(Note: There is an online video for this topic.)*

Open this center and, on the **Vendors** tab, highlight **Southern Garden**. Filter to **Show Item Receipts** for **All** dates (Figure 9:24).

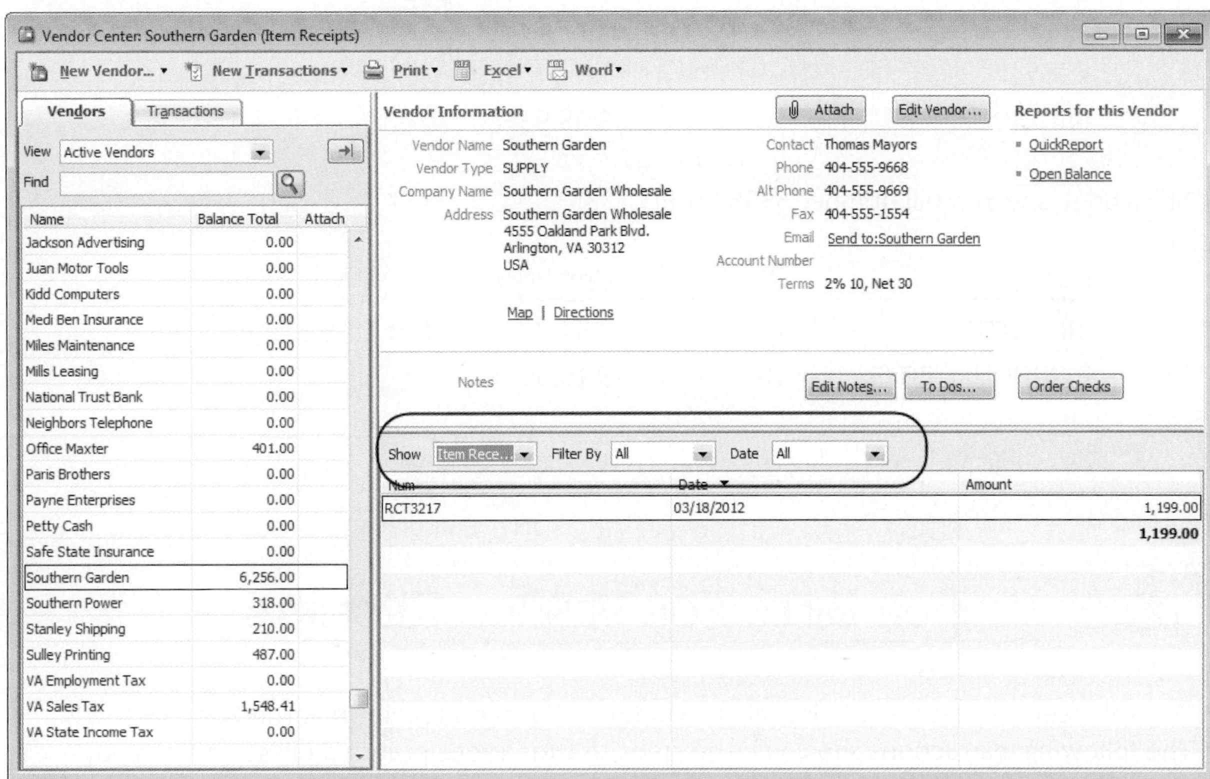

Figure 9:24

After reopening a receipt or bill, you can modify it and save the changes. You can also delete bills and receipts using ***Edit*** on the main menu. After deleting, QBP will reinstate POs used to create the transaction so you can receive items again.

Caution: You should not modify or delete paid bills because the payment will no longer match the bill. Instead, void the payment and then delete the bill. We will show you how to void payments later in the chapter.

Remember Appendix B provides a complete set of instructions on correcting QBP transactions.

ENTER VENDOR RECEIPTS AND BILLS FOR PURCHASE ORDERS

On March 22, Baxter receives the following shipments. Record the transactions.

Receipt: DeJulia Wholesale receipt number RCT750 for PO 132:

Item	Qty	Unit Price
BIRDHOUSE	20	$ 35.95

Bill: Abney and Son bill number 5355 for PO 133:

Item	Qty	Unit Price	
BIRDBATH	10	$ 51.95	(Not all items received)
BIRDHOUSE-POLE	10	$ 19.95	

VENDOR BILLS FOR VENDOR RECEIPTS

You still need to post the vendor bill for Southern Garden's receipt recorded on March 18. The following instructions show you the steps to turn a receipt into a bill so you can pay the vendor.

STEPS TO RECORD A VENDOR BILL FOR A RECEIPT

1. On the **Home** page, click **Enter Bills Against Inventory**. As shown in Figure 9:25, look up and select **Southern Garden**. Highlight the receipt and click **OK**.

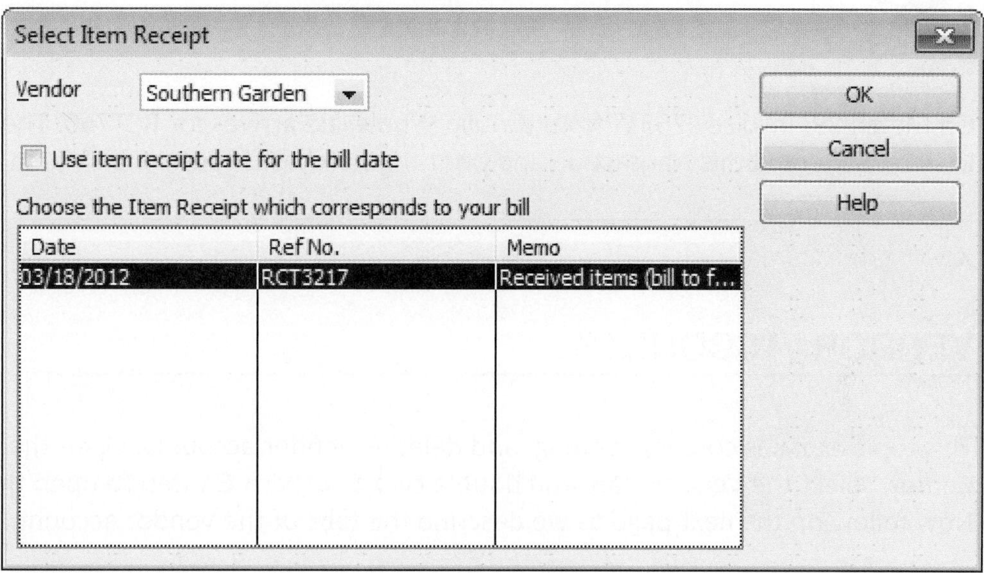

Figure 9:25

2. Change the **Date** to "3/18/12" and enter "97235" as the **Ref. No**.

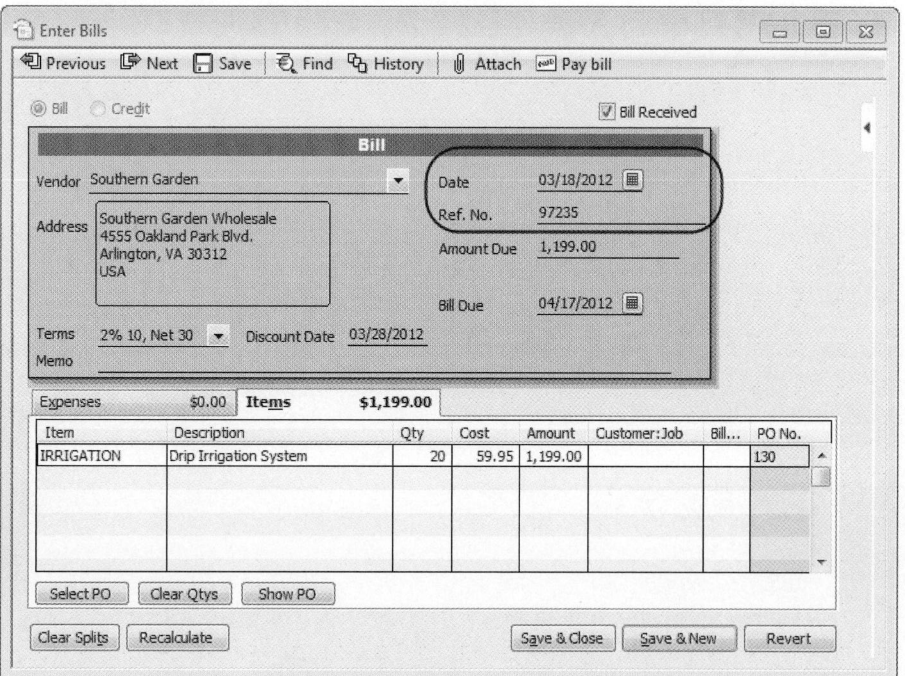

Figure 9:26

3. Click **Save & Close** and click **Yes** to change the transaction.

ENTER VENDOR BILL FOR VENDOR RECEIPT

On March 29, Invoice "7631" from DeJulia Wholesale arrives for RCT750. The bill is dated March 25. Record this transaction and print the Purchases Journal for March 25.

VENDOR ACCOUNTS

This topic explains creating, editing, and deleting vendor accounts. Open the **Vendor Center**, select the **Vendors** tab, and double click **Southern Garden** to open the account. Now follow on the next page as we describe the tabs of the vendor account.

Address Info Tab

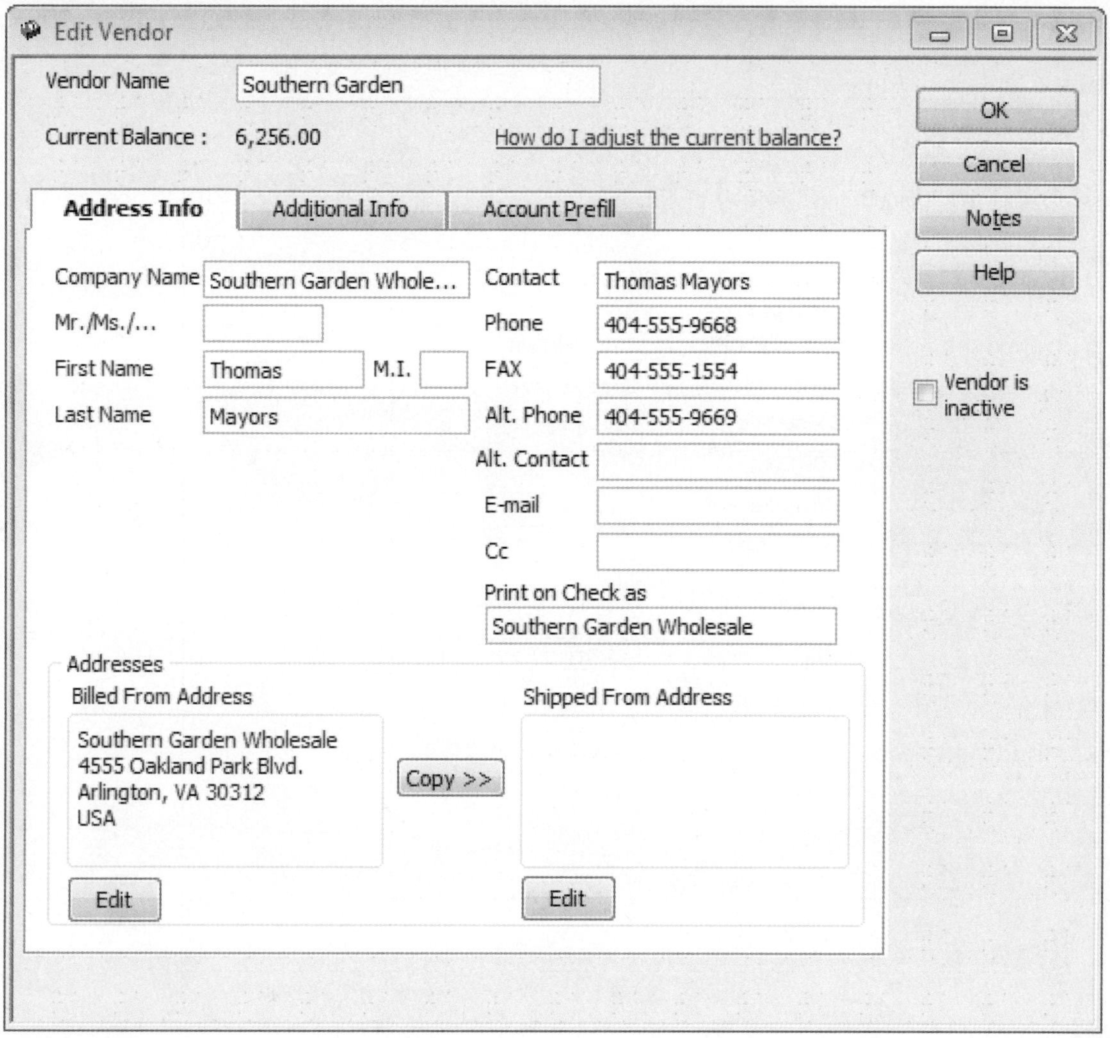

Edit Vendor

Vendor Name: Southern Garden

Current Balance : 6,256.00

How do I adjust the current balance?

OK | Cancel | Notes | Help

Address Info | Additional Info | Account Prefill

Company Name: Southern Garden Whole...
Mr./Ms./...:
First Name: Thomas M.I.:
Last Name: Mayors

Contact: Thomas Mayors
Phone: 404-555-9668
FAX: 404-555-1554
Alt. Phone: 404-555-9669
Alt. Contact:
E-mail:
Cc:
Print on Check as: Southern Garden Wholesale

Vendor is inactive

Addresses

Billed From Address:
Southern Garden Wholesale
4555 Oakland Park Blvd.
Arlington, VA 30312
USA

Copy >>

Shipped From Address:

Edit | Edit

Figure 9:27

This tab stores basic vendor information such as address, phone numbers, and contacts.

Additional Info Tab

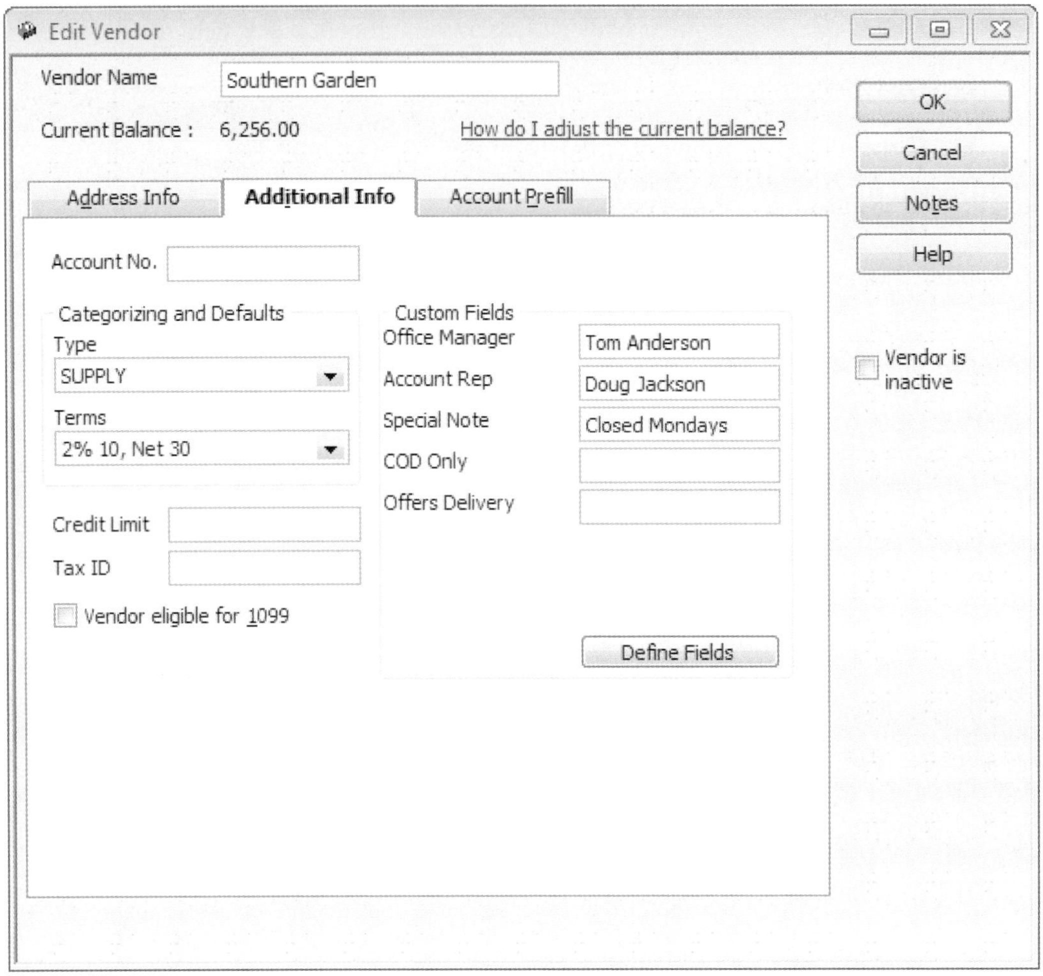

Figure 9:28

This tab stores vendor transaction defaults and fields for reporting.

Account No. is optional and stores the account number used by the vendor.

Type is optional and is used to group reports by vendor characteristics. You can click the dropdown list to view the types used by Baxter.

Terms on the vendor serve the same role as terms on the customer by controlling vendor bill due dates and early payment discounts.

Credit Limit on the vendor serves the same function as on the customer by controlling vendor purchases.

Vendor eligible for 1099 triggers a vendor for IRS tax reporting. When selected, QBP tracks annual payments for reporting on Form 1099. The IRS requires the annual filing of Form 1099 for subcontractor payments that exceed $600. Information on 1099 reporting requirements is available at www.irs.gov.

Tax ID stores a vendor's Social Security number or federal ID number for Form 1099 reporting.

Account Prefill

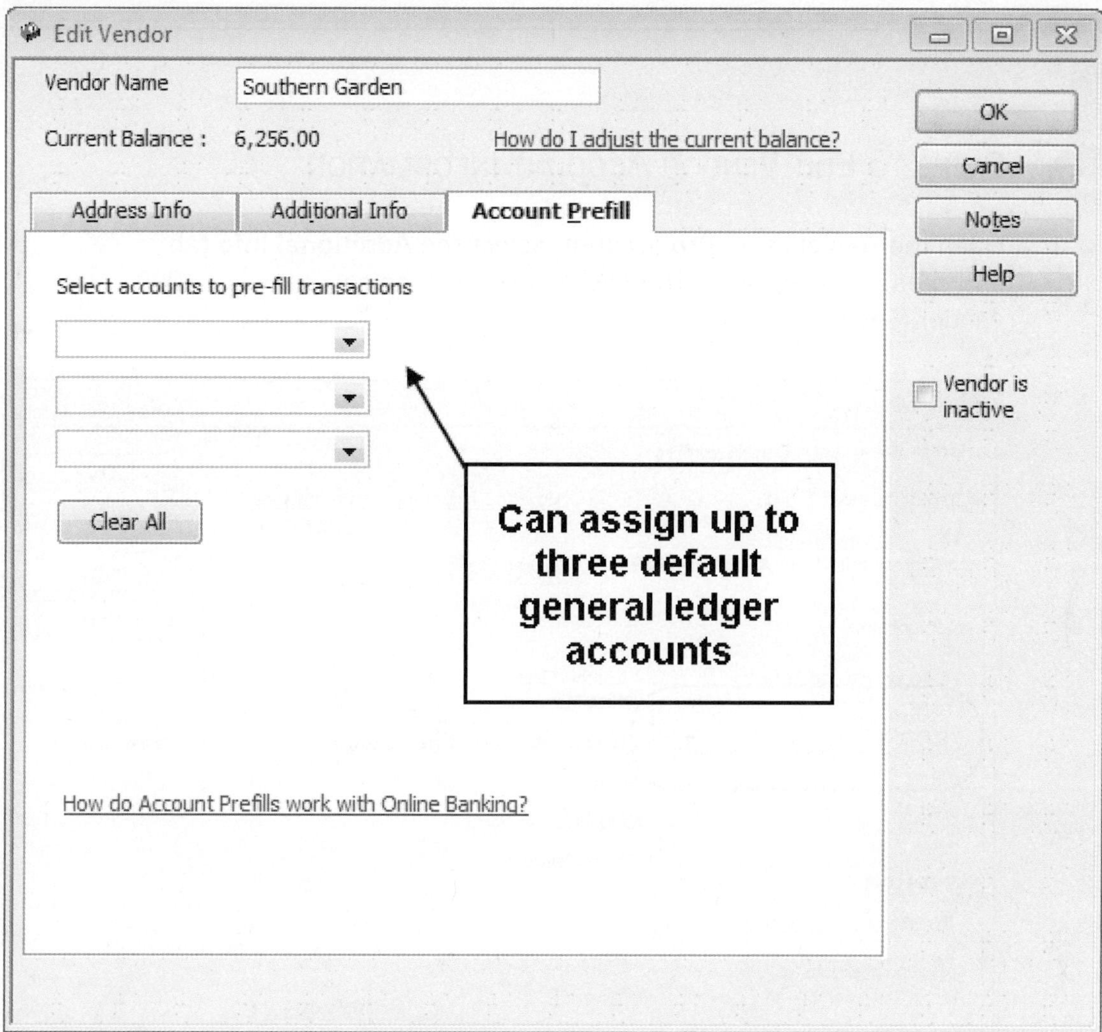

Figure 9:29

This tab assigns multiple default general ledger expense accounts. If a vendor has prefilled accounts, QBP will automatically enter the accounts on the Expenses tab of the Enter Bills window.

Southern Garden does not have prefill accounts because it is a supplier of inventory and purchases from this vendor use the default account assigned to the inventory item. You can open the Petty Cash vendor if you want to view prefilled accounts.

Click **X** to close the account. Now practice editing vendor accounts by completing the next exercise.

Steps to Edit Vendor Account Information

1. Open the **Daniel Lawn Pro** account. Select the **Additional Info** tab and change the **Type** to **SUBCON**. Notice that the company is a 1099 vendor.(See Figure 9:30.)

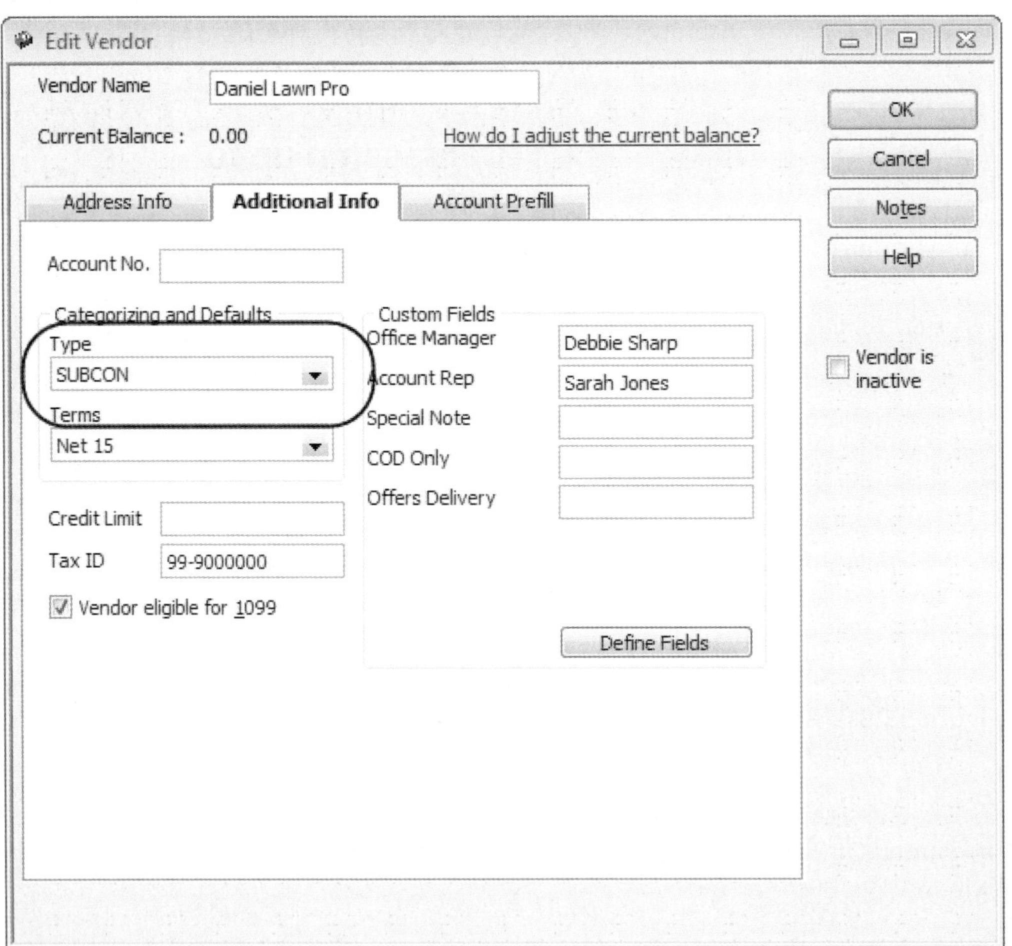

Figure 9:30

2. Click **OK** and click **Yes** if warned about affecting previously posted transactions.

You can delete vendors by highlighting a vendor account and selecting ***Edit>>Delete Vendor*** on the main menu. Like customers, you cannot delete accounts with transaction history, so use the **Vendor is inactive** option if you need to deny future transactions.

Adding vendors is similar to adding customers. Practice creating a new vendor in the exercise that follows.

CREATE A NEW VENDOR ACCOUNT

The following lists information for Baxter's new vendor account added on March 4.

Sullivan Buyer Supplies
P.O. Box 1732
Arlington, VA 30022

Vendor Type:	OFFICE
Terms:	Net 30
Account Prefill:	Office Supplies Expense

VENDOR BILLS FOR EXPENSES

Baxter also receives vendor bills for expenses not originating on POs and not involving inventory. These bills are normally for expenses such as office supplies, utilities, and insurance.

On March 28, Baxter receives a bill for advertising expense. Complete the exercise that follows to record this transaction.

Steps for Entering Vendor Bills for Expenses

1. On the **Home** page, click **Enter Bills**. In **Vendor**, look up and select "Jackson Advertising." Enter "3/28/12" as the **Date**.

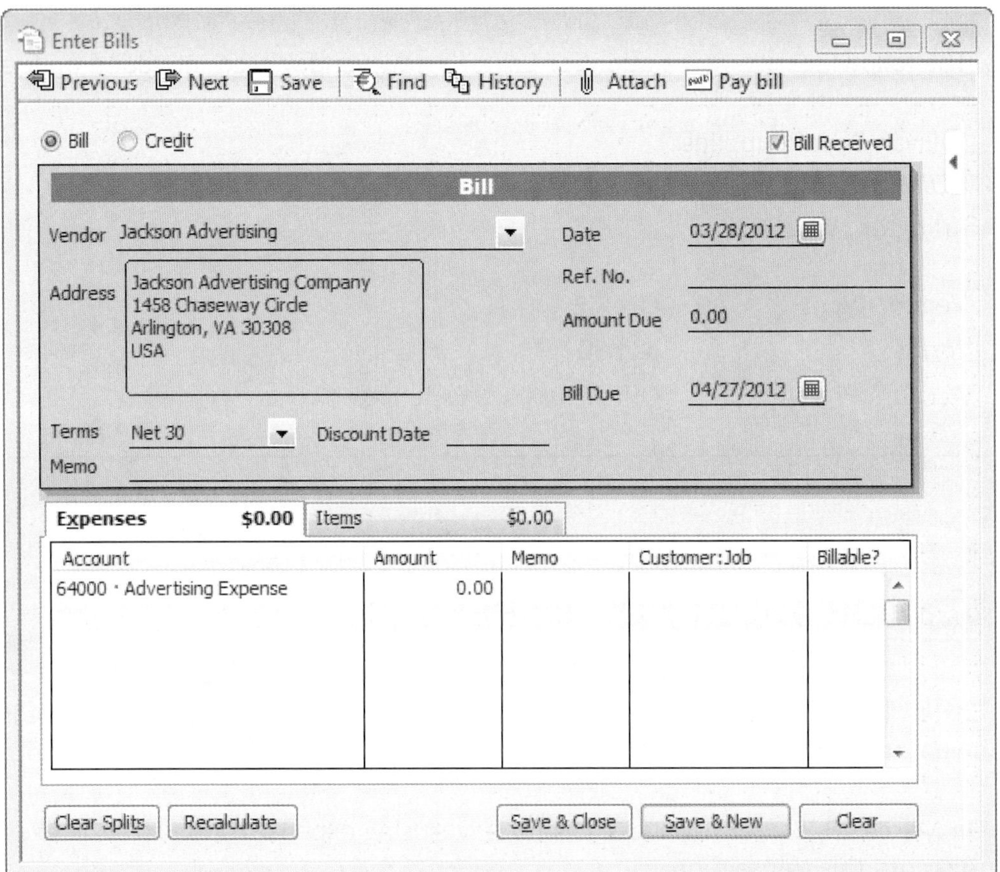

Figure 9:31

2. Enter "6067" as the **Ref. No**.

3. Enter "250.00" as the **Amount.**

4. Notice that the prefilled account of Advertising Expense automatically filled on the **Expenses** tab and the **Amount** automatically filled after entering $250.00 into **Amount Due**. Tab to **Memo** and type "Advertising flyers" into the field.

5. Figure 9:32 shows the completed transaction. Click **Save & Close** to post it.

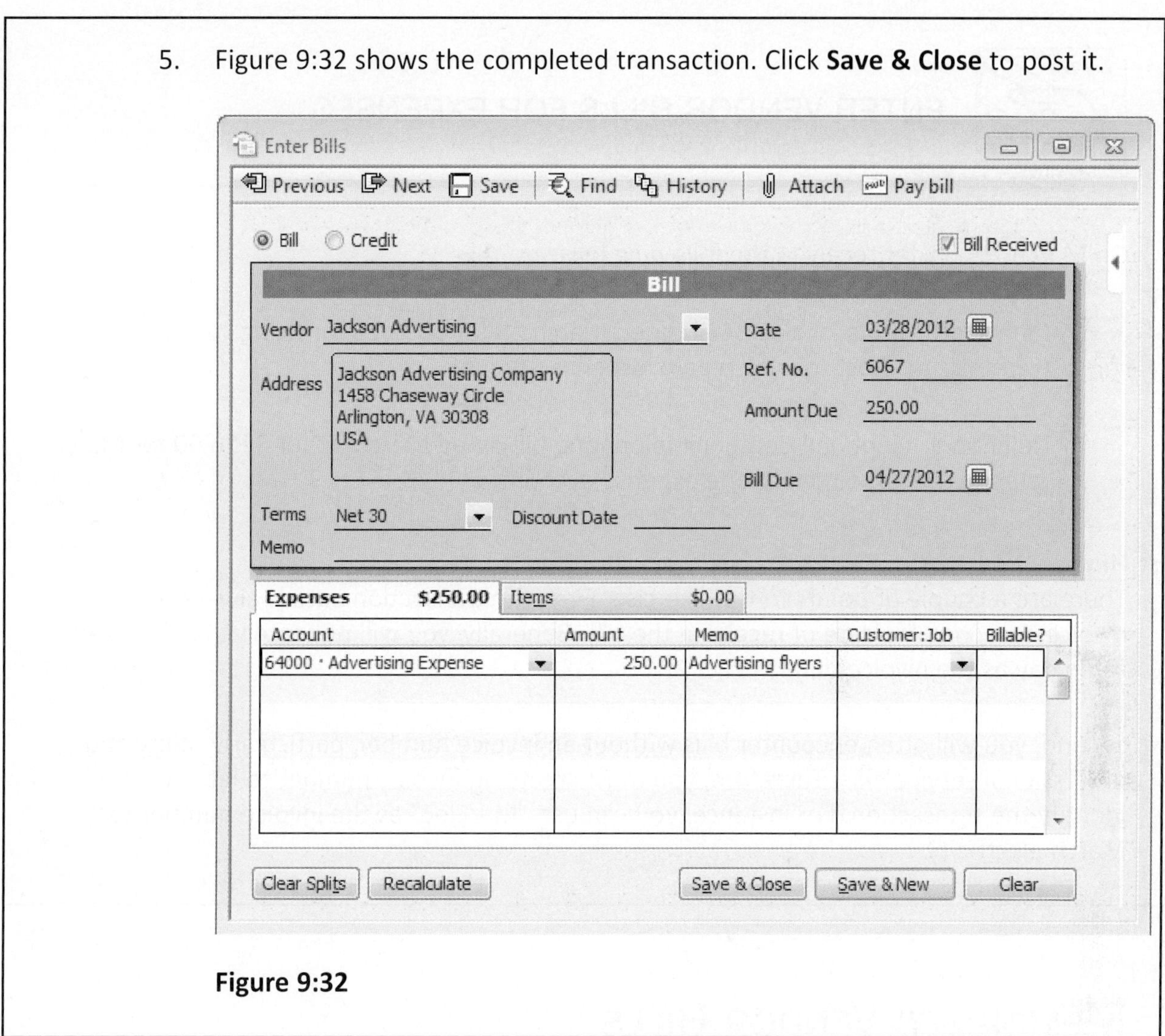

Figure 9:32

The *You Try* exercise that follows provides more practice on entering vendor bills for expenses.

ENTER VENDOR BILLS FOR EXPENSES

On March 29, Baxter received the following bills.

> Juan Motor Tools Invoice 3434 dated March 28 for $603.25 for fixing vehicle transmission. Post to auto repairs expense account.
>
> Neighbors Telephone Company telephone bill dated March 22 for $216.00 for March telephone. Post to telephone expense account.

Hints:
There are a couple of points to this exercise. First, the transaction date is always the invoice date, not the date of receiving the bill. Generally, you will not receive bills on the same day as the invoice date.

Second, you will often encounter bills without an invoice number, particularly utility and professional service bills. Therefore, you must create an invoice number to let you later identify the transaction. For instance, you can use "MarElec" as the invoice number for March electricity.

MEMORIZED VENDOR BILLS

QBP will let you memorize vendor bills. This feature is especially useful with recurring bills. You can memorize while creating a new bill or you can open a posted bill and memorize it.

The accountant has just signed a contract with Miles Maintenance for monthly office cleaning. In the following exercise, you enter the March bill and save it as a memorized bill.

STEPS TO CREATE A MEMORIZED VENDOR BILL

1. Click **Enter Bills** on the Home page and enter the following information.

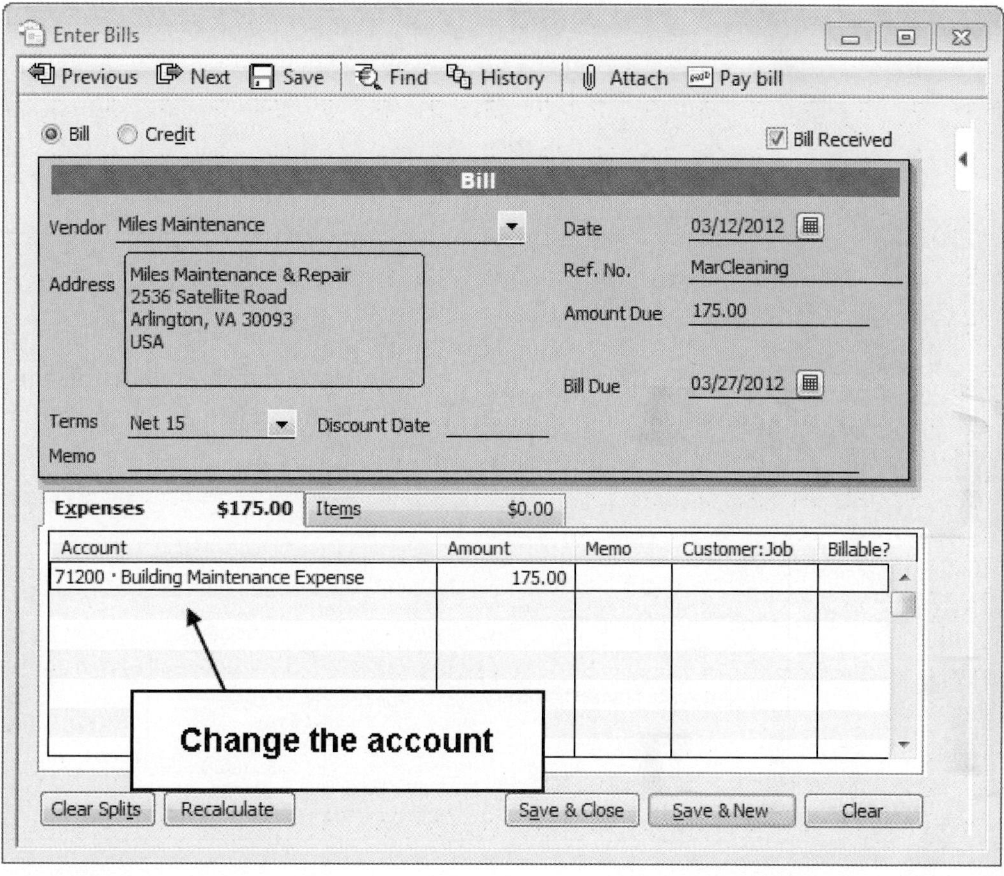

Figure 9:33

2. On the main menu, select ***Edit>>Memorize Bill*** to open the window illustrated in Figure 9:34.

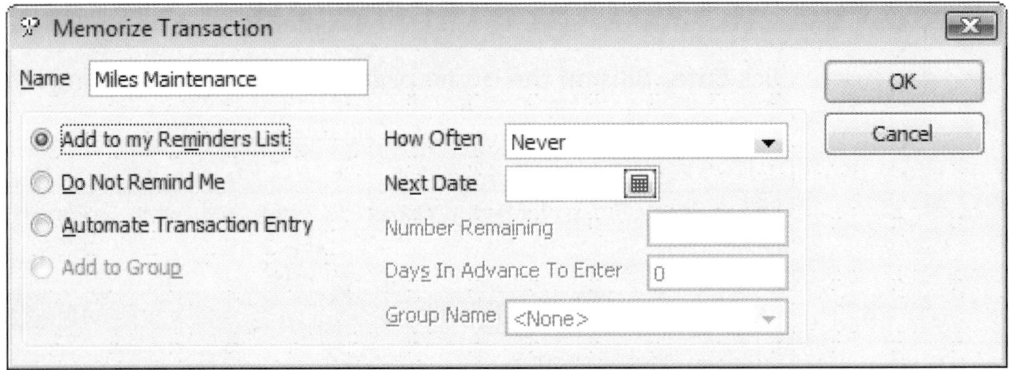

Figure 9:34

You can instruct QBP to remind you to post the bill or tell the software to automatically post it. Select **Don't Remind Me** as illustrated in Figure 9:35.

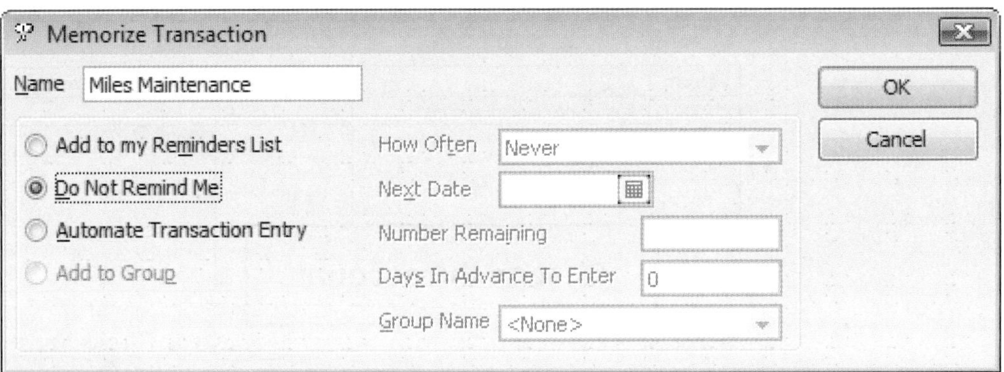

Figure 9:35

Click **OK** and click **Save & Close** on the March bill.

3. You will now locate this memorized transaction. Select ***Lists>>Memorized Transaction List*** on the main menu to open the Memorized Transaction List (Figure 9:36).

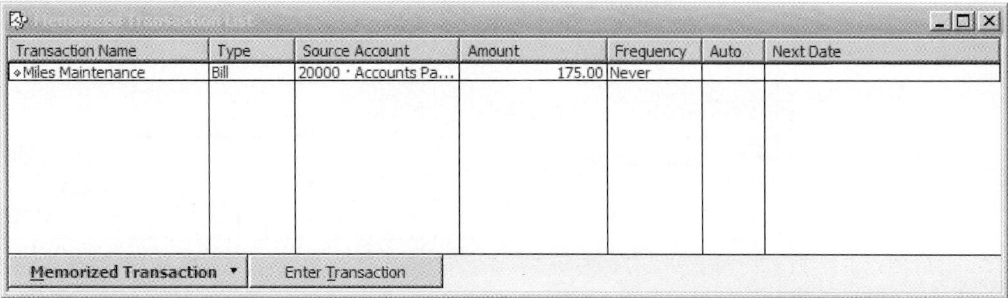

Figure 9:36

4. You can modify the scheduling of a memorized transaction. Highlight the **Miles** bill, click the **Memorized Transaction** button and select **Edit Memorized Transaction**. You have reopened the scheduling window where you reschedule the transaction. Click **Cancel**.

5. You will now record this transaction for April. With the transaction highlighted, click **Enter Transaction**.

   Enter the **Date** indicated and enter the **Ref. No.** of "AprCleaning" as illustrated next. Click **Save & Close**.

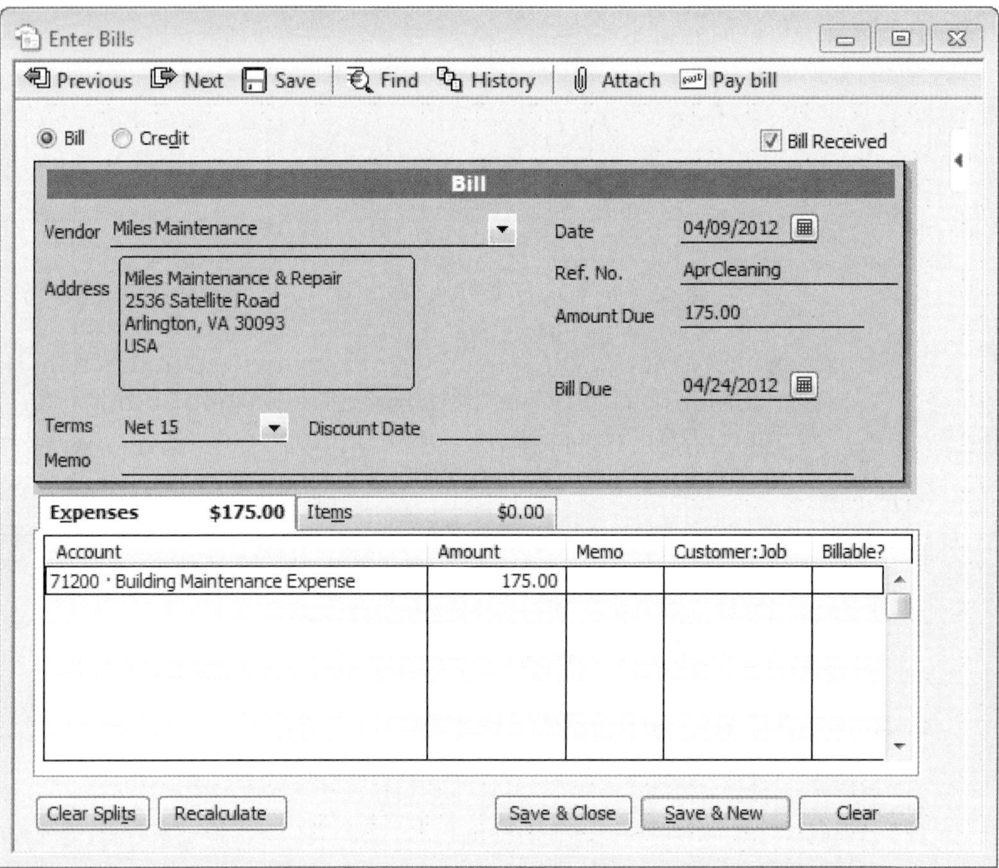

Figure 9:37

6. Click **X** to close the list.

VENDOR PAYMENTS

In this topic, you focus on paying vendor bills. In the following exercise, you create checks dated March 25 for vendor bills due by April 1 and bills having a discount that expires if not paid by March 29. *(Note: There is an online video for this topic.)*

STEPS TO PAY VENDORS

1. Before cutting checks, Melvin prepares an aged payables report to review bill due dates. Create this report by selecting ***Reports>>Vendors & Payables>>A/P Aging Detail*** on the main menu.

   Change the **Date** to April 1, 2012. Click **Customize Report**. On the **Display** tab, change the **Sort by** field to "Due Date." Click **OK**.

   Using the report illustrated in Figure 9:38, you can see the bills due by April 1. Close the report.

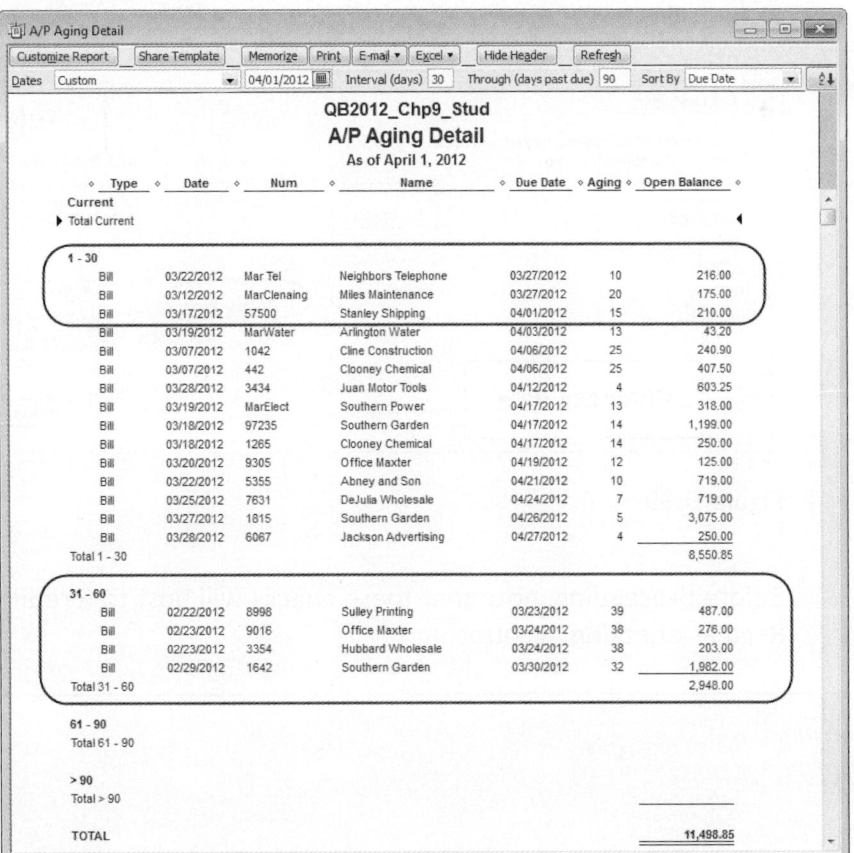

A/P Aging Detail

Customize Report | Share Template | Memorize | Print | E-mail | Excel | Hide Header | Refresh

Dates Custom 04/01/2012 Interval (days) 30 Through (days past due) 90 Sort By Due Date

QB2012_Chp9_Stud
A/P Aging Detail
As of April 1, 2012

Type	Date	Num	Name	Due Date	Aging	Open Balance
Current						
Total Current						
1 - 30						
Bill	03/22/2012	Mar Tel	Neighbors Telephone	03/27/2012	10	216.00
Bill	03/12/2012	MarClenaing	Miles Maintenance	03/27/2012	20	175.00
Bill	03/17/2012	57500	Stanley Shipping	04/01/2012	15	210.00
Bill	03/19/2012	MarWater	Arlington Water	04/03/2012	13	43.20
Bill	03/07/2012	1042	Cline Construction	04/06/2012	25	240.90
Bill	03/07/2012	442	Clooney Chemical	04/06/2012	25	407.50
Bill	03/28/2012	3434	Juan Motor Tools	04/12/2012	4	603.25
Bill	03/19/2012	MarElect	Southern Power	04/17/2012	13	318.00
Bill	03/18/2012	97235	Southern Garden	04/17/2012	14	1,199.00
Bill	03/18/2012	1265	Clooney Chemical	04/17/2012	14	250.00
Bill	03/20/2012	9305	Office Maxter	04/19/2012	12	125.00
Bill	03/22/2012	5355	Abney and Son	04/21/2012	10	719.00
Bill	03/25/2012	7631	DeJulia Wholesale	04/24/2012	7	719.00
Bill	03/27/2012	1815	Southern Garden	04/26/2012	5	3,075.00
Bill	03/28/2012	6067	Jackson Advertising	04/27/2012	4	250.00
Total 1 - 30						8,550.85
31 - 60						
Bill	02/22/2012	8998	Sulley Printing	03/23/2012	39	487.00
Bill	02/23/2012	9016	Office Maxter	03/24/2012	38	276.00
Bill	02/23/2012	3354	Hubbard Wholesale	03/24/2012	38	203.00
Bill	02/29/2012	1642	Southern Garden	03/30/2012	32	1,982.00
Total 31 - 60						2,948.00
61 - 90						
Total 61 - 90						
> 90						
Total > 90						
TOTAL						11,498.85

Figure 9:38

2. Click **Pay Bills** on the Home page. We will not use the filtering option because Baxter wants to pay bills due on or before April 1 and bills with a discount.

   Select **Show all bills** and enter "3/25/12" as the **Payment Date**. Select the **To be printed** option. Now mark the bills shown in Figure 9:39.

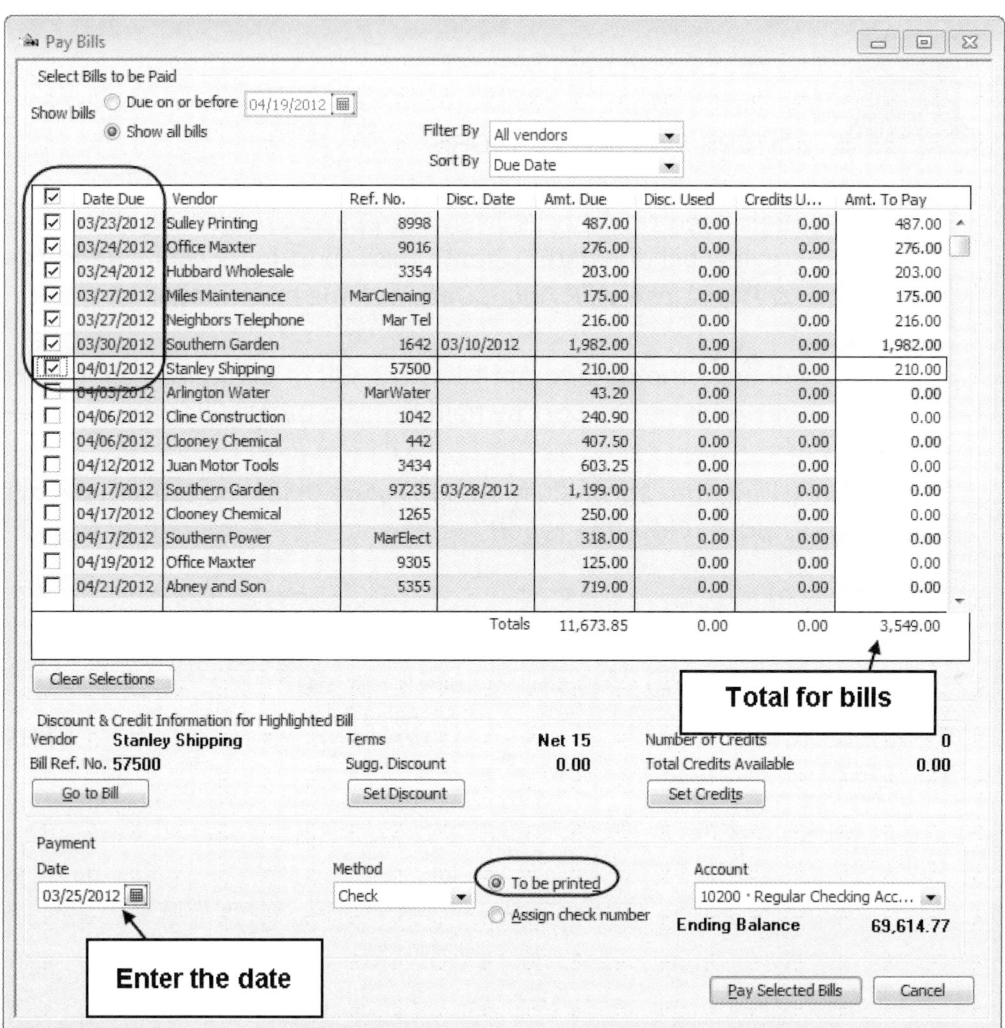

Figure 9:39

Before proceeding, note that these checks will post to (credit) 10200 Regular Checking Account.

3. Next, review the **Disc. Date** column to identify bills with a discount that expire before April 1. Select the invoice illustrated and the total **Amt. to Pay** increases, as illustrated next.

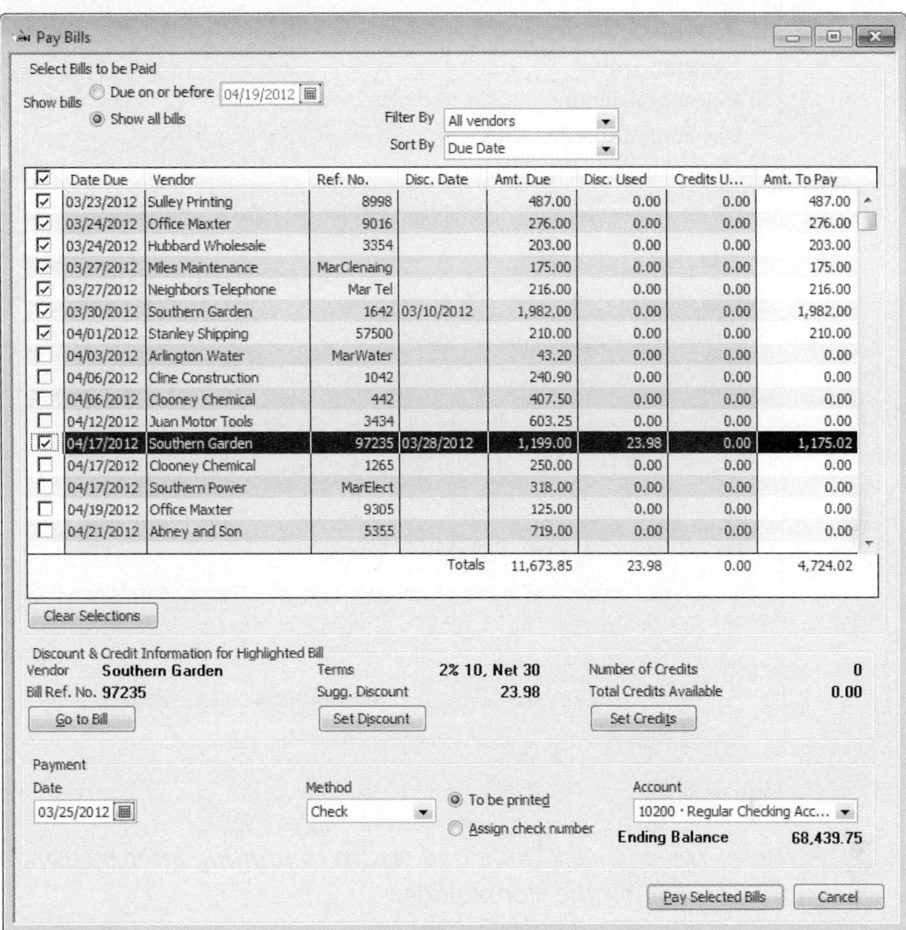

Figure 9:40

You can reduce the payment to a vendor by changing the **Amt. To Pay**. Checks will credit the regular checking account and debit the accounts payable account. The **Disc. Used** column amount will credit the 59500 Purchase Discounts. This account is set on the Company Preferences tab for Bills as illustrated next.

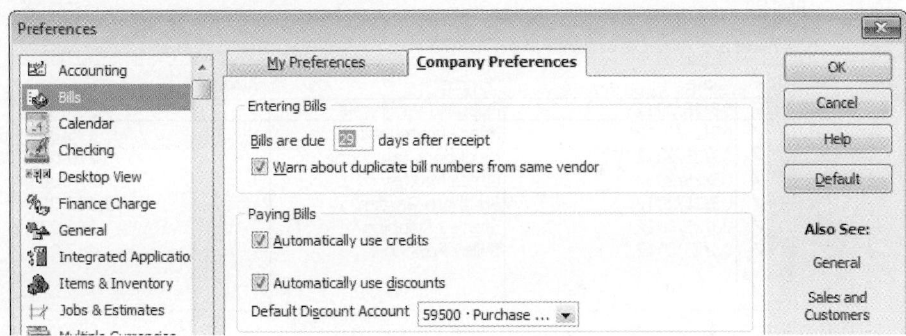

Figure 9:41

4. Click **Pay Selected Bills** to open the window illustrated in Figure 9:42.

Payment Summary

Payment Details

Payment Date 03/25/2012

Payment Account 10200 · Regular Checking Account

Payment Method Check

Payments have been successfully recorded for the following 8 of 8 bills:

Date Due	Vendor	Amount Paid
03/24/2012	Hubbard Wholesale	203.00
03/27/2012	Miles Maintenance	175.00
03/27/2012	Neighbors Telephone	216.00
03/24/2012	Office Maxter	276.00
	Total	4,724.02

How do I find and change a bill payment?

You can print checks now or print them later from Print Forms on the File menu.

Pay More Bills | Print Checks | Done

Figure 9:42

Note: You can click Done and return to printing later by using the Print Checks icon on the Home page.

5. Click **Print Checks** and the window in Figure 9:43 opens. Keep the **First Check Number** illustrated.

   Notice that QBP has combined vendor bills so that seven checks will print.

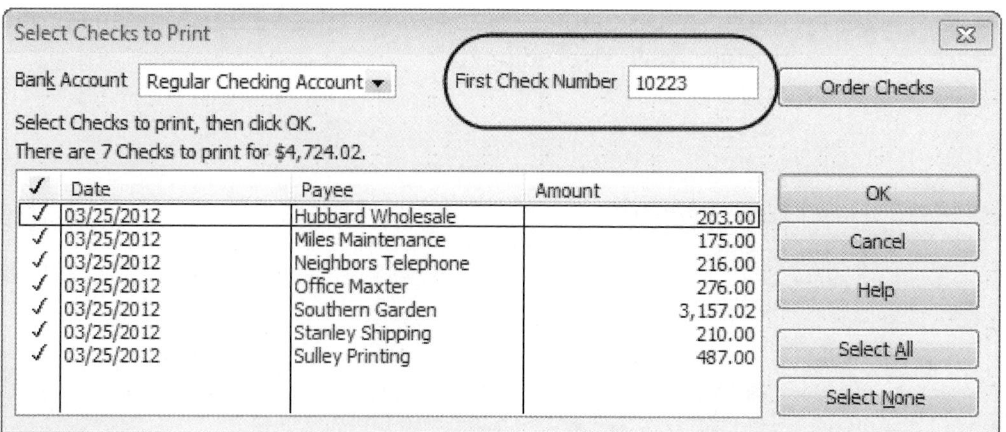

Figure 9:43

6. Click **OK** and the printer selection window opens. Select a printer and click **Print**. Figure 9:44 shows the first check printed.

3/25/2012

Hubbard Wholesale **203.00

Two Hundred Three and 00/100***

Hubbard Wholesale
1500 Pavilion Place
Arlington, VA 30093
USA

Hubbard Wholesale 3/25/2012

Date	Type	Reference	Original Amt.	Balance Due	Discount	Payment
2/23/2012	Bill	3354	203.00	203.00		203.00
					Check Amount	203.00

Regular Checking Acc 203.00

Hubbard Wholesale 3/25/2012

Date	Type	Reference	Original Amt.	Balance Due	Discount	Payment
2/23/2012	Bill	3354	203.00	203.00		203.00
					Check Amount	203.00

Regular Checking Acc 203.00

Figure 9:44

Note: This check illustrates printing on a two-part check where Baxter can send the top portion to the vendor and attach the bottom portion to the paid bill.

7. QBP next confirms check printing (Figure 9:45). If checks did not print properly, you can click Select All and click Cancel so that check numbers are not assigned. You would then return to printing by using the Print Checks icon on the Home page.

   Click **OK**.

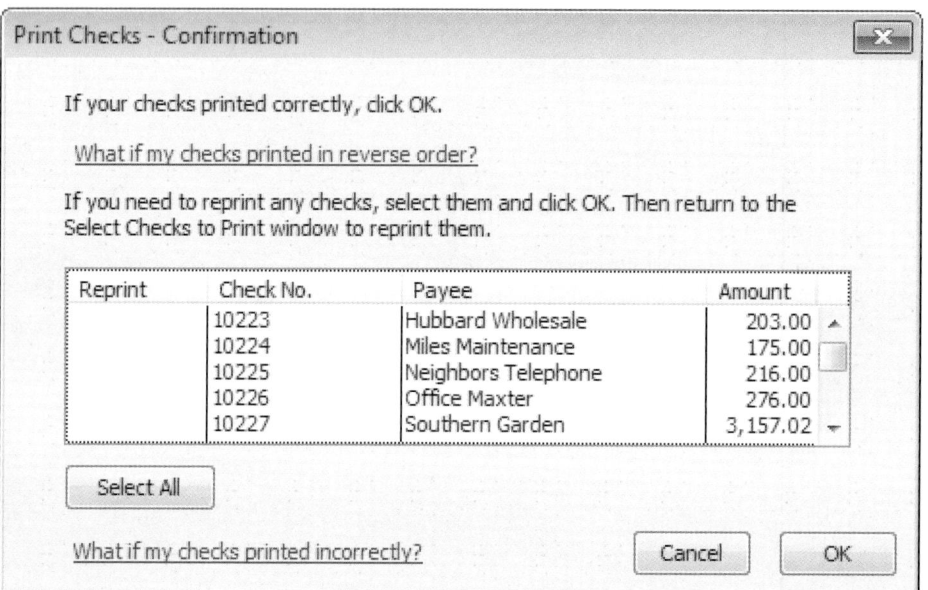

Figure 9:45

Behind the Keys of a Posted Vendor Payment

Now trace the audit trail for the checks printed in the previous topic. On the main menu, select ***Reports>>Memorized Reports>>Accounting Journals>>Cash Disbursement Journal.*** Change the date range to "**3/25/12.**" (See Figure 9:46.)

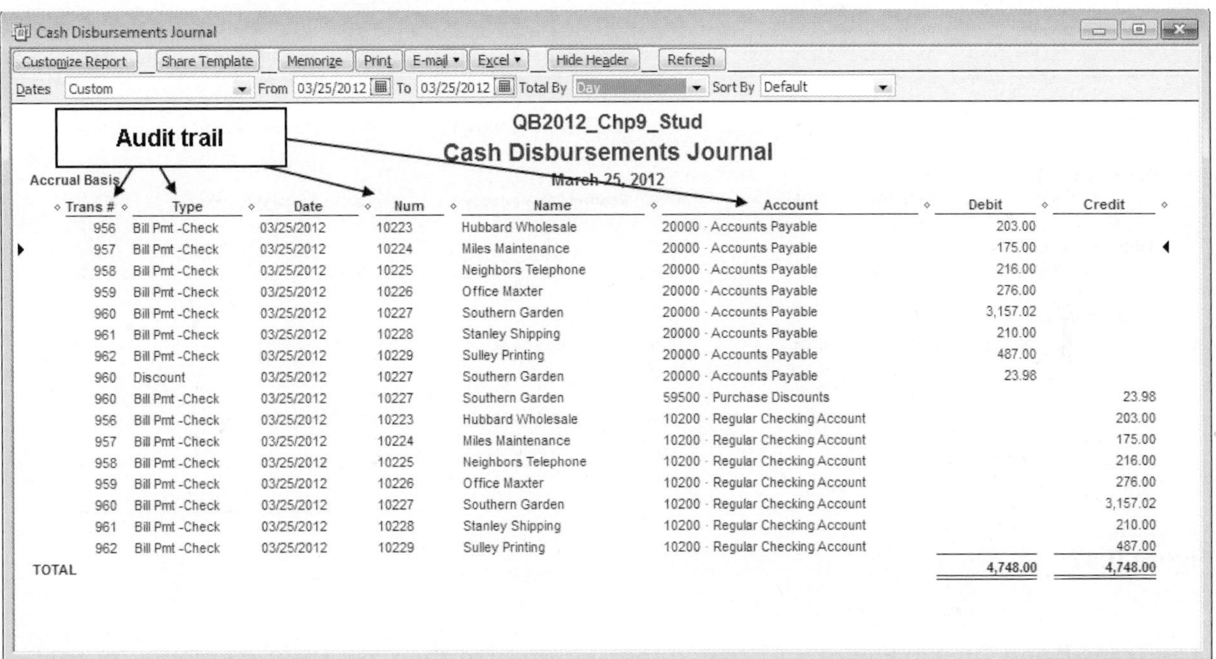

Cash Disbursements Journal

Dates Custom From 03/25/2012 To 03/25/2012 Total By Day Sort By Default

QB2012_Chp9_Stud
Cash Disbursements Journal
March 25, 2012
Accrual Basis

Trans #	Type	Date	Num	Name	Account	Debit	Credit
956	Bill Pmt -Check	03/25/2012	10223	Hubbard Wholesale	20000 · Accounts Payable	203.00	
957	Bill Pmt -Check	03/25/2012	10224	Miles Maintenance	20000 · Accounts Payable	175.00	
958	Bill Pmt -Check	03/25/2012	10225	Neighbors Telephone	20000 · Accounts Payable	216.00	
959	Bill Pmt -Check	03/25/2012	10226	Office Maxter	20000 · Accounts Payable	276.00	
960	Bill Pmt -Check	03/25/2012	10227	Southern Garden	20000 · Accounts Payable	3,157.02	
961	Bill Pmt -Check	03/25/2012	10228	Stanley Shipping	20000 · Accounts Payable	210.00	
962	Bill Pmt -Check	03/25/2012	10229	Sulley Printing	20000 · Accounts Payable	487.00	
960	Discount	03/25/2012	10227	Southern Garden	20000 · Accounts Payable	23.98	
960	Bill Pmt -Check	03/25/2012	10227	Southern Garden	59500 · Purchase Discounts		23.98
956	Bill Pmt -Check	03/25/2012	10223	Hubbard Wholesale	10200 · Regular Checking Account		203.00
957	Bill Pmt -Check	03/25/2012	10224	Miles Maintenance	10200 · Regular Checking Account		175.00
958	Bill Pmt -Check	03/25/2012	10225	Neighbors Telephone	10200 · Regular Checking Account		216.00
959	Bill Pmt -Check	03/25/2012	10226	Office Maxter	10200 · Regular Checking Account		276.00
960	Bill Pmt -Check	03/25/2012	10227	Southern Garden	10200 · Regular Checking Account		3,157.02
961	Bill Pmt -Check	03/25/2012	10228	Stanley Shipping	10200 · Regular Checking Account		210.00
962	Bill Pmt -Check	03/25/2012	10229	Sulley Printing	10200 · Regular Checking Account		487.00
TOTAL						4,748.00	4,748.00

Figure 9:46

The report lists the **Trans #** and **Type** audit trail for each payment. Close the report.

Select ***Reports>>Vendors & Payables>>Transaction List by Vendor*** to open the report listing transactions to vendor accounts. Enter "**3/25/12**" as the date range and **Customize** to add the **Trans #** column. Click **OK**.

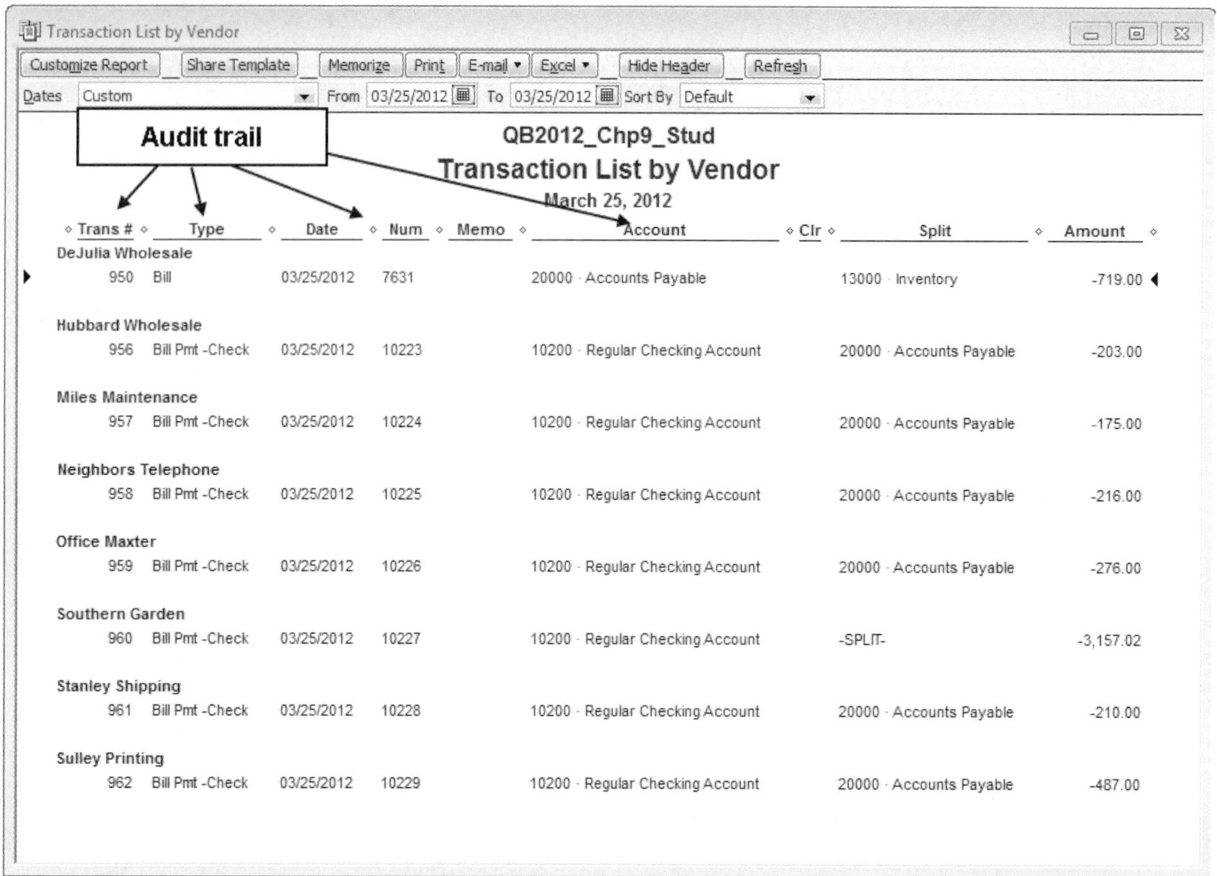

QB2012_Chp9_Stud
Transaction List by Vendor
March 25, 2012

Trans #	Type	Date	Num	Memo	Account	Clr	Split	Amount
DeJulia Wholesale								
950	Bill	03/25/2012	7631		20000 · Accounts Payable		13000 · Inventory	-719.00
Hubbard Wholesale								
956	Bill Pmt -Check	03/25/2012	10223		10200 · Regular Checking Account		20000 · Accounts Payable	-203.00
Miles Maintenance								
957	Bill Pmt -Check	03/25/2012	10224		10200 · Regular Checking Account		20000 · Accounts Payable	-175.00
Neighbors Telephone								
958	Bill Pmt -Check	03/25/2012	10225		10200 · Regular Checking Account		20000 · Accounts Payable	-216.00
Office Maxter								
959	Bill Pmt -Check	03/25/2012	10226		10200 · Regular Checking Account		20000 · Accounts Payable	-276.00
Southern Garden								
960	Bill Pmt -Check	03/25/2012	10227		10200 · Regular Checking Account		-SPLIT-	-3,157.02
Stanley Shipping								
961	Bill Pmt -Check	03/25/2012	10228		10200 · Regular Checking Account		20000 · Accounts Payable	-210.00
Sulley Printing								
962	Bill Pmt -Check	03/25/2012	10229		10200 · Regular Checking Account		20000 · Accounts Payable	-487.00

Figure 9:47

The **Trans #** and **Type** in Figure 9:47 match the audit trail in the **Cash Disbursements Journal.**

Close this report and complete tracing entries by opening the **General Ledger Detail Report.** Locate your entries in accounts 10200 Regular Checking and 20000 Accounts Payable (not illustrated).

Write Checks Without a Vendor Bill

You can write checks without entering a bill first. This is useful if you need to write a check to a vendor that requests cash upon delivery. Sometimes the vendor account will also be new so you add it "on the fly." *(Note: Remember "on the fly" means creating a new account while entering a transaction.)*

Complete the next exercise to write a check for miscellaneous office supplies.

STEPS TO ADD A VENDOR ON THE FLY WHILE WRITING A CHECK WITHOUT A VENDOR BILL

1. Click **Write Checks** under the **Banking** section of the **Home** page. Enter "3/25/12" as the **Date** and mark **To be printed.**

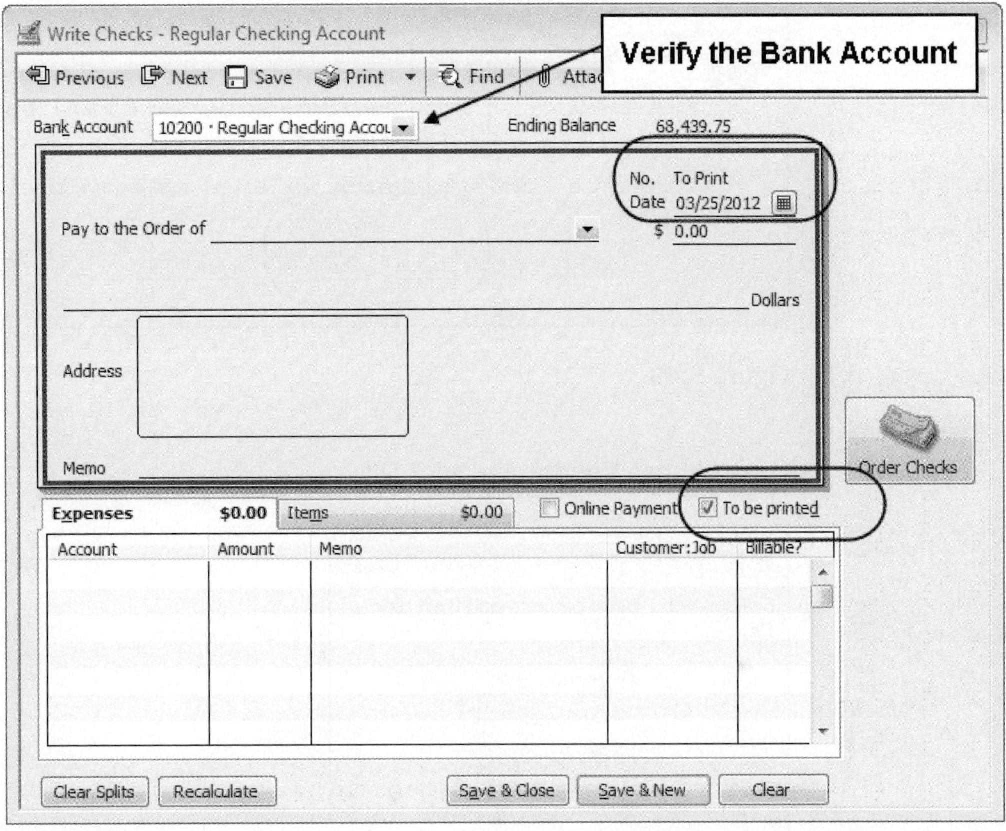

Figure 9:48

2. The vendor is not on file so place your cursor in **Pay to the Order of** and type "Ready Supplies."

   Press Tab. When QBP prompts to create the account (Figure 9:49), click **Set Up**.

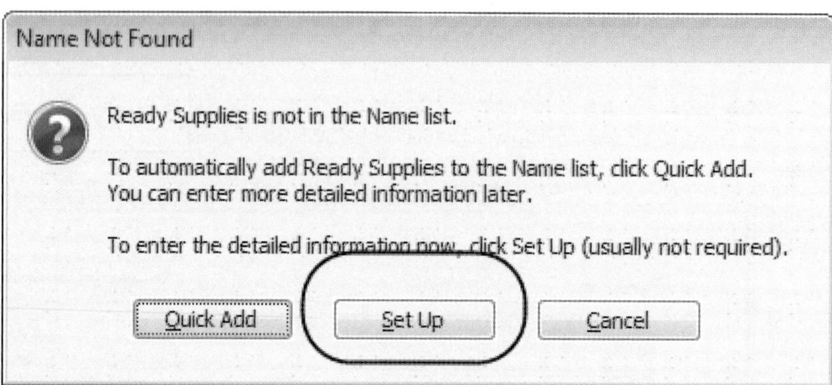

Figure 9:49

Next, choose **Vendor** and click **OK**.

Select Name Type

Select which type of name to add then click OK.

Vendor
Customer
Employee
Other

OK Cancel

Figure 9:50

3. Use information in the next series of figures to create the vendor account.

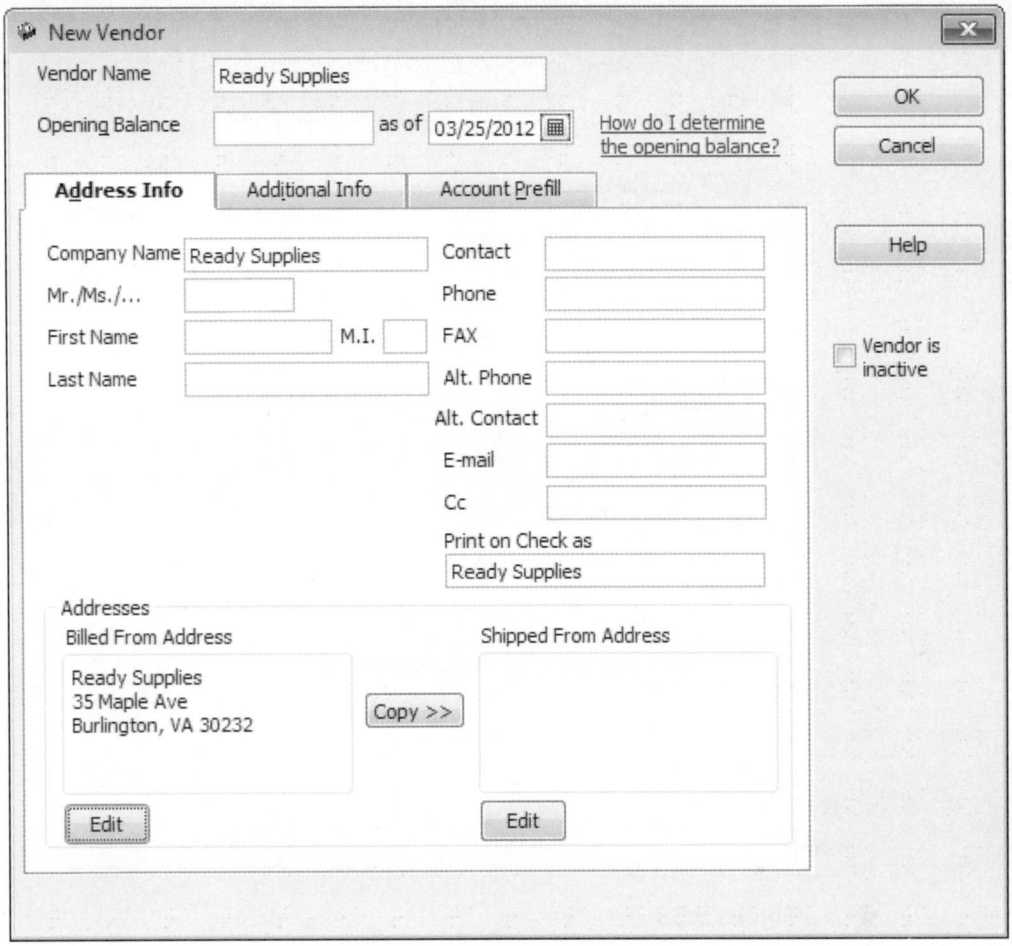

Figure 9:51

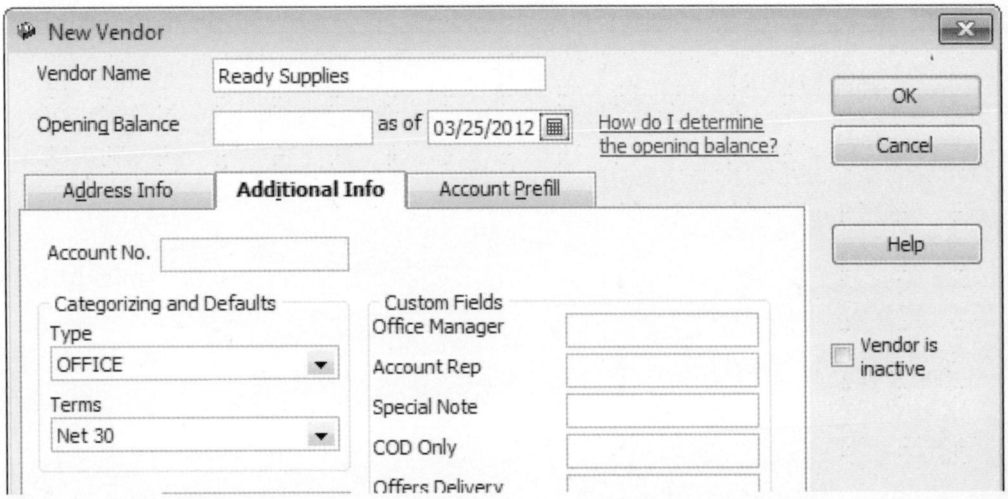

Figure 9:52

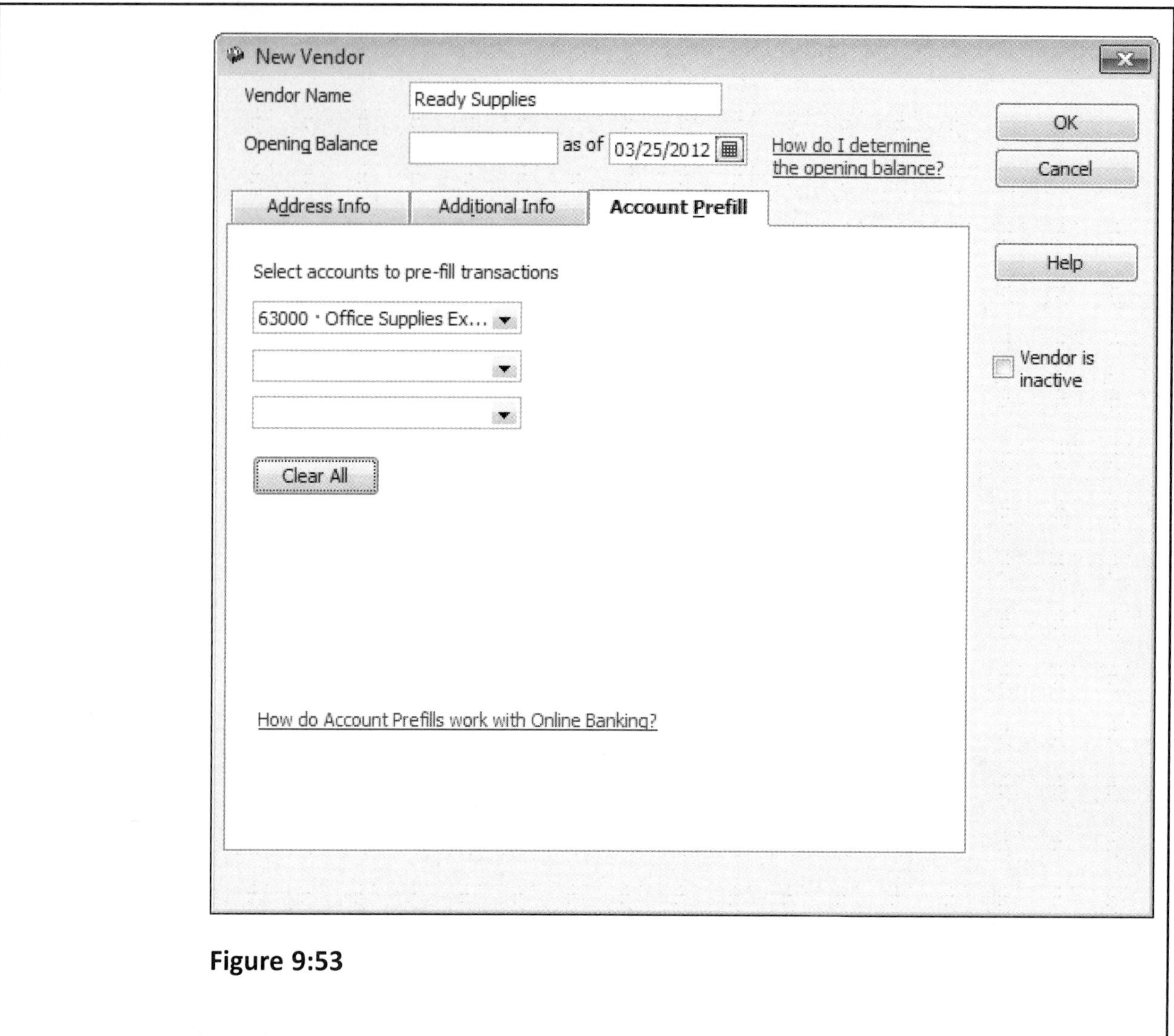

Figure 9:53

Click **OK** and you have just added a vendor "on the fly."

4. Now complete the check as shown in Figure 9:54.

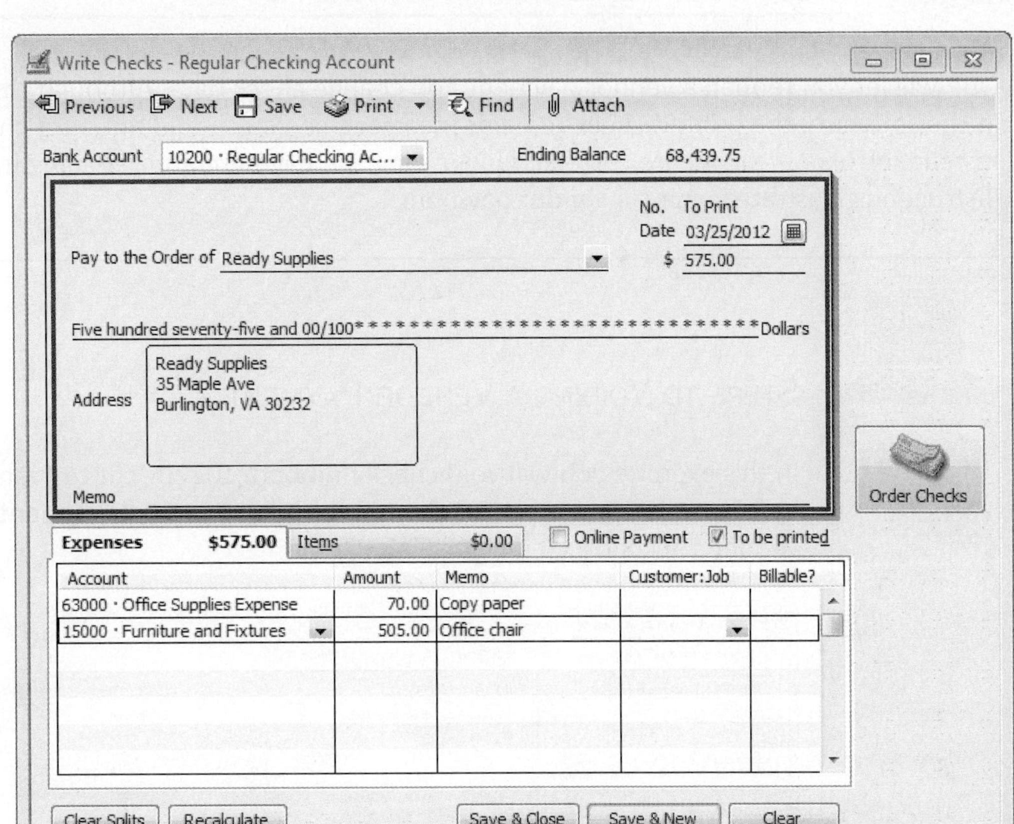

Figure 9:54

You are using two different accounts to record this transaction because office chairs are furniture and fixture assets, not office supplies expense.

5. Click **Print** and confirm that the check number is "10230". Click **OK**, choose a printer, and click **Print**. Click **OK** to confirm that the check printed correctly.

6. Click **Save & Close**.

VOIDING VENDOR PAYMENTS

QBP will let you reopen a vendor payment and change check data. Although this changes data in the software, the printed check remains incorrect, so you should not alter check data. Instead, errors on checks are corrected by voiding the payment and reissuing it. The following instructions illustrate voiding a vendor payment.

STEPS TO VOIDING A VENDOR PAYMENT

1. In this exercise you will void check number "10220" cut to Juan Motor Tools on March 19. Open the **Vendor Center** and locate **Bill Payments** for this vendor's account. (See Figure 9:55.)

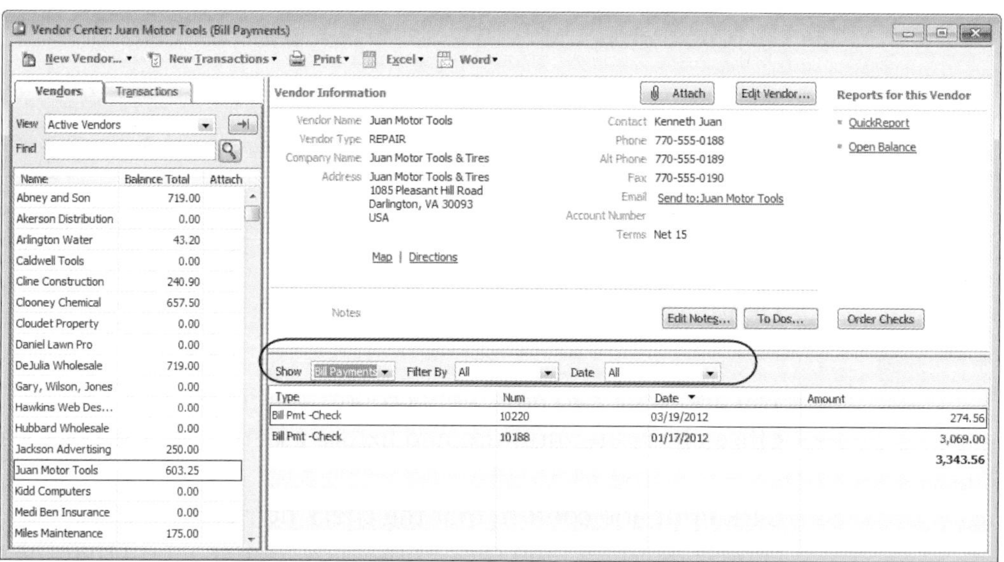

Figure 9:55

2. Double click to reopen the check. On the main menu, select ***Edit>>Void Bill Pmt – Check.***

   Notice that the **Memo** now reads "Void" and the bills are no longer selected for payment.

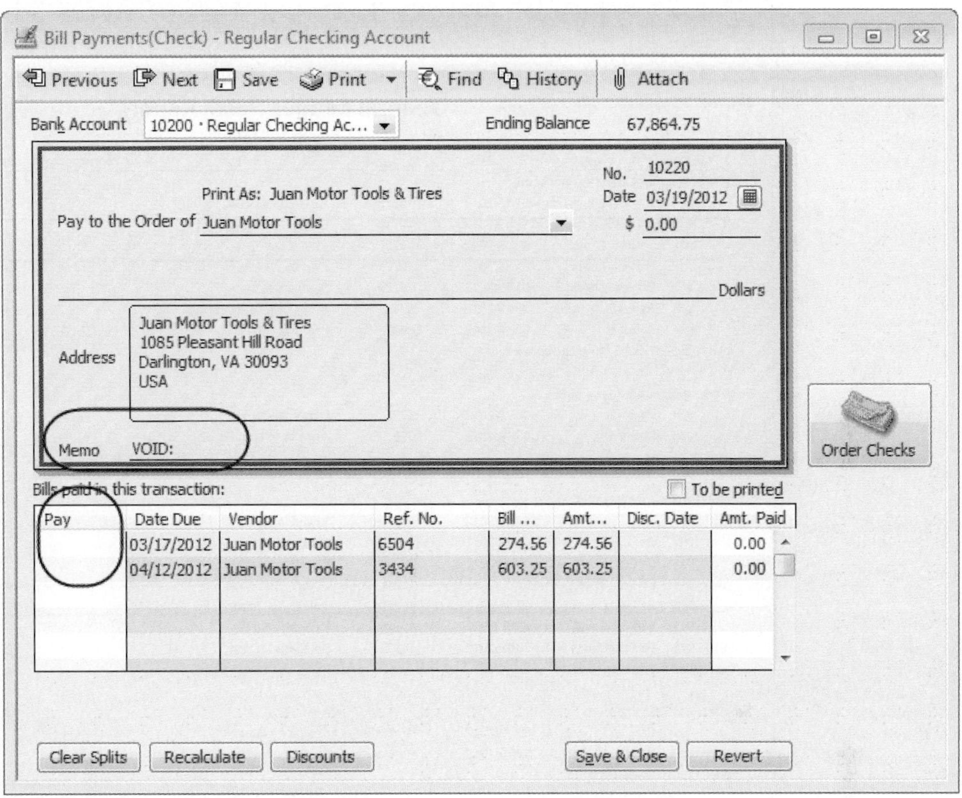

Figure 9:56

You want to be very careful when voiding checks. QBP will always post the entry for a voided check as of the check date. If voiding a check written in a closed accounting period, QBP will prompt to post the entry to the closed period. There is no option choose a date. Therefore, permit the entry to backdate and record a general journal entry to reclassify the amount to the open accounting period.

3. Click **Save & Close.** When prompted (Figure 9:57), click **Yes.**

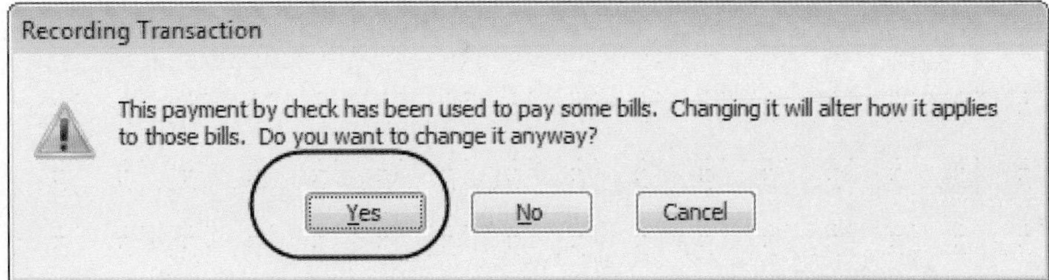

Figure 9:57

4. View the results of your action. Select **Reports>>Memorized Reports>> Accounting Journals>>General Ledger Detail Report** on the main menu. Enter "**3/19/12**" as the date range. Notice that QBP voided the check as of the check date (Figure 9:58). Close the report.

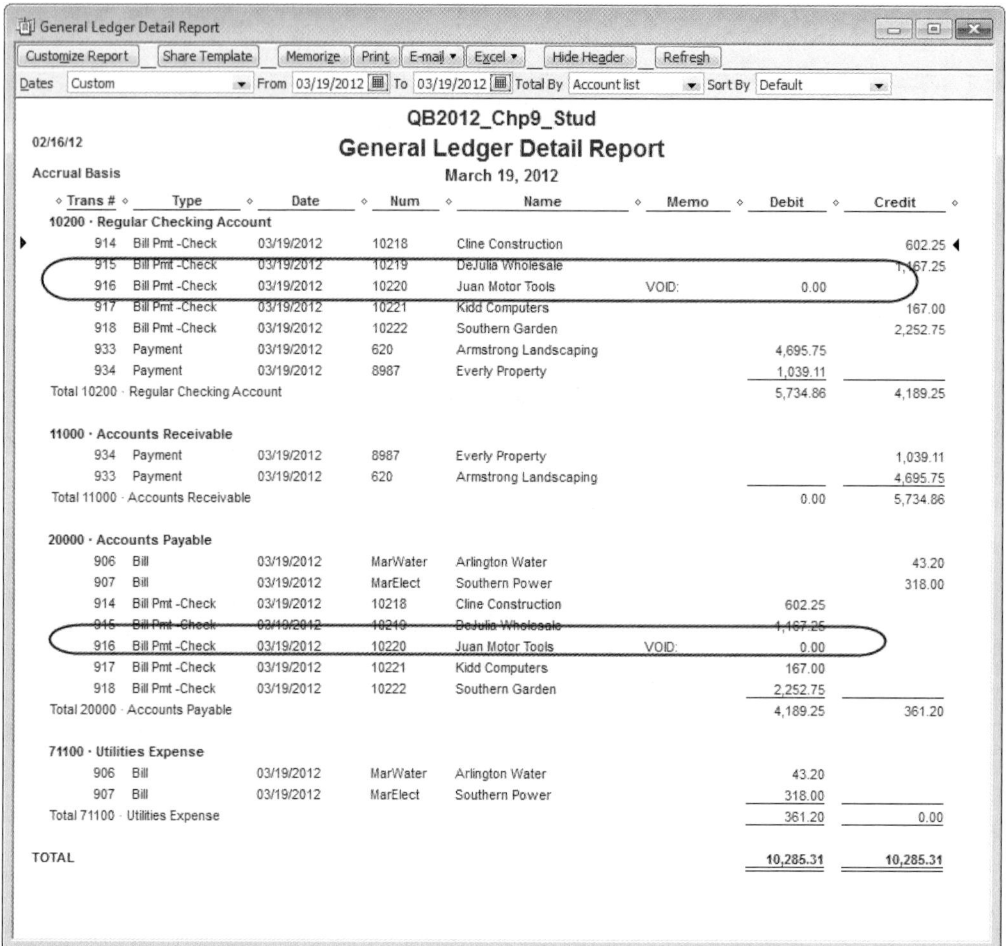

General Ledger Detail Report

Customize Report | Share Template | Memorize | Print | E-mail | Excel | Hide Header | Refresh

Dates Custom From 03/19/2012 To 03/19/2012 Total By Account list Sort By Default

QB2012_Chp9_Stud

02/16/12 General Ledger Detail Report

Accrual Basis March 19, 2012

Trans #	Type	Date	Num	Name	Memo	Debit	Credit
10200 · Regular Checking Account							
914	Bill Pmt -Check	03/19/2012	10218	Cline Construction			602.25
915	Bill Pmt -Check	03/19/2012	10219	DeJulia Wholesale			1,167.25
916	Bill Pmt -Check	03/19/2012	10220	Juan Motor Tools	VOID:	0.00	
917	Bill Pmt -Check	03/19/2012	10221	Kidd Computers			167.00
918	Bill Pmt -Check	03/19/2012	10222	Southern Garden			2,252.75
933	Payment	03/19/2012	620	Armstrong Landscaping		4,695.75	
934	Payment	03/19/2012	8987	Everly Property		1,039.11	
Total 10200 · Regular Checking Account						5,734.86	4,189.25
11000 · Accounts Receivable							
934	Payment	03/19/2012	8987	Everly Property			1,039.11
933	Payment	03/19/2012	620	Armstrong Landscaping			4,695.75
Total 11000 · Accounts Receivable						0.00	5,734.86
20000 · Accounts Payable							
906	Bill	03/19/2012	MarWater	Arlington Water			43.20
907	Bill	03/19/2012	MarElect	Southern Power			318.00
914	Bill Pmt -Check	03/19/2012	10218	Cline Construction		602.25	
915	Bill Pmt -Check	03/19/2012	10219	DeJulia Wholesale		1,167.25	
916	Bill Pmt -Check	03/19/2012	10220	Juan Motor Tools	VOID:	0.00	
917	Bill Pmt -Check	03/19/2012	10221	Kidd Computers		167.00	
918	Bill Pmt -Check	03/19/2012	10222	Southern Garden		2,252.75	
Total 20000 · Accounts Payable						4,189.25	361.20
71100 · Utilities Expense							
906	Bill	03/19/2012	MarWater	Arlington Water		43.20	
907	Bill	03/19/2012	MarElect	Southern Power		318.00	
Total 71100 · Utilities Expense						361.20	0.00
TOTAL						10,285.31	10,285.31

Figure 9:58

5. Return to the vendor's account and view the **Bills**. The March bill has an open balance so it can be reselected for payment. You will pay this bill in the next exercise.

Close the **Vendor Center**.

PAY VENDORS

Create vendor checks dated April 1. Individually select bills to pay based on the following.

All bills with a due date before April 11.
Reduce the payment to Cline Construction to $200.00
All invoices with a discount expiring before April 11.

The selected payments will total $4,643.38. Print the checks using "10231"as the first check number.

Print the Cash Disbursements Journal for April 1.

PAYING SALES TAX

At the end of every month, Baxter must remit sales tax collected from customers. QBP tracks sales tax collections and the following shows you how to remit it.

Steps to Paying Sales Tax

1. Click **Manage Sales Tax** on the **Home** page to open the window shown in Figure 9:59.

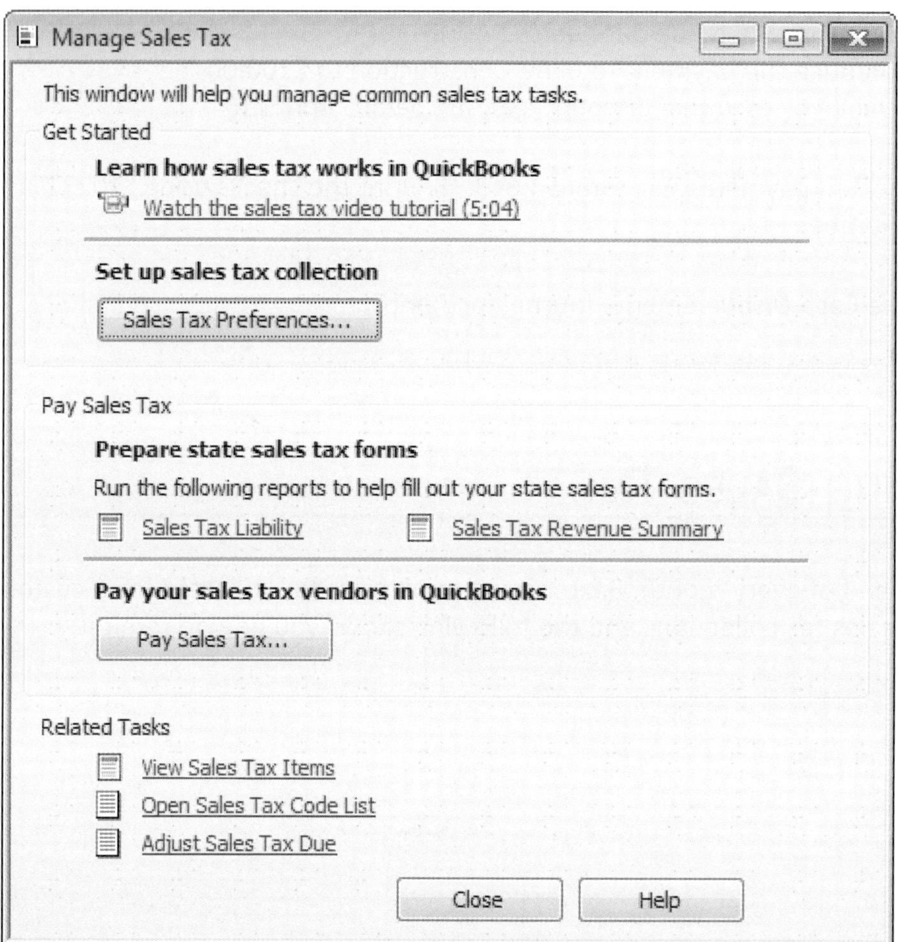

Figure 9:59

2. Click **Sales Tax Preferences.** Figure 9:60 shows that Baxter collects Virginia sales tax, owes the tax after the customer pays the invoice, and remits sales tax monthly.

   Click **Cancel** to exit this window.

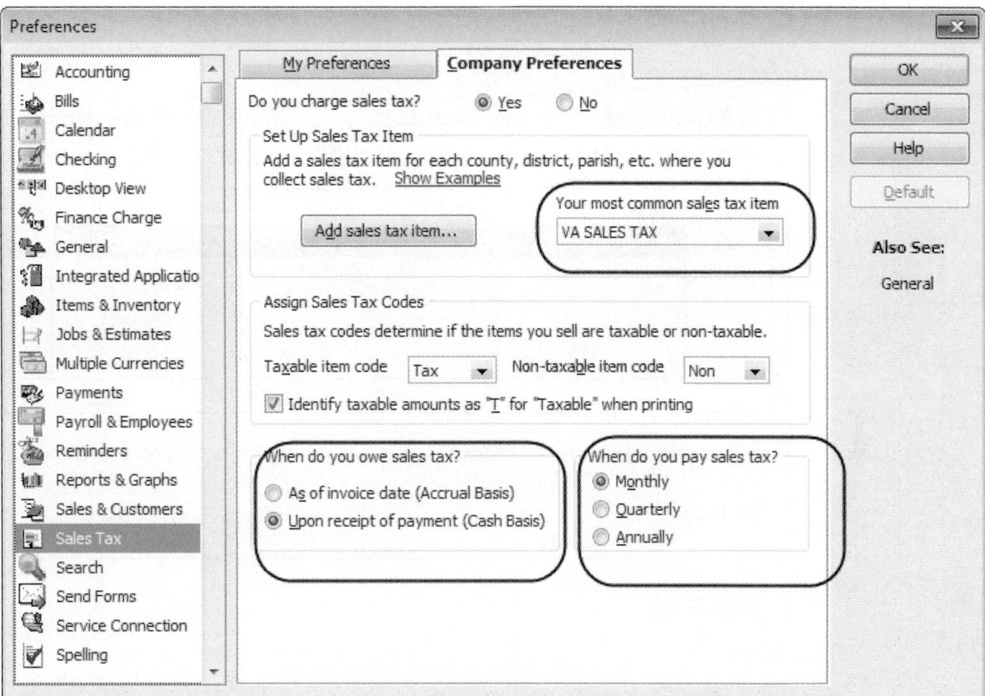

Figure 9:60

3. On the **Manage Sales Tax** window, click the **Sales Tax Liability** link to view a report showing the current sales tax owed.

   Enter the date range of **3/01/12** through **3/31/12.** Close the report after noting the amount under Sales Tax Payable (Figure 9:61).

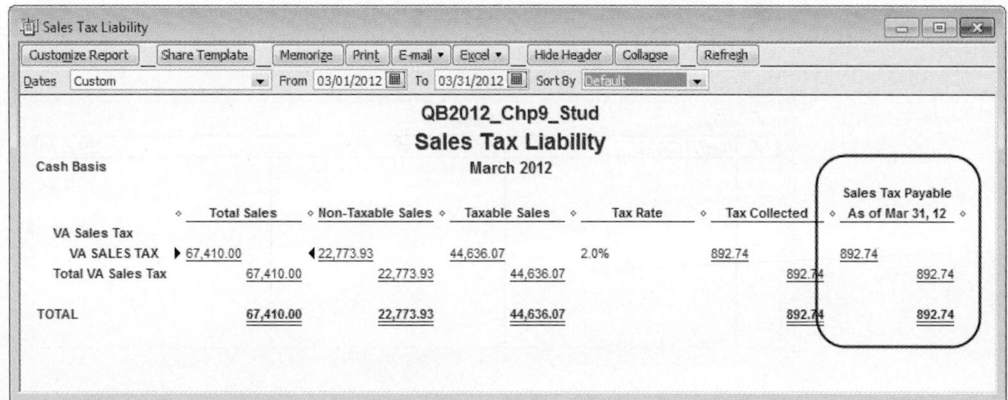

Figure 9:61

4. Click the **Pay Sales Tax** button. Enter the **Check Date** of 4/1/12 and **Show sales tax due through** date of 3/31/12. Click to select the **Pay** column and click to select **To be printed**.

   The **Amt. Due** in Figure 9:62 matches the amount due on the previous report.

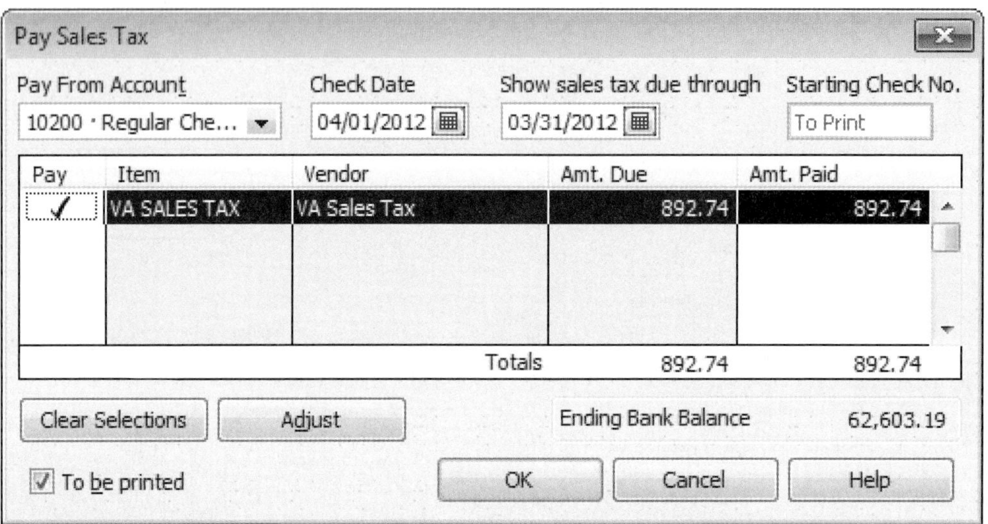

Figure 9:62

5. Click **OK** and **Close** the Pay Sales Tax window.

6. You will now print the check. Click **Print Checks** under the **Banking** section of the Home page and select the Regular Checking Account.

   Confirm that "10237" is the check number and then click **OK**. Click **Print** in the printer selection window. Click **OK** in the confirmation window.

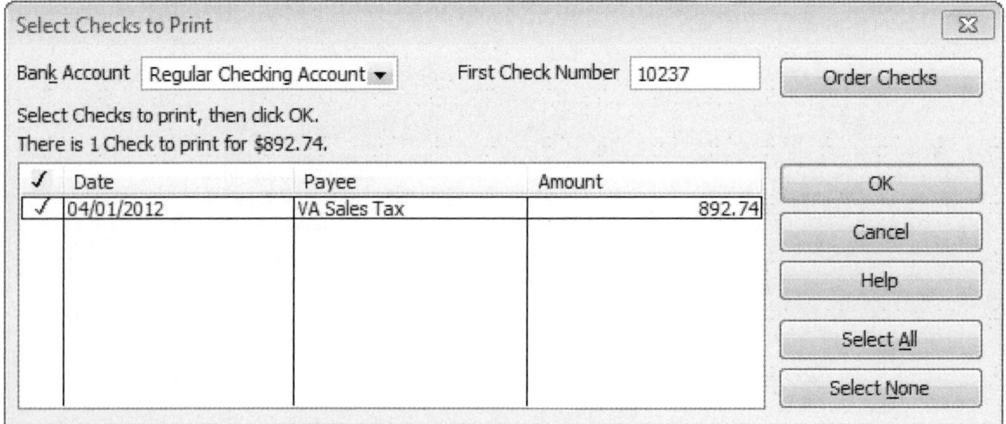

Figure 9:63

VENDOR CREDITS

Just as Baxter issues credits to customers, vendors issue credits to Baxter. Follow the next steps and record a credit for returning two BIRDBATH-2FT-WHITE items on Invoice 1042 from Cline Construction.

STEPS TO ENTER A VENDOR CREDIT MEMO

1. Click **Enter Bills** on the Home page. Select the **Credit** option and select the **Items** tab.

   Now enter the information on Figure 9:64.

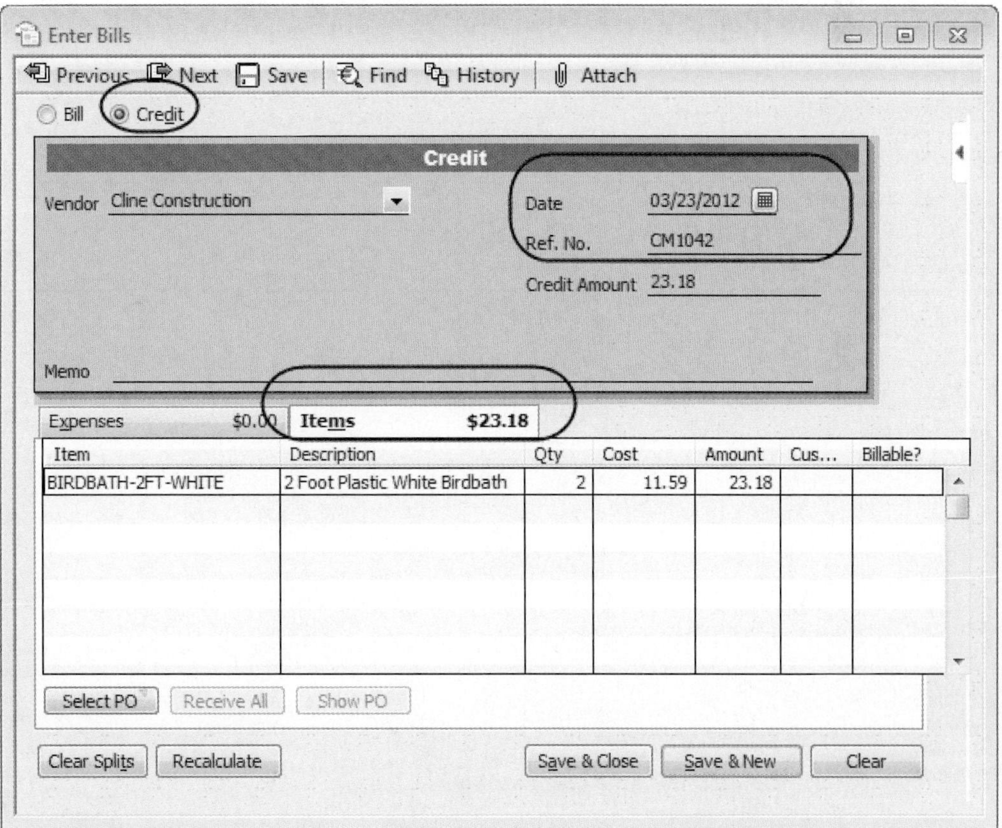

Figure 9:64

2. Click **Save & Close**.

3. Open the **Vendor Center** and view all transactions for Cline Construction's account. The credit memo is circled in Figure 9:65.

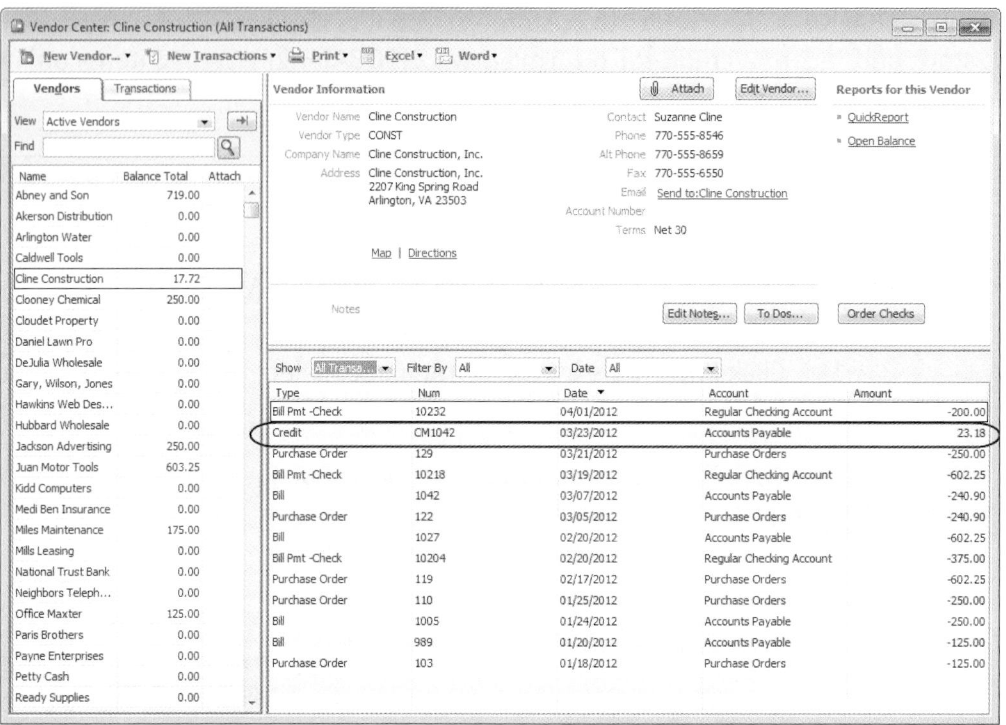

Figure 9:65

4. See what happens the next time you pay Cline Construction. Click the **New Transactions** button on the Vendor Center and select **Pay Bills**.

   Highlight the invoice from Cline Construction and the window will display the available credit of $23.18.

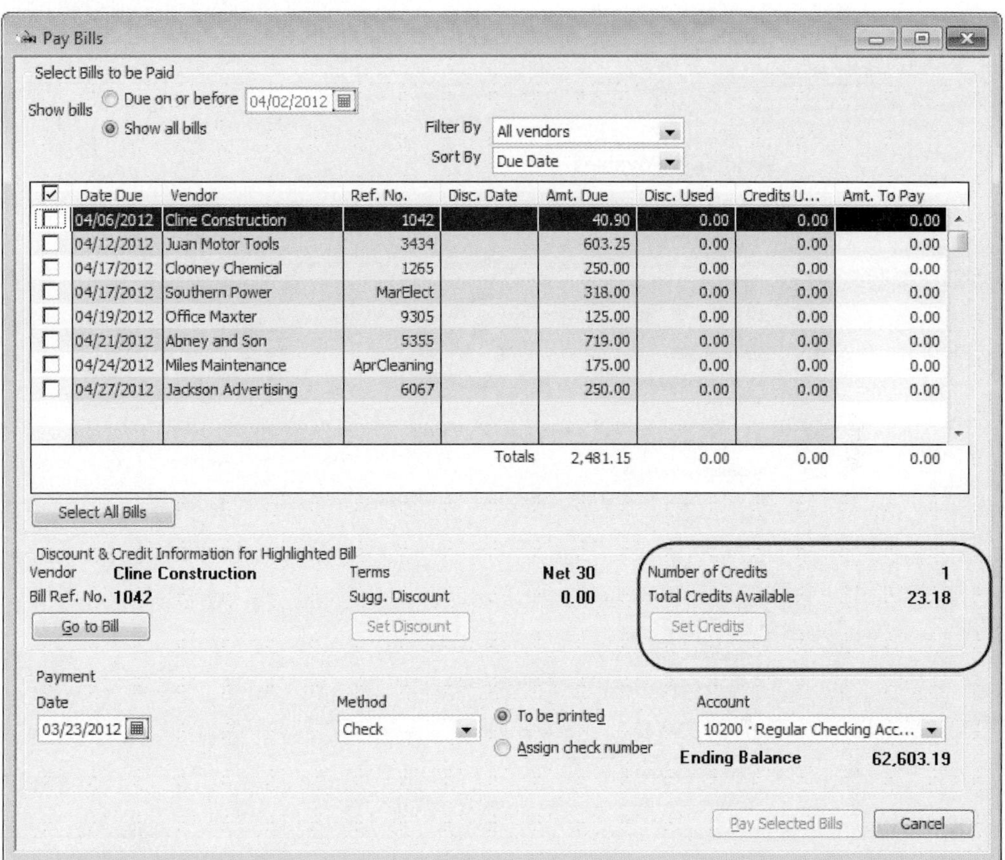

Figure 9:66

Now click to select the invoice and the credit will be applied to the bill and the amount applied appears in the **Credits Used** column. *(Note: You could apply the credit to any invoice from Cline Construction.)*

Click **Cancel** on the window above and close the Vendor Center.

Vendor Reporting and Reconciling Activities

QBP offers a variety of purchasing and vendor reports on the **Report Center**. Open the **Report Center** using the icon on the toolbar and select the **Vendors & Payables** category. You have already opened many of these reports using the Reports menu.

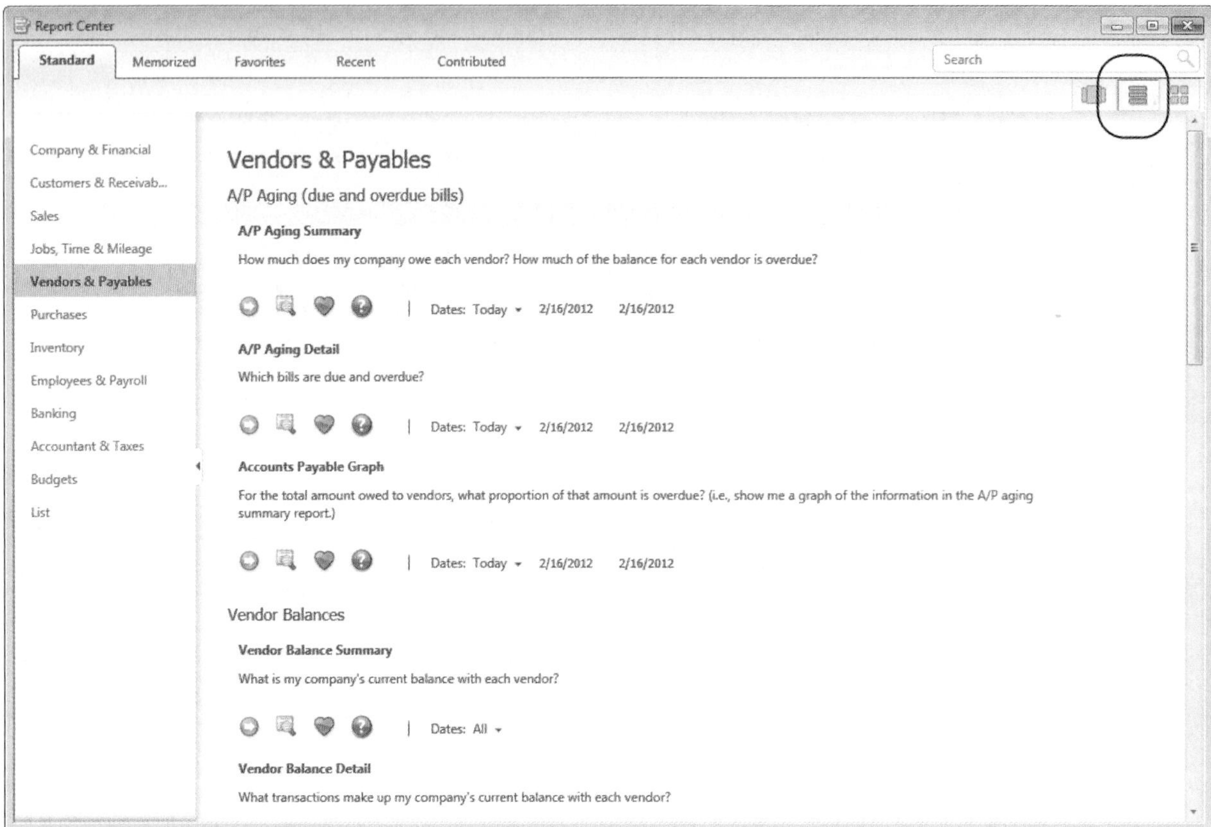

Figure 9:67

We will begin with **A/P Aging** reports. Double click to open the **A/P Aging Summary** report and enter **3/31/12** as the date. The report is illustrated in Figure 9:68.

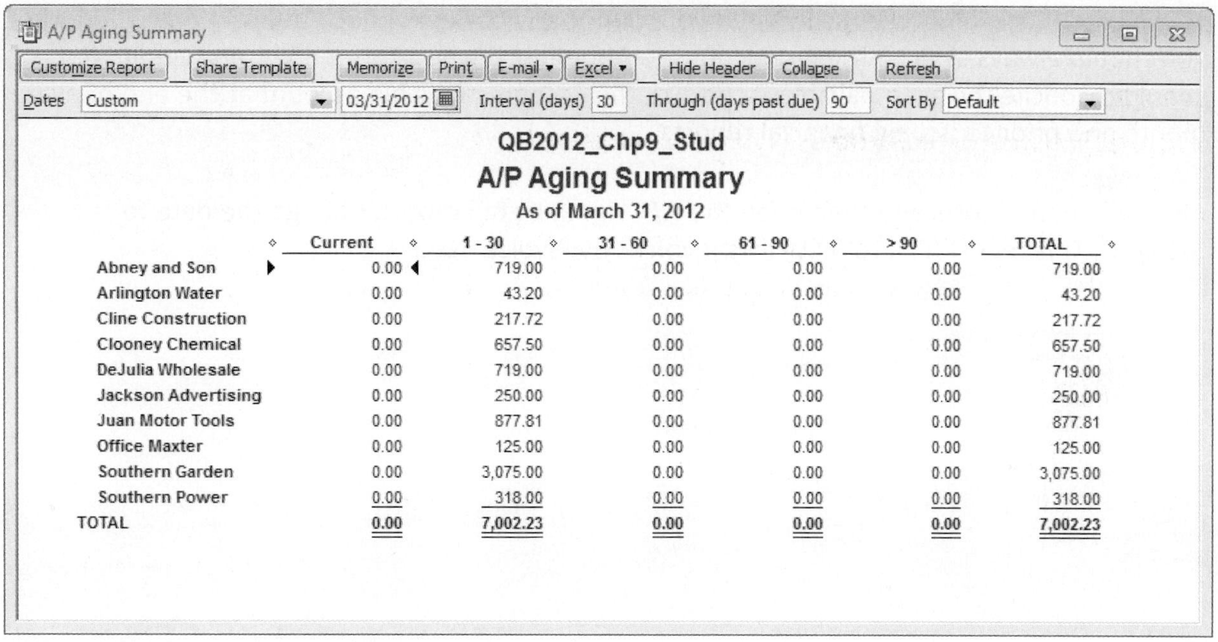

A/P Aging Summary

Customize Report | Share Template | Memorize | Print | E-mail ▾ | Excel ▾ | Hide Header | Collapse | Refresh

Dates Custom | 03/31/2012 | Interval (days) 30 | Through (days past due) 90 | Sort By Default

QB2012_Chp9_Stud
A/P Aging Summary
As of March 31, 2012

	Current	1 - 30	31 - 60	61 - 90	> 90	TOTAL
Abney and Son	0.00	719.00	0.00	0.00	0.00	719.00
Arlington Water	0.00	43.20	0.00	0.00	0.00	43.20
Cline Construction	0.00	217.72	0.00	0.00	0.00	217.72
Clooney Chemical	0.00	657.50	0.00	0.00	0.00	657.50
DeJulia Wholesale	0.00	719.00	0.00	0.00	0.00	719.00
Jackson Advertising	0.00	250.00	0.00	0.00	0.00	250.00
Juan Motor Tools	0.00	877.81	0.00	0.00	0.00	877.81
Office Maxter	0.00	125.00	0.00	0.00	0.00	125.00
Southern Garden	0.00	3,075.00	0.00	0.00	0.00	3,075.00
Southern Power	0.00	318.00	0.00	0.00	0.00	318.00
TOTAL	0.00	7,002.23	0.00	0.00	0.00	7,002.23

Figure 9:68

This report lists outstanding vendor balances by age of the balance. *(Note: Your balances will differ from those illustrated if you have not completed all chapter exercises.)* The report serves two important purposes.

First, Baxter uses it to monitor vendor payments and to manage company cash flow. Second, the report is used to reconcile vendor balances with the accounts payable control account. This task is performed by comparing the aging report total with the March ending balance in general ledger account 20000 Accounts Payable.

Now view the balance in accounts payable. Select ***Reports>>Accountant & Taxes>>Trial Balance*** on the main menu and filter the report for **3/31/12.** Scroll down and locate the balance in 20000 Accounts Payable. The total on the A/P Aging report and the balance in Accounts Payable must agree to ensure proper recording of vendor activities.

These amounts will not reconcile when you improperly correct vendor transactions. Therefore, you should always refer to the instructions in Appendix B when correcting transactions. You should reconcile the aged payables report to the accounts payable account at the end of every month and prior to issuing financial reports.

Close all open reports and then open the **A/P Aging Detail** report. Change the date to **3/31/12.** This report (Figure 9:69) lists invoices by invoice age.

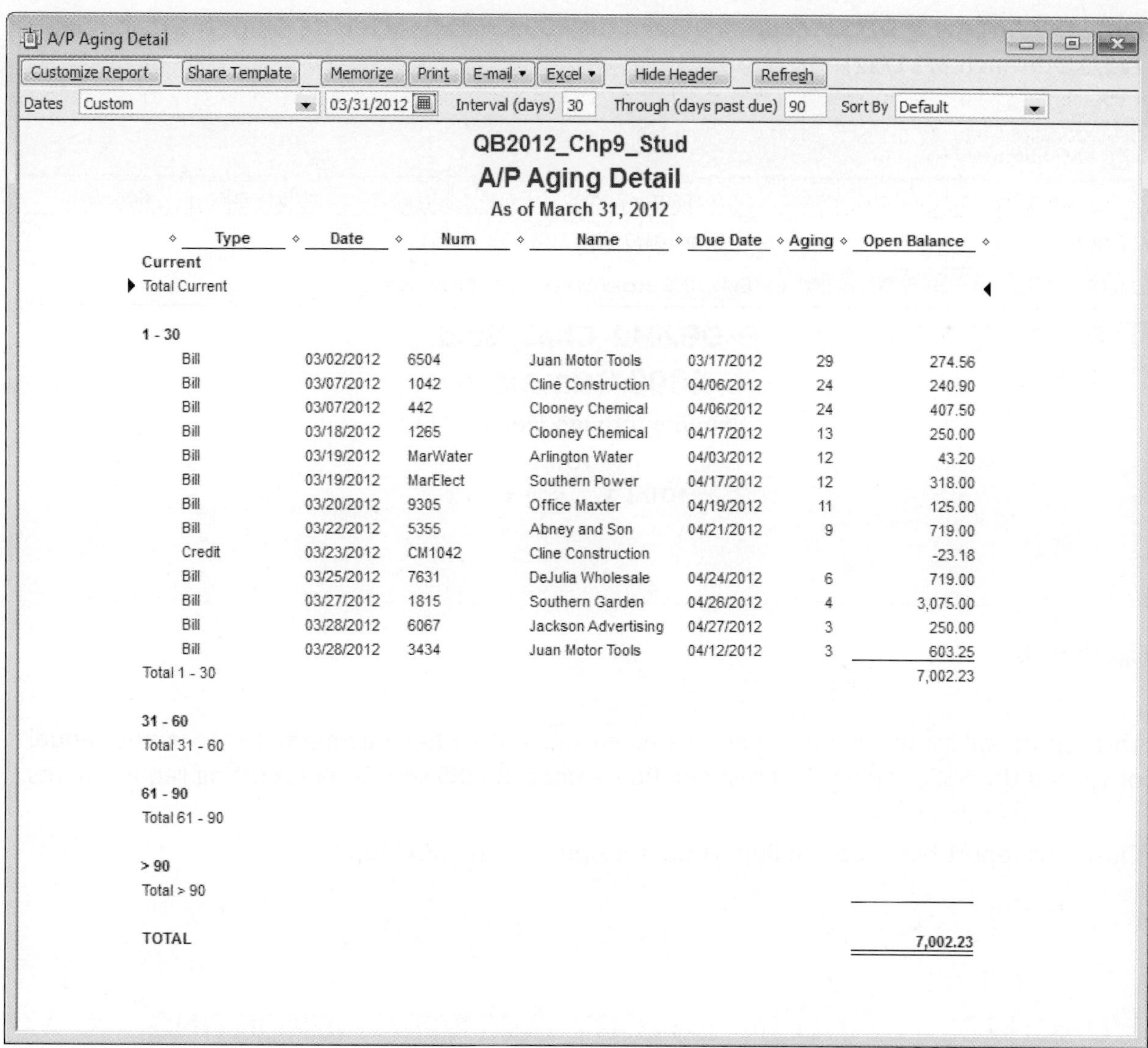

A/P Aging Detail

Customize Report | Share Template | Memorize | Print | E-mail | Excel | Hide Header | Refresh

Dates Custom 03/31/2012 Interval (days) 30 Through (days past due) 90 Sort By Default

QB2012_Chp9_Stud

A/P Aging Detail

As of March 31, 2012

Type	Date	Num	Name	Due Date	Aging	Open Balance
Current						
Total Current						
1 - 30						
Bill	03/02/2012	6504	Juan Motor Tools	03/17/2012	29	274.56
Bill	03/07/2012	1042	Cline Construction	04/06/2012	24	240.90
Bill	03/07/2012	442	Clooney Chemical	04/06/2012	24	407.50
Bill	03/18/2012	1265	Clooney Chemical	04/17/2012	13	250.00
Bill	03/19/2012	MarWater	Arlington Water	04/03/2012	12	43.20
Bill	03/19/2012	MarElect	Southern Power	04/17/2012	12	318.00
Bill	03/20/2012	9305	Office Maxter	04/19/2012	11	125.00
Bill	03/22/2012	5355	Abney and Son	04/21/2012	9	719.00
Credit	03/23/2012	CM1042	Cline Construction			-23.18
Bill	03/25/2012	7631	DeJulia Wholesale	04/24/2012	6	719.00
Bill	03/27/2012	1815	Southern Garden	04/26/2012	4	3,075.00
Bill	03/28/2012	6067	Jackson Advertising	04/27/2012	3	250.00
Bill	03/28/2012	3434	Juan Motor Tools	04/12/2012	3	603.25
Total 1 - 30						7,002.23
31 - 60						
Total 31 - 60						
61 - 90						
Total 61 - 90						
> 90						
Total > 90						
TOTAL						7,002.23

Figure 9:69

Close the **A/P Aging Detail** report and open the **1099 Summary** report. Enter the date range of **1/1/12** through **3/31/12.**

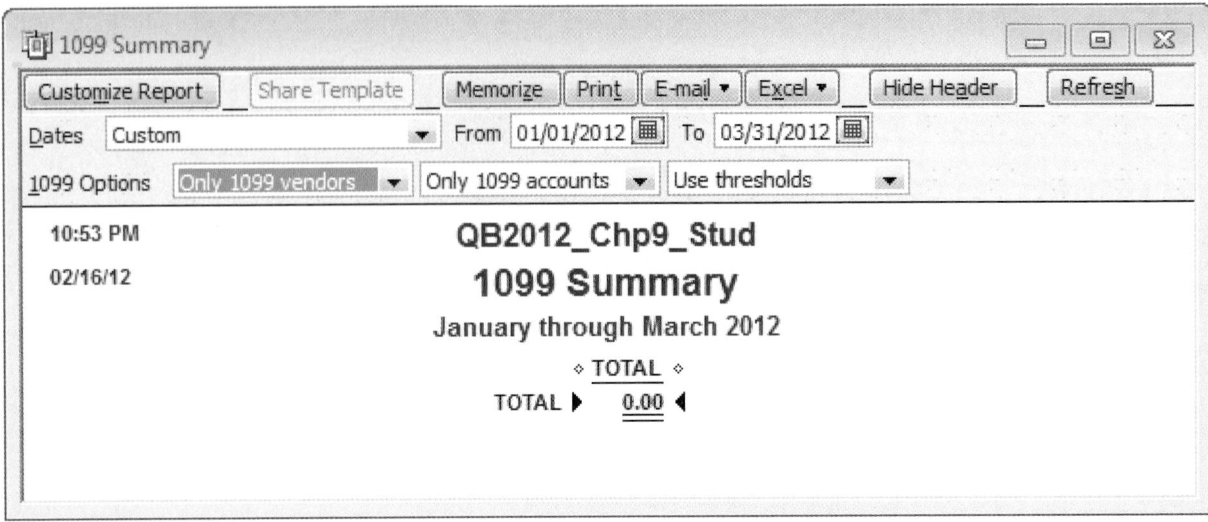

Figure 9:70

This report will list payments to vendors receiving 1099s when payments to the vendor equal or exceed the $600 reporting threshold. Remember the IRS sets 1099 reporting requirements.

Close this report but keep the Report Center open for the next topic.

Purchasing And Inventory Activity Reporting

Select the **Purchases area** of the **Report Center**. These reports let you analyze vendor purchases and monitor open purchase orders.

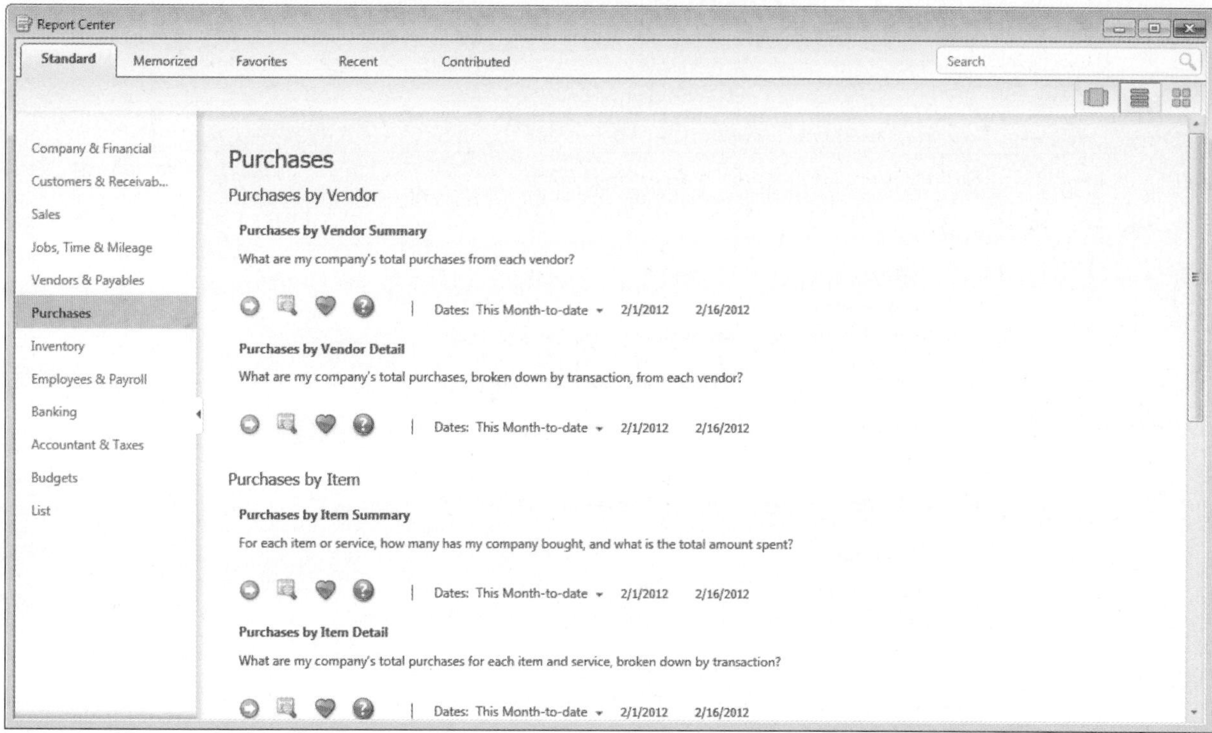

Figure 9:71

Double click to open the **Open Purchase Orders** report to locate the outstanding PO illustrated in Figure 9:72. Companies monitor this report to make sure that inventory is delivered in a timely manner.

QB2012_Chp9_Stud

Open Purchase Orders

All Transactions

	Type	Date	Name	Num	Deliv Date	Amount	Open Balance
	Purchase Order	03/20/2012	DeJulia Wholesale	127	03/20/2012	918.50	918.50
	Purchase Order	03/21/2012	Southern Garden	128	03/21/2012	2,818.65	2,818.65
	Purchase Order	03/21/2012	Cline Construction	129	03/21/2012	250.00	250.00
	Purchase Order	03/21/2012	Abney and Son	133	03/21/2012	978.75	259.75
Total						4,965.90	4,246.90

Figure 9:72

Purchases by Vendor reports can help analyze the volume of items purchased from vendors. Upon finding large volumes of purchases with specific vendors, you could possibly negotiate more favorable discount terms or preferred pricing discounts. Close the report.

Now select the **Inventory** category.

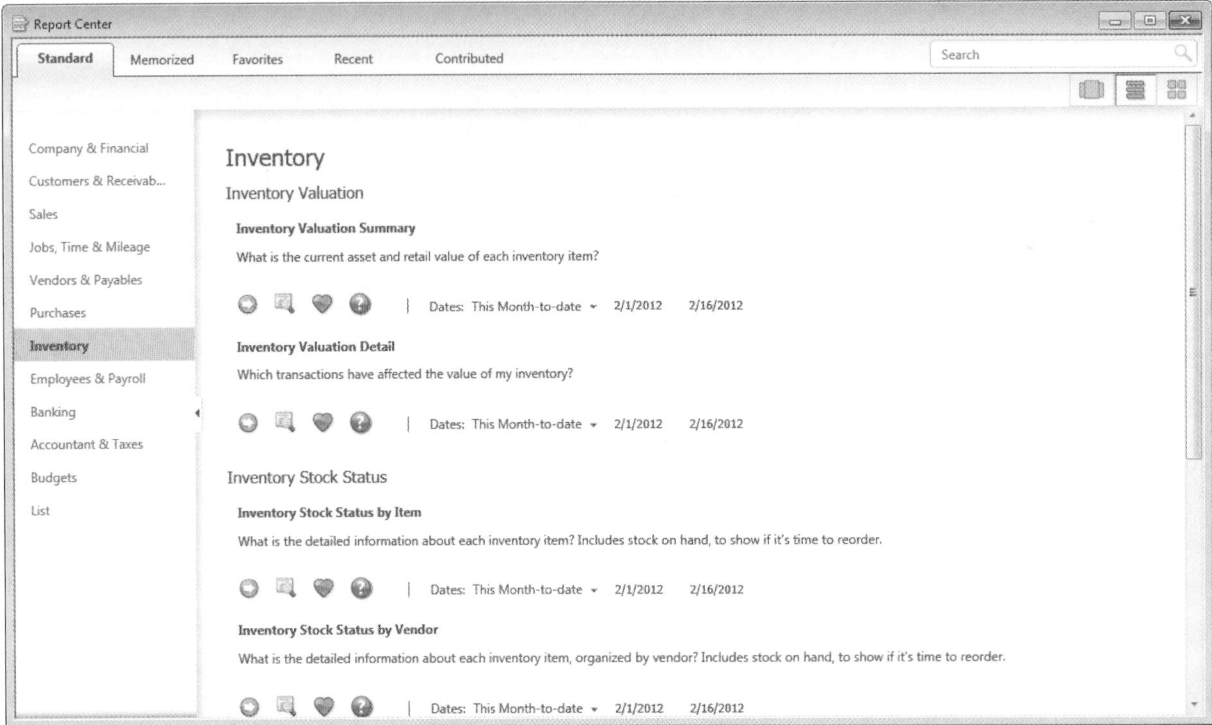

Figure 9:73

Inventory reports let you analyze inventory turnover and stock status and reconcile inventory transactions to the general ledger inventory control account. In Chapter 8, you practiced inventory reconciliation procedures.

Open the **Inventory Stock Status by Item** report and enter the date range of **3/1/12** to **3/31/12.** (See Figure 9:74.)

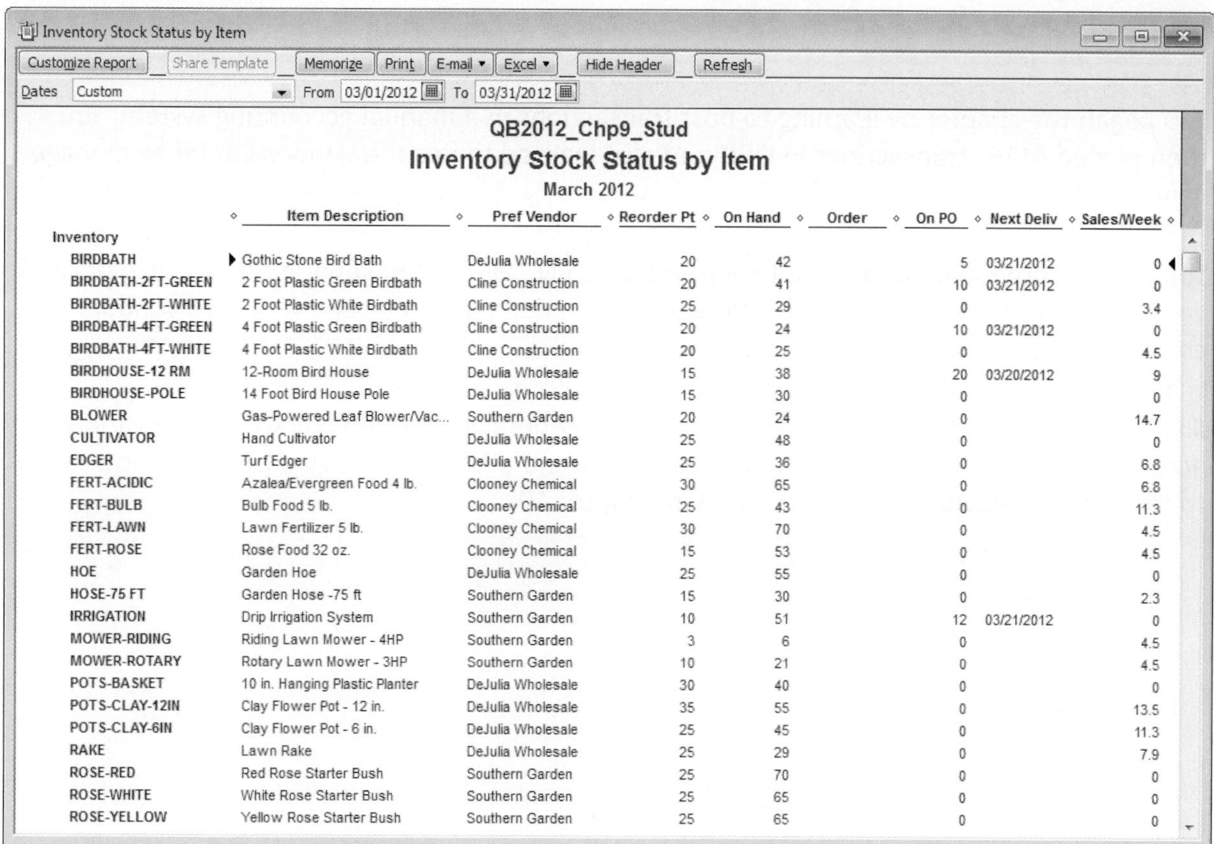

Inventory Stock Status by Item

Customize Report | Share Template | Memorize | Print | E-mail | Excel | Hide Header | Refresh

Dates Custom From 03/01/2012 To 03/31/2012

QB2012_Chp9_Stud

Inventory Stock Status by Item

March 2012

	Item Description	Pref Vendor	Reorder Pt	On Hand	Order	On PO	Next Deliv	Sales/Week
Inventory								
BIRDBATH	Gothic Stone Bird Bath	DeJulia Wholesale	20	42		5	03/21/2012	0
BIRDBATH-2FT-GREEN	2 Foot Plastic Green Birdbath	Cline Construction	20	41		10	03/21/2012	0
BIRDBATH-2FT-WHITE	2 Foot Plastic White Birdbath	Cline Construction	25	29		0		3.4
BIRDBATH-4FT-GREEN	4 Foot Plastic Green Birdbath	Cline Construction	20	24		10	03/21/2012	0
BIRDBATH-4FT-WHITE	4 Foot Plastic White Birdbath	Cline Construction	20	25		0		4.5
BIRDHOUSE-12 RM	12-Room Bird House	DeJulia Wholesale	15	38		20	03/20/2012	9
BIRDHOUSE-POLE	14 Foot Bird House Pole	DeJulia Wholesale	15	30		0		0
BLOWER	Gas-Powered Leaf Blower/Vac...	Southern Garden	20	24		0		14.7
CULTIVATOR	Hand Cultivator	DeJulia Wholesale	25	48		0		0
EDGER	Turf Edger	DeJulia Wholesale	25	36		0		6.8
FERT-ACIDIC	Azalea/Evergreen Food 4 lb.	Clooney Chemical	30	65		0		6.8
FERT-BULB	Bulb Food 5 lb.	Clooney Chemical	25	43		0		11.3
FERT-LAWN	Lawn Fertilizer 5 lb.	Clooney Chemical	30	70		0		4.5
FERT-ROSE	Rose Food 32 oz.	Clooney Chemical	15	53		0		4.5
HOE	Garden Hoe	DeJulia Wholesale	25	55		0		0
HOSE-75 FT	Garden Hose -75 ft	Southern Garden	15	30		0		2.3
IRRIGATION	Drip Irrigation System	Southern Garden	10	51		12	03/21/2012	0
MOWER-RIDING	Riding Lawn Mower - 4HP	Southern Garden	3	6		0		4.5
MOWER-ROTARY	Rotary Lawn Mower - 3HP	Southern Garden	10	21		0		4.5
POTS-BASKET	10 in. Hanging Plastic Planter	DeJulia Wholesale	30	40		0		0
POTS-CLAY-12IN	Clay Flower Pot - 12 in.	DeJulia Wholesale	35	55		0		13.5
POTS-CLAY-6IN	Clay Flower Pot - 6 in.	DeJulia Wholesale	25	45		0		11.3
RAKE	Lawn Rake	DeJulia Wholesale	25	29		0		7.9
ROSE-RED	Red Rose Starter Bush	Southern Garden	25	70		0		0
ROSE-WHITE	White Rose Starter Bush	Southern Garden	25	65		0		0
ROSE-YELLOW	Yellow Rose Starter Bush	Southern Garden	25	65		0		0

Figure 9:74

This report shows on-hand quantities and quantities on POs. A checkmark in the **Order** column is a quick indicator that an item needs to be ordered. The checkmark appears when the **On Hand** quantity falls below the **Reorder Pt**.

The report also helps analyze sales by item. The **Sales/Week** column lists the average quantity sold in March.

Close this report and the Report Center.

Remember that inventory reports can be exported to Excel. After exporting, you can further analyze transactions such as computing inventory turnover ratios.

The key point is that reports are the basic means for analyzing company performance. Take the time to review other inventory and purchasing reports to see the wide range of information that is available.

You have now completed the chapter. ***Make a backup of the data file to a backup file named "QB2012_Chp9_Stud_Completed."***

SUMMARY

You began the chapter by learning to post transactions in a manual accounting system. You then posted *MAPS* transactions in QBP. You also learned to use the Vendor Center to manage vendor activities.

You have recorded POs and receipts of items on a PO. You posted vendor bills for receipts and vendor bills for expenses. You also paid vendors, voided payments, and recorded vendor credits.

Finally, you reconciled vendor transactions to the general ledger and worked with a variety of accounts payable, purchasing, and inventory reports that analyze activities. You are now ready to focus on the payroll activities covered in Chapter 10.

END-OF-CHAPTER QUESTIONS

TRUE/FALSE

_____ 1. You can identify open POs using a report.

_____ 2. The Enter Bills icon is used to record PO receipts.

_____ 3. QBP will let you change information on a posted vendor payment.

_____ 4. Vendor bills for expenses are entered as vendor receipts.

_____ 5. When entering a vendor bill, QBP prompts to select a PO if the vendor has an open PO.

_____ 6. After recording a vendor bill for the receipt of all items on a PO, QBP marks the PO as Received.

_____ 7. When deleting a vendor receipt, QBP will reinstate the PO so that you can receive the items again.

_____ 8. You can reopen a vendor bill using the Vendor Center.

_____ 9. The Write Checks icon will let you pay a vendor without entering a vendor bill.

_____ 10. You must delete a check issued to the wrong vendor.

_____ 11. A vendor credit memo is entered in the Enter Bills window.

_____ 12. The Vendor Balance Summary report is found under the Vendors & Payables area of the Report Center.

_____ 13. You can use the Manage Sales Tax window to view sales tax preferences.

_____ 14. You will use the Receive Inventory icon to enter a bill for a posted vendor receipt.

_____ 15. You can pay vendor receipts in the Pay Bills window.

MULTIPLE CHOICE

_____ 1. QBP will post an item receipt as a __________.

a. Debit to inventory, credit to accounts payable
b. Debit to inventory, credit to accounts payable, debit to cost of goods sold
c. Debit to inventory, credit to accounts receivable
d. None of the above

_____ 2. QBP posts entries for vendor payments as a ________.

a. Debit to inventory, credit to checking
b. Debit to checking, credit to accounts payable
c. Credit to checking, debit to accounts payable
d. Credit to checking, debit to accounts receivable

_____ 3. QBP will post a PO as a _________.
   a. Debit to inventory, credit to accounts payable
   b. Debit to inventory, credit to accounts payable, debit to cost of goods sold
   c. Debit to inventory, credit to accounts receivable
   d. None of the above

_____ 4. Which report will display items that need to be reordered?
   a. Physical Inventory Worksheet
   b. Inventory Stock Status by Vendor
   c. Inventory Stock Status by Item
   d. Both b and c

_____ 5. Payments to vendors are listed on the _________ report.
   a. Transaction List by Vendor
   b. Check Detail
   c. Vendor Balance Detail
   d. All of the above

_____ 6. Which report will age by vendor invoice?
   a. A/P Aging Summary
   b. A/P Aging Detail
   c. Vendor Balance Detail
   d. All of the above

_____ 7. In the Manage Sales Tax window, you can _________.
   a. View sales tax preferences
   b. View the Sales Tax Liability report
   c. Pay sales taxes
   d. All of the above

_____ 8. The Enter Bills window contains all the following, except _________.
   a. An Expenses tab
   b. A Discount Date
   c. A Vendor field
   d. Bill Due field

_____ 9. The Pay Bills window contains all the following, except ________.
   a. A Show all bills option
   b. A Filter By option
   c. A Payment Date field
   d. A Bill Date field

_____ 10. You can run a ________ report to view the total purchases by vendor.
   a. A/P Aging Summary
   b. A/P Aging Detail
   c. Purchases by Vendor Summary
   d. None of the above

PRACTICE SET

In this practice set, you will record vendor activities for April 2012. Keep the following in mind:

- Unless otherwise instructed, accept all defaults assigned from the vendor account.
- You will print reports in Step 2, so do not print transactions unless otherwise instructed.

Begin by:

- Opening the software.
- Opening the **QB2012_Chp8_PracSet_Stud** data file. Add your initials to the end to the Company Name by clicking ***Company>>Company Information*** on the main menu. Click **OK** to save the changes.
- **Toggling the software to the PRO EDITION** by selecting ***File>>Toggle to Another Edition*** on the main menu and choosing **QuickBooks Pro** as the edition.

1. Record the following transactions.

2012

Apr 1 Post Mills Leasing bill dated April 1 for office rent, $600.00.

Post Safe State Insurance bill dated April 1 for 6 months of vehicle insurance, $600.00. Post to prepaid expenses.

Apr 2 Create the following POs. Be sure to select the ***To be printed*** option so you can later print the documents.

PO 130 for $602.25 to Cline Construction for the following items.

Item	Qty	Unit Price
BIRDBATH-2FT-GREEN	25	$ 12.50
BIRDBATH-2FT-WHITE	25	$ 11.59

PO 131 for $1,074.75 to Abney and Son for the following items.

Item	Qty	Unit Price
SEED-BLUEGRASS	90	$ 7.95
SPREADER	15	$ 23.95

PO 132 for $557.25 to DeJulia Wholesale for the following items.

Item	Qty	Unit Price
EDGER	25	$ 7.95
SHOVEL-SCOOP	30	$ 11.95

PO 133 for $837.75 to Clooney Chemical for the following items.

Note: The price for one item has increased so enter the new price and click Yes when prompted.

Item	Qty	Unit Price	
TRIMMER	20	$ 25.00	Price increase
SPRINKLER	35	$ 9.65	

Apr 4 Post DeJulia Wholesale Invoice 590 dated April 3, $918.50, for all items on PO 127 issued March 20.

Apr 7 Post Abney and Son Invoice 871 dated April 5, $1,074.75, for all items on PO 131 issued April 2.

Post DeJulia Wholesale receipt number RCT6932 dated April 7, $557.25, for all items on PO 132 issued April 2.

Apr 8 Post DeJulia Wholesale Invoice 605 dated April 7, $557.25, for receipt number RCT6932.

Post Clooney Chemical Invoice 480 dated April 6, $712.75, for the following items received on PO 133 issued April 2.

Item	Qty	Unit Price	
TRIMMER	15	$ 25.00	Partial shipment
SPRINKLER	35	$ 9.65	

Post Cline Construction Invoice 1053 dated April 7, $250.00, for all items on PO 129 issued March 21.

Apr 12 Post Cline Construction Invoice 1055 dated April 9, $602.25, for all items on PO 130 issued April 2.

Apr 13 Post Clooney Chemical Invoice 495 dated April 12, $125.00, for the remaining 5 items of TRIMMER on PO 133 issued April 2.

Apr 14 Pay vendors for bills with a due date before April 28 and a discount date expiring before April 28. Total bills selected, $9,113.70. First check number is 10223. Verify that the ***To be printed*** option is selected.

Apr 17 Enter bills dated April 16 for the following expenses dated.

Southern Power	April electric	$153.00
Neighbors Telephone	April telephone	$205.00
Arlington Water	April water	$125.00

Post Cline Construction credit memo CM1053 dated April 12, $62.50, for returning 5 items of BIRDBATH-2FT-GREEN on Invoice 1053.

Apr 19 Write check number 10235 to Postmaster for postage expense, $250.00. Add this account “on the fly” using the following information. Verify that the check is written on Bank Account 10200 Regular Checking Account.

Company Name:	Postmaster
Address:	317 W. Main St., Arlington, VA 23135
Type:	OFFICE
Prefill Account:	63100 Postage Expense

Apr 20 Create the following POs.

PO 134 for $585.25 to Southern Garden for the following items.

Item	Qty	Unit Price
HOSE-75 FT	20	$15.95
ROSE-WHITE	15	$ 5.25
SOIL-STRAW	50	$ 3.75

PO 135 for $416.25 to Clooney Chemical for the following items.

Item	Qty	Unit Price
SPRAYER-HOSE	40	$ 5.20
SPRAYER-HAND	25	$ 3.95
FERT-BULB	30	$ 3.65

PO 136 for $101.25 to DeJulia Wholesale for the following items.

Item	Qty	Unit Price
HOE	15	$ 6.75

Apr 21 Create the following new vendor.

Wilmort Hotel
173 E. Rutherford St.
Newport, RI 32653

Type:	OFFICE
Payment terms:	Net 5
Prefill Account:	76000 Travel Expense

Enter the following bills dated April 20.

Wilmort Hotel, Invoice 713	April travel expense	$ 225.00
Office Maxter, Invoice 3131	Office supply expense	$ 108.00
Juan Motor Tools, Invoice 137	Repairs auto expenses	$ 325.00
Kidd Computers, Invoice 431	Repairs equipment expense	$ 178.25

Post Southern Garden Invoice 1899 dated April 20, $2,818.65, for all items on PO 128 issued March 21.

Apr 24 Post DeJulia Wholesale receipt number RCT8032 dated April 23, $101.25, for all items on PO 136 issued April 20.

Apr 25 Post Clooney Chemical Invoice 650 dated April 23, $416.25, for all items on PO 135 issued April 20.

Apr 26 Post Southern Garden Invoice 1903 dated April 23, for $510.25 for the following items on PO 134 issued April 20.

Item	Qty	Unit Price	
HOSE-75 FT	20	$ 15.95	
ROSE-WHITE	15	$ 5.25	
SOIL-STRAW	30	$ 3.75	Partial shipment

Apr 27 Pay vendors for bills with a due date before May 10 or a discount date expiring before May 10. Total bills selected, $7,791.07. First check number is 10246.

Apr 30 Write check number 10246 for $892.74 for sales tax due through April.

2. Print the following reports.

   a. Print POs 130 to 136.

   b. Purchases Journal for April transactions.

   c. Cash Disbursements Journal for April transactions. Customize the report and, on the Filters tab, change the Transaction Type filter to include Check, Bill Payment, and Sales Tax Payment.

   d. Open Purchase Orders report for All dates.

   e. Detailed A/P Aging Detail report for April 30.

3. ***Back up the data file to a backup file named "QB2012_Chp9_PracSet_Stud_Completed."***

INTERNET MINI-PROJECT

To complete this mini-project, go to the Website at ***www.pearsonhighered.com/brunsdon/*** and download the instruction file named **Every Gadget.pdf** and the data file named **Every Gadget.QBW.**

CHAPTER 10 PAYROLL ACTIVITIES FOR A MERCHANDISING BUSINESS

LEARNING OBJECTIVES

In this chapter, you will process payroll by:

1. Learning the *MAPS* for processing employee paychecks before processing paychecks in QBP
2. Reviewing the set up of payroll in the software to understand its impact on processing payroll transactions
3. Learning to use the Employee Center to manage employees and paycheck transactions
4. Paying employees
5. Going *Behind the Keys* of posted paychecks to trace the entries
6. Learning to correct paychecks
7. Remitting payroll tax liabilities to government taxing agencies
8. Creating and interpreting payroll reports, including Form 941 and Form W-2 and W-3

Begin by:

- Opening the software.
- Opening the **QB2012_Chp10_Stud** data file. Add your initials to the end to the Company Name by clicking ***Company>>Company Information*** on the main menu. Click **OK** to save the changes.
- **Toggling the software to the PRO EDITION** by selecting ***File>>Toggle to Another Edition*** on the main menu and choosing **QuickBooks Pro** as the edition.

MANUAL ACCOUNTING PROCEDURES

Baxter pays employees biweekly (every two weeks) so the number of pay periods for the year is 26 (i.e., 52 weeks divided by 2). Employees are paid either an annual salary or an hourly wage. Salaried employees are paid the same gross pay amount each pay period, which is calculated by dividing the annual salary by the number of pay periods in the year. Hourly employees are paid for the hours worked during the pay period.

You will soon learn that processing payroll in a manual accounting system is tedious and time consuming. You first calculate gross wages for hourly employees by multiplying the total hours worked times the hourly pay rate. As explained above, the gross pay for salaried employees is the same each pay period. You next calculate net pay for each employee. Net pay is gross pay minus payroll tax withholdings and voluntary deductions.

The following tables explain payroll tax withholdings and voluntary deductions.

Employee Tax Withholdings	**Description**
Federal Income Tax	Employee federal income taxes withheld on taxable wages. Taxable wages exclude employee contributions to a 401K or IRA retirement plan. IRS Circular E sets the guidelines for withholding federal income taxes and using this table is explained later.
Social Security (FICA)	Employee taxes withheld on gross wages and paid to the federal government to fund Social Security retirement. Gross wages include employee contributions to a 401K or IRA retirement plan. The IRS has historically taxed gross wages, below the annual cap, at 6.2 percent (0.062). This cap is changed each year. For 2012, the cap is $110,100. *(Note: In 2011 and 2012, a 2 percent reduction is in effect, making the percentage 4.2 percent (.042). The text will continue to use the 6.2 percent rate.)*
Medicare (FICA)	Employee taxes withheld on gross wages and paid to the federal government to fund Medicare health insurance. Gross wages include employee contributions to a 401K or IRA retirement plan. The IRS taxes gross wages at 1.45 percent (0.0145) with no annual wage cap.
State Income Tax	Employee state income taxes withheld on taxable wages (i.e., gross wages minus contributions to a 401K or IRA retirement plan). Each state publishes guidelines for withholding state income taxes. ***Baxter withholds 3 percent (0.03) of gross wages.***

Employee Voluntary Deductions	**Description**
Retirement Plans	Employee voluntary contributions to an employer-sponsored retirement plan. Retirement plans include 401K and IRA plans. These contributions are deducted from gross wages to determine federal and state taxable wages. ***Baxter sponsors a 401K retirement plan and employees may elect to participate.***
Health Insurance	Health insurance premiums deducted from pay when the employer requires its employees to pay for a portion of health insurance costs. ***Baxter does not require employees to share this cost.***
Contributions	Deductions from net pay for charitable contributions made by the employee.

Baxter also pays taxes on employee compensation and provides additional compensation by paying the full cost of health insurance and matching employee contributions to a company sponsored 401K plan. The next tables explain typical employer tax liabilities and other forms of employee compensation.

Employer Payroll Taxes	Description
Social Security (FICA) and Medicare (FICA)	Employer portion of Social Security and Medicare taxes paid on gross wages. The employer tax equals the tax paid by employees. *(Exception: In 2011 and 2012, the employer does not receive the 2% reduction given to employees.)*
Federal Unemployment (FUTA)	Employer tax on gross wages paid to the federal government for subsidizing state unemployment compensation funds. Historically, employers have paid 0.8 percent (0.008) on the first $7,000 of annual gross wages paid to each employee. In July 2011, the rate was reduced to 0.6 percent (0.006); however, employers in states with higher than normal unemployment pay an adjusted rate that is higher. For simplicity, the text will continue to illustrate the historical rate.
State Unemployment (SUTA)	Employer tax on gross wages paid to the state for funding compensation for unemployed workers. Typically the tax rate is based on an employer's unemployment history and/or business type and will be capped after reaching an annual limit on gross wages. ***For Baxter, the rate is 1.5 percent (0.015) of the first $8,000 of annual wages paid to each employee.***
Worker's Compensation	Employer tax paid to the state to fund compensating injured workers. Typically, states set the tax rates based on risk factors in an employee's job. ***The text does not illustrate worker's compensation tax.***

Additional Compensation	Description
Retirement Plans	Employer contributions to a company-sponsored 401K or IRA retirement plan. Typically, companies match contributions based on employee participation in the plan. ***Baxter matches employee 401K contributions $.50 for every dollar contributed by the employee, up to a maximum of 5 percent (0.05) of the employee's annual pay.***
Health Insurance	Employer premiums for health insurance. Employers may pay all premiums or require employees to share in this cost. ***Baxter pays all health insurance premiums for employees eligible to participate in the plan.***

Each pay period the accountant prepares the following Excel spreadsheet, called the **Payroll Register,** to calculate employee net pay. The register illustrated in Figure 10:1 covers the two-week pay period of February 20 to March 4, 2012.

Baxter Garden Supply
Paychecks for Pay Period 2/20/2012 thru 3/04/2012

Check No.	Employee	Filing Status	Allow	Pay Type	Pay Rate	Regular Hrs	OT Hrs	Gross Pay	Taxable Pay	Federal Income Tax	Soc. Sec. (FICA) Tax	Medicare Tax	VA State Tax	401K Deduc.	Net Pay
1180	Beck, Dorothy L.	Married	2	Hourly wage	9.00	80.00		720.00	720.00	15.00	44.64	10.44	21.60	0.00	628.32
1181	Chester, Amanda W.	Single	1	Hourly wage	14.00	80.00		1,120.00	1,075.20	110.00	69.44	16.24	32.26	44.80	847.26
1182	Frost, Melvin H.	Single	1	Salary	1,461.54			1,461.54	1,373.85	155.00	90.62	21.19	41.22	87.69	1,065.82
1183	Hecter, Anthony H.	Single	1	Hourly wage	13.00	80.00		1,040.00	1,040.00	107.00	64.48	15.08	31.20	0.00	822.24
1184	Nunnley, Brandee M.	Married	1	Salary	1,211.54			1,211.54	1,211.54	85.00	75.12	17.57	36.35	0.00	997.50
1185	Prather, Samuel R.	Married	1	Salary	1,584.62			1,584.62	1,489.54	127.00	98.25	22.98	44.69	95.08	1,196.62
	Totals					240.00	0.00	7,137.70		599.00	442.55	103.50	207.32	227.57	5,557.76
	Tax Basis									Circular E	6.20%	1.45%	3.00%		
	G/L Accounts							60000		23400	23400	23400	23600	23300	10300

Figure 10:1

The Payroll Register shows that Amanda Chester claims the federal filing status of Single (S) with one withholding allowance. Amanda's federal income tax withholding for this pay period is calculated by referring to the payroll tax withholding table illustrated in Figure 10:2.

(Note: These tables are for instructional purposes only and are excerpted from the Internal Revenue Service's Circular E publication, which is updated annually. To obtain a current edition of this publication, visit www.irs.gov.)

SINGLE Persons—**BIWEEKLY** Payroll Period

(For Wages Paid in)

If the wages are–		And the number of withholding allowances claimed is—										
At least	But less than	0	1	2	3	4	5	6	7	8	9	10
		The amount of income tax to be withheld is—										
$800	$820	$92	$71	$51	$31	$17	$4	$0	$0	$0	$0	$0
820	840	95	74	54	34	19	6	0	0	0	0	0
840	860	98	77	57	37	21	8	0	0	0	0	0
860	880	101	80	60	40	23	10	0	0	0	0	0
880	900	104	83	63	43	25	12	0	0	0	0	0
900	920	107	86	66	46	27	14	0	0	0	0	0
920	940	110	89	69	49	29	16	2	0	0	0	0
940	960	113	92	72	52	32	18	4	0	0	0	0
960	980	116	95	75	55	35	20	6	0	0	0	0
980	1,000	119	98	78	58	38	22	8	0	0	0	0
1,000	1,020	122	101	81	61	41	24	10	0	0	0	0
1,020	1,040	125	104	84	64	44	26	12	0	0	0	0
1,040	1,060	128	107	87	67	47	28	14	1	0	0	0
1,060	1,080	131	110	90	70	50	30	16	3	0	0	0
1,080	1,100	134	113	93	73	53	33	18	5	0	0	0
1,100	1,120	137	116	96	76	56	36	20	7	0	0	0
1,120	1,140	140	119	99	79	59	39	22	9	0	0	0
1,140	1,160	143	122	102	82	62	42	24	11	0	0	0
1,160	1,180	146	125	105	85	65	45	26	13	0	0	0
1,180	1,200	149	128	108	88	68	48	28	15	1	0	0
1,200	1,220	152	131	111	91	71	51	30	17	3	0	0
1,220	1,240	155	134	114	94	74	54	33	19	5	0	0
1,240	1,260	158	137	117	97	77	57	36	21	7	0	0
1,260	1,280	161	140	120	100	80	60	39	23	9	0	0
1,280	1,300	164	143	123	103	83	63	42	25	11	0	0
1,300	1,320	167	146	126	106	86	66	45	27	13	0	0

Figure 10:2

Figure 10:2 is the IRS table for employees paid biweekly and claiming the Single (S) filing status. There are separate IRS tables for employees claiming the Married (M) filing status and separate tables for married and single employees paid on a weekly or monthly basis.

Amanda's $110.00 federal income tax withholding amount is found at the point where her taxable pay of $1,075.20 intersects with her one claimed withholding allowance. Federal income taxes are calculated on taxable pay, which is equal to gross pay minus 401K deductions.

Amanda's Social Security tax withholding of $69.44 equals her gross pay times 6.2 percent (.062). Her Medicare tax withholding of $16.24 equals gross pay times 1.45 percent (.0145). *(Note: 401K contributions are not deducted from FICA and Medicare tax calculations*.)

The state tax withholding amount of $32.26 is based on a state tax rate of 3 percent (.03) of taxable pay. 401K contributions are deducted from gross pay to determine taxable pay for state purposes.

Baxter sponsors a 401K retirement plan that allows employees to elect participation by contributing a percentage of gross pay. Employees can choose to contribute any percentage up to 11 percent of gross pay and Baxter will match contributions by the same percentage up to 5 percent of gross pay. Amanda has chosen to contribute 4 percent (.04) of gross pay each pay period.

Amanda has no deductions for health insurance premiums or charitable contributions. In fact, premiums are not deducted from any employee's paycheck because Baxter pays the full cost of health insurance. Finally, there are no employees making charitable contributions through payroll.

Accordingly, Amanda's net pay of $847.26 equals her gross pay of $1,120.00 minus the sum of her tax withholdings and voluntary deductions.

In addition to preparing the payroll register, the accountant computes the following employer payroll tax liabilities for the pay period.

Baxter Garden Supply
Employer Costs for Pay Period 2/20/2012 thru 3/04/2012

Employee	401K Match	ER Soc. Sec. (FICA)	ER Medicare	ER FUTA	ER SUTA	Health Insurance
Beck, Dorothy L.	0.00	44.64	10.44	5.76	10.80	0.00
Chester, Amanda W.	22.40	69.44	16.24	8.96	16.80	90.00
Frost, Melvin H.	43.85	90.62	21.19	4.58	21.92	125.00
Hecter, Anthony H.	0.00	64.48	15.08	8.32	15.60	90.00
Nunnley, Brandee M.	0.00	75.12	17.57	9.69	18.17	125.00
Prather, Samuel R.	47.54	98.25	22.98	5.28	23.77	125.00
Totals	**113.79**	**442.55**	**103.50**	**42.59**	**107.06**	**555.00**
Tax Basis	**50% Match**	**6.20%**	**1.45%**	**0.8%**	**1.5%**	
G/L Accounts	**23300 / 60500**	**23400 / 61000**	**23400 / 61000**	**23500 / 61000**	**23700 / 61000**	**23750 / 60300**

Figure 10:3

After computing employee pay and employer payroll tax expenses, the accountant creates paychecks and records the general journal entries illustrated in Figure 10:4.

Audit Trail

Baxter Garden Supply
General Journal **Page 7**

Date	Account Post Ref	Description	Debit	Credit
3/5/2012	60000	Salaries and Wages Expense	7,137.70	
	23400	Federal Payroll Taxes Payable		1,145.05
	23600	State Payroll Taxes Payable		207.32
	23300	401K Deductions Payable		227.57
	10300	Payroll Checking Account		5,557.76
To record employee paychecks				
3/5/2012	61000	Payroll Tax Expense	695.70	
	60500	Pension/Profit-Sharing Expense	113.79	
	60600	Employee Benefit Expense	555.00	
	23400	Federal Payroll Taxes Payable		546.05
	23500	FUTA Tax Payable		42.59
	23700	SUTA Tax Payable		107.06
	23300	401K Deductions Payable		113.79
	23750	Health Insurance Payable		555.00
To record employer payroll tax expense				

Figure 10:4

These journal entries are then posted to the general ledger accounts illustrated next. *(Note: Only two general ledger accounts are illustrated.)* As explained in previous chapters, the audit trail is recorded while posting to general ledger accounts.

General Ledger					
Payroll Checking Account					**Account No. 10300**
Date	**Description**	**Post Ref**	**Debit**	**Credit**	**Balance**
3/4/2012	Balance Forward				6,325.00
3/5/2012		GJ 7		5,557.76	767.24

Audit Trail

General Ledger					
Federal Payroll Taxes Payable					**Account No. 23400**
Date	**Description**	**Post Ref**	**Debit**	**Credit**	**Balance**
3/4/2012	Balance Forward				-
3/5/2012		GJ 7		1,145.05	1,145.05
3/5/2012		GJ 7		546.05	1,691.10

Figure 10:5

With an understanding of *MAPS* for paycheck activities, you are now ready to perform these activities in QBP.

UNDERSTANDING PAYROLL ITEMS

A series of setup steps is performed before a company can use QBP to process payroll. The accountant has already completed these steps; however, it will help you to understand the process.

Begin by opening the Payroll Item List. Select ***Lists>>Payroll Item List*** on the main menu to open the window illustrated next.

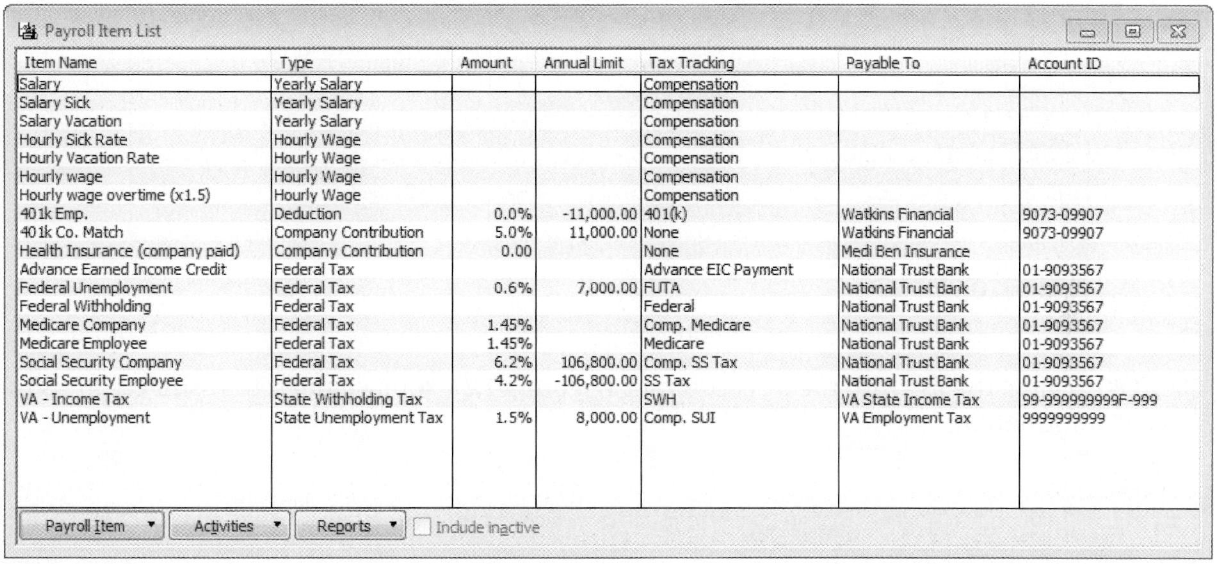

Payroll Item List

Item Name	Type	Amount	Annual Limit	Tax Tracking	Payable To	Account ID
Salary	Yearly Salary			Compensation		
Salary Sick	Yearly Salary			Compensation		
Salary Vacation	Yearly Salary			Compensation		
Hourly Sick Rate	Hourly Wage			Compensation		
Hourly Vacation Rate	Hourly Wage			Compensation		
Hourly wage	Hourly Wage			Compensation		
Hourly wage overtime (x1.5)	Hourly Wage			Compensation		
401k Emp.	Deduction	0.0%	-11,000.00	401(k)	Watkins Financial	9073-09907
401k Co. Match	Company Contribution	5.0%	11,000.00	None	Watkins Financial	9073-09907
Health Insurance (company paid)	Company Contribution	0.00		None	Medi Ben Insurance	
Advance Earned Income Credit	Federal Tax			Advance EIC Payment	National Trust Bank	01-9093567
Federal Unemployment	Federal Tax	0.6%	7,000.00	FUTA	National Trust Bank	01-9093567
Federal Withholding	Federal Tax			Federal	National Trust Bank	01-9093567
Medicare Company	Federal Tax	1.45%		Comp. Medicare	National Trust Bank	01-9093567
Medicare Employee	Federal Tax	1.45%		Medicare	National Trust Bank	01-9093567
Social Security Company	Federal Tax	6.2%	106,800.00	Comp. SS Tax	National Trust Bank	01-9093567
Social Security Employee	Federal Tax	4.2%	-106,800.00	SS Tax	National Trust Bank	01-9093567
VA - Income Tax	State Withholding Tax			SWH	VA State Income Tax	99-999999999F-999
VA - Unemployment	State Unemployment Tax	1.5%	8,000.00	Comp. SUI	VA Employment Tax	9999999999

Payroll Item ▼ | Activities ▼ | Reports ▼ | Include inactive

Figure 10:6

This list shows payroll items for posting compensation, payroll tax withholdings, and payroll tax liabilities. Salary and wage types post employee compensation whereas federal and state types post employee tax withholdings and employer tax liabilities.

You will now add columns to the list so that general ledger accounts display for each item. Click **Payroll Item** at the bottom of the list and select **Customize Columns.**

Under Available Columns, highlight **Expense Account** under **Available Columns** and click **Add.** Do the same for **Liability Account.** Under Chosen Columns, highlight **Account ID** and click **Remove.** The completed window is illustrated in Figure 10:7.

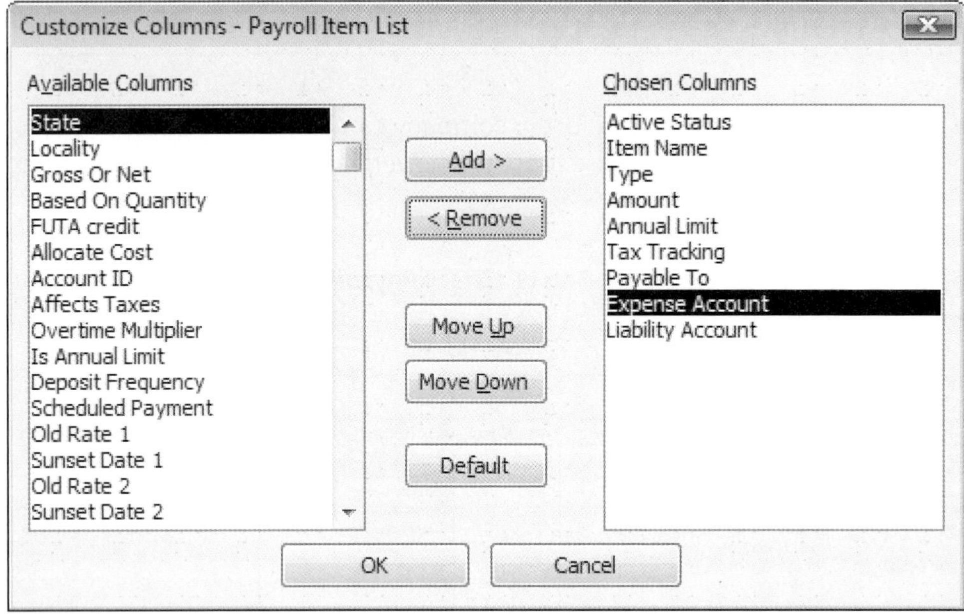

Figure 10:7

Click **OK** to view the list with the new columns (Figure 10:8). You will need to resize columns to view all information.

Payroll Item List

Item Name	Type	Amount	Annual Limit	Tax Tracking	Payable To	Expense Account	Liability Account
Salary	Yearly Salary			Compensation		60000 · Salaries and Wages Expense	
Salary Sick	Yearly Salary			Compensation		60300 · Payroll Expenses	
Salary Vacation	Yearly Salary			Compensation		60300 · Payroll Expenses	
Hourly Sick Rate	Hourly Wage			Compensation		60300 · Payroll Expenses	
Hourly Vacation Rate	Hourly Wage			Compensation		60300 · Payroll Expenses	
Hourly wage	Hourly Wage			Compensation		60000 · Salaries and Wages Expense	
Hourly wage overtime (x1.5)	Hourly Wage			Compensation		60000 · Salaries and Wages Expense	
401k Emp.	Deduction	0.0%	-11,000.00	401(k)	Watkins Financial		23300 · 401 K Deductions Payable
401k Co. Match	Company Contribution	5.0%	11,000.00	None	Watkins Financial	60500 · Pension/Profit-Sharing Expense	23300 · 401 K Deductions Payable
Health Insurance (company paid)	Company Contribution	0.00		None	Medi Ben Insurance	60600 · Employee Benefits Expense	23750 · Health Insurance Payable
Advance Earned Income Credit	Federal Tax			Advance EIC Payment	National Trust Bank		23400 · Federal Payroll Taxes Payable
Federal Unemployment	Federal Tax	0.6%	7,000.00	FUTA	National Trust Bank	61000 · Payroll Tax Expense	23500 · FUTA Tax Payable
Federal Withholding	Federal Tax			Federal	National Trust Bank		23400 · Federal Payroll Taxes Payable
Medicare Company	Federal Tax	1.45%		Comp. Medicare	National Trust Bank	61000 · Payroll Tax Expense	23400 · Federal Payroll Taxes Payable
Medicare Employee	Federal Tax	1.45%		Medicare	National Trust Bank		23400 · Federal Payroll Taxes Payable
Social Security Company	Federal Tax	6.2%	106,800.00	Comp. SS Tax	National Trust Bank	61000 · Payroll Tax Expense	23400 · Federal Payroll Taxes Payable
Social Security Employee	Federal Tax	4.2%	-106,800.00	SS Tax	National Trust Bank		23400 · Federal Payroll Taxes Payable
VA - Income Tax	State Withholding Tax			SWH	VA State Income Tax		23600 · State Payroll Taxes Payable
VA - Unemployment	State Unemployment Tax	1.5%	8,000.00	Comp. SUI	VA Employment Tax	61000 · Payroll Tax Expense	23700 · SUTA Tax Payable

Payroll Item ▾ Activities ▾ Reports ▾ Include inactive

Figure 10:8

Refer to these accounts as we go through the setup of payroll items.

Double click to open the **Salary** item. The window illustrated in Figure 10:9 is used to define an item's name or to inactivate the item.

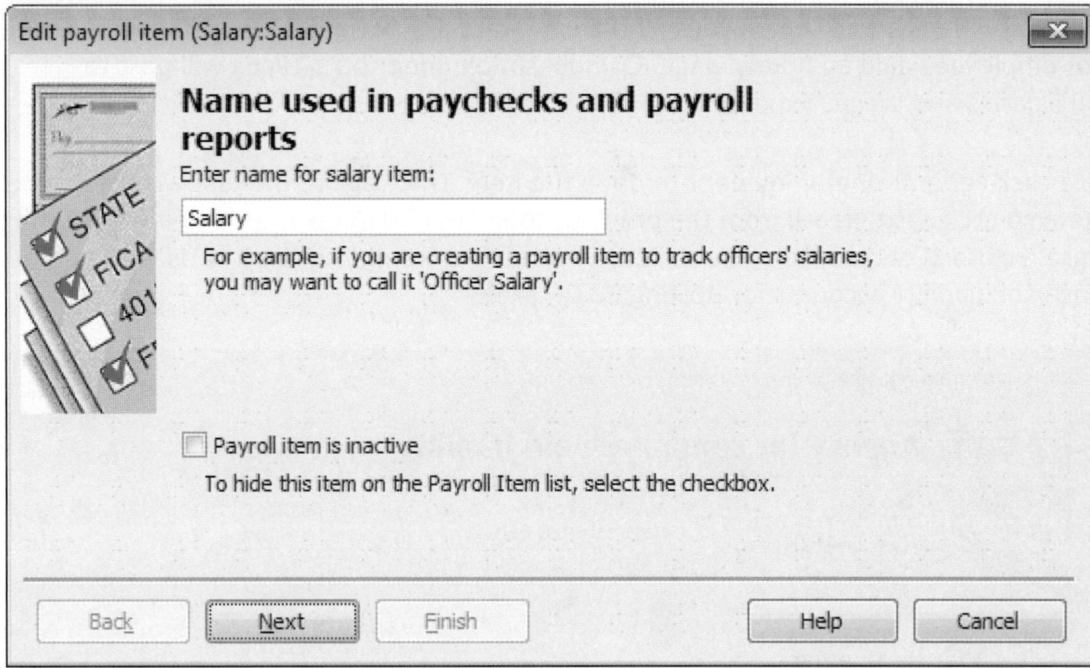

Figure 10:9

Click **Next** to move to the window illustrated in Figure 10:10. This is where you set the default general ledger account used when posting salaried employee gross pay. The account displayed in the window agrees to the expense account for this item on the Payroll Item List.

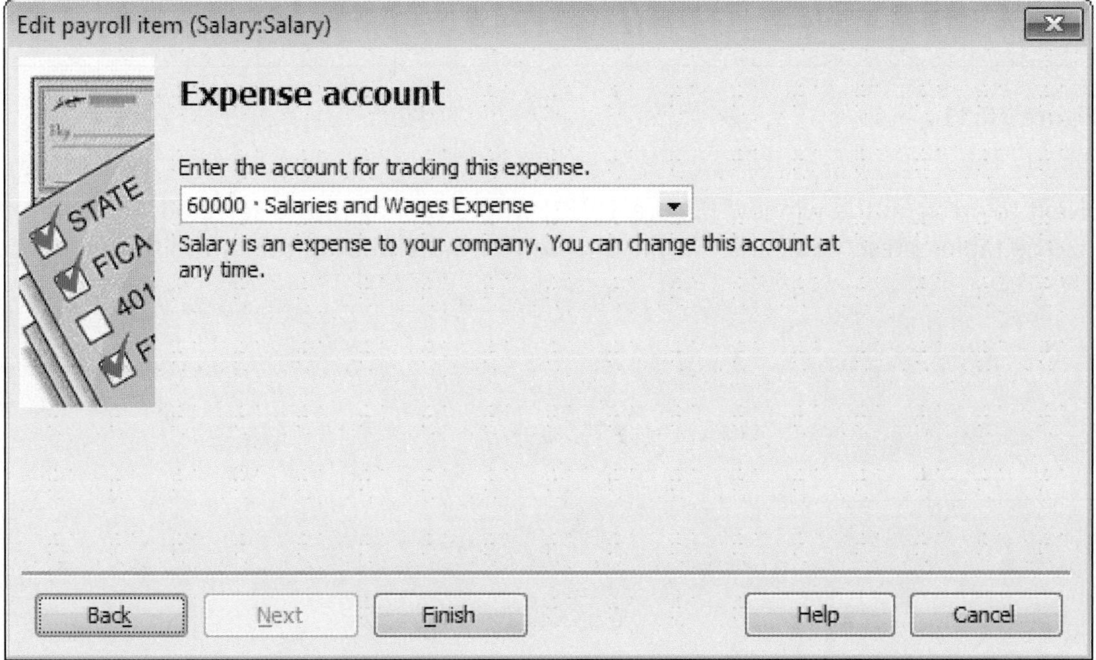

Figure 10:10

Click **Cancel** and now review the **Payroll Item List** to note that Baxter has a separate category for hourly wage compensation.

Yearly Salary types are for employees paid an annual salary whereas **Hourly Wage** types are for employees paid an hourly wage. Compensation under both types will post to 60000 Salaries and Wages Expense.

Double click **Federal Unemployment** to open the item. Once again, the first window names the item so click **Next.** Recall from the previous topic that FUTA tax is an employer payroll tax expense. Figure 10:11 is where you select the vendor for remitting taxes to as well as the expense and liability accounts for posting FUTA taxes.

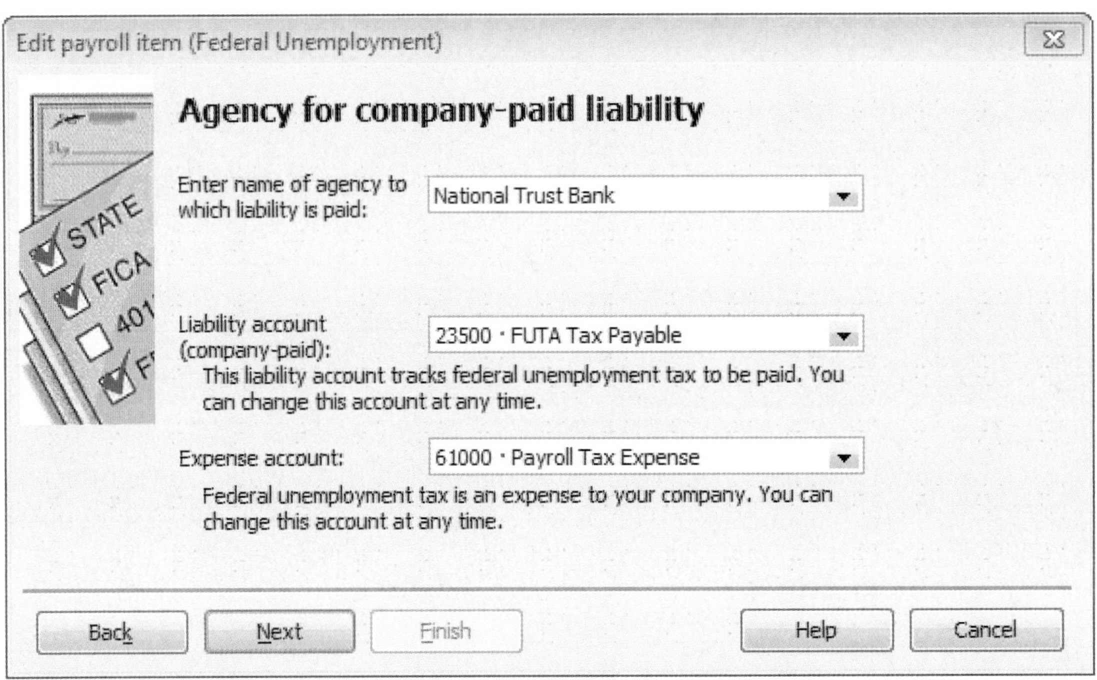

Figure 10:11

Click **Next** to arrive at the window (Figure 10:12) where the tax rate is selected. You can refer back to the tables presented earlier in the chapter for more information on this rate.

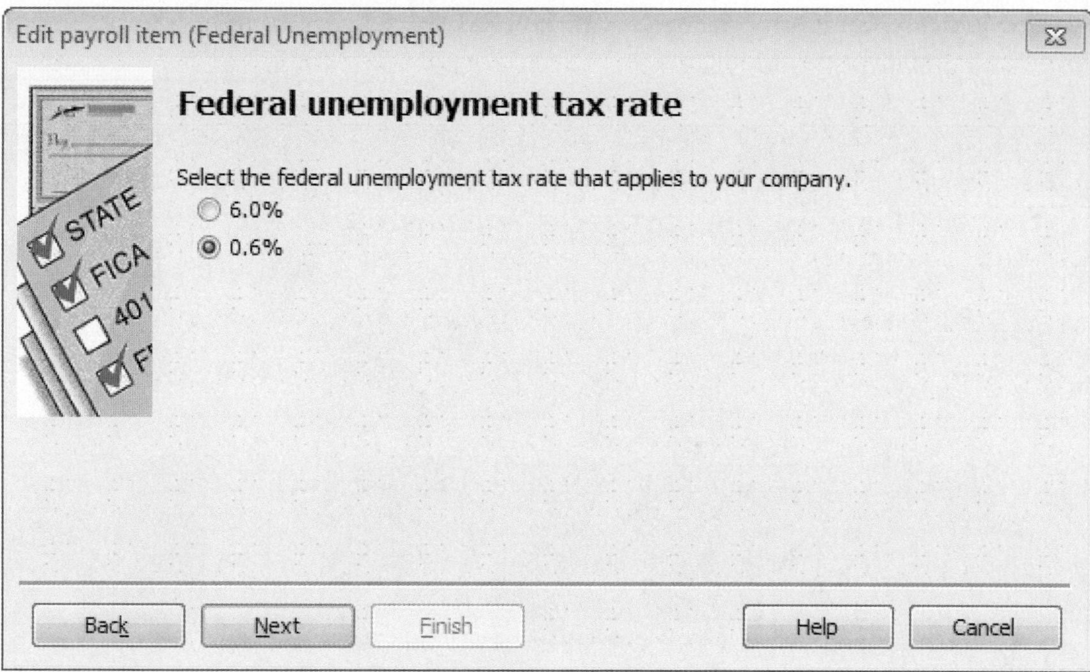

Figure 10:12

Click **Next** and you are at the window (Figure 10:13) for choosing compensation items that are subject to FUTA tax. Generally, all wage compensation will be FUTA taxable. For more information on FUTA taxes, visit www.irs.gov.

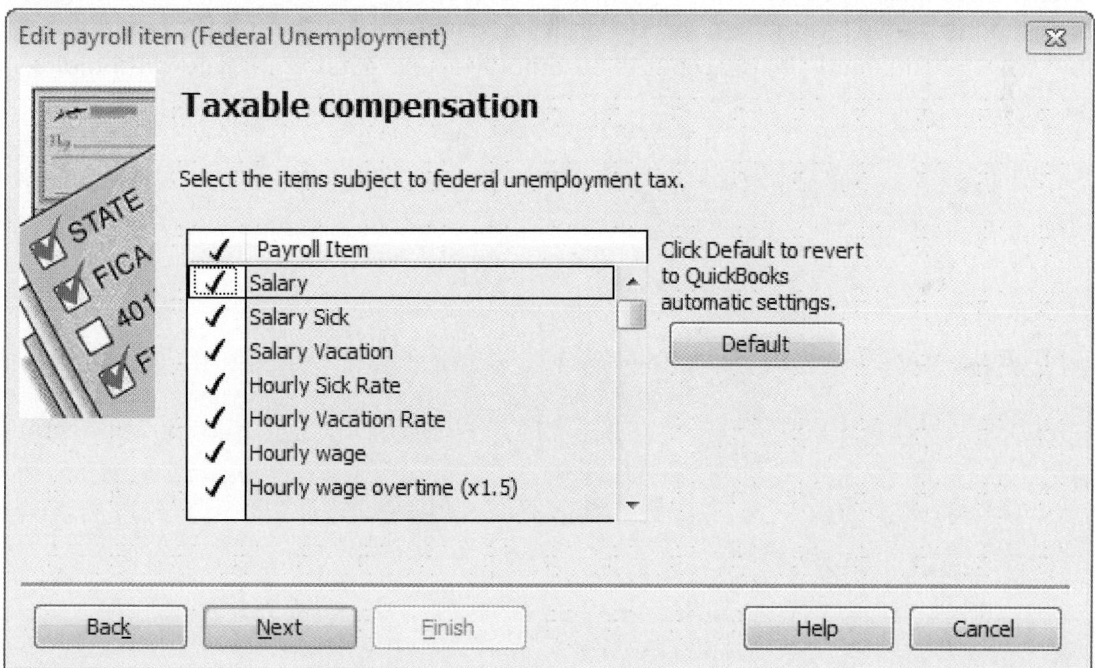

Figure 10:13

Click **Cancel**.

Now open **Medicare Company.** The screen in Figure 10:14 names two items because both the employee and employer pay Medicare.

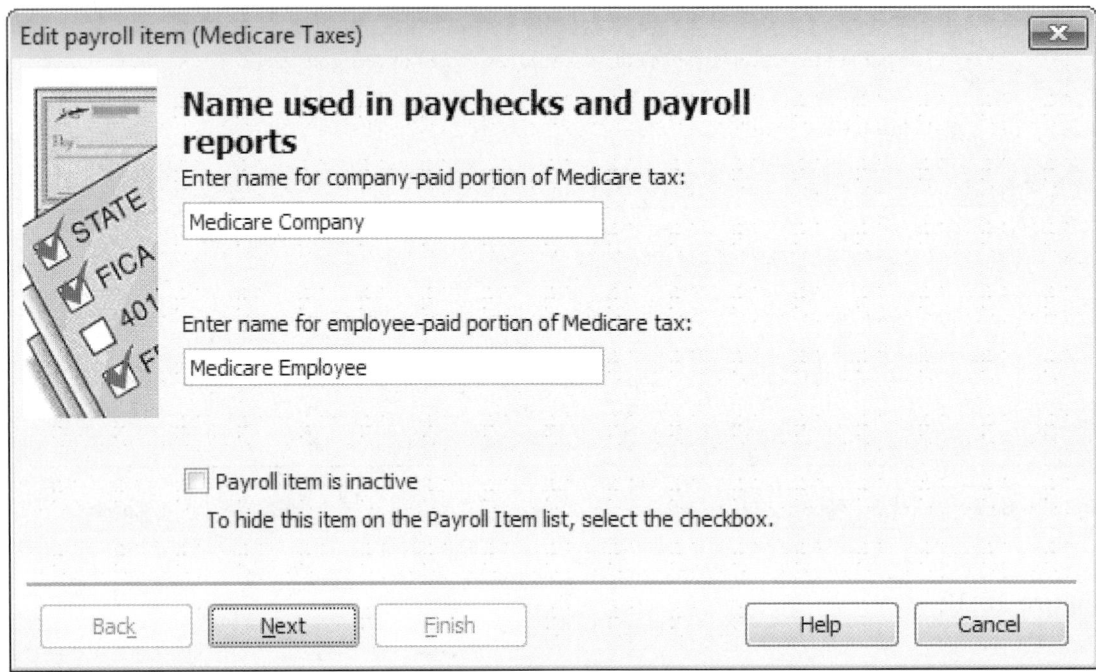

Figure 10:14

Click **Next.** Once again, you find a window (Figure 10:15) for selecting the general ledger posting accounts as well as the vendor for remitting payment. However, this time the window sets only default liability accounts for employer taxes and employee withholdings.

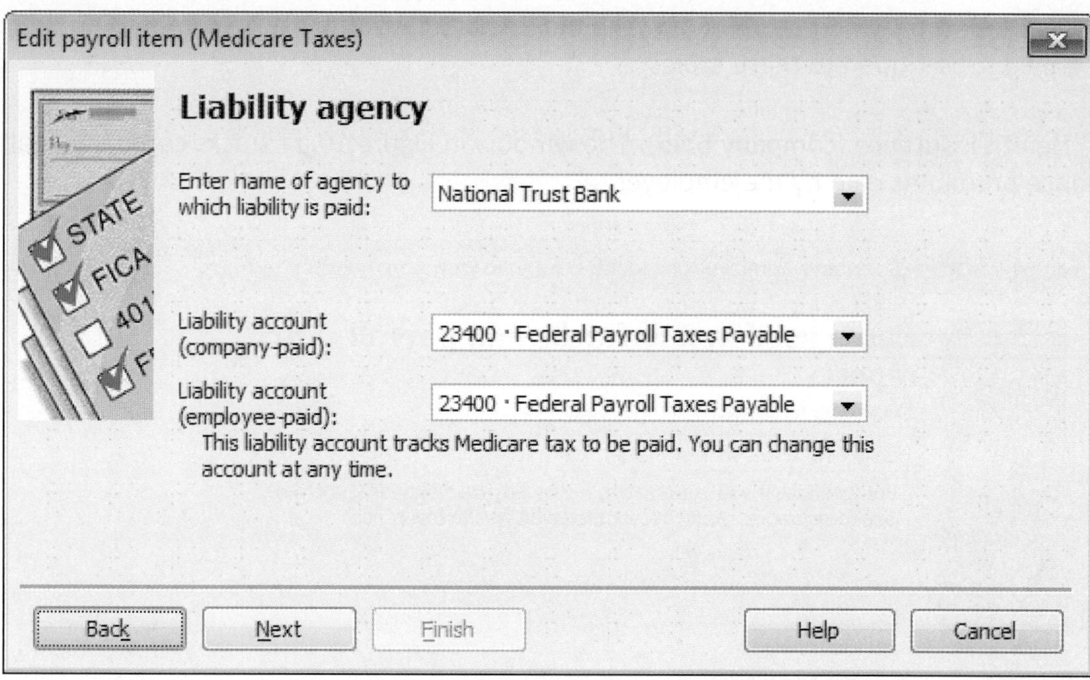

Figure 10:15

Click **Next.** The window in Figure 10:16 is where you select the employer tax expense account.

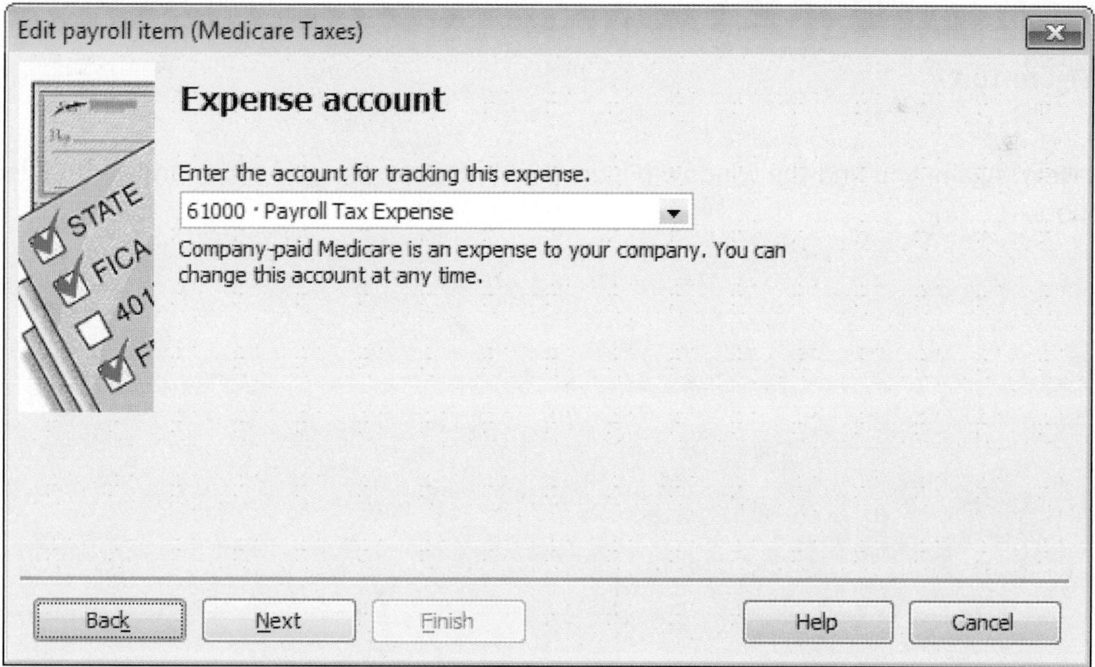

Figure 10:16

Click **Cancel.**

Notice that you were unable to set the tax rate on the previous item. In fact, you will be unable to set tax rates for any Federal Tax types, other than FUTA, or State Withholding Tax types.

QBP sets these rates when downloading the online payroll tax tables. Remember you do not have a paid subscription to these tables.

Open **Health Insurance (company paid).** The window in Figure 10:17 tracks company health insurance premiums paid by the employer.

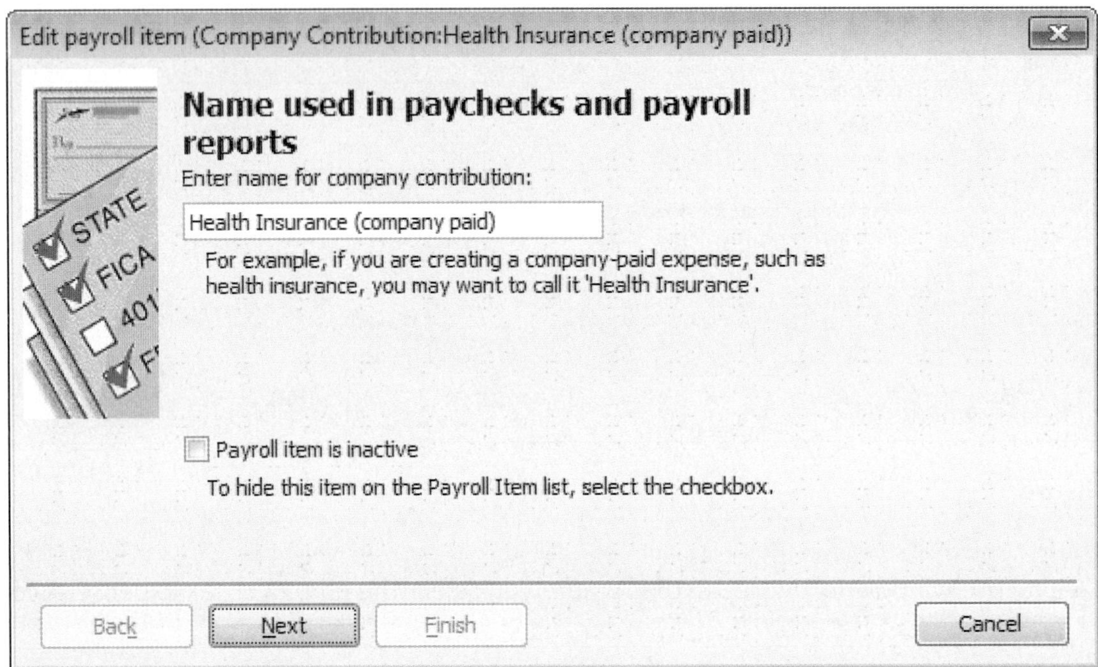

Figure 10:17

Click **Next**. Again, you find the window (Figure 10:18) for selecting a vendor and general ledger accounts.

Edit payroll item (Company Contribution:Health Insurance (company paid))

Agency for company-paid liability

Enter name of agency to which liability is paid: Medi Ben Insurance

Enter the number that identifies you to agency:

Liability account (company-paid): 23750 · Health Insurance Payable

This liability account tracks company contributions to be paid. You can change this account at any time.

Expense account: 60600 · Employee Benefits Expense

Company-paid contributions are an expense to your company. You can change this account at any time.

Back Next Finish Cancel

Figure 10:18

Click **Next.** On this window (Figure 10:19) you can opt to print company contributions for health insurance on employee W-2s. Baxter has elected not to print this information.

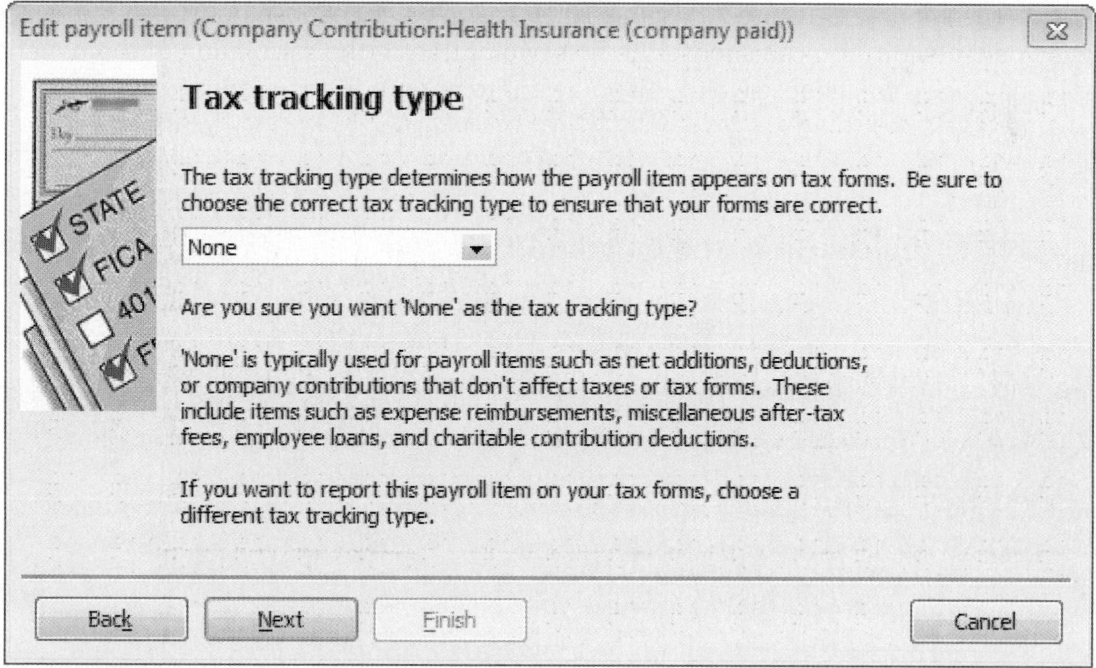

Figure 10:19

Click **Next.** This window (Figure 10:20) determines when a company-paid benefit is subject to employer and/or employee payroll taxes. Remember, these benefits are deemed additional compensation, which may or may not be taxable. Typically, employer-paid health insurance premiums are not subject to tax.

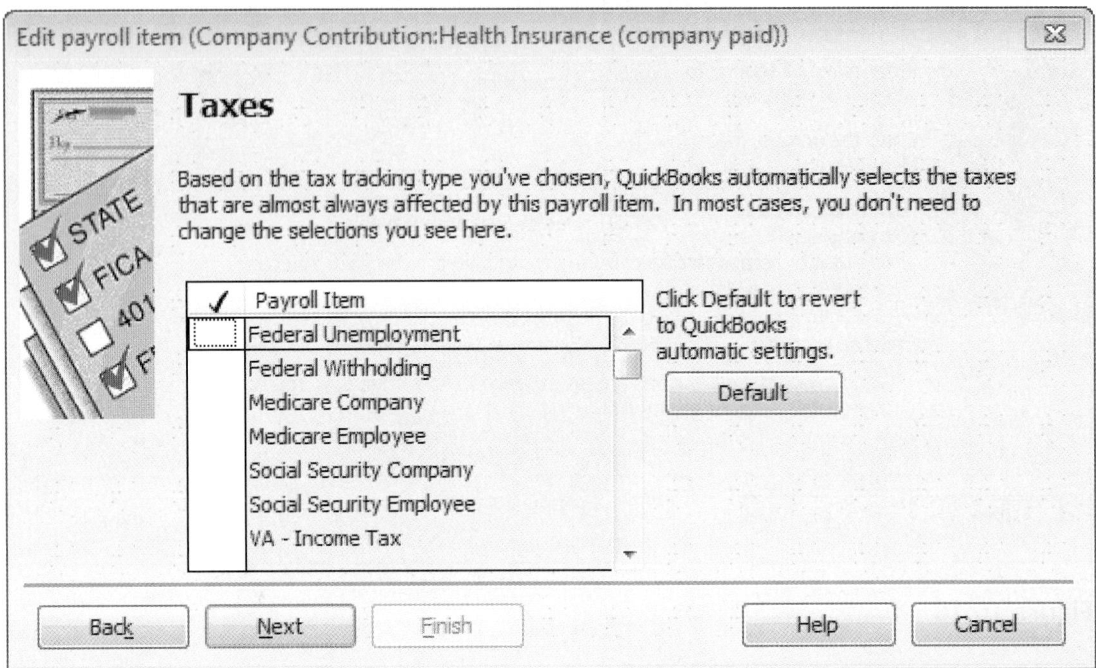

Figure 10:20

Click **Next**. The window illustrated in Figure 10:21 is where you choose how to calculate the company-paid benefit. You can choose the first two options if the calculation of the benefit varies by paycheck. You choose Neither if you want to enter a fixed amount.

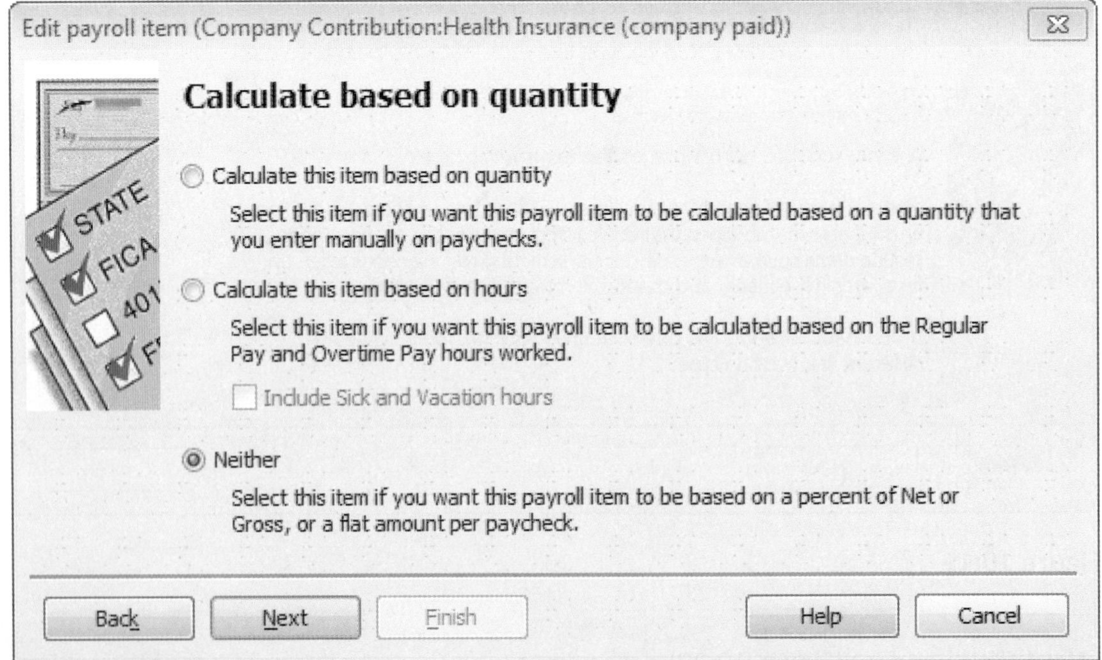

Figure 10:21

Click **Next**. On the window illustrated in Figure 10:22, the default rate or percentage can be entered. Baxter has not entered an amount because it varies by employee so the amount has been stored on the employee account.

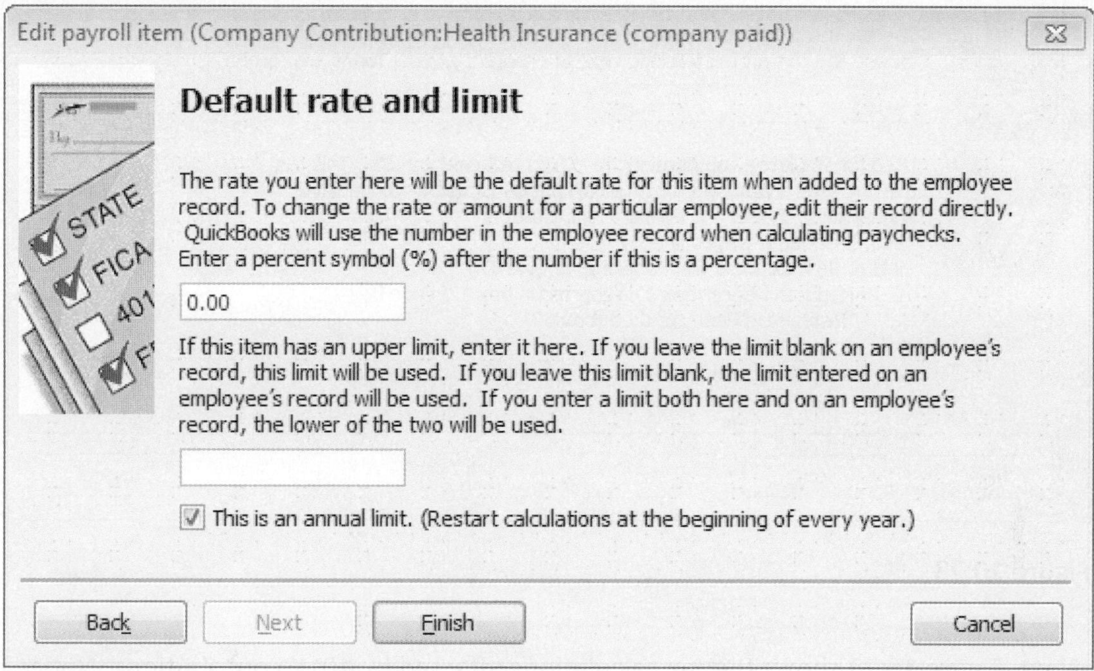

Figure 10:22

Click **Cancel.**

Now open **401k Emp**. This item is for employee 401K contributions. Click **Next** on the window that names the item and **Next** on the window that sets the vendor and general ledger account to arrive at the window (Figure 10:23) that reports the item on W-2s and lists the annual contribution limit.

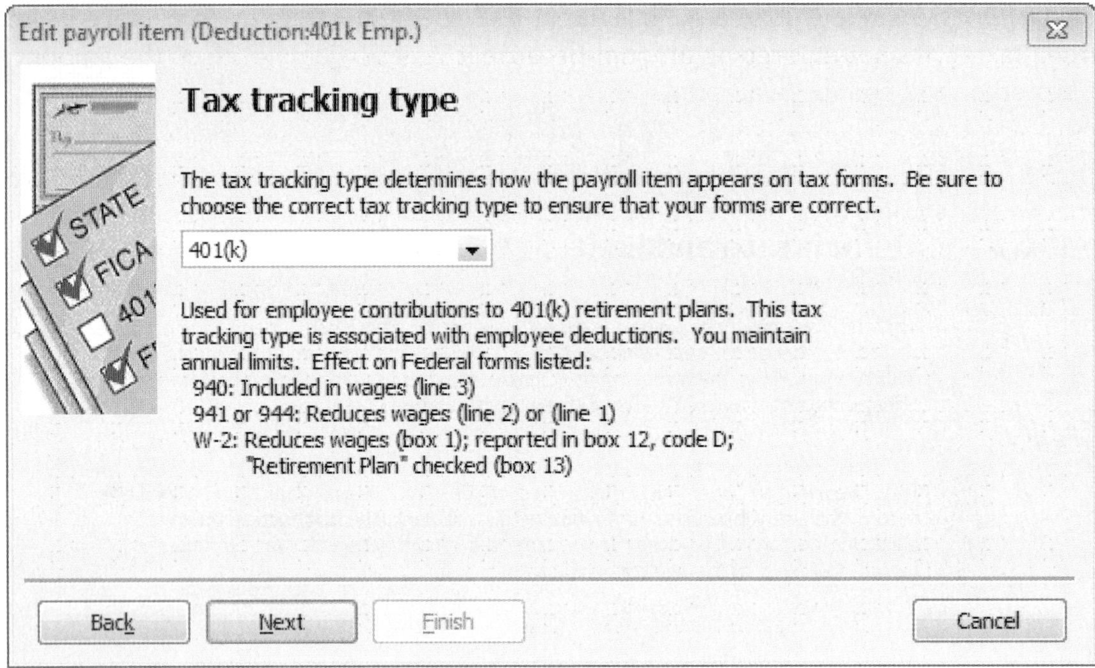

Figure 10:23

Click **Next.** Figure 10:24 shows the tax calculations affected by 401K contributions. Notice that only federal and state income tax withholdings are affected. Gross wages will be reduced by employee 401K contributions before calculating Federal Withholding and VA-Income Tax.

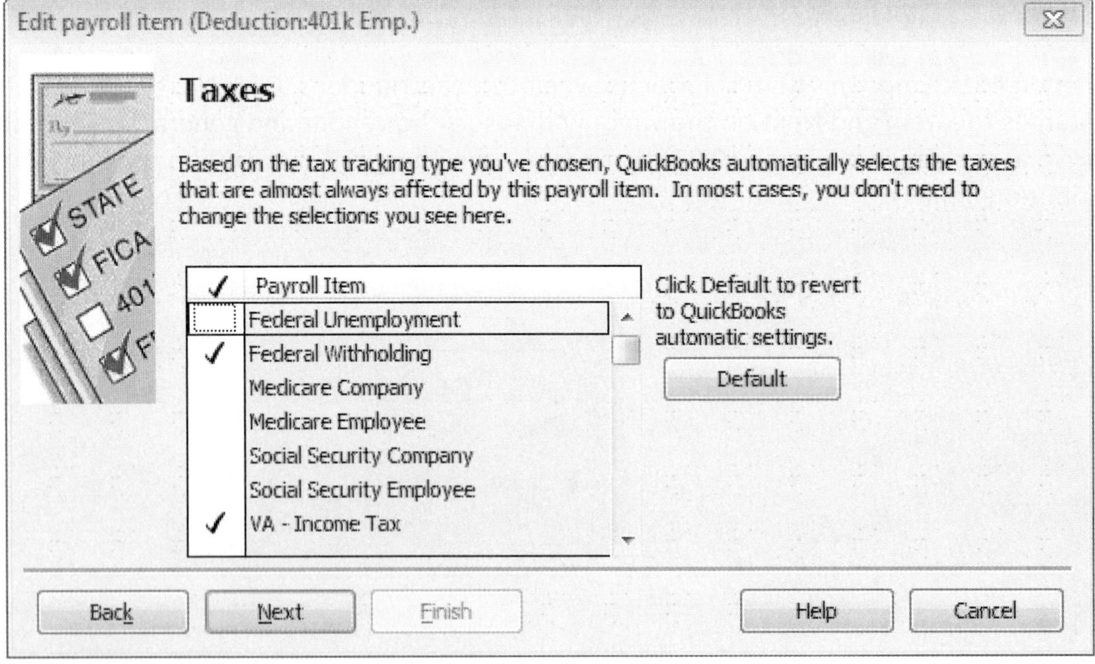

Figure 10:24

Click **Next** and then **Next** on the calculation basis window to arrive at the window illustrated in Figure 10:25. Baxter has not set a default percentage because employee contribution rates vary.

In addition to a rate, this window stores the annual limit imposed by the IRS for the tax deductibility of 401K contributions. The $11,000 limit shown is not current. This is an example of why companies subscribe to Intuit's payroll tax service to receive updates. Information on retirement plan annual limits is available on the IRS website.

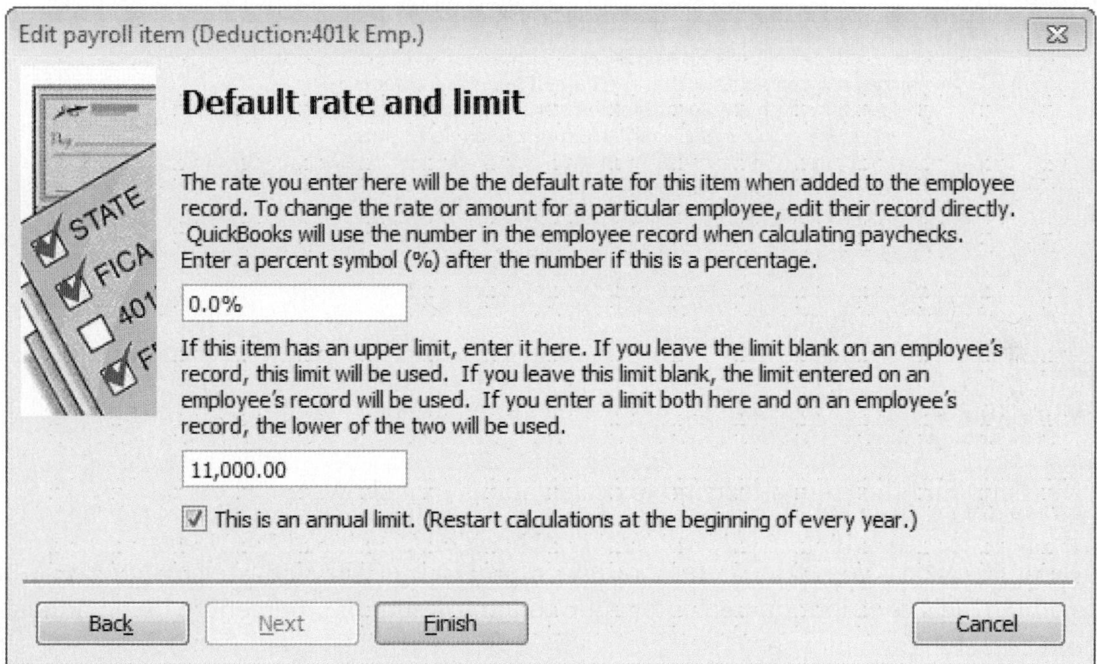

Figure 10:25

Click **Cancel** and you will now open the employer 401K matching contribution item.

Open **401k Co. Match.** Click **Next** and **Next** to arrive at the window illustrated in Figure 10:26. This item will not print on employee W-2s. Employer contributions are not taxable at the time of contribution because the employee pays tax on contributions when receiving retirement benefits.

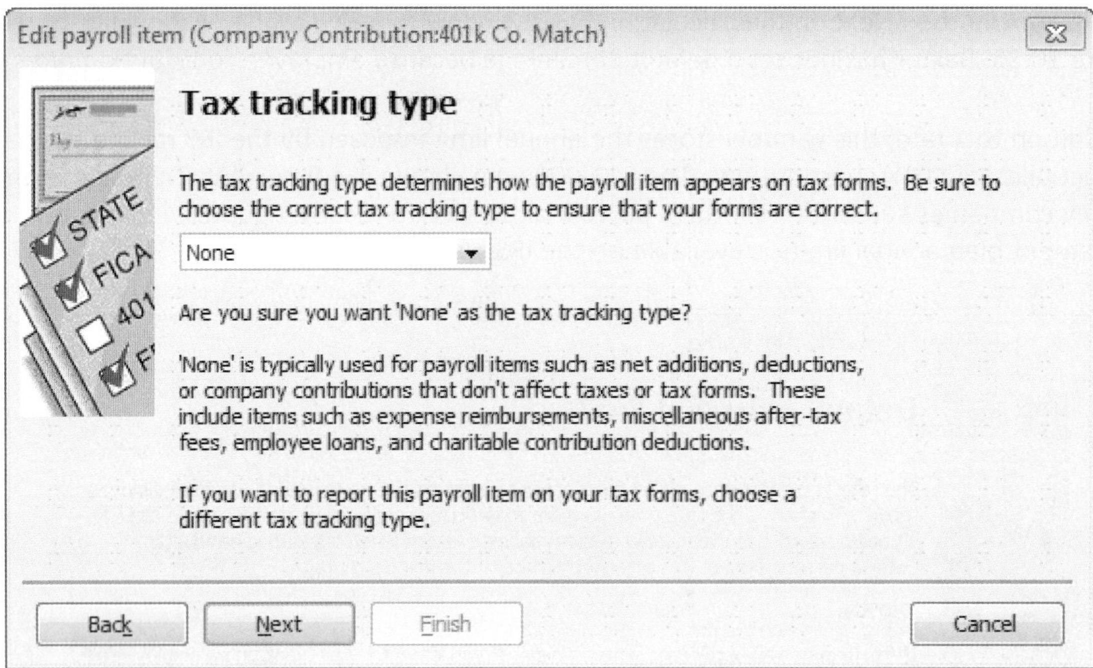

Figure 10:26

Click **Next** and find this item affects no tax calculations (not shown).

Click **Next** and **Next** to open the default rate window (Figure 10:27). Baxter matches one-half of the employee's contribution percentage, up to a maximum of 5 percent, with an annual limit of $11,000 per employee.

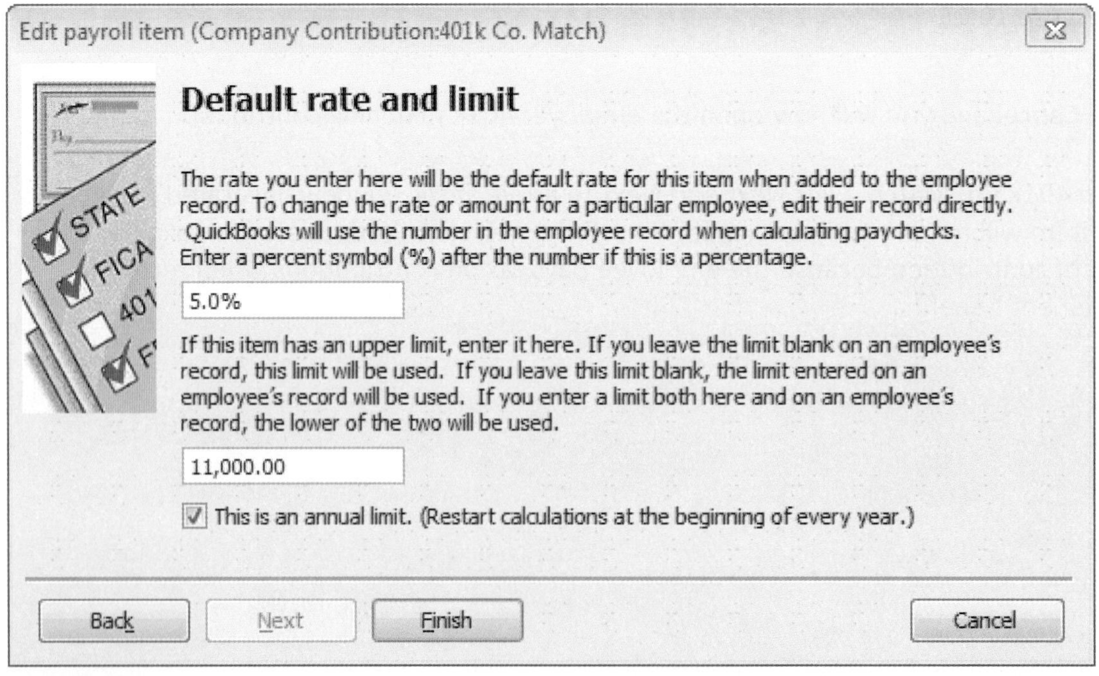

Figure 10:27

Click **Cancel** and close the Payroll Item List.

With all the complexities just illustrated, you can see why many companies outsource payroll. Now that you understand the purpose of payroll items, you will next learn to manage the employee accounts linked to these items.

EMPLOYEE CENTER

In this topic, you use the Employee Center to manage employee accounts and locate payroll transactions.

Click the **Employees** icon on the toolbar to open the **Employees Center.** Select the **Employees** tab, **Amanda Chester,** and the filtering options illustrated in Figure 10:28.

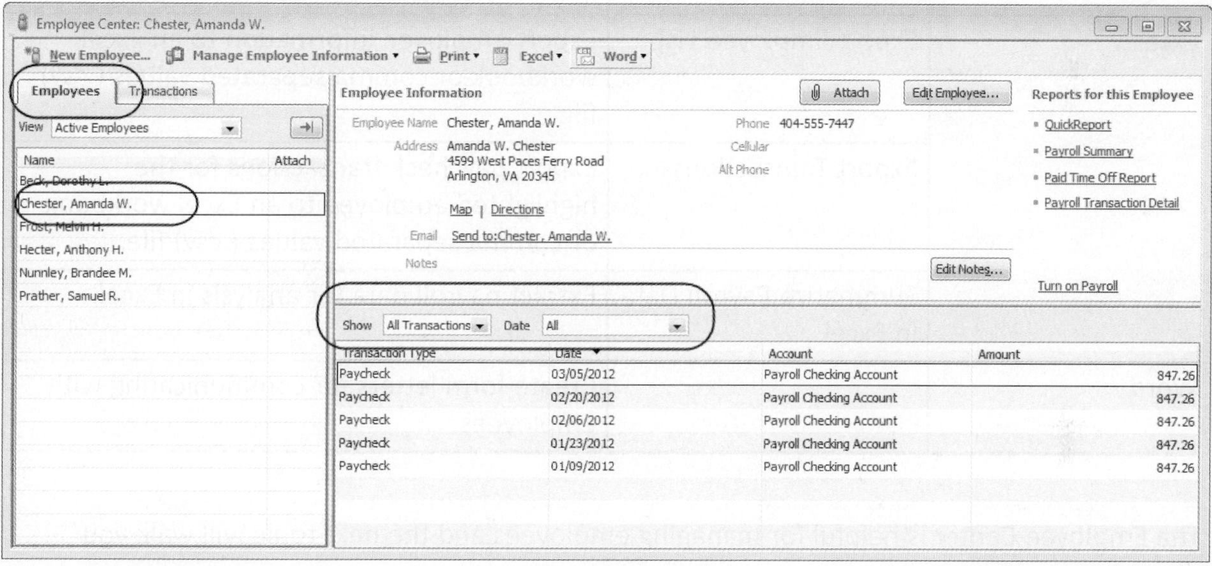

Figure 10:28

The **Transactions** tab serves the same purpose served on other centers. The table that follows explains activities and tasks on the **Employees** toolbar. Remember that actions are performed on the account highlighted to the left.

Employee Activities	Task	Description
New Employee		Create a new employee account.
Manage Employee Information	Add/Edit Sales Rep	Manage existing employee accounts.
	Change New Employee Default Settings	Create employee defaults that will be assigned to new employee accounts.
Print	Print Paychecks	Print paychecks.
	Print/Send Paystubs	Print only pay stubs. This is used when checks are deposited directly to employee bank accounts.
	Employee List/Employee Information/Employee Transaction List	Print an employee list, account information, or paycheck transactions. These reports cannot be customized so use the Reports menu to print this information.
Excel	Export Employee List	Export employee information to an Excel workbook or comma separated values (.csv) file.
	Export Transactions	Export paycheck transactions for the highlighted employee to an Excel workbook or comma separated values (.csv) file.
	Summarize Payroll Data in Excel	Extract payroll data for analysis in Excel.
Word		Create form letters for communicating with employees.

The Employee Center is helpful for managing employees and the next topic will walk you through this activity.

MANAGING EMPLOYEES

Double click Amanda Chester's account to open it. *(Note: You can also click the Edit Employee button to the right.)*

An employee account contains three different tabs for entering information. You choose a tab by selecting it from the dropdown list on **Change tabs.** (See Figure 10:29.) As illustrated, the tab names are **Personal Info, Payroll and Compensation Info,** and **Employment Info.**

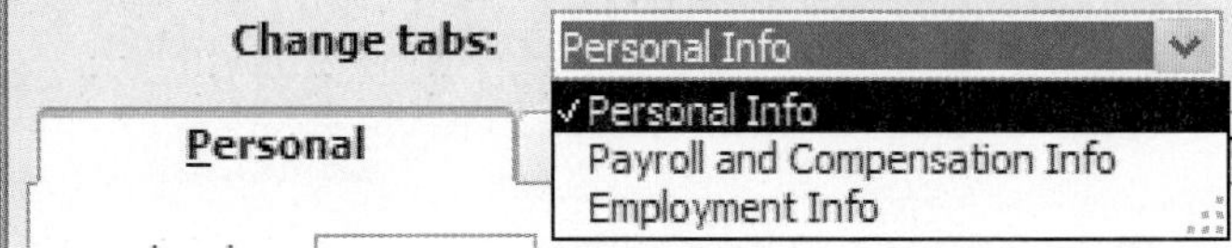

Figure 10:29

Select the **Personal Info** tab. As illustrated next, this tab contains three sub-tabs, namely **Personal, Address and Contact,** and **Additional Info.** We next illustrate the information stored on each sub-tab.

Personal Tab

Figure 10:30

This tab stores employee Social Security number and birth date.

Address and Contact Tab

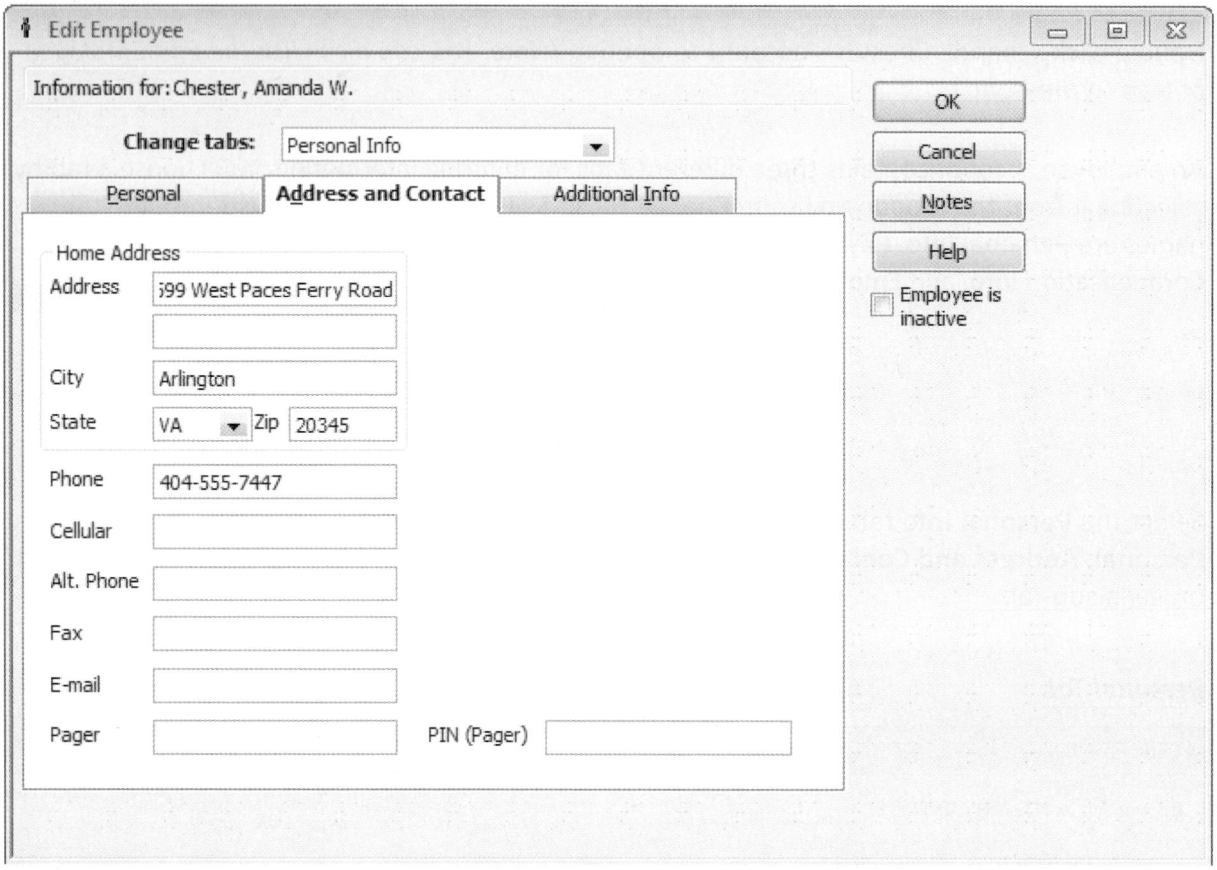

Edit Employee

Information for: Chester, Amanda W.

Change tabs: Personal Info

Personal | Address and Contact | Additional Info

Home Address

Address: 599 West Paces Ferry Road

City: Arlington

State: VA Zip: 20345

Phone: 404-555-7447

Cellular

Alt. Phone

Fax

E-mail

Pager PIN (Pager)

OK

Cancel

Notes

Help

Employee is inactive

Figure 10:31

This tab stores basic contact information for the employee.

Additional Info Tab

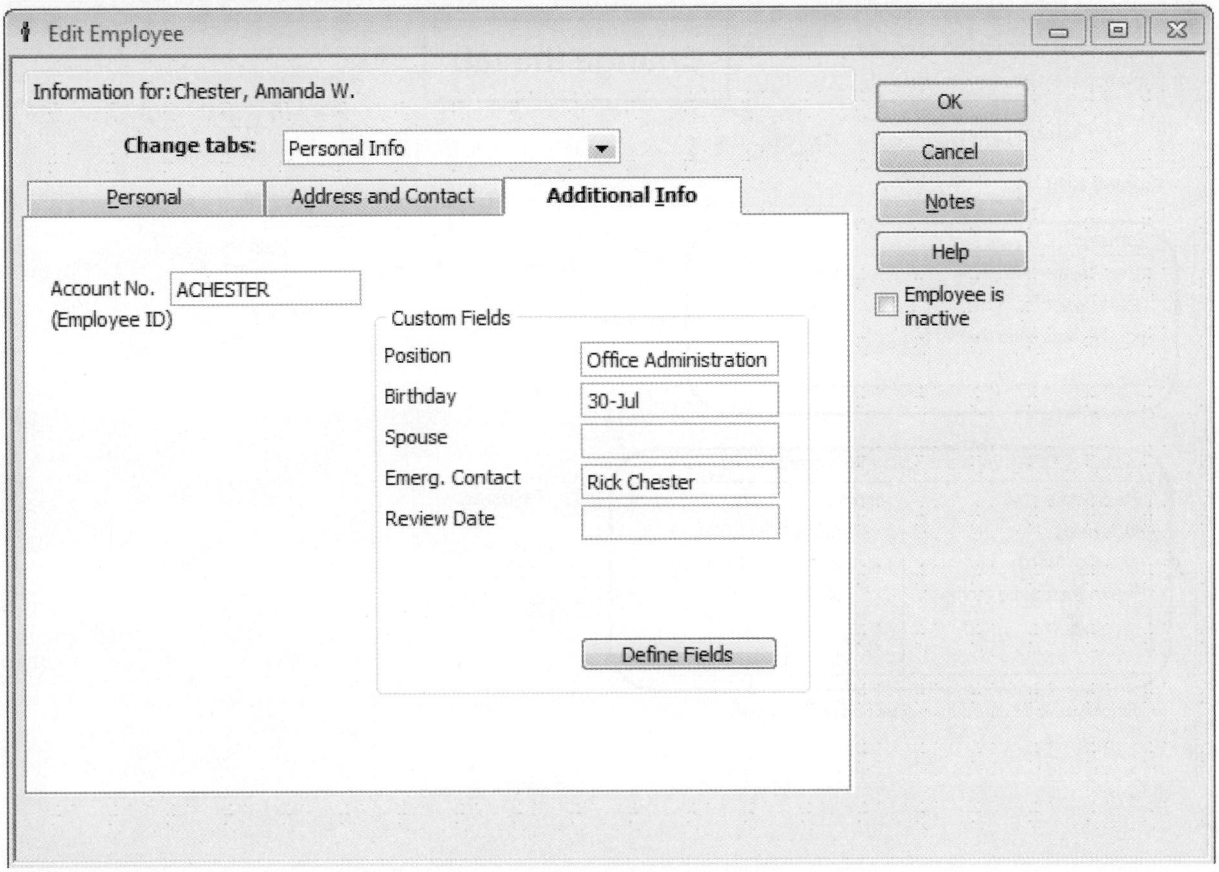

Edit Employee

Information for: Chester, Amanda W.

Change tabs: Personal Info

Personal | Address and Contact | Additional Info

Account No. (Employee ID): ACHESTER

Custom Fields

Position	Office Administration
Birthday	30-Jul
Spouse	
Emerg. Contact	Rick Chester
Review Date	

Define Fields

OK

Cancel

Notes

Help

Employee is inactive

Figure 10:32

This tab stores miscellaneous information such as job position.

Now change the tab to **Payroll and Compensation Info.**

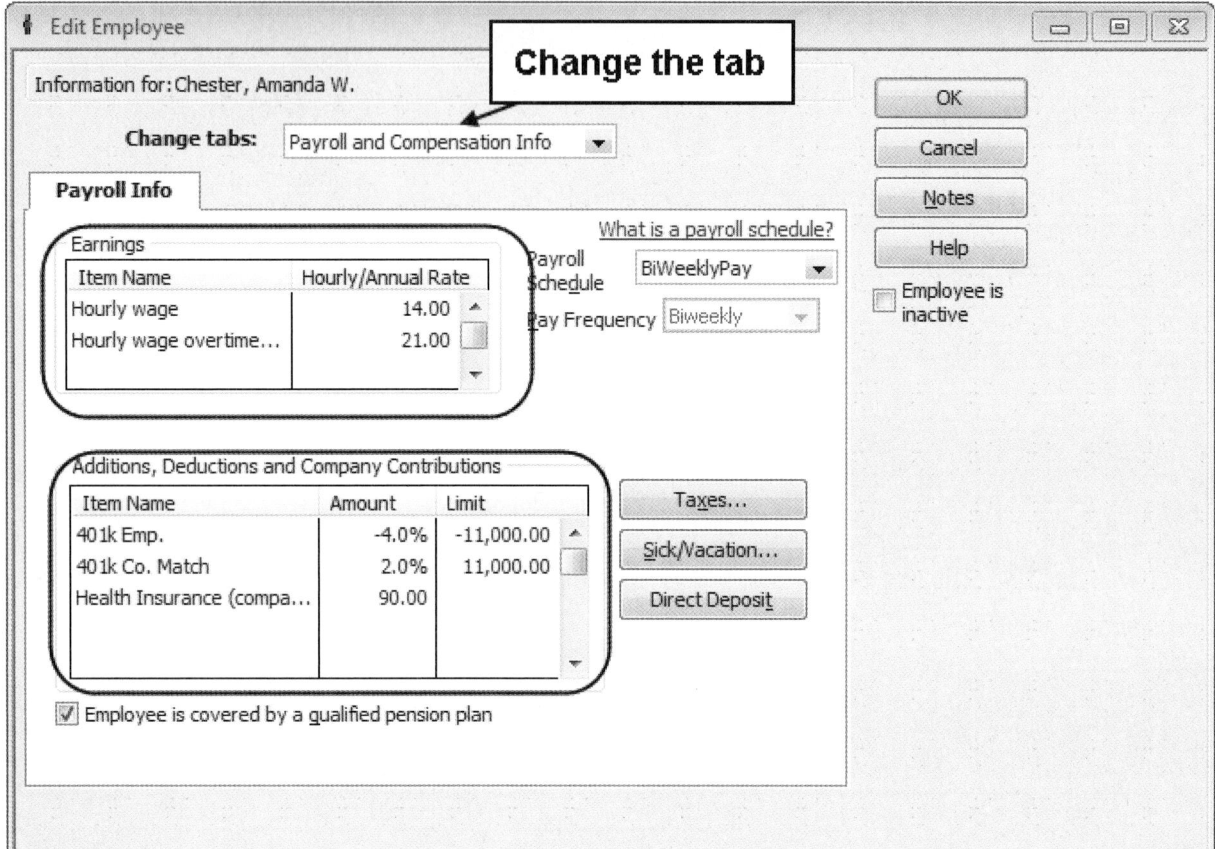

Figure 10:33

Figure 10:33 is where you enter **Earnings** information, **Taxes,** and other deductions and benefits. You also set a **Payroll Schedule** for paying the employee.

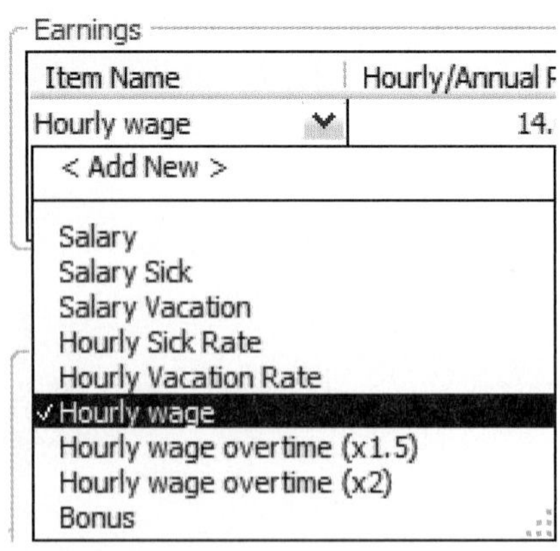

Figure 10:34

Now focus on **Item Name** under **Earnings.** Notice that Amanda is paid biweekly at $14.00 per hour for regular time and $21.00 per hour for overtime. Click **Hourly wage** and open the dropdown list. Figure 10:34 shows the payroll items we reviewed in the Payroll Items topic. Amanda's account has been assigned to Hourly wage, so you know that her compensation is based on hours worked during the pay period.

Click the **Taxes** button. The tab illustrated in Figure 10:35 is where you enter filing statuses and withholding allowances for federal, state, and other taxes.

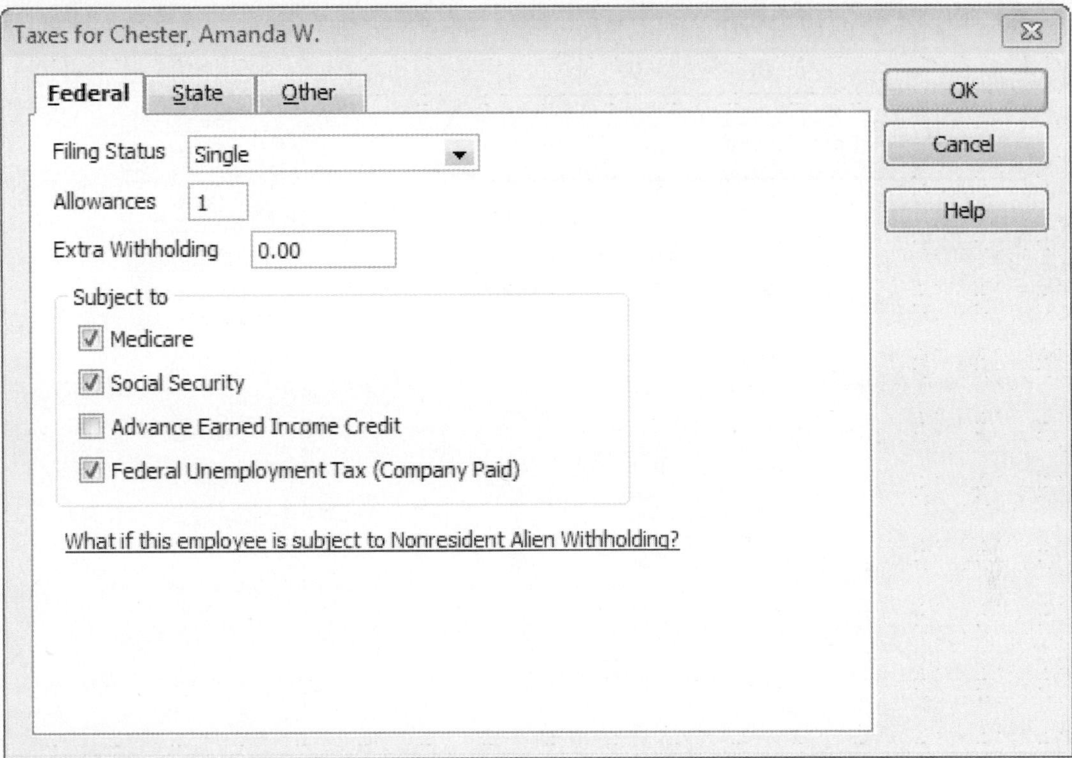

Figure 10:35

The **Federal** tab shows Amanda's federal **Filing Status** as **Single** with one withholding **Allowance.** At the bottom, you see that Amanda's wages are subject to Medicare and Social Security tax withholdings. In addition, wages are subject to employer Medicare, Social Security, and FUTA taxes.

The **State** tab is used to enter state withholding information. The **Other** tab is used when employees must also pay city or local taxes.

Click **Cancel** to exit the tax window.

Finally, change the tab to **Employment Info.** This tab (Figure 10:36) stores an employee's hire date as well as the last day an employee worked for the company.

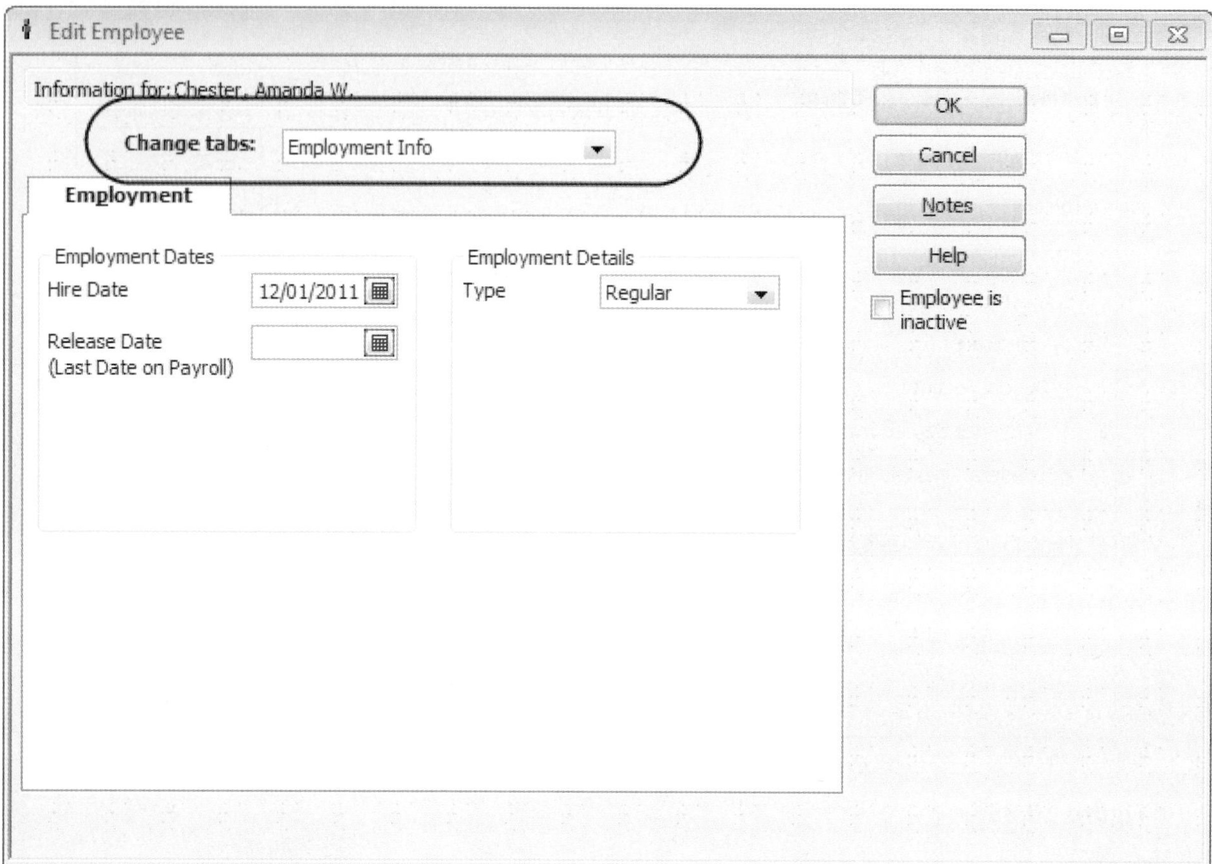

Figure 10:36

Click **Cancel** to close Amanda's account.

Before leaving this topic, review pay information for a salaried employee. Open the account for **Melvin Frost** and change the tab to **Payroll and Compensation Info.** (See Figure 10:37.)

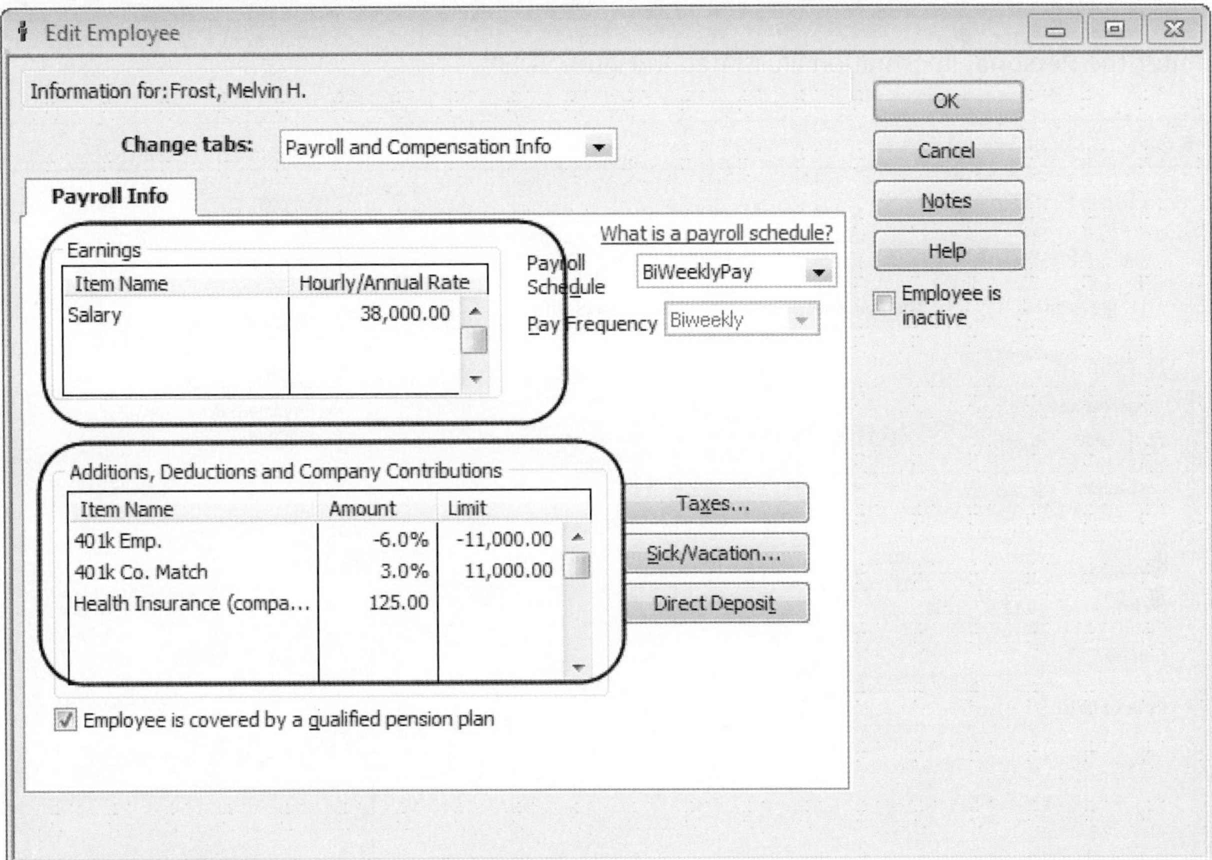

Figure 10:37

Salaried employee pay rates are entered as annual compensation. For Melvin, the annual salary is $38,000. Also notice that Melvin is paid biweekly, so he will receive 26 paychecks during the year (52 weeks per year / 2 weeks per pay period). Based on this information, QBP will calculate Melvin's gross pay for each pay period as $38,000 / 26.

Melvin's account is also linked to other payroll items. Melvin contributes 6 percent to his 401K account and the company matches 3 percent. The company also accrues $125 each pay period for Melvin's health insurance.

Click **Cancel** to exit Melvin's account.

You are now ready to create a new employee. Click the **New Employee** button on the Employee Center. Baxter hired Susan Sharpton to work as a retail clerk, so follow the next steps to create her account.

Enter the **Personal** information illustrated in Figure 10:38.

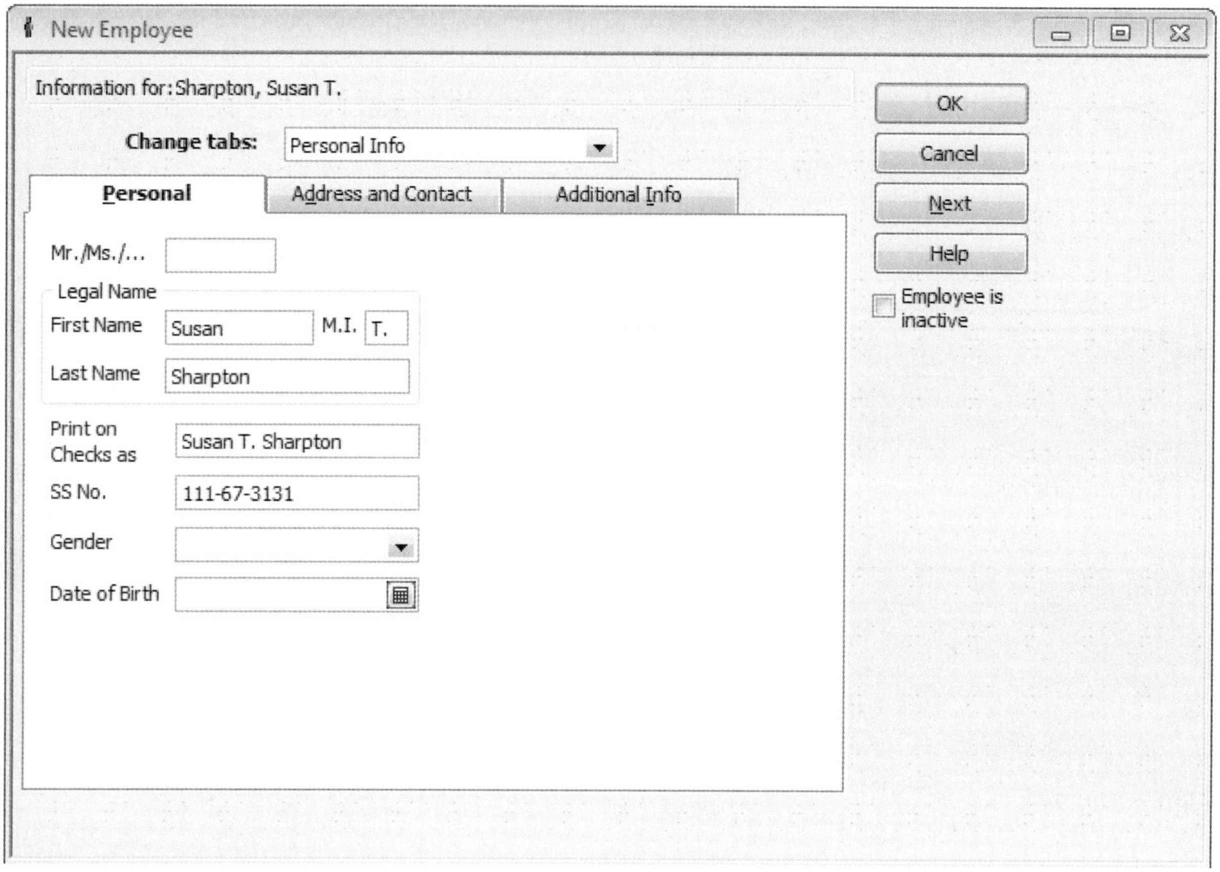

New Employee

Information for: Sharpton, Susan T.

Change tabs: Personal Info

Personal | Address and Contact | Additional Info

Mr./Ms./...

Legal Name

First Name: Susan M.I.: T.

Last Name: Sharpton

Print on Checks as: Susan T. Sharpton

SS No.: 111-67-3131

Gender

Date of Birth

OK

Cancel

Next

Help

Employee is inactive

Figure 10:38

Click **Address and Contact** and enter the information shown in Figure 10:39.

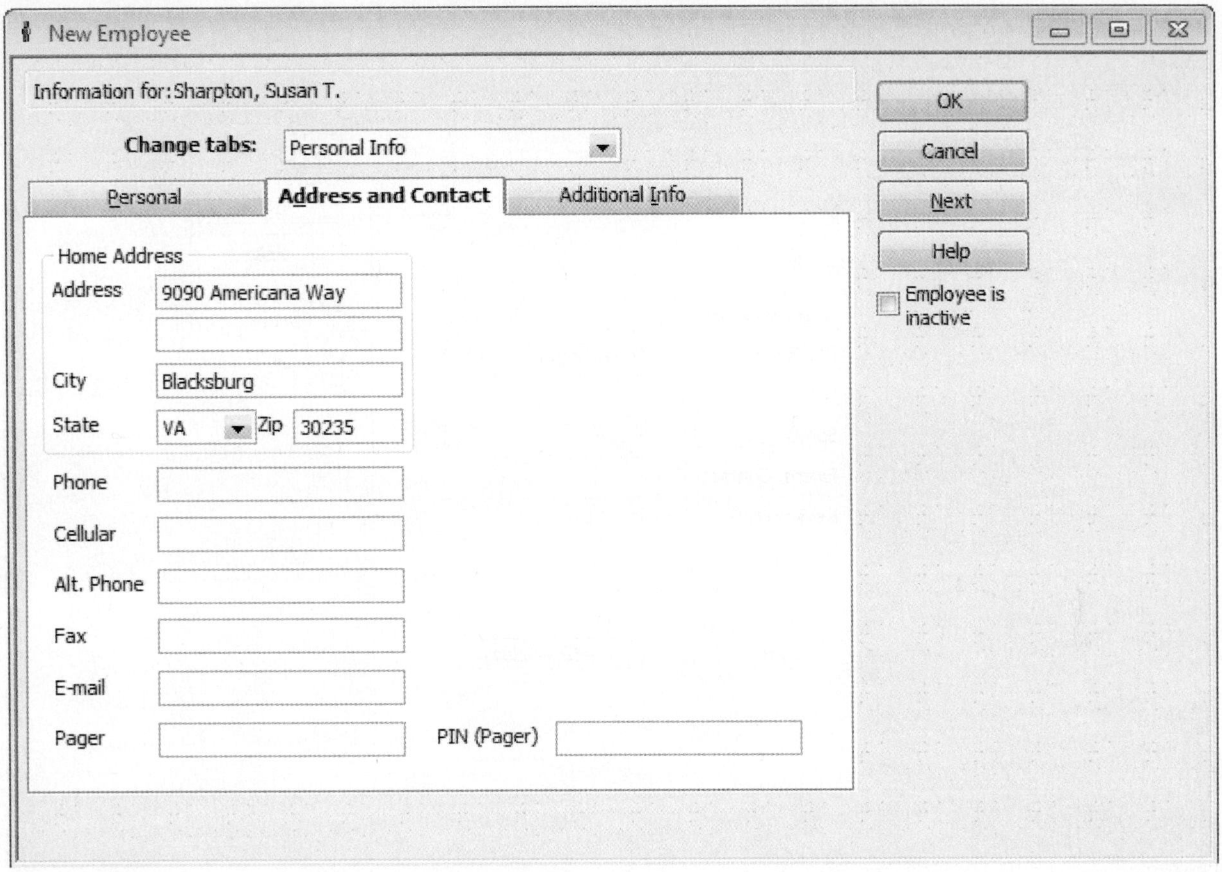

Figure 10:39

Click **Additional Info** and enter the information shown in Figure 10:40.

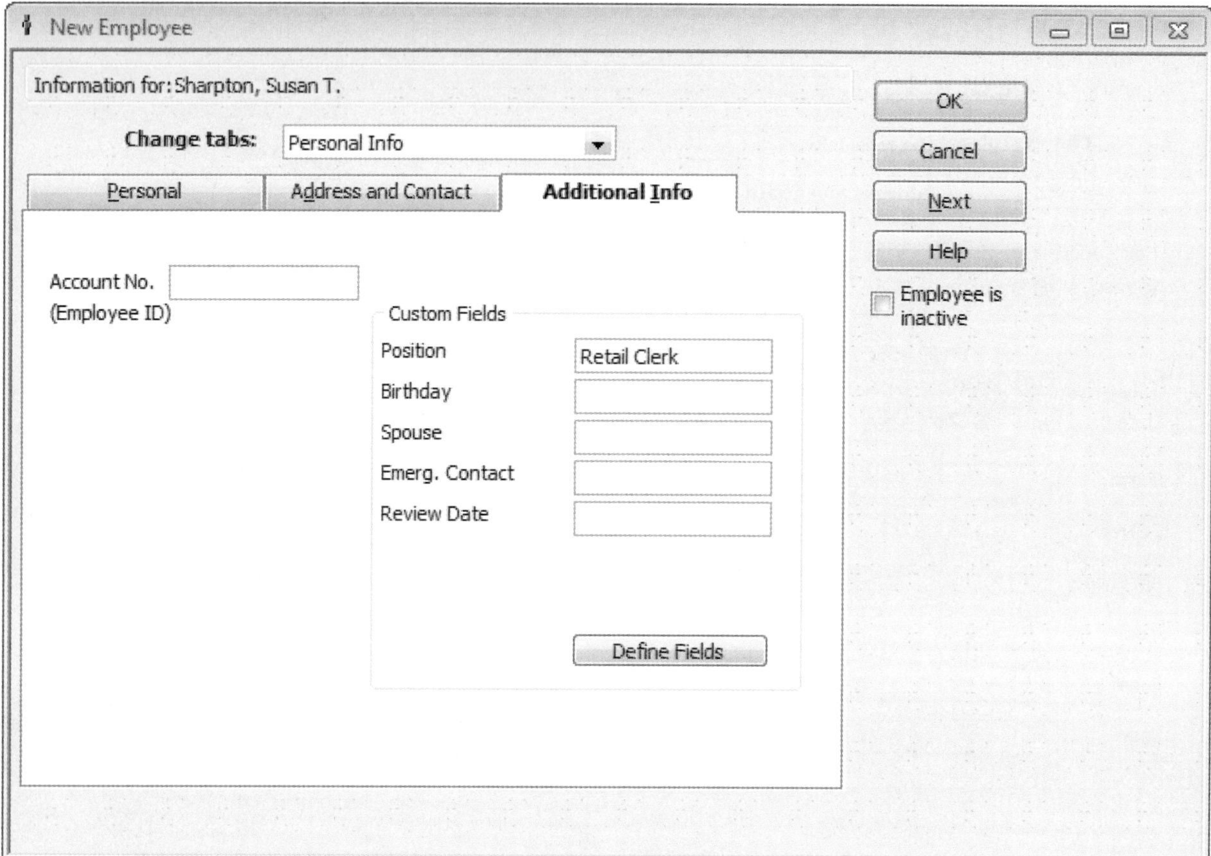

Figure 10:40

Now change the tab to **Payroll and Compensation Info.** (See Figure 10:41.) Instructions for completing this window follow the figure.

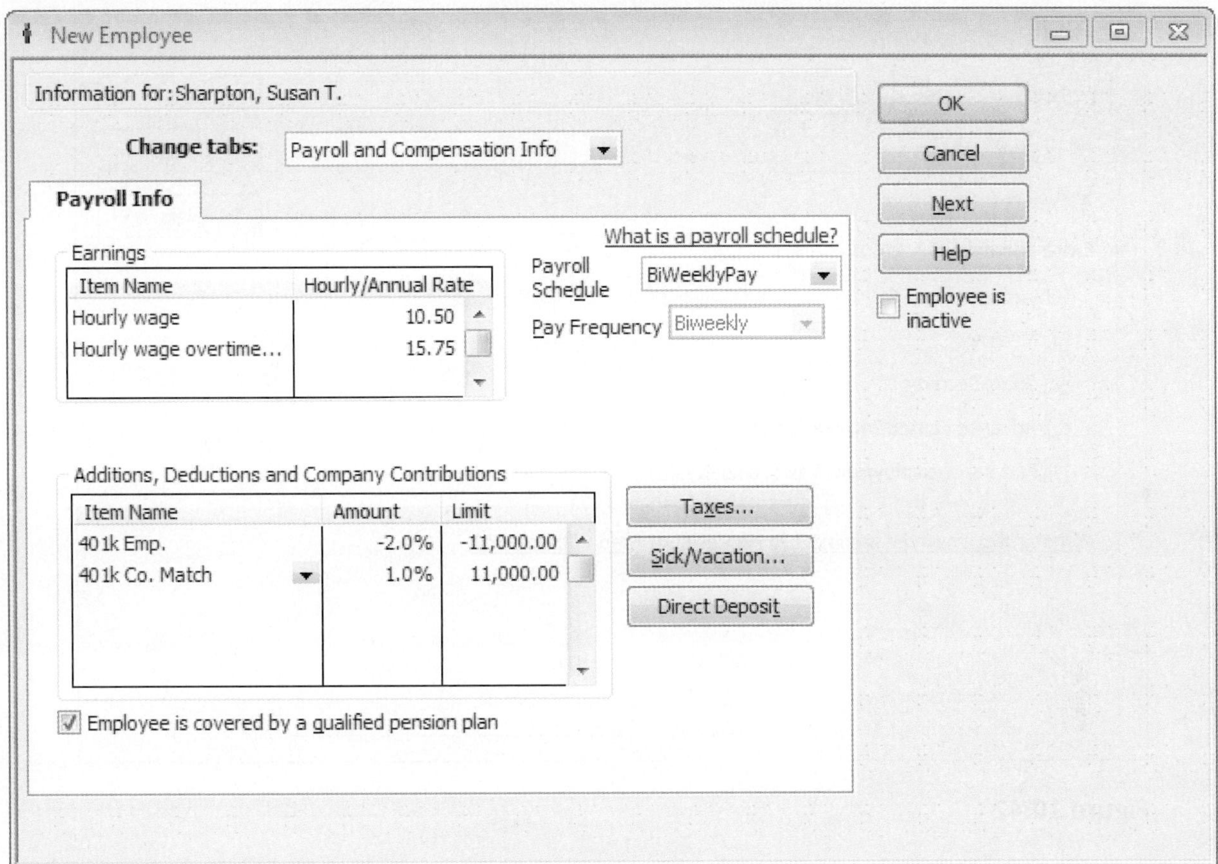

Figure 10:41

Enter Susan's salary information by following the next steps.

1. Place your cursor in **Item Name** and look up **Hourly wage.**
2. Tab to **Hourly/Annual Rate** and enter 10.50.
3. Place your cursor in the next row for **Item Name** and select **Hourly wage overtime (x1.5).** QBP will fill in the rate of $15.75.
4. Use your cursor and select **BiWeeklyPay** in the **Payroll Schedule.**
5. At the bottom, look up and select **401k Emp.** Tab to **Amount** and enter "2%".
6. Add the employer match by looking up and selecting **401k Co. Match.** Tab to **Amount** and enter "1%".

Click the **Taxes** button and follow the next steps to enter Susan's federal and state withholding information.

1. On the **Federal** tab illustrated in Figure 10:42, look up and select **Married** as the **Filing Status.**
2. Enter "0" in **Allowances.**

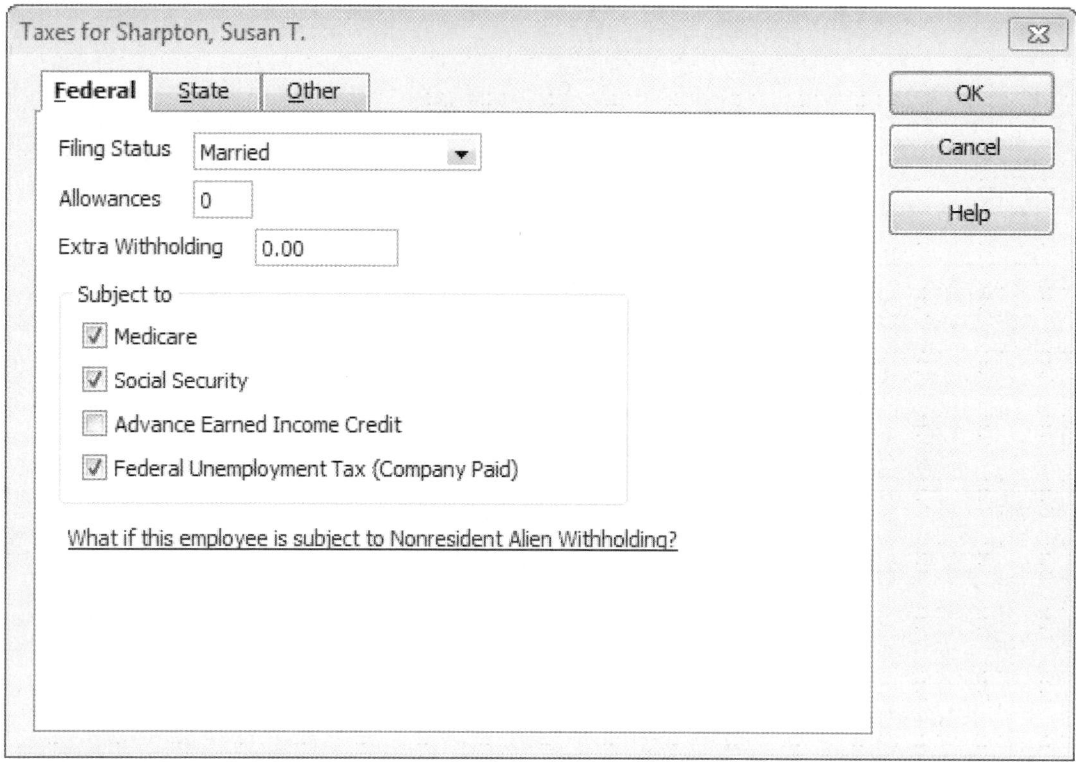

Figure 10:42

3. Click the **State** tab and verify that the information matches Figure 10:43. When finished, click **OK.**

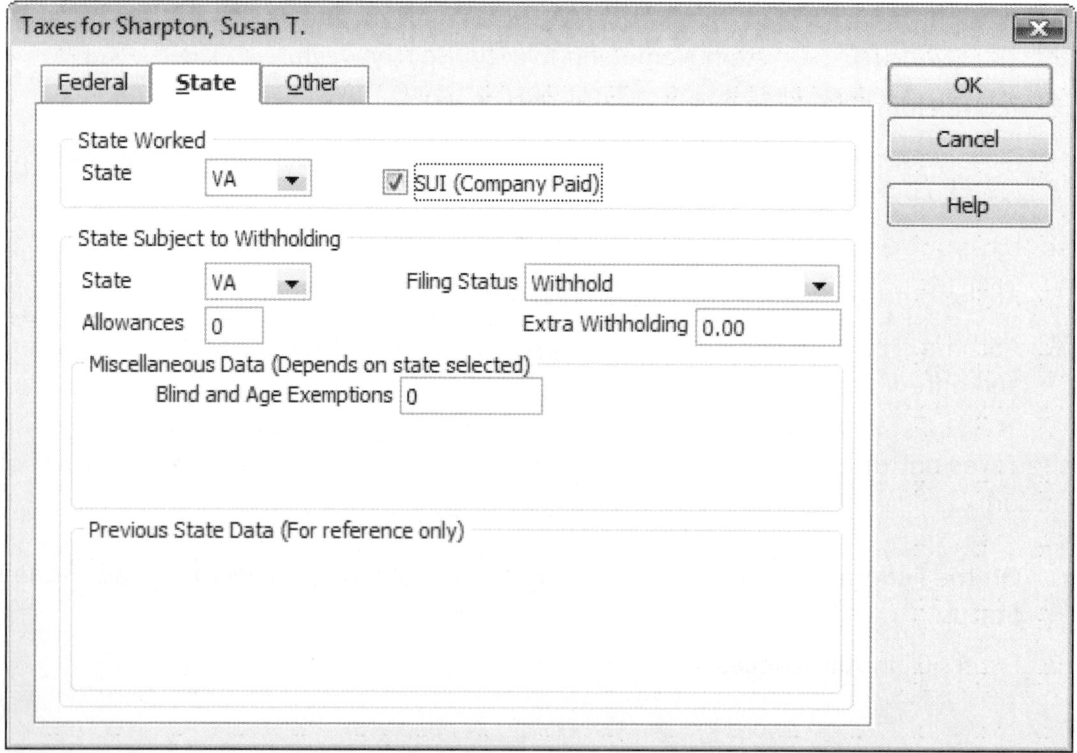

Figure 10:43

Now change the tab to **Employment Info** and enter Susan's hire date.

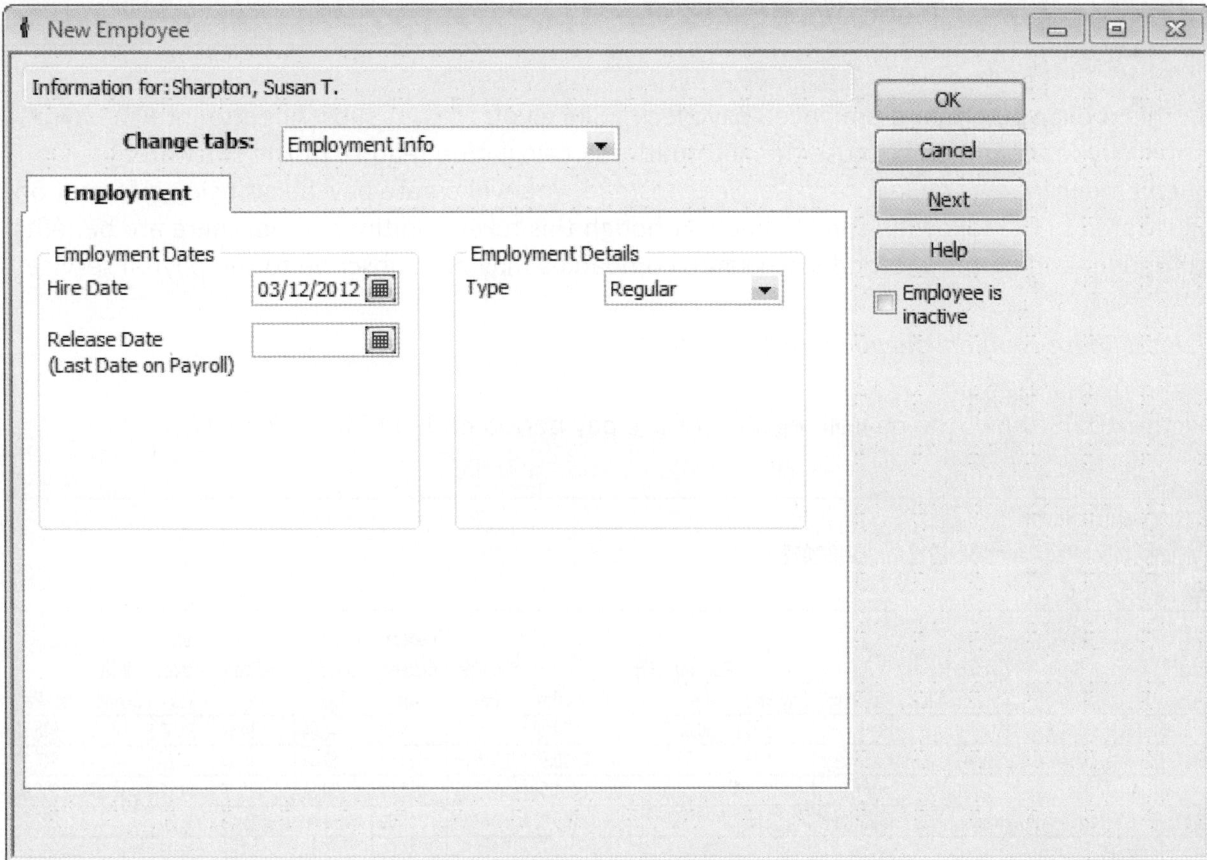

Figure 10:44

Click **OK** to save Susan's account. If prompted to set up local taxes and sick/vacation time, click **Leave As Is.**

Close the Employee Center.

Besides creating, you also need to know how to terminate an employee. You cannot delete an employee account with paycheck history. Instead, you enter a termination date under **Release Date** on the **Employment** tab and mark the **Employee is inactive** option.

Now that you understand managing employee accounts, you are ready to pay employees.

Note: In Chapter 4, the topic that followed this topic covered recording employee time because that chapter illustrated a service-based business using time to bill its customers. Because Baxter is a merchandising business, you do not need to enter timesheets. You can enter employee hours directly into the Enter Payroll Information window.

PAYING EMPLOYEES

In this topic, you prepare employee paychecks. Since you are not subscribed to Intuit's payroll service, you are not able to use the automatic tax calculation feature of the software. *(Remember there is a fee for this service.)* Instead, you will create paychecks using information illustrated in the following spreadsheet. Although this takes additional time, there are benefits to understanding this method since some companies may not subscribe to the payroll service.

(Note: There is an online video for this topic.)

Figure 10:45 shows the payroll register for the pay period ended March 18, 2012.

Baxter Garden Supply
Paychecks for Pay Period 3/5/2012 thru 3/18/2012

Check No.	Employee	Filing Status	Allow	Pay Type	Pay Rate	Regular Hrs	OT Hrs	Gross Pay	Taxable Pay	Federal Income Tax	Soc. Sec. (FICA) Tax	Medicare Tax	VA State Tax	401K Deduc.	Net Pay
1186	Beck, Dorothy L.	Married	2	Hourly wage	9.00	80.00		720.00	720.00	15.00	44.64	10.44	21.60	0.00	628.32
1187	Chester, Amanda W.	Single	1	Hourly wage	14.00	80.00		1,120.00	1,075.20	110.00	69.44	16.24	32.26	44.80	847.26
1188	Frost, Melvin H.	Single	1	Salary	1,461.54			1,461.54	1,373.85	155.00	90.62	21.19	41.22	87.69	1,065.82
1189	Hecter, Anthony H.	Single	1	Hourly wage	13.00	80.00		1,040.00	1,040.00	107.00	64.48	15.08	31.20	0.00	822.24
1190	Nunnley, Brandee M.	Married	1	Salary	1,211.54			1,211.54	1,211.54	85.00	75.12	17.57	36.35	0.00	997.50
1191	Prather, Samuel R.	Married	1	Salary	1,584.62			1,584.62	1,489.54	127.00	98.25	22.98	44.69	95.08	1,196.62
1192	Sharpton, Susan T.	Married	0	Hourly wage	10.50	40.00		420.00	411.60	11.00	26.04	6.09	12.35	8.40	356.12
	Totals					280.00	0.00	7,557.70		610.00	468.59	109.59	219.67	235.97	5,913.88
	Tax Basis									Circular E	6.20%	1.45%	3.00%		
	G/L Accounts							60000		23400	23400	23400	23600	23300	10300

Figure 10:45

Figure 10:46 shows the payroll register for employer costs.

Baxter Garden Supply Employer Costs for Pay Period 3/5/2012 thru 3/18/2012						
Employee	401K Match	ER Soc. Sec. (FICA)	ER Medicare	ER FUTA	ER SUTA	Health Insurance
Beck, Dorothy L.	0.00	44.64	10.44	5.76	10.80	0.00
Chester, Amanda W.	22.40	69.44	16.24	8.96	16.80	90.00
Frost, Melvin H.	43.85	90.62	21.19	0.00	10.40	125.00
Hecter, Anthony H.	0.00	64.48	15.08	8.32	15.60	90.00
Nunnley, Brandee M.	0.00	75.12	17.57	7.55	18.17	125.00
Prather, Samuel R.	47.54	98.25	22.98	0.00	1.15	125.00
Sharpton, Susan T.	4.20	26.04	6.09	3.36	6.30	0.00
Totals	117.99	468.59	109.59	33.95	79.22	555.00
Tax Basis	50% Match	6.20%	1.45%	0.8%	1.5%	
G/L Accounts	23300 / 60500	23400 / 61000	23400 / 61000	23500 / 61000	23700 / 61000	23750 / 60600

Figure 10:46

Now follow the next steps to create employee paychecks using the spreadsheet information.

Steps to Create Employee Paychecks

1. Click **Pay Employees** on the **Home** page to open the Enter Payroll Information window illustrated in Figure 10:47.

   Set the **Pay Period Ends** date to 3/18/12; **Check Date** to 3/19/12; and verify that the **Bank Account** is 10300 Payroll Checking. Click **Check All** to select all employees.

   Baxter does not use timesheets, so you must verify that employee hours agree with the hours reported in Figure 10:45. You can enter hours for each employee directly in this window.

   This is the first paycheck for Susan Sharpton, so scroll down to Susan's record and enter "40" in the **Hourly wage** column.

   Do not worry that the payroll checking balance does not show enough to cover payroll. Companies normally do not carry large balances in the payroll account. Instead, funds are transferred on payday to cover the amount of payroll. In the next chapter, you will transfer funds from the regular checking account into this account.

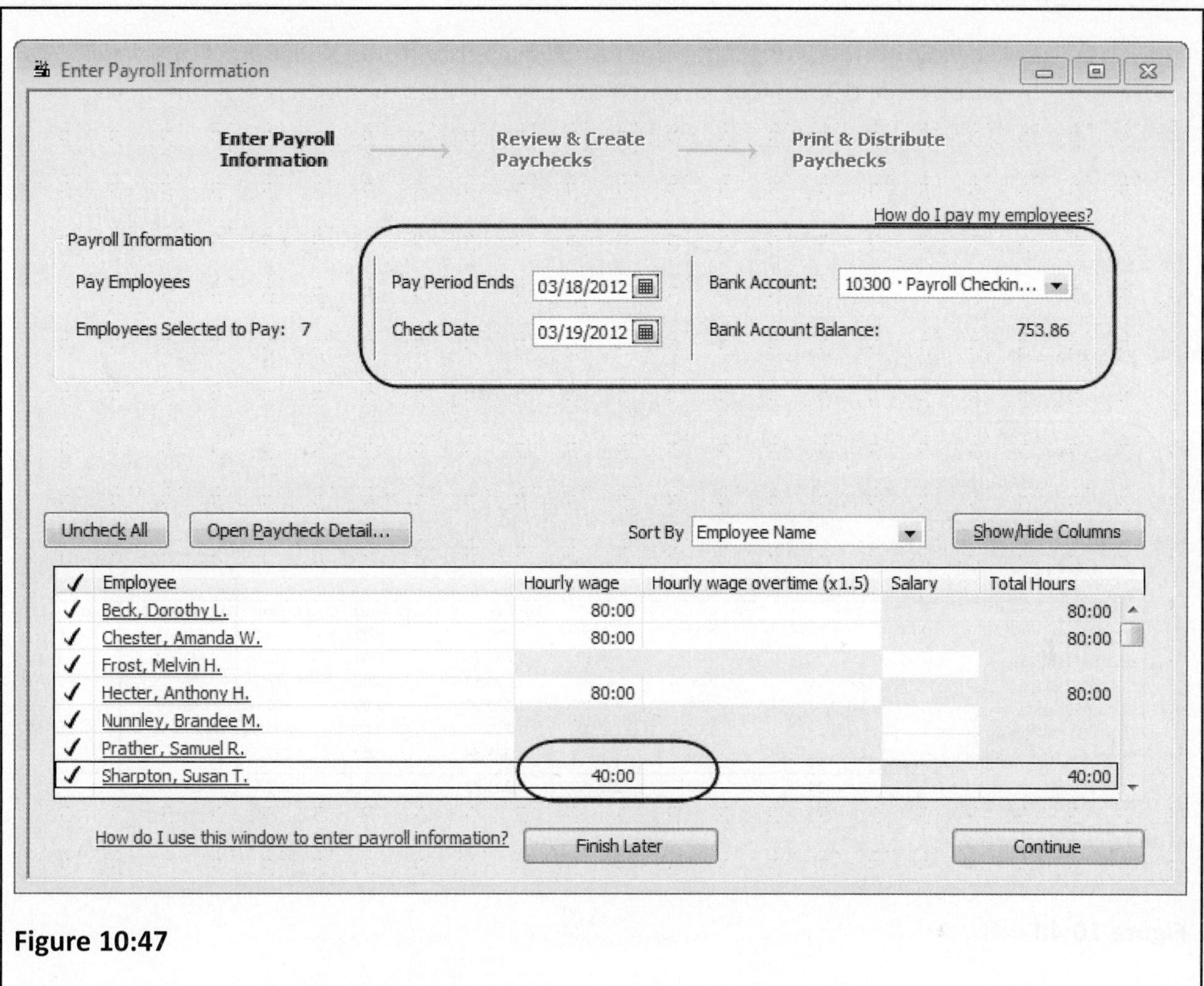
Enter Payroll Information
Enter Payroll Information
Review & Create Paychecks
Print & Distribute Paychecks
How do I pay my employees?
Payroll Information
Pay Employees
Employees Selected to Pay: 7
Pay Period Ends 03/18/2012
Check Date 03/19/2012
Bank Account: 10300 · Payroll Checkin...
Bank Account Balance: 753.86
Uncheck All
Open Paycheck Detail...
Sort By Employee Name
Show/Hide Columns
Employee
Hourly wage
Hourly wage overtime (x1.5)
Salary
Total Hours
Beck, Dorothy L. 80:00 80:00
Chester, Amanda W. 80:00 80:00
Frost, Melvin H.
Hecter, Anthony H. 80:00 80:00
Nunnley, Brandee M.
Prather, Samuel R.
Sharpton, Susan T. 40:00 40:00
How do I use this window to enter payroll information?
Finish Later
Continue

Figure 10:47

2. Click **Continue**. Verify that the **Print paychecks from QuickBooks** option is selected and **Total Hours** match the payroll register. (See Figure 10:48.)

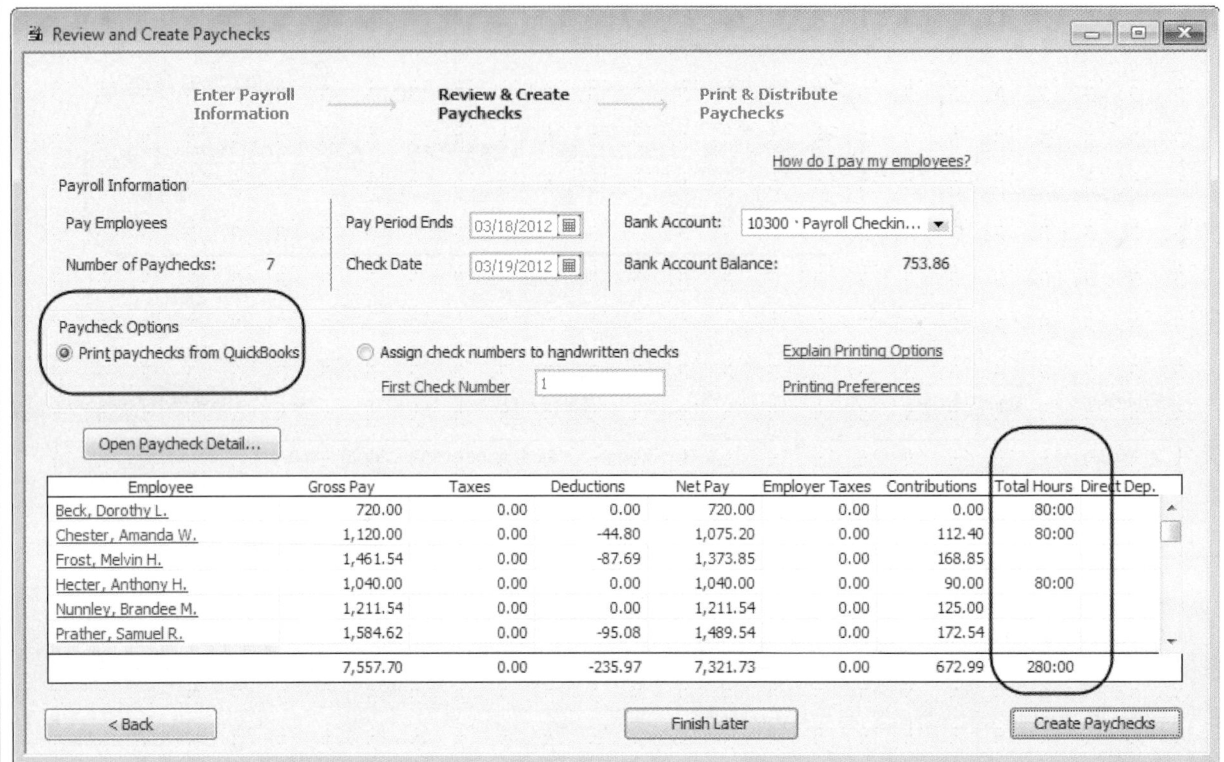

Figure 10:48

Preliminary check totals appear at the bottom. Notice that the total for **Gross Pay** agrees with gross pay on the worksheet.

No tax tables are loaded in the software, so totals for taxes and deductions are not displayed. You will manually enter the taxes in the following steps.

3. Click **Beck, Dorothy L.** or click **Open Paycheck Detail** to open paycheck details. Step 4 illustrates entering information in the fields circled in Figure 10:49. *(Note: This information is gathered from the payroll spreadsheets.)*

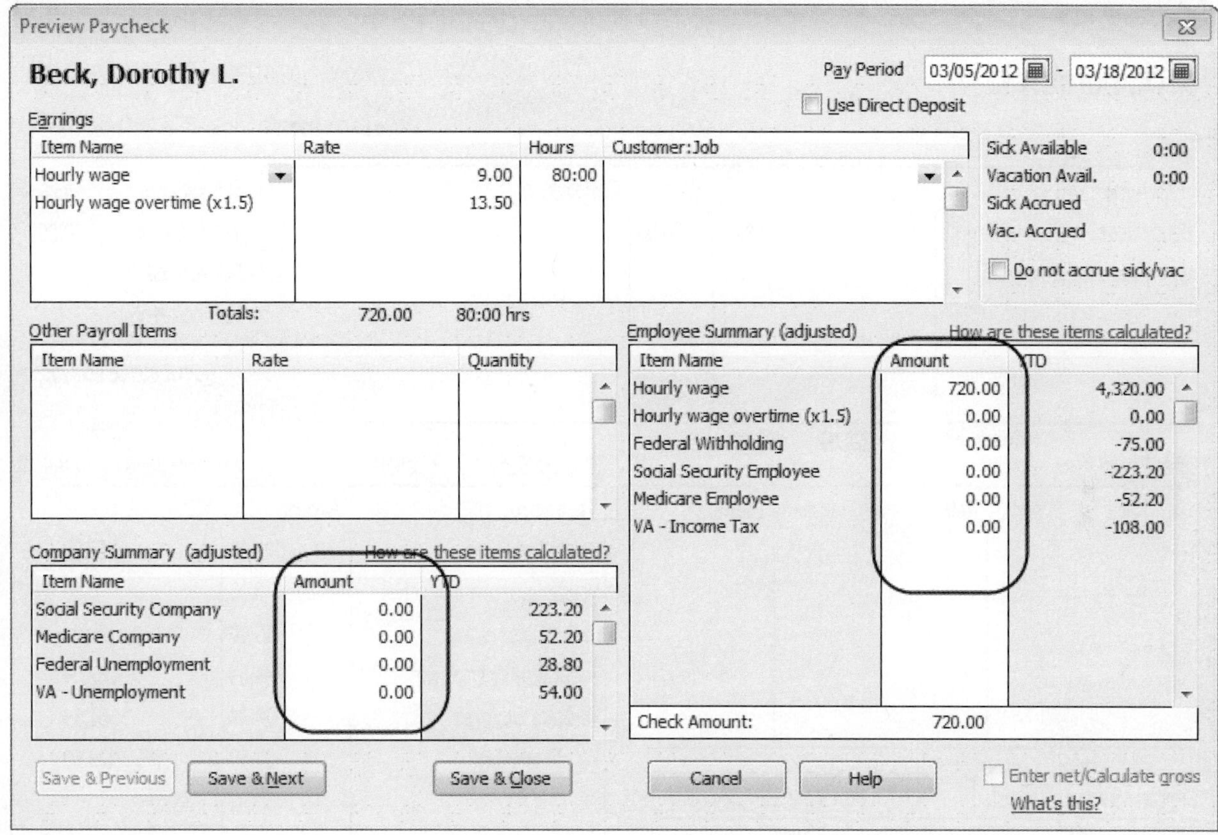

Figure 10:49

4. Notice that Dorothy does not contribute to the 401K plan or participate in the health insurance plan. When an employee does participate, you will not enter amounts for these items because QBP will already calculate the amount.

   Under **Company Summary**, place your cursor in **Social Security Company** and enter "44.64." Tab to **Medicare Company** and enter "10.44." Now enter the remaining employer taxes as follows.

Federal Unemployment (FUTA)	5.76
VA-Unemployment (SUTA)	10.80

5. Tab to **Employee Summary** and enter the amounts on the worksheet. *(Note: You will enter a positive amount and then QBP converts it to a negative amount.)*

Federal Withholding	15.00
Social Security Employee	44.64
Medicare Employee	10.44
VA – Income Tax	21.60

6. Dorothy's completed paycheck is shown in Figure 10:50. Her **Check Amount** agrees with the net pay amount on the worksheet.

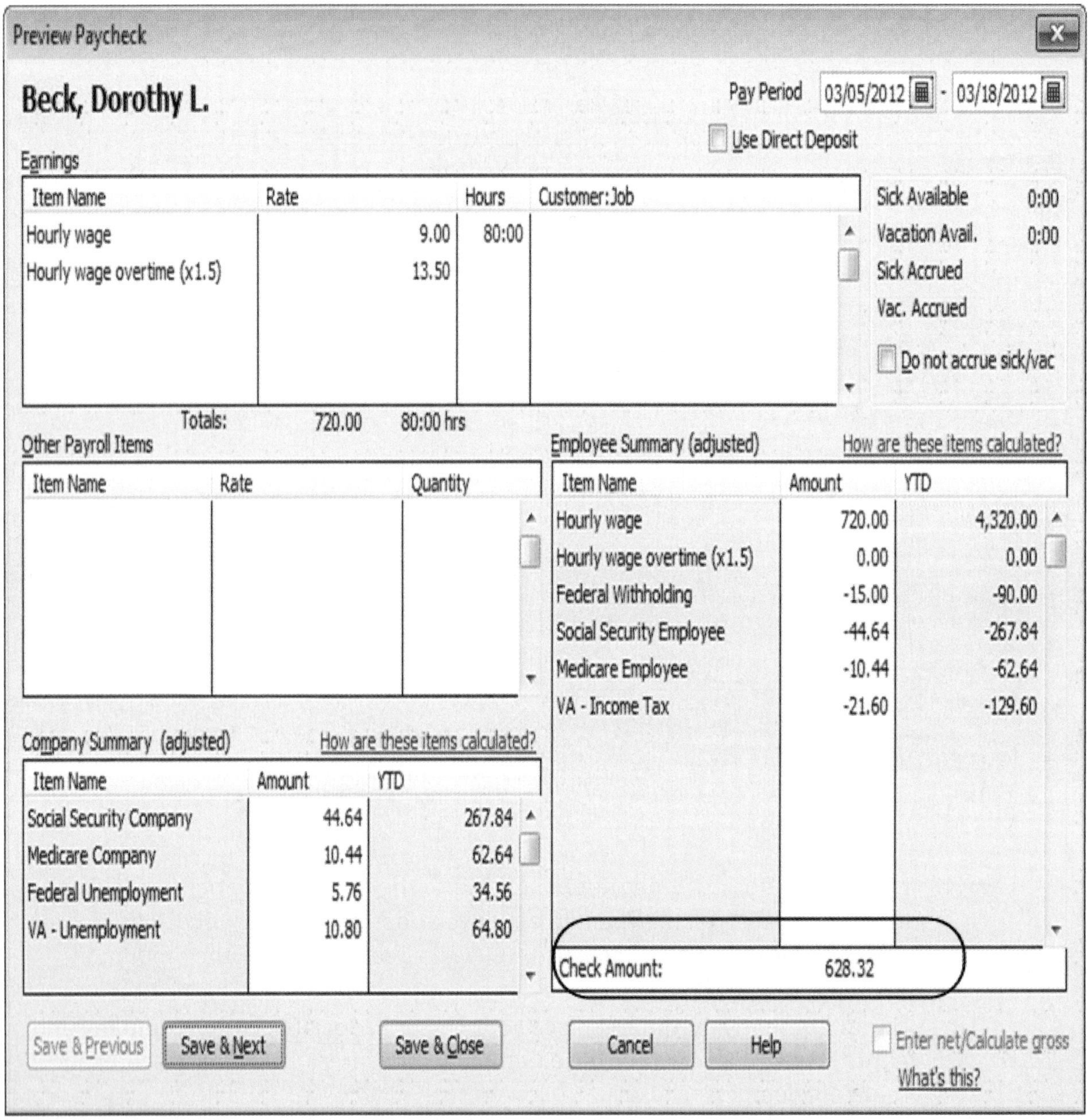

Preview Paycheck

Beck, Dorothy L.

Pay Period 03/05/2012 - 03/18/2012

Use Direct Deposit

Earnings

Item Name	Rate	Hours	Customer:Job
Hourly wage	9.00	80:00	
Hourly wage overtime (x1.5)	13.50		
Totals:	720.00	80:00 hrs	

Sick Available	0:00
Vacation Avail.	0:00
Sick Accrued	
Vac. Accrued	

Do not accrue sick/vac

Other Payroll Items

Item Name	Rate	Quantity

Employee Summary (adjusted) How are these items calculated?

Item Name	Amount	YTD
Hourly wage	720.00	4,320.00
Hourly wage overtime (x1.5)	0.00	0.00
Federal Withholding	-15.00	-90.00
Social Security Employee	-44.64	-267.84
Medicare Employee	-10.44	-62.64
VA - Income Tax	-21.60	-129.60
Check Amount:	628.32	

Company Summary (adjusted) How are these items calculated?

Item Name	Amount	YTD
Social Security Company	44.64	267.84
Medicare Company	10.44	62.64
Federal Unemployment	5.76	34.56
VA - Unemployment	10.80	64.80

Save & Previous | Save & Next | Save & Close | Cancel | Help | Enter net/Calculate gross | What's this?

Figure 10:50

7. Click **Save & Next** and enter the following paycheck information for **Amanda W. Chester.** *(Note: Since you will not enter 401K or health insurance amounts, we have scrolled to the bottom of Company Summary items so that all tax amounts display.)*

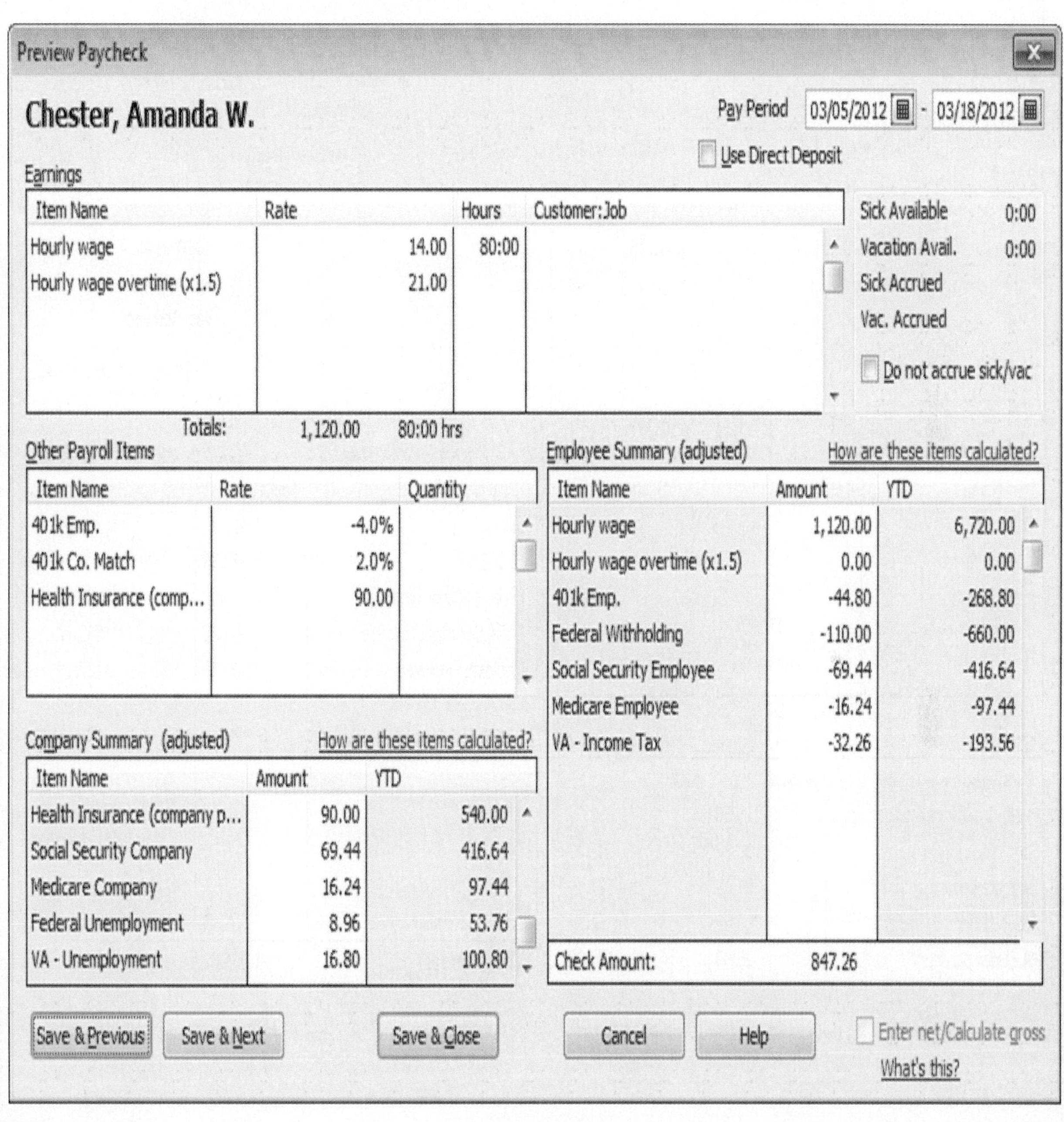

Figure 10:51

8. Continue clicking **Save & Next** until you have entered the remaining paychecks illustrated next.

Frost, Melvin H.

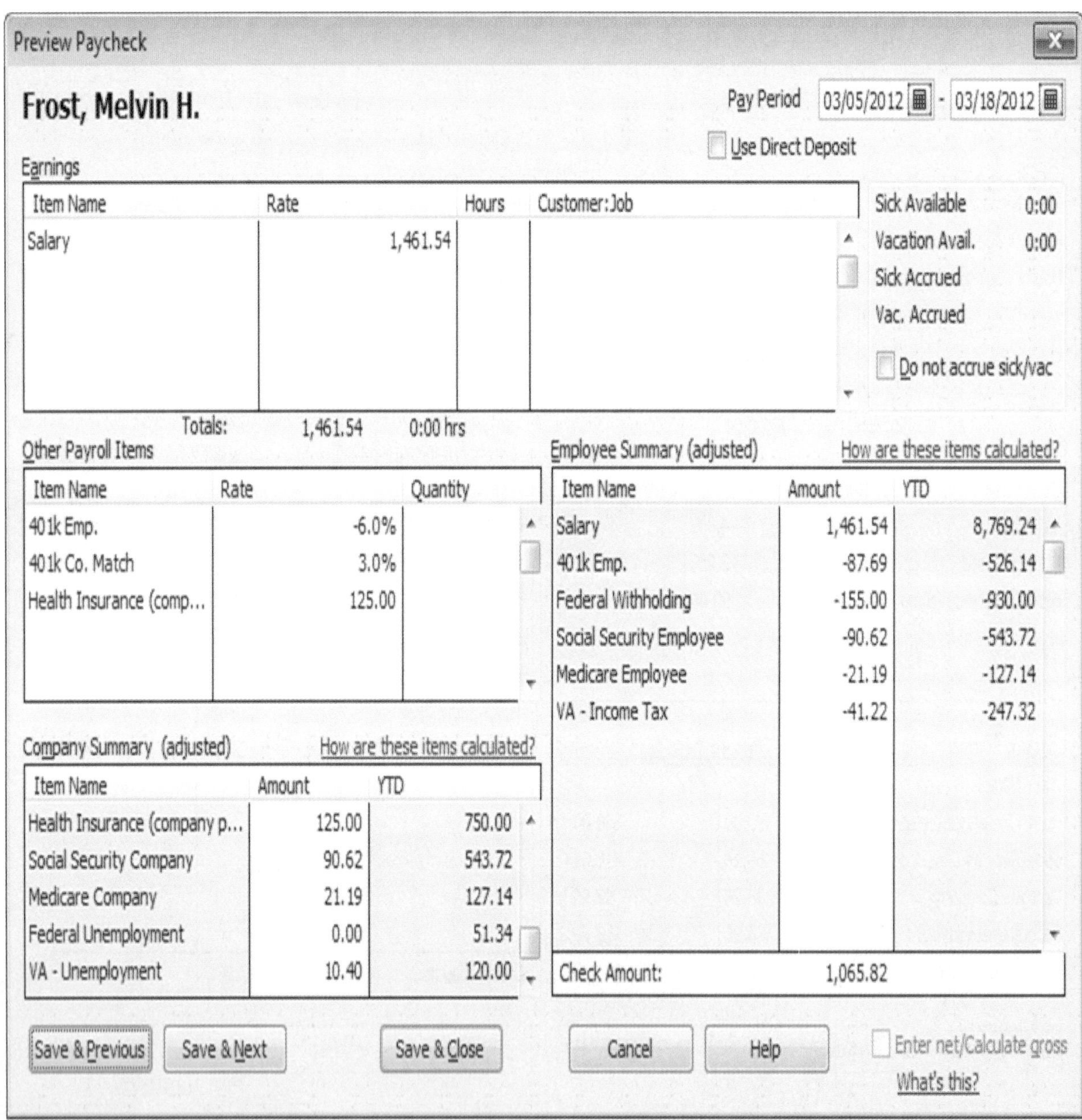

Figure 10:52

(Notice that unemployment taxes are zero because his year-to-date wages exceed the taxable limit for this year.)

Hecter, Anthony H.

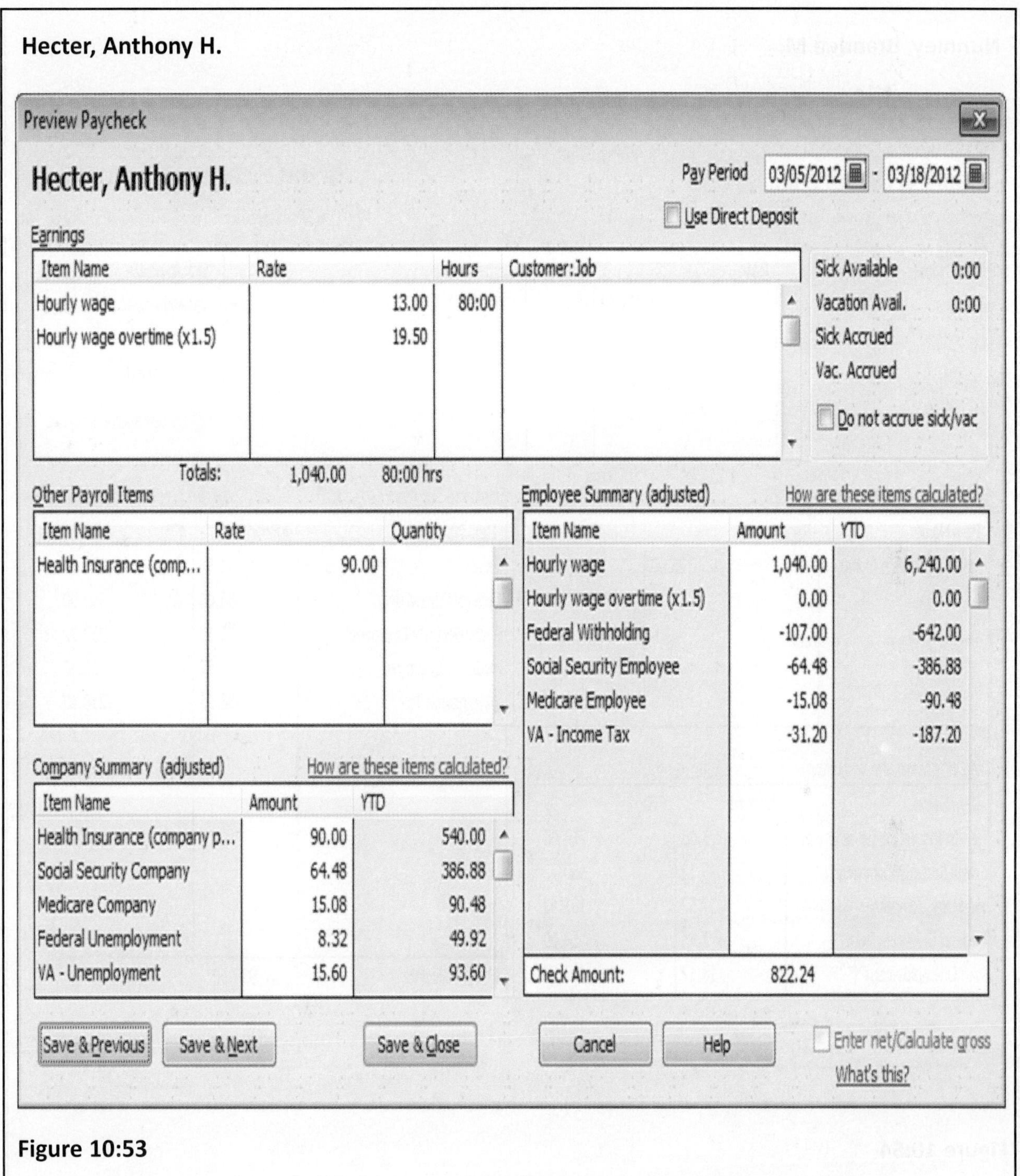

Preview Paycheck

Hecter, Anthony H.

Pay Period 03/05/2012 - 03/18/2012

Use Direct Deposit

Earnings

Item Name	Rate	Hours	Customer:Job
Hourly wage	13.00	80:00	
Hourly wage overtime (x1.5)	19.50		
Totals:	1,040.00	80:00 hrs	

Sick Available	0:00
Vacation Avail.	0:00
Sick Accrued	
Vac. Accrued	

Do not accrue sick/vac

Other Payroll Items

Item Name	Rate	Quantity
Health Insurance (comp...	90.00	

Employee Summary (adjusted) How are these items calculated?

Item Name	Amount	YTD
Hourly wage	1,040.00	6,240.00
Hourly wage overtime (x1.5)	0.00	0.00
Federal Withholding	-107.00	-642.00
Social Security Employee	-64.48	-386.88
Medicare Employee	-15.08	-90.48
VA - Income Tax	-31.20	-187.20

Check Amount: 822.24

Company Summary (adjusted) How are these items calculated?

Item Name	Amount	YTD
Health Insurance (company p...	90.00	540.00
Social Security Company	64.48	386.88
Medicare Company	15.08	90.48
Federal Unemployment	8.32	49.92
VA - Unemployment	15.60	93.60

Save & Previous | Save & Next | Save & Close | Cancel | Help

Enter net/Calculate gross

What's this?

Figure 10:53

Nunnley, Brandee M.

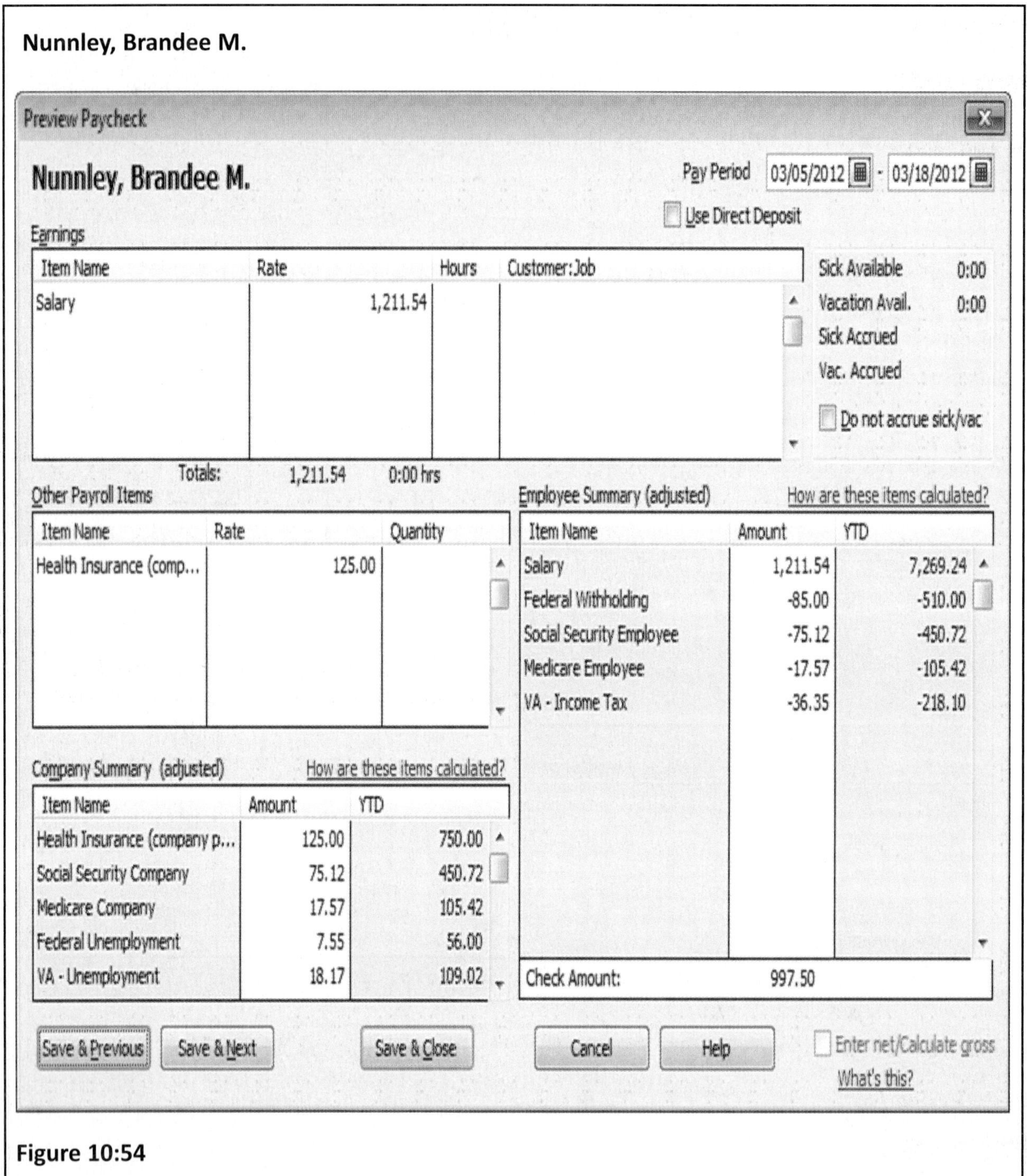

Figure 10:54

Prather, Samuel R.

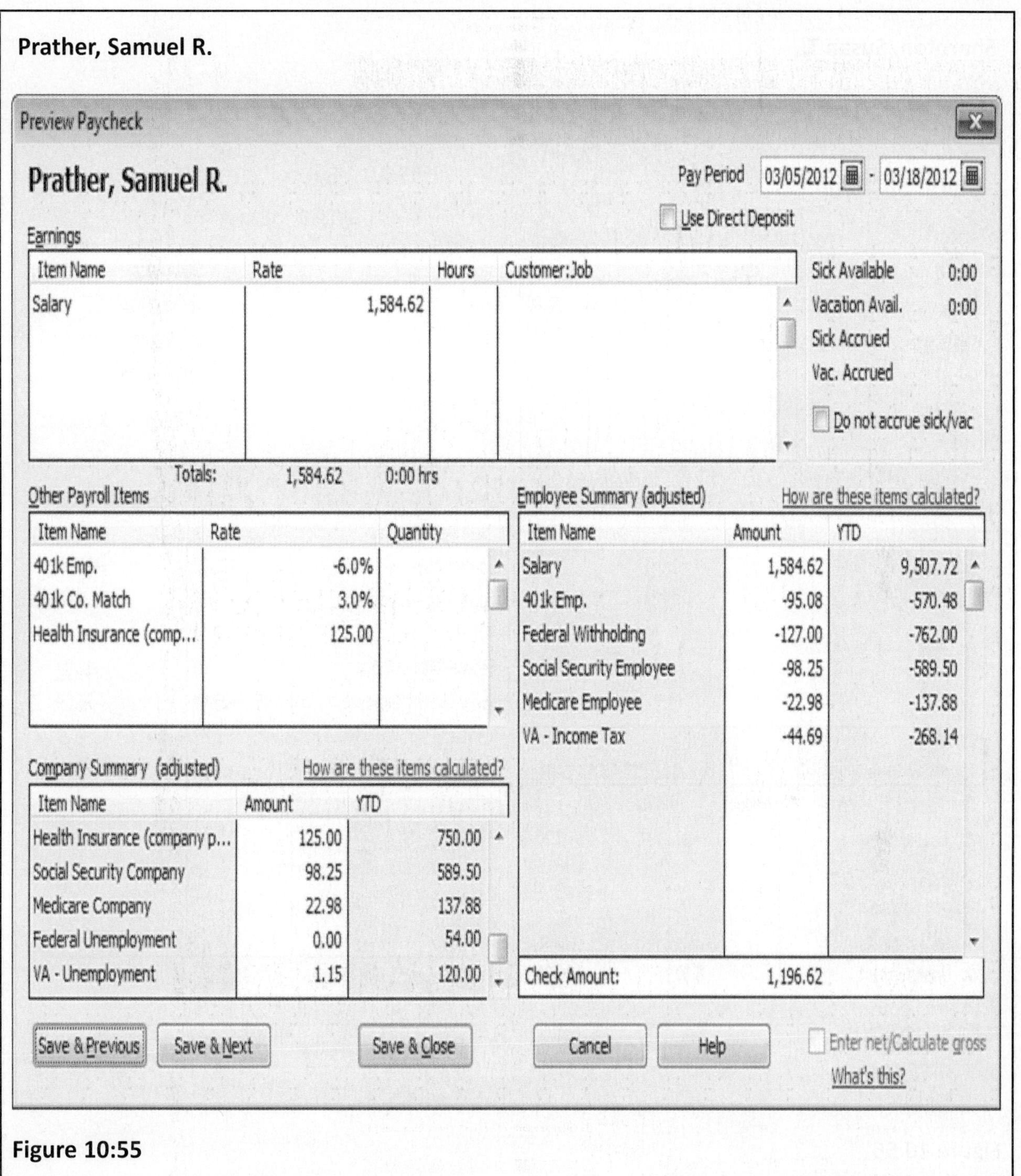

Figure 10:55

Sharpton, Susan T.

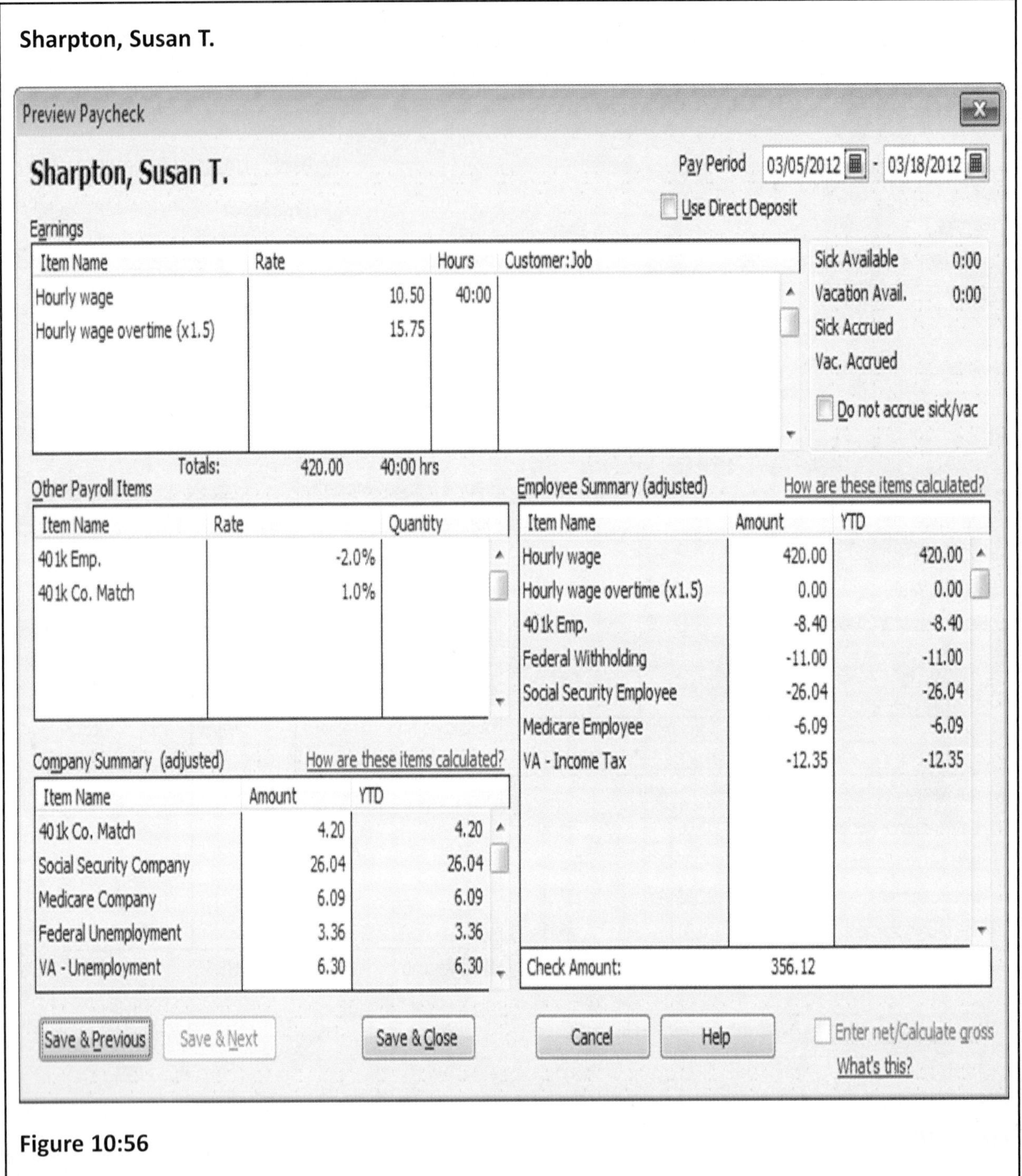

Figure 10:56

9. Click **Save & Close.** Your totals should agree with those illustrated next. If you find an error, click the employee's paycheck and make corrections.

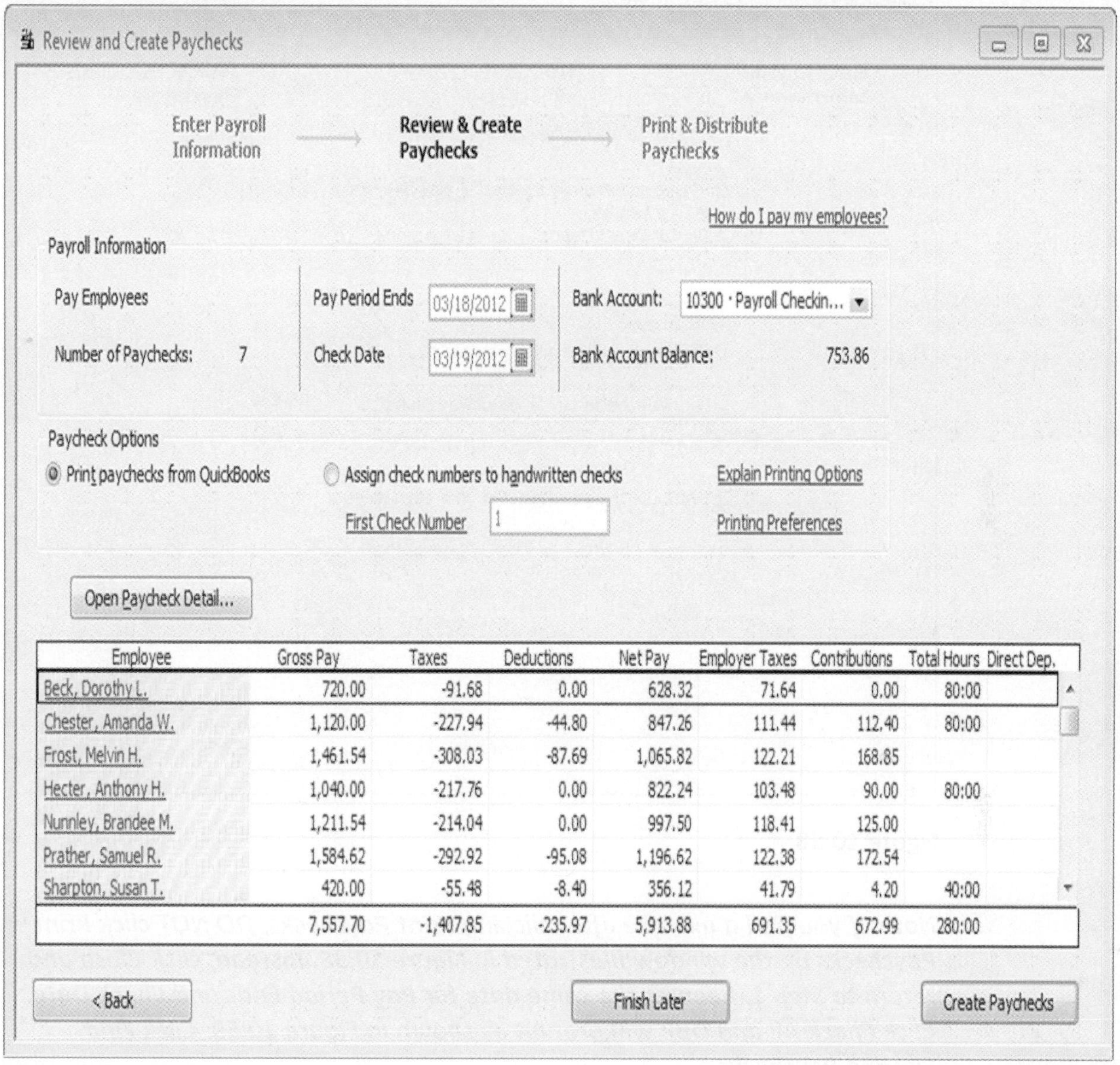

Review and Create Paychecks

Enter Payroll Information → **Review & Create Paychecks** → Print & Distribute Paychecks

How do I pay my employees?

Payroll Information

Pay Employees | Pay Period Ends 03/18/2012 | Bank Account: 10300 · Payroll Checkin...

Number of Paychecks: 7 | Check Date 03/19/2012 | Bank Account Balance: 753.86

Paycheck Options

Print paychecks from QuickBooks | Assign check numbers to handwritten checks | Explain Printing Options

First Check Number 1 | Printing Preferences

Open Paycheck Detail...

Employee	Gross Pay	Taxes	Deductions	Net Pay	Employer Taxes	Contributions	Total Hours	Direct Dep.
Beck, Dorothy L.	720.00	-91.68	0.00	628.32	71.64	0.00	80:00	
Chester, Amanda W.	1,120.00	-227.94	-44.80	847.26	111.44	112.40	80:00	
Frost, Melvin H.	1,461.54	-308.03	-87.69	1,065.82	122.21	168.85		
Hecter, Anthony H.	1,040.00	-217.76	0.00	822.24	103.48	90.00	80:00	
Nunnley, Brandee M.	1,211.54	-214.04	0.00	997.50	118.41	125.00		
Prather, Samuel R.	1,584.62	-292.92	-95.08	1,196.62	122.38	172.54		
Sharpton, Susan T.	420.00	-55.48	-8.40	356.12	41.79	4.20	40:00	
	7,557.70	-1,407.85	-235.97	5,913.88	691.35	672.99	280:00	

< Back | Finish Later | Create Paychecks

Figure 10:57

10. Click **Create Paychecks** and seven paychecks are created and ready for printing.

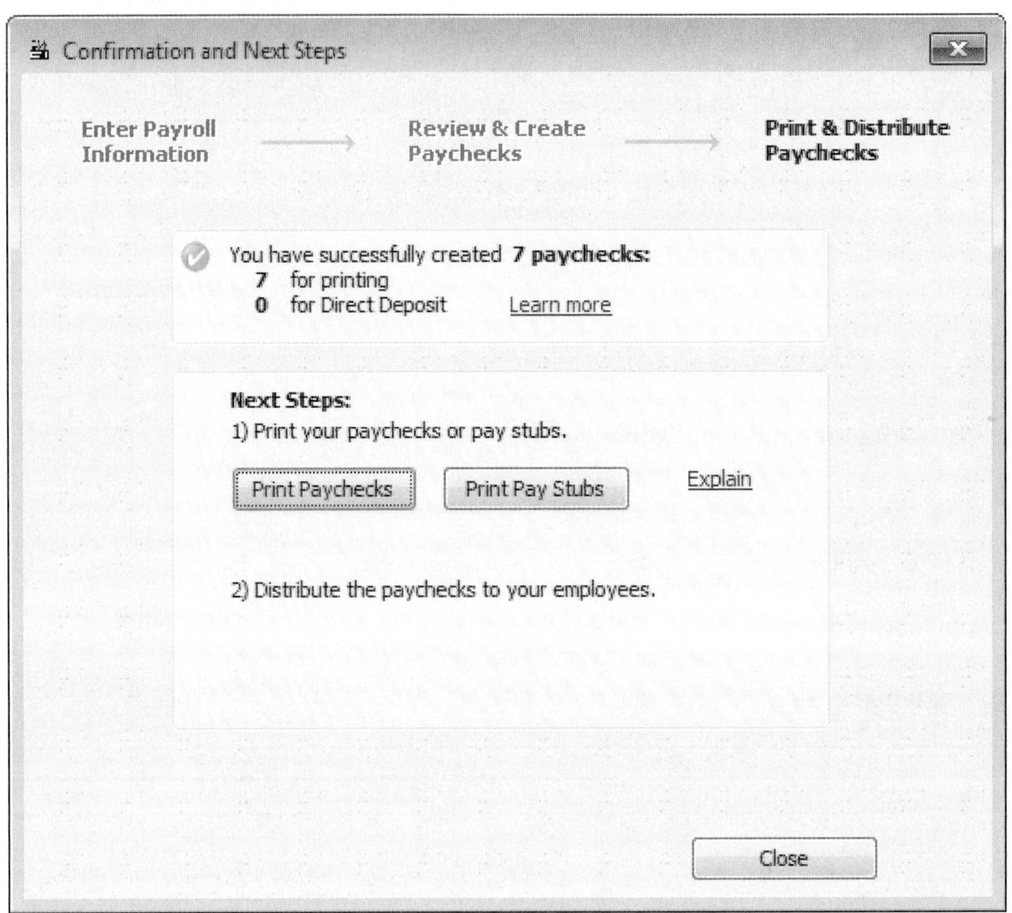

Figure 10:58

Note: If you find a mistake after clicking Print Paychecks, DO NOT click Print Paychecks on the window illustrated in Figure 10:58. Instead, click Close and return to Step 1. Reenter the same date for Pay Period Ends and Check Date. Click Check All and QBP will prompt as shown in Figure 10:59. Click Find Existing Paychecks.

If there are no mistakes, proceed to Step 11.

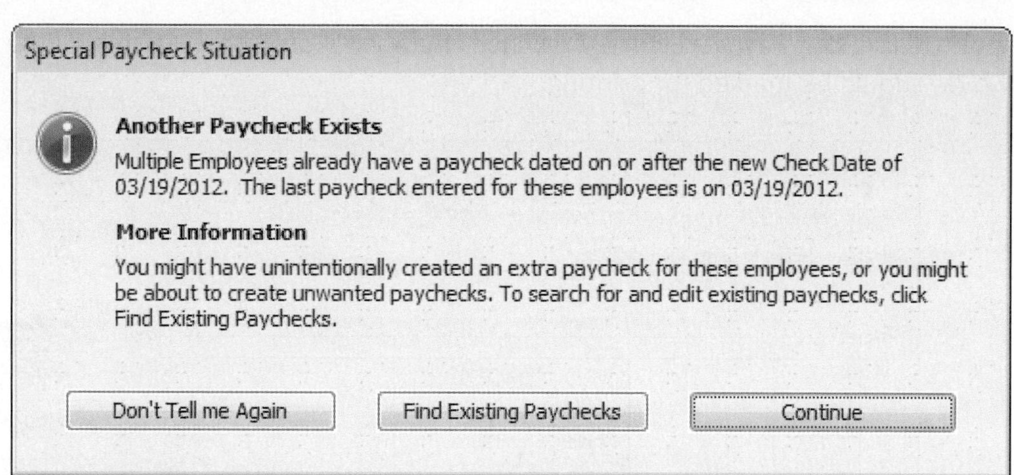

Figure 10:59

When the window illustrated in Figure 10:60 opens, highlight a paycheck and click **Edit.** Open the **Paycheck Detail,** make corrections, and **Save & Close.** When finished, click **Done**. Close the Enter Payroll Information window.

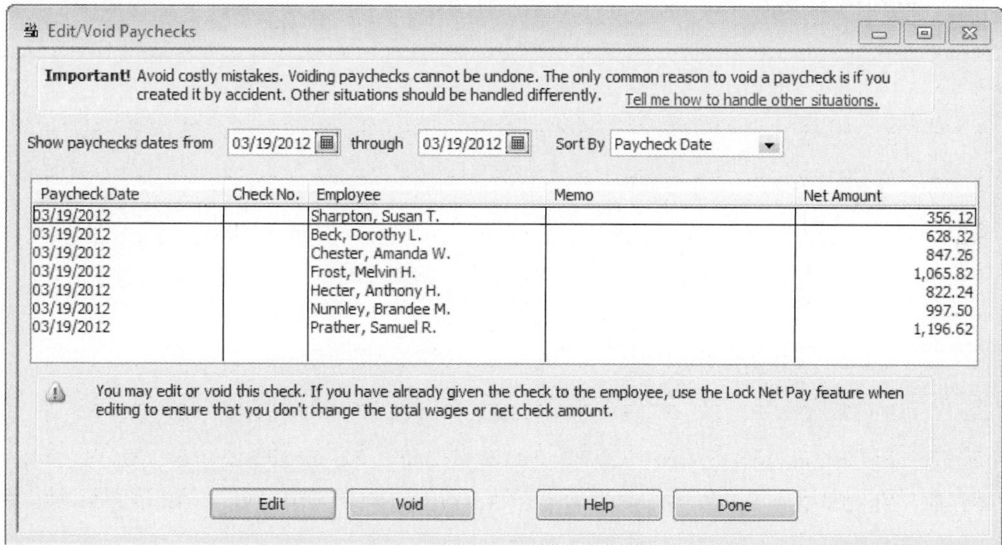

Figure 10:60

To return to printing paychecks, click ***File>>Print Forms>>Paychecks*** on the main menu. This opens the window illustrated in the next step.

11. Click **Print Paychecks.** The first check number should be 1186 and all the checks should be marked for printing.

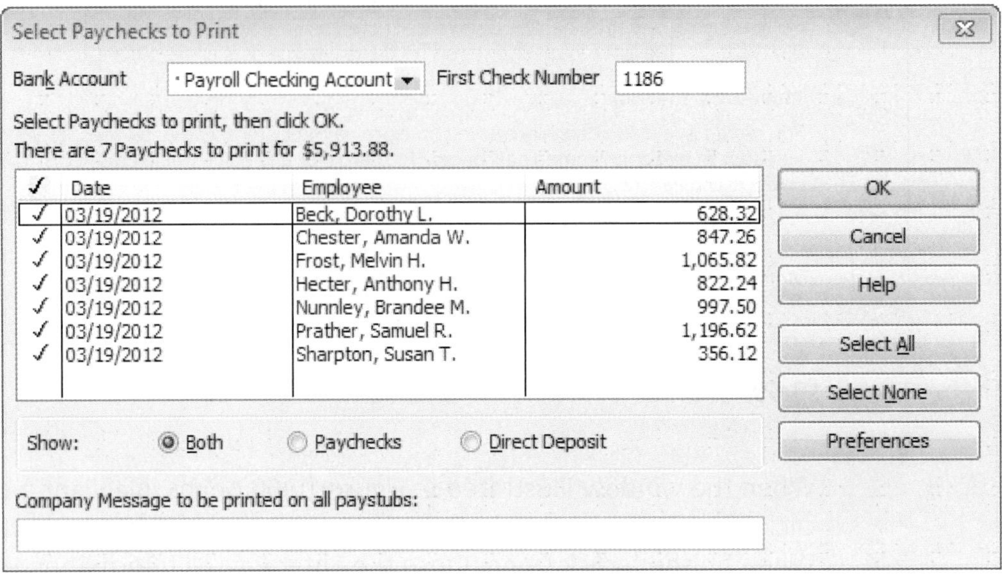

Figure 10:61

12. Click **OK.** Select a printer and then click **Print.** Figure 10:62 shows the first paycheck.

3/19/2012

Dorothy L. Beck **628.32

Six Hundred Twenty-Eight and 32/100***

Dorothy L. Beck
3743 North Druid Hills Road
Arlington, VA 23045

Pay Period: 03/05/2012 - 03/18/2012

Employee: Dorothy L. Beck, 3743 North Druid Hills Road, Arlington, VA 23045
Status (Fed/State): Married/Withhold
Pay Period: 03/05/2012 - 03/18/2012
Allowances/Extra: Fed-2/0/VA-0
Pay Date: 03/19/2012

Earnings and Hours	Qty	Rate	Current	YTD Amount
Hourly wage	80:00	9.00	720.00	4,320.00

Taxes	Current	YTD Amount
Federal Withholding	-15.00	-90.00
Social Security Employee	-44.64	-267.84
Medicare Employee	-10.44	-62.64
VA - Income Tax	-21.60	-129.60
	-91.68	-550.08
Net Pay	628.32	3,769.92

Baxter Garden Supply, 1352 W. Maple Ave, Arlington, VA 23523 Powered by Intuit Payroll

Employee: Dorothy L. Beck, 3743 North Druid Hills Road, Arlington, VA 23045
Status (Fed/State): Married/Withhold
Pay Period: 03/05/2012 - 03/18/2012
Allowances/Extra: Fed-2/0/VA-0
Pay Date: 03/19/2012

Earnings and Hours	Qty	Rate	Current	YTD Amount
Hourly wage	80:00	9.00	720.00	4,320.00

Taxes	Current	YTD Amount
Federal Withholding	-15.00	-90.00
Social Security Employee	-44.64	-267.84
Medicare Employee	-10.44	-62.64
VA - Income Tax	-21.60	-129.60
	-91.68	-550.08
Net Pay	628.32	3,769.92

Baxter Garden Supply, 1352 W. Maple Ave, Arlington, VA 23523 Powered by Intuit Payroll

Figure 10:62

13. After printing, QBP confirms that checks printed correctly. Click **OK.** *(Note: If prompted to subscribe to a payroll service, select* **No, and don't show me this message again** *and click* ***OK.)*** Click **Close** on the confirmation window.

You have just printed paychecks. Now trace the entries that posted.

BEHIND THE KEYS OF A POSTED PAYCHECK

You will now trace the entries made after printing the paychecks by following the next steps.

STEPS TO TRACING PAYCHECK ENTRIES

1. Click **Reports** on the Icon bar. Select the **Employees & Payroll** category and open the **Payroll Transaction Detail** report. Enter **3/19/12** as the date range.

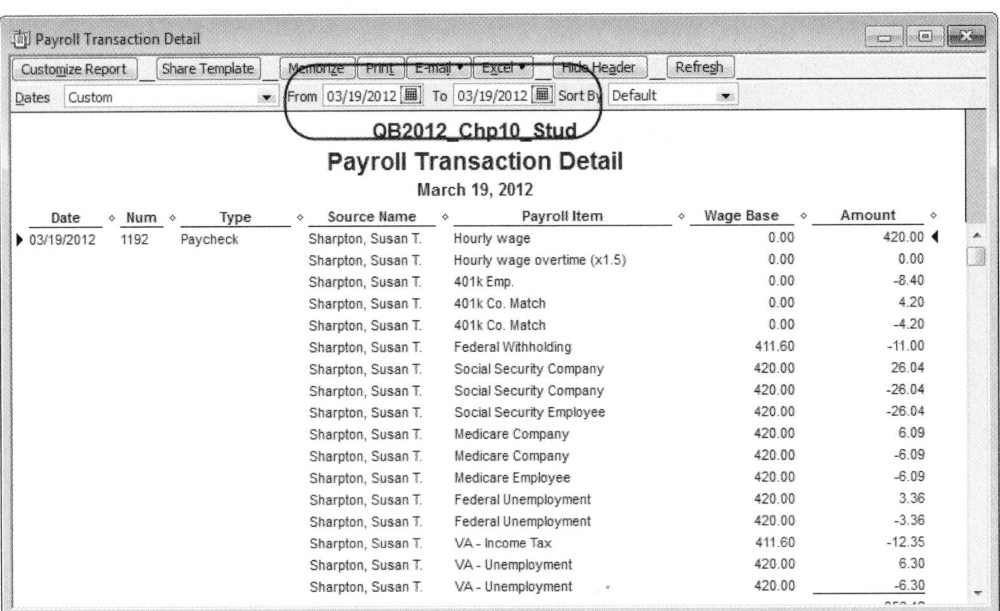

QB2012_Chp10_Stud

Payroll Transaction Detail

March 19, 2012

Date	Num	Type	Source Name	Payroll Item	Wage Base	Amount
03/19/2012	1192	Paycheck	Sharpton, Susan T.	Hourly wage	0.00	420.00
			Sharpton, Susan T.	Hourly wage overtime (x1.5)	0.00	0.00
			Sharpton, Susan T.	401k Emp.	0.00	-8.40
			Sharpton, Susan T.	401k Co. Match	0.00	4.20
			Sharpton, Susan T.	401k Co. Match	0.00	-4.20
			Sharpton, Susan T.	Federal Withholding	411.60	-11.00
			Sharpton, Susan T.	Social Security Company	420.00	26.04
			Sharpton, Susan T.	Social Security Company	420.00	-26.04
			Sharpton, Susan T.	Social Security Employee	420.00	-26.04
			Sharpton, Susan T.	Medicare Company	420.00	6.09
			Sharpton, Susan T.	Medicare Company	420.00	-6.09
			Sharpton, Susan T.	Medicare Employee	420.00	-6.09
			Sharpton, Susan T.	Federal Unemployment	420.00	3.36
			Sharpton, Susan T.	Federal Unemployment	420.00	-3.36
			Sharpton, Susan T.	VA - Income Tax	411.60	-12.35
			Sharpton, Susan T.	VA - Unemployment	420.00	6.30
			Sharpton, Susan T.	VA - Unemployment	420.00	-6.30

Figure 10:63

2. Now customize the report to show additional information. Click **Customize Report** and

   On the Display tab:

Add columns:	Trans #, Account, Debit, Credit
Remove columns:	Wage Base, Amount

   On the Filters tab, under Current Filter Choices:
   Click **Detail Level** and remove the filter
   Click **Payroll Item** and remove the filter

   On the Header/Footer tab:
   Type "Payroll Journal" as the **Report Title.** Click **OK.**

   Figure 10:64 shows the customized report listing all accounts affected by an employee's paycheck. Notice that the accounts affected match payroll item settings discussed in the *Payroll Items* topic. You also see the audit trail code under **Tran #** and **Type.**

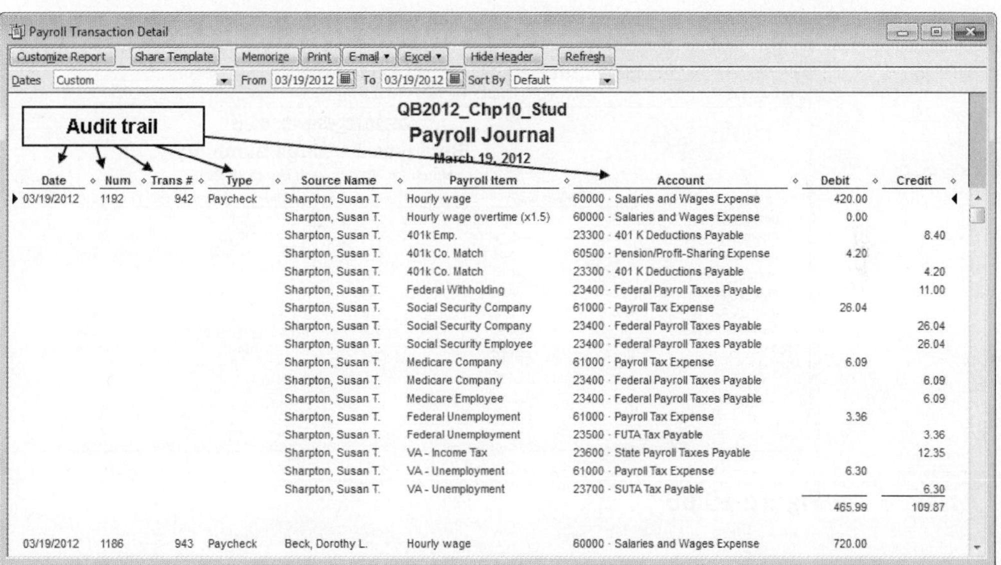

Date	Num	Trans #	Type	Source Name	Payroll Item	Account	Debit	Credit
03/19/2012	1192	942	Paycheck	Sharpton, Susan T.	Hourly wage	60000 · Salaries and Wages Expense	420.00	
				Sharpton, Susan T.	Hourly wage overtime (x1.5)	60000 · Salaries and Wages Expense	0.00	
				Sharpton, Susan T.	401k Emp.	23300 · 401 K Deductions Payable		8.40
				Sharpton, Susan T.	401k Co. Match	60500 · Pension/Profit-Sharing Expense	4.20	
				Sharpton, Susan T.	401k Co. Match	23300 · 401 K Deductions Payable		4.20
				Sharpton, Susan T.	Federal Withholding	23400 · Federal Payroll Taxes Payable		11.00
				Sharpton, Susan T.	Social Security Company	61000 · Payroll Tax Expense	26.04	
				Sharpton, Susan T.	Social Security Company	23400 · Federal Payroll Taxes Payable		26.04
				Sharpton, Susan T.	Social Security Employee	23400 · Federal Payroll Taxes Payable		26.04
				Sharpton, Susan T.	Medicare Company	61000 · Payroll Tax Expense	6.09	
				Sharpton, Susan T.	Medicare Company	23400 · Federal Payroll Taxes Payable		6.09
				Sharpton, Susan T.	Medicare Employee	23400 · Federal Payroll Taxes Payable		6.09
				Sharpton, Susan T.	Federal Unemployment	61000 · Payroll Tax Expense	3.36	
				Sharpton, Susan T.	Federal Unemployment	23500 · FUTA Tax Payable		3.36
				Sharpton, Susan T.	VA - Income Tax	23600 · State Payroll Taxes Payable		12.35
				Sharpton, Susan T.	VA - Unemployment	61000 · Payroll Tax Expense	6.30	
				Sharpton, Susan T.	VA - Unemployment	23700 · SUTA Tax Payable		6.30
							465.99	109.87
03/19/2012	1186	943	Paycheck	Beck, Dorothy L.	Hourly wage	60000 · Salaries and Wages Expense	720.00	

Figure 10:64

Click **Memorize,** enter the following information, and close the report.

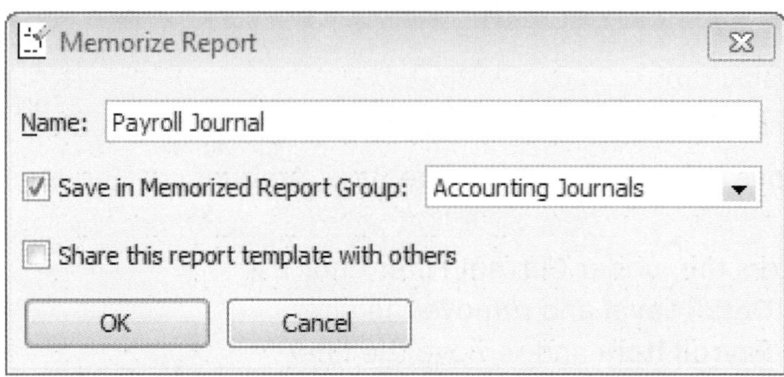

Figure 10:65

3. To view a report that looks something like our payroll register in Excel, open the **Employee Earnings Summary** report. Enter **3/19/12** as the date range.

   Use the scroll bars to view additional information. This report should reconcile to the Excel payroll register.

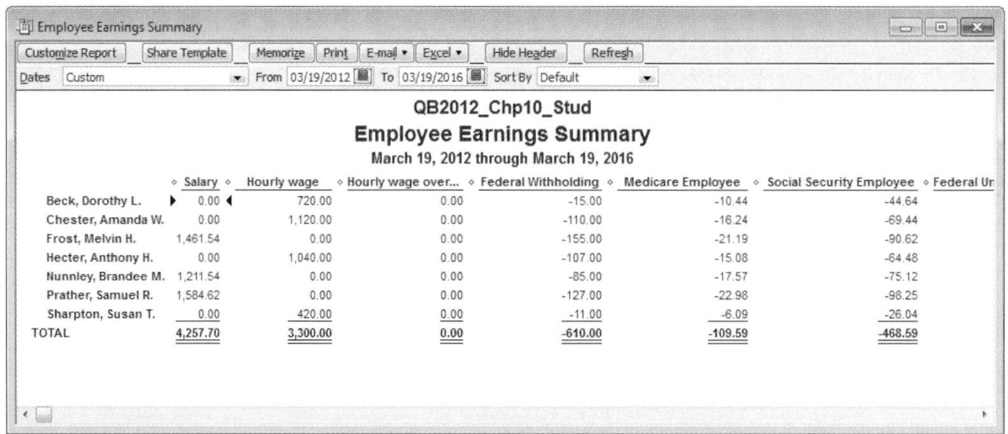

QB2012_Chp10_Stud
Employee Earnings Summary
March 19, 2012 through March 19, 2016

	Salary	Hourly wage	Hourly wage over...	Federal Withholding	Medicare Employee	Social Security Employee	Federal Ur
Beck, Dorothy L.	0.00	720.00	0.00	-15.00	-10.44	-44.64	
Chester, Amanda W.	0.00	1,120.00	0.00	-110.00	-16.24	-69.44	
Frost, Melvin H.	1,461.54	0.00	0.00	-155.00	-21.19	-90.62	
Hecter, Anthony H.	0.00	1,040.00	0.00	-107.00	-15.08	-64.48	
Nunnley, Brandee M.	1,211.54	0.00	0.00	-85.00	-17.57	-75.12	
Prather, Samuel R.	1,584.62	0.00	0.00	-127.00	-22.98	-98.25	
Sharpton, Susan T.	0.00	420.00	0.00	-11.00	-6.09	-26.04	
TOTAL	4,257.70	3,300.00	0.00	-610.00	-109.59	-468.59	

Figure 10:66

4. Remember that you complete tracing entries to the general ledger by displaying the ***Reports>>Memorized Reports>>Accounting Journals>>General Ledger Detail Report.***

5. Close all open reports and the Report Center.

CORRECTING EMPLOYEE PAYCHECKS

We told you how to correct a paycheck before printing it while you were entering paycheck data. But what happens when you find an error after printing? Well, you must then void the paycheck and issue a replacement.

Practice voiding a printed check by voiding and reissuing Susan Sharpton's March 19 paycheck in the steps that follow.

STEPS TO VOIDING A PRINTED PAYCHECK

1. Select **Employees>>Edit/Void Paychecks** on the main menu. Enter the date range of **3/19/12.** You now see the paychecks issued on this date (Figure 10:67).

   Highlight Susan's check and click **Void.**

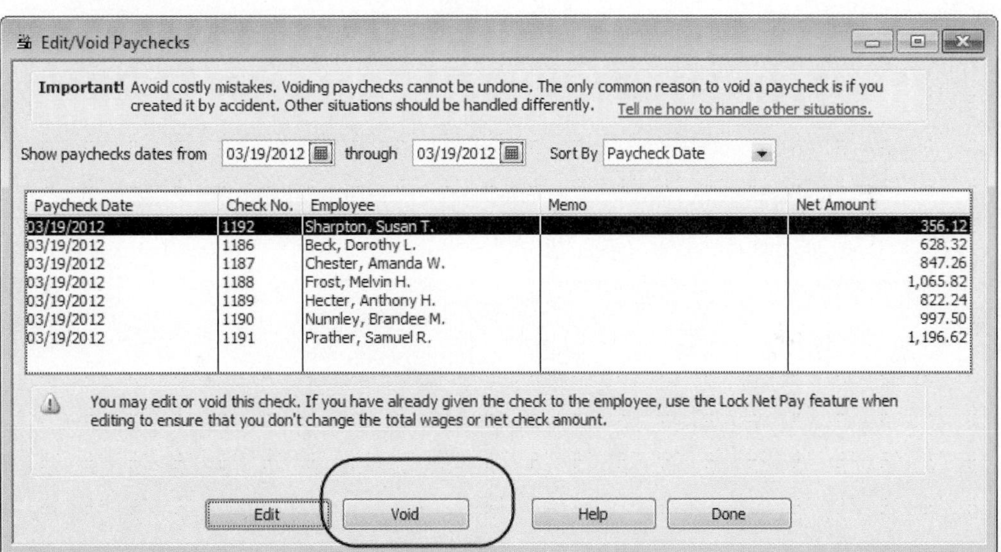

Figure 10:67

2. The void paychecks window updates, showing the paycheck as void. Click **Done.**

Edit/Void Paychecks

Important! Avoid costly mistakes. Voiding paychecks cannot be undone. The only common reason to void a paycheck is if you created it by accident. Other situations should be handled differently. Tell me how to handle other situations.

Show paychecks dates from 03/19/2012 through 03/19/2012 Sort By Paycheck Date

Paycheck Date	Check No.	Employee	Memo	Net Amount
03/19/2012	1192	Sharpton, Susan T.	VOID:	0.00
03/19/2012	1186	Beck, Dorothy L.		628.32
03/19/2012	1187	Chester, Amanda W.		847.26
03/19/2012	1188	Frost, Melvin H.		1,065.82
03/19/2012	1189	Hecter, Anthony H.		822.24
03/19/2012	1190	Nunnley, Brandee M.		997.50
03/19/2012	1191	Prather, Samuel R.		1,196.62

This check has already been voided.

Edit Void Help Done

Figure 10:68

3. You will now reissue Susan's check. Click **Pay Employees** on the Home page and enter the dates shown in Figure 10:69. Click to select **Sharpton, Susan T.**

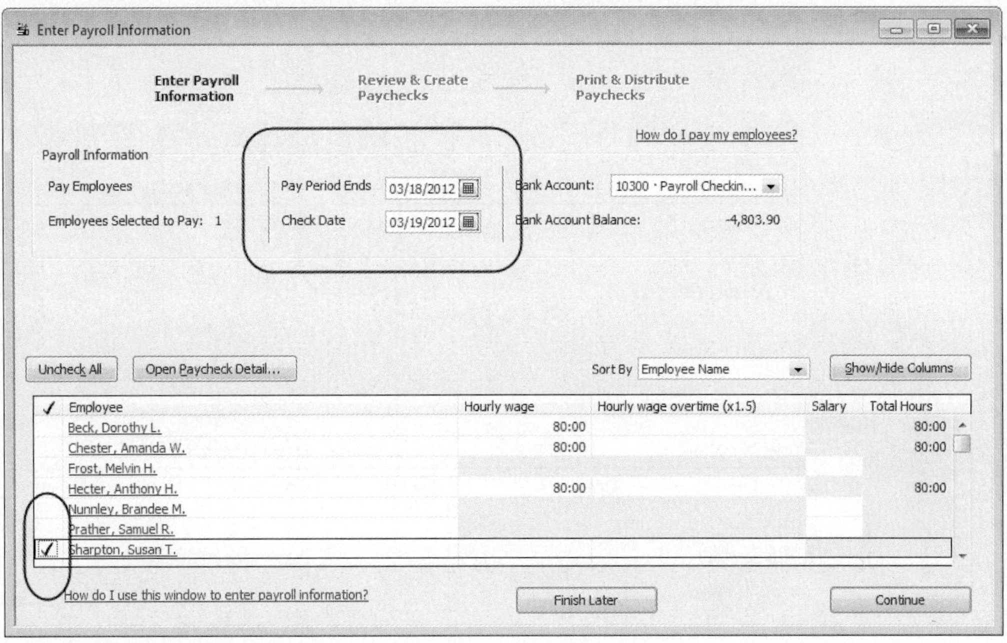

Figure 10:69

4. Click **Continue**. Click to open Susan's paycheck and enter her paycheck information again as illustrated in Figure 10:70. *(Note: You will have to enter her hours and taxes.)*

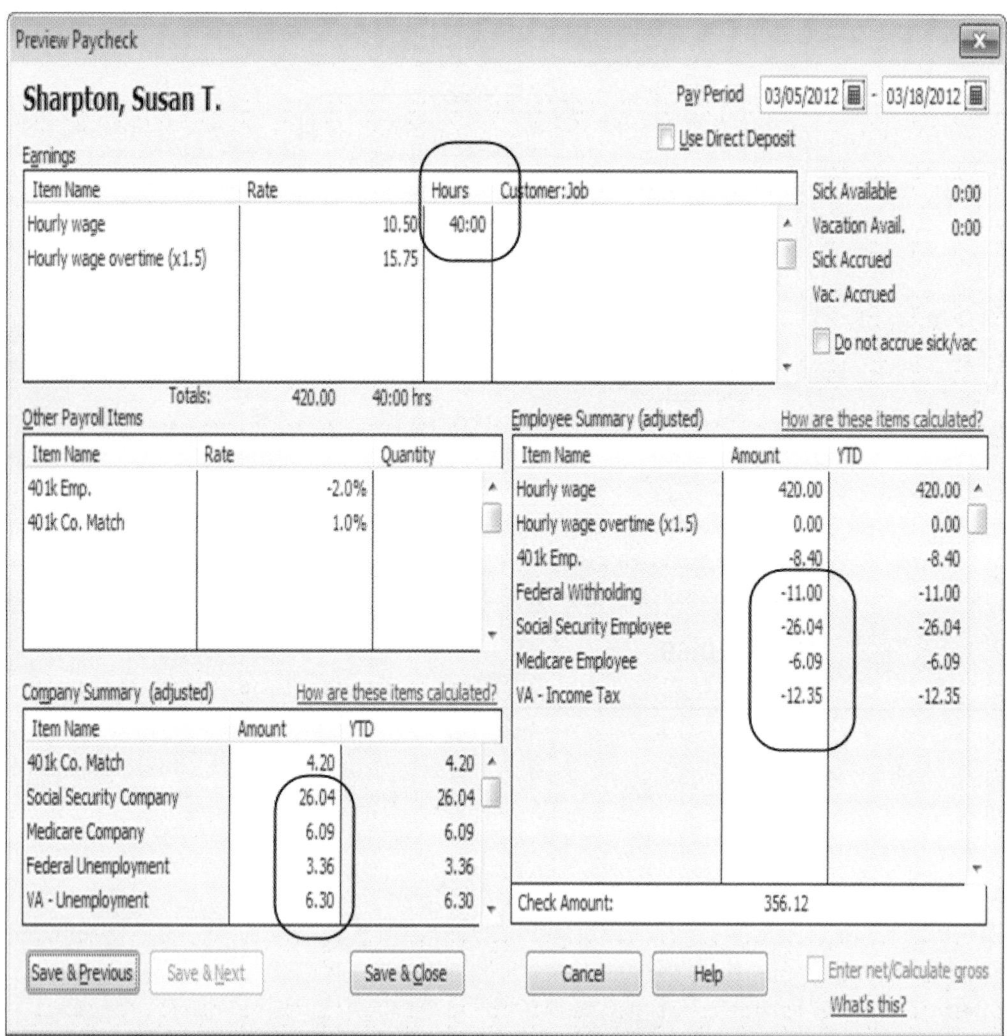

Figure 10:70

5. Click **Save & Close** and Figure 10:71 shows the updated check.

Review and Create Paychecks

Enter Payroll Information → **Review & Create Paychecks** → Print & Distribute Paychecks

How do I pay my employees?

Payroll Information

Pay Employees | Pay Period Ends 03/18/2012 | Bank Account: 10300 · Payroll Checkin...

Number of Paychecks: 1 | Check Date 03/19/2012 | Bank Account Balance: -4,803.90

Paycheck Options

Print paychecks from QuickBooks | Assign check numbers to handwritten checks | Explain Printing Options

First Check Number 1 | Printing Preferences

Open Paycheck Detail...

Employee	Gross Pay	Taxes	Deductions	Net Pay	Employer Taxes	Contributions	Total Hours	Direct Dep.
Sharpton, Susan T.	420.00	-55.48	-8.40	356.12	41.79	4.20	40:00	
	420.00	-55.48	-8.40	356.12	41.79	4.20	40:00	

< Back | Finish Later | Create Paychecks

Figure 10:71

6. Click **Create Paychecks** and then click **Print Paychecks.** The first check number should be 1193. Click **OK,** select a printer, and click **Print.**

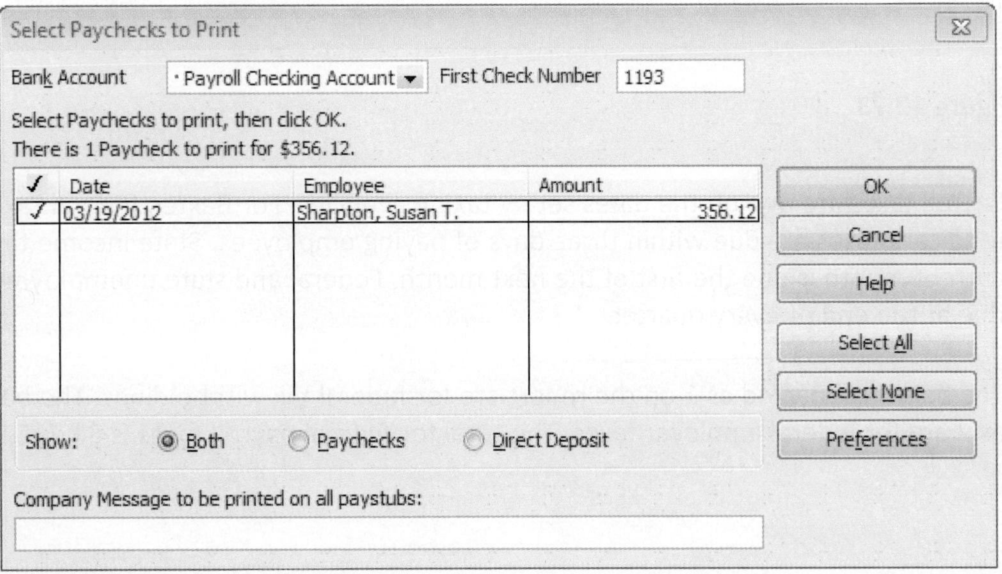

Figure 10:72

7. Click **OK** in the print confirmation window and then **Close** the print confirmation window.

Paying Employer and Employee Payroll Taxes

In this topic, you remit employee tax withholdings and employer payroll taxes. But before that, you should prepare a Payroll Liability Balances report.

Open the **Report Center** and then open the **Payroll Liability Balances** report under the **Employees & Payroll** category.

Enter the date range of **1/01/12** to **3/31/12** to view the report illustrated in Figure 10:73.

Payroll Liability Balances

Customize Report | Share Template | Memorize | Print | E-mail ▾ | Excel ▾ | Hide Header | Refresh

Dates Custom | From 01/01/2012 | To 03/31/2012 | Columns Month | Sort By Default

QB2012_Chp10_Stud

Payroll Liability Balances

January through March 2012

	Jan 12	Feb 12	Mar 12	BALANCE
Payroll Liabilities				
Federal Withholding	0.00	0.00	610.00	610.00
Medicare Employee	0.00	0.00	109.59	109.59
Social Security Employee	0.00	0.00	468.59	468.59
Federal Unemployment	114.20	112.20	76.54	302.94
Medicare Company	0.00	0.00	109.59	109.59
Social Security Company	0.00	0.00	468.59	468.59
VA - Income Tax	0.00	0.00	426.99	426.99
VA - Unemployment	214.12	214.12	186.28	614.52
401k Emp.	455.14	-455.14	463.54	463.54
401k Co. Match	227.58	-227.58	231.78	231.78
Health Insurance (company paid)	0.00	0.00	1,110.00	1,110.00
Total Payroll Liabilities	1,011.04	-356.40	4,261.49	4,916.13

(1: Federal Withholding, Medicare Employee, Social Security Employee; 2: Medicare Company, Social Security Company)

Figure 10:73

Payroll taxes are due on the dates set by taxing agencies. For Baxter, federal tax, FICA, and Medicare taxes are due within three days of paying employees. State income tax for the current month is due the first of the next month. Federal and state unemployment taxes are due at the end of every quarter.

The balances marked as 1 on the report are for federal tax withholdings. The balances marked as 2 are for federal employer taxes. The total for federal payroll taxes is $1,766.36.

Now verify that report totals reconcile with balances in the general ledger accounts. Press **Ctrl + A** on the keyboard to open the chart of accounts. (See Figure 10:74.)

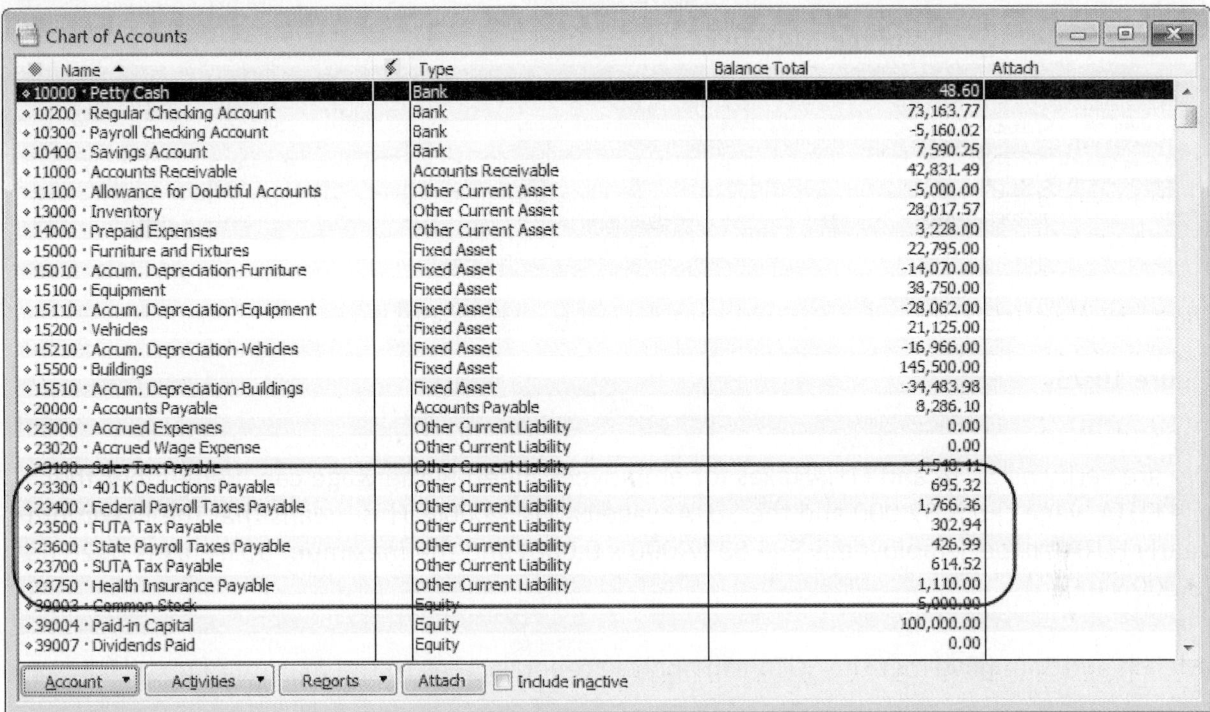

Name	⚡	Type	Balance Total	Attach
10000 · Petty Cash		Bank	48.60	
10200 · Regular Checking Account		Bank	73,163.77	
10300 · Payroll Checking Account		Bank	-5,160.02	
10400 · Savings Account		Bank	7,590.25	
11000 · Accounts Receivable		Accounts Receivable	42,831.49	
11100 · Allowance for Doubtful Accounts		Other Current Asset	-5,000.00	
13000 · Inventory		Other Current Asset	28,017.57	
14000 · Prepaid Expenses		Other Current Asset	3,228.00	
15000 · Furniture and Fixtures		Fixed Asset	22,795.00	
15010 · Accum. Depreciation-Furniture		Fixed Asset	-14,070.00	
15100 · Equipment		Fixed Asset	38,750.00	
15110 · Accum. Depreciation-Equipment		Fixed Asset	-28,062.00	
15200 · Vehicles		Fixed Asset	21,125.00	
15210 · Accum. Depreciation-Vehicles		Fixed Asset	-16,966.00	
15500 · Buildings		Fixed Asset	145,500.00	
15510 · Accum. Depreciation-Buildings		Fixed Asset	-34,483.98	
20000 · Accounts Payable		Accounts Payable	8,286.10	
23000 · Accrued Expenses		Other Current Liability	0.00	
23020 · Accrued Wage Expense		Other Current Liability	0.00	
23100 · Sales Tax Payable		Other Current Liability	1,540.41	
23300 · 401 K Deductions Payable		Other Current Liability	695.32	
23400 · Federal Payroll Taxes Payable		Other Current Liability	1,766.36	
23500 · FUTA Tax Payable		Other Current Liability	302.94	
23600 · State Payroll Taxes Payable		Other Current Liability	426.99	
23700 · SUTA Tax Payable		Other Current Liability	614.52	
23750 · Health Insurance Payable		Other Current Liability	1,110.00	
39003 · Common Stock		Equity	5,000.00	
39004 · Paid-in Capital		Equity	100,000.00	
39007 · Dividends Paid		Equity	0.00	

Figure 10:74

Scroll down to 23400 Federal Payroll Tax Liabilities to find that the account balance equals the report balance. You can also compare other payroll liability balances to the report.

Close the report and the Chart of Accounts.

Because March is the end of a quarter, it is time to pay FUTA and SUTA taxes. You will now run a report to check those taxes. Return to the **Report Center** and open the **Employee Earnings Summary** report. Enter **1/01/12** to **3/31/12** as the date range. (See Figure 10:75.)

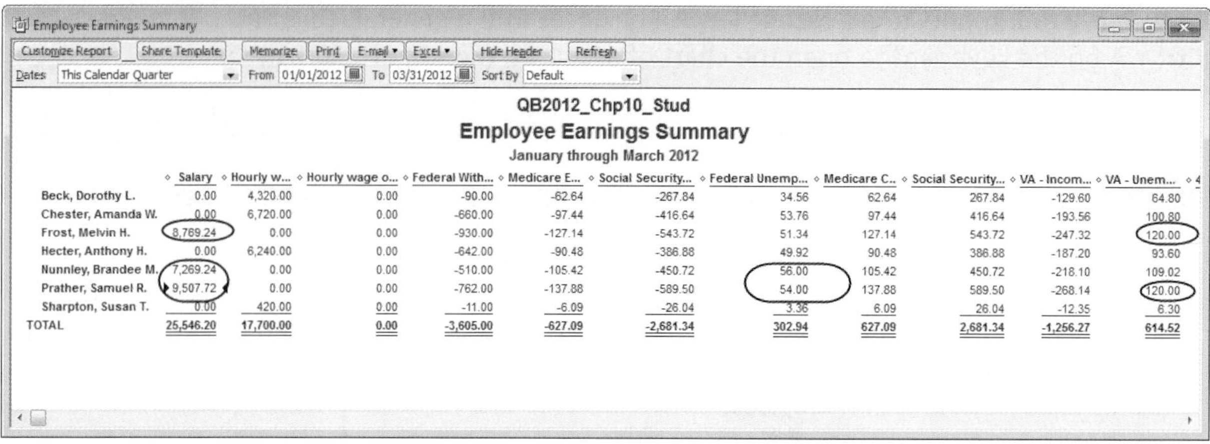

QB2012_Chp10_Stud

Employee Earnings Summary

January through March 2012

	Salary	Hourly w...	Hourly wage o...	Federal With...	Medicare E...	Social Security...	Federal Unemp...	Medicare C...	Social Security...	VA - Incom...	VA - Unem...
Beck, Dorothy L.	0.00	4,320.00	0.00	-90.00	-62.64	-267.84	34.56	62.64	267.84	-129.60	64.80
Chester, Amanda W.	0.00	6,720.00	0.00	-660.00	-97.44	-416.64	53.76	97.44	416.64	-193.56	100.80
Frost, Melvin H.	8,769.24	0.00	0.00	-930.00	-127.14	-543.72	51.34	127.14	543.72	-247.32	120.00
Hecter, Anthony H.	0.00	6,240.00	0.00	-642.00	-90.48	-386.88	49.92	90.48	386.88	-187.20	93.60
Nunnley, Brandee M.	7,269.24	0.00	0.00	-510.00	-105.42	-450.72	56.00	105.42	450.72	-218.10	109.02
Prather, Samuel R.	9,507.72	0.00	0.00	-762.00	-137.88	-589.50	54.00	137.88	589.50	-268.14	120.00
Sharpton, Susan T.	0.00	420.00	0.00	-11.00	-6.09	-26.04	3.36	6.09	26.04	-12.35	6.30
TOTAL	25,546.20	17,700.00	0.00	-3,605.00	-627.09	-2,681.34	302.94	627.09	2,681.34	-1,256.27	614.52

Figure 10:75

We are verifying SUTA and FUTA taxes for employees meeting the wage cap. Remember that the FUTA wage cap is $7,000 and the SUTA wage cap is $8,000. This means that the maximum yearly FUTA tax per employee is $56.00 (7,000 x 0.008) and the maximum SUTA tax is $120.00 (8,000 x 0.015).

Melvin and Sam have met the SUTA cap and the report agrees to the maximum tax.

Now focus on FUTA tax. Melvin, Brandee, and Sam have all met the FUTA cap; however, the FUTA taxes for Sam are incorrect. The total shows $54.00 when it should be $56.00. This is one of the disadvantages to not subscribing to the payroll service. It is very easy to make a mistake when recording paychecks.

You will now correct this error. Select ***Employees>>Payroll Taxes and Liabilities>>Adjust Payroll Liabilities*** on the main menu to open the Liability Adjustments window.

Because this error does not affect the employee's W-2, we will adjust it as of the end of March. Enter **3/31/12** as the **Date** for posting the adjustment. Also, use the same date in the **Effective Date.** (See Figure 10:76.)

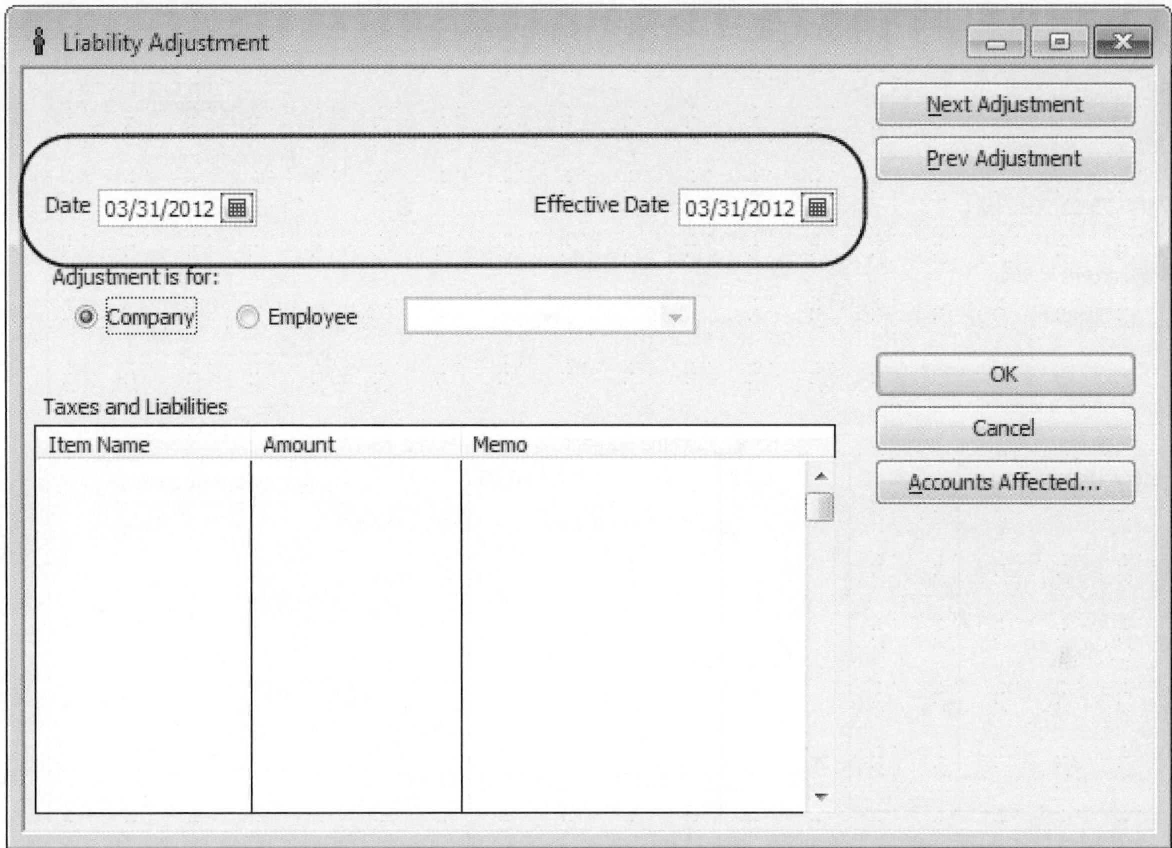

Figure 10:76

Because we want the adjustment to appear on the Employee Earnings Summary report, look up Sam Prather as the **Employee.** Place your cursor in **Item Name** and select **Federal Unemployment.** Tab to **Amount** and enter "2.00" (i.e., $56.00 - $54.00).

Click the **Accounts Affected** button and verify that **Affect liability and expense accounts** is selected so that the adjustment increases FUTA liability and posts to the general ledger account. Click **OK** to exit the Accounts Affected window.

Figure 10:77 shows the completed entry. Click **OK.**

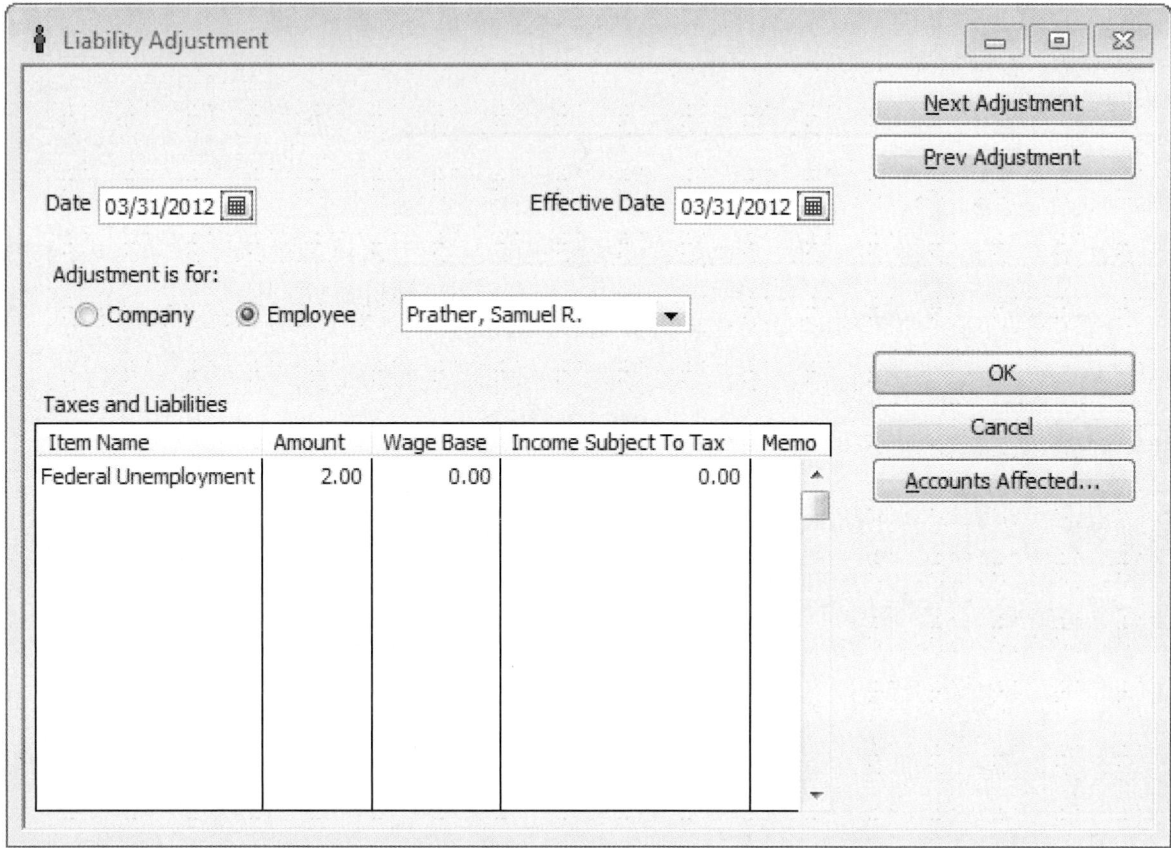
Liability Adjustment
Next Adjustment
Prev Adjustment
Date 03/31/2012
Effective Date 03/31/2012
Adjustment is for:
Company
Employee
Prather, Samuel R.
OK
Cancel
Accounts Affected...
Taxes and Liabilities
Item Name
Amount
Wage Base
Income Subject To Tax
Memo
Federal Unemployment
2.00
0.00
0.00

Figure 10:77

Return to the **Employee Earnings Summary** report and note that FUTA tax is adjusted to $56.00. You can also check the chart of accounts to find that the balance in the liability account has increased.

Close the report and the Report Center.

After reconciling balances, you are ready to pay these taxes. In the next exercise, you create a check to pay employee federal tax, FICA, and Medicare withholdings and employer FICA and Medicare taxes. In the "You Try" exercise that follows, you will pay the remaining liabilities.

STEPS TO PAYING PAYROLL TAXES

1. Click **Pay Liabilities** on the **Home** page. Enter the date range of **1/01/12** to **3/31/12** to view all liabilities for the quarter and then click **OK**.

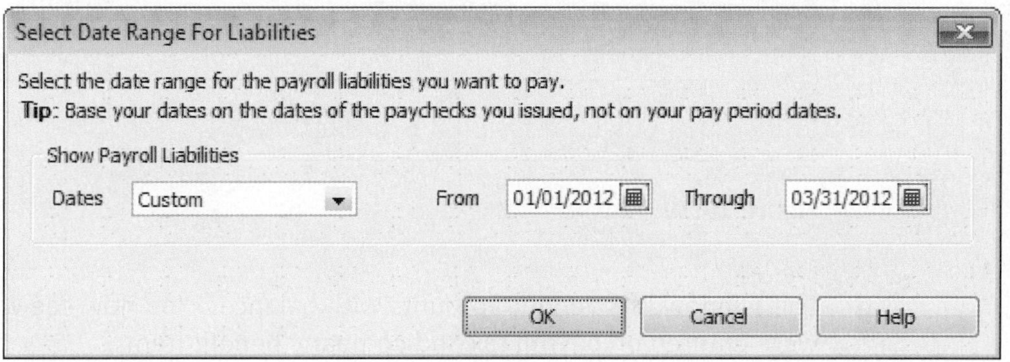

Figure 10:78

2. Enter **3/19/12** as the **Check Date.** Verify that the options of **To be printed** and **Review Liability check to enter expenses/penalties.** Also, confirm that 10200 Regular Checking is the **Bank Account.**

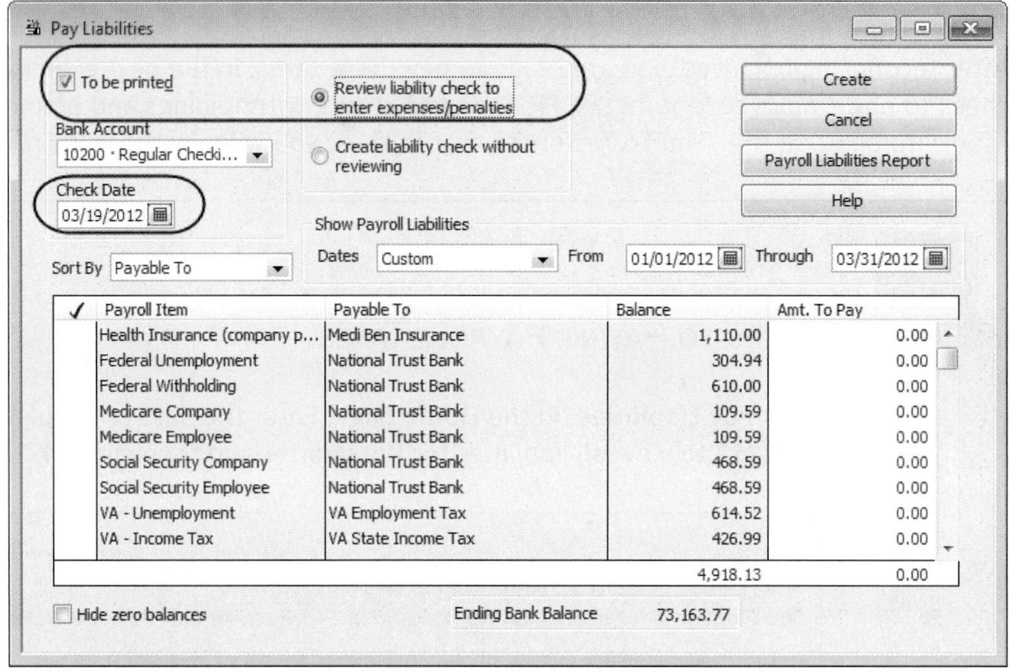

✓	Payroll Item	Payable To	Balance	Amt. To Pay
	Health Insurance (company p...	Medi Ben Insurance	1,110.00	0.00
	Federal Unemployment	National Trust Bank	304.94	0.00
	Federal Withholding	National Trust Bank	610.00	0.00
	Medicare Company	National Trust Bank	109.59	0.00
	Medicare Employee	National Trust Bank	109.59	0.00
	Social Security Company	National Trust Bank	468.59	0.00
	Social Security Employee	National Trust Bank	468.59	0.00
	VA - Unemployment	VA Employment Tax	614.52	0.00
	VA - Income Tax	VA State Income Tax	426.99	0.00
			4,918.13	0.00

Figure 10:79

This window lists vendor accounts with balances. You now see why vendors were entered on payroll tax and company benefit items.

Also, notice that you can print payroll liability reports from this window by clicking the **Payroll Liabilities Report** button.

3. You will now select the taxes to pay. You are paying the **Health Insurance (company paid), Federal Withholding,** and all **Medicare** and **Social Security** liabilities. Click each item to select it for payment.

   Confirm the total in the **Amt. To Pay** column. (See Figure 10:80.)

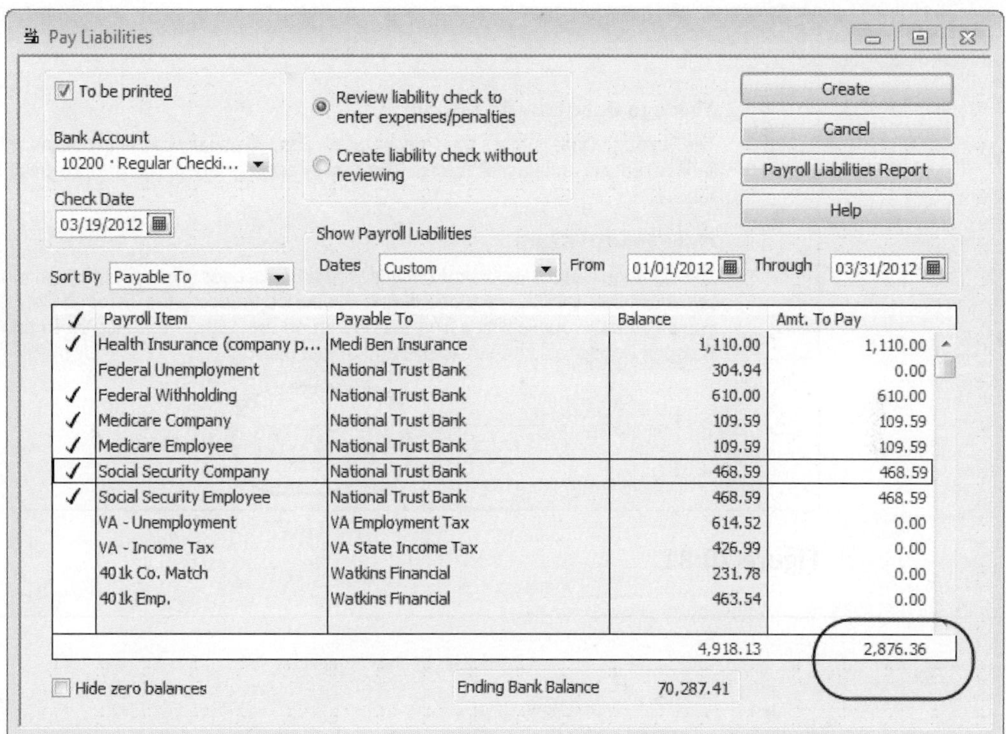

✓	Payroll Item	Payable To	Balance	Amt. To Pay
✓	Health Insurance (company p...	Medi Ben Insurance	1,110.00	1,110.00
	Federal Unemployment	National Trust Bank	304.94	0.00
✓	Federal Withholding	National Trust Bank	610.00	610.00
✓	Medicare Company	National Trust Bank	109.59	109.59
✓	Medicare Employee	National Trust Bank	109.59	109.59
✓	Social Security Company	National Trust Bank	468.59	468.59
✓	Social Security Employee	National Trust Bank	468.59	468.59
	VA - Unemployment	VA Employment Tax	614.52	0.00
	VA - Income Tax	VA State Income Tax	426.99	0.00
	401k Co. Match	Watkins Financial	231.78	0.00
	401k Emp.	Watkins Financial	463.54	0.00
			4,918.13	2,876.36

Figure 10:80

4. Click **Create.** The warning in Figure 10:81 is issued because the check date comes before the Through date on Figure 10:80. However, notice that the message states this can be appropriate, especially when prepaying a liability.

   Click **Continue.**

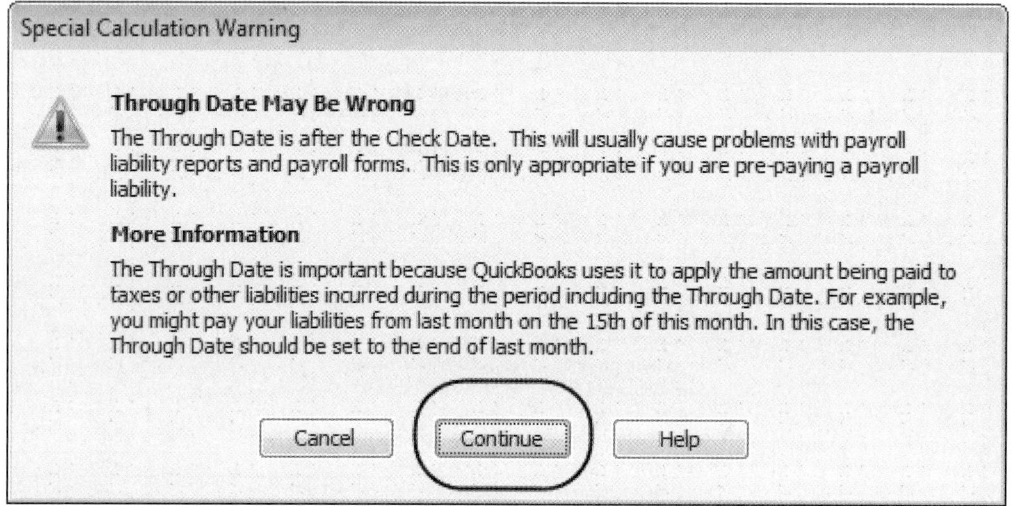

Figure 10:81

5. Because the Review option was selected in the Pay Liabilities window, the check for health insurance opens (Figure 10:82) for you to review it and enter additional information if needed. For instance, if the bill contained additional fees, you could add these fees to the Expenses tab.

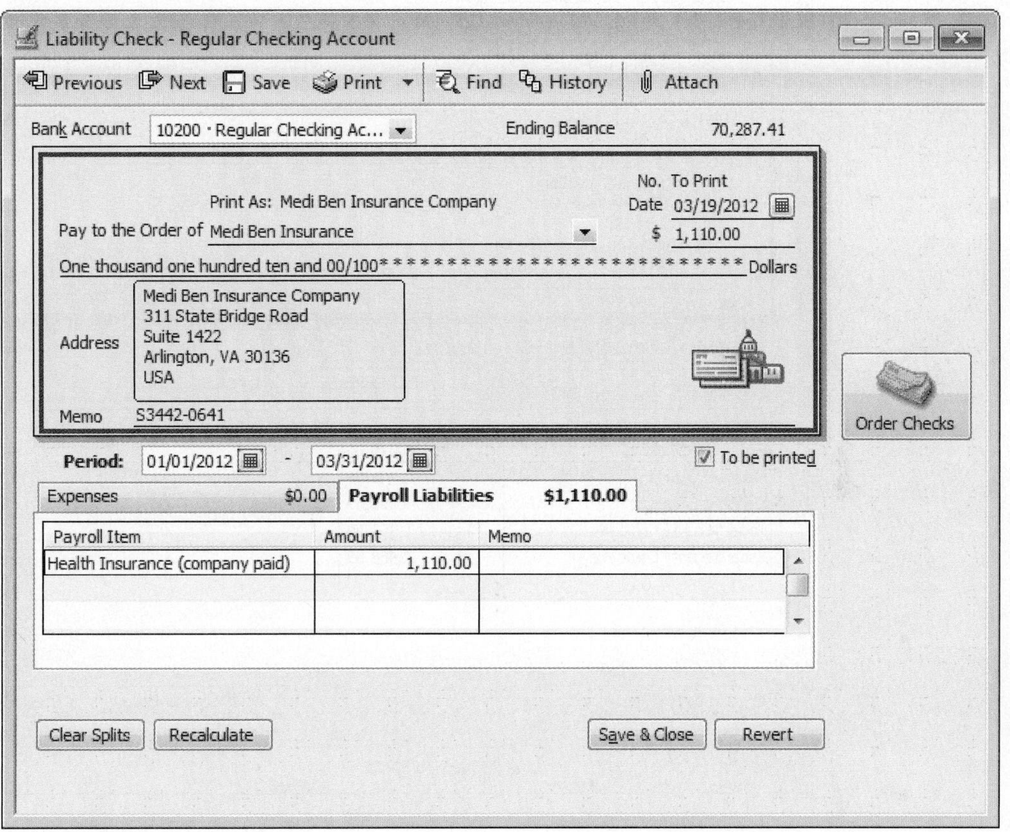

Figure 10:82

6. Click **Next** and the second check opens. Click **Save & Close.**

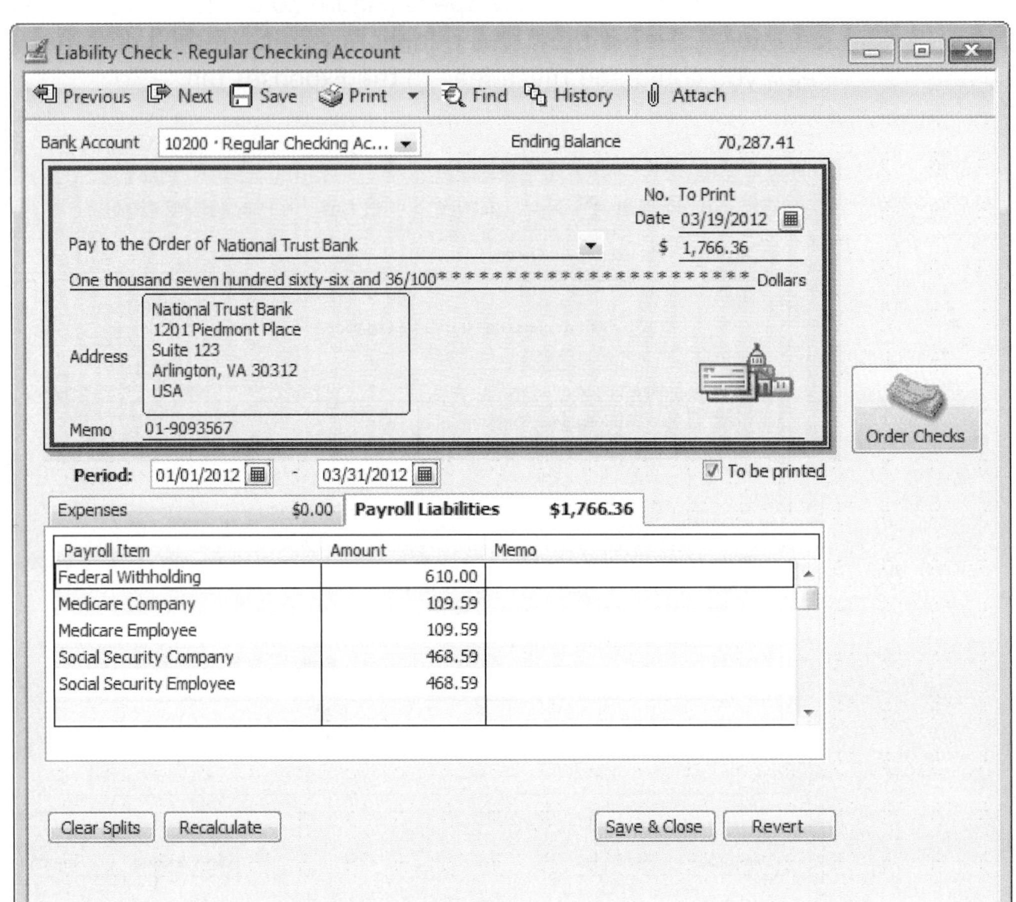

Figure 10:83

7. You will now print the checks. Click **Print Checks** on the **Home** page and verify that the **Bank Account** is the Regular Checking Account. Confirm that two payments are marked and the first check number is 10223.

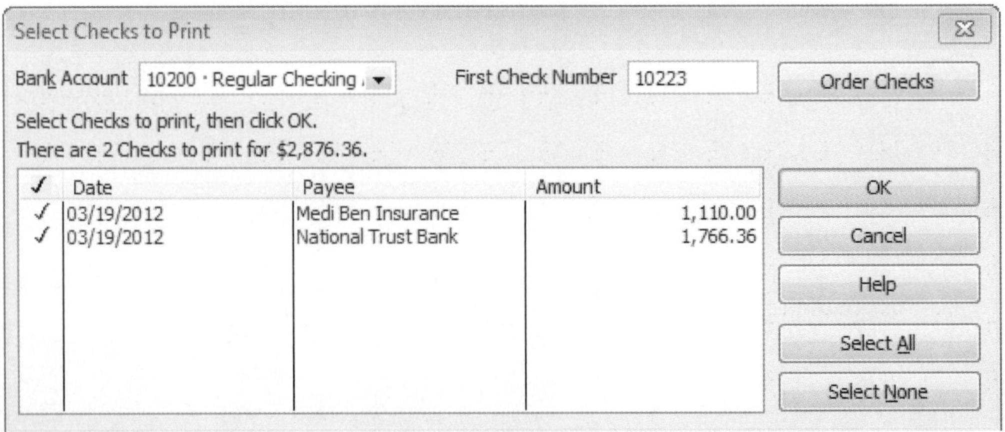

Figure 10:84

8. Click **OK**. Select a printer and click **Print**. Click **OK** in the print confirmation window.

Now complete the next exercise to pay the remaining tax liabilities for the month of March and the first quarter of the year.

CREATE CHECKS FOR PAYROLL TAXES

Reopen the Pay Liabilities window and enter the date range of 1/01/12 to 3/31/12.

Create checks dated 4/2/12 to pay FUTA, SUTA, state tax withholdings, and 401k liabilities.

Print the checks using the first check number of 10225. The checks will total $2,041.77.

Print the Check Detail report for April 1.

QUARTERLY AND YEAR-END PAYROLL REPORTING

At the end of each quarter, Baxter prepares payroll tax reports for each taxing agency. These reports list employee wages and reconcile employee tax withholdings and employer tax liabilities with taxes paid during the quarter.

For federal taxes, the quarterly report is called Form 941. We will now show you how to prepare this report based on information from QBP.

Open the **Report Center** and run the **Employee Earnings Summary** for 1/01/12 to 3/31/12 (See Figure 10:85.) Print and close the report.

QB2012_Chp10_Stud

Employee Earnings Summary

January through March 2012

	Salary	Hourly wage	Hourly wage overtime ...	Federal Withholding	Medicare Employee	Social Security Employee
Beck, Dorothy L.	0.00	4,320.00	0.00	-90.00	-62.64	-267.84
Chester, Amanda W.	0.00	6,720.00	0.00	-660.00	-97.44	-416.64
Frost, Melvin H.	8,769.24	0.00	0.00	-930.00	-127.14	-543.72
Hecter, Anthony H.	0.00	6,240.00	0.00	-642.00	-90.48	-386.88
Nunnley, Brandee M.	7,269.24	0.00	0.00	-510.00	-105.42	-450.72
Prather, Samuel R.	9,507.72	0.00	0.00	-762.00	-137.88	-589.50
Sharpton, Susan T.	0.00	420.00	0.00	-11.00	-6.09	-26.04
TOTAL	25,546.20	17,700.00	0.00	-3,605.00	-627.09	-2,681.34
	1	1	1	2	4	3

	Federal Unemployment	Medicare Company	Social Security Company	VA - Income Tax	VA - Unemployment
Beck, Dorothy L.	34.56	62.64	267.84	-129.60	64.80
Chester, Amanda W.	53.76	97.44	416.64	-193.56	100.80
Frost, Melvin H.	51.34	127.14	543.72	-247.32	120.00
Hecter, Anthony H.	49.92	90.48	386.88	-187.20	93.60
Nunnley, Brandee M.	56.00	105.42	450.72	-218.10	109.02
Prather, Samuel R.	56.00	137.88	589.50	-268.14	120.00
Sharpton, Susan T.	3.36	6.09	26.04	-12.35	6.30
TOTAL	304.94	627.09	2,681.34	-1,256.27	614.52
		4	3		

	401k Emp.	401k Co. Match	Health Insurance (com...	TOTAL
Beck, Dorothy L.	0.00	0.00	0.00	4,199.76
Chester, Amanda W.	-268.80	134.40	540.00	6,426.60
Frost, Melvin H.	-526.14	263.10	750.00	8,250.22
Hecter, Anthony H.	0.00	0.00	540.00	6,094.32
Nunnley, Brandee M.	0.00	0.00	750.00	7,456.16
Prather, Samuel R.	-570.48	285.24	750.00	9,118.34
Sharpton, Susan T.	-8.40	4.20	0.00	402.11
TOTAL	-1,373.82	686.94	3,330.00	41,947.51

Figure 10:85

Next run the **Payroll Transactions by Payee** for 1/01/12 to 3/31/12, listing total federal tax payments for the first quarter. (See Figure 10:86.) Print and close the report.

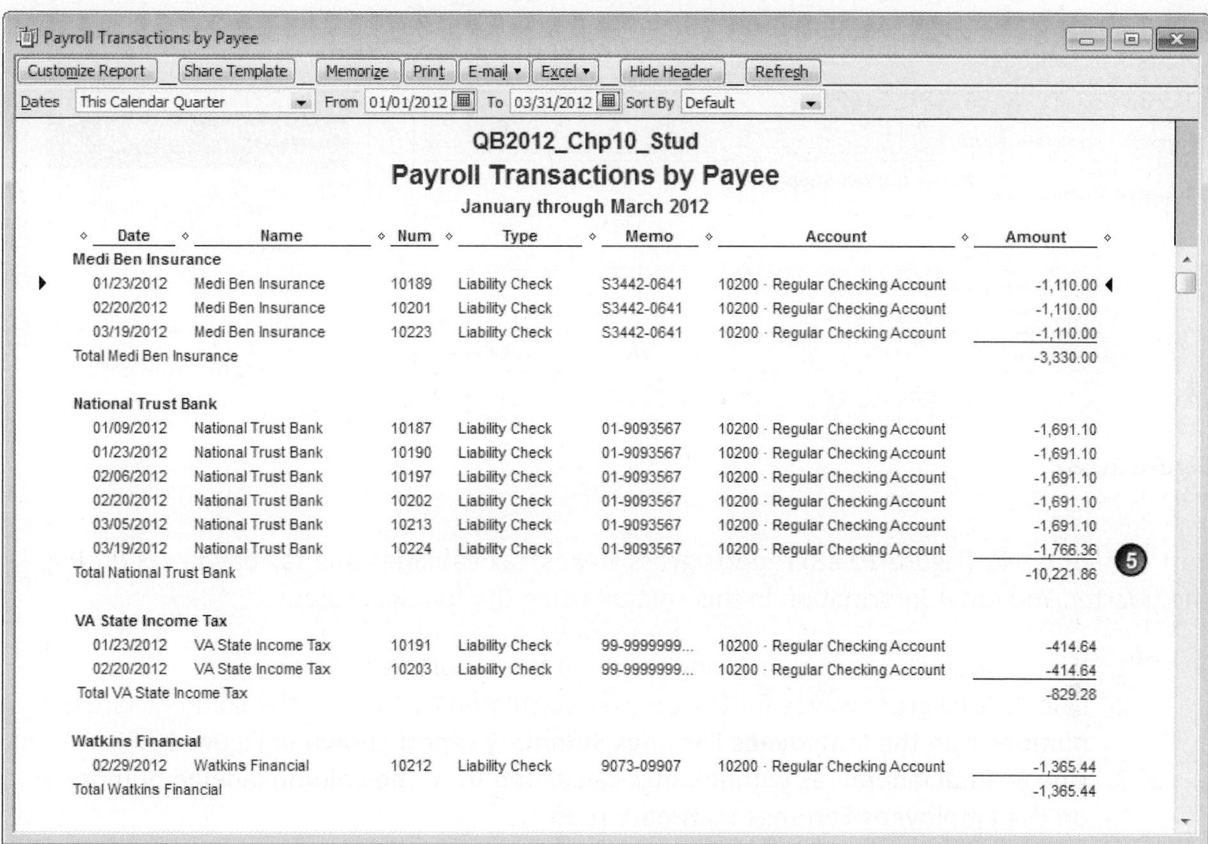

Payroll Transactions by Payee

Customize Report | Share Template | Memorize | Print | E-mail | Excel | Hide Header | Refresh

Dates: This Calendar Quarter | From 01/01/2012 | To 03/31/2012 | Sort By: Default

QB2012_Chp10_Stud

Payroll Transactions by Payee

January through March 2012

Date	Name	Num	Type	Memo	Account	Amount
Medi Ben Insurance						
01/23/2012	Medi Ben Insurance	10189	Liability Check	S3442-0641	10200 · Regular Checking Account	-1,110.00
02/20/2012	Medi Ben Insurance	10201	Liability Check	S3442-0641	10200 · Regular Checking Account	-1,110.00
03/19/2012	Medi Ben Insurance	10223	Liability Check	S3442-0641	10200 · Regular Checking Account	-1,110.00
Total Medi Ben Insurance						-3,330.00
National Trust Bank						
01/09/2012	National Trust Bank	10187	Liability Check	01-9093567	10200 · Regular Checking Account	-1,691.10
01/23/2012	National Trust Bank	10190	Liability Check	01-9093567	10200 · Regular Checking Account	-1,691.10
02/06/2012	National Trust Bank	10197	Liability Check	01-9093567	10200 · Regular Checking Account	-1,691.10
02/20/2012	National Trust Bank	10202	Liability Check	01-9093567	10200 · Regular Checking Account	-1,691.10
03/05/2012	National Trust Bank	10213	Liability Check	01-9093567	10200 · Regular Checking Account	-1,691.10
03/19/2012	National Trust Bank	10224	Liability Check	01-9093567	10200 · Regular Checking Account	-1,766.36
Total National Trust Bank						-10,221.86
VA State Income Tax						
01/23/2012	VA State Income Tax	10191	Liability Check	99-9999999...	10200 · Regular Checking Account	-414.64
02/20/2012	VA State Income Tax	10203	Liability Check	99-9999999...	10200 · Regular Checking Account	-414.64
Total VA State Income Tax						-829.28
Watkins Financial						
02/29/2012	Watkins Financial	10212	Liability Check	9073-09907	10200 · Regular Checking Account	-1,365.44
Total Watkins Financial						-1,365.44

Figure 10:86

We will next explain entering information from these two reports onto Form 941. For purposes of this example, we downloaded a Form 941 from the Internal Revenue Service website (www.irs.gov).

The top of Form 941 (Figure 10:87) contains basic company information such as EIN, Business name, Business address, and the reporting quarter.

Form **941 for** : **Employer's QUARTERLY Federal Tax Return** 950108
(Rev. January) Department of the Treasury — Internal Revenue Service OMB No. 1545-0029

(EIN) Employer identification number: 0 1 – 9 0 9 3 5 6 7

Name (not your trade name): Baxter Garden Supply

Trade name (if any):

Address: 1352 W. Maple Ave
Number Street Suite or room number

Arlington VA 23523
City State ZIP code

Read the separate instructions before you fill out this form. Please type or print within the boxes.

Report for this Quarter of (Check one.)

- [x] 1: January, February, March
- [ ] 2: April, May, June
- [ ] 3: July, August, September
- [ ] 4: October, November, December

Figure 10:87

Part I of Form 941 (Figure 10:88) reports gross wages, tax liabilities and tax payments during the quarter. You enter information in this section using the following steps.

1. Line 1: Total employees receiving wages in the reporting quarter.
2. Line 2: Total gross wages for the quarter calculated by totaling the columns labeled number 1 on the **Employees Earnings Summary** report shown in Figure 10:85.
3. Line 3: Total federal tax withholdings calculated from the column labeled number 2 on the **Employees Earnings Summary** report.
4. Line 5a:
    a. Column 1: Gross wages from Form 941 Line 2 minus wages over the Social Security annual limit. Recall that taxes stop after wages exceed the annual taxable limit.
    b. Column 2: Calculated by multiplying Column 1 wages by the percentage provided. The 12.4 percent (0.124) rate represents the employee rate of 6.2 percent (0.062) plus the employer rate of 6.2 percent (0.062). This amount should equal the total for columns labeled number 3 on the **Employees Earnings Summary** report, disregarding any rounding differences in the cents.
5. Line 5c:
    a. Column 1: Gross wages from Form 941 Line 2.
    b. Column 2: Calculated by multiplying Column 1 wages by the percentage provided. The 2.9 percent (0.029) rate represents the employee rate of 1.45 percent (0.0145) plus the employer rate of 1.45 percent (0.0145). This amount should equal the total for columns labeled number 4 on the **Employees Earnings Summary** report, disregarding any rounding differences in the cents.
6. Line 5d: The total of Lines 5a plus 5c, column 2. This is the total FICA and Medicare taxes due this quarter.
7. Line 7a: The rounding difference that occurs because Form 941 calculates FICA and Medicare as a percentage of total wages whereas the taxes were actually calculated on individual paychecks.
8. Line 11: The total payroll tax payments labeled number 5 on the **Payroll Transactions by Payee** report (Figure 10:86).

Part 1: Answer these questions for this quarter.

1 Number of employees who received wages, tips, or other compensation for the pay period including: *Mar. 12* (Quarter 1), *June 12* (Quarter 2), *Sept. 12* (Quarter 3), *Dec. 12* (Quarter 4)		1	7
2 Wages, tips, and other compensation		2	(1) 43,246.20
3 Total income tax withheld from wages, tips, and other compensation		3	(2) 3605.00
4 If no wages, tips, and other compensation are subject to social security or Medicare tax			☐ Check and go to line 6.
5 Taxable social security and Medicare wages and tips:	Column 1	Column 2	
5a Taxable social security wages	(1) 43,246.20 × .124 =	(3) 5,362.53	
5b Taxable social security tips	× .124 =		
5c Taxable Medicare wages & tips	(1) 43,246.20 × .029 =	(4) 1,254.14	
5d Total social security and Medicare taxes (*Column 2*, lines 5a + 5b + 5c = line 5d)		5d	6,616.67
6 Total taxes before adjustments (lines 3 + 5d = line 6)		6	10,221.67
7 **TAX ADJUSTMENTS** (read the instructions for line 7 before completing lines 7a through 7g):			
7a Current quarter's fractions of cents		0.19	
7b Current quarter's sick pay			
7c Current quarter's adjustments for tips and group-term life insurance			
7d Current year's income tax withholding (attach Form 941c)			
7e Prior quarters' social security and Medicare taxes (attach Form 941c)			
7f Special additions to federal income tax (attach Form 941c)			
7g Special additions to social security and Medicare (attach Form 941c)			
7h **TOTAL ADJUSTMENTS** (combine all amounts: lines 7a through 7g)		7h	0.19
8 Total taxes after adjustments (combine lines 6 and 7h)		8	10,221.86
9 Advance earned income credit (EIC) payments made to employees		9	
10 Total taxes after adjustment for advance EIC (line 8 – line 9 = line 10)		10	10,221.86
11 Total deposits for this quarter, including overpayment applied from a prior quarter		11	(5) 10,221.86
12 Balance due (If line 10 is more than line 11, write the difference here.) For information on how to pay, see the instructions.		12	0.00
13 Overpayment (If line 11 is more than line 10, write the difference here.)		Check one	☐ Apply to next return. ☐ Send a refund.

▶ You **MUST** fill out both pages of this form and **SIGN** it. **Next ➔**

For Privacy Act and Paperwork Reduction Act Notice, see the back of the Payment Voucher. Cat. No. 17001Z Form **941** (Rev.

Figure 10:88

After completing Part 1, you complete Parts 2 through 5 using the next instructions. (See Figure 10:89.)

1. Part 2:
   a. Line 14: The code for the state where the company makes tax deposits.
   b. Line 15: Check the box that the company was a semiweekly depositor for the quarter. This also means that Schedule B must be completed and attached to Form 941. (See Figure 10:90.)
2. Part 5: Sign and date.

Name *(not your trade name)*
Baxter Garden Supply

Employer identification number (EIN)
01-9093567

Part 2: Tell us about your deposit schedule and tax liability for this quarter.

If you are unsure about whether you are a monthly schedule depositor or a semiweekly schedule depositor, see *Pub. 15 (Circular E)*, section 11.

14 [V][A] **Write the state abbreviation for the state where you made your deposits** OR **write "MU" if you made your deposits in *multiple* states.**

15 Check one: ☐ **Line 10 is less than $2,500.** Go to Part 3.

☐ **You were a monthly schedule depositor for the entire quarter. Fill out your tax liability for each month.** Then go to Part 3.

Tax liability: Month 1 ______ .

Month 2 ______ .

Month 3 ______ .

~~**Total liability for quarter**~~ ______ . ~~**Total must equal line 10.**~~

☑ **You were a semiweekly schedule depositor for any part of this quarter.** Fill out *Schedule B (Form 941): Report of Tax Liability for Semiweekly Schedule Depositors,* and attach it to this form.

Part 3: Tell us about your business. If a question does NOT apply to your business, leave it blank.

16 If your business has closed or you stopped paying wages . . . . ☐ Check here, and

enter the final date you paid wages ___ / ___ / ___ .

17 If you are a seasonal employer and you do not have to file a return for every quarter of the year . . ☐ Check here.

Part 4: May we speak with your third-party designee?

Do you want to allow an employee, a paid tax preparer, or another person to discuss this return with the IRS? See the instructions for details.

☐ Yes. Designee's name and phone number ______ ( ) –

Select a 5-digit Personal Identification Number (PIN) to use when talking to IRS. ☐☐☐☐☐

☐ No.

Part 5: Sign here. You MUST fill out both pages of this form and SIGN it.

Under penalties of perjury, I declare that I have examined this return, including accompanying schedules and statements, and to the best of my knowledge and belief, it is true, correct, and complete.

X Sign your name here ______

Print your name here ______

Print your title here ______

Date ___ / ___ / ___

Best daytime phone ( ) –

Part 6: For paid preparers only (optional)

Paid Preparer's Signature ______

Firm's name (or yours if self-employed) ______

Address ______ EIN ______

ZIP code ______

Date ___ / ___ / ___ Phone ( ) – SSN/PTIN ______

☐ Check if you are self-employed.

Page **2** Form **941** (Rev. 1-)

Figure 10:89

Finally, Schedule B (Figure 10:90) is completed when a company makes semi-weekly deposits. The information for this form is gathered from the **Payroll Transactions by Payee** report (Figure 10:86). The IRS will use this information to verify that employers pay all taxes by the due date. Baxter is required to pay tax liabilities within 3 days of paying employees. You should know that failure to pay taxes by the due date will result in IRS-imposed penalties and interest.

Schedule B (Form 941):

990306

Report of Tax Liability for Semiweekly Schedule Depositors

(Rev. . Department of the Treasury — Internal Revenue Service OMB No. 1545-0029

(EIN) Employer identification number: 0 1 – 9 0 9 3 5 6 7

Name (not your trade name): Baxter Garden Supply

Calendar year: 2 0 1 2 (Also check quarter)

Report for this Quarter ... (Check one.)

- [x] 1: January, February, March
- [ ] 2: April, May, June
- [ ] 3: July, August, September
- [ ] 4: October, November, December

Use this schedule to show your TAX LIABILITY for the quarter; DO NOT use it to show your deposits. You must fill out this form and attach it to Form 941 (or Form 941-SS) if you are a semiweekly schedule depositor or became one because your accumulated tax liability on any day was $100,000 or more. Write your daily tax liability on the numbered space that corresponds to the date wages were paid. See Section 11 in *Pub. 15 (Circular E), Employer's Tax Guide,* for details.

Month 1

Day	Amount	Day	Amount	Day	Amount	Day	Amount
1	.	9	1,691.10	17	.	25	.
2	.	10	.	18	.	26	.
3	.	11	.	19	.	27	.
4	.	12	.	20	.	28	.
5	.	13	.	21	.	29	.
6	.	14	.	22	.	30	.
7	.	15	.	23	1,691.10	31	.
8	.	16	.	24	.		

Tax liability for Month 1: 3,382.20

Month 2

Day	Amount	Day	Amount	Day	Amount	Day	Amount
1	.	9	.	17	.	25	.
2	.	10	.	18	.	26	.
3	.	11	.	19	.	27	.
4	.	12	.	20	1,691.10	28	.
5	.	13	.	21	.	29	.
6	1,691.10	14	.	22	.	30	.
7	.	15	.	23	.	31	.
8	.	16	.	24	.		

Tax liability for Month 2: 3,382.20

Month 3

Day	Amount	Day	Amount	Day	Amount	Day	Amount
1	.	9	.	17	.	25	.
2	.	10	.	18	.	26	.
3	.	11	.	19	1,766.36	27	.
4	.	12	.	20	.	28	.
5	1,691.10	13	.	21	.	29	.
6	.	14	.	22	.	30	.
7	.	15	.	23	.	31	.
8	.	16	.	24	.		

Tax liability for Month 3: 3,457.46

Fill in your total liability for the quarter (Month 1 + Month 2 + Month 3) = Total tax liability for the quarter ▶
Total must equal line 10 on Form 941 (or line 8 on Form 941-SS).

Total liability for the quarter: 10,221.86

For Paperwork Reduction Act Notice, see separate instructions. Cat. No. 11967Q **Schedule B (Form 941)** Rev.

Figure 10:90

Close all open reports and the Report Center.

We just illustrated preparing one quarterly report. There are additional quarterly reporting requirements for state tax withholdings and state unemployment tax that were not illustrated.

Besides quarterly reports, Baxter files annual reports in January. Form 940 reporting FUTA taxes must be prepared and submitted to the IRS. In addition, W-2s must be printed and distributed to employees by January 31.

Figure 10:91 shows an uncompleted Form W-2. These forms are mailed to the Social Security Administration along with a Form W-3 (Figure 10:92), which serves to reconcile total wages and taxes on the W-2 forms.

When you subscribe to QBP's payroll tax service, you can then prepare quarterly and annual tax reports in the software.

22222	Void ☐	a Employee's social security number	For Official Use Only ▶ OMB No. 1545-0008	
b Employer identification number (EIN)			1 Wages, tips, other compensation	2 Federal income tax withheld
c Employer's name, address, and ZIP code			3 Social security wages	4 Social security tax withheld
			5 Medicare wages and tips	6 Medicare tax withheld
			7 Social security tips	8 Allocated tips
d Control number			9 Advance EIC payment	10 Dependent care benefits
e Employee's first name and initial	Last name	Suff.	11 Nonqualified plans	12a See instructions for box 12
			13 Statutory employee ☐ Retirement plan ☐ Third-party sick pay ☐	12b
			14 Other	12c
				12d
f Employee's address and ZIP code				

15 State	Employer's state ID number	16 State wages, tips, etc.	17 State income tax	18 Local wages, tips, etc.	19 Local income tax	20 Locality name

Form **W-2** **Wage and Tax Statement**

Department of the Treasury—Internal Revenue Service

For Privacy Act and Paperwork Reduction Act Notice, see back of Copy D.

Copy A For Social Security Administration — Send this entire page with Form W-3 to the Social Security Administration; photocopies are not acceptable.

Cat. No. 10134D

Do Not Cut, Fold, or Staple Forms on This Page — Do Not Cut, Fold, or Staple Forms on This Page

Figure 10:91

DO NOT STAPLE

33333	a Control number	For Official Use Only ▶ OMB No. 1545-0008	
b Kind of Payer: 941 ☐ Military ☐ 943 ☐ 944 ☐ CT-1 ☐ Hshld. emp. ☐ Medicare govt. emp. ☐ Third-party sick pay ☐		1 Wages, tips, other compensation	2 Federal income tax withheld
		3 Social security wages	4 Social security tax withheld
c Total number of Forms W-2	d Establishment number	5 Medicare wages and tips	6 Medicare tax withheld
e Employer identification number (EIN)		7 Social security tips	8 Allocated tips
f Employer's name		9 Advance EIC payments	10 Dependent care benefits
		11 Nonqualified plans	12 Deferred compensation
		13 For third-party sick pay use only	
g Employer's address and ZIP code		14 Income tax withheld by payer of third-party sick pay	
h Other EIN used this year			
15 State	Employer's state ID number	16 State wages, tips, etc.	17 State income tax
		18 Local wages, tips, etc.	19 Local income tax
Contact person		Telephone number ( )	For Official Use Only
Email address		Fax number ( )	

Under penalties of perjury, I declare that I have examined this return and accompanying documents, and, to the best of my knowledge and belief, they are true, correct, and complete.

Signature ▶ Title ▶ Date ▶

Form **W-3** Transmittal of Wage and Tax Statements

Department of the Treasury Internal Revenue Service

Send this entire page with the entire Copy A page of Form(s) W-2 to the Social Security Administration.

Figure 10:92

You have now completed the chapter. ***Make a backup of the data file to a backup file named "QB2012_Chp10_Stud_Completed."***

SUMMARY

You began this chapter with an overview of payroll processing in a manual system. We first explained the types of employee withholdings and voluntary deductions as well as the types of employer payroll taxes and additional forms of compensation. You also learned to calculate payroll taxes and withholdings.

You next looked at the different types of payroll items in QBP. This helped you to understand how item types track wages, employee withholdings, and employer taxes. You also saw that items determine the general ledger account used when posting paychecks.

You then worked with the Employee Center to manage employee accounts and view payroll transactions. You also created a new employee and learned the procedures for terminating an employee.

With this knowledge, you were ready to begin processing payroll. You entered data to create paychecks and then printed the checks. You also printed checks for payroll tax liabilities and reviewed quarterly and annual tax filing requirements. You learned to prepare Form 941 and reviewed W-2s.

In the next chapter, you will focus on finalizing Baxter's March accounting period by recording adjusting entries, printing financial statements, and closing the accounting period.

END-OF-CHAPTER QUESTIONS

TRUE/FALSE

______ 1. Employee state tax withholdings can be calculated by referring to Circular E.

______ 2. Employers pay Social Security and Medicare taxes equal to employee withholdings for these taxes.

______ 3. Government taxing agencies set the due date for employer tax payments.

______ 4. You must void a paycheck to properly correct errors discovered after printing.

______ 5. Deductions are mandatory employee tax withholdings.

______ 6. Employer tax expense includes unemployment taxes.

______ 7. Gross pay for a salaried employee equals hours worked in the pay period times the pay rate.

______ 8. You should contribute to a 401K plan when possible to reduce your federal and state taxes while saving for future retirement.

______ 9. A Form W-2 is provided to employees every year and reports to the employee his/ her gross wages and tax withholdings for the year.

______ 10. Employers prepare a Form 941 every quarter to report gross wages, federal tax withholdings, a federal employer taxes to the Internal Revenue Service.

MULTIPLE CHOICE

______ 1. The ________ report can be used to reconcile the employer's FUTA tax liability for the quarter. *(Hint: Explore optional fields.)*

   a. Employee State Taxes Detail
   b. Employee Earnings Summary
   c. Payroll Liability Balances
   d. Both b and c

______ 2. Form 940 reports _________ taxes and is filed ______.

   a. FUTA, annually
   b. Employee withholdings and employer FICA and Medicare taxes, annually
   c. FUTA, quarterly
   d. Employee withholdings and employer FICA and Medicare taxes, quarterly

______ 3. An employee's Medicare taxes equal ________ of an employee's gross pay.
   a. 1.45 percent
   b. 6.2 percent
   c. 7.65 percent
   d. Employees do not pay Medicare taxes.

______ 4. Per the IRS tax table, an employee must withhold ______ for federal taxes when paid biweekly for taxable pay of $960 and claiming Single with 2 allowances. *(Note: See Appendix D for complete payroll tax withholding tables.)*
   a. $72
   b. $75
   c. $37
   d. $39

______ 5. An employee with gross pay of $1,295 will have a net pay of. Assume the employee is paid biweekly, claims Single with 0 allowances, contributed $35 to a 401k plan, and pays state taxes at 3 percent of taxable pay.
   a. $965.13
   b. $962.13
   c. $959.13
   d. $1,006.13

______ 6. When preparing a Form 941, you should refer to the _______ report(s).
   a. Employees Earnings Summary
   b. Payroll Transactions by Payee
   c. Both a and b
   d. None of the above

______ 7. Employee gross wages are reported on the ________.
   a. Form W-2
   b. Form 941
   c. Form W-3
   d. All the above

______ 8. When making a payroll liability adjustment, you will need to.
   a. Enter an effective date
   b. Choose if it is a company or an employee adjustment
   c. Choose the payroll item to be effected
   d. All the above

______ 9. When correcting an error on an employee paycheck that has already been printed, all the following are true, except _________.
   a. Make corrections to the paycheck
   b. Use the Edit/Void Paychecks window to void the check with the errors
   c. You can make corrections to the printed paycheck and reprint it
   d. Print a corrected paycheck

_____ 10. In the chapter, we created a payroll journal report by customizing the _______ report.

a. Employee Earnings Summary
b. Payroll Transaction Detail
c. Payroll Liability Balances
d. Employee Earnings Detail

PRACTICE SET

In this Practice Set, you complete the following payroll activities for March and April.

Begin by:

- Opening the software.
- Opening the **QB2012_Chp10_PracSet_Stud** data file. Add your initials to the end to the Company Name by clicking ***Company>>Company Information*** on the main menu. Click **OK** to save the changes.
- **Toggling the software to the PRO EDITION** by selecting ***File>>Toggle to Another Edition*** on the main menu and choosing **QuickBooks Pro** as the edition.

1. Record the following transactions.

2012

Mar 19	Create the following paychecks for the Pay Period ending 3/18/12. Be sure to confirm all hours.

Baxter Garden Supply
Paychecks for Pay Period 3/05/2012 thru 3/18/2012

Check No.	Employee	Filing Status	Allow	Pay Type	Pay Rate	Regular Hrs	OT Hrs	Gross Pay	Taxable Pay	Federal Income Tax	Soc. Sec. (FICA) Tax	Medicare Tax	VA State Tax	401K Deduc.	Net Pay
1186	Beck, Dorothy L.	Married	2	Hourly wage	9.00	80.00		720.00	720.00	15.00	44.64	10.44	21.60	0.00	628.32
1187	Chester, Amanda W.	Single	1	Hourly wage	14.00	80.00		1,120.00	1,075.20	110.00	69.44	16.24	32.26	44.80	847.26
1188	Frost, Melvin H.	Single	1	Salary	1,461.54			1,461.54	1,373.85	155.00	90.62	21.19	41.22	87.69	1,065.82
1189	Hecter, Anthony H.	Single	1	Hourly wage	13.00	80.00	5.00	1,137.50	1,137.50	107.00	70.53	16.49	34.13	0.00	909.35
1190	Nunnley, Brandee M.	Married	1	Salary	1,211.54			1,211.54	1,211.54	85.00	75.12	17.57	36.35	0.00	997.50
1191	Prather, Samuel R.	Married	1	Salary	1,584.62			1,584.62	1,489.54	127.00	98.25	22.98	44.69	95.08	1,196.62
	Totals					240.00	5.00	7,235.20		599.00	448.60	104.91	210.25	227.57	5,644.87
	Tax Basis									Circular E	6.20%	1.45%	3.00%		
	G/L Accounts							60000		23400	23400	23400	23600	23300	10300

Baxter Garden Supply
Employer Costs for Pay Period 3/05/2012 thru 3/18/2012

Employee	401K Match	ER Soc. Sec. (FICA)	ER Medicare	ER FUTA	ER SUTA	Health Insurance
Beck, Dorothy L.	0.00	44.64	10.44	5.76	10.80	0.00
Chester, Amanda W.	22.40	69.44	16.24	8.96	16.80	90.00
Frost, Melvin H.	43.85	90.62	21.19	4.66	10.40	125.00
Hecter, Anthony H.	0.00	70.53	16.49	9.10	17.06	90.00
Nunnley, Brandee M.	0.00	75.12	17.57	7.55	18.17	125.00
Prather, Samuel R.	47.54	98.25	22.98	0.00	1.15	125.00
Totals	**113.79**	**448.60**	**104.91**	**36.03**	**74.38**	**555.00**
Tax Basis	**50% Match**	**6.20%**	**1.45%**	**0.8%**	**1.5%**	
G/L Accounts	**23300 / 60500**	**23400 / 61000**	**23400 / 61000**	**23500 / 61000**	**23700 / 61000**	**23750 / 60600**

The next illustration shows your totals after entering the paychecks. Print the paychecks on first check number 1186.

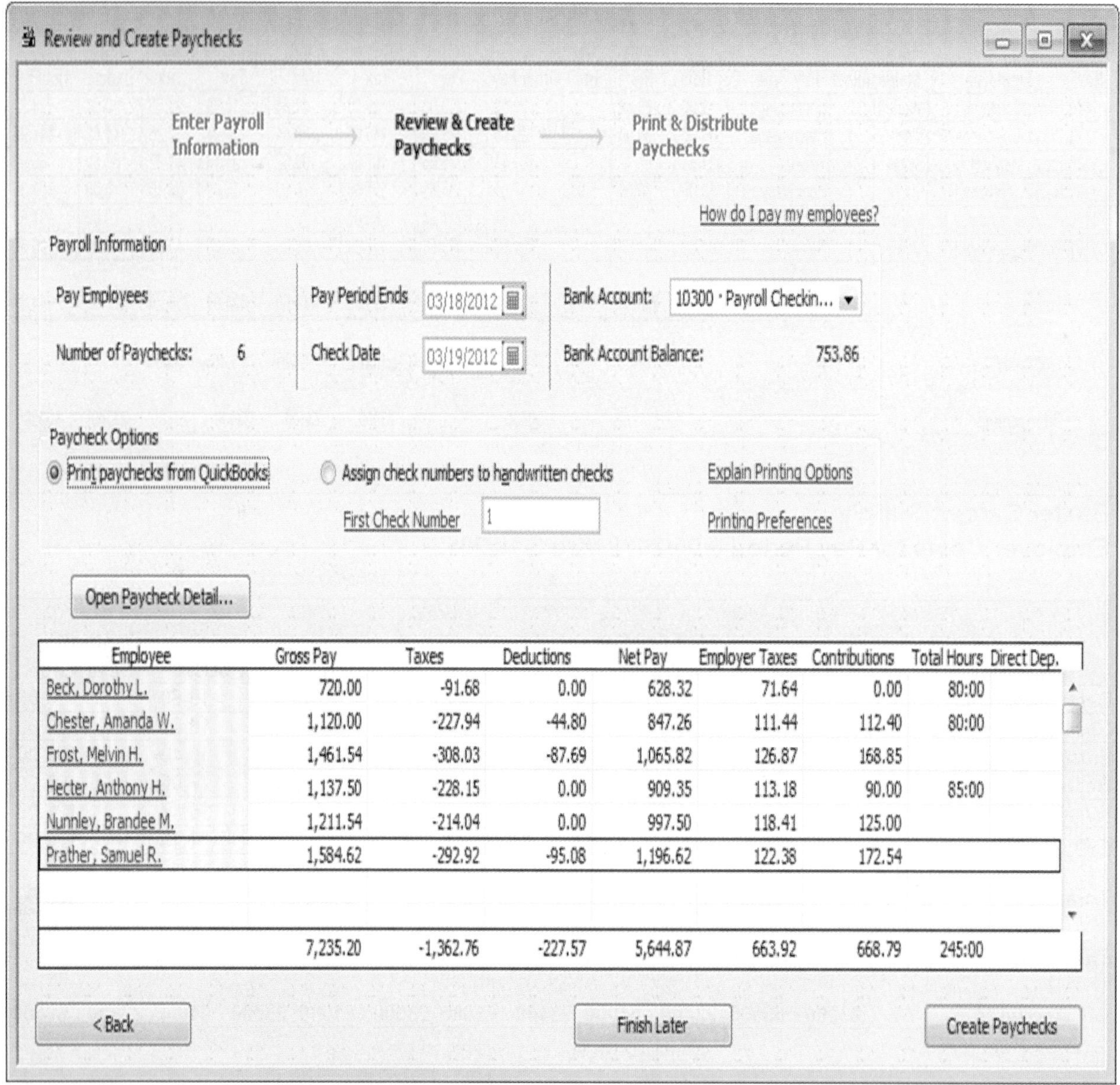

Mar 19 Print check number 10223 to National Trust Bank for $1,706.02 for federal withholdings, Medicare, and Social Security taxes for the liability period of 1/01/12 to 3/19/12.

2012

Apr 1 Print the following checks for payroll liabilities from 1/01/12 to 3/31/12. First check number is 10224 and checks total $3,126.99.

Medi Ben Insurance for health insurance	$1,110.00
National Trust Bank for FUTA taxes	$307.02
VA Employment Tax for unemployment	$609.68
VA State Income Tax for VA income tax	$417.57
Watkins Financial for 401K liabilities	$682.72

Apr 2 Create the following paychecks for the Pay Period ending 4/01/12. Verify the hours.

Baxter Garden Supply
Paychecks for Pay Period 3/19/2012 thru 4/01/2012

Check No.	Employee	Filing Status	Allow	Pay Type	Pay Rate	Regular Hrs	OT Hrs	Gross Pay	Taxable Pay	Federal Income Tax	Soc. Sec. (FICA) Tax	Medicare Tax	VA State Tax	401K Deduc.	Net Pay
1192	Beck, Dorothy L.	Married	2	Hourly wage	9.00	80.00		720.00	720.00	15.00	44.64	10.44	21.60	0.00	628.32
1193	Chester, Amanda W.	Single	1	Hourly wage	14.00	80.00		1,120.00	1,075.20	110.00	69.44	16.24	32.26	44.80	847.26
1194	Frost, Melvin H.	Single	1	Salary	1,461.54			1,461.54	1,373.85	155.00	90.62	21.19	41.22	87.69	1,065.82
1195	Hecter, Anthony H.	Single	1	Hourly wage	13.00	80.00		1,040.00	1,040.00	107.00	64.48	15.08	31.20	0.00	822.24
1196	Nunnley, Brandee M.	Married	1	Salary	1,211.54			1,211.54	1,211.54	85.00	75.12	17.57	36.35	0.00	997.50
1197	Prather, Samuel R.	Married	1	Salary	1,584.62			1,584.62	1,489.54	127.00	98.25	22.98	44.69	95.08	1,196.62
	Totals					240.00	0.00	7,137.70		599.00	442.55	103.50	207.32	227.57	5,557.76
	Tax Basis									Circular E	6.20%	1.45%	3.00%		
	G/L Accounts							60000		23400	23400	23400	23600	23300	10300

Baxter Garden Supply
Employer Costs for Pay Period 3/19/2012 thru 4/01/2012

Employee	401K Match	ER Soc. Sec. (FICA)	ER Medicare	ER FUTA	ER SUTA	Health Insurance
Beck, Dorothy L.	0.00	44.64	10.44	5.76	10.80	0.00
Chester, Amanda W.	22.40	69.44	16.24	2.24	16.80	90.00
Frost, Melvin H.	43.85	90.62	21.19	0.00	0.00	125.00
Hecter, Anthony H.	0.00	64.48	15.08	5.30	15.60	90.00
Nunnley, Brandee M.	0.00	75.12	17.57	0.00	10.98	125.00
Prather, Samuel R.	47.54	98.25	22.98	0.00	0.00	125.00
Totals	**113.79**	**442.55**	**103.50**	**13.30**	**54.18**	**555.00**
Tax Basis	**50% Match**	**6.20%**	**1.45%**	**0.8%**	**1.5%**	
G/L Accounts	**23300 / 60500**	**23400 / 61000**	**23400 / 61000**	**23500 / 61000**	**23700 / 61000**	**23750 / 60600**

The next illustration shows your totals after entering the paychecks. Print the paychecks on first check number 1192.

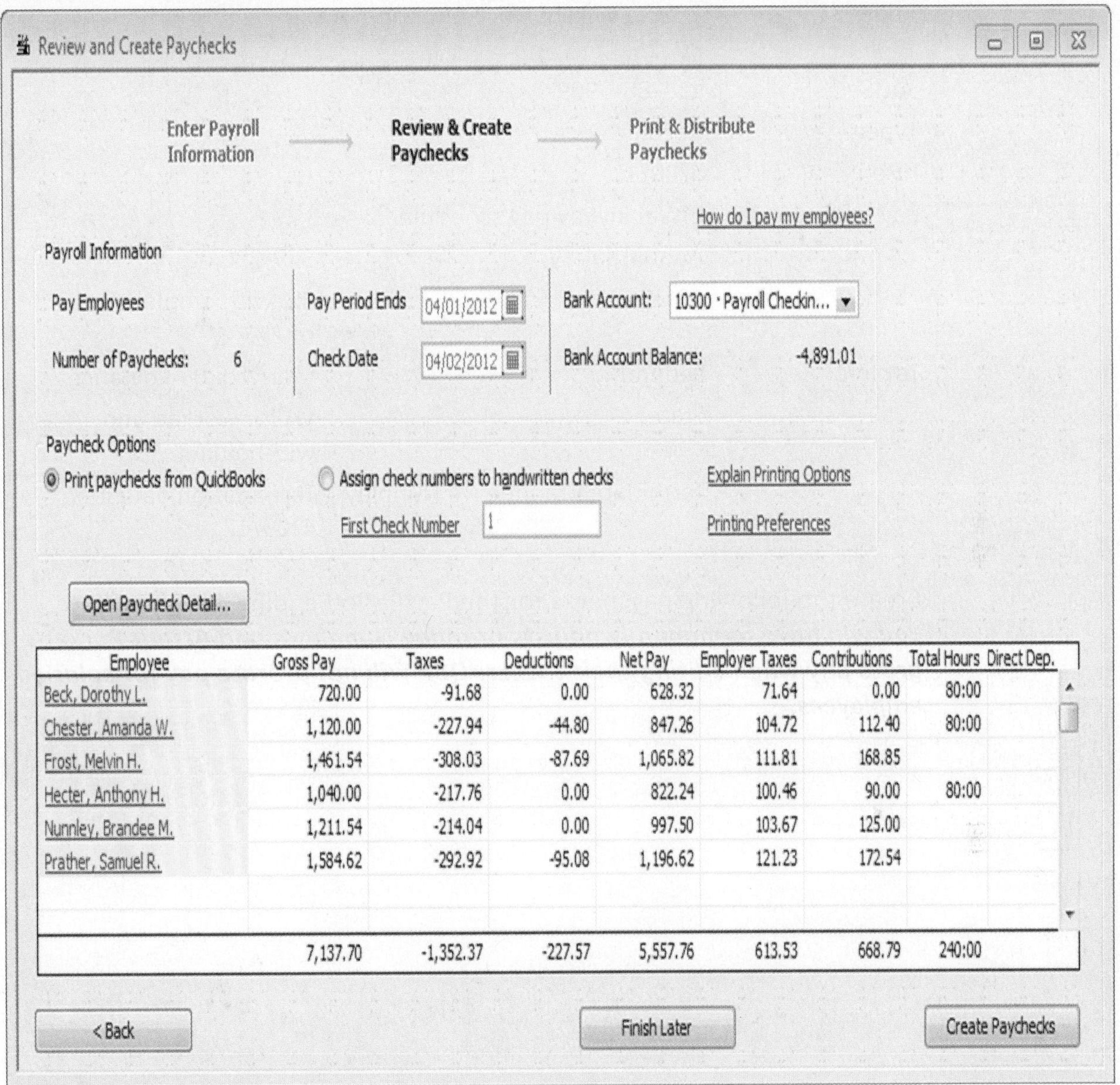

Apr 2 Print check number 10229 to National Trust Bank for $1,691.10 for federal withholding, Medicare, and Social Security taxes for the payroll liability period of 1/01/12 to 4/02/12.

Apr 9	Add the following new employee.		
	Name:	Arthur C. Parker	
	Address:	782 Sewickly Blvd, Arlington, VA 30025	
	Soc Sec:	111-88-0909	
	Type:	Regular	
	Hired:	4/09/12	
	Pay Info:	BiWeeklyPay pay schedule	
		Annual salary:	$27,690.00
		401K:	4% with employer match of 2%
	Tax Info:	Federal	Married, 0 Allowances
		State:	VA for worked and withholding
		Terminate Brandee M. Nunnley.	Termination date is 4/09/12.
Apr 16	Create the following paychecks for the Pay Period ending 4/15/12. ***Note: You will have to manually adjusts Brandee Nunnley's and Arthur Parker's gross pay when editing their checks. QBP will not prorate pay for salaried employees.***		

Baxter Garden Supply
Paychecks for Pay Period 4/02/2012 thru 4/15/2012

Check No.	Employee	Filing Status	Allow	Pay Type	Pay Rate	Regular Hrs	OT Hrs	Gross Pay	Taxable Pay	Federal Income Tax	Soc. Sec. (FICA) Tax	Medicare Tax	VA State Tax	401K Deduc.	Net Pay
1198	Beck, Dorothy L.	Married	2	Hourly wage	9.00	80.00		720.00	720.00	15.00	44.64	10.44	21.60	0.00	628.32
1199	Chester, Amanda W.	Single	1	Hourly wage	14.00	80.00		1,120.00	1,075.20	110.00	69.44	16.24	32.26	44.80	847.26
1200	Frost, Melvin H.	Single	1	Salary	1,461.54			1,461.54	1,373.85	155.00	90.62	21.19	41.22	87.69	1,065.82
1201	Hecter, Anthony H.	Single	1	Hourly wage	13.00	80.00		1,040.00	1,040.00	107.00	64.48	15.08	31.20	0.00	822.24
1202	Nunnley, Brandee M.	Married	1	Salary	605.77			605.77	605.77	17.00	37.56	8.78	18.17	0.00	524.26
1203	Parker, Arthur C.	Married	0	Salary	537.50			537.50	516.00	20.00	33.33	7.79	15.48	21.50	439.40
1204	Prather, Samuel R.	Married	1	Salary	1,584.62			1,584.62	1,489.54	127.00	98.25	22.98	44.69	95.08	1,196.62
	Totals					240.00	0.00	7,069.43		551.00	438.32	102.50	204.62	249.07	5,523.92
	Tax Basis									Circular E	6.20%	1.45%	3.00%		
	G/L Accounts							60000		23400	23400	23400	23600	23300	10300

Baxter Garden Supply
Employer Costs for Pay Period 4/02/2012 thru 4/15/2012

Employee	401K Match	ER Soc. Sec. (FICA)	ER Medicare	ER FUTA	ER SUTA	Health Insurance
Beck, Dorothy L.	0.00	44.64	10.44	5.76	10.80	0.00
Chester, Amanda W.	22.40	69.44	16.24	0.00	2.40	90.00
Frost, Melvin H.	43.85	90.62	21.19	0.00	0.00	125.00
Hecter, Anthony H.	0.00	64.48	15.08	0.00	9.34	90.00
Nunnley, Brandee M.	0.00	37.56	8.78	0.00	0.00	125.00
Parker, Arthur C.	10.75	33.33	7.79	4.30	8.06	0.00
Prather, Samuel R.	47.54	98.25	22.98	0.00	0.00	125.00
Totals	124.54	438.32	102.50	10.06	30.60	555.00
Tax Basis	50% Match	6.20%	1.45%	0.8%	1.5%	
G/L Accounts	23300 / 60500	23400 / 61000	23400 / 61000	23500 / 61000	23700 / 61000	23750 / 60600

The next illustration shows your totals after entering the paychecks. Print the paychecks on first check number 1198.

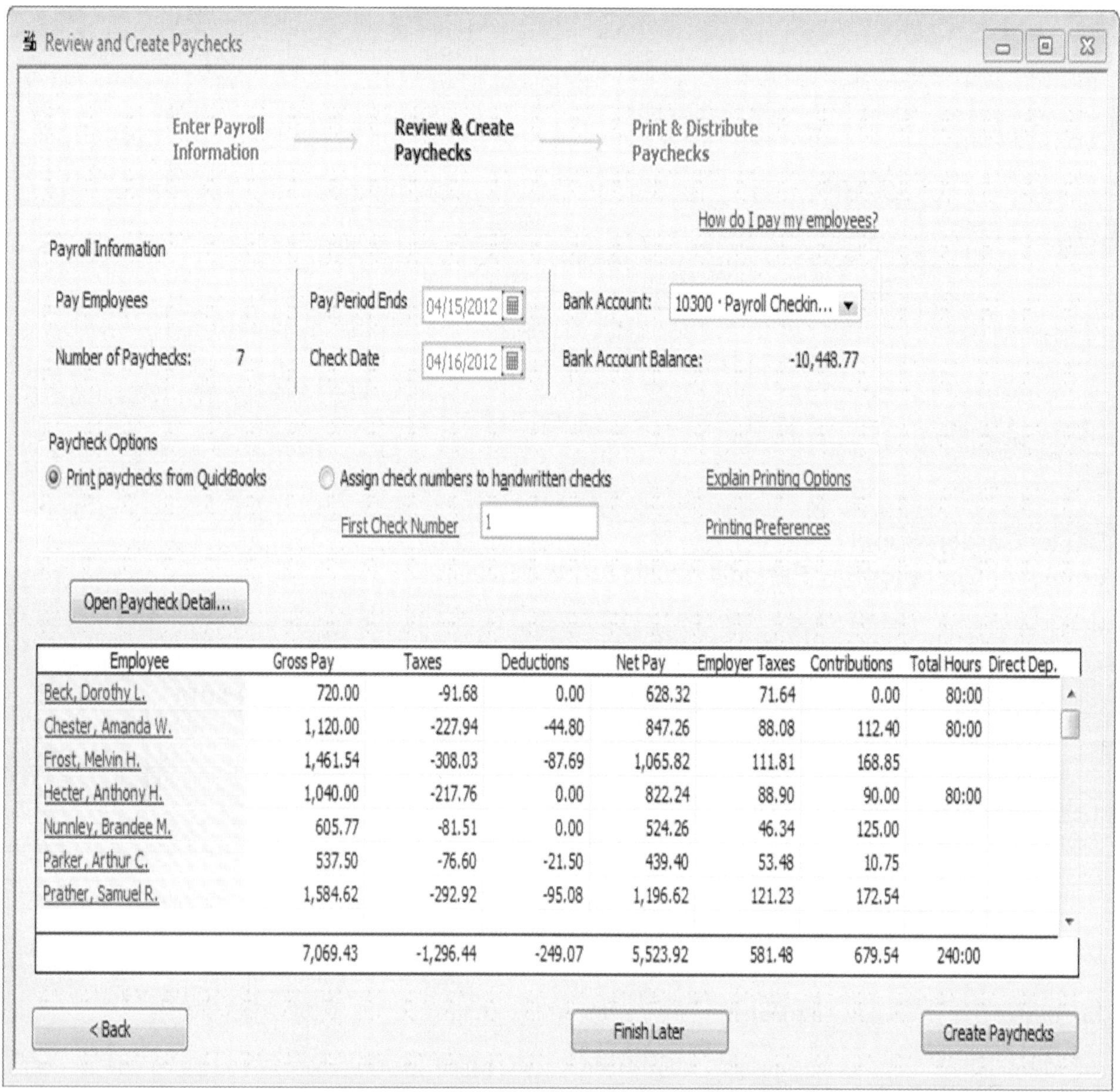

Apr 16 Print check number 10230 to National Trust Bank for $1,632.64 for federal withholdings, Medicare, and Social Security taxes for the payroll liability period of 1/01/12 to 4/16/12.

Apr 30 Print the following checks for payroll liabilities from 1/01/12 to 4/30/12 First check number is 10231 and checks total $2,236.91.

Medi Ben Insurance for health insurance	$1,110.00
VA State Income Tax for VA income tax	$411.94
Watkins Financial for 401K liabilities	$714.97

2. Print the following reports to document activities.

   a. Payroll Transactions by Payee filtered for 3/19/12 to 4/30/12.

   b. Payroll Liability Balances report filtered for 1/01/12 to 4/30/12.

3. ***Back up the data file to a backup file named "QB2012_Chp10_PracSet_Stud_Completed."***

Internet Mini-Project

This mini-project asks you to prepare a Form 941 and the instructions are downloaded from the textbook Website at ***www.pearsonhighered.com/brunsdon/.*** Download the files named **PrepareForm941.pdf** and **JacksonForm941.pdf.**

CHAPTER 11 CLOSE THE ACCOUNTING PERIOD FOR A MERCHANDISING BUSINESS

LEARNING OBJECTIVES

In this chapter, you complete the accounting cycle for March 2012 by performing the following:

1. Analyzing the transactions posted in March to review for accuracy and to identify missing transactions
2. Reviewing a preclosing checklist
3. Posting adjusting entries
4. Reconciling bank accounts
5. Preparing financial statements
6. Closing the accounting period

Begin by:

- Opening the software.
- Opening the **QB2012_Chp11_Stud** data file. Add your initials to the end to the Company Name by clicking ***Company>>Company Information*** on the main menu. Click **OK** to save the changes.
- **Toggling the software to the PRO EDITION** by selecting ***File>>Toggle to Another Edition*** on the main menu and choosing **QuickBooks Pro** as the edition.

ANALYZE TRANSACTIONS

You will begin the process of closing the March accounting period by analyzing transactions posted for the month. It is important to analyze posted transactions. First, you need to review the accuracy of postings so you can correct any errors. Next, you need to review for adjusting entries that need to be posted before preparing financial statements.

You begin this analysis by reviewing the **General Ledger** report that follows. Open this report by selecting ***Reports>>Accountant and Taxes>>General Ledger*** General Ledger Report Reports: General Ledger on the main menu. Enter the date range of **3/01/12** to **3/31/12.**

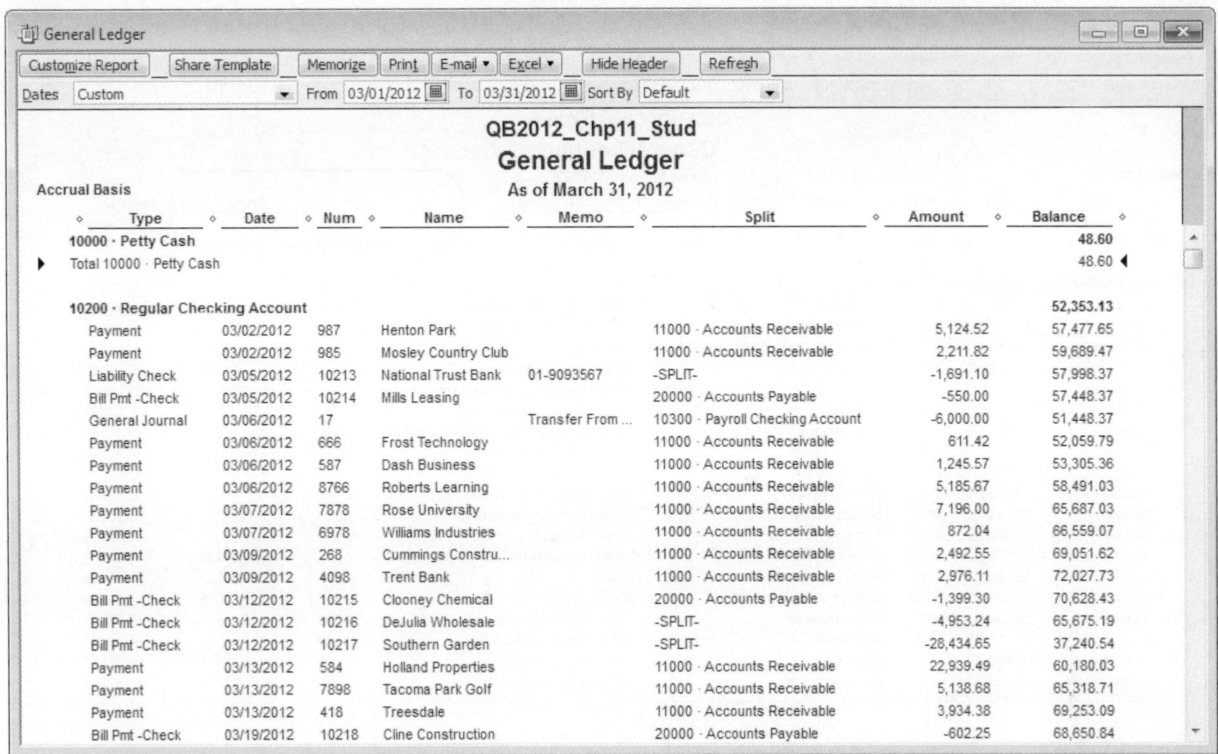

Figure 11:1

This report differs from the General Ledger Detail report you used to document the audit trail because it also lists beginning and ending account balances.

Next, customize the report so that transactions appear in debit and credit columns. Click **Customize Report**, add the **Debit** and **Credit** columns and then remove the **Amount** column. (See Figure 11:2.)

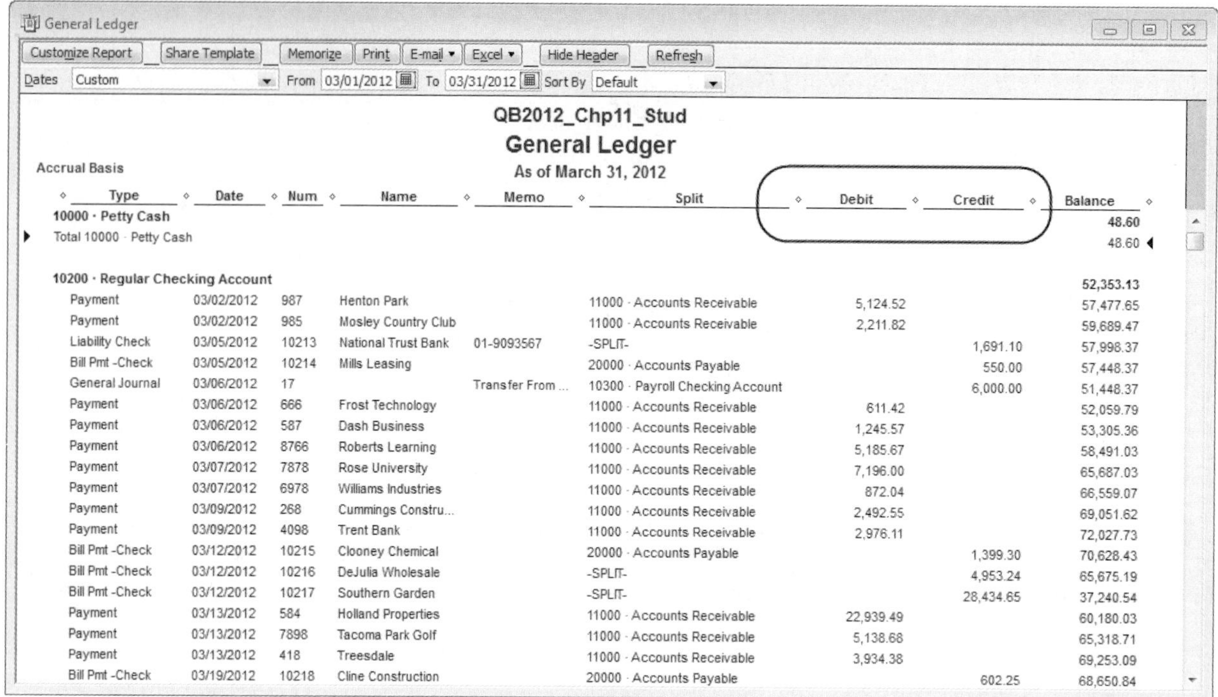

QB2012_Chp11_Stud
General Ledger
As of March 31, 2012

Accrual Basis

Type	Date	Num	Name	Memo	Split	Debit	Credit	Balance
10000 · Petty Cash								48.60
Total 10000 · Petty Cash								48.60
10200 · Regular Checking Account								52,353.13
Payment	03/02/2012	987	Henton Park		11000 · Accounts Receivable	5,124.52		57,477.65
Payment	03/02/2012	985	Mosley Country Club		11000 · Accounts Receivable	2,211.82		59,689.47
Liability Check	03/05/2012	10213	National Trust Bank	01-9093567	-SPLIT-		1,691.10	57,998.37
Bill Pmt -Check	03/05/2012	10214	Mills Leasing		20000 · Accounts Payable		550.00	57,448.37
General Journal	03/06/2012	17		Transfer From ...	10300 · Payroll Checking Account		6,000.00	51,448.37
Payment	03/06/2012	666	Frost Technology		11000 · Accounts Receivable	611.42		52,059.79
Payment	03/06/2012	587	Dash Business		11000 · Accounts Receivable	1,245.57		53,305.36
Payment	03/06/2012	8766	Roberts Learning		11000 · Accounts Receivable	5,185.67		58,491.03
Payment	03/07/2012	7878	Rose University		11000 · Accounts Receivable	7,196.00		65,687.03
Payment	03/07/2012	6978	Williams Industries		11000 · Accounts Receivable	872.04		66,559.07
Payment	03/09/2012	268	Cummings Constru...		11000 · Accounts Receivable	2,492.55		69,051.62
Payment	03/09/2012	4098	Trent Bank		11000 · Accounts Receivable	2,976.11		72,027.73
Bill Pmt -Check	03/12/2012	10215	Clooney Chemical		20000 · Accounts Payable		1,399.30	70,628.43
Bill Pmt -Check	03/12/2012	10216	DeJulia Wholesale		-SPLIT-		4,953.24	65,675.19
Bill Pmt -Check	03/12/2012	10217	Southern Garden		-SPLIT-		28,434.65	37,240.54
Payment	03/13/2012	584	Holland Properties		11000 · Accounts Receivable	22,939.49		60,180.03
Payment	03/13/2012	7898	Tacoma Park Golf		11000 · Accounts Receivable	5,138.68		65,318.71
Payment	03/13/2012	418	Treesdale		11000 · Accounts Receivable	3,934.38		69,253.09
Bill Pmt -Check	03/19/2012	10218	Cline Construction		20000 · Accounts Payable		602.25	68,650.84

Figure 11:2

Remember that the Split column lists the corresponding account used on the transaction. If the term "SPLIT" appears, multiple accounts were involved. What follows are steps performed to analyze the report.

First, scroll through the report looking for transactions that may indicate a posting error. In particular, scroll to **72100 Repairs - Equipment Expense** to locate an entry for shipping. The accountant recalls that this transaction involved shipping a package to a customer and should have posted to **57500 Freight.**

You will now reclassify the expense. Double click the entry to reopen it. Using the lookup on **Account,** change the account to **57500 Freight.** (See Figure 11:3.)

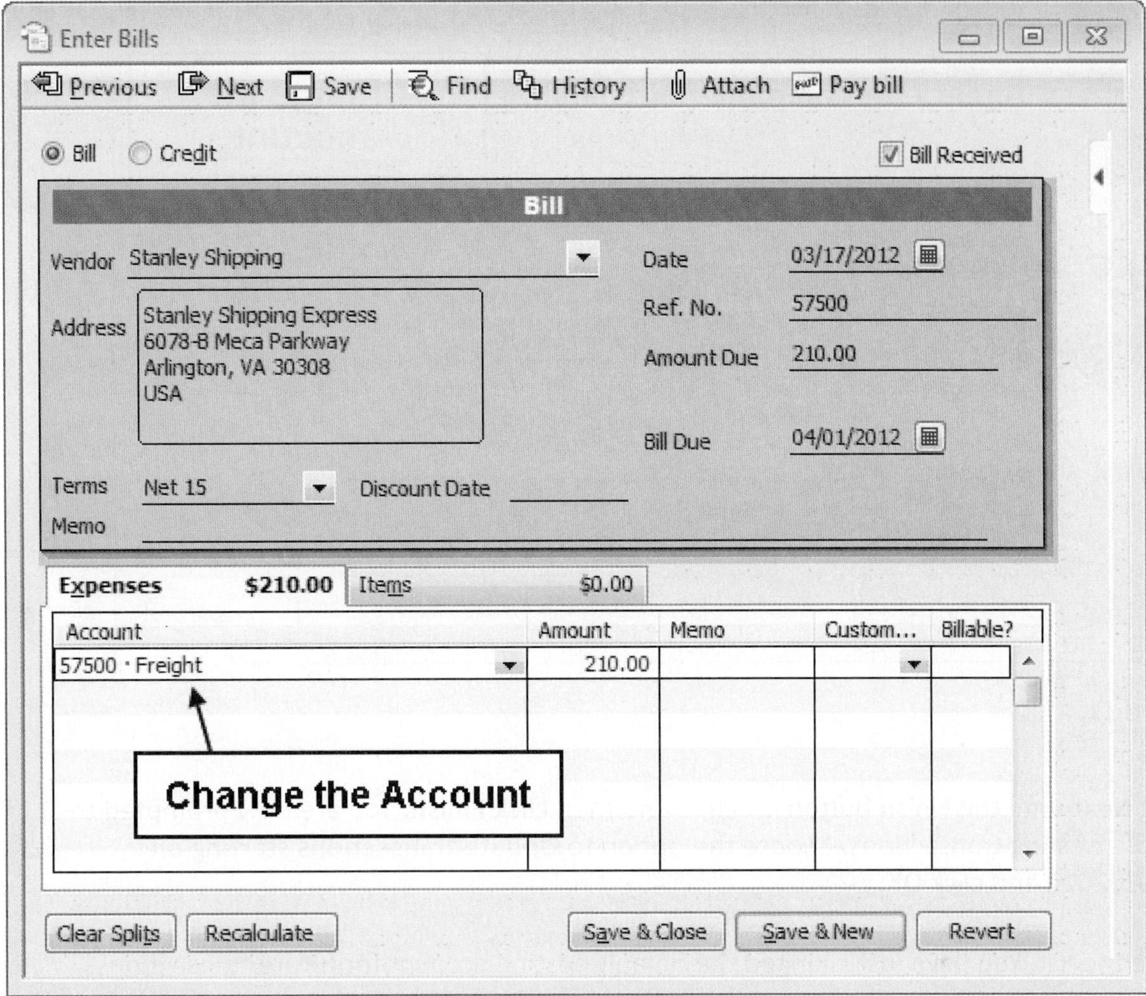

Figure 11:3

Click **Save & Close** and **Yes** when prompted to confirm your changes. That is how easy it is to reclassify a posting error for expenses.

It is not so easy to correct a posting error if another record is linked to the transaction, such as an inventory or payroll item. Scroll to **60300 Payroll Expenses,** which contains entries for employee health insurance costs. The accountant wanted this expense to post to **60600 Employee Benefits Expense.** You cannot simply open each payroll check to change the posting account because this will not correct future posting errors. Instead, you must change the payroll item's default posting account.

To change the default account open the Payroll Item List using ***Lists>>Payroll Item List*** on the main menu. Double click to open the **Health Insurance (company paid)** item. Click **Next** and change the **Expense account** as shown in Figure 11:4.

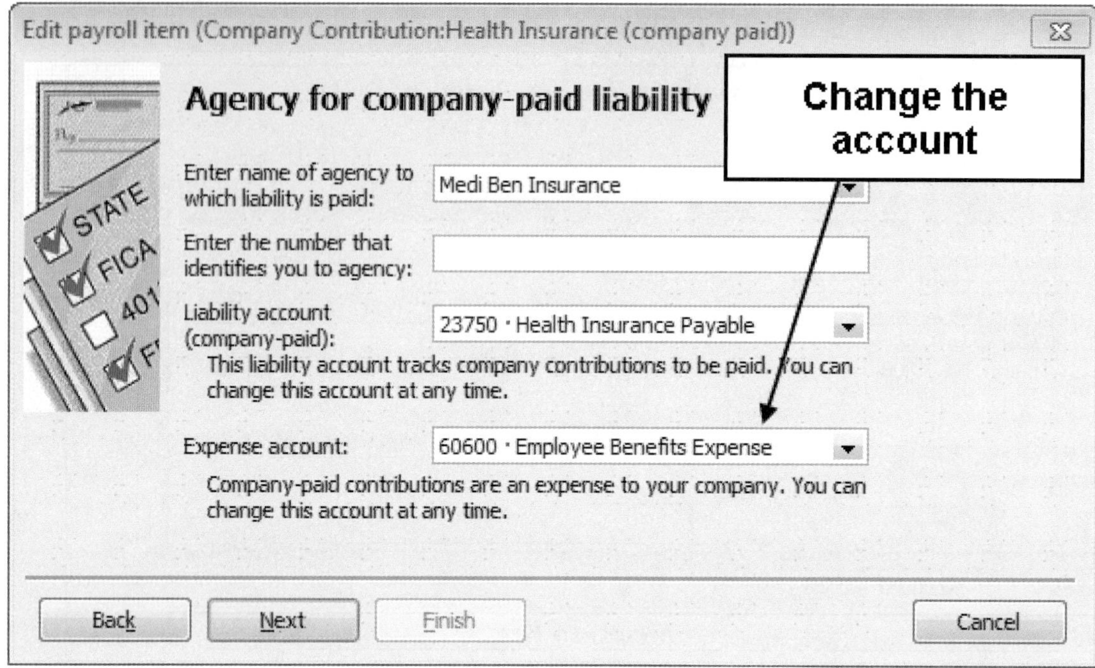

Figure 11:4

Click **Next** until the Finish button is active and then click **Finish.** You are now prompted to handle existing transactions. Choose the option to **Update transactions starting on 01/01/2012** and click **OK.**

Close the list. You have just changed the default posting account for future transactions. Moreover, return to the General Ledger report and notice that QBP has reclassified existing transactions into 60600 Employee Benefits Expense, so error correction is complete.

The next step in analyzing the General Ledger involves reviewing the report for missing transactions. In particular, scroll to account **10300 Payroll Checking** to find that the March 19 bank transfer covering payroll checks has not been recorded. (See Figure 11:5.)

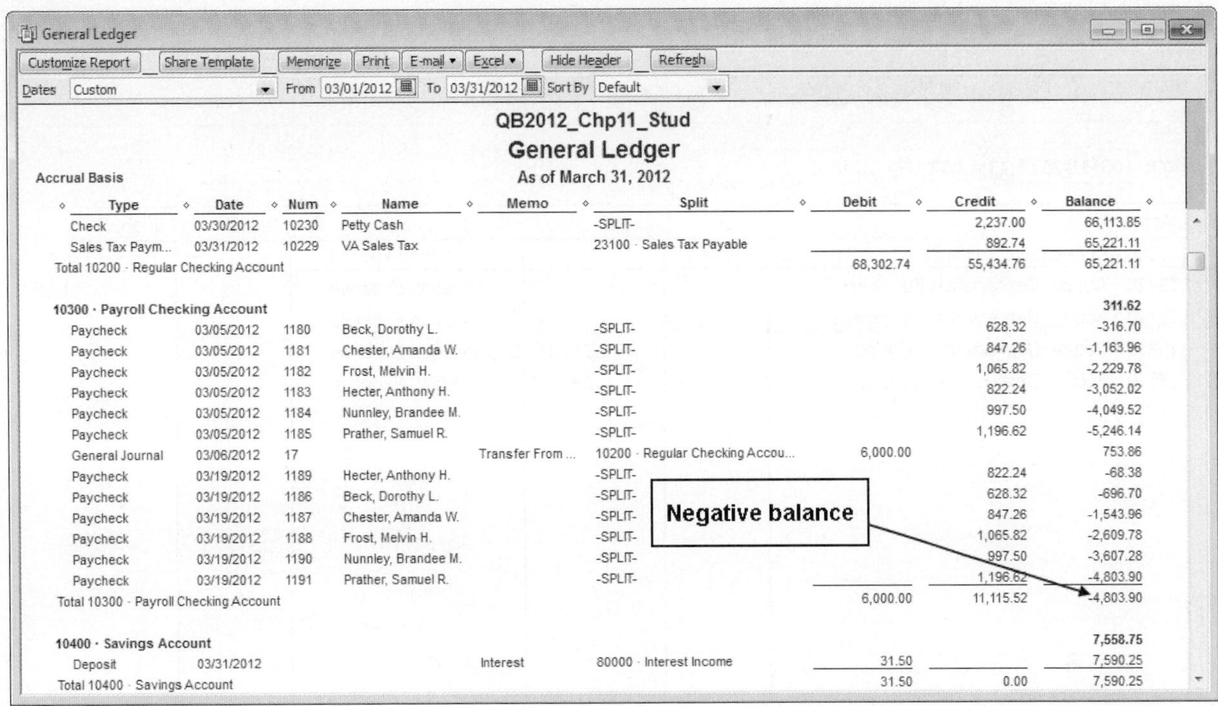

QB2012_Chp11_Stud
General Ledger
As of March 31, 2012
Accrual Basis

Type	Date	Num	Name	Memo	Split	Debit	Credit	Balance
Check	03/30/2012	10230	Petty Cash		-SPLIT-		2,237.00	66,113.85
Sales Tax Paym...	03/31/2012	10229	VA Sales Tax		23100 · Sales Tax Payable		892.74	65,221.11
Total 10200 · Regular Checking Account						68,302.74	55,434.76	65,221.11
10300 · Payroll Checking Account								311.62
Paycheck	03/05/2012	1180	Beck, Dorothy L.		-SPLIT-		628.32	-316.70
Paycheck	03/05/2012	1181	Chester, Amanda W.		-SPLIT-		847.26	-1,163.96
Paycheck	03/05/2012	1182	Frost, Melvin H.		-SPLIT-		1,065.82	-2,229.78
Paycheck	03/05/2012	1183	Hecter, Anthony H.		-SPLIT-		822.24	-3,052.02
Paycheck	03/05/2012	1184	Nunnley, Brandee M.		-SPLIT-		997.50	-4,049.52
Paycheck	03/05/2012	1185	Prather, Samuel R.		-SPLIT-		1,196.62	-5,246.14
General Journal	03/06/2012	17		Transfer From ...	10200 · Regular Checking Accou...	6,000.00		753.86
Paycheck	03/19/2012	1189	Hecter, Anthony H.		-SPLIT-		822.24	-68.38
Paycheck	03/19/2012	1186	Beck, Dorothy L.		-SPLIT-		628.32	-696.70
Paycheck	03/19/2012	1187	Chester, Amanda W.		-SPLIT-		847.26	-1,543.96
Paycheck	03/19/2012	1188	Frost, Melvin H.		-SPLIT-		1,065.82	-2,609.78
Paycheck	03/19/2012	1190	Nunnley, Brandee M.		-SPLIT-		997.50	-3,607.28
Paycheck	03/19/2012	1191	Prather, Samuel R.		-SPLIT-		1,196.62	-4,803.90
Total 10300 · Payroll Checking Account						6,000.00	11,115.52	-4,803.90
10400 · Savings Account								7,558.75
Deposit	03/31/2012			Interest	80000 · Interest Income	31.50		7,590.25
Total 10400 · Savings Account						31.50	0.00	7,590.25

Figure 11:5

Next scroll to **14000 Prepaid Expenses** to find that the entry recognizing this month's expired prepaid insurance must also be recorded. You will record these entries in the exercises that follow.

Scroll to **15010 Accum Depreciation – Furniture.** The accountant has already posted the entry for March depreciation. Double click the entry to open it. (See Figure 11:6.) *(Note: Click **OK** if you receive a message on automatically assigning journal entry numbers.)*

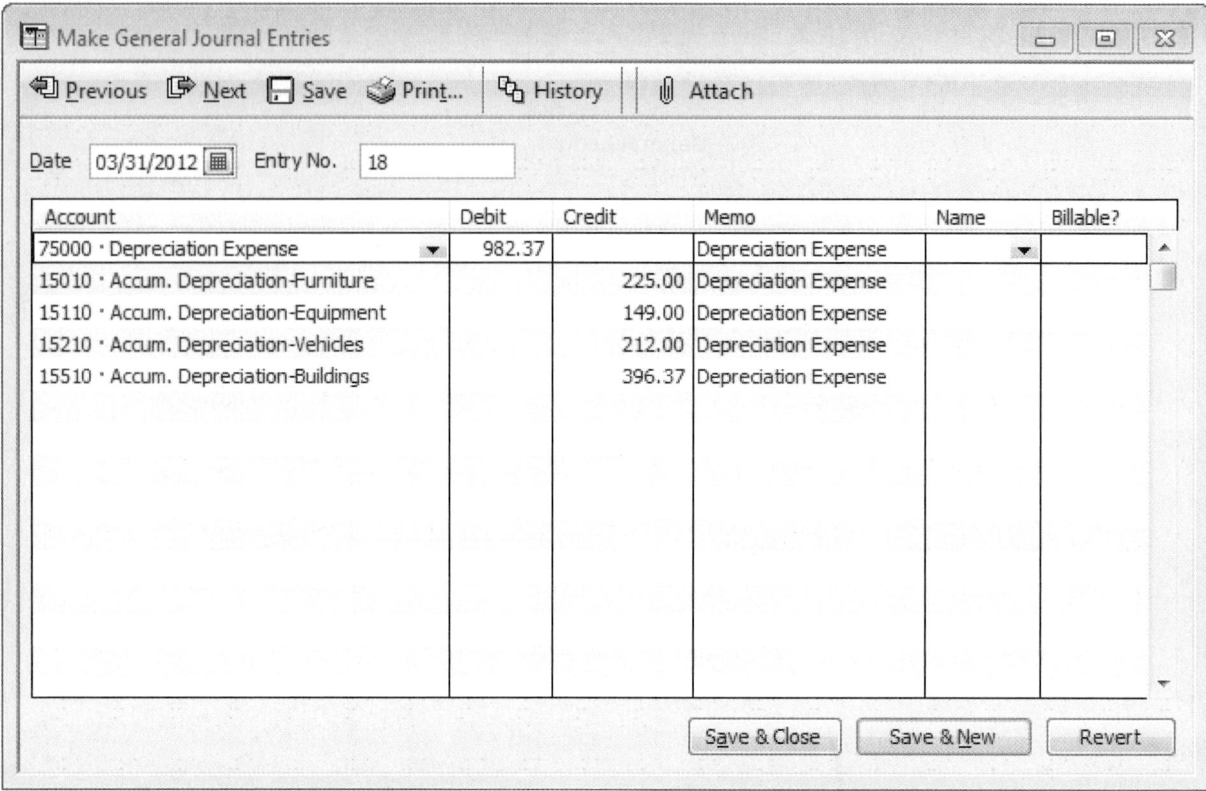

Figure 11:6

Figure 11:6 illustrates recording an adjusting entry for depreciation. Furthermore, adjusting entries are often saved as memorized transactions when the transaction repeats every month. Before closing the entry, see if the accountant has created a memorized transaction for depreciation.

Select ***Lists>>Memorized Transactions List*** on the main menu.

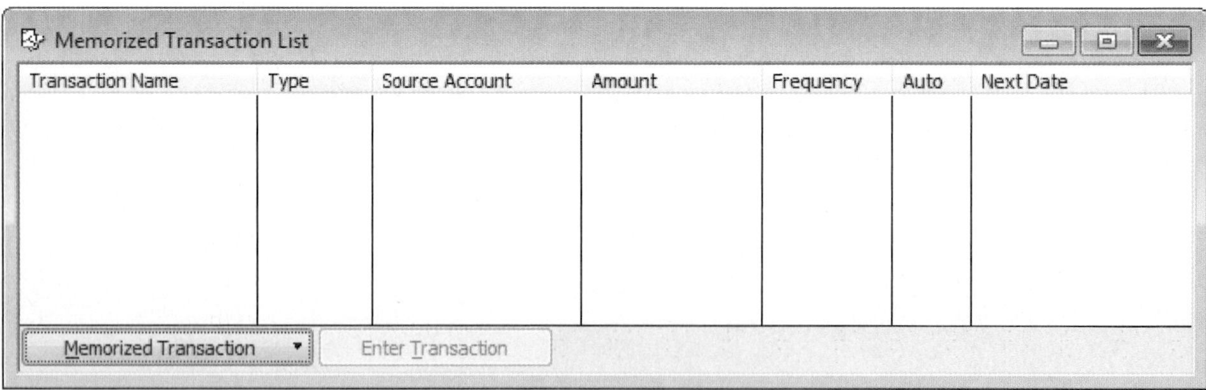

Figure 11:7

There are no memorized transactions. You will now memorize the depreciation entry.

Return to the open journal entry and select ***Edit>>Memorize General Journal*** on the main menu. Next, enter the information shown in Figure 11:8 and click **OK.**

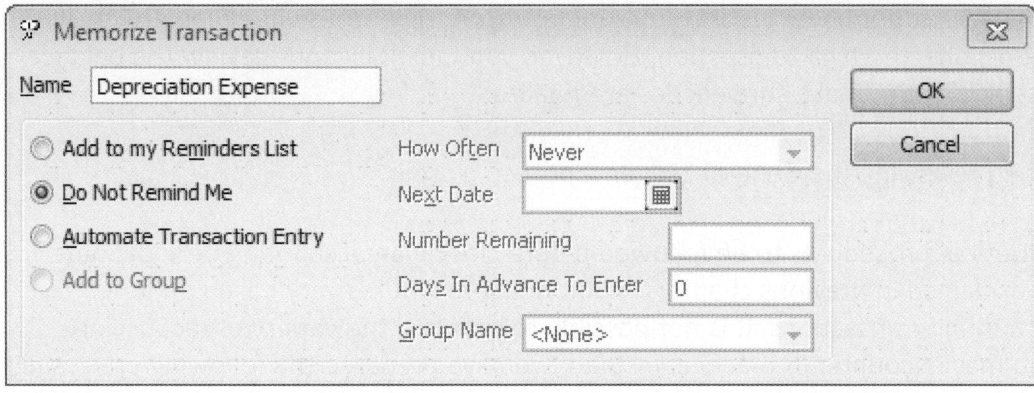

Figure 11:8

Click **X** to close the journal entry window. Return to the Memorized Transaction List and notice your memorized entry before clicking **X** to close the list.

Now is a good time to talk about using a suspense account. Scroll to the bottom of the General Ledger report to locate the **99999 Suspense** account. This account is used when you need to post an entry but do not have all the information necessary to complete it.

For instance, assume the company sold a vehicle costing $3,000 and received $500 in cash. You cannot delay recording cash on the sale; however, you do not have final depreciation on the vehicle to finalize gain or loss on the sale. This is where the entry can be posted using the suspense account. The following illustrates the journal entry to post the transaction using the suspense account.

	Debit	Credit
10200 Regular Checking Account	$ 500	
99999 Suspense	$2,500	
15200 Vehicles		$3,000

When you later calculate that $1,000 was previously recorded to the accumulated vehicle depreciation account and that final depreciation is $1,200, the following journal entry records the depreciation adjustment.

	Debit	Credit
75000 Depreciation Expense	$200	
15210 Accum. Depreciation – Vehicles		$200

You would then reclassify the earlier suspense account entry by recording the next journal entry.

	Debit	Credit
15210 Accum. Depreciation – Vehicles	$1,200	
90000 Gain/Loss on Sale of Assets	$1,300	
99999 Suspense		$2,500

Thus, the suspense account becomes a useful tool for recording entries when you are unsure of all the accounts affected by a transaction. However, you must diligently review the balance in the suspense account to make sure entries are finalized.

You have finished reviewing the General Ledger report so close it.

There are a variety of procedures to be followed before closing an accounting period. Some of these were explained in previous chapters. Additional procedures vary based on a company's accounting transactions. It is not possible to simulate the variety of reconciling procedures you may encounter in practice. Instead, we have prepared the following preclosing checklist to help guide you in the future.

Preclosing Checklist	
Review Pending Transactions	Review pending sales to verify all sales income has been recognized.
	Review pending purchases to verify all expenses have been recognized.
	Review payroll tax liability accounts to ensure timely payment.
Reconciliation Procedures	Reconcile all bank statements.
	Reconcile the A/R aging report to the accounts receivable control account. (Performed in Chapters 4 and 8.)
	Reconcile the inventory valuation report to the inventory control account. (Performed in Chapter 8.)
	Reconcile fixed asset reports to fixed asset control accounts. Often fixed asset costs and depreciation will be tracked outside the software. QBP can track fixed asset costs and depreciation but this feature is not illustrated.
	Reconcile the A/P aging report to the accounts payable control account. (Performed in Chapters 5 and 9.)
Adjusting Entries	Post petty cash transactions.
	Review prepaid expenses for expired costs.
	Review accrued liability accounts such as wages and taxes payable.
	Review expenses in the prior period to identify expenses that need to be recognized in the current period. For example, missing utility bills or recurring rent transactions.
	Review posted expenses for prepaid costs and for fixed assets expensed to office supplies.

ADJUSTING ENTRIES

In this topic, you post the remaining adjusting entries for March. The accountant has already posted entries for depreciation expense. When posting depreciation, keep in mind that this is an estimate of expense based on ending assets held in the prior year. Actual depreciation expense is then adjusted at year-end to take into account asset additions and deletions during the year.

All that remains is transferring funds from the regular checking account to the payroll checking, expensing expired prepaid expense, accruing wage expense, and writing a check to reimburse petty cash. In the next exercise, you post accrued wages and petty cash. In the *You Try* exercise that follows, you post entries for expired prepaid insurance and the bank transfer.

STEPS TO ENTER ADJUSTING ENTRIES

1. You will be recording accrued wages for March. The steps for calculating the amount to accrue are as follows:

    a. Open the **Employee Earnings Summary** report to determine the average weekly wage expense. Enter **3/1/12** to **3/31/12** as the date range. Total the salary and hourly wage amounts and divide by 4. The weekly average, rounded to the nearest dollar, is $3,569.00, computed as (8,515.40 + 5,760.00) / 4.

    b. Next, compute a daily average wage by dividing the weekly average by 5 working days. The daily average, rounded up to the nearest hundred, is $800.00.

    c. Finally, multiply the daily average by the number of days to accrue. For March, this is 10 days because the last pay period ended March 18. Thus, the amount to accrue is $8,000.00.

2. Close the report. Select ***Company>>Make General Journal Entries*** on the main menu and enter the information illustrated in Figure 11:9. Click **Save & New.**

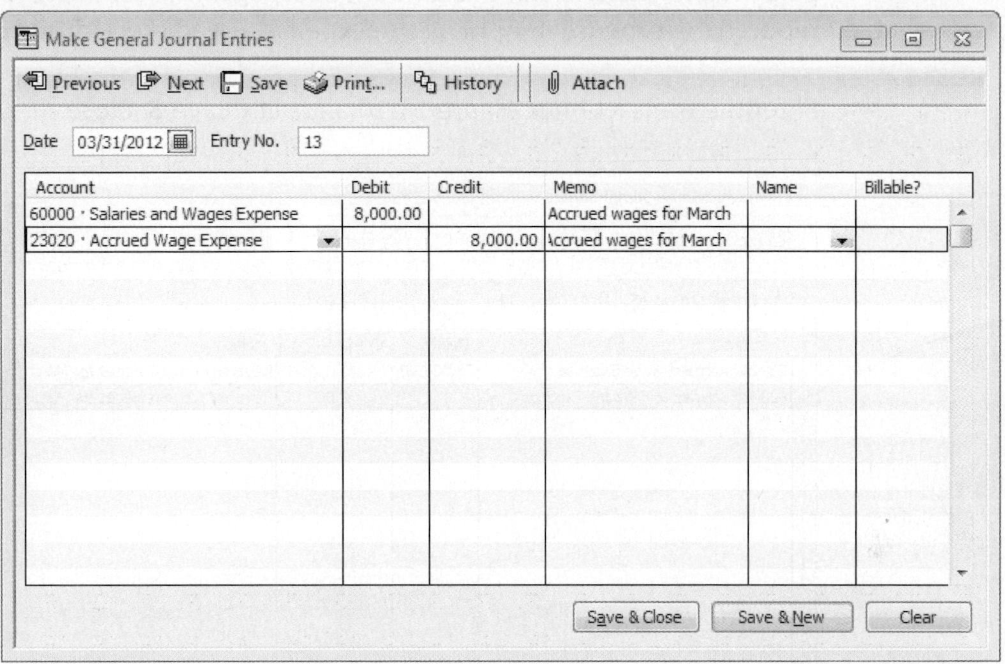

Figure 11:9

3. You will now record an entry on April 1 that reverses the payroll accrued in the previous step. Remember that the amount accrued in March will actually be paid in April. When paid, this amount posts again. Thus, the reversing entry reduces the expense in April by the expense already recognized in March.

   Enter the transaction in Figure 11:10 and click **Save & Close.**

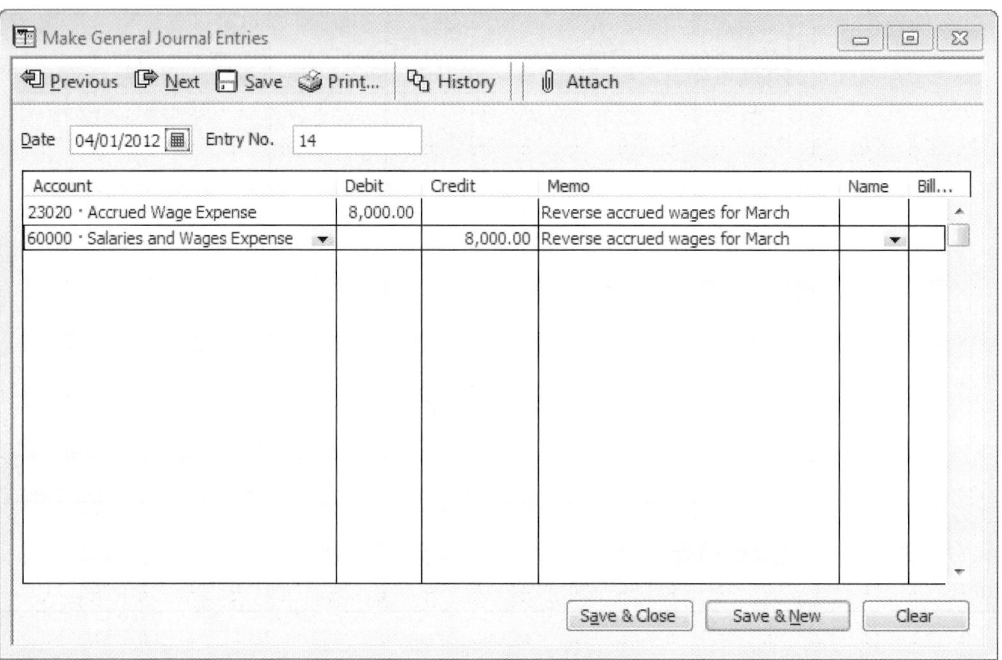

Figure 11:10

4. Now create a check that reimburses petty cash. Click the **Write Checks** icon and complete the check as illustrated in Figure 11:11. Verify that the **To be printed** option is unchecked and enter **10231** as the check **No.**

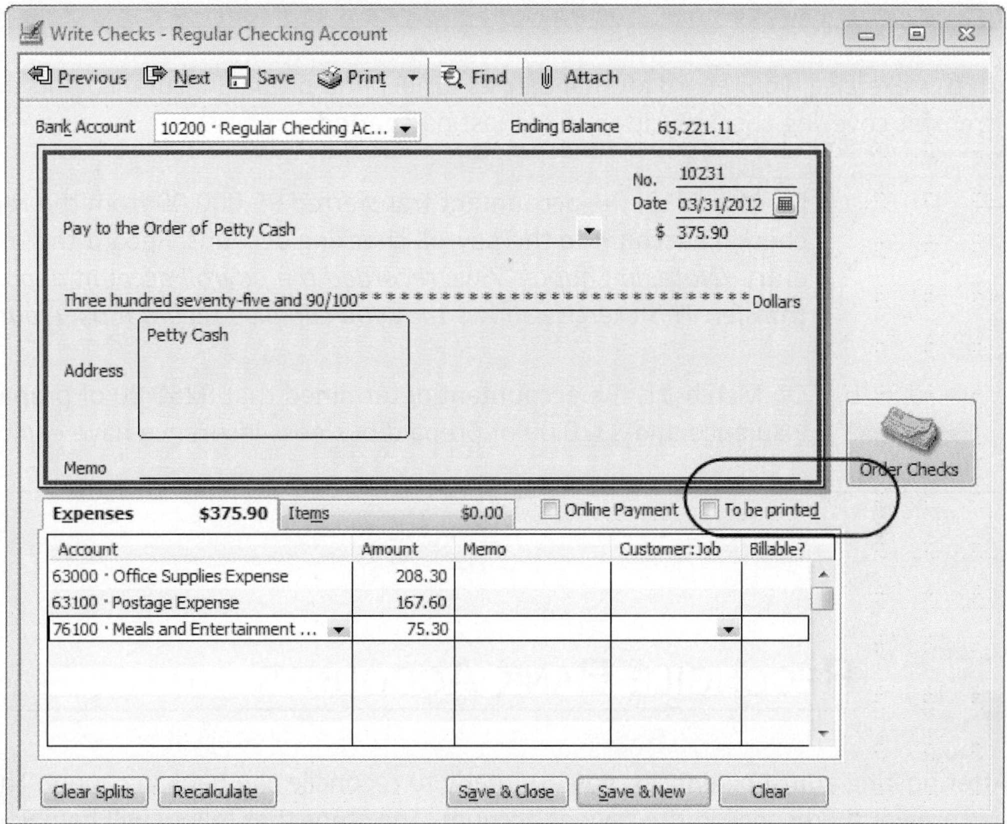

Figure 11:11

5. Click **Save & Close.**

FINISH RECORDING MARCH ADJUSTING ENTRIES

In this exercise, you record journal entries for expired prepaid insurance and the bank transfer covering checks written in the last pay period.

a. On March 19, the accountant transferred $5,000.00 from the regular checking account to the payroll checking account. Record this as a journal entry. *(Note: In Chapter 7 we recorded the payroll account deposit as a bank transfer. This exercise shows that you can also record it as a journal entry.)*

b. On March 31, the accountant determined that $250.00 of prepaid auto insurance and $310.00 of prepaid business insurance have expired.

Reconcile Bank Accounts

After posting adjusting entries, you are ready to reconcile the bank accounts. The accountant has previously reconciled the savings account. The steps that follow will help you reconcile the regular checking account. Thereafter, you will reconcile the payroll checking account in the *You Try* exercise. *(Note: There is an online video for this topic.)*

On the Home page, click **Reconcile** under **Banking.** The reconciliation process always begins by selecting the bank account. Select the **10200 Regular Checking Account.** (See Figure 11:12.)

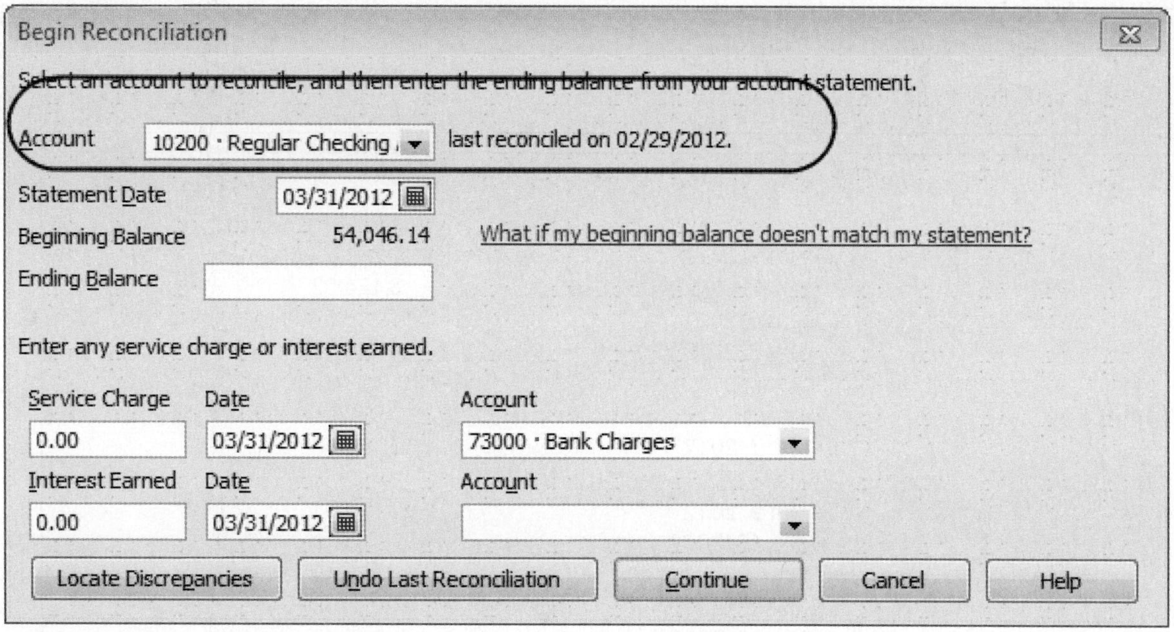

Begin Reconciliation	
Select an account to reconcile, and then enter the ending balance from your account statement.	
Account	10200 · Regular Checking last reconciled on 02/29/2012.
Statement Date	03/31/2012
Beginning Balance	54,046.14 What if my beginning balance doesn't match my statement?
Ending Balance	

Enter any service charge or interest earned.

Service Charge	Date	Account
0.00	03/31/2012	73000 · Bank Charges
Interest Earned	**Date**	**Account**
0.00	03/31/2012	

Locate Discrepancies | Undo Last Reconciliation | Continue | Cancel | Help

Figure 11:12

Baxter received the March bank statement for the regular checking account. The next exercise walks through reconciling this account to the March bank statement that follows.

Baxter Garden Supply
Bank Statement March 31, 2012

Beginning Balance from February Statement				$ 54,046.14
March Deposits				
	Mar 2, 2012		2,211.82	
	Mar 2, 2012		5,124.52	
	Mar 6, 2012		1,245.57	
	Mar 6, 2012		611.42	
	Mar 6, 2012		5,185.67	
	Mar 7, 2012		872.04	
	Mar 7, 2012		7,196.00	
	Mar 9, 2012		2,492.55	
	Mar 9, 2012		2,976.11	
	Mar 13, 2012		3,934.38	
	Mar 13, 2012		22,939.49	
	Mar 13, 2012		5,138.68	
	Mar 19, 2012		4,695.75	
	Mar 19, 2012		1,039.11	
	Mar 20, 2012		1,469.86	
	Mar 20, 2012		1,169.77	
Total Deposits for March				68,302.74
March Checks Cleared				
	Mar 3, 2012	10211	327.57	
	Mar 3, 2012	10212	1,365.44	
	Mar 10, 2012	10213	1,691.10	
	Mar 10, 2012	10214	550.00	
	Mar 18, 2012	10215	1,399.30	
	Mar 18, 2012	10216	4,953.24	
	Mar 18, 2012	10217	28,434.65	
	Mar 23, 2012	10218	602.25	
	Mar 23, 2012	10219	1,167.25	
	Mar 23, 2012	10220	274.56	
	Mar 23, 2012	10221	167.00	
	Mar 23, 2012	10222	2,252.75	
	Mar 27, 2012	10223	1,706.02	
	Mar 29, 2012	10225	291.32	
	Mar 31, 2012	10230	2,237.00	
	Mar 31, 2012	10231	451.20	
Total Cleared Checks for March				47,870.65
Less Bank Transfers				
	Mar 6, 2012		6,000.00	
	Mar 19, 2012		5,000.00	
Total March Transfers				11,000.00
March Service Charges				75.00
Ending Bank Balance March 31, 2012				$ 63,403.23

Figure 11:13

STEPS TO RECONCILE THE CHECKING ACCOUNT

1. Verify **10200 Regular Checking** as the **Account.**

   Referring to the bank statement, enter the **Ending Balance, Date,** and **Service Charge** as shown in Figure 11:14. Verify that the service charge will post to **73000 Bank Charges.**

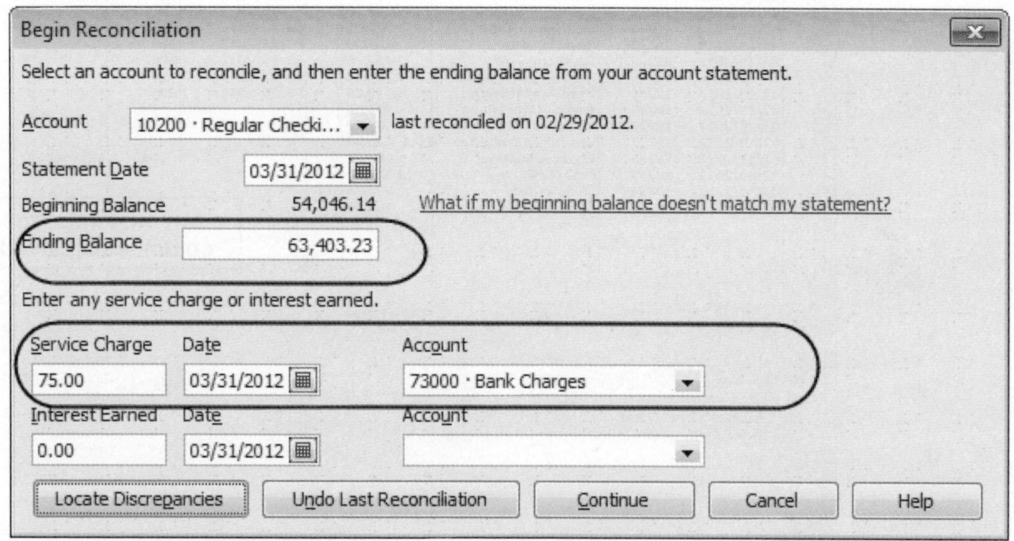

Figure 11:14

2. Click **Continue** to proceed to the screen for selecting deposits and checks clearing the March bank statement.

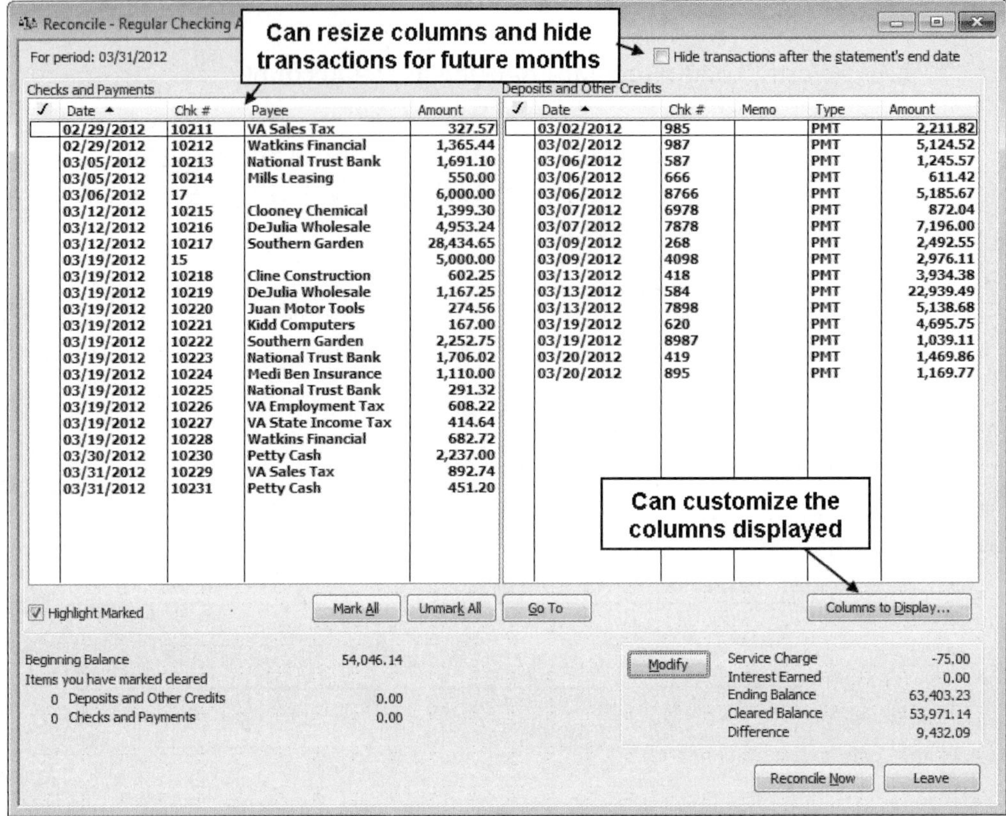

Figure 11:15

3. We will now explain using this window.

Modify reopens the Begin Reconciliation window illustrated in Step 1 to change entries.

Outstanding checks and bank transfers are listed on the left. On the right are deposits and void checks.

Click a transaction to clear it. *(Note: You can also click the Mark All button and then click individual checks and deposits that have not cleared.)*

You can double click a transaction to reopen it.

The **Columns to Display** button customizes the columns.

The **Hide transactions after the statement's end date** option removes transactions posted in future months from the window.

4. Click **Mark All** and refer to the totals listed at the bottom of the window. (See Figure 11:16.) The total for **Deposits** and **Other Credits** equals the total cleared deposits on the bank statement. You will now work on the checks.

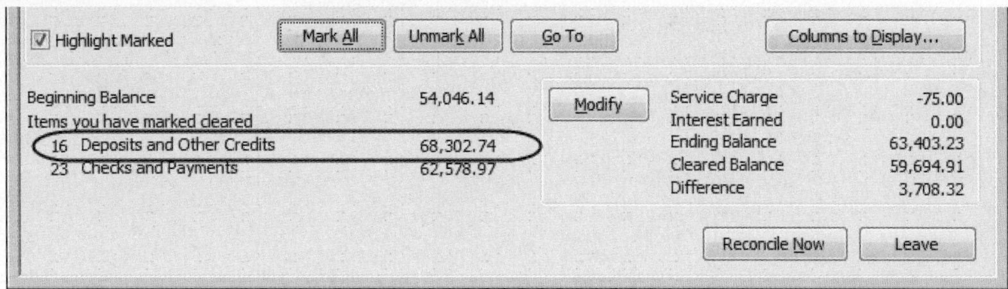

Figure 11:16

5. Refer again to the bank statement and click to deselect checks in the Reconcile window that have not cleared the statement. When finished, your results will compare to the results illustrated in Figure 11:17. *(Hint: Click the Chk # column header on the left to sort by check number.)*

   The total for **Checks, Payments,** and **Service Charges** now equals the sum of bank transfers, service charges, and cleared checks on the bank statement.

   You cannot complete the next step until the **Difference** equals zero.

   If you have difficulty reconciling an account, the **Leave** button saves your work and closes the reconciliation window. You can return later to complete the reconciliation.

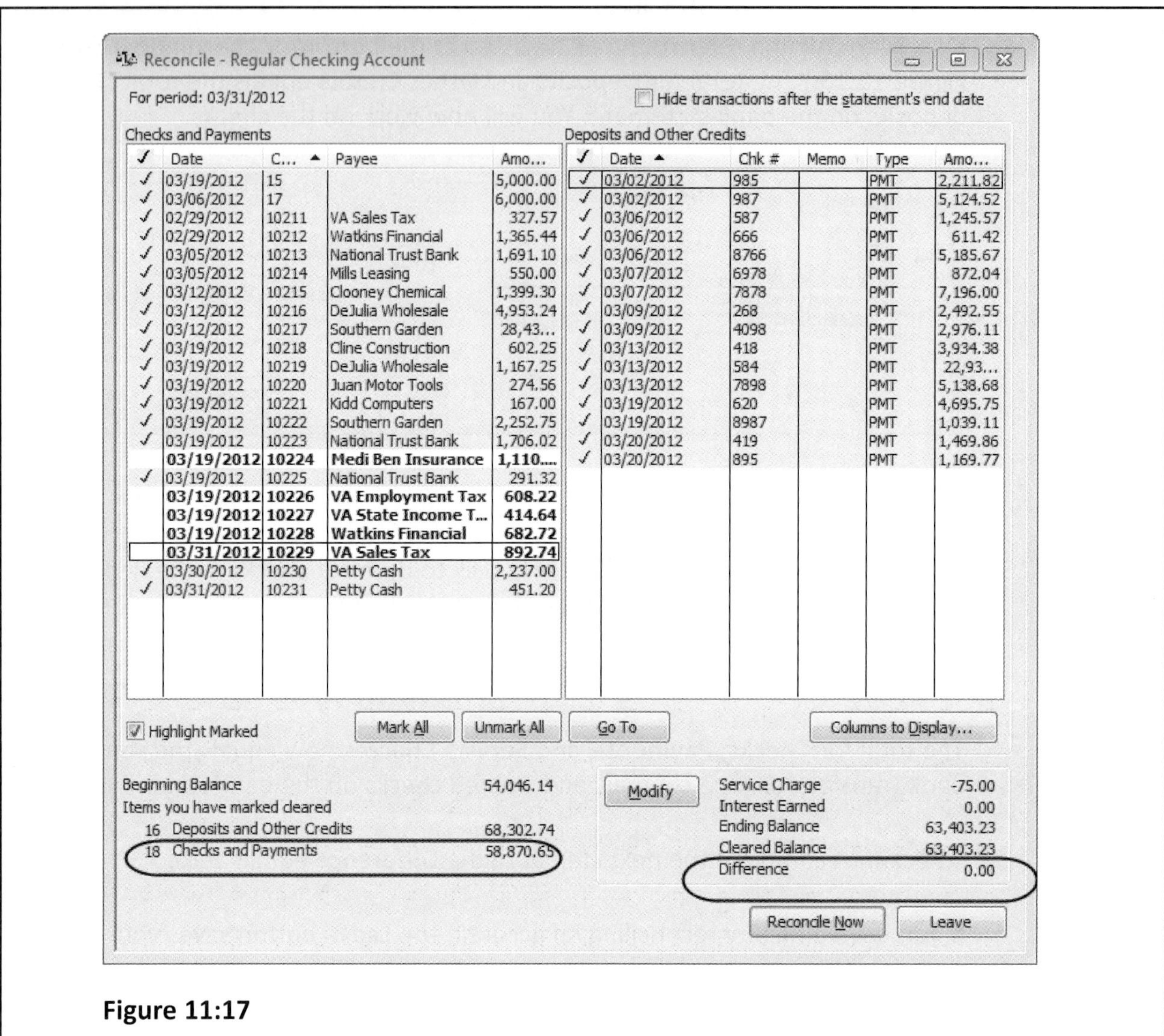
Reconcile - Regular Checking Account
For period: 03/31/2012
Hide transactions after the statement's end date
Checks and Payments
✓ Date C... Payee Amo...
✓ 03/19/2012 15 5,000.00
✓ 03/06/2012 17 6,000.00
✓ 02/29/2012 10211 VA Sales Tax 327.57
✓ 02/29/2012 10212 Watkins Financial 1,365.44
✓ 03/05/2012 10213 National Trust Bank 1,691.10
✓ 03/05/2012 10214 Mills Leasing 550.00
✓ 03/12/2012 10215 Clooney Chemical 1,399.30
✓ 03/12/2012 10216 DeJulia Wholesale 4,953.24
✓ 03/12/2012 10217 Southern Garden 28,43...
✓ 03/19/2012 10218 Cline Construction 602.25
✓ 03/19/2012 10219 DeJulia Wholesale 1,167.25
✓ 03/19/2012 10220 Juan Motor Tools 274.56
✓ 03/19/2012 10221 Kidd Computers 167.00
✓ 03/19/2012 10222 Southern Garden 2,252.75
✓ 03/19/2012 10223 National Trust Bank 1,706.02
03/19/2012 10224 Medi Ben Insurance 1,110....
✓ 03/19/2012 10225 National Trust Bank 291.32
03/19/2012 10226 VA Employment Tax 608.22
03/19/2012 10227 VA State Income T... 414.64
03/19/2012 10228 Watkins Financial 682.72
03/31/2012 10229 VA Sales Tax 892.74
✓ 03/30/2012 10230 Petty Cash 2,237.00
✓ 03/31/2012 10231 Petty Cash 451.20
Deposits and Other Credits
✓ Date Chk # Memo Type Amo...
✓ 03/02/2012 985 PMT 2,211.82
✓ 03/02/2012 987 PMT 5,124.52
✓ 03/06/2012 587 PMT 1,245.57
✓ 03/06/2012 666 PMT 611.42
✓ 03/06/2012 8766 PMT 5,185.67
✓ 03/07/2012 6978 PMT 872.04
✓ 03/07/2012 7878 PMT 7,196.00
✓ 03/09/2012 268 PMT 2,492.55
✓ 03/09/2012 4098 PMT 2,976.11
✓ 03/13/2012 418 PMT 3,934.38
✓ 03/13/2012 584 PMT 22,93...
✓ 03/13/2012 7898 PMT 5,138.68
✓ 03/19/2012 620 PMT 4,695.75
✓ 03/19/2012 8987 PMT 1,039.11
✓ 03/20/2012 419 PMT 1,469.86
✓ 03/20/2012 895 PMT 1,169.77
Highlight Marked
Mark All
Unmark All
Go To
Columns to Display...
Beginning Balance 54,046.14
Items you have marked cleared
16 Deposits and Other Credits 68,302.74
18 Checks and Payments 58,870.65
Modify
Service Charge -75.00
Interest Earned 0.00
Ending Balance 63,403.23
Cleared Balance 63,403.23
Difference 0.00
Reconcile Now
Leave

Figure 11:17

6. Click **Reconcile Now** and Figure 11:18 opens. Keep the report option of **Both** and click **Display.** *(Note: Turn off future messages when QBP prompts with information about reports.)*

Figure 11:18

7. Figure 11:19 is the **Reconciliation Summary** report. The **Cleared Balance** agrees with the ending balance on the March bank statement. You will not print this statement because there is no information on individual items, so close it.

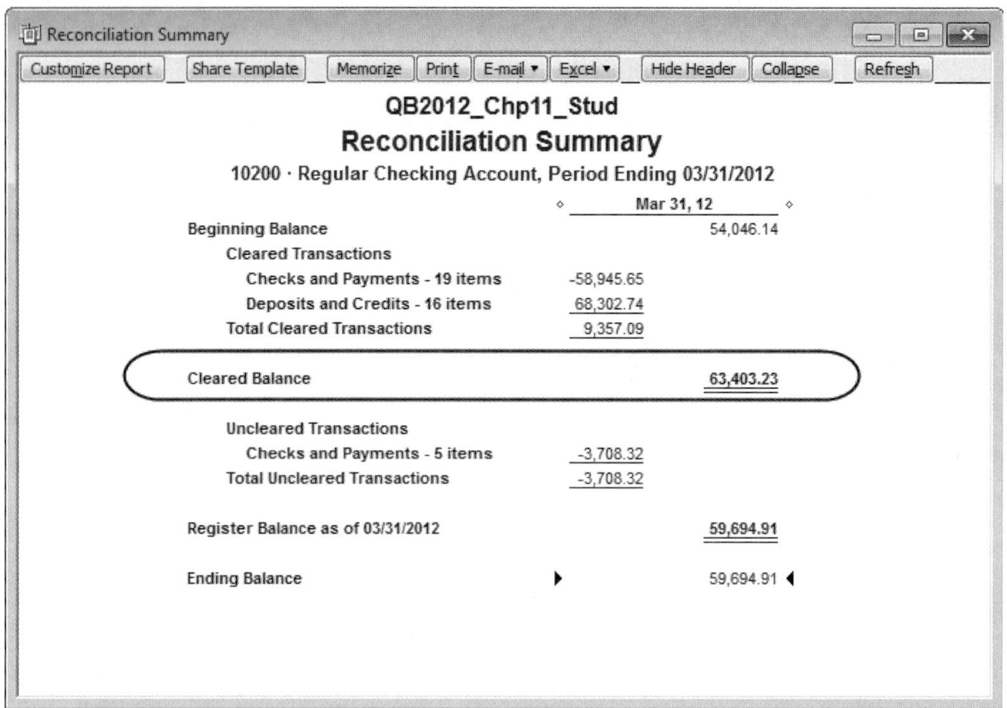

Figure 11:19

8. You now see the **Reconciliation Detail** report, which was located behind the summary report. You will always want to print this report because it provides information on individual transactions.

   Scroll down to where the report lists the **Cleared Balance.** Again, this amount will agree with the ending balance on the March bank statement. Beneath this are transactions that should clear the April bank statement.

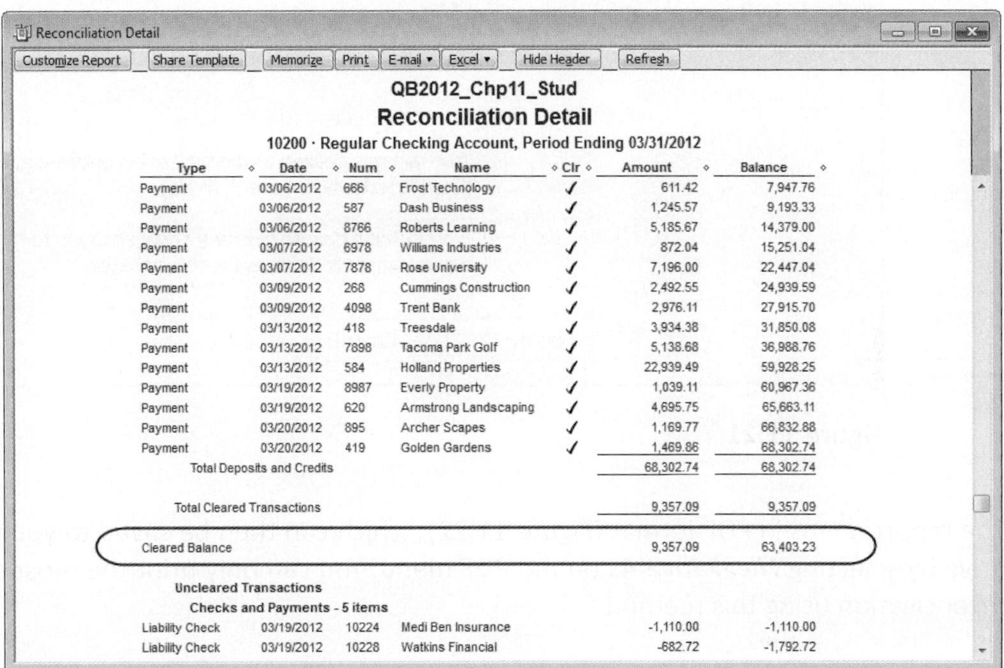

Reconciliation Detail

Customize Report | Share Template | Memorize | Print | E-mail ▾ | Excel ▾ | Hide Header | Refresh

QB2012_Chp11_Stud

Reconciliation Detail

10200 · Regular Checking Account, Period Ending 03/31/2012

Type	Date	Num	Name	Clr	Amount	Balance
Payment	03/06/2012	666	Frost Technology	✓	611.42	7,947.76
Payment	03/06/2012	587	Dash Business	✓	1,245.57	9,193.33
Payment	03/06/2012	8766	Roberts Learning	✓	5,185.67	14,379.00
Payment	03/07/2012	6978	Williams Industries	✓	872.04	15,251.04
Payment	03/07/2012	7878	Rose University	✓	7,196.00	22,447.04
Payment	03/09/2012	268	Cummings Construction	✓	2,492.55	24,939.59
Payment	03/09/2012	4098	Trent Bank	✓	2,976.11	27,915.70
Payment	03/13/2012	418	Treesdale	✓	3,934.38	31,850.08
Payment	03/13/2012	7898	Tacoma Park Golf	✓	5,138.68	36,988.76
Payment	03/13/2012	584	Holland Properties	✓	22,939.49	59,928.25
Payment	03/19/2012	8987	Everly Property	✓	1,039.11	60,967.36
Payment	03/19/2012	620	Armstrong Landscaping	✓	4,695.75	65,663.11
Payment	03/20/2012	895	Archer Scapes	✓	1,169.77	66,832.88
Payment	03/20/2012	419	Golden Gardens	✓	1,469.86	68,302.74
Total Deposits and Credits					68,302.74	68,302.74
Total Cleared Transactions					9,357.09	9,357.09
Cleared Balance					9,357.09	63,403.23
Uncleared Transactions						
Checks and Payments - 5 items						
Liability Check	03/19/2012	10224	Medi Ben Insurance		-1,110.00	-1,110.00
Liability Check	03/19/2012	10228	Watkins Financial		-682.72	-1,792.72

Figure 11:20

9. If needed, you can click the **Print** button on the Reconciliation Detail report, select a printer, and click **Print.** Close the report.

You can reprint reconciliation reports by selecting ***Reports>>Banking>>Previous Reconciliation*** on the main menu. Open the window illustrated in Figure 11:21 and choose the options shown. Click **Display.**

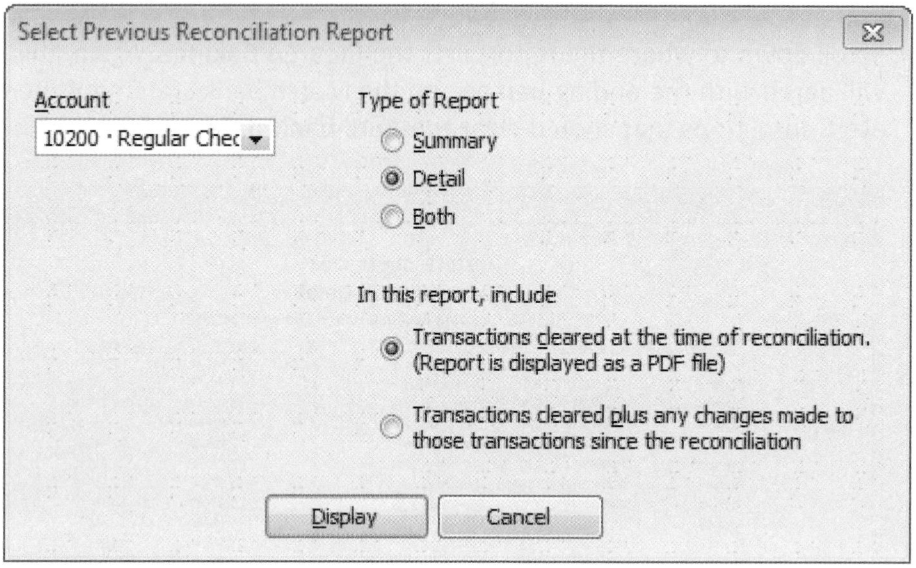

Select Previous Reconciliation Report

Account

10200 · Regular Chec

Type of Report

Summary

Detail

Both

In this report, include

Transactions cleared at the time of reconciliation. (Report is displayed as a PDF file)

Transactions cleared plus any changes made to those transactions since the reconciliation

Display Cancel

Figure 11:21

The report opens in PDF format (Figure 11:22), which can then be saved to your local hard drive by selecting ***File>>Save As*** on the PDF menu. You can only print the most recent reconciliation using this method.

Close the report.

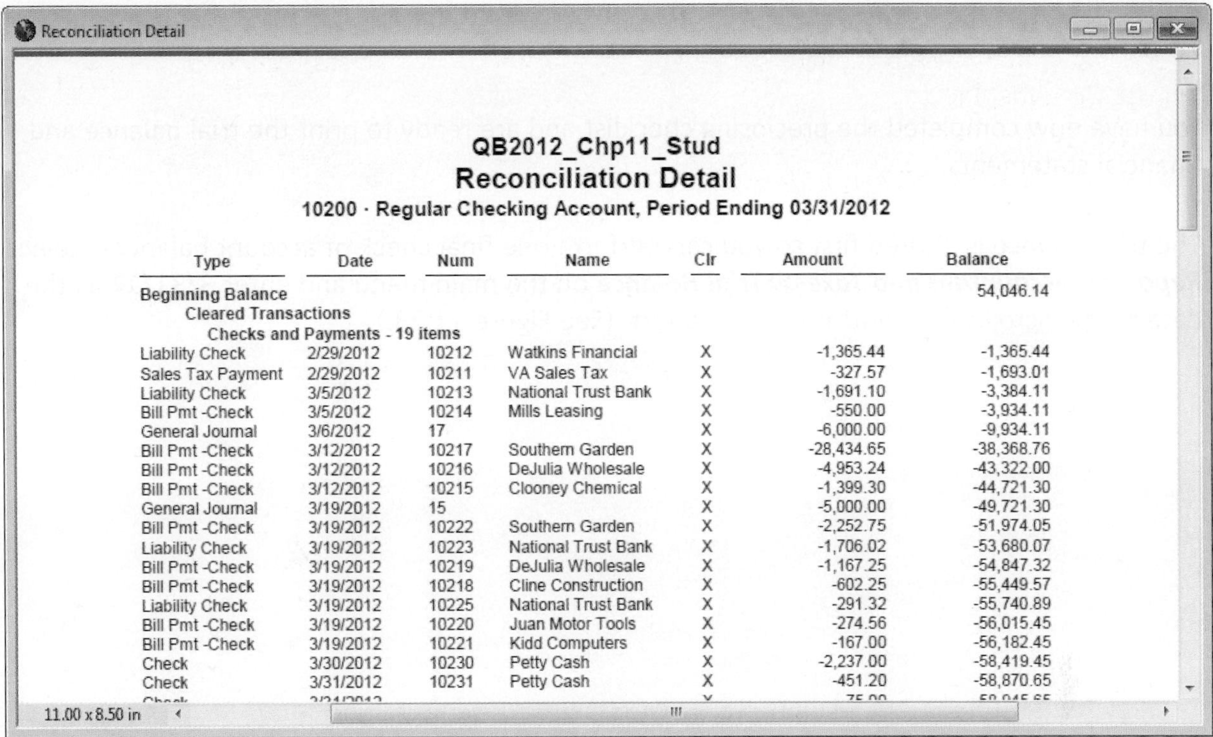
Reconciliation Detail

QB2012_Chp11_Stud
Reconciliation Detail
10200 · Regular Checking Account, Period Ending 03/31/2012

Type	Date	Num	Name	Clr	Amount	Balance
Beginning Balance						54,046.14
Cleared Transactions						
Checks and Payments - 19 items						
Liability Check	2/29/2012	10212	Watkins Financial	X	-1,365.44	-1,365.44
Sales Tax Payment	2/29/2012	10211	VA Sales Tax	X	-327.57	-1,693.01
Liability Check	3/5/2012	10213	National Trust Bank	X	-1,691.10	-3,384.11
Bill Pmt -Check	3/5/2012	10214	Mills Leasing	X	-550.00	-3,934.11
General Journal	3/6/2012	17		X	-6,000.00	-9,934.11
Bill Pmt -Check	3/12/2012	10217	Southern Garden	X	-28,434.65	-38,368.76
Bill Pmt -Check	3/12/2012	10216	DeJulia Wholesale	X	-4,953.24	-43,322.00
Bill Pmt -Check	3/12/2012	10215	Clooney Chemical	X	-1,399.30	-44,721.30
General Journal	3/19/2012	15		X	-5,000.00	-49,721.30
Bill Pmt -Check	3/19/2012	10222	Southern Garden	X	-2,252.75	-51,974.05
Liability Check	3/19/2012	10223	National Trust Bank	X	-1,706.02	-53,680.07
Bill Pmt -Check	3/19/2012	10219	DeJulia Wholesale	X	-1,167.25	-54,847.32
Bill Pmt -Check	3/19/2012	10218	Cline Construction	X	-602.25	-55,449.57
Liability Check	3/19/2012	10225	National Trust Bank	X	-291.32	-55,740.89
Bill Pmt -Check	3/19/2012	10220	Juan Motor Tools	X	-274.56	-56,015.45
Bill Pmt -Check	3/19/2012	10221	Kidd Computers	X	-167.00	-56,182.45
Check	3/30/2012	10230	Petty Cash	X	-2,237.00	-58,419.45
Check	3/31/2012	10231	Petty Cash	X	-451.20	-58,870.65

11.00 x 8.50 in

Figure 11:22

RECONCILE THE PAYROLL CHECKING ACCOUNT

The March bank statement for the payroll checking account has arrived. All paychecks and deposits have cleared. Bank charges for March are $10.00 and the ending balance on the statement is $186.10.

Reconcile the account and print the Detail Reconciliation report.

FINANCIAL REPORTS

You have now completed the preclosing checklist and are ready to print the trial balance and financial statements.

The trial balance is printed first so you can perform one final check of account balances. Select ***Reports>>Accountant and Taxes>>Trial Balance*** on the main menu and enter **3/31/12** as the date range. Scroll to the bottom of the report. (See Figure 11:23.)

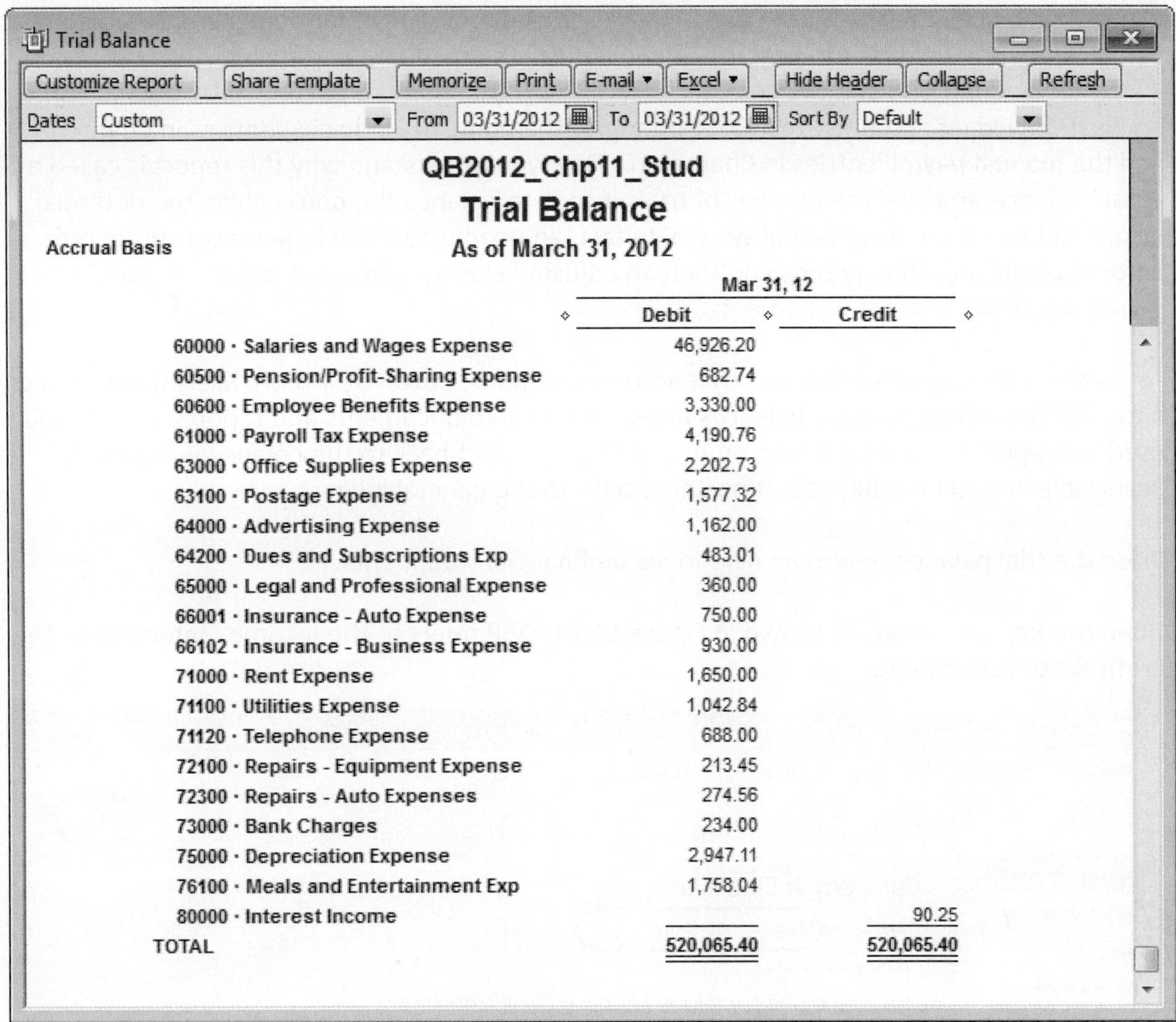

Trial Balance

Customize Report | Share Template | Memorize | Print | E-mail | Excel | Hide Header | Collapse | Refresh

Dates Custom From 03/31/2012 To 03/31/2012 Sort By Default

QB2012_Chp11_Stud

Trial Balance

Accrual Basis As of March 31, 2012

	Mar 31, 12	
	Debit	Credit
60000 · Salaries and Wages Expense	46,926.20	
60500 · Pension/Profit-Sharing Expense	682.74	
60600 · Employee Benefits Expense	3,330.00	
61000 · Payroll Tax Expense	4,190.76	
63000 · Office Supplies Expense	2,202.73	
63100 · Postage Expense	1,577.32	
64000 · Advertising Expense	1,162.00	
64200 · Dues and Subscriptions Exp	483.01	
65000 · Legal and Professional Expense	360.00	
66001 · Insurance - Auto Expense	750.00	
66102 · Insurance - Business Expense	930.00	
71000 · Rent Expense	1,650.00	
71100 · Utilities Expense	1,042.84	
71120 · Telephone Expense	688.00	
72100 · Repairs - Equipment Expense	213.45	
72300 · Repairs - Auto Expenses	274.56	
73000 · Bank Charges	234.00	
75000 · Depreciation Expense	2,947.11	
76100 · Meals and Entertainment Exp	1,758.04	
80000 · Interest Income		90.25
TOTAL	520,065.40	520,065.40

Figure 11:23

In a manual accounting system, this report was critical to proving that debits equaled credits before preparing financial statements. You will recall the manual sales journal entries illustrated in Chapter 8 and the cross footing of this journal before posting entries to customer and general ledger accounts. You also remember the manual purchasing entries in Chapter 9 and the manual payroll entries in Chapter 10. Now you understand why this report is called a "trial" balance. Imagine the number of trials it took to balance the books given the potential errors that can occur in a manual system. In fact, an unadjusted trial balance was prepared before posting adjusting entries and then an adjusted closing trial balance was prepared before preparing financial statements.

Today the trial balance still verifies that accounts balance; however, it more likely functions as a tool for reconciling account balances to external source documents and reports. In fact, you used the report to tie the balance on the A/R aging report back to the balance in Accounts Receivable and to tie other report balances back to the general ledger.

Close the trial balance so we can next focus on financial statements.

Open the **Report Center.** As shown in Figure 11:24, QBP refers to the Income Statement as the **Profit & Loss** statement.

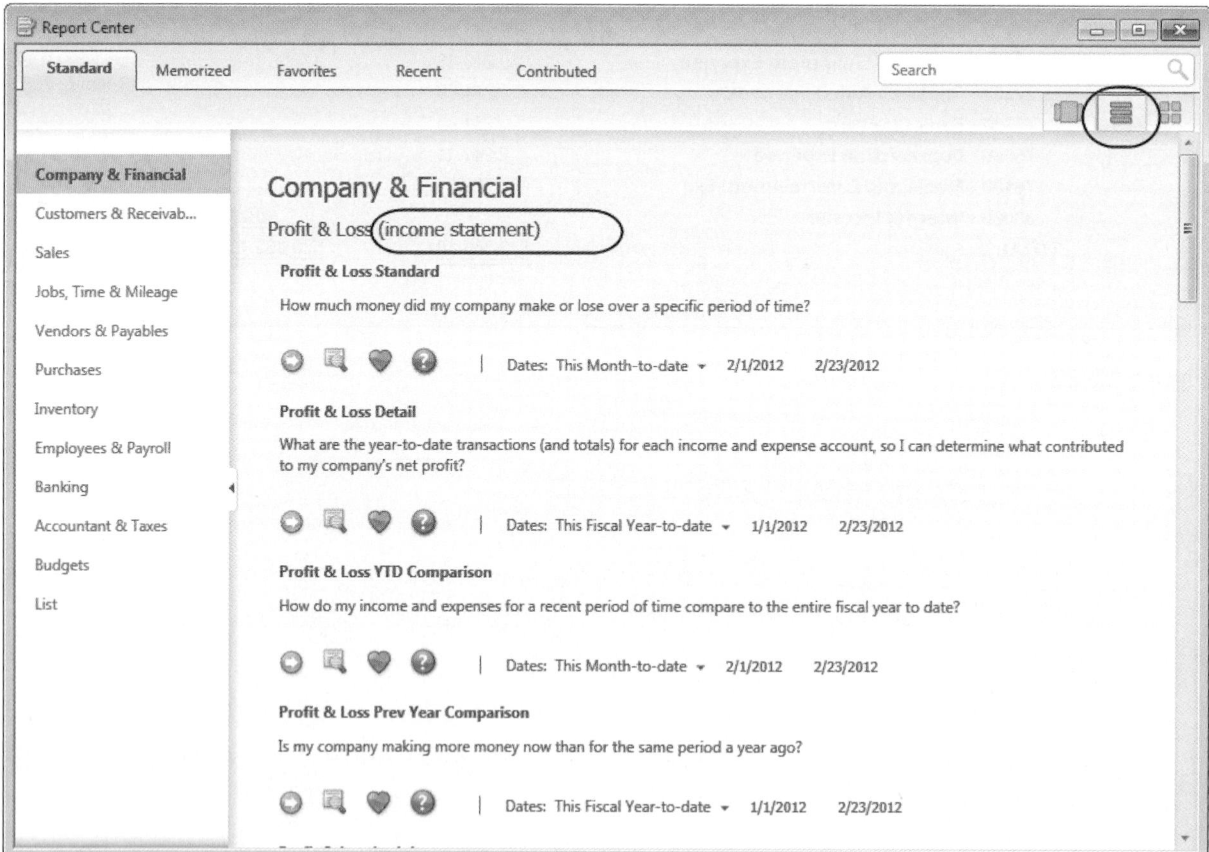

Figure 11:24

Open the **Profit & Loss Standard** statement and enter the date range of **1/01/12** to **3/31/12.** Scroll to the bottom and locate year-to-date net income. (See Figure 11:25.) *(Note: This statement is on the Accrual Basis. If the company reports on the Cash Basis, you would need to click Customize Report and choose the Cash option.)*

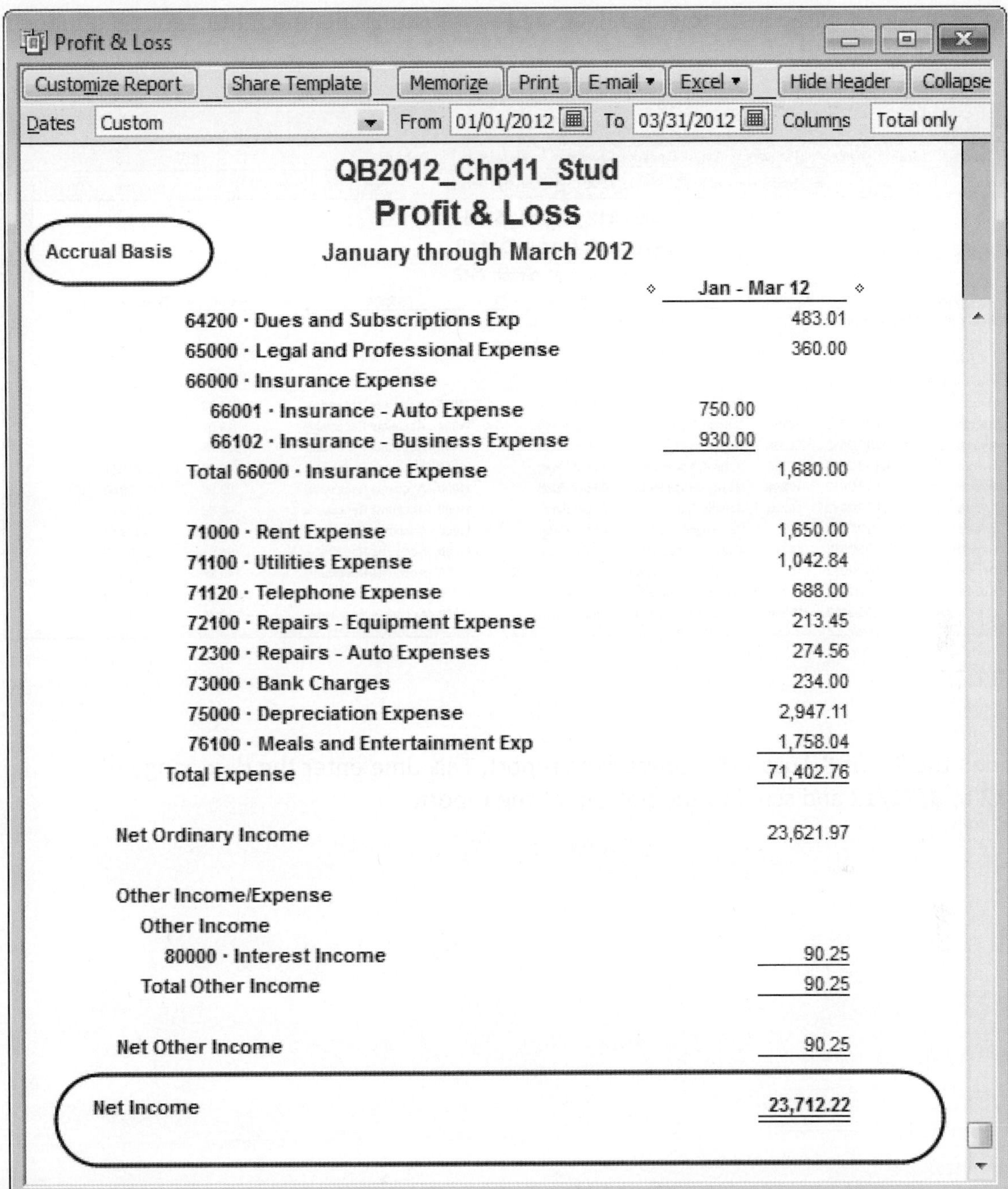

Figure 11:25

Close this report and open the **Profit & Loss Detail** report. Again enter the date range of **1/01/12** to **3/31/12**.

The report in Figure 11:26 lists individual transactions affecting Income Statement accounts. Close this report.

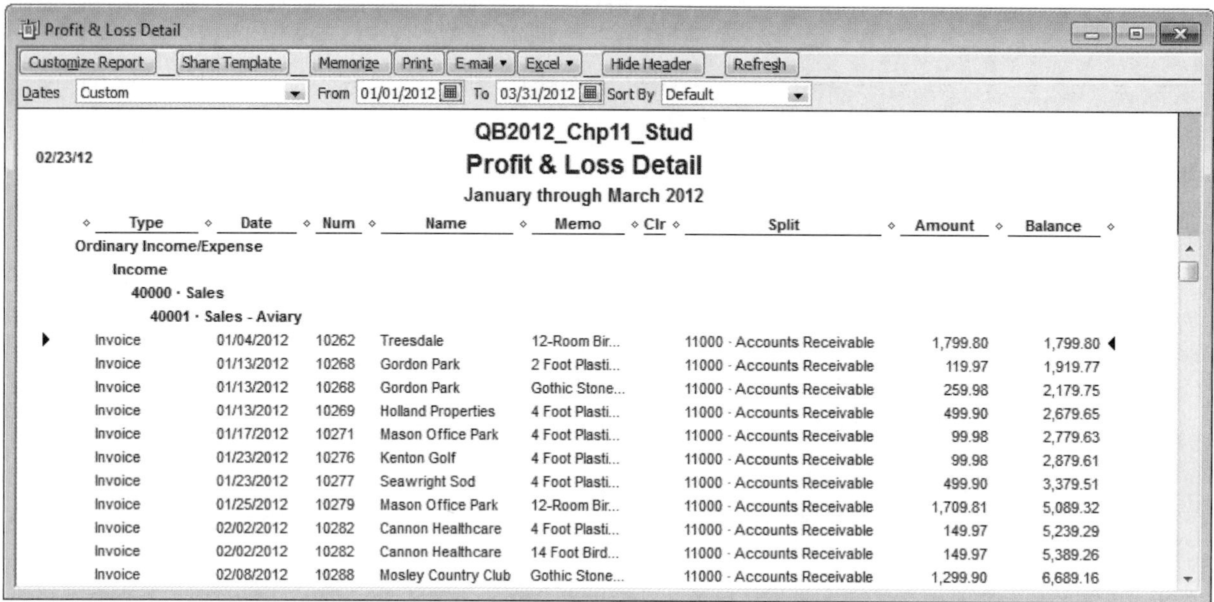

02/23/12

QB2012_Chp11_Stud

Profit & Loss Detail

January through March 2012

Type	Date	Num	Name	Memo	Clr	Split	Amount	Balance
Ordinary Income/Expense								
Income								
40000 · Sales								
40001 · Sales - Aviary								
Invoice	01/04/2012	10262	Treesdale	12-Room Bir...		11000 · Accounts Receivable	1,799.80	1,799.80
Invoice	01/13/2012	10268	Gordon Park	2 Foot Plasti...		11000 · Accounts Receivable	119.97	1,919.77
Invoice	01/13/2012	10268	Gordon Park	Gothic Stone...		11000 · Accounts Receivable	259.98	2,179.75
Invoice	01/13/2012	10269	Holland Properties	4 Foot Plasti...		11000 · Accounts Receivable	499.90	2,679.65
Invoice	01/17/2012	10271	Mason Office Park	4 Foot Plasti...		11000 · Accounts Receivable	99.98	2,779.63
Invoice	01/23/2012	10276	Kenton Golf	4 Foot Plasti...		11000 · Accounts Receivable	99.98	2,879.61
Invoice	01/23/2012	10277	Seawright Sod	4 Foot Plasti...		11000 · Accounts Receivable	499.90	3,379.51
Invoice	01/25/2012	10279	Mason Office Park	12-Room Bir...		11000 · Accounts Receivable	1,709.81	5,089.32
Invoice	02/02/2012	10282	Cannon Healthcare	4 Foot Plasti...		11000 · Accounts Receivable	149.97	5,239.29
Invoice	02/02/2012	10282	Cannon Healthcare	14 Foot Bird...		11000 · Accounts Receivable	149.97	5,389.26
Invoice	02/08/2012	10288	Mosley Country Club	Gothic Stone...		11000 · Accounts Receivable	1,299.90	6,689.16

Figure 11:26

Now open the **Profit & Loss YTD Comparison** report. This time enter the date range of **3/01/12** to **3/31/12** and scroll to the bottom of the report.

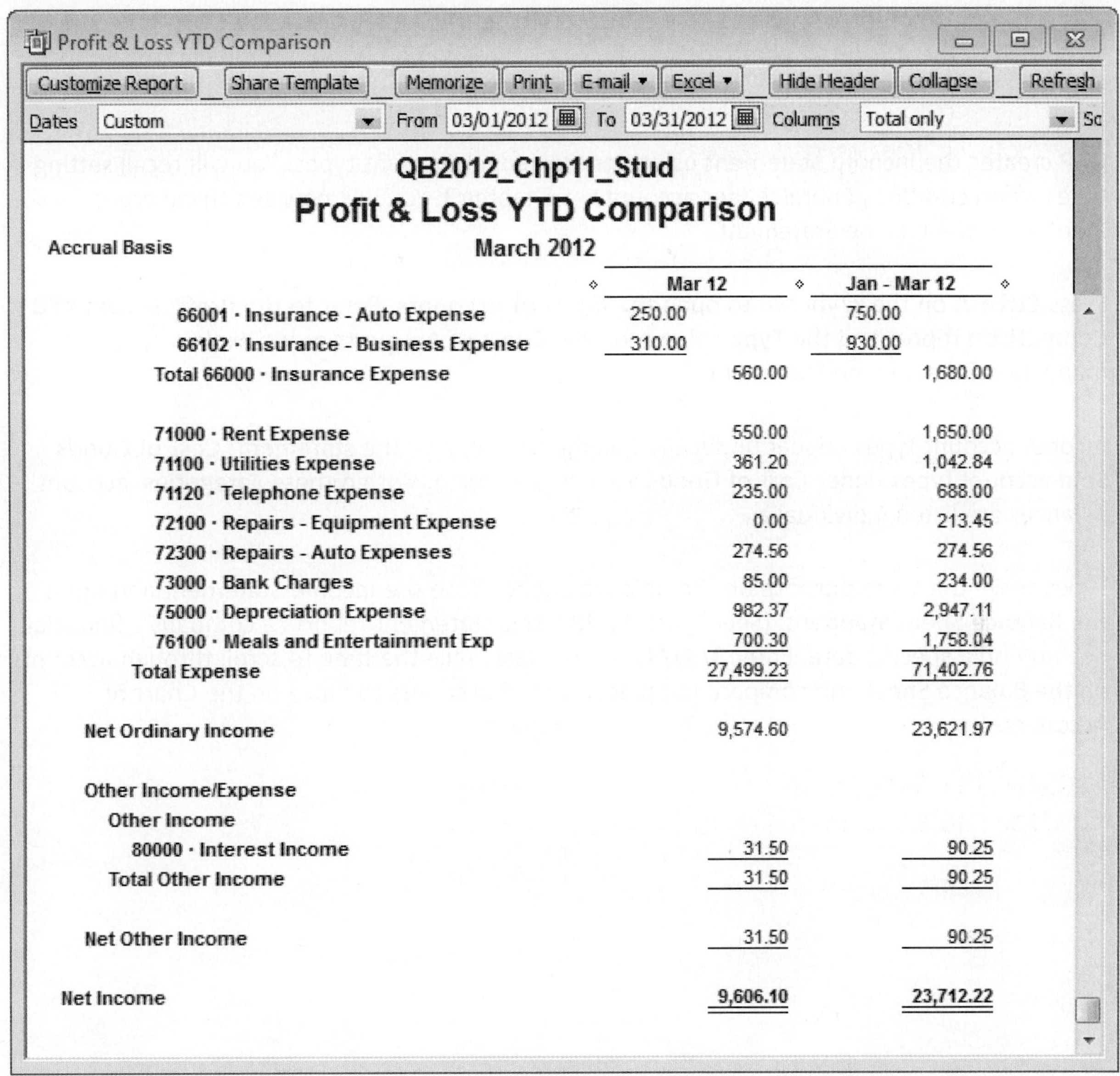

Profit & Loss YTD Comparison

Customize Report | Share Template | Memorize | Print | E-mail | Excel | Hide Header | Collapse | Refresh

Dates Custom From 03/01/2012 To 03/31/2012 Columns Total only

QB2012_Chp11_Stud

Profit & Loss YTD Comparison

Accrual Basis March 2012

	Mar 12		Jan - Mar 12	
66001 · Insurance - Auto Expense	250.00		750.00	
66102 · Insurance - Business Expense	310.00		930.00	
Total 66000 · Insurance Expense		560.00		1,680.00
71000 · Rent Expense		550.00		1,650.00
71100 · Utilities Expense		361.20		1,042.84
71120 · Telephone Expense		235.00		688.00
72100 · Repairs - Equipment Expense		0.00		213.45
72300 · Repairs - Auto Expenses		274.56		274.56
73000 · Bank Charges		85.00		234.00
75000 · Depreciation Expense		982.37		2,947.11
76100 · Meals and Entertainment Exp		700.30		1,758.04
Total Expense		27,499.23		71,402.76
Net Ordinary Income		9,574.60		23,621.97
Other Income/Expense				
Other Income				
80000 · Interest Income		31.50		90.25
Total Other Income		31.50		90.25
Net Other Income		31.50		90.25
Net Income		9,606.10		23,712.22

Figure 11:27

This comparison report compares March income to year-to-date income. As you know, the Income Statement paints a company's financial picture over a period of time and this report informs company owners that 40 percent of year-to-date income year was generated in March.

QBP creates the Income Statement using general ledger account types. You will recall setting types when creating general ledger accounts in Chapter 3. You will now see these types mapped to the Income Statement.

Press **Ctrl + A** on the keyboard to open the **Chart of Accounts**. Refer to the **Profit & Loss YTD Comparison** report and the **Type** column on the **Chart of Accounts** as we explain type mapping on the Income Statement.

Income account types appear under the Income category on the statement; **Cost of Goods Sold** account types under Cost of Goods Sold, and so forth. Within these categories, account balances are listed individually.

Types serve the same purpose on the Balance Sheet. Close the Income Statement and open the **Balance Sheet Standard.** (See Figure 11:28.) This statement reports a company's financial position on a specific date. Enter **3/31/12** as the date. Take the time to scroll through accounts on the Balance Sheet and compare the placement of accounts to types on the Chart of Accounts.

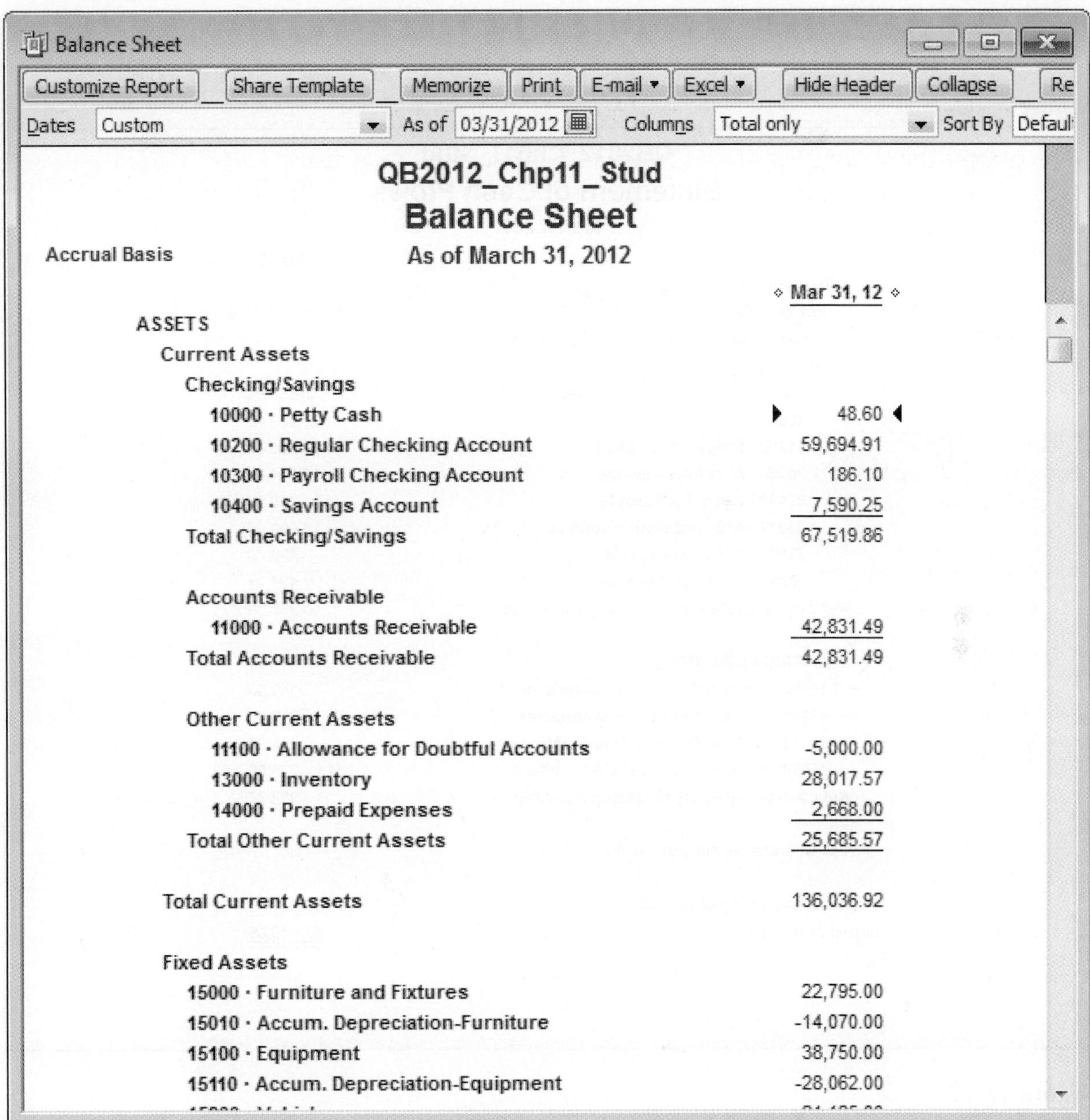

Figure 11:28

Close the Balance Sheet and the Chart of Accounts.

Next open the **Statement of Cash Flows** and enter the date range of **3/01/12** to **3/31/12.**

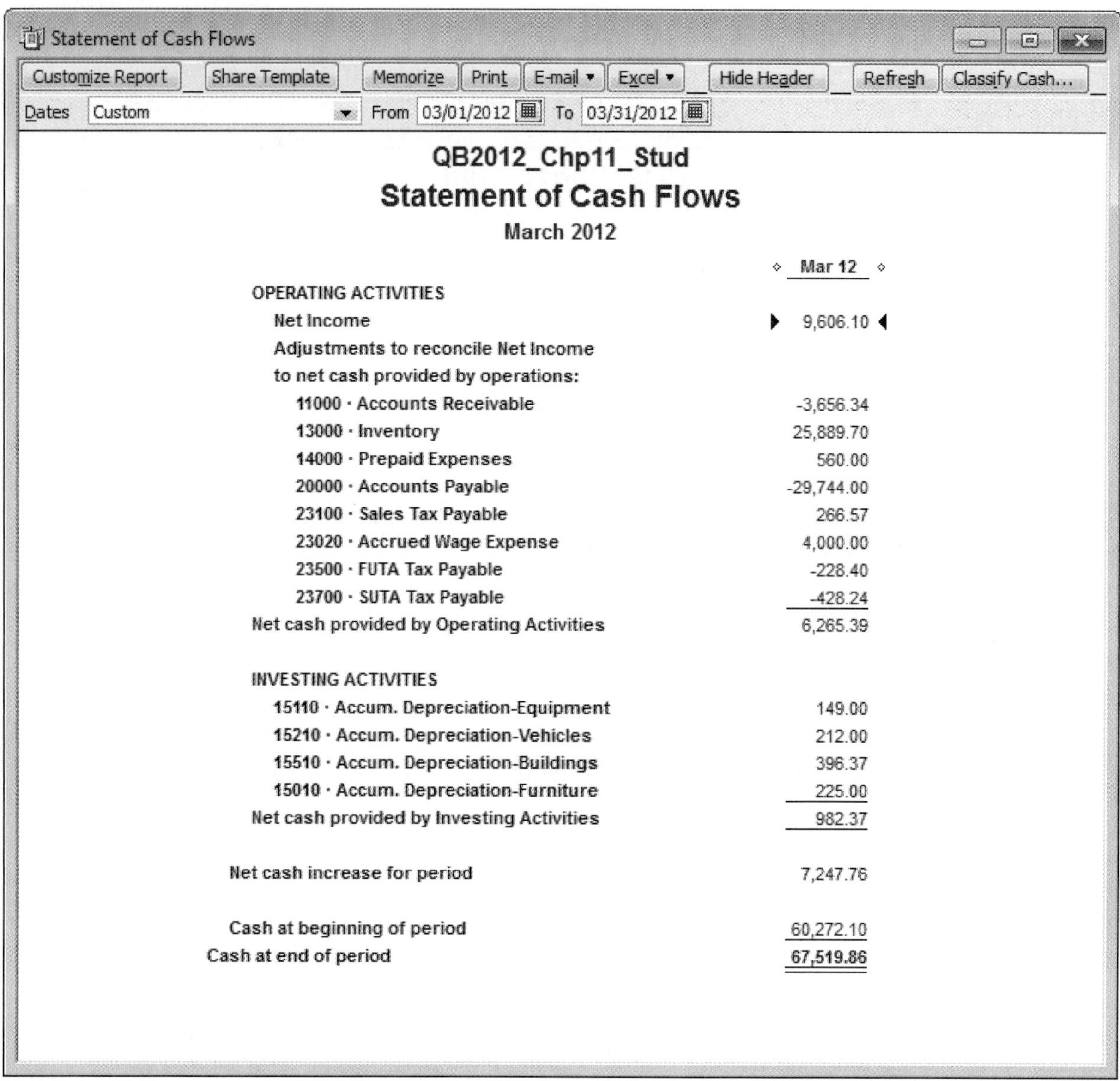

QB2012_Chp11_Stud
Statement of Cash Flows
March 2012

	Mar 12
OPERATING ACTIVITIES	
Net Income	9,606.10
Adjustments to reconcile Net Income	
to net cash provided by operations:	
11000 · Accounts Receivable	-3,656.34
13000 · Inventory	25,889.70
14000 · Prepaid Expenses	560.00
20000 · Accounts Payable	-29,744.00
23100 · Sales Tax Payable	266.57
23020 · Accrued Wage Expense	4,000.00
23500 · FUTA Tax Payable	-228.40
23700 · SUTA Tax Payable	-428.24
Net cash provided by Operating Activities	6,265.39
INVESTING ACTIVITIES	
15110 · Accum. Depreciation-Equipment	149.00
15210 · Accum. Depreciation-Vehicles	212.00
15510 · Accum. Depreciation-Buildings	396.37
15010 · Accum. Depreciation-Furniture	225.00
Net cash provided by Investing Activities	982.37
Net cash increase for period	7,247.76
Cash at beginning of period	60,272.10
Cash at end of period	67,519.86

Figure 11:29

This may be your first exposure to the Statement of Cash Flows so we will spend some time explaining its importance.

This statement reports cash activities by operations, investing, and financing. Operating cash is generated by day-to-day activities such as collecting on accounts receivable and reducing accounts payable. Investing is the cash effect of buying or selling company assets such as equipment or buildings. Finally, financing is the cash effect of borrowing or repaying loans.

After reviewing the report, the accountant notices that accumulated depreciation accounts are appearing under investing activities when these accounts should appear under operating activities because depreciation is a noncash activity added back to net income. Follow the next steps to correct the reporting of these accounts.

Select ***Edit>>Preferences*** on the main menu or click the [Classify Cash...] button on the Statement of Cash Flows. When the **Preferences** window opens, click the **Classify Cash** button on the **Company Preferences** tab for the **Reports and Graphs** category. (See Figure 11:30.)

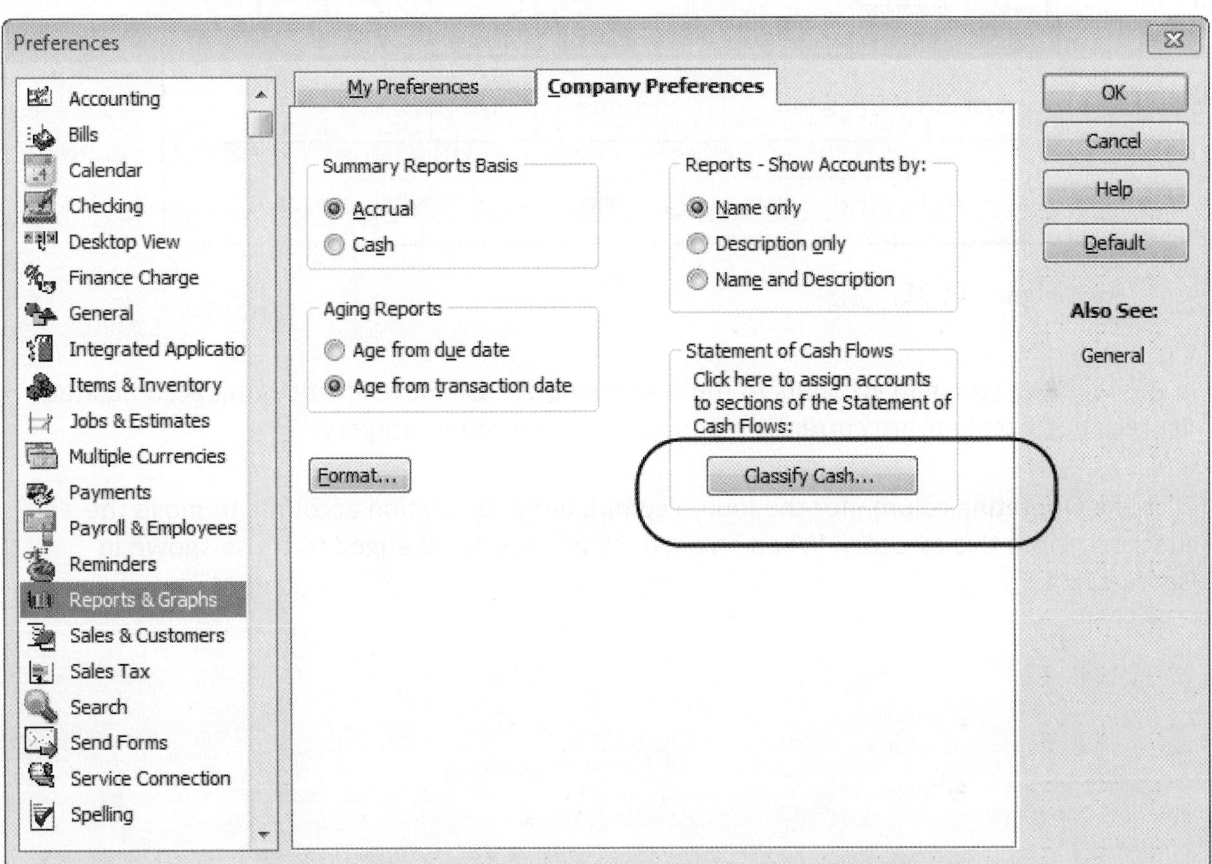

Figure 11:30

After clicking **Classify Cash**, the window in Figure 11:31 opens. Scroll down to the accounts indicated.

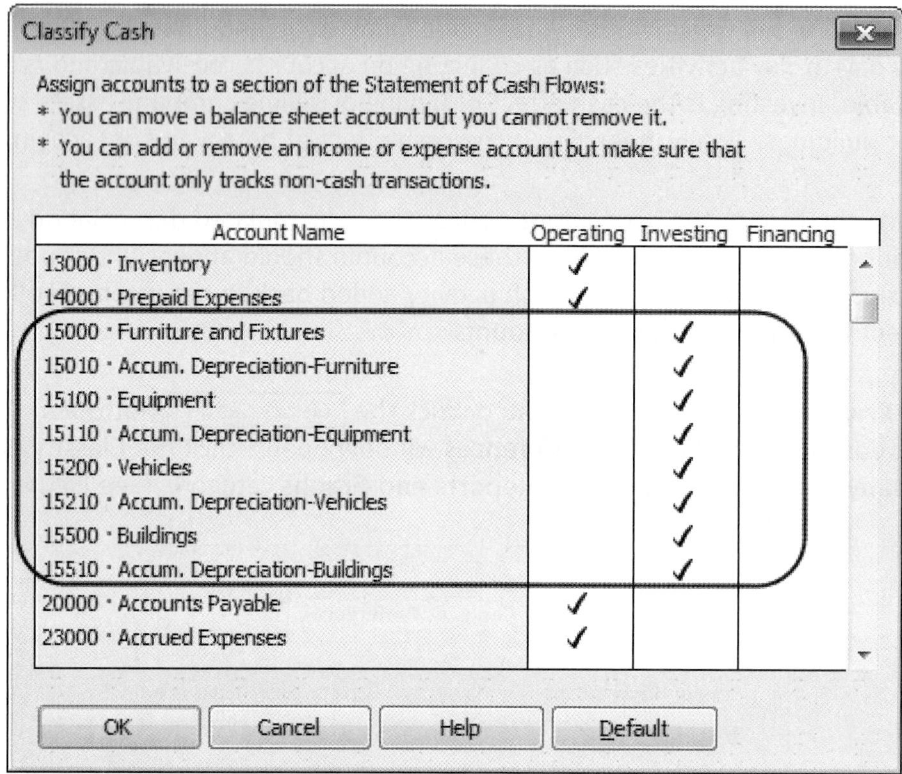

Figure 11:31

In this window, you map accounts to the Statement of Cash Flows. Notice that accumulated depreciation accounts are currently mapped to the Investing category.

Click the **Operating** column for the four accumulated depreciation accounts to move the checkmark into this category. When finished, categories are changed to those shown in Figure 11:32.

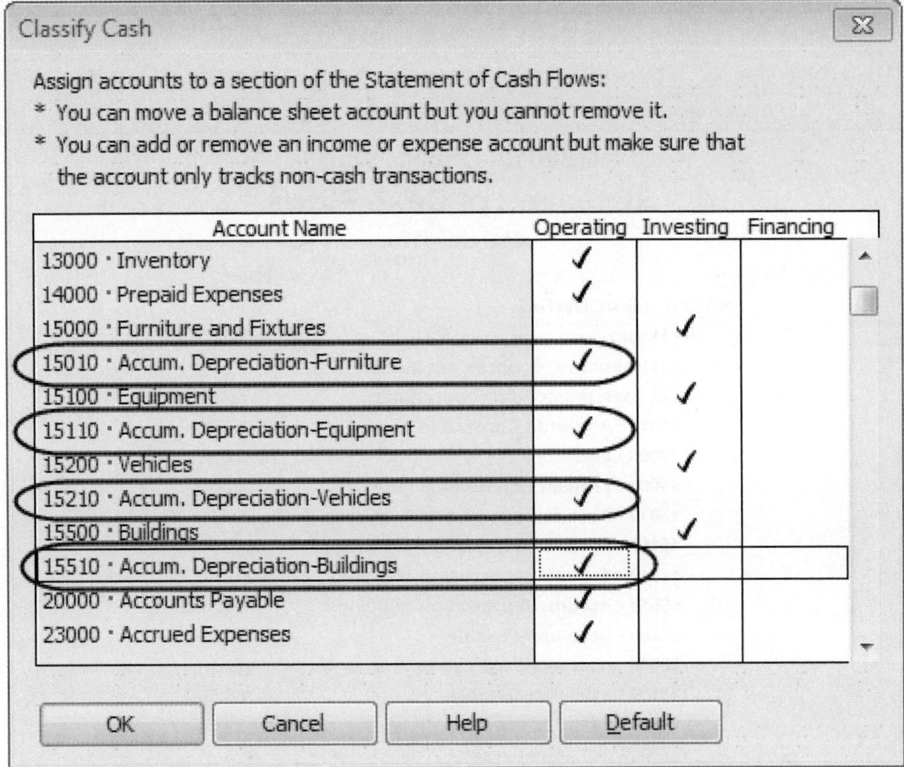

Figure 11:32

Before saving the changes, scroll down and notice that you do not map Income Statement accounts to the Statement of Cash Flows. Instead, these accounts already appear in the Net Income line of the statement.

Click **OK** to save these changes and click **OK** to close the Preferences window.

Return to the Statement of Cash Flows and note the changes. (See Figure 11:33.)

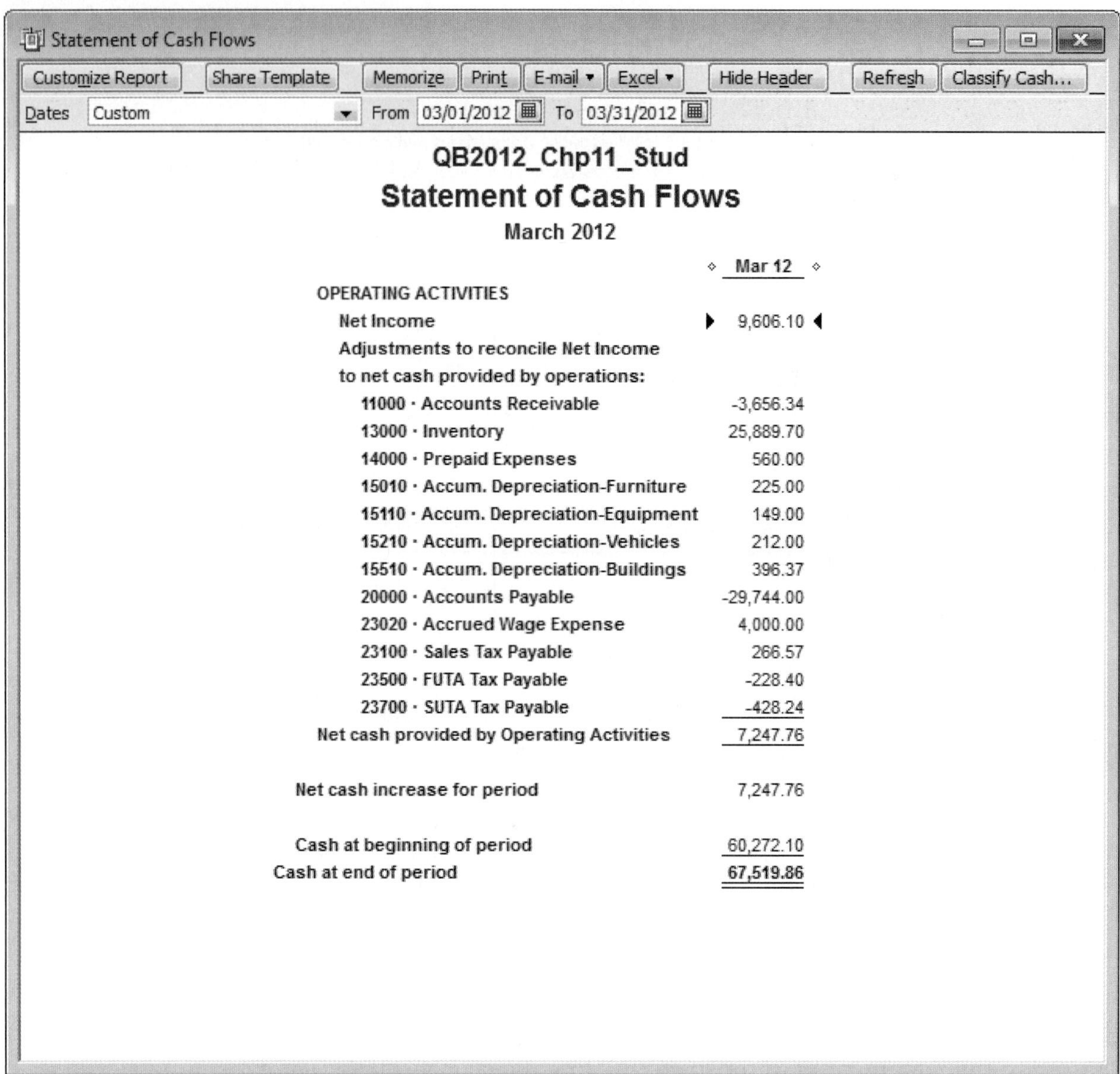
Statement of Cash Flows

Customize Report | Share Template | Memorize | Print | E-mail | Excel | Hide Header | Refresh | Classify Cash...

Dates Custom From 03/01/2012 To 03/31/2012

QB2012_Chp11_Stud

Statement of Cash Flows

March 2012

	Mar 12
OPERATING ACTIVITIES	
Net Income	9,606.10
Adjustments to reconcile Net Income	
to net cash provided by operations:	
11000 · Accounts Receivable	-3,656.34
13000 · Inventory	25,889.70
14000 · Prepaid Expenses	560.00
15010 · Accum. Depreciation-Furniture	225.00
15110 · Accum. Depreciation-Equipment	149.00
15210 · Accum. Depreciation-Vehicles	212.00
15510 · Accum. Depreciation-Buildings	396.37
20000 · Accounts Payable	-29,744.00
23020 · Accrued Wage Expense	4,000.00
23100 · Sales Tax Payable	266.57
23500 · FUTA Tax Payable	-228.40
23700 · SUTA Tax Payable	-428.24
Net cash provided by Operating Activities	7,247.76
Net cash increase for period	7,247.76
Cash at beginning of period	60,272.10
Cash at end of period	67,519.86

Figure 11:33

We now focus on interpreting this statement. The statement begins with **Net Income** from the March Income Statement and adjusts this number to arrive at net income on a cash basis.

Noncash items, such as depreciation, are added back and the cash changes for operating asset and liability accounts are calculated to obtain the **Net cash provided by Operating Activities.** Net positive cash from operations is a critical point of analysis. Companies that continually fail to generate cash from operations will eventually need to borrow to fund day-to-day activities, such as paying employees and vendors.

Net cash flow from operations is then adjusted for cash changes from investing and financing activities to arrive at the **Net cash increase for period.** *(Note: This could be a net cash decrease.)*

Focus now on the bottom section of the report. **Cash at beginning of period** equals the February 29 total for all cash accounts on the **Balance Sheet.** (See Figure 11:34.)

Figure 11:34

Cash at end of Period equals the total for all cash accounts on the March 31 **Balance Sheet** shown in Figure 11:35.

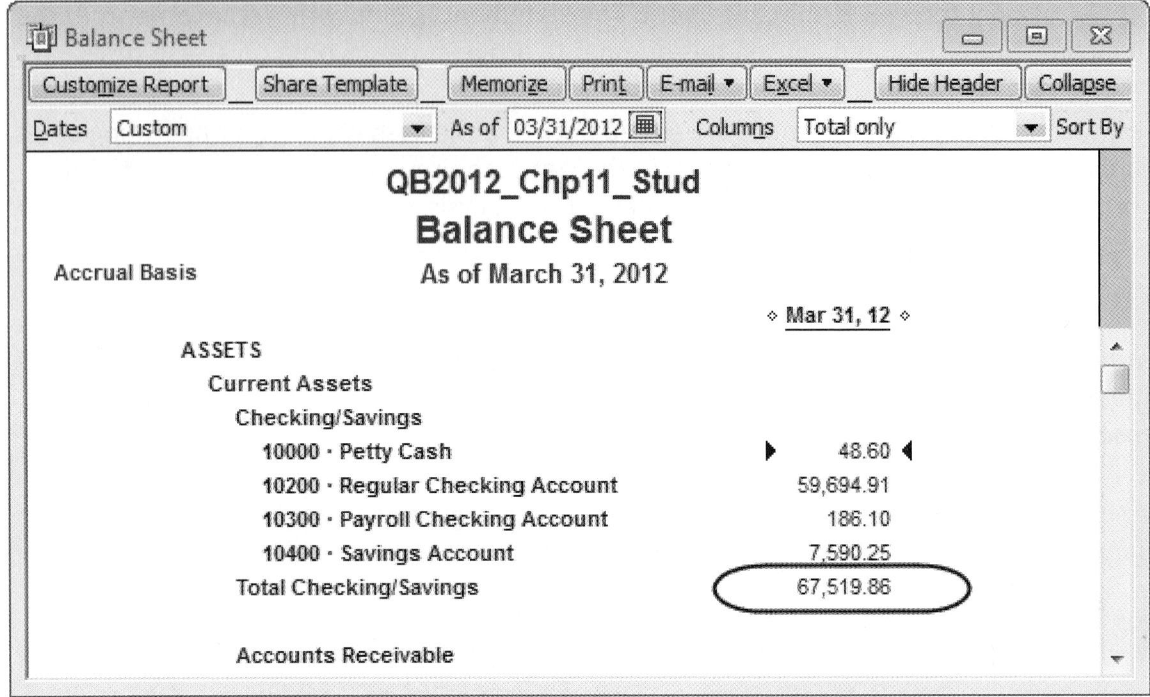

Figure 11:35

The difference between these amounts matches the **Net cash increase for period.**

Close this statement and the Report Center. After printing financial statements, you are ready to close the accounting period.

Closing the Accounting Period

Closing the period is important to prevent posting transactions that affect issued financial statements. You do not want to send March financial statements to owners or the bank and subsequently have an entry erroneously posted to March.

You should always back up a data file before closing a period so create a ***backup of the data file to a backup file named "QB2012_Ch11_Stud_Completed."***

Now click ***Company>>Set Closing Date*** on the main menu to open the window illustrate in Figure 11:36.

Preferences
Accounting
Bills
Calendar
Checking
Desktop View
Finance Charge
General
Integrated Applicatio
Items & Inventory
Jobs & Estimates
Multiple Currencies
Payments
Payroll & Employees
Reminders
Reports & Graphs
Sales & Customers
Sales Tax
Search
Send Forms
Service Connection
Spelling
My Preferences
Company Preferences
Accounts
Use account numbers
Require accounts
Show lowest subaccount only
Use class tracking
Prompt to assign classes
Automatically assign general journal entry number
Warn when posting a transaction to Retained Earnings
Date Warnings
Warn if transactions are 90 day(s) in the past
Warn if transactions are 30 day(s) in the future
Closing Date
Date through which books are closed: 02/29/2012
Set Date/Password
OK
Cancel
Help
Default
Also See:
General
Payroll and Employees

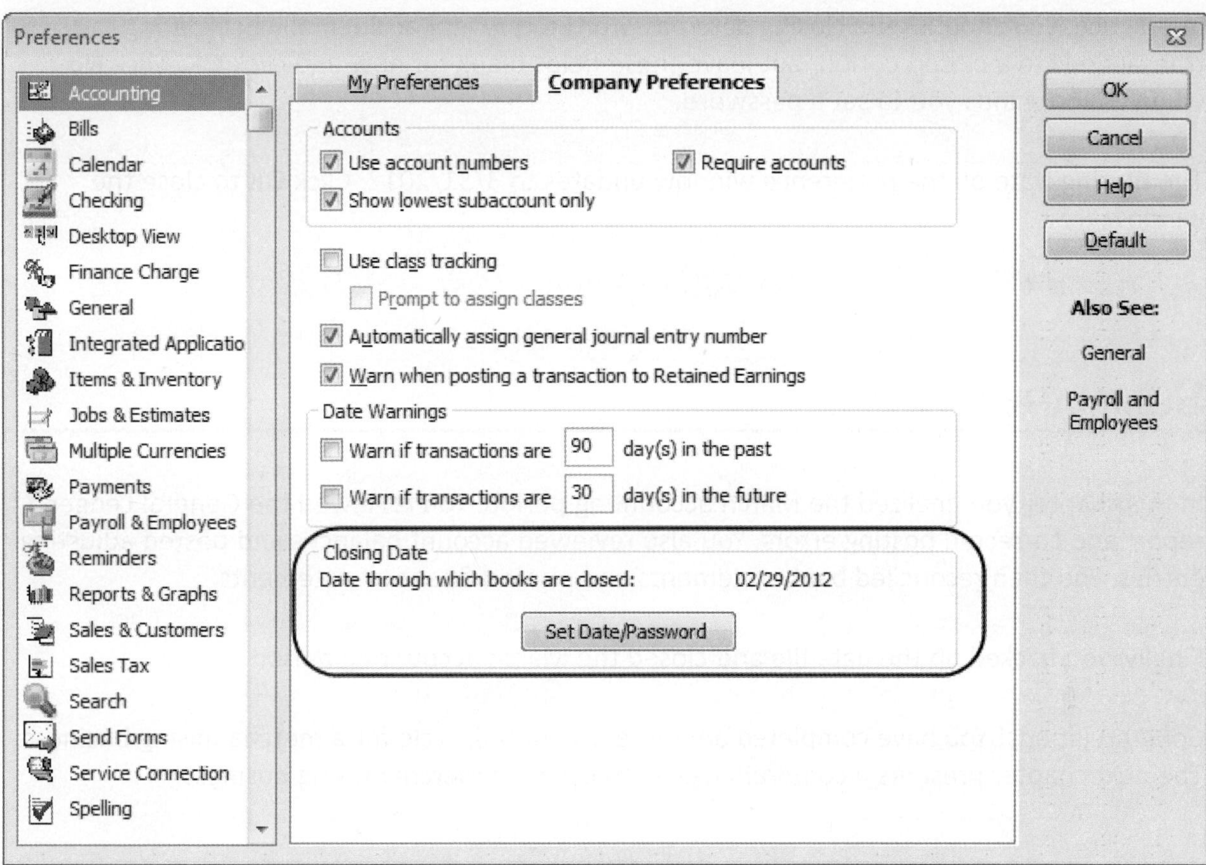

Figure 11:36

This window shows that the books are closed through February 29. Click **Set Date/Password** and enter **3/31/12** as illustrated in Figure 11:37.

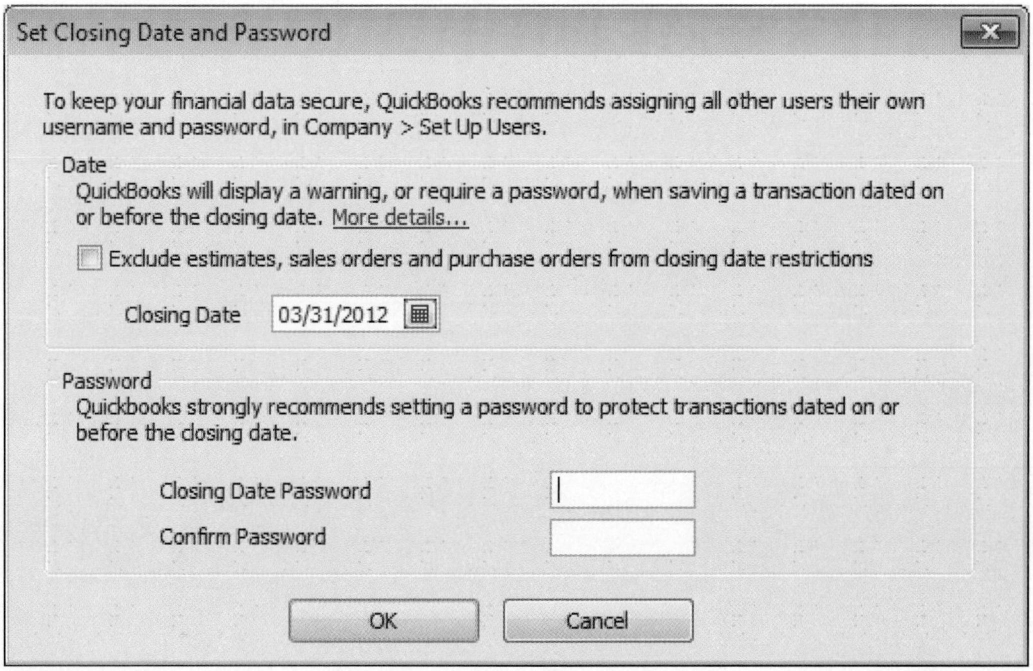

Set Closing Date and Password
To keep your financial data secure, QuickBooks recommends assigning all other users their own username and password, in Company > Set Up Users.
Date
QuickBooks will display a warning, or require a password, when saving a transaction dated on or before the closing date. More details...
Exclude estimates, sales orders and purchase orders from closing date restrictions
Closing Date 03/31/2012
Password
Quickbooks strongly recommends setting a password to protect transactions dated on or before the closing date.
Closing Date Password
Confirm Password
OK
Cancel

Figure 11:37

In practice, you should set a closing date password to prevent accidentally backdating transactions to a closed period, but leave these fields blank for now and click **OK.** Click **No** when QBP reminds you to set a password.

The Closing Date on the preference window updates to 3/31/2012. Click **OK** to close the window.

Summary

In this chapter you finalized the March accounting period. You reviewed the General Ledger report and corrected posting errors. You also reviewed account balances and posted adjusting entries. You then reconciled bank statements and printed financial statements.

Finally, you backed up the data file and closed the March accounting period.

Congratulations! You have completed an entire accounting cycle for a merchandising business. The next chapter presents a comprehensive project for a merchandising business.

END-OF-CHAPTER QUESTIONS

TRUE/FALSE

_____ 1. The accounting period is closed only at the end of the year.

_____ 2. The Standard Profit & Loss report will report March income compared to year-to-date income.

_____ 3. Accrued wages should be reversed in the following month.

_____ 4. To print a Balance Sheet for March, you entered the date range of 3/01/12 to 3/31/12.

_____ 5. The Cash Flow Statement begins with net income or loss for the period.

_____ 6. Net income is only reported on the Profit and Loss report.

_____ 7. The balances in the cash accounts are reported on the Balance Sheet.

_____ 8. You open the Make General Journal Entries window from the Customers menu.

MULTIPLE CHOICE

_____ 1. Which statement reports a company's financial position at a specific point in time?
   a. Statement of Cash Flows
   b. Balance Sheet
   c. Statement of Retained Earnings
   d. Income Statement

_____ 2. The owner wants to see cash generated from accounts receivable. Which report(s) would you print?
   a. Cash Receipts Journal
   b. Statement of Cash Flows
   c. Income Statement
   d. Both a and b

_____ 3. Net income/net loss for March will affect the _____ statement(s).
   a. Balance Sheet
   b. Income Statement
   c. Statement of Retained Earnings
   d. All of the above

_____ 4. Which report demonstrates that the inventory general ledger account reconciles to the inventory costs?
   a. Inventory Stock Status by Item report
   b. Inventory Valuation Summary report
   c. Both a and b
   d. None of the above

_____ 5. Which report would you use for spotting missing or out-of-sequence accounts payable checks?
   a. Missing Checks
   b. Check Detail
   c. Cash Disbursements Journal
   d. All of the above

_____ 6. On the Statement of Cash Flows, all the following are true except _____.
   a. Depreciation expense is not reported on the statement
   b. Net income is reported on the statement
   c. The cash at the end of the period matches the cash on the Balance Sheet
   d. The statement lists operating, investing, and financing activities

_____ 7. On the Balance Sheet, total assets must equal _____.
   a. Total liabilities
   b. Total equity
   c. Total liabilities plus total equity
   d. Total cash

_____ 8. Management wants to know if operations are having a positive effect on cash. Which report would you prepare?
   a. Profit & Loss
   b. Balance Sheet
   c. Statement of Cash Flows
   d. All of the above

PRACTICE SET

In this practice set, you will perform the activities needed to close the March and April accounting periods.

Begin by:

- Opening the software.
- Opening the **QB2012_Chp11_PracSet_Stud** data file. Add your initials to the end to the Company Name by clicking ***Company>>Company Information*** on the main menu. Click **OK** to save the changes.
- **Toggling the software to the PRO EDITION** by selecting ***File>>Toggle to Another Edition*** on the main menu and choosing **QuickBooks Pro** as the edition.

1. Record the following transactions to close the March accounting period.

2012

Mar 19 Post the transfer of $5,500.00 from the regular checking account to the payroll checking account.

Mar 31 Reconcile the Regular Checking account for March using the statement that follows. Use **the Hide transactions after the statement's end date** option to hide April transactions. *(Note: This statement is different from the statement illustrated in the chapter.)* Print the Detail Reconciliation report.

Reconcile the Payroll Checking Account for March. The ending statement balance is $679.30. All checks and deposits for the month have cleared and the monthly bank charge is $16.80. *(Remember that April transactions are also in this account.)* Print the Detail Reconciliation report.

Post an entry that expenses the following prepaid expenses.

66001 Insurance - Auto Expense $200.00

66102 Insurance - Business Expense $800.00

Accrue wages of $5,000.00 to Salaries expense.

Print the Balance Sheet Standard, Profit & Loss Standard, and Statement of Cash Flows for March.

Close the March accounting period.

Baxter Garden Supply
Bank Statement March 31, 2012

Beginning Balance from February Statement				$ 54,046.14
March Deposits				
	Mar 2, 2012		2,211.82	
	Mar 2, 2012		5,124.52	
	Mar 6, 2012		1,245.57	
	Mar 6, 2012		611.42	
	Mar 6, 2012		5,185.67	
	Mar 7, 2012		872.04	
	Mar 7, 2012		7,196.00	
	Mar 9, 2012		2,492.55	
	Mar 9, 2012		2,976.11	
	Mar 13, 2012		3,934.38	
	Mar 13, 2012		22,939.49	
	Mar 13, 2012		5,138.68	
	Mar 19, 2012		4,695.75	
	Mar 19, 2012		1,039.11	
	Mar 20, 2012		1,469.86	
	Mar 20, 2012		1,169.77	
Total Deposits for March				68,302.74
March Checks Cleared				
	Mar 3, 2012	10211	327.57	
	Mar 3, 2012	10212	1,365.44	
	Mar 10, 2012	10213	1,691.10	
	Mar 10, 2012	10214	550.00	
	Mar 18, 2012	10215	1,399.30	
	Mar 18, 2012	10216	4,953.24	
	Mar 18, 2012	10217	28,434.65	
	Mar 23, 2012	10218	602.25	
	Mar 23, 2012	10219	1,167.25	
	Mar 23, 2012	10220	274.56	
	Mar 23, 2012	10221	167.00	
	Mar 23, 2012	10222	2,252.75	
	Mar 31, 2012	10230	2,237.00	
Total Cleared Checks for March				45,422.11
Less Bank Transfers				
	Mar 6, 2012		6,000.00	
	Mar 19, 2012		5,500.00	
Total March Transfers				11,500.00
March Service Charges				55.00
Ending Bank Balance March 31, 2012				$ 65,371.77

2. Perform the following accounting activities to close the April accounting period.

2012

Apr 1 Reverse the March 31 journal entry for $5,000.00 of accrued wages.

Apr 2 Record a journal entry transferring $5,000.00 from the Regular Checking Account to the Payroll Checking account to cover paychecks printed on April 2.

Apr 16 Record a journal entry transferring $6,000.00 from the Regular Checking Account to the Payroll Checking account to cover paychecks printed on April 16.

Apr 20 Post a journal entry for the following sale of a vehicle.

Vehicle cost	$13,500.00
Accumulated Depreciation on vehicles	$10,700.00
Cash deposited to regular checking	$ 1,000.00

Apr 30 Post the following adjusting journal entries.

Accrued wages	$ 6,000.00
Expired prepaid auto insurance	$ 200.00
Expired prepaid business insurance	$ 800.00

Post April depreciation expense.

Accum Depr Furniture	$ 225.00
Accum Depr Equipment	$ 149.00
Accum Depr Vehicles	$ 198.00
Accum Depr Buildings	$ 400.00

Reconcile the Regular Checking account using the statement that follows. Print the Detail Reconciliation report.

Reconcile the Payroll Checking Account. The ending statement balance is $545.03. All checks and deposits have cleared and the monthly bank charge is $18.75. Print the Detail Reconciliation report.

Reconcile the Savings Account. Interest income is $37.50 and the ending statement balance is $7,627.75. Do not print the reconciliation report.

Print the Balance Sheet Standard, Profit & Loss Standard, and Statement of Cash Flows for April.

Create a backup file named "QB2012_Chp11_PracSet_Stud_Completed" and close the April accounting period.

Baxter Garden Supply
Bank Statement April 30, 2012

Beginning Balance from March Statement				$ 65,371.77
April Deposits				
	Apr 1, 2012		1,864.40	
	Apr 1, 2012		211.54	
	Apr 1, 2012		4,299.35	
	Apr 4, 2012		3,228.90	
	Apr 4, 2012		5,303.19	
	Apr 10, 2012		22,021.60	
	Apr 10, 2012		17,780.68	
	Apr 10, 2012		2,085.52	
	Apr 17, 2012		1,835.80	
	Apr 20, 2012		1,000.00	
	Apr 25, 2012		22,939.49	
	Apr 25, 2012		3,816.99	
Total Deposits for April				86,387.46
April Checks Cleared				
	Apr 3, 2012	10223	1,691.10	
	Apr 6, 2012	10224	1,110.00	
	Apr 6, 2012	10225	306.24	
	Apr 6, 2012	10226	608.22	
	Apr 6, 2012	10227	414.64	
	Apr 6, 2012	10228	682.72	
	Apr 9, 2012	10229	892.74	
	Apr 9, 2012	10231	1,691.10	
	Apr 9, 2012	10232	43.20	
	Apr 9, 2012	10233	240.90	
	Apr 12, 2012	10234	407.50	
	Apr 12, 2012	10235	203.00	
	Apr 12, 2012	10236	276.00	
	Apr 12, 2012	10237	550.00	
	Apr 12, 2012	10238	235.00	
	Apr 20, 2012	10239	4,995.50	
	Apr 20, 2012	10240	210.00	
	Apr 22, 2012	10241	487.00	
	Apr 23, 2012	10242	1,691.10	
	Apr 27, 2012	10245	125.00	
Total Cleared Checks for April				16,860.96
Less Bank Transfers				
	Apr 2, 2012		5,000.00	
	Apr 16, 2012		6,000.00	
Total April Transfers				11,000.00
April Service Charges				65.00
Ending Bank Balance April 30, 2012				$ 123,833.27

PROJECT 2 COMPREHENSIVE EXAM FOR A MERCHANDISING BUSINESS

In this exam, you will record February transactions for a company we call Olsen Office Furniture. Olsen specializes in selling mid-range office furniture to wholesale distributors and businesses. You will be entering all transactions for the month of February, including month-end adjusting entries.

All checks received from customers are deposited into the Regular Checking Account. You will only print when instructed and will not be asked to print POs and invoices.

Begin by:

- Opening the software.
- Opening the **QB2012_Proj2_Stud** data file. Add your initials to the end to the Company Name by clicking ***Company>>Company Information*** on the main menu. Click **OK** to save the changes.
- **Toggling the software to the PRO EDITION** by selecting ***File>>Toggle to Another Edition*** on the main menu and choosing **QuickBooks Pro** as the edition.

<table>
<tr><td rowspan="4">Feb 1</td><td>Issue the following sales invoices.

Invoice 1790 to Winetraub Office Furniture for $2,999.80.
<table><tr><th>Qty</th><th>Item</th><th>Unit Price</th></tr><tr><td>20</td><td>SmallDesk</td><td>$149.99</td></tr></table>
Invoice 1791 to Anderson & Anderson, Attorneys at Law for $9,523.00 with tax.
<table><tr><th>Qty</th><th>Item</th><th>Unit Price</th></tr><tr><td>10</td><td>ChairClothBlack</td><td>$185.00</td></tr><tr><td>12</td><td>ChairLeatherBlack</td><td>$375.00</td></tr><tr><td>3</td><td>ConfTableOak</td><td>$850.00</td></tr></table></td></tr>
<tr><td>Received the following checks. (Note: Verify that checks will deposit into the Regular Checking Account.)

Check number 1835 for $8,774.88 from Arbrook Office Supply for Invoice 1783.
Check number 3078 for $30,575.25 from Parker Office Building for Invoice 1784.</td></tr>
<tr><td>New vendor:
Pearson Property Management
3075 W. 7th Street
Fort Worth, TX 76022
Terms: Net 3
Account Prefill: 74000 Rent or Lease Expense

Enter a rent bill for $800.00 to Pearson Property Management for February office and warehouse rental.</td></tr>
<tr><td>Print checks totaling $8,897.58, paying all bills due on or before February 5. First check number is 8938.</td></tr>
</table>

<table>
<tr><td>Feb 3</td><td>Issue the following POs.

PO 1040 to Brothers Furniture Mfg for $1,875.00 for the following item.
<table><tr><th>Item</th><th>Qty</th><th>Price</th></tr><tr><td>ChairLeatherBlack</td><td>25</td><td>$75.00</td></tr></table>PO 1041 to Planter Interiors for $2,600.00 for the following item.
<table><tr><th>Item</th><th>Qty</th><th>Price</th></tr><tr><td>SmallDesk</td><td>40</td><td>$65.00</td></tr></table></td></tr>
<tr><td></td><td>Received bills for the following inventory that was received.

All items on PO 1038 to Tollman Table Manufacturing. Invoice 68534 for $5,500.00 dated Feb 3.

All items on PO 1039 to Willis Office Supplies. Invoice 2378 for $1,910.00 dated Feb 3.</td></tr>
<tr><td></td><td>Received the following checks.
Check number 8053 for $34,595.00 from Ernst Furniture for Invoice 1785.
Check number 3478 for $5,403.50 from Poseiden Landscaping for Invoice 1786.</td></tr>
</table>

<table>
<tr><td rowspan="3">Feb 4</td><td>Issue the following sales invoices.

Invoice 1792 to Arbrook Office Supply for $3,599.78.
<table><tr><th>Qty</th><th>Item</th><th>Unit Price</th></tr><tr><td>15</td><td>ChairErgo</td><td>$169.99</td></tr><tr><td>7</td><td>SmallDesk</td><td>$149.99</td></tr></table>
Invoice 1793 to Parker Office Building for $12,224.75 with tax.
<table><tr><th>Qty</th><th>Item</th><th>Unit Price</th></tr><tr><td>8</td><td>ConfTableMaple</td><td>$850.00</td></tr><tr><td>5</td><td>ExecDeskMaple</td><td>$925.00</td></tr></table></td></tr>
<tr><td>Issue Credit Memo CM1787 for $4,012.50, with tax, to Anderson and Anderson for the return of 10 ChairLeatherBrown on Invoice 1787.</td></tr>
<tr><td>Received check number 5768 for $4,825.57 from Anderson and Anderson for balance due on Invoice 1787.</td></tr>
</table>

<table>
<tr><td rowspan="3">Feb 6</td><td>

Issue the following sales invoices.

Invoice 1794 to Wellman and Wellman, CPA for $27,017.50, with tax. *(You checked with Mr. Olsen and he approved exceeding the customer's credit limit.)*

Qty	Item	Unit Price
20	ChairLeatherBrown	$375.00
10	ExecDeskAsh	$925.00
10	ConfTableAsh	$850.00

Invoice 1795 to Ernst Furniture for $11,799.85.

Qty	Item	Unit Price
15	ChairErgo	$169.99
10	ExecDeskOak	$925.00

</td></tr>
<tr><td>

Issue the following POs.

PO 1042 to Brothers Furniture Mfg for $1,500.00 for the following item.

Item	Qty	Price
ChairLeatherBrown	20	$75.00

PO 1043 to Oregon Oak Furniture for $21,000.00 for the following items.

Item	Qty	Price
ExecDeskAsh	25	$350.00
ExecDeskMaple	15	$350.00
ExecDeskOak	20	$350.00

PO 1044 to Planter Interiors for $700.00 for the following item.

Item	Qty	Price
ChairErgo	20	$35.00

PO 1045 to Tollman Table Manufacturing for $2,500.00 for the following item.

Item	Qty	Price
ConfTableAsh	10	$250.00

</td></tr>
<tr><td>

Received the following inventory.

Invoice 3479 dated Feb 4 from Brothers Furniture for $1,125.00 for 15 of the ChairLeatherBlack items on PO 1040.

All items on PO 1041 to Planter Interiors. Invoice not included. Receipt number RCT89007 dated Feb 4.

</td></tr>
</table>

Feb 6	Prepare payroll for the biweekly pay period ended Feb 5. Daniel Anderson worked 4 hours of overtime and remaining hourly paid employees worked 80 hours. Create the paychecks using the spreadsheets that follow. Print the paychecks on beginning check number 1109. Pay the liabilities from 1/01/12 to 2/06/12 for all Federal Withholding, Medicare, and Social Security taxes. Print as check number 8943 for $2,186.42 from the Regular Checking Account. Transfer $8,500.00 from the Regular Checking Account to the Payroll Checking Account to cover payroll.
	Enter Invoice 100378 for $2,600.00 dated Feb 4 from Planter Interiors for receipt number RCT89007.

Olsen Office Furniture
Pay Period 1/23/2012 thru 2/05/2012

Employee	Filing Status	Allow	Pay Type	Pay Rate	Regular Hrs	OT Hrs	Gross Pay	Federal Income Tax	Soc. Sec. (FICA) Tax	Medicare Tax	Net Pay
Anderson, Daniel	Married	3	Hourly	15.00	80.00	4.00	1,290.00	56.00	79.98	18.71	1,135.31
Jenkins, Charles	Married	2	Hourly	15.00	80.00		1,200.00	65.00	74.40	17.40	1,043.20
Olsen, David	Married	4	Salary	2,500.00			2,500.00	220.00	155.00	36.25	2,088.75
Olsen James	Married	3	Salary	2,500.00			2,500.00	240.00	155.00	36.25	2,068.75
Vavra, Wesley	Married	4	Hourly	16.00	80.00		1,280.00	44.00	79.36	18.56	1,138.08
Wilson, Brian	Married	4	Hourly	15.00	80.00		1,200.00	36.00	74.40	17.40	1,072.20
Totals					**320.00**	**4.00**	**9,970.00**	**661.00**	**618.14**	**144.57**	**8,546.29**
Tax Basis								**Circular E**	**6.20%**	**1.45%**	
G/L Accounts							**60000**	**23400**	**23400**	**23400**	**10300**

Olsen Office Furniture
Employer Costs for Period 1/23/2012 thru 2/05/2012

Employee	ER Soc. Sec. (FICA)	ER Medicare	ER FUTA	ER SUTA
Anderson, Daniel	79.98	18.71	10.32	38.70
Jenkins, Charles	74.40	17.40	9.60	36.00
Olsen, David	155.00	36.25	20.00	75.00
Olsen James	155.00	36.25	20.00	75.00
Vavra, Wesley	79.36	18.56	10.24	38.40
Wilson, Brian	74.40	17.40	9.60	36.00
Totals	**618.14**	**144.57**	**79.76**	**299.10**
Tax Basis	**6.20%**	**1.45%**	**0.8%**	**3.0%**
G/L Accounts	23400 / 60100	23400 / 60100	23500 / 60100	23700 / 60100

Feb 10	Issue Invoice 1796 to Baker Hardware for $7,998.25, with tax, for the following items. Qty / Item / Unit Price 10 / ChairClothBlack / $185.00 15 / ChairLeatherBlack / $375.00
	Received the following inventory. The remaining items on PO 1040 to Brothers Furniture. Invoice 3501 for $750.00 dated Feb 9. All items on PO 1044 issued to Planter Interiors. Invoice 100425 for $700.00 dated Feb 9. All items on PO 1042 issued to Brothers Furniture. Invoice 3502 for $1,500.00 dated Feb 9.
Feb 11	New vendor: DFW Equipment 3300 Camp Bowie Blvd. Fort Worth, TX 76022 Terms: Net 3 Account Prefill: 74500 Repairs Expense Enter Invoice 5663 dated Feb 10 for $859.87 from DFW Equipment for repair of equipment. Pay bill on check number 8944.
	Received the following inventory. All items on PO 1045 issued to Tollman Tables Manufacturing. Invoice 68578 for $2,500.00 dated Feb 10. All items on PO 1043 issued to Oregon Oak Furniture. Invoice 98873 for $21,000.00 dated Feb 10.

Feb 14

Mr. Olsen sent a memo instructing you to raise the credit limit for Art Decoraters, Arbrook Office Supply, and Ernst Furniture to $85,000.

Issue the following Sales Invoices.

Invoice 1797 to Art Decoraters for $37,824.70.

Qty	Item	Unit Price
30	SmallDesk	$149.99
25	ExecDeskAsh	$925.00
12	ConfTableAsh	$850.00

Invoice 1798 to Arbrook Office Supply for $35,774.80.

Qty	Item	Unit Price
20	ExecDeskOak	$925.00
15	ExecDeskMaple	$925.00
20	ChairErgo	$169.99

Issue the following POs.

PO 1046 to Oregon Oak Furniture for $21,000.00 for the following items.

Item	Qty	Price
ExecDeskAsh	25	$350.00
ExecDeskMaple	15	$350.00
ExecDeskOak	20	$350.00

PO 1047 to Planter Interiors for $3,300.00 for the following items.

Item	Qty	Price
ChairErgo	20	$35.00
SmallDesk	40	$65.00

PO 1048 to Tollman Table Manufacturing for $2,500.00 for the following item.

Item	Qty	Price
ConfTableAsh	10	$250.00

Received the following checks.

Check number 2057 for $5,950.00 from Art Decoraters for Invoice 1788.
Check number 90087 for $2,549.85 from Winetraub Office Furniture for Invoice 1789.

<table>
<tr><td>Feb 16</td><td>Received the following inventory.

All items on PO 1046 to Oregon Oak Furniture. Invoice 98899 for $21,000.00 dated Feb 15.

All items on PO 1047 to Planter Interiors. Invoice 100863 for $3,300.00 dated Feb 15.</td></tr>
<tr><td></td><td>Issue the following Sales Invoices.

Invoice 1799 to Ernst Furniture for $36,250.00.
<u>Qty</u> <u>Item</u> <u>Unit Price</u>
30 ExecDeskAsh $925.00
10 ConfTableOak $850.00

Invoice 1800 to Winetraub Office Furniture for $12,749.30.
<u>Qty</u> <u>Item</u> <u>Unit Price</u>
20 ChairErgo $169.99
10 ChairClothBlack $185.00
50 SmallDesk $149.99</td></tr>
</table>

<table>
<tr><td>Feb 18</td><td>Received all items on PO 1048 to Tollman Tables Manufacturing. Invoice 68883 for $2,500.00 dated Feb 17.</td></tr>
<tr><td></td><td>Issue the following POs.

PO 1049 to Brothers Furniture Mfg for $1,300.00 for the following item.

Item | Qty | Price
ChairClothBlack | 20 | $65.00

PO 1050 to Oregon Oak Furniture for $8,750.00 for the following item.

Item | Qty | Price
ExecDeskAsh | 25 | $350.00

PO 1051 to Planter Interiors for $3,300.00 for the following items.

Item | Qty | Price
ChairErgo | 20 | $35.00
SmallDesk | 40 | $65.00

PO 1052 to Tollman Table Manufacturing for $2,500.00 for the following item.

Item | Qty | Price
ConfTableOak | 10 | $250.00</td></tr>
<tr><td>Feb 20</td><td>Prepare payroll for the biweekly pay period ended Feb 19. All hourly paid employees worked 80 hours.

Create the paychecks using the spreadsheets that follow. Print the paychecks on beginning check number 1115.

Pay the liabilities from 1/01/12 to 2/20/12 for all Federal Withholding, Medicare, and Social Security taxes. Print as check number 8945 for $2,166.64 from the Regular Checking Account.

Transfer $8,500.00 from the Regular Checking Account to the Payroll Checking Account to cover payroll.</td></tr>
<tr><td></td><td>Pay all vendor invoices, totaling $11,135.00, due on or before March 7. Print checks on beginning check number 8946.</td></tr>
</table>

Olsen Office Furniture
Pay Period 2/06/2012 thru 2/19/2012

Employee	Filing Status	Allow	Pay Type	Pay Rate	Regular Hrs	OT Hrs	Gross Pay	Federal Income Tax	Soc. Sec. (FICA) Tax	Medicare Tax	Net Pay
Anderson, Daniel	Married	3	Hourly	15.00	80.00		1,200.00	50.00	74.40	17.40	1,058.20
Jenkins, Charles	Married	2	Hourly	15.00	80.00		1,200.00	65.00	74.40	17.40	1,043.20
Olsen, David	Married	4	Salary	2,500.00			2,500.00	220.00	155.00	36.25	2,088.75
Olsen James	Married	3	Salary	2,500.00			2,500.00	240.00	155.00	36.25	2,068.75
Vavra, Wesley	Married	4	Hourly	16.00	80.00		1,280.00	44.00	79.36	18.56	1,138.08
Wilson, Brian	Married	4	Hourly	15.00	80.00		1,200.00	36.00	74.40	17.40	1,072.20
Totals					**320.00**	**0.00**	**9,880.00**	**655.00**	**612.56**	**143.26**	**8,469.18**
Tax Basis								**Circular E**	**6.20%**	**1.45%**	
G/L Accounts							**60000**	**23400**	**23400**	**23400**	**10300**

Olsen Office Furniture
Employer Costs for Period 2/06/2012 thru 2/19/2012

Employee	ER Soc. Sec. (FICA)	ER Medicare	ER FUTA	ER SUTA
Anderson, Daniel	74.40	17.40	9.60	36.00
Jenkins, Charles	74.40	17.40	9.60	36.00
Olsen, David	155.00	36.25	4.00	45.00
Olsen James	155.00	36.25	4.00	45.00
Vavra, Wesley	79.36	18.56	10.24	38.40
Wilson, Brian	74.40	17.40	9.60	36.00
Totals	**612.56**	**143.26**	**47.04**	**236.40**
Tax Basis	**6.20%**	**1.45%**	**0.8%**	**3.0%**
G/L Accounts	**23400 / 60100**	**23400 / 60100**	**23500 / 60100**	**23700 / 60100**

Feb 23	Received the following checks. Check number 90133 for $2,999.80 from Winetraub Office Furniture for Invoice 1790. Check number 5773 for $9,523.00 from Anderson & Anderson for Invoice 1791.
Feb 24	Received the following inventory. 20 ExecDeskAsh items on PO 1050 to Oregon Oak Furniture. Invoice 98903 for $7,000.00 dated Feb 23. All items on PO 1051 to Planter Interiors. Invoice 100984 for $3,300.00 dated Feb 23. All items on PO 1052 to Tollman Table Manufacturing. Invoice 68885 for $2,500.00 dated Feb 23.
	Pay February sales tax liability of $3,292.44 due through February 29 to Texas Comptroller and print on check number 8950.
	Write check number 8951 for $625.00 to Reliant Electric for the February electricity bill. Write check number 8952 for $237.50 to Fort Worth Water Utilities for the February water bill.

<table>
<tr><td>EOM</td><td>Prepare the following end-of-month adjusting entries.

Refer to the Jan 31 entry for depreciation expense and record the February depreciation entry.

Accrue $4,940 for wages. Reverse this entry on Mar 1.

Write and print check number 8953 to Cash for $154.50 to replenish petty cash fund. Debit the following expense accounts.
Office Supplies $ 27.50
Meals and Entertainment $127.00

Expense one month of Prepaid expenses to insurance expense, $300.00.

Prepare the following bank reconciliations and print the detail reconciliation report.

Regular Checking Account statement balance using the statement that follows.

Payroll Checking Account statement balance is $296.17. All items have cleared.

Print the following reports for February.

Trial Balance report. Review for accuracy.

Aged Receivables and Aged Payables Detail reports as of February 29 and Inventory Valuation Detail report for month of February. Reconcile these reports to the appropriate account balances on the Trial Balance report.

Payroll Liability report dated Jan 1 to Feb 29. Reconcile report totals to the appropriate payroll liability and expense accounts on the trial balance.

Open Purchase Orders report.

Print the following February financial statements.
Profit & Loss Standard
Balance Sheet Standard
Statement of Cash Flows</td></tr>
<tr><td colspan="2">Backup the company data file to a backup file named QB2012_Proj2_Stud_Completed.</td></tr>
</table>

Olsen Office Furniture
Bank Statement February 29, 2012

Beginning Balance from January Statement				$ 89,258.36
February Deposits				
	Feb 1, 2012		8,774.88	
	Feb 1, 2012		30,575.25	
	Feb 3, 2012		5,403.50	
	Feb 3, 2012		34,595.00	
	Feb 4, 2012		4,825.57	
	Feb 14, 2012		2,549.85	
	Feb 14, 2012		5,950.00	
	Feb 23, 2012		2,999.80	
	Feb 23, 2012		9,523.00	
Total Deposits for February				105,196.85
February Checks Cleared				
	Feb 1, 2012	8936	2,166.64	
	Feb 1, 2012	8938	1,875.00	
	Feb 1, 2012	8939	147.58	
	Feb 1, 2012	8940	800.00	
	Feb 1, 2012	8941	575.00	
	Feb 1, 2012	8942	5,500.00	
	Feb 7, 2012	8943	2,186.42	
	Feb 11, 2012	8944	859.87	
	Feb 20, 2012	8945	2,166.64	
	Feb 20, 2012	8946	1,125.00	
	Feb 20, 2012	8947	2,600.00	
	Feb 20, 2012	8948	5,500.00	
	Feb 20, 2012	8949	1,910.00	
Total Cleared Checks for February				27,412.15
Less Bank Transfers				
	Feb 6, 2012		8,500.00	
	Feb 20, 2012		8,500.00	
Total February Transfers				17,000.00
February Service Charges				75.00
Ending Bank Balance February 29, 2012				$ 149,968.06

CHAPTER 12 CREATE A NEW COMPANY

LEARNING OBJECTIVES

In this chapter, you create a company data file for a merchandising business. We will call this company Electronics Supply. To perform this task, you will:

1. Create a new data file for the company using QBP's wizard
2. Setup the chart of accounts and enter beginning balances
3. Set preferences for the new company data file
4. Create customer accounts and enter beginning balances
5. Create vendor accounts and enter beginning balances
6. Create inventory items and enter beginning balances
7. Setup payroll and enter employee information
8. Customize forms for the company
9. Complete a practice set at the end of the chapter where you post transactions and print financial statements for the new company

Begin by:

- Opening the software.
- Closing any company currently open in the software by clicking ***File>>Close Company*** on the main menu.
- **Toggling the software to the PRO EDITION** by selecting ***File>>Toggle to Another Edition*** on the main menu and choosing **QuickBooks Pro** as the edition.

NEW COMPANY DATA FILE WIZARD

To begin creating a new company data file, click ***File>>New Company*** on the main menu. In the window illustrated in Figure 12:1, click **Express Start.**

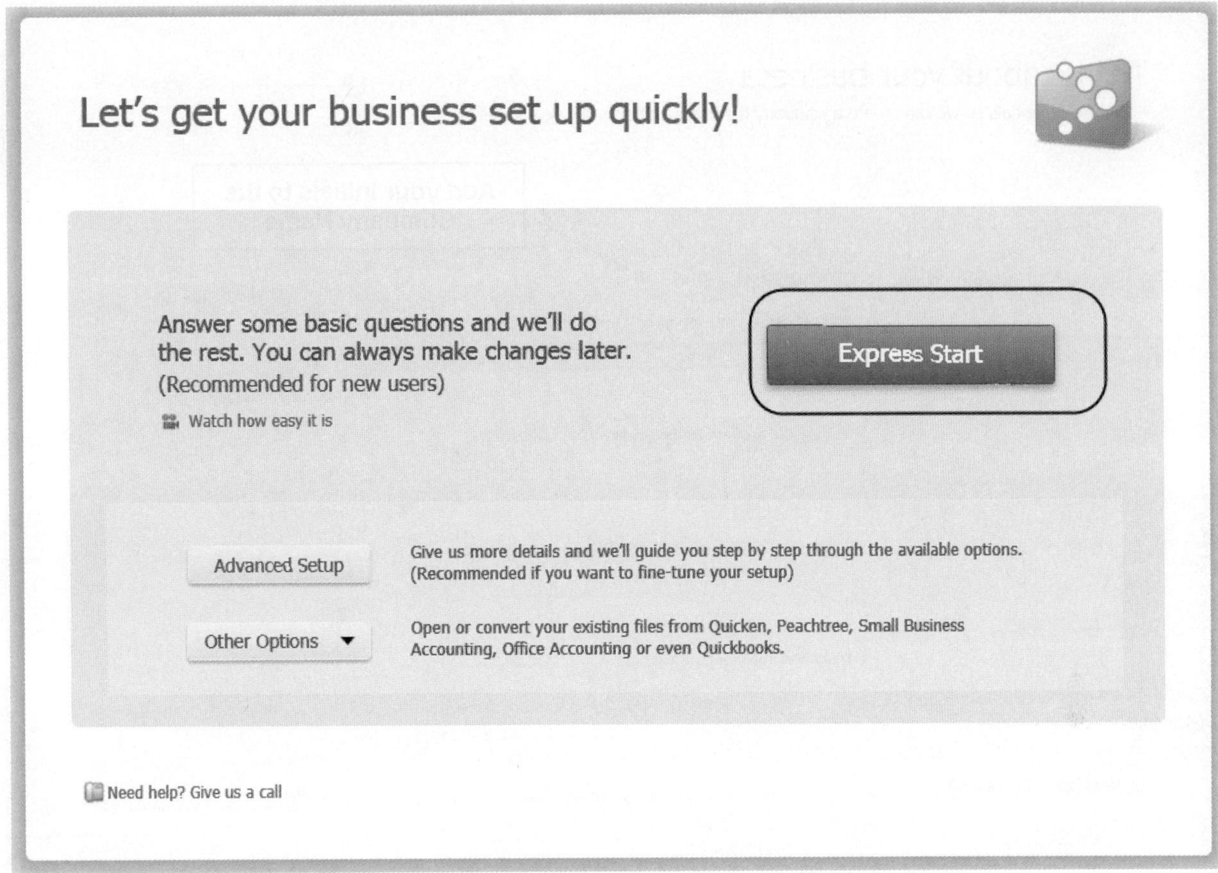

Figure 12:1

Enter the **Company Name** illustrated in Figure 12:2. ***Add your initials to the end of the Company Name.***

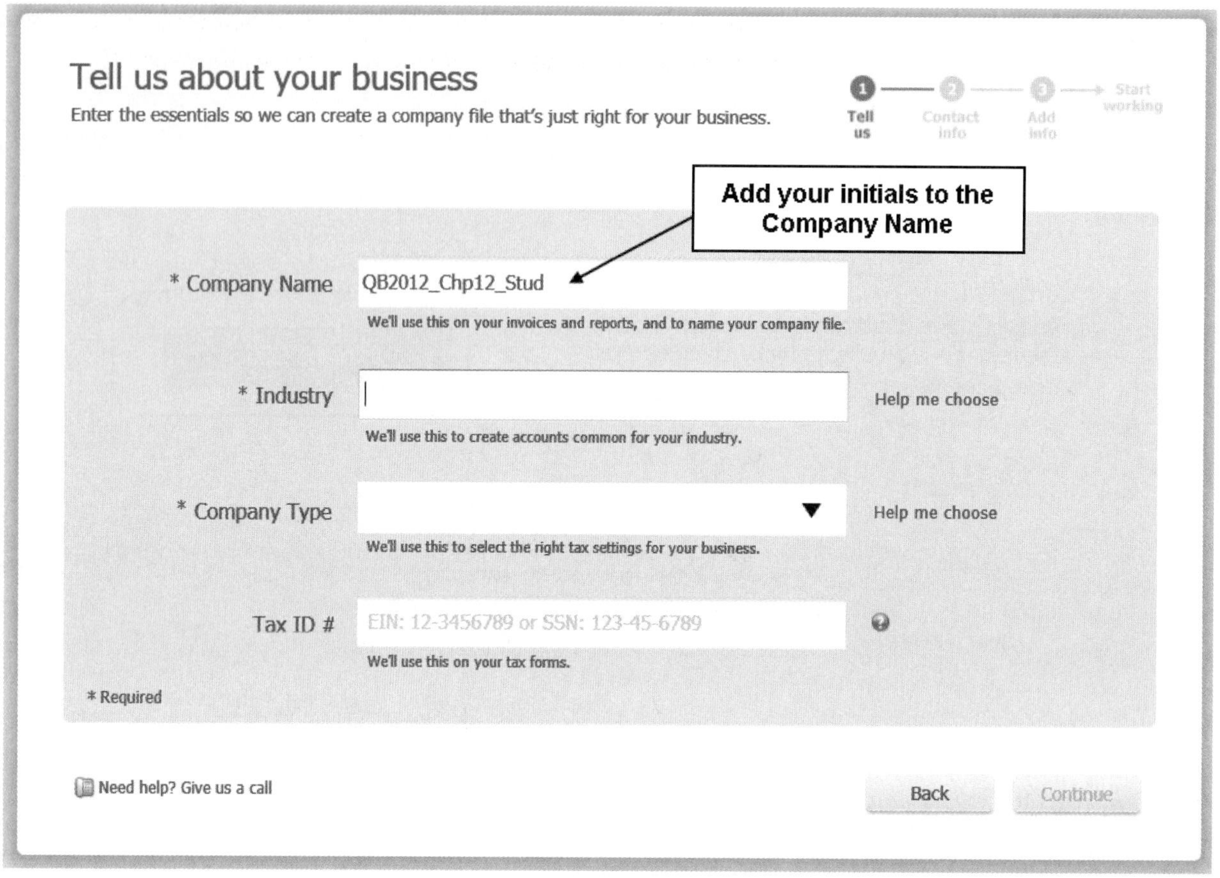

Tell us about your business

Enter the essentials so we can create a company file that's just right for your business.

Tell us — Contact info — Add info — Start working

Add your initials to the Company Name

* Company Name QB2012_Chp12_Stud

We'll use this on your invoices and reports, and to name your company file.

* Industry Help me choose

We'll use this to create accounts common for your industry.

* Company Type Help me choose

We'll use this to select the right tax settings for your business.

Tax ID # EIN: 12-3456789 or SSN: 123-45-6789

We'll use this on your tax forms.

* Required

Need help? Give us a call

Back Continue

Figure 12:2

On the **Industry** field, click the **Help me choose** link to open the window illustrated in Figure 12:3. Choose the **General Product-based Business,** which will create the chart of accounts listed on the right. Click **OK.**

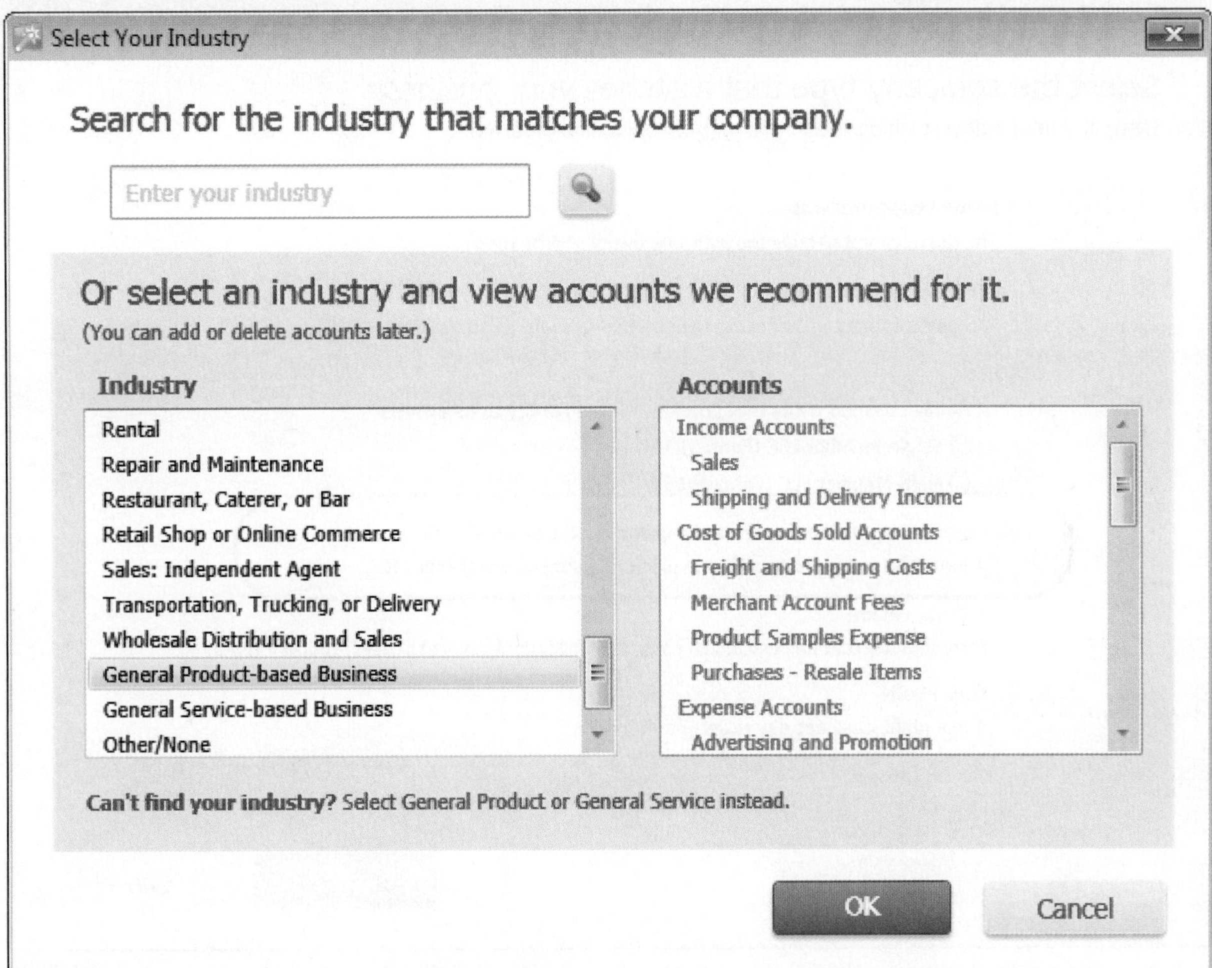

Figure 12:3

Upon returning to the Tell us about your business window, click the **Help me choose** link on the **Company Type** field. As illustrated in Figure 12:4, choose **Corporation.** Click **OK.**

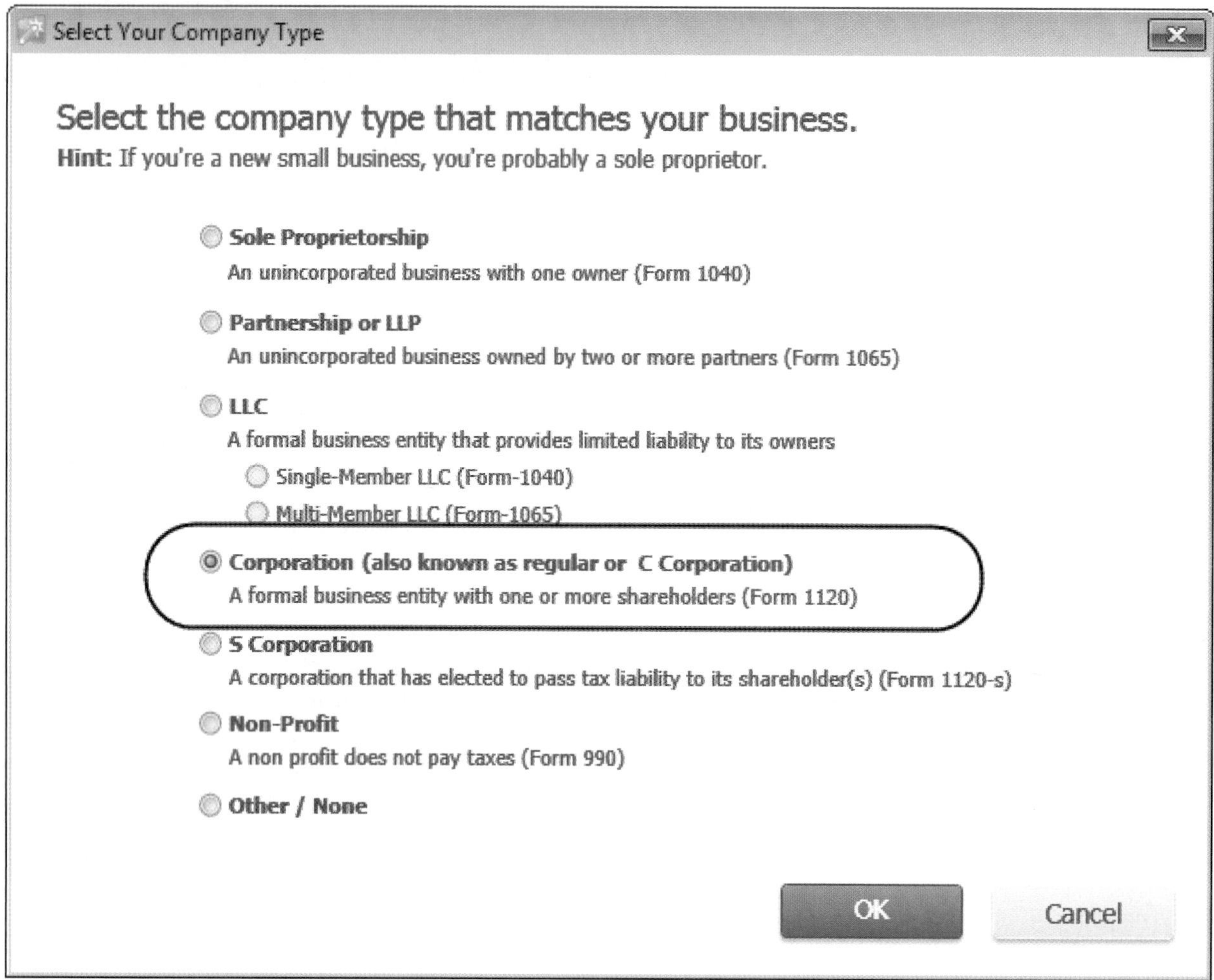

Figure 12:4

Click **Continue** and enter the information illustrated in Figure 12:5. When finished, click **Create Company File.**

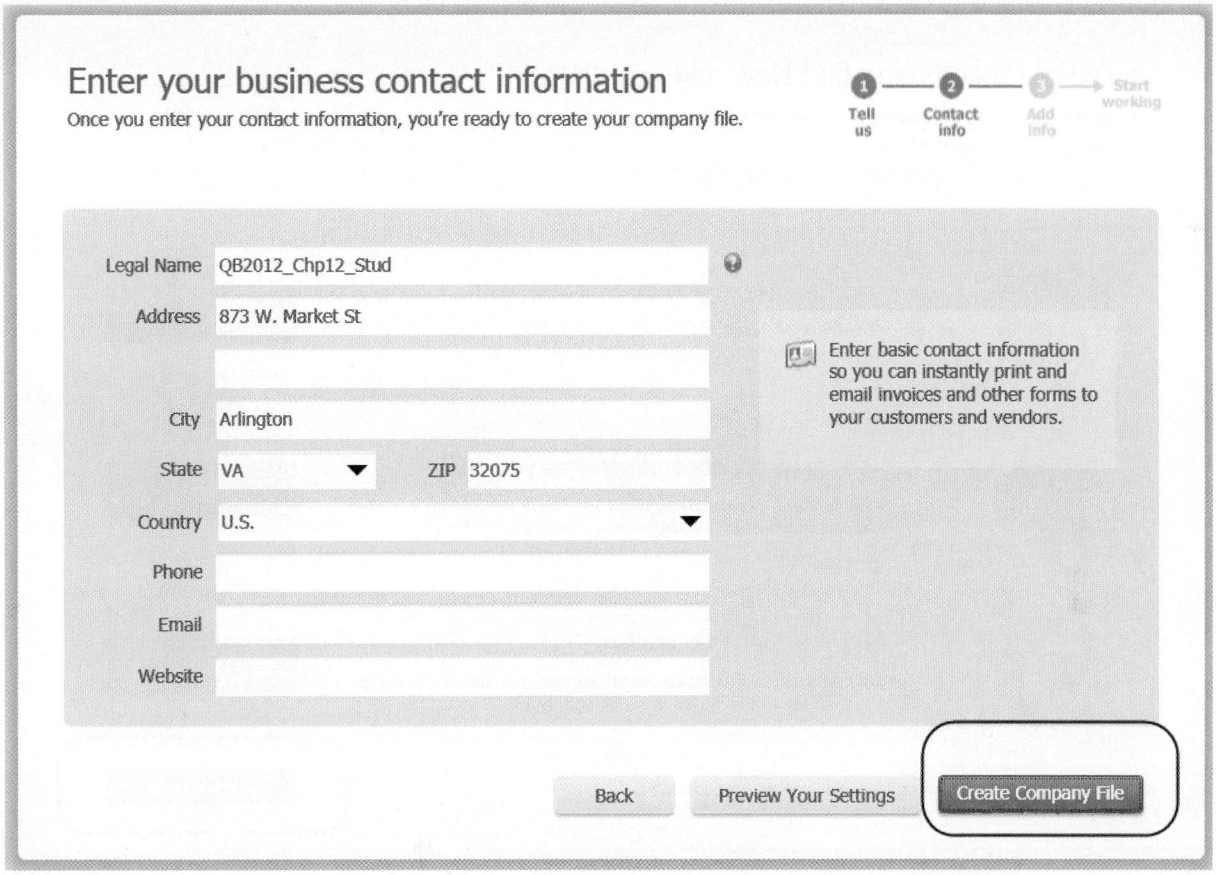

Figure 12:5

In the window illustrated in Figure 12:6, you could add customers, products, and bank accounts. We are not ready to create these items so click **Start Working.**

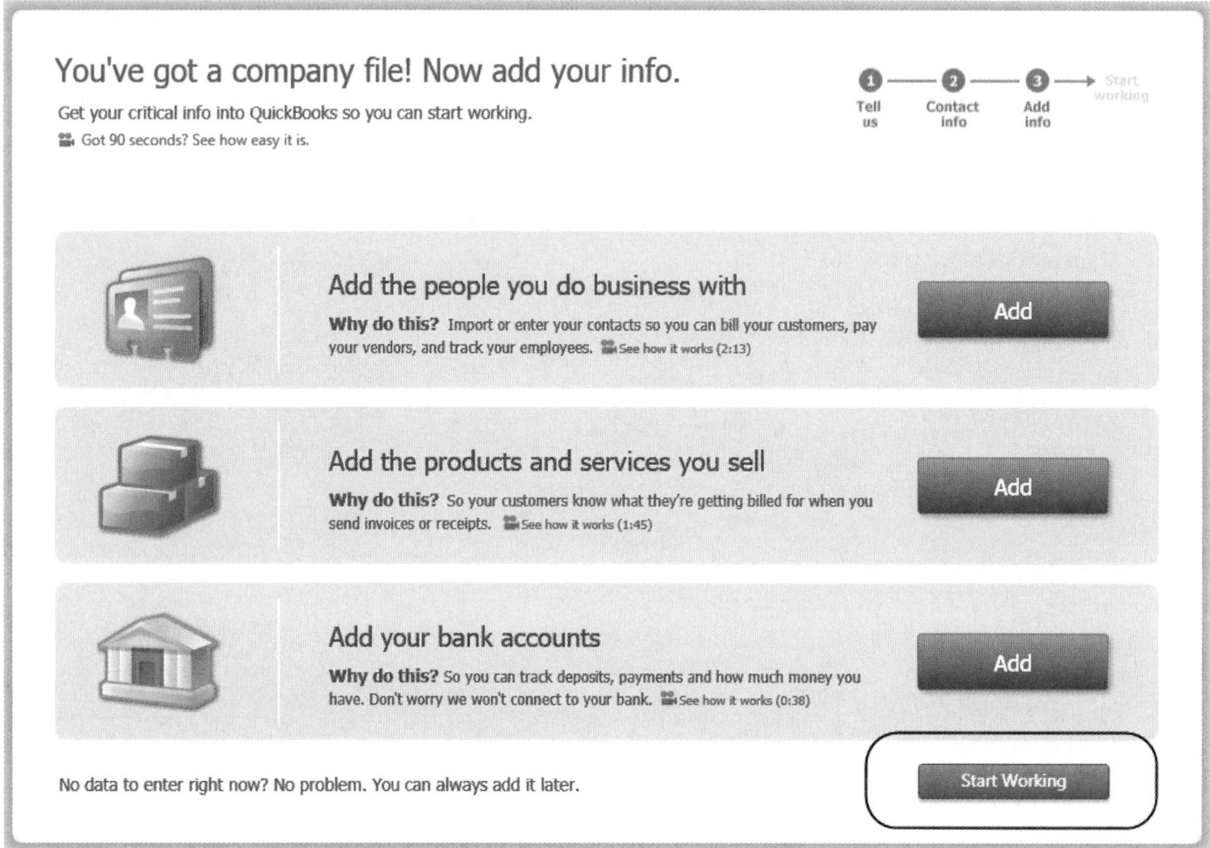

Figure 12:6

When the **Quick Start Center** window opens (not illustrated), click **x** to close it.

The Home page now opens and we are ready to finish creating the chart of accounts. Press **Ctrl + A** on the keyboard to view accounts already created by the software. (See Figure 12:7.)

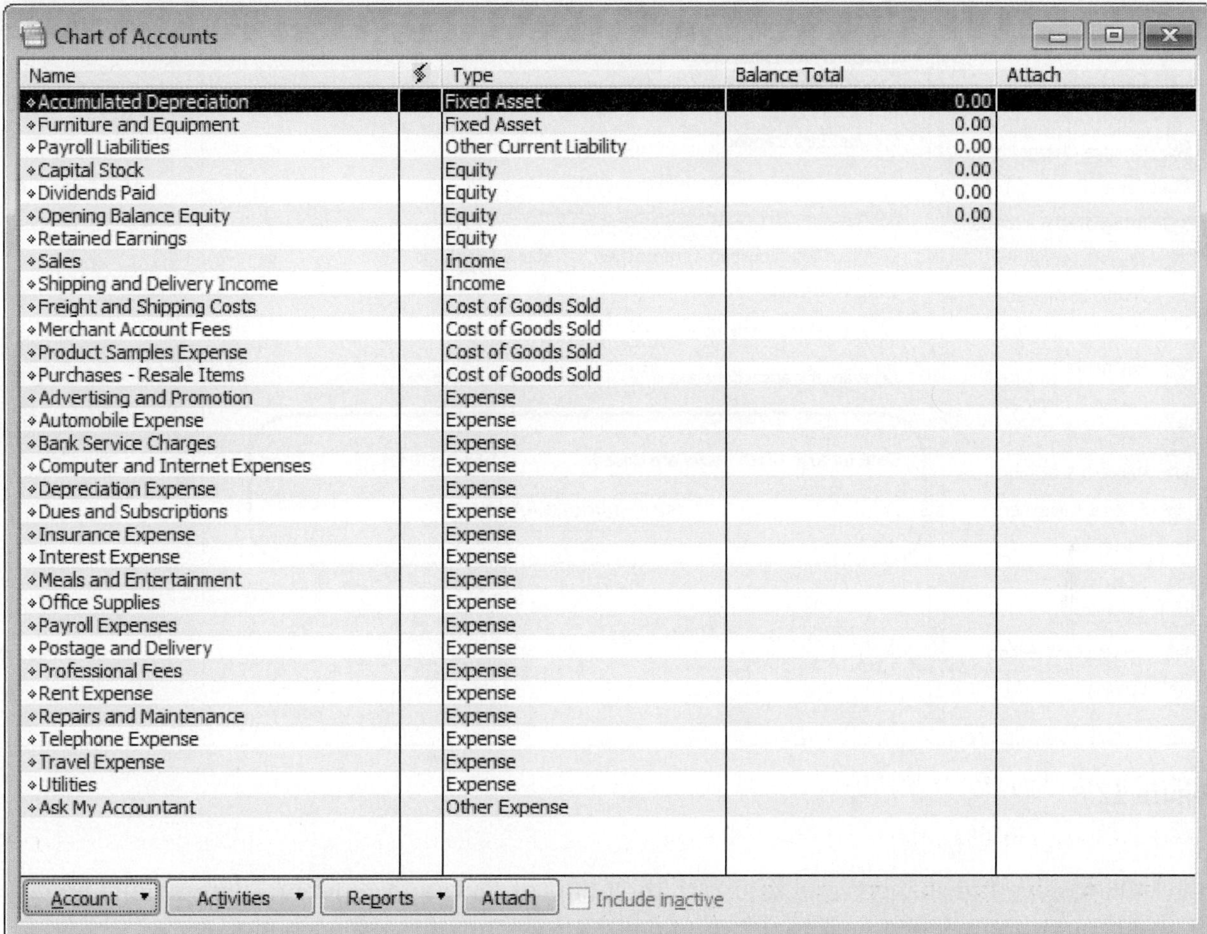
Chart of Accounts

Name	⚡	Type	Balance Total	Attach
◆Accumulated Depreciation		Fixed Asset	0.00	
◆Furniture and Equipment		Fixed Asset	0.00	
◆Payroll Liabilities		Other Current Liability	0.00	
◆Capital Stock		Equity	0.00	
◆Dividends Paid		Equity	0.00	
◆Opening Balance Equity		Equity	0.00	
◆Retained Earnings		Equity		
◆Sales		Income		
◆Shipping and Delivery Income		Income		
◆Freight and Shipping Costs		Cost of Goods Sold		
◆Merchant Account Fees		Cost of Goods Sold		
◆Product Samples Expense		Cost of Goods Sold		
◆Purchases - Resale Items		Cost of Goods Sold		
◆Advertising and Promotion		Expense		
◆Automobile Expense		Expense		
◆Bank Service Charges		Expense		
◆Computer and Internet Expenses		Expense		
◆Depreciation Expense		Expense		
◆Dues and Subscriptions		Expense		
◆Insurance Expense		Expense		
◆Interest Expense		Expense		
◆Meals and Entertainment		Expense		
◆Office Supplies		Expense		
◆Payroll Expenses		Expense		
◆Postage and Delivery		Expense		
◆Professional Fees		Expense		
◆Rent Expense		Expense		
◆Repairs and Maintenance		Expense		
◆Telephone Expense		Expense		
◆Travel Expense		Expense		
◆Utilities		Expense		
◆Ask My Accountant		Other Expense		

Figure 12:7

Before customizing the Chart of Accounts, we will add the company preference that turns on account numbers.

Select ***Edit>>Preferences*** on the main menu and choose the **Accounting** preference. On the **Company Preferences** tab, mark the option to **Use account numbers.** Click **Set Date/Password** and enter **12/31/2011** as the **Closing Date.** Remember to click **OK** and **No** to setting a password. (See Figure 12:8.)

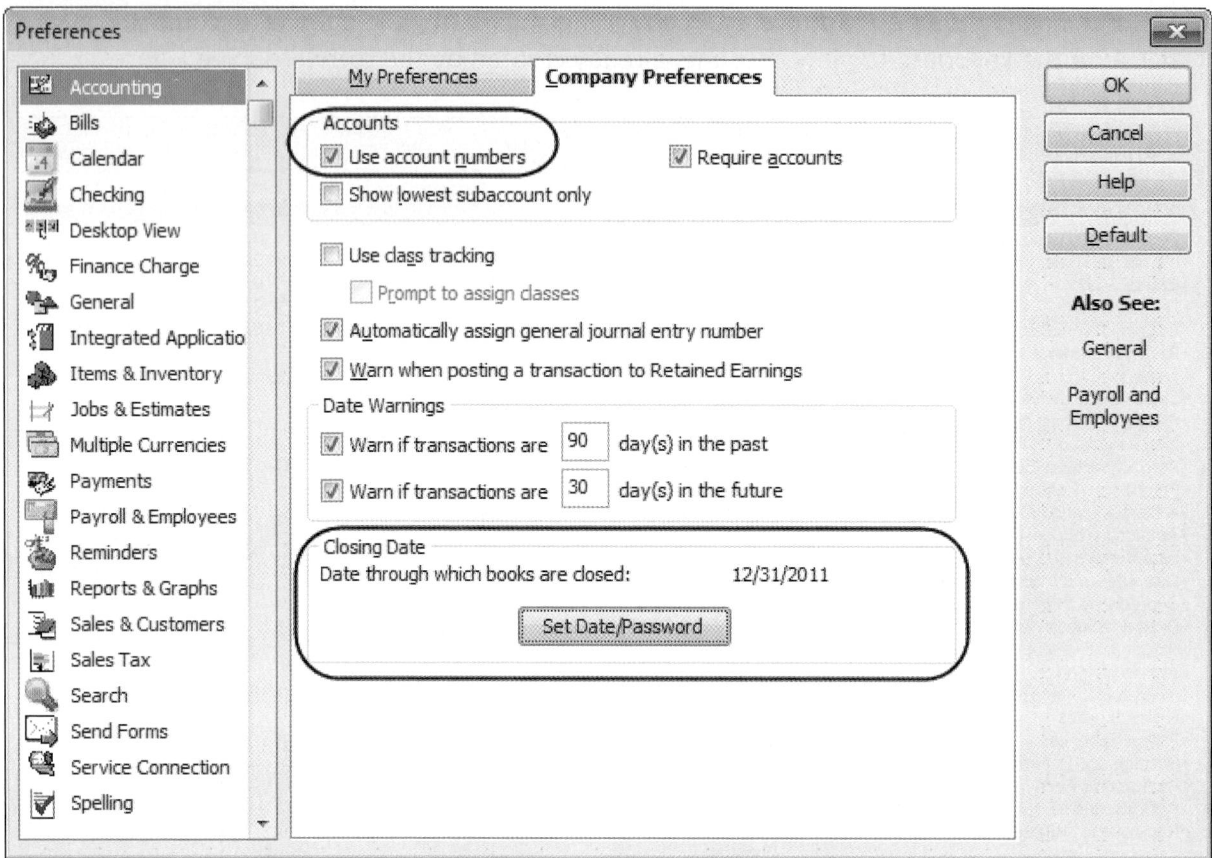

Figure 12:8

Click **OK** to save the changes and return to the Chart of Accounts window. The accounts now have account numbers. In next topic, you finalize the setup of these accounts.

CHART OF ACCOUNTS SETUP

You will now finish setting up the chart of accounts. If the Chart of Accounts window is not open from the previous topic, press **Ctrl + A** on the keyboard to open it. You will begin by editing existing accounts.

You will first change some of the fields on a few accounts. Click the **15000 Furniture and Equipment** account. Click the **Account** button and select **Edit Account.** *(Note: You can also use the shortcut key of **Ctrl + E** after clicking an account.)*

Change the **Account Name** to **Furniture and Fixtures** as illustrated in Figure 12:9.

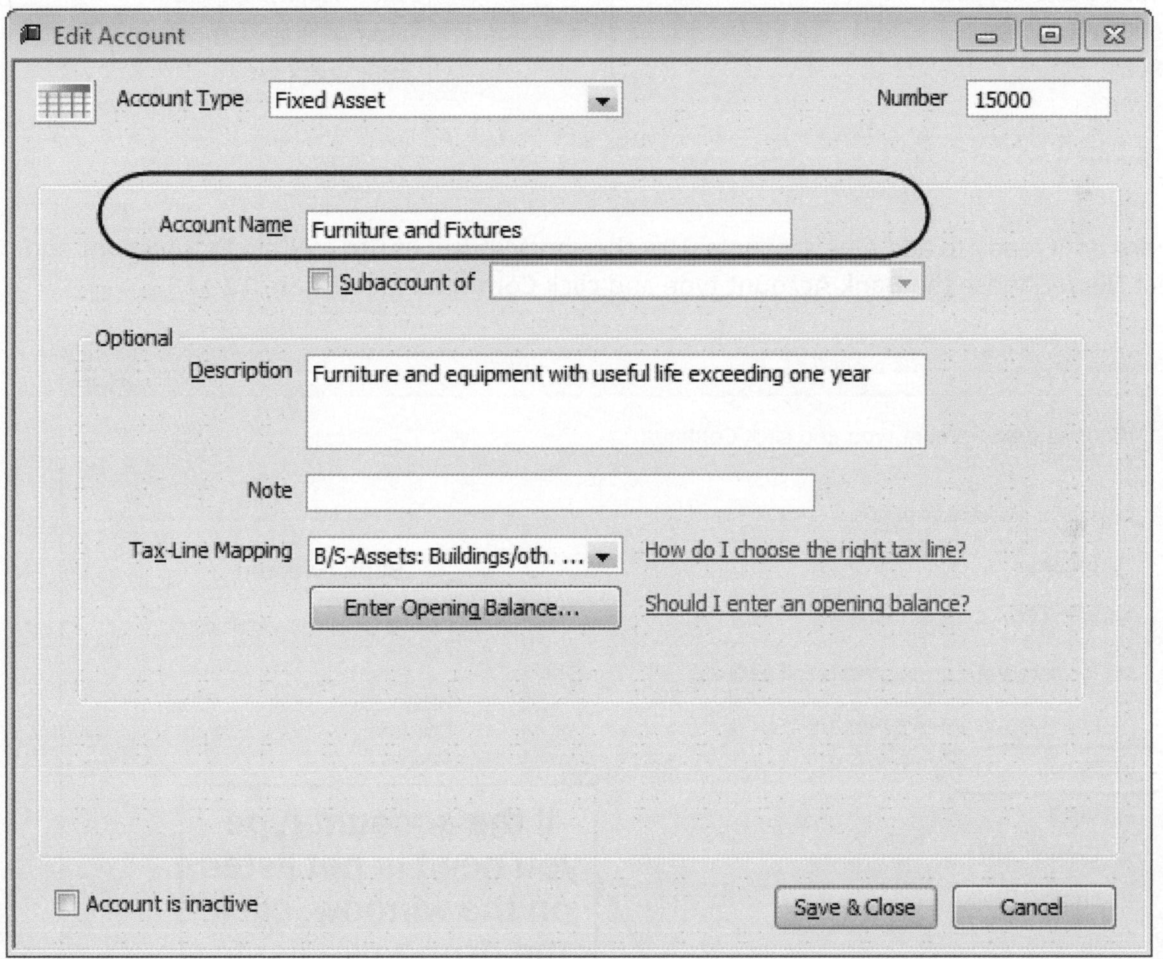

Figure 12:9

Click **Save & Close.**

Continue making changes to existing accounts by referring to information in the following figure.

Additional Account Changes

Existing Account	New Account Type	New Number	New Account Name
24000 Payroll Liabilities			Federal Withholding Tax Payable
47900 Sales		40000	
63400 Interest Expense	Other Expense	85000	
64900 Office Supplies			Office Supplies Expense
66000 Payroll Expenses			Salary & Wage Expense
68600 Utilities			Utilities Expense

Figure 12:10

You are now ready to add new accounts. Use the shortcut key of **Ctrl + N** or click **Account** and select **New.** Choose the **Bank Account** type and click **Continue.** (See Figure 12:11.)

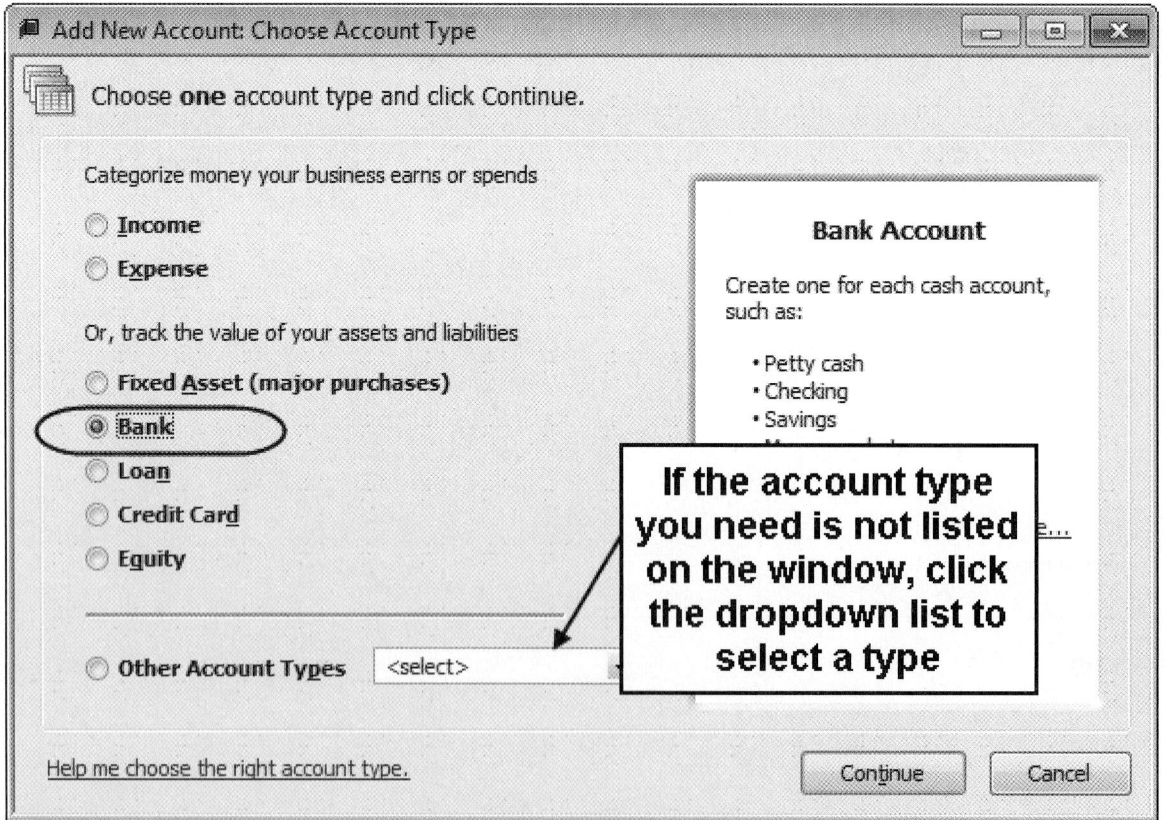

Figure 12:11

Type in the **Number** and **Account Name** illustrated in Figure 12:12.

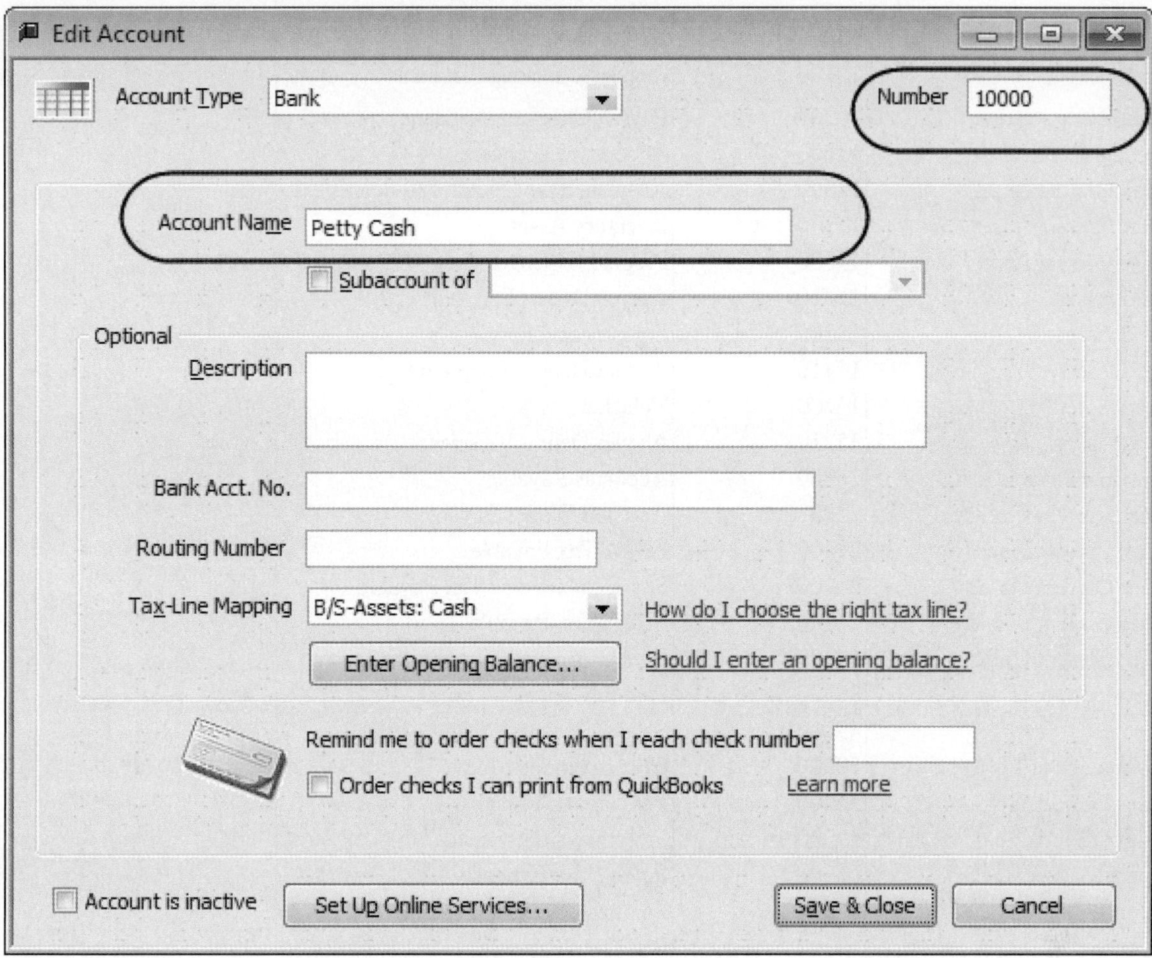

Figure 12:12

We will not enter opening balances at this time because we will post a journal entry later in the chapter to record these balances. Click **Save & New** and add the remaining accounts listed in Figure 12:13.

Additional Accounts Added

Account Type	Number	Account Name
Bank	10100	Regular Checking Account
Bank	10200	Payroll Checking Account
Accounts Receivable	11000	Accounts Receivable
Other Current Asset	11500	Allowance for Doubtful Accounts
Other Current Asset	12100	Inventory Asset
Other Current Asset	13000	Prepaid Expenses
Fixed Asset	15010	Accum Depr - Furn and Fixt
Fixed Asset	15100	Equipment
Fixed Asset	15110	Accum Depr - Equipment
Fixed Asset	15200	Vehicles
Fixed Asset	15210	Accum Depr - Vehicles
Accounts Payable	20000	Accounts Payable
Other Current Liability	22000	Accrued Wages Payable
Other Current Liability	24100	FUTA Tax Payable
Other Current Liability	24200	State Withholding Tax Payable
Other Current Liability	24300	SUTA Tax Payable
Other Current Liability	24400	Health Insurance Payable
Equity	30300	Paid-in Capital
Income	49000	Sales Discounts
Cost of Goods Sold	50000	Cost of Goods Sold
Cost of Goods Sold	55000	Purchases Discount
Cost of Goods Sold	59000	Inventory Adjustments
Expense	66100	Payroll Tax Expense
Expense	66200	Employee Benefit Expense
Expense	69100	Bad Debt Expense
Other Income	81000	Interest Income
Other Income	82000	Gain or Loss on Asset Sales
Other Expense	99000	Suspense Account

Figure 12:13

Finally, return to the Chart of Accounts window to delete the following accounts. (See Figure 12:14.) You delete an account by highlighting it, clicking **Account** and selecting **Delete Account.**

Accounts to Delete
17000 Accumulated Depreciation
48900 Shipping and Delivery Income
51800 Merchant Account Fees
52300 Product Samples Expense
52900 Purchases - Resale Items
80000 Ask My Accountant

Figure 12:14

After making all changes, print an Account Listing to verify the changes.

Select ***Reports>>Accountant and Taxes>>Account Listing*** on the main menu. Click **Customize Report** and remove the **Description**, **Accnt. #**, and **Tax Line** columns. Compare your results to those in Figure 12:15.

QB2012_Chp12_Stud

Account Listing

Account	Type	Balance Total
10000 · Petty Cash	Bank	0.00
10100 · Regular Checking Account	Bank	0.00
10200 · Payroll Checking Account	Bank	0.00
11000 · Accounts Receivable	Accounts Receivable	0.00
11500 · Allowance for Doubtful Accounts	Other Current Asset	0.00
12100 · Inventory Asset	Other Current Asset	0.00
13000 · Prepaid Expenses	Other Current Asset	0.00
15000 · Furniture and Fixtures	Fixed Asset	0.00
15010 · Accum Depr - Furn and Fixt	Fixed Asset	0.00
15100 · Equipment	Fixed Asset	0.00
15110 · Accum Depr - Equipment	Fixed Asset	0.00
15200 · Vehicles	Fixed Asset	0.00
15210 · Accum Depr - Vehicles	Fixed Asset	0.00
20000 · Accounts Payable	Accounts Payable	0.00
24000 · Federal Withholding Tax Payable	Other Current Liability	0.00
24100 · FUTA Tax Payable	Other Current Liability	0.00
24200 · State Withholding Tax Payable	Other Current Liability	0.00
24300 · SUTA Tax Payable	Other Current Liability	0.00
24400 · Health Insurance Payable	Other Current Liability	0.00
30000 · Opening Balance Equity	Equity	0.00
30100 · Capital Stock	Equity	0.00
30200 · Dividends Paid	Equity	0.00
30300 · Paid-in Capital	Equity	0.00
32000 · Retained Earnings	Equity	
40000 · Sales	Income	
49000 · Sales Discounts	Income	
50000 · Cost of Goods Sold	Cost of Goods Sold	
51100 · Freight and Shipping Costs	Cost of Goods Sold	
55000 · Purchases Discount	Cost of Goods Sold	
59000 · Inventory Adjustments	Cost of Goods Sold	
60000 · Advertising and Promotion	Expense	
60200 · Automobile Expense	Expense	
60400 · Bank Service Charges	Expense	
61700 · Computer and Internet Expenses	Expense	
62400 · Depreciation Expense	Expense	
62500 · Dues and Subscriptions	Expense	
63300 · Insurance Expense	Expense	
64300 · Meals and Entertainment	Expense	
64900 · Office Supplies Expense	Expense	
66000 · Salary & Wage Expense	Expense	
66100 · Payroll Tax Expense	Expense	
66200 · Employee Benefit Expense	Expense	
66500 · Postage and Delivery	Expense	
66700 · Professional Fees	Expense	
67100 · Rent Expense	Expense	
67200 · Repairs and Maintenance	Expense	
68100 · Telephone Expense	Expense	
68400 · Travel Expense	Expense	
68600 · Utilities Expense	Expense	
69100 · Bad Debt Expense	Expense	
81000 · Interest Income	Other Income	
82000 · Gain or Loss on Asset Sales	Other Income	
85000 · Interest Expense	Other Expense	
99000 · Suspense Account	Other Expense	

Figure 12:15

If you find a mistake, double click the account on the report to reopen it. Make any changes and resave. **Close** the **Account Listing** report and the **Chart of Accounts** window.

You will now post beginning balances. *(Note: You will not post balances for accounts receivable, inventory, or accounts payable because these balances are posted when creating the accounts and items.)*

Click ***Company>>Make General Journal Entries*** on the main menu and enter the following information. (See Figure 12:16.) *(Note: when prompted about assigning numbers to journal entries, click the option to turn off future messages and click OK.)*

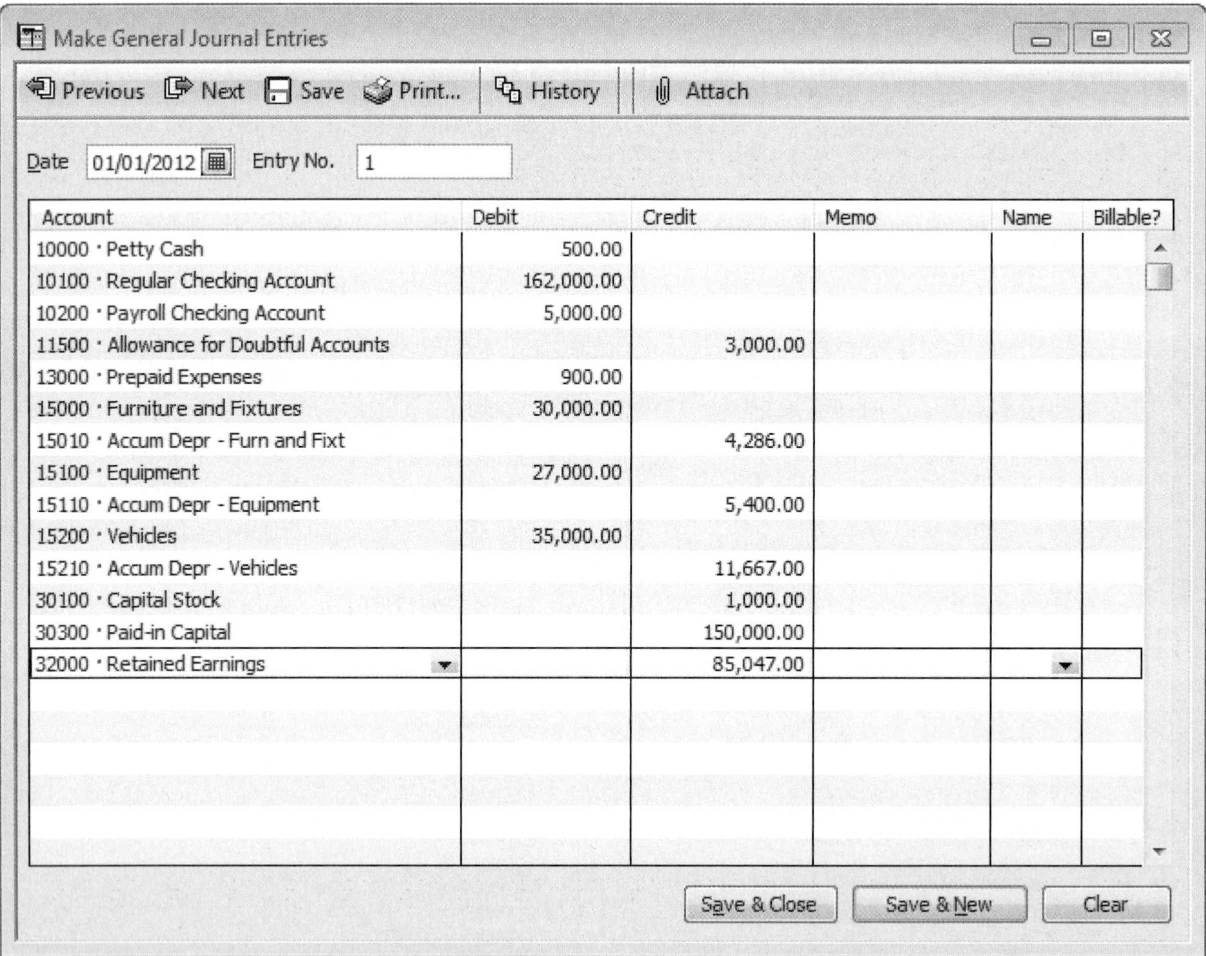

Account	Debit	Credit	Memo	Name	Billable?
10000 · Petty Cash	500.00				
10100 · Regular Checking Account	162,000.00				
10200 · Payroll Checking Account	5,000.00				
11500 · Allowance for Doubtful Accounts		3,000.00			
13000 · Prepaid Expenses	900.00				
15000 · Furniture and Fixtures	30,000.00				
15010 · Accum Depr - Furn and Fixt		4,286.00			
15100 · Equipment	27,000.00				
15110 · Accum Depr - Equipment		5,400.00			
15200 · Vehicles	35,000.00				
15210 · Accum Depr - Vehicles		11,667.00			
30100 · Capital Stock		1,000.00			
30300 · Paid-in Capital		150,000.00			
32000 · Retained Earnings		85,047.00			

Figure 12:16

Click **Save & Close.** When prompted about tracking fixed assets, turn off future messages and click **OK.** When prompted about posting to retained earnings, click **OK.**

You are now ready for the next topic that discusses company preferences.

Company Preferences Setup

Select ***Edit>>Preferences*** on the main menu and follow the next series of illustrations to configure preferences for the new company. Select the **Preference** category and tab illustrated in the figures. Click **Yes** whenever prompted to save your changes.

Bills

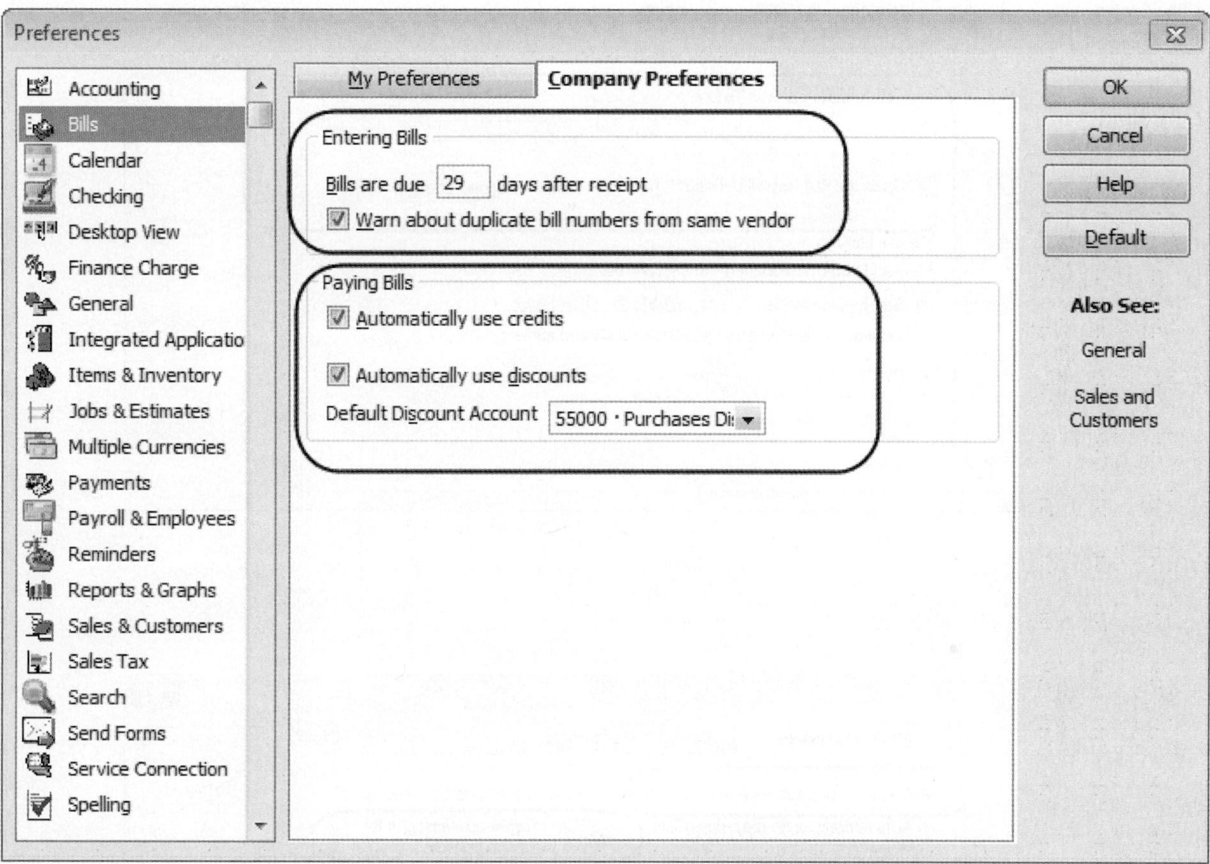

Figure 12:17

Checking

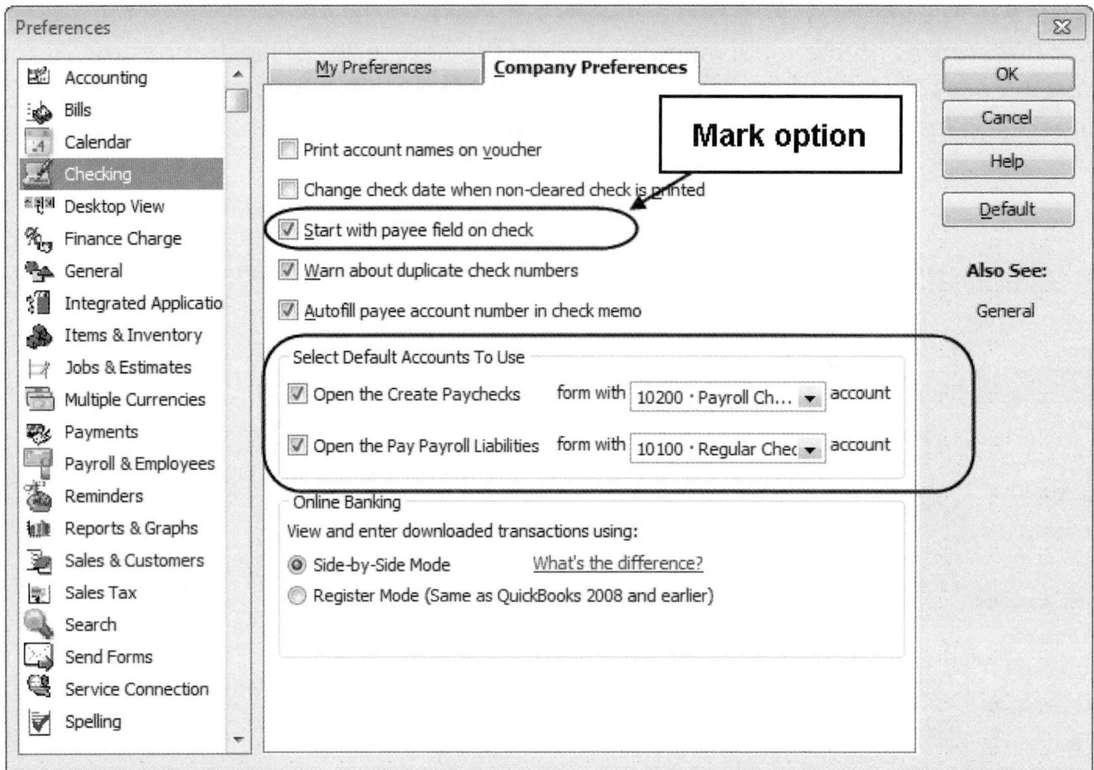

Figure 12:18

General

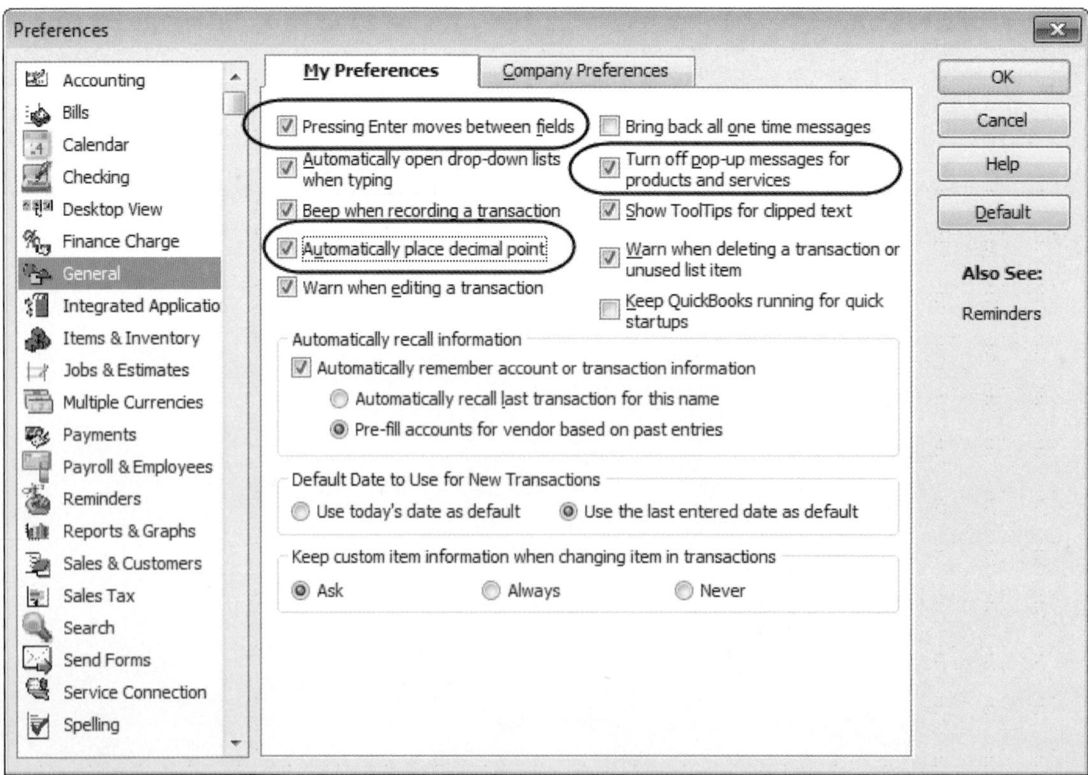

Figure 12:19

Items & Inventory

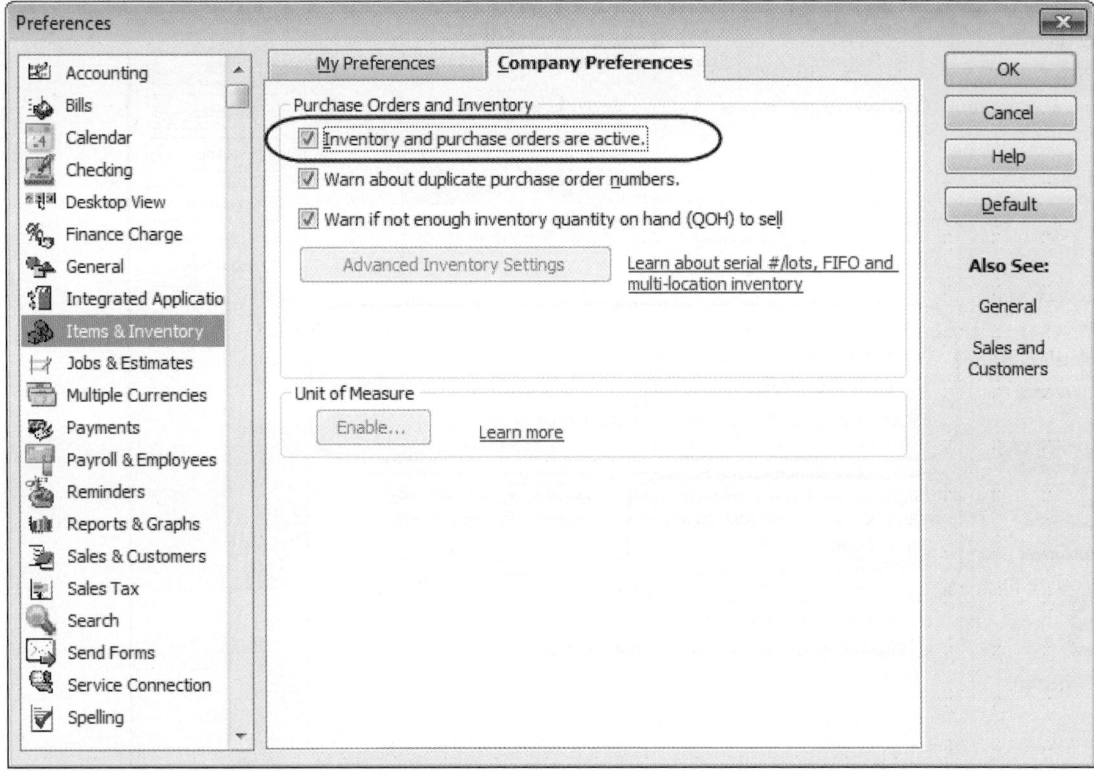

Figure 12:20

Jobs & Estimates

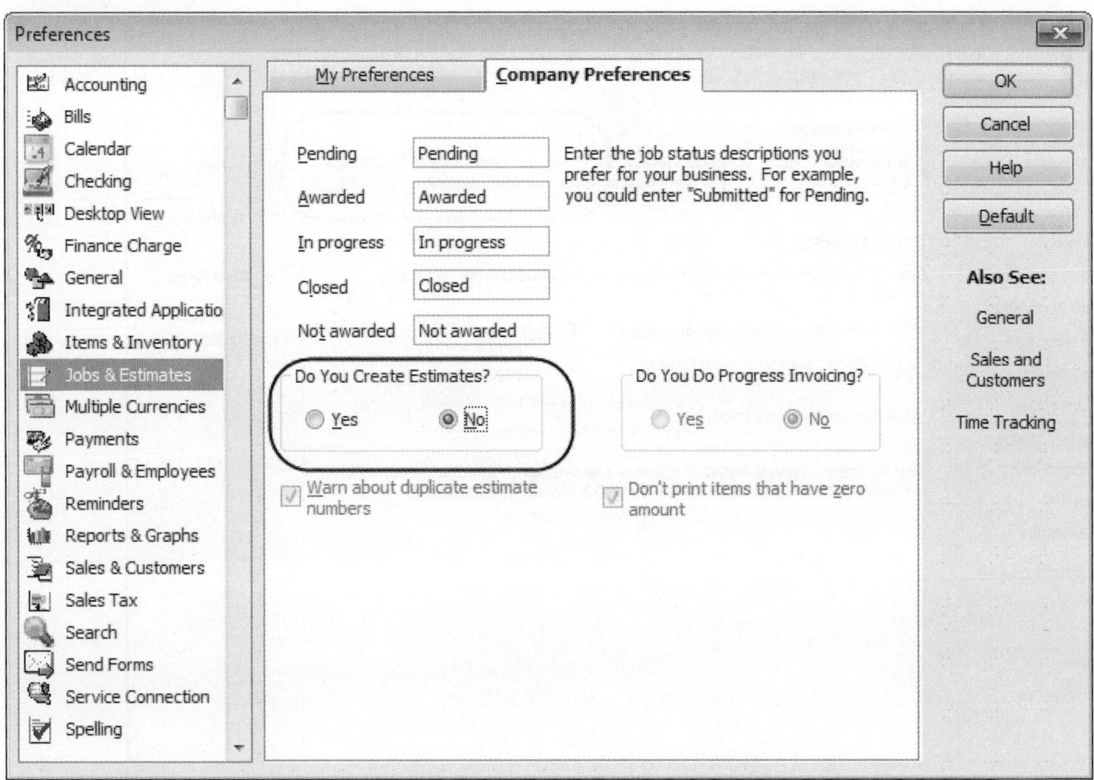

Figure 12:21

Payroll & Employees

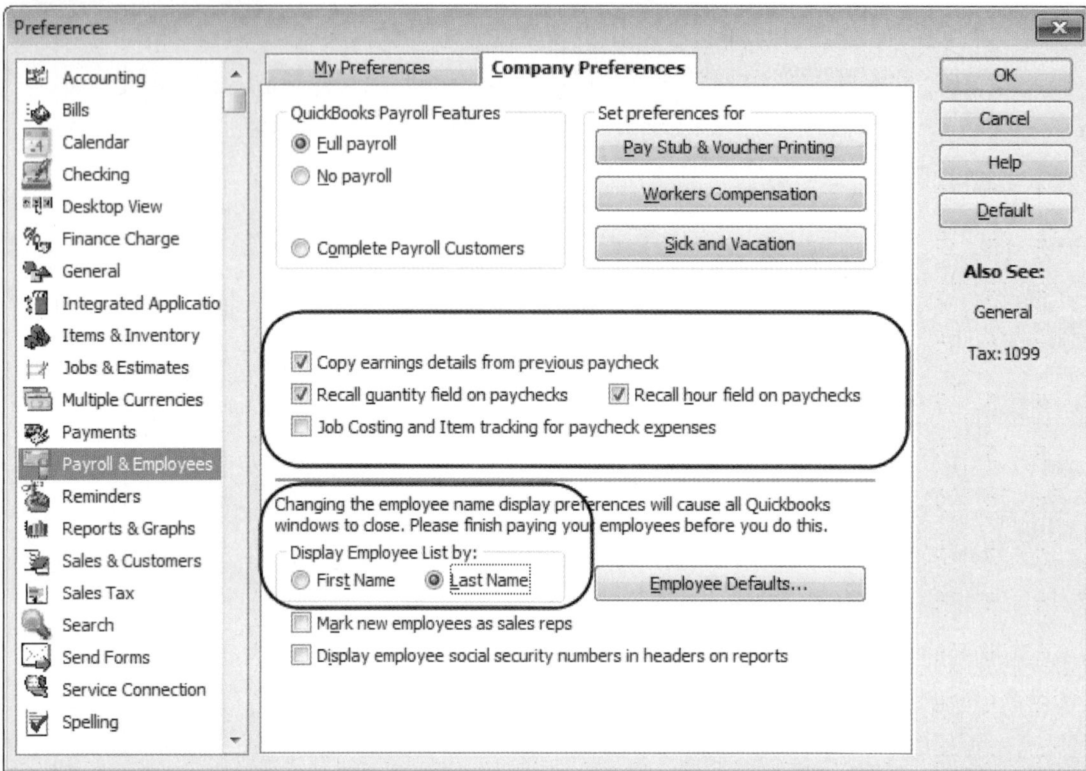

Figure 12:22

Payments

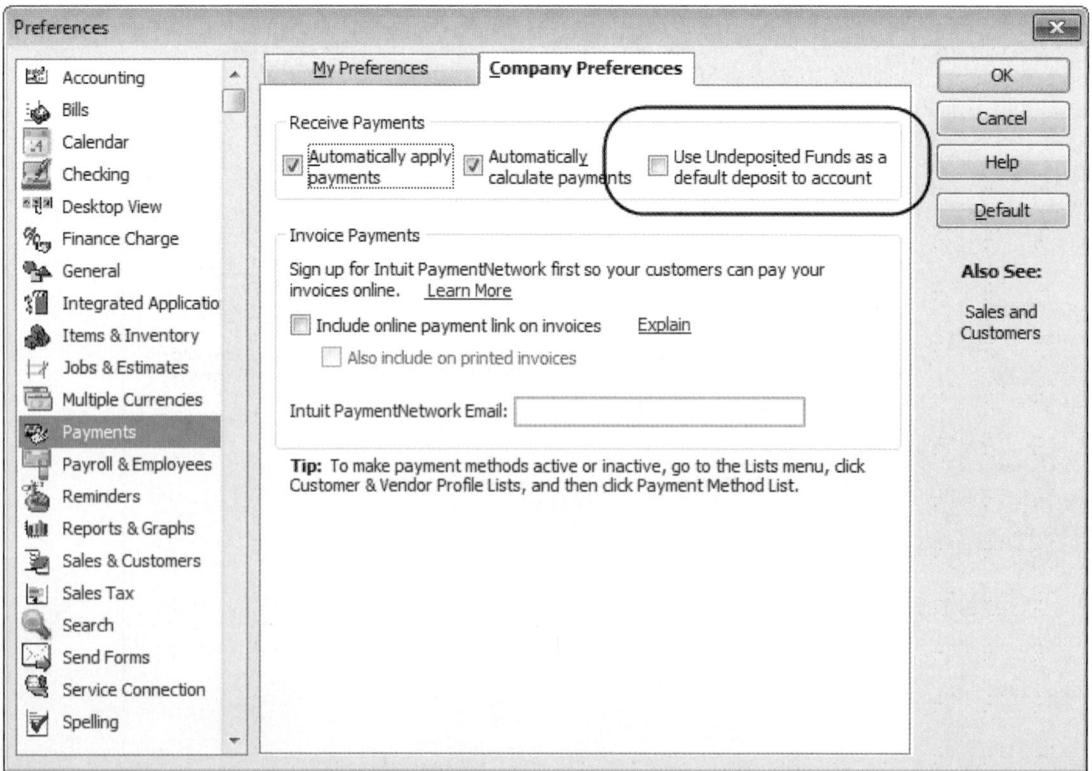

Figure 12:23

Reports & Graphs

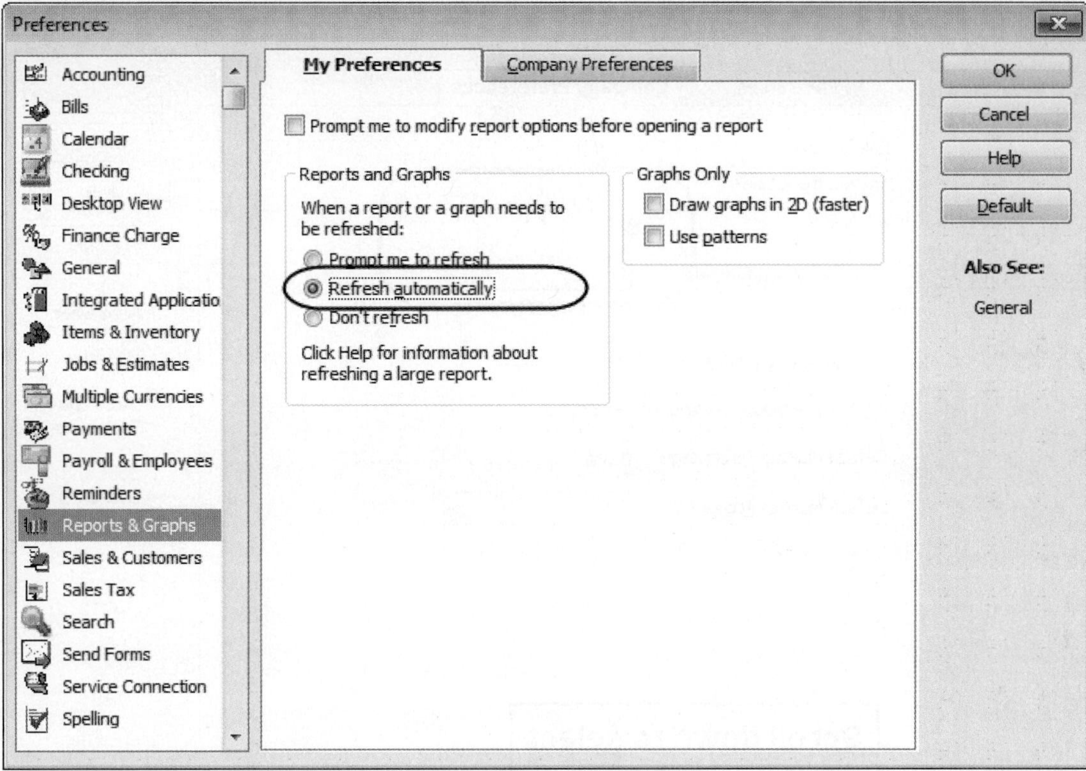

Figure 12:24

Sales & Customers

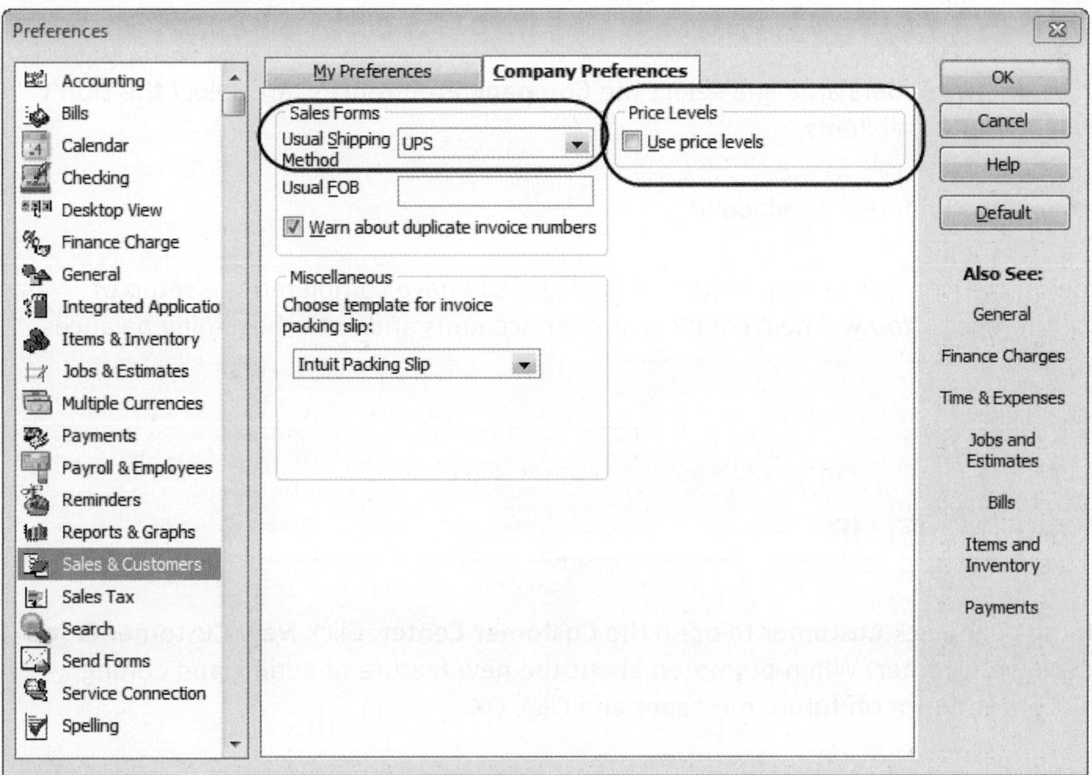

Figure 12:25

Time & Expenses

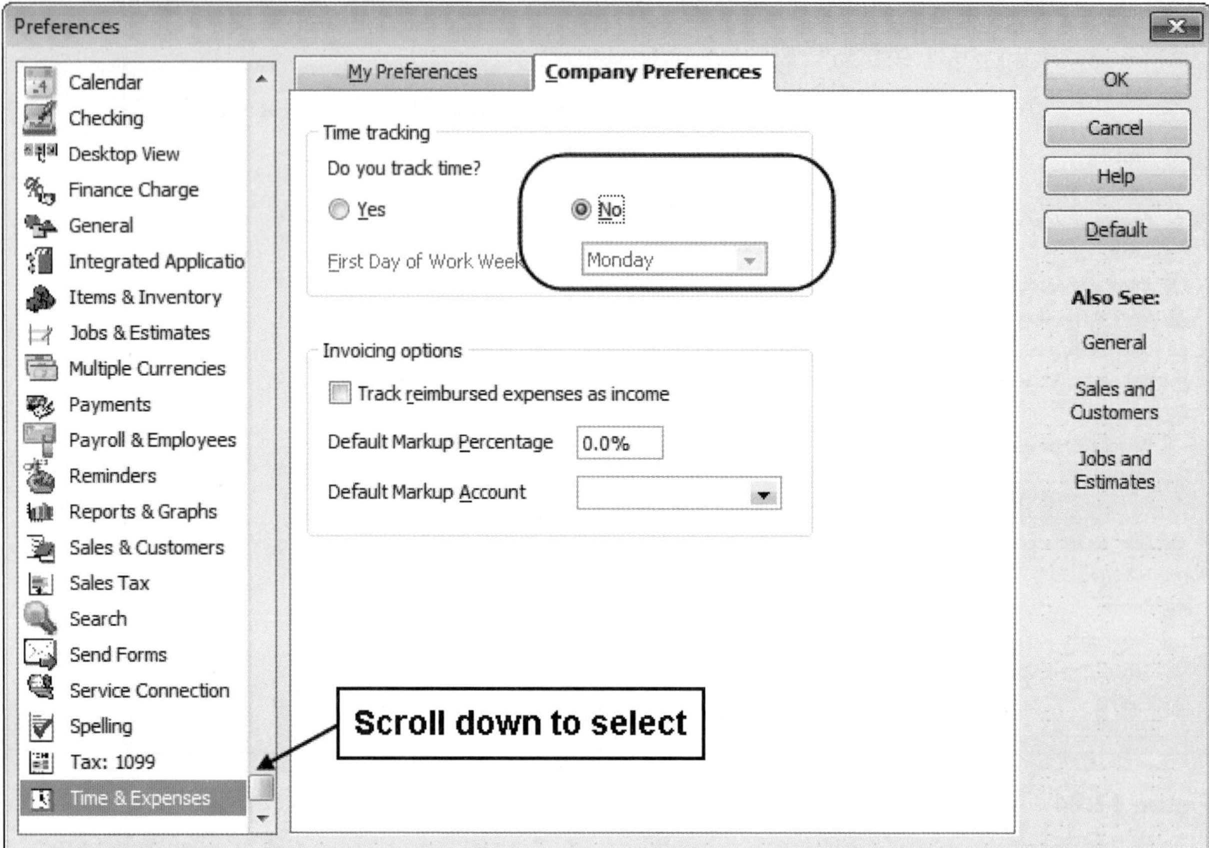

Figure 12:26

Finally, go to the **Reminders** area and select the **Company Preferences** tab. Select the **Don't Remind Me** option for all items.

Click **OK** to exit the Preferences window.

Click **Home** on the Icon bar to reopen the Home page. You have completed the setup of company preferences. You will next create customer accounts and enter beginning balances for these accounts.

Customer Setup

On the **Home** page, click **Customer** to open the **Customer Center.** Click **New Customer & Job** and select **New Customer.** When prompted about the new feature of adding and editing multiple list entries, turn off future messages and click **OK.**

Figure 12:27 illustrates creating the **Address Info** tab on the first customer. Make sure to enter the **Opening Balance** and the **as of** date. Also, copy the **Bill to** address into the **Ship to** address.

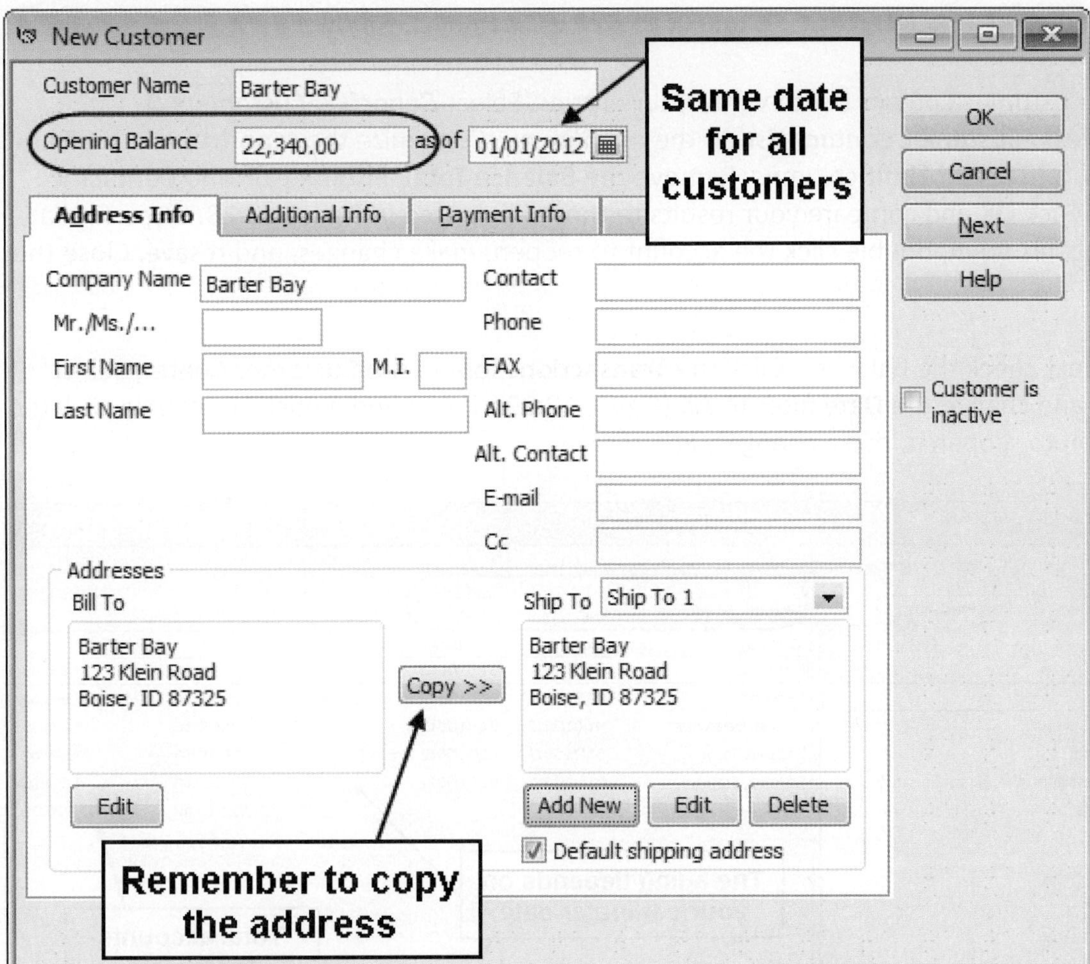

Figure 12:27

Complete the Barter Bay account by referring to Figure 12:28. Remember that **Terms** are entered on the **Additional Info** tab and the **Credit Limit** on the **Payment Info** tab.

When finished, click **Next** to save the account so you can enter the next account. Continue entering accounts and opening balances until you have created all the accounts illustrated in to Figure 12:28.

Customer Listing

Customer Name	Address	City, State, Zip	Terms	Credit Limit	Opening Balance
Barter Bay	123 Klein Road	Boise, ID 87325	Net 30	30,000.00	22,340.00
Better Buy	825 W. Exchange St.	Chicago, IL 60609	2% 10 Net 30	50,000.00	27,000.00
Discount Electronics	33 Rodeo Drive	Berstow, CA 65841	Net 30	30,000.00	9,670.00
Electronic Town	3454 Broadway Ave.	Aliquippa, PA 42251	Net 30	30,000.00	23,500.00
GG Hregg Stores	454 Sanford St.	Lansing, MI 60543	Net 30	30,000.00	9,600.00
Television World	25 Saturday Ave.	New York, NY 36544	Net 30	30,000.00	-

Figure 12:28

After entering all accounts, click **OK** to exit the New Customer window.

Print the Customer Contact List to verify your entries. Select ***Reports>>Customers & Receivables>>Customer Contact List*** on the main menu. Customize the report to add the **Ship to**, **Terms**, and **Credit Limit** columns. Remove the **Balance Total**, **Phone**, **Fax**, and **Contact** columns. Click **OK** and compare your results to those illustrated in Figure 12:28. If you find a mistake at this point, double click the account to reopen, make changes, and resave. Close the report.

You will next check the balances. Click the **Transactions** tab on the **Customer Center**, select **Invoices**, and change the **Date** filter to **All** (Figure 12:29). If you find a mistake, double click the transaction to reopen it, make changes, and resave.

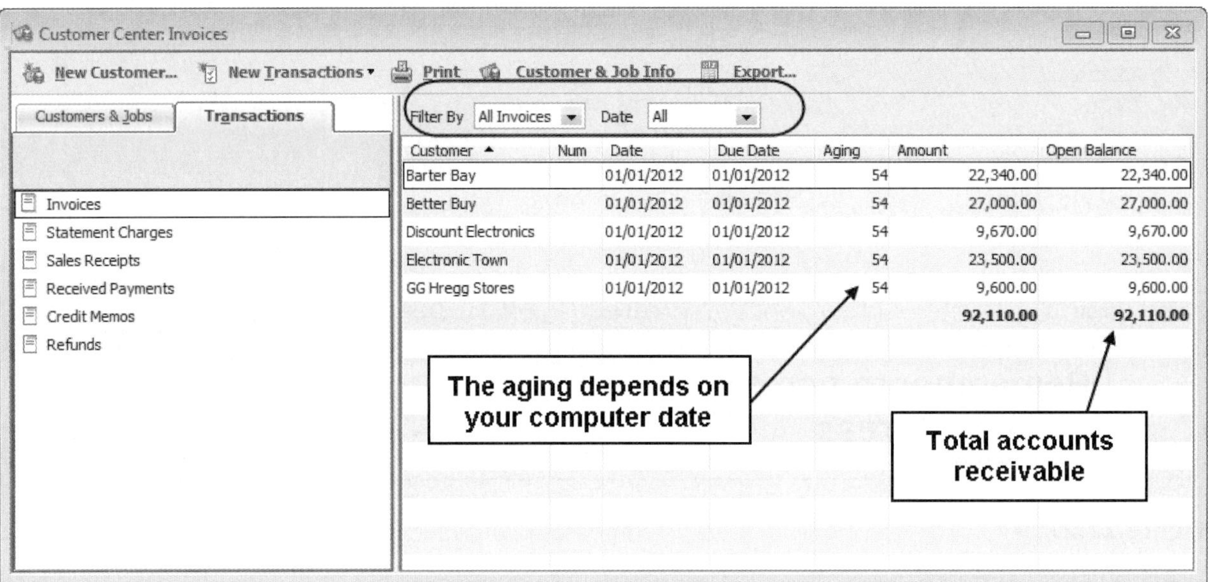

Figure 12:29

Close the Customer Center. You will next create vendor accounts.

VENDOR SETUP

Open the **Vendor Center** and click **New Vendor** to select **New Vendor.** Figure 12:30 illustrates creating the first vendor account and opening balance. Refer to Figure 12:31 to create vendors and opening balances. Terms are added on the **Additional Info** tab. *(Note: The Net 5 payment terms can be added "on the fly" from the vendor account.)* General ledger accounts are selected on the **Account Prefill** tab.

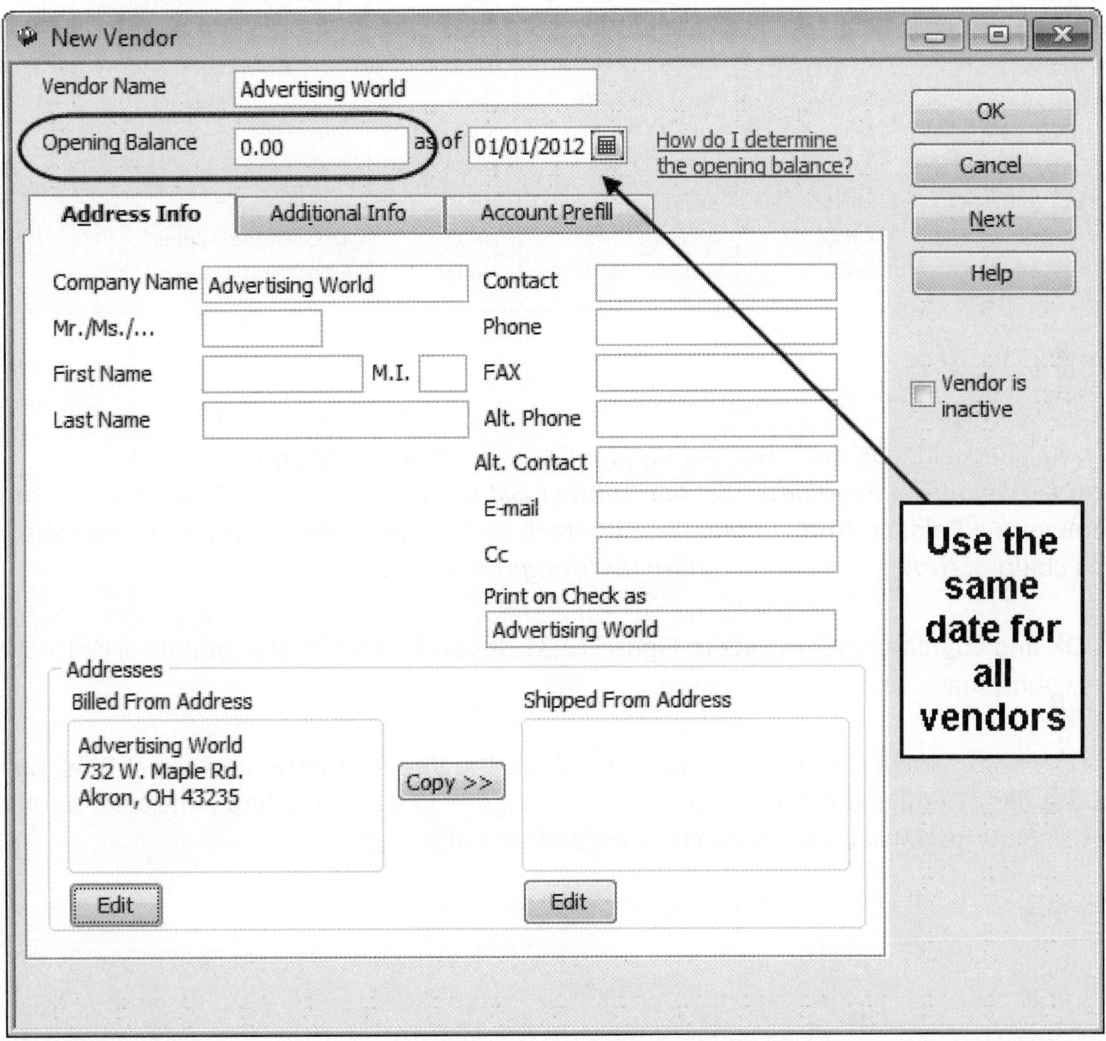

Figure 12:30

Vendor Listing					
Vendor Name	**Address**	**City, State, Zip**	**Terms**	**Account Prefill**	**Opening Balance**
Advertising World	732 W. Maple Rd.	Akron, OH 43235	Net 30	60000 Advertising and Promotion	0.00
Bank Amerex	2332 Arlington Dr.	Arlington, VA 23532	Net 5		0.00
Canyon Cam	8754 Anthony Lane	Harrisburg, PA 15237	2% 10 Net 30		7,740.00
Cooleys Repair	8 Ripley Ave.	Blacksburg, VA 43253	Net 30	67200 Repairs and Maintenance	0.00
CSB Telephone	2 Rich St.	Arlington, VA 45235	Net 15	68100 Telephone Expense	0.00
Federal Xpert	903 Mulberry Ave.	Montpelier, NH 17325	Net 15	66500 Postage and Delivery	0.00
Javix Cam	898 Main St.	Albany, NY 09325	Net 30		7,760.00
Mutual Health Insurance	7542 Golf Way	Concord, NH 45789	Net 15	24400 Health Insurance Payable	0.00
Neer Pio	896 Angel Rd.	Salem, OR 23456	Net 30		41,400.00
Office Rex	105 Curl Ave.	Arlington, VA 44333	Net 30	64900 Office Supplies Expense	0.00
Petty Cash			Due on receipt	64900 Office Supplies Expense	0.00
SumSang Corporation	78123 Mulberry Ave.	Santa Anita, CA 09827	Net 30		0.00
Travelor's Insurance	7895 Cat Dr.	Salem, OR 78453	Net 15	13000 Prepaid Expenses	0.00
Virginia Electric	41 Cala Rd.	Arlington, VA 42353	Net 15	68600 Utilities Expense	0.00

Figure 12:31

When finished, click **OK** and print the Vendor Contact List to verify entries. Select ***Reports>>Vendors & Payables>>Vendor Contact List*** on the main menu. Customize the report to remove the **Balance Total**, **Phone**, **Fax**, **Contact**, and **Account No.** columns and add the **Terms** column. *(Note: There is no option for listing the Account Prefill.)*

Click **OK** and compare your results to Figure 12:31. If you find a mistake, double click to open the account, make changes, and resave.

Close the report. Now click the **Transactions** tab on the **Vendor Center** and select **Bills**. Change the **Date** filter to **All** and compare your results to Figure 12:32. If you find a mistake, double click to open the transaction, make changes, and resave.

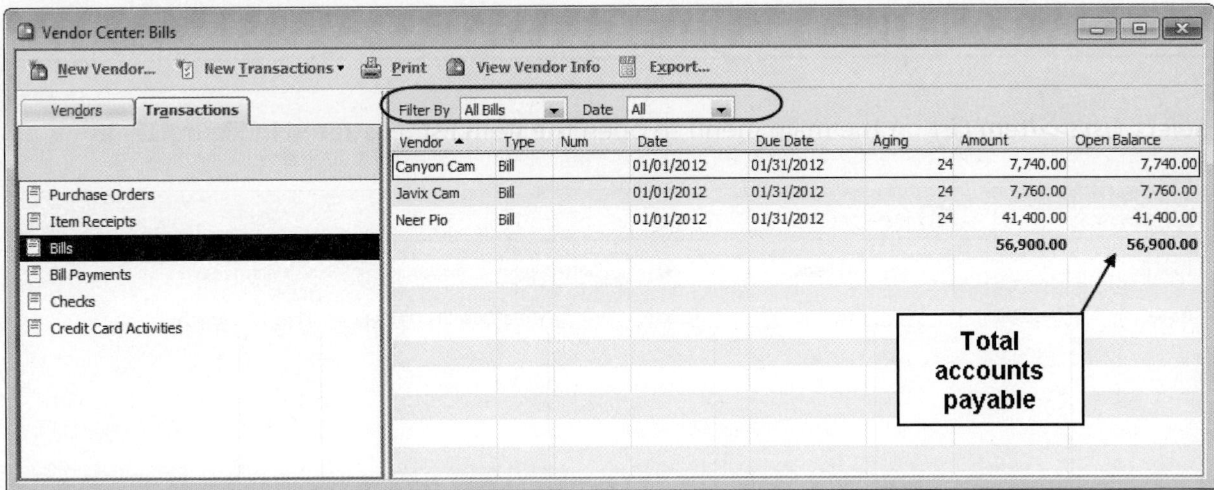

Figure 12:32

Close the Vendor Center. You will next create inventory items.

INVENTORY SETUP

Select ***Lists>>Item List*** on the main menu to open the Item list illustrated in Figure 12:33.

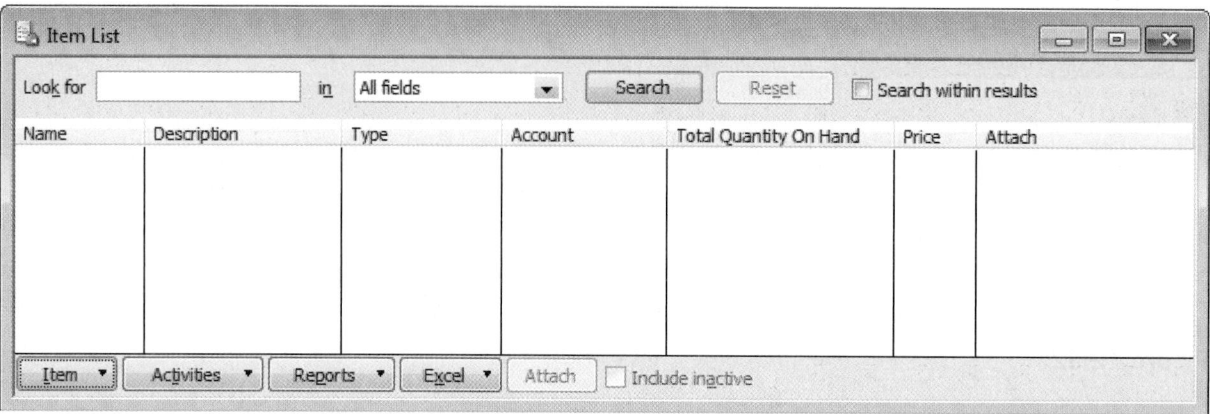

Figure 12:33

Click **Item** and select **New** or use the **Ctrl+N** shortcut key. Select **Inventory Part** as the **Type.**

Notice that QBP has overridden your chart of accounts by creating a new cost of goods sold and inventory account (i.e., 50001 *Cost of Goods Sold and 12101 Inventory Asset). (See Figure 12:34.) Do not use these accounts because we will delete the accounts in a subsequent topic. Instead, use the **50000 Cost of Goods Sold** and **12000 Inventory Asset**, which are the accounts you created earlier.

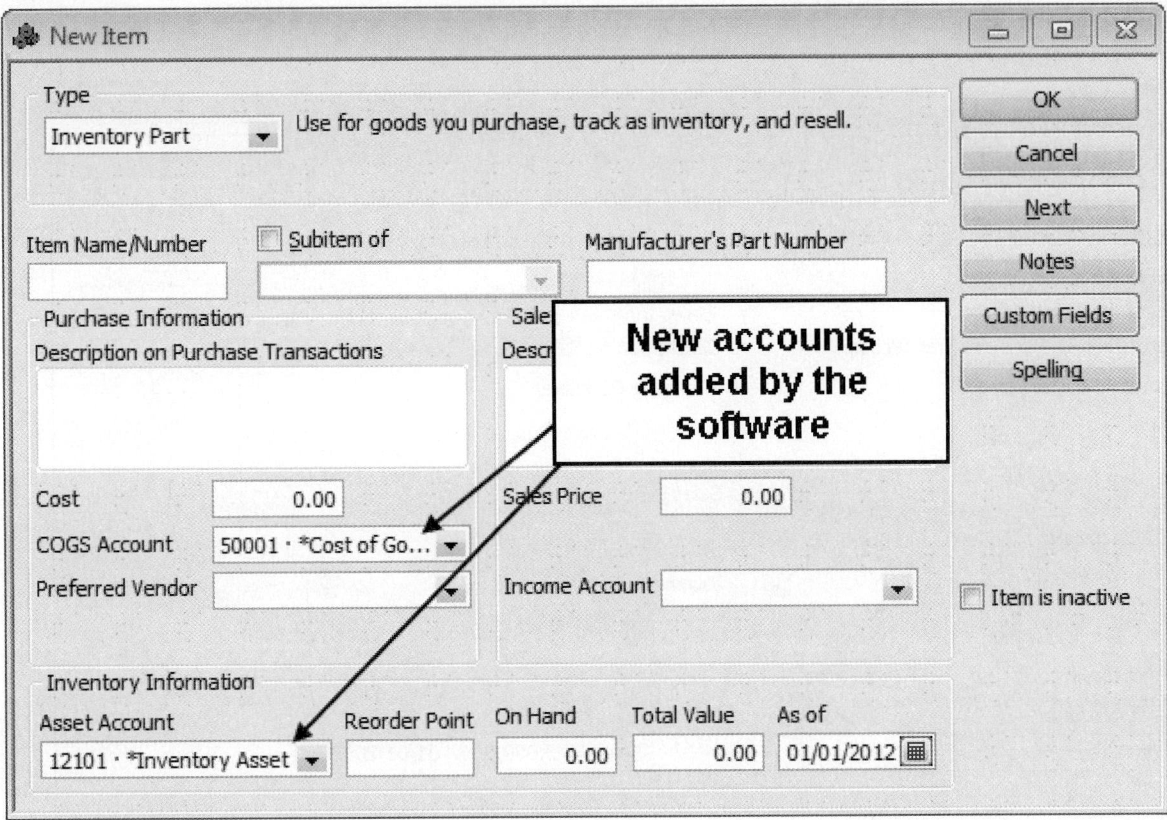

Figure 12:34

Add the first item by referring to Figure 12:35. Click **Next** and continue entering the items listed in Figure 12:36. All items are of the **Inventory Part** type and use the **COGS Account**, **Income Account**, **Asset Account**, and **As of date** illustrated in Figure 12:35.

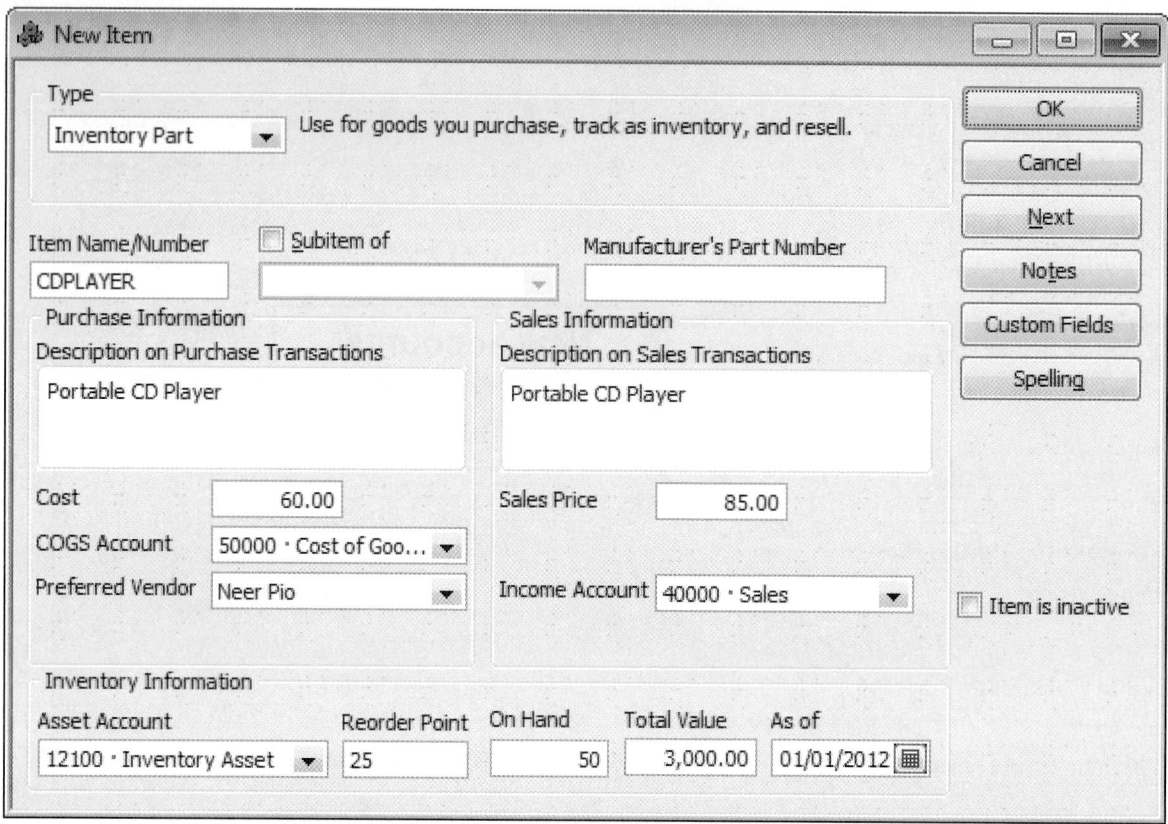

Figure 12:35

Item List

Item Name / Number	Description on Purchase and Sales Transactions	Cost	Preferred Vendor	Sales Price	Reorder Point	On Hand	Total Value
CDPLAYER	Portable CD Player	60.00	Neer Pio	85.00	25	50	3,000.00
DIGCAM	Digital Camera	191.00	Canyon Cam	285.00	25	50	9,550.00
DIGCORD	Digital Camcorder	394.00	Javix Cam	588.00	20	60	23,640.00
DVDPLAY	DVD Player	131.00	SumSang Corporation	195.00	25	50	6,550.00
DVRREC	DVR Recorder	67.00	SumSang Corporation	95.00	30	80	5,360.00
ENTSYS	Dolby Surround System	837.00	Neer Pio	1,350.00	15	25	20,925.00
HDTV	HD Television	1,620.00	SumSang Corporation	2,700.00	15	20	32,400.00
HOMSTER	Home Stereo	600.00	Neer Pio	895.00	25	30	18,000.00
LCDTV	LCD Television	2,700.00	SumSang Corporation	4,500.00	15	20	54,000.00
PRINTER	Color Printer	175.00	SumSang Corporation	250.00	20	90	15,750.00

Figure 12:36

When finished, click **OK** and return to the **Item List**. Click **Item** and select **Customize Columns**. Now add, remove, and rearrange columns to match Figure 12:37.

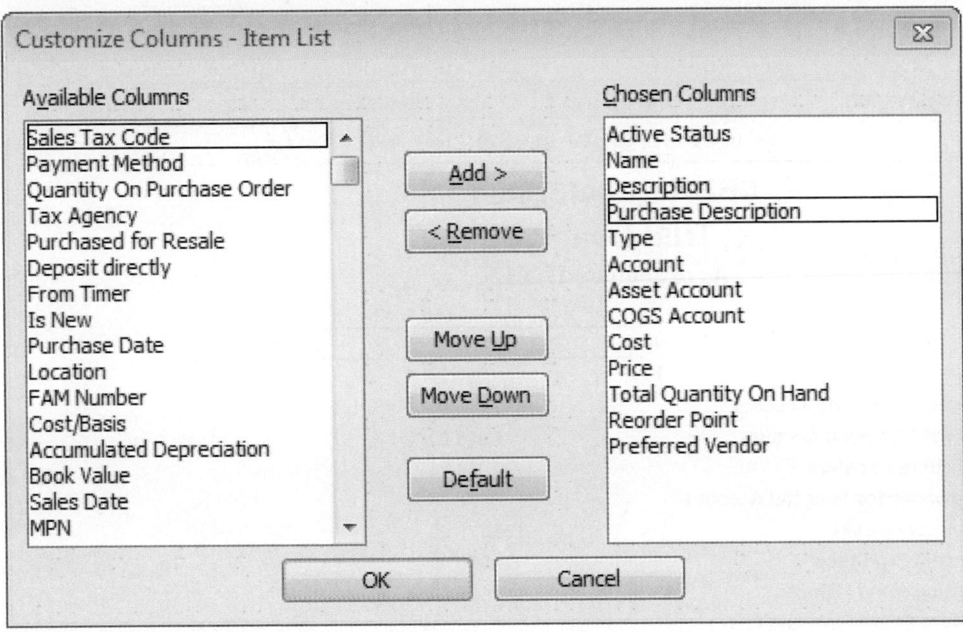

Figure 12:37

Click **OK** and compare your results with the next illustration.

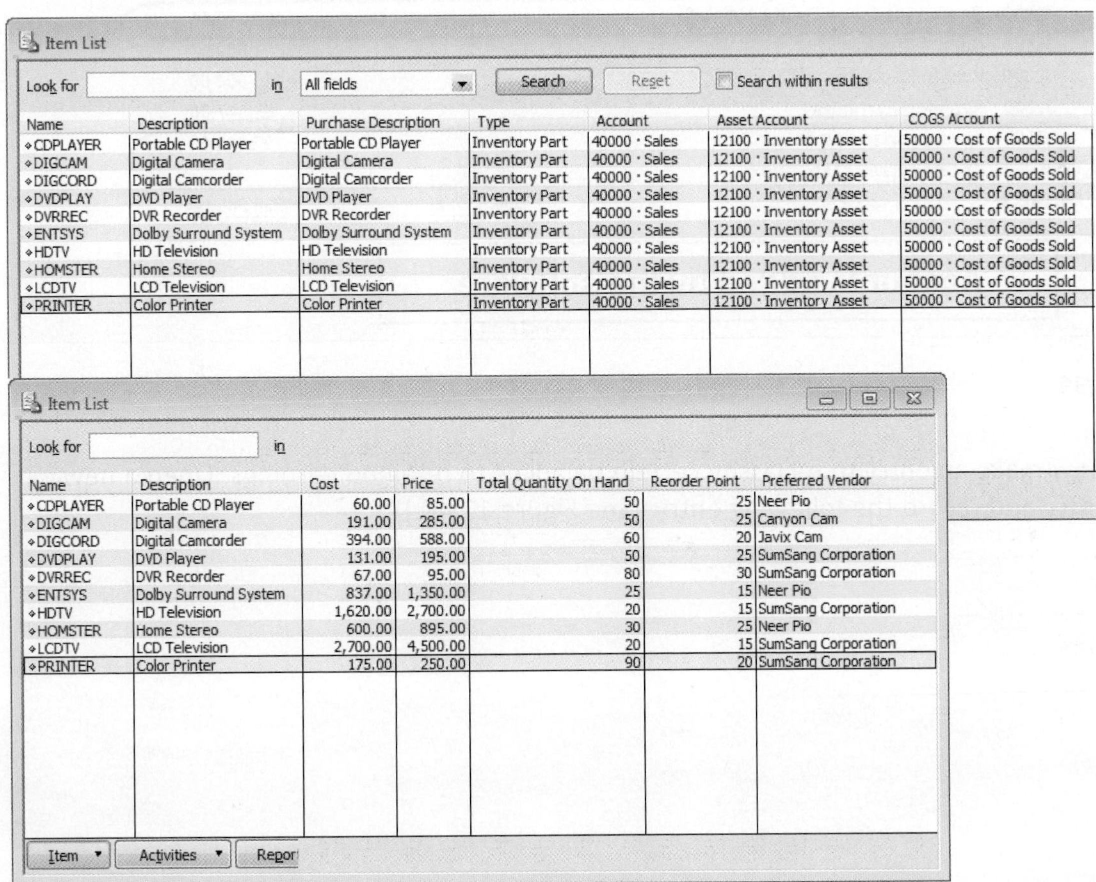

Name	Description	Purchase Description	Type	Account	Asset Account	COGS Account
◆CDPLAYER	Portable CD Player	Portable CD Player	Inventory Part	40000 · Sales	12100 · Inventory Asset	50000 · Cost of Goods Sold
◆DIGCAM	Digital Camera	Digital Camera	Inventory Part	40000 · Sales	12100 · Inventory Asset	50000 · Cost of Goods Sold
◆DIGCORD	Digital Camcorder	Digital Camcorder	Inventory Part	40000 · Sales	12100 · Inventory Asset	50000 · Cost of Goods Sold
◆DVDPLAY	DVD Player	DVD Player	Inventory Part	40000 · Sales	12100 · Inventory Asset	50000 · Cost of Goods Sold
◆DVRREC	DVR Recorder	DVR Recorder	Inventory Part	40000 · Sales	12100 · Inventory Asset	50000 · Cost of Goods Sold
◆ENTSYS	Dolby Surround System	Dolby Surround System	Inventory Part	40000 · Sales	12100 · Inventory Asset	50000 · Cost of Goods Sold
◆HDTV	HD Television	HD Television	Inventory Part	40000 · Sales	12100 · Inventory Asset	50000 · Cost of Goods Sold
◆HOMSTER	Home Stereo	Home Stereo	Inventory Part	40000 · Sales	12100 · Inventory Asset	50000 · Cost of Goods Sold
◆LCDTV	LCD Television	LCD Television	Inventory Part	40000 · Sales	12100 · Inventory Asset	50000 · Cost of Goods Sold
◆PRINTER	Color Printer	Color Printer	Inventory Part	40000 · Sales	12100 · Inventory Asset	50000 · Cost of Goods Sold

Name	Description	Cost	Price	Total Quantity On Hand	Reorder Point	Preferred Vendor
◆CDPLAYER	Portable CD Player	60.00	85.00	50	25	Neer Pio
◆DIGCAM	Digital Camera	191.00	285.00	50	25	Canyon Cam
◆DIGCORD	Digital Camcorder	394.00	588.00	60	20	Javix Cam
◆DVDPLAY	DVD Player	131.00	195.00	50	25	SumSang Corporation
◆DVRREC	DVR Recorder	67.00	95.00	80	30	SumSang Corporation
◆ENTSYS	Dolby Surround System	837.00	1,350.00	25	15	Neer Pio
◆HDTV	HD Television	1,620.00	2,700.00	20	15	SumSang Corporation
◆HOMSTER	Home Stereo	600.00	895.00	30	25	Neer Pio
◆LCDTV	LCD Television	2,700.00	4,500.00	20	15	SumSang Corporation
◆PRINTER	Color Printer	175.00	250.00	90	20	SumSang Corporation

Figure 12:38

Close the **Item List** and open the **Trial Balance** report for **1/1/12.** Compare your balances to those illustrated in Figure 12:39.

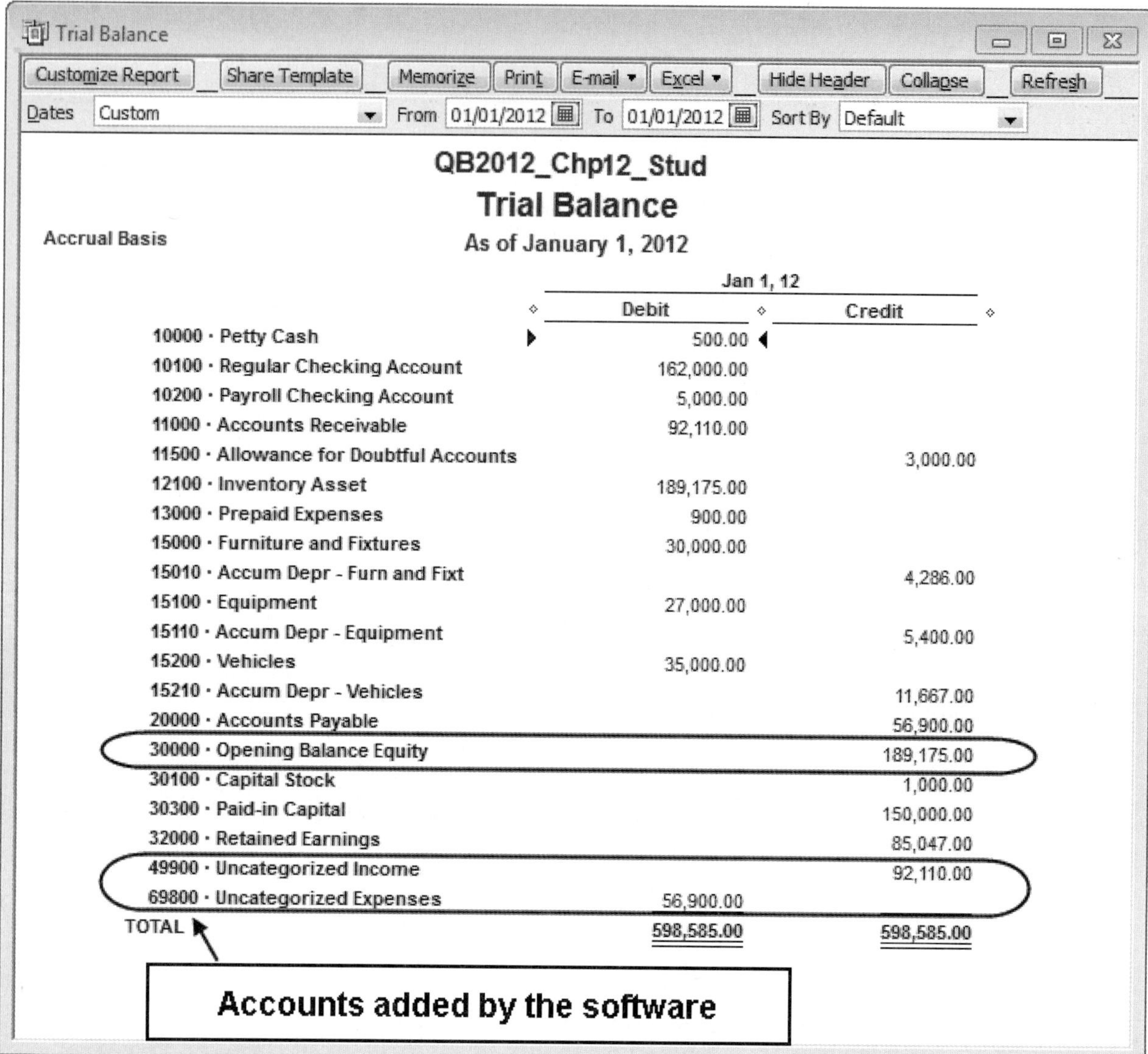

Trial Balance

Customize Report | Share Template | Memorize | Print | E-mail | Excel | Hide Header | Collapse | Refresh

Dates Custom From 01/01/2012 To 01/01/2012 Sort By Default

QB2012_Chp12_Stud

Trial Balance

Accrual Basis — As of January 1, 2012

	Jan 1, 12	
	Debit	Credit
10000 · Petty Cash	500.00	
10100 · Regular Checking Account	162,000.00	
10200 · Payroll Checking Account	5,000.00	
11000 · Accounts Receivable	92,110.00	
11500 · Allowance for Doubtful Accounts		3,000.00
12100 · Inventory Asset	189,175.00	
13000 · Prepaid Expenses	900.00	
15000 · Furniture and Fixtures	30,000.00	
15010 · Accum Depr - Furn and Fixt		4,286.00
15100 · Equipment	27,000.00	
15110 · Accum Depr - Equipment		5,400.00
15200 · Vehicles	35,000.00	
15210 · Accum Depr - Vehicles		11,667.00
20000 · Accounts Payable		56,900.00
30000 · Opening Balance Equity		189,175.00
30100 · Capital Stock		1,000.00
30300 · Paid-in Capital		150,000.00
32000 · Retained Earnings		85,047.00
49900 · Uncategorized Income		92,110.00
69800 · Uncategorized Expenses	56,900.00	
TOTAL	598,585.00	598,585.00

Figure 12:39

We will now make an entry to reclassify certain balances to retained earnings. Open a new journal entry and record the following entry. (See Figure 12:40.)

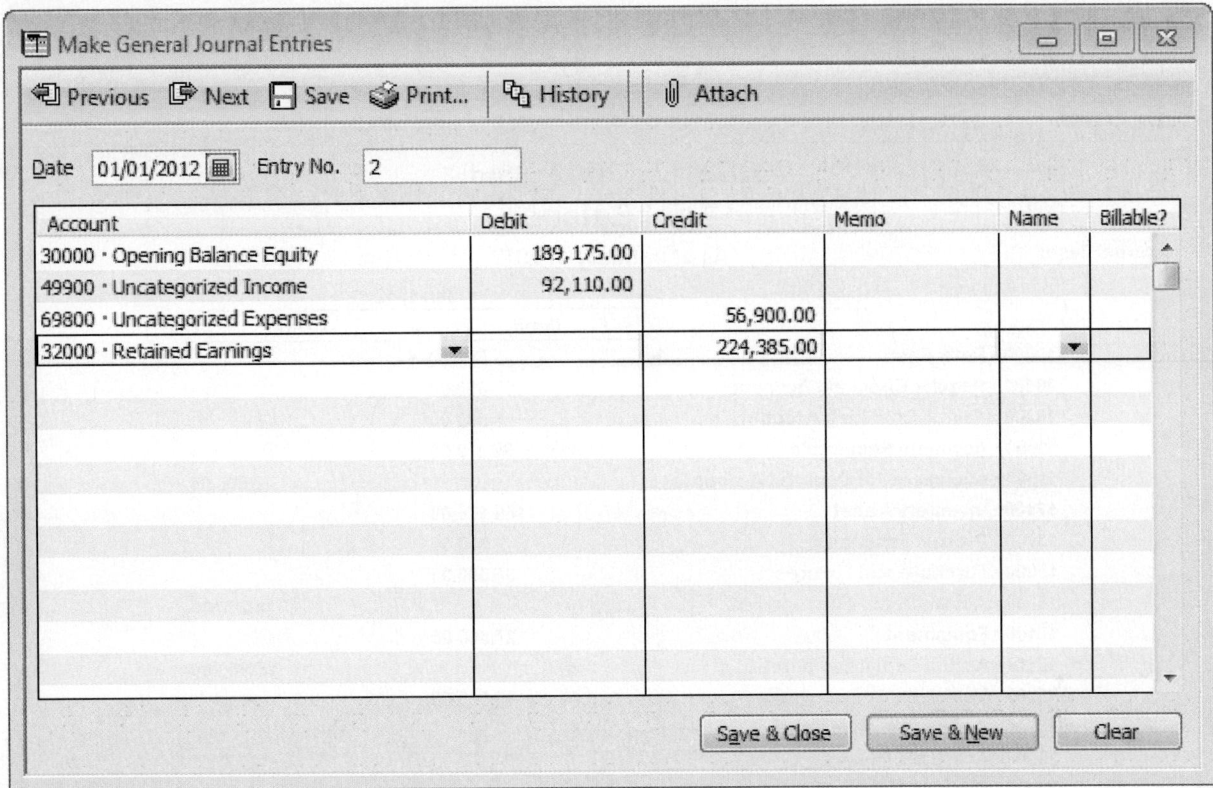

Figure 12:40

Click **Save & Close** and **OK** to post the entry to Retained Earnings.

Return to the Trial Balance and compare yours to the one illustrated in Figure 12:41.

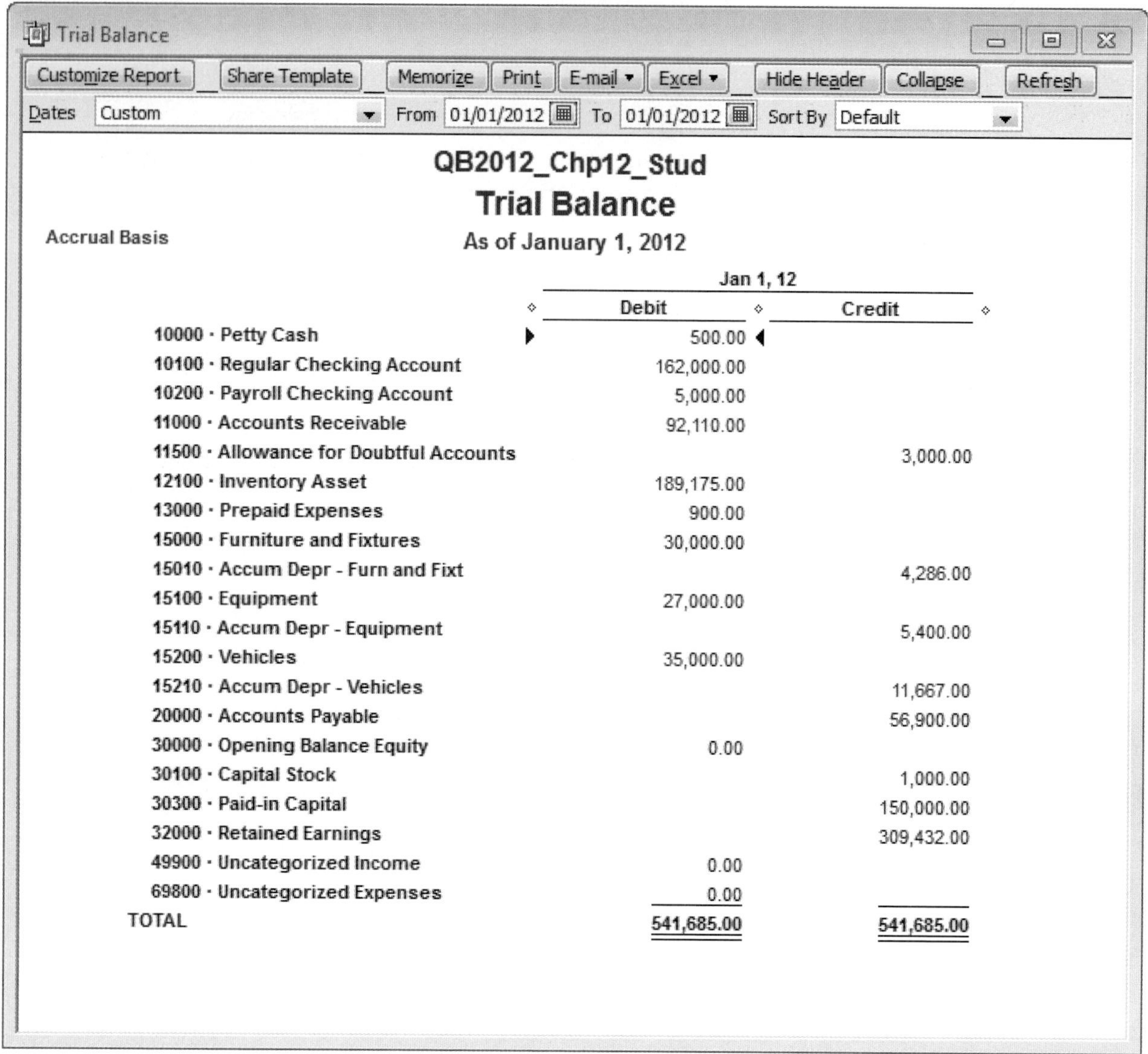

Trial Balance

Customize Report | Share Template | Memorize | Print | E-mail | Excel | Hide Header | Collapse | Refresh

Dates: Custom | From 01/01/2012 | To 01/01/2012 | Sort By Default

QB2012_Chp12_Stud

Trial Balance

Accrual Basis

As of January 1, 2012

	Jan 1, 12	
	Debit	Credit
10000 · Petty Cash	500.00	
10100 · Regular Checking Account	162,000.00	
10200 · Payroll Checking Account	5,000.00	
11000 · Accounts Receivable	92,110.00	
11500 · Allowance for Doubtful Accounts		3,000.00
12100 · Inventory Asset	189,175.00	
13000 · Prepaid Expenses	900.00	
15000 · Furniture and Fixtures	30,000.00	
15010 · Accum Depr - Furn and Fixt		4,286.00
15100 · Equipment	27,000.00	
15110 · Accum Depr - Equipment		5,400.00
15200 · Vehicles	35,000.00	
15210 · Accum Depr - Vehicles		11,667.00
20000 · Accounts Payable		56,900.00
30000 · Opening Balance Equity	0.00	
30100 · Capital Stock		1,000.00
30300 · Paid-in Capital		150,000.00
32000 · Retained Earnings		309,432.00
49900 · Uncategorized Income	0.00	
69800 · Uncategorized Expenses	0.00	
TOTAL	541,685.00	541,685.00

Figure 12:41

Reopen the **Account List.** Right click the following accounts and select **Make Account Inactive.**

12101 *Inventory Asset
30000 Opening Balance Equity
49900 Uncategorized Income
50001 *Cost of Goods Sold
69800 Uncategorized Expenses

Close the Chart of Accounts and Trial Balance. You are now ready to begin setting up payroll and creating employees.

Payroll and Employee Setup

Before creating employees, you need to set up the data file to pay employees. Select ***Help>>QuickBooks Help*** on the main menu. Refer to Figure 12:42 as we explain the steps.

1. On the **Search** tab, type in "manual payroll" and press enter.
2. Click the first topic to **process payroll manually without a subscription.**
3. In the window that opens, click the **manual payroll calculations** link.
4. In the window that opens, click the **Set my company file to use manual calculations** link. Close the Help windows and you will find a prompt to confirm your action. Click **OK.**

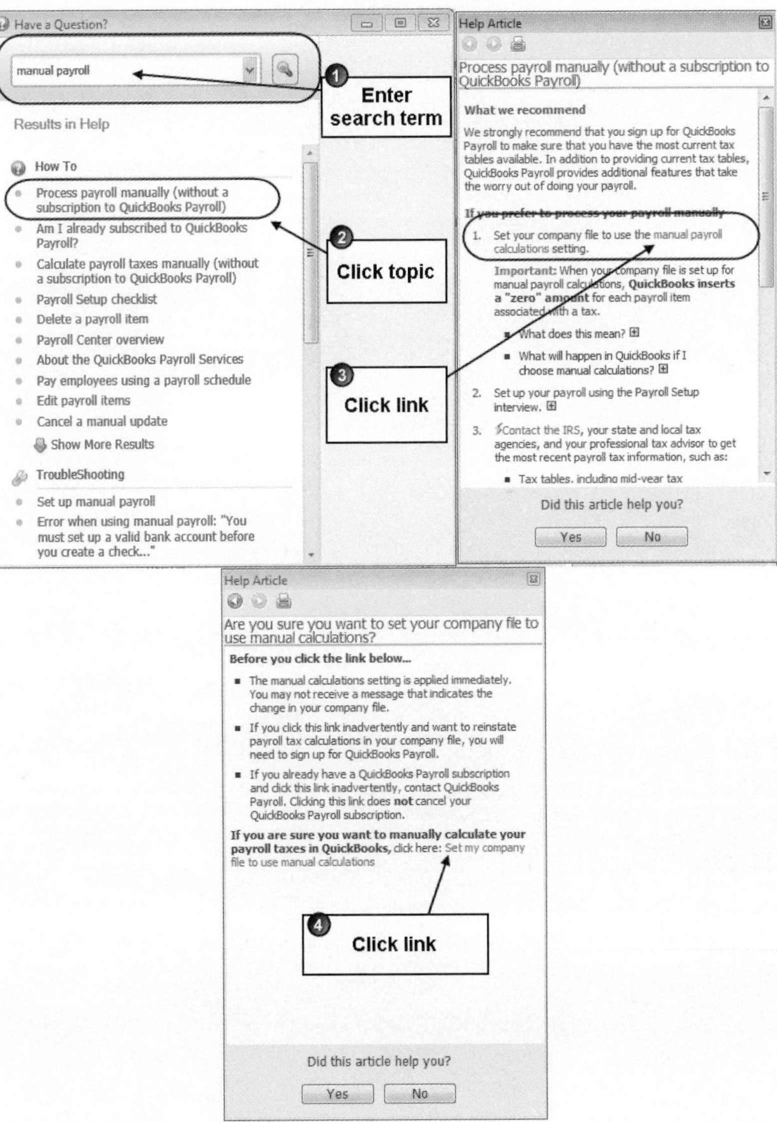

Figure 12:42

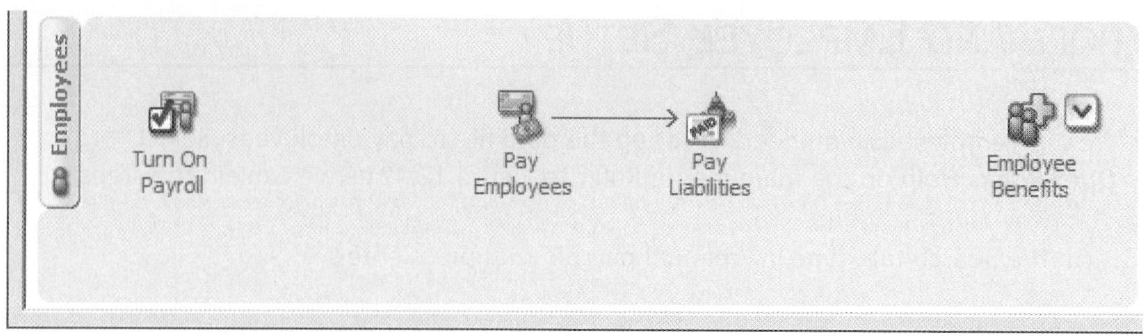

Figure 12:43

Now select ***Employees>>Payroll***

Setup on the main menu to begin the setup interview. (See Figure 12:44.)

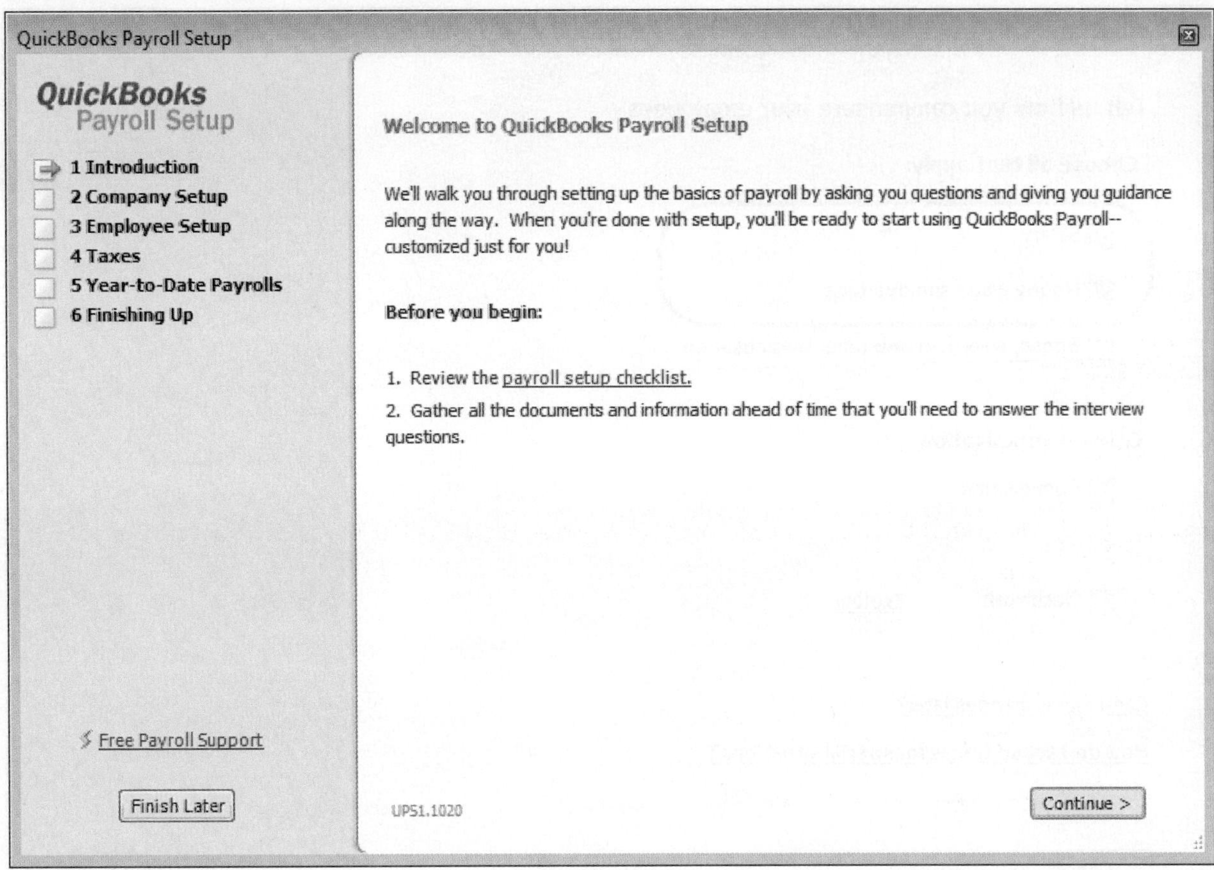

Figure 12:44

Click **Continue** and **Continue.** Mark the options illustrated in Figure 12:45 and click **Finish.**

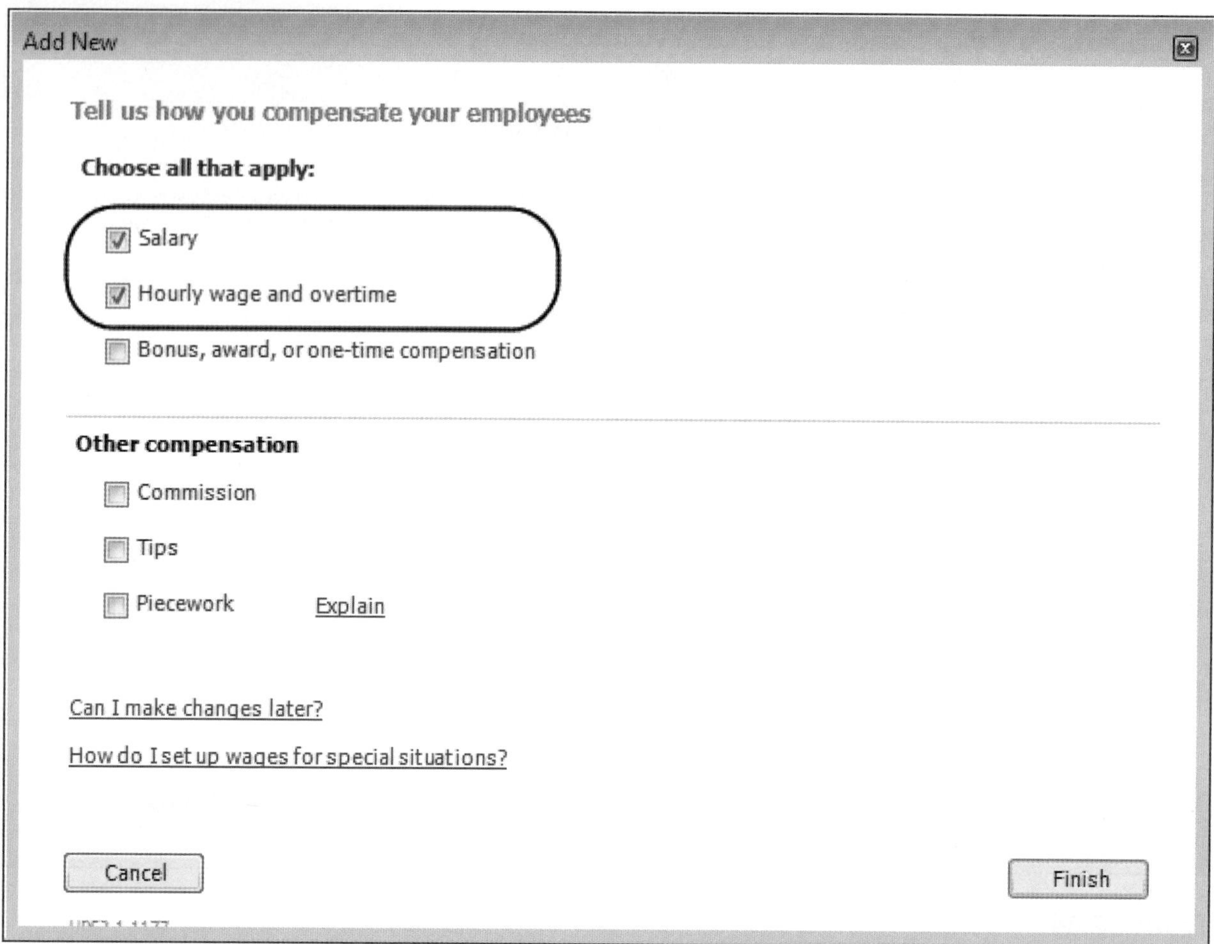

Figure 12:45

When the compensation list appears, highlight **Double-time Hourly**, click **Delete**, and **Yes** to confirm. You now have the items illustrated in Figure 12:46.

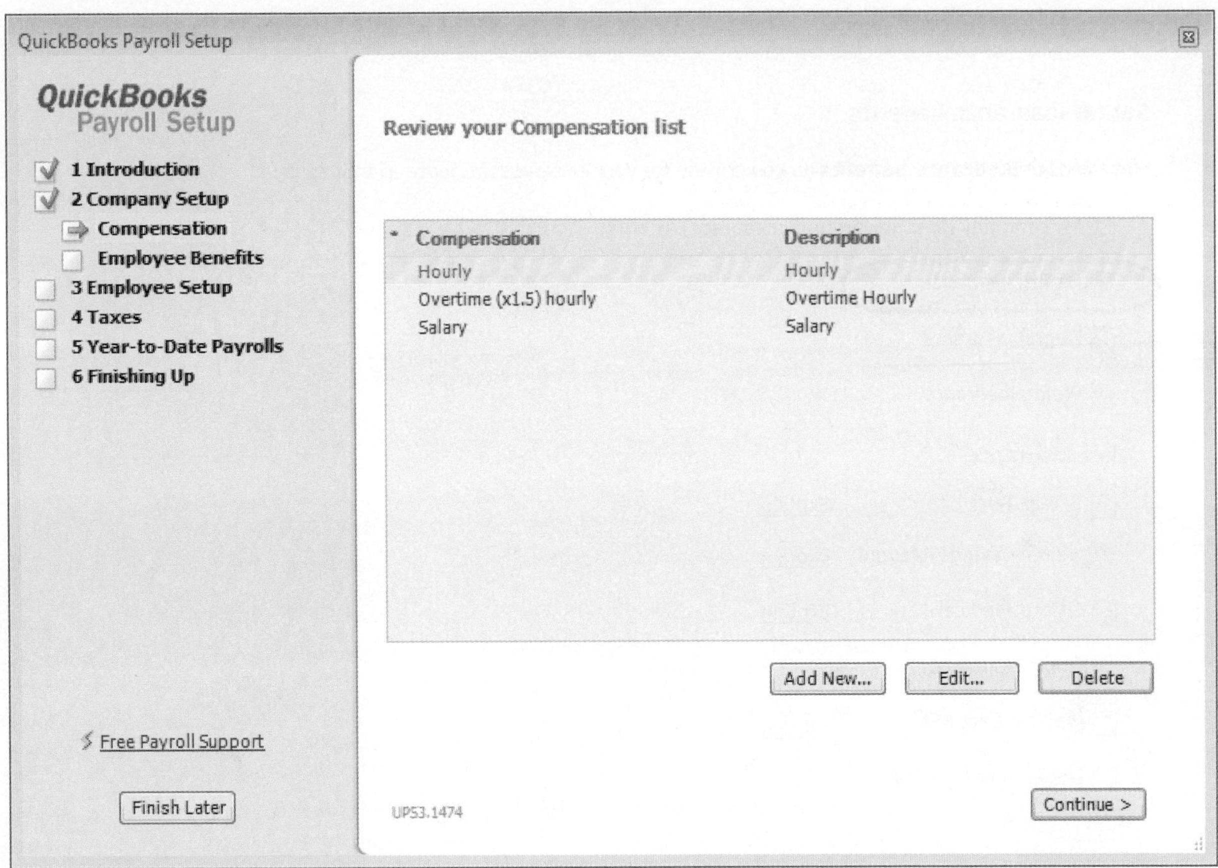

Figure 12:46

Click **Continue** and **Continue** again. Click **Health insurance** (Figure 12:47) and click **Next.**

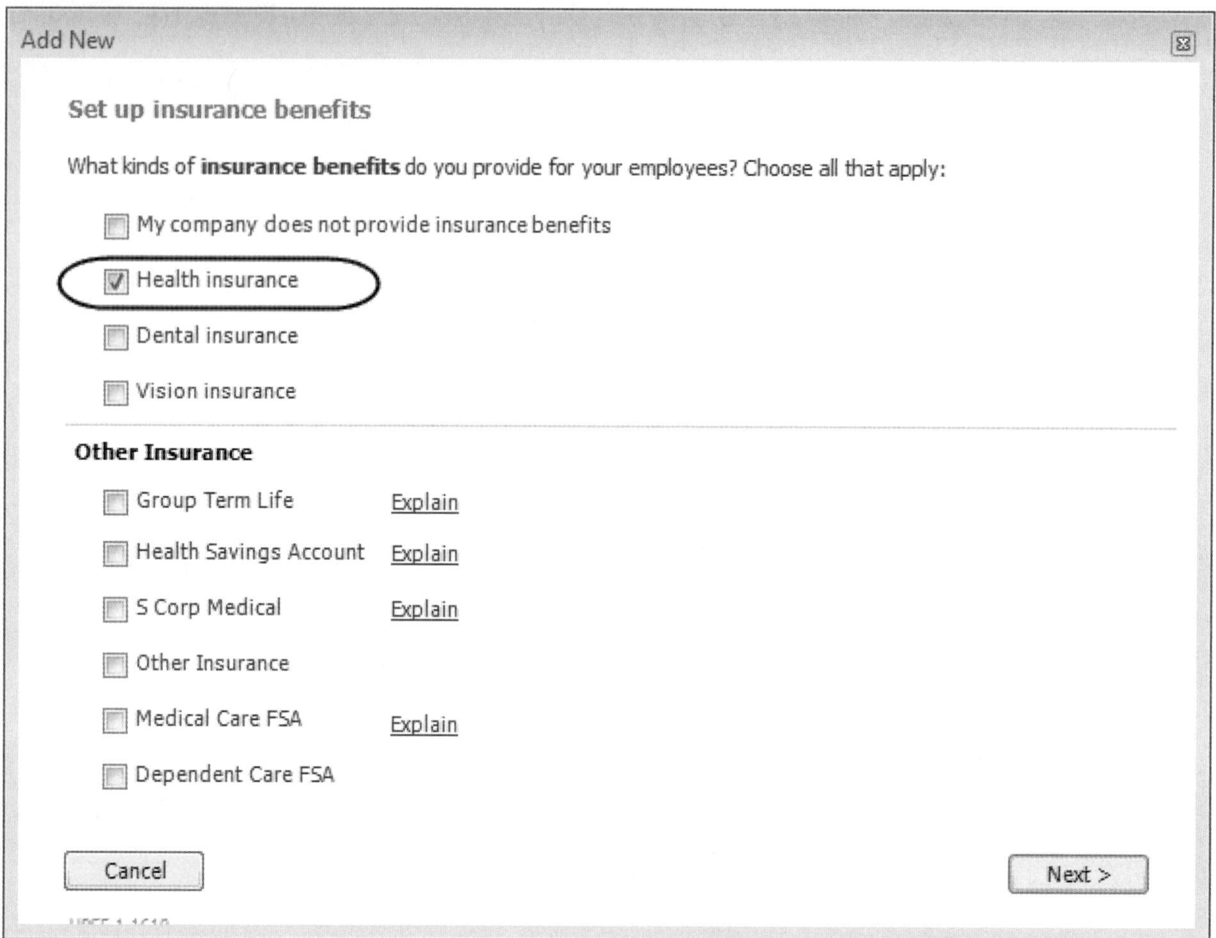

Figure 12:47

On the next screen (not illustrated) keep the option provided so that the company pays for all insurance costs and click **Next.** Fill out the payment schedule as illustrated in Figure 12:48.

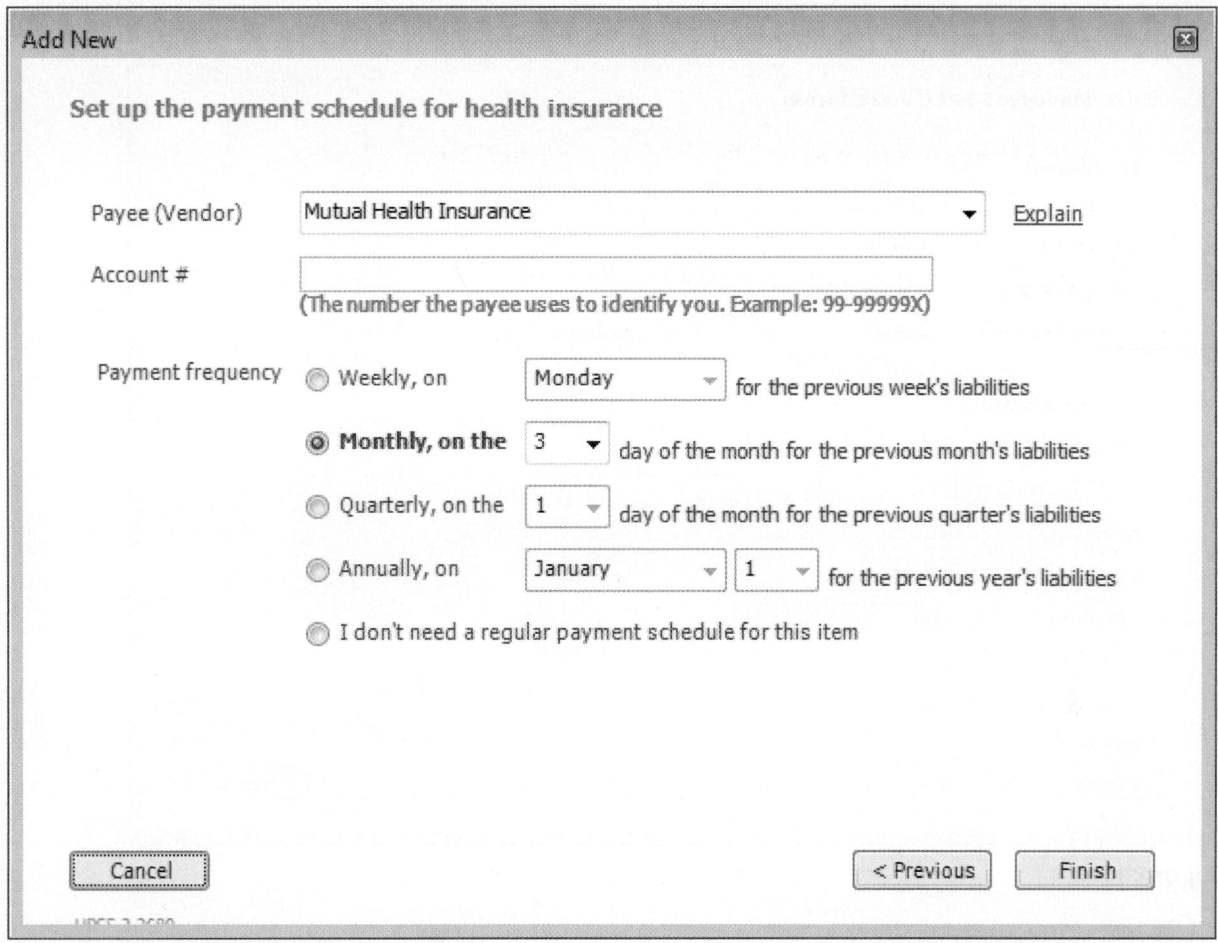

Figure 12:48

Click **Finish** and then **Continue.** Click **Finish** on the retirement benefits screen and click **Continue.**

Click **Finish** without setting up paid time off options and click **Continue.** Click **Finish** on setting up additions and deductions and click **Continue.**

You will now create employee accounts. Click **Continue.** The next series of illustrations helps you set up the first employee.

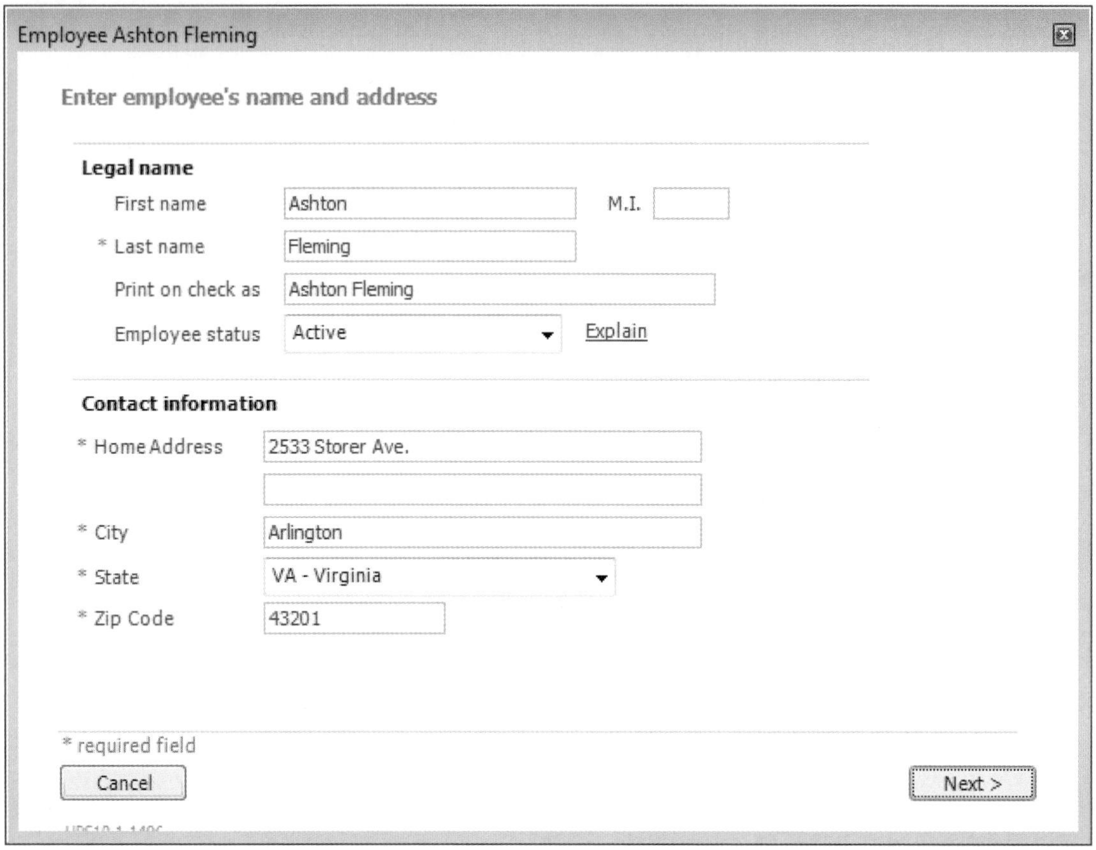

Employee Ashton Fleming

Enter employee's name and address

Legal name

First name: Ashton M.I.

* Last name: Fleming

Print on check as: Ashton Fleming

Employee status: Active Explain

Contact information

* Home Address: 2533 Storer Ave.

* City: Arlington

* State: VA - Virginia

* Zip Code: 43201

* required field

Cancel Next >

Figure 12:49

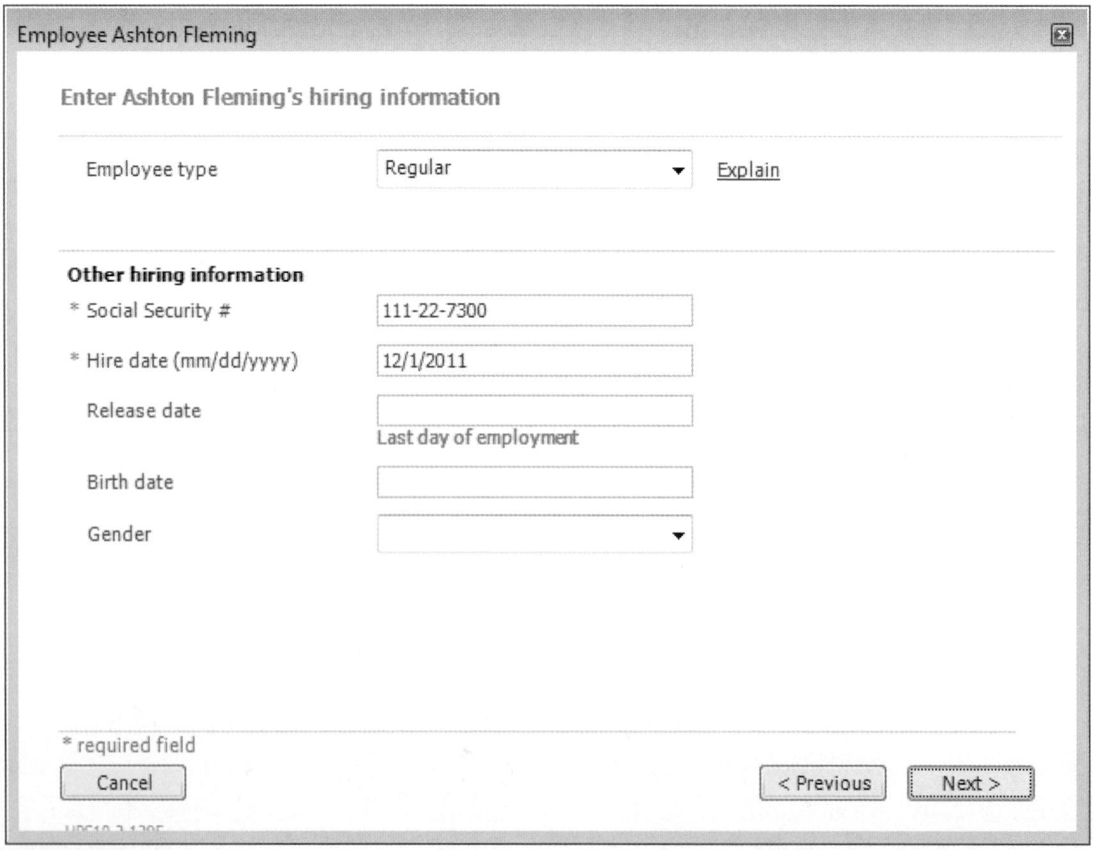

Employee Ashton Fleming

Enter Ashton Fleming's hiring information

Employee type: Regular Explain

Other hiring information

* Social Security #: 111-22-7300

* Hire date (mm/dd/yyyy): 12/1/2011

Release date: Last day of employment

Birth date

Gender

* required field

Cancel < Previous Next >

Figure 12:50

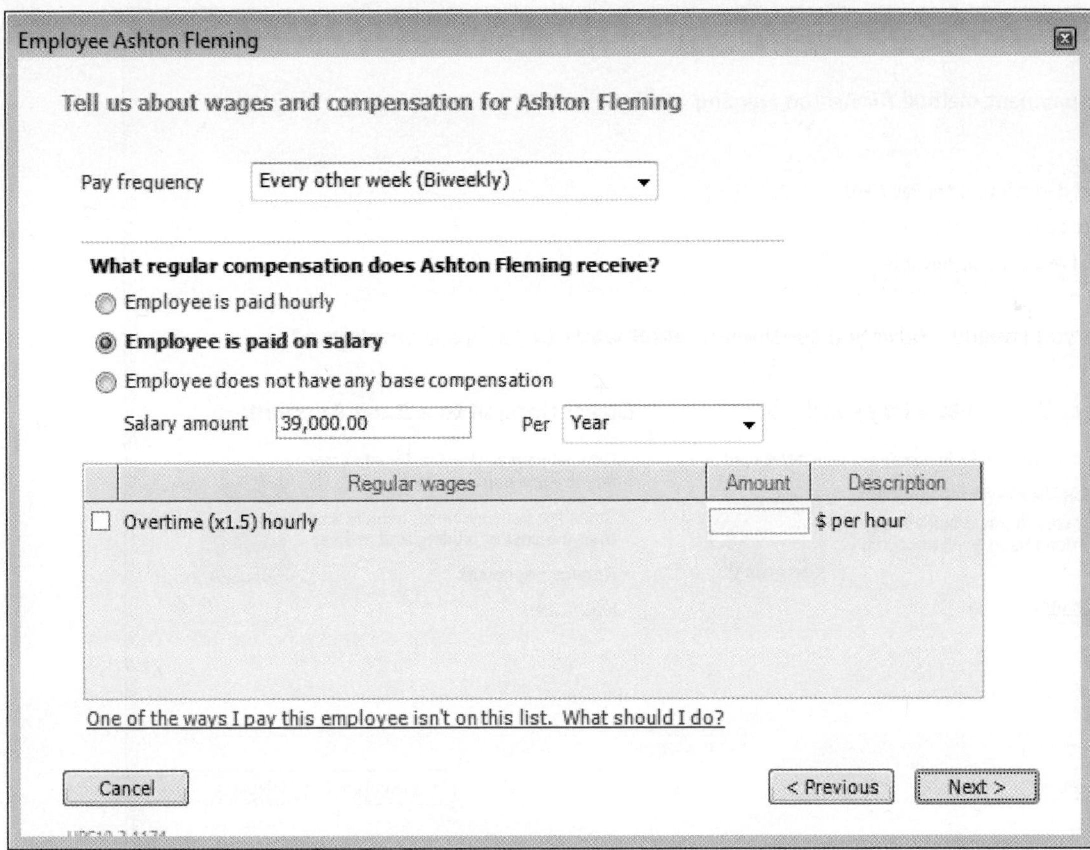

Figure 12:51

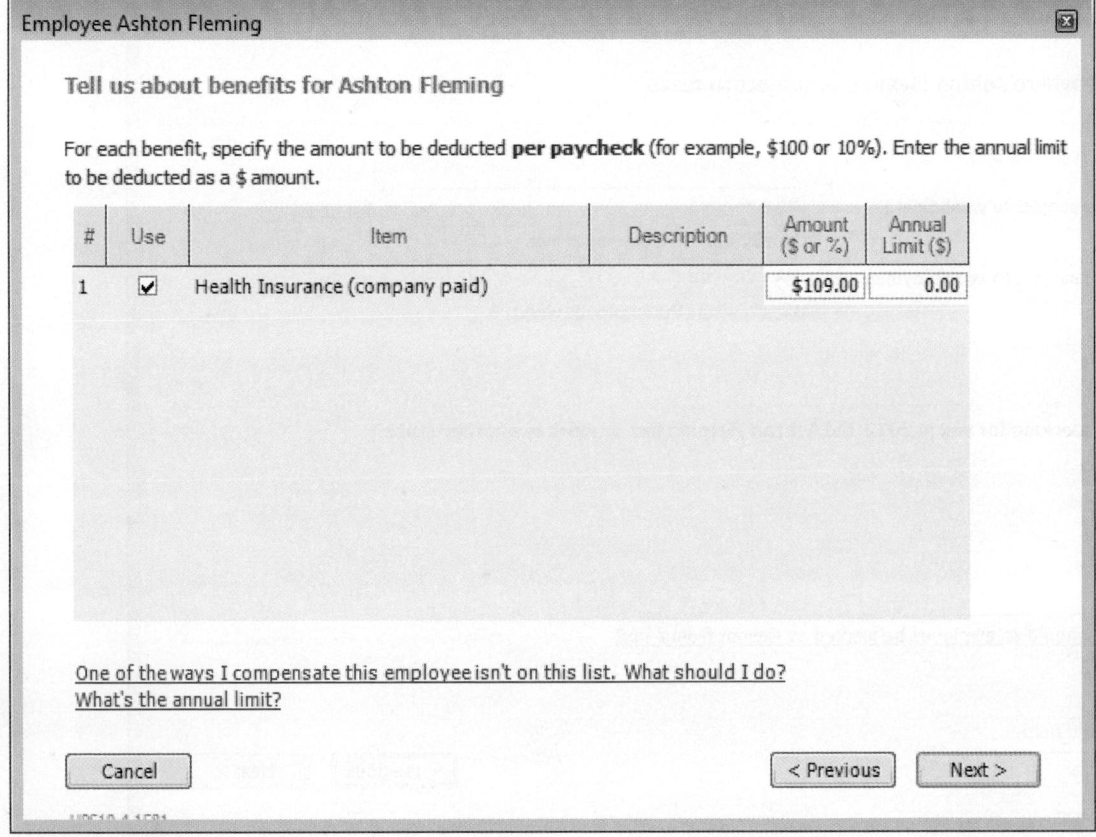

Figure 12:52

Employee Ashton Fleming
Set up payment method for Ashton Fleming
Check
Direct deposit to Intuit Pay Card
Direct deposit to bank account
Split direct deposit amounts
Before you continue, have you considered faster ways to pay your employee?
Direct Deposit to a Pay Card:
• Deposit paychecks to a prepaid Visa debit card
• No cost to you as the employer
• Easy way to pay employees who don't have bank accounts
Learn more
Direct Deposit to a Bank Account:
• Deposit paychecks directly into your employee's bank account
• Small fee per paycheck, usually less than the cost of printing and mailing
• Reduce paperwork
Learn more
* required field
Cancel
< Previous
Next >

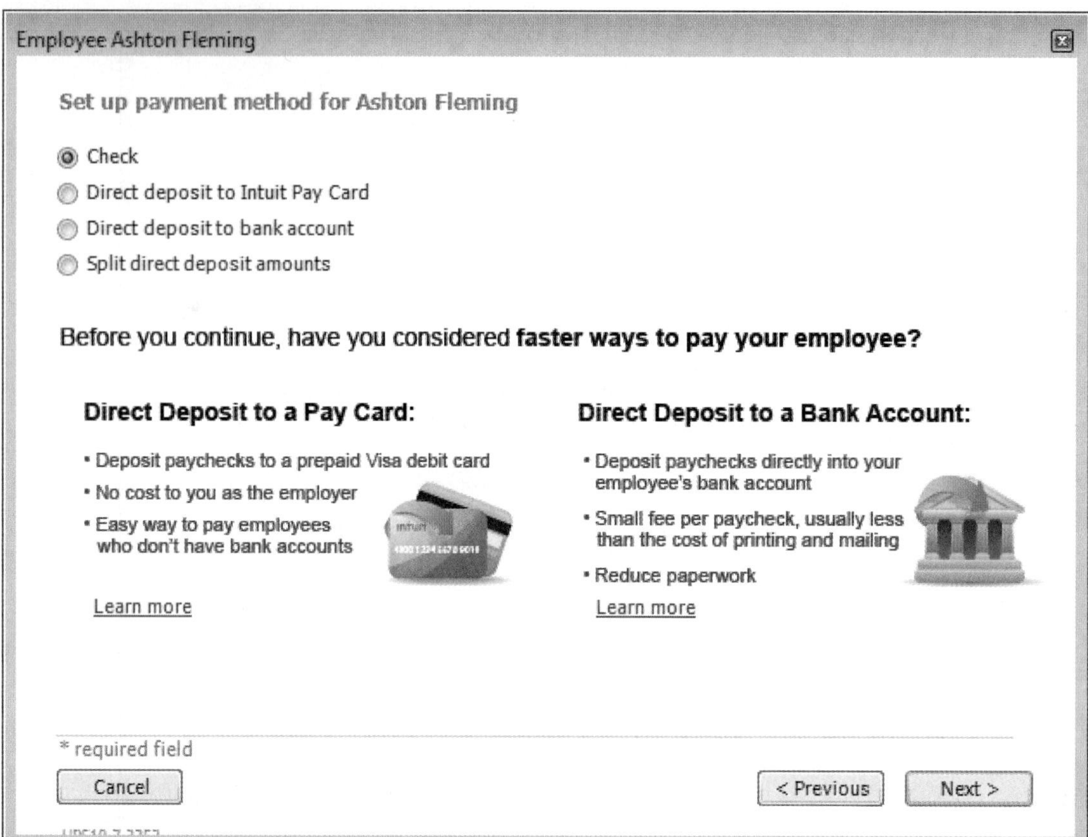

Figure 12:53

Employee Ashton Fleming
Tell us where Ashton Fleming is subject to taxes
* State subject to withholding
VA - Virginia
Usually where the employee lives
Explain
* State subject to unemployment tax
VA - Virginia
Usually where the employee works
Explain
While working for you in 2012, did Ashton Fleming live or work in another state?
No
Yes
When should an employee be marked as exempt from a tax?
* required field
Cancel
< Previous
Next >

Figure 12:54

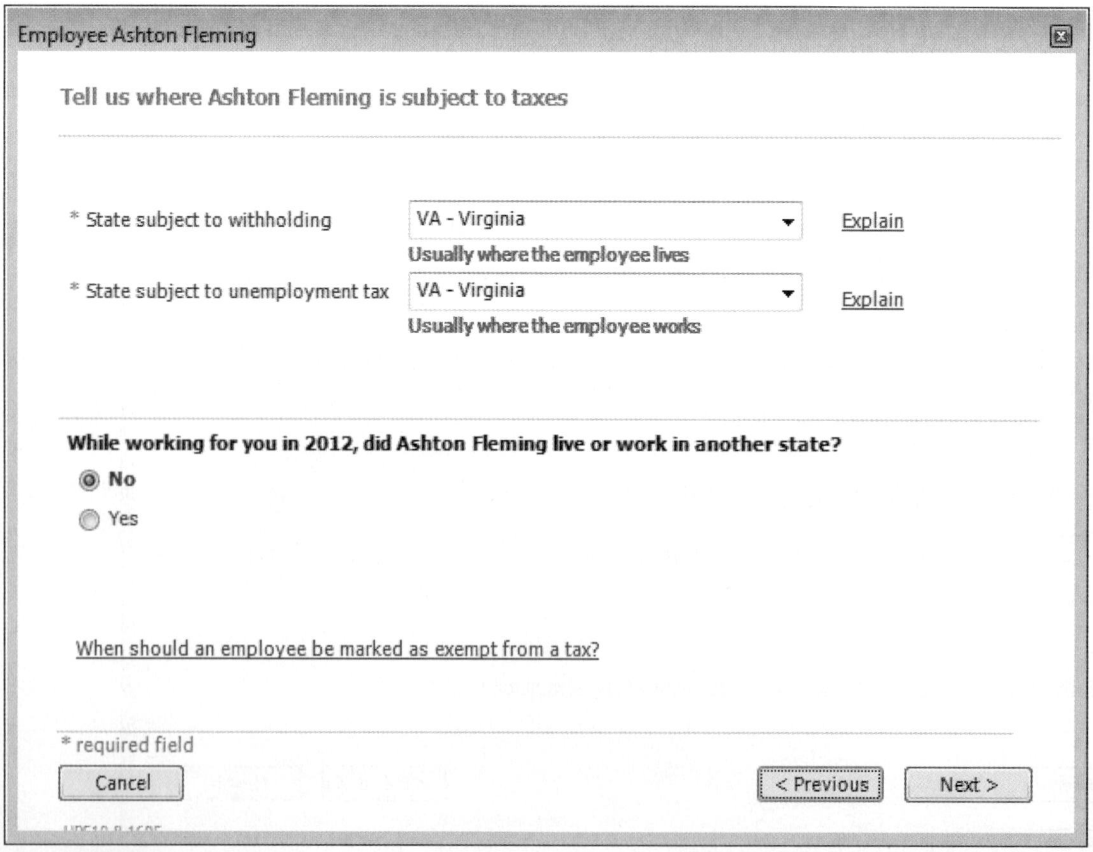

Employee Ashton Fleming

Enter federal tax information for Ashton Fleming

Filing Status: Single — Explain

Allowances: 0 — Explain

Extra Withholding: 0.00 — Explain

Nonresident Alien Withholding: Does not apply — Explain

HIRE Act Exemption: Not a qualified employee — Explain

Withholdings and Credits:
Most employees' wages are **subject to** the following withholdings; also, most employees are **not eligible** for the Advance Earned Income Credit. Incorrectly changing the selections below will cause your taxes to be calculated incorrectly, resulting in penalties; be sure to check with your tax agency or accountant if you are unsure.

- [x] Subject to Medicare — Explain
- [x] Subject to Social Security — Explain
- [x] Subject to Federal Unemployment
- [ ] Subject to Advance Earned Income Credit — Explain

Cancel | < Previous | Next >

Figure 12:55

Employee Ashton Fleming

Enter state tax information for Ashton Fleming

VA - Virginia state taxes

Filing Status: Withhold

Personal Exemptions: 0 — Explain

Blind and Age Exemptions: 0 — Explain

Extra Withholding:

Most employees' wages are **subject to** the following withholdings. Incorrectly changing the selections below will cause your taxes to be calculated incorrectly, resulting in penalties; be sure to check with your tax agency or accountant if you are unsure.

- [x] Subject to VA - Unemployment

Is this employee subject to any special local taxes not shown above?

(•) **No**

( ) Yes

Some of the taxes for employees who changed locations aren't listed here. Why?

Cancel | < Previous | Finish

Figure 12:56

Click **Finish** and then click **Add New** to enter the three remaining employees listed in Figure 12:57. All employees have zero allowances for state tax purposes and have the same hire date of 12/1/11.

Employee List

Employee	Address	City	State	Zip	SS No
Ashton Fleming	2533 Storer Ave.	Arlington	VA	43201	111-22-7300
Susan Gonzales	18 Birdlane Dr.	Blacksburg	VA	43231	011-08-3253
Lebron Johns	873 Star Ave.	Arlington	VA	43232	110-09-0098
April Levine	998 Maplewood Dr.	Gunther	VA	43235	011-10-0939

Employee	Frequency	Annual Salary	Hourly Regular	Hourly Overtime	Health Insurance	Federal Filing Status	Federal Allowances
Ashton Fleming	Biweekly	39,000.00			109.00	Single	0
Susan Gonzales	Biweekly	67,600.00			109.00	Married	2
Lebron Johns	Biweekly		12.50	18.75	109.00	Single	1
April Levine	Biweekly		18.00	27.00	109.00	Married	0

Figure 12:57

Click **Continue** and **Continue** again to arrive at the following federal payroll tax items (Figure 12:58).

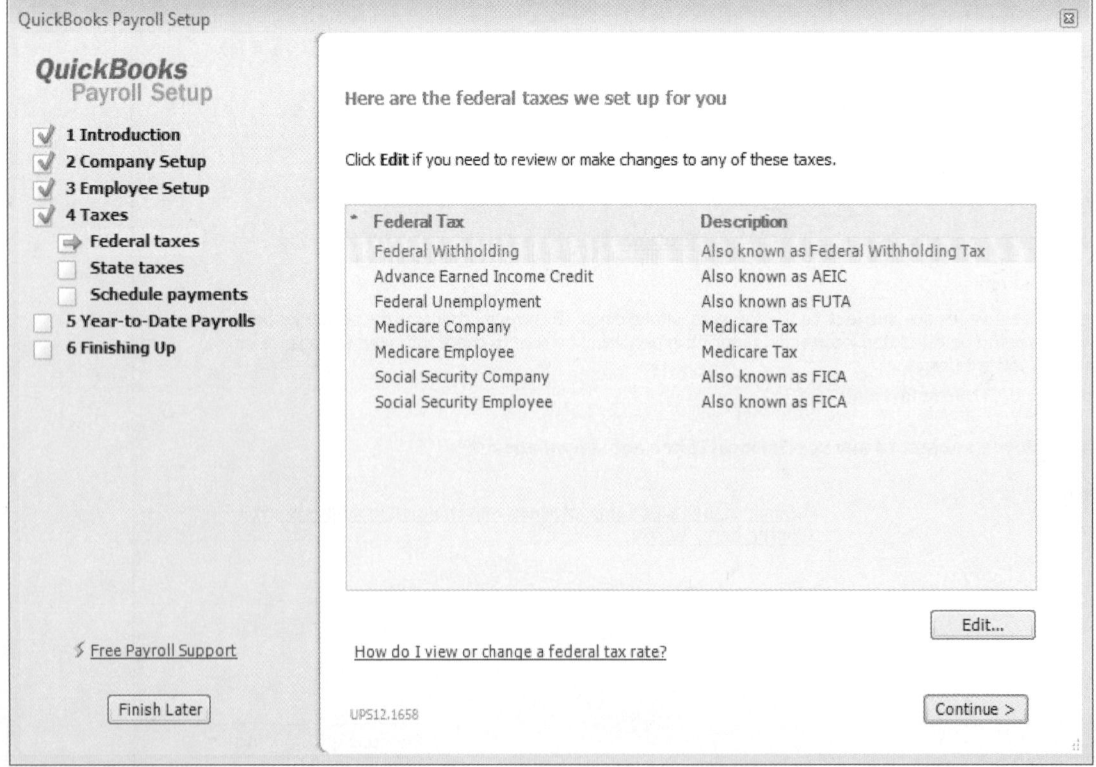

Figure 12:58

Click **Continue** and enter the information on Figure 12:59 for Virginia unemployment tax.

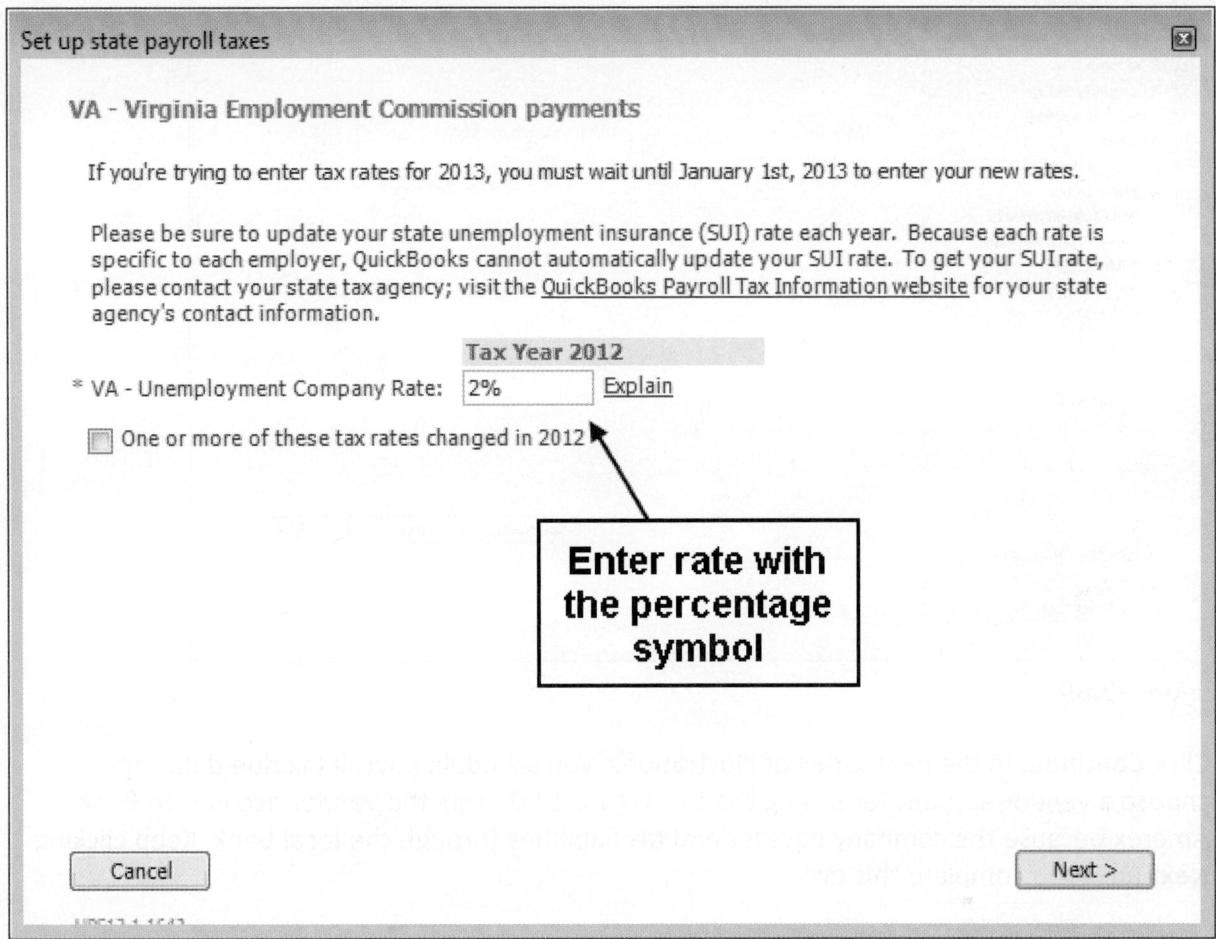

Figure 12:59

Click **Finish** and the window displays the following state payroll tax items (Figure 12:60).

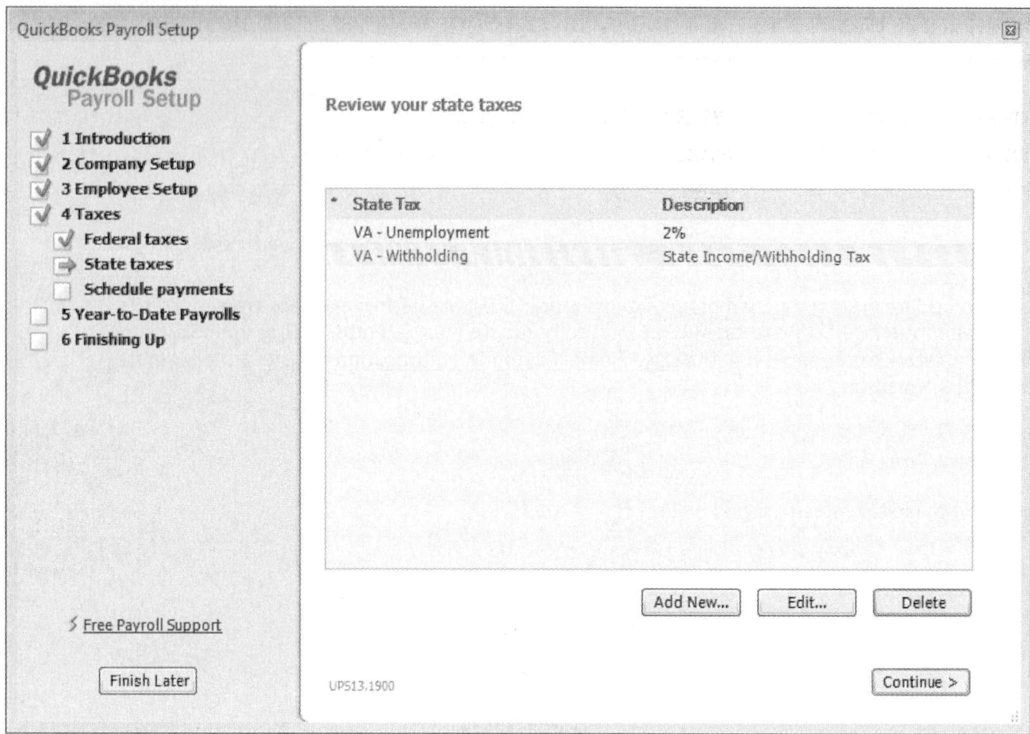

Figure 12:60

Click **Continue.** In the next series of illustrations, you schedule payroll tax due dates and choose a vendor account for paying the tax. Figure 12:61 sets the vendor account to Bank Amerex because the company pays federal tax liabilities through the local bank. Keep clicking **Next** until you complete this task.

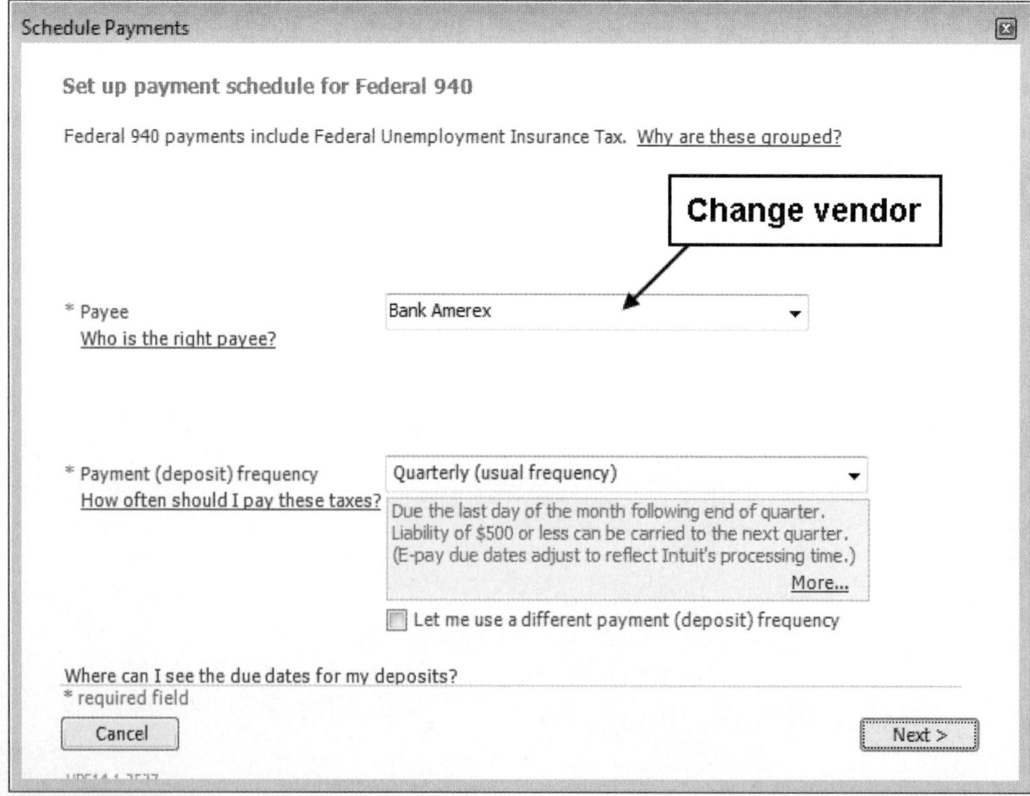

Figure 12:61

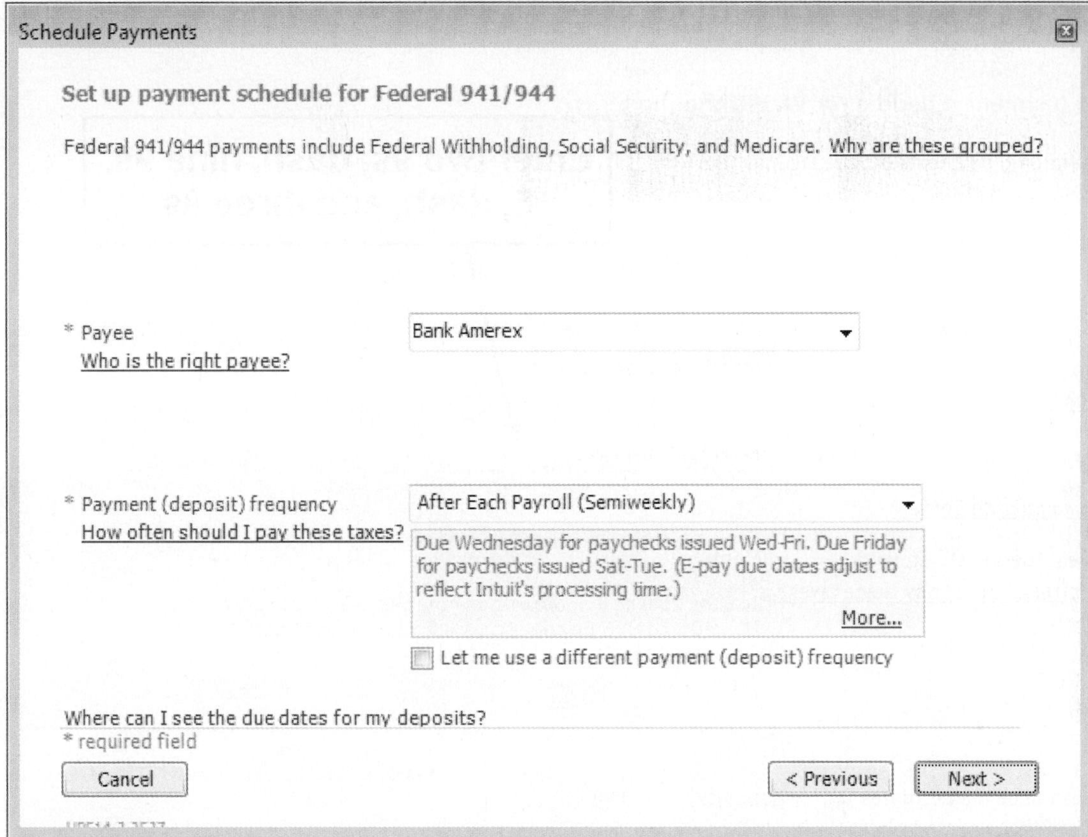

Figure 12:62

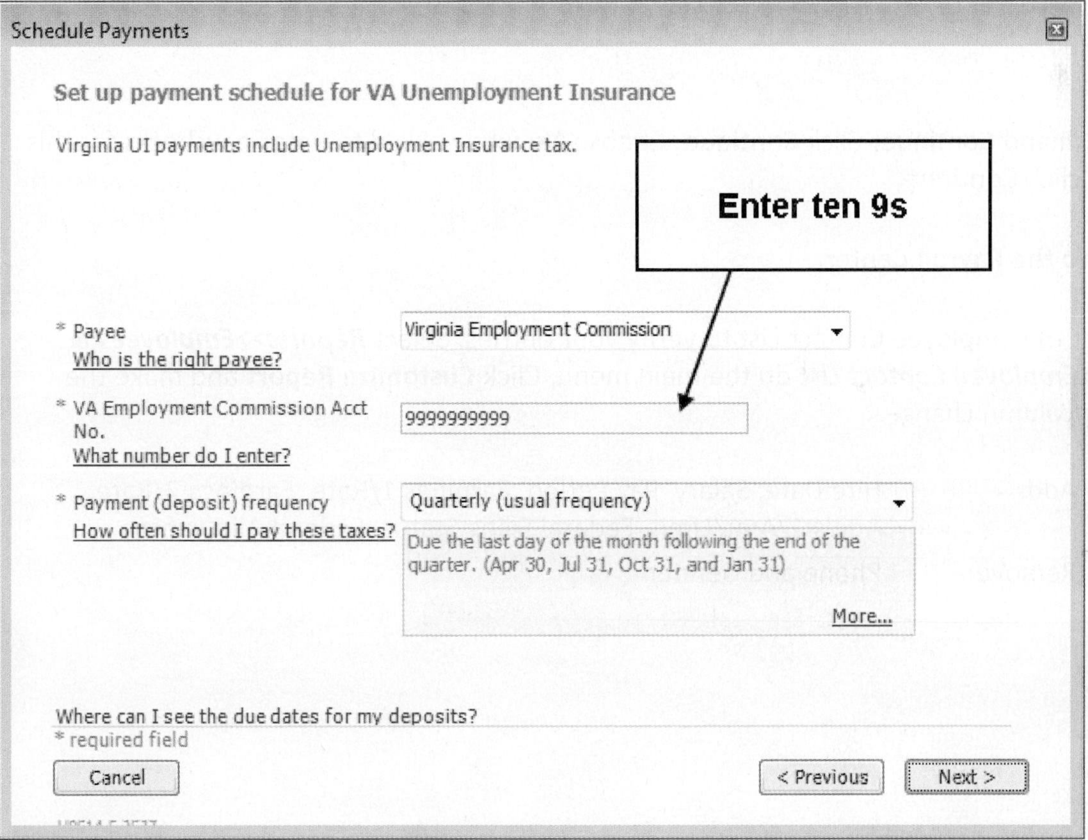

Figure 12:63

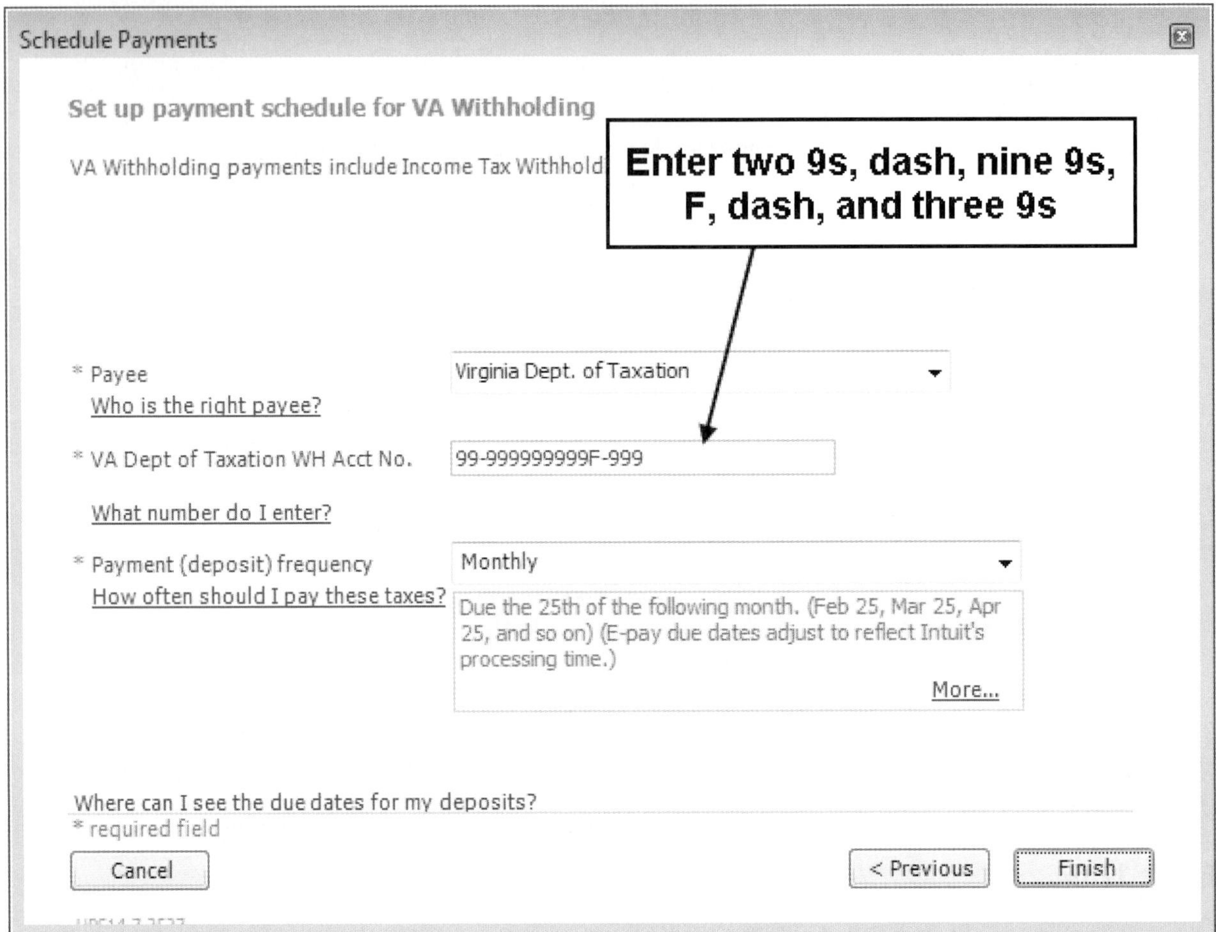

Figure 12:64

Click **Finish** and **Continue.** Click **Continue.** Choose **No** when asked to enter paychecks for this year and click **Continue.**

Click **Go to the Payroll Center.**

Now print the Employee Contact List to verify your entries. Select ***Reports>>Employees & Payroll>>Employee Contact List*** on the main menu. Click **Customize Report** and make the following column changes.

Add:	Hire Date, Salary, Pay Period, Earnings 1/Rate, Earnings 2/Rate, Adjust1/Amt/Limit, Federal Filing Status, Federal Allowances
Remove:	Phone and Gender

The report is illustrated in Figure 12:65 for you to compare results. If you find a mistake, double click the employee to reopen, make changes, and resave.

QB2012_Chp12_Stud

Employee Contact List

Employee	SS No.	Address	Hire Date	Salary	Pay Period	Earnings 1/Rate
Fleming, Ashton	111-22-7300	2533 Storer Ave. Arlington, VA 43201	12/01/2011	39,000.00	Biweekly	Salary 39,000.00
Gonzales, Susan	011-08-3253	18 Birdlane Dr. Blacksburg, VA 43231	12/01/2011	67,600.00	Biweekly	Salary 67,600.00
Johns, Lebron	110-09-0098	998 Maplewood Dr Arlington, VA 43232	12/01/2011	0.00	Biweekly	Hourly 12.50
Levine, April	011-10-0939	998 Maplewood Dr. Gunther, VA 43235	12/01/2011	0.00	Biweekly	Hourly 18.00

Employee	Earnings 2/Rate	Adjust 1/Amt/Limit	Federal Filing Status	Federal Allowances
Fleming, Ashton		Health Insurance (company paid) 109.00 0.00	Single	0
Gonzales, Susan		Health Insurance (company paid) 109.00 0.00	Married	2
Johns, Lebron	Overtime (x1.5) hourly 18.75	Health Insurance (company paid) 109.00 0.00	Single	1
Levine, April	Overtime (x1.5) hourly 27.00	Health Insurance (company paid) 109.00 0.00	Married	0

Figure 12:65

Close the report and open the Payroll Item List by selecting ***Lists>>Payroll Item List*** on the main menu. Click **No** to using QBP's payroll service.

We will now customize posting accounts for a few of these items. Double click the **Health Insurance** item and click **Next.** Change the **Liability** account and **Expense** account to the accounts shown in Figure 12:66.

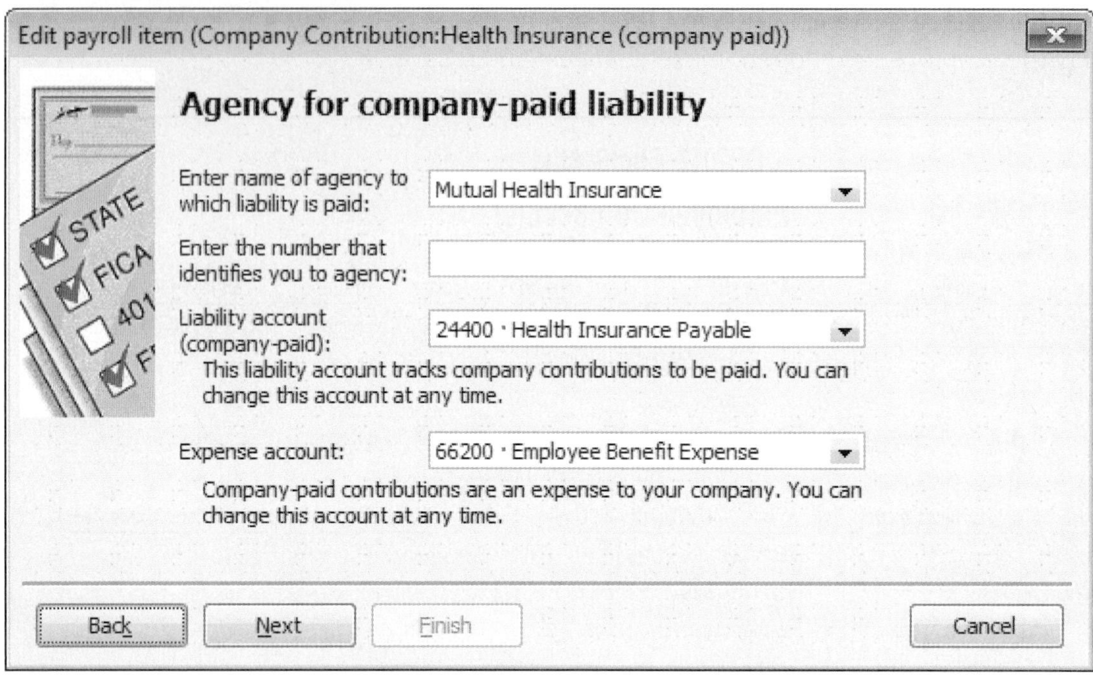

Figure 12:66

Click **Next** until you can click **Finish.**

Use the same steps to change the general ledger accounts on the following payroll items.

Item Name	Liability Account	Expense Account
Medicare Company		66100 Payroll Tax Expense
Social Security Company		66100 Payroll Tax Expense
Federal Unemployment	24100 FUTA Tax Payable	66100 Payroll Tax Expense
VA – Withholding	24200 State Withholding Tax Payable	
VA – Unemployment	24300 SUTA Tax Payable	66100 Payroll Tax Expense

Close the list and the Employee Center. Reopen the **Home** page and return to the **Vendor Center**. You need to adjust vendor accounts created by QBP when adding payroll tax items.

First, delete the **United States Treasury** account by highlighting it and clicking ***Edit>>Delete Vendor*** on the main menu. Click **OK** to confirm.

Next, open the following vendor accounts to enter the vendor information provided.

Virginia Dept. of Taxation

PO Box 8721, Arlington, VA 32513

Terms: Net 5

Account Prefill: 24200 State Withholding Tax Payable

Virginia Employment Commission

PO Box 8181, Arlington, VA 32513

Terms: Net 5

Account Prefill: 24300 SUTA Tax Payable

Close the Vendor Center.

CUSTOMIZING FORM TEMPLATES

Customizing the forms used by a company is the last step to finalizing a new data file. Select ***Lists>>Templates*** on the main menu to access QBP's form templates (Figure 12:67).

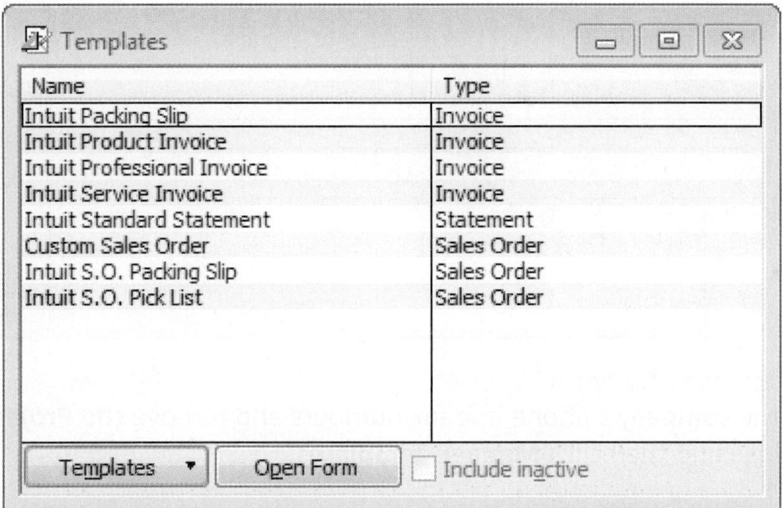

Figure 12:67

We will customize the product invoice first. Double click the **Intuit Product Invoice** and click the **Print Preview** button. Click **Zoom In** to enlarge the view and the form appears as illustrated in Figure 12:68.

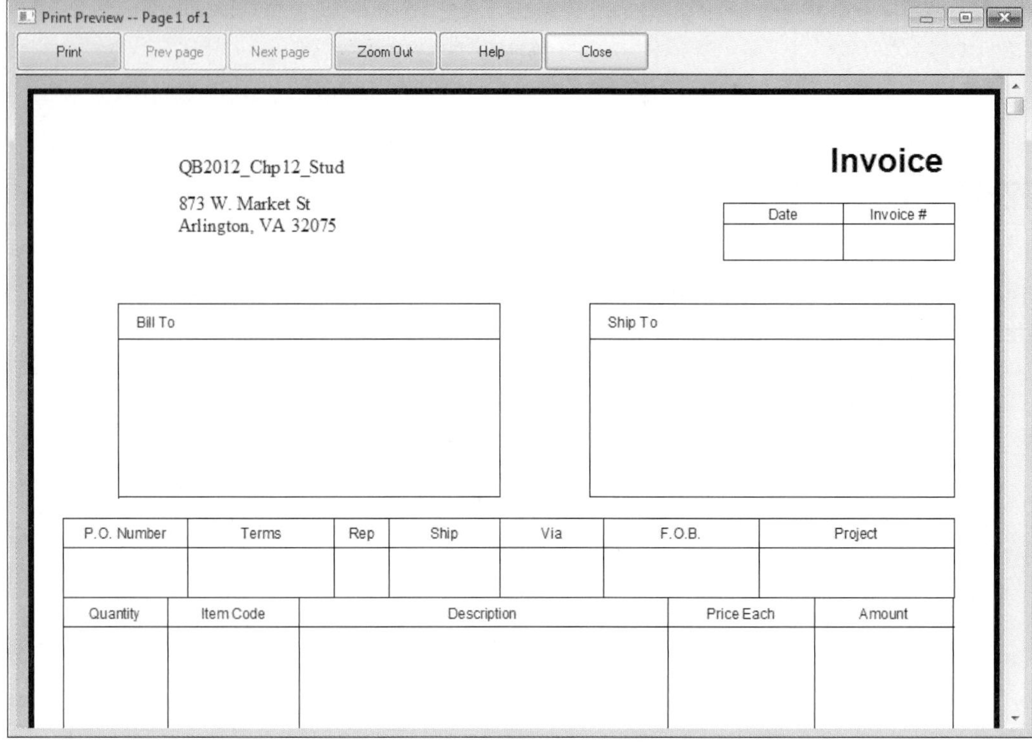

Figure 12:68

We want to add the company's phone and fax numbers and remove the **Project** field from the form. Click **Close** and then click **Manage Templates.**

Highlight **Intuit Product Invoice,** click **Copy,** and change the name to **Electronic Invoice** (Figure 12:69). Click **OK.**

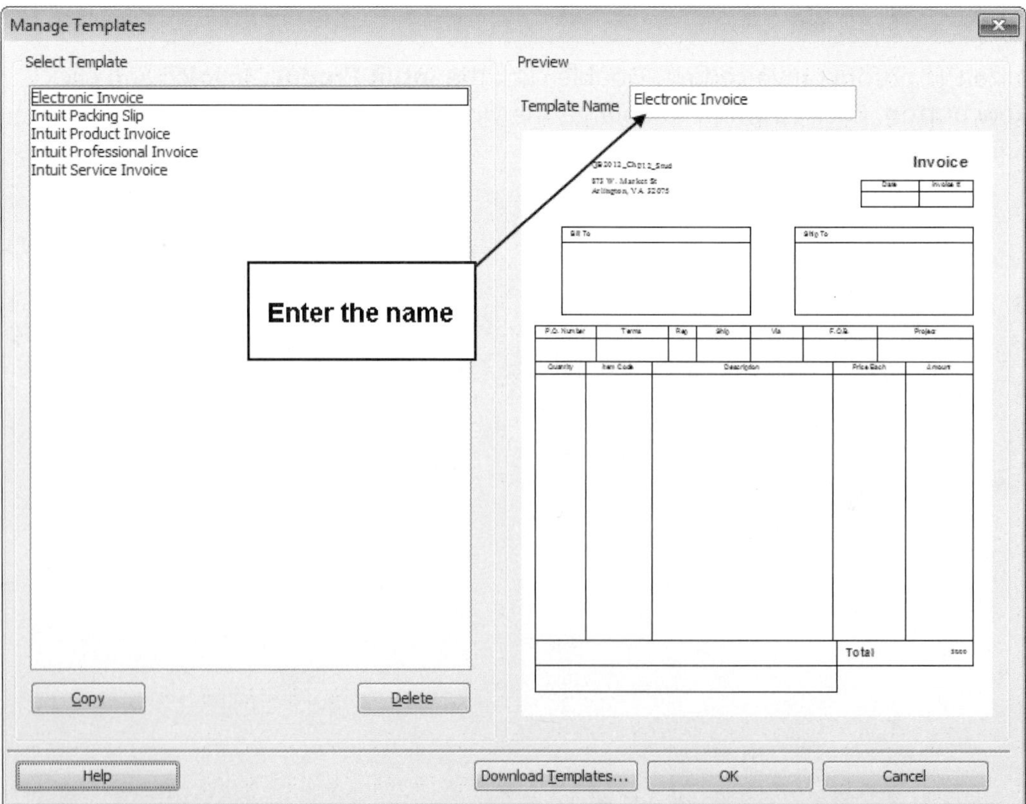

Figure 12:69

Click the **Phone Number** field (Figure 12:70), causing QBP to prompt to use the **Layout Designer.** Select the option to turn off future messages and click **OK.** Also, click the **Fax Number** field.

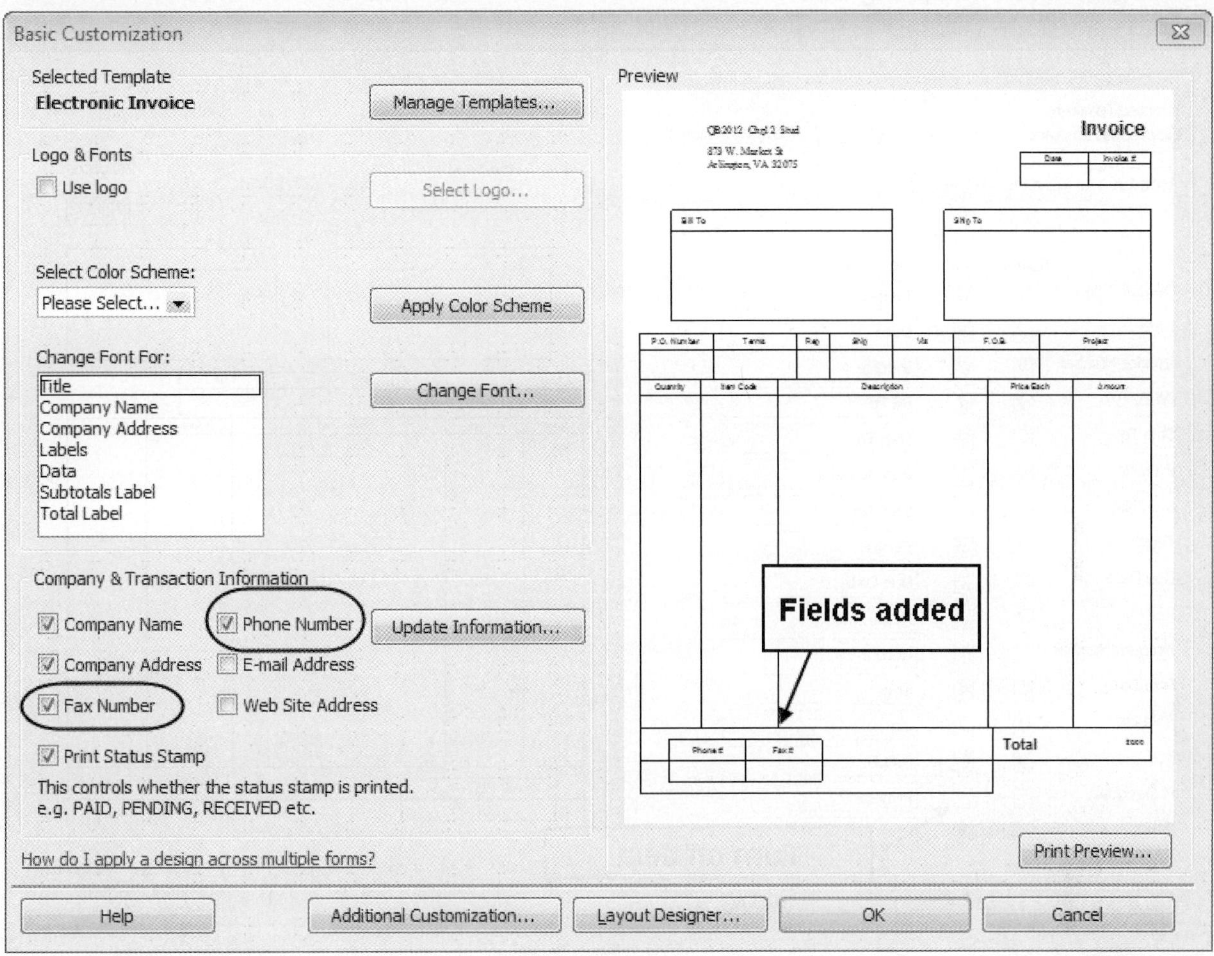

Figure 12:70

The new fields were added to the bottom of the form so you will move them to the top. Before that, click **Additional Customization** to remove the **Project** field. With the **Header** tab selected, turn off the **Project/Job** field. (See Figure 12:71.) Click **Continue** when you receive a message about overlapping fields.

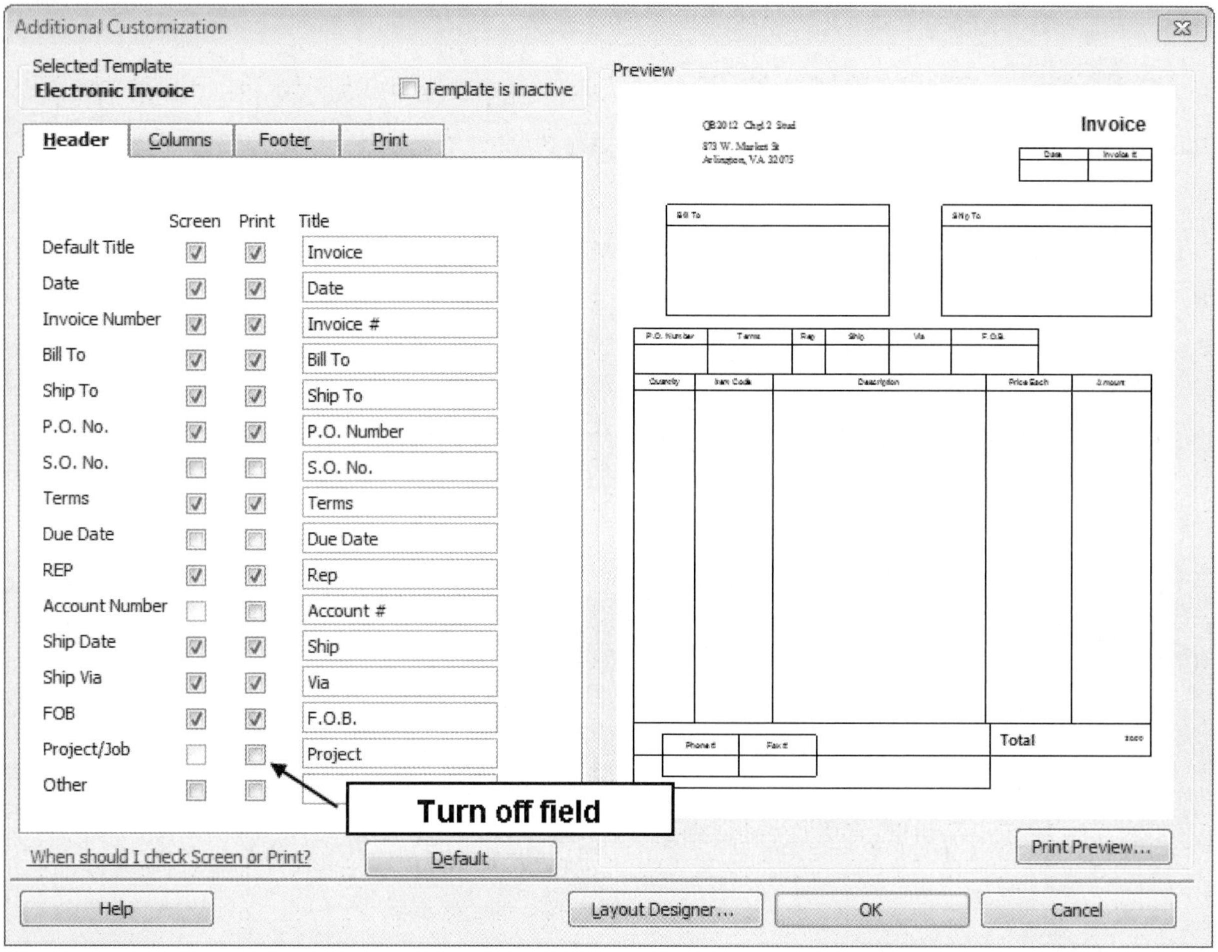

Additional Customization

Selected Template
Electronic Invoice
Template is inactive

Header | Columns | Footer | Print

	Screen	Print	Title
Default Title	☑	☑	Invoice
Date	☑	☑	Date
Invoice Number	☑	☑	Invoice #
Bill To	☑	☑	Bill To
Ship To	☑	☑	Ship To
P.O. No.	☑	☑	P.O. Number
S.O. No.	☐	☐	S.O. No.
Terms	☑	☑	Terms
Due Date	☐	☐	Due Date
REP	☑	☑	Rep
Account Number	☐	☐	Account #
Ship Date	☑	☑	Ship
Ship Via	☑	☑	Via
FOB	☑	☑	F.O.B.
Project/Job	☐	☐	Project
Other	☐	☐	

Turn off field

Preview

Invoice

Total

When should I check Screen or Print? | Default | Print Preview...

Help | Layout Designer... | OK | Cancel

Figure 12:71

The **Header** tab sets the fields and titles that print at the top of the form. The **Columns** tab (not shown) sets the fields and titles that appear in the body of the form. The **Footer** tab sets information for the bottom of the form. Finally, the **Print** tab sets printing attributes.

Click **Print Preview** and scroll to the bottom of the form. Notice that the phone fields you added are at the bottom of the form. (See Figure 12:72.) We will reposition them next.

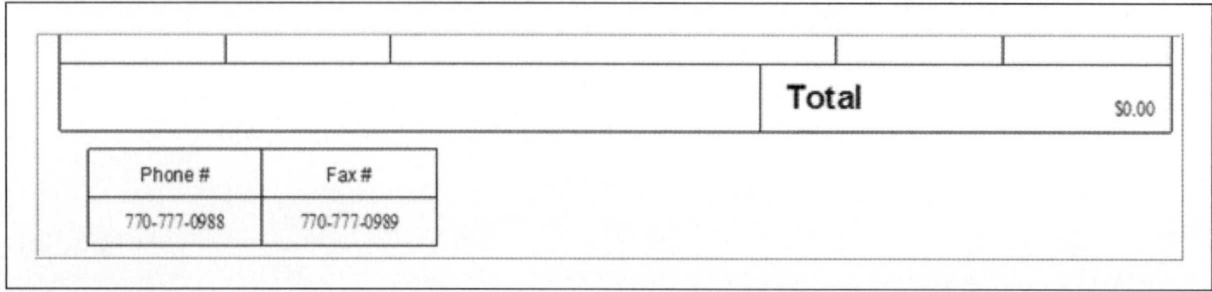

Figure 12:72

Click **Close** to exit the preview pane and click **Layout Designer** so you can reposition these fields.

Scroll to the bottom of the form and locate the phone fields. Each field is comprised of a field title and the field value. You can move all four fields simultaneously using the next instructions.

Click the **Phone #** title first and then hold down the Shift key as you click the three remaining fields. When finished, the four fields are grouped together. (See Figure 12:73.)

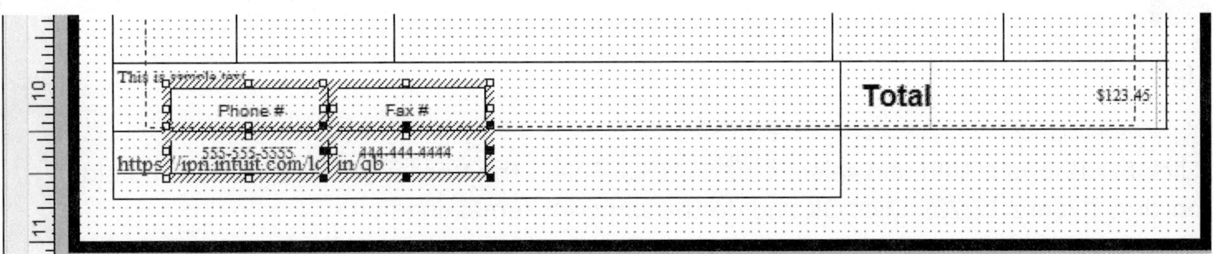

Figure 12:73

Using your mouse, drag the fields to reposition them at the top of the form (Figure 12:74). *(Note: The arrows on your keyboard will move the fields.)*

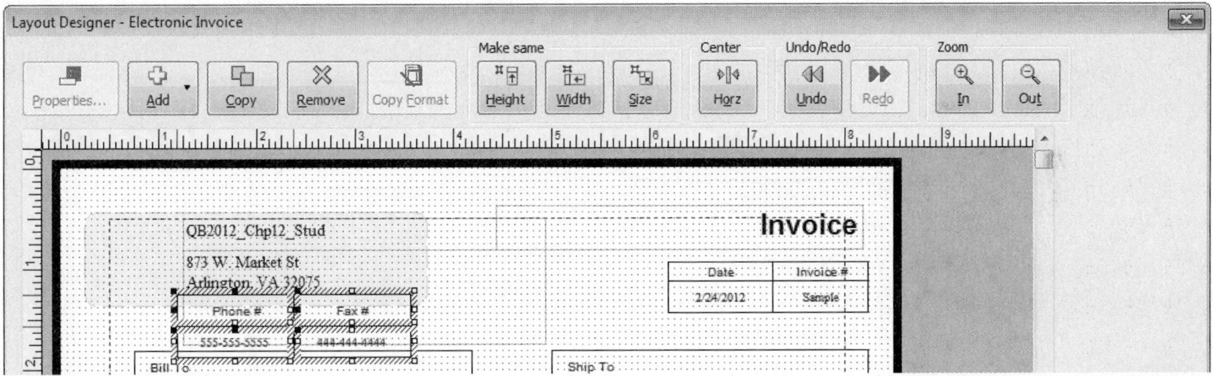

Figure 12:74

Click on the body of the form to ungroup the fields. Now resize and reposition each field individually so each appears as shown in the next illustration.

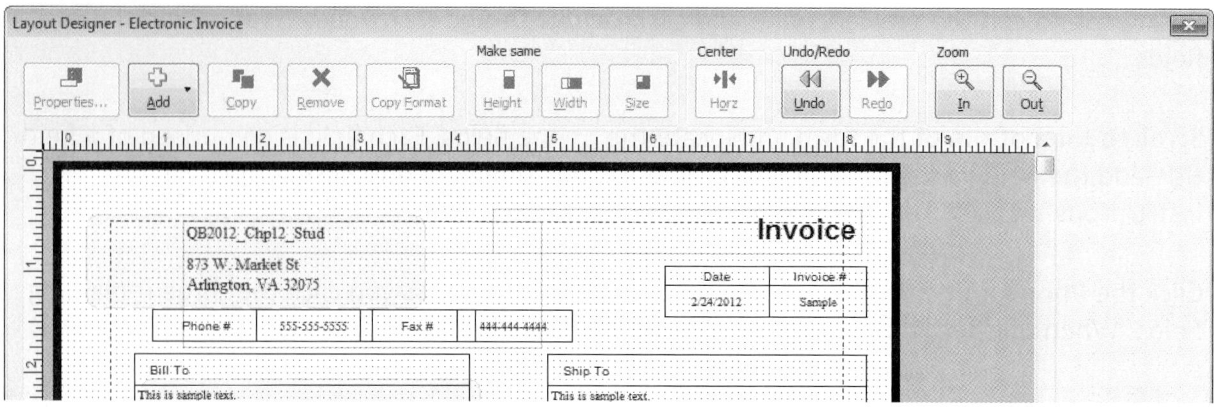

Figure 12:75

Click the **Phone #** field and select Properties... . Select the **Border** tab to turn off the field borders (Figure 12:76). Click **OK** and do the same for remaining fields.

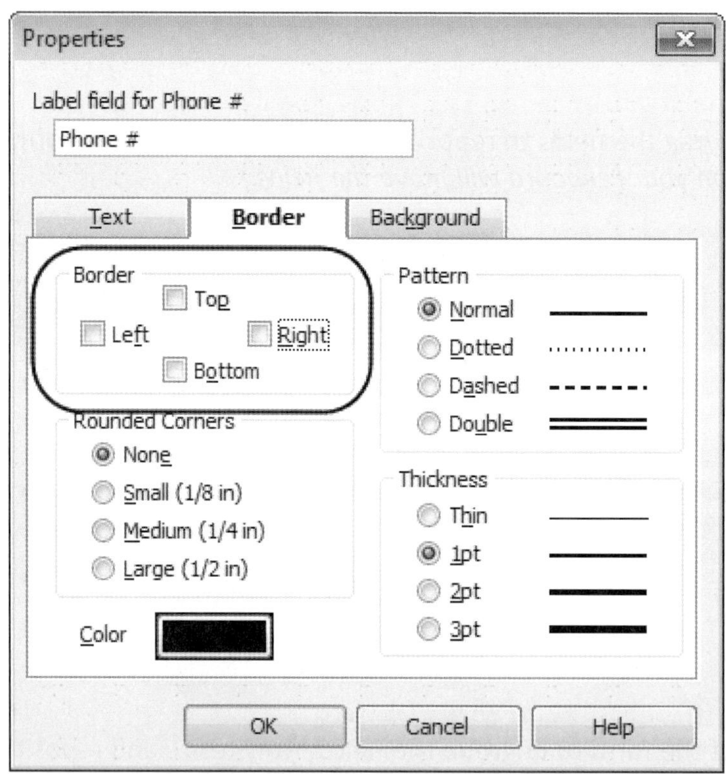

Figure 12:76

Click **OK** to save the changes. Click **Print Preview** to view the redesigned form. (See Figure 12:77.)

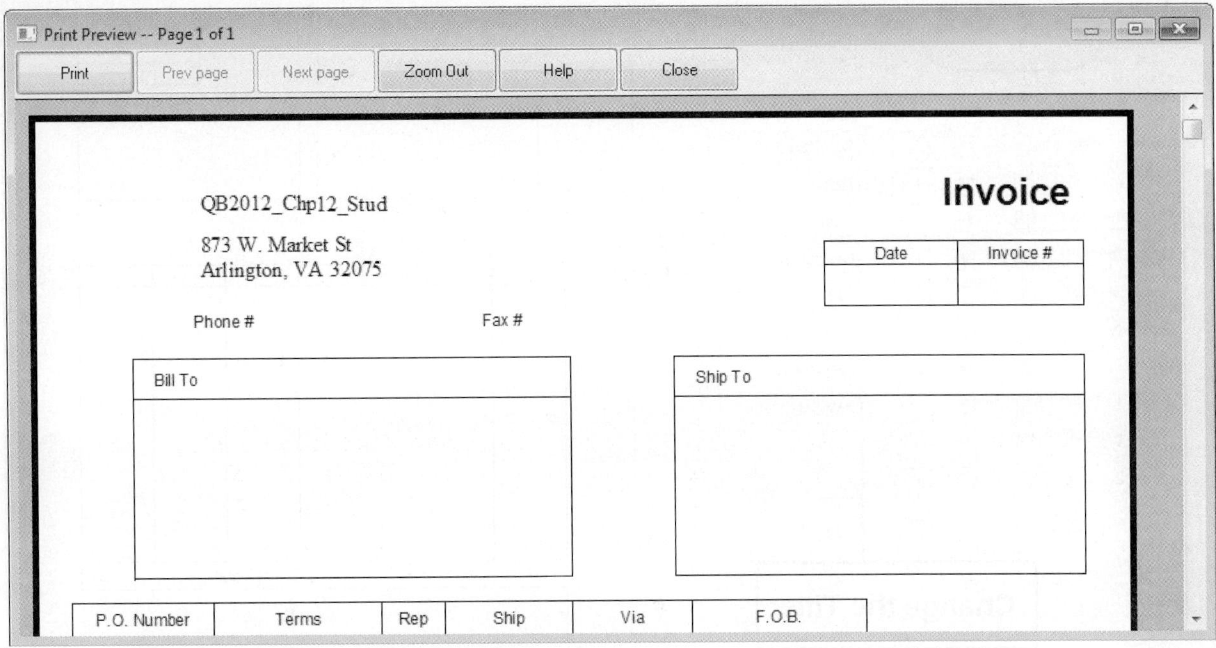

Figure 12:77

Click **Close** and then **OK** on the **Layout Designer** window. Click **OK** on the **Basic Customization** window. The Electronic Invoice template now appears at the top of the template list.

You also need to redesign the PO form. The template does not appear on the list so click ***Vendors>>Create Purchase Orders*** on the main menu. Click **X** to close the PO.

Return to the Templates list and open the **Custom Purchase Order** form. Click **Additional Customization** and select the **Columns** tab. Change the **Title** of "Rate" to "Unit Price" as illustrated in Figure 12:78.

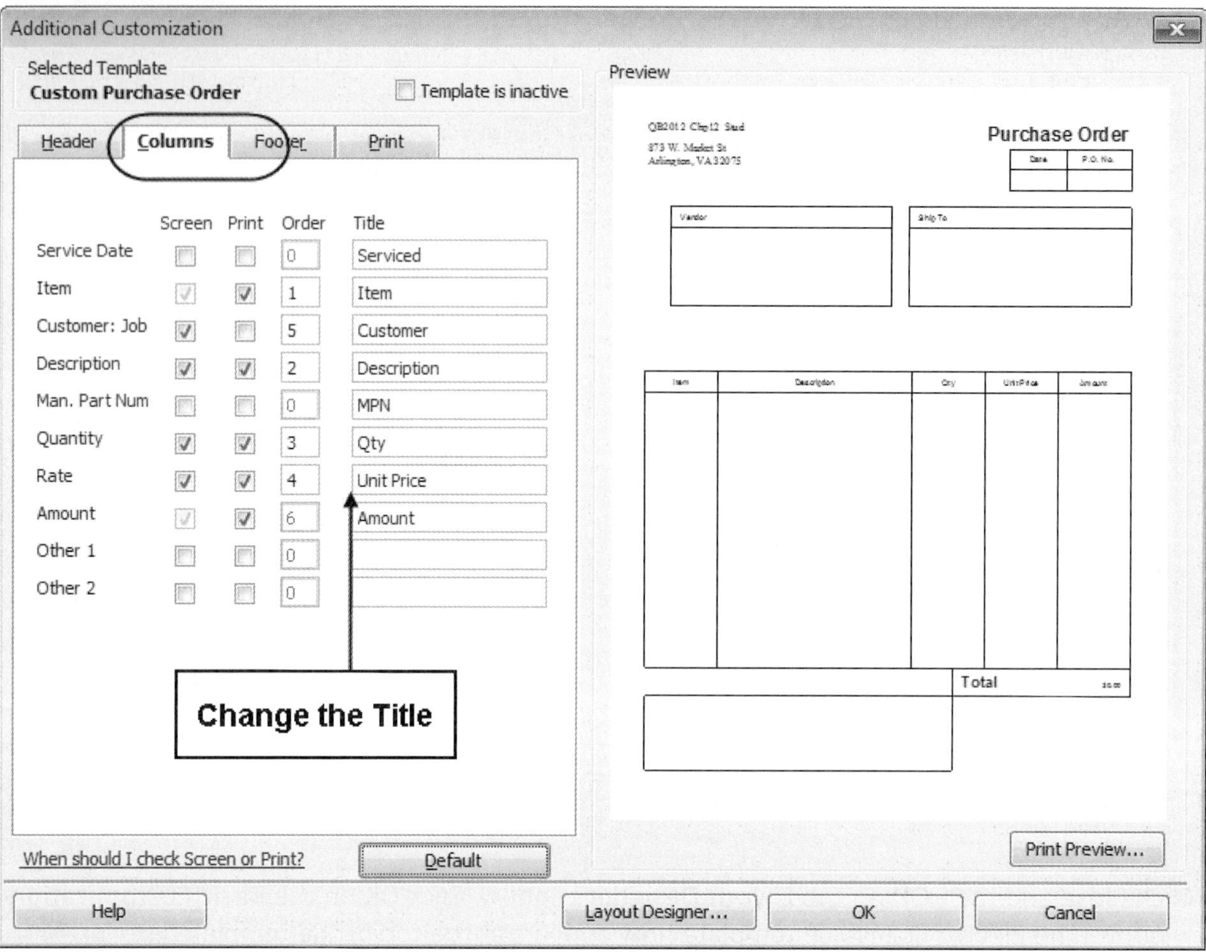

Figure 12:78

Click **OK** and **OK** again. Click **X** to close the Templates list.

You have finished creating the new company file. ***Create a backup of it using the backup filename of "QB2012_Chp12_Stud_Completed."***

Summary

Congratulations! You have created a new company. You first established the company data file and then created the chart of accounts and entered opening balances. You then set the company's preference options. From there you created customers, vendors, and inventory items, making sure to verify opening balances after creating. Finally, you established the company's payroll options, created employees, and customized forms. You are now ready to complete the following Practice Set where you record Electronics' accounting transactions for January.

PRACTICE SET

In this practice set, you record January 2012 transactions for the new company you created in the chapter. When completing the tasks, keep the following in mind:

- Click OK if a transaction exceeds the customer credit limit because the owner has approved the transaction.
- Print transactions only when instructed. Reports are printed in Steps 2 and 3.

Begin by:

- Opening the software.
- Opening the **QB2012_Chp12_Stud** data file you created in the chapter.
- **Toggling the software to the PRO EDITION** by selecting ***File>>Toggle to Another Edition*** on the main menu and choosing **QuickBooks Pro** as the edition.

1. Record the following transactions.

Jan. 2	Sales Invoice 2000 for $11,400 to Barter Bay for 40 items of DIGCAM, unit sales price $285. ***Change the template to Electronic Invoice.***
	Check number 783 from Discount Electronics for $9,670 paying opening balance in full. *(Note: If asked to calculate payments automatically, turn off future messages and click Yes.)* Change the **Deposit to** field to 10100 Regular Checking Account.
	PO 101 for $41,850 to Neer Pio for 50 items of ENTSYS, unit price $837. PO 102 for $48,600 to SumSang Corporation for 30 items of HDTV, unit price $1,620.
	Vendor Invoice 1235 for $3,000 from Travelor's Insurance; $1,200 for 6 months of prepaid auto insurance and $1,800 for 6 months of prepaid business insurance.
Jan. 4	Check number 132 from GG Hregg Stores for $9,600 that pays the opening balance in full.
	Sales Invoice 2001 for $90,000 to Television World for 20 items of LCDTV, unit sales price $4,500.
	PO 103 for $108,000 to SumSang Corporation for 40 items of LCDTV, unit price $2,700.
	Vendor Invoice 3729 for $48,600 for all items on SumSang Corporation PO 102.

Jan. 5	Vendor Invoice 3733 for $108,000 for all items on SumSang Corporation PO 103.
	Sales Invoice 2002 for $38,500 to Better Buy for 50 items of DVRREC, unit sales price $95, and 25 units of ENTSYS, unit sales price $1,350.
	Check number 888 from Electronic Town for $23,500 that pays the opening balance in full. Check number 632 from Better Buy for $27,000 that pays the opening balance in full.
Jan. 6	Vendor Receipt RCT3253 from Neer Pio for all items on PO 101. Make sure the Memo field reads Received items (bill to follow).
	Check number 772 from Barter Bay for $22,340 that pays the opening balance in full.
Jan. 7	Vendor Invoice 7333 for $41,850 from Neer Pio for Receipt RCT3253. *(Remember to change the transaction date and document number.)* Vendor Invoice 45 for $350 from Advertising World for January advertising expense.
	Credit Memo CM2000 for $1,425 to Barter Bay for returning 5 items of DIGCAM on Invoice 2000. Apply to the invoice.

Jan. 9	Create the following payroll checks for the biweekly pay period ended January 8. Be sure to enter the hours. Print checks from Payroll Checking Account on starting check number 1236.

Electronics Supply
Paychecks for Pay Period 12/26/2011 thru 1/08/2012

Check No.	Employee	Filing Status	Allow	Pay Type	Pay Rate	Regular Hrs	OT Hrs	Gross Pay	Federal Income Tax	Soc. Sec. (FICA) Tax	Medicare Tax	VA State Tax	Net Pay
1236	Fleming, Ashton	Single	0	Salary	1,500.00			1,500.00	217.00	93.00	21.75	60.00	1,108.25
1237	Gonzalez, Susan	Married	2	Salary	2,600.00			2,600.00	275.00	161.20	37.70	104.00	2,022.10
1238	Johns, Lebron	Single	1	Hourly	12.50	80.00		1,000.00	101.00	62.00	14.50	40.00	782.50
1239	Levine, April	Married	0	Hourly	18.00	80.00		1,440.00	141.00	89.28	20.88	57.60	1,131.24
	Totals					160.00	0.00	6,540.00	734.00	405.48	94.83	261.60	5,044.09
	Tax Basis								Circular E	6.20%	1.45%	4.00%	
	G/L Accounts							6000	2330	2330	2330	2350	1030

Electronics Supply
Employer Costs for Pay Period 12/26/2011 thru 1/08/2012

Employee	ER Soc. Sec. (FICA)	ER Medicare	ER FUTA	ER SUTA	Health Insurance
Fleming, Ashton	93.00	21.75	12.00	30.00	109.00
Gonzalez, Susan	161.20	37.70	20.80	52.00	109.00
Johns, Lebron	62.00	14.50	8.00	20.00	109.00
Levine, April	89.28	20.88	11.52	28.80	109.00
Totals	405.48	94.83	52.32	130.80	436.00
Tax Basis	6.20%	1.45%	0.8%	2.0%	
G/L Accounts	2330 / 6100	2330 / 6100	2340 / 6100	2360 / 6100	2370 / 6110

Check your totals before printing.

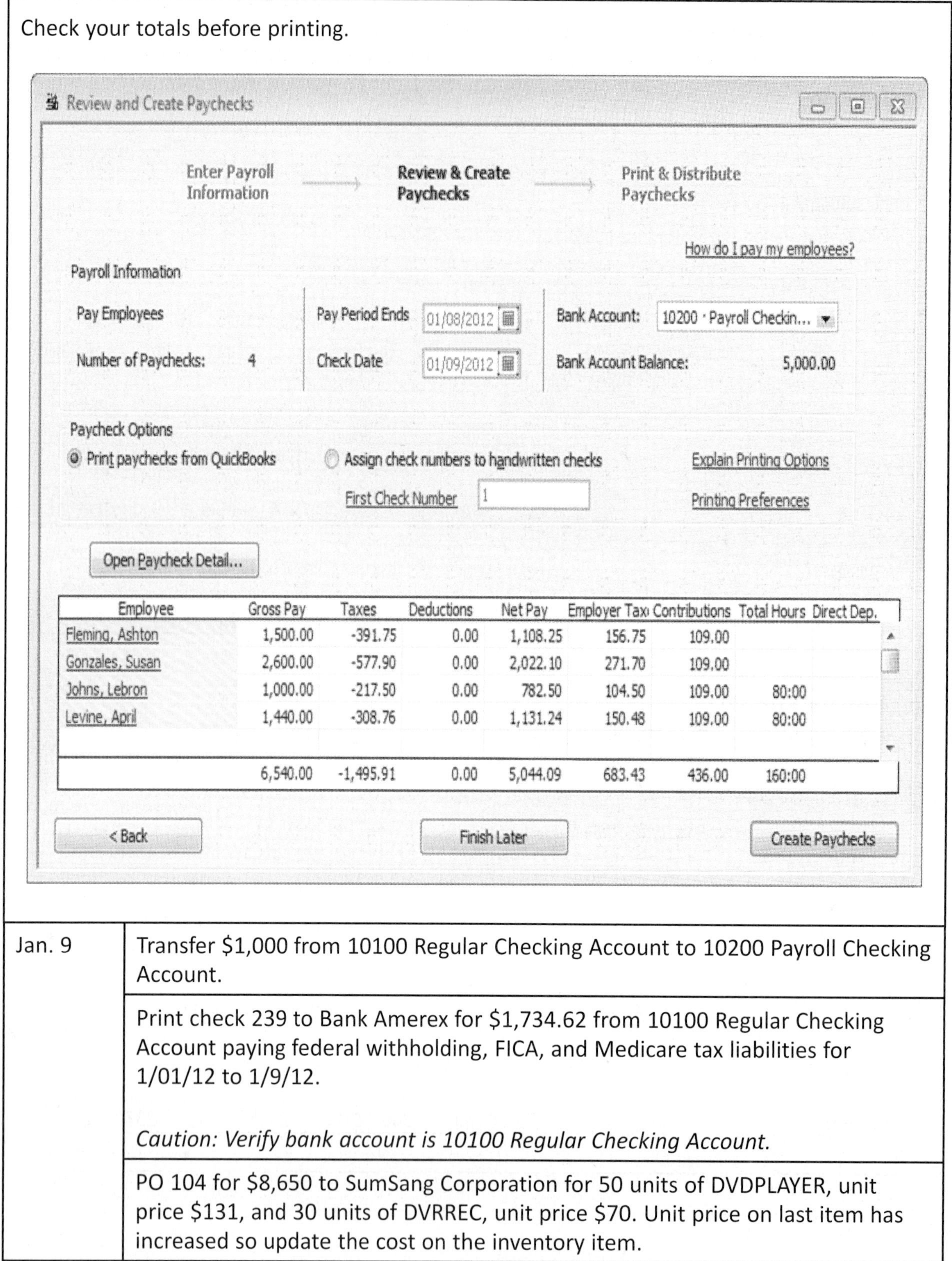

Employee	Gross Pay	Taxes	Deductions	Net Pay	Employer Tax	Contributions	Total Hours	Direct Dep.
Fleming, Ashton	1,500.00	-391.75	0.00	1,108.25	156.75	109.00		
Gonzales, Susan	2,600.00	-577.90	0.00	2,022.10	271.70	109.00		
Johns, Lebron	1,000.00	-217.50	0.00	782.50	104.50	109.00	80:00	
Levine, April	1,440.00	-308.76	0.00	1,131.24	150.48	109.00	80:00	
	6,540.00	-1,495.91	0.00	5,044.09	683.43	436.00	160:00	

Jan. 9	Transfer $1,000 from 10100 Regular Checking Account to 10200 Payroll Checking Account.
	Print check 239 to Bank Amerex for $1,734.62 from 10100 Regular Checking Account paying federal withholding, FICA, and Medicare tax liabilities for 1/01/12 to 1/9/12. *Caution: Verify bank account is 10100 Regular Checking Account.*
	PO 104 for $8,650 to SumSang Corporation for 50 units of DVDPLAYER, unit price $131, and 30 units of DVRREC, unit price $70. Unit price on last item has increased so update the cost on the inventory item.

Jan. 13	Print checks from the 10100 Regular Checking Account paying vendors for bills due on or before January 31. Starting check number is 240. Selected bills total $59,900.
	PO 105 for $1,500 to Neer Pio for 25 units of CDPLAYER, unit price $60.
	Check number 6323 from Better Buy for $37,730 paying Invoice 2002 with a discount of $770. Post the discount to 49000 Sales Discount. Check number 2223 from Barter Bay for $9,975 paying Invoice 2000.
Jan. 16	Sales Invoice 2003 for $112,500 to GG Hregg Stores for 25 units of LCDTV, unit sales price $4,500.
	Vendor Receipt RCT332 for all items on Neer Pio PO 105.
	Vendor Invoice 88935 for $8,650 for all items on SumSang Corporation PO 104.
	Check number 7325 from Television World for $90,000 paying Invoice 2001.
Jan. 19	PO 106 for $9,550 to Javix Cam for 50 units of DIGCAM, unit price $191.
	Post the following vendor bills dated January 19. CSB Telephone for January telephone, $230 Virginia Electric for January electric, $370 Cooleys Repair, Invoice 7722 for $275 for furnace repair expense Office Rex, Invoice 4234 for $673 for office supplies expense
Jan. 20	PO 107 for $24,000 to Neer Pio for 40 units of HOMSTER, unit price $600.
	Sales Invoice 2004 for $53,850 to Electronic Town for 30 of HOMSTER, unit sales price $895 and 10 units of HDTV, unit sales price $2,700.
	Vendor Receipt RCT55533 for all items on Javix Cam PO 106.
	Vendor Invoice 7395 for $1,500 from Neer Pio for Receipt RCT332.
Jan. 21	Sales Invoice 2005 for $33,270 to Discount Electronics for 40 units of DIGCORD, unit sales price $588, and 50 units of DVDPLAYER, unit sales price $195. Sales Invoice 2006 for $20,000 to Barter Bay for 80 units of PRINTER, unit sales price $250. Sales Invoice 2007 for $14,310 to Better Buy for 30 units of CDPLAYER, unit sales price $85, and 20 units of DIGCORD, unit sales price of $588.
	PO 108 for $15,760 to Canyon Cam for 40 units of DIGCORD, unit price $394.

Jan. 23	Create the following payroll checks for the biweekly pay period ended January 22 Print checks from Payroll Checking Account on starting check number 1240.

Electronics Supply
Paychecks for Pay Period 1/09/2012 thru 1/22/2012

Check No.	Employee	Filing Status	Allow	Pay Type	Pay Rate	Regular Hrs	OT Hrs	Gross Pay	Federal Income Tax	Soc. Sec. (FICA) Tax	Medicare Tax	VA State Tax	Net Pay
1240	Fleming, Ashton	Single	0	Salary	1,500.00			1,500.00	217.00	93.00	21.75	60.00	1,108.25
1241	Gonzalez, Susan	Married	2	Salary	2,600.00			2,600.00	275.00	161.20	37.70	104.00	2,022.10
1242	Johns, Lebron	Single	1	Hourly	12.50	80.00	2.00	1,037.50	104.00	64.33	15.04	41.50	812.63
1243	Levine, April	Married	0	Hourly	18.00	80.00		1,440.00	141.00	89.28	20.88	57.60	1,131.24
	Totals					160.00	2.00	6,577.50	737.00	407.81	95.37	263.10	5,074.22
	Tax Basis								Circular E	6.20%	1.45%	4.00%	
	G/L Accounts							6000	2330	2330	2330	2350	1030

Electronics Supply
Employer Costs for Pay Period 1/09/2012 thru 1/22/2012

Employee	ER Soc. Sec. (FICA)	ER Medicare	ER FUTA	ER SUTA	Health Insurance
Fleming, Ashton	93.00	21.75	12.00	30.00	109.00
Gonzalez, Susan	161.20	37.70	20.80	52.00	109.00
Johns, Lebron	64.33	15.04	8.30	20.75	109.00
Levine, April	89.28	20.88	11.52	28.80	109.00
Totals	407.81	95.37	52.62	131.55	436.00
Tax Basis	6.20%	1.45%	0.8%	2.0%	
G/L Accounts	2330 / 6100	2330 / 6100	2340 / 6100	2360 / 6100	2370 / 6110

Check your totals.

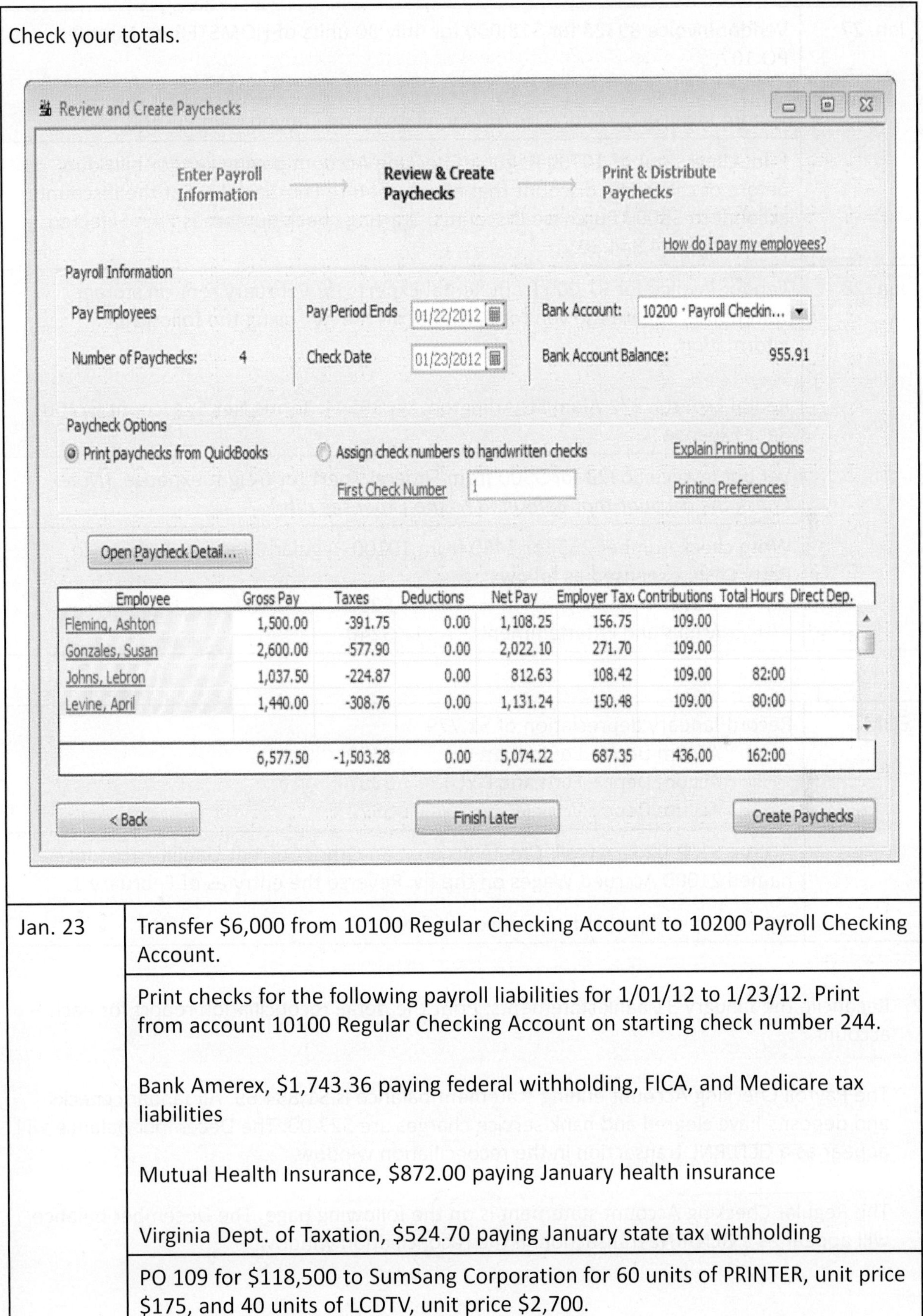

Jan. 23	Transfer $6,000 from 10100 Regular Checking Account to 10200 Payroll Checking Account.
	Print checks for the following payroll liabilities for 1/01/12 to 1/23/12. Print from account 10100 Regular Checking Account on starting check number 244. Bank Amerex, $1,743.36 paying federal withholding, FICA, and Medicare tax liabilities Mutual Health Insurance, $872.00 paying January health insurance Virginia Dept. of Taxation, $524.70 paying January state tax withholding
	PO 109 for $118,500 to SumSang Corporation for 60 units of PRINTER, unit price $175, and 40 units of LCDTV, unit price $2,700.

Jan. 27	Vendor Invoice 89323 for $18,000 for only 30 units of HOMSTER on Neer Pio PO 107. Vendor Invoice 2232 for $15,760 for all items on Canyon Cam PO 108.
	Print checks out of 10100 Regular Checking Account paying vendor bills due before or carrying a discount that expires before February 12. Set the discount account to 55000 Purchase Discounts. Starting check number is 247. Selected bills total $214,844.80.
Jan. 28	Vendor Invoice for $1,000 from Rental Experts for February rent on storage warehouse. Create the vendor account "on the fly" using the following information. Rental Experts, 872 Alum St, Arlington, VA 36544, Terms Net 5, account 67100 Rent Expense.
	Vendor Invoice 66323 for $500 from Federal Xpert for freight expense. *(Note: Check the account that defaulted to the Expenses tab.)*
	Write check number 253 for $450 from 10100 Regular Checking Account to Petty Cash, expensed as follows: Travel $210 Meals and Entertainment $240

EOM	Record January depreciation of $1,779. Accum Depr – Equipment $450 Accum Depr – Furn and Fixt $357 Accum Depr – Vehicle $972
	Accrue $1,400 for payroll. Create account an Other Current Liability account named 21000 Accrued Wages on the fly. Reverse the entry as of February 1.
	Record expired prepaid insurance of $500.

2. Reconcile the January 31 bank statements. Print the detail reconciliation report for each account.

   The Payroll Checking Account ending statement balance is $1,854.69. All January checks and deposits have cleared and bank service charges are $27.00. The December balance will appear as a GENJRNL transaction in the reconciliation window.

   The Regular Checking Account statement is on the following page. The December balance will appear as a GENJRNL transaction in the reconciliation window.

Electronic Supply, Inc.
Bank Statement January 31, 2012

Beginning Balance from December Statement				$ 162,000.00
January Deposits				
	Jan 2, 2012		9,670.00	
	Jan 4, 2012		9,600.00	
	Jan 5, 2012		23,500.00	
	Jan 5, 2012		27,000.00	
	Jan 6, 2012		22,340.00	
	Jan 13, 2012		37,730.00	
	Jan 13, 2012		9,975.00	
	Jan 16, 2012		90,000.00	
Total Deposits for January				229,815.00
January Checks Cleared				
	Jan 9, 2012	239	1,734.62	
	Jan 13, 2012	240	7,740.00	
	Jan 13, 2012	241	7,760.00	
	Jan 13, 2012	242	41,400.00	
	Jan 13, 2012	243	3,000.00	
	Jan 23, 2012	244	1,743.36	
Total Cleared Checks for January				63,377.98
Less Bank Transfers				
	Jan 9, 2012		1,000.00	
	Jan 23, 2012		6,000.00	
Total January Transfers				7,000.00
January Service Charges				102.00
Ending Bank Balance January 31, 2012				$ 321,335.02

3. Print the following reports.
   a. Trial Balance as of January 31
   b. Sales by Customer Detail for the month of January
   c. Deposit Detail for month of January
   d. A/R Aging Detail as of January 31
   e. Purchases by Vendor Detail for month of January
   f. Open Purchase Orders Detail for month of January. Customize the Filters tab to change the Received filter to Either and the Display tab to remove the Source Name, Deliv Date, and Backordered columns
   g. Missing Checks for Checking Account
   h. Missing Checks for Payroll Checking Account
   i. A/P Aging Detail as of January 31
   j. Inventory Valuation Detail for month of January
   k. Payroll Liability Balances for month of January
   l. Profit & Loss Standard for month of January
   m. Balance Sheet Standard as of January 31
   n. Cash Flow Statement for month of January

4. ***Back up the data file to a backup file named "QB2012_Chp12_PracSet_Stud_Completed."***

APPENDIX A INSTALLING QUICKBOOKS PRO & PREMIER ACCOUNTANT EDITION 2012

You begin by verifying that your computer meets the following minimum system requirements for a single-user installation.

Hardware/Software	**Requirements**
Computer processor	2 GHz Intel Pentium 4 or equivalent (2.4GHz recommended)
Memory	At least 1 GB of RAM
Hard disk	2.5 GB of available disk space to install plus additional space for data files
Internet functionality	Broadband service or dial-up with at least 56 Kbps modem and Internet Explorer 6.0 or later
Operating system	Windows XP with Service Pack 2 or later, Windows 7, or Vista
Display	Minimum 1024 x 768 screen resolution. 16-bit or higher color
CD ROM	4x CD-ROM drive
Optional Items	
Microsoft Office Outlook with Business Contacts	190 MB of additional hard disk space required
Integration functionality	Microsoft Word, Excel, and Outlook versions 2002, 2003, 2007, 2010

To locate your computer's processor, RAM information, and operating system version, right click the **Computer** icon on your desktop and select the **Properties** menu (Figure: A:1).

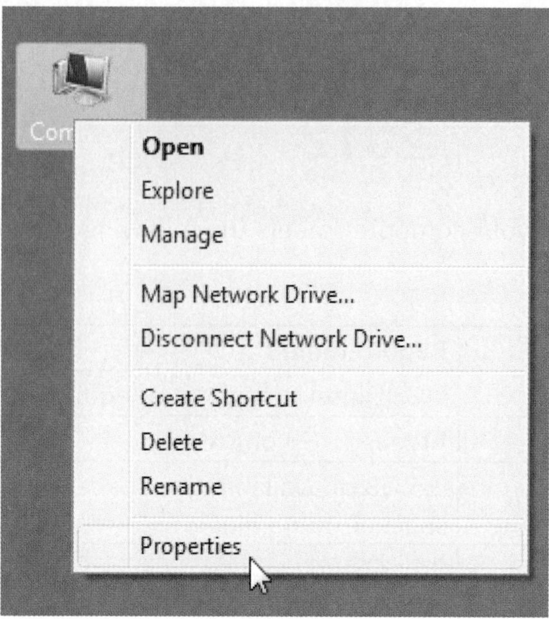

Figure: A:1

The window that opens (Figure: A:2) lists your computer's system information. *(Note: The window view is based on the computer operating system; therefore, your view may vary from the illustration.)* After reviewing, click **X** to close the System Properties window.

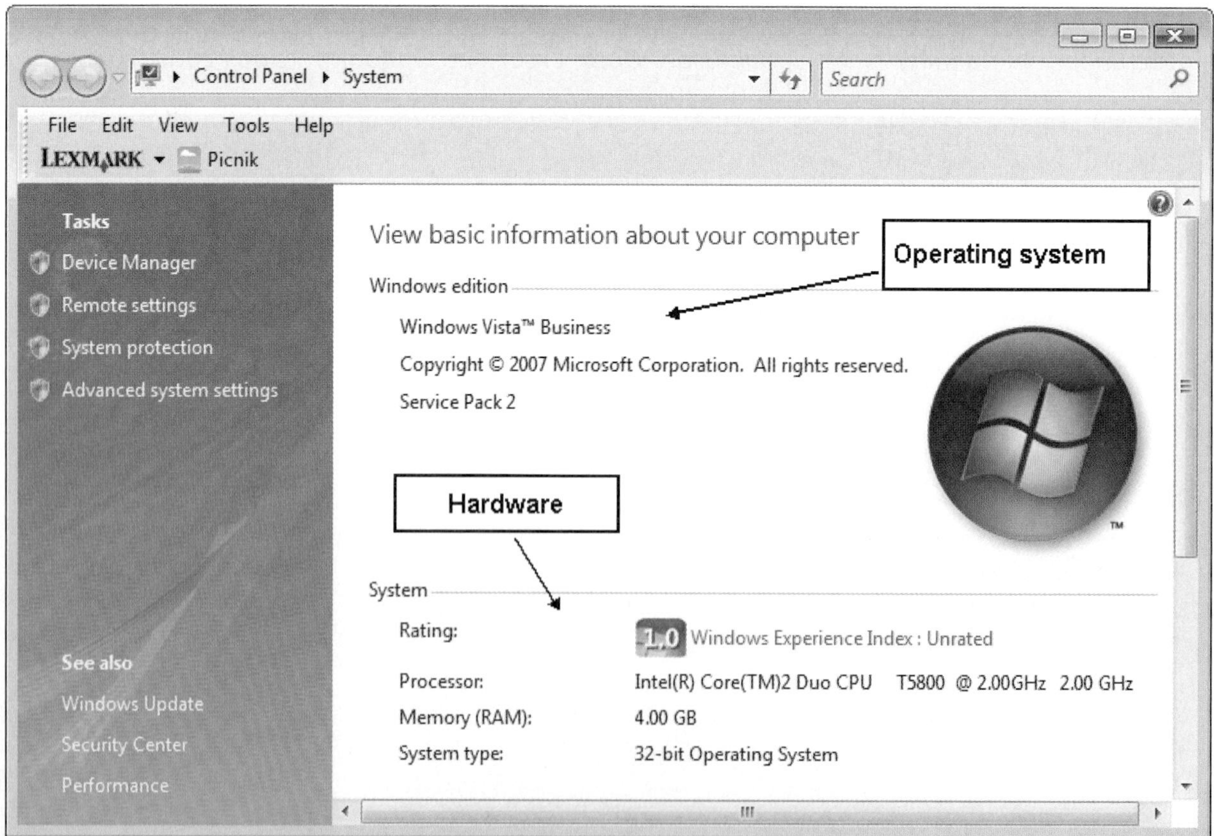

Figure: A:2

To review your computer's available hard disk space, double click the **Computer** icon and locate the drive labeled **C** (Figure: A:3). *Note: Your window may list folder content different from that illustrated. You can click the Views menu to change the view.*

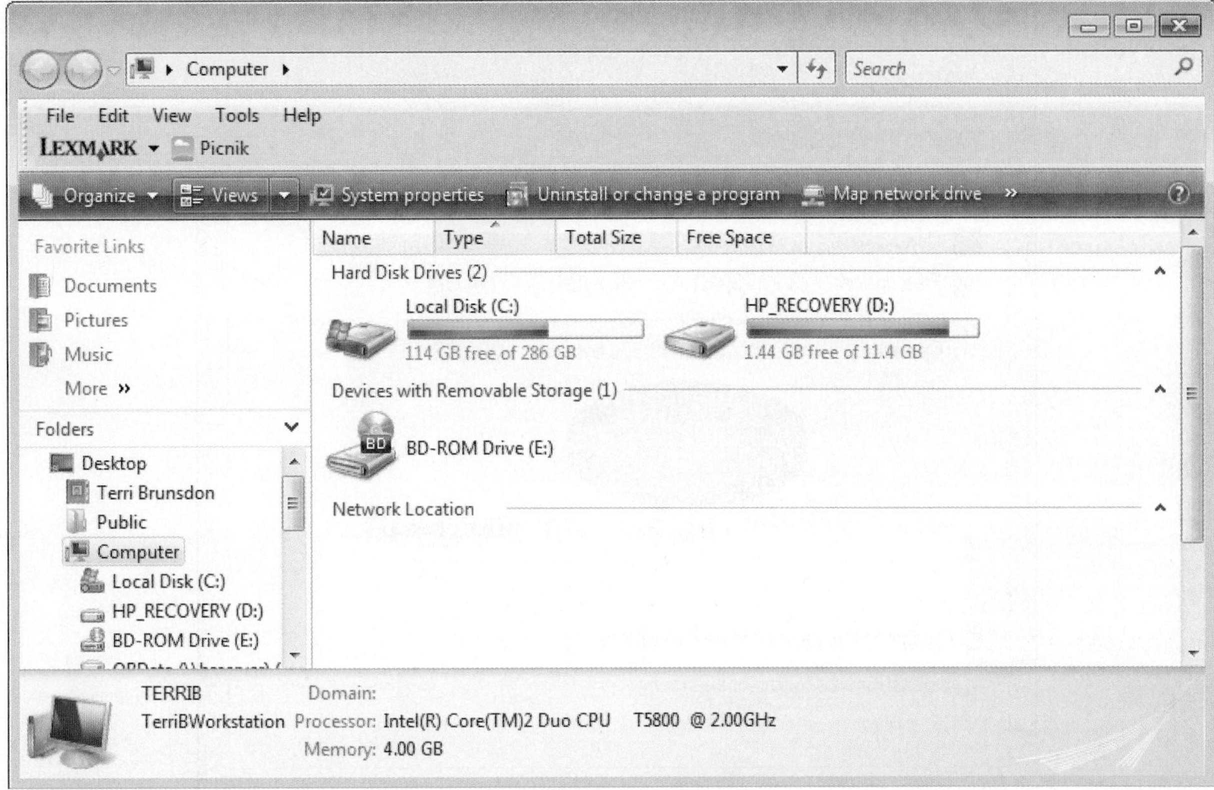

Figure: A:3

Notice that free space on a drive is listed under that drive. You can view additional information for the **C** drive by right clicking it and selecting **Properties**. (See Figure: A:4.) When finished, close any open windows by clicking **X**.

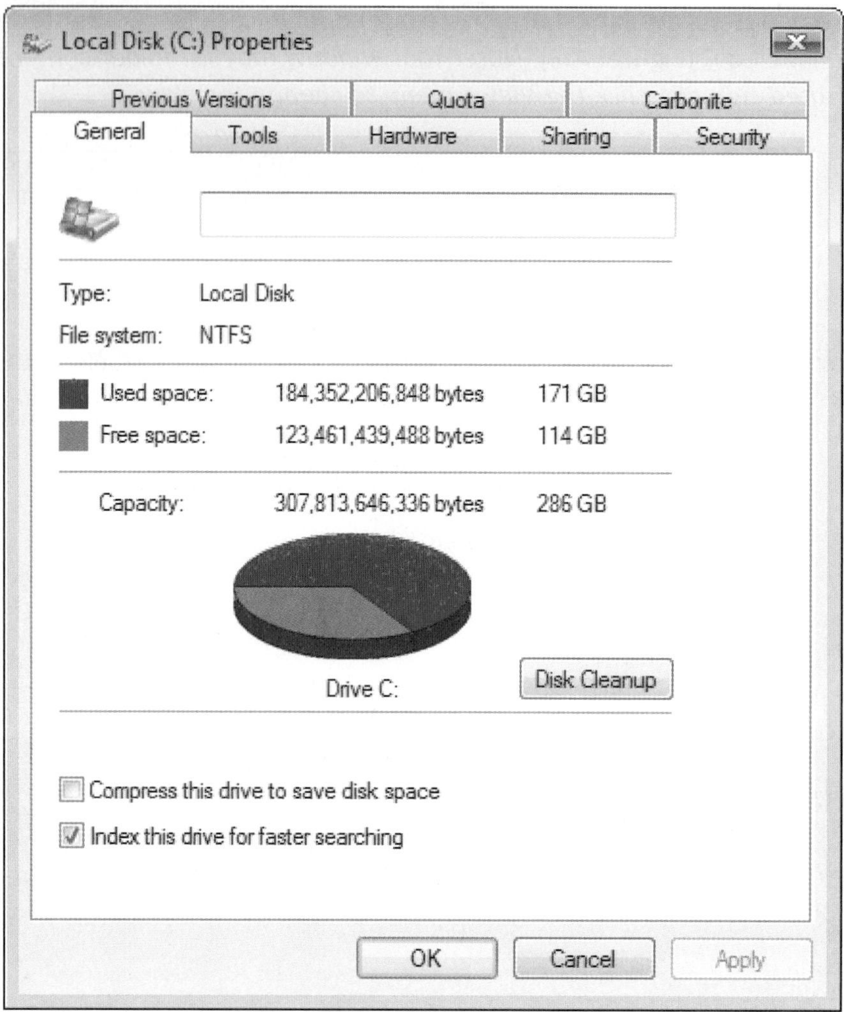

Figure: A:4

After confirming that your computer meets minimum system requirements, close all programs currently running and insert the **QuickBooks** software CD into your computer's CD drive.

The instructions for completing installation appear on the following pages.

The first window to appear is the Welcome to QuickBooks screen. Click **Next** to continue.

The next window displays the **License Agreement** illustrated next. You must accept this agreement before continuing. Before accepting, you can read the agreement by scrolling the window with the scroll bar on the right.

After reading, click the **I accept the terms of the license agreement** option and click **Next** to continue.

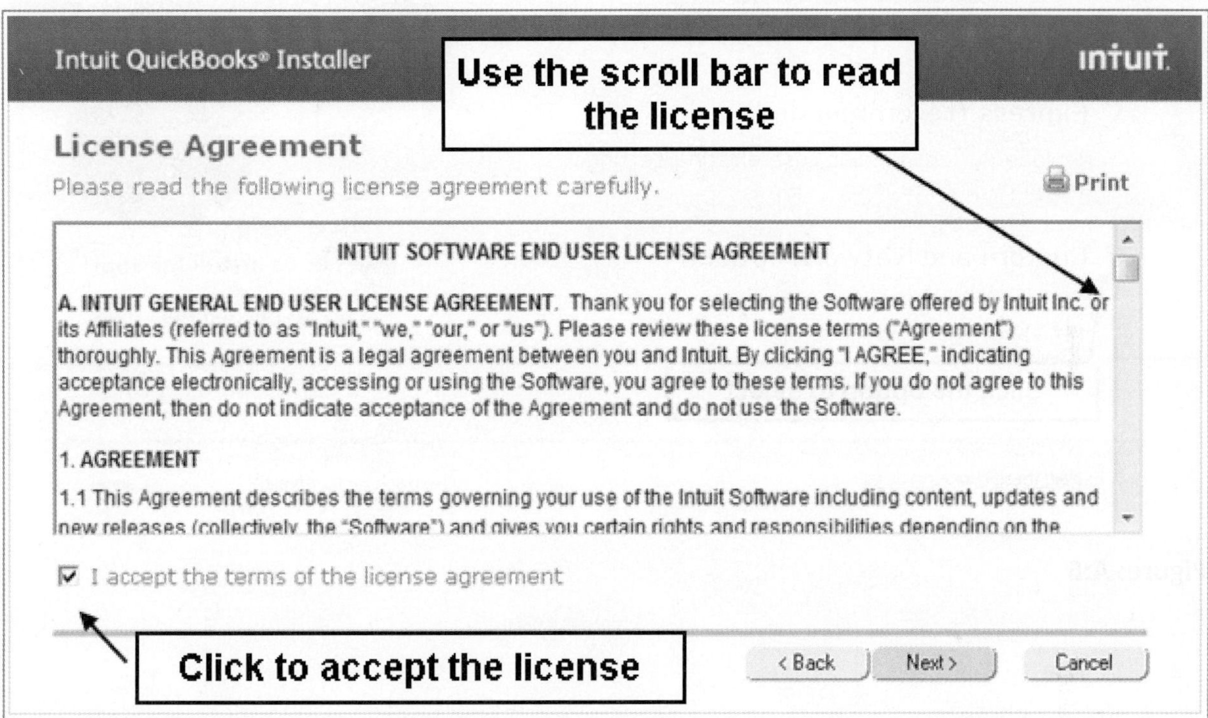

Figure: A:5

In the window illustrated in Figure: A:6, choose the **Custom and Network options** if you have an earlier version of QuickBooks installed on your computer. Otherwise, choose the **Express** option. Click **Next.**

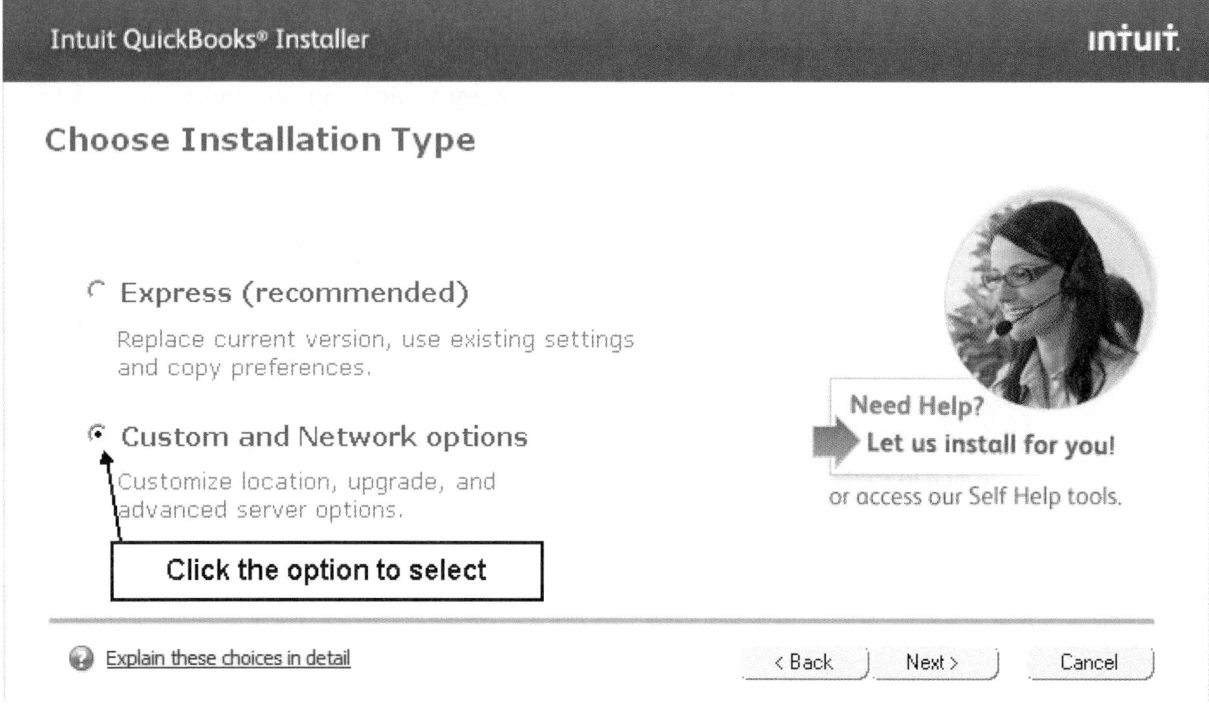

Figure: A:6

The next window appears (Figure: A:7) if you chose **Custom and Network** options in the previous window. Choose the option indicated. Click **Next** to continue.

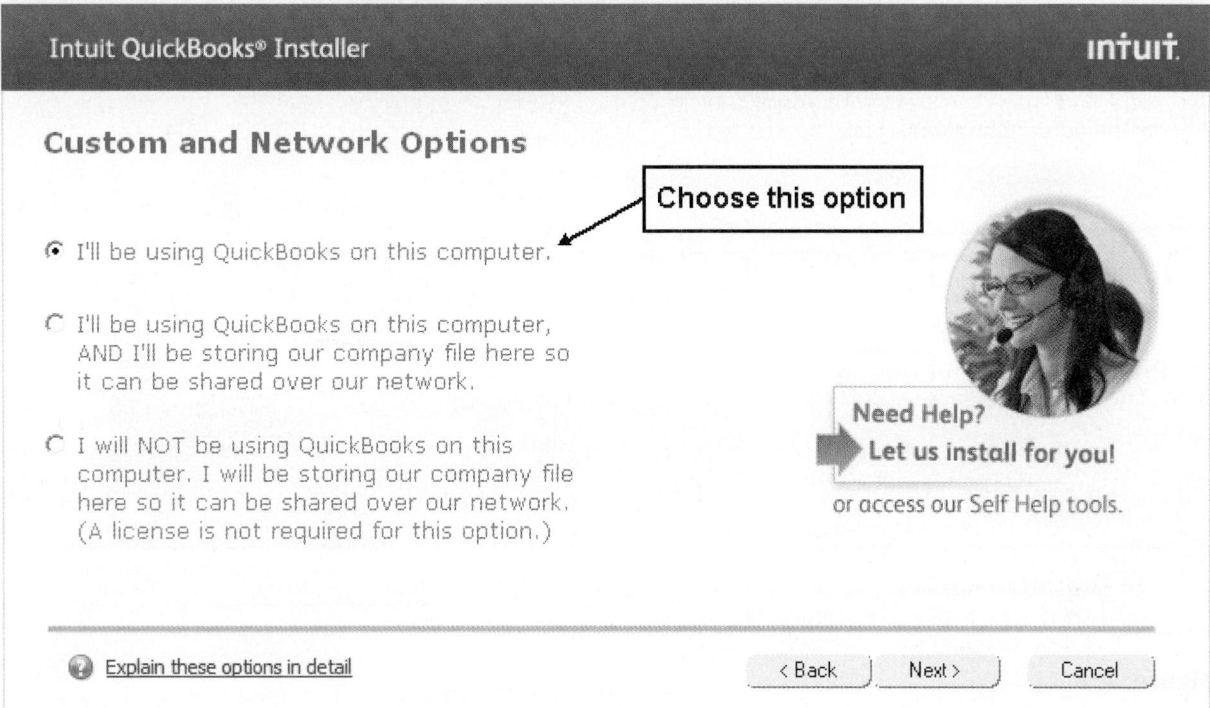

Figure: A:7

Now enter the **License Number** and **Product Number** that came with your software. (See Figure: A:8.) Click **Next.**

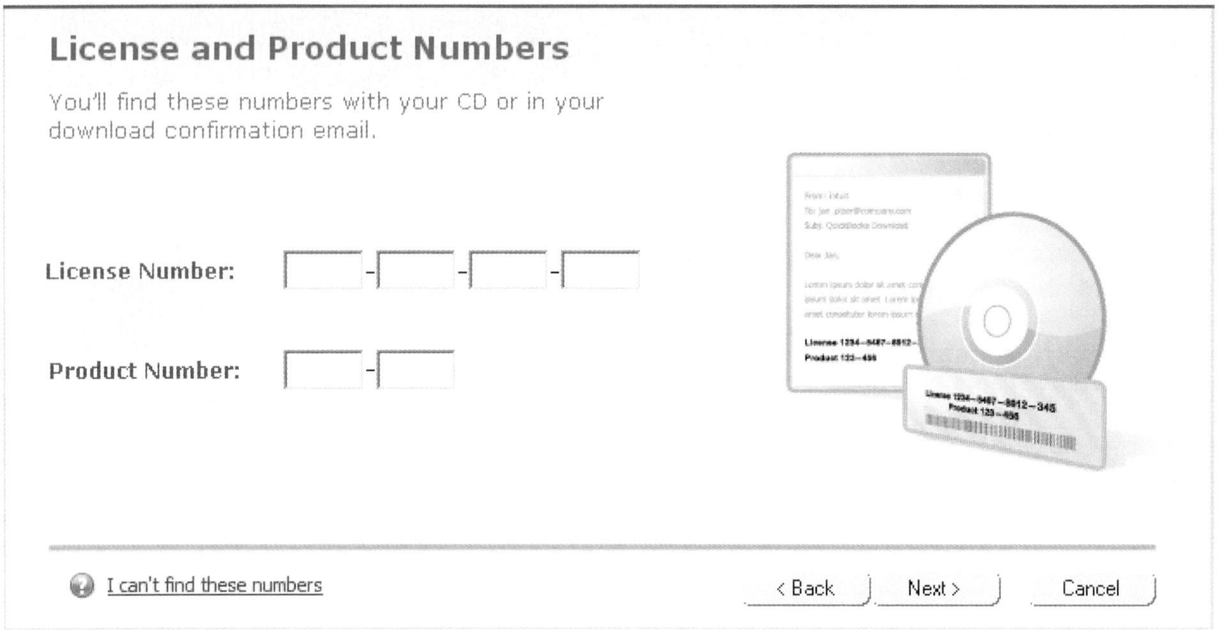

License and Product Numbers

You'll find these numbers with your CD or in your download confirmation email.

License Number: - - -

Product Number: -

I can't find these numbers

< Back Next > Cancel

Figure: A:8

The next window (Figure: A:9) appears if you chose **Custom and Network** options. It allows you to change the install location. Enter the path shown. Click **Next.**

Figure: A:9

The next window (Figure: A:10) confirms your selections and explains that installation may take up to twenty minutes. Click **Install** to begin.

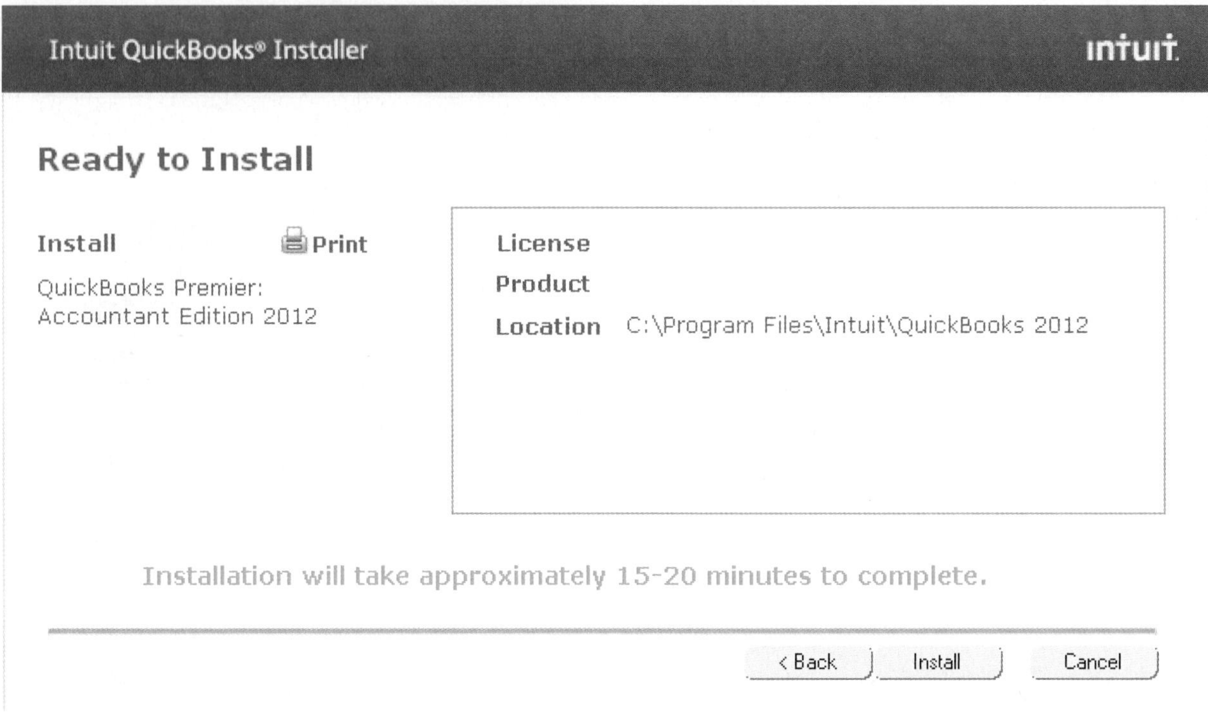

Figure: A:10

You have completed installation when the next window opens. (See Figure: A:11.)

Deselect the options indicated and click **Finish.** You may need to reboot your computer.

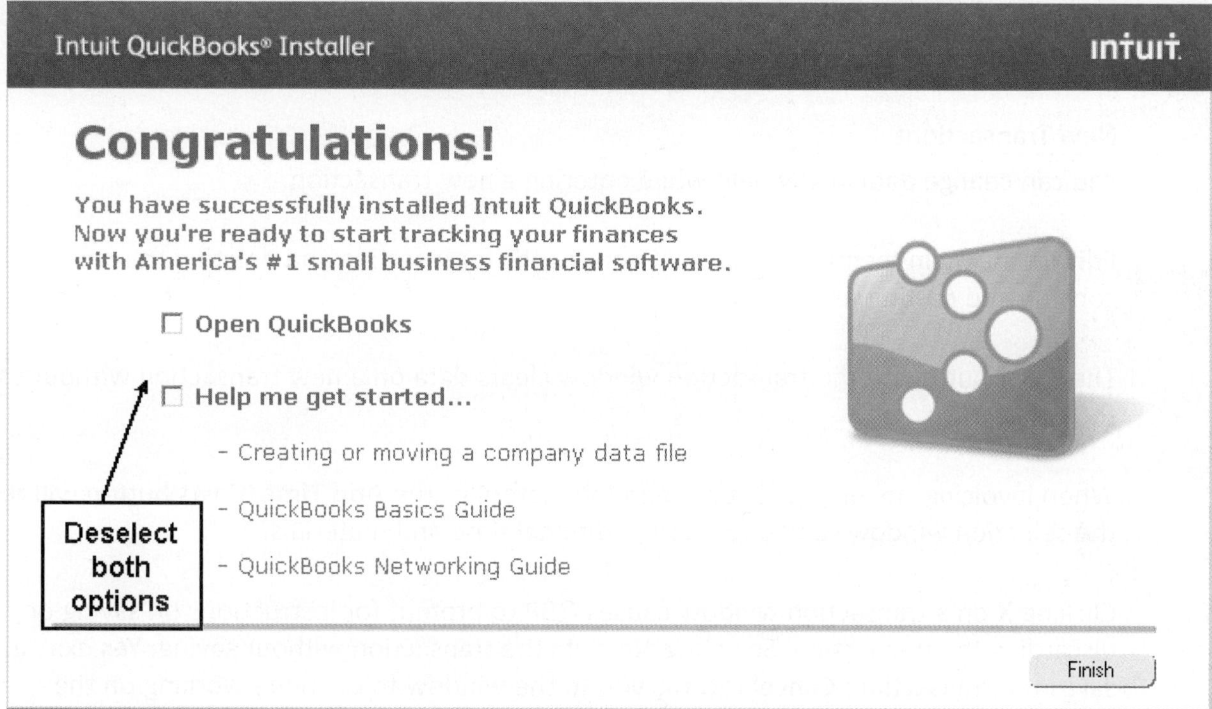

Figure A:11

Remove the software CD from the drive and store it in a safe place. Return to Chapter 1 to load the sample company data files into QuickBooks.

APPENDIX B CORRECTING TRANSACTIONS

The information in this topic appears throughout the text and is repeated here to provide a central location for locating instructions on correcting transactions.

New Transactions

You can change data in any field while entering a new transaction.

Edit on the main menu accesses data commands for inserting and deleting transaction lines or copying and pasting text.

The **Clear** button on the transaction window clears data on a new transaction without saving the transaction.

When invoicing customers for time and job materials, the **Add Time/Costs** button will reopen the selection window so you can add additional time and materials.

Clicking **X** on a transaction window causes QBP to prompt for instructions on saving or discarding the transaction. Selecting **No** exits the transaction without saving; **Yes** exits and saves the transaction; **Cancel** returns you to the window to continue working on the transaction.

Posted Transactions

Although the software will let you change and delete a saved transaction, you must be careful when altering posted transactions that have interacted with other transactions, such as changing a customer invoice that has been paid. The transaction categories below guide you on correcting posted transactions.

- Sales Invoices

  You can modify, delete, or void a posted sales invoice ***as long as you have not posted a customer payment against the invoice.*** The first step is locating the posted invoice. This is done by opening the Customer Center and locating the invoice on the customer account. You then double click to reopen.

  After reopening you can modify, delete, or void the invoice. When modifying you repost the transaction by clicking **Save & Close.** Invoices are deleted by selecting ***Edit>>Delete Invoice*** on the main menu. You void an invoice by selecting ***Edit>>Void Invoice*** on the main menu and then clicking **Save & Close.**

  When the posted invoice involves employee time or job materials, deleting or voiding the invoice will not reinstate hours or materials. This means that you cannot reuse previously invoiced employee timesheets or vendor bills to reinvoice the customer.

Before deleting or voiding an invoice of this nature, print the invoice to use as a reference for reinvoicing the customer.

After posting a customer payment against an invoice you should not alter the invoice without first deleting or voiding the customer payment. (Caution: Read the instructions that follow before deleting a customer payment.)

❖ Customer Payments

You can modify or delete a posted customer payment by opening the payment on the customer account. You can use Edit on the main menu to delete the payment.

Modifying or deleting a transaction appearing on a reconciled bank account will alter the reconciliation report. QBP will warn you prior to making such changes. To track changes made to a reconciled bank account, print the ***Reports>>Banking>> Reconciliation Discrepancy*** report.

❖ Purchase Orders

Purchase orders do not post so these transactions do not interact with other vendor transactions ***until after you apply a vendor bill or receipt to the PO.*** You can modify or delete a PO after locating the transaction on a vendor account. Use the Vendor Center to locate the transaction. You then double click to reopen the transaction.

POs are deleted by selecting ***Edit>>Delete Purchase Order*** on the main menu.

After receiving all items on a PO, the PO's status changes to **Closed PO** and you cannot make changes to the transaction without first deleting the vendor transaction used to receive the items. *(Caution: Read the topic that follows before deleting a posted vendor bill or receipt.)* After deleting the vendor transaction, the PO status will be reinstated to open and you can make changes or delete the PO. If you receive all items or only some items on the PO then only those items are closed to editing.

❖ Vendor Bills and Receipts

Vendor receipts can be changed, deleted, and voided. Vendor bills can also be changed, deleted, and voided ***as long as you have not paid the bill.*** Locate the vendor bill or receipt on the vendor account using the Vendor Center and then double click to reopen. To delete or void, select the appropriate command on the Edit menu.

After paying a vendor bill, you should not change, delete, or void it without first deleting or voiding the vendor payment. (Caution: Read the topic that follows before deleting a vendor payment.) After deleting or voiding a payment, the bill will be reinstated so you can repay the vendor.

❖ Vendor Payments

You can change, delete, or void a vendor's check by using the Vendor Center to locate the transaction on the vendor account. Double click to reopen the transaction and then select the appropriate command from the Edit menu. In the real world, checks that have been printed are not changed because altering data does not affect the printed check. After voiding, you can reselect the vendor bill to print a new check.

If you select the wrong vendor bills to pay but have not printed the checks then you can delete the unprinted checks by opening them under the Bill Payments section of the Vendor center. You can then return to selecting bills to pay.

Modifying, voiding or deleting a check on a reconciled bank account will alter the reconciliation report. QBP will warn you prior to making such changes. To track changes to a reconciled bank account, print the ***Reports>>Banking>>Reconciliation Discrepancy*** report.

- Employee Time and Paychecks

  You can correct employee timesheets ***as long as you have not paid employees for the time.*** After paying the employee for recorded time, you must void the paycheck to release the time. Timesheets are changed by clicking the Enter Time icon to reopen the Weekly Timesheet window and then scrolling to the week containing the error.

  If you find an error prior to printing paychecks and are still in the Confirmation and Next Steps window, click Close to exit the window and then reopen the window. Select the same pay ending date and then click Find Existing Paychecks. QBP will open the Edit/Void Paychecks window for you to double click an employee check to open it for changes. After entering changes, click Save & Close. You are then returned to the Edit/Void Paychecks window. Reopen any listed paycheck and then click the dropdown menu for Print to select Print Batch for printing the paychecks.

  If you find an error after printing paychecks, void the check by selecting ***Employees>>Edit/Void Paychecks*** on the main menu. Enter the check date, highlight the check with errors, and click Void. To reissue the paycheck, click Pay Employees and complete the window by entering the pay period end date and check date. If you voided a paycheck for an hourly paid employee, then reenter pay period hours. (Note: QBP will not repay previously paid timesheet hours.) Click the employee's name to reopen paycheck data. Reenter the data and then complete the steps that print the paycheck.

- General Journal Entries

  You can change, delete, or void general journal entries by reopening the entry, Entries are voided or deleted by selecting the appropriate command from the Edit menu.

APPENDIX C BACKING UP AND RESTORING DATA FILES

For your convenience, the instructions for backing up and restoring company data files from Chapter 1 are repeated below. You will also find the instructions for creating and restoring a portable backup file. Portable backup files are used if you need to reduce a backup file size to fit on a removable storage device but these files store only financial data, not related data such as customized templates.

All instructions assume that you are either backing up or restoring the **QB2012_Chp1_Stud** data file.

Regular Backup and Restore Procedures

❖ ***Backup Step 1***

Click the **Backup** icon on the Icon bar to open the window illustrated in Figure: C.1. *(Note: You can also choose File>>Create Backup on the main menu, but the window that opens will not begin at the next illustration.)* Choose the option shown and click **Next.**

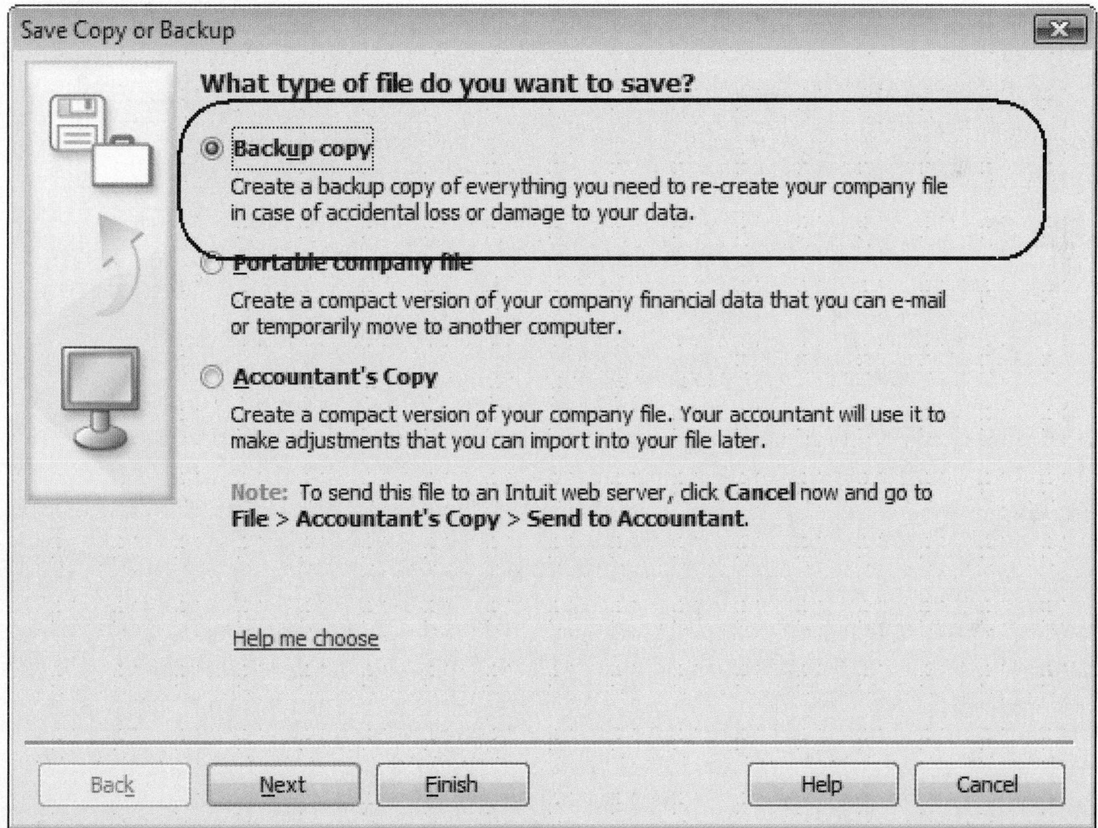

Figure: C:1

❖ ***Backup Step 2***

On the screen illustrated in Figure: C:2, select **Local backup.**

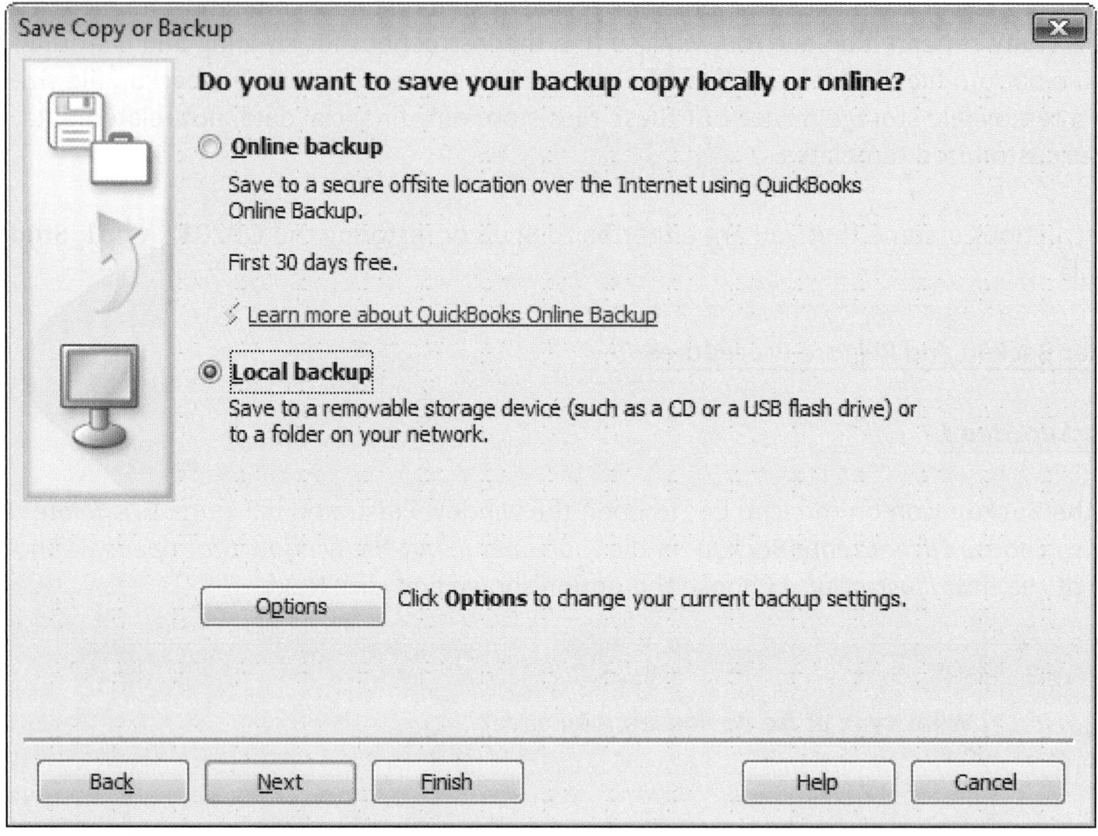

Figure: C:2

❖ *Backup Step 3*

Click **Options** to set options for storing the backup (Figure: C:3).

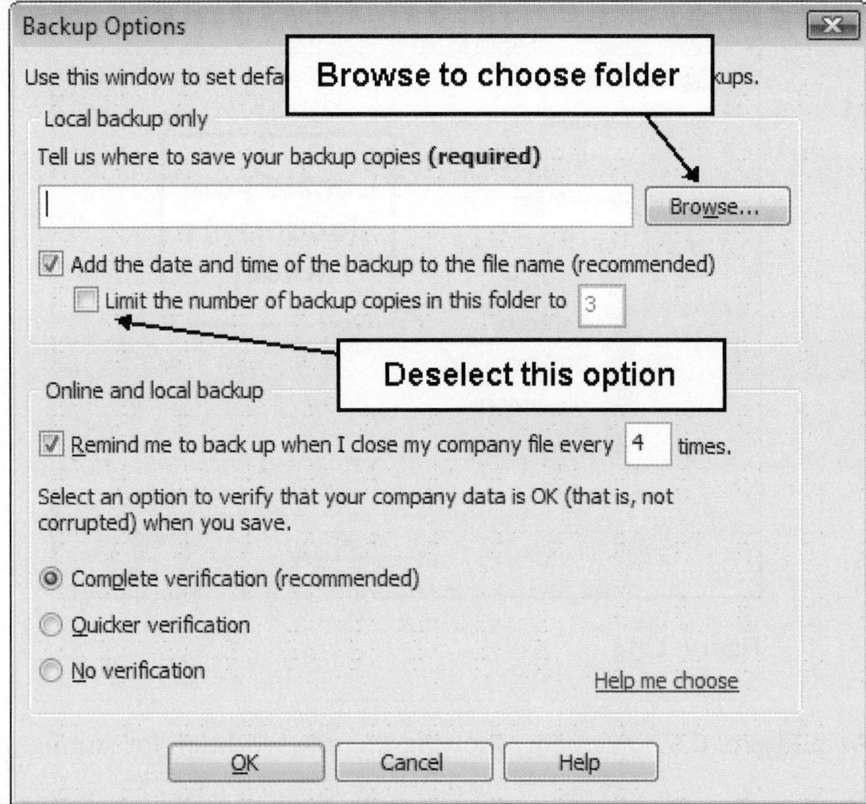

Figure: C:3

Click **Browse** to choose a path for storing the backup file. To make it easy to locate the file in the future, select the **Documents** or **My Documents** folder, depending on your operating system. (See Figure: C:4.) Click **OK.**

Note: You can also select the drive labeled CD-RW Drive. You can also select a USB drive, which is normally labeled "E." However, when storing backups to these devices you may need to use the instructions in Appendix C and create a portable backup to reduce the backup file size.

Figure: C:4

The window in Figure: C:5 now opens, showing the exact location for storing the backup file.

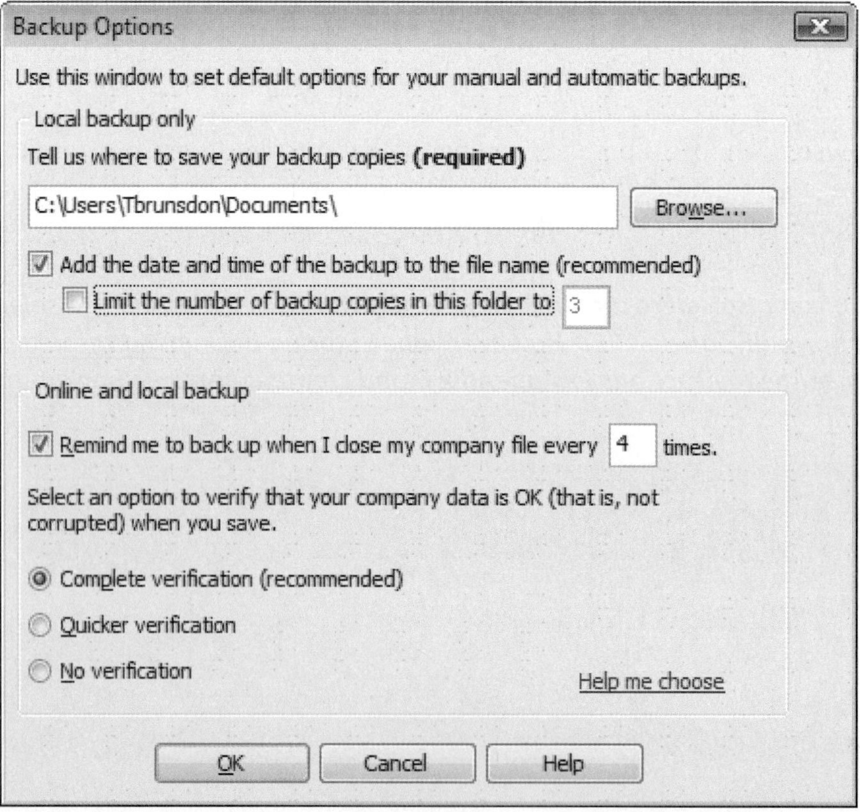

Figure: C:5

Click **OK** and you are prompted to change the location (Figure: C:6). Click **Use this location.**

Figure: C:6

❖ ***Backup Step 4***

Click **Next**, select **Save it now** (Figure: C:7), and click **Next.**

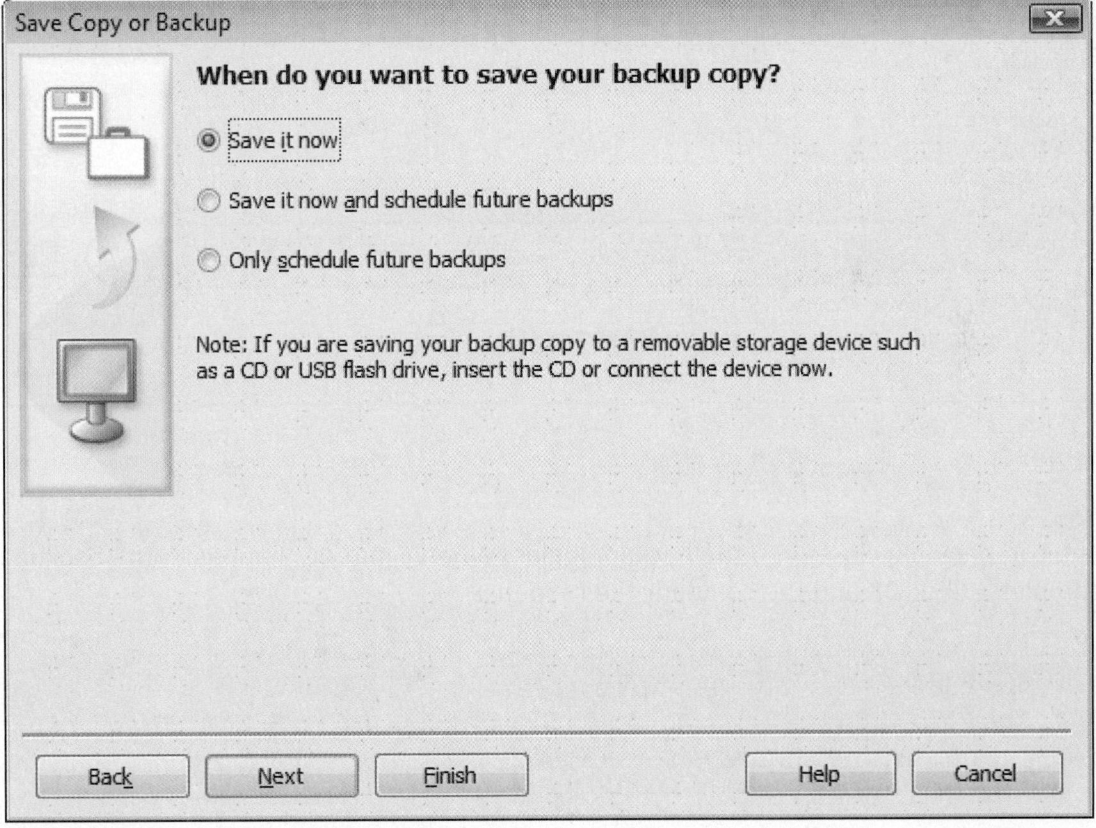

Figure: C:7

❖ *Backup Step 5*

We suggest replacing the date portion of the backup file name with an extension that identifies the point where you stopped working in the file. This example assumes you have finished a chapter. Therefore, in the window illustrated in Figure: C:8, the **File name** is changed to QB2012_Chp1_Stud_Completed. After entering a file name, click **Save.** *(Note: QBP adds the QBB extension to a backup file name.)*

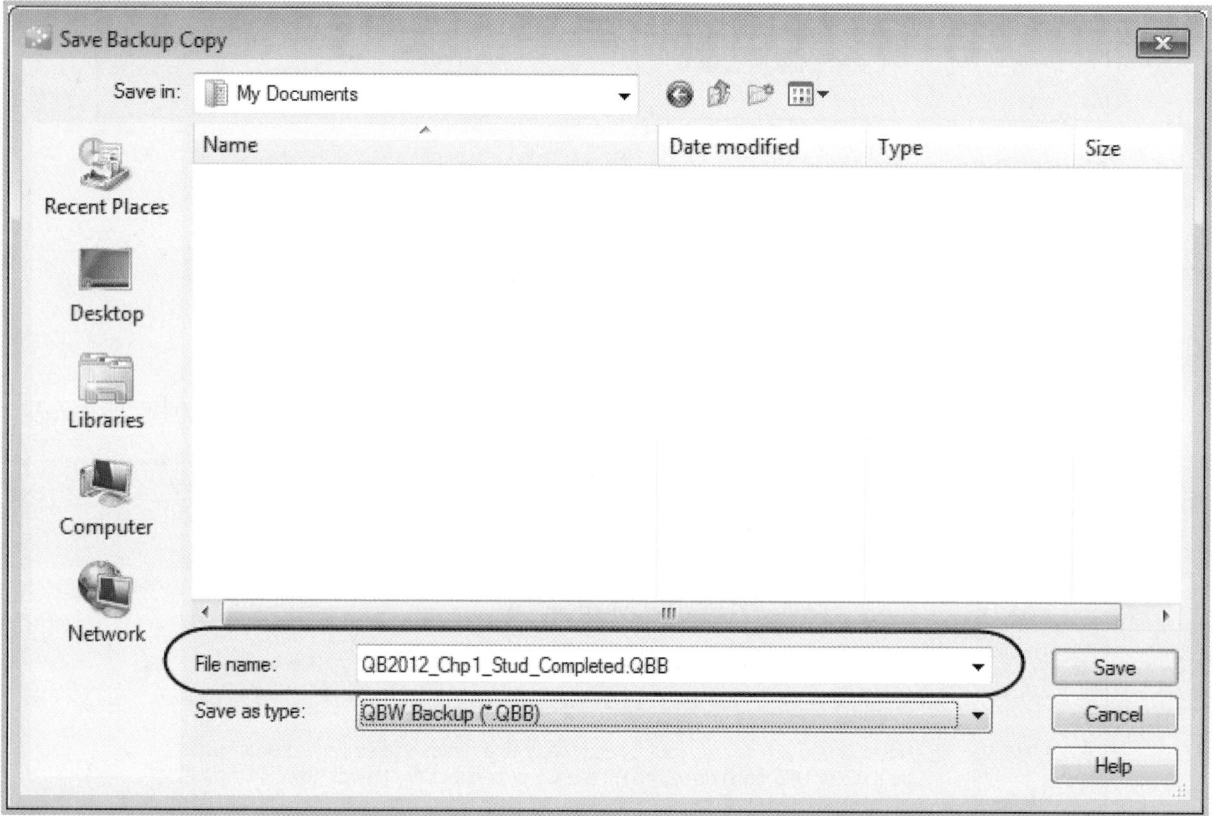

Figure: C:8

The company file closes and the backup begins. When Figure: C:9 appears, the backup is complete. Click **OK** and the company file reopens.

Figure: C:9

❖ ***Restore Step 1***

Note: You cannot restore previous work unless you have created a backup file; however, you can always return to using the original data files downloaded from the textbook's Website.

Note: Restoring a backup file overwrites all existing data. Therefore, you should backup existing data using a unique filename before restoring a backup file.

Open the company to be restored by selecting ***File>>Open or Restore Company*** on the main menu. *(Note: You can actually open any company file.)* Choose the option illustrated in Figure: C:10 and click **Next.**

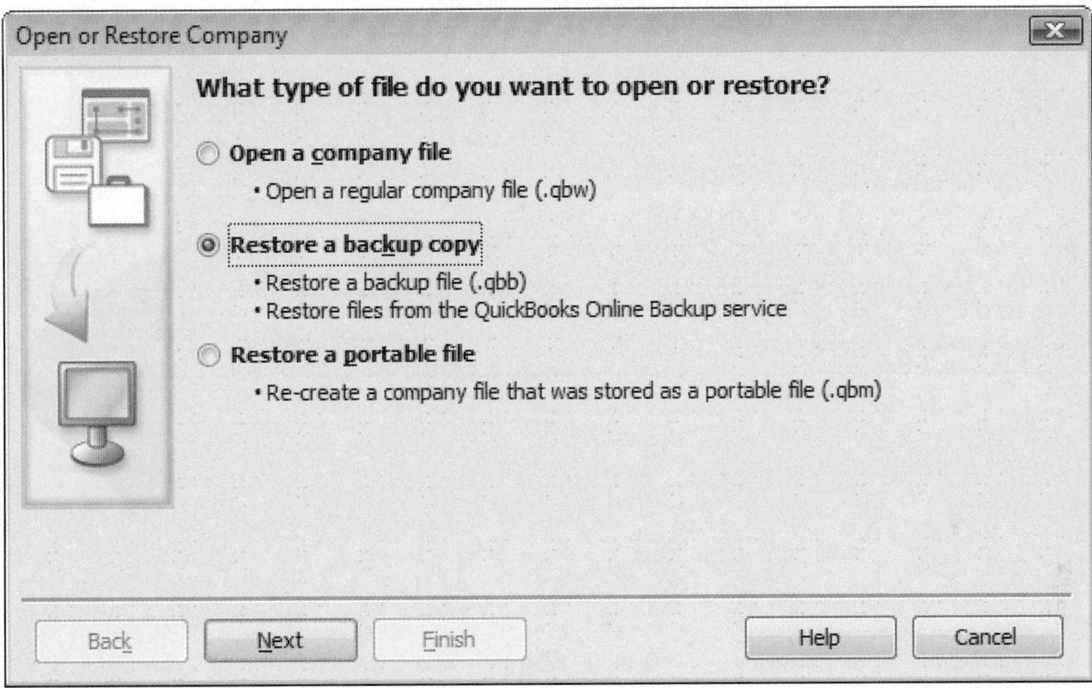

Figure: C:10

❖ *Restore Step 2*

Select **Local backup** and click **Next** (Figure: C:11).

Figure: C:11

❖ ***Restore Step 3***

Highlight the backup file name and click **Open** (Figure: C:12).

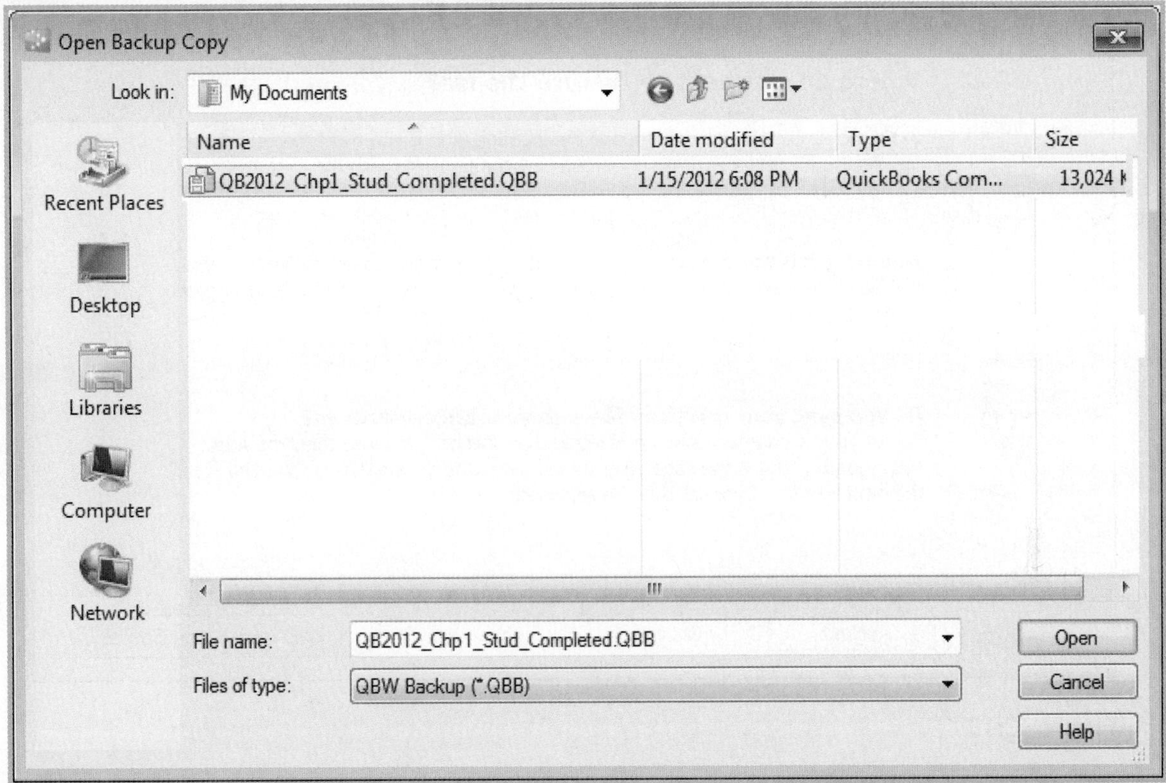

Figure: C:12

❖ *Restore Step 4*

On the window illustrated in Figure: C:13 click **Next.**

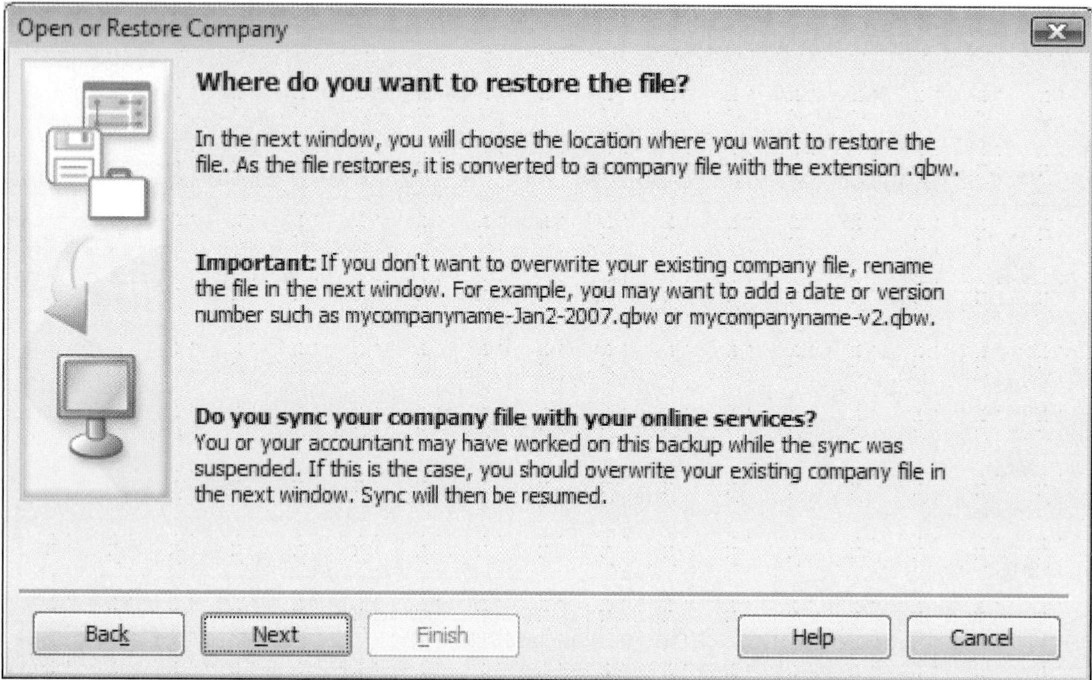

Figure: C:13

In the window that opens (not illustrated) highlight **QB2012_Chp1_Stud** and click **Save.** When QBP warns that the file already exists, click **Yes** to replace it.

The company closes and opens a confirmation screen to delete existing data by restoring data from the backup file (Figure: C:14). Type "YES" in all caps and click **OK.**

Delete Entire File

Caution! You are about to permanently delete this data file. Are you sure?

Type 'YES' to confirm. YES

OK

Cancel

Figure: C:14

Click **OK** when QBP prompts and the company reopens.

Creating Portable Backup Files and Restoring These Files

If you are using a USB or CD drive, you may need to create a portable backup file of your company. Portable backup files are small enough to fit on a removable storage device because they store only financial data, not related files like templates. The following provides the steps for creating and restoring a portable backup file.

Be aware that portable backups do not fully protect company data so you should still create regular backup files.

❖ *Portable Backup Step 1*

Click the **Backup** icon on the Icon Bar and in the window that opens (Figure: C:15), choose the option shown and click **Next.** *(Note: You must use the Backup icon to open the window illustrated.)*

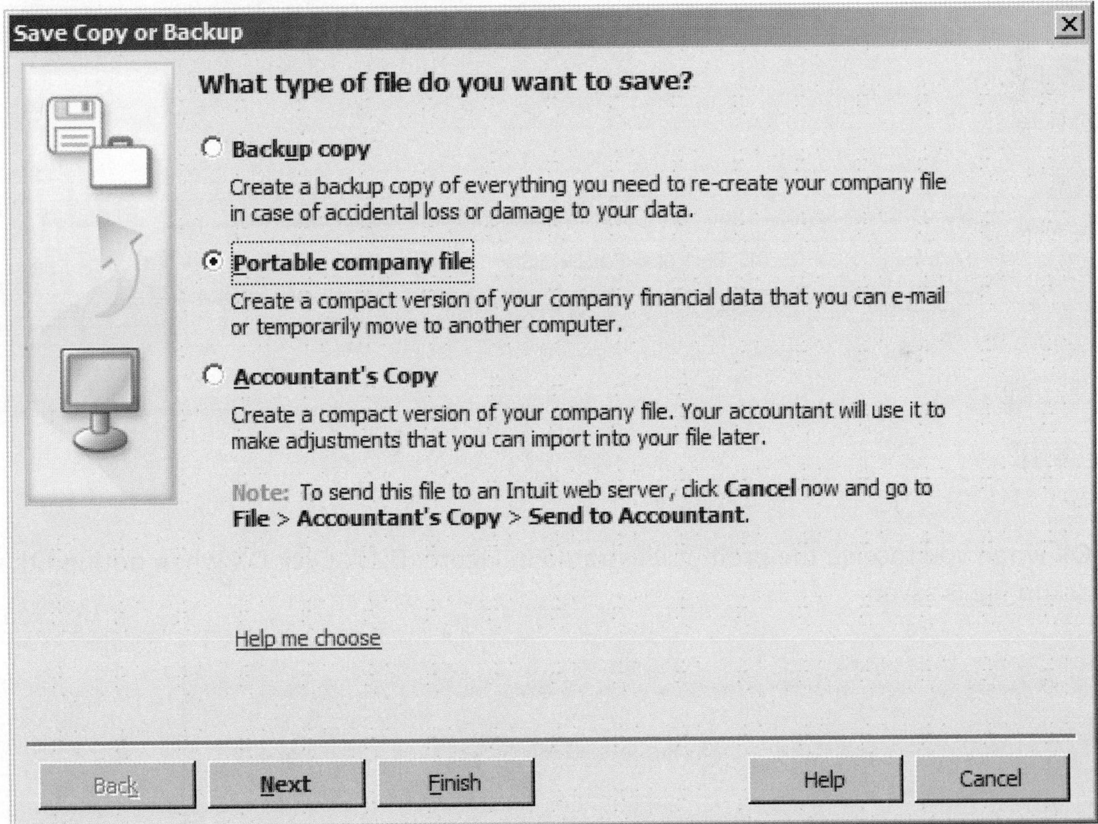

Figure: C:15

❖ ***Portable Backup Step 2***

Set the path for storing the backup file by using the **Save in** dropdown list, enter a name for the backup file, and click **Save** (Figure: C:16). *Note that QBP assigns QBM as the file extension for a portable backup file.*

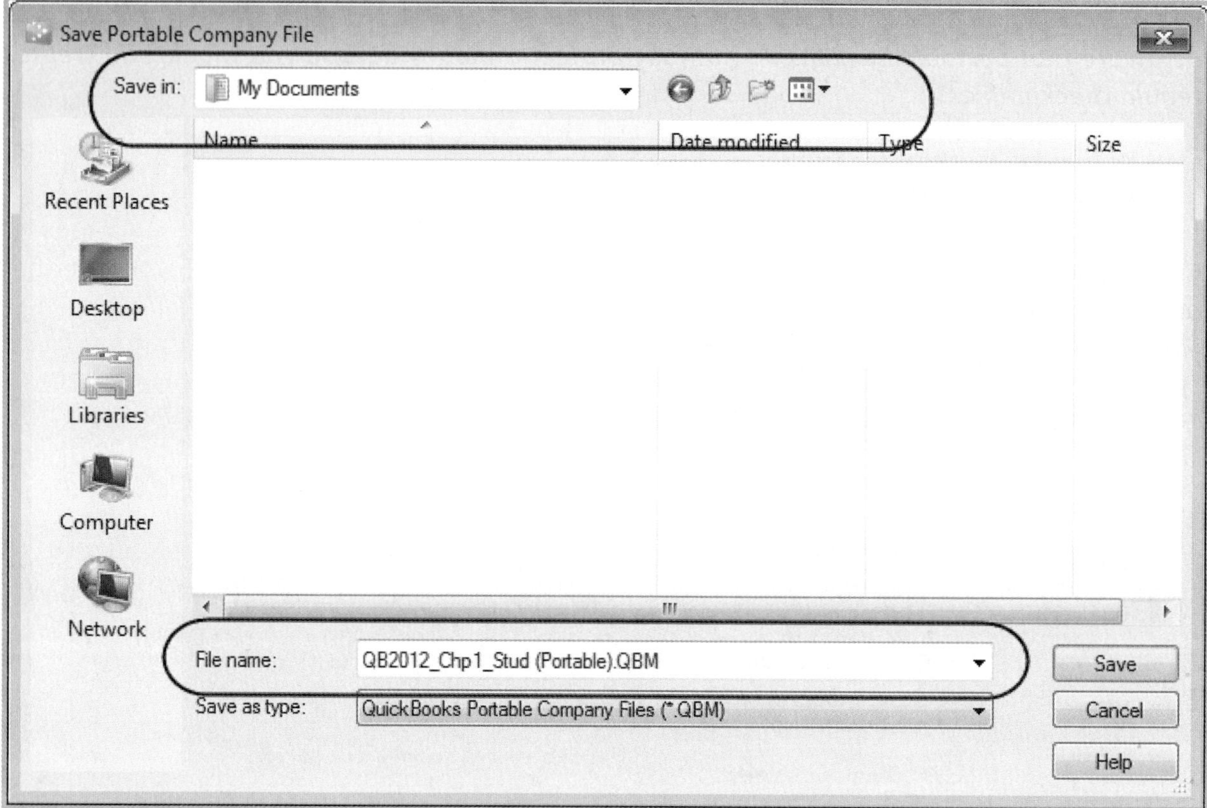

Figure: C:16

Click **OK** when you receive the prompt illustrated in Figure: C:17. Click **OK** when notified that the backup file is saved.

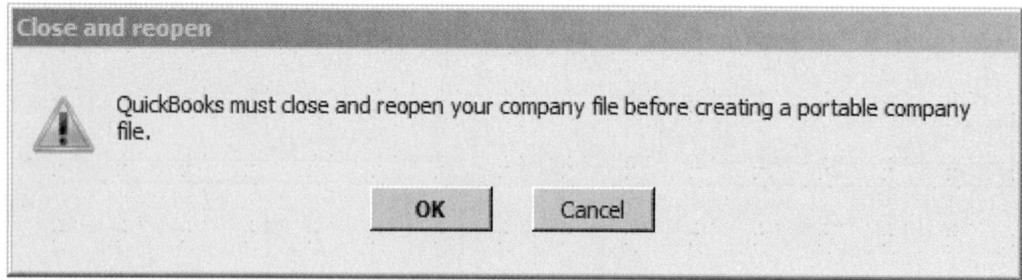

Figure: C:17

❖ ***Restore Portable Backup Step 1***

Open the company to restore. In this example, it is **QB2012_Chp1_Stud**. Click ***File>>Open or Restore Company*** on the main menu. Select the option illustrated in Figure: C:18 and click **Next**.

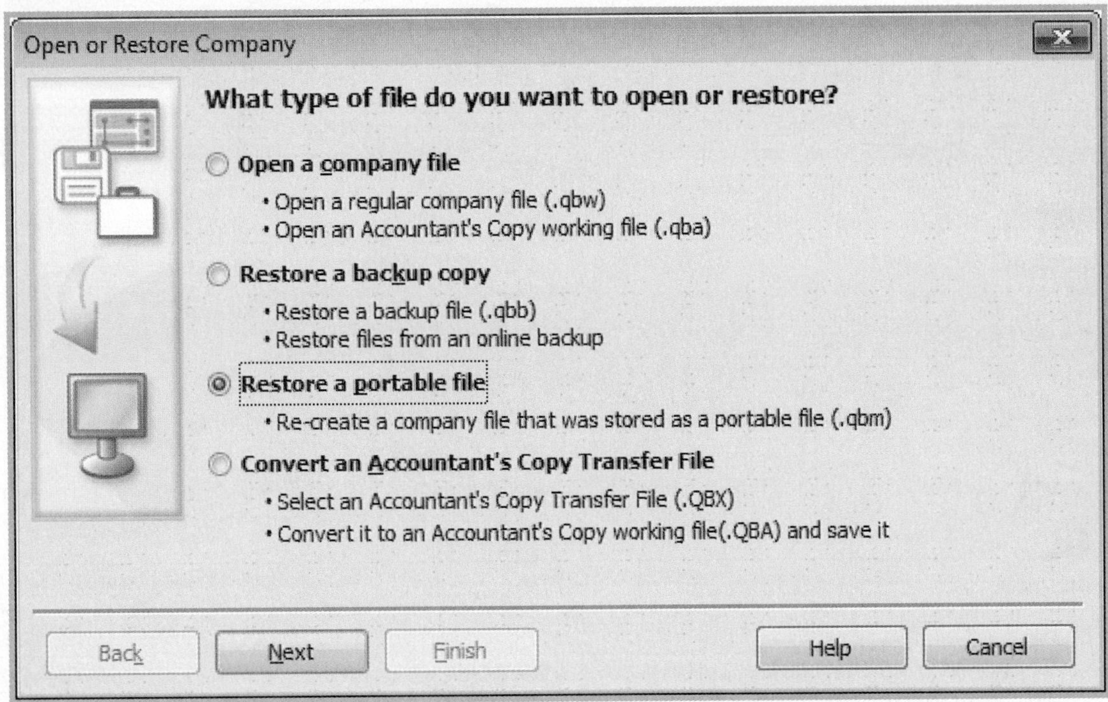

Figure: C:18

❖ ***Restore Portable Backup Step 2***

In the window illustrated in Figure: C:19, highlight the backup file and click **Open**. *(Note: The file name must have a QBM extension.)*

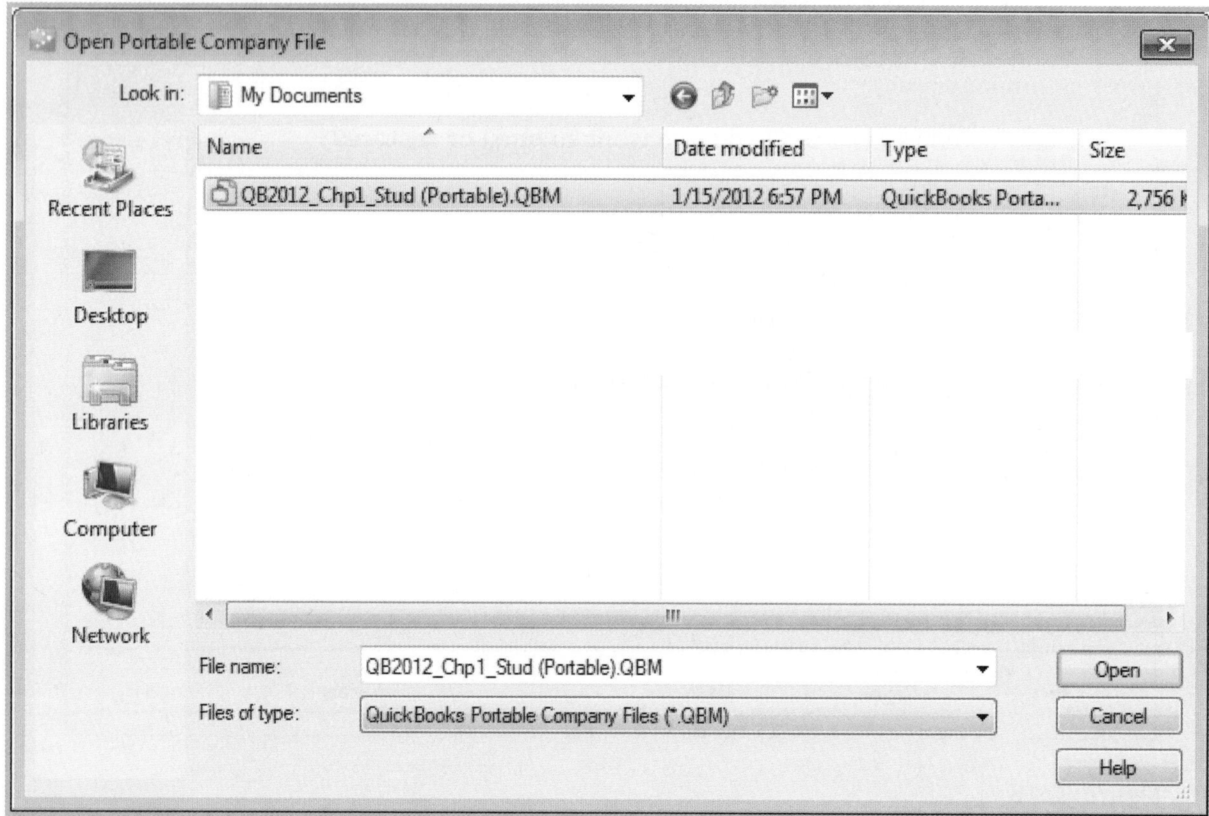

Figure: C:19

❖ *Restore Portable Backup Step 3*

In the window illustrated in Figure: C:20, click **Next.**

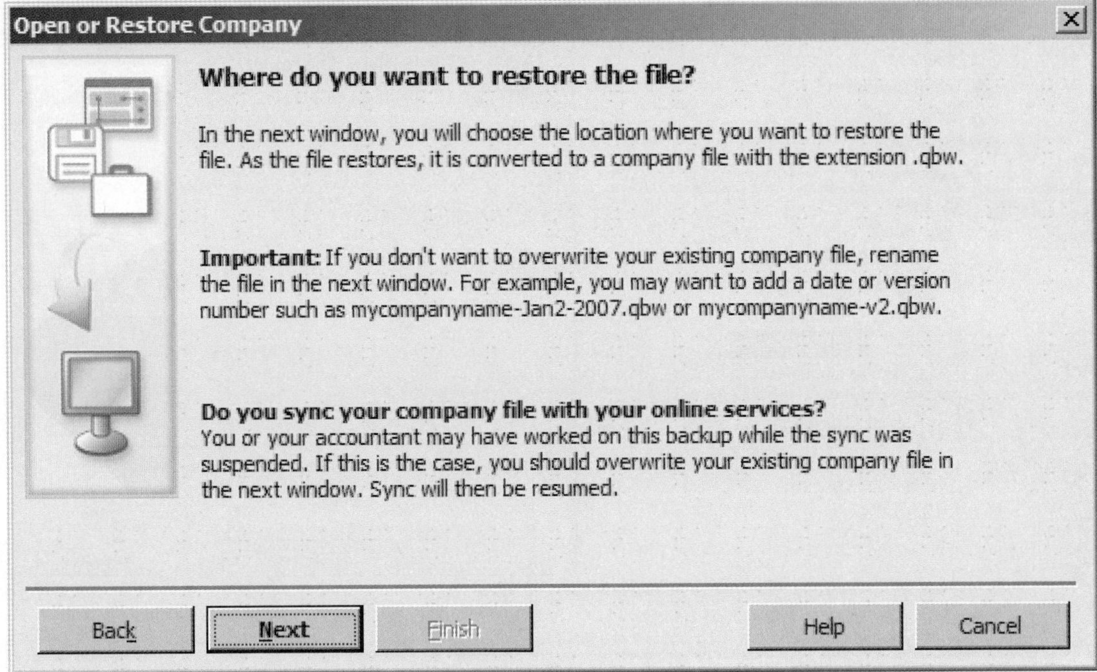

Figure: C:20

❖ *Restore Portable Backup Step 4*

In the window that opens (Figure: C:21), set the **Save in** location to the folder location you used to install the data files.

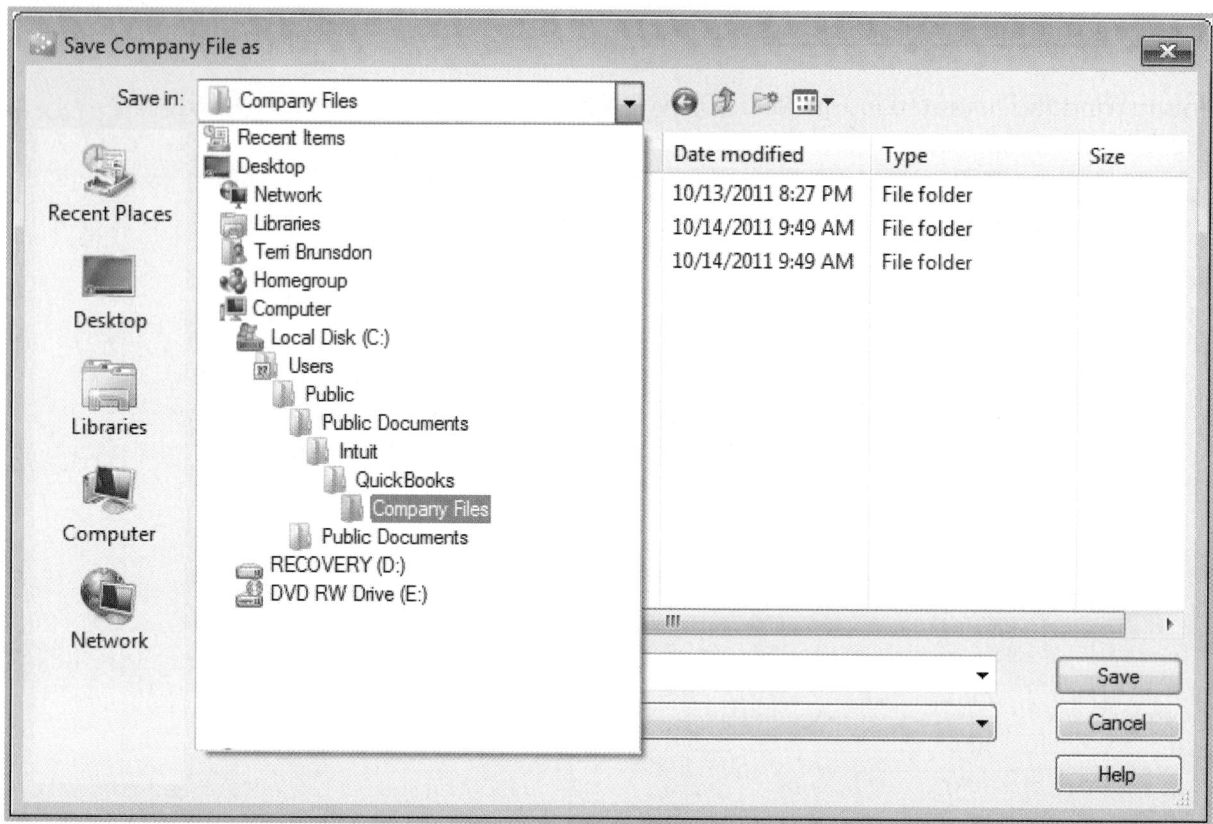

Figure: C:21

Highlight the **QB2012_Chp1_Stud** file and click **Save.** When QBP warns that the file already exists, click **Yes** to replace it.

The company closes and QBP opens the window in Figure: C:22. Type **YES** in all caps and then click **OK.**

Delete Entire File

Caution! You are about to permanently delete this data file. Are you sure?

Type 'YES' to confirm. YES

OK

Cancel

Figure: C:22

Moving Data Between Home and School

You can use the regular backup and restore procedures or the portable backup and restore procedures to move your data files between home and school by following the next steps.

1. On the current machine, open each company to be moved and follow the steps for creating a regular backup or portable backup file. Remember to set the path for saving the file to your USB or CD drive.

2. On the second machine, follow the steps for restoring a regular backup file or a portable backup file. Open the file from your USB or CD drive and restore it to the second machine, making sure to select the correct the company name that you are restoring.

APPENDIX D IRS CIRCULAR E TAX TABLES

The payroll tax withholding tables used in the text begin on the next page. These tables are for instructional purposes only and are excerpted from the Internal Revenue Service's Circular E publication, which is updated annually. To obtain a current edition of this publication, visit www.irs.gov.

SINGLE Persons—BIWEEKLY Payroll Period

(For Wages Paid in)

If the wages are–		And the number of withholding allowances claimed is—										
At least	But less than	0	1	2	3	4	5	6	7	8	9	10
		The amount of income tax to be withheld is—										
$0	$105	$0	$0	$0	$0	$0	$0	$0	$0	$0	$0	$0
105	110	1	0	0	0	0	0	0	0	0	0	0
110	115	1	0	0	0	0	0	0	0	0	0	0
115	120	2	0	0	0	0	0	0	0	0	0	0
120	125	2	0	0	0	0	0	0	0	0	0	0
125	130	3	0	0	0	0	0	0	0	0	0	0
130	135	3	0	0	0	0	0	0	0	0	0	0
135	140	4	0	0	0	0	0	0	0	0	0	0
140	145	4	0	0	0	0	0	0	0	0	0	0
145	150	5	0	0	0	0	0	0	0	0	0	0
150	155	5	0	0	0	0	0	0	0	0	0	0
155	160	6	0	0	0	0	0	0	0	0	0	0
160	165	6	0	0	0	0	0	0	0	0	0	0
165	170	7	0	0	0	0	0	0	0	0	0	0
170	175	7	0	0	0	0	0	0	0	0	0	0
175	180	8	0	0	0	0	0	0	0	0	0	0
180	185	8	0	0	0	0	0	0	0	0	0	0
185	190	9	0	0	0	0	0	0	0	0	0	0
190	195	9	0	0	0	0	0	0	0	0	0	0
195	200	10	0	0	0	0	0	0	0	0	0	0
200	205	10	0	0	0	0	0	0	0	0	0	0
205	210	11	0	0	0	0	0	0	0	0	0	0
210	215	11	0	0	0	0	0	0	0	0	0	0
215	220	12	0	0	0	0	0	0	0	0	0	0
220	225	12	0	0	0	0	0	0	0	0	0	0
225	230	13	0	0	0	0	0	0	0	0	0	0
230	235	13	0	0	0	0	0	0	0	0	0	0
235	240	14	0	0	0	0	0	0	0	0	0	0
240	245	14	1	0	0	0	0	0	0	0	0	0
245	250	15	1	0	0	0	0	0	0	0	0	0
250	260	15	2	0	0	0	0	0	0	0	0	0
260	270	16	3	0	0	0	0	0	0	0	0	0
270	280	17	4	0	0	0	0	0	0	0	0	0
280	290	18	5	0	0	0	0	0	0	0	0	0
290	300	19	6	0	0	0	0	0	0	0	0	0
300	310	20	7	0	0	0	0	0	0	0	0	0
310	320	21	8	0	0	0	0	0	0	0	0	0
320	330	22	9	0	0	0	0	0	0	0	0	0
330	340	23	10	0	0	0	0	0	0	0	0	0
340	350	24	11	0	0	0	0	0	0	0	0	0
350	360	25	12	0	0	0	0	0	0	0	0	0
360	370	26	13	0	0	0	0	0	0	0	0	0
370	380	27	14	0	0	0	0	0	0	0	0	0
380	390	28	15	1	0	0	0	0	0	0	0	0
390	400	29	16	2	0	0	0	0	0	0	0	0
400	410	31	17	3	0	0	0	0	0	0	0	0
410	420	32	18	4	0	0	0	0	0	0	0	0
420	430	34	19	5	0	0	0	0	0	0	0	0
430	440	35	20	6	0	0	0	0	0	0	0	0
440	450	37	21	7	0	0	0	0	0	0	0	0
450	460	38	22	8	0	0	0	0	0	0	0	0
460	470	40	23	9	0	0	0	0	0	0	0	0
470	480	41	24	10	0	0	0	0	0	0	0	0
480	490	43	25	11	0	0	0	0	0	0	0	0
490	500	44	26	12	0	0	0	0	0	0	0	0
500	520	47	27	14	0	0	0	0	0	0	0	0
520	540	50	29	16	2	0	0	0	0	0	0	0
540	560	53	32	18	4	0	0	0	0	0	0	0
560	580	56	35	20	6	0	0	0	0	0	0	0
580	600	59	38	22	8	0	0	0	0	0	0	0
600	620	62	41	24	10	0	0	0	0	0	0	0
620	640	65	44	26	12	0	0	0	0	0	0	0
640	660	68	47	28	14	1	0	0	0	0	0	0
660	680	71	50	30	16	3	0	0	0	0	0	0
680	700	74	53	33	18	5	0	0	0	0	0	0
700	720	77	56	36	20	7	0	0	0	0	0	0
720	740	80	59	39	22	9	0	0	0	0	0	0
740	760	83	62	42	24	11	0	0	0	0	0	0
760	780	86	65	45	26	13	0	0	0	0	0	0
780	800	89	68	48	28	15	2	0	0	0	0	0

SINGLE Persons—BIWEEKLY Payroll Period

(For Wages Paid in)

If the wages are–		And the number of withholding allowances claimed is—										
At least	But less than	0	1	2	3	4	5	6	7	8	9	10
		The amount of income tax to be withheld is—										
$800	$820	$92	$71	$51	$31	$17	$4	$0	$0	$0	$0	$0
820	840	95	74	54	34	19	6	0	0	0	0	0
840	860	98	77	57	37	21	8	0	0	0	0	0
860	880	101	80	60	40	23	10	0	0	0	0	0
880	900	104	83	63	43	25	12	0	0	0	0	0
900	920	107	86	66	46	27	14	0	0	0	0	0
920	940	110	89	69	49	29	16	2	0	0	0	0
940	960	113	92	72	52	32	18	4	0	0	0	0
960	980	116	95	75	55	35	20	6	0	0	0	0
980	1,000	119	98	78	58	38	22	8	0	0	0	0
1,000	1,020	122	101	81	61	41	24	10	0	0	0	0
1,020	1,040	125	104	84	64	44	26	12	0	0	0	0
1,040	1,060	128	107	87	67	47	28	14	1	0	0	0
1,060	1,080	131	110	90	70	50	30	16	3	0	0	0
1,080	1,100	134	113	93	73	53	33	18	5	0	0	0
1,100	1,120	137	116	96	76	56	36	20	7	0	0	0
1,120	1,140	140	119	99	79	59	39	22	9	0	0	0
1,140	1,160	143	122	102	82	62	42	24	11	0	0	0
1,160	1,180	146	125	105	85	65	45	26	13	0	0	0
1,180	1,200	149	128	108	88	68	48	28	15	1	0	0
1,200	1,220	152	131	111	91	71	51	30	17	3	0	0
1,220	1,240	155	134	114	94	74	54	33	19	5	0	0
1,240	1,260	158	137	117	97	77	57	36	21	7	0	0
1,260	1,280	161	140	120	100	80	60	39	23	9	0	0
1,280	1,300	164	143	123	103	83	63	42	25	11	0	0
1,300	1,320	167	146	126	106	86	66	45	27	13	0	0
1,320	1,340	172	149	129	109	89	69	48	29	15	2	0
1,340	1,360	177	152	132	112	92	72	51	31	17	4	0
1,360	1,380	182	155	135	115	95	75	54	34	19	6	0
1,380	1,400	187	158	138	118	98	78	57	37	21	8	0
1,400	1,420	192	161	141	121	101	81	60	40	23	10	0
1,420	1,440	197	164	144	124	104	84	63	43	25	12	0
1,440	1,460	202	168	147	127	107	87	66	46	27	14	0
1,460	1,480	207	173	150	130	110	90	69	49	29	16	2
1,480	1,500	212	178	153	133	113	93	72	52	32	18	4
1,500	1,520	217	183	156	136	116	96	75	55	35	20	6
1,520	1,540	222	188	159	139	119	99	78	58	38	22	8
1,540	1,560	227	193	162	142	122	102	81	61	41	24	10
1,560	1,580	232	198	165	145	125	105	84	64	44	26	12
1,580	1,600	237	203	170	148	128	108	87	67	47	28	14
1,600	1,620	242	208	175	151	131	111	90	70	50	30	16
1,620	1,640	247	213	180	154	134	114	93	73	53	33	18
1,640	1,660	252	218	185	157	137	117	96	76	56	36	20
1,660	1,680	257	223	190	160	140	120	99	79	59	39	22
1,680	1,700	262	228	195	163	143	123	102	82	62	42	24
1,700	1,720	267	233	200	166	146	126	105	85	65	45	26
1,720	1,740	272	238	205	171	149	129	108	88	68	48	28
1,740	1,760	277	243	210	176	152	132	111	91	71	51	31
1,760	1,780	282	248	215	181	155	135	114	94	74	54	34
1,780	1,800	287	253	220	186	158	138	117	97	77	57	37
1,800	1,820	292	258	225	191	161	141	120	100	80	60	40
1,820	1,840	297	263	230	196	164	144	123	103	83	63	43
1,840	1,860	302	268	235	201	167	147	126	106	86	66	46
1,860	1,880	307	273	240	206	172	150	129	109	89	69	49
1,880	1,900	312	278	245	211	177	153	132	112	92	72	52
1,900	1,920	317	283	250	216	182	156	135	115	95	75	55
1,920	1,940	322	288	255	221	187	159	138	118	98	78	58
1,940	1,960	327	293	260	226	192	162	141	121	101	81	61
1,960	1,980	332	298	265	231	197	165	144	124	104	84	64
1,980	2,000	337	303	270	236	202	169	147	127	107	87	67
2,000	2,020	342	308	275	241	207	174	150	130	110	90	70
2,020	2,040	347	313	280	246	212	179	153	133	113	93	73
2,040	2,060	352	318	285	251	217	184	156	136	116	96	76
2,060	2,080	357	323	290	256	222	189	159	139	119	99	79
2,080	2,100	362	328	295	261	227	194	162	142	122	102	82
$2,100 and over		Use Table 2(a) for a **SINGLE person** on page 38. Also see the instructions on page 36.										

MARRIED Persons—**BIWEEKLY** Payroll Period

(For Wages Paid in)

If the wages are–		And the number of withholding allowances claimed is—										
At least	But less than	0	1	2	3	4	5	6	7	8	9	10
		The amount of income tax to be withheld is—										
$0	$250	$0	$0	$0	$0	$0	$0	$0	$0	$0	$0	$0
250	260	0	0	0	0	0	0	0	0	0	0	0
260	270	0	0	0	0	0	0	0	0	0	0	0
270	280	0	0	0	0	0	0	0	0	0	0	0
280	290	0	0	0	0	0	0	0	0	0	0	0
290	300	0	0	0	0	0	0	0	0	0	0	0
300	310	0	0	0	0	0	0	0	0	0	0	0
310	320	1	0	0	0	0	0	0	0	0	0	0
320	330	2	0	0	0	0	0	0	0	0	0	0
330	340	3	0	0	0	0	0	0	0	0	0	0
340	350	4	0	0	0	0	0	0	0	0	0	0
350	360	5	0	0	0	0	0	0	0	0	0	0
360	370	6	0	0	0	0	0	0	0	0	0	0
370	380	7	0	0	0	0	0	0	0	0	0	0
380	390	8	0	0	0	0	0	0	0	0	0	0
390	400	9	0	0	0	0	0	0	0	0	0	0
400	410	10	0	0	0	0	0	0	0	0	0	0
410	420	11	0	0	0	0	0	0	0	0	0	0
420	430	12	0	0	0	0	0	0	0	0	0	0
430	440	13	0	0	0	0	0	0	0	0	0	0
440	450	14	0	0	0	0	0	0	0	0	0	0
450	460	15	1	0	0	0	0	0	0	0	0	0
460	470	16	2	0	0	0	0	0	0	0	0	0
470	480	17	3	0	0	0	0	0	0	0	0	0
480	490	18	4	0	0	0	0	0	0	0	0	0
490	500	19	5	0	0	0	0	0	0	0	0	0
500	520	20	7	0	0	0	0	0	0	0	0	0
520	540	22	9	0	0	0	0	0	0	0	0	0
540	560	24	11	0	0	0	0	0	0	0	0	0
560	580	26	13	0	0	0	0	0	0	0	0	0
580	600	28	15	1	0	0	0	0	0	0	0	0
600	620	30	17	3	0	0	0	0	0	0	0	0
620	640	32	19	5	0	0	0	0	0	0	0	0
640	660	34	21	7	0	0	0	0	0	0	0	0
660	680	36	23	9	0	0	0	0	0	0	0	0
680	700	38	25	11	0	0	0	0	0	0	0	0
700	720	40	27	13	0	0	0	0	0	0	0	0
720	740	42	29	15	2	0	0	0	0	0	0	0
740	760	44	31	17	4	0	0	0	0	0	0	0
760	780	46	33	19	6	0	0	0	0	0	0	0
780	800	48	35	21	8	0	0	0	0	0	0	0
800	820	50	37	23	10	0	0	0	0	0	0	0
820	840	52	39	25	12	0	0	0	0	0	0	0
840	860	54	41	27	14	0	0	0	0	0	0	0
860	880	56	43	29	16	2	0	0	0	0	0	0
880	900	58	45	31	18	4	0	0	0	0	0	0
900	920	60	47	33	20	6	0	0	0	0	0	0
920	940	63	49	35	22	8	0	0	0	0	0	0
940	960	66	51	37	24	10	0	0	0	0	0	0
960	980	69	53	39	26	12	0	0	0	0	0	0
980	1,000	72	55	41	28	14	1	0	0	0	0	0
1,000	1,020	75	57	43	30	16	3	0	0	0	0	0
1,020	1,040	78	59	45	32	18	5	0	0	0	0	0
1,040	1,060	81	61	47	34	20	7	0	0	0	0	0
1,060	1,080	84	64	49	36	22	9	0	0	0	0	0
1,080	1,100	87	67	51	38	24	11	0	0	0	0	0
1,100	1,120	90	70	53	40	26	13	0	0	0	0	0
1,120	1,140	93	73	55	42	28	15	1	0	0	0	0
1,140	1,160	96	76	57	44	30	17	3	0	0	0	0
1,160	1,180	99	79	59	46	32	19	5	0	0	0	0
1,180	1,200	102	82	62	48	34	21	7	0	0	0	0
1,200	1,220	105	85	65	50	36	23	9	0	0	0	0
1,220	1,240	108	88	68	52	38	25	11	0	0	0	0
1,240	1,260	111	91	71	54	40	27	13	0	0	0	0
1,260	1,280	114	94	74	56	42	29	15	2	0	0	0
1,280	1,300	117	97	77	58	44	31	17	4	0	0	0
1,300	1,320	120	100	80	60	46	33	19	6	0	0	0
1,320	1,340	123	103	83	63	48	35	21	8	0	0	0
1,340	1,360	126	106	86	66	50	37	23	10	0	0	0
1,360	1,380	129	109	89	69	52	39	25	12	0	0	0

MARRIED Persons—BIWEEKLY Payroll Period

(For Wages Paid in)

If the wages are–		And the number of withholding allowances claimed is—										
At least	But less than	0	1	2	3	4	5	6	7	8	9	10
		The amount of income tax to be withheld is—										
$1,380	$1,400	$132	$112	$92	$72	$54	$41	$27	$14	$1	$0	$0
1,400	1,420	135	115	95	75	56	43	29	16	3	0	0
1,420	1,440	138	118	98	78	58	45	31	18	5	0	0
1,440	1,460	141	121	101	81	61	47	33	20	7	0	0
1,460	1,480	144	124	104	84	64	49	35	22	9	0	0
1,480	1,500	147	127	107	87	67	51	37	24	11	0	0
1,500	1,520	150	130	110	90	70	53	39	26	13	0	0
1,520	1,540	153	133	113	93	73	55	41	28	15	1	0
1,540	1,560	156	136	116	96	76	57	43	30	17	3	0
1,560	1,580	159	139	119	99	79	59	45	32	19	5	0
1,580	1,600	162	142	122	102	82	61	47	34	21	7	0
1,600	1,620	165	145	125	105	85	64	49	36	23	9	0
1,620	1,640	168	148	128	108	88	67	51	38	25	11	0
1,640	1,660	171	151	131	111	91	70	53	40	27	13	0
1,660	1,680	174	154	134	114	94	73	55	42	29	15	2
1,680	1,700	177	157	137	117	97	76	57	44	31	17	4
1,700	1,720	180	160	140	120	100	79	59	46	33	19	6
1,720	1,740	183	163	143	123	103	82	62	48	35	21	8
1,740	1,760	186	166	146	126	106	85	65	50	37	23	10
1,760	1,780	189	169	149	129	109	88	68	52	39	25	12
1,780	1,800	192	172	152	132	112	91	71	54	41	27	14
1,800	1,820	195	175	155	135	115	94	74	56	43	29	16
1,820	1,840	198	178	158	138	118	97	77	58	45	31	18
1,840	1,860	201	181	161	141	121	100	80	60	47	33	20
1,860	1,880	204	184	164	144	124	103	83	63	49	35	22
1,880	1,900	207	187	167	147	127	106	86	66	51	37	24
1,900	1,920	210	190	170	150	130	109	89	69	53	39	26
1,920	1,940	213	193	173	153	133	112	92	72	55	41	28
1,940	1,960	216	196	176	156	136	115	95	75	57	43	30
1,960	1,980	219	199	179	159	139	118	98	78	59	45	32
1,980	2,000	222	202	182	162	142	121	101	81	61	47	34
2,000	2,020	225	205	185	165	145	124	104	84	64	49	36
2,020	2,040	228	208	188	168	148	127	107	87	67	51	38
2,040	2,060	231	211	191	171	151	130	110	90	70	53	40
2,060	2,080	234	214	194	174	154	133	113	93	73	55	42
2,080	2,100	237	217	197	177	157	136	116	96	76	57	44
2,100	2,120	240	220	200	180	160	139	119	99	79	59	46
2,120	2,140	243	223	203	183	163	142	122	102	82	62	48
2,140	2,160	246	226	206	186	166	145	125	105	85	65	50
2,160	2,180	249	229	209	189	169	148	128	108	88	68	52
2,180	2,200	252	232	212	192	172	151	131	111	91	71	54
2,200	2,220	255	235	215	195	175	154	134	114	94	74	56
2,220	2,240	258	238	218	198	178	157	137	117	97	77	58
2,240	2,260	261	241	221	201	181	160	140	120	100	80	60
2,260	2,280	264	244	224	204	184	163	143	123	103	83	63
2,280	2,300	267	247	227	207	187	166	146	126	106	86	66
2,300	2,320	270	250	230	210	190	169	149	129	109	89	69
2,320	2,340	273	253	233	213	193	172	152	132	112	92	72
2,340	2,360	276	256	236	216	196	175	155	135	115	95	75
2,360	2,380	279	259	239	219	199	178	158	138	118	98	78
2,380	2,400	282	262	242	222	202	181	161	141	121	101	81
2,400	2,420	285	265	245	225	205	184	164	144	124	104	84
2,420	2,440	288	268	248	228	208	187	167	147	127	107	87
2,440	2,460	291	271	251	231	211	190	170	150	130	110	90
2,460	2,480	294	274	254	234	214	193	173	153	133	113	93
2,480	2,500	297	277	257	237	217	196	176	156	136	116	96
2,500	2,520	300	280	260	240	220	199	179	159	139	119	99
2,520	2,540	303	283	263	243	223	202	182	162	142	122	102
2,540	2,560	306	286	266	246	226	205	185	165	145	125	105
2,560	2,580	309	289	269	249	229	208	188	168	148	128	108
2,580	2,600	312	292	272	252	232	211	191	171	151	131	111
2,600	2,620	315	295	275	255	235	214	194	174	154	134	114
2,620	2,640	318	298	278	258	238	217	197	177	157	137	117
2,640	2,660	321	301	281	261	241	220	200	180	160	140	120
2,660	2,680	324	304	284	264	244	223	203	183	163	143	123
2,680	2,700	327	307	287	267	247	226	206	186	166	146	126
$2,700 and over		Use Table 2(b) for a **MARRIED person** on page 38. Also see the instructions on page 36.										

APPENDIX E Solutions for You Try Exercises

Chapter 1

No in-chapter exercises presented.

Chapter 2

The Chart of Accounts reports for sample companies are not illustrated.

CHAPTER 3

RECORD TEK'S JANUARY TRANSACTIONS

Journal report listing January transactions.

QB2012_Chp3_Stud
Journal
January 1 - 24, 2012

Trans #	Type	Date	Num	Name	Memo	Account	Debit	Credit
1	General Journal	01/02/2012	1		Cash sale	10100 · Regular Checking Account	1,000.00	
					Cash fees	40000 · Consulting Income		1,000.00
							1,000.00	1,000.00
2	General Journal	01/02/2012	2		Owner deposit	10100 · Regular Checking Account	5,000.00	
					Owner deposit	39006 · Owner's Contribution		5,000.00
							5,000.00	5,000.00
3	General Journal	01/03/2012	3		Check no 171	61400 · Office Supplies Expense	250.00	
					Check no 171	10100 · Regular Checking Account		250.00
							250.00	250.00
4	General Journal	01/05/2012	4		Check no 172, 2 mos rent	14100 · Prepaid Expenses	500.00	
					Check no 172, 2 mos rent	10100 · Regular Checking Account		500.00
							500.00	500.00
5	General Journal	01/07/2012	5		Cash fees earned	10100 · Regular Checking Account	1,375.00	
					Cash fees earned	40000 · Consulting Income		1,375.00
							1,375.00	1,375.00
6	General Journal	01/13/2012	6		Check no 173	39007 · Owner's Draw	700.00	
					Check no 173	10100 · Regular Checking Account		700.00
							700.00	700.00
7	General Journal	01/18/2012	7		Cash fees earned	10100 · Regular Checking Account	625.00	
					Cash fees earned	40000 · Consulting Income		625.00
							625.00	625.00
8	General Journal	01/21/2012	8		Check no 174	61600 · Telephone Expense	195.00	
					Check no 174	10100 · Regular Checking Account		195.00
							195.00	195.00
9	General Journal	01/24/2012	9		Check no 175	60000 · Salaries and Wages	975.00	
					Check no 175	10100 · Regular Checking Account		975.00
							975.00	975.00
TOTAL							10,620.00	10,620.00

Figure: E:1

RECORD ADDITIONAL JOURNAL ENTRIES

Journal report filtered for dates specified.

QB2012_Chp3_Stud
Journal
January 25 - 28, 2012

Trans #	Type	Date	Num	Name	Memo	Account	Debit	Credit
10	General Journal	01/28/2012	10		Owner cash contribution	10100 · Regular Checking Account	7,000.00	
					Owner car contribution	15200 · Vehicle	10,000.00	
					Owner computer contribution	15000 · Office Equipment	12,000.00	
					Owner contribution cash, car, computer	39006 · Owner's Contribution		29,000.00
							29,000.00	29,000.00
11	General Journal	01/25/2012	11		Check no 176, 6 mos vehicle insurance	14100 · Prepaid Expenses	1,200.00	
					Check no 176, 6 mos vehicle insurance	10100 · Regular Checking Account		1,200.00
							1,200.00	1,200.00
12	General Journal	01/26/2012	12		Check no 177	61400 · Office Supplies Expense	210.00	
					Check no 177, 4 desks	15100 · Office Furniture & Fixtures	3,250.00	
					Check no 177	10100 · Regular Checking Account		3,460.00
							3,460.00	3,460.00
13	General Journal	01/27/2012	13		Check no 178, Jan electric	61500 · Utilities Expense	375.00	
					Check no 178, Jan electric	10100 · Regular Checking Account		375.00
							375.00	375.00
14	General Journal	01/28/2012	14		Cash fees earned	10100 · Regular Checking Account	2,376.00	
					Cash fees earned	40000 · Consulting Income		2,376.00
							2,376.00	2,376.00
TOTAL							36,411.00	36,411.00

Figure: E:2

RECORD JANUARY ADJUSTING ENTRIES

Journal report.

QB2012_Chp3_Stud
Journal
January 31, 2012

Trans #	Type	Date	Num	Name	Memo	Account	Debit	Credit
15	General Journal	01/31/2012	15		Expense one month of rent	61300 · Rent Expense	250.00	
					Expense one month of rent	14100 · Prepaid Expenses		250.00
							250.00	250.00
16	General Journal	01/31/2012	16		January depreciation	62800 · Depreciation Expense	235.00	
					January depreciation	15010 · Accum Depr - Office Equipm...		120.00
					January depreciation	15110 · Accum Depr - Office Furniture		30.00
					January depreciation	15220 · Accum Depr - Vehicle		85.00
							235.00	235.00
TOTAL							485.00	485.00

Figure: E:3

CHAPTER 4

CREATE A NEW CUSTOMER ACCOUNT

Graphic Printing Services' Address Info tab.

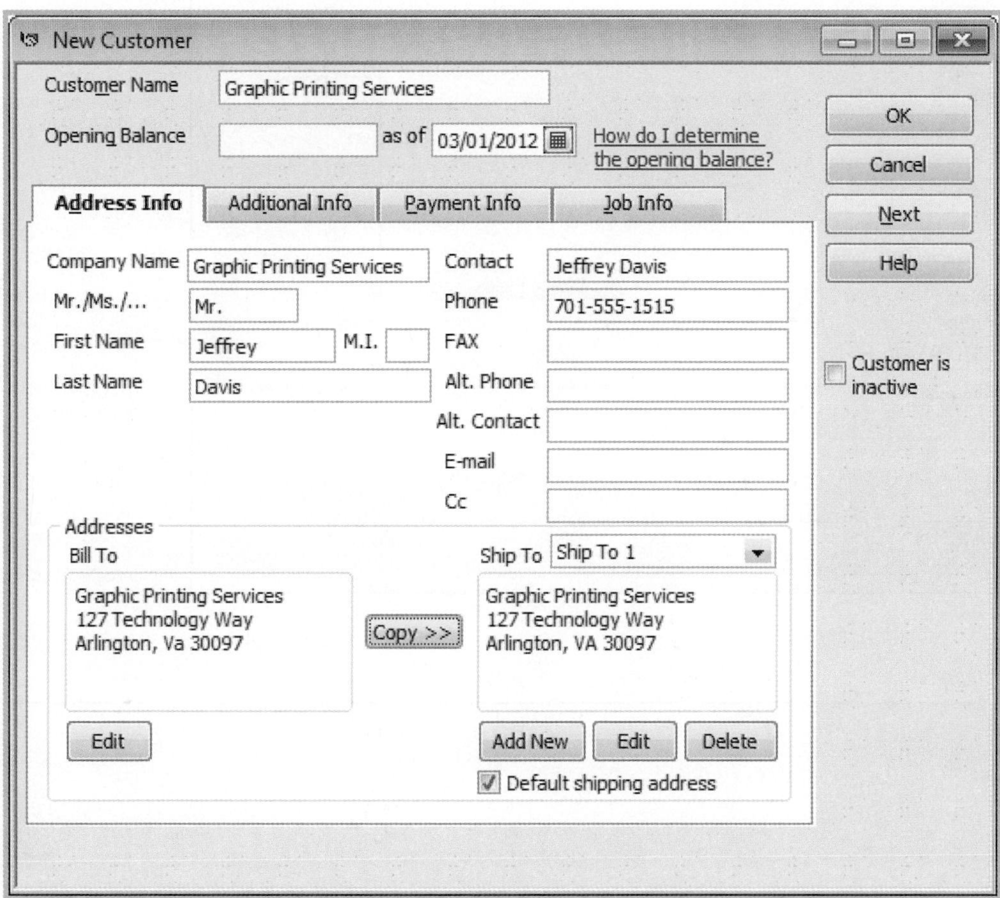

Figure: E:4

Graphic Printing Services' Additional Info tab.

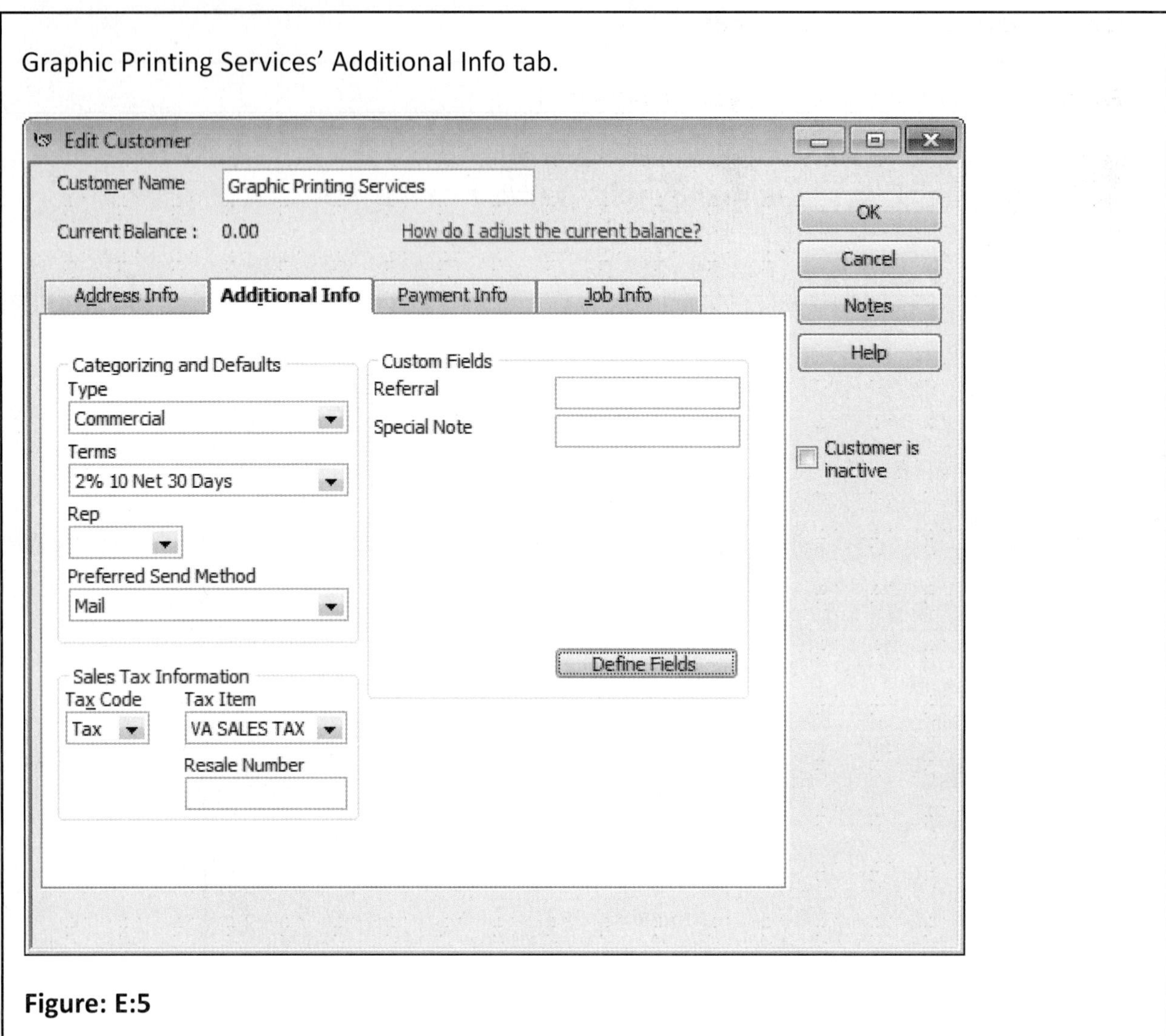

Figure: E:5

Graphic Printing Services' Payment Info tab.

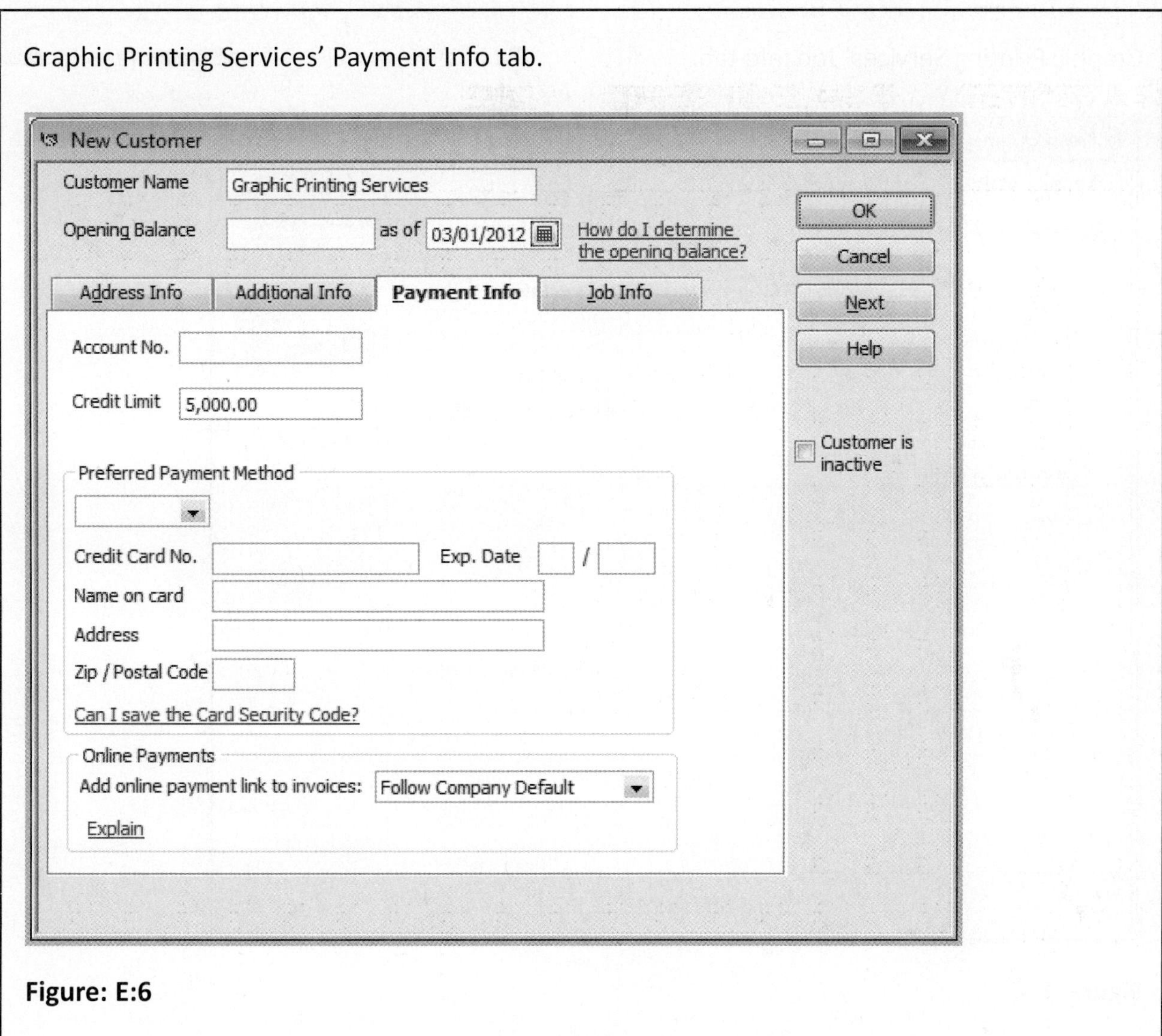

Figure: E:6

Graphic Printing Services' Job Info tab.

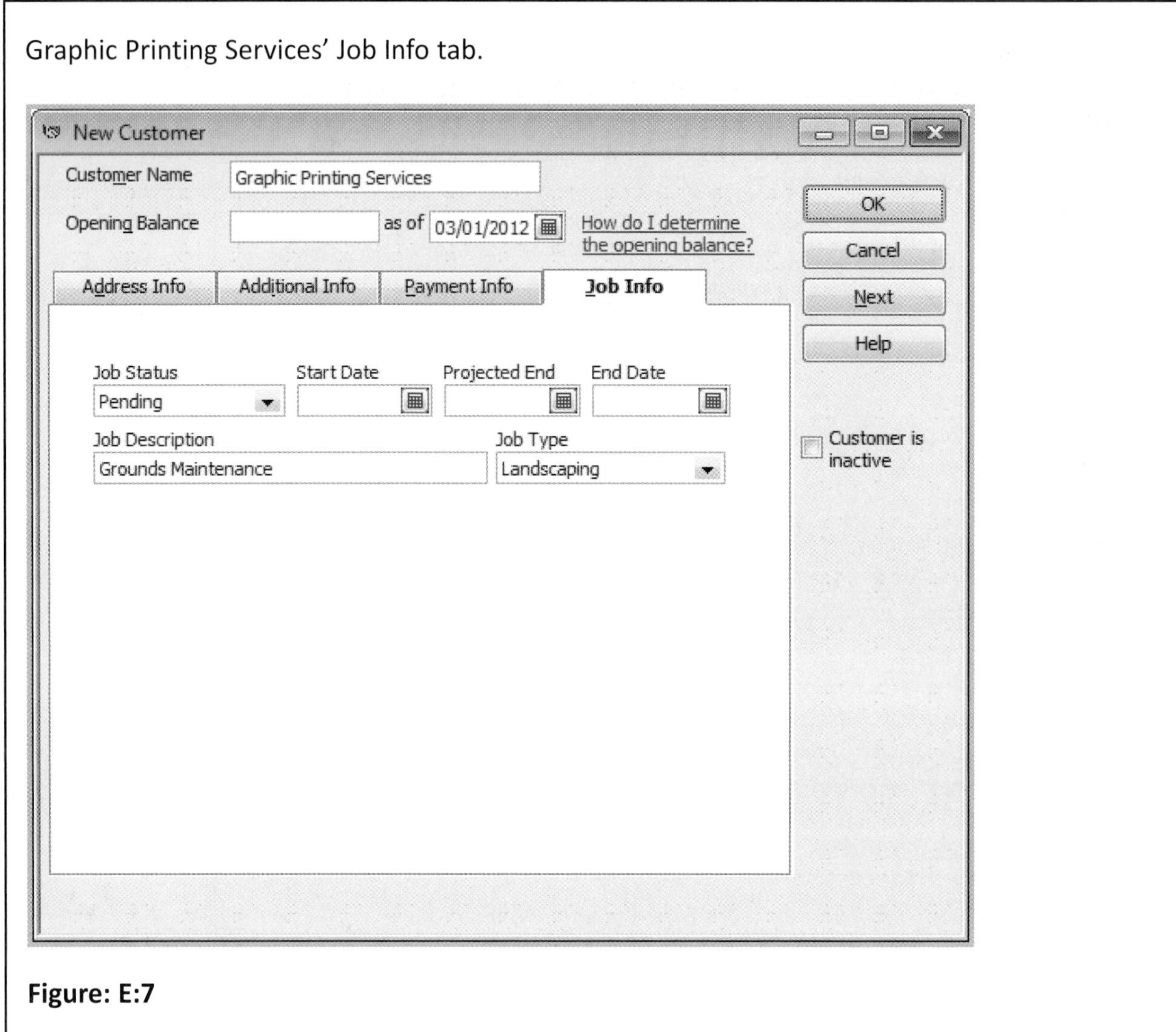

Figure: E:7

INVOICE A CUSTOMER FOR JOB COSTS

Time ticket selected for invoicing.

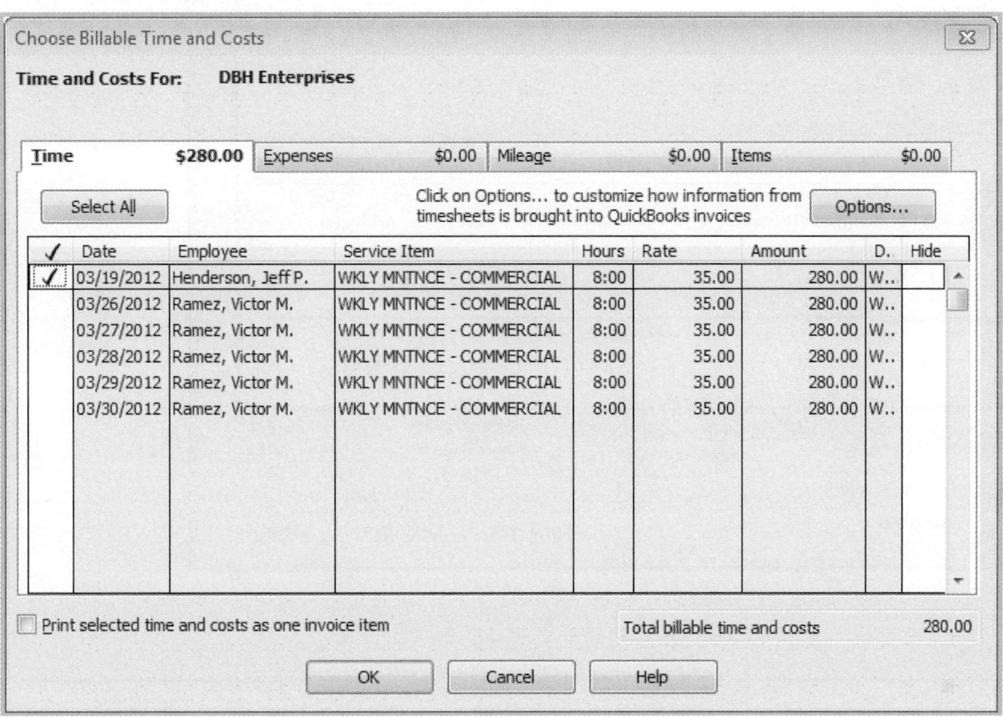

Figure: E:8

Invoice created.

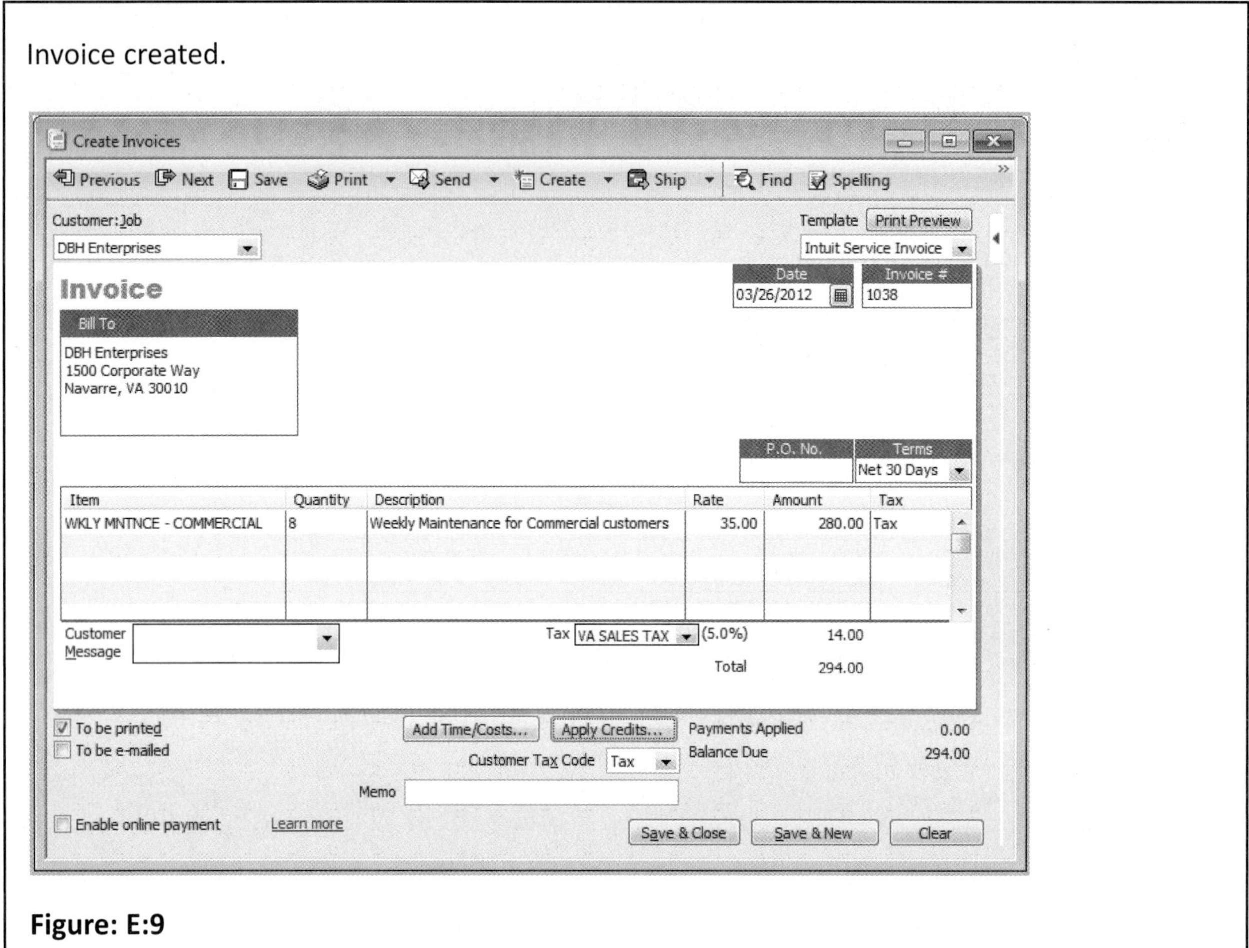

Figure: E:9

CREATE A JOB REPORT

Time by Job Summary report.

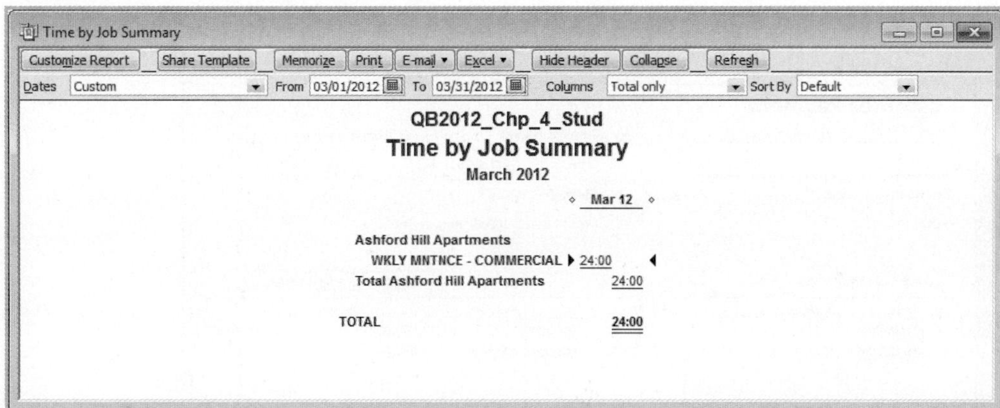

Figure: E:10

How to use: After customizing the report, it shows time that needs to be invoiced to Ashford Hill Apartments. You can use the report to create invoices for customers.

RECORD CUSTOMER PAYMENTS

Ashford Hill Apartments' payment.

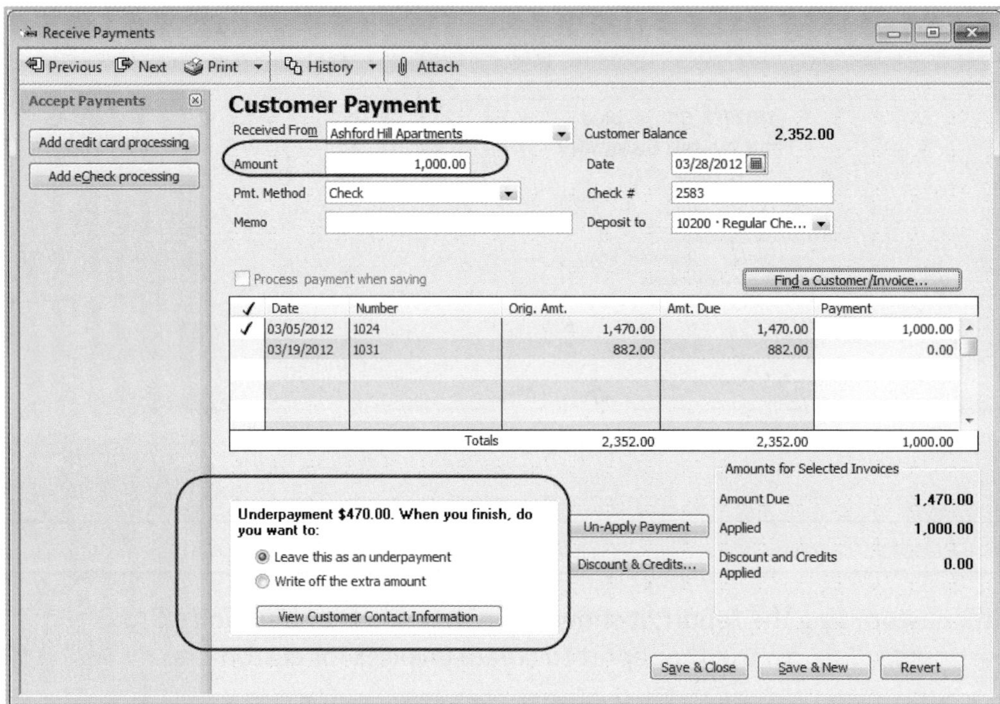

Figure: E:11

Sycamore Homes' payment.

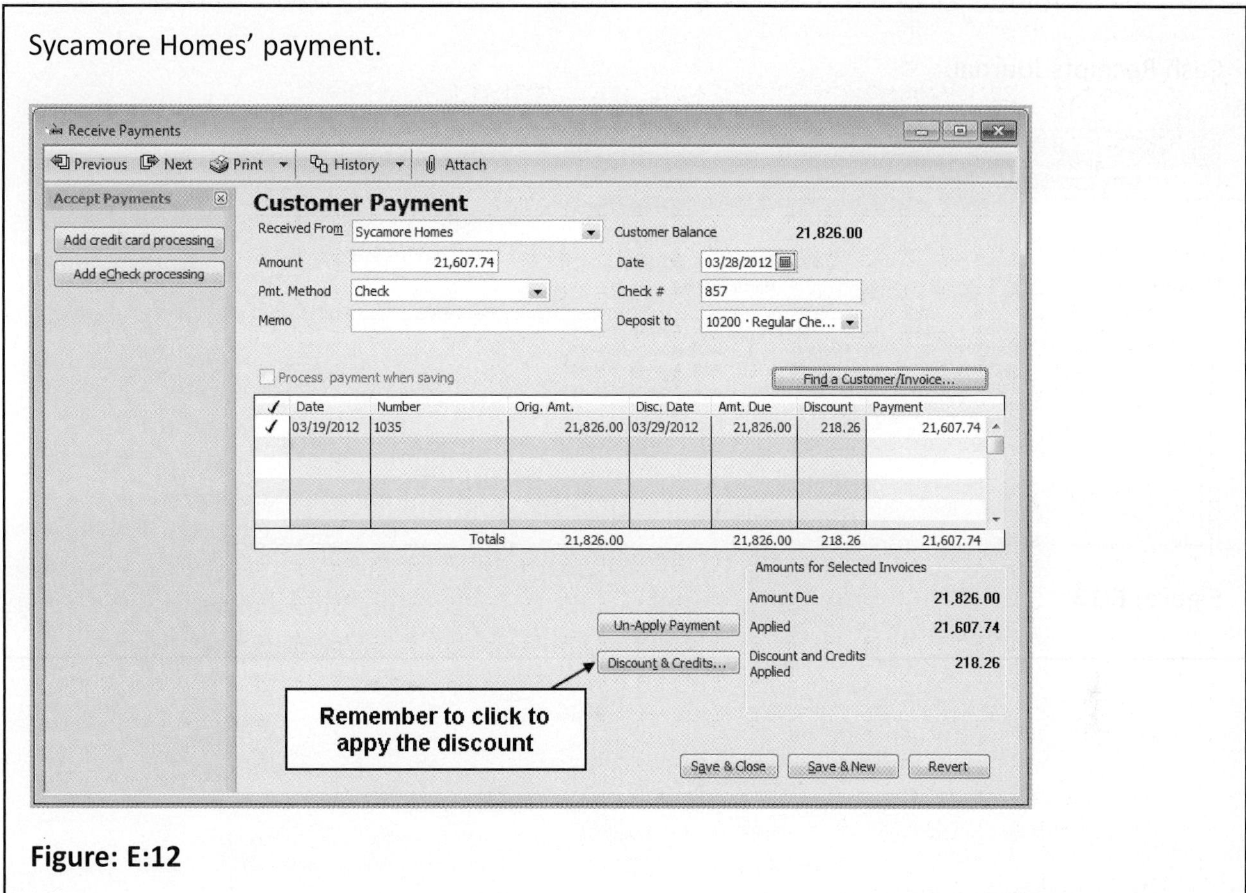

Figure: E:12

Cash Receipts Journal.

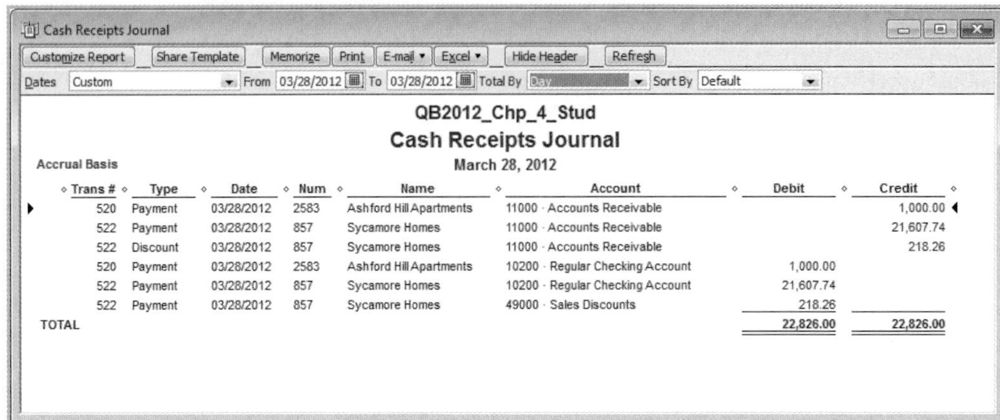

QB2012_Chp_4_Stud

Cash Receipts Journal

Accrual Basis

March 28, 2012

Trans #	Type	Date	Num	Name	Account	Debit	Credit
520	Payment	03/28/2012	2583	Ashford Hill Apartments	11000 · Accounts Receivable		1,000.00
522	Payment	03/28/2012	857	Sycamore Homes	11000 · Accounts Receivable		21,607.74
522	Discount	03/28/2012	857	Sycamore Homes	11000 · Accounts Receivable		218.26
520	Payment	03/28/2012	2583	Ashford Hill Apartments	10200 · Regular Checking Account	1,000.00	
522	Payment	03/28/2012	857	Sycamore Homes	10200 · Regular Checking Account	21,607.74	
522	Payment	03/28/2012	857	Sycamore Homes	49000 · Sales Discounts	218.26	
TOTAL						22,826.00	22,826.00

Figure: E:13

CHAPTER 5

ENTER PURCHASE ORDERS

Calvert Stone Supplies' PO.

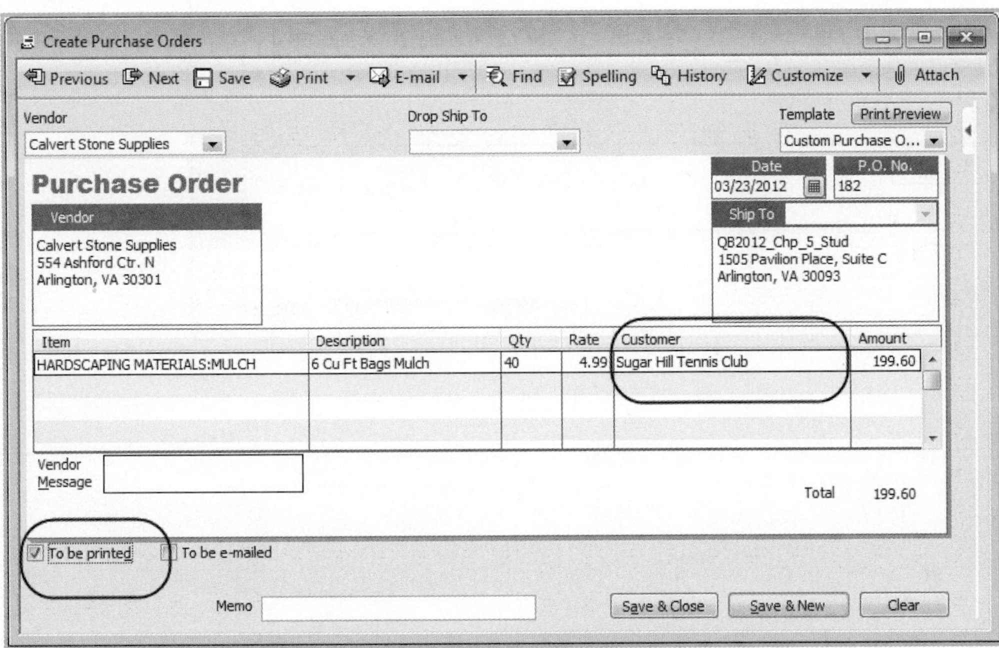

Figure: E:14

Southern Garden Wholesale's PO.

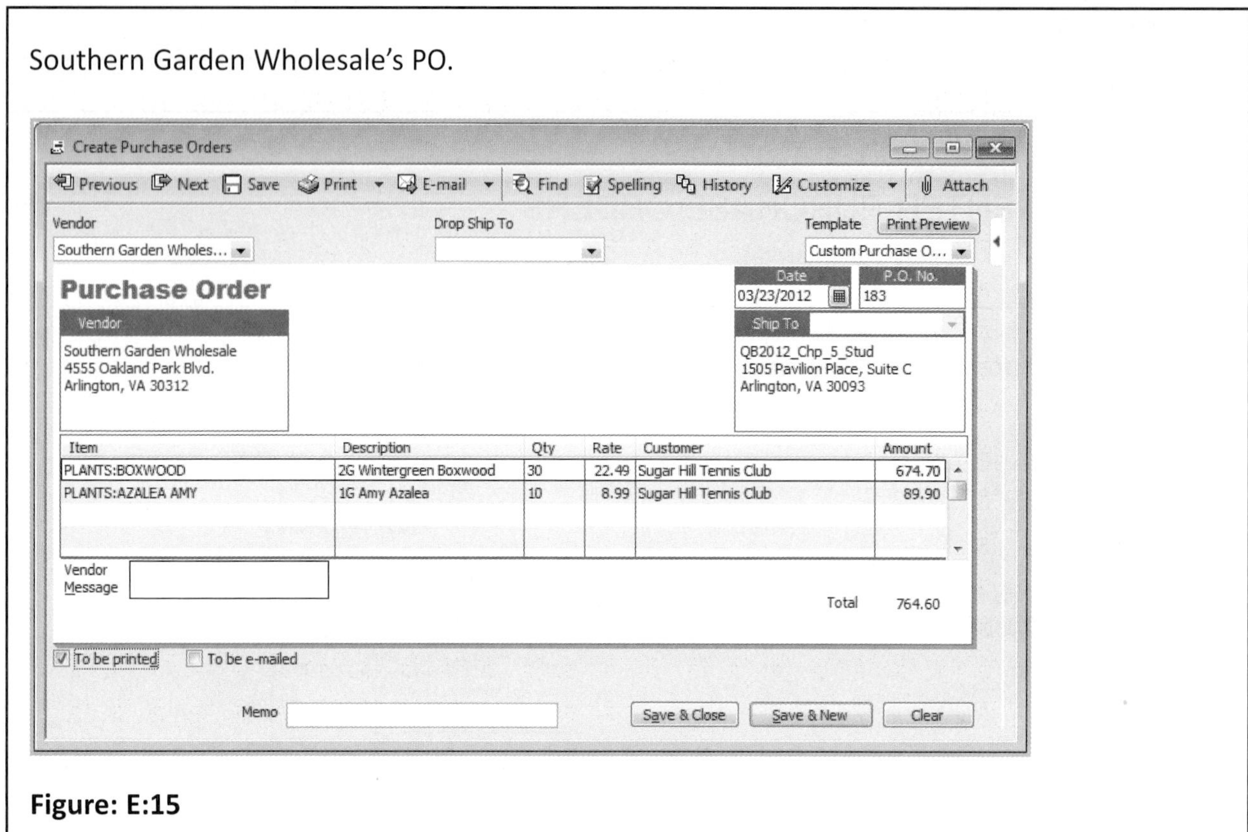

Figure: E:15

ENTER VENDOR RECEIPTS AND BILLS FOR PURCHASE ORDERS

Calvert Stone Supplies' vendor bill.

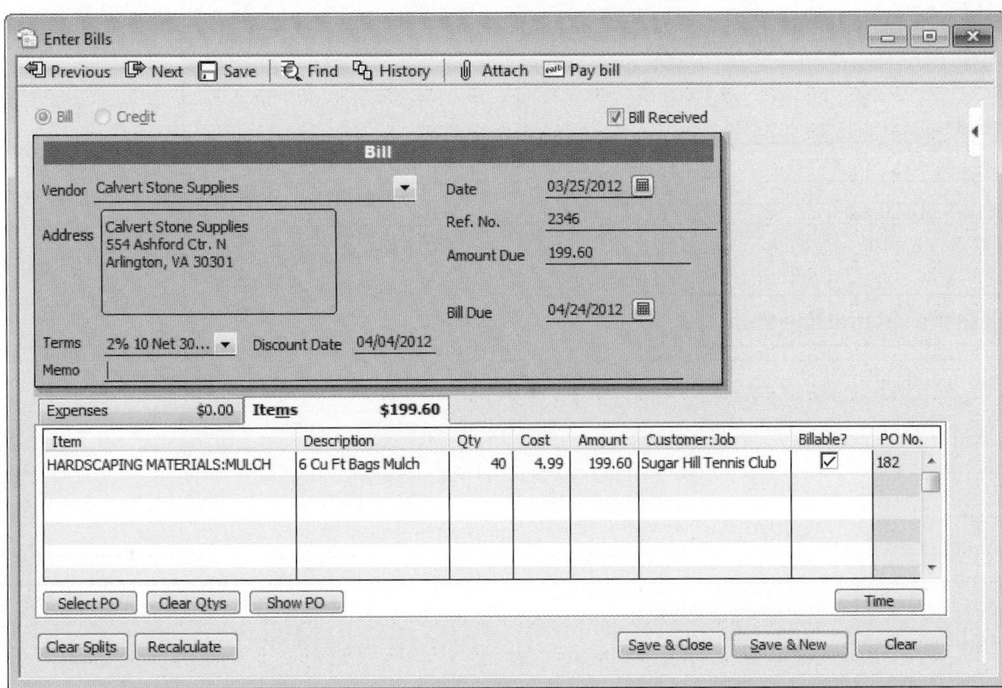

Figure: E:16

Southern Garden Wholesale's Receipt. *Note: Astor did not receive any of the Amy Azaleas so remove this line item by highlighting the row and clicking Edit>>Delete Line on the main menu.*

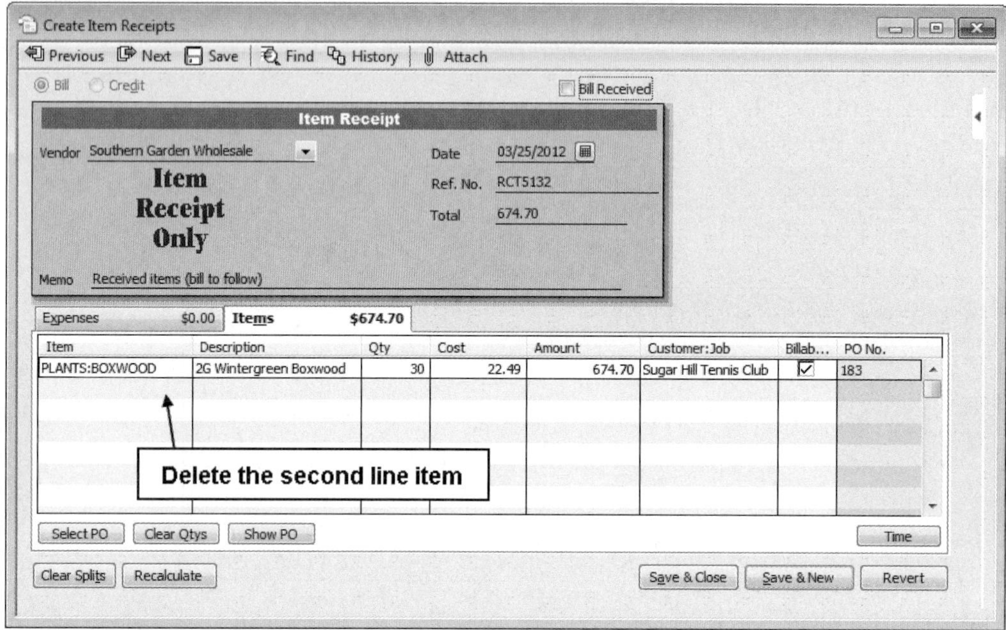

Figure: E:17

Purchases Journal.

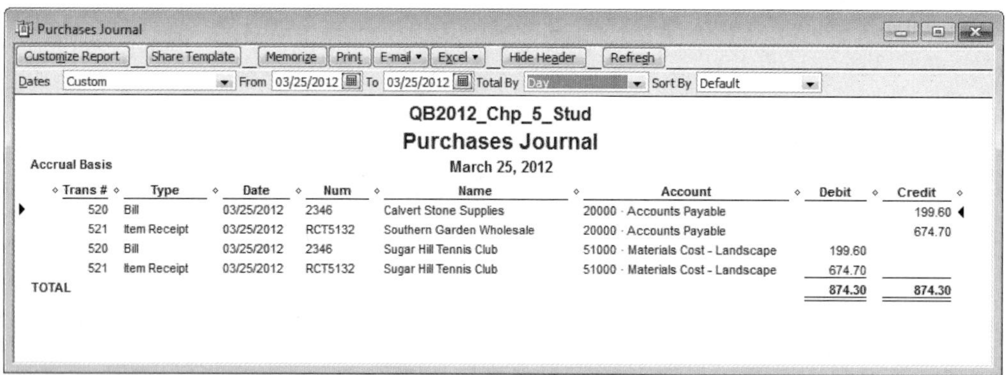

QB2012_Chp_5_Stud
Purchases Journal
March 25, 2012
Accrual Basis

Trans #	Type	Date	Num	Name	Account	Debit	Credit
520	Bill	03/25/2012	2346	Calvert Stone Supplies	20000 · Accounts Payable		199.60
521	Item Receipt	03/25/2012	RCT5132	Southern Garden Wholesale	20000 · Accounts Payable		674.70
520	Bill	03/25/2012	2346	Sugar Hill Tennis Club	51000 · Materials Cost - Landscape	199.60	
521	Item Receipt	03/25/2012	RCT5132	Sugar Hill Tennis Club	51000 · Materials Cost - Landscape	674.70	
TOTAL						874.30	874.30

Figure: E:18

ENTER VENDOR BILL FOR VENDOR RECEIPT

Southern Garden Wholesale's bill. *Note: Click Show PO to reopen the PO and enter "1" as the Qty received. Also, change the Date, Ref. No., and Amount Due.*

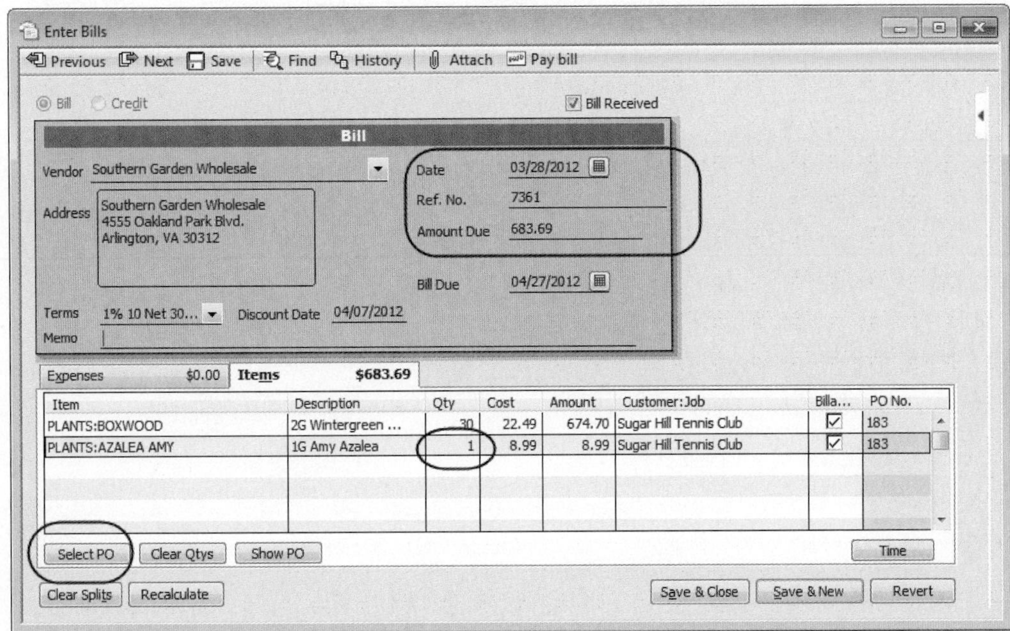

Figure: E:19

Purchases Journal.

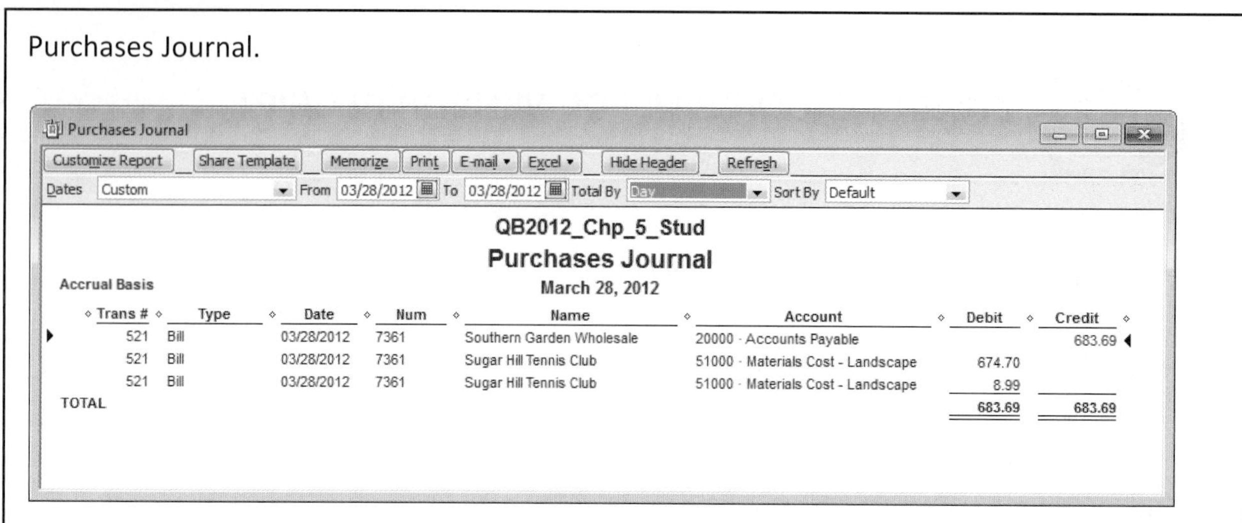

Purchases Journal

Customize Report | Share Template | Memorize | Print | E-mail ▾ | Excel ▾ | Hide Header | Refresh

Dates Custom From 03/28/2012 To 03/28/2012 Total By Day Sort By Default

QB2012_Chp_5_Stud

Purchases Journal

Accrual Basis

March 28, 2012

Trans #	Type	Date	Num	Name	Account	Debit	Credit
521	Bill	03/28/2012	7361	Southern Garden Wholesale	20000 · Accounts Payable		683.69
521	Bill	03/28/2012	7361	Sugar Hill Tennis Club	51000 · Materials Cost - Landscape	674.70	
521	Bill	03/28/2012	7361	Sugar Hill Tennis Club	51000 · Materials Cost - Landscape	8.99	
TOTAL						683.69	683.69

Figure: E:20

CREATE A NEW VENDOR ACCOUNT

Jackson Hyland Tax Service's Address Info information.

New Vendor

Vendor Name: Jackson Hyland Tax Service

Opening Balance ___ as of ___ How do I determine the opening balance?

OK | Cancel | Next | Help

Address Info | Additional Info | Account Prefill

Company Name: Jackson Hyland Tax Ser...
Mr./Ms./...
First Name ___ M.I. ___
Last Name

Contact
Phone
FAX
Alt. Phone
Alt. Contact
E-mail
Cc
Print on Check as: Jackson Hyland Tax Service

Vendor is inactive

Addresses

Billed From Address:
Jackson Hyland Tax Service
P.O. Box 8276
Arlington, VA 30010

Copy >>

Shipped From Address

Edit | Edit

Figure: E:21

Jackson Hyland Tax Service's Additional information.

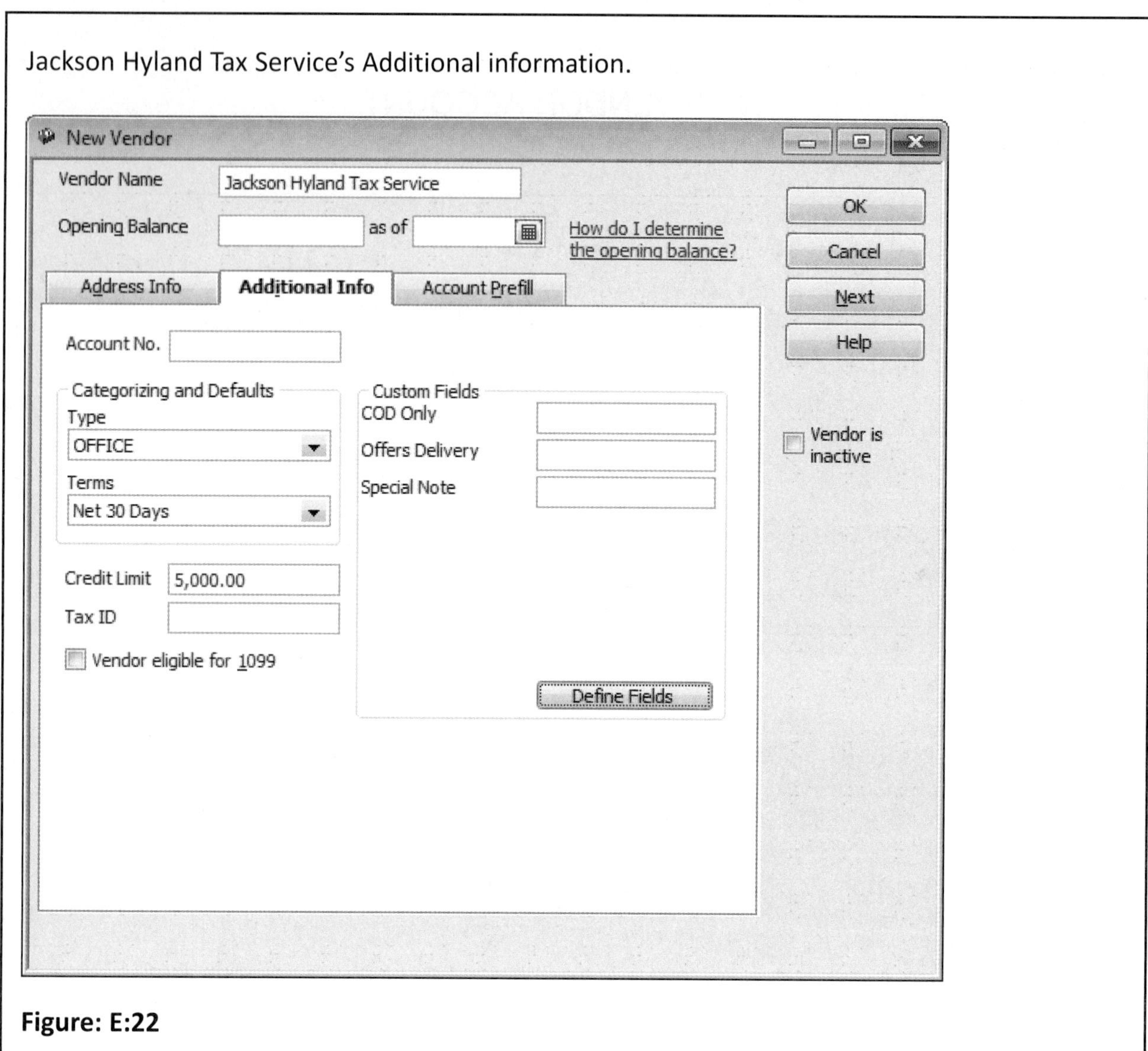

Figure: E:22

Jackson Hyland Tax Services' Account Prefill information.

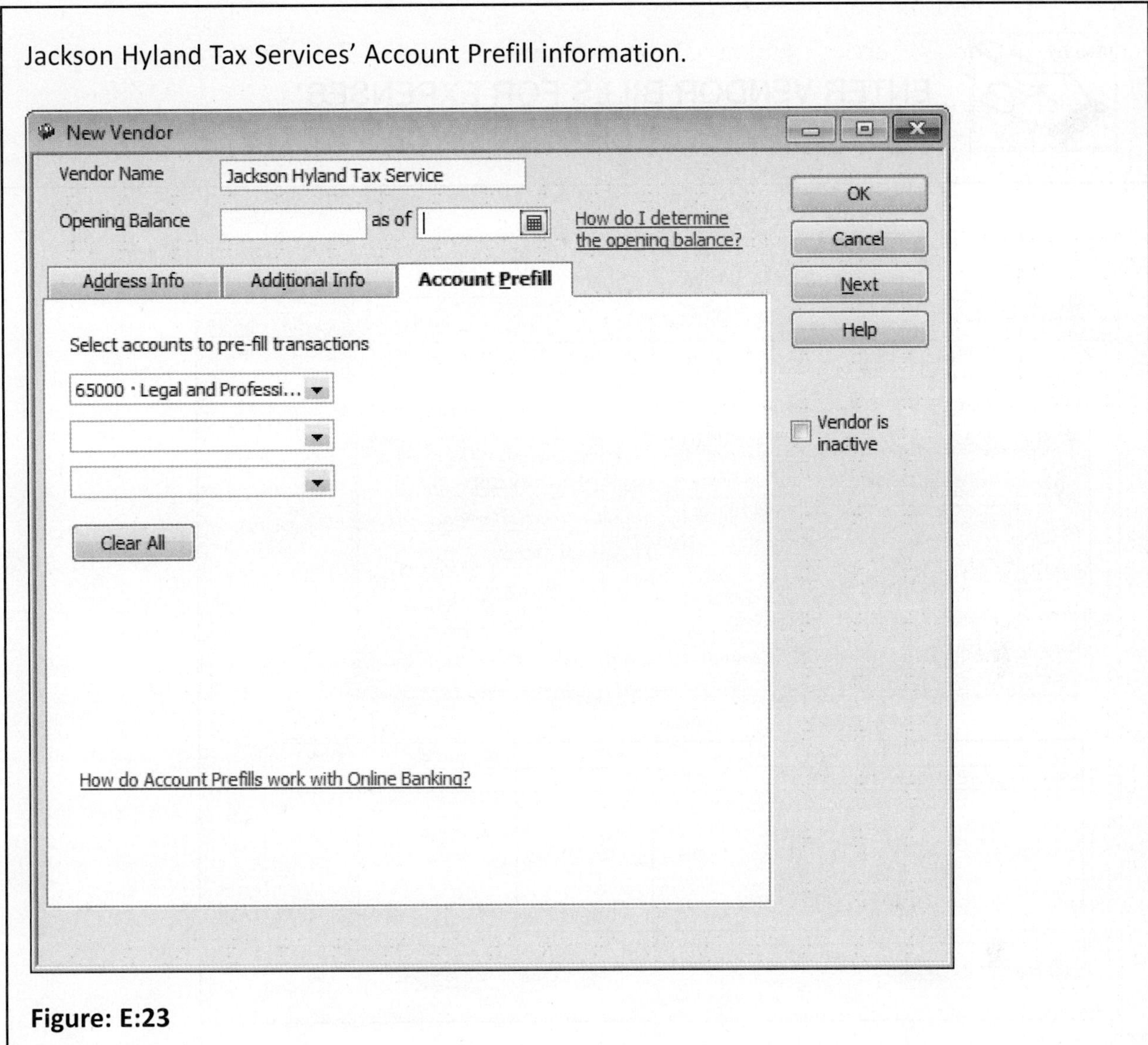

Figure: E:23

ENTER VENDOR BILLS FOR EXPENSES

Jackson Hyland's posted transaction.

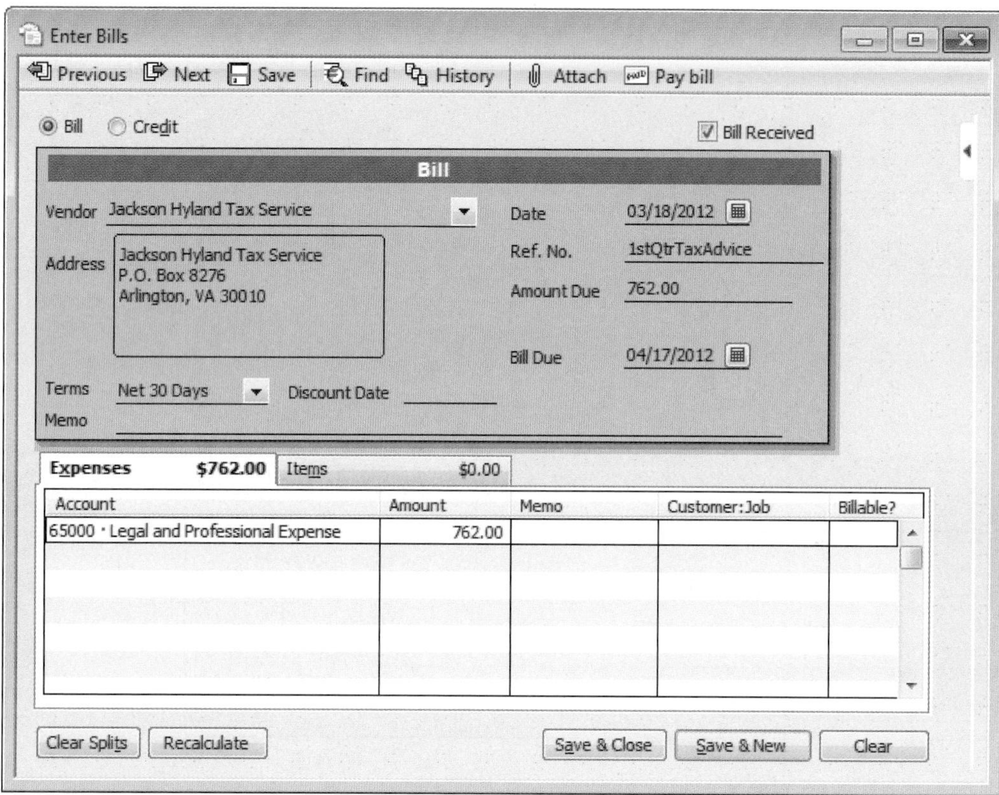

Figure: E:24

PAY VENDORS

Cash Disbursements Journal.

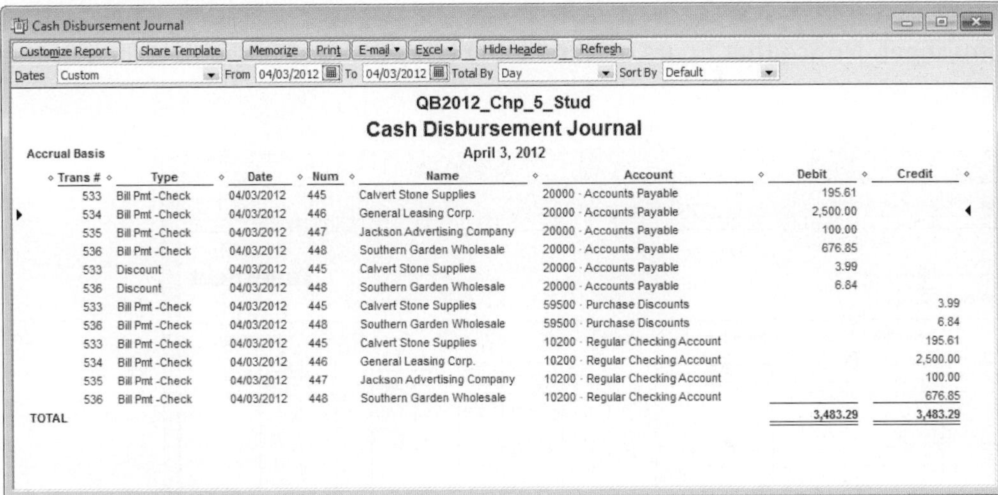

Cash Disbursement Journal

Customize Report | Share Template | Memorize | Print | E-mail | Excel | Hide Header | Refresh

Dates Custom From 04/03/2012 To 04/03/2012 Total By Day Sort By Default

QB2012_Chp_5_Stud

Cash Disbursement Journal

Accrual Basis April 3, 2012

Trans #	Type	Date	Num	Name	Account	Debit	Credit
533	Bill Pmt -Check	04/03/2012	445	Calvert Stone Supplies	20000 · Accounts Payable	195.61	
534	Bill Pmt -Check	04/03/2012	446	General Leasing Corp.	20000 · Accounts Payable	2,500.00	
535	Bill Pmt -Check	04/03/2012	447	Jackson Advertising Company	20000 · Accounts Payable	100.00	
536	Bill Pmt -Check	04/03/2012	448	Southern Garden Wholesale	20000 · Accounts Payable	676.85	
533	Discount	04/03/2012	445	Calvert Stone Supplies	20000 · Accounts Payable	3.99	
536	Discount	04/03/2012	448	Southern Garden Wholesale	20000 · Accounts Payable	6.84	
533	Bill Pmt -Check	04/03/2012	445	Calvert Stone Supplies	59500 · Purchase Discounts		3.99
536	Bill Pmt -Check	04/03/2012	448	Southern Garden Wholesale	59500 · Purchase Discounts		6.84
533	Bill Pmt -Check	04/03/2012	445	Calvert Stone Supplies	10200 · Regular Checking Account		195.61
534	Bill Pmt -Check	04/03/2012	446	General Leasing Corp.	10200 · Regular Checking Account		2,500.00
535	Bill Pmt -Check	04/03/2012	447	Jackson Advertising Company	10200 · Regular Checking Account		100.00
536	Bill Pmt -Check	04/03/2012	448	Southern Garden Wholesale	10200 · Regular Checking Account		676.85
TOTAL						3,483.29	3,483.29

Figure: E:25

CHAPTER 6

WORKING WITH TIMESHEETS

Roy Dillion's timesheet. Notice that hours on the first line have already been invoiced to the customer.

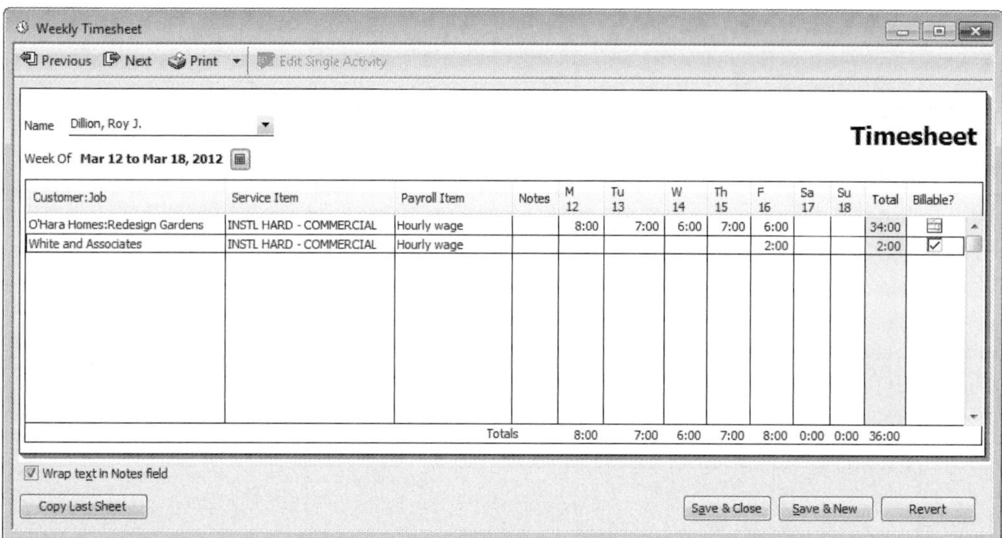

Figure: E:26

Jan Folse's timesheets for the biweekly pay period.

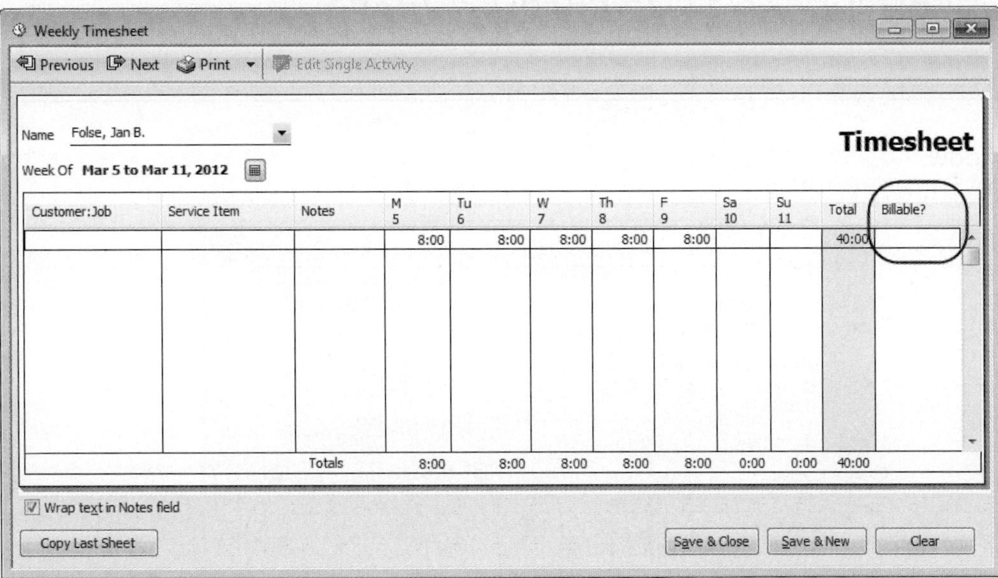

Figure: E:27

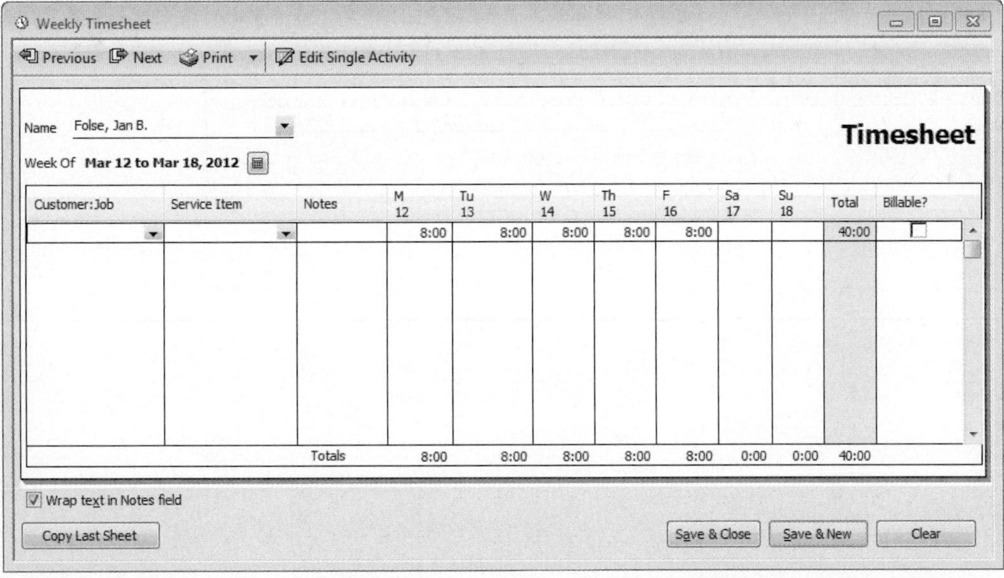

Figure: E:28

CREATE CHECKS FOR PAYROLL TAXES

Pay Liabilities window.

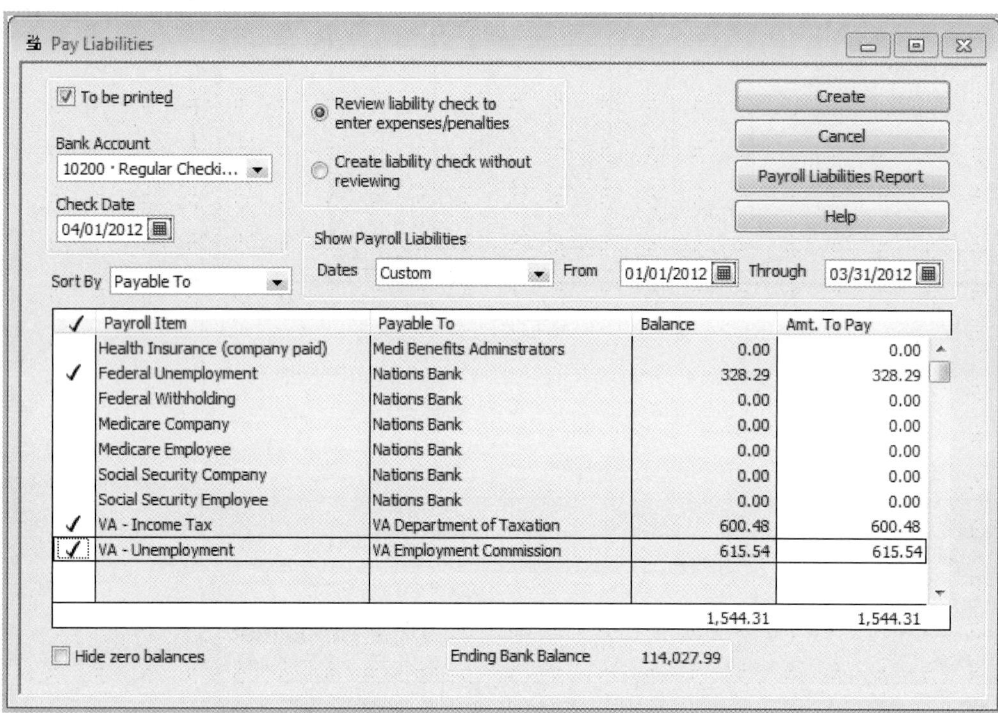

Figure: E:29

Check Detail report.

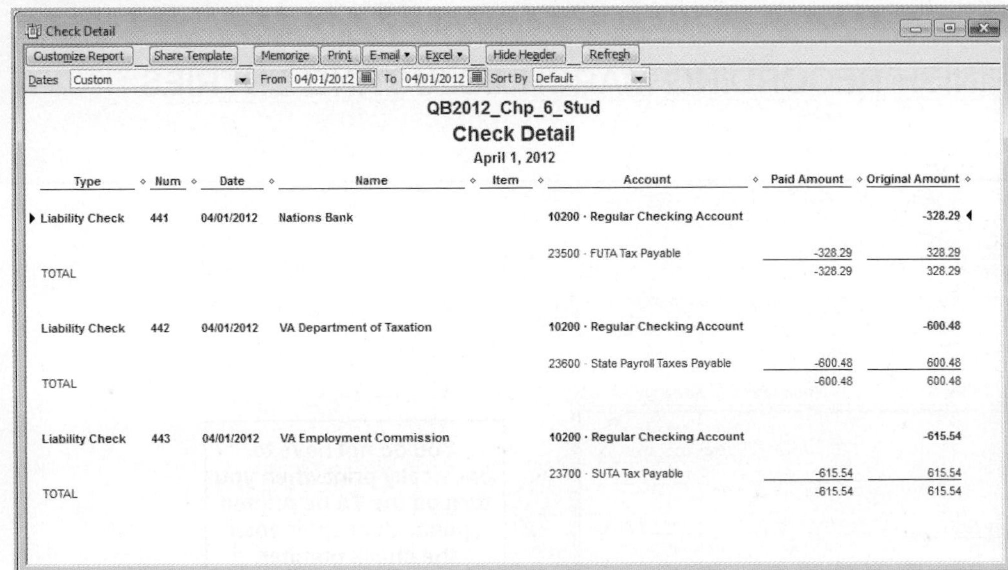

Check Detail

Customize Report | Share Template | Memorize | Print | E-mail | Excel | Hide Header | Refresh

Dates Custom From 04/01/2012 To 04/01/2012 Sort By Default

QB2012_Chp_6_Stud

Check Detail

April 1, 2012

Type	Num	Date	Name	Item	Account	Paid Amount	Original Amount
Liability Check	441	04/01/2012	Nations Bank		10200 · Regular Checking Account		-328.29
					23500 · FUTA Tax Payable	-328.29	328.29
TOTAL						-328.29	328.29
Liability Check	442	04/01/2012	VA Department of Taxation		10200 · Regular Checking Account		-600.48
					23600 · State Payroll Taxes Payable	-600.48	600.48
TOTAL						-600.48	600.48
Liability Check	443	04/01/2012	VA Employment Commission		10200 · Regular Checking Account		-615.54
					23700 · SUTA Tax Payable	-615.54	615.54
TOTAL						-615.54	615.54

Figure: E:30

CHAPTER 7

FINISH RECORDING MARCH ADJUSTING ENTRIES

Petty Cash Check.

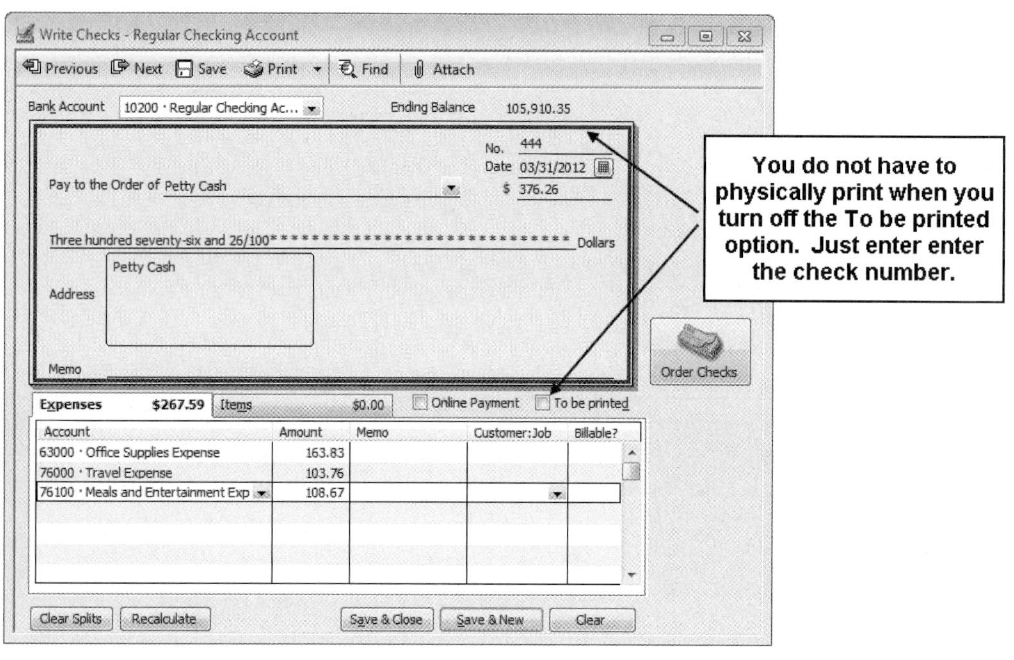

Figure: E:31

Accrued wages entry.

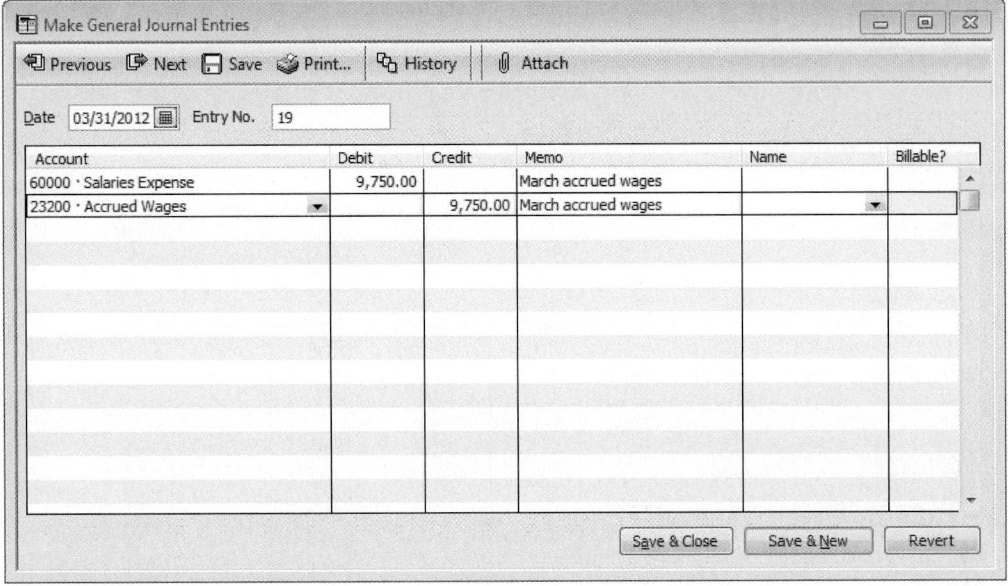

Figure: E:32

Note: In practice, you would also post a reversing entry dated April 1 in the following month to reverse the accrued expense because the March accrued expense will post as actual expense when paying wages in April. In essence, the reversing entry reduces the April actual expense for the expense already recorded in March.

Here is an example of the reversing entry. Do not post this entry.

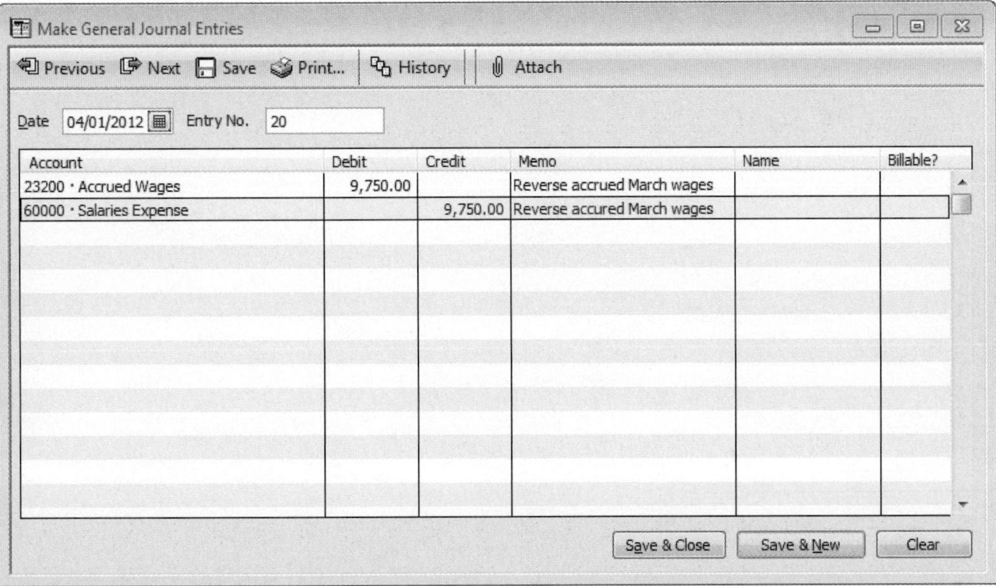

Figure: E:33

RECONCILE THE PAYROLL CHECKING ACCOUNT

Bank reconciliation window.

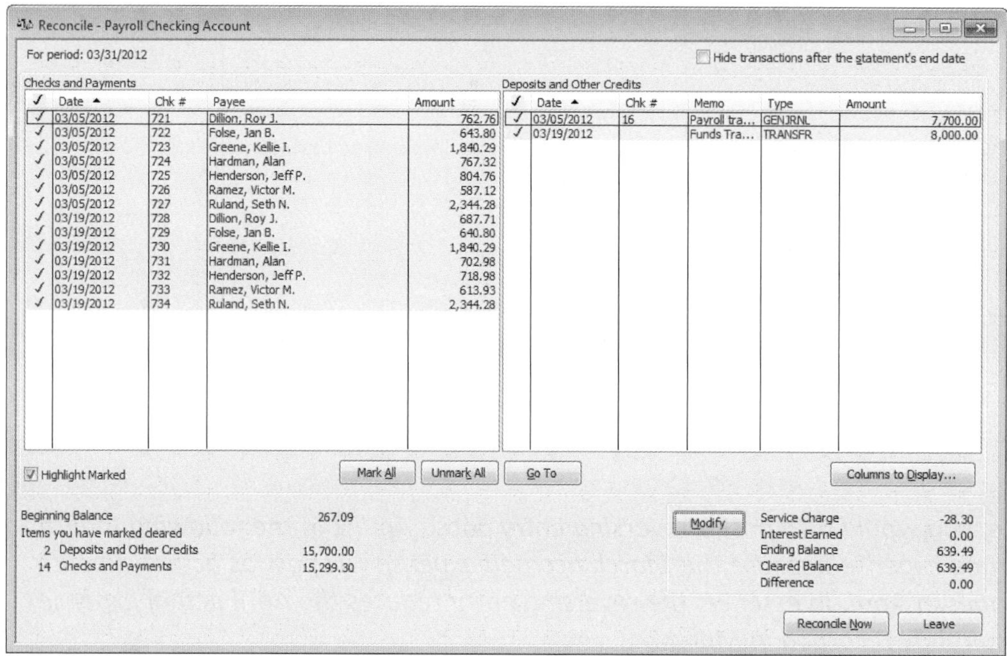

Figure: E:34

Reconciliation Detail report.

Reconciliation Detail

Customize Report | Share Template | Memorize | Print | E-mail ▾ | Excel ▾ | Hide Header | Refresh

QB2012_Chp_7_Stud

Reconciliation Detail

10300 · Payroll Checking Account, Period Ending 03/31/2012

Type	Date	Num	Name	Clr	Amount	Balance
Beginning Balance						**267.09**
Cleared Transactions						
Checks and Payments - 15 items						
Paycheck	03/05/2012	727	Ruland, Seth N.	✓	-2,344.28	-2,344.28
Paycheck	03/05/2012	723	Greene, Kellie I.	✓	-1,840.29	-4,184.57
Paycheck	03/05/2012	725	Henderson, Jeff P.	✓	-804.76	-4,989.33
Paycheck	03/05/2012	724	Hardman, Alan	✓	-767.32	-5,756.65
Paycheck	03/05/2012	721	Dillion, Roy J.	✓	-762.76	-6,519.41
Paycheck	03/05/2012	722	Folse, Jan B.	✓	-643.80	-7,163.21
Paycheck	03/05/2012	726	Ramez, Victor M.	✓	-587.12	-7,750.33
Paycheck	03/19/2012	734	Ruland, Seth N.	✓	-2,344.28	-10,094.61
Paycheck	03/19/2012	730	Greene, Kellie I.	✓	-1,840.29	-11,934.90
Paycheck	03/19/2012	732	Henderson, Jeff P.	✓	-718.98	-12,653.88
Paycheck	03/19/2012	731	Hardman, Alan	✓	-702.98	-13,356.86
Paycheck	03/19/2012	728	Dillion, Roy J.	✓	-687.71	-14,044.57
Paycheck	03/19/2012	729	Folse, Jan B.	✓	-640.80	-14,685.37
Paycheck	03/19/2012	733	Ramez, Victor M.	✓	-613.93	-15,299.30
Check	03/31/2012			✓	-28.30	-15,327.60
Total Checks and Payments					-15,327.60	-15,327.60
Deposits and Credits - 2 items						
General Journal	03/05/2012	16		✓	7,700.00	7,700.00
Transfer	03/19/2012			✓	8,000.00	15,700.00
Total Deposits and Credits					15,700.00	15,700.00
Total Cleared Transactions					372.40	372.40
Cleared Balance					372.40	639.49
Register Balance as of 03/31/2012					372.40	639.49
Ending Balance					**372.40**	**639.49**

Figure: E:35

CHAPTER 8

CREATE A NEW CUSTOMER ACCOUNT

Frost Garden Center's Address Info.

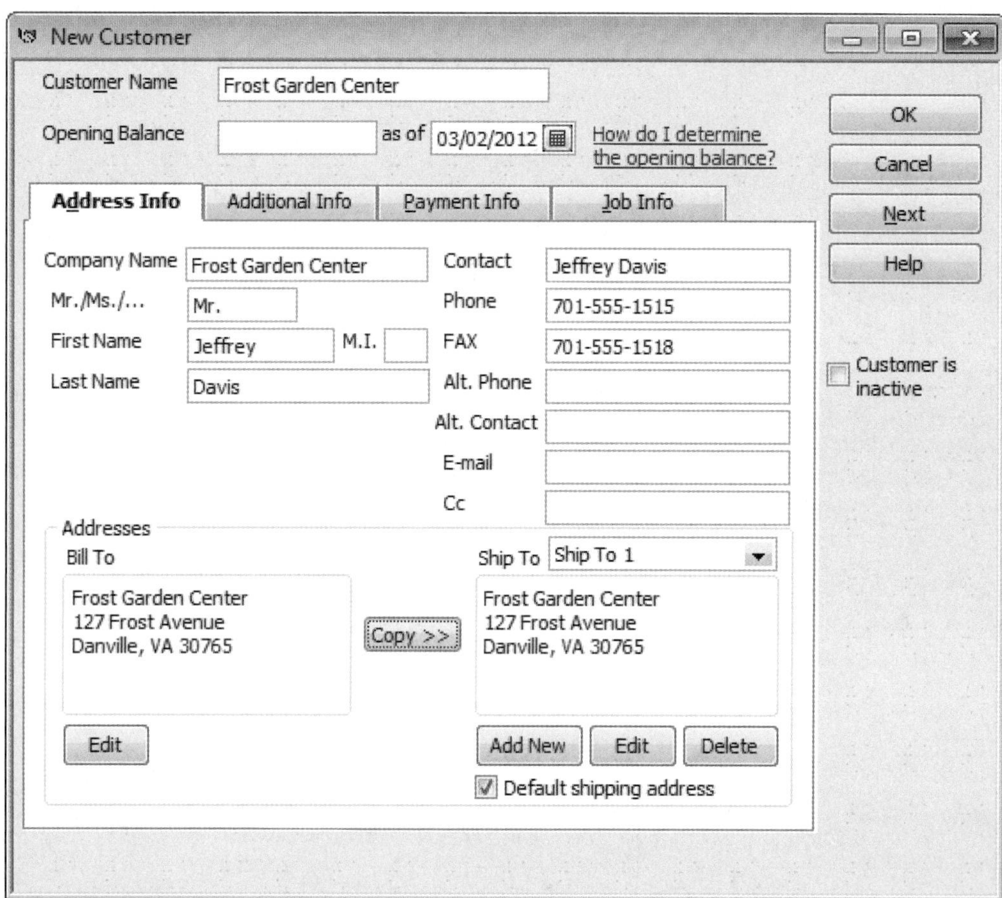

Figure: E:36

Frost Garden Center's Additional Info.

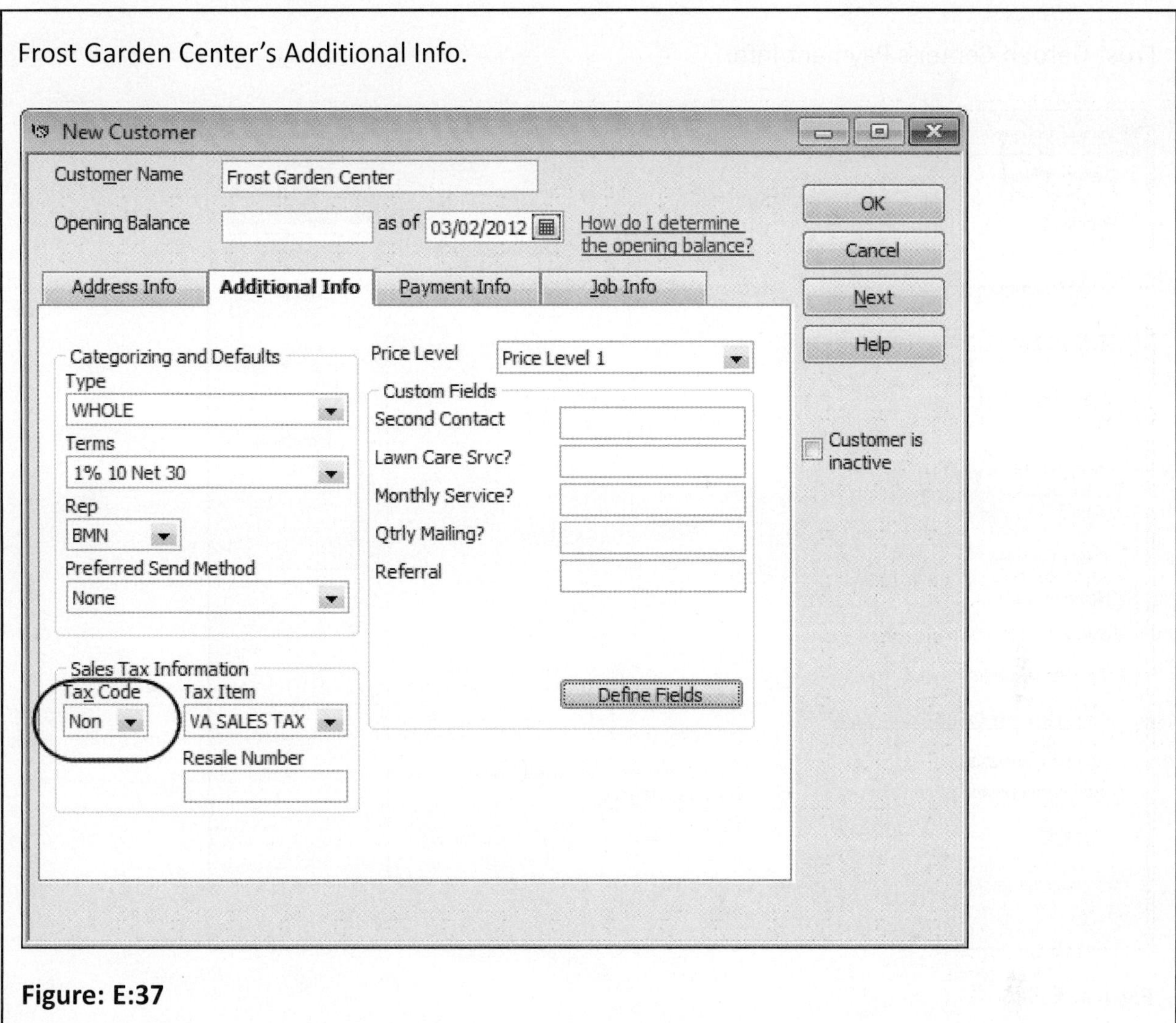

Figure: E:37

Frost Garden Center's Payment Info.

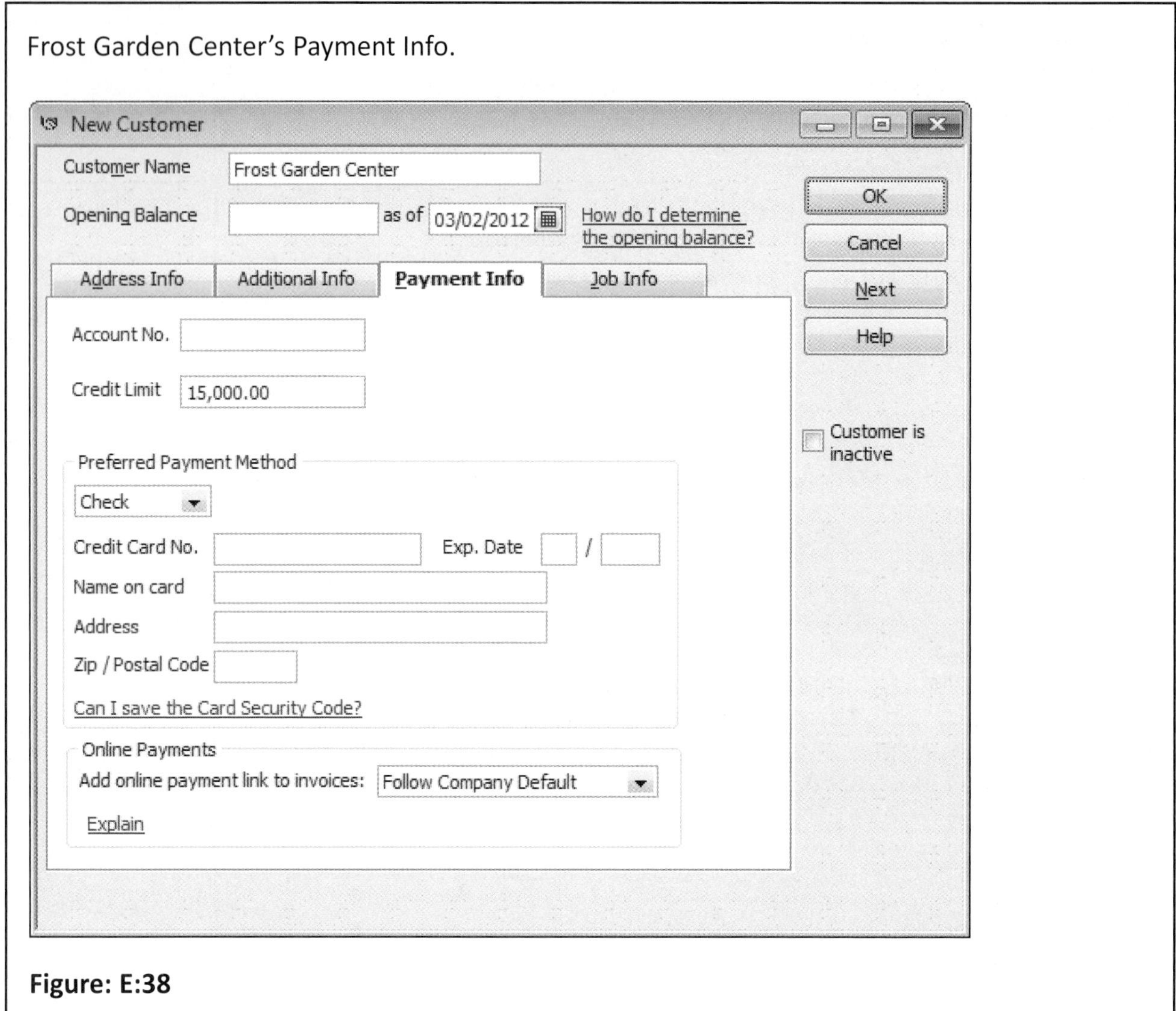

Figure: E:38

CREATE A NEW INVENTORY ITEM

New item and Item Listing report.

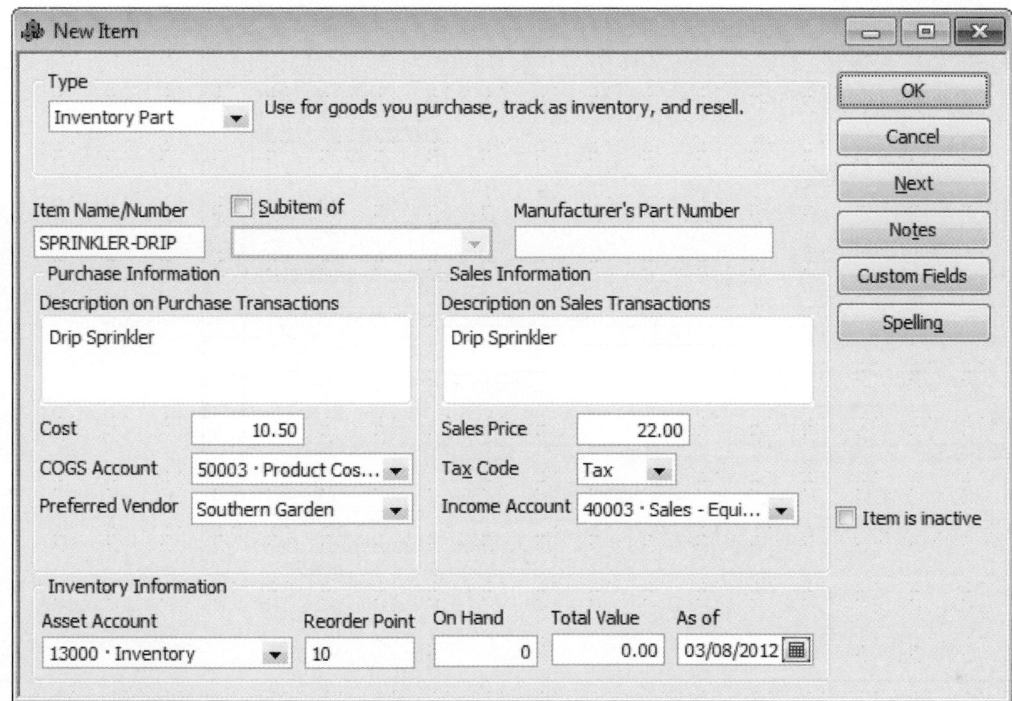

Figure: E:39

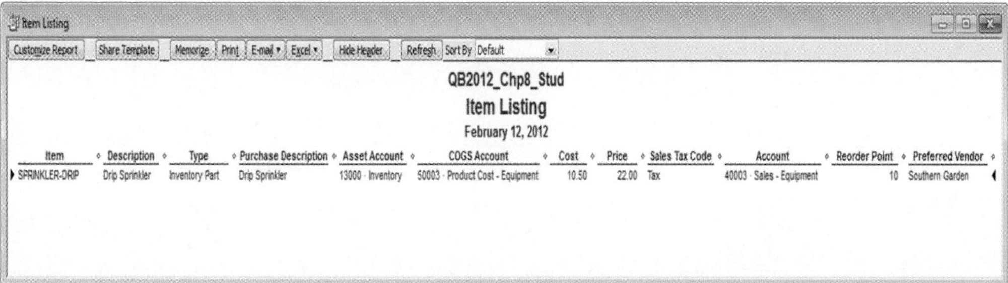

QB2012_Chp8_Stud

Item Listing

February 12, 2012

Item	Description	Type	Purchase Description	Asset Account	COGS Account	Cost	Price	Sales Tax Code	Account	Reorder Point	Preferred Vendor
SPRINKLER-DRIP	Drip Sprinkler	Inventory Part	Drip Sprinkler	13000 · Inventory	50003 · Product Cost - Equipment	10.50	22.00	Tax	40003 · Sales - Equipment	10	Southern Garden

Figure: E:40

ENTER A STOREFRONT SALE OF MERCHANDISE

Freemond Country Club's sale.

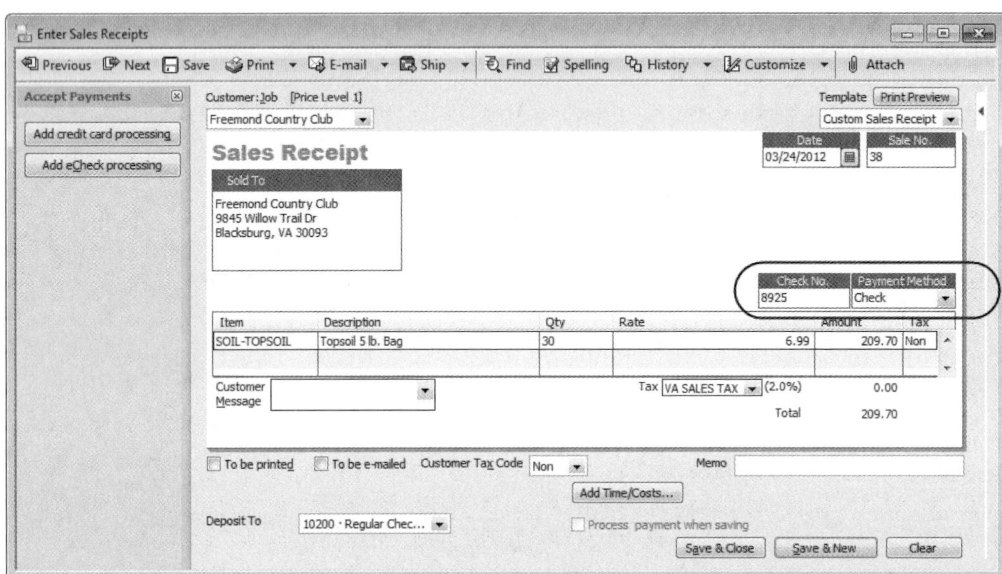

Figure: E:41

RECORD CUSTOMER PAYMENTS

Everly Property's payment. Note the option of applying an underpayment because the customer underpaid the invoice.

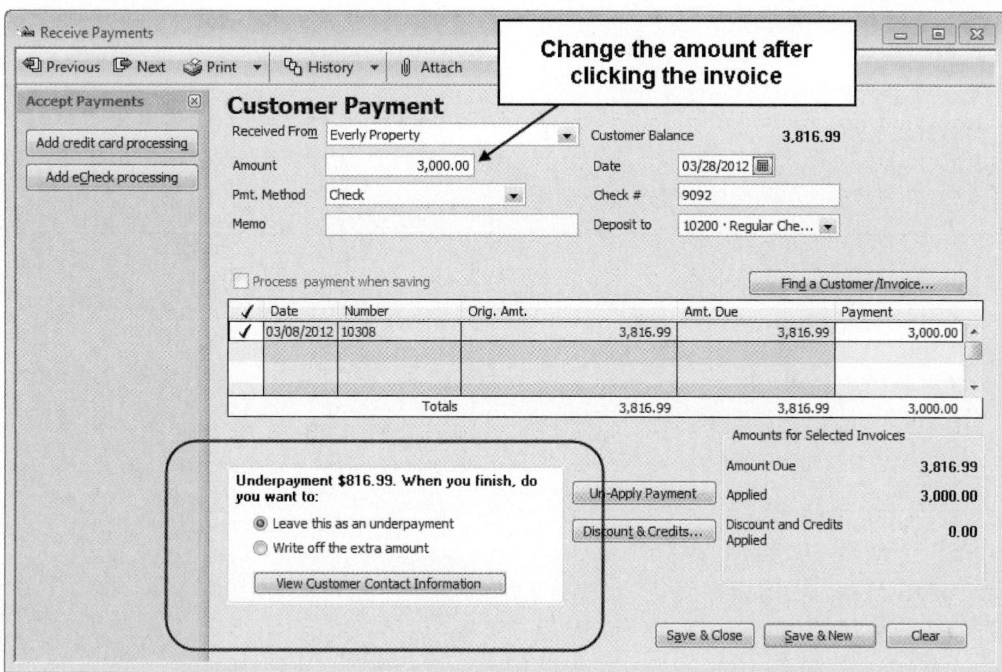

Figure: E:42

Cash Receipts Journal.

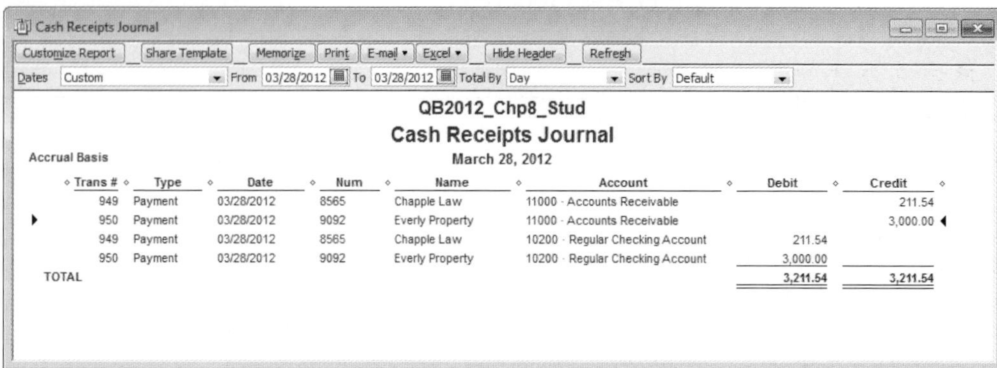

QB2012_Chp8_Stud

Cash Receipts Journal

March 28, 2012

Accrual Basis

Trans #	Type	Date	Num	Name	Account	Debit	Credit
949	Payment	03/28/2012	8565	Chapple Law	11000 · Accounts Receivable		211.54
950	Payment	03/28/2012	9092	Everly Property	11000 · Accounts Receivable		3,000.00
949	Payment	03/28/2012	8565	Chapple Law	10200 · Regular Checking Account	211.54	
950	Payment	03/28/2012	9092	Everly Property	10200 · Regular Checking Account	3,000.00	
TOTAL						3,211.54	3,211.54

Figure: E:43

CHAPTER 9

ENTER PURCHASE ORDERS

DeJulia Wholesale Suppliers' PO.

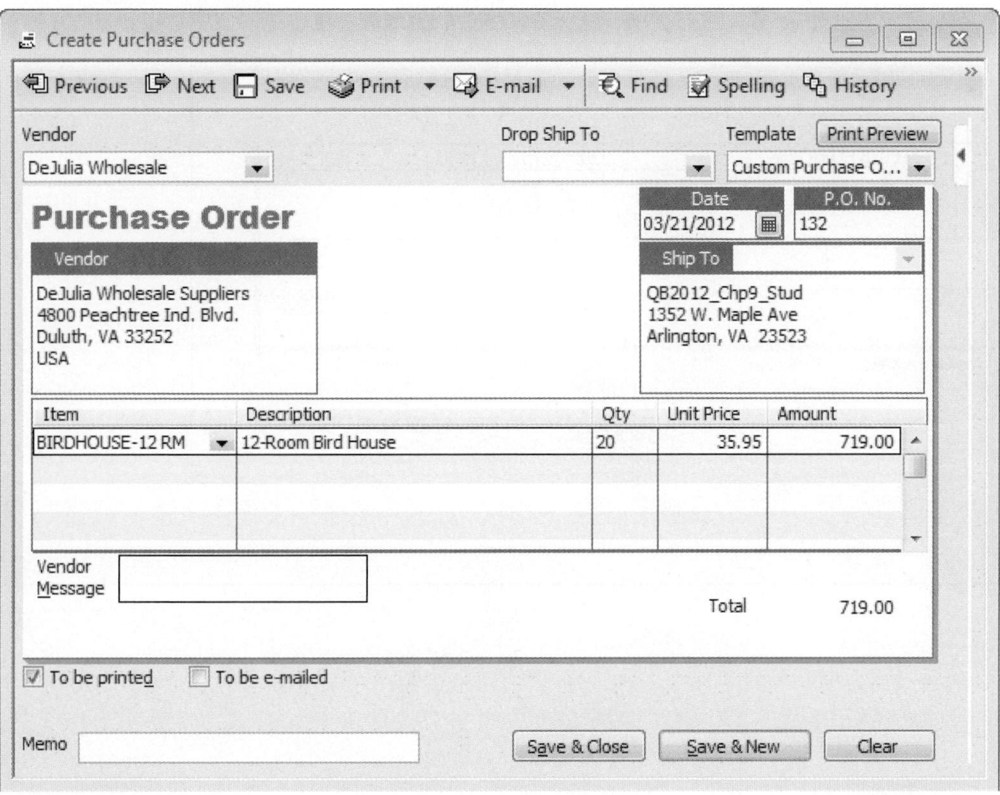

Figure: E:44

Abney and Son Contractors' PO.

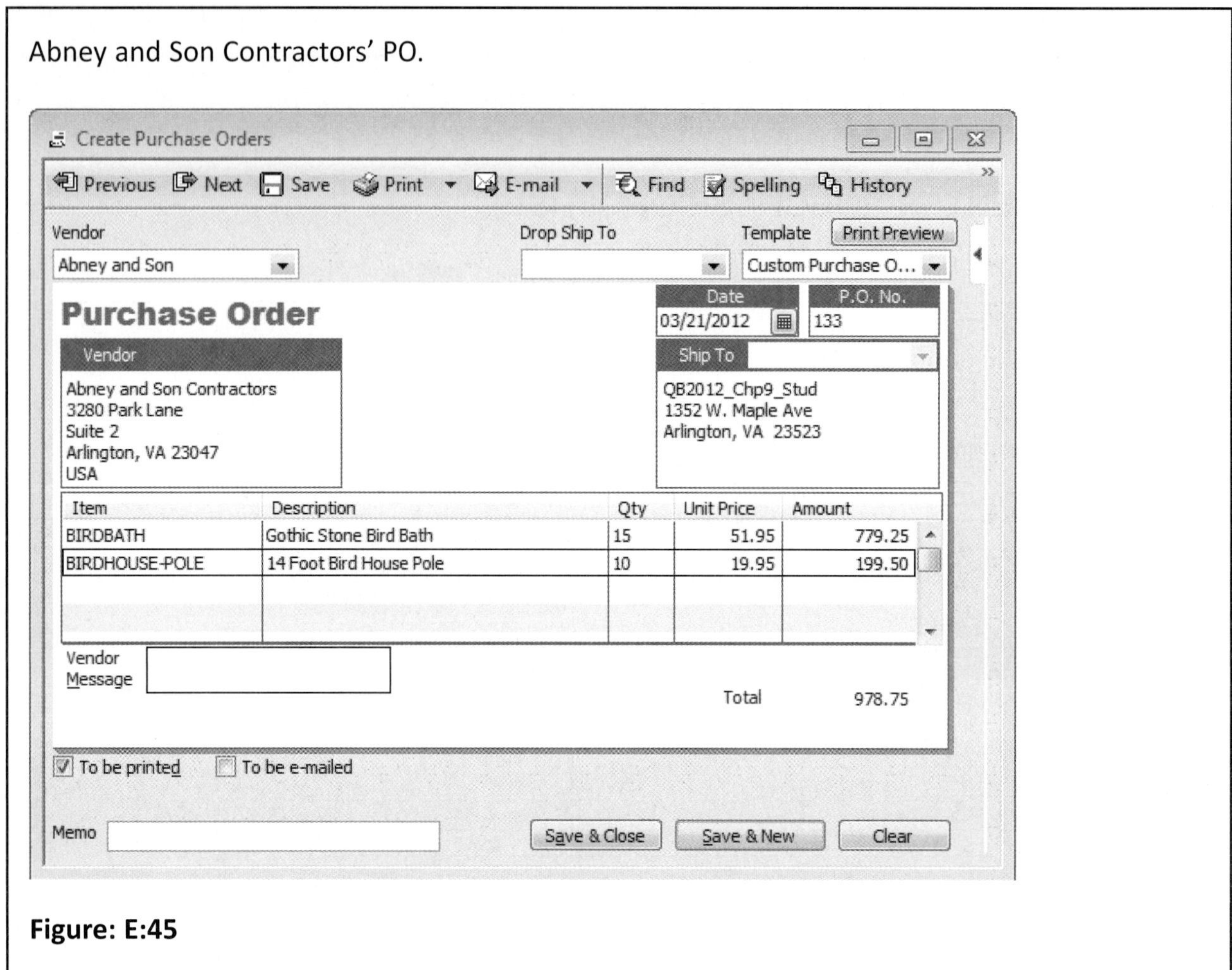
Create Purchase Orders

Previous | Next | Save | Print | E-mail | Find | Spelling | History

Vendor: Abney and Son
Drop Ship To:
Template: Custom Purchase O... | Print Preview

Purchase Order

Date	P.O. No.
03/21/2012	133

Vendor

Abney and Son Contractors
3280 Park Lane
Suite 2
Arlington, VA 23047
USA

Ship To

QB2012_Chp9_Stud
1352 W. Maple Ave
Arlington, VA 23523

Item	Description	Qty	Unit Price	Amount
BIRDBATH	Gothic Stone Bird Bath	15	51.95	779.25
BIRDHOUSE-POLE	14 Foot Bird House Pole	10	19.95	199.50

Vendor Message

Total 978.75

To be printed | To be e-mailed

Memo

Save & Close | Save & New | Clear

Figure: E:45

ENTER VENDOR RECEIPTS FOR A PO

DeJulia Wholesale Suppliers' receipt.

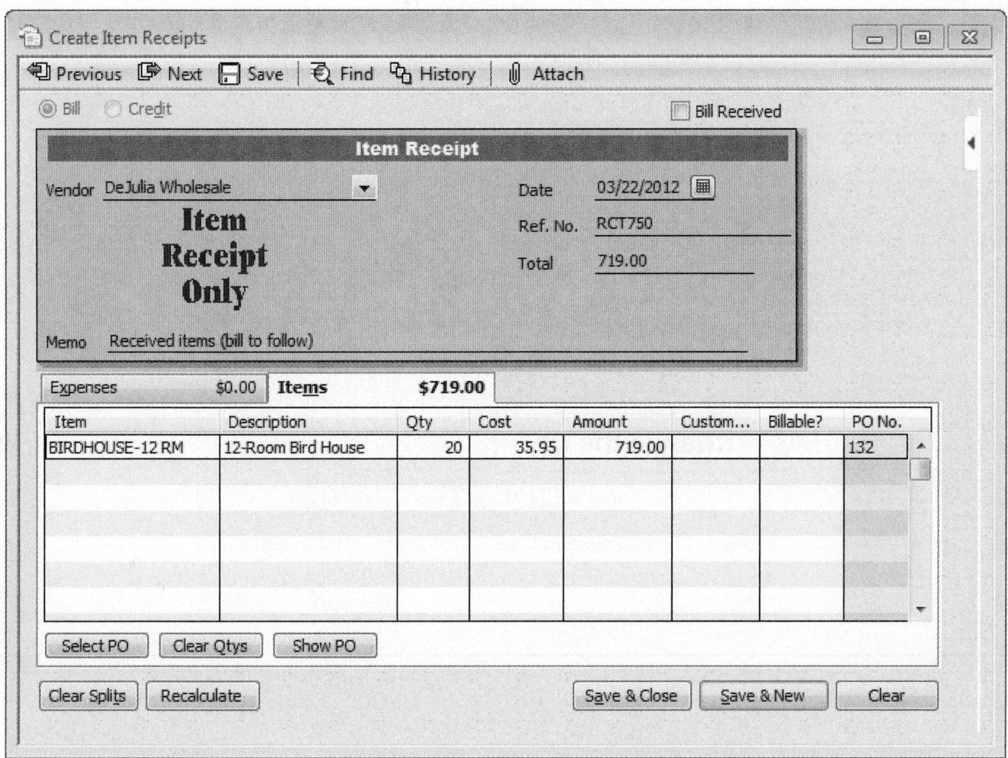

Figure: E:46

Abney and Son Contractors' receipt.

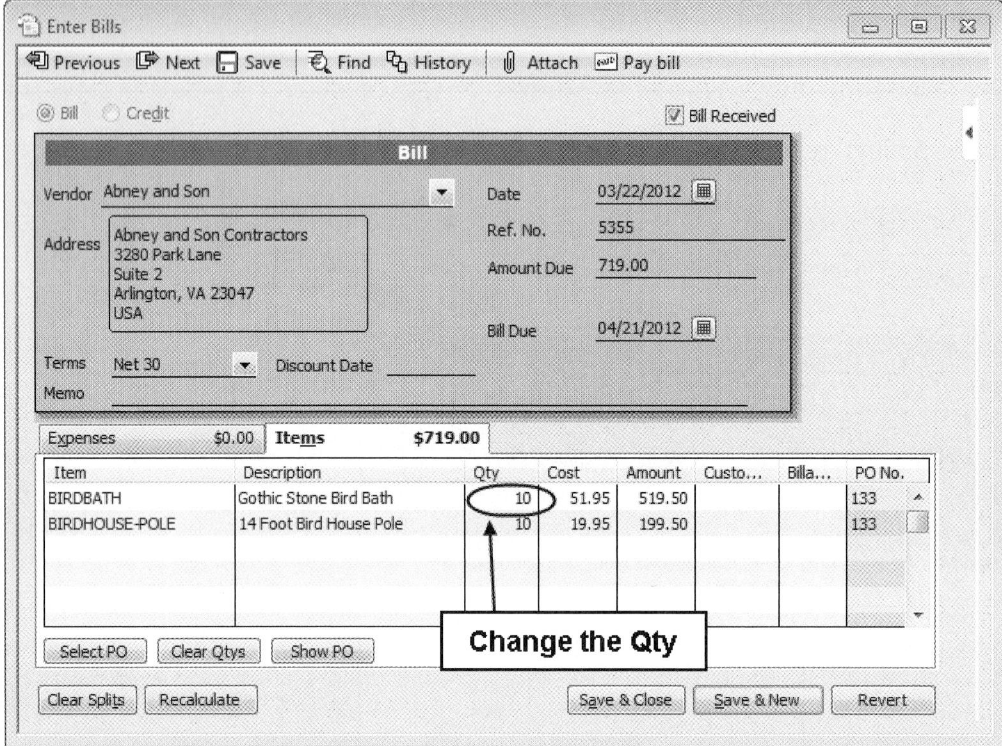

Figure: E:47

Abney's PO remains open because only 10 items of BIRDBATH were received.

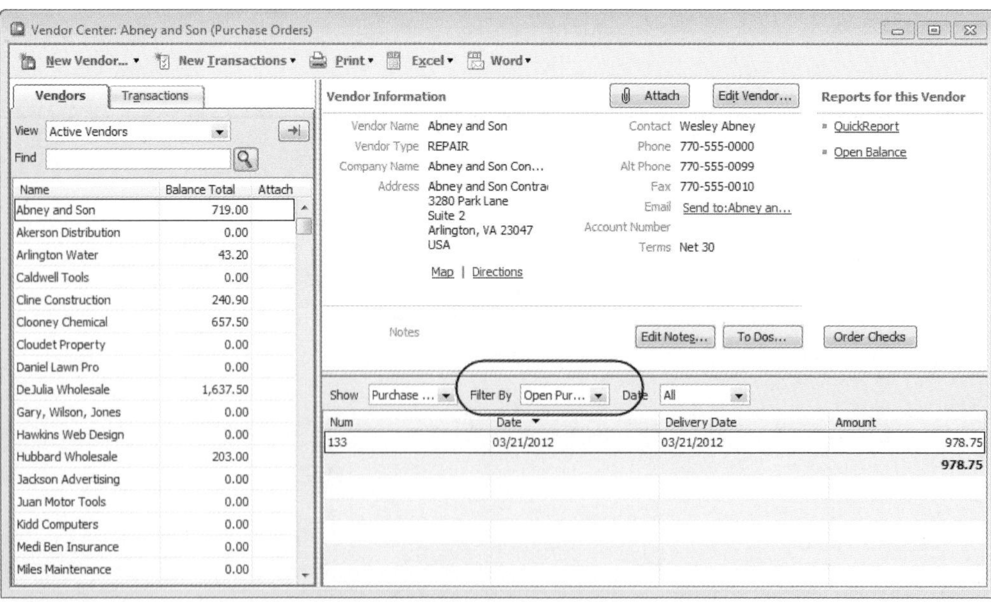

Figure: E:48

ENTER VENDOR BILL FOR VENDOR RECEIPT

DeJulia Wholesale Suppliers' invoice.

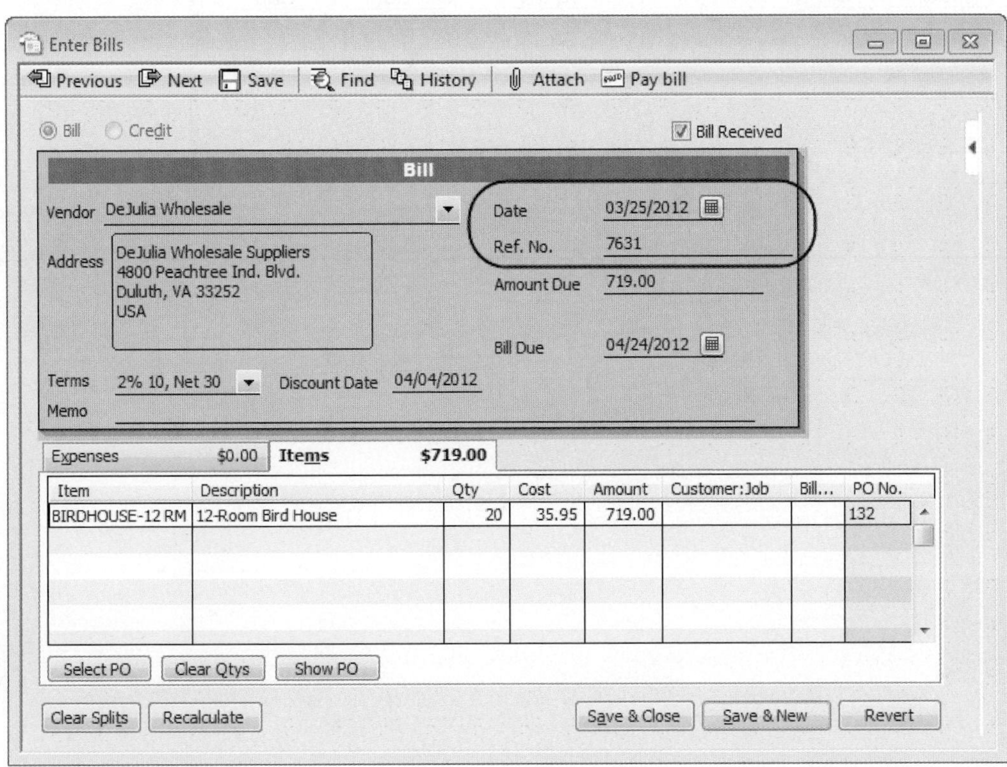

Figure: E:49

Purchases Journal. *(Note: Southern Garden's transaction already existed.)*

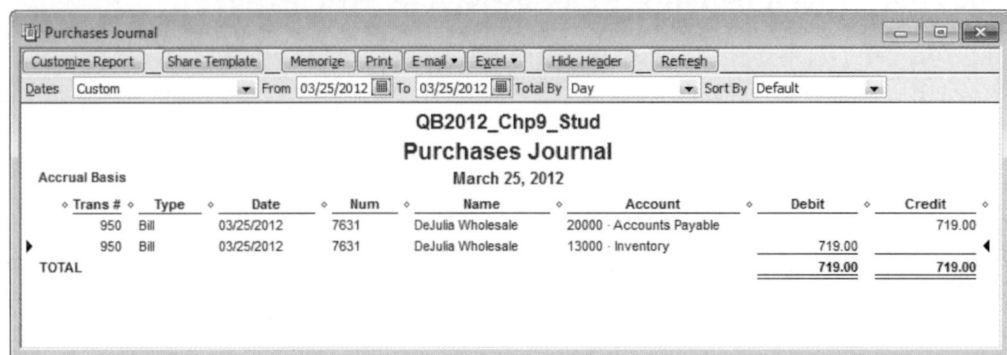

QB2012_Chp9_Stud

Purchases Journal

Accrual Basis

March 25, 2012

Trans #	Type	Date	Num	Name	Account	Debit	Credit
950	Bill	03/25/2012	7631	DeJulia Wholesale	20000 · Accounts Payable		719.00
950	Bill	03/25/2012	7631	DeJulia Wholesale	13000 · Inventory	719.00	
TOTAL						719.00	719.00

Figure: E:50

CREATE A NEW VENDOR ACCOUNT

Sullivan Buyer Supplies' Address Info.

New Vendor

Vendor Name: Sullivan Buyer Supplies

Opening Balance: as of 03/04/2012 — How do I determine the opening balance?

OK | Cancel | Next | Help

Address Info | Additional Info | Account Prefill

Company Name: Sullivan Buyer Supplies

Mr./Ms./...

First Name / M.I.

Last Name

Contact

Phone

FAX

Alt. Phone

Alt. Contact

E-mail

Cc

Print on Check as: Sullivan Buyer Supplies

Vendor is inactive

Addresses

Billed From Address:
Sullivan Buyer Supplies
P.O. box 1732
Arlington, VA 30022

Copy >>

Shipped From Address:
Sullivan Buyer Supplies
P.O. box 1732
Arlington, VA 30022

Edit | Edit

Figure: E:51

Sullivan Buyer Supplies' Additional Info.

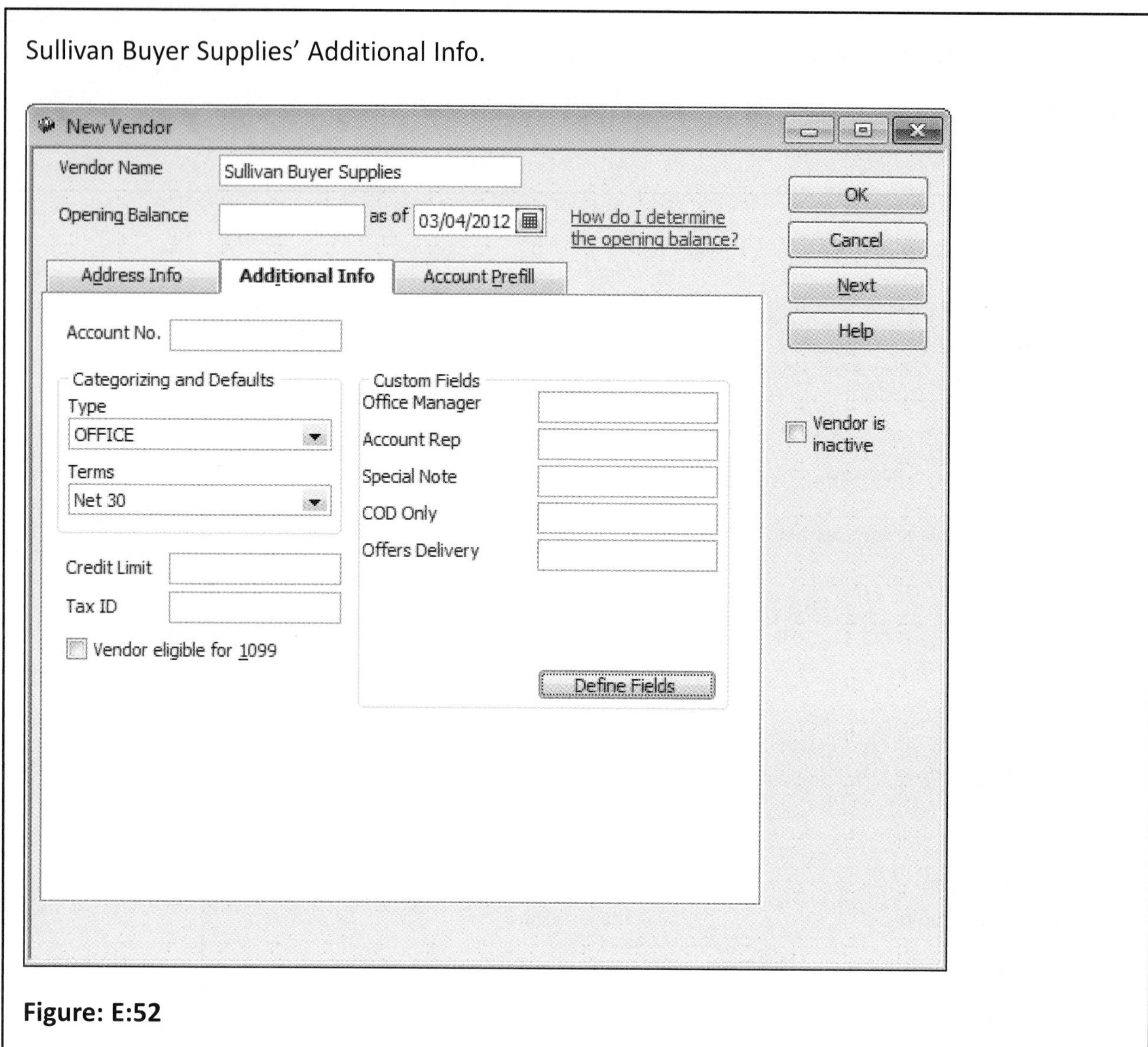

Figure: E:52

Sullivan Buyer Supplies' Account Prefill.

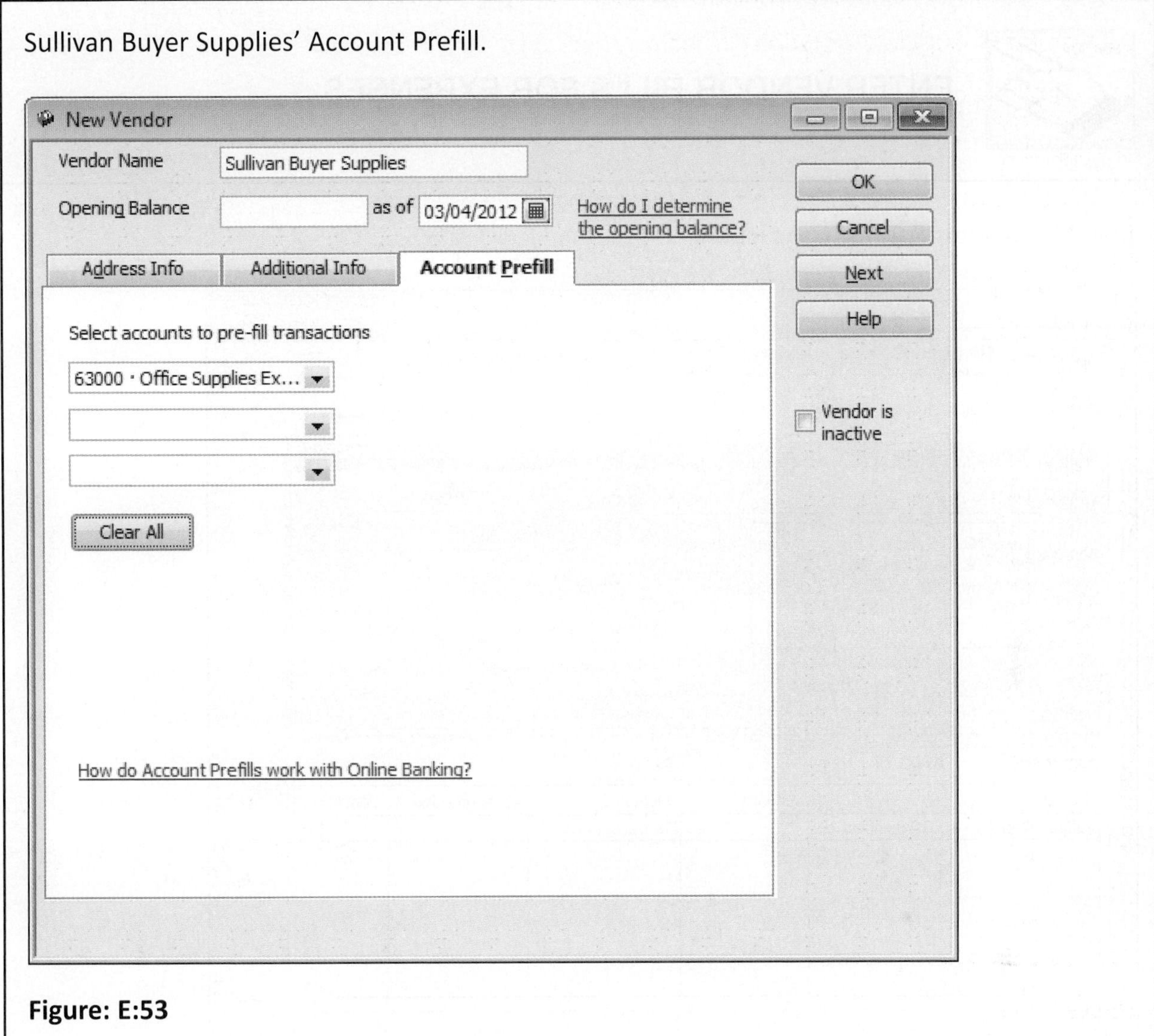

Figure: E:53

ENTER VENDOR BILLS FOR EXPENSES

Juan Motor Tools & Tires' transaction.

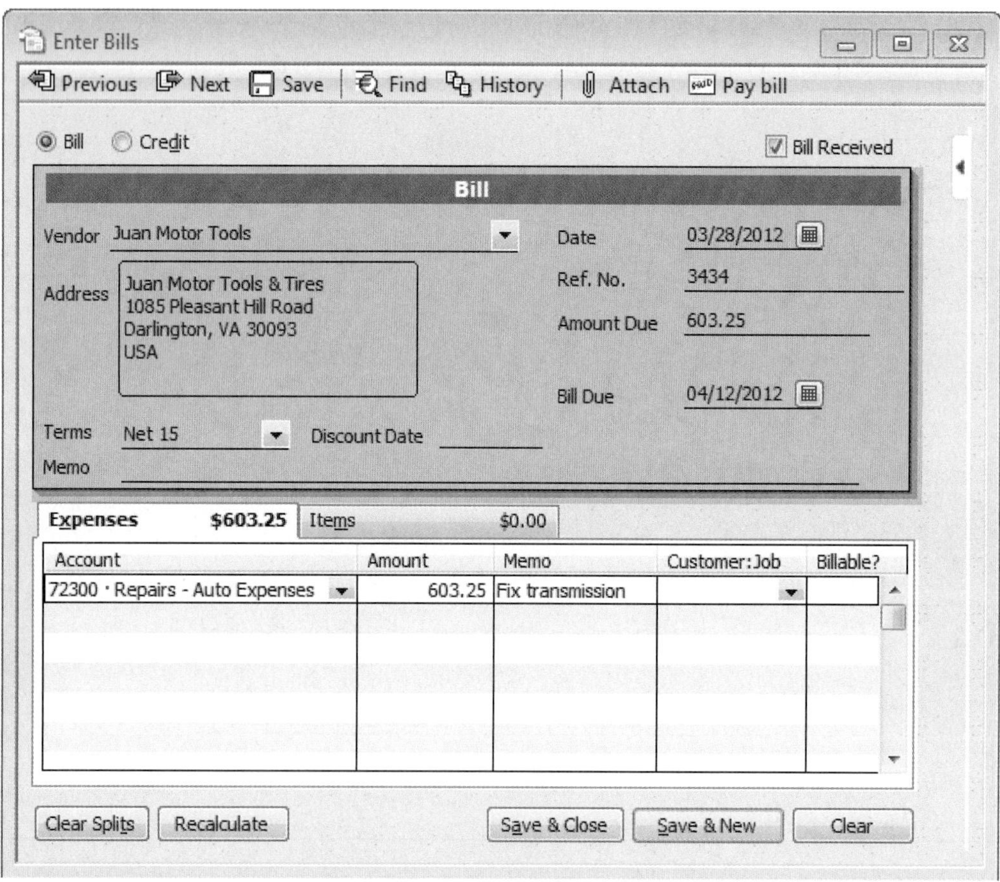

Figure: E:54

Neighbors Telephone Company's bill.

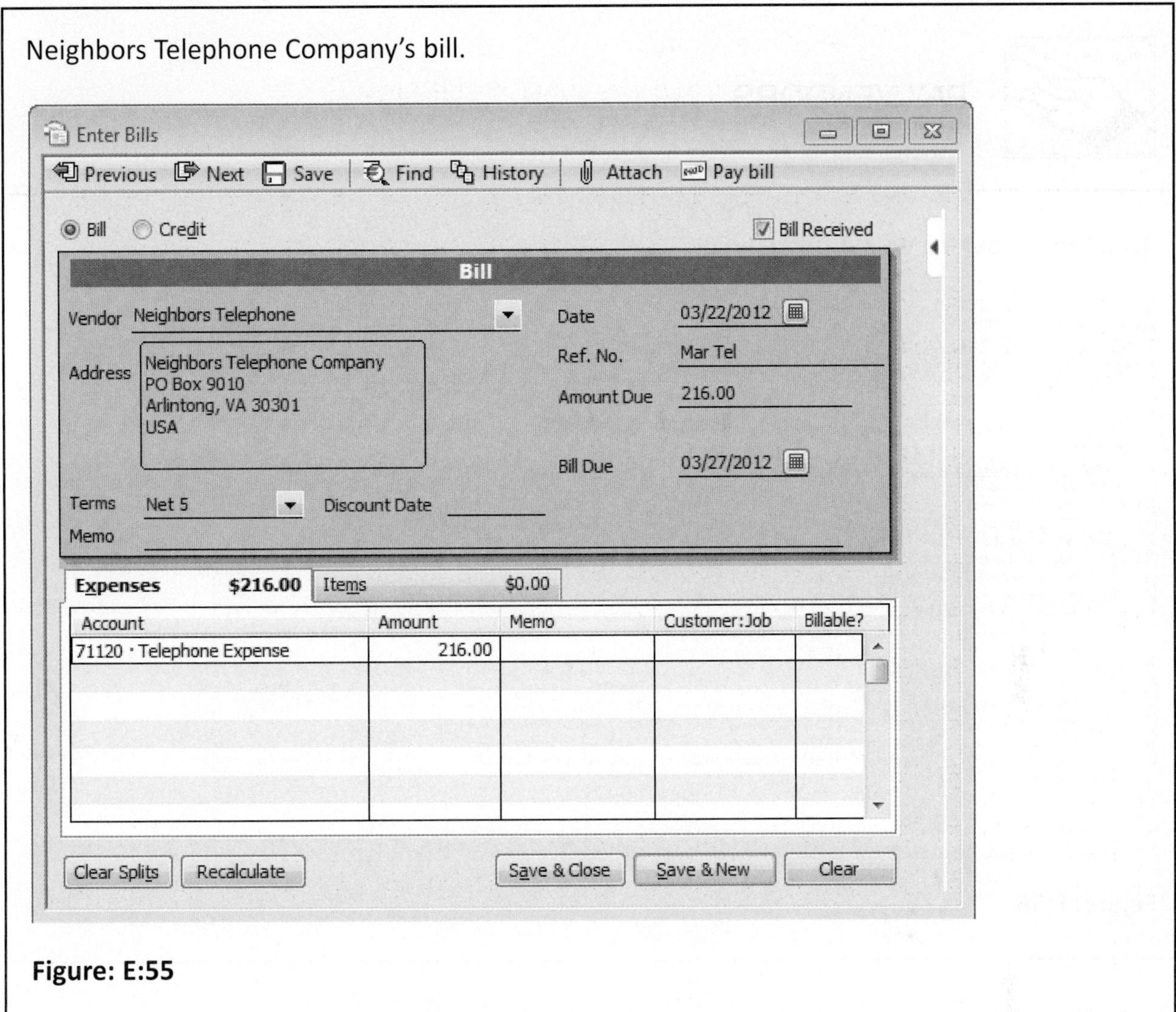

Figure: E:55

PAY VENDORS

The Cash Disbursements Journal.

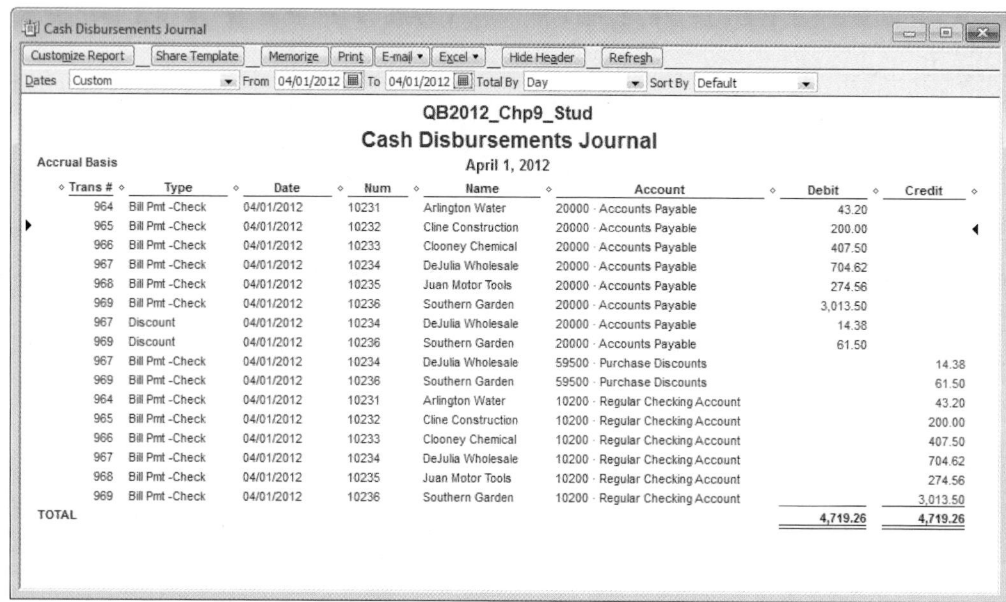

QB2012_Chp9_Stud

Cash Disbursements Journal

Accrual Basis

April 1, 2012

Trans #	Type	Date	Num	Name	Account	Debit	Credit
964	Bill Pmt -Check	04/01/2012	10231	Arlington Water	20000 · Accounts Payable	43.20	
965	Bill Pmt -Check	04/01/2012	10232	Cline Construction	20000 · Accounts Payable	200.00	
966	Bill Pmt -Check	04/01/2012	10233	Clooney Chemical	20000 · Accounts Payable	407.50	
967	Bill Pmt -Check	04/01/2012	10234	DeJulia Wholesale	20000 · Accounts Payable	704.62	
968	Bill Pmt -Check	04/01/2012	10235	Juan Motor Tools	20000 · Accounts Payable	274.56	
969	Bill Pmt -Check	04/01/2012	10236	Southern Garden	20000 · Accounts Payable	3,013.50	
967	Discount	04/01/2012	10234	DeJulia Wholesale	20000 · Accounts Payable	14.38	
969	Discount	04/01/2012	10236	Southern Garden	20000 · Accounts Payable	61.50	
967	Bill Pmt -Check	04/01/2012	10234	DeJulia Wholesale	59500 · Purchase Discounts		14.38
969	Bill Pmt -Check	04/01/2012	10236	Southern Garden	59500 · Purchase Discounts		61.50
964	Bill Pmt -Check	04/01/2012	10231	Arlington Water	10200 · Regular Checking Account		43.20
965	Bill Pmt -Check	04/01/2012	10232	Cline Construction	10200 · Regular Checking Account		200.00
966	Bill Pmt -Check	04/01/2012	10233	Clooney Chemical	10200 · Regular Checking Account		407.50
967	Bill Pmt -Check	04/01/2012	10234	DeJulia Wholesale	10200 · Regular Checking Account		704.62
968	Bill Pmt -Check	04/01/2012	10235	Juan Motor Tools	10200 · Regular Checking Account		274.56
969	Bill Pmt -Check	04/01/2012	10236	Southern Garden	10200 · Regular Checking Account		3,013.50
TOTAL						4,719.26	4,719.26

Figure: E:56

CHAPTER 10

CREATE CHECKS FOR PAYROLL TAXES

Pay Liabilities window.

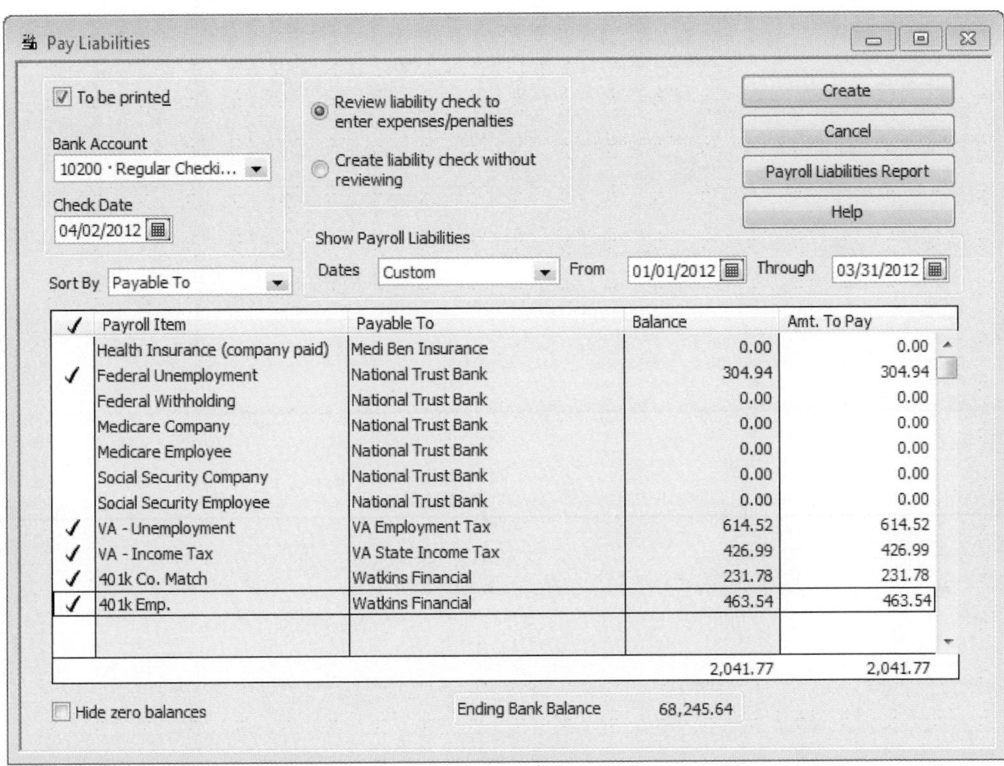

Figure: E:57

Check Detail report.

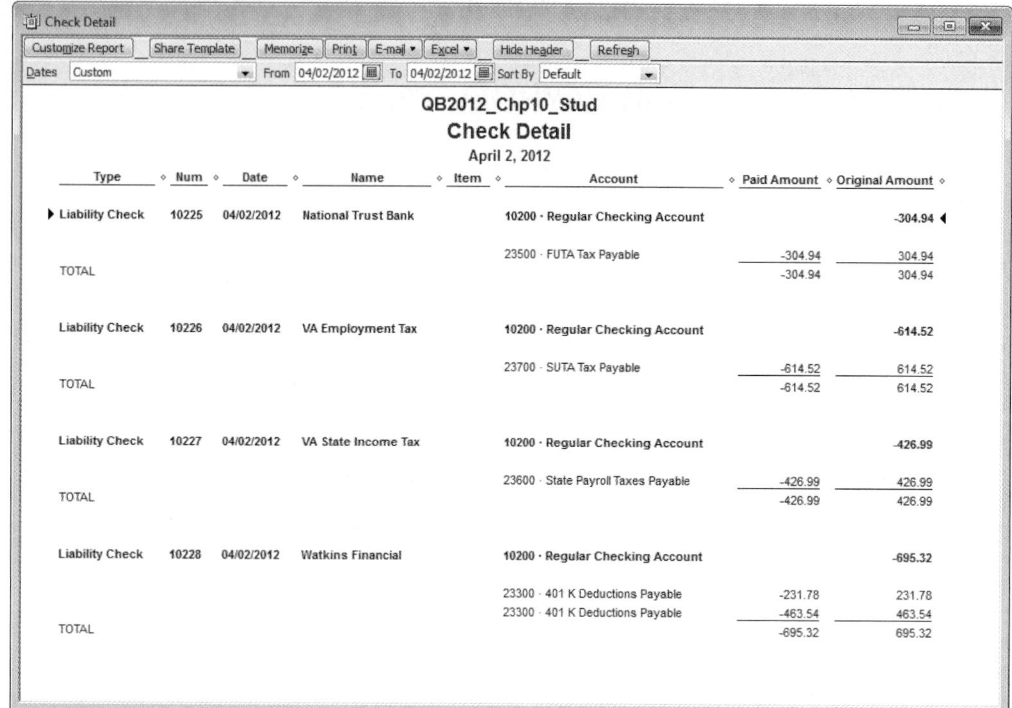

QB2012_Chp10_Stud

Check Detail

April 2, 2012

Type	Num	Date	Name	Item	Account	Paid Amount	Original Amount
Liability Check	**10225**	**04/02/2012**	**National Trust Bank**		**10200 · Regular Checking Account**		**-304.94**
					23500 · FUTA Tax Payable	-304.94	304.94
TOTAL						-304.94	304.94
Liability Check	**10226**	**04/02/2012**	**VA Employment Tax**		**10200 · Regular Checking Account**		**-614.52**
					23700 · SUTA Tax Payable	-614.52	614.52
TOTAL						-614.52	614.52
Liability Check	**10227**	**04/02/2012**	**VA State Income Tax**		**10200 · Regular Checking Account**		**-426.99**
					23600 · State Payroll Taxes Payable	-426.99	426.99
TOTAL						-426.99	426.99
Liability Check	**10228**	**04/02/2012**	**Watkins Financial**		**10200 · Regular Checking Account**		**-695.32**
					23300 · 401 K Deductions Payable	-231.78	231.78
					23300 · 401 K Deductions Payable	-463.54	463.54
TOTAL						-695.32	695.32

Figure: E:58

Chapter 11

FINISH RECORDING MARCH ADJUSTING ENTRIES

Bank transfer entry.

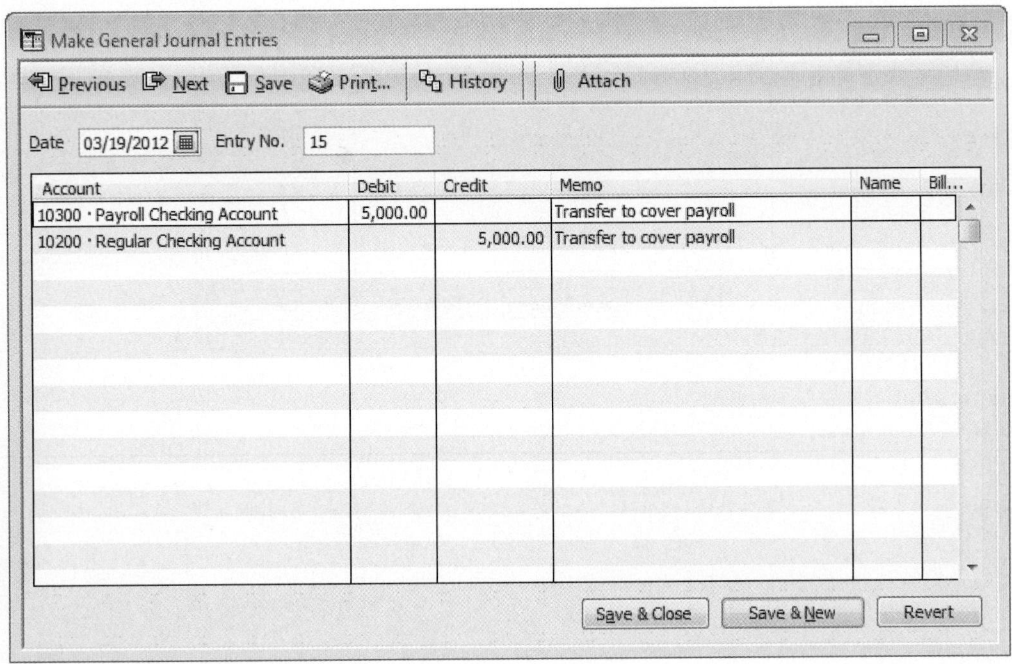

Figure: E:59

Expired prepaid expense entry.

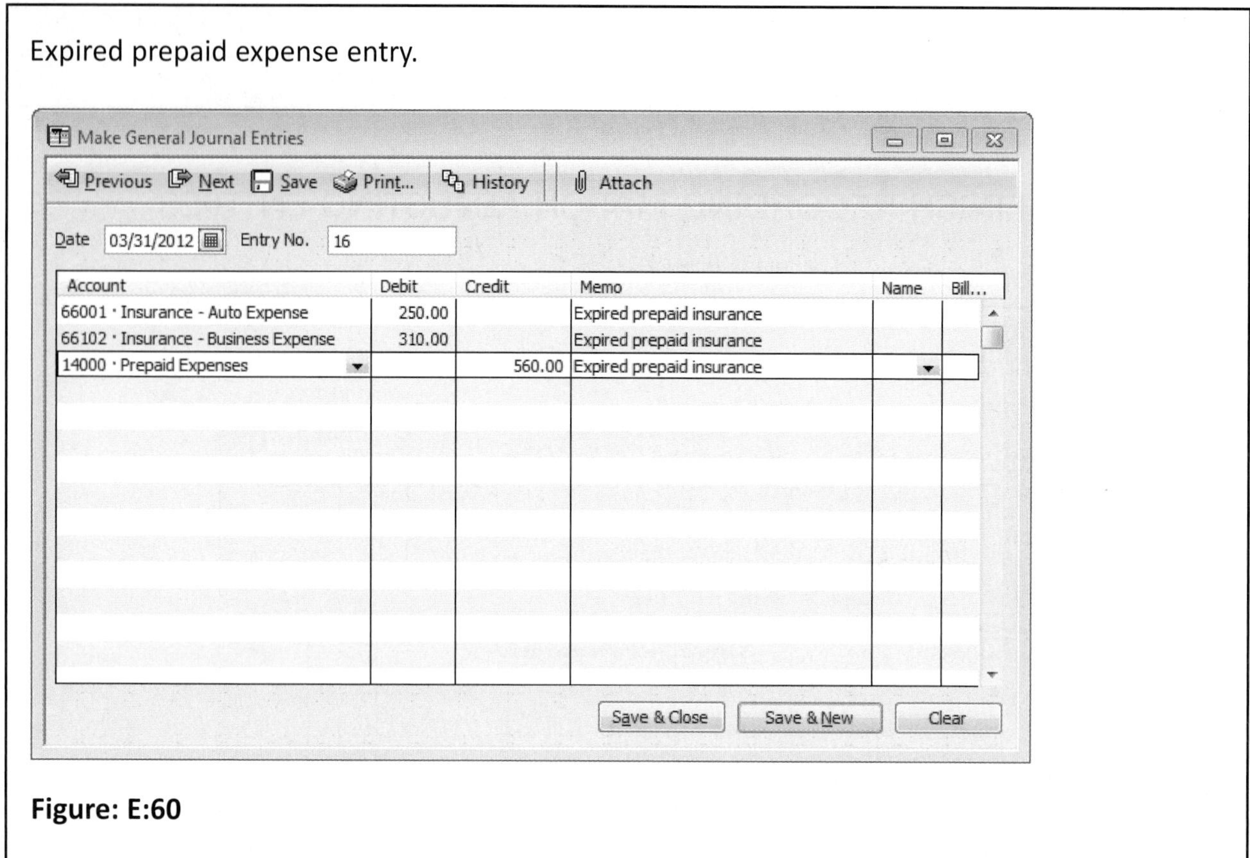

Figure: E:60

RECONCILE THE PAYROLL CHECKING ACCOUNT

Payroll Checking Account reconciliation window.

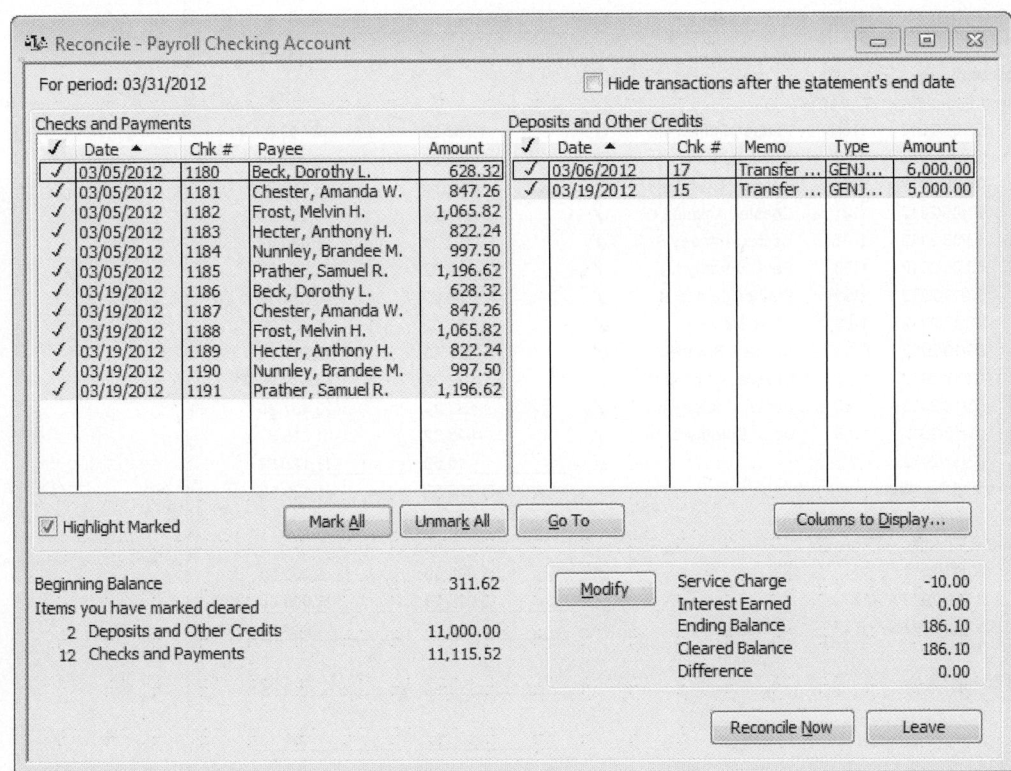

Figure: E:61

Payroll Checking Account bank reconciliation.

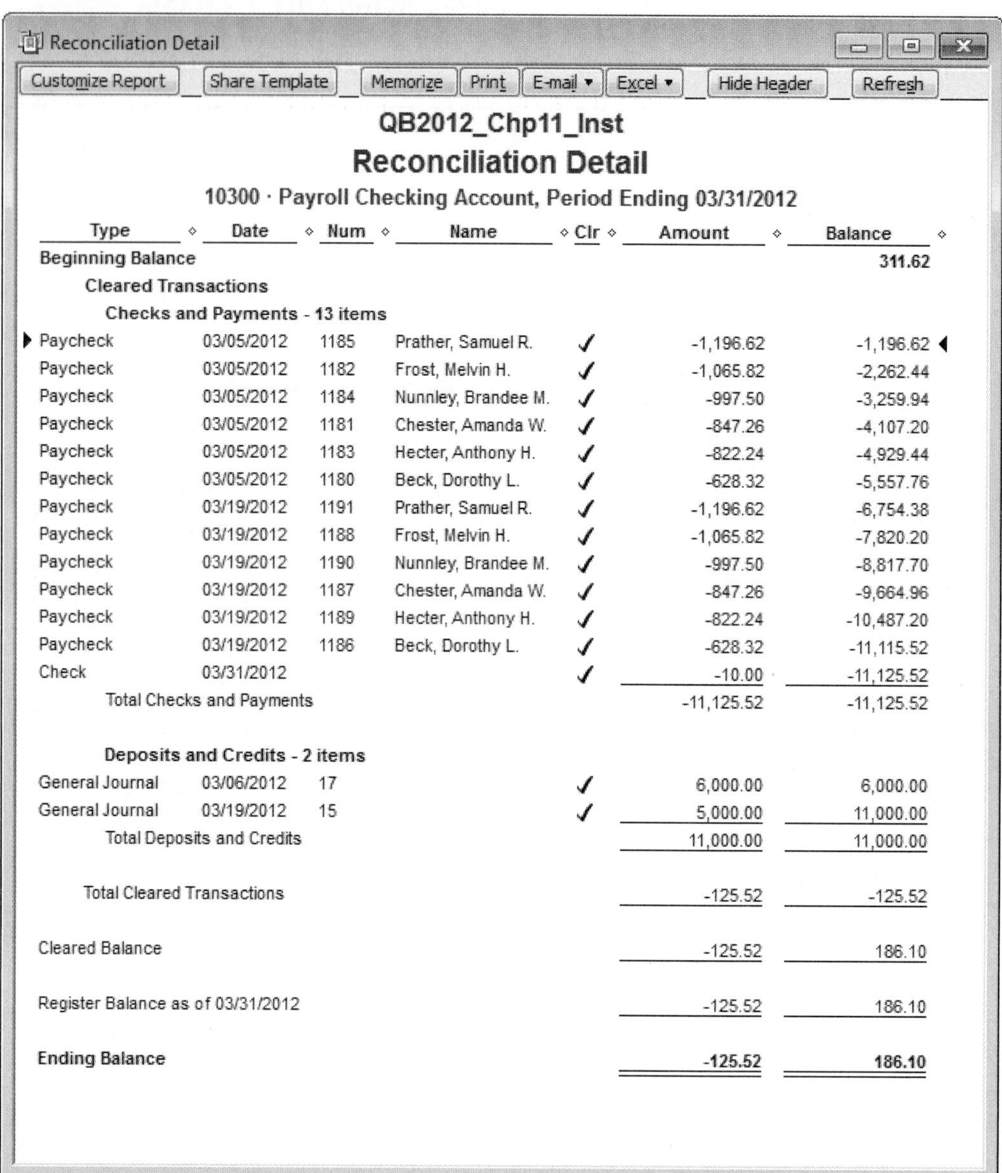

Reconciliation Detail

Customize Report | Share Template | Memorize | Print | E-mail ▾ | Excel ▾ | Hide Header | Refresh

QB2012_Chp11_Inst

Reconciliation Detail

10300 · Payroll Checking Account, Period Ending 03/31/2012

Type	Date	Num	Name	Clr	Amount	Balance
Beginning Balance						**311.62**
Cleared Transactions						
Checks and Payments - 13 items						
Paycheck	03/05/2012	1185	Prather, Samuel R.	✓	-1,196.62	-1,196.62
Paycheck	03/05/2012	1182	Frost, Melvin H.	✓	-1,065.82	-2,262.44
Paycheck	03/05/2012	1184	Nunnley, Brandee M.	✓	-997.50	-3,259.94
Paycheck	03/05/2012	1181	Chester, Amanda W.	✓	-847.26	-4,107.20
Paycheck	03/05/2012	1183	Hecter, Anthony H.	✓	-822.24	-4,929.44
Paycheck	03/05/2012	1180	Beck, Dorothy L.	✓	-628.32	-5,557.76
Paycheck	03/19/2012	1191	Prather, Samuel R.	✓	-1,196.62	-6,754.38
Paycheck	03/19/2012	1188	Frost, Melvin H.	✓	-1,065.82	-7,820.20
Paycheck	03/19/2012	1190	Nunnley, Brandee M.	✓	-997.50	-8,817.70
Paycheck	03/19/2012	1187	Chester, Amanda W.	✓	-847.26	-9,664.96
Paycheck	03/19/2012	1189	Hecter, Anthony H.	✓	-822.24	-10,487.20
Paycheck	03/19/2012	1186	Beck, Dorothy L.	✓	-628.32	-11,115.52
Check	03/31/2012			✓	-10.00	-11,125.52
Total Checks and Payments					-11,125.52	-11,125.52
Deposits and Credits - 2 items						
General Journal	03/06/2012	17		✓	6,000.00	6,000.00
General Journal	03/19/2012	15		✓	5,000.00	11,000.00
Total Deposits and Credits					11,000.00	11,000.00
Total Cleared Transactions					-125.52	-125.52
Cleared Balance					-125.52	186.10
Register Balance as of 03/31/2012					-125.52	186.10
Ending Balance					**-125.52**	**186.10**

Figure: E:62

APPENDIX F FEATURES IN QUICKBOOKS ACCOUNTANT

This Appendix provides an overview of features in the Accountant edition of QuickBooks. Professional accountants use this edition for several reasons. First, it allows the accountant to open data files created in earlier versions of the software and, as you have seen, toggle to different editions. Second, it also comes with the fixed asset manager feature and many other features that simplify working on client data files.

For instance, the accountant can post a reversing journal entry while recording the original journal entry. (See Figure: F:1).

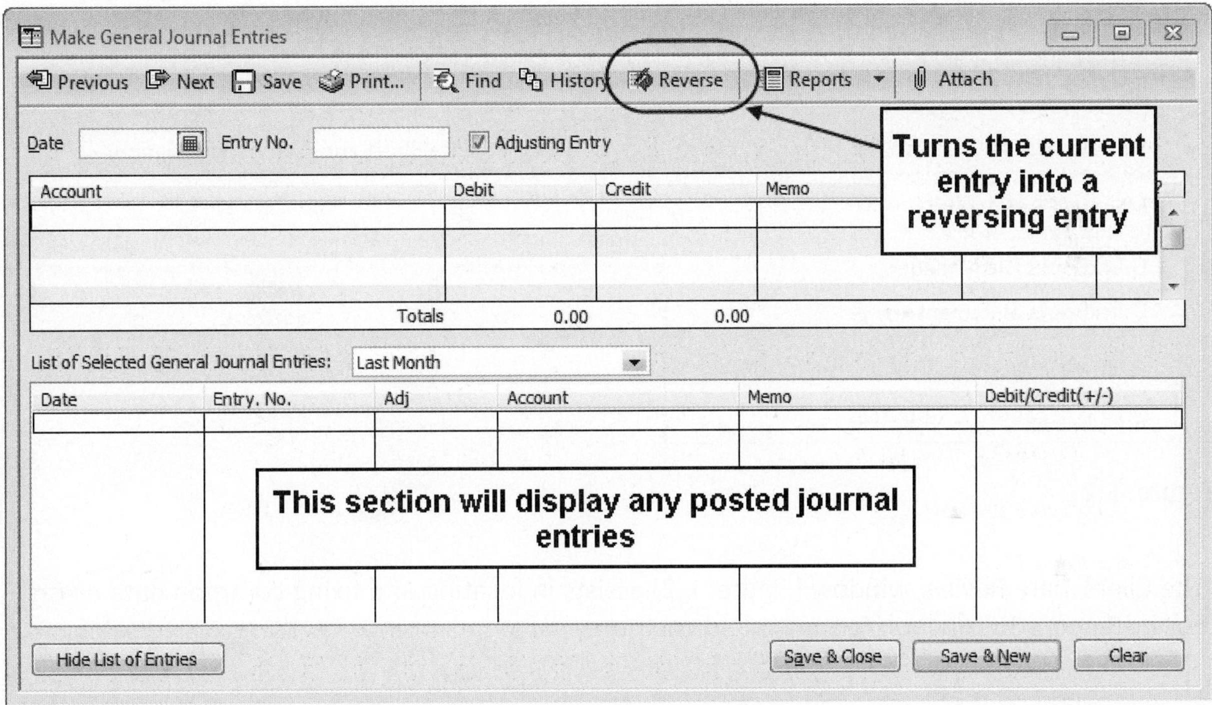

Figure: F:1

Another big feature in this edition is the Accountant's Copy, which works as follows. The client creates an Accountant's Copy of their data file by selecting ***File>>Accountant's Copy>>Send to Accountant*** on the main menu. This copy can be created in any edition of the software, but can only be imported in the Accountant edition. After importing the copy, the accountant makes adjusting entries and sends the file back to the client, who imports the changes. All of this is done without interrupting the client's continued use of the data file.

Another beneficial feature for accountants is Client Data Review. This feature is accessed from the following menu.

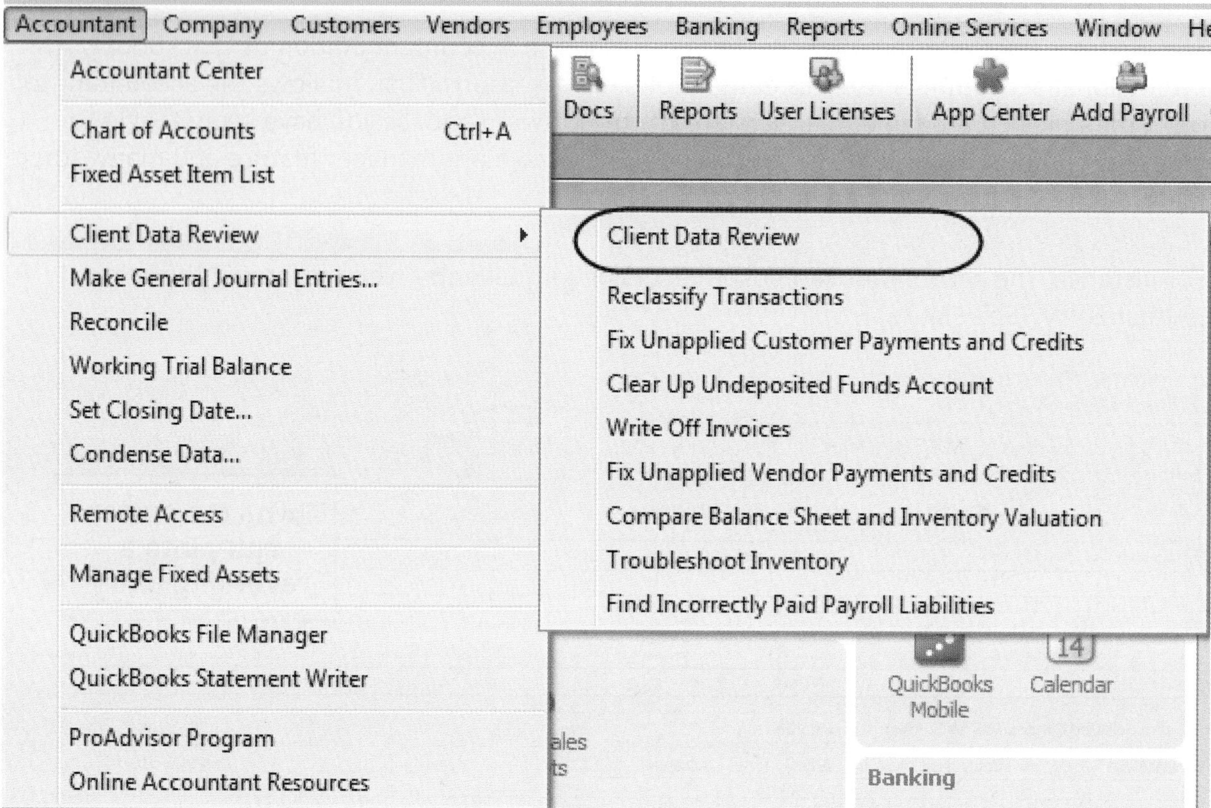

Figure: F:2

The Client Data Review window (Figure: F:3) assists in locating and fixing common data errors. For instance, you can look for unapplied customer payments or incorrectly recorded sales tax.

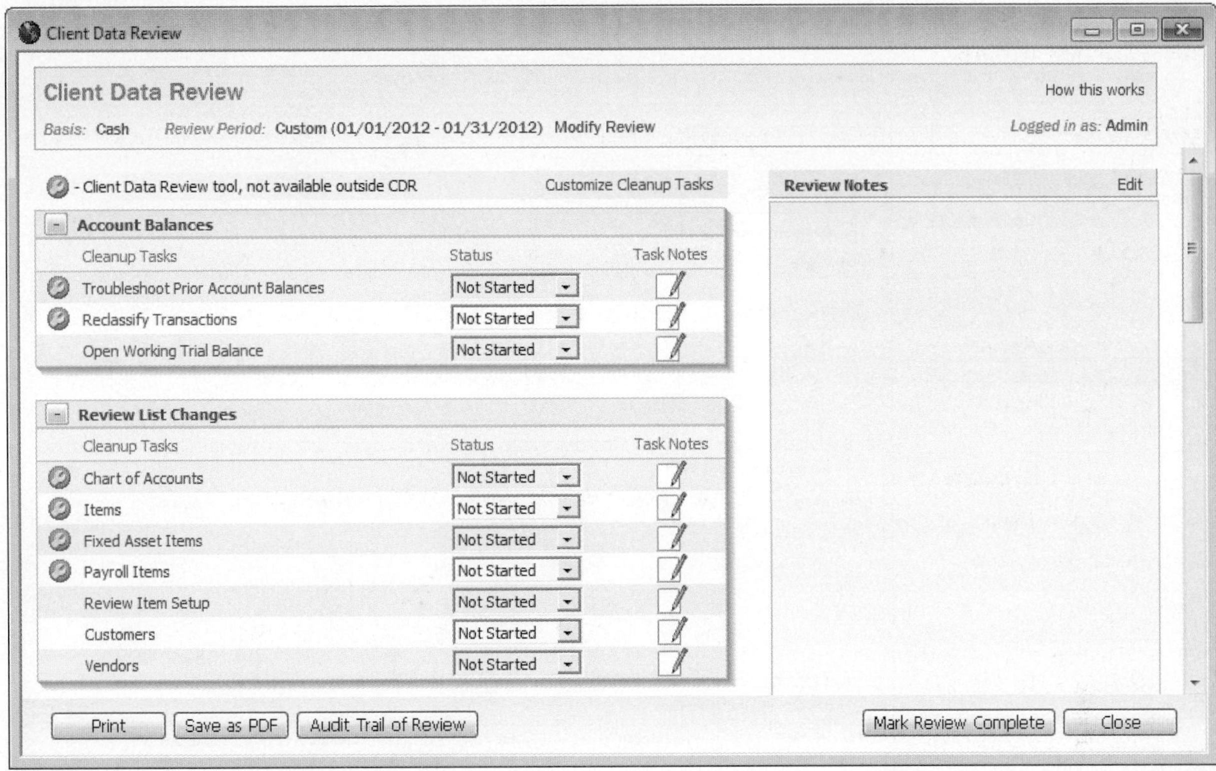

Figure F:3

Another plus is the QuickBooks File Manager feature. You may have noticed the icon in Figure: F:4 on your desktop. If you double click the icon, the window illustrated next opens. *(Note: The first time you open the file manager, you may be prompted for the path to your data files.)*

Figure F:4

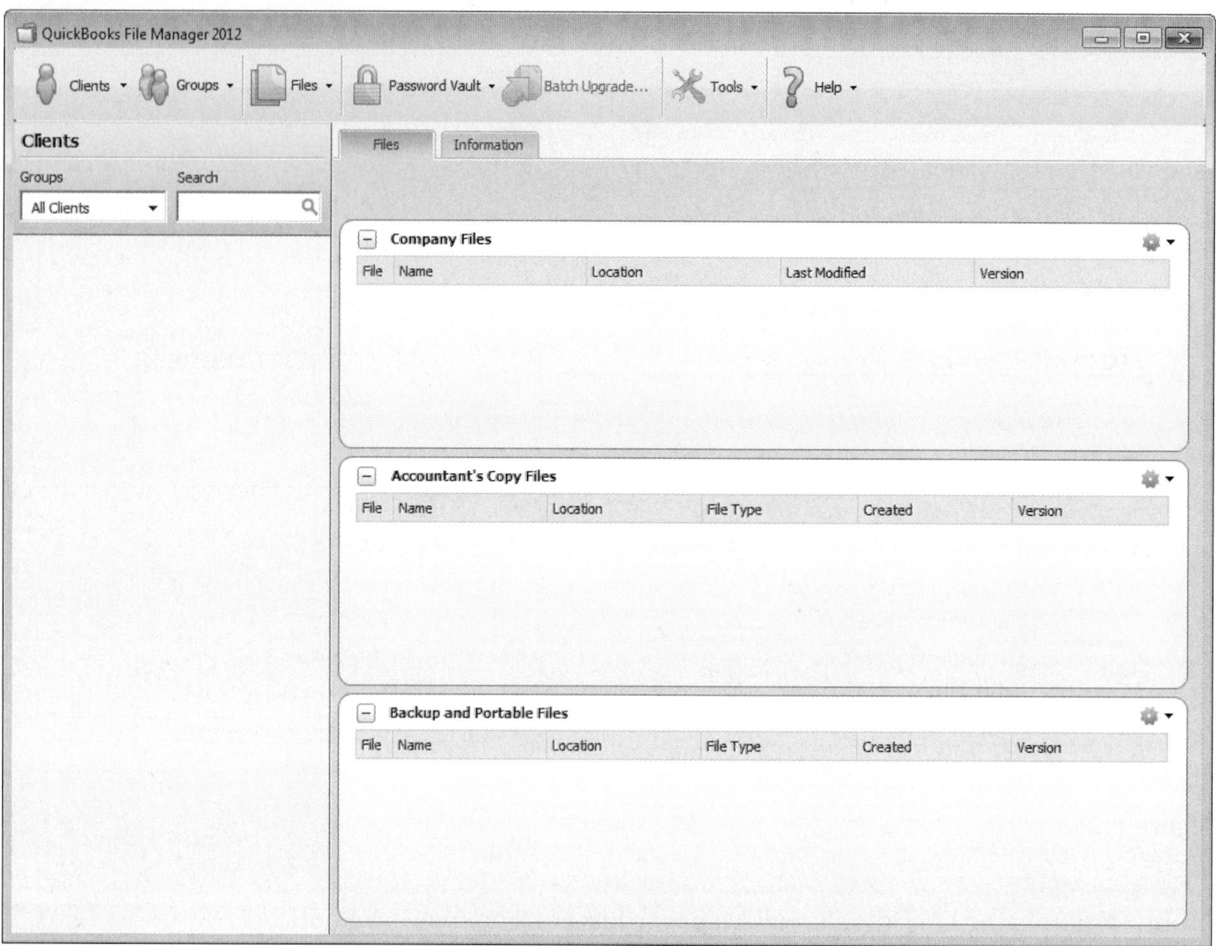

Figure: F:5

Click the **Clients** button and choose **Add Client Via>>Update Client List Wizard** to open the window illustrated in Figure: F:6. Keep the From QuickBooks file names option and click **Next**.

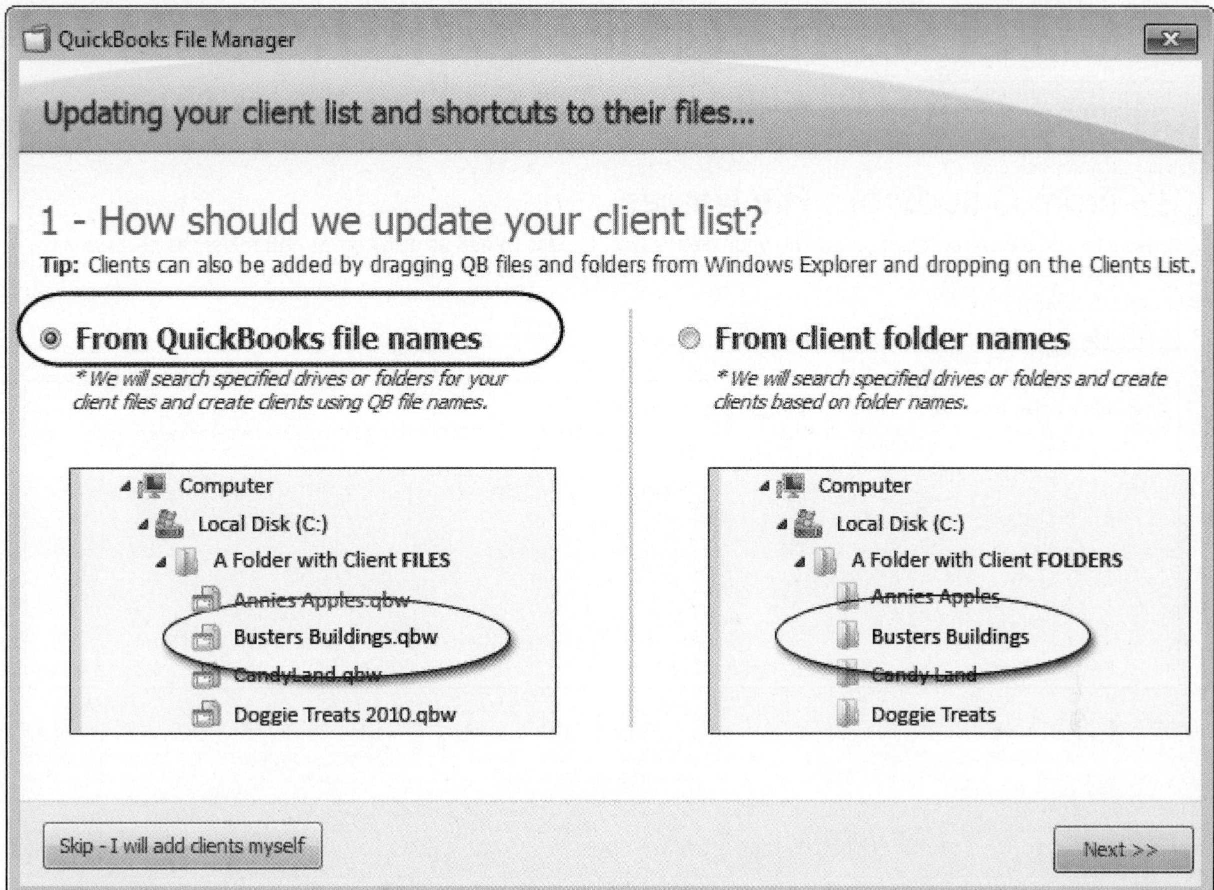

Figure F:6

In the window that opens (Figure: F:7), click **Browse** to select the path for your data files. Click **Finish** after selecting.

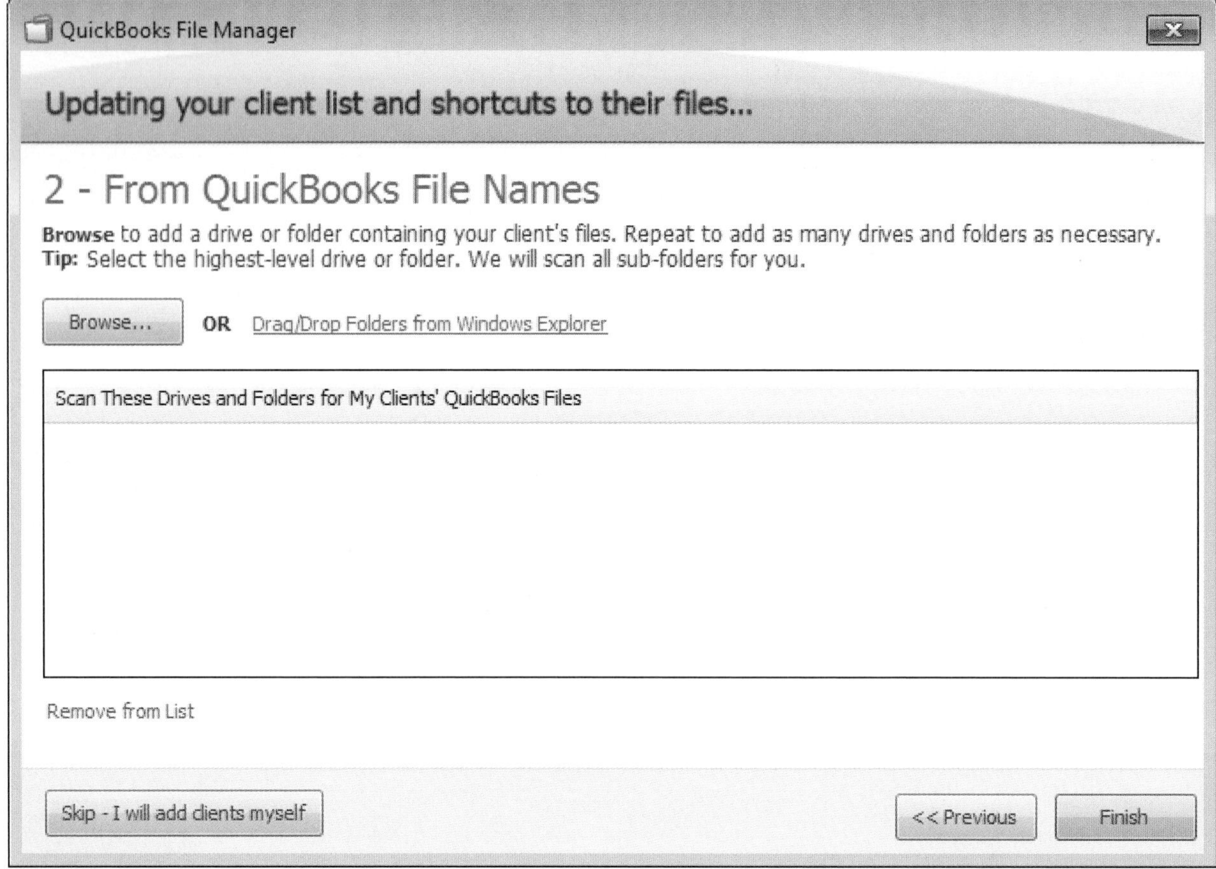

Figure F:7

The software begins updating the client list. When finished, the files are displayed in the window as illustrated next. You can now use this window to open your data files. The window will also display any accountant's copies and backup files. You can also store client passwords in the Password Vault and can upgrade company files to a newer edition.

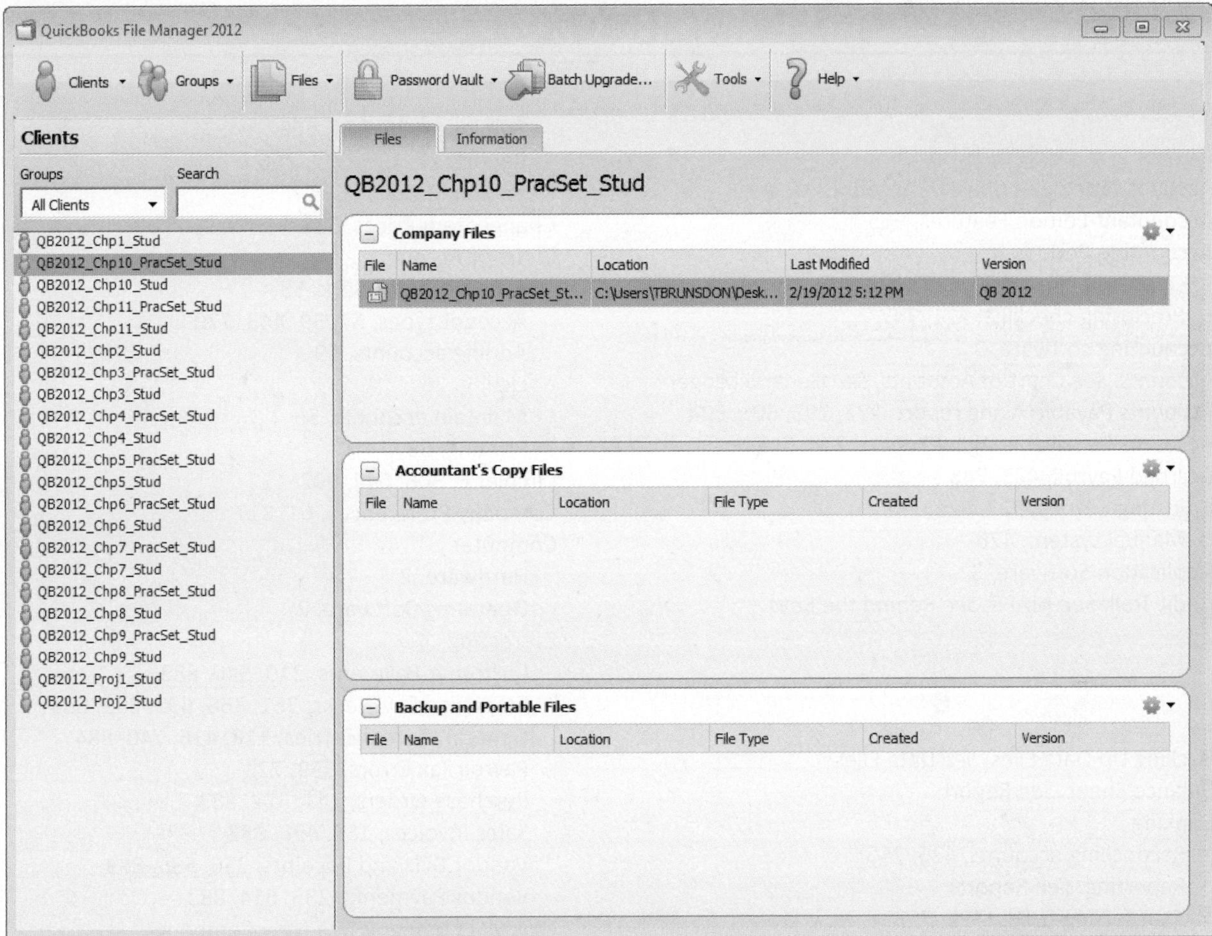

Figure F:8

This brief overview is just a few of the reasons why accountants like to use this edition of the software. With this edition, you have the added tools that make working on client files more efficient.

Index

L

M

N

P

Q

R

S

T